CRIMINAL LAW

Text, Cases, and Materials

SECOND EDITION

Jonathan Herring

OXFORD

UNIVERSITY PRESS

OXFORD
UNIVERSITY PRESS

Great Clarendon Street, Oxford OX2 6DP

Oxford University Press is a department of the University of Oxford.
It furthers the University's objective of excellence in research, scholarship,
and education by publishing worldwide in

Oxford New York

Auckland Cape Town Dar es Salaam Hong Kong Karachi
Kuala Lumpur Madrid Melbourne Mexico City Nairobi
New Delhi Shanghai Taipei Toronto

With offices in

Argentina Austria Brazil Chile Czech Republic France Greece
Guatemala Hungary Italy Japan Poland Portugal Singapore
South Korea Switzerland Thailand Turkey Ukraine Vietnam

Oxford is a registered trade mark of Oxford University Press
in the UK and in certain other countries
Published in the United States
by Oxford University Press Inc., New York

© Jonathan Herring 2006

First edition, 2004
Second edition, 2006

British Library Cataloguing in Publication Data

Data available

Library of Congress Cataloging in Publication Data

Data available

Typeset by RefineCatch Limited, Bungay, Suffolk
Printed in Great Britain
on acid-free paper by
Ashford Colour Press Limited, Gosport, Hampshire

ISBN 978–0–19–928935–6

3 5 7 9 10 8 6 4

CRIMINAL LAW

For Kirsten, Laurel, Joanna, and Darcy

PREFACE

Usually, students greatly enjoy criminal law. The facts of the cases are readily understandable and provide a revealing insight into the bizarre and grotesque. But many students miss out on the intellectual fascination that the subject has to offer. This is in part because much of the theoretical material on criminal law has been presented with such sophistication that it is inaccessible to students. It is one of the primary aims of this book to make the theoretical material on criminal law more readily comprehensible to undergraduates. Therefore, each chapter (apart from the first) has two parts. The first sets out the law, with extracts from the leading cases. The second part describes some of the theoretical material, extracting some of the writing from leading commentators. The hope is that the reader will have a secure grasp of the law itself, but also an introduction to the complex philosophical and ethical debates concerning criminal law.

The selection of materials in books of this kind is far harder than might be thought. The articles and books which might be the leading authorities on the topics are sometimes not readily susceptible to having short passages extracted. I have therefore included throughout the book suggestions for further reading. These will enable a reader who wishes to pursue a particular issue in further detail to do so.

The book seeks to set out the law as at 1 December 2005

Jonathan Herring
Exeter College

OUTLINE TABLE OF CONTENTS

1	An introduction to criminal law	1
2	*Actus reus*: the conduct element	85
3	*Mens rea*: the mental element	146
4	Strict liability	223
5	Homicide	245
6	Non-fatal non-sexual offences against the person	336
7	Sexual offences	426
8	Theft, handling, and robbery	501
9	Deception	570
10	Burglary and blackmail	621
11	Criminal damage	645
12	Defences	664
13	The criminal liability of corporations	789
14	Inchoate offences	816
15	Complicity	887

CONTENTS

Abbreviations	*xxvii*
Acknowledgements	*xxix*
Source Acknowledgements	*xxxi*
Table of Cases	*xxxv*
Table of Statutes	*lv*
Table of Statutory Instruments	*lxi*

1 | AN INTRODUCTION TO CRIMINAL LAW — 1

1 What is a crime?	1
2 The role of criminal law	6
3 The statistics of criminal behaviour	9
4 'Principles' of criminal law	10
4.1 The principle of legality	11
4.2 The principle of responsibility	11
4.3 The principle of minimal criminalization	12
4.4 The principle of proportionality	16
4.5 The principle of fair labelling	19
5 The 'need' for a Criminal Code	19
5.1 Arguments in favour of a Code	20
5.2 Disadvantages of the Code	21
6 What conduct should be criminal?	21
6.1 Autonomy	22
6.2 The harm principle	23
6.3 Practicality	33
7 Culpability	36
7.1 The subjectivism/objectivism debate	41
8 The victim in criminal law	49
9 The criminal process	52
10 Criminal law and the Human Rights Act 1998	55
10.1 The significance of the Human Rights Act 1998	55
10.2 The important Articles in the European Convention	57
10.3 Potential consequences of the HRA on the criminal law	60
11 Critical criminal law	69

12 Feminist legal thought   72

13 Punishment   77
    13.1 Consequentialist theories of punishment   77
    13.2 Non-consequentialist theories   79
    13.3 Mixed theories   81

14 Sentencing   81

2 ACTUS REUS: THE CONDUCT ELEMENT   85

I THE LAW   85

1 Distinguishing the component elements of a crime   85

2 The voluntary act 'requirement'   86
   2.1 Omissions   87
   2.2 Situational offences   100
   2.3 Liability for the acts of other people   101

3 Causation   101
   3.1 Factual or 'but for' causation   102
   3.2 The key test for legal causation   103
   3.3 Acts of third parties breaking the chain of causation   104
   3.4 Omissions of third parties breaking the chain of causation   111
   3.5 Cases which do not fit into the traditional analysis   111
   3.6 Acts of the victim breaking the chain   115
   3.7 The 'thin skull' rule   118
   3.8 A natural event ('Acts of God')   119
   3.9 Intended results   119

II ACTUS REUS: THEORY   120

4 Classification of defences   120

5 The need for a voluntary act   121
   5.1 Why might the law have a voluntary act requirement?   122
   5.2 What is the 'voluntary act requirement'?   122

6 Omissions   126
   6.1 Should the criminal law punish omissions?   126

7 Causation: should consequences matter?   132
   7.1 Arguments against holding people responsible for the consequences of their
        actions   132
   7.2 Arguments that consequences do matter   133

8 Seeking a coherent approach to causation   135
   8.1 'Causal minimalism'   136
   8.2 Hart and Honoré   136

8.3 Reasonable forseeability 137

8.4 Natural consequences 140

8.5 Narrowness of causation approach 142

3 | *MENS REA*: THE MENTAL ELEMENT 146

I THE LAW 146

1 The meaning of *mens rea* 146

2 Intention 147

2.1 The core meaning of intention 147

2.2 Borderline cases of intention 150

2.3 Intoxication and intent 156

3 Recklessness 156

3.1 *Cunningham* recklessness 156

3.2 *Caldwell* recklessness 159

4 Negligence 169

5 Gross negligence 170

6 Distinguishing between intention, recklessness, and negligence 170

7 Intoxication 171

7.1 Involuntary and voluntary intoxication 171

7.2 Offences of basic and specific intent 172

7.3 Stating the present law 173

8 Knowledge and belief 174

9 Transferred *mens rea* 175

10 Coincidence of *actus reus* and *mens rea* 176

10.1 'Exceptions' to the coincidence requirement 177

II *MENS REA* THEORY 181

11 General discussion on *mens rea* 181

12 Choice/capacity character theory 183

13 Subjective/objective 184

14 Normal meaning 184

15 Intent 187

15.1 Distinguishing indirect intention and direct intention 187

15.2 Is intention an issue of fact or an issue of moral responsibility? 194

16 Recklessness 198

16.1 Subjective and objective forms of recklessness and inadvertence 198

16.2 An insufficient regard for the interests of others: Victor Tadros   199

16.3 Practical indifference: Anthony Duff   202

17 Negligence   204

17.1 Opposition to the use of negligence in criminal law   204

17.2 Support for the use of negligence in criminal law   205

18 Intoxication   207

18.1 Intoxication and crime   207

18.2 Alcoholism and drug dependency: illness or weakness?   208

18.3 Explaining the present law on intoxication   208

18.4 Alternatives to *Majewski*   210

19 Motive   213

19.1 Is motive relevant in the criminal law?   213

19.2 Arguments in favour of taking motive into account   214

19.3 Arguments against taking motives into account   215

20 The 'correspondence principle'   216

20.1 Which principle best reflects the law?   217

20.2 Which principle is most justifiable in theory?   217

21 Individualism and *mens rea*   220

4   STRICT LIABILITY   223

I THE LAW   223

1 What is a strict liability offence?   223

2 Which offences are strict liability?   224

3 When will a court not presume *mens rea*?   230

4 What *mens rea* will be presumed?   231

5 The Human Rights Act and strict liability offences   232

6 Common law defences and strict liability offences   232

7 Possession offences   232

II THE THEORY OF STRICT LIABILITY OFFENCES   234

8 The arguments for and against strict liability   234

8.1 Arguments for strict liability offences   235

8.2 Arguments against strict liability offences   236

8.3 Analysing the arguments   239

5 HOMICIDE 245

I THE LAW 245

1 General 245

2 Murder 245
2.1 *Actus reus* 245
2.2 *Mens rea* 247

3 Manslaughter: an introduction 248

4 Provocation 249
4.1 The defendant was provoked to lose his self-control and kill 250
4.2 Would a reasonable person have acted as the defendant did? 254

5 Diminished responsibility 265
5.1 'Abnormality of mind' 267
5.2 The cause of the abnormality of mind 269
5.3 Substantial impairment of responsibility 269
5.4 Diminished responsibility and intoxication 270

6 Suicide pact 272

7 Mercy killing and euthanasia 273

8 Infanticide 274

9 Constructive manslaughter 274
9.1 An unlawful act 277
9.2 Dangerous act 278
9.3 Causation 279

10 Gross negligence manslaughter 280
10.1 A duty 286
10.2 A breach of a duty 287
10.3 Causing the death 287
10.4 Gross negligence 287

11 Subjective reckless manslaughter 288

12 Protecting life on the roads 288
12.1 Causing death by dangerous driving 288
12.2 Causing death by careless driving when under the influence of drink or drugs 289
12.3 Manslaughter and driving 290

13 Causing or allowing the death of a child or vulnerable adult 290

II THEORETICAL ISSUES IN HOMICIDE LAW 291

14 Homicide: the statistics 291

15 The structure of homicide   292
    15.1 Creating a wide range of kinds of homicide   293
    15.2 Leaving distinctions to sentencing   293
    15.3 Distinguishing on the basis of the victims   293
    15.4 Labelling the method of killing used   294

16 The *actus reus* of homicide   294

17 Non-homicidal killings   294

18 The *mens rea* for murder   295
    18.1 The meaning of intention   295
    18.2 Is intention the appropriate *mens rea*?   295
    18.3 The fact that intention to cause grievous bodily harm is sufficient   296

19 Defining the *mens rea* for manslaughter   308

20 Provocation   313
    20.1 Theory   313
    20.2 The provocative act must be something said or done   316
    20.3 The reasonable person requirement   316
    20.4 The gendered nature of the defence   319
    20.5 The case for the abolition of the defence   321
    20.6 Reform of provocation   325

21 Diminished responsibility   328
    21.1 Diminished responsibility in practice   328
    21.2 The theoretical basis of the diminished responsibility defence   329
    21.3 Reform of diminished responsibility   334

6   NON-FATAL NON-SEXUAL OFFENCES AGAINST THE PERSON

                                                                                 336

I   THE LAW   336

1   Introduction   336

2   Assault and battery   337
    2.1 Assault   337
    2.2 Battery   343

3   Assault occasioning actual bodily harm   347

4   Malicious wounding   349

5   Wounding with intent   355

6   Mixing and matching the offences   357

7   Poisoning   357
    7.1 The meaning of 'poison' or 'noxious substance'   358

7.2 The meaning of 'administer'   360

7.3 The meaning of 'maliciously'   360

7.4 The meaning of 'endangerment of life' or 'cause grievous bodily harm'   361

7.5 The meaning of 'with intent to injure, aggrieve, or annoy'   361

8 Other assault crimes   362

9 Racially and religiously aggravated crimes   362

10 Protection from Harassment Act 1997   364

10.1 Section 1: harassment   364

10.2 Section 4 of the Protection from Harassment Act 1997   368

11 Threats offences   369

12 Transmitting disease   369

13 Consent and assault   376

13.1 To what offences against the person is consent a defence?   376

13.2 What is consent?   387

13.3 What if there is no consent but the defendant believes that there is consent?   390

II THEORETICAL ISSUES ON ASSAULTS   391

14 The true nature and extent of violent crime   391

15 The nature of an assault   396

16 Objections to and reform of the Offences Against the Person Act 1861   398

17 Proposed reforms to the Offences Against the Person Act   404

18 Consent   406

18.1 Defence or *actus reus*?   406

18.2 The dispute over *Brown*   407

19 Stalking   417

20 Transmitting disease and the criminal law   421

7 SEXUAL OFFENCES   426

I THE LAW ON SEXUAL OFFENCES   426

1 Rape   426

1.1 Who can commit rape?   427

1.2 Who can be the victim of rape?   428

1.3 What is penetration?   428

1.4 What is consent?   428

1.5 *Mens rea*: an intent to penetrate   445

1.6 *Mens rea*: the defendant does not reasonably believe that the victim consents   445

1.7 Intoxication and the law of rape   448

1.8 How the 2003 Act changed the law on rape   448
1.9 Assessment of the Sexual Offences Act 2003   448

2 Assault by penetration   454

3 Sexual assault   454

4 Causing sexual activity without consent   457

5 Preparatory offences   458

6 Sexual offences designed to protect children   458
   6.1 Offences which are versions of the general offences   458
   6.2 Offences designed specifically to protect children from sexual abuse   459
   6.3 Abuse of position of trust offences   460
   6.4 Familial child sex offences   461
   6.5 Child prostitution and child pornography   462

7 Offences against those with a mental disorder   463

8 Prostitution and trafficking   463

9 Incest   463

10 Miscellaneous offences   464

II THE THEORY OF SEXUAL OFFENCES   465

11 Background of sexual crimes   465

12 Statistics on rape   467

13 The nature of rape   469
    13.1 The historical explanation   469
    13.2 The autonomy explanation   469
    13.3 Rape as violence   469
    13.4 Rape as invasion of integrity   470
    13.5 Rape as moral injury   473
    13.6 The radical feminist explanation of rape   476

14 Consent and sexual activity   478
    14.1 What is consent: is it objective or subjective?   478
    14.2 What is consent: to waive or intend?   479
    14.3 What is consent: is a failure to voice opposition consent?   479
    14.4 Consent: what is the status of a mistaken consent?   483
    14.5 Consent and pressure   488
    14.6 Consent: intoxicated mistake   489

15 Mens rea for rape   490

16 The actus reus of rape   496

8 | THEFT, HANDLING, AND ROBBERY   501

I THE LAW   501

1 Theft   501
   1.1 Property   502
   1.2 Belonging to another   507
   1.3 Appropriation   511
   1.4 Intention permanently to deprive   523
   1.5 Dishonesty   529

2 Robbery   534

3 Assault with intent to rob   536

4 Handling stolen goods   536
   4.1 It must be shown that the goods have been already stolen   538
   4.2 It must be shown that the defendant handled the property   538
   4.3 It must be shown that the defendant knew or believed that the goods were stolen   541
   4.4 The defendant was dishonest   541

5 Money laundering offences   541

II THEFT AND THEORY   542

6 Introduction to property offences   542
   6.1 In what way do property offences harm victims?   542
   6.2 Structure of property offences   545
   6.3 The civil law/criminal law interface   546
   6.4 Theft: the statistics   548
   6.5 What is property?   549

7 The debate over *Gomez*   550
   7.1 The case for *Gomez*   550
   7.2 The case against *Gomez*   552

8 The *Hinks* debate   555
   8.1 The arguments against *Hinks*   555

9 Temporary appropriation   560

10 Dishonesty   562

11 Robberies   567

9 | DECEPTION   570

I THE LAW ON DECEPTION   570

1 What is a deception?   570

2 Obtaining property by deception 576
2.1 The elements of the offence 577
2.2 Distinguishing between obtaining property by deception and theft 581

3 Obtaining a money transfer 581

4 Obtaining a pecuniary advantage by deception 582
4.1 Deception 582
4.2 Obtaining 582
4.3 A pecuniary advantage 582

5 Obtaining services by deception 583

6 Section 2 of the Theft Act 1978: evasion of a liability by deception 585
6.1 Distinguishing between the offences in section 2 586
6.2 Section 2(1)(a) 587
6.3 Section 2(1)(b) 587
6.4 Section 2(1)(c) 588

7 Making off without payment: section 3 of the Theft Act 1978 589
7.1 Making off from the place where payment was expected 590
7.2 Goods supplied or services done 591
7.3 Without having paid as required or expected 591
7.4 Dishonesty 592
7.5 Knowing that payment on the spot is required or expected of him 592
7.6 Intent to avoid payment 592

8 Cheques, credit cards, and credit balances 595

II THE THEORY OF DECEPTION OFFENCES 606

9 Deception offences in practice 606

10 What is a deception? 606

11 What is wrong with a deceit? 608

12 Deception offences and civil law 612

13 Standards of honesty among the general public 612

14 Reform of the present law on fraud and deception offences 614

10 BURGLARY AND BLACKMAIL 621

I THE LAW 621

1 Burglary 621
1.1 Building or part of a building 622
1.2 Entry 622
1.3 Trespasser 623
1.4 The *mens rea* for burglary 627

2 Aggravated burglary 628

3 Trespass with intent to commit a sexual offence 629

4 Blackmail 629
4.1 A demand 630
4.2 With a view to a gain or loss 630
4.3 Menaces 631
4.4 The demand must be unwarranted 633

II BURGLARY AND BLACKMAIL: THEORY 635

5 Burglary: theory 635
5.1 Burglary in practice 635
5.2 Why is burglary an offence? 635

6 Blackmail theory 639
6.1 The incidence of blackmail 639
6.2 Why is blackmail a crime? 639

11 CRIMINAL DAMAGE 645

I THE LAW ON CRIMINAL DAMAGE 645

1 Basic criminal damage 645
1.1 Damage 646
1.2 Property 647
1.3 Belonging to another 647
1.4 *Mens rea* 648
1.5 Defences 648

2 Arson 651

3 Aggravated criminal damage 652
3.1 Defences 653

4 Racially aggravated criminal damage 654

5 Computer crime: Computer Misuse Act 1990 654
5.1 Section 1: unauthorized access to computer material 655
5.2 Section 2: unauthorized access with intent 656
5.3 Section 3: unauthorized modification of computer material 656

II THEORETICAL ISSUES ON CRIMINAL DAMAGE 657

6 Criminal damage theory 657
6.1 Statistics 657
6.2 What is special about damaging property 657
6.3 Should it be an offence to damage your own property? 658

6.4 The definition of damage 658

6.5 The justification for aggravated criminal damage 659

7 The theory of computer crimes 661

12 DEFENCES 664

I THE LAW 664

1 Private defence and the prevention of crime 665

1.1 The legal source of the defence 665

1.2 To what crimes is private defence a defence? 666

1.3 What needs to be shown to establish the defence? 666

1.4 What about defendants who think they are being attacked but are not? 672

1.5 Self-induced private defences 672

1.6 Excessive use of force 672

1.7 Has the Human Rights Act 1998 changed the law? 673

2 Necessity 675

2.1 The meaning of necessity 675

2.2 Cases denying the existence of a general defence of necessity 675

2.3 The limited defence of necessity at common law 676

2.4 Implied recognition of necessity 682

2.5 Duress of circumstances 683

3 Chastisement 684

4 Consent 685

5 Duress 685

5.1 Terminology 685

5.2 To what crimes is duress a defence? 685

5.3 What are the elements of the defence of duress? 687

6 Coercion 704

7 Entrapment 705

8 Superior orders 706

9 Automatism 706

9.1 A complete loss of voluntary control 706

9.2 An external factor 709

9.3 The defendant was not at fault in causing the condition 710

10 Insanity 710

10.1 Insanity at the time of the alleged offence 711

10.2 A claim that the defendant was insane at the time of the trial 717

11 Diminished responsibility 721

12 Provocation 721

13 Children   721
   13.1 Children below the age of 10   721
   13.2 A child aged 10 to 14   722

14 Intoxication   722

15 Mistake   726
   15.1 A mistake which may negate *mens rea*   726
   15.2 Mistakes and defences   727
   15.3 Mistakes of law   729

II THE THEORY OF DEFENCES   730

16 Defining defences   730
   16.1 The traditional approach   730
   16.2 Alternatives to the traditional classification   731
   16.3 Does any of this matter?   731

17 Justifications and excuses   732
   17.1 Justifications   734
   17.2 Excuses   737
   17.3 Does the distinction between justifications and excuses really matter?   741
   17.4 Should justifications be objective and excuses subjective?   742
   17.5 Problems with justifications and excuses   746

18 Character, choice, and capacity   747
   18.1 The capacity theory   750
   18.2 The character theory   751

19 Determinism   754

20 The rejection of an overarching theory   757

21 Insanity   760
   21.1 Problems with the present law   760
   21.2 Reform of the present law   762

22 Private defence   765
   22.1 The moral basis of private defence   765
   22.2 Mistaken private defence   769

23 Duress   772

24 Necessity   776

25 Issues which fall between the gaps of the defences   779
   25.1 *Kingston*   780
   25.2 Battered women   782
   25.3 The Zeebrugge disaster   785

13 THE CRIMINAL LIABILITY OF CORPORATIONS   789

I   THE LAW ON CORPORATE CRIMINALITY   789

1   The difficulty in convicting companies of crimes   789

2   Vicarious liability   790

3   Identification   790

4   Reform of the law on corporate killing   796

5   Vicarious liability   797
    5.1   What is vicarious liability?   797
    5.2   Which crimes can be committed vicariously?   797
    5.3   For whose act can the defendant be vicariously liable?   798
    5.4   What *mens rea* must be proved?   798

II   THE THEORY OF CORPORATE LIABILITY   799

6   Theoretical issues in corporate liability   799
    6.1   The reality of corporate crime   799
    6.2   The clamour for corporate liability   799
    6.3   Should a company be guilty of a crime?   800
    6.4   If there is to be corporate crime, what form should it take?   810

14 INCHOATE OFFENCES   816

I   THE LAW ON INCHOATE OFFENCES   816

1   Inchoate offences   816

2   Attempt   817
    2.1   *Mens rea*   817
    2.2   *Actus reus*   823
    2.3   Impossible attempts   827
    2.4   Attempts and abandonment   833

3   Incitement   834
    3.1   The nature of the offence of incitement   834
    3.2   What is the *actus reus* of incitement?   838
    3.3   What must be incited?   839
    3.4   When does the offence take place?   840
    3.5   The *mens rea* for incitement   840
    3.6   Incitement and impossibility   842

4   Conspiracy   843
    4.1   The nature of conspiracy   843

4.2 Statutory conspiracies   844
4.3 Impossibility and statutory conspiracies   853
4.4 Common law conspiracies   854
4.5 Impossibility and common law offences   858

II THEORY   858

5 Inchoate offences   858

6 The theory of criminal attempts   861
   6.1 Why do we punish attempts?   861
   6.2 'The problem of moral luck'   862
   6.3 *Actus reus* of attempt   869
   6.4 *Mens rea* for attempt   874
   6.5 Impossible attempts   877

7 Conspiracy theory   880

15 COMPLICITY   887

I THE LAW OF COMPLICITY   887

1 Principals and accomplices   887
   1.1 Who is the principal?   888
   1.2 'Innocent agency'   889

2 Complicity: the *actus reus*   890
   2.1 Aiding   892
   2.2 Abetting   892
   2.3 Counselling   892
   2.4 Procuring   894
   2.5 Joint enterprise   895
   2.6 Time issues   895
   2.7 Omissions and accomplice liability   896

3 *Mens rea*   900
   3.1 *Mens rea* in cases of aiding, abetting, counselling, and procuring   900
   3.2 *Mens rea* in cases of joint enterprise   904
   3.3 Is there a special rule for procuring?   915
   3.4 Is there a special rule for offences of strict liability?   915
   3.5 The effect of provocation on accessories   915
   3.6 The selling of dangerous items   916

4 Secondary participation and inchoate offences   917

5 Conviction of secondary party and acquittal of principal   917

6 Can a secondary party ever be guilty of a greater offence than the
   principal?   918

7	Withdrawal by a secondary party	919
8	Accessories and victims	922
9	Assistance after offence	923

II ACCESSORIES AND THEORY — 923

10	General theories of accessorial liability	923
	10.1 Derivative theory of accessorial liability	924
	10.2 Causation and accomplice liability	928
	10.3 Inchoate model	934
11	Theories of accessorial *mens rea*	937
	11.1 Purpose	937
	11.2 Recklessness	939
	11.3 The accomplice's *mens rea* should be the same as that required for the principal	939
12	The theory of joint enterprise	941
13	*Actus reus* issues	942
14	Withdrawal	943

Bibliography	947
Index	1007

ABBREVIATIONS

AC	Appeal Cases
ALJR	Australian Law Journal Reports
All ER	All England Reports
ASBO	Anti-social behaviour order
BCS	British Crime Survey
BHRC	Butterworths Human Rights Cases
BMLR	Butterworths Medico-Legal Reports
BWS	Battered Women's Syndrome
C & P	Craig & Phillips
CA	Court of Appeal
CAR	Commonwealth Arbitration Reports (Aust.)
CCA	Criminal Court of Appeal
CCR	Crown Cases Reserved
CLR	Commonwealth Law Reports (Aust.)
CPS	Crown Prosecution Service
Cr App R	Criminal Appeal Reports
Crim LR	Criminal Law Review
D & B	Dearsley & Bell
DC	Divisional Court
DLR	Dominion Law Reports (Can.)
DPP	Director of Public Prosecutions
ECHR	European Convention on Human Rights
ECtHR	European Court of Human Rights
EHRR	European Human Rights Reports
ER	English Reports
EWCA	England and Wales Court of Appeal
EWHC	England and Wales High Court
FCR	Family Court Reporter
FD	Family Division
GM	Generically Modified
HL	House of Lords
HRA	Human Rights Act 1998
HRLR	Human Rights Law Reports
JP	Justice of the Peace Reports
KB	King's Bench
LR	Law Reports (New South Wales)
LT	Law Times Reports
NI	Northern Ireland Law Reports
NZLR	New Zealand Law Reports

P & CR	Property, Planning & Compensation Reports
PC	Privy Council
QB	Queen's Bench
QBD	Queen's Bench Division
RTR	Road Traffic Reports
SCR	Supreme Court Reports (Can.)
TLR	Times Law Reports
UKHL	United Kingdom House of Lords
UKPC	United Kingdom Privy Council
VLR	Victorian Law Reports (Aust.)
WLR	Weekly Law Reports

ACKNOWLEDGEMENTS

I am very grateful to many colleagues who have offered intellectual and practical support in the writing of this book. I am particularly grateful to several anonymous reviewers who with great care provided comments on the first edition. I have also greatly benefited from conversations with the following who have (sometimes unknowingly) assisted in the writing of the book: Andrew Ashworth, Alan Bogg, John Cartwright, John Eekelaar, and Sandra Fredman. The many students to whom I have taught criminal law have greatly influenced this book by their constant questioning of the accepted view on a topic and their insistence on no-nonsense answers. I also owe a great debt, as do countless other students, to Roy Stuart who as my tutor introduced me to the study of criminal law. The team at Oxford University Press have been excellent in their advice, assistance, and attention to detail. Above all I am grateful to my wife, Kirsten Johnson, and children, Laurel, Joanna, and Darcy, for their encouragement, love, and laughter.

Jonathan Herring
Exeter College

SOURCE ACKNOWLEDGEMENTS

Grateful acknowledgement is made to all the authors and publishers of copyright material which appears in this book, and in particular to the following for permission to reprint material from the sources indicated:

Extracts from *Law Commission Reports* (LCR) 177, 237, & 276; *House of Lords Reports* (UKHL) 10, 22, 37, & 41; P Roberts: Consultation paper 177; and Home Office reports are Crown copyright material and are reproduced under Class Licence Number C01P0000148 with the permission of the Controller of HMSO and the Queen's Printer for Scotland.

FRED J ABBATE: extract from 'The Conspiracy Doctrine: A Critique' in *Philosophy and Public Affairs*, Vol. 11, Spring 1974.

PETER ARENELLA: extracts from 'Convicting the Morally Blameless: Reassessing the Relationship between Legal and Moral Accountability', 39 *UCLA Law Review* 1151 (1992).

ARIZONA LAW REVIEW, College of Law, University of Arizona: extracts from Douglas N Husak: 'The Nature and Justifiability of Nonconsummate Offenses', 37 *Arizona Law Review* 151 (1995), copyright © 1995 by the Arizona Board of Regents.

ASHGATE PUBLISHING: extract from Joan MacGregor: *Is it Rape?* (Ashgate, 2005), copyright © Joan MacGregor 2005.

BLACKWELL PUBLISHING: extracts from *Modern Law Review*: Nicola Lacey: 'A Clear Concept of Intention: Elusive or Illusory?', 56 *MLR* 621 (1993); Barry Mitchell: 'Multiple Wrongdoing and Offence Structure: A Plea for Consistency and Fair Labelling', 64 *MLR* 394 (2001); and Stephen Shute and Jeremy Horder: 'Thieving and Deceiving: What is the Difference?', MLR 548 (1993); and extracts from *Legal Studies*: Alan L Bogg and John Stanton-Ife: 'Theft as exploitation', *Legal Studies* (2003).

BUFFALO CRIMINAL LAW REVIEW, SUNY Buffalo Law School: extracts from *Buffalo Criminal Law Review*: A Duff: 'Harms and Wrongs', 5 *BCLR* 13 (2001), copyright © Buffalo Criminal Law Review 2001; V Norse: 'Heart and Minds: Understanding the New Culpability', 8 *BCLR* 361 (2002), copyright © Buffalo Criminal Law Review 2002; and A P Simester: 'On the So-called Requirement for Voluntary Action', 1 *BCLR* 403 (1998), copyright © Buffalo Criminal Law Review 1998.

CAMBRIDGE LAW JOURNAL and the authors: extracts from *Cambridge Law Journal*: John Gardner: 'Rationality and the Rule of Law in Offences Against Person', *CLJ* 502 (1994); G R Sullivan: 'The Attribution of Culpability to Limited Companies', 55 *CLJ* 515 (1996); and Glanville Williams: 'Oblique Intention' *CLJ* 417 (1987).

CAMBRIDGE UNIVERSITY PRESS and the author: extract from John Keown: *Euthanasia, Ethics and Public Policy* (CUP, 2002).

THE CANADIAN JOURNAL OF LAW & JURISPRUDENCE, Faculty of Law, The University of Western Ontario: extracts from *The Canadian Journal of Law & Jurisprudence*: Jeremy Horder: 'Self-Defence, Necessity and Duress: Understanding the Relationship', 11 *CJLJ* 143 (1998); Dennis Klimchuck: 'Causation, Thin Skulls and Equality', 11 *CJLJ* 115 (1998); Nicola Lacey: 'Unspeakable Subjects, Impossible Rights: Sexuality, Integrity and Criminal Law', 11 *CJLJ* 47 (1998); and S E Marshall and R A Duff: 'Criminalization and Sharing Wrongs', 11 *CJLJ* 7 (1998).

CAVENDISH PUBLISHING LTD: extracts from D Nicolson and L Bibbings (eds) *Feminist Perspectives in Criminal Law* (Cavendish Press, 1996): Nicola Lacey: 'General Principles of Criminal Law? A Feminist View', and Aileen McColgan: 'General Defences'.

CORNELL LAW REVIEW, Cornell Law School: extract from Laurie L Levenson: 'Good Faith Defenses: Reshaping Strict Liability Crimes', 78 *Cornell Law Review* 401 (1993).

GEORGE FLETCHER: extract from G P Fletcher: *Rethinking Criminal Law* (Little Brown, 1978).

HART PUBLISHING: extracts from A P Simester and G Sullivan: *Criminal Law Theory and Doctrine* (Hart, 2000); William Wilson: *Central Issues in Criminal Theory* (Hart, 2002); and extract from J Horder: 'Between Provocation and Diminished Responsibility', *Kings College Law Journal* 143 (1999).

HASTINGS COLLEGE OF LAW, University of California, O'Brien Center for Scholarly Publications: extracts from Joshua Dressler: 'Reassessing the Theoretical Underpinnings of Accomplice Liability: New Solutions to an Old Problem', 37:1 *Hastings Law Journal* 91 (September 1985), © 1985 by University of California, Hastings College of Law; and Stuart P Green: 'Lying, Misleading, and Falsely Denying: How Moral Concepts Inform the Law of Perjury, Fraud and False Statements', 53:1 *Hastings Law Journal* 157 (November 2001), © 2001 by University of California, Hastings College of Law.

INCORPORATED COUNCIL OF LAW REPORTING: extracts from the *Queen's Bench Reports* (QB), the *Appeal Court Reports* (AC) and *Family Court Reports* (Fam).

KLUWER ACADEMIC PUBLISHERS and the authors: extracts from Stephen Schullhofer: 'Taking Sexual Autonomy Seriously: Rape Law and Beyond' 11 *Law and Philosophy* 35 (1992); and Alan Wertheimer: 'Intoxicated Consent to Sexual Relations' 20:4 *Law and Philosophy* 373 (2001).

LEXISNEXIS UK: extract from J Spencer: 'Trying to help another person commit a crime' in *Criminal Law: Essays in Honour of J C Smith* (Butterworths, 1987); and from *All England Law Reports* (All ER) and *England & Wales Court of Appeal: Criminal* (EWCA Crim).

LOYOLA LAW SCHOOL: extract from Samuel H Pillsbury: 'Crimes Against the Heart: Recognizing the Wrongs of Forced Sex', 35 *Loyola of Los Angeles Law Review* 845 (2002).

MICHAEL MOORE: extracts from Michael Moore: 'The Moral Worth of Retribution' in A von Hirsch and Andrew Ashworth (eds): *Principled Sentencing* (Hart, 1998).

NEWS INTERNATIONAL SYNDICATION: article 'Widow gave poisoned sherry to man who rejected her', *The Times*, 4 April 2003, copyright © The Times 2003.

NORTHWESTERN UNIVERSITY SCHOOL OF LAW: extract from Sanford Kadish: 'Reckless Complicity', 87:2 *Journal of Criminal Law and Criminology* 369 (1997).

OXFORD UNIVERSITY PRESS: extracts from Andrew Ashworth: *Principles of Criminal Law* (4e, OUP, 2003); Anthony Duff: *Criminal Attempts* (OUP, 1996); H L A Hart: *Punishment and Responsibility: Essays in the Philosophy of Law* (OUP, 1968); H L A Hart and Tony Honoré: *Causation in the Law* (2e, OUP, 1985); A von Hirsch: *Censure and Sanctions* (OUP, 1993); J Horder: *Excusing Crime* (OUP, 2003); Michael Moore: *Act and Crime* (OUP, 1993); Michael Moore: *Placing Blame* (OUP, 1997); V Tadros: *Criminal Responsibility* (OUP, 2005); Nigel Walker: *Crime and Criminology* (OUP, 1987); Celia Wells: *Corporations and Criminal Responsibility* (2e, OUP, 2001); and Lucia Zedner: *Criminal Justice* (OUP, 2005); and extracts from Nicola Lacey: 'Partial Defences to Homicide', and William Wilson: 'Murder and the Structure of Homicide', in A Ashworth and B Mitchell (eds.): *Rethinking English Homicide Law* (OUP, 2001); A Simester and G Sullivan: 'The Nature and Rational of Property', and V Tadros: 'The Distinctiveness of Domestic Abuse', in R A Duff and S P Green (eds): *Defining Crimes: Essays on the Special Part of*

Criminal Law (OUP, 2005); Andrew Ashworth: 'Belief, Intent and Criminal Liability', in J Eekelaar and J Bell: *Oxford Essays in Jurisprudence* (OUP, 1987); John Gardner and Stephen Shute: 'The Wrongness of Rape', and Nicola Lacey: 'Philosophical Foundations of the Common Law: Social not Metaphysical', in J Horder (ed): *Oxford Essays in Jurisprudence* (4th Series, OUP, 2000); Rob Allen: 'Alternatives to Prosecution', Nicola Lacey: 'Legal Constructions of Crime', and Lucia Zedner: 'Victims', in M Maguire, R Morgan and R Reiner (eds): *The Oxford Handbook of Criminology* (OUP, 2002); R A Duff: 'Rule-violations and Wrongdoings', and V Tadros: 'Recklessness and the Duty to take Care', in S Shute and A Simester (eds): *Criminal Law Theory* (OUP, 2002); A Simester: 'Is Strict Liability Always Wrong?' in A Simester (ed): *Appraising Strict Liability* (OUP, 2005); R A Duff: 'Subjectivism, Objectivism, and Criminal Attempts', J Gardner: 'Justifications and Reasons', Grant Lamond: 'Coercion, Threats, and Blackmail', and G R Sullivan: 'Making Excuses', in A Simester and A Smith (eds): *Harm and Culpability* (OUP, 1996); also extracts from *Oxford Journal of Legal Studies*: Simon Gardner: 'Importance of Majewski', 26 *OJLS* 279 (1994) and 'Necessities Newest Inventions', *OJLS* (1991) 125; A P Simester: 'Mistakes in Defences', *OJLS* (1992) 295; G R Sullivan: 'Is Criminal Law Possible?', *OJLS* (2002) 747; and Victor Tadros: 'The Characters of Excuses', 21 *OJLS* (2001) 495.

Oxford University Press Australia: extract from Rob White and Fiona Haines: *Crime and Criminology* (2e, OUP, 2000), copyright © Oxford University Press, www.oup.com.au.

Oxford University Press, Inc: extract from George Fletcher: *Basic Concepts of Criminal Law* (OUP, 1998), copyright © 1998 by George Fletcher.

Pax Forlag: extracts from N Jareborg: 'What kind of Criminal Law do we want?' in A Snare: *Beware of Punishment* (Pax Forlag, 1995).

Pearson Education Ltd: extract from William Wilson: *Criminal Law* (Longman, 2003).

Routledge/Taylor & Francis Books, Inc: extract from Elizabeth Schneider: 'The Violence of Privacy' in Martha Albertson Fineman and R Mykitiuk (eds.): *The Public Nature of Private Violence* (Routledge, 1994).

Santa Clara Law Review, Santa Clara University School of Law: extract from Joshua Dressler: 'Some Brief Thoughts (Mostly Negative) about 'Bad Samaritan' Laws', 40 *Santa Clara Law Review* 971 (2000).

Southern California Law Review, The Law School, University of Southern California: extract from Grace E Mueller: 'The *Mens Rea* of Accomplice Liability', 61 *Southern California Law Review* 2169 (1998).

Sweet & Maxwell Ltd: extract from C M V Clarkson: *Understanding Criminal Law* (3e, Sweet & Maxwell, 2001); extracts from *Criminal Appeal Reports*; extracts from *Law Quarterly Review*: Andrew Ashworth: 'Is Criminal Law a Lost Cause?', 116 *LQR* 225 (2000), and 'The Scope of Criminal Liability for Omissions', 105 *LQR* 424 (1989); Tony Honoré: 'Responsibility and Luck', 104 *LQR* 530 (1988); and Simon Gardner: 'Appropriation in Theft: The Last Word?', 109 *LQR* 194; and extracts from *Criminal Law Review*: Andrew Ashworth: 'Robbery Re-assessed', *Crim LR* 851 (2002); Andrew Ashworth and Jennifer Temkin: 'The Sexual Offences Act 2003: (1) Rape, Sexual Acts and the Problems of Consent', *Crim LR* 328 (2004); Simon Bronitt: 'Spreading Disease and the Criminal Law'. *Crim LR* 21 (1994); I Dennis: 'Reverse Onuses and the Presumption of Innocence: In Search of Principle', *Crim LR* 901 (2005); D Elliot: 'Endangering Life by Destroying or Damaging Property', *Crim LR* 382 (1997); Emily Finch: 'Stalking the Perfect Stalking Law: An Evaluation of the Efficacy of the Protection from Harassment Act 1997', *Crim LR* 703 (2002); S Gardner: 'Direct Action and the Defence of Necessity', *Crim LR* 371 (2005); E Griew: 'Dishonesty: The Objections to Feely and Ghosh', *Crim LR* 341 (1985); R Heaton: 'Cheques and Balances', *Crim LR* 752 (2005); J Herring: 'Mistaken Sex', *Crim LR* 511 (2005); Jeremy Horder: 'How Culpability Can, and Cannot, be Denied in Under-Age Sex Crimes', *Crim*

LR 15 (2001), and 'Reconsidering Psychic Assault', *Crim LR* 392 (1998); F Leverick: 'Is English Self-defence Law Incompatible with Article 2 of the ECHR?', *Crim LR* 347 (2002); D Ormerod: 'Drug Suppliers as Manslaughterers (Again)',*Crim LR* 819 (2005); A Pedain: 'Intention and the Terrorist Example', *Crim LR* 579 (2003); S Shute: 'The Second Law Commission Consultation Paper on Consent (1) Something Old, Something Borrowed: Three Aspects of the Project', *Crim LR* 684 (1996), and 'Appropriation and the Law of Theft', *Crim LR* 445 (2002); K J M Smith: 'Withdrawal in Complicity: A Restatement of Principles', *Crim LR* 769 (2001); M Weait: 'Knowledge, Autonomy and Consent: R v Konzani', *Crim LR* 763 (2005); Glanville Williams: 'Temporary Appropriation should be Theft', *Crim LR* 129 (1981); and William Wilson: 'The Structure of Criminal Defences', *Crim LR* 108 (2005).

SYDNEY LAW REVIEW, University of Sydney Faculty of Law: extracts from Neil McCormick: 'What is Wrong with Deceit?', *Sydney Law Review* 5 (1983).

UNIVERSITY OF CHICAGO PRESS: extracts from C A Mackinnon: 'Feminism, Marxism, Method and the State: Toward Feminist Jurisprudence', 8 *Signs* 635 (1983).

UNIVERSITY OF MICHIGAN LAW SCHOOL: extracts from M A Gomez: 'The writing on our walls: Finding solutions through distinguishing graffiti art from graffiti vandalism', 26 *University of Michigan Law Journal of Law Reform* 633 (1993).

UNIVERSITY OF MINNESOTA LAW SCHOOL and the authors: extracts from Beverley Balos and Mary Louise Fellows: 'Guilty of the Crime of Trust: Nonstranger Rape', 75 *Minnesota Law Review* 599 (1991); and Joshua Dressler: 'Why Keep the Provocation Defense?: Some Reflections on a Difficult Subject', 86 *Minnesota Law Review* 959 (2002).

UNIVERSITY OF PENNSYLVANIA LAW SCHOOL: extracts from Neal Kumar Katyal: 'Criminal Law in Cyberspace', 149 *University of Pennsylvania Law Review* 1003 (2001); and Kimberly Kessler: 'The Role of Luck in the Criminal Law', 142 *University of Pennsylvania Law Review* 2183 (1994).

VIRGINIA LAW REVIEW ASSOCIATION via Copyright Clearance Center: extracts from *Virginia Law Review*: S Wallerstein: 'Justifying the Right to Self-Defense: A Theory of Forced Circumstances', 91 VLR (2005) 999.

WILLAN PUBLISHING: extract from E Burney: *Making People Behave* (Willan, 2005).

THE YALE LAW JOURNAL COMPANY and WILLIAM S HEIN COMPANY: extracts from Neal Kumar Katyal: 'Conspiracy Theory', 112 *Yale Law Journal* 101 (2003); and Victoria Nourse: 'Passions' Progress: Modern Law Reform and the Provocation Defense', 106 *Yale Law Journal* 1331(1997).

Every effort has been made to trace and contact copyright holders prior to publication but this has not been possible in every case. If notified, the publisher will undertake to rectify any errors or omissions at the earliest opportunity. **An updated version of this Acknowledgments page is available on the book's accompanying Online Resource Centre (www.oxfordtextbooks.co.uk/ orc/herringcriminal2e/).**

TABLE OF CASES

Where extracts from cases are reproduced, the cases and relevant page numbers are shown in **bold**.

A v United Kingdom [1998] 2 FLR 959; [1998] 3 FCR 597; (1999) 27 EHRR 611, ECHR . . . 56, 684

A, re [1992] 3 Med LR 303 . . . 246

A (A Juvenile) v R [1978] Crim LR 689 . . . 646

A (Children) (Conjoined Twins: Medical Treatment) (No.1), re; sub nom. A (Children) (Conjoined Twins: Surgical Separation), re [2001] Fam 147; [2001] 2 WLR 480; [2000] 4 All ER 961 (CA) . . . 21, 674, 675, 676, **677–682**, 777

A (FC) v Secretary of State for the Home Department [2004] UKHL 56 . . . 778

Abbott v R [1977] AC 755; [1976] 3 WLR 462; [1976] 3 All ER 140; (1976) 63 Cr App R 241 (PC) (Trin) . . . 686

Adams v Camfoni [1929] 1 KB 95 (KBD) . . . 798

Adams v The Queen [1995] 1 WLR 52 (PC) . . . 855

Adams (Bodkins) v Dunne [1978] RTR 281; [1978] Crim LR 365 . . . 213, 246

ADT v United Kingdom [2000] Crim LR 1009 . . . 465

Airedale NHS Trust v Bland [1993] AC 789; [1993] 2 WLR 316; [1993] 1 All ER 821 (HL) . . . **95–100**, 130, 273

Albert v Lavin [1982] AC 546; [1981] 3 WLR 955; [1981] 3 All ER 878; (1982) 74 Cr App R 150 . . . 770

Allen v Whitehead [1930] 1 KB 211 . . . 798

Alphacell Ltd v Woodward [1972] AC 824 (HL) . . . 231, 235, 790

Anderton v Ryan [1985] AC 560 (HL) . . . 830, 831, 832, 833, 878, 879

Andrews v DPP *sub nom* R v Andrews [1937] AC 576 (HL) . . . 277, 280, 282

Andronicou and Constantinou v Cyprus (25052/94) (1998) 25 EHRR 491; 3 BHRC 389; [1998] Crim LR 823, ECHR . . . 673

Applin v Race Relations Board [1975] AC 259; [1974] 2 WLR 541; [1974] 2 All ER 73; 72 LGR 479; 118 SJ 311 (HL) [1973] QB 815 (CA) . . . 838

Armhouse Lee Ltd v Chappell (1996) *The Times*, 7 August 1996; *The Independent*, 26 July 1996 (CA) . . . 857, 858

Arrowsmith v Jenkins [1963] 2 QB 561; [1963] 2 WLR 856; [1963] 2 All ER 210 . . . 190

Attorney-General v Able [1984] QB 795 (CA) . . . 891, 892, 911

Attorney-General for Jersey v Holley [2005] UKPC 23; [2005] 3 WLR 29; [2005] 3 All ER 371; [2005] 2 Cr App R 36 . . . **257–264**, 265

Attorney-General of Northern Ireland v Gallagher (Patrick) [1963] AC 349 (HL) . . . 173, 519

Attorney-General of Northern Ireland's Reference (No.1 of 1975), re [1977] AC 105 (HL) . . . 670, 671

Attorney-General of South Australia v Brown [1960] AC 432 . . . 725

Attorney-General's Reference (No.1 of 1974), re [1974] QB 744; [1974] 2 WLR 891; [1974] 2 All ER 899; (1974) 59 Cr App R 203 (CA) . . . 538

Attorney-General's Reference (No.1 of 1975), re [1975] QB 773; [1975] 3 WLR 11; [1975] 2 All ER 684 (CA) . . . 891, 892, 894, 901, 915, 943

Attorney-General's Reference (Nos.1 and 2 of 1979), re [1980] QB 180; [1979] 3 WLR 577; [1979] 3 All ER 143 (CA) . . . 628, 823

Attorney-General's Reference (No.4 of 1980), re [1981] 1 WLR 705 (CA) . . . 180

Attorney-General's Reference (No.6 of 1980), re [1981] QB 715; [1981] 1 WLR 705 (CA) . . . 380, 386, 389

Attorney-General's Reference (No.2 of 1982), re [1984] QB 624 (CA) . . . 515

Attorney-General's Reference (No.1 of 1983), [1985] QB 182 (CA) . . . 510

Attorney-General's Reference (No.2 of 1983), re [1984] QB 456 (CA) . . . 670

Attorney-General's Reference (No.1 of 1991), re [1993] QB 94 (CA) . . . 654

Attorney-General's Reference (No.1 of 1992), re [1993] 1 WLR 274; [1993] 2 All ER 190 (CA) . . . 817, 826

Attorney-General's Reference (No.2 of 1992), re [1994] QB 91; [1993] 3 WLR 982; [1993] 4 All ER 683; (1993) 97 Cr App R 429 (CA) . . . **706–709**

Attorney-General's Reference (No.3 of 1992), re [1994] 1 WLR 409; (1994) 98 Cr App R 383; [1994] RTR 122; [1994] Crim LR 348 (CA) . . . 653, 660, **819–821**, 822

Attorney-General's Reference (No.3 of 1994), re [1998] AC 245; [1997] 3 WLR 421; [1997] 3 All ER 936; [1998] 1 Cr App R 91; [1997]

Crim LR 829 (HL) . . . 176, 178, 248, **275–277,** 277, 279, 296

Attorney-General's Reference (No.3 of 1998), re [2000] QB 401 (CA) . . . 718

Attorney-General's Reference (No.2 of 1999), re [2000] QB 796; [2000] 3 WLR 195; [2000] 3 All ER 182; [2001] BCC 210; [2000] 2 BCLC 257; [2000] 2 Cr App R 207; [2000] IRLR 417; [2000] Crim LR 475 (CA) . . . 284, 288, **790–795**

Attorney-General's Reference (No.4 of 2002) [2005] 1 AC 264 . . . **63–67**

Attorney-General's Reference (Nos.4 and 7 of 2002), re [2002] EWCA Crim 127; [2002] 2 Cr App R (S) 77; [2002] Crim LR 333 (CA) . . . 78, 568

Attorney-General's Reference (No.3 of 2003) [2004] 2 Cr App R 367 . . . 168

Attorney-General's Reference (No.3 of 2004) [2005] EWCA Crim 1882 . . . 915

Attorney-General's Reference (No.4 of 2004) [2005] Crim LR 799 (CA) . . . 364

Atwal v Massey [1971] 3 All ER 881 . . . 541

Ayliffe v DPP [2005] 3 All ER 330 . . . 671

B (A Child) v DPP [1998] 4 All ER 265 (DC) . . . 227, 228

B (A Child) v DPP [2000] 2 AC 428; [2000] 2 WLR 452; [2000] 1 All ER 833; [2000] Crim LR 403 (HL) . . . 46, 47, 165, 182, **224–228,** 229, 230, 231, 726

B (Consent to Treatment: Capacity), re; *sub nom* B v NHS Hospital Trust; B (Adult: Refusal of Medical Treatment), re [2002] EWHC 429; [2002] 2 All ER 449 . . . 273

B and S v Leathley [1979] Crim LR 314 . . . 622

Bank of New South Wales v Piper [1897] AC 383 (PC) (Aus) . . . 225

Banks v State (1919) 211 SW 217 . . . 300

Barber v Superior Court of State of California 195 Cal Rptr 484 . . . 99

Barnfather v Islington LBC [2003] EWHC 418 (Admin); [2003] All ER (D) 89; [2003] ELR 263; [2003] ACD 57 (QBD) . . . 224, 230, 231, 232

Baron v Crown Prosecution Service CO/1569/00 (QBD) . . . 366, 420

Beatty v Gillbanks (1881–82) 9 QBD 308 (QBD) . . . 894

Beckford v R [1988] AC 130 (PC) . . . 246, 667, 670, 672, 726, 727, 769, 771, 772

Bedder v DPP [1954] 1 WLR 1119 (HL) . . . 255, 331

Bell v Lever Brothers Ltd [1932] AC 161 . . . 517

Bellinger v Bellinger [2003] UKHL 21 (HL) . . . 55

Belmont Finance Corporation Ltd v Williams Furniture Ltd [1979] Ch 250 (CA) . . . 515

Bently (1850) 4 Cox 406 . . . 356

Blake v Barnard (1840) 9 C & P 626; 173 ER 985 . . . 342

Blake v DPP [1993] Crim LR 586 (DC) . . . 648, 666

Blakely v DPP; Sutton v DPP [1991] RTR 405; [1991] Crim LR 763 (DC) . . . 911, 915

Boggeln v Williams [1978] 1 WLR 873 . . . 532

Bolam v Friern Hospital Management Committee [1957] 1 WLR 582 . . . 96

Bratty v Attorney-General of Northern Ireland [1963] AC 386 (HL) . . . 87, 708, 713, 714, 715, 716

Brock and Wyner [2001] 1 WLR 1159; [2001] 2 Cr App R 3 . . . 131

Broom v Crowther (1984) 148 JP 592 (DC) . . . 522

Broome v Perkins (1987) 85 Cr App R 321; [1987] RTR 321 . . . 708, 709, 710

Brutus v Cozens [1973] AC 854 (HL) . . . 184

Burrell v Harmer [1967] Crim LR 169 . . . 388

Bush v Commonwealth 78 Ky 268 (1880) (Kentucky Court of Appeals) . . . 111

C v DPP [1996] AC 1 . . . 795

C (A Minor) v Eisenhower *see* JJC (A Minor) v Eisenhower

C (Adult: Refusal of Treatment), re [1994] 1 WLR 290; [1994] 1 All ER 819; [1994] 1 FLR 31; [1994] 2 FCR 151 (FD) . . . 388, 441

Callow v Tillstone (1900) 83 LT 411; (1900) 64 JP 823 . . . 223, 911, 915, 939

Cambridge County Council v Associated Lead Mills Ltd [2005] EWHC Civ 1627 . . . 798

Canadian Dredge Co v The Queen (1985) 19 DLR 314 (Canada) . . . 791

Caurti v DPP [2001] EWHC Admin 867; [2002] Crim LR 131 (DC) . . . 368

Chamberlain v Lindon [1998] 1 WLR 1252 . . . 648, 649

Chan Wing-Siu v The Queen [1985] AC 168 . . . 905, 906, 907, 908

Chapman v DPP (1989) 89 Cr App R 190 (CA) . . . 671

Charles *see* Metropolitan Police Commissioner v Charles (Derek Michael)

Chief Constable of Avon and Somerset v Shimmen (1987) 84 Cr App R 7 . . . 200–201

Chiu-Cheung v The Queen; *sub nom* Yip Chiu-Cheung v The Queen [1995] 1 AC 111; [1994] 3 WLR 514; [1994] 2 All ER 924 (PC) . . . 706

Chorherr v Austria (A/266-B) (1994) 17 EHRR 358, ECHR . . . 61

Churchill (Victor George) (Senior) v Walton [1967] 2 AC 224 (HL) . . . 846

Cichon v DPP [1994] Crim LR 918 . . . 675, 683

Cole v Turner (1704) 6 Mod Rep 149; 90 ER 958 . . . 345

Collins v Wilcock [1984] 1 WLR 1172; [1984] 3 All ER 374; (1984) 79 Cr App R 229 . . . 343, **345–346**, 380, 388

Commissioner of Police for the Metropolis v Streeter (1980) 71 Cr App R 113 . . . 538

Commonwealth v Ashburn 331 A.2d 167 (Pa.1975) . . . 300

Coppen v Moore (No.2) [1898] 2 QB 306 (QBD) . . . 797

Corbyn v Saunders [1978] 2 All ER 697; [1978] 1 WLR 400 . . . 594

Corcoran v Anderton (1980) 71 Cr App R 104 . . . 535

Cordas v Peerless Transportation Co (1941) 27 NYS 2d 198 . . . 770

Cote v R [1986] 1 SCR 2 (Canada) . . . 856

Coward v Baddeley [1859] 4 H & N 478; 157 ER 927 . . . 346

Cox v Riley (1986) 83 Cr App R 54 (DC) . . . 646

CR v United Kingdom [1996] 1 FLR 434 (ECtHR) . . . 94, 427

Cundy v Le Cocq (1884) 13 QBD 207 . . . 230

Cunliffe v Goodman [1950] 2 KB 237 (CA) . . . 148

Customs and Excise Commissioners v City of London Magistrates Court [2000] 1 WLR 2020 . . . 720

Davey v Lee [1968] 1 QB 366 . . . 870

Davies v Flackett [1973] RTR 8 . . . 571

Director of Public Prosecutions *see* DPP

Dobson v North Tyneside Health Authority [1996] 4 All ER 474 . . . 506

Donoghue v Stevenson [1932] AC 562 . . . 360

Doodeward v Spence (1908) 6 CLR 406; 15 ALR 105; 9 SR (NSW) 107 . . . 506

DPP for Northern Ireland v Lynch *see* Lynch v DPP [1975]

DPP v A [2001] Crim LR 140 (DC) . . . 351

DPP v Andrews *see* Andrews v DPP *sub nom* R v Andrews [1937] AC 576 (HL)

DPP v Armstrong [2000] Crim LR 379 (QBD) . . . **834–838**, 841, 842, 843

DPP v Bayer [2004] Crim LR 663 . . . 666

DPP v Beard and Pagett [1920] AC 479 . . . 303

DPP v Bell [1992] RTR 335 . . . 688

DPP v Braun (Klaus Armstrong); *sub nom* DPP v Armstrong-Braun (1999) 163 JP 271; [1999] Crim LR 416 . . . 670

DPP v Camplin *see* R v Camplin (Paul); *sub nom* DPP v Camplin [1978] AC 705 (HL)

DPP v Collins [2005] Crim LR 794 . . . 341

DPP v Gomez (Edwin) [1993] AC 442; [1992] 3 WLR 1067; [1993] 1 All ER 1; (1993) 96 Cr App R 359; (1993) 157 JP 1; [1993] Crim LR 304 (HL) . . . **512–516**, 516, 517, 518, 519, 550, 551, 552, 555, 556, 557, 581, 605, 611

DPP v Harper; DPP v H [1997] 1 WLR 1406; (1997) 161 JP 697; [1998] RTR 200; (1998) 39

BMLR 91; (1997) 94(18) LSG 31; [1998] RTR 200; *The Times*, 2 May 1997 . . . 232, 715, 717

DPP v Hicks [2002] EWHC 1638; [2002] All ER (D) 285 (QBD) . . . 688

DPP v K [1990] 1 WLR 1067; [1990] 1 All ER 331 (DC) . . . 344, 399

DPP v K and B; *sub nom* DPP v K and C [1997] 1 Cr App R 36 . . . 427, 890, 918

DPP v Lavender (Melvyn) [1994] Crim LR 297 . . . 525, **526–527**

DPP v Little [1992] QB 645 (DC) . . . 347

DPP v McFarlane [2002] EWHC 485 (Admin Ct) . . . 364

DPP v Majewski; R v Majewski (Robert Stefan) [1977] AC 443; [1976] 2 WLR 623; [1976] 2 All ER 142 (HL) . . . 156, 161, 167, 172, 209, 210, 211, 212, 213, 906

DPP v Morgan (William Anthony); *sub nom* R v Morgan (William Anthony) [1976] AC 182 (HL) . . . 46, 165, 226, 447, 491, 726, 728, 769, 770

DPP v Newbury (Neil) [1977] AC 500 . . . 276

DPP v Nock [1978] AC 979; [1978] 3 WLR 57; [1978] 2 All ER 654 (HL) . . . 836, 842, 845, 858

DPP v Pal [2000] Crim LR 756 (DC) . . . 364

DPP v Ramsdale [2001] EWHC Admin 106 . . . 366, 420

DPP v Ray [1974] AC 370; [1973] 3 WLR 359; [1973] 3 All ER 131; (1974) 58 Cr App R 130 (CA) . . . 571, 572, **574–576**

DPP v Rogers [1998] Crim LR 202 (QBD) . . . 689

DPP v Santa-Bermudez [2003] EWHC 2908; [2004] Crim LR 417 . . . 344

DPP v SJ, PI, RC [2002] EWHC 291 . . . 526

DPP v Smith (Jim) [1961] AC 290 (HL) . . . 147, 247, 303, 350

DPP v Stonehouse [1978] AC 55 (HL) . . . 577

DPP v Taylor (Keith Richard); DPP v Little [1992] QB 645; 1 All ER 708 (CA) . . . 337

DPP v Woods [2002] EWHC 85 (Admin Ct) . . . 363

Drake v DPP (1994) 158 JP 828; [1994] RTR 411 . . . 646

Du Cros v Lambourne [1907] 1 KB 40 . . . 91, 896, 899

Edgington v Fitzmaurice (1885) 29 ChD 459 (CA) . . . 573

Edwards (alias David Christopher Murray) v The Queen [1973] AC 648 (PC) . . . 254

Eldredge v US (1932) 62 F 2d 449 (US) . . . 922

Elliott v C (A Minor) [1983] 1 WLR 939; [1983] 2 All ER 1005; (1983) 77 Cr App R 103 (DC) . . . 160, 162, 163, 167, 168, 170, 183, 199

Ellis v DPP (No.1) [2001] EWHC Admin 362 . . . 656

Empress Car Co (Abertillery) Ltd v National Rivers Authority [1998] *see* Environmental Agency (formerly National Rivers Authority) v Empress Car Co (Abertillery) Ltd

Environment Agency (formerly) National Rivers Authority) v Empress car Co (Abertillery) Ltd [1999] 2 AC 22; [1998] 2 WLR 350; [1998] 1 All ER 481 (HL) . . . 102

Environment Agency (formerly National Rivers Authority) v Empress car Co (Abertillery) Ltd [1999] 2 AC 22; [1998] 2 WLR 350; [1998] 1 All ER 481 (HL) . . . 102

Evans v Hughes [1972] 1 WLR 1452 (DC) . . . 670

F v West Berkshire HA; *sub nom* F (Mental Patient: Sterilisation), re [1990] 2 AC 1; [1989] 2 WLR 1025; [1989] 2 All ER 545 (HL) . . . 95, 99, 346, 676, 680, 681

Fagan v Commissioner of Police of the Metropolis [1969] 1 QB 439; [1968] 3 All ER 441 (QBD) . . . 91, 93, **179–180**, 233, 339, 342, 343

Faulkner v Talbot [1981] 1 WLR 1528; [1981] 3 All ER 468 (CA) . . . 347

Ferens v O'Brien (1883) 11 QBD 21 . . . 504

Ferguson v Weaving [1951] 1 KB 814 (DC) . . . 798

Galloway v Guardian Royal Exchange (UK) Ltd [1999] Lloyd's Insurance Rep IR 209 (CA) . . . 613

Gammon (Hong Kong) Ltd v Attorney-General of Hong Kong [1985] AC 1 (HL) . . . 230

Gardner v Akeroyd [1952] 2 QB 743 (DC) . . . 798

Garrett v Arthur Churchill (Glass) Ltd [1970] 1 QB 92 (CA) . . . 916

Gayford v Chouler [1898] 1 QB 316 (DC) . . . 646

Gillick v West Norfolk and Wisbech AHA [1986] AC 112; [1985] 3 WLR 830; [1985] 3 All ER 402 (HL) . . . 214, 215, 388, 441, 683, 902

Giorgianni v R (1985) 156 CLR 473 . . . 898

Green v Burnett [1955] 1 QB 78 . . . 798

Hardman v Chief Constable of Avon and Somerset [1986] Crim LR 330 . . . 646

Harrow LBC v Shah [2000] 1 WLR 83; [1999] 3 All ER 302; [1999] 2 Cr App R 457; (1999) 163 JP 525; [2000] Crim LR 692 (DC) . . . 223

Hashman v United Kingdom (25594/94) (2000) 30 EHRR 241; (2000) 8 BHTC 104; [2000] Crim LR 185 (ECtHR) . . . **60–62**

Haughton v Smith [1975] AC 476 (HL) . . . 538, 828, 842

Haystead v Chief Constable of Derbyshire; *sub nom* Haystead v DPP [2000] 3 All ER 890; [2000] 2 Cr App R 339; (2000) 164 JP 396; [2000] Crim LR 758 . . . 344

Hibbert v McKiernan [1948] 2 KB 142 . . . 507

Hill v Baxter [1958] 1 QB 277; [1958] 2 WLR 76; [1958] 1 All ER 193 . . . 706, 707

Hillen v ICI (Alkali) Ltd; Pettigrew v ICI (Alkali) Ltd [1936] AC 65 (HL) . . . 627

HL Bolton Engineering Co Ltd v TJ Graham & Sons Ltd [1957] 1 QB 159 (CA) . . . 791, 792

Hobbs v Winchester Corporation [1910] 2 KB 471 (CA) . . . 243

Hobson v Impett (1957) 41 Cr App R 138 . . . 539

Holmes, re [2005] Crim LR 229 DC

Holmes v DPP [1946] AC 588 (HL) . . . 331

Hui Chi-Ming v The Queen [1992] 1 AC 34; [1991] 3 WLR 495; [1991] 3 All ER 897 (PC) (HK) . . . 917

Hussain, Bhatti and Bhatti [2002] Crim LR 405 (CA) . . . 845

Hyam v DPP [1975] AC 55 (HL) . . . 147, 149, 190, 192, 193, 195, 293, 300, 303, 856

Information Commissioner v Islington LBC [2002] EWHC 1036 . . . 795

Invicta Plastics Ltd v Clare [1976] Crim LR 131; [1976] RTR 251 . . . 838, 839, 841, 936

Isaac v DPP [2002] EWHC 2448 . . . 552

Jaggard v Dickenson [1981] QB 527; [1981] 2 WLR 118; [1980] 3 All ER 716 (DC) . . . 648, 728

Jaggard and Brown v United Kingdom [1997] 24 EHRR 39 . . . 371, 408

JJC (A Minor) v Eisenhower; *sub nom* C (A Minor) v Eisenhower [1984] QB 331; (1984) 78 Cr App R 48 (DC) . . . 349

Johnson v Phillips [1976] 1 WLR 65; [1975] 3 All ER 682 . . . 677

Johnson v Youden [1950] 1 KB 544; [1950] 1 All ER 300 (DC) . . . 898, 901, 914

Kay v Butterworth (1945) 61 TLR 452; (1945) 173 LT 191 . . . 87, 177

Kelly v DPP [2003] Crim LR 43 (DC) . . . 365

King v DPP [2000] unreported, 20 June 2000 . . . 366

Kite v OLL Ltd (1994) unreported, 8 December 1994 . . . 796

Knuller (Publishing, Printing and Promotions) Ltd v DPP [1973] AC 435 (HL) . . . 857

Kumar, re [2000] Crim LR 504 . . . 510

Large v Mainprize [1989] Crim LR 213 . . . 580

Laskey, Jaggard and Brown v United Kingdom (1997) 24 EHRR 39 . . . 371, 408

Lau v DPP [2000] 1 FLR 799; [2000] Crim LR 586 (CA) . . . 365

Lee Chun-Chuen v R [1963] AC 220 (PC) (HK) . . . 252

Lennard's Carrying Co Ltd v Asiatic Petroleum Co Ltd [1915] AC 705 (HL) . . . 791

Lewin v CPS (2003) unreported,
24 May 2002 . . . 283

Lim Chin Aik v R [1963] AC 160 (PC) . . . 231, 729

Lloyd v DPP [1992] 1 All ER 982 . . . 646

Logdon v DPP [1976] Crim LR 121 . . . 341

Low v Blease [1975] Crim LR 513 . . . 504

Luc Thiet Thuan v The Queen [1997] AC 131 . . . 257, 258, 259, 261, 262, 331

Lynch v DPP [1975] AC 653 (HL) . . . 213, 686, 697, 755, 772, 901

McAuliffe v The Queen 69 ALJR 621 . . . 905

McCann v United Kingdom (A/324) (1996) 21 EHRR 97 . . . 673

McCrone v Riding [1938] 1 All ER 721 . . . 170

Macklin and Murphy's Case (1838) 2 Lew CC 225 . . . 888

McLoughlin v O'Brien [1983] AC 410 . . . 701

Majewski see DPP v Majewski; R v Majewski (Robert Stefan)

Malnik v DPP [1989] Crim LR 451 (DC) . . . 672

Martin v City of Indianapolis 192 F 3d 608(7th Circ 1999) . . . 658

Masterson v Holden [1986] 1 WLR 1017 . . . 11

Maxwell v DPP (1979) 68 Cr App R 128 (HL) . . . 913

MB (An Adult: Medical Treatment), re [1997] 2 FLR 426; [1997] 2 FCR 541 (CA) . . . 388, **441**

Meli v The Queen [1954] 1 WLR 228 . . . 177

Melias v Preston [1957] 2 QB 380 (CA) . . . 798

Meridian Global Funds Management Asia Ltd v Securities Commission [1995] 2 AC 500 . . . 790, 792, 793, 794, 795

Metropolitan Police Commissioner v Charles (Derek Michael); *sub nom* R v Charles (Derek Michael) [1977] AC 177 (HL) . . . 578, 595, 596, 598, 599

Moberley v Allen (1991) *The Times*, 13 December 1991 . . . 590

Mohan (Ramnath) v The Queen [1967] 2 AC 187 (PC) (Trin) . . . 888

Morphitis v Salmon (1990) 154 JP 365; [1990] Crim LR 48 (DC) . . . 646

Mousell Brothers Ltd v London and North Western Railway Co [1917] 2 KB 836, KBD . . . 797

Nancy B v Hotel-Dieu de Quebec (1992) 86 DLR (4th) 385 . . . 97

National Coal Board v Gamble [1959] 1 QB 11 . . . 892, 899, 901, 902, 916

NHS Trust A v M; NHS Trust B v H [2001] Fam 348; [2001] 2 WLR 942; [2001] 1 All ER 801; [2001] 2 FLR 367 . . . 273

NHS Trust v H [2001] 2 FLR 501; [2002] 1 FCR 713; [2001] Fam Law 664; *The Times*, 17 May 2001 . . . 56

Norfolk Constabulary v Seekings and Gould [1986] Crim LR 167 . . . 622

O'Shea v Coventry Magistrates' Court *ex p* CPS CO/6342/2003 . . . 839

Oxford v Moss (1979) 68 Cr App R 183 . . . 504

Palmer (Sigismund) v The Queen [1971] AC 814 (PC) . . . 671

Papadimitropoulos (1957) 31 ALJ 784; (1957) 98 CLR 249 (Aus HC) . . . 432, 485

Parker v British Airways Board [1982] QB 1004; [1982] 2 WLR 503; [1982] 1 All ER 834 (CA) . . . 538

Parker v R [1964] AC 1369 . . . 252

Parry v DPP [2004] EWHC 3112 . . . 363

People v Beardsley (1967) 113 NW 1128 . . . 88

Percy v DPP [2001] EWHC Admin 1125 . . . 61

Perka v R (1984) 13 DLR (4th) 1 . . . 680

Pharmaceutical Society of Great Britain v Storkwain Ltd [1986] 1 WLR 903 (HL) . . . 230

Phillips v United Kingdom (41087/98) 11 BHRC 280; [2001] Crim LR 217, ECHR . . . 63

Pinkerton v US (1946) 328 US 640 . . . 924

Postermobile plc v Brent LBC (1997) *The Times*, 8 December 1997 (QBD) . . . 729

Practice Statement (Judicial Precedent) [1966] 1 WLR 1234 . . . 161

Practice Statement Note [1996] 3 All ER 77; [1966] 1 WLR 1234 . . . 832

Pretty v United Kingdom (2346/02) [2002] 2 FLR 45; [2002] 2 FCR 97 . . . 273

Pretty *see also* R (On the application of Pretty) v DPP

Quality Dairies (York) Ltd v Pedley [1952] 1 KB 275 (DC) . . . 798

R (Farnell) v Criminal Cases Review Commission [2003] EWHC 835 (Admin) . . . 262

R (On the application of Brenda Rowley) v DPP [2003] EWHC 693 . . . 284, 287

R (on the application of Smeaton) v Secretary of State for Health [2002] EWHC 610; [2002] 2 FLR 146; [2002] 2 FCR 193; [2002] Crim LR 664 . . . 246

R (On the application of Stephens) v DPP CO/2506/2000, 19 October 2000 . . . 312

R (On the application of Pretty) v DPP [2001] UKHL 61; [2002] 1 AC 800; [2001] 3 WLR 1598; [2002] 1 All ER 1; [2002] 2 Cr App R 1; [2002] 1 FLR 268; [2002] 1 FCR 1 (HL) . . . 273

R v A, 12 May 2003 (CA) . . . 688

R v Abdul-Hussain; Aboud; Hasan; Naji; Muhssin; Hosham [1999] Crim LR 570 (CA) . . . 681, 689, **694–696**, 701

R v Acott (Brian Gordon) [1997] 1 WLR 306; [1997] 1 All ER 706; [1997] 2 Cr App R 94 (HL) . . . 251, 254

R v Adams [1957] Crim LR 365 . . . 247

R v Adams (Christopher) [2003] EWCA Crim 3620 . . . 602

R v Adomako (John Asare) [1995] 1 AC 171; [1994] 3 WLR 288; [1994] 3 All ER 79; [1994] Crim LR 757 (HL) . . . 170, **280–282**, 283, 284, 286, 287, 288, 290, 311, 793, 794, 795

R v Ahluwalia [1992] 4 All ER 889; (1993) 96 Cr App R 133; [1993] Crim LR 63 (CA) . . . **252–253**, 261, 320

R v Ahmad (Zafar) (1987) 84 Cr App R 64; (1986) 18 HLR 416; (1986) 52 P & CR 346 (CA) . . . 88, 826

R v Aitken (Thomas Adam) [1992] 1 WLR 1006; [1992] 4 All ER 541; (1992) 95 Cr App R 304 . . . 387, 411

R v Ali [2001] 2 WLR 211 (CA) . . . 266

R v Ali [2005] Crim LR 864 . . . 846

R v Allan (George Donald) [1965] 1 QB 130 (CA) . . . 896

R v Allen (Christopher) [1985] AC 1029; [1985] 3 WLR 107; [1985] 2 All ER 641; (1985) 81 Cr App R 200; (1985) 149 JP 587; [1985] Crim LR 739 (HL) . . . **592–594**, 612

R v Allen (Kevin) [1988] Crim LR 698 (CA) . . . 172

R v Allen (Tony John) [2005] EWCA Crim 1344 . . . 149

R v Allsop (Anthony Adward) (1977) 64 Cr App R 29 (CA) . . . 855, 856, 857

R v Anderson (Lascelles Fitzalbert); R v Morris (Emmanuel) [1966] 2 QB 110l [1966] 2 WLR 1195 . . . 905, 907, 908

R v Anderson (William Ronald) [1986] AC 27; [1985] 3 WLR 268; [1985] 2 All ER 961; (1985) 81 Cr App R 253; [1985] Crim LR 651 (HL) . . . **848–851**, 852

R v Andrews see Andrews v DPP sub nom R v Andrews [1937] AC 576 (HL)

R v Andrews (Christopher Kenneth) [2002] EWCA Crim 3021; [2003] Crim LR 477 . . . 278, 389

R v Andrews and Hedges [1981] Crim LR 106 (CCC) . . . 587

R v Antar [2004] EWCA Crim 2708 . . . 693

R v Antoine (Pierre Harrison) [2001] 1 AC 340; [2000] 2 WLR 703; [2000] 2 All ER 208 (HL) . . . 266, 718, 720

R v Ardalan (Siamak) [1972] 1 WLR 463; [1972] 2 All ER 257 (CA) . . . 845

R v Arnold (Lydon Ewart) [1997] 4 All ER 1; [1997] Crim LR 833 (CA) . . . 596

R v Ashbee (David) [1989] 1 WLR 109 (CA) . . . 577

R v Asher (1981) The Times, 9 June 1981 . . . 269

R v Ashford and Smith (1988) unreported, 26 May 1988 . . . 649, 650

R v Ashton [1992] Crim LR 667 (CA) . . . 852

R v Associated Octel Co Ltd [1996] 1 WLR 1543; [1996] 4 All ER 846; [1996] ICR 972; [1997] IRLR 123 (HL) . . . 793, 794, 795

R v Atakpu (Austin) and Abrahams [1994] QB 69 (CA) . . . 522, 539

R v Atkinson (1869) 11 Cox CC 330 . . . 896

R v Austin (Christopher Timothy) [1981] 1 All ER 374 (CA) . . . 918

R v Ayres (David Edward) [1984] AC 447 (HL) . . . 844

R v Aziz [1993] Crim LR 708 (CA) . . . 591, 592

R v Backshall (David Anthony) [1998] 1 WLR 1506; [1999] 1 Cr App R 35; [1998] RTR 423; [1999] Crim LR 662 (CA) . . . 232

R v Bailey (1800) Russ & Ry 1 . . . 729

R v Baillie (John Dickie) [1995] 2 Cr App R 31; [1995] Crim LR 739 (CA) . . . 253

R v Bainbridge (Alan) [1960] 1 QB 129; (1959) Cr App R 194 (CA) . . . 892, 902, 913, 936

R v Baker [1994] Crim LR 444 (CA) . . . 919

R v Baker (Janet); R v Wilkins (Carl) [1997] Crim LR 497 (CA) . . . 648, 672, 689

R v Ball [1989] Crim LR 730 (CA) . . . 279

R v Barnard (1837) 7 C & P 784; 173 ER 342 . . . 571

R v Barnard (Philip Charles) (1980) 70 Cr App R 28 (CA) . . . 847

R v Barnes [2005] 1 WLR 910 . . . 374, 386

R v Barrow (1868) 1 CCR 158 . . . 432

R v Bassett (Albert); R v Jeff (Edwin Albert Gordon) (1967) 51 Cr App R 28 (CA) . . . 571

R v Bastian (Stephen) [1958] 1 WLR 413 . . . 711

R v Bateman (Percy) (1925) 19 Cr App R 8 (CCA) . . . 280, 282

R v Bates (Jason Alan) [1999] 1 Cr App R 126 (CA) . . . 912, 913

R v Becerra (Antonio) (1976) 62 Cr App R 212 (CA) . . . 919, 921

R v Becker (Ferdinand) No.199905228/75, 19 June 2000 (CA) . . . 287

R v Beech (Hugh Sadler) (1912) 7 Cr App R 197 (CA) . . . 115

R v Belfon (Horace Adrian) [1976] 1 WLR 741; [1976] 3 All ER 46; (1976) 63 Cr App R 59 (CA) . . . 184

R v Benge (1965) 4 F & F 504 . . . 103

R v Bennett (Christine) [1995] Crim LR 877 (CA) . . . 159, 209

R v Bevan (David John) (1987) 84 Cr App R 143; [1987] ECC 372; [1987] Crim LR 129 (CA) . . . 582

R v Bevans (Ronald George Henry) (1988) 87 Cr App R 64 (CA) . . . 631

R v Bird (Debbie) [1985] 1 WLR 816; [1985] 2 All ER 513 (CA) . . . 670, 671

R v Blackburn [1995] Crim LR 323 (CA) . . . 508

R v Bland (1987) 151 JP 857; [1988] Crim LR 41 (CA) . . . 897

R v Blaue (Robert Konrad) [1975] 1 WLR 1411; [1975] 3 All ER 446; (1975) 61 Cr App R 271 (CA) . . . 115, **116–117**, 118

R v Bloxham (Albert John) [1983] 1 AC 109; [1982] 2 WLR 392; [1982] 1 All ER 582; (1982) 74 Cr App R 279 (HL) . . . **539–541**

R v Bodin and Bodin [1979] Crim LR 176 . . . 840

R v Bollom [2003] EWCA Crim 2846 . . . 350

R v Bonner (George Andrew) [1970] 1 WLR 838; [1970] 2 All ER 97 (Note) (CA) . . . 507

R v Bonnyman (1942) 28 Cr App R 131 (CA) . . . 89

R v Booth (Stephen) (Arson or Criminal Damage) [1999] Crim LR 144 (CA) . . . 843

R v Bosson [1999] Crim LR 596 (CA) . . . 539

R v Bourne [1938] 3 All ER 615 . . . 683

R v Bourne [1976] QB 217 . . . 841

R v Bourne (Sydney Joseph) (1952) 36 Cr App R 125 (CCA) . . . 918, 927

R v Bournewood Community and Mental Health NHS Trust ex p L [1999] 1 AC 458; [1998] 3 WLR 107; [1998] 3 All ER 289 (HL) . . . 677, 681

R v Bow Street Metropolitan Stipendiary Magistrate ex p United States (No.2) [2000] 2 AC 216 (HL) . . . 656

R v Bowden [1993] Crim LR 379 (CA) . . . 173

R v Bowden (Stephen Robert) [2002] EWCA Crim 1279 (CA) . . . 522

R v Bowen (Cecil) [1997] 1 WLR 372; [1996] 4 All ER 837; [1996] 2 Cr App R 157 (CA) . . . 165, **690–693**

R v Boyea (1992) 156 JP 505; [1992] Crim LR 574 (CA) . . . 371, 389, 390

R v Bradley (John William) (1980) 2 Cr App R (S) 12 (CA) . . . 208

R v Brain (1834) 6 C & P 349 . . . 246

R v Brennan [1990] Crim LR 118 . . . 533

R v Brewster (Alex Edward) [1998] 1 Cr App R 220 (CA) . . . 636

R v Briggs (Basil Ian) [1977] 1 WLR 605; [1977] 1 All ER 475; (1976) 63 Cr App R 215 . . . 158

R v Bristol Magistrates' Court ex p E [1999] 1 WLR 390; [1998] 3 All ER 798 (QBD) . . . 827

R v British Steel plc [1995] 1 WLR 1356; [1995] ICR 586; [1995] IRLR 310 (CA) . . . 793, 794, 795

R v Broad (Christopher) [1997] Crim LR 666 (CA) . . . 847

R v Brooks (Edward George); R v Brooks (Julie Ann) (1983) 76 Cr App R 66 (CA) . . . 590, 592

R v Brown (1776) 168 ER 11 . . . 255

R v Brown (1841) Car & M 314 . . . 896

R v Brown (Anthony Joseph); R v Laskey (Colin);

R v Jaggard (Roland Leonard); R v Lucas (Saxon); R v Carter (Christopher Robert); R v Cadman (Graham William) [1994] 1 AC 212; [1993] 2 WLR 556; [1993] 2 All ER 75; (1993) 1 Cr App R 44 (HL) . . . 371, 373, 375, 376, **377–383**, 384, 385, 387, 389, 390, 406, 407, 408, 409, 410, 411, 416

R v Brown (Michael Thomas Ernest) [1970] 1 QB 105 (CA) . . . 539

R v Brown (Vincent) [1985] Crim LR 212 (CA) . . . 622

R v Brown and Stratton [1998] Crim LR 484 (CA) . . . 350

R v Bruzas (John) [1972] Crim LR 367 . . . 250

R v Bryce [2004] EWCA Crim 1231; 2 Cr App R 35 (CA) . . . 892, 893, 895, **900–903**, 915

R v Bullock (1954) 38 Cr App R 151 . . . 902

R v Burgess (Barry Douglas) [1991] 2 QB 92 (CA) . . . 708, 709, 762

R v Burke [1986] QB 626 . . . 918, 926

R v Burke (Leslie Robert) [2000] Crim LR 413 (CA) . . . 597

R v Burns (James) (1984) 79 Cr App R 173 (CA) . . . 717

R v Burstow see R v Ireland (Robert Matthew)

R v Buzalek; R v Schiffer [1991] Crim LR 130 (CA) . . . 533

R v Byrne (Patrick Joseph) [1960] 2 QB 396; [1960] 3 WLR 440; [1960] 3 All ER 1; (1960) 44 Cr App R 246 (CA) . . . **267–269**, 270

R v C (David Alexander) [2005] EWCA Crim 2827; [2006] 1 Cr App R 20 . . . 840, 842

R v C (Sean Peter) [2001] EWCA Crim 1251; [2001] 2 FLR 757; [2001] 3 FCR 409; [2001] Crim LR 845; [2001] Fam Law 732 (CA) . . . **366–368**, 447

R v Cairns (John) [1999] 2 Cr App R 137 (CA) . . . 689

R v Cairns (Robert Emmett) (No.2) [2002] EWCA Crim 533 (CA) . . . 912

R v Cakmak (Kenan) [2002] EWCA Crim 500; [2002] 2 Cr App R 10; [2002] Crim LR 581 (CA) . . . 645

R v Caldwell (James); sub nom Commissioner of Police of the Metropolis v Caldwell [1982] AC 341; [1981] 2 WLR 509; [1981] 1 All ER 961; (1981) 73 Cr App R 13 (HL) . . . 44, 156, 159, 160, 161, 162, 163, 164, 165–166, 167, 168, 172, 212, 353, 580, 771, 794

R v Calhaem (Kathleen Nell) [1985] QB 808; [1985] 2 WLR 826; [1985] 2 All ER 226; (1985) 81 Cr App R 131; [1985] Crim LR 303 (CA) . . . **892**, 894

R v Callender (Robert Albert) [1993] QB 303; [1992] 3 WLR 501; [1992] 3 All ER 51 (CA) . . . 583

R v Cambridge (David John) [1994] 1 WLR 971; [1994] 2 All ER 760; (1994) 99 Cr App R 142; [1994] Crim LR 690 (CA) . . . 250

R v Campbell [1997] Crim LR 495
(CA) . . . 266

R v Campbell (Colin Frederick) (1987) 84 Cr App
R 255; [1986] Crim LR 257 (CA) . . . 266

R v Campbell (Colin Frederick) [1997] 1 Cr App R
199 (CA) . . . 256

R v Campbell (Tony) (1991) 93 Cr App R 350
(CA) . . . 824, 826

R v Camplin (Paul); *sub nom* DPP v Camplin
[1978] AC 705 (HL) . . . 255, 256, 257, 261, 262,
263, 265, 317, 331

R v Candy; R v Wise (1990) *The Independent*,
21 August 1990 (CA) . . . 571

R v Cascoe (Handel Barrington) [1970]
2 All ER 833; (1970) 54 Cr App R 401
(CA) . . . 250

R v Case (1850) 4 Cox CC 220 . . . 430

R v Cato (Ronald Philip) [1976] 1 WLR 110;
[1976] 1 All ER 260; (1976) Cr App R 41
(CA) . . . 103, 277, 279, 300, 358, 359

R v Chan-Fook (Mike) [1994] 1 WLR 689; [1994]
99 Cr App R 147 (CA) . . . 348, 350

R v Cheshire (David William) [1991] 1 WLR 844;
[1991] 3 All ER 670; (1991) 93 Cr App R 251
(CA) . . . 103, 104, 106–108, 110, 141

R v Chrastny (Charlotte Barbara) (No.1) [1991]
1 WLR 1381 (CA) . . . 845

R v Church (Cyril David) [1966] 1 QB 59
(CCA) . . . 178, 279

R v Clarence (Charles James) (1888) 22 QBD 23
(CCR) . . . 344, 351, 370, 373, 431–432, 434,
435

R v Clark (Brian James Hemmings) [2001] EWCA
Crim 884; [2002] 1 Cr App R 14 (CA) . . . 597,
603, 604, 605

R v Clarke [1991] Crim LR 383 (CA) . . . 265

R v Clarke (Dennis Geoffrey) (1985) 80 Cr App R
344 (CA) . . . 911

R v Clarke (May) [1972] 1 All ER 219 (CA) . . . 715

R v Clarkson (David George) [1971] 1 WLR 1402;
[1971] 3 All ER 344; (1971) 55 Cr App R 449
(CMCA) . . . 894, 896, 898

R v Clear (Thomas Walter) [1968] 1 QB 670;
[1968] 2 WLR 122; [1968] 1 All ER 74
(CA) . . . 631, 632

R v Clegg (Lee William) [1995] 1 AC 482; [1995]
2 WLR 80; [1995] 1 All ER 334 (HL) . . . 672,
706

R v Clouden [1987] Crim LR 56 (CA) . . . 535

R v Clowes (Peter) (No.2) [1994] 2 All ER 316
(CA) . . . 546

R v Cocker [1989] Crim LR 740 (CA) . . . 251, 273,
296, 320

R v Codère (Georges) (1916) 12 Cr App R 21,
CCA . . . 715

R v Coffey [1987] Crim LR 498 (CA) . . . 525

R v Cogan (John Rodney); R v Leak (Michael
Edward), [1976] QB 217 (CA) . . . 427, 842, 890,
917, 927

R v Cole [1994] Crim LR 582 (CA) . . . 685, 694

R v Coles (Lee Henry) [1995] 1 Cr App R 157
(CA) . . . 199

R v Collins (1864) 9 Cox CC 497 . . . 830, 831

R v Collins (Stephen William George) [1973] QB
100; [1972] 3 WLR 243; [1972] 2 All ER 1105;
(1972) 56 Cr App R 554 (CA) . . . 622, 623–625,
626, 627

R v Collis-Smith [1971] Crim LR 716 (CA) . . . 578

R v Collister (Thomas James); R v Warhurst (John)
(1955) 39 Cr App R 100 (CA) . . . 630

R v Colohan *see* R v C (Sean Peter)

R v Concannon (John) [2002] Crim LR 213
(CA) . . . 68

R v Coney (1882) 8 QBD 534 (QBD) . . . 380, 896,
898

R v Constanza (Gaetano) [1997] Crim LR 576
(DC); [1997] 2 Cr App R 492 (CA) . . . 338,
341

R v Conway (Francis Gerald) [1989] QB 290;
[1988] 3 WLR 1238; [1988] 3 All ER 1025;
(1989) 88 Cr App R 159 (CA) . . . 685, 697

R v Cooke (Anthony Martin) [1986] AC 909
(HL) . . . 578, 848, 857

R v Corbett (Christopher) [1996] Crim LR 594
(CA) . . . 118

R v Cort [2004] QB 388 . . . 370

R v Cotter (Christopher James) [2002] EWCA
Crim 1033; [2003] QB 951; [2003] 2 WLR 115;
[2002] 2 Cr App R 29; [2002] Crim LR 824
(CA) . . . 62

R v Court (Robert Christopher) [1989] AC 28
(HL) . . . 455

R v Cousins (Robert William) [1982] QB 526;
[1982] 2 All ER 115 (CA) . . . 665, 666

R v Cox (1992) 12 BMLR 38 . . . 213, 246

R v Cox (1992) unreported,
18 September 1992 . . . 98

R v Cramp (1880) 5 QBD 307 . . . 358

R v Croft (William James) [1944] KB 295; (1944)
29 Cr App R 169, CCA . . . 920

R v Cunningham (Anthony Barry) [1982]
AC 566; (1981) 73 Cr App R 253
(HL) . . . 247

R v Cunningham (Roy) [1957] 2 QB 396; [1957]
2 All ER 412 (CA) . . . 156–168, 212, 343, 353,
354, 360, 580, 626, 628

R v Curley (James) (1909) 2 Cr App
R 96 . . . 105

R v Curr (Patrick Vincent) [1968] 2 QB 944
(CA) . . . 834, 835, 837, 842

R v Currier [1998] SCR (Canada) 371 . . . 421

R v D [2005] EWCA Crim 1981 . . . 913

R v Dalby (Derek Shaun) [1982] 1 WLR 621;
[1982] 1 All ER 916; (1982) 74 Cr App R 348
(CA) . . . 279

R v Dale (1852) 6 Cox CC . . . 360

R v Dalloway (1847) 2 Cox 273 . . . 94, 102

R v Davies (Peter John Brinley) [1975] QB 691 (CA) . . . 253

R v Davis (Gary) (1989) 88 Cr App R 347 . . . 597

R v Dawson [1976] RTR 533; [1976] Crim LR 692 (CA) . . . 535

R v Dawson (Brian) (1985) 81 Cr App R 150 (CA) . . . 278, 279

R v Day (1841) 9 C & P 722 . . . 442

R v Day (Martin); R v Day (Simon) [2001] EWCA Crim 572; [2001] EWCA Crim 1594 (CA) . . . 912, **914–915**

R v Dear [1996] Crim LR 595 (CA) . . . 118

R v Dee (1884) 15 Cox CC 579 . . . 432

R v Deller (Charles Avon) (1952) 36 Cr App R 184 (CA) . . . 570

R v Dica (Mohammed) [2004] EWCA Crim 1103; [2004] QB 1257 . . . 351, 356, **369–373**, 374, 375, 387, 424

R v Dietschmann (Anthony) (Appeal against Conviction) [2003] UKHL 10; [2003] 1 AC 1209; [2003] 2 WLR 613; [2003] 1 All ER 897 (HL) . . . **270–272**

R v Ditchfield [2005] EWCA Crim 1415; [2005] 1 WLR 3642; [2005] 2 Cr App R 34 . . . 703

R v Ditta [1988] Crim LR 43 (CA) . . . 704

R v Dix (Trevor Glyn) (1981) 74 Cr App R 306 (CA) . . . 269

R v Donovan [1934] 2 KB 498 (CCA) . . . 348, 371, 384, 385, 389

R v Doring (Petra) [2002] EWCA Crim 1695 (CA) . . . 230

R v Doughty (Stephen Clifford) (1986) 83 Cr App R 319 (CA) . . . 251, 254, 316

R v Doukas (Joseph Davis) [1978] 1 WLR 372; [1978] 1 All ER 1061; (1978) 66 Cr App R 228; [1978] Crim LR 177 (CA) . . . **579–580**

R v Downes (1983) 77 Cr App R 260 . . . 605

R v DPP [2001] Crim LR 397 (DC) . . . 368

R v DPP ex p Kebilene [2000] 2 AC 326; [1999] 3 WLR 972; [1999] 4 All ER 801 (HL) . . . 63, 716

R v DPP ex p Moseley and others, 23 June 1999, CO/664/99 . . . 367

R v Drew (Martin Ralph) [2000] 1 Cr App R 91 (CA) . . . 845

R v Dryden [1995] 4 All ER 987 (CA) . . . 256, 261, 263

R v Dudley [1989] Crim LR 57 (CA) . . . 652, 660, 661

R v Dudley (Thomas); R v Stephens (Edward) (1884–85) 14 QBD 273 (QBD) . . . 676, 678, 680, 682, 686, 687, 741, 786

R v Duffy (Elizabeth Lilian) [1967] 1 QB 63 (CA) . . . 665

R v Dume (Constantine) (1986) The Times, 16 October 1986 (CA) . . . 341

R v Dunbar [1988] Crim LR 693 (CA) . . . 914

R v Dunbar [1995] 1 Cr App R 280 (CA) . . . 508

R v Dunbar (Ronald Patrick) [1958] 1 QB 1 . . . 266

R v Dunnington (Kevin Vincent) [1984] QB 472 (CA) . . . 827

R v Duru (Ignatius Chima) [1974] 1 WLR 2; [1973] 3 All ER 715; (1974) 58 Cr App R 151 (CA) . . . 528, 604, 614

R v Dyke and Munro [2001] EWCA Crim 2184; [2002] 1 Cr App R 30 (CA) . . . 508

R v Dyson [1908] 2 KB 454 (CA) . . . 102

R v Dytham (Philip Thomas) [1979] QB 722; [1979] 3 WLR 467; [1979] 3 All ER 641; (1979) 69 Cr App R 387 (CA) . . . 88

R v Eagleton (1855) Dears 315; (1855) 6 Cox CC 559 . . . 824, 826, 870

R v Easom (John Arthur) [1971] 2 QB 315; [1971] 3 WLR 82; [1971] 2 All ER 945 (CA) . . . 524

R v Edwards [1991] Crim LR 45 (CA) . . . 852

R v Egan (Shaun Daniel) [1992] 4 All ER 470 (CA) . . . 269

R v Elbekkay [1995] Crim LR 163 (CA) . . . 435, 436

R v Ellis (Ian); R v Street (Edward James); R v Smith (Gloria Marie) (1987) 84 Cr App R 235 (CA) . . . 726

R v Emery (Sally Lorraine) (1993) 14 Cr App R (S) 394 (CA) . . . 89, 691

R v Emmett (1999) 18 June 1999 (CA), The Times 15 October 1999 . . . 371, 385

R v Enoch (1830) 5 C & P 539 . . . 246

R v Erisman [1988] 1 Hong Kong Law Reports 370 . . . 386

R v Evans and Gardiner (No.2) [1976] VR 523 . . . 108

R v Fagan [1972] NI 80 . . . 670

R v Fancy [1980] Crim LR 171 . . . 647

R v Feely (David) [1973] QB 530 (CA) . . . 562, 563, 564, 565

R v Fenton (1975) 61 Cr App R 261 . . . 270

R v Fernandes (Roland Anthony) [1996] 1 Cr App R 175 (CA) . . . 526, 528

R v Field [1972] Crim LR 435 (CA) . . . 672

R v Firth (Peter Stanley) (1990) 91 Cr App R 217; (1990) 154 JP 576; [1990] Crim LR 326 (CA) . . . 574

R v Fitzmaurice (Robert) [1983] QB 1083; [1983] 2 WLR 227; [1983] 1 All ER 189; (1983) 76 Cr App R 17 (CA) . . . 838, 842

R v Flatt (David Sean) [1996] Crim LR 576 (CA) . . . 693

R v Flattery (John) (1877) 2 QBD 410 . . . 431, 432, 435

R v Forbes (Giles) [2001] UKHL 40; [2002] 2 AC 512; [2001] 3 WLR 428; [2001] 4 All ER 97 (HL) . . . 174

R v Forman and Ford [1988] Crim LR 677 (Crown Ct) . . . 896

R v Forrester [1992] Crim LR 793 (CA) . . . 535

R v Forsyth (Elizabeth) [1997] 2 Cr App R 299 (CA) . . . 174, 538, 541

R v Fotheringham (William Bruce) (1989) 88 Cr App R 206 (CA) . . . 390, 728

R v Francis [1982] Crim LR 363 (CA) . . . 629

R v Francom (Mark Frank) [2001] 1 Cr App R 17 (CA) . . . 896

R v Franklin (1883) 15 Cox CC 163 . . . 277

R v Fritschy [1985] Crim LR 745 (CA) . . . 514

R v G and R [2002] EWCA Crim 1992; [2003] UKHL 50; [2004] 1 AC 1034; [2003] 3 WLR 1060; [2003] 4 All ER 765; [2004] 1 Cr App R 21; [2004] Crim LR 369 (HL) . . . **160–167**, 168, 170, 282, 284

R v Gamble [1989] NI 268 . . . 907, 908

R v Garwood (Patrick Augustus) [1987] 1 WLR 319; [1987] 1 All ER 1032; (1987) 85 Cr App R 85; [1987] Crim LR 476 (CA) . . . **631–632**

R v Gateway Food Market [1997] 3 All ER 78 . . . 795

R v Geddes (Gary William) (1996) 160 JP 697; [1996] Crim LR 894; (1996) 160 JPN 730 (CA) . . . **823–825**

R v Gee (Stephen James) [1999] Crim LR 397 (CA) . . . 586

R v Ghosh (Deb Baran) [1982] QB 1053; [1982] 3 WLR 110; [1982] 2 All ER 689; (1982) 75 Cr App R 154 (CA) . . . 557, 562, 564–567, 592

R v Giannetto (Robert Vincent) [1997] 1 Cr App R 1 (CA) . . . 888, **889**, 892

R v Giaquinto (Andrew Pasquale) [2001] EWCA Crim 2696 (CA) . . . 685

R v Gibbons and Proctor (1919) 13 Cr App R 134 (CA) . . . 89

R v Gibson (Richard Norman) [1990] 2 QB 619 (CA) . . . 854

R v Gilks (Donald) [1972] 1 WLR 1341; [1972] 3 All ER 280; (1972) 56 Cr App R 734 (CA) . . . 508

R v Gillard (Simon Paul) (1988) 87 Cr App R 189; [1988] Crim LR 531 (CA) . . . 360

R v Gilmour (Thomas Robert) [2000] NI 367; [2000] 2 Cr App R 407 (CA) (NI) . . . 914

R v Gittens [1984] 3 All ER 252 . . . 271

R v Gleeson [2003] 1 Cr App R (S) 484 . . . 65

R v Goldman (Nigel) [1997] Crim LR 894 (CA) . . . 533, 838, 839

R v Gomez see DPP v Gomez (Edwin)

R v Goodfellow (Kevin) (1986) 83 Cr App R 23 (CA) . . . 277, 300, 303

R v Goodwin (Phillip) [1996] Crim LR 262 (CA) . . . 571

R v Gotts (Benjamin) [1992] 2 AC 412 (HL) . . . 687, 697, 704

R v Graham (Hemamali Krishna) [1997] 1 Cr App R 302 (CA) . . . 585

R v Graham (Paul Anthony) [1982] 1 WLR 294; [1982] 1 All ER 801; (1982) 74 Cr App R 235 (CA) . . . 165, 603, 604, 687, 688, 689, 690, 693, 695, 698, 728

R v Grainge (Albert Robert Burns) [1974] 1 WLR 619; [1974] 1 All ER 928 (CA) . . . 174

R v Grant (Heather) [2001] EWCA Crim 2611; [2002] QB 1030; [2002] 2 WLR 1409 (CA) . . . 718

R v Greatrex (David Anthony) [1999] 1 Cr App R 126 (CA) . . . 912, 913

R v Greenstein (Allan) [1975] 1 WLR 1353; [1976] 1 All ER 1; (1975) 61 Cr App R 296 . . . 532, 595

R v Griffin [1993] Crim LR 514 . . . 826

R v Griffiths (1965) Cr App R 94 (CA) . . . 845

R v Griffiths (Leslie George) (1974) 60 Cr App R 14 (CA) . . . 174, 541

R v Grundy [1977] Crim LR 543 (CA) . . . 350

R v Gullefer (Ian John) [1990] 1 WLR 1063; [1990] 3 All ER 882; [1991] Crim LR 576 (CA) . . . 824, 825, 826

R v H [2001] EWCA Crim 104; [2001] 2 Cr App R (S) 59 (CA) . . . 68, 684

R v H (Deb Baran) [1982] QB 1053; [1982] 3 WLR 110; [1982] 2 All ER 689; (1982) 75 Cr App R 154 (CA) . . . **531–533**, 533, 534, 580, 583, 857

R v H (Fitness to Plead) [2003] UKHL 1; [2003] 1 WLR 411; [2003] 1 All ER 497; [2003] 2 Cr App R 2; (2003) 167 JP 125; [2003] HRLR 19 (HL) . . . **719–721**

R v H (Karl Anthony) [2005] EWCA 732; [2005] 1 All ER 859; [2005] 2 Cr App R 9; [2005] 1 WLR 2005; [2005] Crim LR 735 . . . **456–457**

R v Hadjou (George) (1989) 11 Cr App R (S) 29 (CA) . . . 639

R v Halai [1983] Crim LR 624 (CA) . . . 585, 614

R v Hale (Robert Angus) (1979) 68 Cr App R 415; [1979] Crim LR 596 (CA) . . . **535–536**

R v Hales (Ricky) [2005] EWCA Crim 118 . . . 148, 149

R v Hall (1928) 21 Cr App R 48 . . . 252

R v Hall (Edward Leonard) (1985) 81 Cr App R 260 (CA) . . . 541

R v Hall (Geoffrey) [1973] QB 126; [1972] 3 WLR 381; [1972] 2 All ER 1009; (1972) 56 Cr App R 547 (CA) . . . **508–510**

R v Hallam and Blackburn [1995] Crim LR 323 (CA) . . . 508, 511

R v Hancock (Reginald Dean); R v Shankland (Russell) [1986] AC 455 (HL) . . . 147, 149, 186, 300, 303, 905

R v Hapgood (Elijah); R v Wyatt (Aaron) (1865–72) 1 CCR 221 . . . 917

R v Hardie (Paul Deverall) [1985] 1 WLR 64; [1984] 3 All ER 848 (CA) . . . 167, 172

R v Harley (1830) 4 C & P 396 . . . 360

R v Harling [1938] 1 All ER 307, CCA . . . 441

R v Harmer (Geoffrey Clive) [2001] EWCA Crim 2930; [2002] Crim LR 401 (CA) . . . 693

R v Harmer (Roy Peter) [2005] EWCA Crim 1; [2005] 2 Cr App R 2 . . . 846

R v Harry [1974] Crim LR 32 . . . 634

R v Hart [1986] 2 NZLR 408 (NZCA) . . . 119

R v Harvey (Alfred Alphonsus); R v Ulyett (Ernest); R v Plummer (Lucius Everard) (1981) 72 Cr App R 139; [1981] Crim LR 104 (CA) . . . **633–634**

R v Harvey (Ian) (No.1) [1999] Crim LR 70 (CA) . . . 852

R v Hassan [2005] 4 All ER 685 . . . **696–700**, 701

R v Hatton (Jonathan) [2005] EWCA 2951; [2006] 1 Cr App R 16 . . . 727

R v Hayes [2002] All ER (D) 6 (CA) . . . 150, 154, 156

R v Hayward (1833) 6 C & P 157 . . . 260

R v Hayward (1908) 21 Cox CC 692 . . . 118, 287

R v Heath (Patrick Nicholas) [2000] Crim LR 109 (CA) . . . 693, 694

R v Hegarty [1994] Crim LR 353 (CA) . . . 691

R v Henderson (1984) unreported, 29 November 1984 . . . 646

R v Henley (Clifford James) (Appeal against Conviction) [2000] Crim LR 582 (CA) . . . 368

R v Hennessy (Andrew Michael) [1989] 1 WLR 287; [1989] 2 All ER 9; (1989) 89 Cr App R 10 (CA) . . . 232, 708, 710, 717, 762

R v Hennigan (James) [1971] 3 All ER 133 (CA) . . . 103

R v Hensler (1870) 11 Cox CC 570 . . . 570

R v Herbert (1960) *The Times*, 22 December 1960 . . . 505

R v Hibbert (1865–72) 1 CCR 184 . . . 223

R v Hibbert (1995) 99 CCC (3rd) 193 . . . 697

R v Higgins (1801) 2 East 5 . . . 834

R v Hill (Frederick Philip) (1986) 83 Cr App R 386; [1986] Crim LR 815 (HL) . . . 361

R v Hill (Valerie Mary); R v Hall (Jennifer) (1989) 89 Cr App R 74; [1989] Crim LR 136 (CA) . . . **649–651**

R v Hills [2001] Crim LR 318 (CA) . . . 365

R v Hinks (Karen Maria) [2001] 2 AC 241; [2000] 3 WLR 1590; [2000] 4 All ER 833 (HL) . . . 511, 512, **516–522**, 546, 555, 556, 557, 558, 560, 562, 581, 595, 605, 611, 612

R v HM Coroner for East Kent *ex p* Spooner (1987) 3 BCC 636; (1989) 88 Cr App R 10 (DC) . . . 790, 793, 794

R v HM Coroner for West London *ex p* Gray [1988] QB 467 . . . 281, 283, 288

R v Hobson (Kathleen) [1998] 1 Cr App R 31 (CA) . . . 269

R v Holden [1991] Crim LR 478 (CA) . . . 530

R v Holland (1841) 2 Mood & R 351 . . . 117

R v Holley [2005] UKPC 23 . . . 329, 693

R v Hollinshead (Peter Gordon) [1985] AC 975; [1985] 3 WLR 159; [1985] 2 All ER 769; (1985) 81 Cr App R 365; [1985] Crim LR 653; (1985) 82 LSG 2739; (1985) 135 NLJ 631; (1985) 129 SJ 447 (HL); [1985] 1 All ER 850 (CA) . . . 846, 855, 917

R v Hollis [1971] Crim LR 525 (CA) . . . 622

R v Holmes [2005] Crim LR 229 (DC) . . . 571, 582

R v Holt (Victor Reginald); R v Lee (Julian Dana) [1981] 1 WLR 1000; [1981] 2 All ER 854; (1981) 73 Cr App R 96 (CA) . . . 588

R v Horne [1994] Crim LR 584 (CA) . . . 691

R v Howard (Robert Lesarian) [1966] 1 WLR 13; [1965] 3 All ER 684, CCA . . . 441

R v Howe (Michael Anthony) [1987] AC 417; [1987] 2 WLR 568; [1987] 1 All ER 771; (1987) 85 Cr App R 32; (1987) 151 JP 265; [1987] Crim LR 480 (HL) . . . 165, 292, 676, 678, 680, 685, **686–687**, 688, 690, 694, 697, 698, 728, 786, 919, 926

R v Howells (Colin David) [1977] QB 614 (CA) . . . 231

R v Hudson (Linda) and Taylor [1971] 2 QB 202; [1971] 2 WLR 1047; [1971] 2 All ER 244; (1972) 56 Cr App R 1 (CA) . . . 694, 695, 772, 775

R v Hudson (Terence) [1966] 1 QB 448 (CA) . . . 170

R v Humphreys (Emma) [1995] 4 All ER 1008 . . . 261, 263

R v Hunt (Anthony Gerald) (1978) 66 Cr App R 105 (CA) . . . 649, 650

R v Hurst (Marnie Michelle) [1995] 1 Cr App R 82 (CA) . . . 691, 694

R v Hussey (1924) 18 Cr App R 160 . . . 669

R v Husseyn (1978) 67 Cr App R 131 (CA) . . . 822, 823

R v Hyde (David Charles) [1991] 1 QB 134 (CA) . . . 906, 907, 914

R v Instan [1893] 1 QB 450 (QBD) . . . 89

R v Ireland (Robert Matthew); R v Burstow (Anthony Christopher) [1998] AC 147; [1997] 3 WLR 534; [1997] 4 All ER 225; [1998] 1 Cr App R 177; (1997) 161 JP 569; [1998] 1 FLR 105; [1997] Crim LR 810 (HL) . . . 278, **338–340**, 344, 348, 350, 351, 355, 356, 370, 396, 397, 417, 689

R v Isitt (Douglas Lance) (1978) 67 Cr App R 44; [1978] RTR 211 (CA) . . . 232, 710

R v Jackson (1983) 147 JP 715; [1983] Crim LR 617 (CA) . . . 587

R v Jackson [1985] Crim LR 444 (CA) . . . 847, 848

R v James (1837) 8 C & P 131; (1837) ER 429 . . . 706

R v James (Alan Michael); R v Ashford (John Phillip) (1986) 82 Cr App R 226 (CA) . . . 839

R v Janjua (Nadeem Ahmed) [1999] 1 Cr App R 91 (CA) . . . 247, 350

R v Jennings [1990] Crim LR 588 (CA) . . . 277

R v JF Alford Transport Ltd [1997] 2 Cr App R 326; [1999] RTR 51; [1997] Crim LR 745 (CA) . . . 896, **897–899**, 911, 914

R v Jobidon [1991] 2 SCR 714 . . . 386

R v Johnson (Christopher Richard) [1989] 1 WLR 740 (CA) . . . 254

R v Johnstone (Robert Alexander) [2003] UKHL 28; [2003] 1 WLR 1736 HL . . . 63, 64

R v Jones (1993) *The Times*, 15 February 1993 . . . 576

R v Jones (John); R v Smith (Christopher) [1976] 1 WLR 672; [1976] 3 All ER 54; (1976) 63 Cr App R 47 (CA) . . . **626–627**

R v Jones (Jonathan Nigel) [2001] EWCA Crim 2235; [2002] 1 Cr App R (S) 127 (CA) . . . 366

R v Jones (Kenneth Henry) [1990] 1 WLR 1057; [1990] 3 All ER 886 (CA) . . . 823, 826

R v Jones (Margaret) [2005] QB 259 . . . 649, 669, 777

R v Jones (Terence) (1986) 83 Cr App R 375 (CA) . . . 386, 387, 390

R v Jordan (James Clinton) (1956) 40 Cr App R 152 (CA) . . . 107, 110

R v Jordan (Shirley) [2001] 2 WLR 211 (CA) . . . 266

R v K (Age of Consent: Reasonable Belief) [2001] UKHL 41; [2002] 1 AC 462; [2001] 3 WLR 471; [2001] 3 All ER 897 (HL) . . . 46, 165, **228–230**, 230

R v Kaitamaki [1985] AC 147 (PC) . . . 428

R v Kanwar (Rena Louise) [1982] 1 WLR 845; [1982] 2 All ER 528; (1982) 75 Cr App R 87 (CA) . . . 539

R v Kelly [1992] Crim LR 181 (CA) . . . 826

R v Kelly (Anthony Noel) [1999] QB 621; [1999] 2 WLR 384; [1998] 3 All ER 741 (CA) . . . **505–506**, 507

R v Kelly (Ronnie Peter) (1993) 97 Cr App R 245; [1993] Crim LR 763 (CA) . . . 629

R v Kemp (Albert) [1957] 1 QB 399 . . . 713, 714, 715

R v Kennedy (Simon) [1999] Crim LR 65 (CA) . . . 277, 279

R v Kennedy (Simon) (No.2) [2005] EWCA Crim 685; [2005] 1 WLR 2159; [2005] 2 Cr App R 23 (CA) . . . **112–114**, 360

R v Kenny [2005] EWCA Crim 1415; [2005] 1 WLR 3642; [2005] 2 Cr App R 34 . . . 703

R v Khan (Mohammed Iqbal); R v Mohammed Iqbal Khan; R v Dhokia (Mahesh); R v Banga (Jaswinder Singh); R v Faiz (Navaid) [1990] 1 WLR 813; [1990] 2 All ER 783; (1990) 91 Cr App R 29 (CA) . . . 490, **818–819**, 820, 821, 822

R v Khan (Nazaqat); R v H (Tahir); H (Jangheer); H (Kadeer) [2001] EWCA Crim 104; [2001] 2 Cr App R (S) 59 (CA) . . . 68, 684

R v Khan (Rungzabe); R v Khan (Tahir) [1998] Crim LR 830 (CA) . . . 94, 278

R v Kimsey [1996] Crim LR 35 (CA) . . . 103

R v King [1979] Crim LR 122 (CA) . . . 573

R v King (Hugo Allen) [1992] QB 20 (CA) . . . 614

R v King (Vincent) [1965] 1 QB 443 (CA) . . . 269

R v Kingston (Barry) [1995] 2 AC 355; [1994] 3 WLR 519; [1994] 3 All ER 353; (1994) 99 Cr App R 286; (1994) 158 JP 717; [1994] Crim LR 846 (HL) . . . 159, **722–725**, 727, 780, 781, 782

R v Kirk (Craig); R v Russell (Steven John) [2002] EWCA Crim 1580; [2002] Crim LR 756 (CA) . . . 230

R v Kitson (Herbert) (1955) 39 Cr App R 66 (CCA) . . . 676

R v Klineberg (Jonathan Simon) and Marsden [1999] 1 Cr App R 427 (CA) . . . 510

R v Konzani [2005] EWCA Crim 706 . . . **373–375**, 422, 423, 424

R v Kovacs (Stephanie Janika) [1974] 1 WLR 370 (CA) . . . 596

R v Kumar [2005] 1 Cr App R 34 . . . 230

R v Lamb (Terence Walter) [1967] 2 QB 981 (CA) . . . 278, 279

R v Lambert (1919) VLR 205 . . . 433

R v Lambert (Steven); R v Ali (Mudassir Mohammed); R v Jordan (Shirley) [2001] UKHL 37; [2002] 2 AC 545; [2001] 3 WLR 206 (HL) . . . 63, 64, 65, **233–234**

R v Lambie (Shiralee Ann) [1982] AC 449 (HL) . . . 578, 595, 596, 598

R v Lane (Linda Joan); R v Lane (James) (1986) 82 Cr App R 5; [1985] Crim LR 789 (CA) . . . 888

R v Lang (Christopher Michael) (1976) 62 Cr App R 50 (CA) . . . 442

R v Larkin (1943) 29 Cr App R 18 . . . 276, 294

R v Larsonneur (1933) 149 LT 542 . . . 100

R v Larter [1995] Crim LR 75 (CA) . . . 440

R v Latif (Khalid) [1996] 1 WLR 104; [1996] 1 All ER 353 (HL) . . . 109, 705

R v Lavallee [1990] 1 SCR 852 . . . 321

R v Laverty (Charles) [1970] 3 All ER 432 (CA) . . . 578

R v Lawrence (Alan) [1972] AC 626 (HL) . . . 512, 513, 514, 515, 516, 517, 518, 519, 551, 558

R v Lawrence (Rodney Brian); R v Pomroy (Norman Albert) (1973) 57 Cr App R 64 (CA) . . . 631, 632

R v Lawrence (Stephen Richard) [1982] AC 510; [1981] 2 WLR 524; [1981] 1 All ER 974 (HL) . . . 161, 167, 280, 281, 282, 794

R v Le Brun [1991] 4 All ER 673 (CA) . . . 178

R v Leak (Michael Edward), [1976] QB 217 (CA) . . . 427, 842, 890, 917, 927

R v Leather (Nicola Jane) (1993) 14 Cr App R (S) 736 (CA) . . . 465

R v Lee [2005] EWCA Crim 1415; [2005] 1 WLR 3642; [2005] 2 Cr App R 34 . . . 703

R v Letenock (1917) 12 Cr App R 221 . . . 255, 728, 729

R v Lewis [1970] Crim LR 647 . . . 115

R v Lewis [2005] Crim LR 797 . . . 705

R v Lidar (no.99/0339/Y4) . . . 288

R v Linekar (Gareth) [1995] QB 250; [1995] 2 WLR 237; [1995] 3 All ER 69; [1995] 2 Cr App R 49; [1995] Crim LR 320 (CA) . . . **431–434**, 434, 453, 486

R v Lipman (Robert) [1970] 1 QB 152 (CA) . . . 710, 717

R v Litchfield [1998] Crim LR 507 (CA) . . . 286

R v Lloyd (Derek William) [1967] 1 QB 175 (CA) . . . 270

R v Lloyd (Sidney Douglas); R v Bhuee (Ranjeet); R v Ali (Mohammed) [1985] QB 829; [1985] 2 All ER 661 (CA) . . . 528

R v Lomas (1913) 9 Cr App R 220 . . . 902

R v Looseley [2001] 4 All ER 897 (HL) . . . 705

R v Loughnan [1981] VR 443 . . . 694

R v Loukes [1996] Crim LR 341 (CA) . . . 918

R v Lowe (Robert) [1973] QB 702 (CA) . . . 89, 278

R v Lowe (Terry) [2003] EWCA Crim 677 (CA) . . . 257

R v Lunderbech [1991] Crim LR 784 (CA) . . . 854

R v Lynsey (Jonathan Simon) [1995] 3 All ER 654 (CA) . . . 337

R v McAllister (Geoffrey Victor) [1997] Crim LR 233 (CA) . . . 445

R v McCarthy [1954] 2 QB 105 . . . 261

R v McCarthy (Michael Reginald) [1967] 1 QB 68 (CA) . . . 718

R v McCrudden [2005] EWCA 466 . . . 231

R v McDavitt [1981] Crim LR 843 (CA) . . . 590

R v McDonnell [1966] 1 QB 233 . . . 845

R v McFall [1994] Crim LR 226 . . . 440

R v McHugh (Eileen Cecilia) (1989) 88 Cr App R 385 (CA) . . . 515

R v McInnes (Walter) [1971] 1 WLR 1600; [1971] 3 All ER 295 (CA) . . . 670

R v McKechnie (Roy Maurer) (1992) 94 Cr App R 51; [1992] Crim LR 194 (CA) . . . 118, 915

R v McKnight and Groark [1999] Crim LR 669 . . . 173

R v McNaghten (1843) 10 Cl & F 200; (1843–60) All ER Rep 229 . . . 712, 714

R v McNamara (James) (1988) 87 Cr App R 246 . . . 233, 234, 270

R v McNiff [1986] Crim LR 57 (CA) . . . 583

R v McShane (Yolande Tregenna) (1977) 66 Cr App R 97 (CA) . . . 273

R v Mahmood (Asaf) [1995] RTR 48; [1994] Crim LR 368 (CA) . . . 913

R v Malcherek (Richard Tadeusz); R v Steel (Anthony) [1981] 1 WLR 690; [1981] 2 All ER 422 (CA) . . . 102, 107, 109, 110, 246

R v Malone (Thomas Patrick) [1998] 2 Cr App R 447 (CA) . . . 440

R v Mandair (Singh Mandair) [1995] 1 AC 208 (HL) . . . 351

R v Mandry (Michael John); R v Wooster (Roger John) [1973] 1 WLR 1232 (CA) . . . 570

R v Manjdadria [1993] Crim LR 73 (CA) . . . 614

R v Marby (1882) 8 QBD 571 . . . 95

R v Marcus (Lily) [1981] 1 WLR 774; [1981] 2 All ER 833; (1981) 73 Cr App R 49; [1981] Crim LR 490; 125 SJ 396 (CA) . . . 358, **359–360**

R v Marison (Lee John) [1997] RTR 457; [1996] Crim LR 909 (CA) . . . 710

R v Marjoram [2000] Crim LR 372 (CA) . . . 116

R v Marks (Errington Lloyd) [1998] Crim LR 676 (CA) . . . 250, 916

R v Marlow (1964) 49 Cr App R 49 . . . 358

R v Marlow (Michael David) [1998] 1 Cr App R (S) 273; [1997] Crim LR 897 (CA) . . . 834, 839, 841

R v Marriott (Charles Percival) [1971] 1 WLR 187; [1971] 1 All ER 595 (CA) . . . 233

R v Marshall (Adrian John) [1998] 2 Cr App R 282 (CA) . . . 507, **527–529**, 605

R v Martin (1827) 172 ER 390 . . . 111

R v Martin (1832) 5 C & P 128 . . . 117

R v Martin (1881–82) 8 QBD 54, CCR . . . 344

R v Martin [1989] 1 All ER 652; (1989) 88 Cr App R 343 (CA) . . . 165, 685, 728

R v Martin (Anthony Edward) (1989) Cr App R 343 . . . 675

R v Martin (Anthony Edward) [2001] EWCA Crim 2245; [2003] QB 1; [2002] 2 WLR 1 (CA) . . . **666–668**, 669, 671, 696

R v Martin (Colin) [1989] 1 All ER 652; (1989) 88 Cr App R 343 (CA) . . . 701

R v Masciantonio (1994–5) 183 CLR (HC Aust) . . . 318, 322

R v Matthews (Darren John) [2003] EWCA Crim 192 (CA) . . . 153, 154

R v Matudi (Misanki Kuranku) [2003] EWCA Crim 697 (CA) . . . 230, 231

R v Mavji (Ramniklal Nathoo) [1987] 1 WLR 1388; [1987] 2 All ER 758; [1986] STC 508; (1987) 84 Cr App R 34; [1987] Crim LR 39; (1987) 131 SJ 1121 (CA) . . . 88

R v Maxwell (Nolan Andrew) (1994) 158 JP 877; [1994] Crim LR 848 (CA) . . . 357

R v Maxwell-King (Paul John) [2001] 2 Cr App R (S) 28; (2001) 98(4) LSG 49; (2001) 145 SJLB 21 (CA) . . . 654, 656

R v MD [2004] EWCA Crim 1391

R v Mead and Belt (1823) 1 Lew 184 . . . 339

R v Mellor (Gavin Thomas) [1996] 2 Cr App R 245 . . . 103

R v Mensah-Lartey (Godso Ni Boye); R v Relevy (Devora) [1996] 1 Cr App R 143 (CA) . . . 502, 614

R v Merrick (David Stephen) [1995] Crim LR 802; [1996] 1 Cr App R 130 (CA) . . . 652

R v Meyrick (1929) 21 Cr App R 523 (CA) . . . 845

R v Michael (1840) 9 C & P 356 . . . 119, 890

R v Millard and Vernon [1987] Crim LR 393 (CA) . . . 817

R v Miller [1968] 3 All ER 442; [1968] 3 WLR 1120; (1968) 52 Cr App R 700 . . . 178

R v Miller (James) [1983] 2 AC 161; [1983] 2 WLR 539; [1983] 1 All ER 978; (1983) 77 Cr App R 17 (HL) . . . 85, **91–94**, 574

R v Miller (Steven Henry) (1992) 95 Cr App R 421; [1993] RTR 6; [1992] Crim LR 744 (CA) . . . 578

R v Mills (Thomas Leonard Lantey) [1963] 1 QB 522; [1963] 2 WLR 137; [1963] 1 All ER 202; (1963) 47 Cr App R 49 (CA) . . . 845

R v Millward (Sidney Booth) (1994) 158 JP 1091; [1994] Crim LR 527 (CA) . . . 841, 842, 894, 918

R v Misra [2004] EWCA Crim 2375; [2005] 1 Cr App R 21 . . . **282–286**

R v Mitchell [1993] Crim LR 788 (CA) . . . 528, 614

R v Mitchell (Frank) (1999) 163 JP 75; [1999] Crim LR 496 (CA) . . . 922

R v Mitchell (Ronald James) [1983] QB 741; [1983] 2 WLR 938; [1983] 2 All ER 427; (1983) 76 Cr App R 293 (CA) . . . 175, 279

R v Mkosiyana (1966) 4 SA 655 (SA) . . . 838

R v M'Loughlin (1838) 173 ER 651 . . . 349

R v Mohammed (Faqir) [2005] EWCA Crim 1880 . . . 257, 265

R v Moloney (Alistair Baden) [1985] AC 905 (HL) . . . 147, 149, 150, 151, 153, 156, 186, 300, 905

R v Moor (1999) unreported, 11 May 1999 . . . 273

R v Moore and Dorn [1975] Crim LR 229, (PC) . . . 178

R v Morhall (Alan Paul) [1996] AC 90 (HL) . . . 255, 256, 257, 261, 262, 318, 320, 331, 691

R v Morris (Clarence Barrington) [1998] 1 Cr App R 386 (CA) . . . 348

R v Morris (David Alan); *sub nom* Anderton v Burnside [1984] AC 320 (HL) . . . 512, 513, 514, 515, 516

R v Morris (Emmanuel) [1966] 2 QB 110; [1966] 2 WLR 1195 . . . 905, 907, 908

R v Morrison (Lawrence Andrew) (1989) 89 Cr App R 17 (CA) . . . 356

R v Moseley, 21 April 1999 (CA) . . . 693

R v Moses and Ansbro [1991] Crim LR 617 (CA) . . . 854

R v Mowatt (Sidney Linton) [1968] 1 QB 421; [1967] 3 All ER 47 (CA) . . . 353, 354

R v Muhamad (Mithum) [2002] EWCA Crim 1856 . . . 230, 232

R v Nabina (Fizeal) [2000] Crim LR 481 (CA) . . . **597–600**

R v Nash (Denis Arthur) [1999] Crim LR 308 (CA) . . . 826

R v Nathan (Ronald Stephen) [1997] Crim LR 835 (CA) . . . 584

R v Naviede (Mohammed) [1997] Crim LR 662 (CA) . . . 585

R v Neary (Graham Robert) [2002] EWCA Crim 1736 (CA) . . . 912

R v Nedrick (Ransford Delroy) [1986] 1 WLR 1025 (CA) . . . 150, 151, 152, 153, 154, 186, 196

R v Newell (1980) 71 Cr App R 331 . . . 261, 263

R v O'Connell (Christopher Jermiah) [1997] Crim LR 683 (CA) . . . 269

R v O'Connell (Michael John) (1992) 94 Cr App R 39 (CA) . . . 580

R v O'Connor (1980) 54 AJLR 349 . . . 209

R v O'Connor [1991] Crim LR 135 (CA) . . . 727

R v O'Flaherty [2004] EWCA Crim 526 . . . 922

R v O'Grady (Patrick Gerald) [1987] QB 995; [1987] 3 WLR 321 (CA) . . . 727

R v O'hAdhmaill [1996] Crim LR 509 (CA) . . . 845, 848

R v Okosi [1996] Crim LR 666 . . . 21

R v Olan [1978] 2 SCR 1175 (Canada) . . . 856

R v O'Leary (Michael) (1986) 82 Cr App R 341 (CA) . . . 629

R v Olugboja (Stephen Olubumni) [1982] QB 320; [1981] 3 WLR 585; [1981] 3 All ER 443; (1981) 73 Cr App R 344 (CA) . . . **442–444**

R v Ortiz (Fernando) (1986) 83 Cr App R 173 (CA) . . . 689

R v Osborn (1919) 84 JP 63 . . . 825

R v Osolin [1993] 4 SCR 595 . . . 467

R v Owino (Nimrod) [1996] 2 Cr App R 128; [1995] Crim LR 743 (CA) . . . 671, 672

R v P&O European Ferries (Dover) Ltd (1991) 93 Cr App R 72; [1991] Crim LR 695, CCC . . . 794, 802

R v Paddison see R v Quick (William George) and Paddison [1973]

R v Pagett (David Keith) (1983) 76 Cr App R 279; [1983] Crim LR 393 (CA) . . . 102, **104–106**, 109

R v Papadimitropoulos (1957) 31 ALJ 784; (1957) 98 CLR 249 (Aus HC) . . . 432, 485, 486

R v Paquette (1997) 70 DLR (3d) 129 (Canada) . . . 773

R v Parker [1977] 1 All ER 760 (CA) . . . 171

R v Parker (Daryl Clive) [1977] 1 WLR 600; [1977] 2 All ER 37; (1977) 63 Cr App R 211 . . . **157–158**, 159, 198

R v Parkes [1973] Crim LR 358 . . . 631

R v Parks (1992) 95 DLR (4th) 27 (Canada) . . . 709

R v Pattni, Dhunna, Soni and Poopalarajah [2001] Crim LR 570 . . . 533

R v Pearce [2001] EWCA Crim 2834 . . . 257

R v Pearman (Stephen Dennis) (1985) 80 Cr App R 259 (CA) . . . 817

R v Pearson (William) [1992] Crim LR 193 (CA) . . . 253, 254

R v Pembiliton (1874) 2 CCC 119 . . . 175

R v Percival 13 May 2003 (CA) . . . 895

R v Perman (Sam) [1996] 1 Cr App R 24; [1995] Crim LR 736 (CA) . . . 913

R v Peters; R v Parfitt [1995] Crim LR 501 (CA) . . . 888

R v Pickford (John Andrew) [1995] QB 203 (CA) . . . 840

R v Pitchley (Abraham Joseph) (1973) 57 Cr App R 30; [1972] Crim LR 705 (CA) . . . 539

R v Pitham (Charles Henry); R v Hehl (Brian Robert) (1977) 65 Cr App R 45 (CA) . . . 511

R v Pitts (1842) C & M 284 . . . 105

R v Pittwood (1902) 19 TLR 37 . . . 88

R v Podola (Guenther Fritz Erwin) [1960] 1 QB 325 (CA) . . . 717

R v Pommell (Fitzroy Derek) [1995] 2 Cr App R 607 (CA) . . . 676, 694, 695

R v Ponting (1985) unreported, 11 February 1985 . . . 214

R v Poulton (1832) 5 C & P 329 . . . 246

R v Powell (Anthony Glassford); R v Daniels (Antonio Eval); R v English (Philip) [1999] 1 AC 1; [1997] 3 WLR 959; [1997] 4 All ER 545; [1998] 1 Cr App R 261; (1998) 162 JP 1; [1998] Crim LR 48 (HL) . . . 296, 903, **904–909**, 910, 913, 914, 921, 925, 926, 941

R v Preddy (John Crawford) [1996] AC 815 (HL) . . . 527, 528, 529, 597, 600, 601, 603, 604, 614

R v Prentice [1993] 4 All ER 935 (CA) . . . 283, 284, 286

R v Quail (1866) 4 F & F 1876 . . . 838

R v Quayle [2005] EWCA Crim 1415; [2005] 1 WLR 3642; [2006] 1 All ER 988 . . . 675, **700–704**, 703

R v Quick (William George) and Paddison [1973] QB 910 (CA) . . . 172, 708, 710, 741

R v R (Rape: Marital Exemption) [1992] 1 AC 599; [1991] 3 WLR 767; [1991] 4 All ER 481 (HL) . . . 427

R v Rabey (1980) 15 CR (3d) 225 (Canada) . . . 709

R v Rai (Thomas) [2000] 1 Cr App R 242 (CA) . . . 574

R v Ram (1893) 17 Cox CC 609 . . . 918

R v Ransford (1874) 13 Cox CC 9 . . . 840

R v Rashid (Abdul) [1977] 1 WLR 298; [1977] 2 All ER 237; (1977) 64 Cr App R 201 (CA) . . . 578, 579, 580

R v Raven, 6 October 1981 (CCC) . . . 261

R v Read [1982] Crim LR 819 (CA) . . . 846

R v Reader (Alfred Raymond) (1978) 66 Cr App R 33 (CA) . . . 174, 541

R v Reardon (Sean) [1999] Crim LR 392 (CA) . . . 912

R v Reid (John Joseph) [1992] 1 WLR 793; [1992] 3 All ER 673; (1992) 95 Cr App R 391 (HL) . . . 161, 167, 199, 212

R v Reigate Justices *ex p* Counsell (1984) 148 JP 193 (QBD) . . . 348

R v Renouf (John William) [1986] 1 WLR 522; [1986] 2 All ER 449 (CA) . . . 666

R v Richards (Isabelle Christina) [1974] QB 776 (CA) . . . 919

R v Richardson (Diane) [1999] QB 444 (CA) . . . 434, 435, 436

R v Richardson and Irwin [1999] 1 Cr App R 392 (CA) . . . 387, 390, 728

R v Richens (Andrew Ronald) [1993] 4 All ER 877 (CA) . . . 251

R v Rimmington [2005] 3 WLR 982 (HL) . . . 68

R v Roberts [1855] 6 Cox CC 559; (1855) 169 ER 836 . . . 870

R v Roberts [1990] Crim LR 122 (CA) . . . 256, 913

R v Roberts [2005] EWCA 155 . . . 272

R v Roberts (David Geraint); R v George (Graham Harold), [1997] RTR 462; [1997] Crim LR 209 (CA) . . . 289

R v Roberts (John Joseph) (1984) 78 Cr App R 41 (CA) . . . 846

R v Roberts (Kenneth Joseph) (1972) 56 Cr App R 95; [1972] Crim LR 27; (1971) 115 SJ 809 (CA) . . . **115–116**, 117, 118, 348, 353, 354

R v Roberts (William) (1987) 84 Cr App R 117 (CA) . . . 541

R v Robertson (Eric John) [1968] 1 WLR 1767 (CA) . . . 717

R v Robinson (2000) 3 February 2000 (CA) . . . 922

R v Rodger (Andrew); R v Rose (Keith John) [1998] 1 Cr App R 143 (CA) . . . 689, 695, 701, 702

R v Roebuck (1856) D & B 24; (1856) 169 ER 900 . . . 578

R v Roffel [1985] VR 511 . . . 515

R v Rogers [2005] EWCA Crim 2863 . . . 364

R v Rook (Adrian) [1993] 1 WLR 1005; [1993] 2 All ER 955; (1993) 97 Cr App R 327 (CA) . . . 901, 915, **920–922**

R v Rothery (Henry Michael) (1976) 63 Cr App R 231; [1976] RTR 550 . . . 505

R v Rowley (Michael) [1991] 1 WLR 1020; [1991] 4 All ER 649; (1992) 94 Cr App R 95 (CA) . . . 823, 854

R v Rozeik (Rifaat Younan) [1996] 1 WLR 159 (CA) . . . 570

R v Rushworth (Gary Alan) (1992) 95 Cr App R 252 (CA) . . . 351

R v Russell [1933] VLR 59 . . . 896

R v Russell (Raymond) (1985) 81 Cr App R 315 (CA) . . . 629

R v Ryan (Lee Bernard) (1996) 160 JP 610; [1996] Crim LR 320 (CA) . . . 623

R v S [2005] EWCA Crim 819 . . . 833

R v Safi [2003] Crim LR 721 (CA) . . . 689, 699, 701

R v Sainsbury and Lewis [1990] Crim LR 903 . . . 274

R v St George (1840) 9 C & P 483 . . . 180

R v Sakavickas [2004] EWCA Crim 2686

R v Sanders (William John) (1982) 75 Cr App R 84 (CA) . . . 539

R v Sanderson (Lloyd) (No.2) (1994) 98 Cr App R 325 (CA) . . . 269

R v Sang [1980] AC 402; [1979] 3 WLR 263; [1979] 2 All ER 1222; (1979) 69 Cr App R 282 (HL) . . . 705

R v Sangha (Sukhvinder Singh) [1988] 1 WLR 519; [1988] 2 All ER 385 (CA) . . . 652

R v Sargeant [1997] Crim LR 50 (CA) . . . 458

R v Saskavickas [2004] EWCA Crim 2686 . . . 846

R v Saunders and Archer (1573) 2 Plowd 473 . . . 913

R v Savage (Susan); *sub nom* DPP v Parmenter (Philip Mark) [1992] 1 AC 699; [1991] 3 WLR 914; [1991] 4 All ER 698; (1992) 94 Cr App R 193; [1992] Crim LR 288 (HL) . . . 212, 340, 343, 344, 348, **352–354**, 353, 354, 379, 398

R v Schaub (Mark Tony); R v Cooper (Joey) [1994] Crim LR 531 . . . 428

R v Schofield [1784] Cald 397 . . . 870

R v Scott (Christopher Ian) [1997] Crim LR 597 (CA) . . . 250

R v Searle [1971] Crim LR 592; (1971) 115 SJ 739 (CA) . . . 896

R v Seers (John Samuel) (1984) 79 Cr App R 261 (CA) . . . 269

R v Senior (1832) 1 Mood CC 346 . . . 246

R v Senior [1899] 1 QB 283 . . . 278

R v Shadrokh-Cigari (Hamid) [1988] Crim LR 465 (CA) . . . 511

R v Shankland (Russell) [1986] AC 455 (HL) . . . 147, 149, 186, 300, 303, 905

R v Sharpe (1857) Dears & B 160 . . . 505

R v Shaw (Obtaining by Deception: Incitement) [1994] Crim LR 365 (CA) . . . 834, 835, 837, 841

R v Shayler (David Michael) [2001] EWCA Crim 1977; [2001] 1 WLR 2206 (CA) . . . 676, 701

R v Shayler (David Michael) [2002] UKHL 11; [2003] 1 AC 247; [2002] 2 WLR 754; [2002] 2 All ER 477; [2002] HRLR 33; [2002] UKHRR. 603; [2002] ACD. 58; (2002) 99(17) LSG 34; (2002) 146 SJLB. 84 (HL) . . . 689

R v Sheehan (Michael) R v Moore (George Alan) [1975] 1 WLR 739; [1975] 2 All ER 960; (1974) 60 Cr App R 308 (CA) . . . 173

R v Shelton (1993) 15 Cr App R (S) 415 (CA) . . . 537

R v Sheppard (James Martin) [1981] AC 394 (HL) . . . 89

R v Shimmen *see* Chief Constable of Avon and Somerset v Shimmen

R v Shivpuri (Pyare) [1987] AC 1; [1986] 2 WLR 988; [1986] 2 All ER 334; (1986) 83 Cr App R 178; (1986) 150 JP 353; [1986] Crim LR 536 (HL) . . . **829–833**, 877, 878, 879

R v Shortland (Malena Iris) [1996] 1 Cr App R 116 (CA) . . . 705

R v Sibartie [1983] Crim LR 470 (CA) . . . 586, **588–589**

R v Silverman (Michael John) (1988) 86 Cr App R 213; (1987) 151 JP 657; [1987] Crim LR 574 (CA) . . . 551, **571–573**, 576

R v Simpson (Trevor John) [2002] EWCA Crim 25 . . . 117

R v Singh (Gurphal) [1999] Crim LR 582 (CA) . . . 94, 283, 286

R v Singh (Narinder) (1992) 13 Cr App R (S) 123 (CA) . . . 319

R v Siracusa (1990) 90 Cr App R 340 . . . 846

R v Siracusa (Francesco); R v di Carlo (Francesco); R v Monteleone (Filippo); R v Luciani (Antonio) (1990) 90 Cr App R 340; [1989] Crim LR 712 (CA) . . . **852–853**

R v Sirat (Mohammed) (1986) 83 Cr App R 41; [1986] Crim LR 245 (CA) . . . 840, 842

R v Skipp [1975] Crim LR 114 (CA) . . . 514

R v Skivington (Jim) [1968] 1 QB 166 (CA) . . . 530

R v Slack (Martin Andrew) [1989] QB 775 (CA) . . . 914

R v Slimmings (Richard Gareth) [1999] Crim LR 69 (CA) . . . 176

R v Slingsby (Simon) [1995] Crim LR 570 . . . 278, 389, 390

R v Small (Adrian Anthony) (1988) 86 Cr App R 170 (CA) . . . 530

R v Smethurst (John Russell) [2001] EWCA Crim 772; [2002] 1 Cr App R 6; (2001) 165 JP 377; [2001] Crim LR 657 (CA) . . . 68

R v Smith (1826) 172 ER 203 . . . 89

R v Smith (1866) 176 ER 910 . . . 343

R v Smith [2006] EWHC 94 . . . 348

R v Smith (Charlotte) (1865) 10 Cox CC 82 . . . 89

R v Smith (David Raymond) [1974] QB 354 (CA) . . . 729

R v Smith (KA) [1983] Crim LR 739 . . . 274

R v Smith (Morgan James) [1998] 4 All ER 387 . . . 329, 331, 334

R v Smith (Morgan James) [2001] 1 AC 146; [2000] 3 WLR 654; [2000] 4 All ER 289; [2001] 1 Cr App R 5; [2000] Crim LR 1004 (HL) . . . 46, 165, 256, 257, 258, 259, 260, 262, 263, 264, 313, 317, 318, 329, 447, 668, 693

R v Smith (Sandie) [1982] Crim LR 531 (CA) . . . 269

R v Smith (Thomas Joseph) [1959] 2 QB 35 . . . 107

R v Smith (Wesley) [1963] 1 WLR 1200; [1963] 3 All ER 597 (CCA) . . . 905, 941

R v Smurthwaite [1998] Crim LR 751 . . . 705

R v Speck (Harry) [1977] 2 All ER 859 (CA) . . . 95

R v Spratt [1991] 2 All ER 210 . . . 353

R v Spriggs [1958] 1 QB 270 . . . 268

R v Springer (Robert) [1999] 1 Cr App R (S) 217 (CA) . . . 705

R v Squire [1990] Crim LR 341 (CA) . . . 533

R v Staines (Linda Irene) (1974) 60 Cr App R 160 (CA) . . . 580

R v Steane (Anthony Cedric Sebastian) [1947] KB 997 (CA) . . . 213, 688

R v Steer (Dennis) [1988] AC 111; [1987] 3 WLR 205; [1987] 2 All ER 833; (1987) 85 Cr App R 352 (HL) . . . **652–653**

R v Stephen (Malcolm R) (1984) 79 Cr App R 334 . . . 160, 162

R v Stephenson (Brian Keith) [1979] QB 695 (CA) . . . 157, 162, 167, 183

R v Stewart (1988) 59 DLR (Canada) . . . 504

R v Stewart (Heather); R v Schofield (Barry John) [1995] 3 All ER 159; [1995] 1 Cr App R 441 (CA) . . . 914

R v Stone (John Edward); R v Dobinson (Gwendoline) [1977] QB 354; [1977] 2 WLR 169; [1977] 2 All ER 341; (1977) 64 Cr App R 186 (CA) . . . **89–91**, 94, 96, 281, 283, 288

R v Stones (James) [1989] 1 WLR 156; (1989) 89 Cr App R 26 (CA) . . . 629

R v Stringer (Neil Bancroft); R v Banks (1992) 94 Cr App R 13; [1991] Crim LR 639 (CA) . . . 890

R v Stripp (David Peter) (1979) 69 Cr App R 318 (CA) . . . 709, 710

R v Strong [1995] Crim LR 428 (CA) . . . 289

R v Sullivan; R v Ballion [2002] Crim LR 758 . . . 507

R v Sullivan [1981] Crim LR 46 (CA) . . . 351, 354

R v Sullivan (Patrick Joseph) [1984] AC 156; [1983] 3 WLR 123; [1983] 2 All ER 673; (1983) 77 Cr App R 176 (HL) . . . 708, 709, **711–714**, 715, 762

R v T [1990] Crim LR 256 . . . 709, 710

R v Taaffe (Paul Desmond) [1983] 1 WLR 627; [1983] 2 All ER 625; [1984] AC 539; [1984] 2 WLR 326; [1984] 1 All ER 747; (1984) 78 Cr App R 301; (1984) 148 JP 510; [1984] Crim LR 356; (1984) 81 LSG 1051; (1984) 128 SJ 203 (HL) . . . 827, 843

R v Tabassum (Naveed) [2000] 2 Cr App R 328; [2000] Lloyd's Rep Med 404 (CA) . . . 370, **434–435**

R v Tacey (1821) Russ & Ry 452 . . . 646

R v Tagg (Heather Susan) [2001] EWCA Crim 1230 (CA) . . . 62

R v Tait [1993] Crim LR 538 (CA) . . . 896

R v Talbott [1995] Crim LR 396 (CA) . . . 578

R v Tandy (Linda Mary) [1989] 1 WLR 350; [1989] 1 All ER 267; (1988) 87 Cr App R 45 (CA) . . . 271, 272

R v Taylor (Anthony) [2005] EWCA Crim 1415; [2005] 1 WLR 3642; [2005] 2 Cr App R 34 . . . 703

R v Taylor (Paul Simon) [2001] EWCA Crim 2263 (CA) . . . 68

R v Taylor (Robert John) [2001] EWCA Crim 1044; [2002] Crim LR 205 (CA) . . . 847

R v Terry [1984] AC 374 (HL) . . . 857

R v Thomas (Emyrs) (1985) 81 Cr App R 331 (CA) . . . 336, 343

R v Thomas (Sharon) (1996) 29 BMLR 120; [1995] Crim LR 314 (CA) . . . 711

R v Thornton [1992] 1 All ER 306 (CA) . . . 320

R v Thornton (Sara Elizabeth) (No.2) [1996] 1 WLR 1174; [1996] 2 All ER 1023 (CA) . . . 261, 320

R v Tokeley-Parry (Jonathon Aidan) [1999] Crim LR 578 (CA) . . . 537

R v Tolson (Martha Ann) (1889) 23 QBD 168 . . . 225

R v Toothill (Peter Kendall) [1998] Crim LR 876 (CA) . . . 826

R v Tosti (Andre) [1997] Crim LR 746 (CA) . . . 826

R v Turner (Frank Richard) (No.2) [1971] 1 WLR 901; [1971] 2 All ER 441; (1971) 55 Cr App R 336 (CA) . . . 507

R v Tyrrell [1894] 1 QB 710 . . . 840

R v Uddin (Rejan) [1999] QB 431; [1998] 3 WLR 1000; [1998] 2 All ER 744; [1999] 1 Cr App R 319; [1999] Crim LR 987 (CA) . . . **909–911**, 913

R v Valderrama-Vega [1985] Crim LR 220 (CA) . . . 688

R v Van Dongen (Anthony Gerrard) [2005] Crim LR 971 (CA) . . . 265

R v Velumyl [1989] Crim LR 299 (CA) . . . 524

R v Venna (Henson George) [1976] QB 421; [1975] 3 WLR 737; [1975] 3 All ER 788 (CA) . . . 343, 352

R v Vickers (John Wilson) [1957] 2 QB 664; [1957] 3 WLR 326; [1957] 2 All ER 741 (CA) . . . 248, 303

R v Vinagre (Orlando Jose Gonzales) (1979) 69 Cr App R 104 (CA) . . . 266, 269, 329

R v Vincent (Christopher James) [2001] EWCA Crim 295; [2001] 1 WLR 1172 (CA) . . . 590, 592

R v Wacker (Perry) [2002] EWCA Crim 1944; [2003] QB 1207; [2003] 2 WLR 374; [2003] 1 Cr App R 22; [2003] 1 Cr App R (S) 92; [2003] Crim LR 108 (CA) . . . 286, 287, 387, 545

R v Wain (Peter) [1995] 2 Cr App R 660 (CA) . . . 510

R v Waites [1982] Crim LR 369 (CA) . . . 582, 596

R v Wakely [1990] Crim LR 119 . . . 905, 906

R v Wales [2005] EWCA Crim 1415; [2005] 1 WLR 3642; [2005] 2 Cr App R 34 . . . 703

R v Walker [1962] Crim LR 458, CCA . . . 845

R v Walkington (Terence John) [1979] 1 WLR 1169; [1979] 2 All ER 716 (CA) . . . 622, 627

R v Waltham (1849) 3 Cox CC 442 . . . 350

R v Wan; R v Chan [1995] Crim LR 296 (PC) . . . 914

R v Warner (Brian William) (1971) 55 Cr App R 93 (CA) . . . 528, 561

R v Watson (Clarence Archibald) [1989] 1 WLR 684; [1989] 2 All ER 865 (CA) . . . 118, 278

R v Webster (Andrew) [1995] 2 All ER 168 (CA) . . . 653, 660, 661

R v Weekes (Stephen) [1999] 2 Cr App R 520 . . . 668

R v Wellard (Mike Colin) [1978] 1 WLR 921; [1978] 3 All ER 161; (1978) 67 Cr App R 364 (CA) . . . 444

R v Weller [2004] 1 Cr App R 1 . . . 263

R v Wheelhouse [1994] Crim LR 756 (CA) . . . 623

R v White (1853) 169 ER 696 . . . 504

R v White [1910] 2 KB 124 (CA) . . . 102

R v White (Anthony Delroy) [2001] EWCA Crim 216; [2001] 1 WLR 1352 (CA) . . . 363

R v Whitefield (Arthur Armour) (1984) 79 Cr App R 36 (CA) . . . 921

R v Whitehouse [1941] 1 WLR 112 . . . 920

R v Whitehouse (Arthur) [1977] QB 868; [1977] 2 WLR 925; [1977] 3 All ER 737; (1977) 65 Crim App R 33 (CA) . . . 840

R v Whiteley (Nicholas Alan) (1991) 93 Cr App R 25 (CA) . . . 646

R v Whiteside and Antoniou [1989] Crim LR 436 (CA) . . . 613

R v Whybrow (Arthur George) (1951) 35 Cr App R 141 (CA) . . . 817

R v Widdowson (Stanley) (1986) 82 Cr App R 314 (CA) . . . 584

R v Willer (Mark Edward) (1986) 83 Cr App R 225; [1987] RTR 22 (CA) . . . 685

R v Williams (Barry Anthony); R v Davis (Frank O'Neill) [1992] 1 WLR 380; [1992] 2 All ER 183 (CA) . . . 116, 117

R v Williams (Gladstone) [1987] 3 All ER 411; (1984) 78 Cr App R 276; [1984] Crim LR 163; (1984) 81 LSG 278 (CA) . . . 121, 226, 672, 689, 727, 769, 770, 771

R v Williams (Owen Richard) [1923] 1 KB 340 (CA) . . . 430, 431

R v Williams (Roy) [2001] Crim LR 253; [2001] Cr App R 362 (CA) . . . 597

R v Williams and Davis (1991) 95 Cr App R 1 . . . 140

R v Willoughby [2004] EWCA Crim 3365 . . . 279, 286

R v Wills (Graham George) (1991) 92 Cr App R 297 . . . 602

R v Wilson (Alan Thomas) [1997] QB 47; [1996] 3 WLR 125; [1996] 2 Cr App R 241; [1996] Crim LR 573 (CA) . . . **384–385**, 387, 390, 411

R v Wilson (Clarence George); R v Jenkins (Edward John); R v Jenkins (Ronald Patrick) [1984] AC 242; [1983] 3 WLR 686; [1983] 3 All ER 448 (HL) . . . 351, 352, 628

R v Windle (Francis Wilfred) [1952] 2 QB 826 (CA) . . . 715

R v Winson [1969] 1 QB 371 (CA) . . . 798

R v Wood [1999] Crim LR 564 (CA) . . . 580

R v Wood (William) and M'Mahon (James) (1830) 1 Mood CC 278 . . . 350

R v Woodman (George Eli) [1974] QB 754 (CA) . . . 507

R v Woods (Patrick Thomas) [1969] 1 QB 447, CCA . . . 174

R v Woods (Walter) (1982) 74 Cr App R 312 (CA) . . . 448

R v Woollin (Stephen Leslie) [1999] 1 AC 82; [1998] 3 WLR 382; [1998] 4 All ER 103; [1999] 1 Cr App R 8; [1998] Crim LR 890 (HL) . . . 147, **150–152**, 153, 154, 155, 170, 247, 295, 356, 817, 841, 848, 902, 903, 904

R v Woolven (Johnathan Robert) (1983) 77 Cr App R 231 (CA) . . . 580

R v Wright (Glenn Paul) [2000] Crim LR 928; *The Times*, 17 May 2000 (CA) . . . 148

R v Wright (Shani Ann) [2000] Crim LR 510 . . . 697

R v Wyatt (Aaron) (1865–72) 1 CCR 221 . . . 917

R v Z [2005] UKHL 22 . . . 689, 694, **696–700**

R v Zezev [2002] EWHC 589; [2002] Crim LR 648; [2002] 2 Cr App R 33 (CA) . . . 845

Race Relations Board v Applin [1973] *see* Applin v Race Relations Board

Rawlings v Till (1837) 3 M & W 28 . . . 346

Read v Coker (1853) 138 ER 1437 . . . 342

Rekvenyi v Hungary (25390/94) (2000) 30 EHRR 519; 6 BHRC 554, ECHR . . . 61

Roberts v Ramsbottom [1980] 1 WLR 823; [1980] 1 All ER 7 . . . 708

Robinson v California 370 US 660 (1962) . . . 122

Robson v Hallett [1967] 2 QB 939 (CA) . . . 623

Roe v Kingerlee [1986] Crim LR 735 . . . 646

Roe v Wade (1973) 410 US 479 (US SCt) . . . 392

Royall v The Queen (1991) 65 ALJR 451 . . . 140

Rubie v Faulkner [1940] 1 KB 571, KBD . . . 896

S (Children) (Care Order: Implementation of Care Plan), re; *sub nom* W and B (Children) (Care Plan), re; W (Children) (Care Plan), re; W (Children) (Care Order: Adequacy of Care

Plan), re [2002] UKHL 10; [2002] 2 AC 291; [2002] 2 WLR 720; [2002] 2 All ER 192; [2002] 1 FLR 815; [2002] 1 FCR 577 (HL) . . . 55

S v McC [1972] AC 24; [1970] 3 WLR 366; [1970] 3 All ER 107 . . . 97

S v Robinson (1968) (1) SA 666 . . . 923

St George's Healthcare NHS Trust v S (Guidelines) [1999] Fam 26; [1998] 3 All ER 673 (CA) . . . 95, 336, 677, 681

Salabiaku v France (A/141-A) (1991) 13 EHRR 379 (ECtHR) . . . 63, 66

Satnam *see* R v S (Kewal); R v S (Satnam)

Schloendorff v Society of New York Hospital (1914) 105 NE 92, 93 . . . 97

Scott (Anthony Peter) v Commissioner of Police of the Metropolis; *sub nom* R v Scott (Anthony Peter) [1975] AC 819; [1974] 3 WLR 741; [1974] 3 All ER 1032 (HL) . . . 854, 855, 857

Scott v Shepherd (1773) 96 ER 525 . . . 109

Seaboard Offshore v Secretary of State for Transport [1994] 1 WLR 541 (HL) . . . 793, 796, 797

Shaw (Norman) v The Queen [2001] UKPC 26; [2001] 1 WLR 1519; [2002] 1 Cr App R 10; [2002] Crim LR 140 (PC) (Bze) . . . 671

Shaw v DPP [1962] AC 220 (HL) . . . 857

Sheldrake v DPP [2005] 1 AC 264 . . . **63–65**, 67

Sherras v De Rutzen [1895] 1 QB 918 (DC) . . . 230

Sidaway v Board of Governors of the Bethlem Royal Hospital and the Maudsley Hospital [1985] AC 871 . . . 97

Silver v United Kingdom (A/161) (1983) 5 EHRR 347 . . . 60

Simpson v Peat [1952] 2 QB 24 (CA) . . . 169

Smedleys Ltd v Breed [1974] AC 839 (HL) . . . 236

Smith v Land & House Property Corp (1884) 28 Ch D 7 (CA) . . . 574

Smith v Littlewoods [1987] AC 241; [1987] 2 WLR 480; [1987] 1 All ER 710 (HL) . . . 91

Smith v Newsam (1674) 3 Keble 283 . . . 396, 397

Smith v Superintendent of Woking Police Station (1983) 76 Cr App R 234 . . . 340, 342, 397

Sooklal (Narine) v Trinidad and Tobago [1999] 1 WLR 2011 (PC) (Trin) . . . 912

Southwark LBC v Williams [1971] Ch 734 (CA) . . . 675, 676, 694, 703

State v Dufield 549 A 2d 1205, 1208 (NH 1988) . . . 210

State v Preslar (1856) 48 NC 417 (USA) . . . 141

Steel v United Kingdom (1999) 28 EHRR 603 (ECtHR) . . . 61, 62

Stephen Malcolm *see* R v R (Stephen Malcolm)

The Sunday Times v United Kingdom (No.2) (1992) 14 EHRR 229 . . . 61

Supply of Ready Mixed Concrete (No.2), re [1995] 1 AC 456 (HL) . . . 792, 793

SW v United Kingdom (A/355-B); CR v United Kingdom [1996] 1 FLR 434 . . . 427

Sweet v Parsley [1970] AC 132 (HL) . . . 225, 226, 227, 231, 284

T (Adult: Refusal of Treatment), re [1993] Fam 95 . . . 97

T v DPP [2003] EWHC 266; [2003] Crim LR 622 . . . 348

T v United Kingdom (24724/94) [2000] 2 All ER 1024 (Note); (2000) 30 EHRR 121; 7 BHRC 659; 12 Fed Sent R 266; [2000] Crim LR 187, ECHR . . . 722

Talkington v Magee [1902] 2 KB 427 . . . 529

Teixeira de Castro v Portugal (1999) 28 EHRR 101; 4 BHRC 533; [1998] Crim LR 751, EHCR . . . 705

Tesco Stores Ltd v Brent LBC [1993] 1 WLR 1037; [1993] 2 All ER 718 . . . 797

Tesco Supermarkets Ltd v Nattrass [1972] AC 153 (HL) . . . 790, 791, 792, 793, 794

Thomas v News Group Newspapers Ltd [2001] EWCA Civ 1233 (CA) . . . 366

Thomas v NUM [1985] 2 All ER 1 . . . 397

Thorne v Motor Trade Association [1937] AC 797 (HL) . . . 631

Thornton v Mitchell [1940] 1 All ER 339, KBD . . . 798, 918

Tison v Arizona 107 S Ct 1676 (1987) . . . 940

Treacy v DPP [1971] AC 537 (HL) . . . 630

Troughton v Metropolitan Police [1987] Crim LR 138 (DC) . . . 591

Tuberville v Savage (1669) 1 Mood Rep 3; 86 ER 684 . . . 342, 345, 397

Tuck v Robson [1970] 1 WLR 741; [1970] 1 All ER 1171 (DC) . . . 91, 896, 899

United States v King (1888) 34 F.302 (USA) . . . 451

Vane v Yiannopoulos [1965] AC 486 (HL) . . . 798

Vezina v R [1986] 1 SCR 2 (Canada) . . . 856

W v W [1972] AC 24 . . . 97

Wai Yu-Tsang v The Queen [1992] 1 AC 269; [1991] 3 WLR 1006; [1991] 4 All ER 664; (1992) 94 Cr App R 264; [1992] Crim LR 425; (1991) 135 SJLB 164 (PC) (HK) . . . **855–857**, 857

Warner v Commissioner of Police of the Metropolis [1969] 2 AC 256 (HL) . . . 233

Wass v DPP CO/1101/00, 11 May 2000 (QBD) . . . 365

Watmore v Jenkins [1962] 2 QB 572 . . . 708

Webley v Buxton [1977] QB 481 . . . 827

Welham v DPP [1961] AC 103; [1960] 2 WLR 669; [1960] 1 All ER 805 (HL) . . . 855, 857

West Deutsche Landesbank Girozentrale v
  Islington LBC [1985] 1 All ER 740 . . . 601
Westminster City Council v Croyalgrange Ltd
  [1986] 1 WLR 674; [1986] 2 All ER 353
  (HL) . . . 174
Whittaker v Campbell [1984] QB 318 . . . 551
Wiffin v Kincard (1807) 2 Bos & PNR 471; 127 ER
  713 . . . 346
Wilcox v Jeffery [1951] 1 All ER 464 (DC) . . . 896,
  929
Williams v Phillips (1957) 41 Cr App R 5 . . . 507
Wilson v Pringle [1987] QB 237 (CA) . . . 347
Wilsons & Clyde Coal Co Ltd v English [1938]
  AC 57 (HL) . . . 794
Winterwerp v Netherlands (A/33) (1979–80)
  2 EHRR 387, ECHR . . . 715, 716
Winzar v Chief Constable of Kent (1983)

The Times, 28 March 1983 . . . 100
Wise v Dunning [1902] 1 KB 167 . . . 109
Woolmington v DPP [1935] AC 462
  (HL) . . . 62
Workman v Cowper [1961] 2 QB 143 . . . 669

X v Netherlands (A/91); *sub nom* X and Y v
  Netherlands (8978/80) (1986) 8 EHRR 235
  (ECrtHR) . . . 674

Yip Chiu-Cheung v The Queen [1995] 1 AC 111
  (HL) . . . 146, 852

Zezev v Governor of Brixton Prison; *sub nom*
  Zezev v United States; Yarimaka v United States
  [2002] EWHC 589; [2002] 2 Cr App R 33;
  [2002] Crim LR 648 . . . 655

TABLE OF STATUTES

Where sections are reproduced in full, the page number is shown in **bold**.

Abortion Act 1967 . . . 246
  s.1(1)(d) . . . 680
Accessories and Abettors Act 1861
  s.8 . . . 849, **890**, 897
Adoption of Children Act 2002
  s.67 . . . 462
Age of Marriage Act 1929
  s.1 . . . 229
Anti-terrorism, Crime and Security
    Act 2001 . . . 22, 363

Bills of Exchange Act 1882
  s.27(1) . . . 600
British Nationality Act 1948
  s.3 . . . 246

Children Act 1961
  s.11(1) . . . 165
Children Act 1989
  s.23(2)(a) . . . 462
  s.59(1)(a) . . . 462
  s.82(5) . . . 461
Children Act 2004
  s.58 . . . 684
Children and Young Persons Act 1933
  s.1 . . . 89, 95
  s.50 . . . 721
Civil Aviation Act 1982
  s.61 . . . 62
Communications Act 2003 . . . 341
Computer Misuse Act 1990 . . . 504, 506, 546, 646,
    654–657, 661
  s.1 . . . **655**
  s.1(2) . . . 655, 656
  s.2 . . . 656
  s.3 . . . 656
  s.3(1) . . . **656**
  s.3(5) . . . 657
  s.17 . . . 655
  s.17(2) . . . **655**
  s.17(5) . . . 656
County Courts Act 1984
  s.14(1)(b) . . . 362
Crime and Disorder Act 1998 . . . 15
  s.1 . . . 13, 14
  s.28 . . . 362
  s.28(1)(a) . . . 363
  s.28(1)(b) . . . 214, 363
  s.29 . . . 362
  s.30 . . . 362

  s.30(1) . . . **654**
  ss.31–32 . . . 362
  s.34 . . . **722**
Crime (Sentences) Act 1997
  ss.2–4 . . . 82
Criminal Appeal Act 1968
  s.2(1) . . . 533, 634
  s.3(2) . . . 354
  s.33(2) . . . 512
Criminal Attempts Act 1981 . . . 817, 824, 831, 849,
    879
  s.1 . . . 819, 829
  s.1(1) . . . 817, 823, 830
  s.1(2) . . . 538, 820, 821, **828**, 830, 833
  s.1(3) . . . **828**, 832
  s.1(4) . . . 827
  s.1(4)(b) . . . 917
  s.4(3) . . . 823
  s.5 . . . 844
Criminal Damage Act 1971 . . . 163, 164, 167, 645,
    665
  s.1 . . . 158, 160, 161, 162, 165, **645**, 653
  s.1(1) . . . 92, 161, 162, 164, 167, 284, 648, 650,
    654
  s.1(2) . . . 161, 284, 647, 652, **652**, 653,
    660
  s.1(2)(a) . . . 660
  s.1(2)(b) . . . 652, **653**, 659, 660
  s.1(3) . . . **651**
  s.2 . . . 369, 645
  s.3 . . . 645, 649
  s.4 . . . 645, 652
  s.5 . . . **648**, 653
  s.5(2) . . . 648, 650, 728
  s.5(2)(b) . . . 648, 649, 650, 688
  s.5(3) . . . **728**
  s.10 . . . **647**
Criminal Justice Act 1925
  s.47 . . . 697, 704
Criminal Justice Act 1967
  s.8 . . . 153, 165, 209
Criminal Justice Act 1987
  s.12(1) . . . **854**
Criminal Justice Act 1988 . . . 541
  s.39 . . . 337
  s.93A(1) . . . 174
Criminal Justice Act 1991 . . . 622
Criminal Justice Act 1993
  Part III . . . 541
Criminal Justice Bill 2003 . . . 81

Criminal Justice and Public Order Act 1994
   s.35 . . . 897
   s.61 . . . 636
   ss.68–69 . . . 636
Criminal Law Act 1967
   s.1 . . . 891
   s.3 . . . **665**, 666, 672
   s.4 . . . 923
   s.4(1) . . . 827
   s.5 . . . 630, 923
   s.5(1) . . . 827
   s.6(4) . . . 826, 827
Criminal Law Act 1977 . . . 845, 849, 890
   s.1 . . . 853
   s.1(1) . . . **844**, 847, 849, 851, 853
   s.1(1)(b) . . . 853
   s.1(2) . . . 848
   s.2(2)(a)–(c) . . . 845
   s.4(1) . . . 843
   s.5(1)–(2) . . . **844**
   s.5(7) . . . 839
   s.5(8)–(9) . . . 846
   s.6 . . . 369
   s.51(1) . . . 369
Criminal Law Amendment Act 1885 . . . 432
Criminal Lunatics Act 1800 . . . 712
Criminal Procedure (Insanity) Act
     1964 . . . 720
   s.4 . . . 717
   s.4(5)–(6) . . . 718
   s.4A . . . 717, 719, 720, 721
   s.4A(1) . . . 719
   s.5(3) . . . 717
   s.6 . . . 711
Criminal Procedure (Insanity and
     Unfitness to Plead) Act 1991 . . . 266, 717,
     762
   s.1 . . . 716
Customs and Excise Management Act
     1979
   s.170(1)(b) . . . 829
   s.170(2) . . . 853
   s.170(2)(b) . . . 852

Dangerous Dogs Act 1991 . . . 22
Domestic Violence, Crime and Victims
     Act 2004
   s.5 . . . 290

Explosive Substances Act 1883 . . . 645
   s.4 . . . 670
Explosives Act 1875 . . . 670

Family Allowance Act 1945 . . . 837
Firearms Act 1968
   s.1(1)(a) . . . 231
   s.16 . . . 653
   s.25 . . . 174
Forgery and Counterfeiting Act 1981
   s.3 . . . 174
Fraud Bill 2005 . . . **618–620**

Health and Safety at Work etc Act 1974
   s.3(1) . . . 791
   s.33(1)(a) . . . 791
Homicide Act 1957 . . . 328
   s.1 . . . 248
   s.2 . . . 262, 271
   s.2(1) . . . 266, 267, 270, 271
   s.2(2)–(3) . . . 266
   s.2(4) . . . 916
   s.3 . . . 250, 259, 262, 263, 264, 271
   s.4 . . . 272
   s.4(2)–(3) . . . 272
Homicide (Jersey) Law 1986
   Art.3 . . . 262
   Art.4 . . . 262, 264
Human Fertilisation and Embryology Act 1990
   s.37(1)(a) . . . 246
Human Rights Act 1998 . . . 11, 18, 21, 52, 55–56,
     63, 68, 234, 273, 328, 615, 673, 705, 716, 778,
     897
   s.3 . . . 55, 63, 65, 67
   s.6 . . . **55–56**
   s.6(3)(a) . . . 56
Human Tissue Act 1961 . . . 506

Incitement to Disaffection Act 1934 . . . 834
Incitement to Mutiny Act 1797 . . . 834
Indecency with Children Act 1960
   s.1 . . . 224, 226, 227
   s.1(1) . . . 46, 48, 224, 226, 227, 229
   s.6(3) . . . 228
Infant Life (Preservation) Act 1929 . . . 246
Infanticide Act 1938
   s.1(1) . . . 274
Insolvency Act 1986
   s.216 . . . 230
Interpretation Act 1978
   s.5 . . . 789

Larceny Act 1916
   s.33 . . . 540
Law Reform (Year and a Day Rule) Act 1996 . . .
     102, 247, 275
Licensing Act
   s.59(1) . . . 797

Magistrates Courts Act 1980
   s.2 . . . 834
   s.44 . . . 890
   s.45 . . . 834
   s.101 . . . 67
   Sch.1 . . . 839
Malicious Communications Act 1988 . . . 630
Malicious Damage Act 1861 . . . 44
   s.2 . . . 645
   s.51 . . . 164
Marriage Act 1753 (Hardwicke's Marriage Act) . . .
     433

Marriage Act 1949
  s.2 . . . 229

Mental Capacity Act 2005
  s.3 . . . 388
  s.44 . . . 89

Mental Health Act 1983 . . . 77, 677, 725
  s.1 . . . 463

Metropolitan Police Act 1839
  s.54(13) . . . 11

Misuse of Drugs Act 1971 . . . 100, 232, 234, 700
  s.5 . . . 64, 234
  s.5(3) . . . 233
  s.5(4) . . . 234
  s.8 . . . 131, 174
  s.19 . . . 839
  s.28 . . . 64, 233, 234

Offences Against the Person Act 1861 . . . 359, 373, 377, 380, 381, 382, 383, 396, 398–405, 628, 689
  s.4 . . . 834
  s.8 . . . 891
  s.9 . . . 246
  s.16 . . . 340, 369
  s.18 . . . 217, 351, **355**, 356, 357, **363**, 373, 375, 391, 398–404, 684, 686, 919
  s.20 . . . 115, **349**, 350, 351, 352, 353, 354, 355, 356, 357, 362, 369, 370, 373, 375, 377–383, 391, 398–404, 684, 919
  s.23 . . . 113, 279, **357**, 358, 361, 846
  s.24 . . . **357**, 359, 361, 846
  s.29 . . . 363
  s.36 . . . 21, 362
  ss.38–46 . . . 402
  s.47 . . . 115, 338, 339, 347, 349, 354, 357, 362, 377–383, 384, 385, 391, 398–404, 431, 684
  s.58 . . . 176, 246, 358, 683
  s.59 . . . 935

Police Act 1964
  s.51 . . . 402
  s.51(1) . . . 345

Police Act 1996
  s.89 . . . 362

Police and Criminal Evidence Act 1984
  s.78 . . . 705

Powers of Criminal Courts (Sentencing) Act 2000 . . . 542
  ss.109–111 . . . 82

Prevention of Crime Act 1953 . . . 100, 232

Prohibition of Female Circumcision Act 1985 . . . 387, 843

Protection of Children Act 1978
  s.1 . . . 839

Protection from Eviction Act 1977 . . . 88
  s.1 . . . 826

Protection from Harassment Act 1997 . . . 175, 341, 367, 417, 418, 419, 420, 447
  s.1 . . . **364–365**, 367
  s.1(2) . . . 367

s.1(3) . . . 367
s.1(3)(c) . . . 367
s.2 . . . 362, 367, 418
s.3 . . . 417, 418
s.4 . . . 363, **368**
s.7(2) . . . 366
s.7(3) . . . 365, 418
s.7(4) . . . 365

Public Health Act 1875 . . . 243

Public Order Act 1986
  s.1 . . . 369, 924
  ss.2–3 . . . 369
  s.4 . . . 363, 369
  s.4A . . . 363
  s.5 . . . 11, 363, 369
  s.6(5) . . . 171

Road Traffic Act 1972
  s.6(1) . . . 894

Road Traffic Act 1988 . . . 827
  s.1 . . . **288–289**
  s.2A . . . **289**
  s.2A(2)–(3) . . . 289
  s.3A(1) . . . **289**
  s.4(2) . . . 100, 171
  s.5 . . . 894
  s.5(1)(a) . . . 717
  s.5(1)(b) . . . 63, 65
  s.5(2) . . . 63, 65, 66
  s.6 . . . 88
  s.7 . . . 289

Road Traffic Act 1991 . . . 288

Road Traffic Regulation Act 1984
  s.5(1) . . . 798

Sale of Food and Drugs Acts . . . 242
Sale of Goods Act 1979 . . . 571

Securities Amendment Act 1988
  s.20 . . . 793

Sex Offenders Act 1997
  Pt I . . . 226
  Sch.1
    para.1(1)(b) . . . 226

Sexual Offences Act 1956 . . . 426, 443
  s.2 . . . 453
  s.3 . . . 434, 453
  s.5 . . . 229, 230
  s.6 . . . 229, 230
  s.6(3) . . . 229
  s.14 . . . 227, **228–229**, 229, 230
  s.14(1) . . . 228, 229
  s.14(2) . . . 229
  s.14(4) . . . 229
  s.15 . . . 227

Sexual Offences Act 1967 . . . 383

Sexual Offences Act 2003 . . . 428, 429, 434, 440, 441, 448, 491, 496
  s.1 . . . **426**, 428, **445–446**, 448
  s.1(1)(c) . . . 450
  s.1(2) . . . 415, 447, 451

Sexual Offences Act 2003 – *continued*
s.1(3) . . . 415
s.2 . . . 427, 428, **454**
s.3 . . . 427, **454**, 456
s.4 . . . **457**
s.5 . . . 441, 458, 459
ss.6–7 . . . 458, 459
s.8 . . . 458
s.9 . . . 459
s.9(1) . . . **459**
s.10 . . . 459, 840
ss.11–14 . . . 459
s.15 . . . 459, **460**
s.15(2) . . . **420**
s.16 . . . 441, 460
s.16(1) . . . **460**, 461
s.17 . . . 441, 460
s.17(1) . . . 461
s.18 . . . 399, 441, 460
s.18(1) . . . 461
s.19 . . . 399, 441, 460
ss.20–21 . . . 399, 441
s.22 . . . 399, 441, 460
s.22(2) . . . 461
s.23 . . . 441, 460, 461
s.24 . . . 441, 461
ss.25–26 . . . 461
s.27 . . . **461–462**
ss.30–41 . . . 463
ss.47–49 . . . 462
ss.52–53 . . . 462
ss.57–59 . . . 463
s.61 . . . 357, 458
s.62 . . . 362, 629
s.62(2) . . . 629
s.63 . . . 458, **629**
s.64 . . . **463–464**
ss.65–67 . . . 464
ss.69–70 . . . 464
s.74 . . . **429**, 442, 444, 453, 454
s.75 . . . **437**, 439, 448, 450, 452, 454
s.75(1) . . . **437**, 446
s.75(2) . . . **437**, 442, 446
s.75(2)(a)–(b) . . . 438, 453
s.75(2)(c)–(d) . . . 438
s.75(2)(e) . . . 438, 441
s.75(2)(f) . . . 438, 442, 449
s.75(3) . . . **437**
s.76 . . . **429–430**, 436, 439, 444, 446, 448, 449, 452, 454
s.76(2) . . . 435
s.76(2)(a) . . . 430, 435, 438
s.77 . . . 399
s.78 . . . **455**
s.78(a) . . . 455
s.78(b) . . . 455, 456
s.79(2) . . . 428
s.79(3) . . . 427, 428
s.79(6) . . . 463
s.79(8) . . . 455, 457
s.79(8)(c) . . . 457
s.79(9) . . . 428

Statutory Instruments Act 1946
s.3(2) . . . 729

Suicide Act 1961 . . . 273
s.2(1) . . . 272, 827

Tattooing of Minors Act 1969 . . . 388
Telecommunications Act 1984
ss.42–43 . . . 369
Terrorism Act 2000
s.11(1) . . . 64, 65
s.11(2) . . . 64
Theft Act 1968 . . . 32, 185, 443, 513, 516, 517, 528, 532, 555, 558, 570, 580, 615
s.1 . . . 401, **501**, 515, 552, **583**
s.1(1) . . . 512, 513, 514, 516, 517
s.1(2) . . . 524
s.1(3) . . . 515
s.2 . . . 186, 529, **530**, 532, 580
s.2(1) . . . 531, 532
s.2(1)(a) . . . 518, 521, 530, 531, 556, 729
s.2(1)(b) . . . 514, 519, 530
s.2(1)(c) . . . 530
s.2(2) . . . 531, 532
s.3 . . . 506, 522, 523, 527, 571
s.3(1) . . . **511**, 513, 517, 522, 602
s.3(2) . . . **522**
s.4 . . . 515, 577
s.4(1) . . . **502**, 515, 596, 603
s.4(2) . . . **502**, 515
s.4(2)(a) . . . 502
s.4(2)(b) . . . **502**
s.4(2)(c) . . . 503
s.4(3) . . . **503**
s.4(4) . . . **504**
s.5 . . . 515, 521
s.5(1) . . . **507**, 508, 511, 515, 521, 580, 601
s.5(2) . . . **507–508**
s.5(3) . . . **508**, 509, 601, 602
s.5(4) . . . **510**, 511, 521, 551, 601
s.6 . . . 521, 524–525, 528, 560, 596, 604
s.6(1) . . . 525, 527, 528, 529
s.6(2) . . . 526, 528
s.8 . . . 362, **534–535**
s.8(1) . . . 554
s.8(2) . . . 536
s.9 . . . **621**, 624, 637
s.9(1) . . . 626, 627
s.9(1)(a) . . . 621, 622, 627, 628, 636, 637, 638
s.9(1)(b) . . . 622, 627, 628, 636, 637, 638
s.9(4) . . . 622
s.10 . . . **628**, 637
s.11(1) . . . 514, 529
s.12 . . . 546
s.12(1) . . . 514, 529
s.13 . . . 504, 514, 571
s.15 . . . 515, 532, 551, 552, 553, 576–577, 580, 581, 595, 596, 611, 612, 790
s.15(1) . . . 513, 531, 537, 572, **576**
s.15(2) . . . 577
s.15(4) . . . **570**, 580
s.15A . . . **581**, 597
s.16 . . . 574, **582**, 588, 596, 790
s.16(1) . . . 574, 598
s.16(2)(a) . . . 582
s.17 . . . 401, 790

Theft Act 1968 – *continued*
  s.18 . . . **790**
  s.20(2) . . . 531, 597
  s.21 . . . 369, **630**, 633
  s.21(1) . . . **633**
  s.22 . . . **536–537**
  s.22(1) . . . **540**
  s.24(2) . . . **537**, 538
  s.24(3) . . . 537, 538
  s.24A . . . 542
  s.25 . . . 232, 579, 628, 935
  s.34 . . . 630
  s.34(1) . . . 515, 580
  s.34(2)(a) . . . **630–631**
  s.34(2)(b) . . . **537**, 591
Theft Act 1978 . . . 570
  s.1 . . . 571, 596
  s.1(2) . . . 591
  s.1(3) . . . 596
  s.2 . . . 584, 585–589, **585**, 588, 592
  s.2(1)(a) . . . 586, 587, 588
  s.2(1)(b) . . . 587, 588, 591, 612
  s.2(1)(c) . . . 574, 586, 588
  s.2(2) . . . 586
  s.2(3) . . . 591
  s.3 . . . 587, **589**, 590, 591, 592
  s.3(1) . . . 590, 593
  s.3(3) . . . 591
  s.5(2) . . . 591

Theft (Amendment) Act 1996 . . . 581, 583, 597
Trade Marks Act 1994
  s.92 . . . 64
Transport Act 1968
  s.99(5) . . . 897

Visual Rights Act 1990 (US) . . . 658

Wireless Telegraphy Act 1949
  s.1(1) . . . 839

Youth Justice and Criminal Evidence
  Act 1999 . . . 50
  s.41 . . . 452

United States Law

California Penal Code
  s.646.9(e) . . . 419–450

International Law

Convention on the Rights of the Child
  Art.40.1 . . . 164
International Covenant of Civil and Political
  Rights 1966 . . . 97

TABLE OF STATUTORY INSTRUMENTS

Air Navigation (No.2) Order (SI 1995/1970)
   Art.57 . . . 62
Aliens Order 1920
   Art.1(3) . . . 100
   Art.18(1)(b) . . . 100

Money Laundering Regulations (SI 1993/1933) . . .
   542

AN INTRODUCTION TO CRIMINAL LAW

1 WHAT IS A CRIME?

You probably think you know what crimes are: murder, rape, theft, and so forth. But is it possible to define a crime? A wide range of conduct can be the basis for criminal offences. Everything from murder to shoplifting, from pollution offences to speeding. So is it possible to define 'a crime' in a way which includes all these offences?

As the following extract demonstrates, the answer to the question 'what is a crime?' depends on your perspective:[1]

R. White and F. Haines, *Crime and Criminology* (2nd edn., Oxford: OUP, 2000), 4–5

Legal and sociological definitions of crime

There are many diverse conceptions of crime, each of which reflects a different scientific and ideological viewpoint. . . . For present purposes, we can summarise broad differences in definition in the following way:

- A **formal legal** definition of crime is one which says that what the state identifies as a crime is a crime. That is, if something is written into the criminal law, and is subject to state sanction in the form of a specific penalty, then that activity is a crime.

- A **social harm** conception of crime says that crime involves both criminal offences (e.g., assault) and civil offences (e.g., negligence), in that each type of action or inaction brings with it some type of harm. Each should therefore attract some sort of penalty.

- A **cross-cultural universal norm** argument states that crime, in essence, does not vary across different cultures. Thus, murder is murder regardless of the society, and we can postulate conduct norms that cut across diverse cultural backgrounds.

- A **labelling approach** to the definition of crime argues that crime only really exists when there has been a social response to particular activity that labels that activity as criminal. If there is no label, there is in effect no crime.

- A **human rights** approach says that crime occurs whenever a human right has been

---

[1] Lacey (1998a). For the benefits of considering the law from different perspectives see: Lacey (2001) on history; Nelken (1987) on economics, Ainsworth (2000) on psychology, and Fletcher (2001) on philosophy.

violated, regardless of the legality or otherwise of the action. Such a conception also expands the definition of crime to include oppressive practices such as racism, sexism, and class-based exploitation.

- A **human diversity** approach defines crime in terms of the manner in which deviance represents a normal response to oppressive or unequal circumstances. A major focus here is on power relations, and the attempts by dominant groups to restrict human diversity of experience, language, and culture.

. . . [T]he variation in definition often has real consequences upon how different types of behaviour are dealt with at a practical level. For example, we might consider the issue of violence.

'In the home, parents hit children; on the playing field, sportsmen assault each other; at work, industrial "accidents" occur; in our community, dangerous chemicals are dumped; our governments turn a blind eye to the practices of some police officers; and our governments are responsible for the mass violence of war' (Alder, 1991, p. 61).

How violence is perceived and responded to by criminal justice institutions depends very much upon a range of political and social factors. Crime is not inherent in an activity: it is defined under particular material circumstances and in relation to specific social processes.

As this extract suggests, whether a particular kind of conduct should be regarded as criminal can change over time as a response to political and social factors and depends on where in the world you live. For example, the legal response to homosexual activity[2] has changed over the decades in response to a variety of social, political, and legal influences.

The definition of a crime comes into focus when it is necessary to distinguish crimes from civil wrongs. If you hit someone you may be prosecuted for the criminal offence of assault and receive a fine. You may also be sued by the victim for damages in the civil law of tort. Both proceedings in a sense result in the same outcome for the defendant: a loss of money; but these legal proceedings have crucial differences. It is the censure and punishment that are attached to a criminal conviction which can explain the difference between civil and criminal proceedings.[3] A fine carries with it moral blame, while an award of damages may signify that a person is responsible for the loss, but not carry the sense of condemnation that a criminal sanction does. This has led Andrew von Hirsch and others to suggest that it is censure that attaches to a criminal penalty which most clearly distinguishes criminal wrongs from other legal wrong.[4] Not everyone is convinced by this argument. It is, for example, possible to award punitive damages in civil proceedings if the court regards the tort or breach of contract as a particularly blameworthy one. A different explanation of the difference between civil and criminal proceedings is provided by Andrew Simester and Bob Sullivan:

Assault involves an interference with fundamental rights of the victim, rights which the State is perceived to have a duty to protect. By contrast, individuals are normally able to protect themselves against breach of contract, and can satisfactorily undo any damage suffered with the aid of the civil law.[5]

---

[2] Lesbian sexual behaviour has not been the subject of specific prohibition under the criminal law.

[3] G. Williams (1955); Fitzgerald (1960). Punishment is what defines criminal proceedings for the purposes of Art. 6 of the European Convention on Human Rights (Ashworth 2001).

[4] von Hirsch (1993: 9–12).   [5] Simester and Sullivan (2003: 2).

They, therefore, argue that the state intervenes with the criminal law to protect citizens when people are unable to protect themselves or receive adequate compensation through the civil courts.

In the following passage Lucia Zedner warns against defining crimes simply in terms of the official legal response. She starts by setting out the official legal classification of what crimes are, before challenging them.

L. Zedner, *Criminal Justice* (Oxford: OUP, 2005), 58–63.

Thinking about crime as a legal category poses problems for students of criminal justice. It tends to downplay the contingency of crime and, by imposing fixed definitions, to deny its open and contested nature. Understanding the central components of the legal classification of crime is indispensable but it is also fraught with difficulties.

First, central to the legal classification of crime is its public quality. A wrong that arises primarily in respect of the rights and duties owed only to individuals is the subject of civil law, whether as a tort, a breach of contract or trust and property rights. A crime is differentiable by the fact that the wrong is deemed to offend against duties owed to society. Just to complicate matters, the same conduct (or inaction) may be both a civil and a criminal wrong; in which case proceedings may generally be taken in both civil and criminal court simultaneously. For example, an assault is potentially both a tort and a crime, and a deception may entail a tort, a breach of contract or trust or be treated as a crime. Given this overlap it is important to identify the differences that determine whether civil or criminal liability, or both, arise. The liability of the civil wrongdoer is based principally upon the loss he or she has occasioned, whereas the criminal wrong resides, in principle at least, in the voluntary action of the perpetrator, their culpability, and the harm caused. And whereas in civil law proceedings are generally brought by the injured party in order to secure compensation or restitution, it is generally the state that prosecutes and punishes crime. A serious problem with the legal classification of crime as public wrong is that it is uninformative: a crime is that which is legally designated as criminal. But the classification does not tell us how, why, or to what end that legal designation has arisen. It cannot explain why some forms of deviance attract the response of the law and not others. It does not explain what determines whether that response is criminal, or civil, or both.

A second facet of the legal classification of crime is that every crime must be so designated by statute or case law and its component parts clearly specified. Every crime consists of a conduct element and, unless it is a crime of strict liability, an accompanying mental element. The conduct element specifies the act or conduct, omission, consequence, or state of affairs that is the substance of the offence. The mental element specifies the state of mind that the prosecution must prove the defendant had at the time of committing the offence. Both must be set down in law to define an offence and both must be proven in order to secure a conviction. For lawyers, this definition has some important attractions. It honours the principle that there be no crime without law and that liability arises only in respect of actions or omissions already proscribed by law as criminal. This principle allows people to go about their daily business free from fear of arbitrary punishment. It gives fair warning to those who choose to offend against the law that they may expect punishment to ensue. It respects the presumption of innocence by making it improper to speak of someone as a criminal until all aspects of liability for a crime have been proven in a court of law. If it is right to refer to suspects, not offenders, in the pre-trial process, then it must be right also to talk only of alleged crimes and alleged victims until the case has been proven in court.

As a substantive definition of crime, however, legal classification is problematic. Although it specifies the structural conditions (principally the mental and conduct elements) that must be met before a court of law will convict, it provides little purchase on the social phenomenon that is crime. To say both that criminal law responds to crime and that crime is defined by the criminal law creates an unfortunate circularity. Taken at face value, it suggests that without criminal law there can be no crime or even that the criminal law, in some bizarre sense, is the formal cause of Crime.

A third aspect is that legal ideology makes certain claims as to the objectivity and political neutrality of legal doctrine and the autonomy of legal reasoning by which judgment is reached. Critical scrutiny of the criminal law allows the student of criminal justice to understand that doctrinal framework and the larger values and political factors that underlie it. For example, attention to the centrality of the mental element in the general part of the criminal law attests to its importance as a mechanism for assigning responsibility. But legal ideology can be problematic too. The proclaimed authority of the judgment and bringing in of the guilty verdict are brutal techniques for imposing order on social strife or messy disputes in which attribution of blame is often far less clear-cut than the law pretends.

A fourth aspect of legal classification is the requirement that crime be subject to a distinctive set of procedures. The rules of evidence, the standard of proof, the requirement that crime be adjudicated in a designated forum, subject to its own procedural rules, and staffed by its own personnel, are all intrinsic to the legal definition of crime. The requirement of proof beyond all reasonable doubt, the principle of orality, and the rules and conventions of the adversarial system combine with the legal institutions of the magistracy, judiciary, and lay jury as distinctive features of the criminal process. Understood this way, crime can be defined as that which is the subject of the criminal process: without prosecution and conviction, no liability for crime can be said to have occurred. The chief problem with this approach is that it is doubtful whether defining crime by reference to laws of evidence and procedure takes one much further.

For the student of criminal justice, the larger problem lies less in the elements so far discussed than the fact that most criminal law scholarship does not address the ways in which law is in practice applied by police, prosecutors, defence lawyers, magistrates, and judges. A simple application of legal definitions misses important variations in social attitudes and moral judgments that determine how those definitions are in practice imposed. And it cannot account for disparities in the application of the law according to the age, sex, class, and race of the supposed perpetrator.

To think about crime, as some criminal law textbooks still do, as comprising discrete, autonomous legal categories remote from the social world, is to engage in an absorbing but esoteric intellectual activity. The exercise of the law is not an arcane clerical task of filing different behaviours in discrete and precisely labelled boxes to achieve nothing more than a semblance of order. Of course, conceptual clarification and normative critique are essential elements of criminal law. Criminal law must define crimes clearly and crimes so defined should be worthy of their label. But the emphasis given by some textbooks to the legal requirements of mental and conduct elements is at odds with the practice of the criminal law, where these concepts play a more marginal role. To illustrate, students of criminal law typically begin their studies by minute examination of the intricacies of the mental elements of crime. They are less often asked to begin by reflecting upon the fact that the great bulk of the 8,000 offences in English criminal law are crimes of strict liability and, as such, require no intention. The sheer number of offences of strict liability raises doubts about the centrality of intention to criminal liability and about the centrality of individual responsibility. It might even be said to place in question what the criminal law is for. With respect to offences of strict liability at least, it is difficult to sustain the notion that crime is principally defined by culpable wrongdoing.

The misapprehension that practising lawyers devote their energies to tortured discussion about the degree of certainty needed to infer or find intention from evidence of foresight would similarly be dispelled by observation of the caseload and working patterns of magistrates' courts where intention is rarely at issue. Likewise, although university courses generally focus on serious offences such as murder, manslaughter, assault, and rape, in practice petty property, public order, and driving offences are the staple work of the lower courts. It is not surprising that generations of students of criminal law are misled into thinking that serious offences and jury trials are the norm, and that sentences of imprisonment are common punishment. Attention to the statistics of recorded crime; to the proportion of cases going to magistrates' and Crown courts; and to patterns of punishment quickly reveals another truth.

Most importantly, for a criminologist to accept that crime is that which is defined by law would lead to some perverse results. To proceed from the idea that crime exists only in law and only insofar as it has been proven in a court of law would excise from criminology a good part of its present subject matter, scope, and interest. By this definition there could be no dark figure of unrecorded crime since, legally, it is not crime at all. It would also require that the *British Crime Survey* be renamed the British Survey of Alleged Crime and its respondents called not victims but claimants. Official criminal statistics, on the other hand, would enjoy a perfect fit with crime. For by definition only those acts and omissions proven to satisfy the legal requirements of crime before a court of law and recorded as such would count as crime. Studies of attrition rates would also need to be re-conceptualized. There could be no gap between the commission and reporting of crime, nor between reporting of crime and recording by police, and no failure of clear-up rates either. Likewise there could be no offenders other than those convicted, nor any victim whose offender has not been so convicted. In sum, the possibility of hidden crime, of unreported crime, of unsolved crime, or of unknown or undisclosed victims would evaporate and much criminological endeavour with it.

This emphatically doctrinal account of criminal law is diminishing as legal and criminological scholarship converge. Criminal lawyers have fruitfully extended their scrutiny to the social world in which the laws they study are constructed, applied, and enforced. And criminologists reflect more and more upon the legal categorization of activities as criminal: to ask not only why people offend, but also why this behaviour, but not that, is legally designated criminal. If, as is currently the case in England, the study of criminal justice increasingly takes place within law schools, then a conception of crime that speaks little to its legally trained students must be undesirable. But convergence is not union and criminal justice scholars sitting at the margins of the two disciplines have to hold two different definitions of crime, the criminological and the legal, simultaneously in play. Those reading their work had better be quite clear which meaning they employ on each occasion. The crime that is the verdict of a jury persuaded beyond all reasonable doubt of the guilt of the offender is, of necessity, a different phenomenon from the crime concealed in the dark field that has yet to face the bright light of the legal process.

FURTHER READING

Finkelstein, C. (2000), 'Positivism and the Notion of an Offense', *California Law Review* 88: 335.

Husak, D. (2002), 'Limitations on Criminalization and the General Part of the Criminal Law' in S. Shute and A. Simester (eds.), *Criminal Law Theory* (Oxford: OUP).

Williams, G. (1955), 'The Definition of Crime', *Current Legal Problems* 107.

2 THE ROLE OF CRIMINAL LAW

What should the aim of the criminal law be?

The American Model Penal Code, section 1.02

(1) The general purposes of the provisions governing the definition of offenses are:

   (a) to forbid and prevent conduct that unjustifiably and inexcusably inflicts or threatens substantial harm to individual or public interests;

   (b) to subject to public control persons whose conduct indicates that they are disposed to commit crimes;

   (c) to safeguard conduct that is without fault from condemnation as criminal;

   (d) to give fair warning of the nature of the conduct declared to constitute an offense;

   (e) to differentiate on reasonable grounds between serious and minor offenses.

Of course, not everyone will agree with all of these. Even if they are accepted these principles will often conflict, and where they do there will be disagreement over how these should be balanced.[6] Take the example of stalking. This is behaviour which clearly falls within (a) as conduct which harms another. But there is great difficulty in defining precisely what stalking is as is required by (d). The law must then decide to either enact legislation which is rather vague but will mean that stalkers can be prosecuted, or enact legislation which is precise, but might allow some stalkers to 'get away' with their wrongdoing.

In the following passage William Wilson seeks to define the purposes of the criminal law by summarizing the interests that the law seeks to protect:

W. Wilson, *Criminal Law* (Harlow: Longman, 2003), 6

The major concerns of the criminal law may be expressed, therefore, as follows:

A The support of public interests in:

1. preventing physical injury. This accounts for the crimes of murder, manslaughter, arson and other crimes of violence; also certain road traffic offences and those relating to public health and safety.

2. proscribing personal immorality deemed injurious to society's well-being. This accounts for crimes such as bigamy, incest, sado-masochism, bestiality and obscenity, drug possession and supply.

---

[6] Robinson (2002: 79) argues that inevitably conflicts will arise between these aims.

3. preventing the moral corruption of the young through crimes such as gross indecency with children and unlawful sexual intercourse.

4. maintaining the integrity of the state and the administration of justice through crimes such as treason, perjury, perverting the course of justice, tax evasion.

5. maintaining public order and security through offences such as riot, affray, breach of the peace, public drunkenness.

B The support of private interests in:

Remaining free from:

(a) undesired physical interference through crimes such as rape, assault, indecent assault, false imprisonment, harassment;

(b) offence through crimes such as indecent exposure, indecency in public, solicitation;

(c) undesired interference with property through crimes such as theft, robbery, taking and driving away a road vehicle, deception.

So far the aims of criminal law have been proposed in a positive light. In the following passage Nils Jareborg warns against demanding too much from the criminal law. He proposes what he calls the 'defensive model' of criminal law which sees as a primary purpose the protection of the public from misuse of state power:

N. Jareborg, 'What Kind of Criminal Law Do we Want?' in A. Snare (ed.), *Beware of Punishment* (Oslo: Pax Forlag, 1995), 24–6

The defensive model

All criminal law aims at protecting the interests of individuals, collective or public interests, or state interests, by using threats of punishment and by using execution of punishment to make the threat credible. But the defensive model (and classical criminal law too) also aims at *protecting individuals against power abuse*, against abuse of state power, excessive repression in legal or illegal forms, as well as against abuse of private, informal power, of which 'lynch justice' is the most obvious form. One could say that an important purpose is to prevent spontaneous social control and replace it with formalized social control. The scope of protection includes not only suspected offenders but also, e.g., witnesses. A central feature of this version of criminal law is that it aims at cooling down conflicts and emotions; legal certainty and justice are values that must not be subordinated to perceived needs for crime prevention. The defensive model does not regard state power as necessarily benevolent.

The distinguishing features of the defensive model as presented here concern principles for criminalization, procedural safeguards and principles for sentencing.

As regards *principles for criminalization* the following ten principles have been selected as the most important:

- A crime presupposes that a legitimate interest or value, capable of concrete specification, is violated or threatened.

- A crime presupposes that the offender is morally responsible for his deed. Criminal responsibility presupposes culpability.

- A crime consists in a separate event of wrongdoing (an evil or bad deed). The criminal law is directly concerned with an act or omission, and only indirectly concerned with the offender.
- Criminalization must be general, it must concern types of deeds; it must not concern particular cases or individuals.
- The crime types must be defined by statutory law, i.e. in general norms easily accessible to the public.
- The crime type descriptions must be understandable and determinate.
- Retroactive criminalization to the detriment of the accused is not allowed.
- The degree of reprehensibility of the crime type should be reflected in the attached penalty scale (or maximum penalty).
- Punishment is society's most intrusive and degrading sanction. Criminalization should accordingly be used only as a last resort or for the most reprehensible types of wrongdoing.
- The general threat of punishment as reflected in actual sentencing (the level of repression) should not be severer than what is proved necessary for keeping criminality at a tolerable level.

A consequence of respecting these principles is that criminalization acquires a pronounced *value-expressive function:* the criminal code may be seen as a list of worldly sins, of socially sanctioned basic moral demands.

A further, very important aspect of the classical criminal law concerns *procedural safeguards*, primarily

- The existence of independent courts.
- The prohibition of retroactive application of the law to the detriment of the accused.
- The prohibition of analogical application of the law to the detriment of the accused.
- The placing of the burden of proof on the prosecutor.
- Requiring proof beyond a reasonable doubt.
- Providing for access to independent legal counsel.
- Allowing appeal of both conviction and sentence.
- Providing for judicial review of pre-trial detention, etc.

As far as *sentencing* is concerned, in the classical criminal law it is, of course, guided by the principles of *proportionality* (between crime and punishment) and *parity* (between the punishments for equally reprehensible crimes). The courts cannot have an independent function in 'combating' crime, even if there is some room for a general change of the repression level (for general-preventive reasons) without legislation. As I mentioned above and will return to below, in addition the defensive model demands that *punishment is used parsimoniously*, that excessive suffering is avoided.

It might be protested that it is misleading to present this picture of (ideal) criminal law as resisted and on its way to losing importance. Is it not still a living ideal, yet to be realized, but gaining ground because of, among other things, the bankruptcy of the so-called treatment ideology and the increasing significance of legal documents concerning human rights? There is some truth in this. In some respects the defensive model still has a strong ideological position. Nevertheless, I want to argue that there is a strong ideological counter-current that is undermining its dominance.

As I indicated in the beginning, the question 'Why punish?' is to be answered differently, depending on what level of the criminal justice system we are dealing with, i.e. depending on what kind of punishment we are talking about: criminalization or sentencing or executing a punishment. We now turn to a fourth interpretation of the question. It concerns the existence of the criminal justice system as a whole.

The basic question is this: *Should the criminal law primarily aim at solving emerging social problems?* The answer given by the defensive model is 'No!'. Certainly, the criminalizations are there in order to help suppress different sorts of behaviour, but the exact degree of efficiency is of minor interest. (We would discuss the abolition of the criminal justice system only if it were much less efficient than it now seems to be.) For the defensive model, the point of having a criminal justice system as a response to unwanted behaviour is rather to protect the offending individual from power abuse. There are many ways of dealing with unwanted behaviour. The defensive model wants to do it in a morally acceptable way, by restraining the state and the public by giving impartial organs a decision monopoly concerning punishments. At best, the criminal law may in addition offer a consistent moral view. To sum up, the defensive model does not deny that the criminal law has a social task or function, but its criminal law policy implies that criminal law is meant to be an obstacle, not only for offenders, but also for authorities and politicians. Criminal law differs from practically all other types of law. Its function is not to solve conflicts, or to facilitate social engineering. . . .

A defensive criminal law policy is not, however, the same as a defensive criminal policy or a defensive policy concerning unwanted behaviour. There are so many methods to use other than criminalization and punishment if one really wants to accomplish something. The problem is that criminalization in itself is very cheap, and since criminality is regarded as something 'unnecessary' the different costs of enforcing the law are normally disregarded. (But at some stage the taxpayers and some offenders will, of course, experience the cost.) In contrast, one knows in advance that efficient crime control is expensive, not only in money but also in terms of personal freedom. Efficient crime prevention presupposes a reduction in the possibilities to commit crime and organized control of a kind that many would regard as too intrusive, as involving serious violations of personal integrity. Much of what would be needed for a substantial reduction of crime rates is politically unthinkable. For example, to make only women eligible as car drivers would mean a lot for the crime rate (and for the level of apparent transvestism). Few would regard this as a politically viable option.

3 THE STATISTICS OF CRIMINAL BEHAVIOUR

We will consider the statistics for particular offences when we deal with them separately. But here are some general statistics which give a picture of criminal behaviour in England and Wales. It should be noted that there is a significant difference between reported offences (those reported to the police and officially recorded) and the British Crime Survey (BCS) (where randomly selected people are interviewed and asked whether they have been the victim of violence). The BCS statistics seek to include those crimes which have not been reported to the police.

(1) The BCS estimates that for the years 2004/2005 there were 10.8 million crimes committed. Of these 5.6 million were reported to the police.[7]

---

[7] Nicholas *et al.* (2005).

(2) In 2004, 1.8 million offenders were found guilty or cautioned.[8]

(3) According to the BCS violent crime in 2004/2005 had fallen by 11% from 2003/2004.[9]

(4) The risk of being a victim of crime in a given year is 24%.[10]

(5) Property offences make up 75% of reported crime and 78% of crimes noted by the BCS.[11]

(6) The detection rate of reported offences was 19% for 2004/2005.[12]

(7) '33% of males and nine per cent of females born in 1953 had been convicted of a standard list offence before the age of 46'.[13]

(8) A recent study found 48.5% of 11- to 16-year-old children admitted to breaking the law.[14]

(9) The most recent BCS findings reveal that 45% of women have experienced some form of domestic violence, sexual assault, or stalking.[15]

(10) Over half of Britain's motorists break the speed limit every day, according to a survey by the RAC.[16]

(11) From people questioned, 47% thought the police did a good or excellent job. Also, 76% had confidence that the criminal justice system treated suspects fairly. Perhaps surprisingly, the figure was even higher amongst members of ethnic minorities.[17]

(12) The general public grossly overestimates the incidence of violent crime and grossly underestimates the length of sentences that are typically awarded.[18]

QUESTIONS

1. Do any of these statistics surprise you? Why?

2. Why is it that the general public appears to have such an inaccurate view of criminal behaviour?

FURTHER READING

Home Office (2002c), *Statistics on Race and Criminal Justice System* (London: Home Office).

—— (2002d), *Statistics on Women and the Criminal Justice System* (London: Home Office).

—— (2005), *Criminal Statistics England and Wales 2005* (London: Home Office).

Maguire, M. (2002), 'Crime Statistics, Patterns and Trends' in M. Maguire, R. Morgan, and R. Reiner, *The Oxford Handbook of Criminology* (Oxford: OUP).

4 'PRINCIPLES' OF CRIMINAL LAW

We will now turn to some of the so-called principles of criminal law. These are principles which some academic commentators and some judges have suggested underpin the English and Welsh criminal law. It must be emphasized that these are not in any sense strict rules

---

[8] Home Office (2005: 10).   [9] Nicholas *et al.* (2005: 1).   [10] Nicholas *et al.* (2005: 1).
[11] Nicholas *et al.* (2005: 15).   [12] BBC Newsonline (2005).   [13] Home Office (2002a: 18).
[14] Carvel (2003).   [15] Walby and Allen (2004).   [16] BBC Newsonline (2005d).
[17] Whitehead and Taylor (2003: 119).   [18] Mattinson and Mirrlees Black (2000: vii).

which are followed throughout the criminal law. Rather they are proposed by some as principles to which the law should aspire. It should be stressed that some commentators are wary of stating principles that apply across the whole of criminal law.

4.1 THE PRINCIPLE OF LEGALITY

This is the principle that criminal offences should be clearly enough defined to enable people who wish to be law-abiding to live their lives confident that they will not be breaking the law.[19] Consider living in a state which had a criminal law: 'It is a criminal offence to behave badly.' You would not know what 'behaving badly' meant. You may try as hard as you could to live a lawful life but still find that the authorities have regarded a particular piece of conduct as 'bad'. This principle is often viewed as a key aspect of the 'Rule of Law', a notion many constitutional lawyers promote as a central plank of a sound legal system. The principle is now enshrined in our criminal law through the Human Rights Act 1998, as we shall see.

This principle has a number of specific aspects, including the following:

(1) The law must be clear.

(2) The law must be capable of being obeyed. A law which prohibited breathing in public would clearly infringe the principle.

(3) The law must be readily available to the public. If all the laws were kept secret, then even if they were written in the clearest language you would not be able to keep them.

An example of an offence which arguably infringes this principle is section 5 of the Public Order Act 1986 which states that it is an offence to engage in disorderly behaviour or threatening, abusive, or insulting behaviour, likely to cause 'harassment, alarm or distress'. This is a potentially very wide offence, and indeed it provides a discretion for police officers to arrest people for conduct of which they do not approve.[20] One study found that it is commonly used to deal with people who swear at police officers,[21] which is different from the kind of thing that the offence was originally designed for.

4.2 THE PRINCIPLE OF RESPONSIBILITY

This is the principle that people should only be guilty in respect of conduct for which they are responsible. So, people should not be guilty for conduct over which they had no control. This principle might be infringed if the criminal law punished a person for behaviour he carried out while suffering from an epileptic fit, for example.

---

[19] See Ashworth (1991) for a discussion of how this principle should be implemented in the interpretation of criminal statutes.

[20] See e.g. *Masterson v Holden* [1986] 1 WLR 1017 (DC) where the Divisional Court held that the magistrates were entitled to say that two men kissing were 'insulting' passers-by. The defendants were charged under the Metropolitan Police Act 1839, s. 54(13).

[21] Brown and Ellis (1994).

4.3 THE PRINCIPLE OF MINIMAL CRIMINALIZATION

This principle suggests that the criminal law should prohibit something only if absolutely necessary.[22] There are practical reasons for such a principle: our courts and prisons are overcrowded enough as it is without creating an ever increasing number of offences. But there is also a principled one. A criminal sanction conveys the message that the conduct was not just bad, but bad enough to involve criminal proceedings. This censure function will be lost if less serious conduct is criminalized.[23] The criminal law, it should be remembered, is only one way of influencing behaviour that is seen as undesirable. Education, rewarding good behaviour, shaming, and civil proceedings are alternatives that the law has at its disposal for dealing with bad behaviour.[24] So, it must be asked whether it is necessary to have, according to Andrew Simester and G.R. Sullivan, 8,000 statutes which create criminal offences.[25]

In the following extract Andrew Ashworth argues that the state has become too keen to use the criminal law to deal with 'troublesome' behaviour:[26]

A. Ashworth, 'Is Criminal Law a Lost Cause?' (2000) 116 *Law Quarterly Review* 225

The number of offences in English criminal law continues to grow year by year. Politicians, pressure groups, journalists and others often express themselves as if the creation of a new criminal offence is the natural, or the only appropriate, response to a particular event or series of events giving rise to social concern. At the same time, criminal offences are tacked on to diverse statutes by various government departments, and then enacted (or, often, re-enacted) by Parliament without demur. There is little sense that the decision to introduce a new offence should only be made after certain conditions have been satisfied, little sense that making conduct criminal is a step of considerable social significance. It is this unprincipled and chaotic construction of the criminal law that prompts the question whether it is a lost cause. From the point of view of governments it is clearly not a lost cause: it is a multi-purpose tool, often creating the favourable impression that certain misconduct has been taken seriously and dealt with appropriately. But from any principled viewpoint there are important issues—of how the criminal law ought to be shaped, of what its social significance should be, of when it should be used and when not—which are simply not being addressed in the majority of instances.

. . .

Despite the disorderly state of English criminal law, it appears that the Government does profess some principles for criminalisation. In response to a parliamentary question, Lord Williams of Mostyn has stated that offences 'should be created only when absolutely necessary', and that

'In considering whether new offences should be created, factors taken into account include whether:

---

[22] Kadish (1958); Wasik, Gibbons, and Redmayne (1999: ch. 6).

[23] Feinberg (1986: ch. 5).

[24] Card and Ashworth (2000).

[25] Simester and Sullivan (2003: 44).

[26] Dennis (1997) makes a similar point, arguing that the creation of *ad hoc* criminal statutes has left the criminal law in a critical condition. For an article making some similar points, but from an American point of view, see Mann (1992).

— the behaviour in question is sufficiently serious to warrant intervention by the criminal law;

— the mischief could be dealt with under existing legislation or by using other remedies;

— the proposed offence is enforceable in practice;

— the proposed offence is tightly-drawn and legally sound; and

— the proposed penalty is commensurate with the seriousness of the offence.

The Government also takes into account the need to ensure, as far as practicable, that there is consistency across the sentencing framework.'

. . .

Although I have tried in this essay to give some flavour of the proliferation of legal forms and structures for the guidance of conduct, and thereby to demonstrate a blurring of the boundaries between criminal and regulatory and between criminal and civil, the main purpose has been to develop two lines of argument.

The first is that the criminal law is indeed a lost cause, from the point of view of principle. The Government's purported criteria for creating new crimes are not followed in practice, nor have they been in the recent past. *Pace* Lord Williams, new offences have been created to penalise non-serious misbehaviour, sometimes with maximum sentences out of pro-portion to other maxima. The empirical basis for this claim was illustrated by examples from the 1997 statute book, and particularly the offence in section 1 of the Crime and Disorder Act 1998 of breaching an anti-social behaviour order. The plain fact is that governments often take the view that the creation of a new crime sends out a symbolic message that, in blunt terms, may 'get them off a political hook'—even though the new crime fails to satisfy Lord Williams' criteria on one or more grounds.

The second line of argument is more constructive, in seeking to identify a principled core of criminal law. The core consists, it is submitted, of four interlinking principles:

The principle that the criminal law should be used, and only used, to censure persons for substantial wrongdoings. The principle recognises that the prevention of such mis-conduct is a reason for criminalising it: if serious wrongdoing can be identified, it is of social importance that its incidence be reduced. However, this should be distinguished from the less acceptable propositions *(a)* that the prevention of misconduct is a sufficient reason for criminalisation, and *(b)* that the criminal law is, either on its own or in combination with other social policies, necessarily an effective means of prevention. The tendency to over-estimate the deterrent efficacy of criminal sentencing has already been mentioned. As for crime prevention strategies, these are usually designed to minimise the risk that certain situations or opportunities will come about, or that certain individuals will find it attractive to behave in particular ways. Appropriately targeted social, educational and housing policies may well have a greater preventive effect than the enactment of a criminal offence and the conviction of (what is likely to be) a relatively small proportion of offenders, a point rarely acknowledged in the political and media discussions that lead to the creation of new crimes. However, methods of crime prevention also raise questions of moral and social principle that should be kept in view.

The principle that criminal laws should be enforced with respect for equal treatment and proportionality. The implication is that enforcement authorities and their policies ought to be reorganised so as to reflect the relative seriousness of the wrongdoing with which they are dealing, and should not remain hidebound by traditional divisions of responsibility that fail to reflect proper assessments of the culpable wrongs involved.

The principle that persons accused of substantial wrongdoing ought to be afforded the protections appropriate to those charged with criminal offences, i.e. *at least the minimum protections declared by Articles 6.2 and 6.3 of the European Convention on Human Rights.* These minimum protections ought to be regarded as an inherent element of criminal procedure, and this principle as interlinked with the others. Thus, if wrongdoing is regarded as serious enough to warrant the creation of an offence, and if it is thought so serious as to require a substantial maximum sentence, it would be a violation of this principle for a government to avoid or whittle down the protections that a person facing such a charge ought to be accorded. This, it will be recalled, is one objection to the offence of failing to comply with an anti-social behaviour order contrary to section 1 of the Crime and Disorder Act 1998. A maximum penalty of five years' imprisonment has been provided for what is a strict liability offence, all the substantive issues having been determined in earlier civil proceedings without the Article 6 safeguards. Civil-criminal hybrids designed to circumvent Convention rights are wrong in principle.

The principle that maximum sentences and effective sentence levels should be proportionate to the seriousness of the wrongdoing. The implication here, as with the second principle, is that there needs to be a root-and-branch change—a thorough revision of maximum penalties and a re-assessment of sentence levels and of differentials between them.

These are put forward as core principles. It is not claimed that they should be regarded as absolute rules, and indeed at various points above some possible qualifications to them have been discussed. Derogations from them should be argued as derogations, and should be principled in themselves.

The principles also lead in other directions that cannot be examined fully in this context. At the core is the idea that, if a particular wrong is thought serious enough to justify the possibility of a custodial sentence, that wrong should be treated as a crime, with fault required and proper procedural protection for defendants. This has implications for those minor wrongs that are presently made the subject of criminal offences simply because the criminal courts offer themselves as a quick and cheap means of dealing with them: many of the 1997 offences fall into this category, as do hundreds of other strict liability offences. A fine solution would be to create a new category of 'civil violation' or 'administrative offence' which would certainly be non-imprisonable and would normally attract a financial penalty; procedures would be simplified but would preserve minimum rights for defendants, such as access to a criminal court. Another implication of the principles should be that any new criminal code for this country ought to declare the most serious offences in English law, rather than simply those traditional offences that have been the focus of textbooks over the years.

What are the prospects for thus re-structuring and restoring integrity to the criminal law? Political reality suggests that they are unpromising: in this sense, the criminal law may be a lost cause. Even governments with large parliamentary majorities, and which profess certain criteria for the creation of new offences, may either give way to the allure of media popularity or simply not care sufficiently to adhere to their own principles. In such political circumstances it is all the more necessary to re-kindle debate about the functions and characteristics that the criminal law ought to have, and to ensure that the close interconnections between criminal law, criminal procedure and sentencing are kept at the forefront of that debate.

In the following extract Elizabeth Burney develops some of these ideas in considering the topical issue of the use of criminal sanctions to combat problems with low-level anti-social behaviour with so-called ASBOs (anti-social behaviour orders).

E. Burney, *Making People Behave* (Cullompton: Willan, 2005), 164–6

There is indeed a symmetry . . . between the erosion of civil liberties and the rule of law in the context of terrorism, and the same process at the opposite end of the scale of seriousness, involving control of disorderly and anti-social conduct. In the early twenty-first century Britain displays the syndrome to an unprecedented degree. *The Economist* (5 February 2005), in a leading article entitled 'Taking Britain's liberties', noted that '[t]he state has given itself new powers to deal with minor offences and other crimes which are scarcely less draconian than those to deal with suspected terrorism'. At least there was a public outcry and strong political resistance to the Home Secretary's intention to use executive powers to impose house arrest and other significant restrictions on terrorist suspects. There was little protest when a 13-year-old boy was subject to similar restrictions following his admittedly insupportable behaviour in his neighbourhood. In this case a court was involved, but acting in a civil capacity as it always does in such cases. The procedure has become so commonplace, and so similar to other adaptations of civil law to suit the purposes of crime control, that objections do not make headlines. In any case, the government knows that clamping down on neighbourhood pests is always popular and critics who raise principled objections are cast as enemies of community well-being.

This is a pity, because it has been important, and overdue, to recognise the more painful effects of the erosion of the quality of life in neighbourhoods that have borne the brunt of civil and economic decay. Labour politicians have been one conduit for channelling this awareness into policy-making circles. There had to be a response, but the form it has taken, and especially the accompanying rhetoric, consistently relies upon blame, enforcement and exclusion, as well as dubious adaptations of the law. One label—'anti-social behaviour'—is used to cover any number of different troubles and annoyances which in reality require quite distinct and focused responses graded and tailored to the matter in hand, be it an aggressive alcoholic neighbour, a crowd of young people gathering outside a shop, a drug-addicted beggar, a flat used for prostitution or a vandalised playground. 'Tough action on criminal neighbours' goes beyond the particular: it has a deeply symbolic meaning combining a law and order message with the creation of a powerful and disturbing image of the enemy within.

Seeing a social problem, the gut instinct in Whitehall is always to add to the statute book. Yet social action, rather than legal action, has always been the main need—sometimes, of course, backed up by legal powers, but these were already plentiful prior to 1998. As Hughes (2000: 191) remarks:

'The 1998 Act stands in a well-established British tradition of passing new legislation to deal with each perceived public order problem as it comes along, so that the law is a series of uncomfortable accretions lying, in geological terms, frequently uncomfortably one on top of another. This is because there is rarely [an] examination of what existing law can do to deal with the problem, how much existing law is relevant, and whether there is anything particularly new in the situation which actually makes a tailor-made response imperative.'

Since the Crime and Disorder Act 1998 there have been, as described in previous chapters, still further statutory accretions in the name of dealing with anti-social behaviour, and the process continues. The emphasis forcefully projected by central government at local authorities and police is that by neglecting to use all the new powers they are failing to serve the public in the manner that people are demanding. Making the authorities more responsive to local needs must be a good thing—New Labour has rightly picked up on failures in dealing with long-standing disorders in vulnerable communities. But to assume that the right way to reverse these failures is to focus legal enforcement on a few individuals whose behaviour is itself often the consequence of public service failure (or at least exacerbated by it) is manifestly the wrong way to go about it.

The thinking behind the enforcement mantra involves several distinct strands of behaviour control which have developed since Labour came to power in 1997. Defending defenceless neighbourhoods ravaged by a minority of aggressive families and individuals is one. A belief that with a bit of encouragement communities (however defined) will learn to re-establish informal social control is another. An expectation that formal, cooperative, arrangements at local government level, always under the watchful eye of central government, will solve the problems of crime and disorder that residents, voluntary organisations and businesses identify, is a third. Fourthly, reduction of visible signs of disorder (whether human or inanimate) by means of the third strand is expected to reduce fear of crime and assist the community solidarity intended in the second strand. Fifthly, the process is to be fostered through new styles of policing (or the reintroduction of old styles) that favour visibility, attention to petty crime and disorder, and direct engagement with the populace.

4.4 THE PRINCIPLE OF PROPORTIONALITY

The sentence accorded to a crime should reflect the seriousness of the offence. This is in a way obvious. It would clearly be wrong if murder carried a less serious sentence than assault, say. But there are more complex arguments over whether one offence is more or less serious than another: is rape more or less serious than having a hand cut off?

To deal with such harder cases we need a way of grading the seriousness of the harm suffered by the victim. Joel Feinberg suggests focusing on the victim's loss of opportunity or range of choices. Clearly, therefore, murder is the most serious offence as it completely destroys the victim's range of opportunities or choices. Andrew von Hirsch and Nils Jareborg have suggested another.[27] In the following extract Andrew Ashworth summarizes and analyses their proposals:

A. Ashworth, *Principles of Criminal Law* (4ᵗʰ edn., Oxford: OUP, 2003), 39–42

Is it possible to identify any agreed interests that ought to be protected by the criminal law? Some core interests are not difficult to state in general terms (e.g. physical integrity), and there are other widely-accepted interests such as personal property. Whether there is a sufficient interest in maintaining a fair financial market (insider trading), or in maintaining the integrity of marriage records (bigamy), for example, is a more difficult issue. In order to take the subject further, the path-breaking work of Andrew von Hirsch and Nils Jareborg should be introduced. Their essay is confined to assessing the seriousness of crimes with individual

---

[27] von Hirsch and Jareborg (1991).

victims, and their method is to assess the effect of the typical case of particular crimes upon the living standard of typical victims. First, in order to determine what interests are violated or threatened by the standard case of the crime, they identify four generic interests:

(1) physical integrity: health, safety, and the avoidance of physical pain;

(2) material support and amenity: includes nutrition, shelter, and other basic amenities;

(3) freedom from humiliation or degrading treatment;

(4) privacy and autonomy.

The interests affected by the typical case of the crime are then analysed in these terms. Once the nature of the interest(s) violated has been settled, the second step is to estimate the degree to which the living standard of the typical victim would be affected by a typical case of the crime. The idea of 'living standard' refers to the means and capabilities that would ordinarily conduce to the achievement of a good life. Four degrees of effect are set out:

(1) subsistence: survival with maintenance of elementary human functions;

(2) minimal well-being: maintenance of a minimal level of comfort and dignity;

(3) adequate well-being: maintenance of an adequate level of comfort and dignity;

(4) significant enhancement: significant enhancement in quality of life above the merely adequate level.

The question then is: would the typical case affect the typical victim's interests at the level of significant enhancement, adequate well-being, minimal well-being, or subsistence? One benefit of this approach is that it moves away from traditional assumptions by rating conduct such as the maintenance of an unsafe workplace or an unsafe transport system at the same level as causing serious injury or death. Of course there are other issues to be discussed, as we shall see in the next two paragraphs. But, in terms of harmfulness, the typical cases are on a par.

One further dimension of seriousness, though not of harmfulness, is culpability. [This is not dealt with in this extract.]

Also relevant to seriousness is the question of remoteness. How can one assess the seriousness of offences such as attempts, conspiracies, drunk driving, or possession, which may cause no actual harm? Attempts and conspiracies may be dealt with on the basis of the intended harm, together with the culpability, perhaps making some reduction in the level of seriousness to reflect the fact that no harm was caused and that the danger was more or less remote. However, the scale of the reduction in seriousness would vary according to whether one adopts a harm-based or a fault-based approach. ... For the present, it is sufficient to note that there are degrees of remoteness: an attempted crime may be very close to being a completed crime, whereas an offence of risk-creation such as drunk driving may be fairly remote, and an offence of possession (e.g. of an offensive weapon) may be very remote from the occurrence of actual harm.

In essence, then, we may distinguish five stages in the calculation of offence-seriousness that von Hirsch and Jareborg propose. First, the interests violated by the offence are identified. Secondly, the effect on a typical victim's living standard is quantified on the scale ranging from offences that merely affect significant enhancement to those that affect subsistence. Thirdly, the culpability of the offender is taken into account. Fourthly, the level of seriousness may be reduced to reflect the remoteness of the offence from the actual harm. The fifth stage is to transfer this assessment on to a scale that in some way quantifies the degree of seriousness. It would be possible to devise an elaborate 100-point scale for this but von Hirsch and Jareborg say that this would give the impression of a 'misleading sense of precision', and their preference is for a scale with five broad bands. This both allows further adjustment within each band and signifies that it remains a rather approximate enterprise.

Inexact it may be, but the enterprise is essential. Judgements of relative seriousness are made frequently in all walks of life—not just by legislators when deciding whether to criminalize and what maximum penalty to assign to an offence, but also by judges and magistrates when sentencing, and also by lay people in commenting on whether the official response is proportionate. The value of the von Hirsch–Jareborg approach is that it identifies the stages of thought through which it is desirable to pass when making these judgements. In practice many of the judgements are made impressionistically, often on the basis of traditional assumptions about the ranking of offences. The von Hirsch–Jareborg approach urges one to dig deeper, and to look more closely at the interests affected. However, their approach is confined to harms with individual victims. It awaits development to deal with the myriad other *forms* of conduct that modern systems of criminal law tend to criminalize. For example, what about offences of theft or deception committed against a wealthy company, or against the State? It would hardly make sense to refer to the typical effect on the living standard of the victim here, since many small or even moderate thefts have, at least taken individually, no significant effect. What about offences against the State and against the administration of justice? It is one thing to argue that offences of espionage may pose a threat to national security; it is quite another thing to transfer this assessment on to a scale of gravity, such as the scale that runs *from* threats to significant enhancement up to threats to subsistence. Similarly with an offence such as perjury: telling lies in court is a 'serious matter', but it cannot always be related to a scale of seriousness constructed with reference to harms to individual victims.

The task of assessing the seriousness of offences is therefore as complex and problematic as it is unavoidable and fundamental. The Human Rights Act has added a further dimension, in that the Convention declares a number of rights that member States are bound to protect, and some require protection through the criminal law. The right to life is guaranteed by Article 2, and States must ensure that they protect this by, for example, having appropriately restricted rules on self-defence. Article 3 declares that no-one should be subjected to torture or to inhuman or degrading treatment, and this requires the States to ensure that they have laws that give adequate protection to individuals, e.g. to children from physical beatings (of a certain magnitude) by their parents. Article 8 declares the right to respect for one's private life, which includes sexuality and sexual relations, and this means that the law ought to provide protection from sexual molestation for the young and the mentally handicapped. Article 8 in combination with Article 14 also requires that the criminal law should respect the right to engage in consensual sexual activities in private and not to discriminate between males and females by reference to age. Articles 8, 9, 10, and 11 may also be important in ensuring that any interference with those rights by criminalizing certain conduct (typically, conduct likely to cause a breach of the peace, or to cause harassment, alarm, or distress) does not restrict the rights disproportionately. It is not argued here that the European Convention is a perfect instrument, containing all the rights for which one would wish to make a strong case. But its elevated status has now been recognized by the Human Rights Act, and Parliament and the courts should therefore regard it as one source of principles for criminalization and non-criminalization, for creating offences, and for recognizing defences.

4.5 THE PRINCIPLE OF FAIR LABELLING

This principle requires that the description of the offence should match the wrong done.[28] For example, if a defendant is convicted of rape then his conduct should be fairly described as rape. Hence there has been debate whether non-consensual anal intercourse should be described as rape or have another title. In defining the offence it is necessary to distinguish between the losses suffered by the victim and the wrongs done to the victim. This point can be made by way of this example: Alf steals Ben's book; Catherine destroys Davina's book. Both Ben and Davina suffer the same loss: their books are gone. But the wrongs done to them are different: the way their property was lost matters in moral terms. Hence the criminal law distinguishes between criminal damage and theft.[29] There is more to this point than that. Imagine that both Edward and Fred are pushed over, but Fred was deliberately pushed over and Edward accidentally. They may have suffered the same harm, but the wrong done to them was different. Edward might laugh the event off as an accident, expecting an apology at most. However, Fred would regard the incident as a serious invasion of his right to bodily integrity.[30] So the state of mind of the defendant is an important aspect of the wrong done to the victim.

FURTHER READING

Ashworth, A. (2000d), 'Is the Criminal Law a Lost Cause?', *Law Quarterly Review* 116: 225.

—— (2003), *Principles of Criminal Law* (4th edn., Oxford: OUP), ch. 3.

—— (2004), 'Social Control and Anti-Social Behaviour', *Law Quarterly Review* 120: 263.

Jareborg, N. (1995), 'What Kind of Criminal Law Do We Want?' in A. Snare (ed.), *Beware of Punishment* (Oslo: Pax Forlag).

Mitchell, B. (2001), 'Multiple Wrongdoing and Offence Structure: A Plea for Consistency and Fair Labelling', *Modern Law Review* 64: 393.

Padfield, N. (2004), 'The Anti-Social Behaviour Act 2003: The Ultimate Nanny-State Act?', *Criminal Law Review* 712

Williams, G. (1983b), 'Convictions and Fair Labelling', *Cambridge Law Review* 42: 85.

5 THE 'NEED' FOR A CRIMINAL CODE

The failure of English and Welsh criminal law to live up to these principles has led some to suggest that the government should produce a Criminal Code. This would be a single statute which would seek to describe the criminal law (or the important parts of criminal law) in one document in clear language.[31] In drafting such a Code it would be possible to seek to adhere to the principles mentioned above as much as possible. Indeed the Law Commission has undertaken the job of drafting such a Code.[32] As yet there are no clear indications that the government is minded to implement it.[33] Although at first the idea of a Code might be

---

[28] Mitchell (2001).   [29] Duff (2002: 6).   [30] J. Gardner (1998a: 211).

[31] Spencer (2000) calls for a code of criminal procedure.

[32] For another version of a code see Robinson (1997) (criticized in Mitchell (2001) and Duff (2002)).

[33] Although the Home Office (2001a: 55) indicates that the government has not given up on the suggestion.

thought an unmitigated blessing (especially for law students!), in fact it has not proved universally popular.

5.1 ARGUMENTS IN FAVOUR OF A CODE

(1) Certainty. The argument in favour of codification is that it will create a pre-existing legal norm which will govern whether a person is guilty. This avoids the common law approach of having rather vaguely defined offences whose interpretation can be expanded or contracted by the judge to fit the justice of the particular case. Of course codification will not produce a criminal law which is absolutely clear in every regard and it would be wrong to think that all common law offences are utterly vague, but the argument is that a Criminal Code should reduce the circumstances in which the principle of legality is breached. The point can also be made in constitutional terms—that a Code would help uphold the separation of powers: that the creation of the law should be for Parliament not the judiciary.

(2) Accessibility. If a member of the public wanted to find out what the criminal law was at present he or she could not find one document that sets out the criminal law. To get hold of all the statutes and all the case law to provide an effective guide to the present law would be a marathon task.[34] In theory if the entire criminal law could be found in a Code it could become readily available to the general public at all good booksellers.

Such arguments have led Paul Robinson[35] to propose a code which distinguishes between rules of conduct and rules of attribution.[36] He sees the rules of conduct as primarily aimed at sending clear messages[37] to citizens telling them what they can and cannot do in simple terms.[38] Controversially this means that the conduct rules do not include references to the results that arise from the acts or to states of mind.[39] By contrast, rules of attribution are directed towards judges or juries telling them when a particular person should be convicted for infringing a rule of attribution. This distinction has the benefit, he claims, of keeping the rules of conduct (which are directed to the general public) as brief and clear as possible.

Critics of Robinson's approach have argued that rules of conduct can be of little use if they do not include an indication of a state of mind.[40] Take rape: a citizen who was seeking to obey the law would conduct his or her sex life quite differently if the law on rape was a strict liability offence than if it was an intention-based offence.[41] Anthony Duff has suggested that it is more important that the Code makes moral sense in that it reflects community values rather than that it is linguistically clear.[42]

(3) Efficiency. The benefits mentioned so far—certainty and accessibility—would also work, it is argued, to make courts more efficient. The judge will be able to give a clear direction on the law to the jury, making the jury's job easier and lessening the need for appeals to the Court of Appeal following a misdirection by judges.

(4) Consistency. Proponents of a Code argue that in drafting it the contradictions and ambiguities in the law can be removed.

---

[34] Purchasing a textbook on the criminal law would be much easier!
[35] Robinson (1997); Robinson (1990).   [36] Robinson (1997). See also Dan-Cohen (2002: ch. 2).
[37] He describes rules of conduct as having a 'communicative function'.
[38] Robinson (1997: 128).   [39] For criticism of this see Husak (1999a).
[40] Alldridge (2002) argues that a diligent, law-abiding citizen would want to know not only the requirements of the criminal law, but also those of the law of tort and contract.
[41] Duff (2002: 69).   [42] Duff (2002). For arguments against Duff's view see Alldridge (2002).

(5) Updating. The Code would provide the opportunity to rid the law of 'old fashioned offences' which might have made sense when they were passed, but seem bizarre in the twenty-first century.[43] Is it really appropriate to have the offence of 'assaulting a clergyman in the discharge of his duties in a place or worship or burial place'?[44]

5.2 DISADVANTAGES OF THE CODE

The following are some of the alleged disadvantages of a Criminal Code:

(1) Obsession with 'consistency'. There is a concern that if the Code were to become obsessed with guiding principles and internal consistency this might overlook the fact that apparent contradictions within the criminal law in fact reflect the complexity of the many political, ethical, and practical issues involved in developing the law for a particular offence.[45] Apparently contradictory aspects of the criminal law may in fact prove to be a workable compromise for those areas of the law. Further, the views of the public on what may be an acceptable criminal law are not always consistent or rational. This may justify a criminal law which although 'irrational' perhaps reflects the public morality.

(2) The benefits of a Code are over-emphasized.[46] It is not realistic that *The Code* will hit the bestseller list. Further, hard cases are hard cases because they involve a clash of important principles. For example, the infamous conjoined twins case[47] (see Chapter 12) raised extremely difficult questions for law and morality. That case would have been no easier were there a Code in place.

FURTHER READING

de Búrca, G., and Gardner, S. (1990), 'The Codification of the Criminal Law', *Oxford Journal of Legal Studies* 10: 559.

Robinson, P. (1998), *Structure and Function of Criminal Law* (Oxford: OUP).

6 WHAT CONDUCT SHOULD BE CRIMINAL?

How should the state decide which conduct should, or should not, be criminal? Why should Parliament not make swearing in a public place an offence?[48] We shall shortly consider the extensive academic analysis of this question. But before doing so it is worth emphasizing that in practice a government's decision on whether to criminalize something is normally a matter of political expediency, rather than fine-sounding principles.[49] For example, in 1990 there was a media campaign against the horrors of 'killer dogs', featuring horrific

---

[43] e.g. *Okosi* [1996] Crim LR 666, where a taxi driver was charged with 'causing bodily injury through wanton or furious driving'.

[44] Offences Against the Person Act 1861, s. 36.

[45] De Búrca and Gardner (1990). Gardner and Jung (1991: 559) complain of the 'passion for uniformity' permeating much writing on criminal law.

[46] Clarkson (1994).

[47] *Re A (Conjoined Twins: Medical Treatment)* [2000] 4 All ER 961 (CA).

[48] Although it might be necessary first to repeal the Human Rights Act 1998 (which protects the freedom of speech).

[49] See Ashworth (2000d).

photographs of children attacked by vicious dogs. The campaign called upon Parliament to 'do something'. In the light of such a campaign it is hard for politicians not to react, not least for fear that in due course there might be other children harmed by dogs and the press would then say 'if only you had passed legislation this child would have been saved'. Indeed in due course the Dangerous Dogs Act 1991 was passed.[50]

These are some of the principles academics have suggested should govern Parliament's decisions on criminalization.

6.1 AUTONOMY

To many commentators the right of autonomy, the right to live one's life as one likes, is of fundamental importance.[51] Making decisions for ourselves means that we can be proud of the good things that we do, but also that we can be ashamed of, and deserve blame for, the bad things we do. Autonomy plays three crucial roles in defining the criminal law:

(1) It justifies the existence of the criminal law. Without the criminal law other people could, without punishment, interfere with my right to live my life as I choose. In other words the criminal law is necessary to prevent one person's exercise of autonomy interfering with another's.

(2) It restricts the extent of the criminal law. The criminal law impinges on people's autonomy. If the criminal law made it illegal for same-sex couples to engage in consenting sexual relationships this would interfere with how many people would like to live their lives. The autonomy principle therefore explains why it is only where the activity causes a significant amount of harm to others or to society that the law is justified in prohibiting it.

(3) It justifies censure. If we are autonomous citizens, able to live our lives as we choose, then we should be responsible for the bad choices we make as well as the good ones. In other words the autonomy principle explains why people should be liable for making the wrong choice, and also explains that where people do not have a free choice to act as they should the criminal law provides a defence (e.g. where they are acting under duress).

It should not be thought that the autonomy principle is uncontroversial. First, there are some who point out that the right to choose how to live our lives may be available for the rich, the able, and advantaged, but it may be regarded as a chimera for the poor, the disabled, and the disadvantaged.[52] Indeed, one of the leading proponents of the importance of autonomy, Joseph Raz, has argued that if the state wants to take the right of autonomy seriously it must ensure that the social conditions necessary for the exercise of full autonomy are provided.[53]

For others there are concerns that the autonomy principle over-emphasizes individualism.[54] It talks about the right for *me* to pursue *my* vision of the 'good life'; but for many people their vision of the good life is tied up with families, friends, and communities. For them the promotion of the good life might mean the promotion of the good of groups of people.

[50] Arguably another example is the Anti-Terrorism, Crime and Security Act 2001 which was passed as a swift response to the events of 11 Sept. 2001 (for discussion see Fenwick (2002)).

[51] Raz (1985). Braithwaite and Pettit (1990: ch. 5) prefer the concept of dominion.

[52] Hudson (1994).   [53] Raz (1986).   [54] Fineman (2004); Harré, Clarke, and DeCarlo (1985).

There are many offences which appear to protect people from themselves and cannot readily be justified by the autonomy principle.[55] One well-known example is the requirement that people in cars wear seat belts.[56] We feel that although we respect people's choices, there comes a point where the law states 'we will not allow you to do such a dangerous thing'.[57]

The autonomy principle is behind one of the most popular theories explaining when a state may criminalize: the harm principle.

6.2 THE HARM PRINCIPLE

The leading exposition of the harm principle is provided by John Stuart Mill with his famous essay, *On Liberty*. At the heart of his argument is the following:

> The only purpose for which power can be rightfully exercised over any member of a civilized community against his will is to prevent harm to others. His own good, either physical or moral, is not sufficient warrant. He cannot rightfully be compelled to do or forbear . . . because in the opinion of others to do so would be wise or even right.[58]

Essentially, then, the harm principle is that each person should be allowed to do and say what he or she likes provided that this does not harm the interests of others. Simply because an activity is seen as immoral or harmful to the actor is not a good enough reason to justify criminalizing it. The harm principle tells us what sorts of behaviour should *not* be criminalized. Just because conduct harms others does not mean that supporters of the harm principle would necessarily support criminalizing it.[59]

In recent times the harm principle has received powerful support from the work of Joel Feinberg, who in three highly influential books has sought to interpret and justify a modern understanding of the principle. In the following extract Douglas Husak summarizes and discusses Feinberg's theory:

D. Husak, 'The Nature and Justifiability of Nonconsummate Offences' (1995) 37 *Arizona Law Review* 151 at 155–9

> Most theorists agree that the criminal sanction should be imposed only for blameworthy and wrongful conduct. This necessary condition of justified criminal legislation might be called the *wrongfulness* requirement. The most persuasive of many possible arguments in support of this requirement focuses on the institution of criminal punishment. Violations of the criminal law, by definition, are subject to the penal sanction. This sanction involves the deliberate infliction of a hardship. The deliberate infliction of a hardship requires a justification. It is hard to see how punishment could be justified unless a person deserves to be

---

[55] This leads Dan-Cohen (2000) to argue that the concept of dignity, rather than autonomy or welfare, should be the basis of the law.

[56] Husak (1989).

[57] Ashworth (1999: 30) writes of the 'welfare principle'.   [58] Mill (1991).

[59] Gardner (1998: 229) suggests that an activity needs to be both harmful and base or worthless to justify criminalization.

punished, and it is unclear how a person could deserve to be punished unless his conduct is blameworthy and wrongful.

There are principled reasons not to criminalize all wrongful and blameworthy conduct, even if the practical difficulties of enforcement could be overcome. Immorality is a necessary, but not a sufficient condition for criminalization. Commentators have struggled to identify that subclass of wrongful conduct that is eligible for punishment. The *harm* requirement provides the most plausible solution to this problem. Joel Feinberg's work represents the most ambitious and impressive defense of what he calls a *liberal* theory of law, characterized as the thesis that the only good reason to subject persons to criminal punishment is to prevent them from wrongfully causing harm to others.

According to Feinberg, 'the sense of "harm" as that term is used in the harm principle must represent the overlap of [normative and non-normative senses]: only setbacks of interests that are wrongs, and wrongs that are setbacks to interest, are to count as harms in the appropriate sense.' In the 'normative' sense of harm, A harms B 'by wronging B, or by treating him unjustly.' In the 'non-normative' sense of harm, A harms B 'by invading, and thereby setting back, his interest.' The need for an overlap of these two senses should be apparent. Harmful but permissible conduct is not eligible for criminal penalties because it fails to satisfy the wrongfulness requirement. Person A might set back the interests of person B—thereby placing B in a 'harmed condition'—through a legitimate competition, for example. But A's conduct should not be criminalized because B has not been wronged or treated unjustly. The interests of B may have been set back and *infringed*, but they have not been *violated*. Conversely, harmless but impermissible conduct is not eligible for criminal penalties because it does not set back anyone's interests. Person A might behave immorally without victimizing anyone. But A's conduct should not be criminalized because no one has been harmed.

The 'overlap' of these two senses of harm can be expressed succinctly by invoking the concept of rights: All wrongful conduct that sets back the interests of others violates their rights. Thus Feinberg's liberal framework establishes the moral limits of the criminal law by reference to the rights of persons. As expressed succinctly, 'criminal prohibitions are legitimate only when they protect individual rights.'

Feinberg claims no originality on behalf of his general thesis, which he locates squarely in the tradition of John Stuart Mill. The novelty of his approach lies in the details of his explication of the harm principle. In particular, Feinberg's interpretation provides a response to two reservations that have long been expressed about the harm requirement, even by theorists who tend to sympathize with it. First, many commentators have feared that the harm requirement is empty, trivial, tautological, or vacuous. If *any* undesirable consequence can be countenanced as a harm, all serious candidates for criminal legislation will satisfy the harm requirement. Second, many commentators have endorsed the harm principle because they believe that the criminal law should not be used to enforce morality. According to these theorists it is harm, rather than immorality, that should be prevented by the criminal law. Thus harm is sometimes thought to represent an alternative to the proposal that the criminal law should enforce morality.

Among Feinberg's central achievements are his responses to each of these two reservations. He interprets the harm requirement as nontrivial and full of substantive content, much of which is clearly moral in nature. Applications of his liberal theory entail that criminal intervention is unjustified in principle unless (a) the rights of someone are set back by (b) wrongful conduct. According to this view, the harm requirement cannot function as a genuine alternative to the claim that the criminal law should enforce morality, but rather identifies that subclass of immoral conduct that the criminal law should proscribe.

A detailed account of the specific instances of legislation that should be rejected as incompatible with a liberal theory of law requires at least two supplementary theories: first, a theory of moral rights, and second, a theory of wrongful conduct. Feinberg is well aware of the need for these two supplementary theories. He is equally aware that neither of these theories is easy to produce, and he does not pretend to have completed the task. Still, a virtue of Feinberg's account is that it clearly identifies the kinds of work that remain to be completed in order to provide a comprehensive theory of the moral limits of the criminal law.

Even without these two supplementary theories, one would anticipate few difficulties in applying Feinberg's views to justify enactment of the most familiar criminal offenses in Anglo-American law. Consider theft. Rights in personal property that are set back by acts of theft are a familiar part of virtually all theories of rights. In addition, the wrongfulness of theft is widely acknowledged. Thus the application of a liberal theory to justify the creation and enforcement of the offense of theft seems unproblematic.

Moreover, Feinberg's views are equally plausible when applied to reveal the deficiencies in proposals to create new criminal legislation that most everyone would denounce as an unjustifiable exercise of state authority. Consider a hypothetical proposal to enact criminal legislation to prohibit persons from dropping out of school prior to graduation. No one doubts the utility of an educated citizenry. But does someone who fails to complete his education act wrongfully (as opposed to foolishly or imprudently)? Does he set back anyone's rights (apart from his own long-term interests)? Unless both of these questions can be answered affirmatively, a liberal theory of law, as explicated by Feinberg, would preclude enacting criminal legislation for this purpose.

Of course, a sponsor of such legislation could always insist that rights *are* set back, and that conduct *is* wrongful, whenever persons drop out of school. It may be impossible to persuade such a sponsor without actually providing supplementary theories of rights and wrongful conduct. In the absence of these two supplementary theories, one can only hope that the intuitive implausibility of these claims would be recognized. In this context, this hope seems reasonable. The judgment that persons should be punished for failing to graduate is not easily brought into 'reflective equilibrium' with other judgments about rights and wrongful conduct, both specific and general, that persons tend to endorse. Thus Feinberg's liberal theory of law, when accompanied by widely shared judgments about the supplementary theories required by its application, seems to escape the charge that the harm principle is trivial and vacuous. His theory supports criminal legislation of which most everyone approves, and condemns criminal legislation of which most everyone disapproves. A liberal theory—according to which the criminal law should not be used except to prevent persons from violating the moral rights of others—is enormously valuable to help identify the moral limits of the criminal law.

As this passage indicates, the harm principle itself is fairly straightforward. But at its heart is the concept of harm, and it is far from clear what that means. There is little disagreement that cuts, bruises, and death count as harms,[60] but other issues are less straightforward.

(1) *Is offence harm?*

If Edna goes shopping and sees someone walking down the street naked she may be very offended. Is this offence 'harm' for the purposes of the harm principle?[61] Joel Feinberg supports the prohibition of conduct that causes offence. But he uses a strict

---

[60] Although, as Stanko (2003) demonstrates, it is far from easy to define violence.
[61] See Simester and von Hirsch (2002) and Feinberg (1986b).

definition of 'offence'. Offence involves more than concern or disapproval. An example might be the feelings relatives would have if they found that the body of their loved one had been horribly desecrated. For other academics no degree of offence is sufficient to constitute a 'harm'. To permit offence to be harm enables one set of people to impose their moral values on others. Indeed the more hardline they are, the more likely they are to be profoundly disturbed, and so the more likely to fall within Feinberg's definition of 'offence'.

(2) *Is harm to future generations harm?*

This issue is relevant in particular to environmental legislation. If it is demonstrated that an activity will not harm anyone presently living but will have long-term environmental damage which might harm future generations; would this be harm for the purposes of the harm principle?

(3) *Are potential harms harm?*

What about conduct which in itself is not harmful but which carries the risk of causing harm? For example, the criminal law prohibits possession of a firearm. The prohibition is not based on the fact that possession itself harms society; rather the possession of firearms generally is likely to increase their use, which can be regarded as a harm.[62] To some there are grave dangers in accepting potential harms as harms.[63] All kinds of activity are potentially harmful.

(4) *Is damage to the public good a harm?*

What about offences which are designed not to prevent the harm to individuals, but harm to society generally?[64] Some traffic laws, building regulations, and state security regulations cannot be said to protect identifiable people, but rather are justified for the good running of society as a whole.[65] Are these reconcilable with the harm principle? Robin West, writing from a feminist perspective, has argued that the law should recognize harms to groups and to society. She complains that too often the law sees harm in terms of the harm to individuals rather than harm to people as connected individuals in relationships.[66] Others are concerned that once 'harms' to groups are taken into account the floodgates may be opened.

In the following passage Susan Marshall and Anthony Duff discuss the way in which a criminal offence harms not just the victim but the wider community:

S.E. Marshall and R.A. Duff, 'Criminalization and Sharing Wrongs' (1998) 11 *Canadian Journal of Law and Jurisprudence* 7 at 17–21

Consider rape as an example. Why should rape be a crime? We can agree that it should be socially proscribed and condemned. It is not a 'private' matter in which the community has no proper interest (and English law has, at last, recognised that this is true even of intra-marital rape); nor is the rape victim simply involved in a 'conflict' with her attacker, which they need to 'negotiate' and resolve: leaving aside problem cases on the borderlines of rape, we should say that rape is a non-negotiable wrong which the community should declare to be so. This has to do in part with the seriousness of the harm wrought by rape—both the harm contingently consequent upon rape, and

---

[62] von Hirsch (1996).   [63] von Hirsch (1985).   [64] Howe (1991).
[65] Duff and Green (2005: 8); Brudner (1993).   [66] West (1988).

the harm intrinsic to it. It also has to do, we suppose, with the idea that it is not difficult for a 'reasonable' man to refrain from rape (indeed, that any 'reasonable' man should not need to *refrain* from rape); and that any woman ought to be able confidently to expect not to be thus attacked as she goes about her normal life. To say that rape should be criminal is also to say that rapists are (presumptively) responsible for what they do, and can properly be held answerable, and be censured, for it: whatever we may say about the kinds of social structure and attitude which encourage men to see women as mere sexual objects and may thus be said to encourage rape, this does not negate the individual rapist's responsible, culpable agency.

But why should rape be dealt with by a 'criminal' rather than by a 'civil' process? Why should rape not be defined simply as a civil wrong, so that it is for the victim to bring a case herself (if but only if she wishes) against her attacker? Part of the answer will be that the rapist should be punished, rather than being liable only to pay compensation to his victim—and we must ask why we should think that. But there is, we think, more to it than that; and that 'more' has to do with the kind of interest the community as a whole should take in such wrongdoing—with, we will argue, the sense in which the community should see the wrong done to her as a wrong done to 'us.'

Of course even if we envisaged rape as only a civil wrong, there are different possibilities. At one extreme it would be for the victim to find the resources herself to bring and pursue the case: the community provides the structure (the civil court) through which she can do so, declares the norms to which she appeals, and will enforce the decision; but no further help is offered. The first step towards some greater community involvement is then to say that the community should at least also offer her resources (advice, help in identifying her assailant and collecting evidence, legal counsel . . .) to help her bring the case. If we ask why this should be so, we might refer again to the seriousness of the injury she has suffered. We may also say that there is a stronger case for offering such help to citizens when the wrong or harm they have suffered is not one they should be seen as having voluntarily risked suffering, or one that they should be willing to risk suffering (subject to a right to compensation if it is actualised) as a part of their ordinary lives. That is to say, there are certain kinds of wrongful harm which we should be able to expect, categorically, to be safe from; and if we suffer such a harm we should at least be able to expect the community to help us pursue its perpetrator.

Perhaps it is the categorical nature of this requirement which makes the difference here, and points us towards a 'criminal,' rather than a 'civil,' process. In a civil case, there is room for the idea of 'contributory negligence': the defendant can admit that he caused the harm, culpably, but argue that the plaintiff was also at fault—and should thus bear part of the cost. Now judges have, notoriously, sometimes talked explicitly of, or (more often) appealed implicitly to, a rape victim's 'contributory negligence': the rapist's culpability (and so his sentence) is thought to be properly reduced by the fact that his victim put herself in danger, or acted in a way which increased the risk of being raped. It is also clearly true that some kinds of conduct—how she dresses, where she goes, how she behaves—in fact create or increase the risk that a woman will be raped; and friends might tell her that she is stupid to behave like that, or criticise her morally if her conduct is intended to stimulate sexual desire or to encourage the prospects of sexual intercourse in a man with whom she has no intention of having sexual intercourse. We might analogously criticise householders who 'encourage' burglary by leaving their houses obviously insecure, or a car owner who 'encourages' theft by leaving valuables in view in an unlocked car. But we do not think that this reduces the culpability of the thief, burglar or rapist: for we think that people should categorically refrain (and should be able to refrain, even if they are tempted) from such wrongs, even if the victim has in fact made it possible or tempting for them to commit such a wrong.

But there is more to the 'criminal' process than this. We still need to ask why the community should not merely offer assistance to a victim who wants to pursue a civil case against her assailant, but also take that case over. Does this amount to 'stealing' her 'conflict' from her; or are there reasons why the case should become the community's ('ours') rather than just hers? We have noted the inadequacy of some answers to this question: answers which appeal to a 'public' good distinct from the victim's own individual good, and which thus fail to do justice to the wrong that *she* has suffered: that wrong must, surely, be integral to the rationale for criminalising rape and for subjecting the rapist to a criminal process.

But we can offer a more plausible account of the sense in which rape is a wrong against the community, which does not involve ignoring or denigrating the wrong done to the individual victim. Consider how a group of women might respond to a sexual attack on one of them (or how a self-conscious racial group might respond to a racial attack on one of them). They may see it as a collective, not merely an individual, wrong (as an attack on *them*), insofar as they associate and identify themselves with the individual victim. For they define themselves as a group, in terms of a certain shared identity, shared values, mutual concern—and shared dangers which threaten them: an attack on a member of the group is thus an attack on the group—on their shared values and their common good. The wrong does not cease to be 'her' wrong: but it is also 'our' wrong insofar as we identify ourselves with her. The point is not just that we realise that other members of the group are also vulnerable to such attacks, or that we want to warn other potential assailants that they cannot attack members of the group with impunity (although the thought that any of us could be attacked and the desire to defend all members of the group are clearly involved): it is that the attack on this individual victim is itself also an attack on us—on her as a member of the group and on us as fellow members.

A group can in this way 'share' the wrongs done to its individual members, insofar as it defines and identifies itself as a community united by mutual concern, by genuinely shared (as distinct from contingently coincident) values and interests, and by the shared recognition that its members' goods (and their identity) are bound up with their membership of the community. Wrongs done to individual members of the community are then wrongs against the whole community—injuries to a common or shared, not merely to an individual, good. This, we suggest, provides an appropriate perspective from which we can understand the point and significance of a 'criminal' rather than a 'civil' process. For suppose we understand a political society not merely as a collection of discrete and separate individuals bound to each other by an imagined social contract, but as a community in this sense (which is what is implied by the communitarian framework of our argument): suppose, that is, that citizens see (or should see) each other as bound together in a way analogous to the way in which members of the women's group or the racial group mentioned in the previous paragraph see each other as bound together (even if those bonds may be somewhat less intimate). We can then also see how wrongs against individual citizens can be understood as shared wrongs, as wrongs against the whole community, insofar as the individual goods which are attacked are goods in terms of which the community identifies and understands itself.

We can from this perspective begin to see both why the community should bring the case 'on behalf of' the individual victim—rather than leaving her to bring it for herself; and why it might sometimes *insist* on bringing the case even if she is unwilling to do so. For, just as we may say that we owe it to her to associate ourselves with her in this way (to take her wrong as also our wrong), so we may say that she owes it to us to recognise that the wrong was done to us as well as to her. This is not yet to say that the outcome of the case should be *punishment*—rather than censure, apology, or compensation to the individual victim; and we noted earlier that to justify a 'criminal' rather than 'civil' process need not be to justify a punitive outcome of that procedure: but we would also suggest that punishment should be understood in terms of the wrongdoer's relationship to the community as well as to the individual victim.

If this is right, it suggests that crimes (as distinct from civil wrongs) must indeed be portrayed as 'public' wrongs, against the community (for if they are not public wrongs it is not clear why they should be dealt with by a criminal rather than a civil process). But it also shows how wrongs done to individuals, attacks on their *Rechtsgüter*, can be understood as being at the same time, and in virtue of their character as wrongs against individuals, wrongs against the community to which the individual belongs. In making the wrong done to the rape victim 'ours,' rather than merely 'hers'; in thus understanding it as an attack on 'our' good, not merely on her individual good: we do not turn our attention *away* from the wrong that she has suffered, towards some distinct 'public' good. Rather, we share *in* the very wrong that she has suffered: it is not 'our' wrong *instead of* hers; it is 'our' wrong *because* it is a wrong done to her, as one of us—as a fellow member of our community whose identity and whose good is found within that community.

(5) *Moral principles*

One of the key elements of the harm principle is that an activity cannot be criminalized simply because it is regarded as immoral.[67] However, some people argue that there are some moral principles which are central to the well-being of society. Consider the current debate over fox-hunting. Leaving aside all the other issues one argument that can be made is that our society is a less civilized and crueller society if we allow fox-hunting. It diminishes society and what it stands for. Many people will disagree. But these kinds of arguments suggest that when thinking about society's welfare there will be a wide range of views on what is good for society. Lord Devlin[68] has argued that there is a 'moral cement' that helps to keep society together, and that the state is entitled to use the criminal law to protect that cement from being damaged by behaviour which infringes those principles. He suggests that the extent of disgust felt by society at a particular kind of activity would indicate whether it challenged a fundamental value that underpinned society.

There is much about this argument which can be challenged. For example, in a multi-cultural, multi-faith society is it true there are moral principles which can be regarded as so fundamental to the way people live their lives that they are society's 'cement'? Even if you think there are, is it true that the fact that a few people break those moral taboos harms that cement? Was Devlin correct to suggest that disgust indicates how precious a moral value is to society?[69] Many people experience great

---

[67] Alldridge (2002).   [68] Devlin (1965).   [69] Hart (1963).

disgust at the picking of a nose, but that does not indicate that it reflects a fundamental moral principle! These issues are discussed further in the following passage:

J.W. Harris, *Legal Philosophies* (2nd edn., London: Butterworths, 1997), 132–42

. . . If society is entitled to use the law to uphold conventional moral standards, then Mill's principle is at least partially false; for then the enforcement of morality can be seen as a distinct warrant for punishment. Interest in this question received an enormous boost in 1957 from the Report of the Committee On Homosexual Offences and Prostitution, under the chairmanship of Sir John Wolfenden. The report includes some general observations which look Mill-like, and were undoubtedly influenced by the Mill libertarian tradition.

'[The function of the criminal law] is to preserve public order and decency, to protect the citizen from what is offensive and injurious, and to provide sufficient safeguards against exploitation and corruption of others, particularly those who are specially vulnerable because they are young, weak in body or mind, inexperienced, or in a state of special physical, official or economic dependence.' (para 13)

'Unless a deliberate attempt is to be made by society, acting through the agency of the law, to equate the sphere of crime with that of sin, there must remain a realm of private morality and immorality which is, in brief and crude terms, not the law's business.' (para 61)

The opposite view, that the law should prohibit conduct simply because it is immoral, has an ancient pedigree. Plato in his *Laws* stated that the lawgiver 'shall lay down what things are ... and bad, and what things are noble and good'. The *Book of Common Prayer* calls for 'the ... ent of wickedness and vice'.

... den Committee made two recommendations which were eventually embodied ... first was that, while prostitution itself should not be punishable, soliciting ... itutes should be punished more effectively than hitherto. Soliciting ... ld be rigorously dealt with. Prostitution in private harmed no one ... e second recommendation was that homosexual acts ... e should no longer be a criminal offence. The harm ... ttee, warrants punishing actions which involve ... al acts with persons under 21, and living off ... ffences. ...

... ict with morality is not enough to ... evlin. In his Hamlyn lecture on ... y has a right to punish any ... nded man'), is grossly ... able individuals or ... tation' or ... the groups. ...

Devlin argues that what is 'indecent' or 'offensive', or what amounts to 'exploi... 'corruption', in Wolfenden terms, can, in many contexts, only be understood if we use ... measure of society's morality. Further, he challenges those who advocate the harm principle to say why the following offences should (if they should) stay on the books: bigamy, bestiality, incest, living off immoral earnings; and to deal with the law's refusal to allow consent as a defence to homicide or serious assault. . . .

Hart's reply to Devlin produced two important qualifications on the harm principle. First, he disagreed with Mill that an adult's self-inflicted harm is no warrant for legal intervention. Hart was opposed to 'legal moralism', to the view that general agreement among the members of society that conduct is immoral is a ground for legal prohibition. But he favoured 'paternalism', the view that society may prevent people from doing themselves physical harm. Paternalism (he argued) justified the criminal law in refusing the defence of consent to homicide and assault. Whereas Mill believed that a man's own good, physical or moral, did not warrant interference, Hart believed that his physical good does.

It is not clear how far paternalism of this sort is to be taken. Does it justify legislation restricting the taking by adults of excessive drink, harmful drugs, or driving without seat-belts? Some would argue that restrictions of this sort can be supported by reference to the harm principle without any need to resort to paternalism. If I get myself injured in a duel, or through drink or drugs or driving without a seat-belt, do I not harm others in that I impose costs on society's medical services and perhaps deprive my dependants of support and the taxman of revenue? 'No man is an island', as John Donne told us. But, on that basis, might not the law prohibit dangerous sports, like pot-holing or mountaineering? If Mill is wrong, and a man's physical well-being is a ground on which society may restrict his liberty—either for Hartian paternalist reasons or on the no-man-an-island argument—no doubt libertarians would insist that the harm must be great in relation to the restriction on liberty involved before interference is justified. Is it practical or desirable to disregard, in this equation, whether the physical harm is self-inflicted in morally neutral or immoral ways?

Hart's second qualification to the harm principle concerns the definition of 'harm' itself, and imports a distinction between offence through public spectacle and offence through knowledge. Hart said that punishment of bigamy can be justified on the ground that, as a public act, it causes offence to religious sentiments; but that, in deciding whether any act inflicts 'harm', we must disregard the distress suffered by X through knowing that Y is doing what X regards as immoral. This is an exclusion to be made as a prior step to any utilitarian balancing. It is justified, seemingly, on distinct libertarian grounds, and is not derived from the principle of utility itself:

'[A] right to be protected from the distress which is inseparable from the bare knowledge that others are acting in ways you think wrong, cannot be acknowledged by anyone who recognises individual liberty as a value . . . If distress incident to the belief that others are doing wrong is harm, so also is the distress incident to the belief that others are doing what you do not want them to do. To punish people for causing this form of distress would be tantamount to punishing them simply because others object to what they do; and the only liberty which could coexist with this extension of the utilitarian principle is liberty to do those things to which no-one seriously objects.'

. . .

Is there any other basis on which someone who values individual liberty can draw the limits which such a belief ought to impose upon legal intervention? In his essay on 'The Enforcement of Morals', Devlin advanced what Basil Mitchell has called the 'social cohesion' argument. Devlin argued that one of the essential elements of a society is a shared morality. Different societies have different moralities, and there is no way in which the legislature can or need choose between them. As it happens, he said, our own society's shared morality is derived from Christianity, even if Christian belief as such is no longer prevalent. If a society's shared morality is weakened, this has a tendency to lead to the destruction of the society itself. Even if an act which is wrong by the society's morality is committed in private and harms no one in the way of offence-to-decency, corruption or exploitation, its very practice weakens the shared morality and so may lead to a weakening of society. Individual freedom of choice is an important value, but it is outweighed by the overriding right of society to survive. No society can be expected to make provision for its own dissolution. Just as treason is punishable because it threatens society's existence, irrespective of the private moral opinions of the traitor; so, Devlin argues, society is entitled to punish any act which, according to popular opinion, is grossly immoral.

Devlin's view is that our society's morality is historically derived from Christianity; but he does not suggest that the way to discover whether any act is immoral is to consult Christian opinion. Indeed, it would be difficult for anyone engaged in rebutting Wolfenden-type pro-grammes to make any such suggestion, since there has been no consensus among leading church figures about the morality or immorality of such matters as homosexuality or obscenity. Devlin himself seems highly suspicious of intellectuals as having any special right to speak on moral issues, whether they are churchmen or not. The Christian nature of society's morality is now beside the point. It should be enforced now, not because it is or was Christian, but because it is (so Devlin supposed) the shared morality of the majority. Hence, the person whose moral opinion is to be consulted is the man in the jury-box. In this respect, Devlin's views march in line with those of many other English judges. Since 1962, the courts have recognised an offence of 'conspiring to corrupt public morals', which gives an important role to jury moral opinion; and the courts have held that the concept of 'dishonesty', employed by the Theft Act 1968, is not a legal term of art but something which the jury is to test by its own moral standards.

'[T]he moral judgment of society must be something about which any 12 men or women drawn at random might after discussion be expected to be unanimous. . . . No society can do without intolerance, indignation and disgust; they are the forces behind the moral law, and indeed it can be argued that if they or something like them are not present, the feelings of society cannot be weighty enough to deprive the individual of freedom of choice.'

Devlin does not suggest that all popular morality is to be enforced. An act must be sufficiently grave as to be likely to cause a jury intolerance, indignation and disgust. Even then there may be grounds which make legal intervention undesirable. The law should be concerned with the minimum necessary for the preservation of society. There must always be a gap between the criminal and the moral law. The practical difficulty of enforcing any law must be taken into account and, as far as possible, privacy is to be respected. Despite the apparent drift of his original lecture, Devlin has since indicated that he is not in favour of punishing homosexual acts between consenting adults in private.

Dworkin argues that, even on the assumption that a society is entitled to enforce the moral opinions of the majority of its members, Devlin's test for what counts as a moral opinion is 'shocking and wrong'. We must, Dworkin claims, distinguish opinions which are supported by moral reasons from opinions based on 'prejudice', 'aversion', or 'rationalisations' (implaus-ible propositions of fact). The conscientious legislator may take account of the former, even if the reasons are controversial, so long as they are sincerely and consistently invoked; but he must ignore the latter. It then becomes a question whether what someone claims to be her 'moral opinion' can be dismissed by her opponent as mere prejudice, aversion or rationalisation. . . .

Hart's criticism of Devlin's social cohesion argument is twofold. First, he denies that a society need have a shared morality in Devlin's sense. Hart believes that there is a morality which every society must have and indeed must embody in law. . . . Every society must have rules restricting violence, theft and deception. This morality is common to all societies, although its detailed implementation varies. Apart from this minimum, a society need have no shared morality peculiar to itself. Our own society is pluralistic, especially in relation to sexual morality. Secondly, Hart argues, even supposing a society does have a shared morality peculiar to itself, there is no good reason to believe that its preservation is necessary to the survival of the society. The fact that people differ from the majority of their fellow citizens on matters of personal morality does not in any way indicate that they are likely to be less loyal citizens. Furthermore, moral experiment—the permitting of activities which the majority now regard as immoral—is positively beneficial. It is always possible that the majority may be wrong, and they will be able to make more informed judgments if they can see other people behaving in deviant ways. . . .

6.3 PRACTICALITY

Although much of the academic debate over criminalization has focused on the controversy surrounding the enforcement of morality, a very important issue is whether or not a law is practically enforceable. This issue is considered further in the following passage by Nigel Walker:

N. Walker, *Crime and Criminology* (Cambridge: Cambridge University Press, 1987), 148–52

An obvious practical consideration is the economics of enforcement. The chief agencies of enforcement are police forces, whose size is restricted by the amount of public money which the society in question is willing to spend on them. Even if this were not a limiting factor, it would be found that the number of suitable men and women willing to be recruited to the police was not large enough to make an enormous expansion possible. Allocating police-men's time to the best advantage will always be a major problem, but the extent to which it regulates the rigour of law-enforcement is not fully appreciated. In many cities a report of a theft involving property of less than a certain amount is not even passed to the detective branch for fear of wasting their time.

Another important consideration is the law-enforcement agencies' need for the assistance of the private citizen. Apart from a selection of driving and parking offences, of revenue offences, and breaches of health or safety regulations which can be detected and brought home to the offenders entirely by the observation and evidence of the police, inspectors, and other officials, very few offences would come to official knowledge if they were not reported by private citizens . . ., and very few of these would be traced to their perpetrators if it were not for the information which the police are able to obtain from the same source.

There are some offences, indeed, which could seldom be prosecuted without the evidence of one of the participators. One of the reasons why women who have resorted to criminal abortionists are so seldom prosecuted in England is that their evidence is usually needed to secure the conviction of the abortionists. Again, most police forces are so deter-mined to convict black-mailers that they will refrain from prosecuting the victims who give evidence against them. One of the dangers inherent in the extension of the criminal law to a multitude of peccadilloes is that by making a larger percentage of the population into targets for law-enforcement agencies it may forfeit the co-operation of this percentage in the enforcement of the more important prohibitions. An obvious example of this possibility is traffic offences, which now account for the great majority of all convictions. It is impossible to assess the amount of co-operation which the law-enforcement agencies forfeit by such prosecutions, but it must be considerable. The same is true of prosecutions for possession of marijuana.

Even when prosecutors could secure convictions without too much trouble they often refrain from doing so in cases where they believe that strict enforcement would alienate the public. In England, youths who can be proved to have had sexual intercourse with girls not far below the statutory age of consent (at present 16) are often not prosecuted, largely because the police feel that public opinion would not support them. Another rather unpopular indictment is bigamy, which in England is not prosecuted nowadays unless there is evidence that the guilty party went through the form of marriage in order to deceive the other party into having sexual intercourse or into parting with property. In countries where private homosexual behaviour between consenting adult men is still criminal, prosecutions for this are often restricted to cases in which there is evidence or suspicion of proselytizing, commercial exploitation, blackmail, or 'orgies'.

Another assumption which seems to underlie some arguments against certain prohibitions is that: A prohibition should not be included in the criminal law if it is unenforceable.

The word 'unenforceable', however, is used very loosely in such arguments. Does it mean 'such that *some* breaches of it would not be detected'? Hardly, for in this sense every prohibition is unenforceable. Does it mean 'such that *some* breaches of it would be undetected'? Again, hardly; for it is no easier to think of any prohibition that would be unenforceable by this criterion. Perhaps the nearest thing to a genuinely unenforceable prohibition in the history of English law was the form of treason which consisted of 'imagining' the death of the king, the queen, or the heir apparent, before it became established by case-law that an overtly treasonable act must be proved. What the principle must mean is that: A prohibition should not be included in the criminal code if only a small percentage of infringements of it could be proved against the infringers.

In this form the principle at once raises the question 'How small must the percentage be?', which is impossible to answer precisely, and not at all easy to answer even roughly until some reply has been given to the more fundamental question 'Why is relative unenforceability an argument against the inclusion of the prohibition?' The stock answer to this is that it 'brings the law into disrepute'.

Like so many stock answers this needs a very close examination. It can hardly mean that a complete absence of attempts to enforce a particular law discredits the whole criminal code, or law-enforcement agencies in general; for the history of every criminal code has plenty of instances in which prohibitions have been allowed to fall into desuetude, without any evidence that this weakened respect for the operative parts of the code. Does it mean that the agencies of law-enforcement make themselves ridiculous by unsuccessful attempts to secure convictions? If so, this could be remedied very easily by taking action only when the prospects of succeeding are very good, as the police do with speeding offences.

A more plausible form of the argument might be that if those who are prosecuted for a given offence are regarded by their fellow citizens as a small and unlucky selection from those who actually committed it, the public may come to, feel that their prosecution is 'unfair'. That such a feeling might well be irrational—especially if the offenders knew that they were risking prosecution—would not prevent it from being widespread. Certainly offenders who are unlucky enough to be prosecuted for a commonly undetected offence—such as exceeding speed limits—seem to feel it.

At most, however, this would be an argument for extreme caution in actually prosecuting detected breaches of the prohibition, and not an argument against including the prohibition in the criminal code. For quite a strong argument can be put forward for retaining, or indeed inserting, even unenforceable prohibitions. The argument is that the law influences conduct not merely because people are deterred by the possible consequences of infringing it, but also because it is taken as a declaration of what the society in question condemns. This the-ory—which I have elsewhere called 'the declaratory theory'—resembles the denunciatory justification of penalties . . . but is distinguishable because it asserts that even if no one were ever penalized for a breach of a prohibition (indeed even if no one knew what the penalty was) it would still help to maintain standards of conduct.

QUESTIONS

1. In the light of the issues discussed so far what arguments can be made for or against fox-hunting? What about incest? (See Temkin (1991).)

2. William Wilson asks (Wilson (2003: 44)): 'How can the state justify censuring and punishing the possession of a few grams of cannabis for one's own use, while the possessing a cellar full of wine for the consumption of the diners of Herefordshire risks only the award of the Michelin rosette?' Do you have a good reply for him?

3. Is the argument 'it is wrong to enforce morality' itself a moral principle which its proponents are seeking to enforce?

4. I suspect that if many people were asked at the end of their lives what had caused them the most harm it would not be those things that concern the criminal law but issues such as broken relationships, which are not covered by the criminal law. Does this mean that the law needs to rethink its understanding of harm?

5. Harcourt (1999) discusses recent attempts in the city of Chicago to prohibit liquor stores. This is not on the basis of the evils of alcohol, but on the harm such stores are said to cause to the atmosphere and ambience of parts of the city. Is this a good reason for criminalization?

FURTHER READING

Devlin, P. (1965), *The Enforcement of Morals* (Oxford: OUP).

Dworkin, G. (1999), 'Devlin was Right: Law and the Enforcement of Morality', *William and Mary Law Review* 40: 927.

Feinberg, J. (1984), *Harm to Others* (New York: OUP).

—— (1986a), *Harm to Self* (New York: OUP).

—— (1986b), *Offense to Others* (New York: OUP).

—— (1988), *Harmless Wrongdoing* (New York: OUP).

Hart, H. (1963), *Law, Liberty and Morality* (Oxford: OUP).

Husak, D. (2002), 'Limitations on Criminalization and the General Part of Criminal Law' in S. Shute and A. Simester (eds.), *Criminal Law Theory* (Oxford: OUP).

Katz, L. (2002) 'A Problem Concerning Criminalization', *Buffalo Criminal Law Review* 6: 451.

Lacey, N. (1995a), 'Contingency and Criminalisation' in I. Loveland (ed.), *The Frontiers of Criminality* (London: Sweet & Maxwell).

MacCormick, N. (1982), *Legal Right and Social Democracy* (Oxford: OUP).

Raz, J. (1988), *The Morality of Freedom* (Oxford: OUP).

Schonsheck, J. (1994), *On Criminalization* (Dordrecht: Kluwer).

Stewart, H. (2001b), 'Harms, Wrongs, and Set-Backs in Feinberg's Moral Limits of the Criminal Law', *Buffalo Criminal Law Review* 5: 47.

Wilson, W. (2002), *Central Issues in Criminal Theory* (Oxford: Hart), ch. 1.

7 CULPABILITY

It is normally not enough to show that the offender caused harm to another; it must also be shown that the defendant was blameworthy in harming the other person. In other words it must be shown that the defendant was responsible for the harm.[70] At a minimum this requires that the defendant was capable of acting differently from the way he or she did.[71]

The traditional way of analysing offences is to divide them up into the harmful act of the accused (the *actus reus*) and the blameworthy state of mind of the accused (the *mens rea*). Even where both the *actus reus* and *mens rea* are present the law provides defences, such as self-defence or duress (e.g. where the defendant commits a crime because he or she has been threatened with death if he or she does not).

In the following extract Nicola Lacey sets out the standard conceptual framework for analysing offences. She explains that through a range of devices the law seeks to ensure that only blameworthy individuals are punished.

N. Lacey, 'Legal Constructions of Crime' in M. Maguire, R. Morgan, and R. Reiner (eds.), *The Oxford Handbook of Criminology* (Oxford: OUP, 2002), 270–2

The Conceptual Framework of Criminal Law

Contemporary codes and commentaries on criminal law in both the common and the civilian traditions tend to be organized around a core framework which sets out the general conditions under which liability may be established. This core framework is often known as the 'general part', or 'general principles', of criminal law—in other words, the set of rules and doctrines which applies across the whole terrain of criminal law rather than to specific offences. In the UK, this framework consists of four main elements: capacity, conduct, responsibility, and (absence of) defence.

Capacity

Only those who share certain basic cognitive and volitional capacities are regarded as the genuine subjects of criminal law. For example, one might regard defences such as insanity as defining certain kinds of people as simply outwith the system of communication embodied by criminal law. Since law operates in terms of general standards, the line between criminal capacity and criminal incapacity is a relatively crude one from the point of view of other disciplines. For instance, almost every criminal law system exempts from criminal liability people under a certain age, whatever their actual capacities.

---

[70] Honoré (1999).

[71] Hart (1968). Pettit (2001) argues that the concept of being capable of acting otherwise is a philosophically difficult concept.

Conduct

Criminal conviction is founded, secondly, in a certain kind of conduct specified in the offence definition: appropriating another person's property in the case of theft; causing a person's death in the case of homicide; having sexual intercourse with a person without his or her consent in the case of rape; driving with a certain level of alcohol in one's blood in the case of driving while intoxicated. Though there are exceptions in this country's criminal law doctrine, it is generally asserted that mere thoughts, being of a certain status rather than doing an act, and—in the absence of a specific duty to act—omitting to do something rather than acting positively, are insufficient to found criminal liability.

Responsibility/fault

Criminal liability is generally said to depend, thirdly, on the capable subject being in some sense responsible for or at fault in committing the conduct specified in the offence definition: we do not hold people liable, to put it crudely, for accidents. Responsibility or fault conditions generally consist of mental states or attitudes such as intention, recklessness, knowledge, belief, dishonesty, and negligence. To revert to the examples above, the relevant conditions consist in a dishonest intention permanently to deprive in the case of theft; an intention to kill or cause some less serious kind of harm, or gross negligence in relation to these results, in the case of homicide; recklessness as to the victim's lack of consent in the case of rape. The fourth example—driving while intoxicated—provides an exception to what is generally represented as the general principle that a discrete responsibility element must be proven by the prosecution: only the driving and the blood alcohol level need be established by the prosecution. Notwithstanding their 'exceptional' status, however, these offences of so-called 'strict' liability are in fact empirically dominant in English criminal law today. This division between offences of 'strict' liability and offences requiring proof of fault is the way in which the division between the 'quasi-moral' and 'instrumental/regulatory' terrains of criminal law is purportedly mapped on to legal doctrine. However, as the example of driving while intoxicated—an offence which thirty years ago was regarded as a quintessentially regulatory offence, yet which today carries a marked moral stigma—illustrates, this line is in fact far from clear.

Defences

Even where a capable subject has committed the relevant conduct with the requisite degree of fault, a range of defences may operate to preclude or mitigate his or her liability. For example, if the defendant has committed a theft while under a threat of violence, she may plead the defence of duress; if a person kills, intentionally, in order to defend himself against an immediate attack, he may plead self-defence; and if that person kills under provocation, he may be convicted of a lesser degree of homicide. These 'general defences' apply not only to crimes which require proof of responsibility, but also to those of strict liability. Hence, for example, a person who drives while intoxicated because of duress, whether in the form of a threat or in the form of highly compelling circumstances, may be able to escape liability. Defences are often thought to fall into three main groups—*exemptions, justifications, and excuses*—each relating to the other three components of liability already mentioned. The defence of insanity, for example, arguably operates to recognize that the defendant's incapacity exempts him or her from the communications of criminal law; the defence of self-defence may be seen as amounting to a claim that the conduct in question was, in the circumstances, *justified* and hence not the sort of conduct which criminal law sets out to proscribe; the defence of duress may be viewed as excusing the defendant on the basis that the conditions under which she formed the relevant fault condition—in cases of duress, this would generally be intention—are such that the usual inference of *responsibility* is blocked. One might, in short, see the defences as a mechanism which fine-tunes, along adequately contextualized and morally sensitive lines, the presumptive inferences of liability produced by the first three elements.

At one level, this conceptual framework is analytic: it simply provides a set of building blocks out of which legislators and lawyers construct criminal liability. On the other hand—as the description of the framework as a set of 'general principles' suggests—it contains an implicit set of assumptions about what makes the imposition of criminal liability legitimate. The ideas, for example, that there should be no punishment for mere thoughts, or that defendants should not be convicted unless they were in some sense responsible for their conduct, or in circumstances in which some internal incapacity or external circumstance deprived them of a fair opportunity to conform to the law, express a normative view of criminal law not merely as an institutionalized system of coercion but rather as a system which is structured around certain principles of justice or morality. This normative aspect of the 'general part' of criminal law becomes yet clearer in the light of two broad procedural standards which characterize most modern systems. The first of these is *the principle of legality* or *rule of law*—the idea that criminal law must be announced clearly to citizens in advance of its imposition. Only those who know the law in advance can be seen as having a fair opportunity to conform to it. Principles such as clarity and non-retroactivity are therefore central tenets of the liberal ideal of the rule of law. The second procedural doctrine is the *presumption of innocence*—*the* idea that a crime must be proven by the prosecution (generally the state, and hence far more powerful than the individual defendant) to a very high standard. Criminal law is therefore implicitly justified not only in terms of its role in proscribing, condemning, and (perhaps) reducing conduct which causes or risks a variety of harms, but also in treating its subjects with respect, as moral agents whose conduct must be assessed in terms of attitudes and intentions, and not merely in terms of effects. And underlying this normative framework is a further set of assumptions about the nature of human conduct: about voluntariness, will, agency, capacity as the basis for genuine human personhood and hence responsibility.

The various assumptions underlying the conceptual framework within which criminal liability is constructed should be of great interest to criminological and criminal justice scholars. First, they give us insight into the processes of interpretation in the courtroom—one key moment in the process of criminalization. Thus, secondly, they also provide some interesting points of both contrast and similarity when compared with the assumptions on the basis of which other practices within the criminal process are founded. Are the assumptions of responsible subjecthood that constitute the core of criminal law thinking the same as, or even consistent with, those that underpin the development of policing strategy, sentencing decision-making, probation practice, or prison regimes? If not, does it matter? And what does it signify?

Having presented the orthodox position Nicola Lacey goes on critically to assess the description of the law she has just provided. As her discussion shows, the position is not as straightforward as might at first appear.

N. Lacey, 'Legal Constructions of Crime' in M. Maguire, R. Morgan, and R. Reiner (eds.), *The Oxford Handbook of Criminology* (Oxford: OUP, 2002), 272–5

'General Principles' of Criminal Law: a Critical Assessment

The need to bring criminal justice and criminal law analyses into relation with one another is therefore clear. However, it is equally clear that criminal justice scholars ought to be wary of taking the 'general principles' of criminal law on lawyers' terms. For the fact is that the 'general principles of criminal law' are honoured in many systems, and certainly in the UK, as much in the breach as in the observance—a fact which suggests that they are as much an ideological as an 'actual' feature of criminal law's operations. In this respect, the criminal justice scholar will get some enlightenment from the more critical genre of criminal law scholarship that has been emerging over the last twenty years, and which has subjected the 'general principles' of criminal law to a searching examination. Early examples of critical criminal law scholarship, notably the work of Mark Kelman (1981), were closely associated with the American 'critical legal studies' movement. The movement embraced a group of scholars who sought to expose the 'politics of law' by means of a close examination of doctrinal principles and categories.

Conventional criminal law scholars, as we have seen, generally provide a brief résumé of the moral/retributive, regulatory/deterrent aspects of criminal justice. They go on to give a terse statement of the competing concerns of fairness and social protection, due process and crime control which are taken to inform the development and implementation of criminal law in liberal societies. From this point on, they take the idea of 'crimes' as given by acts of law-creation. In this way both political and criminological issues are quietly removed from the legal agenda. In contrast, critical criminal lawyers assume that the power and meaning of criminal laws depend on a more complex set of processes and underlying factors than the mere positing of prohibitory norms to be enforced according to a particular procedure. Most obviously, they assume that the influences of political and economic power permeate the practice of doctrinal interpretation. Yet their view is not the reductive, instrumental one of Realism or the Chicago School. Rather, critical criminal lawyers argue that judicial practice is shaped by tensions between competing values whose power infuses all social practices, and which cannot be reconciled by either legislative reform or feats of rationalizing interpretation. From this critical perspective, further links between the legal and social construction of crime appear. For it seems, *a priori*, likely that the evaluative and pragmatic tensions which shape the development of criminal law will also manifest themselves, albeit to different degrees and in different ways, in other criminal justice practices.

The primary aim of early critical criminal law scholarship was to develop an internal or 'immanent' critique of the doctrinal framework within which different areas of law have been taken to be organized. Taking a close interest in the way in which criminal liability is *constructed* within legal discourse, critical scholars took as their focus the structure of 'general principles' which are usually taken to underpin criminal law in liberal societies. These included not only the liberal ideals about the fair terms under which criminal punishment may be imposed upon an individual agent, which we considered above, but also the aspirations of neutrality, objectivity, and determinacy of legal method which are associated with the rule of law (Norrie 2001). For example, Kelman's work scrutinized the basis of the responsibility/fault doctrine which purports to structure and justify the attribution of criminal responsibility to the free individual *via* the employment of standards of fault such as intent and recklessness. He showed that fault requirements veer in an unprincipled way between 'subjective' standards, in which attributions of responsibility depend on what the defendant actually intended or contemplated, and 'objective' standards such as negligence, which impute to the defendant the state of mind of the 'reasonable man'. Following from this, Kelman emphasized the fact that criminal law doctrine evinces no consistent commitment to either a free-will or a determinist model of human behaviour (Kelman 1981). Furthermore, Kelman and others demonstrated the manipulability and indeterminacy of the generally accepted doctrinal framework according to which criminal liability is constructed in terms of the four elements discussed above: capacity, conduct, responsibility or fault, and absence of defence. For example, critical scholars pointed out that the issue of mistake could be conceptualized with equal doctrinal propriety as matter pertaining to the existence of the conduct or fault elements of a crime, or to the existence of a defence (Lacey and Wells 1998: chapter 1). A person who assaults another person in the mistaken belief that that other person is in the process of committing an assault on a third party could, in other words, be regarded as having a defence (of mistaken self-defence), or as lacking the conduct (no 'unlawful' act) or (in certain circumstances) fault/responsibility (no relevant intention) elements of a crime. Since these conceptualizations sometimes affect the outcome of the legal analysis, this entails that doctrinal rules are not as determinate as the conventional theory of legal reasoning assumes. Moreover, critical analysis illustrated the fact that the outcome of legal reasoning is contingent upon factors such as the time frame within which the alleged offence was set. For example, whether or not a person is regarded as negligent, in the sense of having failed to reach a reasonable standard of care or awareness, may well depend on what range of conduct the court is able to examine. What appears an unreasonable lapse judged in itself may look more reasonable if evidence about its history can be admitted. This broadening of the time frame or context is precisely what the defences often effect. How far the time frame is expanded, however, also depends on interpretive and evidential factors: on whether, for example, evidence of a history of domestic violence is seen as relevant to the establishment of the defence of provocation or self-defence. Yet the influence of the framing process is not acknowledged within the doctrinal structure, which accordingly fails to regulate judicial interpretation in the way which is generally supposed.

The critical enterprise here is to hold criminal law up to scrutiny in terms of the standards which it professes to instantiate; and in doing so, to reveal that, far from consisting of a clear, determinate set of norms, based on a coherent set of 'general principles', it rather exemplifies a contradictory and conflicting set of approaches which are obscured by the superficial coherence and determinacy of legal reasoning. By scrutinizing carefully the form which criminal legal reasoning takes, it becomes possible to reveal that practice as having important ideological dimensions, rationalizing and legitimating a system which serves a variety of powerful interests by representing criminal law as a technical and apolitical sphere of judgement (Norrie 2001). An important part of this process is the (re)reading of cases not merely as exercises in formal legal analysis, but also as texts whose rhetorical structure is at least as important as their superficial legal content (Goodrich 1986). In this kind of reading, critical scholars emphasize the significant symbolic aspect of the power of criminal law, along with the implicit yet powerful images of wrongdoing and rightful conduct, normal and abnormal subjects, guilt and innocence which legal discourse draws upon and produces (Lacey 1993).

The early critical focus on the intricacies of doctrinal rationalization and the exposure of conflicts which such rationalization obscures has, however, gradually been supplemented by a further set of questions suggested by the process of immanent critique. If critical criminal law was not to remain a set of observations about the apparent irrationality of legal doctrine, the question of the deeper logics underpinning legal discourse had to be addressed (Norrie 2001). Hence questions about the broad socio-political conditions under which a particular doctrinal framework arises and 'works', and about the historical conditions of existence of particular doctrinal systems of classification (taken as 'given' within conventional scholarship) have begun to claim the attention of criminal law scholars (Norrie 1992; Lacey 1998, 2001a, 2001b).

7.1 THE SUBJECTIVISM/OBJECTIVISM DEBATE

There has been much debate over whether, when assessing the blameworthiness of a defendant, the law should adopt a subjectivist or objectivist perspective.[72] In short, a subjectivist account argues that criminal liability should be determined by looking inside the state of mind of the defendant. The focus should be on the intentions and foresight of the defendant. An objectivist account focuses on the behaviour of the defendant and asks whether the defendant acted as a reasonable person would.

In the following extract Anthony Duff describes the key elements of subjectivism and objectivism:

R.A. Duff, 'Subjectivism, Objectivism and Criminal Attempts' in A. Simester and A. Smith (eds.), *Harm and Culpability* (Oxford: OUP, 1996), 19–22

It is no doubt sometimes unhelpful to portray controversies about the proper principles of criminal liability as controversies between 'subjectivism' and 'objectivism'. Certainly neither term picks out a single, unitary, position. Furthermore, some disagreements rather concern the scope of the 'subjective' itself: for example, should we analyse recklessness in terms of conscious risk-taking or of 'practical indifference', both of which could be portrayed as 'subjective' aspects of the agent's conduct? Nor can we always draw a clear distinction between the 'subjective' and the 'objective'. If we justify an ascription of recklessness by saying that an agent failed to notice some obvious risk because he did not care about it, we are not simply explaining his failure to notice that risk in morally neutral terms: we are, rather, interpreting his conduct in the light of some normative, non-subjective, standard of appropriate care.

In some contexts, however, there does seem to be a clear distinction between 'subjectivist' and 'objectivist' principles of criminal liability, and controversies which embody that distinction. One such context is the law of attempts. . . .

'Subjectivists' and 'objectivists' disagree about the appropriate criteria for action-ascriptions. An agent is criminally liable only if an action matching the law's definition of an offence can justly be ascribed to her. But how should we decide what actions can justly be ascribed to an agent; what criteria should determine our ascriptions? Subjectivists insist that the criteria should be 'subjective'; the actions that are to be ascribed to an agent, for which she is to be held liable, must be described in 'subjective' terms. By contrast objectivists argue that what is 'mine' as an agent cannot be defined or delimited in purely 'subjective' terms, but must be described in partly 'objective' terms.

But what are 'subjective', or 'objective', terms or descriptions? We can say that the 'subjective' is a matter of the agent's psychological states: but that is too vague to be helpful. Any more precise account of the 'subjective', however, would have to be an account of the

---

[72] Lacey (2001) discusses the historical background of the debate.

different conceptions of the 'subjective' expressed in *different* forms of subjectivism. The two most familiar contemporary subjectivist theories, the 'choice' and the 'character' accounts of criminal liability, embody different accounts of the 'subjective'. 'Choice' theorists insist that we can properly ascribe to an agent only those actions that he *chose* to perform; any action for which he is to be held liable must be described in terms of his choices. Choice, as constituting the 'subjective', can then be (minimally) defined in terms of intention and belief; I choose to do what I intend to do, or believe myself to be doing. 'Character' theorists, by contrast, hold that we should ground criminal liability in the character traits manifested in the agent's conduct; for them, the 'subjective' consists in those dispositions, attitudes, or motives which constitute legally relevant character traits.

I will focus in this paper on the 'choice' conception of criminal liability, which is the dominant version of subjectivism. Though the objectivist grounding for the law of attempts which I will sketch is opposed to both types of subjectivism, the implications of each type for the law of attempts differ; and the arguments that I will offer against the 'choice' conception are not the same as those that might be offered against the 'character' conception.

The 'choice' version of subjectivism can be defined by Ashworth's 'intent' and 'belief' principles: agents should be held 'criminally liable for what they intended to do, and not according to what actually did or did not occur', and must be 'judged on the basis of what they believed they were doing, not on the basis of actual facts and circumstances which were not known to them at the time'. This does not mean that agents are to be held liable for their intentions and beliefs *rather than* for their actions. The claim is that the *actions* for which agents are to be held liable should be identified in terms of what they intended to do or believed they were doing: agents are liable for their actions qua chosen.

A subjectivist might argue, or might avow principles which imply, that the action-ascriptions which generate criminal liability should be determined by *purely* subjective criteria: the actions we ascribe to an agent must be described purely in terms of her intentions and beliefs. By contrast, 'objectivists' (as I shall use the notion) do not hold that criminal liability should be based on *purely* objective criteria: that agents' actual intentions or beliefs should be wholly irrelevant to their criminal liability. They deny, rather, that the subjective dimensions of the agent's conduct are all that matter for criminal liability: its 'objective' aspects may also be crucial. But what are these 'objective' aspects?

They are of two kinds. One consists in what actually occurs or is actually the case: for example, in the fact of whether the shot that I intend should hit, or believe will hit, V actually hits or misses; in the fact of whether the woman on whom I press sexual intercourse, believing her to consent to it, actually consents or not. The other consists in what a 'reasonable' person would believe, or realize: in the fact that what I take to be a person is obviously (i.e. would be immediately seen by any reasonable person to be) a tree; or that the means by which I hope to achieve a criminal goal are obviously (i.e. would be seen by any reasonable person to be) utterly inadequate; or that my action creates an obvious risk of harm which would be recognized by any reasonable persons.

Now in many contexts subjectivist principles play an *exculpatory* role, exempting from criminal liability those who might otherwise be held liable, Thus someone who does not realize that her action might damage another's property should not be convicted of criminal damage—even if her act 'in fact creates an obvious risk' (one that would be obvious to the 'ordinary prudent' person) of such damage: for she has not chosen to risk damaging another's property. A man who honestly believed that the woman with whom he had intercourse consented to it should not be convicted of rape—even if his belief was both mistaken and unreasonable: for he did not choose to have, or to take a risk of having, 'intercourse with a woman who [did] not consent to it'.

In the following passage from a Law Commission report on manslaughter the benefits and disadvantages of an objectivist and subjectivist approach are explored:

Law Commission Report No. 237, *Legislating the Criminal Code: Involuntary Manslaughter* (London: HMSO, 1996), paras. 4.4–4.23

Orthodox Subjectivist Theory

4.4 The legal philosophy traditionally applied in mainstream English criminal law and by this Commission is known as 'subjectivist theory'. It rests on the principle that moral guilt, and hence criminal liability, should be imposed only on people who can be said to have *chosen* to behave in a certain way or to cause or risk causing certain consequences. The roots of subjectivism lie in a liberal philosophy that regards individuals as autonomous beings, capable of choice, and each deserving of individual respect. It is called 'subjectivism' because of the significance that it accords to the individual's state of mind at the time of the prohibited conduct.

4.5 Three principles have been identified as inherent in this basis of liability. The first of these is the '*mens rea* principle', which imposes liability only for outcomes which were *intended* or *knowingly risked* by the alleged wrongdoer. The second principle, the 'belief principle', judges a defendant according only to what *she* believed she was doing or risking. Thirdly, according to the 'principle of correspondence', subjectivists insist that the fault element of a crime *correspond* to the conduct element; for example, if the conduct element is 'causing serious injury', the fault element ought to be 'intention or recklessness as to causing serious injury'. This ensures that the defendant is punished only for causing a harm which she *chose* to risk or to bring about.

4.6 Subjectivist philosophy applies widely in the criminal law today. A man cannot be convicted of rape, for example, if he genuinely believed, albeit unreasonably, that his victim consented to sexual intercourse, because this belief would be incompatible with the intention to have intercourse with a woman *without her consent*, or recklessness as to that possibility, which are the mental states required for rape.

. . .

Criticisms of the Subjectivist *Mens Rea* Principle: Can Liability Based on Inadvertence ever be Justified?

4.12 Orthodox subjectivist theory, then, requires the defendant to have been, at least, *aware* of the risk of causing the prohibited harm. However, there is a body of criticism, from very distinguished commentators, of the orthodox subjectivist *mens rea* principle. One ground of criticism is that it is based on a simplistic view of what constitutes knowledge or awareness of risk:

'. . . while we do indeed sometimes make our knowledge of what we are doing explicit to ourselves in . . . silent mental reports, it is absurd to suggest that such knowledge can be actual only if it is made thus explicit. When I drive my car, my driving is guided by my (actual) knowledge of my car and of the context in which I am driving: but my driving is not accompanied by a constant silent monologue in which I tell myself what to do next, what the road conditions are, whether I am driving safely or not, and all the other facts of which I am certainly aware while I am driving. . . . The occurrence or the non-occurrence of certain explicit thoughts is irrelevant to whether I am actually aware of what I am doing: my actions can manifest my awareness even if no explicit thoughts about the relevant facts pass through my mind at the time.'[73]

4.13 On this view of what constitutes a mental state, the contrast between awareness and lack of awareness of risk is not as stark as in conventional subjectivist accounts, and it is less clear why inadvertence ought not to be classified, as mens rea in certain circumstances.

4.14 The main argument in favour of criminalizing some forms of inadvertent risk-taking, however, is that in some circumstances a person is *at fault in failing to consider* the consequences that might be caused by her conduct. The example given by R A Duff is that of a bridegroom who misses his wedding because it slipped his mind when he was in the pub. An orthodox subjectivist would point to his lack of intention or awareness, and deem him consequently less culpable. The bride, however, would rightly condemn him, because it is plain from his conduct that he did not care, and this attitude is sufficient to make him blameworthy. Duff argues that this account retains a subjective element, because attitudes are subjective.

4.15 A similar argument was used by Lord Diplock in the famous case on criminal damage, *Caldwell:*

'If it had crossed his mind that there was a risk that someone's property might be damaged but because his mind was affected by rage or excitement or confused by drink, he did not appreciate the seriousness of the risk or trusted that good luck would prevent it happening, this state of mind would amount to malice in the restricted meaning placed upon that term by the Court of Appeal; whereas if, for any of these reasons, he did not even trouble to give his mind to the question whether there was any risk of damaging the property, this state of mind would not suffice to make him guilty of an offence under the Malicious Damage Act 1861. *Neither state of mind seems to me to be less blameworthy than the other. . . .*'[74]

4.16 Professor Hart some years ago attacked the assumption that to allow criminal liability for negligence would be to set aside the requirement of *mens rea* as a precondition of punishment. His argument was that since 'negligence' implies a failure to do what ought to have been done, it is therefore more than inadvertence, it is *culpable* inadvertence:

'Only a theory that mental operations like attending to, or thinking about, or examining a situation are somehow "either there or not there", and so utterly outside our control, can lead to the theory that we are *never* responsible if, like the signalman who forgets to pull the signal, we fail to think or remember. . . . What is crucial is that those whom we punish should have had, when they acted, the normal capacities, physical and mental, for doing what the law requires and abstaining from what it forbids, and a fair opportunity to exercise these capacities. Where these capacities and opportunities are absent, as they are in different ways in the varied cases of accident, mistake, paralysis, reflex action, coercion, insanity etc, the moral protest is that it is morally wrong to punish because "he could not have helped it" or "he could not have done otherwise" or "he had no real choice". But as we have seen, there is no reason (unless we are to reject the whole business of responsibility and punishment) *always* to make this protest when someone who "just didn't think" is punished for carelessness. For in some cases at least we may say "he could have thought about what he was doing" with just as much rational confidence as one can say of any intentional wrongdoing "he could have done otherwise." '[75]

Professor Ashworth also concedes that negligence may be an appropriate standard for criminal liability where the harm risked was great, the risk obvious and the defendant had the capacity to take the required precautions.

---

[73] Duff (1990: 160).   [74] [1982] AC 341, 352 (emphasis added).   [75] Hart (1968: 151–2).

What Makes Inadvertence *Culpable*?

4.17 In all the sources cited in paragraphs 4.12–4.16, the view is taken that it may be justifiable to impose criminal liability for the *unforeseen* consequences of a person's acts, at any rate where the harm risked is great and the actor's failure to advert to this risk is *culpable*, we are persuaded by this reasoning, in the following paragraphs, therefore, we consider the criteria by which *culpable inadvertence* should be judged if it is to attract the sanctions of the criminal law when death results.

4.18 The first criterion of culpability upon which we must insist is that the harm to which the accused failed to advert was at *least foreseeable*, if not strikingly foreseeable or obvious. If the accused is an ordinary person, she cannot be blamed for failing to take notice *of a* risk if it would not have been apparent to an *average person* in *her position*, because the criminal law cannot require an *exceptional* standard of perception or awareness from her. If the accused held herself out as an expert *of* some kind, however, a higher standard can be expected from her; if she is a doctor, for example, she will be at fault if she fails to advert to a risk that would have been obvious to the average doctor in her position.

4.19 As a matter of strict principle, the accused ought only to be held liable for causing death if the risk to which she culpably failed to avert was a risk of *death*. In practice, however, there is a very thin line between behaviour that risks serious injury and behaviour that risks death, because it is frequently a matter of chance, depending on such factors as the availability of medical treatment, whether serious injury leads to death. Admittedly it is possible for conduct to involve a risk of serious injury (such as a broken limb) though not a risk of death; but intention to cause serious injury constitutes the *mens rea* of murder although the *actus reus* is the causing of death, and we see no compelling reason to distinguish between murder and manslaughter in this respect. We consider, therefore, that it would not be wrong in principle if a person were to be held responsible for causing death through failing to advert to a clear risk of causing death *or* serious injury—subject of course to a second criterion, to which we now turn.

4.20 The second criterion of culpability which we consider to be essential is that the accused herself would have been *capable* of perceiving the risk in question, had she directed her mind to it. Since the fault *of* the accused lies in her failure to consider a risk, she cannot be punished for this failure if the risk in question would never have been apparent to her, no matter how hard she thought about the potential consequences of her conduct. If this criterion is not insisted upon, the accused will, in essence, be punished for being less intelligent, mature or capable than the average person.

. . .

4.22 . . . A person cannot be said to be morally at fault in failing to advert to a risk if she lacked the capacity to do so.

4.23 If the criteria in paragraphs 4.17–4.22 are satisfied, we consider that it is appropriate to impose for inadvertently causing harm in cases where the harm risked is *very serious*. Where a person embarks on a course of conduct which inherently involves a risk of causing death or serious injury to another, society is justified in requiring a higher standard of care from her than from someone whose conduct involves a lesser risk or no risk at all. JL Austin made this point graphically when he wrote 'We may plead that we trod on the snail inadvertently: but not on the baby—you ought to look where you're putting your great feet'.[76]

---

[76] Austin (1956: 1).

The debate between subjectivism and objectivism has influenced several recent cases before the House of Lords. We will consider one case to see how the objectivist/subjectivist dispute can make all the difference between guilt and innocence. In *B v DPP* Lord Nicholls,[77] in upholding the view that in English and Welsh law a subjective state of mind is required, stated:

> By definition the mental element in a crime is concerned with a subjective state of mind, such as intent or belief. To the extent that an overriding objective limit ('on reasonable grounds') is introduced, the subjective element is displaced. To that extent a person who lacks the necessary intent or belief may nevertheless commit the offence. When that occurs the defendant's 'fault' lies exclusively in falling short of an objective standard. His crime lies in his negligence. A statute may so provide expressly or by necessary implication. But this can have no place in a common law principle, of general application, which is concerned with the need for a mental element as an essential ingredient of a criminal offence.

Applying this subjectivist approach the House of Lords held that an accused who believed that he was making an indecent assault on a girl over the age of 14 could not be convicted of inciting a girl under the age of 14 to commit an act of gross indecency with him, contrary to section 1(1) of the Indecency with Children Act 1960. In the following extract Jeremy Horder explains why he rejects the subjectivist approach:

J. Horder, 'How Culpability Can, and Cannot, be Denied in Under-age Sex Crimes'
[2001] *Criminal Law Review* 15

2. The Irrationality of the Subjectivist Approach to B's Belief

Section 1(1) [of the Indecency with Children Act 1960] says that 'Any person who commits an act of gross indecency with or towards a child under the age of fourteen, or who incites a child *under that age* to commit such an act with him or another, shall be liable . . .' (my emphasis). No provision is made for the mental element in the crime, but all the Law Lords in *B. (A Minor) v. DPP were* agreed that, in the absence of express provision for, or necessary implication of, strict liability in a criminal statute, there was a common law presumption of a requirement of *mens rea*. Few would quarrel with the moral and legal importance of this presumption. It is the particular species of *mens rea* presumptively required that is controversial. In this regard, as I have said, the Law Lords were drawn by what they perceived to be the force of the subjectivist understanding of the correspondence principle. On this view, chiefly as a result of the decision in *DPP v. Morgan*, if D honestly believes any element of the *actus reus* is missing, s/he is entitled to be acquitted. The burden is on the prosecution to show that there was no such belief. So, according to this argument, on the facts of *B. (A Minor) v. DPP*, D is entitled to an acquittal if the jury thinks he might have honestly believed, whether reasonably or not, that the victim was aged 14 or more.

---

[77] *Sub nom B (A Child) v DPP* [2000] 2 AC 428 (HL). Other recent House of Lords cases which appear to adopt a more subjectivist analysis include *K* [2001] UKHL 41 and *Smith (Morgan)* [2001] 1 AC 146 (HL). We shall be considering these cases later in this book.

On the face of it, such a holding is capable of producing some unsavoury results. Suppose D, an adult paedophile, invites V, who is in fact 13, to commit an act of gross indecency with him. D believes V is over 14. D's belief is based, however, solely on an inference drawn from the character of previous sexual experiences he has had with V, as compared to his numerous sexual experiences with other children both younger and older than V. The law as it stands after *B. (A Minor) v. DPP* would acquit D in this example, even though it was nothing more than his experience as a paedophile that led him to believe that V was over 14. Nonetheless, the general intellectual case for D's acquittal is made by Smith and Hogan, in the section entitled 'The Variable Nature of *Mens Rea*': 'An ideal rule would seem to be [one] requiring intention or recklessness as to all the elements in the *actus reus*. Presumably, no element is included in the definition of an actus reus unless it contributes to the heinousness of the offence. If the accused is blamelessly inadvertent with respect to *any* one element in the offence . . . is it then proper to hold him responsible for it.' The making of this case, though, is marred by a curious—and I would argue, highly significant—qualification to the 'ideal rule' (outlined above)—the correspondence principle—that subjective *mens rea* must match '*all* the elements in the *actus reus*'.

Immediately following their ringing endorsement of the 'ideal rule', the rule that has become the subjectivists' *leit-motiv* [sic], one finds the following observations (rather less frequently discussed by other subjectivists), which I hope I may be forgiven for citing at some length:

'There is a particular difficulty in requiring *mens rea* as to an element in the *actus reus* of a morally indifferent nature. The definition of a crime sometimes draws an arbitrary line as to a person's age, or as to time, weight, size and other matters of degree . . . a person who is unaware of the law is unlikely to direct his mind to the question whether the arbitrary line has been crossed in the particular case . . . a person taking a girl out of the possession of her parents may give no thought to the question whether she is under or over 16, if he is unaware of the legal significance of that age. The case is different in a material respect from that of the person who has a positive but mistaken belief that the girl is over 16. Williams sought to resolve the difficulty by distinguishing between cases of "mistaken belief" (where there is positive belief) which will negative recklessness and "simple ignorance" (where there is no advertence to the question) which will not . . . D can truly be said to be indifferent as to the circumstance—he does not care whether . . . the girl [is] under or over 16, because he is unaware that it matters.'

So, the 'ideal rule', in which *mens rea* must be proved in relation to all the elements of the *actus reus*, is regarded by Smith and Hogan as subject to an exception where the element of the *actus reus* in question is 'morally indifferent' (this term is not explained). In such a case D may be convicted, even if the prosecution has offered no evidence of *mens rea* on D's part, if D gave no thought to whether or not the 'morally indifferent' element of the *actus reus* was present. However, even when the relevant element of the *actus reus* is 'morally indifferent', if D claims that s/he *positively believed* (whether reasonably or not) that that element of the *actus reus* was absent, then that situation is once again governed by the 'ideal rule'. There will be a burden on the prosecution of disproving the existence of the belief. This particular line of reasoning is not expressly considered by the House of Lords in *B. (A Minor) v. DPP*, but was endorsed by Brooke L.J. in the Divisional Court below.

What is curious about this line of reasoning is the way in which a belief in the existence of, as opposed to ignorance of, an admittedly morally indifferent element of the actus reus comes to be governed by the ideal rule, rather than simply falling, like the 'ignorance case', under the exception. This crucial point—the different treatment of the 'belief case' as against the 'ignorance case'—must be considered in greater depth. At the end of the passage cited above, it looks as if one justification for the distinction is thought by subjectivists to be this. If D is unaware of the legal significance of the relevant element of the *actus reus*, he can be described as *indifferent* to it, given its moral insignificance, and is thus in a state of mind amounting to *mens rea*. It seems that we are invited to conclude, by way of contrast, that if D positively believed that the morally insignificant element of the *actus reus* was absent, he or she could not have been indifferent to it, and thus the *mens* was not *rea*. This line of argument sits uneasily alongside the usual subjectivist insistence that, to be described as indifferent to a circumstance or consequence, D must have been aware of it. As Smith and Hogan themselves put it, 'it is difficult to understand how a man can be indifferent to something the possibility of which he has not envisaged'. More importantly, however, the contrast we are invited to draw between the 'belief case' and the 'ignorance case', in terms of the legitimacy of attributing indifference, is illusory when the relevant element of the *actus reus* is morally indifferent.

In defining terms such as 'indifference', 'recklessness' and '(gross) negligence', the law is concerned with the defendant's disregard for a guiding reason, a reason that bears on what he or she may not do. In cases where a guiding reason is in play, there is indeed some difference between the 'ignorance case' and the 'belief case'. If I have permission to do construction work on your house, but in doing it I fail to acquaint myself with the precautions I should take against accidents, that will amount to culpable disregard. Your safety is a guiding reason that ought to affect the way in which I do the work. Accordingly, if, by way of contrast, I believed that certain steps I had taken would avert any danger, although as it turned out they did not, that belief in itself may have moral significance, precisely because it concerns a guiding reason. I can be plausibly described as indifferent in the case where I fail to acquaint myself with the necessary precautions (the 'ignorance case'), but much less plausibly so described in the case where I mistakenly believe I have averted the danger (the 'belief case'). Notice, though, that in this example, the different way in which one should treat the 'ignorance case' and the 'belief case' hinges entirely on the fact that the ignorance and the mistaken belief concern a guiding reason, your safety. As I shall now argue, where the ignorance or the mistaken belief concern something other than a guiding reason, there is no distinction of significance to be drawn between them, as far as inferring indifference is concerned.

Suppose that I work with a fellow builder, who has given no thought to whether you—the customer—are a reformed alcoholic, whereas I may for some reason mistakenly believe that you are. In the event, however, we will be equally indifferent to whether or not you are a reformed alcoholic, because in the context of what we are doing it is—and ought to be—a matter of no practical significance to either of us. In this context there is no moral question on which my colleague's ignorance, as contrasted with my mistaken belief, or vice versa, has a particular bearing. Now, turning back to section 1(1), D may rightly be said to be indifferent to V's age in the 'ignorance case', because whether V is, say, just under rather than just over 14 years of age is not something that affects whether a guiding reason is in play. That V is aged just over 14 gives D no more reason to propose an act of gross indecency than if V is just under that age. This is because the guiding reason dictating that D ought not to be making such a proposal is that V is *under* 16, *the age of consent* (on which, more shortly), and that reason has equal moral force in either case. So, we can infer indifference to the *actus reus* issue—whether V is aged just under or just over 14—that does not directly concern that very guiding reason. The process of reasoning is just the same, however, in the 'belief case'. D may mistakenly believe that V is over 14. Even so, it will be just as accurate to call him (indifferent as it was in the 'ignorance case', even though D's mistake is about the same issue age) as is at stake in the guiding reason. The simple mistaken belief that V is aged 14, like ignorance that V is aged under 14, does not in itself centre on the guiding reason against doing as D did, that V was under the age of consent.

FURTHER READING

Duff, R.A. (2005a), 'Theorizing Criminal Law: a 25th Anniversary Essay', *Oxford Journal of Legal Studies* 25: 353.

Smith, A. (1978), 'On *Actus Reus* and *Mens Rea*' in P. Glazebrook (ed.), *Reshaping the Criminal Law* (London: Sweet & Maxwell).

Sullivan, G.R. (1996a), 'Making Excuses' in A. Simester and G.R. Sullivan (eds.), *Harm and Culpability* (Oxford: OUP).

Tadros, V. (2005), *Criminal Responsibility* (Oxford: OUP).

Tur, R. (1993), 'Subjectivism and Objectivism: Towards Synthesis' in S. Shute, J. Gardner, and J. Horder (eds.), *Action and Value in Criminal Law* (Oxford: OUP).

Wells, C. (1982), 'Swatting the Subjectivist Bug', *Criminal Law Review* 209.

8 THE VICTIM IN CRIMINAL LAW

Until fairly recently criminal lawyers and criminologists have focused on the defendant and assessments of his or her liability.[78] The victim, in much writing on criminal law, is a shadowy figure who appears to be an irrelevance. Consider a case of alleged rape where a defendant wrongly but reasonably believed that the victim was consenting. This 'easy' case would be dealt with by the law saying that such a defendant lacks the *mens rea* for rape and so no offence is committed. But that is to look at the question entirely from the defendant's point of view. As for the victim, she was raped: she did not consent to the penetration.

Recently, the interest in victims of crime has increased, especially amongst criminologists.[79] In particular, attempts have been made to develop the notion of restorative justice which seeks to give a greater place for victims.[80] In the following extract Lucia Zedner summarizes what the notion of restorative justice means:

L. Zedner, 'Victims' in M. Maguire, R. Morgan, and R. Reiner (eds.), *The Oxford Handbook of Criminology* (Oxford: OUP, 2002), 419 at 443–7

Victims, once on the margins of criminology research, are now a central focus of academic research. Victim surveys, both national and local, and qualitative studies of the impact

---

[78] Edwards (2004); Doak (2003).

[79] The organization Victim Support has done much to assist and offer support to victims (see Victim Support (2002)).

[80] See the concern expressed in Ashworth (2002c) that the involvement of victims in trials may jeopardize the defendant's right to a fair trial. There are especial concerns in the involvement of victims in cases of domestic violence.

of crime and of victim needs have permanently altered the criminological agenda. Victims complicate the old triumvirate of crimes, criminals, and their control. And criminologists have been obliged to recognize that crime has consequences more painful than once acknowledged. Academic research on victims has been mirrored and encouraged by the growth of influential interest groups, cross-party political concern, and international recognition. As a result, the victim has moved from being a 'forgotten actor' to become a key player in the criminal justice process. The promotion of victims' interests at both national and international level has prompted debate about victims' rights and the setting of standards of service. For victims are now the subject of political as much as criminological attention.

. . .

The Rise of Restorative Justice

The proliferation of research about victims has raised larger questions about the very purpose of criminal justice and the place of the victim within it. Victim surveys have consistently revealed that victims are no more punitive than the general public, and many are willing to engage in direct mediation, or to receive monetary or other compensation from their offender (Mattinson and Mirrlees-Black 2000: 41).

Academics, policy-makers, and criminal justice professionals seeking an alternative paradigm to that of punishment have advocated various models of restitution, or reparative or restorative justice with increasing success (Barnett 1977; Wright 1991, 1995; Marshall 1999; Braithwaite 1999). Restorative justice (as it is now predominantly called) is an umbrella term for a variety of theories concerned with the restoration of victim, offender, and community. Other terms used in broadly the same sense include community justice, positive justice, reintegrative justice, relational justice, and transformative justice (Braithwaite 1989; Marshall 1999: 7).

. . .

Restorative Justice in Practice

Restorative justice initiatives have developed across the world—in Australia, Canada, New Zealand, and South Africa, as well as in Britain (Young 2001; Hoyle and Young 2002). Typically, they are intended to involve offenders, their families, victims, other interested members of the community, and a facilitator (often a youth justice co-ordinator, social worker, or police officer). The United Nations defines restorative justice as a process 'in which the victim, the offender and/or any other individuals or community members affected by a crime participate actively together in the resolution of matters arising from the crime' (United Nations 1999b). In contrast to mediation, therefore, bi- or tri-partite resolution is replaced with a meeting of all those involved, however tangentially. The group discusses the offence, the circumstances underlying it, its effects on the victim, and how relationships have been affected by it. The principal purpose is to share information and, collectively, 'to formulate a plan about how best to deal with the offending' (Morris and Maxwell 2000: 209).

In principle the victim is a central actor in restorative justice. In practice, levels of victim participation in restorative justice schemes, in Britain at least, are very low. For example, the Youth Justice and Criminal Evidence Act 1999 set up youth offender panels governed by restorative principles. In 2000–2001, less than 7 per cent of panels were attended by victims: a very low figure even bearing in mind that many of the offences were 'victimless' (Newburn *et al.* 2001: 19; see also Miers *et al.* 2001). Given that responses to the 1998 BCS suggested that 41 per cent of victims were willing to meet with their offender (Mattinson and Mirrlees-Black 2000), it is possible that the problem lies with inadequacies in the means by which victims are involved. In New Zealand, by contrast, victims attended about half of all family group conferences (reasons given for non-attendance included that they were not invited, the time arranged was unsuitable, or inadequate notice was given) (Morris and Maxwell 2000: 211). And rates of victim attendance in Australia are even higher: 73 per cent at conferences in New South Wales and up to 89 per cent for crimes of personal violence in the RISE experiments in Canberra. Aside from actual attendance, victims can have an input to restorative programmes (through victim statements, for example), or benefit from reparative work done for them. Moreover, to judge the success of restorative justice schemes by reference to victim participation rates might encourage wholly undesirable pressure upon victims to take part. But on current evidence it is far from clear that restorative justice is centrally, or even principally, about victims. A review of restorative justice programmes in twelve European countries found that only one country (Denmark) claimed to be victim-oriented; a further five are offender-oriented; in two countries the orientation varies with the particular programme; and in the remaining four the orientation is mixed (Miers 2001a: 79).

The question then arises: how much is restorative justice really about victims? There is some evidence that restorative justice works in the sense of reducing reconviction rates in respect of serious offenders undergoing intensive, long-term intervention (though there is little evidence of success in respect of lesser offenders with whom contact is short and superficial) (Miers *et al.* 2001). But does it serve victims' interests as well? Is there a danger that victims are being used to promote ends that have little to do with their own interests? Ashworth has warned of the dangers of 'victim prostitution' (Ashworth 2000a: 186). In restorative cautioning panels, for example, emphasis is on diversion or reducing re-offending among offenders rather than on the value of the process for victims (Young and Goold 1999). Like victim–offender mediation before them, restorative justice conferences and panels may entail pressure upon victims to participate; burdens upon their time and goodwill; and possible psychological costs inherent in meeting with their offender and talking again about the crime and its impact. Victims may feel responsible for the outcome faced by their offender, such that they feel obliged to cooperate and to accept any apology offered, even when they doubt its sincerity. And a small but significant minority of victims report feeling worse after involvement in a restorative justice conference (Braithwaite 1999: 22).

Fundamental questions remain unresolved: can and should restorative justice challenge the prevailing paradigm of punishment, or should restorative justice remain ancillary to the proper purposes of punishment? How far are developments in restorative justice based on a coherent view of the rights and responsibilities of victim, offenders, and the state? Do they offer sufficient procedural safeguards to victims and offenders? Can they ensure substantive fairness (if, for example, a particular victim is forgiving or vengeful)? What are the implications of restorative justice for the mass of 'victimless' crimes, or for crimes where there is not one victim but many (Young 2001)?

Alongside the rise of restorative justice, recent decades have witnessed a very different trend in criminal justice towards increasingly punitive policies. Prison populations have burgeoned in both America and, to a lesser extent, Britain. Although the victims' movement in general has been careful to avoid political involvement in penal policy, certain victims' organizations have been vociferous in their demand for greater severity in sentencing (Rock 1998: 218). More generally, the idea of the victim has been invoked as a potent rhetorical device or symbolic tool to lever up punitiveness in what Ashworth calls 'victims in the service of severity' and Garland describes as 'the projected, politicized, image of "the victim" . . . as an all-purpose justification for measures of penal repression' (Ashworth 2000a: 186; Garland 2001: 143). Similarly, the naming of criminal laws and penal measures after individual victims (for example, 'Megan's Law' in America, and the campaign for 'Sarah's Law' in Britain) uses the plight of the victim to legitimate more extensive controls and new punitive measures. The power of restorative justice to counter, or even to displace, these punitive tendencies remains to be seen (Levrant *et al.* 1999; Sanders and Young 2000).

The significance of victims is also raised by the Human Rights Act 1998. As we shall see, under the European Convention on Human Rights victims have rights to be protected under the criminal law. The definition of criminal offences will now need to be reconsidered to see if they adequately protects the human rights of victims. A contrary view is that if the rights of victims are to receive weight, so should their responsibilities. Might we, for example, include a discussion of the extent to which individuals should be expected to protect themselves from crime in considering our definition of offences?[81]

FURTHER READING

Cancio Meliá, M. (2004), 'Victim Behavior and Offender Liability', *Buffalo Criminal Law Review* 7: 513.

Johnstone, G. (2002), *Restorative Justice* (Cullompton: Willan).

von Hirsch, A., Roberts, J., Bottoms, A., Roach, K., and Schiff, M. (2003), *Restorative Justice and Criminal Justice* (Oxford: Hart).

Zedner, L. (1994), 'Reparation and Retribution: Are They Reconcilable?', *Modern Law Review* 57: 228.

9 THE CRIMINAL PROCESS

Statistics on the number of convictions for particular offences are a poor guide to which crimes are actually committed.[82] It is estimated that only 2 to 3 per cent of crimes committed result in a conviction.[83] This is because victims often do not report the crimes to the police,[84] and if they do the offender is rarely caught. Even if the offender is found, the police may still decide not to charge him.[85] If the police decide to charge, then the Crown Prosecution Service (CPS) may decide not to pursue a prosecution.[86] There have been concerns over how these decisions not to prosecute are reached. In particular there are concerns that race, sex, and economic background can improperly play a role in the decision.[87] The CPS, even if it does decide to prosecute, may charge a lesser offence than the one committed. This might be done for various reasons: the CPS might believe that it would be easier in order to obtain a conviction to do so; or the defendant might have offered to plead guilty to the lesser

---

[81] Cancio Meliá (2004); Ben-Shahar and Harel (1996).
[82] Maguire (2000). [83] Home Office (1999a). [84] Clarkson *et al.* (1994).
[85] e.g. 61% of known offenders under 18 were cautioned for indictable offences in 1997 (Home Office (1999a: 31)). Although the government has expressed concern that youth crime is not being taken seriously (Home Office (1997a)).
[86] Baldwin (1997). Bucke and James (1998) demonstrate that there are variations in changing practice between police forces.
[87] Ashworth (2003: ch. 1).

charge, but would plead not guilty to the more serious charge;[88] or charging the lesser offence may mean that the case will be heard before magistrates, rather than the Crown Court, and so be cheaper.

As this demonstrates, there are points at which an offender may escape from the route that leads to a criminal conviction. Statistically a suspect is far more likely to escape punishment due to a decision of the police or the CPS than to be acquitted by the jury or magistrates. In the following passage these points are considered in further detail:

R. Allen, 'Alternatives to Prosecution' in M. McConville and G. Wilson (eds.), *The Handbook of the Criminal Justice Process* (Oxford: OUP, 2002), 168–81

Alternatives to Prosecution in England and Wales

In England and Wales, there is a variety of alternatives to prosecution. Unlike in many countries most of the alternatives to prosecution are available *before* the case reaches a prosecutor.

For the most minor offences, there is a system of fixed penalties or on-the-spot fines. These currently apply to a range of motoring offences. The police, or other authorities such as traffic wardens, can issue penalty notices on the spot or at a police station. Such notices provide an opportunity, to discharge any liability to conviction for the offence by payment of a sum of money. There is no criminal conviction or admission of guilt associated with payment, although the alleged offender has the right to opt for trial by a court and risk conviction if he so chooses. Failure to pay the penalty or opting for trial may lead to the imposition of a fine substantially higher than the amount of the penalty. In 1998, 3.4 million fixed penalty notices were issued in England and Wales, of which 78 per cent resulted in payment, 14 per cent were registered as fines, and less than 1 per cent were referred for court proceedings.

Very recently, legislation has expanded substantially the range of offences which can be dealt with in this way. The government considers fixed penalty notices as a simple and swift way of addressing a range of low-level anti-social offending associated with disorderly conduct, though the provisions have been controversial, not least because of the high level of discretion allowed to the police in applying them. The Auld Review has recommended a presumption in favour of fixed penalty notices in all eligible road traffic cases and a systematic review of other kinds of infringements which might be suitably dealt with in this way. It also recommends that the use of a television without a licence be dealt with in the first instance by a fixed penalty—there are currently about 160,000 prosecutions a year for the offence. An analogous system already applies in cases of vehicle excise duty evasion, when people use motor vehicles without registering them or paying tax. There are about 1,000,000 cases a year which could be prosecuted. The Driver Vehicle Licensing Authority (DVLA) operates an out-of-court settlement scheme for those who pay what they owe plus a penalty. Despite this, there are still about 300,000 prosecutions a year, of which 98 per cent result in a guilty plea. A discount for early payment is to be introduced shortly in order to encourage more offenders to pay up prior to prosecution.

In more serious cases, the police enjoy considerable discretion in how to respond to crime. It is the police who usually start proceedings when this is the course of action which is pursued. A survey of what happens to people arrested by the police found that 52 per cent of suspects were charged, 20 per cent had no further action taken against them, 17 per cent were cautioned, and the remaining 13 per cent were dealt with in other ways.

---

[88] This is sometimes called 'plea bargaining'. See McConville (2002); Derbyshire (2000).

When the police do start proceedings, the case is passed to the Crown Prosecution Service (CPS) which reviews it and decides whether to continue or discontinue it.

. . .

There are two clear stages in the decision made by the CPS whether to prosecute. First is the evidential test. The CPS must be satisfied that there is enough evidence to produce a realistic prospect of conviction. The Code requires that prosecutors address two particular questions in making this assessment. Can the evidence be used in court? Is the evidence reliable?

The second stage is the public interest test. Where the evidential test is met, a prosecution will normally continue unless there are public interest factors tending against prosecution which clearly outweigh those tending in favour. The most important public interest factor is the seriousness of the offence. In addition, a prosecution is likely to be needed if:

- a conviction is likely to result in a significant sentence;
- a weapon was used or violence threatened;
- the victim was a public servant;
- the defendant was in a position of trust;
- the offence was premeditated;
- the offender was the organizer;
- the offence was committed by a group;
- the victim was vulnerable;
- the offence was motivated by discrimination on grounds of ethnicity, nationality, sex, religion, politics, or sexual orientation;
- the victim and defendant were different ages or there was any element of corruption;
- the defendant has relevant previous convictions or cautions;
- the offence was committed while the defendant was under a court order;
- the offence formed part of a pattern of conduct;
- the offence, although not serious in itself, is widespread in the community.

On the other hand, a prosecution is less likely if:

- the court is likely to impose a nominal penalty;
- the defendant is already under an order and any further conviction would be unlikely to add a penalty;
- the offence was committed as the result of a genuine mistake;
- the loss or harm is minor;
- there has been a long delay since the offence;
- the prosecution is likely to have a bad effect on the victim's health;
- the defendant is elderly or is or was at the time of the offence suffering from serious physical or mental ill health;
- the defendant has put right the loss or harm;
- details may be made public that could harm sources of information, international relations, or national security.

In 1999, the CPS discontinued about 165,000 cases. It is not known what proportion of these were discontinued for evidential and for public interest reasons.

FURTHER READING

Ashworth, A. (2005a), *The Criminal Process* (Oxford: OUP).

Saunders, A. and Young, R. (2002), 'From Suspect to Trial' in M. Maguire, R. Morgan, and R. Reiner (eds.), *The Oxford Handbook of Criminology* (Oxford: OUP).

10 CRIMINAL LAW AND THE HUMAN RIGHTS ACT 1998

10.1 THE SIGNIFICANCE OF THE HUMAN RIGHTS ACT 1998

At many points throughout this book we will considered the potential impact of the Human Rights Act 1998 (HRA) on the interpretation of the offence. This section will not therefore seek to summarize the impact of the Act on English and Welsh criminal law,[89] but will outline how the Act works. The 1998 Human Rights Act is designed to ensure the protection of individuals' rights under the European Convention on Human Rights (ECHR). The HRA protects the rights in the ECHR in two main ways:

(1) Section 3 requires judges to interpret legislation in a way which complies with the ECHR so far as is possible. It states:

> So far as it is possible to do so, primary legislation and subordinate legislation must be read and given effect in a way which is compatible with the Convention rights.

As section 3 makes clear, if the wording of a statute is ambiguous and can be interpreted either in a way which is compliant with the Convention rights or in a way which is not, then the statute should be read so as to be compliant. The key phrase is 'so far as it is possible'. Only time will tell how far the courts will be willing to stretch the meaning of words to comply with the statute.[90] The House of Lords have given some guidance on this by saying that section 3 is to be used to interpret, but not amend, legislation.[91] If the court is unable to interpret a statute in line with the Convention rights then it must apply the statute as it stands and issue a declaration of incompatibility, as a result of which Parliament should consider whether the legislation needs to be amended.[92]

(2) Section 6 requires public authorities to act in a way which is compatible with the Convention rights. Section 6 states:

> (1) It is unlawful for a public authority to act in a way which is incompatible with a Convention right.

---

[89] See Ashworth and Strange (2003); Herring (2002: ch. 19).
[90] Ashworth (2000c) argues for a non-minimalist approach to the HRA.
[91] *Re S, Re W* [2002] 1 FCR 577 (HL), para. 38.
[92] See *Bellinger v Bellinger* [2003] UKHL 21 for an example of a case where a declaration of incompatibility was issued.

> (2) Subsection (1) does not apply to an act if—
>
> > (a) as the result of one or more provisions of primary legislation, the authority could not have acted differently; or
> >
> > (b) in the case of one or more provisions of, or made under, primary legislation which cannot be read or given effect in a way which is compatible with the Convention rights, the authority was acting so as to give effect to or enforce those provisions.

Importantly for criminal lawyers the definition of a public authority includes the police, the CPS, and a court.[93] The significance of section 6 for criminal lawyers is as follows:

(1) If a defendant has been convicted of an offence in a way which infringes his or her Convention rights[94] it is arguable that under section 6 of the HRA the court must interpret that offence (if possible) in line with the Convention.[95] This is controversial. Some say that the HRA was not intended to alter well-established common law offences.[96] Others say that Article 6 of the European Convention prohibits a court from giving effect to a common law offence in a way which infringes an individual's Convention rights.[97] The one case to consider the issue, *H*,[98] accepted (without detailed discussion) that the HRA could affect common law criminal law.[99]

(2) When the CPS is considering whether or not to bring a prosecution it is bound by section 6, because it is a public body. If a particular criminal offence is in conflict with the defendant's Convention rights (e.g. it improperly interferes with his or her freedom of expression) then it is arguable that section 6 requires the CPS not to bring a prosecution against the defendant.[100]

(3) If a defendant has been convicted of an offence which infringes the Convention rights (e.g. a statutory offence which could not be interpreted in line with the Convention) then it can be argued that the court should impose only a nominal sentence (e.g. an absolute discharge).[101] To impose a substantial sentence would infringe an individual's Convention rights, which section 6 prohibits.

DEFINITION

It is important to appreciate that the Human Rights Act can affect the definition of a criminal offence in two ways:

1. A defendant may argue that to convict him or her of a particular offence would infringe his or her Convention rights.

2. A victim (or potential victim) may argue that the state has infringed his or her rights by not protecting him or her under the criminal law. In *A v UK* the fact that the

---

[93] Human Rights Act 1998, s. 6(3)(a).   [94] If the offence is a statutory one s. 3 applies.
[95] Note that s. 3 applies only when the court is interpreting a statutory offence.
[96] Buxton (2000).
[97] Ashworth (2000c).   [98] [2002] Cr App R 59 (CA). See also *NHS Trust v H, The Times*, 17 May 2001.
[99] The case concerned the defence of chastisement.
[100] Indeed it could be argued that to bring a case would amount to an abuse of process.
[101] Herring (2002: 467).

step-father could hit his step-son without being liable to punishment under the criminal law infringed the step-son's rights under Article 3. This subsequently led the Court of Appeal in *H* to reinterpret the circumstances in which a parent can rely on the defence of reasonable chastisement when facing a charge of assault.

10.2 THE IMPORTANT ARTICLES IN THE EUROPEAN CONVENTION

The following are the most important rights under the ECHR for criminal lawyers:

The European Convention on Human Rights and Fundamental Freedoms

Article 2 Right to Life

1. Everyone's right to life shall be protected by law. No one shall be deprived of his life intentionally save in the execution of a sentence of a court following his conviction of a crime for which this penalty is provided by law.

2. Deprivation of life shall not be regarded as inflicted in contravention of this Article when it results from the use of force which is no more than absolutely necessary:

   (a) in defence of any person from unlawful violence;

   (b) in order to effect a lawful arrest or to prevent the escape of a person lawfully detained;

   (c) in action lawfully taken for the purpose of quelling a riot or insurrection.

Article 3 Prohibition of Torture

No one shall be subjected to torture or to inhuman or degrading treatment or punishment.

Article 5 Right to Liberty and Security

1. Everyone has the right to liberty and security of person. No one shall be deprived of his liberty save in the following cases and in accordance with a procedure prescribed by law:

   (a) the lawful detention of a person after conviction by a competent court;

   (b) the lawful arrest or detention of a person for non-compliance with the lawful order of a court or in order to secure the fulfilment of any obligation prescribed by law;

   (c) the lawful arrest or detention of a person effected for the purpose of bringing him before the competent legal authority on reasonable suspicion of having committed an offence or when it is reasonably considered necessary to prevent his committing an offence or fleeing after having done so;

   (d) the detention of a minor by lawful order for the purpose of educational supervision or his lawful detention for the purpose of bringing him before the competent legal authority;

   (e) the lawful detention of persons for the prevention of the spreading of infectious diseases, of persons of unsound mind, alcoholics or drug addicts or vagrants;

(f) the lawful arrest or detention of a person to prevent his effecting an unauthorised entry into the country or of a person against whom action is being taken with a view to deportation or extradition.

2. Everyone who is arrested shall be informed promptly, in a language which he understands, of the reasons for his arrest and of any charge against him.

3. Everyone arrested or detained in accordance with the provisions of paragraph 1(c) of this Article shall be brought promptly before a judge or other officer authorised by law to exercise judicial power and shall be entitled to trial within a reasonable time or to release pending trial. Release may be conditioned by guarantees to appear for trial.

4. Everyone who is deprived of his liberty by arrest or detention shall be entitled to take proceedings by which the lawfulness of his detention shall be decided speedily by a court and his release ordered if the detention is not lawful.

5. Everyone who has been the victim of arrest or detention in contravention of the provisions of this Article shall have an enforceable right to compensation.

Article 6 Right to a Fair Trial

1. In the determination of his civil rights and obligations or of any criminal charge against him, everyone is entitled to a fair and public hearing within a reasonable time by an independent and impartial tribunal established by law. Judgment shall be pronounced publicly but the press and public may be excluded from all or part of the trial in the interest of morals, public order or national security in a democratic society, where the interests of juveniles or the protection of the private life of the parties so require, or to the extent strictly necessary in the opinion of the court in special circumstances where publicity would prejudice the interests of justice.

2. Everyone charged with a criminal offence shall be presumed innocent until proved guilty according to law.

3. Everyone charged with a criminal offence has the following minimum rights:

    (a) to be informed promptly, in a language which he understands and in detail, of the nature and cause of the accusation against him;

    (b) to have adequate time and facilities for the preparation of his defence;

    (c) to defend himself in person or through legal assistance of his own choosing or, if he has not sufficient means to pay for legal assistance, to be given it free when the interests of justice so require;

    (d) to examine or have examined witnesses against him and to obtain the attendance and examination of witnesses on his behalf under the same conditions as witnesses against him;

    (e) to have the free assistance of an interpreter if he cannot understand or speak the language used in court.

Article 7 No Punishment without Law

1. No one shall be held guilty of any criminal offence on account of any act or omission which did not constitute a criminal offence under national or international law at the time when it was committed. Nor shall a heavier penalty be imposed than the one that was applicable at the time the criminal offence was committed.

2. This Article shall not prejudice the trial and punishment of any person for any act or omission which, at the time when it was committed, was criminal according to the general principles of law recognised by civilised nations.

Article 8 Right to Respect for Private and Family Life

1. Everyone has the right to respect for his private and family life, his home and his correspondence.
2. There shall be no interference by a public authority with the exercise of this right except such as is in accordance with the law and is necessary in a democratic society in the interests of national security, public safety or the economic well-being of the country, for the prevention of disorder or crime, for the protection of health or morals, or for the protection of the rights and freedoms of others.

Article 9 Freedom of Thought, Conscience and Religion

1. Everyone has the right to freedom of thought, conscience and religion; this right includes freedom to change his religion or belief and freedom, either alone or in community with others and in public or private, to manifest his religion or belief, in worship, teaching, practice and observance.
2. Freedom to manifest one's religion or beliefs shall be subject only to such limitations as are prescribed by law and are necessary in a democratic society in the interests of public safety, for the protection of public order, health or morals, or for the protection of the rights and freedoms of others.

Article 10 Freedom of Expression

1. Everyone has the right to freedom of expression. This right shall include freedom to hold opinions and to receive and impart information and ideas without interference by public authority and regardless of frontiers. This Article shall not prevent States from requiring the licensing of broadcasting, television or cinema enterprises.
2. The exercise of these freedoms, since it carries with it duties and responsibilities, may be subject to such formalities, conditions, restrictions or penalties as are prescribed by law and are necessary in a democratic society, in the interests of national security, territorial integrity or public safety, for the prevention of disorder or crime, for the protection of health or morals, for the protection of the reputation or rights of others, for preventing the disclosure of information received in confidence, or for maintaining the authority and impartiality of the judiciary.

Article 11 Freedom of Assembly and Association

1. Everyone has the right to freedom of peaceful assembly and to freedom of association with others, including the right to form and to join trade unions for the protection of his interests.
2. No restrictions shall be placed on the exercise of these rights other than such as are prescribed by law and are necessary in a democratic society in the interests of national security or public safety, for the prevention of disorder or crime, for the protection of health or morals or for the protection of the rights and freedoms of others.

This Article shall not prevent the imposition of lawful restrictions on the exercise of these rights by members of the armed forces, of the police or of the administration of the State.

Article 14 Prohibition of Discrimination

The enjoyment of the rights and freedoms set forth in this Convention shall be secured without discrimination on any ground such as sex, race, colour, language, religion, political or other opinion, national or social origin, association with a national minority, property, birth or other status.

10.3 POTENTIAL CONSEQUENCES OF THE HRA ON THE CRIMINAL LAW

Throughout the book we will mention the potential impact of the HRA on specific offences. But here we will consider some of the general principles of the ECHR which will affect the whole of the criminal law.

1 Certainty

The state is permitted under the ECHR to create criminal offences which interfere with citizens' convention rights, such as rights to private and family life (Article 8) and freedom of expression (Article 10), but only if the interferences are in accordance with a 'law'. The European Court of Human Rights has interpreted 'law' in an interesting way.[102] A rule can be a law only if it is defined with sufficient precision to enable the citizen to know how to behave in accordance with the law. In the following case the European Court of Human Rights held that the power under English law to bind the defendant to keep the peace on the basis that his conduct was *contra bonos mores* ('contrary to the public good') was so imprecise that it did not amount to a law, and therefore was an impermissible infringement of the individual's rights.

Hashman and Harrup v United Kingdom
(Application No. 25594/94) (2000) 30 EHRR 241 (ECtHR)[103]

The applicants were bound over to keep the peace and to be of good behaviour by a UK court after they had disrupted the Portman hunt. They claimed that the finding that they had behaved in a manner *contra bonos mores* and the binding over order interfered with the exercise of their rights under Article 10 in a way which was not 'prescribed by law'.

31. The Court recalls that one of the requirements flowing from the expression 'prescribed by law' is foreseeability. A norm cannot be regarded as a 'law' unless it is formulated with sufficient precision to enable the citizen to regulate his conduct. At the same time, whilst

---

[102] *Silver v UK* (1983) 5 EHRR 347.   [103] (2000) 8 BHRC 104, [2000] Crim LR 185.

certainty in the law is highly desirable, it may bring in its train excessive rigidity and the law must be able to keep pace with changing circumstances. The level of precision required of domestic legislation—which cannot in any case provide for every eventuality—depends to a considerable degree on the content of the instrument in question, the field it is designed to cover and the number and status of those to whom it is addressed. (See generally in this connection, *Rekvenyi v. Hungary*: 20 May 1999, para. 34).

32. The Court further recalls that prior restraint on freedom of expression must call for the most careful scrutiny on its part. (See, in the context of the necessity for a prior restraint, *The Sunday Times v. United Kingdom (No. 2)*, loc. cit., para. 51).

33. The Court has already considered the issue of 'lawfulness' for the purposes of Article 5 of the Convention of orders to be bound over to keep the peace and be of good behaviour. (In *Steel v. United Kingdom*, loc. cit., paras. 71–77.) In that case, the Court found that the elements of breach of the peace were adequately defined by English law. (ibid., para. 75).

. . .

35. It is a feature of the present case that it concerns an interference with freedom of expression which was not expressed to be a 'sanction', or punishment, for behaviour of a certain type, but rather an order, imposed on the applicants, not to breach the peace or behave contra bonos mores in the future. The binding-over order in the present case thus had purely prospective effect. It did not require a finding that here had been a breach of the peace. The case is thus different from the case of *Steel*, in which the proceedings brought against the first and second applicants were in respect of breaches of the peace which were later found to have been committed.

36. The Court must consider the question of whether behaviour contra bonos mores is adequately defined for the purposes of Article 10(2) of the Convention.

37. The Court first recalls that in its *Steel* judgment, it noted that the expression 'to be of good behaviour' was particularly imprecise and offered little guidance to the person bound over as to the type of conduct which would amount to a breach of the order'. (para. 76) Those considerations apply equally in the present case, where the applicants were not charged with any criminal offence, and were found not to have breached the peace.

38. The Court next notes that conduct contra bonos mores is defined as behaviour which is 'wrong rather than right in the judgment of the majority of contemporary fellow citizens'. (para. 13) It cannot agree with the Government that this definition has the same objective element as conduct 'likely to cause annoyance', which was at issue in the case of *Chorherr*. (para. 29) The Court considers that the question of whether conduct is 'likely to cause annoyance' is a question which goes to the very heart of the nature of the conduct proscribed: it is conduct whose likely consequence is the annoyance of others. Similarly, the definition of breach of the peace given in the case of *Percy v. Director of Public Prosecutions* (para. 11).—that it includes conduct the natural consequences of which would be to provoke others to violence—also describes behaviour by reference to its effects. Conduct which is 'wrong rather than right in the judgment of the majority of contemporary citizens', by contrast, is conduct which is not described at all, but merely expressed to be 'wrong' in the opinion of a majority of citizens.

39. Nor can the Court agree that the Government's other examples of behaviour which is defined by reference to the standards expected by the majority of contemporary opinion are similar to conduct contra bonos mores as in each case cited by the Government, the example given is but one element of a more comprehensive definition of the proscribed behaviour.

40. With specific reference to the facts of the present case, the Court does not accept that it must have been evident to the applicants what they were being ordered not to do for the period of their binding over. Whilst in the case of *Steel* the applicants had been found to have breached the peace, and the Court found that it was apparent that the bind over related to similar behaviour, the present applicants did not breach the peace, and given the lack of precision referred to above, it cannot be said that what they were being bound over not to do must have been apparent to them.

41. The Court thus finds that the order by which the applicants were bound over to keep the peace and not to behave contra bonos mores did not comply with the requirement of Article 10(2) of the Convention that it be 'prescribed by law'.

. . .

43. It follows that there has been a violation of Article 10 of the Convention.

Violation of Article 10 found.

It should not be thought that a court will readily find that an offence is too vaguely defined to constitute law and hence potentially infringe the European Convention. In *Steel v UK*[104] it was held that the English offence of breach of the peace (defined as 'when an individual causes harm to persons or property or acts in a manner the natural consequences of which would be to provoke others to violence') was sufficiently precise to amount to 'law'. In *Tagg*[105] the Court of Appeal rejected an argument that the offence of being drunk on an aircraft[106] was insufficiently precise to amount to a law.

2 Burden of proof

Most members of the public know that under English and Welsh criminal law a person should be presumed innocent unless proved guilty. Lord Sankey LC in *Woolmington v DPP*[107] declared that 'throughout the web of the English criminal law one golden thread is always to be seen—that it is the duty of the prosecution to prove the prisoner's guilt'. The principle is justified on the basis that the consequences of a conviction and punishment are so severe that the state prefers to run the risk of acquitting people who may in fact have committed the offence than convicting people who are in fact innocent. The principle also reflects the fact that the prosecution will have all the resources and power of the state on its side, while the defendant will usually have comparatively limited resources.[108]

The reality is that the presumption of innocence is honoured more in the breach than the observance. Even of the more serious offences which are triable in the Crown Court 40 per cent include some form of departure from the presumption of innocence, according to Andrew Ashworth and Meredith Blake.[109] A common way of departing from the presumption is to create strict liability offences (where it is necessary to prove only that the defendant caused a particular result or state of affairs, and it is not necessary to show that the defendant had a particular state of mind or even behaved unreasonably) but then create a defence of 'due diligence' or 'no intent' for which the defendant is obligated to produce evidence.

---

[104] 23 Sept. 1998 RJD VII.

[105] [2001] EWCA Crim 1230. See also *Cotter* [2002] Crim LR 824 (CA) where it was held that the offence of perverting the course of justice was sufficiently clear to be compatible with the European Convention.

[106] Air Navigation (No. 2) Order 1995, Art. 57 and Civil Aviation Act 1982, s. 61.

[107] [1935] AC 462, 481 (HL). [108] Ashworth (2003: 84). [109] Ashworth and Blake (1996).

Any departure from the presumption of innocence must now be considered in the light of the HRA. The presumption of innocence is reinforced by Article 6(2) of the ECHR which declares 'Everyone shall be presumed innocent until proved guilty according to the law'.[110] However, perhaps surprisingly, the European Court of Human Rights has not interpreted that Article as strictly as it might. The Court's approach in *Salabiaku v France*[111] and *Phillips v UK*[112] is that presumption of guilt or the placing of the burden of proof on the defendant does not contravene Article 6 if it is confined within 'reasonable limits'. The House of Lords examined the issue in *Kebilene*[113] and held that the key issue was the difference between persuasive and evidential burdens of proof:

(1) A persuasive burden of proof means that the party must prove the matter at issue.

(2) An evidential burden of proof means that the party must introduce sufficient evidence to establish the reasonable possibility that a particular issue is true.

For example if D faces a charge of assault and wishes to raise the defence of duress, D has an evidential burden of establishing some evidence to show that he might have been acting under duress. If he or she introduces some evidence to show that that might be true the prosecution has the persuasive burden of proof of showing beyond reasonable doubt that the defendant was not acting under duress.

The House of Lords in *Kebilene*[114] explained that reverse burdens of proof were more likely to be compatible with Article 6 if they were evidential rather than persuasive burdens. The court will need to consider the relative difficulty of proving the relevant matter for the defendant and the prosecution, and the seriousness of the threat at which the criminal offence is directed. In other words, a persuasive burden will be justifiable only if it involves an issue which is very easy for the defendant to establish (e.g. to prove that he or she has a licence to perform the activity) or the burden is necessary for the protection of the public. Therefore, in the light of the HRA, section 3, any statutory burden of proof on the defendant would be interpreted to be evidential if at all possible. It will be interpreted as persuasive burden only if there is a 'pressing necessity'[115] for there to be a persuasive burden.

The House of Lords have considered the issue in three cases *Lambert*;[116] *Johnstone*;[117] and *Sheldrake*.

Sheldrake v Director of Public Prosecutions
Attorney-General's Reference (No. 4 of 2002) [2005] 1 AC 264

Two cases concerning burdens of proof were heard by the House of Lords together. In the first Peter Sheldrake was charged with the offence under section 5(1)(b) Road Traffic Act 1988 of being in charge of a motor vehicle after having consumed so much alcohol that the proportion of it in his breath exceeded the prescribed limit. He sought to rely on the defence under section 5(2) which cast upon the defendant the legal burden of proving that there was no likelihood of his driving the vehicle while over the limit. He was convicted by the magistrates. He argued before the House of Lords that this burden

---

[110] D. Lewis (2000).   [111] (1988) 13 EHRR 379.   [112] [2001] Crim LR 217.
[113] *R v DPP, ex parte Kebilene* [1999] 4 All ER 801 (HL).   [114] Ibid.
[115] *Lambert* [2001] 3 WLR 206 (HL).
[116] [2001] 3 WLR 206 (HL) For criticism of the ruling in *Lambert* that the HRA is of prospective effect only see Beyleveld, Kirkham, and Townend (2002).
[117] [2003] 1 WLR 1736.

of proof was not compliant with the presumption of innocence guaranteed by Article 6(2) of the European Convention on Human Rights.

In the Attorney-General's reference case the defendant was charged with belonging to a proscribed organization contrary to section 11(1) of the Terrorism Act 2000. He sought to rely on the defence in section 11(2) that the organization had not been proscribed at the time when he became a member or professed to be member of it and that he had not taken part in any of the organization's activities since it had been proscribed. At the trial the Crown conceded that the defence in section 11(2) imposed an evidential, but not legal burden on the defendant. The Attorney-General referred to the Court of Appeal the question of whether the defence in section 11(2) imposed a legal or evidential burden on the defendant and if a legal one, then whether it was compatible with Article 6(2).

Lord Bingham of Cornhill

[Having reviewed the relevant case law from the European Court of Human Rights Lord Bingham stated:]

21. From this body of authority certain principles may be derived. The overriding concern is that a trial should be fair, and the presumption of innocence is a fundamental right directed to that end. The Convention does not outlaw presumptions of fact or law but requires that these should be kept within reasonable limits and should not be arbitrary. It is open to states to define the constituent elements of a criminal offence, excluding the requirement of *mens rea*. But the substance and effect of any presumption adverse to a defendant must be examined, and must be reasonable. Relevant to any judgment on reasonableness or proportionality will be the opportunity given to the defendant to rebut the presumption, maintenance of the rights of the defence, flexibility in application of the presumption, retention by the court of a power to assess the evidence, the importance of what is at stake and the difficulty which a prosecutor may face in the absence of a presumption. Security concerns do not absolve member states from their duty to observe basic standards of fairness. The justifiability of any infringement of the presumption of innocence cannot be resolved by any rule of thumb, but on examination of all the facts and circumstances of the particular provision as applied in the particular case.

. . .

30. Both *R v Lambert* [2002] 2 AC 545 and *R v Johnstone* [2003] 1 WLR 1736 are recent decisions of the House, binding on all lower courts for what they decide. Nothing said in *R v Johnstone* suggests an intention to depart from or modify the earlier decision, which should not be treated as superseded or implicitly overruled. Differences of emphasis (and Lord Steyn was not a lone voice in *R v Lambert*) are explicable by the difference in the subject matter of the two cases. Section 5 of the Misuse of Drugs Act 1971 and section 92 of the Trade Marks Act 1994 were directed to serious social and economic problems. But the justifiability and fairness of the respective exoneration provisions had to be judged in the particular context of each case. I have already identified the potential consequence to a section 5 defendant who failed, perhaps narrowly, to make good his section 28 defence. He might be, but fail to prove that he was, entirely ignorant of what he was carrying. By contrast, the offences under section 92 are committed only if the act in question is done by a person 'with a view to gain for himself or another, or with intent to cause loss to another.' Thus these are offences committed (if committed) by dealers, traders, market operators, who could reasonably be expected (as Lord Nicholls pointed out) to exercise some care about the provenance of goods in which they deal. The penalty imposed for breaches of section 92 may be severe (see, for

example, *R v Gleeson* [2002] 1 Cr App R (S) 485), but that is because the potential profits of fraudulent trading are often great.

31. The task of the court is never to decide whether a reverse burden should be imposed on a defendant, but always to assess whether a burden enacted by Parliament unjustifiably infringes the presumption of innocence. It may none the less be questioned whether (as the Court of Appeal ruled in para 52d) 'the assumption should be that Parliament would not have made an exception without good reason'. Such an approach may lead the court to give too much weight to the enactment under review and too little to the presumption of innocence and the obligation imposed on it by section 3.

Director of Public Prosecutions v Sheldrake

. . .

41. It may not be very profitable to debate whether section 5(2) infringes the presumption of innocence. It may be assumed that it does. Plainly the provision is directed to a legitimate object: the prevention of death, injury and damage caused by unfit drivers. Does the provision meet the tests of acceptability identified in the Strasbourg jurisprudence? In my view, it plainly does. I do not regard the burden placed on the defendant as beyond reasonable limits or in any way arbitrary. It is not objectionable to criminalise a defendant's conduct in these circumstances without requiring a prosecutor to prove criminal intent. The defendant has a full opportunity to show that there was no likelihood of his driving, a matter so closely conditioned by his own knowledge and state of mind at the material time as to make it much more appropriate for him to prove on the balance of probabilities that he would not have been likely to drive than for the prosecutor to prove, beyond reasonable doubt, that he would. I do not think that imposition of a legal burden went beyond what was necessary. If a driver tries and fails to establish a defence under section 5(2), I would not regard the resulting conviction as unfair, as the House held that it might or would be in *R v Lambert* [2002] 2 AC 545. I find no reason to conclude that the conviction of Mr Sheldrake was tainted by any hint of unfairness.

. . .

44. I would allow the Director's appeal, reinstate the justices' decision and answer the certified question by saying that the burden of proof provision in section 5(2) of the Road Traffic Act 1988 imposes a legal burden on an accused who is charged with an offence contrary to section 5(1)(b) of that Act.

Attorney-General's Reference (No. 4 of 2002)

. . .

54. In penalising the profession of membership of a proscribed organisation, section 11(1) does, I think, interfere with exercise of the right of free expression guaranteed by article 10 of the Convention. But such interference may be justified if it satisfies various conditions. First, it must be directed to a legitimate end. Such ends include the interests of national security, public safety and the prevention of disorder or crime. Section 11(1) is directed to those ends. Secondly, the interference must be prescribed by law. That requirement is met, despite my present doubt as to the meaning of 'profess'. Thirdly, it must be necessary in a democratic society and proportionate. The necessity of attacking terrorist organisations is in my view clear. I would incline to hold subsection (1) to be proportionate, for article 10 purposes, whether subsection (2) imposes a legal or an evidential burden. But I agree with Mr Owen that the question does not fall to be considered in the present context, and I would (as he asks) decline to answer this part of the Attorney General's second question.

. . .

Lord Carswell

79. My Lords, I have had the advantage of reading in draft the opinion of my noble and learned friend, Lord Rodger of Earlsferry. I agree with his reasons and conclusions and wish to add only a few observations of my own.

80. The issue common to these appeals is whether it is unfair to the accused to have to undertake the burden of proving the defence provided for in the governing legislation and, if so, whether the relevant provisions should be 'read down' as an evidential rather than a legal or persuasive burden. My noble and learned friend, Lord Bingham of Cornhill, has reviewed in detail in his opinion the applicable provisions of the European Convention on Human Rights and the decisions of the European Court of Human Rights, together with the domestic decisions which affect the issues before us, and I do not wish to add anything to the discussion of the law set out in his opinion and that of Lord Rodger of Earlsferry. I shall consider in this opinion the application of the law to the two appeals before us, observing only that the objective of article 6 of the Convention is to require a fair trial and that the presumption of innocence contained in article 6(2) is one aspect of that requirement, rather than constituting a free-standing obligation. For that reason, as accepted by the European Court of Human Rights in *Salabiaku v France* 13 EHRR 379, inroads into the obligation of the prosecution to prove beyond reasonable doubt all the matters in issue in a criminal trial may be permissible in certain circumstances. The reversal of the ordinary burden of proof resting upon the prosecution may accordingly be justified in some cases and will not offend against the principle requiring a fair trial. Where the question arises, it has to be determined, first, whether it is fair and reasonable in the achievement of a proper statutory objective for the state to deprive the defendant of the protection normally guaranteed by the presumption of innocence whereby the burden of proof is placed upon the prosecution to prove beyond reasonable doubt all the matters in issue. Secondly, one must determine whether the exception is proportionate, that is to say, whether it goes no further than is reasonably necessary to achieve that objective.

. . .

[Lord Carswell in considering the *Sheldrake* case stated]

84. The ultimate risk may be that the defendant may elect to drive the vehicle, but it is not in my view the gravamen of the offence. Being in charge of a vehicle while over the limit is in itself such an anti-social act that Parliament has long since made it an offence. A person who has drunk more than the limit should take steps to put it out of his power to drive. Section 5(2) gives him an escape route, which it is quite easy for him to take in a genuine case, as he is the person best placed to know and establish whether he was likely to drive the vehicle. Conversely, the prosecution might be able readily enough to establish that the defendant was in a position to drive the vehicle if he elected to do so, but it could well be difficult to prove beyond reasonable doubt that there was a likelihood of his driving it.

85. An example may be posed to test these propositions. The owner of a car, who has drunk enough alcohol to take him over the limit, decides to wash the car. He takes his keys with him, which he uses to open the doors to get access to all the surfaces to be washed and to clean the inside. It is indisputable that during this process he is in charge of the vehicle. He may have started off with the sole intention of confining himself to cleaning the car, but the possibility exists that he may change his intention and drive it on some errand, perhaps to fill the tank with petrol. The person who knows best whether there was a real risk of that occurring is the defendant himself. I see nothing unreasonable or disproportionate in requiring him to prove on the balance of probabilities that there was no likelihood of his doing

so. He should in my opinion have to do so, by adducing evidence which may be duly tested in court.

Appeal allowed. Order of Divisional Court set aside. Order of Court of Appeal (Criminal Division) affirmed in regard to the first question referred and set aside in regard to the second question referred. Defendant's costs on reference in Court of Appeal and House of Lords out of Central Funds.

In the following extract Ian Dennis usefully summarizes the current state of the law:

I. Dennis (2005) 'Reverse Onuses and the Presumption of Innocence: In Search of Principle', *Criminal Law Review* 901 at 912–17

The first stage of the decision-making process deals with the question whether a statute imposes a burden of any kind on the defendant, and, if so, whether it is a legal or an evidential burden. This question is settled by ordinary principles of statutory construction. These include the effect of s.101 of the Magistrates Courts Act 1980, as explained and expanded by Edwards and Hunt. If the burden is an evidential one no problem of compatibility with Art.6 arises. If the burden is a legal one, the issue of compatibility must be considered.

The second stage of decision-making requires a court to decide the issue of compatibility according to whether the reverse onus (legal burden) is justified as a proportionate measure in pursuance of a legitimate aim. It is at this stage that the main problems and uncertainties arise. The debate is almost entirely about proportionality, but analysis of the case law shows considerable disagreement and inconsistency about the use of one or more of six relevant factors in determining this question. If no broader principles for applying the relevant factors can be identified, the decisions as to the justifiability of particular reverse onuses will continue to resemble a forensic lottery. A search for principle suggests that issues of moral blameworthiness should be proved by the prosecution. These issues will include, in addition to the relevant prohibited acts, any requisite culpable mental states, any objective fault such as negligence, and the unavailability of any common law defences raised by the defendant. Exceptionally, legal burdens can be placed on defendants to prove formal qualifications to do certain regulated acts, and in cases where the defendant accepts the burden of proof of exculpation by virtue of voluntarily participating in a regulated activity from which he intends to derive benefit. Lord Bingham in *Sheldrake* adopted a further principle that where the scope of an offence is so wide as to include defendants who are not blameworthy a reverse onus on the defendant to prove lack of culpability is disproportionate. Conversely, an onus to prove facts taking the defendant outside the rationale of the offence, meaning the danger with which the prohibited, morally blameworthy, conduct is intended to deal, may be upheld. There are advantages to Lord Bingham's principle, but also significant problems.

If the reverse onus is justified as proportionate to a legitimate aim no further decision is necessary. If it is not justified according to these criteria the third stage of decision-making requires the court to read down the legal burden to an evidential burden if it is possible to do this using s.3 of the HRA. On the basis of *Sheldrake* it seems that it will almost always be possible to do this; it is hard to envisage a case that would not come within the scope of Lord Bingham's reasoning. Accordingly a declaration of incompatibility of a reverse onus will almost never be necessary.

3 The impact of the HRA and particular offences

As already mentioned, at many points throughout this book we will consider the impact of the HRA on particular offences. Here just a couple of examples will be given. As the following examples indicate, although defendants may often seek to raise a defence on the basis of the HRA, rarely have they been successful:

(1) *Smethurst*:[118] a defendant charged with the creation of an indecent photograph sought to argue that to convict him of the offence interfered with his right to freedom of expression or right to respect for private life. His argument was rejected.

(2) *Taylor*:[119] a Rastafarian defendant unsuccessfully claimed that to convict him of a drugs offence interfered with his right to religious freedom.[120]

(3) *H*:[121] the Court of Appeal interpreted the defence of reasonable chastisement in a way which was compatible with the victim's rights under the ECHR.

(4) *Concannon*:[122] the defendant argued that the law on accessories operated unfairly in the context of murder, and that therefore his right to a fair trial under Article 6 was breached. His argument failed, with the Court of Appeal emphasizing that Article 6 concerned the fairness of criminal trials, not the fairness of the law itself.

(5) *Rimmington*:[123] the House of Lords rejected an argument that the offence of causing a public nuisance was too vague to satisfy the requirements of Article 6.

FURTHER READING

Arden, J. (1999), 'Criminal Law at the Crossroads: The Impact on Human Rights From the Law Commission's Perspective and the Need for a Code', *Criminal Law Review* 439.

Ashworth, A. (2000c), 'The Human Rights Act and the Substantive Criminal Law: A Non-minimalist View', *Criminal Law Review* 564.

—— (2001), 'Criminal Proceedings After the Human Rights Act', *Criminal Law Review* 855.

—— (2002a), *Human Rights, Serious Crime and Criminal Procedure* (London: Sweet & Maxwell).

Buxton, R. (2000), 'The Human Rights Act and the Substantive Criminal Law', *Criminal Law Review* 311.

Centre for Public Law at the University of Cambridge (1999), *The Human Rights Act and the Criminal Justice and Regulatory Process* (Cambridge: Centre for Public Law at the University of Cambridge).

Dingwall, G. (2002), 'Statutory Exceptions, Burdens of Proof and the Human Rights Act 1998', *Modern Law Review* 65: 40.

Duff, R.A. (2005c), 'Strict Liability, Legal Presumptions, and the Presumption of Innocence' Innocence' in A. Simester (ed.), *Appraising Strict Liability* (Oxford: OUP).

Emmerson, B., and Ashworth, A. (2001), *Human Rights and Criminal Justice* (London: Sweet & Maxwell).

---

[118] [2001] Crim LR 657.   [119] [2001] EWCA Crim 2263.
[120] Khaliq and Young (2001) discuss wider issues involving cultural diversity and human rights.
[121] [2002] 1 Cr App R 59.   [122] [2002] Crim LR 213 (CA).   [123] [2005] 3 WLR 982 (HL).

Roberts, P. (2005), 'Strict Liability and the Presumption of Innocence' in A. Simester (ed.), *Appraising Strict Liability* (Oxford: OUP).

11 CRITICAL CRIMINAL LAW

In recent times much attention has been paid to critical analysis of criminal law. Critical analysts claim that the attempts of the judiciary and commentators to paint a picture of a law which is rational and logical have failed and that in fact criminal law is replete with irrationality. This reflects political and social tensions within society.[124] We have already seen a fine example of critical analysis in Nicola Lacey's analysis of the general principles of criminal law excerpted above.

One of England's leading critical criminal lawyers is Alan Norrie, whose work will be excerpted at various points in this book. Here we will extract an analysis of his work by G.R. Sullivan. He focuses on Norrie's claim that criminal law cannot be just because of its failure to consider the potential impact of social and economic inequalities in society.[125] He challenges Norrie—a challenge he often faces—to suggest an alternative criminal law which would be more just. This is a common criticism of critical scholars, they are brilliant deconstructors, but what is to replace the rubble they have created?[126]

G.R. Sullivan, 'Is Criminal Law Possible?' [2002] *Oxford Journal of Legal Studies* 747 at 750-4

... Norrie is right to accord a central place to a concern with the nature of the justice or injustice that the criminal law engenders. For Norrie, the maintenance of order in a 40/30/30 society entails that the criminal law operates in a fundamentally unjust manner, albeit an injustice tempered by a concern with the requirements of (too limited) a model of justice.

Many will agree with Norrie that large inequalities of resources and power are a bad thing and that many civic advantages would flow from establishing a more egalitarian, less materialistic society. The link between social deprivation and the incidence of criminal offending is undeniable. Anyone with the most cursory knowledge of the day to day realities of the criminal justice system will know the questionable nature of many of its decisions and their consequences when assessed in terms of justice and fairness. Norrie argues that if the criminal justice system is to advance the cause of justice for defendants, the grip of the Kantian model must be eased. Norrie does not dismiss as chimeras the Kantian values of autonomy and freedom. He acknowledges that there is a place in moral judgments for responsibility based on personal agency. His argument is that an exclusive stress on personal agency excludes far too much of the whole picture. He emphasizes time and again that conduct is a compound of the social and the personal. Accordingly, the pressures and exigencies of social circumstances and forces should feature in determining criminal liability—a relational account grounded in social reality.

---

[124] Kelman (1981); Norrie (2002).

[125] Of particular concern are the racial aspects of crime: see Phillips and Bowling (2002). On the wider issue of the link between crime and social exclusion see J. Young (2002). Garland (2001) discusses the use of crime as a form of social control.

[126] Wilson (2002: 57) argues that justice is something our society and legal system should be working towards, rather than expecting it to be met exactly.

There is considerable force in Norrie's arguments. Yet it is unclear what consequences for the form and content of the criminal law would be entailed by a relational account. He returns frequently to his contention that the principal role of the criminal law is to maintain the status quo for a society profoundly unequal. This perspective would allow claims that at least certain criminal acts are justified forms of defiance and/or appropriate exercises in distributive justice. A functioning legal order could not accept such claims as the basis of exemption from the norms of the criminal law. Thus his argument moves in the direction of displacing the current legal order. Yet Norrie insists he is not bent on a dismissal of legal ordering and legal values. His project is one of reconstruction, albeit radical reconstruction. In keeping with that, he nowhere claims directly that social disadvantage justifies criminal acts. Indeed, he seems to allow that findings of guilt must be made even within the current dispensation. His position seems to be that social factors should constitute grounds of *excuse* and that these excuses currently go unheard because of the Kantian model. Thus we are not dealing with a macro rejection of the right of the institutions of an unjust society to condemn and punish. We are within the realm of the micro examination of the circumstances of individuals, the realm of excuses.

Thus Norrie requires a theory of excuse which accommodates the exculpatory force of certain kinds of social circumstances and pressures. Yet the possibility of such a theory is unexamined by Norrie. The link between the macro unfairness of society and the micro circumstances of individuals is not made. There is merely a pervasive assumption that exculpation would frequently follow *ipso facto* from an holistic appraisal of all the salient circumstances of disadvantaged defendants. Norrie is aware that an holistic appraisal would be very difficult to fit in with any kind of criminal law which aspired to be a rule based system. He seemingly envisages forms of adjudication which reflect systems of popular justice which have emerged from time to time in certain countries, usually in revolutionary or immediate post-revolution times. Norrie's reconstruction is effectively a dismissal of the possibility of a just and principled criminal law for our current form of liberal capitalist society.

Norrie, with his preoccupation with societal forces, gives little if any attention to the psychological determinants of human agency. It is fair to say that he adopts the Standard Social Science Model of human conduct, allowing pre-dominant effect to the formative influence of social structures and cultural norms. As stated, the individual and individual agency are part of Norrie's ontology and yet the mechanics of individual agency are unexplored. He accepts the premise of free will required by the Kantian paradigm, albeit a free will heavily conditioned by social circumstances. Yet the acceptance of free will, in however socially conditioned a form, makes the accommodation of excuses based on non-exceptional social circumstances very difficult to accommodate.

Undeniably, social deprivation has a vast impact on the range and nature of options available to an agent. But, of course, there is more in the mix than the constriction of resources and legitimate opportunities. Family circumstances, maleness and age clearly correlate with the incidence of offending. And yet the majority of socially disadvantaged males under the age of 25 from single parent households are not consistent offenders. Clearly, the particulars of an individual's psychology and the vagaries of chance and luck are important too. We may be confident that D would not Φ, if he had been placed in different social circumstances, and yet the majority of his contemporaries in similar social and familial circumstances to him do not Φ. Indeed, a focus on the psychological make-up of the individual defendant may open the way for a more destabilizing critique of the foundations of judgments of culpability than the socially orientated account offered by Norrie.

In the past decade, due to developing imaging techniques, remarkable progress has been made into the understanding of the nature of the brain and its processes. It would be foolish to claim that the increase in the scientific understanding of brain processes eliminates the possibility of an empirically grounded account of free-will. Indeed, so complex is the brain and its processes, a full scientific account of human agency and consciousness may never be had. Yet enough information is already to hand to persuade any open minded person that deterministic accounts of human activities, including complex cerebral activities, cannot be refuted by metaphysics alone.

A striking feature arising from what is known of the workings of the brain is the automaticity of the neuro-chemical processes that are triggered by responses to threats and opportunities arising from the agent's environment. These processes may initiate complex behaviours which are non-volitional if volition implies unconditioned, voluntary choice. It becomes entirely plausible to suppose that different agents, otherwise in like case, might respond to the same threat or opportunity according to their brain-conditioned psychology. This does not deny for one moment the salience of social circumstances in the construction of conduct. Agent E may be in a position either to offer immediate resistance to a threat or to seek legal redress thereafter. Agent D may lack the option of legal redress. Clearly such socially conditioned data will affect the brain's responses. Yet whether D resists the threat (and thereby commits an offence) or succumbs to it will be a product of her brain-conditioned psychology in addition to her social situation. Whether her conduct is to be conceived as a natural product or as arising from a capacity for choice which she can exercise within some haven of reasons sequestered from the natural order is moot. Yet even if we still cling to the latter view, we must at least concede that it is a contingent hypothesis. Unfortunately, for many criminal lawyers and theorists, free-will will continue to be a confidently held article of faith, supplying vitality to the malign Kantian heritage of punishment as a good in itself rather than a regrettable and problematic necessity. By contrast, receptiveness to the possibility that determinism, even in its hardest versions, may be true should encourage rethinking about the whole process of punishment and stimulate the pursuit of more rational, humane forms of social control.

Accordingly, for persons coming from a very different direction than Norrie, a great deal of scepticism may arise about the criminal law as a system of justice. But just or otherwise, the criminal law will remain as a system of control for the indefinite future. Popular sentiment, quite understandably, would still be moved to condemn wrongdoing and wrongdoers whatever the level of acceptance among scientists and theorists that a deterministic account was the most plausible account of human conduct. Indeed popular sentiment may be fortified by moral theories which do not make voluntarism a necessary condition of blame. In any event, whatever the ultimate legitimacy of these forms of popular sentiment and varieties of moral theory, an atomistic and conflictual society such as our own could not, for Hobbesian reasons, dispense with State coercion and control in respect of anti-social conduct. As a system of control, Norrie conceives the criminal law as predominantly a resource for the powerful to deploy against the excluded. This, it is suggested, is too monolithic a picture.

It is true, that notwithstanding the advent of the Serious Fraud Office and the Financial Services Authority, the criminal law is of very limited effectiveness in punishing property and fraud offences perpetrated by persons in commercial and professional settings. But then the clear-up rates for domestic burglaries are low, in some police authorities appallingly so. The criminal law and its agencies are not necessarily perceived as an alien occupying force even in the most impoverished of neighbourhoods. Not infrequently, the inhabitants of such neighbourhoods seek more effective protection from the criminal law and explore alternatives to police protection where it is ineffectual. Vulnerable classes of victim such as victims of domestic violence, child abuse, racial attack, corporate disregard for safety look to the criminal law to correct imbalances of power. On occasion, protection may not be forthcoming because the provision of protection may be too disruptive of vested interests. Nonetheless some of the greatest upheavals in doctrine arise when protection is extended to a vulnerable victim in circumstances not obviously within the letter of the law.

The criminal law, its agencies, its punitive infrastructure are problematic, overly politicized facets of modem society. If society is too unfair to command the support of the majority of agents subjected to its criminal law, it follows that the norms of the criminal law will be rejected along with other civic obligations. Yet if the calculus is that the civic order of current society is, all things considered, worth preserving, notwithstanding the unfair distribution of goods in that society,—the question arises of whether a criminal law can be achieved which combines effectiveness with legitimacy. The fact that any system of criminal law currently conceivable must, perforce, cause significant injustice to least advantaged citizens must be compatible with an all things considered judgment favouring the criminal law's legitimacy. We must face too the real possibility that the criminal law employs a model of human conduct at variance with the facts of the natural order. These are large caveats, perhaps too large to be set aside. If they are conceded however, central to its legitimacy is whether criminal law is a legal domain or merely a particular form of political decision making.

QUESTION

1. Lacey and Wells (1998: 57) argue 'At school, we begin to become accustomed to routine and surveillance which prepare us for submission to legal coercion for the rest of our lives'. This continues thereafter and we are controlled through religion, family welfare systems, conventional moralities, cultural assumptions, and the influence of the media. In the light of these constraints on deviant behaviour, does criminal law have a significant role to perform?

FURTHER READING

Duff, R.A. (1998b), 'Principle and Contradiction in the Criminal Law: Motives and Criminal Liability' in A. Duff (ed.), *Philosophy and the Criminal Law* (Cambridge: CUP).

Lacey, N. (1998a), 'Contingency, Coherence and Conceptualism' in A. Duff (ed.), *Philosophy and the Criminal Law* (Cambridge: CUP).

—— and Wells, C. (1998), *Reconstructing Criminal Law* (London: Butterworths).

Norrie, A. (2001), *Crime, Reason and History* (2nd edn., London: Butterworths).

—— (2002), *Punishment, Responsibility and Justice* (Oxford: OUP).

12 FEMINIST LEGAL THOUGHT

Feminist analysis has proved a powerful influence on the study of criminal law.[127] Much work has been done on highlighting injustices to women within the criminal justice system. Consider for example the following recent indictment of the criminal justice system:

---

[127] See Naffine (1997, 2002) and Wells (2004) for a discussion generally on feminist approaches to law.

Domestic violence accounts for a quarter of all crime, and yet only 5 per cent of recorded cases of domestic violence end in conviction, less than 20 per cent of rapes; and sexual assaults are reported to the police, and less than 6 per cent of rapes result in conviction. There are now over 4,500 women in prison, an increase of 194 per cent in the last ten years. Most women are convicted of non-violent offences, such as shoplifting. One woman out of 12 judges in the House of Lords, 5 women out of 43 police Chief Constables, 18 women out of 42 Chief Officers of Probation, 7 women out of 42 Chief Crown Prosecutors, 31 women out of 138 Prison Governors. There was evidence of sexual harassment and discrimination experienced by women working in the system.[128]

It must not be thought that feminism's sole contribution is to point out examples of gender stereotyping amongst the judiciary or lawyers (rape cases are replete with these) or examples of where the law unjustifiably treats men and women differently (coercion may be an example of this in that it is available as a defence for wives but not husbands). As the following extract by Nicola Lacey suggests, there is much more to a feminist perspective than this:

N. Lacey, 'General Principles of Criminal Law? A Feminist View' in D. Nicolson and L. Bibbings (eds.), *Feminist Perspectives in Criminal Law* (London: Cavendish, 1996), 92–9

Probably the most *distinctively* feminist objection to the idea of criminal law as based on general principles lies, however, in the claim that generalisations—appeals to universally valid categories or concepts—tend to obscure important differences between persons, actions or situations. From a liberal point of view, for example, the move from the standard of a 'reasonable man' to that of a 'reasonable person' is an advance. But feminists may question whether the abstract person is implicitly understood in terms of characteristics, contexts and capacities more typical of men's than of women's lives and, moreover, is so understood in generalised terms which render exposure of sex/gender issues yet more difficult than in the days of sex-specific language.

This argument comes in more and less radical forms. The more radical version is summed up by Catharine MacKinnon's witty comment that 'I refer: to women and men because you don't see many persons around'. MacKinnon implies that sex/gender is such a fundamental feature of human identity that the idea of a gender-neutral subjectivity simply makes no sense. This might be taken to mean that the very idea of a standard of 'reasonableness' engages in a totalising discourse, flattening out relevant differences between persons and contexts and brutally assimilating the vast array of human difference to a specific norm. Of course, this is not an *exclusively* feminist argument: it can be (and has been) reproduced around other indices of differentiation, such as ethnicity or class. But it is an argument which has been of sufficient salience in feminist thought to count as one of the distinctive questions posed by feminist scholarship for the general principles.

There are two reasons, however, why this argument fails to generate an entirely convincing critique of the substance of criminal law's general principles. In the first place, the

---

[128] Dustin (2004).

argument proves too much; if it were genuinely persuasive, it would undermine all forms of generalisation, feminist analysis and other forms of critical social theory included. Secondly, a strong form of the argument entails a decisive objection not only to the idea of criminal law as based on general principles, but also to the very idea of criminal law, which is, inevitably, in the business of applying general standards across a range of persons and in a variety of situations. This, of course, does not mean that key political questions about proper respect for relevant differences of history or circumstance do not arise for criminal law. But it does suggest that the implementation of substantive offences and rules of evidence, rather than the general principles, should be the primary object of critical attention. This is because the contextual factors which may be normatively relevant to the application of a general standard to a particular case need to be, understood in relation to the types of situation in which they arise.

A less sweeping version of the argument about the capacity of generalisations to obscure important questions of sexual difference has been articulated by Hilary Allen. In a subtle analysis of interpretations of the reasonable person in a series of provocation cases, Allen has revealed the way in which the gender-neutral person is nonetheless fleshed out in judicial discourse in highly (and often stereotypically) sex-specific terms. The construct of the reasonable person cannot entirely conceal the fact that the judges themselves find it difficult to conceive of a legal standard of reasonable behaviour applicable across the sexes. From Allen's point of view, this is highly problematic, because it is inconsistent with the tenet that women are properly accounted full and equal citizens and legal subjects. This does not imply, however, that the different situations of men and women in certain contexts should not be taken into account by criminal law. In relation to provocation, this cashes out in terms of an argument that the level of self-control to be expected should indeed be that attributable to a reasonable legal subject, irrespective of sex, while sexually-specific aspects affecting the gravity of the provocation to a particular woman or man should, like other salient, social differences, indeed be taken into account. Allen's argument implies the more general, prescriptive proposition that criminal law should show sensitivity to inequalities of impact along sexually patterned lines, but that its basic conceptualisation of its subjects should not be sexually differentiated. This argument has something in common with Donald Nicolson's suggestion that the appropriate approach is to ask what it is reasonable to expect of particular defendants in the light of their history, circumstances and so on.

As Allen's argument suggests, another promising ground for feminist analysis lies in the normative aspect of the appeal to general principles. The post-enlightenment vision of responsible human agency which underpins the normative appeal of the general principles is one which was thought valid for women considerably later than for men. Arguably, the gradual recognition of women's agency represents the crowning triumph of feminism's immanent critique of liberalism. Nonetheless, there remains a significant and disturbing difference of degree in the willingness to interpret women's behaviour as the product of psychological or medical pathology, rather than responsible choice. This point is under-scored by Allen's excellent *Justice Unbalanced*, a study which demonstrates sentencing courts' willingness to interpret female offending as the product of mental disorder and a corresponding unwillingness so to interpret male offending.

It is often argued, however, that liberal legal orders conjure up an inappropriately atomistic vision of the social world—a world peopled by competitive individuals whose relations with one another are structured primarily or even exclusively by the pursuit of self-interest. And some feminists have argued that this vision of the social world has particularly baleful implications in marginalizing the relations of care, nurturing and the relations of care, nurturing and reciprocity which have, as a matter of history, been more central to women's lives than to men's. Interestingly, this is a less salient feature of criminal law than of, say, contract law; criminal law is, after all, in the business of articulating reciprocal responsibilities. One might argue, on the other hand, that the inexorable shift towards subjectivism as the dominant interpretation of the general principles reinforces an individualistic and decontextualised interpretation of human behaviour. By contrast, the reasonableness test, whose allegedly 'objective' nature has been controversial among some feminists, is anything but atomistic. It is, at root, all about a vision of the obligations which human beings owe to one another. Yet again, important feminist questions are likely to arise not merely about the content of these obligations, but also about the kinds of evidence which should be relevant to determining whether they have been breached and about the law's proper response where those obligations have a radically unequal impact on women and men.

. . .

Sexing the Subject of Criminal Law?

In recent years, feminist criminal law theory has shifted away from questions about how a pre-existing category, 'women', are treated (or ignored) by legal doctrine in favour of questions about legal doctrine's dynamic role in *constituting* women and men as legal and social subjects. This shift was presaged in Cousins' argument that: '[A feminist approach] must analyse how particular legal forms of agency are more or less implicated in the organization of sexual difference and what effect they have on that.' differentiation. A good example of this sort of approach is Ngaire Naffine's analysis of the law of rape, which traces a particular and highly sexually differentiated conception of heterosexual relations, even into the 'post-feminist', gender-neutral reconstructed Australian sexual assault provisions. Similarly, one could interpret the critical analysis of the immediacy requirements structuring self-defence and of the loss of self-control model of provocation as contributions to this more recent project.

This sort of argument engages directly with aspects of the general principles of criminal law; it exposes the assumptions which underlie allegedly general concepts, such as consent, belief, foresight or reasonableness and reveals the ways in which they are implicated in the constitution of sexually differentiated social relations. But, crucially, it does so not merely in terms of engagement with the general principles themselves, but rather in terms of the combined effects of a number of much more concrete factors. These include not only widely applied concepts, but also the substance of particular offences; the nature of the time frame and the breadth of the social context defined as relevant by rules of evidence; and the context in which offences are interpreted. Only in relation to this broader set of factors can a specifically feminist analysis of aspects of the general principles be realised. A good example is the well known argument about criminal law's reflection of a dualistic view of human beings as divided between the mental and the material, between mind and body, which is vividly reflected in the distinction between *actus reus* and *mens rea*. This, along with the understanding of *mens rea* in terms of capacities of reason, understanding and self-control has been argued to have distinctively feminist implications. The strong cultural association of men and the masculine with the mind and with reason, and of women and the feminine with the body and with emotion, inevitably, so the argument goes, constructs women as non-standard subjects of the rationalist discourse of criminal law.

This is a potentially important insight, but it takes 'on different complexions according to the context in which it is deployed. It might be argued that the contemporary theoretical emphasis on mental conditions of responsibility—on culpability, rather than harmful conduct—indeed reflects a highly gendered world view, in which the standard model of responsible behaviour is implicitly marked as masculine. Ironically, this might be taken to imply a greater willingness to regard men as potentially criminally responsible and hence to prosecute and punish them. In the context of rape law, the emphasis on the mental linchpin of consent implies something rather different: the doctrinal marginalisation of the embodied aspect of the wrong. At the level of defences based on mental incapacities, it might be expected to lead to a marginalisation of women's full responsibility. These are, of course, questions which are susceptible of empirical research.

In order to interpret the feminist significance of the conceptual building blocks out of which criminal liability is constructed, we therefore have to contextualise those building blocks within the actual offences which they help to create. And, as analysis of the law of rape illustrates, one of the most important issues in tracing criminal law's 'implication in the organisation of sexual difference' will be the relevant rules of evidence, which shape the, relevant context and time frame within which the subject is conceptualised. The sexing of criminal law's subjects—indeed, their subjectification—happens in the enactment and inter- pretation of substantive offences and of the rules of evidence. Though certain aspects of criminal law's normative ideals or conceptual framework may be more often implicated in the construction of sexual difference than are others, their significance varies dramatically across the offences and defences. A dynamic analysis of criminal law's role in maintaining sexual difference is likely to be obstructed, therefore, by the contemporary scholarly practice of placing primary emphasis on the general part.

Finally, it is important to notice that the contours of the general principles, focused as they are on the construction of criminal liability, form an unduly narrow basis for an evaluation of criminal law's sexing of its subjects. For, as feminist analyses of the operation of the law of rape demonstrate, criminal law's constitution of sexed subjects relates not only to defendants, but also to victims and witnesses in the criminal process. To take a doctrinal example, the sexually differentiated position of the incest victim tells us something just as important as the sexually-specific definition of the incest offender's conduct. An adequate feminist analysis of criminal law could never, therefore, confine itself to the conceptual framework or normative underpinnings of liability.

Many feminists have pointed to the obvious, but too easily forgotten, fact that men are responsible for the vast majority of crimes.[129] This has led to an increase in interest in masculinity and what it is that creates such a strong link between the male identity and the commission of crime.[130] There will, no doubt, be an increasing amount of academic interest in that subject.

FURTHER READING

Forell, C., and Matthews, D. (2000), *The Reasonable Woman as a Measure of Man* (New York: New York University Press).

Moran, M. (2003), *Rethinking the Reasonable Person* (Oxford: OUP)

Naffine, N. (1998), *Law and the Sexes* (Sydney: Allen and Unwin).

Nicolson, D., and Bibbings, L. (eds.) (2001), *Feminist Perspectives on Criminal Law* (London: Cavendish).

Smart, C. (1992), 'The Woman of Legal Discourse', *Social and Legal Studies* 1: 29.

---

[129] Heidensohn (2002).   [130] Walklate (2001).

Wells, C. (2004), 'The Impact of Feminist Thinking on Criminal Law and Justice', *Criminal Law Review* 503.

Young, A. (1996), *Imagining Crime* (London: Sage).

13 PUNISHMENT

Theories of why we punish offenders are crucial to the understanding of criminal law.[131] Knowing why we punish people can assist us in knowing what offences should be criminal. After all there is little point in finding guilty of offences people who we do not think deserve any kind of punishment.[132]

In fact it is not easy to define punishment.[133] Why do we regard the payment of taxes as not a punishment; is it really different from a fine? Is detention under the Mental Health Act different from imprisonment? There is, not surprisingly, no agreement over what exactly punishment is. It is generally thought to contain some of the following elements:[134]

(1) it must be unpleasant;

(2) it is inflicted by the state;

(3) it is imposed on those who have broken the law;

(4) its purpose is not to compensate the victim;

(5) it carries censure of what the defendant did.

The starting point is that punishment is something that requires strong justification.[135] For the state to deprive a citizen of his or her liberty by detaining him or her in prison is a huge invasion in respect to that citizen's basic rights and requires the best of reasons.[136]

Theories of punishment can be broken down into those which are consequentialist (that claim that there are good consequences that result from punishment and therefore justify it) and those which are non-consequentialist (that claim that there are other reasons apart from its consequences which justify punishment). As can be imagined, a whole book could easily be written on the theories of punishment and here the topic can only be covered in outline.[137]

13.1 CONSEQUENTIALIST THEORIES OF PUNISHMENT

Consequentialist justifications include the following:

(1) **Personal deterrence**. By punishing the offender he or she will be deterred from committing a crime again.[138]

(2) **General deterrence**. By punishing the offender the general public (and particularly those of a criminal bent), on learning of the punishment, will be deterred from

---

[131] A very useful collection of readings can be found in von Hirsch and Ashworth (1998).

[132] For a good discussion of why people commit crimes see Downes and Rock (2003).

[133] See Lacey (1988: 7–8); Hart (1968: 4–5); and Lucas (1980: 125).

[134] See Lacey (1988: 7–8).   [135] J.G. Murphy (1994).

[136] For some discussion on why we punish see Duff and Garland (1994); Lacey (1988); Honderick (1984).

[137] Often one's views on punishment reflect wider social, political, and even religious views.

[138] Walker (1994).

committing offences.[139] This may be directly (a person deciding not to commit a crime for fear of the punishment) or indirectly (the law and punishment may affect the moral attitudes of society, which thereby leads to people not taking up crime).[140]

(3) **Rehabilitation**. The punishment may reform and educate the offender so that he or she does not commit an offence again.[141]

(4) **Incapacitation**. The offender is removed from society (by imprisonment) and so prevented from causing (for a period of time) more harm to society.[142]

(5) **Restorative justice**. There are two main versions of this theory. One focuses on the notion that the response of the criminal law should be analogous to conflict resolution. The criminal law should seek to mediate and mend the broken relationship between the victim and the offender. The other aims to compensate the victim for the wrong done. The link between these themes is that they seek to undo or rectify the harm or some of the harm done by the defendant to the victim.[143] We have discussed restorative justice in the extract from Lucia Zedner above.[144]

Critics of consequentialist theories claim that they can lead to injustice. They could lead to one offender receiving a far longer sentence than he or she deserved in order to deter others from committing a crime, or to reform the offender him- or herself. Imagine that researchers told the Home Secretary that if she announced that every year ten people who had been convicted of theft would be selected at random and have their hands cut off, this would reduce the number of thefts by half. This research would still not justify the cutting off of the hands of the unlucky few involved.

There are also objections that in fact punishment does not achieve the desired aims. For example:[145]

(1) there is little evidence that imprisonment deters offenders from reoffending;[146]

(2) the evidence that people can be reformed is inconclusive;[147]

(3) there is even evidence that prison may make people more likely to commit offences on their release.[148]

These points, however, should not mean that the consequentialist theories must be abandoned. It may be, for example, that better systems of treating prisoners may improve the reformation rates.[149] Or, if conviction rates were higher it might be that the deterrent effect of punishment would be more effective.

---

[139] See the discussion in Lucas (1980). Posner (1998) discusses deterrence from an economic point of view. For a startling recent example see *Attorney-General's Reference No. 4 of 2002* [2002] Crim LR 333 which suggested sentences of 5 years for robbery of mobile phones in order to deter others.

[140] Edmundson (2002).

[141] Richards (1998); Brody (1998).

[142] Morris (1994). One particularly controversial proposal is that those deemed particularly dangerous should be incapacitated for longer than those deemed non-dangerous who commit similar offences (see von Hirsch (1998a and b) and Prins (2003)).

[143] Christie (1998).

[144] Johnstone (2002).

[145] Brody (1976); Allen (1981).

[146] The evidence is discussed in Beyleveld (1998).

[147] F. Allen (1981); von Hirsch (1976); von Hirsch and Maher (1998).

[148] Martinson (1974).

[149] Brody (1998) discusses the effectiveness of various rehabilitative techniques.

13.2 NON-CONSEQUENTIALIST THEORIES

The most popular non-consequentialist theory is retributive theory.[150] This is that, quite simply,[151] punishment is justified because the offender deserves it.[152] It is good in and of itself to punish, regardless of any consequences of the punishment. Through punishment, the law treats people as human beings who are able to make choices and take the consequences of those choices.[153] To some retributivists punishment is linked to a concept of the offender paying his or her dues to society. Having suffered the penalty the offender can return to society as a fully acceptable member. To others an offender has gained an unfair advantage over law-abiding citizens by breaking the law, and this needs to be removed by imposing the burden of a punishment.[154] This last theory has difficulties in the context of serious crime. It is uncomfortable saying that a rapist has gained an advantage by raping.

Retributive theories would also indicate that the level of punishment should reflect the amount of punishment the offender deserves. This seems obvious, but it is significant in that it means that a person should not be given a longer sentence than he or she might otherwise receive on the basis that to do so would be for his or her own good, or for society's good. We should therefore not, for example, impose an especially high sentence on people who have stolen a mobile phone in order to discourage others from stealing or imprison shoplifters just in order to ensure they receive treatment for their drug addiction. In both these cases we would be imposing a higher sentence than their crimes deserve. Rather, what should be done is to impose a sentence which is proportional to the wrong they have done.[155]

Another non-consequentialist theory of punishment is that punishment is an expression of censure (see the extract at p. 3).[156] Punishment expresses the denunciation by society of the kind of conduct done by the offender.[157] This helps to promote social cohesion and channels public outrage, thereby avoiding vigilantism. This theory provides a clear explanation of why taxation is not equivalent to a fine: a fine, but not a tax demand, carries with it condemnation of the actions of the recipient. The difficulty with the censure theory is that it does not explain why it is necessary to impose a punishment in order to do the censuring task.[158] The censure theory is seen by one of its chief proponents as complementary to retributivism:[159]

M. Moore, 'The Moral Worth of Retribution' in A. von Hirsch and A. Ashworth (eds.), *Principled Sentencing* (Oxford: Hart, 1998), 150 at 153–4

Retributivism is a very straightforward theory of punishment: we are justified in punishing because and only because offenders deserve it. Moral culpability (desert) is in such a view both a sufficient as well as a necessary condition of liability to punitive sanctions. Such justification gives society more than merely a right to punish culpable offenders. It does this, making it not unfair to punish them, but retributivism justifies more than this. For a retributivist, the moral culpability of an offender also gives society the *duty* to punish. Retributivism,

---

[150] Walker (1998).

[151] Moore (1987) claims that retributive theories reflect a natural intuition.

[152] Kant (1965: 100).

[153] Duff (1998a) emphasizes the importance of seeing punishment as a form of communication between the state and offenders.

[154] Morris (1968). There is an element of this suggestion in Ripstein's (1999) argument that reciprocity between citizens underpins the criminal law.

[155] von Hirsch (1985).   [156] von Hirsch (1993); Feinberg (1994).

[157] Morris (1994).   [158] Feinberg (1994).   [159] Feinberg (1994).

in other words, is truly a theory of justice such that, if it is true, we have an obligation to set up institutions so that retributivism is achieved

[Moore then turns to defend retributivism from two common criticisms:]

1. First and foremost there is the popularly accepted belief that punishment for its own sake does no good. 'By punishing the offender you cannot undo the crime', might be the slogan for this point of view. I mention this view only to put it aside, for it is but a reiteration of the consequentialist idea that only further good consequences achieved by punishment could possibly justify the practice. Unnoticed by those who hold this position is that they abandon such consequentialism when it comes to other areas of morals. It is a sufficient justification not to scapegoat innocent individuals, that they do not deserve to be punished; the injustice of punishing those who did not deserve it seems to stand perfectly well by itself as a justification of our practices, without need for further good consequences we might achieve. Why do we not similarly say that the injustice of the guilty going unpunished can equally stand by itself as a justification for punishment, without need of a showing of further good consequences? It simply is not the case that justification always requires the showing of further good consequences.

Those who oppose retributivism often protest at this point that punishment is a clear harm to the one punished, and the intentional causing of this harm requires some good thereby achieved to justify it; whereas *not* punishing the innocent is not a harm and thus does not stand in need of justification by good consequences. Yet this response simply begs the question against retributivism. Retributivism purports to be a theory of justice, and as such claims that punishing the guilty achieves something good—namely, justice—and that therefore reference to any other good consequences is simply beside the point. One cannot defeat the central retributivist claim—that justice is achieved by punishing the guilty—simply by assuming that it is false.

The question-begging character of this response can be seen by imagining a like response in areas of tort, property, or contract law. Forcing another to pay tort or contract damages, or to forgo use and possession of some thing, is a clear harm that corrective justice theories of tort, promissory theories of contract, or natural right theories of property are willing to impose on defendants. Suppose no one gains anything of economic significance by certain classes of such impositions—as, for example, in cases where the plaintiff has died without heirs after his cause of action accrued. 'It does no good to force the defendant to pay', interposed as an objection to corrective justice theories of tort, promissory theories of contract, or natural right theories of property simply denies what these theories assert: that something good *is* achieved by imposing liability in such cases—namely, that justice is done.

This 'harm requires justification' objection thus leaves untouched the question of whether the rendering of justice cannot in all such cases be the good that justifies the harm all such theories impose on defendants. I accordingly put aside this initial objection to retributivism, relying as it does either on an unjustifiable discrimination between retributivism and other deontological theories, or upon a blunderbuss assault on deontological theories as such.

2. A second and very popular suspicion about retributive judgments is that they presuppose an indefensible objectivism about morals. Sometimes this objection is put metaphysically: There is no such thing as desert or culpability (Mackie, 1982). More often the point is put as a more cautious epistemological modesty: 'Even if there is such a thing as desert, we can never know who is deserving'. For religious people, this last variation usually contrasts us to God, who alone can know what people truly deserve. We might call this the 'don't play God' objection.

A striking feature of the 'don't play God' objection is how inconsistently it is applied. Let us revert to our use of desert as a limiting condition on punishment: We certainly seem confident both that it is true and that we can know that it is true, that we should not punish the morally innocent because they do not deserve it. Neither metaphysical scepticism nor epistemological modesty gets in our way when we use lack of moral desert as a reason not to punish. Why should it be different when we use the presence of desert as a reason to punish? If we can know when someone does *not* deserve punishment, mustn't we know when someone *does* deserve punishment? Consider the illogic in the following passages from Karl Menninger (1968):

'It does not advance a solution to use the word justice. It is a subjective emotional word . . . The concept is so vague, so distorted in its applications, so hypocritical, and usually so irrelevant that it offers no help in the solution of the crime problem which it exists to combat but results in its exact opposite—injustice, injustice to everybody' (10–11).

Apparently Dr. Karl knows injustice when he sees it, even if justice is a useless concept. Analogously, consider our reliance on moral desert when we allocate initial property entitlements. We think that the person who works hard to produce a novel deserves the right to determine when and under what conditions the novel will be copied for others to read. The novelist's labour gives him or her, the moral right. How can we know this—how can it be true—if desert can be judged only by those with godlike omniscience, or worse, does not even exist? Such scepticism about just deserts would throw out a great deal that we will not throw out. To me, this shows that no one really believes that moral desert does not exist or that we could not know it if it did. Something else makes us suspect our retributive judgments than supposed moral scepticism or epistemological modesty.

13.3 MIXED THEORIES

One very influential theory, propounded by Herbert Hart, has sought to mix both consequentialist and non-consequentialist theories together. He relies on a retributivist theory in order to explain who should be punished and a consequentialist theory to explain how people should be punished. In other words only those who deserve punishment should be punished, but the form of punishment can be decided on the basis of the consequentialist aims of deterrence, incapacitation, or reform.

FURTHER READING

Duff, R.A. (1986), *Trials and Punishments* (Cambridge: CUP).

—— and Garland, D. (eds.) (1994), *A Reader on Punishment* (Oxford: OUP).

Hart, H. (1968), *Punishment and Responsibility* (Oxford: OUP).

Norrie, A. (2000), *Punishment, Responsibility and Justice* (Oxford: OUP).

von Hirsch, A. (1993), *Censure and Sanctions* (Oxford: OUP).

14 SENTENCING

Of course a conviction is not the end of the trial. If there is a conviction the judge still needs to go on to consider the appropriate sentence to be imposed.[160] In the following extract, Alan

---

[160] A furore surrounded the Criminal Justice Bill 2003 in which the Home Secretary intends to restrict further the sentencing powers of judges in cases of murder.

Norrie argues that the flexibility in matters of sentencing is in marked contrast to the 'strictness' of the criminal law:

A. Norrie, *Crime, Reason and History* (London: Butterworths, 2001), 199–210

Throughout this book, I have probed a particular conception of the criminal law as a systematic attempt to govern human conduct by rules. That conception is central to the legitimacy of the modem state, and is most clearly presented in the work of doctrinal scholars operating within the liberal tradition where values of the rule of law and of individual justice are presented as central. I have sought to show that these values are essentially flawed. This is because the model of the abstract juridical individual at their heart constantly comes into conflict with the socio-political realities of crime on the one hand and the politics of the judiciary, as an arm of the state, on the other. Because of this double tension in the basic elements, the lines of legal doctrine are constantly disrupted as rules are tugged this way then that according to the tensions upon which they are founded. Nonetheless the substantive doctrine of the criminal law is rule-based, even if the nature of those rules cannot be adequately understood within a liberal, positivist framework. The general principles of the criminal law remain the very 'stuff' of legal analysis, even if the orthodox approach to them can never properly capture the law's working.

However, when we come to the sentencing stage of the criminal process, we find that once we get beyond the conviction of the accused, the rules and principles of the criminal law largely evaporate and the system becomes much more discretionary and less regulated by law. In terms of liberal theory, this is surprising. After all, it is the sentence of the court that deprives the individual of the liberty that the rule of law is supposed to protect and respect at the conviction stage. Indeed, as Lacey's comment at the head of the chapter indicates, without the sentence of the court, the hard edge of delivery of the criminal sanction, none of the paraphernalia of law at the earlier stage would make much sense. Yet now we come to 'the moment of penal truth', much of the legitimating symbolism of the rule of law is largely cast aside.

The situation might be compared to one of those competitions on the back of breakfast cereal packs. The questions posed are so easy that everyone knows that it is the tie-breaker ('Explain in no more than ten words why you like Krispy Korn Flakes') that determines who gets the prize, and this is decided according to the subjective preference of the judges. The questions become no more than a backdrop to the real process of determining the winner. Consequently, the competitor becomes cynical because it turns out that the competition is not the real basis for deciding who has won, and also because the actual decision is at the judges' discretion. The same might be said for the criminal law. Conviction does qualify the offender for sentencing but, without a proper set of rules to determine the latter, the most important matter is left in the hands, and at the discretion, of the judge. This overstates the issue, for it is not that discretion is complete. Sentencing maxima exist for many offences and minima are now established for some (Crime (Sentences) Act 1997, ss 2–4, consolidated in Powers of Criminal Courts (Sentencing) Act 2000, ss 109–111). Guideline judgments have also been issued by the Court of Appeal, which 'provide judges with a starting point or range of sentences, and indicate the considerations which ought to be taken into account'. However, such judgments 'do not assign weight to the various factors' (Ashworth, 2000, 34) to be considered and their authority is indicative rather than binding. They 'merely set the general tariff, but judges are free to tailor the sentence to the facts of the particular case' (Taylor, 1993, 130). This leads to 'considerable latitude, some variation and, inevitably, some inconsistency' (Ashworth, 2000, 31). Judges consider sentencing to consist in 'trying to reconcile a number of totally irreconcilable facts' (Lord Lane, quoted in ibid, 34), as art rather than science, and therefore as requiring substantial discretion.

Why should this be so? Why is sentencing only loosely regulated by law, prompting Lacey's suggestion that the system is in bad faith with its own premises as evinced at the stage of conviction? Her answer is to point to the disagreements of principle, the tensions between the underlying values, and the lack of consensus about the proper functions of the criminal law which underlie the sentencing stage. What needs to be added to this is the way in which these disagreements and tensions are generated by the limitations of the ideological forms that underlie the liberal conception of criminal law and criminal punishment.

Problems in the sentencing stage are not just the result of a plurality of competing values, but the product of the organic tensions within the liberal model of the punishable, juridical, individual. Enlightenment thought produced an abstract individual who furnished legal discourse with ideas of rationality, intentionality, voluntariness: in short, of responsibility. But this model was never just legal in a narrow sense. It was always at the core of a broader conception of social order and social control which was premised upon a moral, rational, individual response to the existence of criminal punishment. Homo juridicus lay at the heart of both legal doctrine and a philosophical plan for social order which involved a particular conception of punishment (Norrie, 1991). Just as our homuncular friend has proved an inherently unsound basis for the rational construction of legal doctrine at the level of the general principles of responsibility, so he has undermined any attempt to rationalise a system of punishment.

The criminal law has traditionally operated with four core ideologies of punishment which began to emerge from the time of the Enlightenment. It is these which provide the main rationales for sentencing decisions in the criminal justice system. They return us at the end of this book to our starting point in the philosophies of retributivism and utilitarianism. It is these theories of punishment which both provide the theoretical backdrop to the sentence of the court and generate the tensions which make the system so difficult to govern by law. These establish the primary ideological bases for sentencing, theories of retribution and deterrence. However, we will see that these theories of punishment also set up, by way of negation and opposition, the space for two other rationales of sentencing, reform (or rehabilitation) and incapacitation, to emerge in the late nineteenth century.

These further ideologies were constituted as a result of the *failure* of the classical ideologies to control the problem of crime, and they took as their basis a critique of the abstract individualism of the classical models. In its place, they substituted a model of human conduct as concretely determined by personal circumstance, and therefore treatable through state intervention. The resulting ideology substituted a model of concrete human individuality and individualised treatment for the classical model of abstract individualism. In so doing, it injected further competing and conflictual elements into the penal arena, alongside the conflicts already generated within the classical models. Substantial indeterminacy at the sentencing stage is the product of these multiple conflicts emerging from the historically generated, theoretically and practically unrealistic, ideological forms that govern the official understanding of crime, its control and punishment.

In the light of some of the points made in this extract it is understandable that several commentators[161] have argued that criminal law can only be properly understood by having a secure grasp of not only the definition of criminal offences, but also criminal procedure and

---

[161] e.g. Lacey (2002).

the law on sentencing. That would certainly be an ideal, but for students it would mean that criminal law courses would have to last three times as long as they do at present. Also, criminal law textbooks would be even bigger.

FURTHER READING

Ashworth, A. (2005b), *Sentencing and Criminal Justice* (Cambridge: CUP).

von Hirsch, A., and Ashworth, A. (eds.) (1998), *Principled Sentencing* (Oxford: Hart).

Wasik, M. (2001), *Emmins on Sentencing* (London: Blackstone).

2

ACTUS REUS: THE CONDUCT ELEMENT

PART I: THE LAW

1 DISTINGUISHING THE COMPONENT ELEMENTS OF A CRIME

DEFINITION

Actus reus: the conduct element of the offence. The *actus reus* describes what the defendant must be proved to have done (or sometimes failed to do), in what circumstances, and with what consequences.

Mens rea: the mental element of the offence. This may be, for example, intention, recklessness, or negligence.

The traditional way of analysing criminal offences is to divide a crime up into the conduct of the accused (known as the *actus reus* or conduct element) and the state of mind of the accused (the *mens rea* or mental element).[1] For example, in a murder case the prosecution must show that the defendant caused the death of the victim and that he or she intended to kill or cause grievous bodily harm to the victim. The *actus reus* of murder is causing the death of the victim; the *mens rea* is an intention to kill or cause grievous bodily harm. Only if both the *actus reus* and *mens rea* are proved will the defendant be guilty.[2] In this chapter we will consider the *actus reus*, and in Chapter 3 the *mens rea* will be discussed. In Part II of this chapter we will examine the benefits and disadvantages of dividing crimes into the *mens rea* and *actus reus* elements.

So what is the *actus reus* of a crime? One popular way of explaining it is to define its role;

---

[1] In *Miller* [1983] 2 AC 161, 174 (HL) Lord Diplock suggested that it would be preferable not to use the Latin terminology and refer instead to 'the conduct of the accused and his state of mind'. The Draft Criminal Code also avoids the Latin terminology, preferring the terms 'external element' and 'internal element'. Despite these objections the Latin terminology is still very widely used by the judiciary and commentators.

[2] The Latin maxim is *actus non facit reum nisi mens sit rea*—'an act is not criminal in the absence of a guilty mind'.

namely that it identifies the conduct which the criminal law considers harmful.[3] The *actus reus* of an offence tell us what we can and cannot do: killing; damaging another's property; injuring another person are examples of forbidden kinds of conduct. By contrast the *mens rea* and defences enable us to decide whether the defendant was to blame for his or her wrongful acts. Another popular way of defining an *actus reus* is by describing what it is not: the *actus reus* is that part of the crime which is not concerned with the accused's state of mind.

The exact nature of the *actus reus* depends on the particular crime: in murder it involves killing; in theft it involves taking another's property. The *actus reus* of a crime may involve three different aspects:

(1) proof that the defendant did a particular act;

(2) proof that the act caused a particular result; and

(3) proof that the act or result occurred in certain circumstances.

Not all *actus rei*[4] involve all three of these. For example, the offence of bigamy requires the act of marriage, in certain circumstances (the defendant is already married), but there is no need to prove any result. Some commentators suggest that it is useful to distinguish between conduct crimes and result crimes:

> *Conduct crimes* require proof only that the defendant did an act. There is no need to demonstrate that the act produced a particular result. Possession of prohibited drugs would be an example.
>
> *Result crimes* require proof not only that the defendant performed a particular act but that that act produced certain results. For example, murder requires proof that the defendant's act caused the death of the victim.

Are there any common threads that link the *actus reus* of every crime? There is much debate over this issue and this chapter will now consider three particular questions:

(1) Do all *actus rei* require an act?

(2) Do all *actus rei* require a *voluntary* act?

(3) If the *actus reus* of a crime requires proof that the defendant caused a particular result, what does 'cause' mean?

2 THE VOLUNTARY ACT 'REQUIREMENT'

DEFINITION

The 'voluntary act requirement': many criminal offences require proof that the defendant performed a voluntary act. But not all do: sometimes offences can be committed by an omission; some only require proof of a state of affairs; and sometimes a defendant can be convicted in respect of the actions of another.

Usually you cannot commit a crime without doing an act. Sitting in a room thinking the most evil of thoughts and conjuring up the most heinous of plans is not an offence.[5]

---

[3] Although see p. 39 for arguments against views of this kind.

[4] *Actus rei* is the plural of *actus reus*.   [5] Dan-Cohen (2002: ch. 6).

Indeed, if evil thoughts were to constitute criminal offences, the prisons would be very full indeed! Not only must there be an act; there must be a voluntary act. Lord Denning[6] explained 'the requirement that it should be a voluntary act is essential . . . in every criminal case'.[7] Where the defendant is not acting voluntarily he or she is said to be acting as an automaton and will not be guilty of an offence because the *mens rea* and *actus reus* will not be proved. If Barbara was holding a valuable vase when Andre came up behind her and said 'boo' in a loud voice, causing Barbara to drop the vase, then this (the dropping of the vase) would not be seen as Barbara's act, and so she could not be convicted of unlawfully damaging the vase.[8] Another example of an involuntary act is where a defendant is rendered unconscious, falls over, and injures someone. The detail of the law on automatism, or involuntary acts, is discussed in Chapter 12.

The general principle that a crime must involve an act of the defendant is subject to two important caveats. First, it is far from clear what is meant by the word 'act' here. The question how to define an act will be considered in detail in Part II of this chapter. Secondly, there are a number of crimes which appear to be exceptions to the rule. In fact there are so many exceptions that some commentators argue that the rule does not really exist.[9] In brief, the exceptions include the following:

(1) Sometimes a failure to act, an omission, can give rise to criminal liability. In such cases the failure to act can constitute the *actus reus* of the crime.

(2) Sometimes the *actus reus* of an offence is defined as a state of affairs or set of circumstances, which may or may not involve an actual act. For example, possession of a firearm can, in some circumstances, amount to an offence.

(3) Under some circumstances a defendant can be responsible for the acts of another person.

It should be noted that whether these are or are not true exceptions in part depends on how one defines an act. This question will be considered in detail in Part II of this chapter. Let us now consider these exceptions to the 'rule' that a criminal offence must require an act.

2.1 OMISSIONS

Generally, a person will not be liable for simply failing to act. Criminal lawyers are keen to point out that if a person comes across a child drowning in a pond and simply walks by leaving the child to die, there is no criminal liability. Some countries have statutes that make it a criminal offence not to offer aid to those you come across who are in peril, when it is reasonably practical for you to do so.[10] But, there is no such general duty in English and Welsh law. This is not to say that a defendant is never criminally liable for an omission: a defendant can be criminally liable for an omission where there is a duty to act in a particular way.

---

[6] *Bratty v AG of Northern Ireland* [1963] AC 386 (HL).
[7] See also *Kay v Butterworth* (1945) 173 LT 191.
[8] Indeed it may be seen as Andre's act.   [9] G. Williams (1982: 31).
[10] See e.g. Ashworth and Steiner (1990) which discusses the French law, and the discussion in Part II of this chapter.

DEFINITION

A summary of the criminal law on omissions: a defendant is only guilty of a crime when failing to act where he or she is under a duty to act.

The discussion of liability for omissions will be divided into four sections. First, we will note that there are some crimes which can never be committed by omission. Secondly, we will consider when a defendant will be under a duty to act. Thirdly, we will ask what is required of a defendant who is under such a duty. Fourthly, the difficult question of how acts and omissions can be distinguished will be tackled.

1 Crimes that cannot be committed by omission

There are certain crimes that cannot be committed by an omission. These are statutory crimes which in their definition require an act to be committed. For example in *Ahmad*[11] the defendant was charged with an offence under the Protection from Eviction Act 1977 which required proof of the defendant 'doing acts calculated to interfere with [the victim's] peace and comfort'. The defendant, a landlord, failed to carry out alterations on the victim's house and this left the premises uninhabitable, thereby interfering with the tenant's peace and comfort. The failure to carry out the alterations was not an 'act' and so the landlord was not guilty of the offence.

2 When the defendant is under a duty to act

The duty to act can arise in the following eight ways:

(i) *Statutory duty.* There are a large number of statutory duties requiring people to act in a particular way. For example, under section 6 of the Road Traffic Act 1988 a driver who fails to provide a sample of breath when required to do so by a constable under certain circumstances commits a criminal offence. There are too many examples of statutory duties to act for them all to be listed here.[12]

(ii) *Duties of law enforcement.* Police officers are under a duty to assist members of the public in danger. So, a police officer who failed to protect a citizen who was being kicked to death was held to have committed an offence.[13] Further, if a police officer calls upon a citizen to assist him or her to restore the peace, the citizen is under a duty to offer the assistance.[14]

(iii) *Contractual duty.* Where a person is under a contractual duty to help another he or she may be under a duty under criminal law to do so. For example, in *Pittwood*[15] the defendant was employed as a gate-keeper on a railway line. One day he failed to perform his duties and did not close the gate when required. This led to an accident in which a train hit a cart and a man was killed. It was held that he could be liable for manslaughter, because he was required under his contract of employment to ensure

---

[11] (1986) 52 P & CR 346 (CA).

[12] There are a few common law offences which can be said to involve liability for omission, e.g. cheating the Revenue and misconduct in a public office (*Mavji* [1987] 1 WLR 1388 (CA)).

[13] *Dytham* (1979) 69 Cr App R 387 (CA).

[14] The law is discussed in detail in Nicholson (1992).   [15] (1902) 19 TLR 37.

that the gate was shut. His omission, in failing to shut the gate, was in breach of his contractual duty and so could constitute a criminal offence.[16]

(iv) *Assumed duties.* People who voluntarily assume responsibility for another's welfare will be under a duty to care for him or her. The assumption of responsibility may be express (for example, where a person explicitly agrees to look after a vulnerable person) or implied (a person has regularly offered assistance to another and so a mutual understanding of responsibility can be assumed).[17]

Some duties arise automatically: a parent is automatically responsible for caring for a child. So, if a parent fails to feed a child and the child dies of starvation then the parent might be liable even though the failure to feed was an omission.[18] Similarly, a parent who stands by and lets another person harm his or her child might be guilty of an offence.[19] In *Sheppard*[20] it was held that there was no duty owed by a parent to an 18-year-old daughter. This suggests that once a child reaches majority the legal duty towards the child may come to an end.[21]

Whether a duty will be assumed in the context of other relationships is less clear. It is generally assumed that spouses (and presumably long-term partners[22]) owe a duty to assist each other if they are in peril.[23] It may be that older children owe duties towards their elderly parents, but the existence or extent of such a duty is yet to be tested in the courts.[24] It may be that outside the parent–child relationship the duty that will be imposed will depend on the nature of the relationship between the two parties. The court will be reluctant to impose a duty between two spouses who have separated, but may be very willing to impose a duty if one person is disabled and depends on a friend for their well-being.

Controversially, a duty of care was held to exist in the following case:[25]

R v Stone; R v Dobinson
[1977] QB 354 (CA)[26]

The appellants were John Edward Stone (a man aged 67, of below average intelligence, partially deaf and almost blind) and Gwendoline Dobinson (aged 43 and described by the court as 'ineffectual and inadequate') Stone's sister, Fanny, aged

---

[16] It should be noted that the contractual duty to shut the gate was owed not to the victim but to the employer.

[17] In *Charlotte Smith* (1865) 10 Cox CC 82 a master was found guilty of the homicide of his servant after he failed to give her sufficient food and general care.

[18] *Gibbons and Proctor* (1919) 13 Cr App R 134 (CA); *Lowe* [1973] 1 QB 702 (CA).

[19] *Emery* (1993) 14 Cr App R (S) 394 (CA).   [20] [1981] AC 394 (HL).

[21] It should be noted that under the Children and Young Persons Act 1933, s. 1 there is a duty not to neglect the child which ends when the child reaches the age of 18. There is also an offence under the Mental Capacity Act 2005; s. 44 willfully to neglect a mentally incompetent person.

[22] Although in an American case, *People v Beardsley* (1967) 113 NW 1128, it was held that a man did not owe a duty to his lover who took morphine in his presence.

[23] *Bonnyman* (1942) 28 Cr App R 131 (CA). However, it has been held that a brother does not owe a duty to care for his sisters: *Smith* (1826) 172 ER 203.

[24] Simester and Sullivan (2003: 76) argue that children do not owe their parents a duty, but J.C. Smith (2002: 63) disagrees.

[25] *Instan* [1893] 1 QB 450 (QBD) provides another example.

[26] [1977] 2 All ER 341, [1977] 2 WLR 169, (1977) 64 Cr App R 186.

50, came to live with them and their son Cyril. She suffered from anorexia nervosa and so often denied herself food and stayed in her room for days at a time. Once she was found by the police wandering the street and the appellants then tried to find her doctor but were unable to do so. Fanny grew weaker and became confined to bed. The appellants did nothing to get help for her, despite requests from neighbours. Subsequently she was found dead: naked, very dirty and in appalling conditions. The appellants were convicted of manslaughter and appealed.

Lord Justice Geoffrey Lane

There is no dispute, broadly speaking, as to the matters on which the jury must be satisfied before they can convict of manslaughter in circumstances such as the present. They are: (1) that the defendant undertook the care of a person who by reason of age or infirmity was unable to care for himself; (2) that the defendant was grossly negligent in regard to his duty of care; (3) that by reason of such negligence the person died. It is submitted on behalf of the appellants that judge's direction to the jury with regard to the first two items was incorrect.

At the close of the Crown's case submissions were made to the judge that there was no, or no sufficient, evidence that the appellants, or either of them, had chosen to undertake the care of Fanny.

. . .

This court rejects that proposition. Whether Fanny was a lodger or not she was a blood relation of the appellant Stone; she was occupying a room in his house; Mrs Dobinson had undertaken the duty of trying to wash her, of taking such food to her as she required. There was ample evidence that each appellant was aware of the poor condition she was in by mid-July. It was not disputed that no effort was made to summon an ambulance or the social services or the police despite the entreaties of Mrs Wilson and Mrs West. A social worker used to visit Cyril [Stone's disabled son]. No word was spoken to him. All these were matters which the jury were entitled to take into account when considering whether the necessary assumption of a duty to care for Fanny had been proved.

This was not a situation analogous to the drowning stranger. They did make efforts to care. They tried to get a doctor; they tried to discover the previous doctor. Mrs Dobinson helped with the washing and the provision of food. All these matters were put before the jury in terms which we find it impossible to fault. The jury were entitled to find that the duty had been assumed. They were entitled to conclude that once Fanny became helplessly infirm, as she had by 19th July, the appellants were, in the circumstances, obliged either to summon help or else to care for Fanny themselves. . . .

Appeals against conviction dismissed. Appeal by the appellant Stone against sentence allowed; sentence varied (from three years to twelve months).

At the heart of this decision is the finding that Stone and Dobinson had voluntarily assumed responsibility to care for Fanny. The decision is highly controversial because of the low capabilities of the two accused. It appears they had enough difficulty looking after themselves effectively, let alone being expected to offer a reasonable level of care to Fanny. It is not clear from *Stone and Dobinson* what was crucial to the finding of a duty. Was it the biological relationship, the undertaking of especial responsibility for the victim's welfare, or a combination of these two factors?

(v) *Ownership or control of property*. It may be that if someone owns a piece of property and another person in his or her presence commits a crime using that property the owner is under a duty to seek to prevent the crime in so far as is reasonable.[27] There certainly have been some cases where the courts have found an owner criminally liable under such circumstances, although this is normally based on liability for aiding and abetting the other person.[28] For example, in *Tuck v Robson*[29] a publican failed to intervene to prevent customers on his premises drinking after hours. He was found to have aided and abetted their crime.[30] The precise scope of this duty is unclear until we have further guidance from the courts.[31]

(vi) *Continuing act*. The courts have held that some cases which appear to be cases involving omissions have, in fact, involved a 'continuing act'. This can be best explained by referring to an example. In *Fagan v Metropolitan Police Commissioner*[32] Fagan drove his car accidentally onto a policeman's foot. When the policeman asked him to remove it he refused to do so. Fagan was convicted but appealed on the basis that the only act he did was driving onto the foot and that was performed without *mens rea*. By the time he realized his car was on the foot (and he had *mens rea*) he was not doing an act. The Divisional Court, however, upheld Fagan's conviction on the basis that he was committing the *actus reus* of battery (exercising force on the policeman's foot) for the whole of the time he had his car on the constable's foot. Fagan was guilty once he was aware of the harm he was causing to the policeman because then he had both the *actus reus* and *mens rea* of the offence at the same time.[33]

(vii) *Creation of the danger*. Where someone has created a dangerous situation they may be under a duty to act to prevent harm resulting. The leading case on this is the following:

R v Miller
[1983] 2 AC 161 (HL)[34]

James Miller, who was drunk, fell asleep with a lighted cigarette in his hand in the house in which he was staying. He subsequently woke to discover that his cigarette had set his mattress on fire. He simply moved out of the room into a neighbouring room. He was convicted of arson. The Court of Appeal dismissed his appeal but gave leave to appeal to the House of Lords, certifying the following question of law: 'whether the actus reus of the offence of arson is present when a defendant accidentally starts a fire and thereafter, intending to destroy or

---

[27] Ashworth (1989: 446).
[28] An accessory is someone who, e.g., assists another in the commission of a crime.
[29] [1970] 1 WLR 741.
[30] Another example can be found in *DuCros v Lambourne* (1907) 1 KB 40.
[31] It may be argued that one neighbour owes a limited duty to another neighbour, e.g. to ensure that a fire does not spread from his or her house: Wilson (2003: 88), relying on the tort case of *Smith v Littlewoods* [1987] 1 All ER 710 (HL).
[32] [1969] 1 QB 439.
[33] See p. 176 for a discussion of the requirement that the *mens rea* and *actus reus* coincide in time.
[34] [1983] 1 All ER 978, [1983] 2 WLR 539, (1983) 77 Cr App R 17.

damage property belonging to another or being reckless as to whether any such property would be destroyed or damaged, fails to take any steps to extinguish the fire or prevent damage to such property by that fire?'

Lord Diplock

. . .

The first question to be answered where a completed crime of arson is charged is: did a physical act of the accused start the fire which spread and damaged property belonging to another . . . ?

The first question is a pure question of causation. It is one of fact to be decided by the jury in a trial on indictment. It should be answered No if, in relation to the fire during the period starting immediately before its ignition and ending with its extinction, the role of the accused was at no time more than that of a passive bystander. In such a case the subsequent questions to which I shall be turning would not arise. The conduct of the parabolical priest and Levite on the road to Jericho may have been indeed deplorable, but English law has not so far developed to the stage of treating it as criminal and if it ever were to do so there would be difficulties in defining what should be the limits of the offence.

If, on the other hand, the question, which I now confine to: 'Did a physical act of the accused start the fire which spread and damaged property belonging to another?', is answered 'Yes', as it was by the jury in the instant case, then for the purpose of the further questions the answers to which are determinative of his guilt of the offence of arson, the conduct of the accused, throughout the period from immediately before the moment of ignition to the completion of the damage to the property by the fire, is relevant so is his state of mind throughout that period.

Since arson is a result-crime the period may be considerable, and during it the conduct of the accused that is causative of the result may consist not only of his doing physical acts which cause the fire to start or spread but also of his failing to take measures that lie within his power to counteract the danger that he has himself created. And if his conduct, active or passive, varies in the course of the period, so may his state of mind at the time of each piece of conduct. If, at the time of any particular piece of conduct by the accused that is causative of the result, the state of mind that actuates his conduct falls within the description of one or other of the states of mind that are made a necessary ingredient of the offence of arson by s 1(1) of the Criminal Damage Act 1971 (i.e. intending to damage property belonging to another or being reckless whether such property would be damaged), I know of no principle of English criminal law that would prevent his being guilty of the offence created by that subsection. Likewise I see no rational ground for excluding from conduct capable of giving rise to criminal liability conduct which consists of failing to take measures that lie within one's power to counteract a danger that one has oneself created, if at the time of such conduct one's state of mind is such as constitutes a necessary ingredient of the offence. I venture to think that the habit of lawyers to talk of 'actus reus', suggestive as it is of action rather than inaction, is responsible for any erroneous notion that failure to act cannot give rise to criminal liability in English law.

No one has been bold enough to suggest that if, in the instant case, the accused had been aware at the time that he dropped the cigarette that it would probably set fire to his mattress and yet had taken no steps to extinguish it he would not have been guilty of the offence of arson, since he would have damaged property of another being reckless whether any such property would be damaged.

I cannot see any good reason why, so far as liability under criminal law is concerned, it should matter at what point of time before the resultant damage is complete a person becomes aware that he has done a physical act which, whether or not he appreciated that it would at the time when he did it, does in fact create a risk that property of another will be damaged, provided that, at the moment of awareness, it lies within his power to take steps, either himself or by calling for the assistance of the fire brigade if this be necessary, to prevent or minimise the damage to the property at risk.

. . .

The recorder, in his lucid summing up to the jury (they took 22 minutes only to reach their verdict), told them that the accused, having by his own act started a fire in the mattress which, when he became aware of its existence, presented an obvious risk of damaging the house, became under a duty to take some action to put it out. The Court of Appeal upheld the conviction, but its ratio decidendi appears to be somewhat different from that of the recorder. As I understand the judgment, in effect it treats the whole course of conduct of the accused, from the moment at which he fell asleep and dropped the cigarette onto the mattress until the time the damage to the house by fire was complete, as a continuous act of the accused, and holds that it is sufficient to constitute the statutory offence of arson if at any stage in that course of conduct the state of mind of the accused, when he fails to try to prevent or minimise the damage which will result from his initial act, although it lies within his power to do so, is that of being reckless whether property belonging to another would be damaged.

My Lords, these alternative ways of analysing the legal theory that justifies a decision which has received nothing but commendation for its accord with common sense and justice have, since the publication of the judgment of the Court of Appeal in the instant case, provoked academic controversy. Each theory has distinguished support. Professor J C Smith espouses the 'duty theory' (see [1982] Crim LR 526 at 528) Professor Glanville Williams who, after the decision of the Divisional Court in *Fagan v Metropolitan Police Comr* [1968] 3 All ER 442, [1969] 1 QB 439 appears to have been attracted by the duty theory, now prefers that of the continuous act (see [1982] Crim LR 773). When applied to cases where a person has unknowingly done an act which sets in train events that, when he becomes aware of them, present an obvious risk that property belonging to another will be damaged, both theories lead to an identical result and, since what your Lordships are concerned with is to give guidance to trial judges in their task of summing up to juries, I would for this purpose adopt the duty theory as being the easier to explain to a jury though I would commend the use of the word 'responsibility', rather than 'duty' which is more appropriate to civil than to criminal law since it suggests an obligation owed to another person, i.e. the person to whom the endangered property belongs, whereas a criminal statute defines combinations of conduct and state of mind which render a person liable to punishment by the state itself.

Appeal dismissed.

This case was a difficult one for the House of Lords. The problem was the requirement that the *actus reus* and *mens rea* of the offence must exist at the same moment of time (see p. 176 below). At first sight in *Miller* the *actus reus* was the dropping of the cigarette, setting off the fire, but at that point there was no *mens rea*. However, at the time when the defendant had the *mens rea* (when he realized there was a fire) he was not doing anything. The House of Lords upheld the conviction by finding that Miller was under a duty to stop the fire because he had started it and that on leaving the room in breach of his duty to act he was therefore committing the *actus reus* of the offence.

(viii) *Novel situations.* It seems that the list of exceptions is not necessarily a closed list. The courts may be willing to create new circumstances under which there is a duty to act.[35]

QUESTIONS

1. Lord Diplock in *Miller* acknowledged that there were two ways of explaining why Miller was liable: (a) the duty theory (Miller was under a duty to stop the fire because he had started it (albeit unintentionally)); (b) the continuing act theory (Miller's initial act was regarded as a continuing act until the result was produced). Which of the two theories do you think a jury would more readily understand?

2. In *Khan and Khan* ([1998] Crim LR 830 (CA)) the defendants supplied a 15-year-old girl with some heroin. It seems that she had not tried the drug before. She took twice the normal amount and collapsed in a coma. The defendants left without summoning medical help and she died. Do you think the defendants had a duty to summon help? (Without deciding the question the Court of Appeal suggested that it 'may be correct that such a duty does arise'.)

3 What is required if there is a duty to act?

The simple answer to this question is that the defendant must do what is reasonable. What is reasonable will be decided by the jury. If a mother finds her child drowning in a shallow pond and she can easily save her child she should do so and if she does not she will have committed the offence of murder or manslaughter. If, however, the child is drowning in a tempestuous sea and she can attempt to rescue the child only by placing her own life in grave danger there is no legal obligation to do so. It may be that the reasonable thing to do is not to rescue the victim but to summon help. In *Singh (Gurphal)*[36] a landlord and his agent were responsible for failing to bring in experts when tenants complained that their gas fires were not working properly and subsequently a tenant died from escaping carbon monoxide.

One issue that is not yet resolved is whether the defendant is required to do what is reasonable *for him or her* or what would be reasonable for an ordinary person in his or her shoes. The Court of Appeal in *Stone and Dobinson*,[37] quoted above, did not directly address the issue, but seemed to ignore the defendant's disabilities and require the defendants to act as ordinary people.

It must be shown that the omission caused the harm. In other words, had the defendant acted reasonably in accordance with his or her duty the harm would not have occurred. For example, in *Dalloway*[38] the defendant was driving a cart without keeping a proper grip on

---

[35] Although it might be argued that to do so would constitute retrospective legislation and so be in breach of Art. 6 of the European Convention on Human Rights (ECHR). In *CR v UK* [1996] 1 FLR 434 the European Court of Human Rights held that case-by-case development of the common law by analogy with established cases would not necessarily constitute retrospective legislation.

[36] [1999] Crim LR 58 (CA). [37] [1977] QB 354 (CA). [38] (1847) 2 Cox CC 273.

the reins. A young child ran out in front of the cart and was killed. It was held that if the defendant was to be convicted it had to be shown that had he been driving properly and holding onto the reins he would have been able to avoid injuring the child.[39] Similarly if a father sees his child drowning in a pond and does nothing to help he is not criminally responsible for causing the child's death if it is shown that even if he had tried to save the child it would have been too late to do so.[40]

4 Distinguishing between omissions and acts

Although the law draws a sharp line between acts and omissions there can be great difficulties in distinguishing between the two. This has led some commentators to question whether it is proper to place so much weight on the distinction. Andrew Ashworth argues, 'although there are some clear cases of omission and some cases of act, there are many ambiguous cases in which the act–omission distinction should not be used as a cloak for avoiding the moral issues.'[41] An example of the difficulty in drawing the distinction between acts and omissions is *Speck*.[42] In that case a child innocently placed her hand on a man's genital area and he did nothing to move her hand. Was this an act or an omission by the man? It was held in effect to be an act by the man, although it might more naturally be regarded as an omission.

A leading case demonstrating the difficulty in drawing the distinction between acts and omissions is *Bland*. In order to understand the House of Lords' judgments it is necessary to appreciate two important points of medical law. The first is that a doctor must not force the treatment on a patient who is competent and refuses to consent, even if without the care the patient will die.[43] The second is that if a patient is unable to express a view a doctor must act in the best interests of the patient.[44] As the reasoning in *Bland* demonstrates, this does not mean that everything must be done to prolong the life of the patient. Sometimes it will be in the patient's interests not to receive treatment which could prolong a painful life, but this does not permit a doctor to do an act to end a patient's life.

Airedale NHS Trust v Bland
[1993] AC 789 (HL)[45]

Tony Bland, then aged 17, was horrifically injured at a disaster at the Hillsborough football ground. He was diagnosed as suffering from a condition known as persistent vegetative state. The medical opinion was that there was no hope of any improvement in his condition or recovery. The consultant in charge of his case, with the support of his parents, sought from the court a declaration permitting the discontinuation of all life-sustaining treatment.

---

[39] There is some debate over whether it needs to be shown that if the defendant had acted as he ought the victim would not have suffered the harm, or whether it is enough that there is evidence that the victim might not have suffered the harm. In *Marby* (1882) 8 QBD 571 the defendant was convicted of manslaughter, after failing to summon medical help which *might* have saved the life of the victim.

[40] He may, nevertheless, be guilty of the offence of child neglect (Children and Young Persons Act 1933, s. 1), for failing to ensure that the child did not get into a dangerous situation.

[41] Ashworth (2003: 113).   [42] [1977] 2 All ER 859 (CA).   [43] *St George's v S* [1999] Fam 26 (CA).

[44] *Re F (Mental Patient: Sterilisation)* [1990] 2 AC 1.

[45] [1993] 1 All ER 821, [1993] 2 WLR 316, [1993] Crim LR 877.

Lord Keith of Kinkel

Where one individual has assumed responsibility for the care of another who cannot look after himself or herself, whether as a medical practitioner or otherwise, that responsibility cannot lawfully be shed unless arrangements are made for the responsibility to be taken over by someone else. Thus a person having charge of a baby who fails to feed it, so that it dies, will be guilty at least of manslaughter. The same is true of one having charge of an adult who is frail and cannot look after herself: *Reg. v. Stone* [1977] Q.B. 354. It was argued for the guardian ad litem, by analogy with that case, that here the doctors in charge of Anthony Bland had a continuing duty to feed him by means of the nasogastric tube and that if they failed to carry out that duty they were guilty of manslaughter, if not murder. This was coupled with the argument that feeding by means of the nasogastric tube was not medical treatment at all, but simply feeding indistinguishable from feeding by normal means. As regards this latter argument, I am of opinion that regard should be had to the whole regime, including the artificial feeding, which at present keeps Anthony Bland alive. That regime amounts to medical treatment and care, and it is incorrect to direct attention exclusively to the fact that nourishment is being provided. In any event, the administration of nourishment by the means adopted involves the application of a medical technique. But it is, of course, true that in general it would not be lawful for a medical practitioner who assumed responsibility for the care of an unconscious patient simply to give up treatment in circumstances where continuance of it would confer some benefit on the patient. On the other hand a medical practitioner is under no duty to continue to treat such a patient where a large body of informed and responsible medical opinion is to the effect that no benefit at all would be conferred by continuance. Existence in a vegetative state with no prospect of recovery is by that opinion regarded as not being a benefit, and that, if not unarguably correct, at least forms a proper basis for the decision to discontinue treatment and care: *Bolam v. Friern Hospital Management Committee* [1957] 1 W.L.R. 582.

Given that existence in the persistent vegetative state is not a benefit to the patient, it remains to consider whether the principle of the sanctity of life, which it is the concern of the state, and the judiciary as one of the arms of the state, to maintain, requires this House to hold that the judgment of the Court of Appeal was incorrect. In my opinion it does not. The principle is not an absolute one. It does not compel a medical practitioner on pain of criminal sanctions to treat a patient, who will die if he does not, contrary to the express wishes of the patient. It does not authorise forcible feeding of prisoners on hunger strike. It does not compel the temporary keeping alive of patients who are terminally ill where to do so would merely prolong their suffering. On the other hand it forbids the taking of active measures to cut short the life of a terminally ill patient. In my judgment it does no violence to the principle to hold that it is lawful to cease to give medical treatment and care to a P.V.S. patient who has been in that state for over three years, considering that to do so involves invasive manipulation of the patient's body to which he has not consented and which confers no benefit upon him.

Lord Goff of Chieveley

. . . I start with the simple fact that, in law, Anthony is still alive. It is true that his condition is such that it can be described as a living death; but he is nevertheless still alive. This is because, as a result of developments in modern medical technology, doctors no longer associate death exclusively with breathing and heart beat, and it has come to be accepted that death occurs when the brain, and in particular the brain stem, has been destroyed: see

Professor Ian Kennedy's paper entitled 'Switching off Life Support Machines: The Legal Implications', reprinted in *Treat Me Right, Essays in Medical Law and Ethics*, (1988), especially at pp. 351–352, and the material there cited. There has been no dispute on this point in the present case, and it is unnecessary for me to consider it further. The evidence is that Anthony's brain stem is still alive and functioning and it follows that, in the present state of medical science, he is still alive and should be so regarded as a matter of law.

It is on this basis that I turn to the applicable principles of law. Here, the fundamental principle is the principle of the sanctity of human life—a principle long recognised not only in our own society but also in most, if not all, civilised societies throughout the modern world, as is indeed evidenced by its recognition both in article 2 of the European Convention for the Protection of Human Rights and Fundamental Freedoms (1953) (Cmd. 8969), and in article 6 of the International Covenant of Civil and Political Rights 1966.

But this principle, fundamental though it is, is not absolute. Indeed there are circumstances in which it is lawful to take another man's life, for example by a lawful act of self-defence, or (in the days when capital punishment was acceptable in our society) by lawful execution. We are not however concerned with cases such as these. We are concerned with circumstances in which it may be lawful to withhold from a patient medical treatment or care by means of which his life may be prolonged. But here too there is no absolute rule that the patient's life must be prolonged by such treatment or care, if available, regardless of the circumstances.

First, it is established that the principle of self-determination requires that respect must be given to the wishes of the patient, so that if an adult patient of sound mind refuses, however unreasonably, to consent to treatment or care by which his life would or might be prolonged, the doctors responsible for his care must give effect to his wishes, even though they do not consider it to be in his best interests to do so: see *Schloendorff v. Society of New York Hospital* (1914) 105 N.E. 92, 93, per Cardozo J.; *S. v. McC. (orse S.) and M. (D.S. Intervener); W. v. W.* [1972] A.C. 24, 43, per Lord Reid; and *Sidaway v. Board of Governors of the Bethlem Royal Hospital and the Maudsley Hospital* [1985] A.C. 871, 882, per Lord Scarman. To this extent, the principle of the sanctity of human life must yield to the principle of self-determination (see ante, pp. 826H–827A, per Hoffmann L.J.), and, for present purposes perhaps more important, the doctor's duty to act in the best interests of his patient must likewise be qualified. On this basis, it has been held that a patient of sound mind may, if properly informed, require that life support should be discontinued: see *Nancy B. v. Hotel-Dieu de Quebec* (1992) 86 D.L.R. (4th) 385. Moreover the same principle applies where the patient's refusal to give his consent has been expressed at an earlier date, before he became unconscious or otherwise incapable of communicating it; though in such circumstances especial care may be necessary to ensure that the prior refusal of consent is still properly to be regarded as applicable in the circumstances which have subsequently occurred: see, e.g., *In re T. (Adult: Refusal of Treatment)* [1993] Fam. 95. I wish to add that, in cases of this kind, there is no question of the patient having committed suicide, nor therefore of the doctor having aided or abetted him in doing so. It is simply that the patient has, as he is entitled to do, declined to consent to treatment which might or would have the effect of prolonging his life, and the doctor has, in accordance with his duty, complied with his patient's wishes.

But in many cases not only may the patient be in no condition to be able to say whether or not he consents to the relevant treatment or care, but also he may have given no prior indication of his wishes with regard to it. In the case of a child who is a ward of court, the court itself will decide whether medical treatment should be provided in the child's best interests, taking into account medical opinion. But the court cannot give its consent on behalf of an adult patient who is incapable of himself deciding whether or not to consent to treatment. I am of the opinion that there is nevertheless no absolute obligation upon the doctor who has the patient in his care to prolong his life, regardless of the circumstances. . . .

I must however stress, at this point, that the law draws a crucial distinction between cases in which a doctor decides not to provide, or to continue to provide, for his patient treatment or care which could or might prolong his life, and those in which he decides, for example by administering a lethal drug, actively to bring his patient's life to an end. As I have already indicated, the former may be lawful, either because the doctor is giving effect to his patient's wishes by withholding the treatment or care, or even in certain circumstances in which (on principles which I shall describe) the patient is incapacitated from stating whether or not he gives his consent. But it is not lawful for a doctor to administer a drug to his patient to bring about his death, even though that course is prompted by a humanitarian desire to end his suffering, however great that suffering may be: see *Reg. v. Cox* (unreported), 18 September 1992. So to act is to cross the Rubicon which runs between on the one hand the care of the living patient and on the other hand euthanasia—actively causing his death to avoid or to end his suffering. Euthanasia is not lawful at common law. It is of course well known that there are many responsible members of our society who believe that euthanasia should be made lawful; but that result could, I believe, only be achieved by legislation which expresses the democratic will that so fundamental a change should be made in our law, and can, if enacted, ensure that such legalised killing can only be carried out subject to appropriate supervision and control. It is true that the drawing of this distinction may lead to a charge of hypocrisy; because it can be asked why, if the doctor, by discontinuing treatment, is entitled in consequence to let his patient die, it should not be lawful to put him out of his misery straight away, in a more humane manner, by a lethal injection, rather than let him linger on in pain until he dies. But the law does not feel able to authorise euthanasia, even in circumstances such as these; for once euthanasia is recognised as lawful in these circumstances, it is difficult to see any logical basis for excluding it in others.

At the heart of this distinction lies a theoretical question. Why is it that the doctor who gives his patient a lethal injection which kills him commits an unlawful act and indeed is guilty of murder, whereas a doctor who, by discontinuing life support, allows his patient to die, may not act unlawfully—and will not do so, if he commits no breach of duty to his patient? Professor Glanville Williams has suggested (see his *Textbook of Criminal Law*, 2nd ed. (1983), p. 282) that the reason is that what the doctor does when he switches off a life support machine 'is in substance not an act but an omission to struggle,' and that 'the omission is not a breach of duty by the doctor, because he is not obliged to continue in a hopeless case.'

I agree that the doctor's conduct in discontinuing life support can properly be categorised as an omission. It is true that it may be difficult to describe what the doctor actually does as an omission, for example where he takes some positive step to bring the life support to an end. But discontinuation of life support is, for present purposes, no different from not initiating life support in the first place. In each case, the doctor is simply allowing his patient to die in the sense that he is desisting from taking a step which might, in certain circumstances, prevent his patient from dying as a result of his pre-existing condition; and as a matter of general principle an omission such as this will not be unlawful unless it constitutes a breach of duty to the patient. I also agree that the doctor's conduct is to be differentiated from that of, for example, an interloper who maliciously switches off a life support machine because, although the interloper may perform exactly the same act as the doctor who discontinues life support, his doing so constitutes interference with the life-prolonging treatment then being administered by the doctor. Accordingly, whereas the doctor, in discontinuing life support, is simply allowing his patient to die of his pre-existing condition, the interloper is actively intervening to stop the doctor from prolonging the patient's life, and such conduct cannot possibly be categorised as an omission. The distinction appears, therefore, to be useful in the present context in that it can be invoked to explain how discontinuance of life support can be differentiated from ending a patient's life by a lethal injection. But in the end the reason for that difference is that, whereas the law considers that discontinuance of life support may be consistent with the doctor's duty to care for his patient, it does not, for reasons of policy, consider that it forms any part of his duty to give his patient a lethal injection to put him out of his agony.

Lord Mustill

After much expression of negative opinions I turn to an argument which in my judgment is logically defensible and consistent with the existing law. In essence it turns the previous argument on its head by directing the inquiry to the interests of the patient, not in the termination of life but in the continuation of his treatment. It runs as follows. (i) The cessation of nourishment and hydration is an omission not an act. (ii) Accordingly, the cessation will not be a criminal act unless the doctors are under a present duty to continue the regime. (iii) At the time when Anthony Bland came into the care of the doctors decisions had to be made about his care which he was unable to make for himself. In accordance with *In re F* [1990] 2 A.C. 1 these decisions were to be made in his best interests. Since the possibility that he might recover still existed his best interests required that he should be supported in the hope that this would happen. These best interests justified the application of the necessary regime without his consent. (iv) All hope of recovery has now been abandoned. Thus, although the termination of his life is not in the best interests of Anthony Bland, his best interests in being kept alive have also disappeared, taking with them the justification for the non-consensual regime and the co-relative duty to keep it in being. (v) Since there is no longer a duty to provide nourishment and hydration a failure to do so cannot be a criminal offence.

My Lords, I must recognise at once that this chain of reasoning makes an unpromising start by transferring the morally and intellectually dubious distinction between acts and omissions into a context where the ethical foundations of the law are already open to question. The opportunity for anomaly and excessively fine distinctions, often depending more on the way in which the problem happens to be stated than on any real distinguishing features, has been exposed by many commentators, including in England the authors above-mentioned, together with *Smith & Hogan on Criminal Law*, 6th ed. (1988), p. 51, H. Beynon at [1982] Crim.L.R. 17 and M.J. Gunn and J.C. Smith at [1985] Crim.L.R. 705. All this being granted we are still forced to take the law as we find it and try to make it work. Moreover, although in cases near the borderline the categorisation of conduct will be exceedingly hard, I believe that nearer the periphery there will be many instances which fall quite clearly into one category rather than the other. In my opinion the present is such a case, and in company with Compton J. in *Barber v. Superior Court of State of California*, 195 Cal.Rptr. 484, 490 amongst others I consider that the proposed conduct will fall into the category of omissions.

I therefore consider the argument to be soundly-based. Now that the time has come when Anthony Bland has no further interest in being kept alive, the necessity to do so, created by his inability to make a choice, has gone; and the justification for the invasive care and treatment, together with the duty to provide it have also gone. Absent a duty, the omission to perform what had previously been a duty will no longer be a breach of the criminal law. . . .

Speeches were also given by **Lord Lowry** and **Lord Browne-Wilkinson** agreeing that the appeal should be dismissed.

Appeal dismissed.

QUESTIONS

1. Professor Smith asks: 'If a doctor is keeping a patient alive by cranking the handle of a machine and he stops, this looks like a clear case of omission. So too if the machine is electrically operated but switches it off every 24 hours and the doctor deliberately does not restart it. Switching off a functioning machine looks like an act; but is it any different in substance from the first two cases?' (J.C. Smith (2002: 64).

2. Lord Goff in *Bland* stated: 'I also agree that the doctor's conduct is to be differentiated from that of, for example, an interloper who maliciously switches off a life support machine because, although the interloper may perform exactly the same act as the doctor who discontinues life support, his doing so constitutes interference with the life-prolonging treatment then being administered by the doctor. Accordingly, whereas the doctor, in discontinuing life support, is simply allowing his patient to die of his pre-existing condition, the interloper is actively intervening to stop the doctor from prolonging the patient's life, and such conduct cannot possibly be categorised as an omission.' Does it make sense that a happening which is regarded as an action when done by one person (an interloper) is regarded as an omission when done by another (a doctor)?

2.2 SITUATIONAL OFFENCES

Analogous to offences involving omissions are cases where the defendant is guilty for being in a particular situation or state of affairs.[46] Examples are being drunk while in charge of a vehicle,[47] or possessing a drug[48] or offensive weapon.[49] (Possession offences will be discussed further in Chapter 4.) Such offences can be seen as being compatible with the voluntary act requirement as they will at least involve an earlier act. Take being drunk in charge of a vehicle. It can be said that getting drunk and getting into a vehicle are acts.

A particularly controversial case concerning a situational offence was *Larsonneur*,[50] in which the defendant was convicted of the offence of being found in the United Kingdom while being 'an alien to whom leave to land in the United Kingdom had been refused', contrary to Articles 1(3) and 18(1)(b) of the Aliens Order 1920, as amended. The case was controversial because the defendant was in the UK only because she had been forcibly returned to the UK by the Irish police.[51] Whether it was correct to punish her when she had performed no voluntary act to put herself in the criminal situation is hotly debated.[52]

---

[46] See generally Glazebrook (1978: 108).   [47] Road Traffic Act 1988, s. 4(2).
[48] Misuse of Drugs Act 1971.   [49] Prevention of Crime Act 1953.
[50] (1933) 149 LT 542.   [51] The background to the case is explained in Lanham (1976).
[52] See also *Winzar v Chief Constable of Kent, The Times*, 28 Mar. 1983.

2.3 LIABILITY FOR THE ACTS OF OTHER PEOPLE

There are certain circumstances under which a party is criminally responsible for the acts of a third party. In such a case a defendant is not punished for his or her own acts, but the acts of someone else. Two examples are particularly relevant: vicarious liability and the doctrine of innocent agency. Under vicarious liability an employer, under certain circumstances, may be criminally responsible for the acts of an employee. This is explored further in Chapter 4. Under the doctrine of innocent agency if A causes B (who is insane or a child) to cause harm to another then A can be made criminally responsible for the consequences of B's act. The doctrine of innocent agency is discussed in Chapter 15.

3 CAUSATION

We mentioned earlier that for some crimes it is necessary to show not only that the defendant performed an act, but that that act caused a particular consequence. For example, in murder it must be proved that the accused has caused the death of the victim. In many cases causation will be straightforward. If the defendant chops off the victim's head and the victims dies, it will be hard to deny that the defendant has caused the victim's death. It is only where there is a rather unusual set of facts that there is any dispute over the question. The most difficult cases are ones where it is not clear which of two people caused the result.

Imagine the following scenario:

> David, who was abused by his father as a child, has recently been made redundant by his employer and turned to drink. After a heavy drinking session Victor hurls a racial insult at him. David flies into a rage and stabs Victor. A passer-by phones for an ambulance, which takes a long time to arrive because of traffic jams and bad weather. When Victor arrives at the hospital there is a long delay before he is seen by a doctor because of the staff shortages in the NHS. By then Victor has died.

Who or what caused Victor's death? It would be possible to blame David; David's father; David's employer; the brewery who produced the alcohol he drank or the pub which sold it to him; Victor for the racial insult; the government for failing to prevent traffic congestion or fund the NHS adequately; the NHS trust at the relevant hospital; or even God for the weather! Indeed it would not be surprising if a doctor; a sociologist; a lawyer; a politician; a theologian; a member of the public all answered the question: 'who caused Victor's death?' in different ways. The important point to make is that there is no magic formula to answer the question correctly; rather the law must decide which of the many possible approaches to take.

The courts have consistently stated that causation is simply a matter of common sense and it is not a question of philosophical analysis. Stephen Shute has explained, 'the law tends to regard causation in terms of broad generalisations based on common sense principles, rather than attempting to mimic the more obscure approach to causation often taken by the philosopher or the scientist'.[53] Therefore the courts tend to see causation as a question of fact for the jury. However, it is not always that straightforward and the House of Lords has recently acknowledged that sometimes it is necessary for a judge to direct the jury to apply

---

[53] Shute (1992: 584).

special legal rules and not just leave the causal question to the common sense of the jury.[54] Indeed if it is clear to the judge that in law the defendant could not be said to have caused the result the judge should withdraw the case from the jury.[55]

At the heart of the law's understanding of causation is an assumption that each person is responsible for his or her actions. Arguments such as 'my background made me act this way' or 'society caused me to do this' carry no weight in the law's understanding of causation. The effect of this is that if there is an act of an individual immediately connected to the result the law's analysis stops. The individual caused the result and there is no need to ask if anything made him or her act that way or inquire into the reasons for his or her action.

Although the issue of causation is a legal one the judiciary appears to apply the rules flexibly. Some commentators feel that in fact policy issues and moral judgements affect the law's attitude to causation. In other words the questions 'should the defendant be held responsible for this result?' and 'did the defendant legally cause the result?' merge together. We will consider this further in Part II of this chapter.

It is now necessary to look at the law's understanding of causation and start by considering factual or 'but for' causation.

3.1 FACTUAL OR 'BUT FOR' CAUSATION

DEFINITION

'But for' causation: the defendant's act is a but for cause of a result, if, but for the defendant's act, the result would not have occurred.

'But for' or factual causation is an important aspect of the criminal law on causation.[56] Something cannot be a legal cause unless it is a factual cause; but it does not follow that just because an act is a factual cause that it is also a legal cause. The test for factual causation requires the jury to consider whether 'but for' the defendant's unlawful actions[57] the harm would have occurred at the same time and in the same way that it did. Contrast these two cases:

(1) In *Dyson*[58] the victim was dying from meningitis when Dyson injured him. The victim died as a result of the injuries. The evidence was that because of the injuries the victim died sooner than he would have done from the meningitis. Dyson could be held to have caused the victim's death. But for Dyson's actions the victim would not have died *at the time and place that he did.*[59]

(2) In *White*[60] the defendant put poison into the victim's drink. The victim suffered a heart attack, having taken a few sips. Medical evidence suggested that the poison was

---

[54] *Empress Car Co (Abertillery) Ltd v National Rivers Authority* [1998] 1 All ER 481 (HL) (extracted below). See also *Paggett* (1983) 76 Cr App R 279 (CA) (extracted below).

[55] *Malcherek* [1981] 2 All ER 422 (CA).   [56] This is sometimes known as *sine qua non* causation.

[57] Remember the point made in *Dalloway* (1847) 2 Cox CC 273 that it must be shown that, had the defendant acted lawfully, the harm would not have occurred (see p. 94).

[58] [1908] 2 KB 959 (CA).

[59] There was, however, no conviction for manslaughter because the victim did not die within a year and a day of the defendant's actions. That year and a day rule is no longer part of the law (Law Reform (Year and a Day Rule) Act 1996).

[60] [1910] 2 KB 124 (CA).

unrelated to the heart attack. The victim would have died in exactly the same way and at the same time had the defendant not put the poison in the drink, and therefore it could not be said that the defendant was a factual cause of the death.

Factual causation cannot be used as the general rule for causation, however, because it is far too wide.[61] For example, in a murder case a defendant's parents could be said to have caused a victim's death: 'but for' the defendant's parents bringing him into the world the victim would not have died. However, 'but for' causation is useful in that it tells us who *cannot* be regarded as a cause of death. If the victim would have died in the same way and at the same time had the defendant not been there then the defendant can not be said to have caused the death in the eyes of the law.[62]

3.2 THE KEY TEST FOR LEGAL CAUSATION

From the factual causes the law selects the one or ones which are the legal cause. A legal cause is 'an operating and substantial cause'. The Court of Appeal in *Mellor* stressed that there may be several operating and substantial causes of the result.[63] So, the mere fact that both the defendant and another person contributed to the harm does not mean that the defendant cannot be responsible. What do the two terms substantial and operating mean?

(1) *Substantial.* The defendant's act must be a substantial cause of the result. It must contribute to the end result to a significant extent,[64] not be a 'slight or trifling link'.[65] It must make more than an 'insubstantial or insignificant contribution'.[66] Imagine Edwin stabbed Thelma in the leg and then Fred shot her and medical evidence established that she had died from the shot, but as she had been slightly weakened by the stabbing she died a second earlier than she would have done without the stab wound. In such a case, the stabbing would be regarded as a minimal contribution to the death and so not a cause. The courts have avoided speaking in mathematical terms. In *Hennigan*[67] a judge who directed the jury that a defendant was not guilty if he was less than one-fifth to blame was held to have given a misdirection.

(2) *Operating.* The defendant's act must be an operating cause of the result. The most common way for a defendant to deny that his or her act was an operating cause is to argue that there has been a 'break in the chain of causation' or a *novus actus interveniens*. This means that the act of someone else has taken over responsibility for the chain of events and the defendant is no longer responsible. For example, if Martin stabbed Simon, but then Nick shot Simon dead, Nick's shooting would be a *novus actus interveniens* and Martin would not be responsible for Simon's death. Martin would however still be guilty of the stabbing.

---

[61] Padfield (1995: 684).

[62] Though see Cane (2002: 120) who discusses whether a 'necessary element of a sufficient set' ('a NESS cause') should be regarded as a factual cause. A NESS cause is a cause which was a necessary element in a set of conditions that were together sufficient to amount to the harm. This would mean that if a victim received two fatal wounds at the same time, both wounds could be seen as causes, even though 'but for' each individual wound the victim would have died from the other at the same time.

[63] See also *Benge* (1865) 4 F & F 504.   [64] *Cheshire* [1991] 3 All ER 670 (CA).

[65] *Kimsey* [1996] Crim LR 35 (CA).   [66] *Cato* [1976] 1 All ER 260 (CA).

[67] [1971] 3 All ER 133.

It is necessary to take a further look at the notion of a *novus actus interveniens*. It is useful to distinguish three different situations: where it is the acts of a third party which break the chain; where it is the victim's acts which are said to break the chain; and where it is a 'natural event' or 'act of God' which is said to break the chain.

3.3 ACTS OF THIRD PARTIES BREAKING THE CHAIN OF CAUSATION

EXAMINATION TIP

If you are dealing with a question in which A injured the victim and then B inflicted a further injury on the victim after which the victim died, the following would be four possible results a court could reach:

(i) If the evidence was that the victim died as a combination of both injuries it could be found that both A and B caused the death.

(ii) It could be found that B's act was a *novus actus interveniens* so A no longer could be said to have caused the death, but B could.

(iii) It could be that B's act was of negligible effect (e.g. if B had only scratched the victim), then it may be found that A caused the death, but B did not.

(iv) It could be found that neither of the acts caused the death, for example if the victim died from a heart attack unconnected with either injury.

You should consider which of these possibilities covers the set of facts you are dealing with.

As the above indicates, if two people both harm the victim there are a number of different legal interpretations of what has happened. Here we will concentrate on where one person's act is a *novus actus interveniens* and breaks the chain of causation.

DEFINITION

A *novus actus interveniens*: a free voluntary act of a third party which renders the original act no longer a substantial and operating cause of the result.

The following two cases[68] outline the approach the courts have taken to claims that a third party broke the chain of causation:

R v Pagett
(1983) 76 Cr App R 279 (CA)[69]

The appellant (David Pagett) shot at police officers who were seeking to arrest him for various offences. He used a 16-year-old woman (Gail Kinchen) as a human body shield. The officers returned fire and she was killed. The trial judge directed the jury that if the appellant had fired first and his act caused the officers to fire back lawfully, and as a result Gail was killed, then they could find that the defendant had caused her death. Pagett appealed on the basis that the judge's direction on causation was wrong and that the police officers' actions had broken the chain of causation.

---

[68] For a discussion of *Cheshire* see Stannard (1992).   [69] [1983] Crim LR 393.

Lord Justice Robert Goff (delivering the judgment of the Court)

. . . In cases of homicide, it is rarely necessary to give the jury any direction on causation as such. Of course, a necessary ingredient of the crimes of murder and manslaughter is that the accused has by his act caused the victim's death. But how the victim came by his death is usually not in dispute. What is in dispute is more likely to be some other matter: for example, the identity of the person who committed the act which indisputably caused the victim's death; or whether the accused had the necessary intent; or whether the accused acted in self-defence, or was provoked. Even where it is necessary to direct the jury's minds to the question of causation, it is usually enough to direct them simply that in law the accused's act need not be the sole cause, or even the main cause, of the victim's death, it being enough that his act contributed significantly to that result. It is right to observe in passing, however, that even this simple direction is a direction of law relating to causation, on the basis of which the jury are bound to act in concluding whether the prosecution has established, as a matter of fact, that the accused's act did in this sense cause the victim's death. Occasionally, however, a specific issue of causation may arise. One such case is where, although an act of the accused constitutes a *causa sine qua non* of (or necessary condition for) the death of the victim, nevertheless the intervention of a third person may be regarded as the sole cause of the victim's death, thereby relieving the accused of criminal responsibility. Such intervention, if it has such an effect, has often been described by lawyers as a *novus actus interveniens*. We are aware that this time-honoured Latin term has been the subject of criticism. We are also aware that attempts have been made to translate it into English; though no simple translation has proved satisfactory, really because the Latin term has become a term of art which conveys to lawyers the crucial feature that there has not merely been an intervening act of another person, but that that act was so independent of the act of the accused that it should be regarded in law as the cause of the victim's death, to the exclusion of the act of the accused. At the risk of scholarly criticism, we shall for the purposes of this judgment continue to use the Latin term.

Now the whole subject of causation in the law has been the subject of a well-known and most distinguished treatise by Professors Hart and Honoré, *Causation in the Law*. Passages from this book were cited to the learned judge, and were plainly relied upon by him; we, too, wish to express our indebtedness to it. It would be quite wrong for us to consider in this judgment the wider issues discussed in that work. But, for present purposes, the passage which is of most immediate relevance is to be found in Chapter XII, in which the learned authors consider the circumstances in which the intervention of a third person, not acting in concert with the accused, may have the effect of relieving the accused of criminal responsibility. The criterion which they suggest should be applied in such circumstances is whether the intervention is voluntary, i.e. whether it is 'free, deliberate and informed.' We resist the temptation of expressing the judicial opinion whether we find ourselves in complete agreement with that definition; though we certainly consider it to be broadly correct and supported by authority. Among the examples which the authors give of non-voluntary conduct, which is not effective to relieve the accused of responsibility, are two which are germane to the present case, viz. a reasonable act performed for the purpose of self-preservation, and an act done in performance of a legal duty.

There can, we consider, be no doubt that a reasonable act performed for the purpose of self-preservation, being of course itself an act caused by the accused's own act, does not operate as a *novus actus interveniens*. If authority is needed for this almost self-evident proposition, it is to be found in such cases as *Pitts* (1842) C. & M. 284, and *Curley* (1909) 2 Cr. App. R. 96. In both these cases, the act performed for the purpose of self-preservation consisted of an act by the victim in attempting to escape from the violence of the accused, which in fact resulted in the victim's death. In each case it was held as a matter of law that, if the victim acted in a reasonable attempt to escape the violence of the accused, the death of the victim was caused by the act of the accused. Now one form of self-preservation is self-defence; for present purposes, we can see no distinction in principle between an attempt to escape the consequences of the accused's act, and a response which takes the form of self-defence. Furthermore, in our judgment, if a reasonable act of self-defence against the act of the accused causes the death of a third party, we can see no reason in principle why the act of self-defence, being an involuntary act caused by the act of the accused, should relieve the accused from criminal responsibility for the death of the third party. Of course, it does not necessarily follow that the accused will be guilty of the murder, or even of the manslaughter, of the third party; though in the majority of cases he is likely to be guilty at least of manslaughter. Whether he is guilty of murder or manslaughter will depend upon the question whether all the ingredients of the relevant offence have been proved; in particular, on a charge of murder, it will be necessary that the accused had the necessary intent . . .

In cases where there is an issue whether the act of the victim or of a third party constituted a *novus actus interveniens*, breaking the causal connection between the act of the accused and the death of the victim, it would be appropriate for the judge to direct the jury, of course in the most simple terms, in accordance with the legal principles which they have to apply. It would then fall to the jury to decide the relevant factual issues which, identified with reference to those legal principles, will lead to the conclusion whether or not the prosecution have established the guilt of the accused of the crime of which he is charged. . . .

Appeal dismissed.

QUESTION

In *Pagett* the Court of Appeal suggested that the police officers were not acting voluntarily. In what sense were they not acting voluntarily? Should the court have paid more attention to the question whether the police officers were grossly negligent in killing Gail Kinchen?

R v Cheshire
[1991] 3 All ER 670 (CA)[70]

David Cheshire (the appellant) shot the victim (Trevor Jeffrey) in the leg and stomach during an argument in the Ozone fish and chip shop. The victim was taken to hospital and placed in intensive care. A tracheotomy tube was inserted in his windpipe because he was having breathing difficulties. Two months after the shooting the victim died because the windpipe had narrowed where the tracheotomy had been performed. This was a rare but not unknown complication of such a procedure. The defendant was convicted of murder. He appealed on the basis that the trial judge had wrongly directed the jury that only if the medical treatment could be described as reckless could the appellant be said not to have caused the victim's death.

[70] [1991] 1 WLR 844, (1991) 93 Cr App R 251.

Lord Justice Beldam

In the criminal law, and in particular in the law of homicide, whether the death of a deceased was the result of the accused's criminal act is a question of fact for the jury, but it is a question of fact to be decided in accordance with legal principles explained to the jury by the judge.

[Having quoted from Hart and Honoré's *Causation in the Law*, Bedlam LJ continued] As Professors Hart and Honoré comment, treatment which falls short of the standard expected of the competent medical practitioner is unfortunately only too frequent in human experience for it to be considered abnormal in the sense of extraordinary. Acts or omissions of a doctor treating the victim for injuries he has received at the hands of an accused may conceivably be so extraordinary as to be capable of being regarded as acts independent of the conduct of the accused but it is most unlikely that they will be.

We have not been referred to any English authority in which the terms of the direction which should be given to a jury in such a case have been considered. We were referred to *R v Jordan* (1956) 40 Cr App R 152, in which the appellant, who had been convicted of murder, sought leave to call further evidence about the cause of the victim's death. The application was granted and evidence was received by the court that the stab wound from which the victim died eight days later was not the cause of the victim's death. The deceased had died from the effects of sensitivity to Terramycin which had been given to him after his intolerance to it was established and in abnormal quantity. The court considered that the introduction into the system of the victim of a substance shown to be poisonous to him and in quantities which were so great as to result in pulmonary oedema leading to pneumonia were factors which ought to have been before the jury and which in all probability would have affected their decision.

R v Jordan was described in the later cause of *R v Smith* [1959] 2 QB 35 as a very particular case dependent upon its exact facts. The appellant in *R v Smith* had been convicted at court-martial of the murder of another soldier by stabbing him. The victim had been dropped twice while being taken to the medical reception station and was subsequently given treatment which was said to be incorrect and harmful. Lord Parker CJ, giving the judgment of the Court Martial Appeal Court, rejected a contention that his death did not result from the stab wound. He said ([1959] 2 QB 35 at 42–43):

'It seems to the court that, if at the time of death the original wound is still an operating cause and a substantial cause, then the death can properly be said to be the result of the wound, albeit that some other cause of death is also operating. Only if it can be said that the original wounding is merely the setting in which another cause operates can it be said that the death does not result from the wound. Putting it in another way, only if the second cause is so overwhelming as to make the original wound merely part of the history can it be said that the death does not flow from the wound.'

Both these cases were considered by this court in *R v Malcherek, R v Steel* [1981] 2 All ER 422, in which it had been argued that the act of a doctor in disconnecting a life support machine had intervened to cause the death of the victim to the exclusion of injuries inflicted by the appellants. In rejecting this submission Lord Lane CJ, after considering *R v Jordan* and *R v Smith*, said: ([1981] 2 All ER 422 at 428):

'In the view of this court, if a choice has to be made between the decision in *R v Jordan* and that in *R v Smith*, which we do not believe it does (*R v Jordan* being a very exceptional case), then the decision in *R v Smith* is to be preferred.'

Later in the same judgment Lord Lane CJ said ([1981] 2 All ER 422 at 428–429):

'There may be occasions, although they will be rare, when the original injury has ceased to operate as a cause at all, but in the ordinary case if the treatment is given bona fide by competent and careful medical practitioners, then evidence will not be admissible to show that the treatment would not have been administered in the same way by other medical practitioners. In other words, the fact that the victim has died, despite or because of medical treatment for the initial injury given by careful and skilled medical practitioners, will not exonerate the original assailant from responsibility for the death.'

In those two cases it was not suggested that the actions of the doctors in disconnecting the life support machines were other than competent and careful. The court did not have to consider the effect of medical treatment which fell short of the standard of care to be expected of competent medical practitioners.

[Having considered passages from the judgments in the Supreme Court of Victoria in *R v Evans and Gardiner (No 2)* [1976] VR 523, Bedlam LJ continued:]

. . . It seems to us that these two passages demonstrate the difficulties in formulating and explaining a general concept of causation but what we think does emerge from this and the other cases is that when the victim of a criminal attack is treated for wounds or injuries by doctors or other medical staff attempting to repair the harm done, it will only be in the most extraordinary and unusual case that such treatment can be said to be so independent of the acts of the accused that it could be regarded in law as the cause of the victim's death to the exclusion of the accused's acts.

Where the law requires proof of the relationship between an act and its consequences as an element of responsibility, a simple and sufficient explanation of the basis of such relationship has proved notoriously elusive.

In a case in which the jury have to consider whether negligence in the treatment of injuries inflicted by the accused was the cause of death we think it is sufficient for the judge to tell the jury that they must be satisfied that the Crown have proved that the acts of the accused caused the death of the deceased, adding that the accused's acts need not be the sole cause or even the main cause of death, it being sufficient that his acts contributed significantly to that result. Even though negligence in the treatment of the victim was the immediate cause of his death, the jury should not regard it as excluding the responsibility of the accused unless the negligent treatment was so independent of his acts, and in itself so potent in causing death, that they regard the contribution made by his acts as insignificant.

It is not the function of the jury to evaluate competing causes or to choose which is dominant provided they are satisfied that the accused's acts can fairly be said to have made a significant contribution to the victim's death. We think the word 'significant' conveys the necessary substance of a contribution made to the death which is more than negligible.

. . . Although for reasons we have stated we think that the judge erred when he invited the jury to consider the degree of fault in the medical treatment rather than its consequences, we consider that no miscarriage of justice has actually occurred. Even if more experienced doctors than those who attended the deceased would have recognised the rare complication in time to have prevented the deceased's death, that complication was a direct consequence of the appellant's acts, which remained a significant cause of his death. We cannot conceive that, on the evidence given, any jury would have found otherwise.

Accordingly, we dismiss the appeal.

Appeal dismissed.

So the principles from these cases appear straightforward. If A does an act after which B does an act, then if B's act is:

(1) a free, voluntary, and informed act; and

(2) it renders A's act no longer a substantial and operating cause,

A will not have caused the result.[71] B's act will be a *novus actus interveniens*.
More needs to be said about these requirements.

A free, voluntary, informed act

Only the free, voluntary, and informed acts of a third party will break the chain of causation. What then will constitute a free, voluntary, informed act? The following points will be of some assistance:

(1) Where a person, D, is not acting voluntarily his or her 'action' will not be a *novus actus interveniens*. So if Guy pushes Mary into Ivy who suffers injuries then Guy is said to have caused the injuries, as Mary was not acting in a voluntary way and so her 'act' could not be regarded as a *novus actus interveniens*. It is not quite clear how far this may be taken. In *Wise v Dunning*[72] a religious preacher gave an anti-Catholic speech. He realized that there were Catholics in the audience and that they would react violently to his speech, which they did. The court was willing to accept that the preacher caused the spontaneous violence. It seems the court took the view that the violence was an instinctive reaction of the listeners, and so was not truly voluntary. Some commentators regard this case as stretching the meaning of 'voluntary' too far.

(2) Where a person is acting in a way which is justified her action is not free, voluntary, or informed.[73] To give three examples:

(a) If someone is acting in order to preserve his or her own life or limb the act will not be free, voluntary, or informed. So if Tim throws an object at Penelope who, in order to protect herself, deflects the object but it then hits Fred, Tim will be said to have caused Fred's injuries. Penelope's act will not break the chain of causation, because she was justified in acting as she did.[74]

(b) If someone is acting in order to assist law enforcement this will not be a break in the chain of causation. So where Tom is committing a crime and a police officer, in a genuine attempt to stop the crime taking place, injures a passer-by, Tom will be said to have caused the injuries.[75]

(c) It may be that acts in accordance with a moral obligation will not break the chain of causation. For example, if a passer-by came across an injured person and tried to administer first aid, but did so in such a way that in fact the victim died, the passer-by's act may not break the chain of causation.[76] Certainly sound medical practice will not break the chain of causation. In *Malcherek and Steel*[77] a doctor who switched off a life-support machine in accordance with approved medical procedures was held not to have caused the patient's death.

---

[71] *R v Latif* [1996] 1 All ER 353 (HL) Lord Steyn (at 364) stated: 'The general principle is that the free deliberate and informed intervention of a second person, who intends to exploit the situation created by the first, but is not acting in concert with him, is held to relieve the first actor of criminal responsibility.'

[72] [1902] 1 KB 167.　　　[73] *Latif* [1996] 1 All ER 353 (HL).　　　[74] *Scott v Shepherd* (1773) 96 ER 525.

[75] *Pagett* (1983) 76 Cr App R 279 (CA). Contrast *Latif* [1996] 1 All ER 353 (HL).

[76] Hart and Honoré (1985: 335).　　　[77] [1981] 1 WLR 690 (CA).

(3) If a person does not know the circumstances of his action it may not break the chain of causation. If Charles posts a parcel bomb which is delivered by Tina (a postal worker) and injures someone, Charles will be said to have caused the injury. Although the delivery of the bomb by Tina was free and voluntary it was not 'informed'.[78]

Rendering the defendant's action no longer an operating and substantial cause

To amount to a *novus actus interveniens* the act of the third party must have rendered the defendant's original act no longer an operating and substantial cause. Many of the cases have involved a defendant who has injured a victim, the victim has then received bad medical treatment and died. The defendant then claims that the bad medical treatment the victim subsequently received broke the chain of causation. The courts have been very reluctant to accept such arguments. They have clearly been persuaded by the response that the victim would not have required medical treatment had the defendant not injured him or her. It therefore hardly lies in the mouth of the defendant to complain about the standard of the medical treatment he or she necessitated. Indeed it has been suggested that bad medical treatment cannot be regarded as 'abnormal'. Inevitably in busy hospitals treatment of emergencies cannot always be of the highest possible standard.[79]

One of the very few cases where medical treatment did break the chain of causation was *R v Jordan*.[80] Here the defendant stabbed the victim. The victim was taken to hospital, where the wound had almost healed when a doctor administered a drug to which the victim was allergic. The drug killed the victim. The court heard evidence that the doctor should have known that the victim was intolerant to the drug. The Court of Appeal held that the medical treatment and not the defendant caused the death of the victim. There were two crucial facts in the case which led to this conclusion:

(1) The original wound had virtually healed at the time of death. In medical terms the wound inflicted by the defendant had not contributed to the death of the deceased.

(2) The treatment provided by the hospital was 'abnormal': 'palpably wrong' or 'grossly negligent'. It should have been known by the doctor that the victim was intolerant to the antibiotic.

Of course, although Jordan was held not to be responsible for the death he was still responsible for the original assault.

Jordan has been regarded as exceptional: only in the most unusual of circumstances will medical treatment, however negligent, break the chain of causation. A more representative example of the case law is *Cheshire*,[81] excerpted above, where, even though the treatment was not as it should have been, it did not break the chain of causation. In *Malcherek*[82] D inflicted wounds upon P, who had to be put on a life support machine. Several days later the machine was switched off by doctors. The Court of Appeal accepted that there was no doubt that the injury was an operating and substantial cause of the death. After all, what did the victim die from when the machine was switched off, if not the injuries inflicted by the defendant?

---

[78] Similarly if D is a child or suffers from a mental illness his actions will not be free, voluntary, and informed.

[79] Stannard (1992: 582).   [80] (1956) 40 Cr App R 152 (CA).

[81] *Cheshire* [1991] 3 All ER 670 (CA).   [82] [1981] 2 All ER 422 (CA).

William Wilson[83] has suggested that in a case where a victim suffers death in hospital it is necessary to distinguish two kinds of cases:

(1) the death of the victim was a result of bad medical treatment which was attempting to treat the victim's injuries. In such a case the treatment must be palpably wrong if it is to break the chain of causation; and

(2) the death of the victim was caused by things done in a hospital not connected to treatment of the injuries inflicted by the defendant (e.g. food poisoning from the hospital food; catching a disease from a fellow patient; a doctor deliberately harming a victim out of maliciousness), which do not have to be palpably wrong to break the chain of causation.

The argument behind this distinction is that although the defendant can reasonably be said to have necessitated the provision of medical treatment there is a looser connection between the defendant and other things that may happen to the victim in hospital. Although the courts have not been explicit in drawing such a distinction, they may well be attracted to such an approach in an appropriate case.

QUESTIONS

1. In *Bush v Commonwealth* 78 Ky 268 (1880) (Kentucky Court of Appeals) the defendant injured the victim. A medical officer then attended the victim and inadvertently infected him with scarlet fever and he died of that. Did the defendant cause the victim's death?

2. In *Martin* (1827) 172 ER 390 a father offered his son a sip from his alcoholic drink, but the child took the whole drink and died. This was held not to be foreseeable (perhaps surprisingly!) and so the father had not caused the death. Do you think the same result would be reached today?

3.4 OMISSIONS OF THIRD PARTIES BREAKING THE CHAIN OF CAUSATION

Although the courts have not said so explicitly, it is submitted that omissions of a third party cannot break the chain of causation. This is because an omission cannot render the defendant's act no longer an operating and substantial cause. If the defendant stabbed the victim, who was taken to hospital but died because no medical treatment was offered, then the defendant would be said to have caused the death.[84]

3.5 CASES WHICH DO NOT FIT INTO THE TRADITIONAL ANALYSIS

Although what has been said is widely supported by academic commentators there have been several cases recently which do not sit easily with the law as it has been generally understood. They have all involved cases where drug dealers have given drugs to the victims who have injected themselves and died. The dealers have then been charged with manslaughter. Based on the principles outlined above it might have been thought that the courts would hold that the decision of the victims to inject themselves were free voluntary

---

[83] Wilson (2003: 112–13).   [84] In such a case it is arguable that the hospital trust also caused the death.

and informed acts and therefore broke the chain of causation. But this has not been the line taken by the courts. The leading case is now the following:

R v Kennedy (No. 2)
[2005] EWCA 685 [85]

Simon Kennedy had prepared a syringe of heroin for Marco Bosque. Bosque injected himself and died shortly after. Kennedy was charged with supplying a class A drug and manslaughter and convicted on both charges. On appeal the Court of Appeal held that the crucial question was whether the appellant could be held to be jointly responsible for carrying out the injection. This issue, it was felt, was adequately covered by the trial judge's direction and therefore the appeal was dismissed. Subsequently the Criminal Cases Review Commission referred the case back to the Court of Appeal on the basis that later cases had cast doubt on the reasoning of the original Court of Appeal case and that the judge had failed to adequately explain to the jury that the free voluntary informed act of the victim in injecting himself with heroin would break the chain of causation between the appellant's act of supplying the drugs and the victim's death.

LORD WOOLF CJ

. . .

Conclusions

51. In view of the conclusions that we have come to as a result of our examination of the authorities, it appears to us that it was open to the jury to convict the appellant of manslaughter. To convict, the jury had to be satisfied that, when the heroin was handed to the deceased 'for immediate injection', he and the deceased were both engaged in the one activity of administering the heroin. These were not necessarily to be regarded as two separate activities; and the question that remains is whether the jury were satisfied that this was the situation. If the jury were satisfied of this then the appellant was responsible for taking the action in concert with the deceased to enable the deceased to inject himself with the syringe of heroin which had been made ready for his immediate use.

52. In our view, the jury would have been entitled to find (and indeed it is an appropriate finding) that in these circumstances the appellant and the deceased were jointly engaged in administering the heroin. This was the conclusion of this court on the first appeal, as we understand Waller LJ's judgment, and we do not feel it necessary to take a different view, though we do accept that the issue could have been left by the trial judge to the jury in more clear terms than it was.

53. The point in this case is that the appellant and the deceased were carrying out a 'combined operation' for which they were jointly responsible. Their actions were similar to what happens frequently when carrying out lawful injections: one nurse may carry out certain preparatory actions (including preparing the syringe) and hand it to a colleague who inserts the needle and administers the injection, after which the other nurse may apply a plaster. In such a situation, both nurses can be regarded as administering the drug. They are working as a team. Both their actions are necessary. They are interlinked but separate parts in the overall process of administering the drug. In these circumstances, as Waller LJ stated on the first appeal, they 'can be said to be jointly responsible for the carrying out of that act'.

[85] [2005] 2 Cr App R 23, [2005] 1 WLR 2159.

54. Whether the necessary linkage existed between the actions of the appellant and the deceased was very much a matter for the jury to determine. The question then arises as to whether the trial judge in the summing up expressed the issue in sufficiently clear terms for the jury? As to this, we share similar reservations to those expressed by Waller LJ in his judgment on the first appeal. There was no need for the jury to find the encouragement that Waller LJ thought was necessary. However, the jury did have to find that the appellant and the deceased were acting in concert in administering the heroin.

Appeal dismissed.

It must be admitted that the notion of parties being jointly responsible for each other's actions is a novel one in the law of causation. In the following passage David Ormerod tries to make sense of the judgment, but it is critical of its reasoning.

D. Ormerod and R. Fortson, 'Drug Suppliers As Manslaughterers (Again)' [2005] *Criminal Law Review* 819 at 825–30

Kennedy No.2's 'joint responsibility' approach

Having rejected the radical Empress approach, the decision in *Kennedy* proceeds to sidestep the obstacle to conviction presented by the orthodox approach to causation. The court does so by propounding a controversial, and we submit unworkable approach to liability based on D's 'joint participation'. It suggests that if the role played by D, in concert with the deceased, amounts to a factual cause of the administering of the drug, or causing the drug to be administered to (or taken by) another, then D will have committed an offence under s.23, and the s.23 offence will therefore be the sufficient unlawful act for manslaughter. Despite having rejected the idea that D can be a secondary party to V's acts (there being no crime committed by V), the court then proceeds to adopt the language of participation:

'[If] the defendant participates in an offence involving the administration of the drug, there could be no question of difficulties in relation to causation.'

With respect, this approach is unconvincing and potentially unworkable for a number of reasons. First, it is unclear how this approach will assist the prosecution in proving the s.23 offence, at least if we adopt a natural interpretation of the concept of 'joint responsibility'. How does 'joint responsibility for carrying out that act' of injecting (para.30), or 'one activity of administering the heroin' (para.51) or 'working as a team' in a 'combined operation' (para.53), give rise to liability for D under s.23 if, an offence is only committed under that section if the administration etc. is to 'any other person'? Who is the 'other'? The Lord Chief Justice provides an example of a nursing team working together to prepare and administer an injection. But surely this works against his lordship's conclusion: the nursing 'team' is injecting 'another'—the patient. In the drug administration case D and V are acting in a team to inject one of their number, not 'another'. This objection is supported by the case law relating to supply of drugs.

Secondly, the nursing example demonstrates that the court is creating confusion by adopting not just the language but the reasoning of joint liability. After expressly rejecting the idea that D is liable as a secondary party the court's approach seems to lead to that same result. In the nursing example both nurses would be liable, one as a principal and one as an accessory. It may be that the court has applied its own understanding of what 'administers' means, so that both nurses are principals, and that D in the drug administration cases may also be held liable as a principal. Some jurisdictions have accepted that D can be liable as a principal where he acts in concert with P even though P is the direct perpetrator of the actus reus of the substantive offence. It is surely unthinkable that the Court of Appeal would have adopted such a revolutionary revision of the principles of secondary liability without acknowledging that it was doing so.

Thirdly, the 'joint responsibility' approach attempts to sidestep the causation problem rather than offer a much needed resolution of the scope and application of the general principles of causation in manslaughter cases. What is clear, although not made explicit by the court, is that the joint responsibility approach cannot be squared with the orthodox approach to causation outlined above. An individual, D, might be regarded as a factual cause of the prohibited result where his action combined with others brings about that result. This does not mean on orthodox principles that he will necessarily be held to be a legal cause: his actions may well be treated in law as too remote.

Fourthly, it is unclear to what extent the 'joint responsibility' approach is restricted to the facts of the case. It is important here to note the court's observation that the drugs were prepared 'for immediate injection'. Is the court aware that otherwise it would expose all drug dealers to manslaughter charges where a user died, and is it therefore trying to impose some limits on its novel method of securing convictions for manslaughter? This factual restriction on the limits of liability raises other interesting questions.

Where does liability, according to *Kennedy No.2*, begin? When D opens an injection pack, or when he cooks up the heroin, or when the heroin is loaded into the syringe? In *Kennedy* the trial judge had accepted that if all that could be established was that K had bought the syringe and water and cooked the heroin for MB, he must be acquitted. Most of the cases of this type involving manslaughter reported in the law reports concern heroin, but the principles articulated in *Kennedy* would seem to be relevant if a person dies as a result of ingesting another substance. All noxious substances in tablet form are prepared ready for 'immediate' ingestion—is that enough to found liability for the preparer?

Finally, unless *Kennedy No.2* is regarded as limited to its facts, or at least to this particular context of 'administering', the decision creates problems at a more fundamental level throughout the criminal law. It is unclear how we are to determine if other offences are capable of being committed by a 'team' in such a way as to render one member liable as principal. In addition, the case has serious implications for secondary liability. D who supplies the bullets for P's gun for him to murder V now becomes a murderer as a principal, not as an accessory. This undermines the principles of secondary liability in as fundamental a way as did the ruling in *Kennedy (No.1)*. Again, it is unclear to what extent this turns on the specific facts—the physical and temporal proximity of the supply? And/or whether the act can be said to be a 'team effort'? How significant is the Lord Chief Justice's remark that each element of the conduct is 'necessary' for the completion of the whole?

Further particular problems with the joint responsibility approach arise in the context of homicide. Where V states an intention to commit suicide and D (at V's request) hands him the syringe of morphine for V to self inject, D is liable as a principal of the statutory offence of aiding and abetting suicide. Parliament provided that specific offence in preference to D being made liable as a murderer or a manslaughterer. The result in *Kennedy (No.2)* means that D could be convicted of murder. The Lord Chief Justice denies that such a prosecution would occur, but the fact is that a prosecution might occur, and it is clear Parliament never intended that it would. More generally one might ask is it appropriate or even possible for the Court of Appeal to substitute the clear will of Parliament with a guarantee of a future stay of prosecution?

3.6 ACTS OF THE VICTIM BREAKING THE CHAIN

What about cases where the defendant alleges that the acts of the victim have broken the chain of causation? There are two leading cases on this which need to be contrasted, *Roberts* and *Blaue*:

R v Roberts
(1972) 56 Cr App R 117 (CA)

Kenneth Roberts was giving the victim a lift in his car after a party when he made indecent suggestions to her. He threatened her and started to touch her coat. She jumped out of the car injuring herself. Roberts was convicted of causing her actual bodily harm, contrary to section 47 of the Offences Against the Person Act 1861. The judge directed the jury that if they felt sure that the victim was induced to jump out of the car they should convict the defendant. Roberts appealed on the basis that the judge had misdirected the jury.

Lord Justice Stephenson

We have been helpfully referred to a number of reported cases, some well over a century old, of women jumping out of windows, or jumping or throwing themselves into a river, as a consequence of threats of violence or actual violence. The most recent case is the case of *Lewis* [1970] Crim. L. R. 647. An earlier case is that of *Beech* (1912) 7 Cr. App. R. 197, which was a case of a woman jumping out of a window and injuring herself, and of a man who had friendly relations with her, whom she knew and might have had reason to be afraid of, being prosecuted for inflicting grievous bodily harm upon her, contrary to section 20 of the Offences against the Person Act. In that case the Court of Criminal Appeal (at p. 200) approved the direction given by the trial judge in these terms:

'Will you say whether the conduct of the prisoner amounted to a threat of causing injury to this young woman, was the act of jumping the natural consequence of the conduct of the prisoner, and was the grievous bodily harm the result of the conduct of the prisoner?' That, said the Court, was a proper direction as far as the law went, and they were satisfied that there was evidence before the jury of the prisoner causing actual bodily harm to the woman. "No-one could say", said Darling J. when giving the judgment of the Court, "that if she jumped from the window it was not a natural consequence of the prisoner's conduct. It was a very likely thing for a woman to do as the result of the threats of a man who was conducting himself as this man indisputably was".'

This Court thinks that that correctly states the law, and that Mr. Carus was wrong in submitting to this Court that the jury must be sure that a defendant, who is charged either with inflicting grievous bodily harm or assault occasioning actual bodily harm, must foresee the actions of the victim which result in the grievous bodily harm, or the actual bodily harm. That, in the view of this Court, is not the test. The test is: Was it the natural result of what the alleged assailant said and did, in the sense that it was something that could reasonably have been foreseen as the consequence of what he was saying or doing? As it was put in one of the old cases, it had got to be shown to be his act, and if of course the victim does something so 'daft,' in the words of the appellant in this case, or so unexpected, not that this particular assailant did not actually foresee it but that no reasonable man could be expected to foresee it, then it is only in a very remote and unreal sense a consequence of his assault, it is really occasioned by a voluntary act on the part of the victim which could not reasonably be foreseen and which breaks the chain of causation between the assault and the harm or injury.

Appeal dismissed.

It should be noted that the test in *Roberts* is not whether the victim acted reasonably, but whether the reaction was reasonably foreseeable.[86] The significance of this distinction is that it is foreseeable that, put into an emergency situation, a victim may react irrationally. *Roberts* was approved by the Court of Appeal in *Williams and Davis,*[87] but with a slight modification of the test. It suggested the question for the jury in these kinds of cases was:

whether the deceased's reaction in jumping from the moving car was within the range of responses which might be expected from a victim placed in the situation in which he was. The jury should bear in mind any particular characteristic of the victim and the fact that in the agony of the moment he may act without thought and deliberation.

Roberts was also followed in the Court of Appeal's decision in *Marjoram*[88] which emphasized that when deciding whether the victim's reaction was reasonably foreseeable the question was whether the reaction was foreseeable to an ordinary person and not whether it was reasonably foreseeable to a person of the defendant's age and characteristics.

R v Blaue
[1975] 3 All ER 446 (CA)[89]

Robert Blaue stabbed Jacolyn Woodhead, piercing her lung. She was taken to hospital and was told that a blood transfusion was necessary. She refused to consent to the operation which was contrary to her beliefs as a Jehovah's Witness. She was told that without the transfusion she would die, but she stuck by her refusal and died the next day. The appellant was subsequently convicted of manslaughter, but appealed, arguing that the victim's refusal to have a blood transfusion broke the chain of causation between the stabbing and death.

Lord Justice Lawton

. . . The physical cause of death in this case was the bleeding into the pleural cavity arising from the penetration of the lung. This had not been brought about by any decision made by the deceased girl but by the stab wound.

Counsel for the appellant tried to overcome this line of reasoning by submitting that the jury should have been directed that if they thought the girl's decision not to have a blood transfusion was an unreasonable one, then the chain of causation would have been broken. At once the question arises—reasonable by whose standards? Those of Jehovah's Witnesses? Humanists? Roman Catholics? Protestants of Anglo-Saxon descent? The man

---

[86] Busutill and McCall Smith (1990).   [87] [1992] 2 All ER 183 (CA).
[88] *Marjoram* [2000] Crim LR 372 (CA).   [89] [1975] 1 WLR 1411, (1975) 61 Cr App R 271.

on the Clapham omnibus? But he might well be an admirer of Eleazar who suffered death rather than eat the flesh of swine (See 2 Maccabees, ch 6, vv 18–31) or of Sir Thomas Moore who, unlike nearly all his contemporaries, was unwilling to accept Henry VIII as Head of the Church in England. Those brought up in the Hebraic and Christian traditions would probably be reluctant to accept that these martyrs caused their own deaths.

As was pointed out to counsel for the appellant in the course of argument, two cases, each raising the same issue of reasonableness because of religious beliefs, could produce different verdicts depending on where the cases were tried. A jury drawn from Preston, sometimes said to be the most Catholic town in England, might have different views about martyrdom to [sic] one drawn from the inner suburbs of London. Counsel for the appellant accepted that this might be so; it was, he said, inherent in trial by jury. It is not inherent in the common law as expounded by Sir Matthew Hale and Maule J. It has long been the policy of the law that those who use violence on other people must take their victims as they find them. This in our judgment means the whole man, not just the physical man. It does not lie in the mouth of the assailant to say that his victim's religious beliefs which inhibited him from accepting certain kinds of treatment were unreasonable. The question for decision is what caused her death. The answer is the stab wound. The fact that the victim refused to stop this end coming about did not break the causal connection between the act and death. . . .

Appeal dismissed.

At first sight these two cases seem to be offering different tests. The *Blaue* decision focuses on the rule that defendants must take their victims as they find them, whatever their peculiarities. This is an application of the 'thin skull' rule, which will be discussed below.[90] The *Roberts* decision focuses on whether the victim's response was reasonably foreseeable. The two tests are quite different. Had the *Roberts* test been applied in the *Blaue* decision it might have been decided that it was not reasonably foreseeable that the victim would be a Jehovah's Witness and refuse a blood transfusion. Although the cases appear to conflict commentators have suggested a number of ways to reconcile them:

1. The crucial fact in the *Blaue* decision was that the victim's act was in effect an omission. She failed to consent to the blood transfusion. By contrast, in *Roberts* the victim acted by jumping out of the car. This interpretation suggests that the *Blaue* rule is that an omission of the victim will not break the chain of causation, whereas the *Roberts* rule explains that the act of a victim might, if the act was unforeseeable or 'daft'.[91] Such a position could be readily justified because it would fit in well with the criminal law's general approach of not attaching causal significance to omissions. Indeed the courts have consistently held that a victim who is injured by a defendant, but decides not to seek medical treatment and dies, will be found to have been killed by the defendant.[92] After all, if the victim neglects the injury and dies, what else does the victim die from, but the injury inflicted by the defendant? Although there is much to be said in favour of this argument, based on whether the victim performs an act or an omission, it must be admitted that it is not one that is made explicit by the courts themselves.

2. It might be argued that there is no conflict between the two approaches given the modification of the *Roberts* test in *Williams and Davis* which required the jury to consider

---

[90] *Martin* (1832) 5 C & P 128. For a case where the victim actually had a thin skull, see *Simpson* [2002] EWCA Crim 25, 14 Jan. 2002.

[91] Simester and Sullivan (2003: 95).   [92] *Holland* (1841) 2 Mood & R 351.

whether the response was reasonably foreseeable, *given the victim's characteristics*. In *Blaue* it was reasonably foreseeable that a victim with the characteristic of being a Jehovah's Witness would refuse a blood transfusion. The difficulty with such a test is that it could be argued that it will always be satisfied. In *Corbett*[93] it was held that the victim's conduct in running away and falling in front of a car was foreseeable, given that the victim was 'immensely drunk'. Further in *Blaue* the Court of Appeal did not rely on the argument that the victim acted as a reasonable Jehovah's Witness.

3. It may be argued *Blaue* was a special case which was in fact about freedom of religion. The argument could be that normally the jury should consider whether the victim's response was reasonably foreseeable, but that the court was unwilling to ask that question in *Blaue* because that might require the jury to consider whether the exercise of a religious belief was unreasonable.

A recent rather problematic decision which is not readily reconcilable with either *Roberts* or *Blaue* is *Dear*,[94] where the victim was stabbed by the defendant. The victim died from the wounds, although it was unclear whether the victim had reopened the wounds himself. With a minimum of discussion of the legal issues the Court of Appeal held that the jury were entitled to find that, even if the victim had deliberately reopened the wounds, the defendant's actions could be found to have been an operating and substantial cause of the victim's death. The point is that the victim had died from the blood seeping from the very wounds inflicted by the defendant.

QUESTIONS

1. Marion slashes Steve's face with a knife. Steve is a vain model and is so distressed with the resulting scar that he commits suicide. Has Marion caused Steve's death? Consider how the cases of *Roberts*, *Blaue*, and *Dear* could be relevant to this case.

2. Timothy stabs Yvonne. When Yvonne gets to hospital she is converted to the faith of the Jehovah's Witnesses by a nurse and therefore refuses to consent to a blood transfusion which is needed to save her life. Yvonne dies. Has Timothy caused Yvonne's death?

3.7 THE 'THIN SKULL' RULE

The 'thin skull' rule states that defendants must take their victims as they find them.[95] In other words, it is no defence for a defendant to say that the injuries or death were caused by the physical condition of the victim.[96] In *Hayward*[97] there was a violent argument between the defendant and his wife. Hayward chased his wife out of the house and she collapsed and died. The medical evidence suggested that the wife had an abnormal medical condition which meant that if she suffered fright or physical exertion she might die. Ridley J confirmed that the husband could be said to have caused the wife's death. The fact that the wife's death had resulted in part from her medical condition was irrelevant: the husband's act had caused her death. A less obvious application of the rule was *McKechnie*,[98] where, owing to

---

[93] [1996] Crim LR 594 (CA).   [94] [1996] Crim LR 595 (CA).
[95] Colvin (1991: 84) argues that there is no need for a 'special' rule because in all cases where the 'thin skull' rule is used, applying the 'operating and substantial cause' test would produce the same result.
[96] *Watson* [1989] 2 All ER 385 (CA).   [97] (1908) 21 Cox CC 692.
[98] (1992) 94 Cr App R 51 (CA).

the injuries inflicted by the defendant, the victim was not able to receive the medical treatment that he needed for an ulcer (which had nothing to do with the injuries caused by the defendant) and died as a result. It was held that the defendant had caused the victim's death.

3.8 A NATURAL EVENT ('ACTS OF GOD')

A natural event will not normally break the chain of causation. If the defendant injures the victim and leaves his or her body on the sea shore and the sea comes in and drowns the victim then the sea coming in does not break the chain of causation.[99] However, where there is a freak of nature this may break the chain of causation. Imagine that the defendant had injured the victim and left his body in a field, and a bolt of lightning came down and killed the victim. In such a case the bolt of lightning could constitute a break in the chain of causation because it would be an 'extraordinary' event.

3.9 INTENDED RESULTS

Some commentators have suggested that if a defendant acts intending to produce a particular result and that result occurs then the defendant will automatically be found to have caused that result.[100] It should be stressed that this would be true only if the 'but for' test were satisfied. Mary could not be convicted of John's murder if he died shortly after she had stuck pins into a voodoo doll of him, intending that this should lead to his death (assuming it cannot be proved that the voodoo caused the death!).

Despite some academic support for the proposition there is little case law on the point.[101] In *Michael*[102] the defendant wished her baby dead and so gave a bottle of poison to a nurse, saying that it was medicine for the baby. The nurse placed the medicine on the mantelpiece, unaware that it was poison. A 5-year-old child removed the poison and gave it to the baby. Even though the turn of events was unexpected, the end result was what the defendant wanted, and so she could be said to have caused it. However, the case can also be explained on the basis that the actions of the nurse and child were not free, voluntary, and informed actions and so could not be *novus actus interveniens*.

FURTHER READING

Hart, H., and Honoré, A. (1985), *Causation in the Law* (2nd edn., Oxford: OUP).

Heaton, R. (2003), 'Dealing in Death', *Criminal Law Review* 497.

—— (2004), 'Principals? No Principles!', *Criminal Law Review* 463.

Ormerod, D., and Fortson, R. (2005), 'Drug Suppliers As Manslaughterers (Again)', *Criminal Law Review* 819.

Padfield, N. (1995), 'Clean Water and Muddy Causation', *Criminal Law Review* 683.

---

[99] In *Hart* [1986] 2 NZLR 408 (NZCA) the New Zealand Court of Appeal found the defendant guilty on similar facts.

[100] See the discussion in J.C. Smith (2002: 55).

[101] Simester and Sullivan (2003: 92) argue that this rule is true only where there is no human *novus actus interveniens*.

[102] (1840) 9 C & P 356.

Shute, S. (1992), 'Causation: Foreseeability v Natural Consequences', *Modern Law Review* 55: 584.

Williams, G. (1957), 'Causation in Homicide', *Criminal Law Review* 429.

Williams, R. (2005a), 'Policy and Principle in Drugs Manslaughter Cases' *Cambridge Law Journal* 64: 66.

—— (2005b), 'Drugs Manslaughter and Unorthodox Doctrine on Causation', *Cambridge Law Journal* 64: 537.

PART II: *ACTUS REUS*: THEORY

4 CLASSIFICATION OF DEFENCES

As suggested at the start of this chapter, the most common way of analysing a criminal offence is to divide it into three elements:[103]

(1) the *actus reus*;

(2) the *mens rea*;

(3) defences which the defendant may rely on.

However, this is by no means the only way of separating out the elements of the offence. Andrew Ashworth, for example, uses four requirements:

(1) voluntary act requirements;

(2) absence of justification;

(3) positive fault requirements; and

(4) negative fault requirements.[104]

By contrast Glanville Williams argues that there are only two elements of an offence, the *actus reus* and *mens rea*.[105]

You may well be wondering whether it really matters very much how we divide up the elements of an offence and how we decide into which category a particular requirement falls.[106] Is this not just academics desperately trying to create a tidy picture of the criminal law? Well, there are both practical and theoretical benefits which some claim for such analysis. Here are some:

(1) Evidential rules. Such divisions may assist when considering burdens of proof. As a very basic rule the prosecution must prove beyond reasonable doubt the *actus reus*

---

[103] e.g. Lanham (1976).

[104] Ashworth (2003: 97). See p. 20 for discussion of P. Robinson (1997)'s proposed restructuring of criminal law.

[105] G. Williams (1961: 20) argues that defences are included in the meaning of the *actus reus*. Others claim that the *mens rea* involves blameworthiness and therefore includes both the required mental element and the absence of a defence: see e.g. Kadish (1968).

[106] See the discussion in P. Robinson (1993).

and *mens rea*. However, the defendant has an evidential burden in relation to a defence.[107] Unfortunately there are exceptions to this. For example, a justification (e.g. self-defence) has been regarded by the courts as an element of the *actus reus*,[108] but the defendant carries the evidential burden in relation to the justification.[109]

(2) Substantive law. There are some occasions on which the substantive law requires attention to whether or not the *actus reus* of the crime has occurred. For example, strict liability offences require proof of the *actus reus*, but not the *mens rea*.[110]

(3) It can be claimed that the distinction between *actus reus* and *mens rea* assists in theoretical analysis of offences in that it separates the issues: what is the wrong with which this offence is concerned (the *actus reus* question) and when will the defendant be held sufficiently blameworthy for the offence (the *mens rea* question).

Several commentators have objected to this kind of reasoning and claimed that the wrong done to the victim sometimes depends on the state of mind with which an act is done. Anthony Duff[111] gives an example: 'Robbery is not just a physical attack or threat, *plus* theft: the character of the attack or the threat as a particular kind of wrong is determined in crucial part by the fact that it is made in order to steal.' In his view, then, the definition of the wrong done to the victim can include elements of both the *actus reus* and *mens rea*.

FURTHER READING

Robinson, P. (1993), 'Should the Criminal Law Abandon the *Actus Reus/Mens Rea* Distinction?' in S. Shute, J. Gardner, and J. Horder (eds.), *Action and Value in Criminal Law* (Oxford: OUP).

—— (1997), *Structure and Function in Criminal Law* (Oxford: OUP).

Smith, A. (1978), 'On *Actus Reus* and *Mens Rea*' in P. Glazebrook (ed.), *Reshaping the Criminal Law* (London: Sweet & Maxwell).

5 THE NEED FOR A VOLUNTARY ACT

Contrast these two examples:

(1) Alfred was a mathematician and was so taken up with considering a novel algebraic problem that he did not look where he was going when he bumped into Beth.

(2) Chau was walking along when he was pushed from behind by Danielle, causing him to bump into Edith.

In both cases Alfred and Chau did not intend to bump into anyone. But there is an important difference between the cases. Although we can say that Alfred's acts caused Beth to fall over in case 1, it is not clear that Chau acted at all. Indeed Danielle was the one who acted and Chau was more like an object than a person.[112] Something was done *to him*, rather than

---

[107] i.e. the defendant must introduce some evidence in support of the defence. If he or she does so then the prosecution must prove beyond reasonable doubt that the defendant does not have the defence. See further p. 63 for a more detailed explanation of the different kinds of burdens of proof.

[108] *Williams (Gladstone)* [1987] 3 All ER 411 (CA).

[109] There is in fact a significant debate over whether a justification is better regarded as an aspect of the *actus reus* or as a defence (see p. 732).

[110] *Saunders* (1988).   [111] Duff (2002: 59).   [112] Hart (1968: 91–2).

something being done *by him*.[113] This distinction is reflected in legal terms by the fact that Alfred would be found not guilty because he lacked *mens rea*, while Chau would be found not guilty on the basis that he did not commit the *actus reus*.

As mentioned in Part I it is often stated that a defendant can be convicted of a crime only if he or she has performed a voluntary act.[114] But why might the law have such a requirement?

5.1 WHY MIGHT THE LAW HAVE A VOLUNTARY ACT REQUIREMENT?

One reason the law may require an act is the argument that the criminal law should not punish evil thoughts alone. But why not? Several reasons could be advanced for this:[115]

(1) Those who fantasize about crime have not done anything which is sufficiently harmful to society to justify criminalization. We do not punish people for being bad, but for doing bad things.[116]

(2) There would be enormous difficulties of proof if an offence was directed towards the thoughts of the defendant alone. Requiring an act lessens the chance of a wrongful conviction by demanding some outward manifestation of the wrongful thoughts.

(3) The requirement limits government power. Punishing people for their thoughts is normally associated with the most authoritarian of governments and is too open to manipulation by corrupt governments or officials who wish to punish those they perceive to be a threat to their power.[117]

Why must the act be voluntary? As indicated in our consideration of Alfred and Chau an involuntary action is one for which not only is the defendant not responsible, it is not even properly described as *his* act. It would clearly be unjust to punish a defendant for something he could not have avoided 'doing', even if he had tried his best.

5.2 WHAT IS THE 'VOLUNTARY ACT REQUIREMENT'?

The obvious meaning of the requirement is that any offence must involve proof that the defendant did something. But Donald Husak has argued that the requirement must mean more than that. His point is that an offence of 'thinking evil thoughts while knitting' is objectionable even though it involves proof of an act (namely knitting). The offence is still objectionable because it is the evil thoughts and not the act of knitting which the offence is actually seeking to prevent. Hence Husak argues that that criminal liability must be imposed '*for* an act'.[118]

---

[113] See Finkelstein (2002) for a discussion of defendants who voluntarily put themselves in a position where they act involuntarily.

[114] It is not always clear whether this is meant as a descriptive point (i.e. this is what the present law is) or a prescriptive one (i.e. this is what the present law should be).

[115] P. Robinson (1993) usefully summarizes these.

[116] M. Moore (1993: 51). This is most evident in the law on inchoate attempts which we will discuss in Ch. 14.

[117] In *Robinson v California* 370 US 660 (1962) the US Supreme Court held that a criminal offence of being addicted to drugs infringed the American constitution.

[118] Husak (1995a).

To understand the requirement further we need to consider what we mean by a voluntary act.[119]

The traditional view: acts as 'willed voluntary movements'

The traditional view is that actions are 'willed bodily movements'.[120] Although the traditional view has in recent years rather fallen into disrespect,[121] interest in it has been revitalized by an impressive and complex book in support, namely *Act and Crime* by Michael Moore.[122] In this passage he summarizes the traditional view:

M. Moore, *Act and Crime* (Oxford: OUP, 1993), 44–6

1. Preliminary Overview of the Act Requirement

As I would unpack it, there are four theses to this theory, as it was propounded by Bentham, (John) Austin, Holmes, and Walter Cook, and carried on into our own time by the American Law Institute's Model Penal Code. The four theses are as follows. First, what I shall call the identity thesis holds that the acts required for criminal liability are partially identical to events of a certain kind, namely, bodily movements like moving one's finger or tongue. Such bodily movements on which the act requirement focuses are the simplest things one knows how to do as a means to achieving some end. Raising one's arm, for example, is usually such a simple act because one doesn't do (or know how to do) some even more simple act in order to do it. If, however, one raises one's arm by moving one's foot on a pulley arrangement attached to the arm, then raising the arm on that occasion is not the act focused on by the act requirement of criminal law. *A fortiori*, if one's raising one's arm on some occasion is to signal the start of a race, so that in moving one's arm one was starting a race, the latter act is also not the act focused on by the criminal law's act requirement; for starting a race is far removed from the simplest act one knows how to do.

Secondly, the only acts that exist are the simple acts on which the act requirement focuses. Although there are complex acts of killing, hitting, scaring, telephoning, and the like, and although criminal codes invariably use these complex action descriptions in their substantive prohibitions, these acts in reality are never anything but some acts of bodily movement. I shall call this the exclusivity thesis.

Thirdly, not just any bodily movements (that are the simplest things one knows how to do) are acts satisfying the act requirement. A reflex movement of the leg, for example, is not an act no matter how identical it is behaviourally to simple leg movements that are acts. Thus, the third thesis—what I shall call the mental cause thesis—requires that such bodily movements must be caused by a certain mental event or state. Such event or state is variously styled as an act of willing, a volition, a desire, a simple intention, or a choice. Because all of these ordinary expressions have connotations inappropriate to this third thesis when it is most favourably construed, I shall use the least ordinary of the terms, 'volition'.

The three theses thus far, taken together, assert that the criminal law's act requirement requires that there be a simple bodily movement that is caused by a volition before criminal

---

[119] See Mackie (1977) for a wide-ranging discussion on acts and Hornsby (1993) and B. Williams (1997) for discussion of what an intentional act is.

[120] M. Moore (1993: 28). The theory goes back to Austin and Holmes, but requires a controversial separation to be drawn between the working of the mind and the body: see Ryle (1949).

[121] M. Moore (1994) responds to his many critics.

[122] See also M. Moore (1997) who places his theories of acts in a wider context.

liability attaches, and that such a movement is all the action a person ever performs. This is the positive core of the orthodox view of the criminal law's act requirement. The fourth thesis seeks to accommodate this univocal act requirement of the general part of the criminal law to the multiple, complex action descriptions used in the various prohibitions of the special part. Statutes almost never use simple action descriptions like 'moving one's finger'; they prohibit actions described as 'starting a race without a permit', 'killing', 'disfiguring', 'removing another's property', etc. For the act requirement just described to fit the criminal law as we know it, something must be said about how such diverse, complex action prohibitions are related to the univocal, simple act requirement. This is the burden of the fourth thesis.

This thesis asserts that any complex action description used in the special part of the criminal law is equivalent to (and thus can be replaced by) a description of some simple act (as defined above) of the accused causing a prohibited state of affairs. Murder statutes prohibit the complex action of killing another, for example. The fourth thesis—what I shall call the equivalence thesis—asserts that such a prohibition is equivalent to a prohibition that forbids 'any simple act that causes the death of another'.

Three objections to the traditional view will now be summarized:

(1) Defining an act as a willed voluntary movement can produce an artificial view of the world.[123] It would describe as 'moving a hand to the right' both a person doing an aerobic exercise and a person punching another. In other words by describing an action simply in terms of what movement was done without considering the context or consequences of that movement gives a misleading (or at least not very useful) description of what was done.[124] Indeed in our day-to-day lives we understand ourselves to be doing certain activities: for example, eating, walking, or talking; and not doing the separate bodily movements that make up those activities.[125]

In reply to such arguments Moore has suggested that his definition of an act describes what it is in our power to do. I can intend to move my arm to the left; whether it hits the person next to me is not something over which I have direct control. Therefore, we should not, he insists, include consequences in the definition of an action.

(2) A second objection is that the traditional view would not answer the point that people sometimes act on 'automatic pilot' when engaging in some routine act (e.g. shaving or eating) where it would be artificial to talk about such acts being willed. But it might be said that in such cases there is an 'unconscious will'[126] which is operating or that such actions *could have been* guided by decisions of the actor if he or she had wished, even if in fact they were not.[127]

(3) It can be argued that the traditional definition of an act may be too narrow, in that it excludes some omissions which would be quite properly described as 'acts'.[128] Consider a

---

[123] Husak (1995a) suggests that although the traditional view may have some merit for the purpose of philosophical discussion, it is not a useful one for criminal lawyers.

[124] Shapira (1998). Norrie (2000: ch. 9) argues that responsibility needs to be 'relationized' to give voice to the true context of the wrong.

[125] Hart (1968) and Melden (1968).

[126] Fletcher (1978: 434–9) is willing to include within the definition of a voluntary act defendants who have a conscious or unconscious reason for acting as they did.

[127] Duff and von Hirsch (1997).

[128] If a scientist can show that thoughts involve movement in the brain then the definition may be too wide. See the discussion in Mackay (1995: ch. 1).

meeting at which it was said that if anyone objected to a proposal they should raise their hand and everyone remained still. It would then be generally accepted that by not raising their hands those attending were supporting the motion, even if they had not moved; their non-movement would be regarded as an act of support for the motion.[129] Yet Moore, in requiring a movement, would say that they had not acted.

Alternatives to the traditional view

If we decide that the traditional view of the voluntary act requirement is not accepted what alternatives are there? The most popular has become known as 'the control principle': namely that it would be unjust to impose criminal liability for a state of affairs over which the defendant had no control.[130] In the following passage Andrew Simester summarizes the 'control principle' and then considers some of its practical implications. Notice that the 'control principle' makes it far easier to punish omissions than the 'voluntary act requirement' does:[131]

A.P. Simester, 'On the So-called Requirement for Voluntary Action' (1998) 1 *Buffalo Criminal Law Review* 403 at 414–18

The indispensable minimum, then, is to establish that D is responsible for the explicit or implicit behavior element of the actus reus, regardless of whether the behavior is named as an act or omission, and of whether D was an agent in respect of that behavior. This require-ment is met when D's behavior is voluntary. Recall our opening case scenario. [One fine September morning, Jim is discovered dead in his home. His skull has been crushed by a blow inflicted with a heavy object. The police are called. Upon further investigation, they establish that he was murdered by his daughter, Alice, who killed him in order to receive her inheritance under his will.] Suppose that Alice did in fact cause Jim's death, but that she did so while suffering an epileptic seizure, during which her movements caused a heavy object to fall and crush Jim. Alice's behavior, which causes Jim's death, is not voluntary. She is not morally responsible for his death, and cannot be convicted of murder.

Very often, acquittal in these circumstances need not be based upon involuntariness. Crimes such as murder require proof of some form of mens rea on the part of the defendant. In most jurisdictions, murder itself cannot be committed unless D intends or is reckless about the victim's death. Thus, even though Alice's behavior may have caused death, she lacks the mental element required to be guilty of murder.

But involuntariness is not merely a denial of intention, or of other forms of mens rea, or even a denial of fault in general. Alice does not claim that she killed Jim by accident. Her denial is much more profound. It is a claim that the movements of her body which caused Jim's death do not belong to Alice as a reasoning person.

As part of our conception of what it is to be a human being, we draw a distinction between a deliberative or reasoning person and her body. Not all movements of one's body can be identified with the person whose body it is that moves. When the doctor tests Simon's

---

[129] See for other examples Wilson (2002: 85). Some supporters of the traditional view argue that flexing muscles to stay still (e.g. a gymnast holding a position) can be regarded as movements.

[130] Husak (1999b); Simester (1998).

[131] Note, however, the argument in J. Gardner (1994b: 499) that the voluntary act requirement and the issue of whether liability should attach to omissions should be seen as quite distinct.

reflexes by tapping him on the knee, the swinging of his leg cannot be attributed to Simon. It is merely an event in the history of his body, rather like the lurching of passengers standing in a crowded bus. These are not actions that a person is answerable for doing; they are things that happen to him, over which he has no control, and for which he is not responsible. So it is with Alice. Her behavior is part of her body's history, but is not traceable to her as a reasoning person. It is not produced by any exercise of the capacities which mark Alice out as a moral agent. In the words of H.L.A. Hart:

'What is missing in these cases appears to most people as a vital link between mind and body; and both the ordinary man and the lawyer might well insist on this by saying that in these cases there is not "really" a human action at all and certainly nothing for which anyone should be made criminally responsible however "strict" legal responsibility may be.'

QUESTIONS

1. Is it wrong to assume that an act is either voluntary or involuntary? Would it be better to accept that there is a scale of voluntariness? Would doing so render the law too uncertain? (See Denno (2002).)

2. Is it possible to distinguish 'moral voluntariness' (where a defendant is under intense moral pressure, e.g. duress) and 'physical voluntariness' (where a defendant is physically unable to act otherwise than he did)? (See Norrie (2002: ch. 6).)

FURTHER READING

Hart, H. (1968), 'Acts of Will and Responsibility' in H. Hart, *Punishment and Responsibility* (Oxford: OUP).

Husak, D. (1999b), 'Does Criminal Liability Require an Act?' in A. Duff (ed.), *Philosophy and the Criminal Law* (Cambridge: CUP).

Moore, M. (1993), *Act and Crime* (Oxford: OUP).

Simester, A. (1998), 'On the So-called Requirement for Voluntary Action', *Buffalo Criminal Law Review* 1: 403.

Wilson, W. (2002), *Central Issues in Criminal Theory* (Oxford: Hart).

6 OMISSIONS

As we saw in Part I of this chapter, the criminal law is generally reluctant to impose criminal liability on a defendant who failed to act. It will do so only if there is a legal duty on the defendant to act.

6.1 SHOULD THE CRIMINAL LAW PUNISH OMISSIONS?

Despite the bitter arguments over the punishment of omissions in fact there is less disagreement than appears at first sight. Few people suggest that we should be guilty in relation to every omission, nor do many suggest that omissions should never be punished.[132] The debate is really over which omissions should be punished.[133]

Arguments against criminalizing omissions

It is argued by some that it cannot be said that an omission causes a result.[134] If a person walks past a drowning child in a pond can it be said that that person caused the child's death? Using 'but for' causation it can be argued that had the defendant not been there the child would still have died at the same time and in the same place. The omission failed to alter the status quo.[135] Further it could be argued that the person's failure to save the child was as significant as anyone else's failure to rescue.

Those who support liability for omission have struggled to overcome this argument. Hart and Honoré[136] explain that omissions liability can be supported by their distinction between normal and abnormal events (discussed further below). They suggest that if someone is under a duty to act and fails to do so this will be regarded as 'abnormal' and hence a cause of the result. For example, if several people walk past a child drowning in the pond, including the child's father, the fact that the father is under a duty to save the child in English law means that it is abnormal for him to walk past, while it would be 'normal' for others to walk past. This explanation is, however, problematic. It concerns an ambiguity over the meaning of 'normal'. If 'normal' means that an action is statistically likely, it is far from clear that statistically it is abnormal for people to help children in peril.[137] If normal means what 'ought' to occur then the argument simply becomes that people are punished for omissions because they ought to be.[138]

It is crucial to realize that this causation argument is not a 'knockout argument' for those who do not wish to punish omissions. The argument is simply stating that one cannot sensibly argue that an omission causes a result. That does not mean that the law cannot seek to punish omissions. The causation argument could not be used against a statute which stated that it was a criminal offence not to offer aid to someone you could reasonably be expected to help. Such a statute does not claim that the omission has caused anything—it punishes for the failure to act itself. In the following extract Joshua Dressler considers such laws which are often known as 'Bad Samaritan laws'.[139] You should note that in this passage 'BS laws' is Dressler's (rather unfortunate!) abbreviation for Bad Samaritan laws:[140]

[132] e.g., even Michael Moore, who is generally reluctant to punish omission, accepts that a parent who fails to feed his or her child deserves to be convicted (M. Moore (1993: 32)).
[133] Glazebrook (1960); Hogan (1986).
[134] M. Moore (1993: 267). See also the discussion in Hughes (1958) and Katz (1987b).
[135] Mack (1980).
[136] Hart and Honoré (1995: 31–2).
[137] Benyon (1987).
[138] M. Smith (2001) for further argument.
[139] The reference is to the parable of the Good Samaritan found in the Bible (Luke 10, 30–7) in which two people walked on past a man who had been mugged, but the Good Samaritan stopped to help him.
[140] McCall Smith (1993); Weinrib (1980); Lipkin (1983); Bagby (2000); Yeager (1993). For a more sceptical attitude to the duty to rescue, see Menlowe (1993) and Dressler (2000). Murphy (2001), Tomlinson (2000), and Hayden (2000) look at the existence of such statutes around the world.

J. Dressler, 'Some Brief Thoughts (Mostly Negative) About "Bad Samaritan" Laws'
[2000] *Santa Clara Law Review* 971 at 981–9

2. Refuting the Justifications for Bad Samaritan Laws

. . .

Criticisms of BS laws begin with legalist concerns with retributive overtones. First, why is the offense called a 'Bad Samaritan' law? The name suggests, I think, that we punish the bystander for being a bad person, i.e., for his 'selfishness, callousness, or whatever it was' that caused him not to come to the aid of a person in need. However, the criminal law should not be (and, ordinarily, is not) used that way: criminal law punishes individuals for their culpable acts (or, perhaps here, culpable non-acts), but not generally for bad character. As mortals, we lack the capacity to evaluate another's soul. It is wrongful conduct, and not an individual's status as a bad person or even an individual's bad thoughts, that justify criminal intervention. BS laws may violate this principle. At a minimum, there is a serious risk that juries will inadvertently punish people for being (or seeming to be) evil or 'soulless,' rather than for what occurred on a specific occasion. One need only consider David Cash and the public's intense feelings of disgust and anger toward him to appreciate why jurors might convict Bad Samaritans less on the basis of the 'technicalities' of a statute, and more on the basis of character evaluation.

Second, for retributivists, punishment of an innocent person is always morally wrong, and the risk of false positives—punishing an innocent person—is especially high with BS laws. Consider, for example, the Vermont BS law. To be guilty of this crime the bystander must 'know' that another is at risk of 'grave physical harm,' and must give 'reasonable assistance' if he can do so 'without danger or peril to himself.' If any one of these elements is lacking, the bystander is innocent and, therefore, in a society committed to the principle of legality, does not deserve punishment.

Notice the inherent problem of punishing people for not-doings rather than wrongdoings. When a person points a loaded gun at another and intentionally pulls the trigger, it is reasonable to infer that the actor intended to cause harm. His *mens rea* is obvious. It is far harder to determine why a person does not act. Return to the Bystander and Blind Person example. The facts stated that Bystander knew what was going on and wanted harm to occur. In the real world, however, it would be exceedingly difficult to reliably determine Bystander's potential guilt. How do we know Bystander realized what was about to happen? Did he see BP? Did he realize BP was about to walk into the street? Did Bystander see the truck? Did he realize the truck driver was not paying attention? Beyond that, why did Bystander not act? Maybe he froze up, maybe he didn't think fast enough, or maybe (reasonably or unreasonably) he believed that helping BP would jeopardize his own safety.

For that matter, why did the Genovese bystanders[141] hear the woman scream but fail to act, if in fact that was the case? Is it at least possible that some of the bystanders did not know she was in dire jeopardy? A person who wakes up from a sleep often fails to appreciate her surroundings. Also, perhaps some of them—even all of them—believed that someone else had already called the police. It may be that, despite the condemnation directed at the Genovese bystanders, few, if any, of them were guilty of Bad Samaritanism. In view of the inherent ambiguities in such circumstances, if juries take their duties seriously—

---

[141] The reference is to the following incident referred to earlier in the article: 'Kitty Genovese—a young Queens, New York woman—cried for help for more than half an hour outside an apartment building as her assailant attacked her, fled, and then returned to kill her. According to reports at the time, as many as thirty-eight persons heard her pleas from the safety of their residences, but did nothing to help her.'

including the presumption of innocence—few, if any, BS convictions will result. If emotions and bad character attributions rule the day, however, innocent persons will be improperly convicted.

Third, the threat of convicting innocent persons points to a related danger. BS statutes are so rubbery in their drafting that they grant police and prosecutors too much discretion to determine whether and whom to prosecute. The due process clause prohibits the enforcement of penal laws that 'fail to establish guidelines to prevent "arbitrary and discriminatory enforcement" of the law.' However, even if the issue is seen as a non-constitutional matter, it is difficult to see how a prosecutor can fairly determine when charges are proper.

Again, the distinction between actions and non-actions demonstrates the vagueness problem. BS laws compel people to make the world (or, at least, a small part of it) better, rather than punish actors for actively making it worse. In the latter case, the identifiable conduct of the accused, and the demonstrable harm caused by those actions, serve to single out the actor as a plausible candidate for prosecution. With laws that punish for nothing, rather than something, there is a need for alternative objective criteria. At least with commission-by-omission liability, there are identifiable criteria, such as the status relationship of the parties, contractual understandings, or the suspect's personal connection to the emergency by having created the initial risk. In contrast, with BS laws, which impose a duty to aid strangers (potentially, anyone), criminal responsibility is based on imprecise factors (e.g., the duty to provide 'reasonable assistance') and nearly unknowable circumstances (e.g., that the stranger is exposed to 'grave' physical harm, and that assistance can be rendered without any 'danger or peril' to the actor or others).

As the Genovese case demonstrates, these omission criteria are far less helpful in determining whether and against whom a prosecution should be initiated than are identifiable acts of commission. There is a significant risk with BS laws that the decision to prosecute will be based on a prosecutor's perceived need to respond to public outrage, which in turn, may be based less on the merits of the case and more on media coverage (which, in turn, may be founded on inappropriate factors, such as race, background, or even the physical attractiveness of the victim and/or the supposed poor character of the bystander). Not only may persons guilty of Bad Samaritanism avoid conviction because of selective enforcement, but the process may result in prosecution of persons who, upon cooler reflection, we might realize are innocent of wrongful not-doing.

There are also utilitarian reasons to question the wisdom of BS legislation. First, if such laws are taken seriously, the costs of investigating and potentially prosecuting bystanders might be prohibitive. Imagine the investigation necessary to decide whether to prosecute any of the Genovese bystanders and, if the decision were to proceed, to determine which of them to prosecute. Second, to the extent that BS statutes are narrowly drafted to reduce the risk of unfairness, prosecutions are likely to be rare (and convictions even rarer). Therefore, it is unlikely that the threat of punishment will have the desired effect of inducing bystanders to help persons in peril. The muted threat of a misdemeanor conviction is less likely to promote good behavior than the threat of public scorn that follows the publicity of such cases, or a Samaritan's own conscience.

Third, to the extent that such laws do, in fact, compel 'Good Samaritanism,' there is a risk that the Samaritan will hurt the person she is trying to assist, hurt others in the process, or unforeseeably harm herself. Fourth, since BS statutes are not linked to any prevention-of-harm causal requirement (i.e., it is not necessary to successfully prevent the threatened harm from occurring; it is enough to give it 'the old college try'), the costs of such laws may easily outweigh their limited practical benefits. Even supporters of BS legislation concede that the law only helps at the boundaries.

There is one final reason to question the wisdom of BS statutes. Not only are positive duties morally less powerful than negative ones, but they also restrict human liberty to a greater degree. A penal law that prohibits a person from doing X (e.g., unjustifiably killing another person) permits that individual to do anything other than X (assuming no other negative duty). In contrast, a law that requires a person to do Y (e.g., help a bystander) bars that person from doing anything other than Y. The edict that 'no student may laugh aloud at a fellow student's silly answers to a professor's questions' only marginally restricts a student's autonomy—she can silently laugh at her colleague, sleep through the answer, or walk out of the room to protest the student's stupidity, just to name a few examples. However, a rule requiring a student to 'provide reasonable assistance to a fellow student in jeopardy of offering a silly answer to a professor's question,' not only is less precise, but also prevents students from doing anything other than help.

Arguments in favour of punishing omissions

There are two main arguments in favour of punishing omissions. The first is that the line between an act and an omission is too fine a line on which to place any great weight. Consider a person who drops a vase: is this an act ('dropping the vase') or an omission ('not holding on to it')?[142] We saw in Part I of this chapter that this argument has received some judicial support.[143] In reply those who support the distinction accept that cases on the borderline are complex, but that is often true when one seeks to draw a distinction between two concepts. They argue that the distinction is a basic one in morality: taking food away from a starving person is not the same as failing to provide food to such a person. To these kinds of arguments William Wilson has replied: 'What is morally worse/causally more significant: shooting a child to prevent the agony of her burning to death in a flaming inferno one is powerless to prevent, or failing to save a similar child from a similar fate by the simple mechanism of unlocking the door behind which she is trapped?'[144]

The second argument in favour of punishing omissions is based on the concept of social responsibility. In an important article on this topic Ashworth contrasts two basic approaches to omissions: the conventional view and the 'social responsibility view'. The conventional view suggests that criminal law should not impose omissions except in clear and serious cases. The 'social responsibility view'[145] would draw attention to the need for cooperation in social life.[146] Ashworth supports the 'social responsibility' view and explains his reasoning in the following passage:[147]

A. Ashworth, 'The Scope of Criminal Liability for Omissions' (1989) 105 *Law Quarterly Review* 431

The social responsibility view of omissions liability grows out of a communitarian social philosophy which stresses the necessary interrelationship between individual behaviour and

---

[142] Lacey and Wells (1998: 37).   [143] e.g. Lord Mustill in *Bland* [1993] AC 789.
[144] Wilson (2003: 81).   [145] He relies on Raz (1985).
[146] See Feinberg (1988: 126–85) for further discussion of arguments in favour of imposing liability for omissions.
[147] For the arguments against Ashworth's views see G. Williams (1991a).

collective goods. Individuals need others, or the actions of others, for a wide variety of tasks, which assist each one of us to maximise the pursuit of out personal goals. A community or society may be regarded as a network of relationships which support one another by direct and indirect means. But the community also consists of individuals, each having certain basic rights (such as the right to life). It is therefore strongly arguable that each individual life should be valued both intrinsically and for its contribution (or potential contribution) to the community. It follows that there is a good case for encouraging co-operating at the minimal level of the duty to assist persons in peril, so long as the assistance does not endanger the person rendering it, and a case may be made for reinforcing this duty by the criminal sanction. (There are arguments for other duties too.) The argument does not rest on a simple utilitarian calculation of benefits, ensuring a net saving of lives with comparatively little inconvenience of others members of society. Nor does it rest on the prediction that both respect for the law and the level of social cooperation will be improved if the law encourages morally desirable conduct, although those would be beneficial consequences. The foundation of the argument is that a level of social co-operation and social responsibility is both good and necessary for the realisation of individual autonomy. What this requires is a general moral and legal recognition of people's vital interests. 'Physical integrity . . . is necessary for the accomplishment of any human aim, and so is an appropriate subject for a system of mutually restraining duties.' Each member of society is valued intrinsically, and the value of one citizen's life is generally greater than the value of another citizen's temporary freedom. Thus it is the element of emergency which heightens the social responsibility in 'rescue' cases, and which focuses other people's vital interests into a 'deliberative priority', and it is immediacy to *me* that generates *my* obligation. The concepts of immediacy and the opportunity of help (usually because of physical nearness) can thus be used to generate, and to limit the scope of, the duty of assistance to those in peril. The duty might well be subject to other limitations too. It should only arise in 'easy rescue' cases, where the assistance is unlikely to endanger the safety of the person present. And the duty to render assistance must give way to the individual's right to self-determination: if a person wishes to be left to die, respect for that person's autonomy should prevent any duty of assistance from arising.

QUESTIONS

1. In *Brock and Wyner* [2001] 2 Cr App R 31 (discussed in Padfield (2000) and Glazebrook (2001)) two project workers at a hostel for homeless people were convicted under section 8 of the Misuse of Drugs Act 1971 for not preventing drug selling in the hostel. Is such a conviction appropriate?

2. Is it a greater infringement of your liberty to be required to act in a particular way or to be forbidden to act in a particular way?

3. If a celebrity was seriously injured in a car crash and a photographer took photographs, rather than summoning help, should the photographer be guilty of an offence?

FURTHER READING

Ashworth, A. (1989), 'The Scope of Criminal Liability for Omissions', *Law Quarterly Review* 105: 424.

Fletcher, G. (1994), 'On the Moral Irrelevance of Bodily Movements', *University of Pennsylvania Law Review* 142: 1443.

Freeman, S. (1994), 'Act & Crime: Act & Omission: Criminal Liability and the Duty to Aid the Distressed', *University of Pennsylvania Law Review* 142: 1455.

Glazebrook, P. (1978), 'Situational Liability' in P. Glazebrook (ed.), *Reshaping the Criminal Law* (London: Sweet & Maxwell).

Kamm, M. (1994), 'Action, Omission, and the Stringency of Duties', *University of Pennsylvania Law Review* 142: 1493.

Simester, A. (1995), 'Why Omissions are Special', *Legal Theory* 1: 311.

Williams, G. (1991a), 'Criminal Omissions—the Conventional View', *Law Quarterly Review* 107: 86.

7 CAUSATION: SHOULD CONSEQUENCES MATTER?

There has been much academic debate over whether the law should hold people criminally responsible for their actions. This is a debate to which we will return at several times in this book, but we will outline the arguments now.

7.1 ARGUMENTS AGAINST HOLDING PEOPLE RESPONSIBLE FOR THE CONSEQUENCES OF THEIR ACTIONS

Although students often assume that criminal law must concern itself with causation, it would be possible to construct a system of criminal law where issues of causation were irrelevant. Supporters of such a system argue that the consequences of our acts are beyond our control and a matter of luck. One way of putting the argument is this: Alf, Bertha, and Charles all throw a punch at someone, intending to give her a black eye. Alf's victim jumps out of the way at the last moment and escapes unhurt. Bertha's punch lands on target and gives the victim the hoped-for black eye. Charles's victim tries to jump out of the way of the punch, but falls over, bangs her head, and dies. Did not Alf, Bertha, and Charles all do the same thing? The different consequences were out of their control. Charles was 'unlucky' that his victim died, it was just luck that Alf's escaped. It is therefore only fair, the argument goes, to punish people for what is within their control; that is what they do, and to ignore the things which are outside their control, such as what happens as a result of their actions. The criminal law should therefore only penalize acts and ignore the consequences of those acts. In practical terms the law would punish acts which endangered others, whether any harm actually resulted being a matter of chance.[148] Many leading figures in the academic world are sympathetic to the force of this argument: Joel Feinberg,[149] Andrew Ashworth,[150] and Sanford Kadish,[151] to name but a few.[152]

At first this sounds a thoroughly convincing argument but, as Paul Robinson has pointed out, those who argue that consequence should not matter are 'a breed that exists (and will

---

[148] Ashworth (1987b). Although whether the harm did or did not result would be useful evidentially in indicating whether the conduct was dangerous. See also J. Lewis (1989) for a discussion of the impact of such thinking on sentencing.

[149] Feinberg (1970) and (1995).   [150] Ashworth (1988).   [151] Kadish (1994).

[152] Parker (1984). Many supporters draw on the writing of Kant: see the discussions in A. Moore (1990) and Nagel (1979).

probably always exists) only in academia. I know of no jurisdiction that actually takes such a view'.[153]

Much has been written on the debate over whether people are responsible for the consequences of their actions and it is an issue to which we will return at several points in this book. We will seek here just to outline some of the key arguments that have been made.

7.2 ARGUMENTS THAT CONSEQUENCES DO MATTER

The reactions of the actor and bystanders

The consequences of a person's actions affect the reaction of the actor and passers-by. If A is driving dangerously and kills a child quite different emotions will be felt by all involved from if A just misses a child.[154] A will feel very guilty about the death of the child, but may soon forget the near miss. The fact that such reactions are near universal indicates that they reflect a moral truth that consequences do matter and people feel responsible for the consequences of what they do.[155] Even if there is not a 'logical'[156] argument that can explain why we should be responsible for the consequences of our actions, it is clearly fundamental to our common experience and the way our society works. Kimberly Kessler[157] suggests, however, that such reactions reflect the distress at the harm suffered (or not suffered) by the victim, rather than judgements about the actor's responsibility.

Action reasons and outcome reasons

John Gardner[158] argues that there is an important difference between what he calls 'action reasons' and the 'outcome reasons' against doing something. An action reason is an argument for not performing a certain kind of action, whatever the consequences. An outcome reason sees the reason for not performing the action as the bad consequences that flow from that action. An example will clarify. A person tells a lie to a friend. Telling a lie could be described as wrong simply because lying is wrong (an action reason) but also because lying has bad consequences (it breaks down the trust in the friendship). The consequences of an action therefore do matter in that they provide another (outcome) reason for (or against) acting in a particular way.

The importance of consequences to our humanity

In the following passage Tony Honoré argues that it is part of treating people as human that both the good and bad consequence of their actions are taken into account:

A. Honoré, 'Responsibility and Luck' (1988) 104 *Law Quarterly Review* 530 at 543–5

[O]utcome-allocation is crucial to our identity as persons; and, unless we were persons who possessed an identity, the question of whether it was fair to subject us to responsibility

---

[153] Robinson (1997: 109).   [154] B. Williams (1981).
[155] Jareborg (1993) argues that deciding the appropriate public response to wrongdoing involves considerations that are not relevant in making a moral judgement about the behaviour.
[156] M. Moore (1997: 232) argues that the fact that a defendant is responsible for the consequences of his or her action is self-evident as a 'foundationalist principle'.
[157] Kessler (1994).   [158] Gardner (1998).

could not arise. If actions and outcomes were not ascribed to us on the basis of our bodily movements and their mental accompaniments, we could have no continuing history or character. There would indeed be bodies and, associated with them, minds. Each would possess a certain continuity. They could be labelled A, B, C. But having decided nothing and done nothing these entities would hardly be people.

In the real world, fortunately, human bodily movements and their mental accompaniments are with some exceptions interpreted as actions and decisions. They are ascribed to authors, who accordingly count as persons; and it is by virtue of these ascriptions that each of us has a history, an identity and a character. But there is a price to be paid for being a person. As the counterpart of this status we are responsible for our actions and their consequences, and sometimes this responsibility exposes us to legal sanctions. To ascribe personhood and responsibility to people in this way is to apply normative principles. It is not merely that others attribute to us an identity and a character, but that we are entitled to claim them for ourselves and to ascribe them to others. Others in turn not only hold us responsible for our actions and their outcomes, but are entitled to do so. Of course the balance between personhood and responsibility cannot, any more than the system of outcome-allocation, be said to rest on a social contract. We have never decided to assume responsibility in exchange for the gift of personal identity. Both are natural in the sense that we can neither choose them nor give them up. Considered as a bargain, the exchange would not even, properly speaking, be in our interest; for to be responsible is part of what it means to be a person and hence to have interests. But the normative principles involved may be regarded in a pre-moral sense as well-founded, since they embody a balance between identity and responsibility.

Such are the normative arguments for allocation according to outcomes and, as a corollary, for strict legal liability for the harmful upshot of risky conduct. In practice most ordinary people endorse the former and most lawyers the latter, though either might be hard put to say why. Virtually no one inside or outside the law believes that fault and desert are the sole basis of responsibility. In their off-duty moments even those philosophers and theologians who in theory cleave to fault alone assign credit and discredit for actions and their outcomes in cases where blame and praise are not in point. Take a non-moral example: the contrasting fortunes of X and Y, two footballers playing in a needle match. X miskicks but a gust of wind carries the ball into the opposing goal. He is credited with a goal, but not praised for scoring it. It would be better, of course, had he been skilful as well as lucky, for he would then both be credited with the goal and praised for scoring it. Y aims a skilful shot at goal, but this time a gust of wind diverts it. He is praised for his good shot but not credited with a goal. It would be still worse for him had his shot been a bad one. X is lucky, Y unlucky; but it is the outcome of their actions, not what they deserve, that primarily determines credit or its absence. Desert merely increases or diminishes credit or discredit. Take a legal example. I fire at my rival intending to kill him. It would be murder if I succeeded, but I miss. I am guilty only of an attempt. If fault is to be judged by disposition, my fault is as great as if I had hit him, but my responsibility is less. Now for an extra-legal example. If purely by your fault in darting out into the road I run you over, I must stop, send for the ambulance and give you what help I can in the meantime. My responsibility is not as great as if I had been at fault. It may not be legal: that depends on the applicable system of law. It may not be moral in the sense that I am morally responsible for the accident itself. But, just because I have hurt you, I am responsible, and by virtue of that responsibility bound to take certain stem. Indeed. Unless I am wholly insensitive, I shall feel and express regret for the harm I have done. For it is a myth that fault and desert are essential to responsibility. They serve rather to increase the credit or discredit for the outcome of our behaviour that we incur in any event.

It is only this primary outcome-responsibility that can explain why we (rightly) judge murder more severely than attempted murder and causing death by dangerous driving more severely than dangerous driving. It is said that morally the harmful outcome makes no difference; and indeed the difference between causing death by dangerous driving and mere dangerous driving, like the difference between aiming a good shot at goal and scoring a goal, is causal, a matter of outcomes. On a narrow view of morality the cases are not morally distinguishable. For allocation according to outcomes is not allocation according to effort, talent or disposition. A good outcome can sometimes be achieved with less effort than a bad outcome, and by a person with less talent and a worse character. Outcome-allocation is allocation according to results, whether they constitute achievements or botches. But it does not follow that the system of allocation according to result, in contrast with its application to individual instances, lacks a moral or pre-moral basis. The person concerned, though he cannot be sure what the outcome of his action will be, has chosen to act in the knowledge that he will be credited or debited with whatever it turns out to be. Moreover we cannot opt out of the system by which we obtain credit for favourable outcomes; and so we cannot slough off the burden of discredit either. Finally, it is outcomes that in the long run make us what we are.

Of course, the choice is not just between saying you are not responsible for any of the consequences of your actions and saying you are responsible for all of the consequences. Most commentators take the view that you are responsible for some but not all of them. It is the rules of causation in the criminal law that seek to take this middle path and define for which of the consequences of an accused's actions you are responsible.[159]

FURTHER READING

Ashworth, A. (1988), 'Criminal Attempts and the Role of Resulting Harm Under the Code, and in the Common Law', *Rutgers Law Journal* 19: 725.

Gobert, J. (1993), 'The Fortuity of Consequences', *Criminal Law Forum* 4: 1.

Honoré, A. (1988), 'Responsibility and Luck', *Law Quarterly Review* 104: 530.

Morse, S. (2004), 'Reason, Results and Criminal Responsibility', *University of Illinois Law Review* 363.

8 SEEKING A COHERENT APPROACH TO CAUSATION

One key question about causation in the law is: 'to what extent is causation a question or fact and to what extent is it a question of judgement?' In other words, in causation cases are we asking 'did the defendant cause this result?' or 'should the defendant be held responsible for this consequence'?[160] To some causation should not be regarded as a quasi-scientific question but rather a question about whether it is fair to impute this consequence to the defendant.[161] To others the questions of culpability and causation should be kept quite distinct.[162]

---

[159] For a wider discussion see Cane (2003: ch. 4) and Morse (2000).
[160] Fumerton and Kress (2001).   [161] Brudner (1998).
[162] e.g. Padfield (1995); M. Moore (1999).

It has become common for those examining the case law on causation to conclude that, rather than applying any general principles, the judge simply considers what he or she considers to be the common sense answer on causation and declares that to be the legal position.[163] In other words it is not possible to set out any guiding rules of causation. This section will consider attempts by those who reject such an argument and seek to develop some general principles governing the law on causation.[164]

8.1 'CAUSAL MINIMALISM'

This view is that factual causation ('but for') causation, (as explained above at pp. 102–3) should be the guiding rule for the criminal law. Opponents point out that it could throw the net of potential liability very widely: the stabber's grandmother could be said to be a 'but for' cause of the stabbing. Supporters reply that such concerns are easily dealt with by the law on *mens rea*, which would acquit the grandmother because she clearly lacked it. However, this reply is not available in relation to crimes of strict liability which do not require proof of *mens rea*.[165]

8.2 HART AND HONORÉ

In their important work, *Causation in the Law*,[166] Hart and Honoré suggest an alternative approach. They place much weight on giving causation its ordinary meaning. They focus on the difference between normal and abnormal effects. Only abnormal conditions can be causes; normal conditions cannot. Normal conditions 'are those conditions which are present as part of the usual state or mode of operation of the things under inquiry'.[167] They give an example of a person who lights a match by a haystack, setting it ablaze. The fact that there is oxygen in the air will be a normal condition and so not a cause. The lighting of the match will be abnormal and so can be regarded as a cause. In the following passage they explain that the free, voluntary, and informed act of a human being will be regarded as an abnormal act that 'breaks the chain of causation' and takes over responsibility for resulting harms, rendering earlier actions no longer causes.

H.L.A. Hart and A. Honoré, *Causation in the Law* (2nd edn., Oxford: OUP, 1985), 42–4

If unusual quantities of arsenic are found in a dead man's body, this is up to a point an explanation of his death and so the cause of it: but we usually press for a further and more satisfying explanation and may find that someone deliberately put arsenic in the victim's food. This is a fuller explanation in terms of human agency; and of course we speak of the poisoner's action as the cause of the death; though we do not withdraw the title of cause from the presence of arsenic in the body—this is now thought of as an ancillary, the 'mere way' in which the poisoner produced the effect. Once we have reached this point, however, we have something which has a special *finality* at the level of common sense: for though we

---

[163] As seen in Part I of this chapter, the legal principles relied upon by the courts, such as 'the operating and substantial cause' test, are so vague that they leave the judiciary open to such charges.

[164] See the Draft Criminal Code's proposed rules on causation, critically discussed in G. Williams (1989).

[165] For criticism of causal minimalism see R. Wright (1985) and (1988).

[166] Hart and Honoré (1985).   [167] Hart and Honoré (1985: 35).

may look for and find an explanation of why the poisoner did what he did in terms of motives like greed or revenge, we do not regard his motive or speak of it as the cause of the *death* into which we are inquiring, even if we do (as is perhaps rare) call the poisoner's motive the 'cause' of his action. The causal explanation of the particular occurrence is brought to a stop when the death has been explained by the deliberate act, in the sense that none of the antecedents of that deliberate act will count as the cause of death. This is not to say that causal inquiries may not be pursued further. We may, for example, discover that someone provided a reason or opportunity for the poisoner to do the deed, e.g. by persuading him not to hesitate or by supplying an appropriate dose of poison. In that case a causal relationship *of some sort* may indeed be established between the conduct of the person who supplies the advice or means and the death of the victim. The latter can properly be described as a consequence of the persuasion or the provision of poison. But the fact that what is here unearthed is not the central type of causal relationship but something more tenuous is marked by the fact that we would not happily say that the accomplice had either 'caused' the death or 'caused' the poisoner to kill. We do not therefore trace the *central type* of causal inquiry *through* a deliberate act.

Although Hart and Honoré's approach has received much judicial and academic support it has its critics. Michael Moore, for example, is concerned about their premise that causation should take its meaning from the normal usage of the word.[168] He is not convinced that there is a 'normal usage', at least in difficult cases of causation. Other concerns surround their emphasis on the distinction between 'normal' and 'abnormal' events or conditions.[169] It can be argued that these terms are vague and too easily permit a judge to smuggle in value judgements when considering whether a cause is abnormal or not.[170] In the extract from Alan Norrie's book at the end of this chapter further objections are made to Hart and Honoré's analysis.

8.3 REASONABLE FORESEEABILITY

Some commentators and courts have sought to argue that defendants cause the reasonably foreseeable consequences of their actions.[171] Such a test has a refreshing simplicity. In the following passage Dennis Klimchuk sets out its moral justification:

D. Klimchuk, 'Causation, Thin Skulls and Equality' (1998) 11 *Canadian Journal of Law and Jurisprudence* 115 at 129–35

The standard of reasonable foreseeability gives expression to a powerful moral intuition, namely, that it is unfair to ask others to answer for those consequences of their actions which we could not reasonably have expected them to consider in deciding what actions to perform or to refrain from performing. This suggests that the fact that extraordinary operations of nature would break the causal chain between the actions of a wrongdoer and the victim's eventual injury follows from the fact that to extend my actions through the intervention of such extraordinary operations would in some sense be unfair. The reasonable foreseeability

---

[168] See also Cane (2002: 118).   [169] Christlieb (1993).

[170] An interesting example is Chamallas and Kerber (1990) who (writing from a feminist perspective) criticize the courts' approach to women who die in attempts to escape from threatening circumstances.

[171] See e.g. Yeo (2000).

test makes explicit the reliance of the doctrine of causation on a sense of fairness only implicit in the substantial or operating cause test.

On what does this sense of fairness rely? The key to the answer I defend lies in giving attention to the work done by the concept of reasonableness in the standard of reasonable foreseeability. I want to borrow an idea that John Rawls develops in *Political Liberalism*, namely that reasonableness and equality are correlative: to act rationally is to act so as to further one's own ends; to act reasonably is to interact with others on terms of equality. Thus, the intuition of fairness to which I appealed above relies on the idea that the reasonable foreseeability standard gives expression to what I called the principle of equality, namely the principle that the law should treat persons as equals.

We have to give some content to the principle of equality. What equality requires in a given legal context will be in part a function of the sorts of interests the law protects in that context. As a part of public law, the primary relationship in terms of which criminal law is typically conceptualized is that between the state and citizen. Indeed, this suggests a common means by which the contrast between public and private law is drawn: tort law, for example, may be understood as having as its domain those aspects of wrongful conduct in which the state has no direct interest, but the pursuit of whose remedy is rather left to the private parties involved.

However, along with the relationship between the citizen and the state—most clearly at issue when the question is whether some *type* of action ought to attract the state's interest—criminal law has as its object, no less than tort law, the relationship citizens have as among themselves—most clearly at issue when the question is whether some *particular* action constitutes a violation of the sort of rights the criminal law protects. Thus to ask, for example, whether self-defence should be recognized as a defence at all is to ask whether the state should ever permit persons the right to self-help when the state's agents are not there to protect them, and this is a question of the relationship between the state's interests and the interests of the individual. To ask whether this particular assault was an act of self-defence is to inquire into the structure of the interaction between two individuals at the time of their violent confrontation. At stake here are not the interests of the state versus those of the individual but rather the protection of an individual's interests as against their interference by another. Following Arthur Ripstein, I would suggest that the relevant interests here are liberty and security. The link to equality is provided by an idea—Kantian in spirit—on which I will here rely: to treat persons as equals is to permit them as much exercise of their liberty and security interests as is compatible with everyone else doing the same.

My suggestion, then, is that the reasonable foreseeability test alone among the options I have considered succeeds in doing so. It will be easiest to see this if we begin by seeing how the other options fail to. Along with the substantial or operating cause test, I considered earlier two criteria by which we might answer the question of which of his consequences a wrongdoer must answer for, namely (1) the wrongdoer must answer for all of those consequences which would not have occurred but for his actions, and (2) the wrongdoer must answer for only those consequences which he acted so as to bring about. I suggested above that both of these can be dismissed on grounds of unfairness; now I want to give some content to the intuition to which I there appealed. Then I will return to the substantial or operating cause and reasonable foreseeability tests.

Let's call the view that the wrongdoer must answer for all of those consequences which would not have occurred but for his actions the *objective view* and the view that the wrongdoer must answer for only those consequences which he acted so as to bring about the *subjective view*. As I suggested above, the contrast between these two views can be captured in terms of the degree to which an agent has authority over the question of which

consequences of his actions will count as his doings. On the objective view, the agent has no such authority; on the subjective view, he has the final say. This contrast can also be captured in terms of who must bear the costs of the agent's intervention into the causal chains in which he acts and is acted upon. On the objective view, the agent, we might say, acts at his own peril; on the subjective view he acts at the peril of others.

The second way of making the contrast most clearly illustrates the extent to which the principle of equality, interpreted in the terms I introduced above, is at issue here. To say that on the objective view, A acts at his own peril, is to say that (supposing A wishes not to do wrong) A cannot act even when the foreseeable consequences of his action do not include harm to others, because if harm were to occur, A would have to answer for it anyway. That is to say, the security of those who might be harmed if A acted is purchased at the cost of his liberty. To say that, on the subjective view, A acts at the peril of others is to say that A will not have to consider as reasons against acting a broad range of the consequences of his actions—all those other than those he acted so as to bring about, including consequences which will consist in harms to others. That is to say, our security is purchased at the cost of A's liberty.

Above I suggested that we think of the substantial or operating cause test and the reasonable foreseeability test as attempts to chart a middle ground between the extremes represented by what I am here calling the objective and subjective views. But note that the substantial or operating cause test shares the shortcomings of the objective view on the terms of analysis just introduced. This follows from the fact that the difference between causes *sine qua non* and substantial or operating causes is one of degree. No less than on the objective view, on the substantial or operating cause test the agent is deprived of any say over which of the consequences of his actions will count as his doings. No less than on the objective view, on the substantial or operating cause test the agent acts at his own peril. Thus on the substantial or operating cause test, our security is purchased at the expense of the agent's liberty, and so the substantial or operating cause test violates the principle of equality.

The reasonable foreseeability test splits the difference, as it were, between the objective view and the substantial or operating cause test on the one hand, and the subjective view on the other. On the one hand, by tying the test concerning which consequences a wrongdoer must answer for to foresight, the reasonable foreseeability standard does not deprive the agent of all say whatsoever over which of the consequences of his actions will count as his doings. On the other hand, by tying the answer to what the agent could have *reasonably* foreseen, the reasonable foreseeability standard prevents the agent from having final authority over which of the consequences of his actions will count as his doings. In this sense, the standard of reasonable foreseeability is both public and objective. It is public to the extent that it can operate as a rule which guides conduct (unlike the objective view and the substantial or operating cause test, which both leave the question of which consequences count as my doings to fortune). It is objective to the extent that it prevents the wrongdoer from measuring the rights of others in terms of his judgment (unlike the subjective view, which leaves the question of which of my consequences count as my doings to my say): and the law treats us as equals, in part, precisely by denying us the privilege of so doing.

Critics of reasonable foreseeability claim that it does not operate fairly in 'thin skull' rule cases, and notably Klimchuck goes on in his article to support the existence of the 'thin skull' test in certain cases as an exception to the 'reasonable foreseeability' test.[172] Klimchuk

---

[172] Of course, other supporters of the 'reasonable foreseeability' test would not permit such an exception.

justifies the 'thin skull' rule because it prevents the defendant claiming that the victim must take legal responsibility for her physical weakness or 'protected beliefs'.[173]

8.4 NATURAL CONSEQUENCES

The natural consequence approach claims that the defendant is responsible for the natural consequences of his actions.[174] It may be thought that there is little difference between the reasonable foreseeability test and the natural consequence test. The key difference seems to be this:[175] the 'reasonable foreseeability' test looks at the issue from the defendant's point of view at the time when he or she acted (could he or she have foreseen the result?), while the 'natural consequence' test looks back from the injury inflicted on the victim and attempts to find out which cause or causes were the most legally significant.[176] Michael Moore supports a version of this theory, arguing that a defendant should be responsible for proximate cause (those things caused in the normal routine) but not for 'freakish' results. Critics might reply that the terms 'natural' or 'proximate' are too vague to be useful.

In the following passage Victor Tadros makes a different objection and that is that when making causation assessment the courts do (and should) take into account normative issues (i.e. questions of how people should have behaved). He makes the point here using the example of third party interventions:

V. Tadros (2005) *Criminal Responsibility* (Oxford: OUP), 173–5

It is commonly argued that the actions of third parties at least sometimes break the chain of causation even where those actions would not have happened but for the action of the defendant. If D acts which then gives rise to an action by D2, it is at least sometimes the case that D is not legally responsible for consequences of the action by D2. That normative considerations are significant in assessing whether the activities of third parties break the chain of causation should be relatively familiar to legal scholars. However, the issue is a complex one and it seems implausible that a general test can be developed to determine when actions of third parties break the chain of causation.

The basic issue can be illuminated by a consideration of the facts of *R v Williams and Davis*. In that case the two defendants gave a lift to a hitch-hiker who they allegedly attempted to rob. The hitch-hiker jumped out of the car and died from head injuries sustained by falling into the road. Two considerations might be thought important in assessing whether the defendants caused the death of the hitch-hiker. The first is the factual question of whether the actions of the hitch-hiker were foreseeable. The second is an assessment of the reasonableness (or rightness, or some other normative assessment) of the acts of the hitch-hiker.

Foreseeability is often thought to be an important element of the law of causation. If a consequence is not foreseeable, it is said, it is not caused. There is a general problem with this idea. Due to lack of knowledge, it may not have been foreseeable in 1900 that cancer

---

[173] Klimchuck (1998) argues that in *Blaue* the right to hold religious views (except in so far as they might harm others) means that the victim had the right to exercise her religious beliefs in refusing the blood transfusion and so it should not be said that her decision broke the chain of causation.

[174] Examples of both views could be found in the decision of the High Court of Australia in *Royall v The Queen* (1991) 65 ALJR 451.

[175] Shute (1992).   [176] Colvin (1991: 84).

would result from smoking, but that does not entail that in 1900 smoking was not a cause of cancer. Whether or not D caused E, then, is not sensitive to the knowledge that we have, or could be expected to have, about E. It is quite possible that we do everything that could be done to establish whether D caused E and still be wrong about the answer because there is something about the world that we do not, and even could not, know. This is a sense in which questions of causation are questions of fact.

Whether the actions of the hitch-hiker were reasonable, on the other hand, might well properly be a determining factor in assessing whether the chain of causation was broken by his jumping from the car. Suppose that the actions of the hitch-hiker were spectacularly unreasonable. Suppose that the threat was very trivial, say because the force threatened was only a slap. In that case surely it would be wrong to say that the death was caused by the actions of the defendants. On the other hand, suppose that the-hitch-hiker reasonably thought that he would be killed whether or not he gave over his money, perhaps because the defendants were known to the hitch-hiker to be convicted serial killers on the run. Then it seems quite right to say that the death of the hitch-hiker was caused by the actions of the defendants. Normative considerations, then, clearly play a role in the assessment of whether intervening acts of third parties break the chain of causation.

Wilson [(2002: 181)] is critical of basing accounts of causation on the idea of reasonableness later in the chapter on causation. He suggests that the difficulty here is that even unreasonable intervening acts of third parties may not break the chain of causation. He considers the case of *R v Cheshire*, in which D shot the victim in the leg and abdomen which induced respiratory problems. In attempting to alleviate this, the doctors performed a tracheotomy. It was negligently performed and the victim died. The chain of causation was held not to have been broken. Wilson approves and thinks that this shows that it is strictly not the 'reasonableness' of the response of the third party that is relevant, but rather the 'reactive nature' of the third party's action. The third party, in such cases, the argument goes, is reacting to a state of affairs created by the defendant. Reactive acts do not, it is claimed, break the chain of causation.

Relevant to deciding the case, Wilson rightly argues, is the fact that doctors 'who have emergency surgery thrust upon them cannot be expected to get it right all the time'. There is a difference between what is right and what is reasonable, of course, but that cannot decide the case. Not only can we not expect doctors to get it right all the time, we cannot always expect them to behave reasonably, or at least even if we do expect them to behave reasonably, unreasonable actions of doctors ought not always to break the chain of causation. Holding the defendant criminally responsible for the death in *R v Cheshire* ought not to preclude at least civil liability for the doctor. And for this reason we should not think that the 'reasonableness' test is very strict. But that is not to say that reasonableness is not the right concept to apply here. It is just that the intervening action must have fallen very far below the level of reasonableness to break the chain of causation in these cases. For, if the action of the doctors is bad enough, the chain of causation will be broken, despite the fact that they are reacting to circumstances created by the defendant.

This explains the decision not to attribute liability in another case that Wilson considers: that of *State v Preslar*. In that case, a husband forced his wife out of their home by his violent acts. She died due to the cold close to her father's house, the explanation being that she didn't want to disturb her father to let her in. Presumably it is because her reason for staying outside was so weak that the defendant could hot be held criminally liable. Had there been some, albeit insufficient, good reason for her not to disturb her father (perhaps he had a heart condition, or would likely have attempted to shoot the defendant) then, presumably, the chain of causation would not have been broken. In such cases, much depends upon the reasonableness of the action of the third party, albeit that it is only very unreasonable acts that break the chain of causation.

It is hard to see anything but a specifically legal explanation of this idea. Surely the reason why only very unreasonable acts break the chain of causation is that the scope of legal liability ought not to be restricted by unrealistic expectations of medical professionals and others to behave rightly. In the natural world, on the other hand, we may be inclined to suggest that the chain of causation is broken more easily. For example, suppose that there is a medical condition which always requires an operation. Some operations of this kind will cause scarring and others will not. In establishing whether the disease was the cause of the scarring in a particular case, it may well be appropriate to suggest that the chain of causation was broken if the doctors conducted the operation negligently.

There are good reasons for the law to be more restrictive about how unreasonable the conduct must be for the chain of causation to be broken. The general requirement that reasonableness is the appropriate concept to determine whether the chain of causation is broken applies in legal and in scientific investigations. But it is plausible that the concept applies differently depending on the purpose of the enquiry.

8.5 NARROWNESS OF CAUSATION APPROACH

Critical scholars have argued that the criminal law with its assumption that individuals are responsible for their actions is placing undue focus on one individual and is ignoring the wider exercise of powers within society. Power structures within society; political assumptions; economic inequality; cultural and social factors all play a role in influencing people to commit crime. The law's approach enables the problem of crime to be seen as the results of the actions of a few evil people, rather than recognizing it as a product of an unequal and exclusatory society.[177] In the following extract Alan Norrie develops several of these points in criticizing the approach to causation developed by Hart and Honoré (which was summarized above).

A. Norrie, *Crime, Reason and History* (London: Butterworths, 2002), 137–40

Liberal Principles for the Imputation of Causation

. . .

Hart and Honoré's position is most plausible where they draw their examples from situations in which an individual, isolated and alone, acts to bring about some effect in nature, for example, the lighting of a spark which sets a forest on fire. But even here, the picture that is presented is one-sided, for we are told nothing about the conditions in which the act occurs, or how it is perceived.

This becomes clear in the crucial distinction they draw between abnormal and normal conditions. An individual is only 'the moral/legal cause of those events in the world that are accompanied by the normal range of attendant conditions. Where an abnormal condition ensues, it becomes the cause in place of the human intervention, which in turn becomes an antecedent condition to the abnormal element.' The problem is that what is normal and what

---

[177] See the interesting discussion of metaphysics and causation in Morse (2000).

is abnormal, what is cause and what is condition, is a matter of judgment and perspective. To use one of the authors' own (slightly modified) examples (1985, 35), the effect of a famine in a third world country might appear to a peasant as the consequence of drought, and to a relief agency as the result of the inefficiency and corruption of government. To a charity activist, it would be seen as the product of the meanness of the industrialised countries, and to a radical as the effect of economic underdevelopment resulting from neo-liberal economics. All these different factors could be singled out as the cause, with the others regarded as the background conditions; each could be presented as the factor which 'makes the difference'. Hart and Honoré acknowledge that 'the distinction between cause and condition may be drawn in different ways in one and the same case according to the context' (1985, 37). But if the 'normal' is contingent and subject to development and change according to context, it is a weak, potentially unstable, foundation for legal and moral judgments. Individual responsibility ultimately relies upon a variable evaluation of what is 'normal' in social life.

A good illustration is provided by Lord Scarman (1981) in his report into English inner city riots in the early 1980s. Speaking of the events leading to a particular riot, he stated that—

'Deeper causes undoubtedly existed, and must be probed: but the immediate cause of Saturday's events was a spontaneous combustion set off by the spark of one particular incident.' (1981, 37)

Which factor 'makes the difference', the 'deeper causes' or the 'immediate cause'? If those 'deeper causes' (relating to poor social environment, racial discrimination, police harassment) are part of the 'normal' conditions of life in late twentieth-century England, are they *for that reason* excluded from our account of what caused the riot? It would perhaps be convenient for the law, with its emphasis on the individual, if they were. Elsewhere in his report, Lord Scarman did draw a distinction between the 'causes' and the 'conditions' of the riots (1981, 16). This was shortly before he argued that the *conditions* of young black people cannot exclude their guilt for grave criminal offences which, as causal agents, they have committed (1981, 14). If Hart and Honoré are correct to say it is all a matter of perspective, the example of the Scarman Report reveals that there are competing political views to that of the law.

Second, there is the question of the law's use of the concept of voluntariness. On the face of it, the idea of a new intervening voluntary act by a third party possesses a measure of solidity that the distinction between the normal and the abnormal does not. However, this is illusory since it all depends on how one defines 'voluntary'. Only a voluntary act will break the causal chain, so the act of a third party may not break the chain if it is adjudged 'involuntary'. Hart and Honoré concede that there are narrower and broader uses of the terminology (1985, 138), and much hinges upon their notion of what constitutes a 'fair choice'. This, they say, 'depends in part on what conduct is regarded from a moral or legal point of view as reasonable in the circumstances', an issue that 'raises questions of legal policy' (1985, 42; cf Stapleton, 1988, 124).

This becomes apparent in their discussion of situations which are not regarded as voluntary by the law. These include, in addition to the more obvious situations of unconsciousness and physical duress, the policy-influenced situations of preservation of property, safeguarding of rights and interests, including economic interests, and the carrying out of legal and even moral obligations (1985, 142–62). All may be regarded as situations 'in which an individual did not act voluntarily. Just how broad the concept of the involuntary may go becomes apparent when the authors are discussing legal obligation:

'In ordinary speech we recognise that even a social obligation restricts our freedom, so that if I have accepted an invitation to dine with you I am "not free" to dine with anyone else. So too in the law.' (1985, 138)

With such wide notions of what might constitute involuntariness, the hope that the voluntary intervention of a third party might draw a line across a causal chain in a principled manner is impossible. The definition is too flexible, too open to broad and narrow interpretations of what the term means.

What is voluntary may be subject to a more or less individualistic interpretation. If it is a matter of looking at whether an individual was conscious when he acted, this is a narrow focus on the individual and his mental state. If, on the other hand, it is a question of examining social or legal obligations, this locates the individual in a network of social relations and understandings, and presents a broad view of the voluntary/involuntary line. From this latter, more social view, rooting the individual in a context of interpersonal relations, it is questionable just what significance the voluntariness of human agency should have (see further Norrie, 2000, chs 1, 9).

Hart and Honoré's argument is that voluntary human agency has a special finality about it. While we may look for reasons why a poisoner did what he did in terms of motives like greed or revenge, we do not regard his motive as the cause of death, although we may consider it the cause of his action. The example is perhaps tendentious, but the main point is that it draws upon the illustration of an isolated, asocial individual, alone with his private emotions, and does not locate individual agency in its broader context. A good counter-example is provided by J B Priestley's play, *An Inspector Calls*. The author persuades us to look behind the 'voluntary' act of the young woman's suicide to the conduct of the various members of the well-to-do family, who each in their own way have contributed to the girl's decision to take her life. Priestley forces the family to see that each of its members has in his or her own way caused the girl's death. They cannot conceal behind the girl's 'voluntary' act their own causal roles stemming from the interconnectedness of relations between rich and poor. It is this which ensures that any focus on individual agency can only be falsely narrow. The girl's suicide is 'voluntary', but it is still caused by the acts of the family, so that no special finality is given to her actions. 'Voluntariness' loses its special character when a broader view of events and actions is taken.

QUESTIONS

1. Which of these approaches would (a) make most sense to a jury and (b) be most desirable in theory?

2. Do you think there is a difference in 'thin skull' cases where because of the physical infirmity the victim suffers a worse injury than would otherwise occur and cases where an action which otherwise would be harmless causes a serious injury? (This question is discussed in Gobert (1993).)

3. If Norrie's argument were accepted, would it be possible to have any kind of criminal law that took appropriate account of the political and social forces that influence the commission of crime?

FURTHER READING

Brudner, A. (1998), 'Owning Outcomes: On Intervening Causes, Thin Skulls and Fault-undifferentiated Crimes', *Canadian Journal of Law and Jurisprudence* 11: 90.

Hart, H., and Honoré, A. (1985), *Causation in the Law* (2nd edn., Oxford: OUP).

Hassett, P. (1987), 'Absolutism in Causation', *Syracuse Law Review* 38: 683.

Klimchuck, D. (1998), 'Causation, Thin Skulls and Equality', *Canadian Journal of Law and Jurisprudence* 11: 115.

Mead, G. (1991), 'Contracting into Crime', *Oxford Journal of Legal Studies* 11: 147.

Norrie, A. (1991), 'A Critique of Criminal Causation', *Modern Law Review* 54: 685.

Tadros, V. (2005) *Criminal Responsibility* (Oxford: OUP), ch. 6.

3

MENS REA: THE MENTAL ELEMENT

PART I: THE LAW

1 THE MEANING OF *MENS REA*

Mens rea[1] is the legal term used to describe the element of a criminal offence that relates to the defendant's mental state. Those who suffer from Latin-phobia may prefer the phrase 'the mental element of the crime'. Different crimes have different *mens rea*: some require intention, others recklessness, negligence, or knowledge. Some crimes do not require proof of any mental state of the defendant. These are known as strict liability offences and will be discussed in Chapter 4.

It has often been suggested that *mens rea* plays the crucial role of ensuring that only blameworthy defendants are punished for their crimes. Someone who causes another's death by an unforeseeable accident does not deserve punishment; someone who causes another's death intentionally does. However, in assessing a defendant's blameworthiness his or her state of mind is only part of the picture. A mercy killer and a contract killer may both intend to kill, but most people would not regard their actions as equally wicked. Indeed, the existence of defences such as duress or self-defence demonstrate that *mens rea* is not by any means the law's sole criterion for determining blameworthiness. Also the courts have made it quite clear that *mens rea* is not equivalent to moral guilt. In *Yip Chiu-Cheung*[2] a police officer, as part of an undercover operation, pretended to be a drug dealer and agreed with a drug baron to import drugs. The Privy Council confirmed that the police officer had the *mens rea* for a conspiracy to import drugs. In moral terms his behaviour was not blameworthy (some would even say it was commendable), but in the eyes of the law he had the *mens rea* for the conspiracy because he agreed to import drugs.[3]

This chapter will consider the following concepts that are used throughout criminal law: (a) intention; (b) recklessness; (c) negligence; and (d) knowledge. These are not the only kinds of *mens rea*. Others will be discussed elsewhere in the book in the context of specific offences. For example, dishonesty will be discussed when we consider property offences. Which *mens rea* is required depends on the particular offence. For example, murder requires proof that the defendant intended death or grievous bodily harm, while criminal damage requires proof that the defendant was reckless as to whether the property belonging to another would be damaged. Occasionally an offence will have different *mens rea* in respect

---

[1] This Latin phrase means 'guilty mind'.
[2] [1995] 1 AC 111 (HL).   [3] Although, not surprisingly, he was never charged with the offence.

of different aspects of the *actus reus*. For example, in rape the defendant must intend to commit sexual intercourse, but need only be reckless as to whether the victim was not consenting.

As a general rule intention is seen as the worst kind of *mens rea*,[4] recklessness the next worst, and negligence the least serious. Therefore these concepts will be discussed in that order.

2 INTENTION

DEFINITION

Intention is to be given its normal meaning: purpose or aim. In the majority of cases the judge should just ask the jury to give intention its everyday meaning. In exceptional borderline cases the jury can be directed that they are entitled to find intention if a result was virtually certain to occur and the defendant realized it was virtually certain to occur.

In the criminal law the concept of intention is the most blameworthy state of mind: it is usually worse to kill someone intentionally than to kill someone recklessly or negligently. Despite it being such an important concept, the meaning of intention has caused problems for the courts. Indeed the House of Lords has been called upon to define intention at least once in each of the last four decades.[5] The core meaning of intention is fairly straightforward. What have caused difficulties are cases on the borderline of intention and recklessness. We shall first look at the basic meaning of intention, before moving on to consider such problematic cases.

2.1 THE CORE MEANING OF INTENTION

The House of Lords has made it clear that the legal meaning of the word 'intention' is the ordinary meaning of the word. This has led Lord Bridge in the House of Lords in *R v Moloney*[6] to explain:

> The golden rule should be that, when directing a jury on the mental element necessary in a crime of specific intent, the judge should avoid any elaboration or paraphrase of what is meant by intent, and leave it to the jury's good sense to decide whether the accused acted with the necessary intent, unless the judge is convinced that, on the facts and having regard to the way the case has been presented to the jury in evidence and argument, some further explanation or elaboration is strictly necessary to avoid misunderstanding.

So the 'golden rule' is that judges normally avoid defining intention by telling the jury to give it its ordinary meaning. The Court of Appeal recently praised a trial judge who simply

---

[4] Those writers who are good at Latin use *mentes reae* as the plural of *mens rea*.
[5] *DPP v Smith* [1961] AC 290 (HL); *Hyam v DPP* [1975] AC 55 (HL); *Moloney* [1985] AC 905 (HL); *Hancock and Shankland* [1986] AC 455 (HL); *Woollin* [1999] 1 AC 82 (HL).
[6] [1985] AC 905, 926.

asked the jury in a murder trial to consider whether the defendant intended to kill the victim and avoided 'chameleon-like concepts of purpose, foresight of consequence and awareness of risk'.[7] In *Hales*[8] the Court of Appeal indicated that only in rare cases will the judge need to give further directions to the jury on intention.

But what is the ordinary meaning of intention? The courts have not told us because (presumably) they think it is obvious. The widely accepted view is that the defendant intends a consequence of his action if he acts with the aim or purpose of producing that consequence. Lord Asquith in *Cunliffe v Goodman*[9] explained that intention 'connotes a state of affairs which the party "intending" . . . does more than merely contemplate: it connotes a state of affairs which, on the contrary, he decides, so far as in him lies, to bring about'.

A useful test for seeing whether a result was the purpose of the defendant is to rely on Anthony Duff's *test of failure*:[10] had the result not occurred would the defendant regard himself as having failed in his plan? Consider the following case. David throws a burning rag into Veronica's house, wanting to frighten her by causing a fire. The rag in fact sets fire to the house and Veronica is killed. Here, had the rag not caused a fire and so Veronica had not been frightened, David would have regarded his enterprise as a failure. David therefore intended to cause the fire. However, had Veronica lived, David would not have regarded the enterprise as a failure (he wanted to frighten her, not kill her) and therefore he did not intend to kill Veronica.[11]

Although Duff's test is a very useful one there is one set of cases where it has to be treated with caution. That is where a result is a means to achieve a desired end. Imagine Martin kills his great aunt Alfreda in order to get his inheritance. The purpose of Martin's action was to get the inheritance. Using Duff's test of failure we could say that Martin would be delighted if Alfreda had lived, but he had somehow got hold of her money. However, it is generally agreed that Martin would be said to intend his great aunt Alfreda's death. This is because under his plan the desired result (obtaining the inheritance) will be achieved through the means of killing her. So when we consider the purpose of the defendant this includes not only the aim, but also the means he wants to use to achieve that end.

Further to clarify the core notion of intention it is useful to distinguish it from other concepts.

Distinguishing intention and foresight

In relation to the core meaning of intention, whether the defendant's act was likely to produce the consequence is irrelevant. If Neil sees Mary a long way away and shoots at her, hoping to kill her, but realizing that because Mary is so far away he is unlikely to succeed, Neil will still be found to have intended to kill Mary. That is because it was his purpose to kill her. However, many commentators accept that if the defendant believes that it is impossible for his action to cause the result, he cannot be said to intend it, however much he may have wanted the result to occur.[12] This is because he cannot be said to act with the purpose of producing a result if he did not believe that the result could possibly be caused by his act.

The House of Lords in several recent cases has made it clear that foresight of a consequence is not the same as intention, but it is evidence from which a jury may infer or find

---

[7] *R v Wright, The Times*, 17 May 2000 (CA).   [8] [2005] EWCA Crim 1118.
[9] [1950] 2 KB 237, 253 (CA).   [10] Duff (1990) and (1996: ch. 1).   [11] Duff (1990a).
[12] Duff (1990a: 58).

intention.[13] The defendant may foresee that there is a risk that he will hit a fellow golf player by hitting the ball towards the green when there are people still on it, but that does not mean he intends to hit them. However, the degree of likelihood is evidence from which a jury may infer that a defendant intended a result. As Lord Scarman put it in *Hancock and Shankland*:[14]

> the greater the probability of a consequence the more likely it is that the consequence was foreseen and . . . if that consequence was foreseen the greater the probability is that the consequence was also intended . . . [T]he probability, however high, of a consequence is only a factor.

In other words the jury may reason that, given all the evidence of the case and the fact that the consequence was so likely to occur following the defendant's actions, the consequence must have been the purpose of his actions and therefore he intended the result. If Charlotte points a gun at Emily, fires, and thereby kills Emily, Charlotte may say to the jury 'I did not want to kill Emily, my purpose was to see how loud the bang was when the gun went off.' The jury in such a case are likely to disbelieve Charlotte and decide that she must have wanted to kill Emily.

Distinguishing intention and motive

The courts have consistently stated that 'intention is something quite different from motive or desire'.[15] In other words it is possible to intend a consequence without wanting it to happen. In *Hales*[16] the defendant ran over a police officer in his car in attempting to escape from an arrest. It was not his motive to kill the police officer, but he was, Keene LJ explained, 'prepared to kill in order to escape' and therefore intended to kill. That said, of course, proving that someone had a motive to kill the victim is strong evidence that that person intended to kill the victim. Imagine that Dorothy cooks Agatha a meal and puts rat poison in the food, killing her. If the jury hears evidence that Agatha had recently made a will leaving Dorothy a large legacy, the jury are less likely to believe Dorothy if she claims this was an absent-minded mistake and more likely to decide that Dorothy intended to kill Agatha.

Distinguishing intention and premeditation

A person may act instinctively in the heat of the moment and yet intend to kill.[17] It should not be thought that a person can intend a result only if he has carefully formulated a plan as to how he is going to produce the result. The person who kills in the heat of an argument wanting to kill the victim can be said to intend to kill as much as the premeditated killer.

Most of what has been said so far is uncontroversial and cases of this kind have not greatly troubled the courts. Far more problematic are cases of so-called indirect intention or oblique intention: where it is not the defendant's purpose to produce the result, but the result was a virtually certain consequence of the defendant's actions.

---

[13] *Hyam v DPP* [1975] AC 55 (HL); *Moloney* [1985] AC 905 (HL); *Hancock and Shankland* [1986] AC 455 (HL).
[14] [1986] AC 455, 473.   [15] *Moloney* [1985] AC 905, 926.
[16] [2005] EWCA Crim 1118.   [17] See Cane (2000) for a discussion of 'fleeting' states of mind.

2.2 BORDERLINE CASES OF INTENTION

As we have seen, in the majority of cases it is enough for the judge to direct the jury that they are to give intention its normal meaning and there is no need to give further direction to the jury.[18] Indeed in *MD* it was held to be inappropriate to give further direction in a normal case.[19] Further direction *is* necessary in rare or exceptional[20] cases where, even though it is very likely that the result will occur following the defendant's actions, the result was not the defendant's purpose.[21] In many cases, for example where the defendant shoots the victim, it will be unbelievable that the defendant could have any other purpose in mind other than to kill or cause serious injury. But it is not impossible to think of cases where although the defendant's act was very likely to cause death, that was not the defendant's purpose. An oft-quoted example is where a person plants a bomb on an aeroplane, hoping to destroy items on board which he has insured. Although he does not want the pilot of the plane to die he knows that this will inevitably occur if the bomb goes off in mid-flight. In such cases, it is necessary for the judge to give a further direction to the jury. *Woollin* is the latest in a long line of cases discussing the correct direction to give a jury in these borderline cases. It represents the present law. The key question for the House of Lords was the appropriateness of a direction proposed by Lord Lane CJ in the Court of Appeal case of *Nedrick*:[22]

> Where the charge is murder and in the rare cases where the simple direction is not enough, the jury should be directed that they are not entitled to infer the necessary intention, unless they feel sure that death or serious bodily harm was a virtual certainty (barring some unforeseen intervention) as a result of the defendant's actions and that the defendant appreciated that such was the case.

R v Woollin
[1999] AC 82 (HL)[23]

Stephen Woollin (the appellant) killed his three-month-old son after throwing him on to a hard surface in a fit of temper. At one point in his summing up the judge directed the jury that if they were satisfied that the appellant had realized that there was a substantial risk that the child would suffer serious harm they could convict him of murder. The appellant appealed unsuccessfully to the Court of Appeal. He then appealed to the House of Lords.

Lord Steyn

The Court of Appeal certified the following questions as of general importance:

'1. In murder, where there is no direct evidence that the purpose of a defendant was to kill or to inflict serious injury on the victim, is it necessary to direct the jury that they may only infer

---

[18] Lord Bridge in *Moloney* [1985] AC 905, 926 thought it would be necessary to give a further direction only in 'rare' and 'exceptional' cases.
[19] [2004] EWCA Crim 1391.   [20] *Allen* [2005] EWCA Crim 1344, para. 63.
[21] *R v Hayes* [2002] All ER (D) 6 (CA).   [22] [1986] 1 WLR 1025 (CA).
[23] [1998] 4 All ER 103, [1998] 3 WLR 382, [1999] 1 Cr App R 8, [1998] Crim LR 890.

an intent to do serious injury, if they are satisfied (a) that serious bodily harm was a virtually certain consequence of the defendant's voluntary act and (b) that the defendant appreciated that fact?

'2. If the answer to question 1 is "yes," is such a direction necessary in all cases or is it only necessary in cases where the sole evidence of the defendant's intention is to be found in his actions and their consequence to the victim?'

On appeal to your Lordships' House the terrain of the debate covered the correctness in law of the direction recommended by Lord Lane CJ in *Nedrick* and, if that direction is sound, whether it should be used only in the limited category of cases envisaged by the Court of Appeal. And counsel for the appellant renewed his submission that by directing the jury in terms of substantial risk the judge illegitimately widened the mental element of murder.

[Having quoted extensively from Lord Lane's direction in *Nedrick* Lord Steyn concluded:] The effect of the critical direction is that a result foreseen as virtually certain is an intended result.

. . .

The Crown did not argue that as a matter of policy foresight of a virtual certainty is too narrow a test in murder. Subject to minor qualifications, the decision in *Nedrick* was widely welcomed by distinguished academic writers: see Professor JC Smith QC's commentary on *Nedrick* [1986] Crim LR 742, 743–744; Glanville Williams, 'The *Mens Rea* for Murder: Leave it Alone' (1989) 105 LQR 387; J R Spencer, 'Murder in the Dark: A Glimmer of Light?' [1986] CLJ 366–367; Ashworth, *Principles of Criminal Law*, 2nd ed (1995), p 172. It is also of interest that it is very similar to the threshold of being aware 'that it will occur in the ordinary course of events' in the Law Commission's draft Criminal Code (see *Criminal Law: Legislating the Criminal Code: Offences against the Person and General Principles*, Law Com No 218 (1993) (Cm 2370), App A (Draft Criminal Law Bill with Explanatory Notes), pp 90–91): compare also Professor JC Smith QC, 'A Note on "Intention" ' [1990] Crim LR 85, 86. Moreover, over a period of twelve years since *Nedrick* the test of foresight of virtual certainty has apparently caused no practical difficulties. It is simple and clear. It is true that it may exclude a conviction of murder in the often cited terrorist example where a member of the bomb disposal team is killed. In such a case it may realistically be said that the terrorist did not foresee the killing of a member of the bomb disposal team as a virtual certainty. That may be a consequence of not framing the principle in terms of risk taking. Such cases ought to cause no substantial difficulty since immediately below murder there is available a verdict of manslaughter which may attract in the discretion of the court a life sentence. In any event, as Lord Lane eloquently argued in a debate in the House of Lords, to frame a principle for particular difficulties regarding terrorism 'would produce corresponding injustices which would be very hard to eradicate': Hansard (HL Debates), 6 November 1989, col 480. I am satisfied that the Nedrick test, which was squarely based on the decision of the House in *Moloney*, is pitched at the right level of foresight.

. . . It may be appropriate to give a direction in accordance with *Nedrick* in any case in which the defendant may not have desired the result of his act. But I accept the trial judge is best placed to decide what direction is required by the circumstances of the case.

The disposal of the present appeal

It follows that judge should not have departed from the *Nedrick* direction. By using the phrase 'substantial risk' the judge blurred the line between intention and recklessness, and hence between murder and manslaughter. The misdirection enlarged the scope of the mental element required for murder. It was a material misdirection. . . .

The status of *Nedrick*

In my view Lord Lane CJ's judgment in *Nedrick* provided valuable assistance to trial judges. The model direction is by now a tried-and-tested formula. Trial judges ought to continue to use it. On matters of detail I have three observations, which can best be understood if I set out again the relevant part of Lord Lane's judgment. It was:

'(A) When determining whether the defendant had the necessary intent, it may therefore be helpful for a jury to ask themselves two questions. (1) How probable was the consequence which resulted from the defendant's voluntary act? (2) Did he foresee that consequence?

'If he did not appreciate that death or serious harm was likely to result from his act, he cannot have intended to bring it about. If he did, but thought that the risk to which he was exposing the person killed was only slight, then it may be easy for the jury to conclude that he did not intend to bring about that result. On the other hand, if the jury are satisfied that at the material time the defendant recognised that death or serious harm would be virtually certain (barring some unforeseen intervention) to result from his voluntary act, then that is a fact from which they may find it easy to infer that he intended to kill or do serious bodily harm, even though he may not have had any desire to achieve that result. . . .

'(B) Where the charge is murder and in the rare cases where the simple direction is not enough, the jury should be directed that they are not entitled to infer the necessary intention, unless they feel sure that death or serious bodily harm was a virtual certainty (barring some unforeseen intervention) as a result of the defendant's actions and that the defendant appreciated that such was the case.

'(C) Where a man realises that it is for all practical purposes inevitable that his actions will result in death or serious harm, the inference may be irresistible that he intended that result, however little he may have desired or wished it to happen. The decision is one for the jury to be reached upon a consideration of all the evidence.' (Lettering added)

First, I am persuaded by the speech of my noble and learned friend, Lord Hope of Craighead, that it is unlikely, if ever, to be helpful to direct the jury in terms of the two questions set out in (A). I agree that these questions may detract from the clarity of the critical direction in (B). Secondly, in their writings previously cited Glanville Williams, Professor Smith and Andrew Ashworth observed that the use of the words 'to infer' in (B) may detract from the clarity of the model direction. I agree. I would substitute the words 'to find.' Thirdly, the first sentence of (C) does not form part of the model direction. But it would always be right for the judge to say, as Lord Lane C.J. put it, that the decision is for the jury upon a consideration of all the evidence in the case. . . .

Appeal allowed; conviction of murder quashed; conviction of manslaughter substituted.

This decision makes it clear that in a murder case the jury should usually just be told to give intent its normal meaning. Where it is not the purpose of the defendant to cause death or grievous bodily harm only rarely will the defendant be found to have the *mens rea* for murder (an intention to kill or cause grievous bodily harm). Only if the death or grievous bodily harm was a virtually certain consequence of the defendant's actions and the defendant realized this was so, can the jury find that the defendant intended death or grievous bodily harm.

Parliament has made it clear that just because a defendant foresaw death was a likely result of his actions does not mean that he necessarily intended death.[24] Section 8 of the Criminal Justice Act 1967 states that a jury:

> (a) shall not be bound in law to infer that he intended or foresaw a result of his actions by reason only of its being a natural and probable consequence of those actions; but
>
> (b) shall decide whether he did intend or foresee that result by reference to all the evidence, drawing such inferences from the evidence as appear proper in the circumstances.

EXAMINATION TIP

The following provides a useful chart for deciding whether a defendant has intention:

Was it the result of the defendant's purpose? YES: he intended it
NO: ask the next question:

Was the result a virtually certain result of   YES: then the jury are entitled to find that he
his actions and did the defendant realize   intended the result
that the result was a virtually certain   NO: he did not intend the result.
result of his actions?

The *Woollin* virtual certainty test at first sight appears straightforward, but there are a number of uncertainties about its interpretation:

(1) What does 'virtually certain' mean? It means that the result will occur unless something completely unexpected occurs.[25] For example, if George pushes Edward off the top of a high cliff, it is conceivable that despite the fall Edward will not suffer death or serious injury. Just occasionally there are stories of people falling great heights without serious injury, but it is virtually certain that Edward will suffer death or serious injury. In other words, 'virtually certain' means as certain as we can be about anything.

(2) If it is shown that the event was virtually certain to result from the defendant's acts and the defendant appreciates this, *must* the jury find intent or *may* the jury find intention? There has been much academic debate on this question.[26] It was recently considered by the Court of Appeal in *Matthews*[27] who after a careful analysis of the authorities made it clear that it was a misdirection for a judge to tell a jury that if a result was foreseen as virtually certain then they *must* find intention. Although the Court of Appeal felt that there were cases, including *Matthews* itself, where, having answered the *Nedrick* questions affirmatively, a finding of intent would be 'irresistible'.

(3) How should the jury decide whether or not to find intention? What factors are the jury to take into account? The answer is that they may take into account any factors

---

[24] *R v Moloney* [1985] AC 905 (HL).   [25] *Moloney* [1985] AC 905, 925 (HL).
[26] e.g. compare Allen (2003: 62–5) and Mirfield (1999).   [27] [2003] EWCA Crim 192.

they wish. It is likely that a jury would consider the motives of the defendant and the circumstances of his actions. Compare these cases:

(i) Alice plants a bomb on an aeroplane intending to blow up the plane so that she can claim money for goods on board which she has insured. She knows it is virtually certain that the bomb will cause the death of those on the plane.

(ii) Ben is at the top of a burning building with his baby. As the flames grow closer he is convinced he and the baby are about to be burnt to death. He throws the baby from the rooftop, even though he knows the baby is almost bound to die because he believes that that is only the way the baby's life may be spared.

Although the matter is entirely in the hands of the jury it is likely that the jury would find that Alice, but not Ben, intended to kill. A jury is likely to be sympathetic to a person who is acting from a good motive (like Ben) rather than a person acting from a disreputable motive (like Alice). In fact case (ii) is particularly striking because Ben's purpose was to save the life of the baby. Therefore to find that he intended to kill the baby seems almost perverse.[28]

(4) There is some doubt whether, using the *Woollin* test, it is necessary to show that the result was actually virtually certain, as well as showing that the defendant believed it was. It appears from the approved *Nedrick* direction to the jury that both must be shown. So the bomber who placed the bomb on the plane may not, under the *Woollin* test, be said to intend the result if (unknown to the bomber) the plane was fitted with a special device which meant that it could normally land safely even if a bomb went off in its cargo hold. This is a little odd, in that it suggests that the structure of the plane can affect the legal classification of the defendant's state of mind. However, Professor Allen[29] has argued, relying on Lord Steyn's *dicta*: 'a result foreseen as virtually certain is an intended result', that all that needs to be shown is that the defendant foresaw the result as virtually certain. His view was not taken up by the Court of Appeal in *Hayes*[30] or *Matthews*[31] which, without discussing the issue, assumed that the *Woollin* direction required both that the result was in fact virtually certain to occur and that the defendant realized this.

(5) What is the significance of Lord Steyn changing the word 'infer' in the *Nedrick* direction to the word 'find'? Unfortunately Lord Steyn did not explain the reason for the change. Here are two possible explanations:

(i) He may simply have thought that 'find' was an easier word for juries to understand than 'infer'. This view, then, is that Lord Steyn did not mean to change the meaning of the direction, just to use more everyday language. If this view is correct then it is not surprising that he offers no explanation for the change.

(ii) He may have meant to suggest that foresight of virtual certainty is not just evidence from which one could infer intention, but actually is intention (in the legal sense). The word 'infer' is used when we use one fact to presume the existence of another fact. For example, you infer from the fact that someone is wearing a wedding ring that he or she is married. Being married and wearing a wedding ring are not the same thing, but one is evidence of the other. Therefore talk about inferring intent from

---

[28] It should be added that in many cases where a defendant had a good motive for acting as he or she did, a defence will be available.
[29] Allen (2003: 64).   [30] [2002] All ER (D) 6 (CA).   [31] [2003] EWCA Crim 192.

foresight of virtual certainty indicates that foresight of virtual certainty and intent are different, but that one is evidence of the other. By contrast, saying that you can find intent from foresight of virtual certainty might suggest that a jury is entitled to conclude that foresight of virtual certainty *is* intention. The main argument in favour of this view is that Lord Steyn refers to an article of Professor Smith who was critical of the courts' use of the word inference and argued that foresight of virtual certainty actually is intention.

(6) Is the *Woollin* test just to be used in cases of murder, or does it apply to other crimes which require proof of intention? Notably Lord Steyn expressly restricted his discussion to murder. Therefore, whenever a crime requires proof of intent the court must consider whether the intention is restricted to its core meaning or whether the *Woollin* direction also applies. In Part II we shall consider further the different roles that intention plays in the criminal law.

QUESTION

Bill is suffering from a terminal illness and is in great pain. His doctor gives him a large dose of painkillers which cause Bill's death within 24 hours. Consider the following states of mind the doctor could have. Which would lead to a conviction of murder?

(1) The doctor wants to lessen Bill's pain by the pills, although she knows that the pills will hasten Bill's death.

(2) The doctor believes Bill has suffered enough and wants to end his pain by killing him.

(3) The doctor wants Bill to die because she knows Bill has left her a large sum of money in his will.

Read accounts of the trial of Dr Moor (P. Arlidge, 'The Trial of Dr David Moor' [2000] *Crim LR* 31; J. Smith, 'A Comment on Moor's Case' [2000] *Crim LR* 41) for a discussion of a recent case involving a doctor alleged to have 'mercy killed' his patient.

FURTHER READING

For further reading on the correct interpretation of the *Woollin* decision, read:

Norrie, A. (1999), 'After *Woollin*', *Criminal Law Review* 532.

—— (2000), *Punishment, Responsibility and Justice* (Oxford: OUP), ch. 8.

Pedain, A. (2003), 'Intention and the Terrorist Example', *Criminal Law Review* 579.

Simester, A., and Shute, S. (1999), 'Letter', *Criminal Law Review* 41.

Smith, J.C. (1998), 'Commentary on *R v Woollin*', *Criminal Law Review* 890.

Wilson, W. (1999), 'Doctrinal Rationality after *Woollin*', *Modern Law Review* 62: 448.

See Part II for reading on the theoretical approaches to intention.

2.3 INTOXICATION AND INTENT

What about a case where a defendant is charged with an offence which requires proof of intent, but at the time of the offence he was intoxicated through alcohol or drugs? Where the defendant is intoxicated (involuntarily or voluntarily[32]) the jury or magistrates should consider the intoxication as part of the evidence in deciding whether the result was the defendant's purpose or whether he foresaw the result as virtually certain:[33]

(1) If the drunken defendant had as his purpose the result he intended it: a 'drunken intent is still an intent'.[34]

(2) If the drunken defendant lacked intent he is not guilty of an intent-based crime, although he may be guilty of a recklessness-based offence.

A good example of how intent and intoxication can interrelate is *Moloney*.[35] There the defendant and his step-father had engaged on a long drinking spree. They then decided to engage in a shooting competition to see who could load and fire a gun the fastest. The defendant won, but in so doing shot his step-father dead. His evidence was that he had fired the gun with the purpose of winning the shooting competition. His story would, no doubt, have been disbelieved by the jury had he been sober, but the fact he was intoxicated made his version of events more believable. Note here though that his defence is not the intoxication, but the fact that he lacked *mens rea*. His intoxication was evidence from which the jury could conclude he lacked intent.[36]

3 RECKLESSNESS

If purpose is at the heart of intention, risk-taking is at the heart of recklessness. For many years the law on recklessness was confusing because there were two definitions of recklessness, which have become known as *Cunningham* recklessness and *Caldwell* recklessness. Some crimes used one and some the other. However, recently the House of Lords have abolished *Caldwell* recklessness and so now there is only one kind of recklessness used. For once a change in the law has made it easier for students to understand rather than harder!

3.1 *CUNNINGHAM* RECKLESSNESS

DEFINITION

There are two elements that need to be shown for *Cunningham* recklessness:

(1) The defendant was aware that there was a risk that his or her conduct would cause a particular result.

(2) The risk was an unreasonable one for the defendant to take.

Recklessness is made up of the following two elements.

---

[32] See p. 171 for a discussion of the difference between voluntary and involuntary intoxication.

[33] The question for the jury or magistrates is whether or not the defendant had the intention, not whether or not the defendant, in his drunken state, was capable of forming an intention: *Hayes* [2002] All ER (D) 6 (CA).

[34] *Majewski* [1977] AC 443 (HL).

[35] [1985] AC 905 (HL).   [36] He was still guilty of manslaughter.

The taking of a risk

In *Cunningham*,[37] Byrne J explained that recklessness meant that 'the accused has foreseen that the particular kind of harm might be done and yet has gone on to take the risk of it'.[38] Two points in particular need to be stressed about this definition. First, it is necessary to show only that the accused foresaw that there was *a* risk. It does not have to be foreseen as highly likely to occur. Secondly, the question is whether the accused foresaw the risk, not whether the risk was obvious or would have been foreseen by a reasonable person. This point is demonstrated in *Stephenson*,[39] where the defendant (who suffered from schizophrenia) lit a fire in a haystack and destroyed it. Because of his illness he did not realize that in lighting a match there was a risk to the haystack. Although the risk to the haystack was obvious and most people would have foreseen the risk, the defendant did not, and so he was not *Cunningham* reckless.

This requirement that the defendant consciously took a risk caused problems in the following case:

R v Parker
[1977] 2 All ER 37[40]

Daryl Parker was fined £10 plus 75p compensation to the Post Office, after causing criminal damage to a telephone kiosk.[41] He had had a terrible evening. He had overslept on the train home after a function in London and missed his station. He was charged an excess fare for travelling further than his ticket permitted. He tried to telephone for a taxi but the telephone did not work. He was seen by the police to 'smash down' a telephone handset onto the dialling box of the public telephone and thereby damage it.

Lord Justice Geoffrey Lane

What was in dispute was, first of all, whether it was the appellant who had caused the damage to the telephone receiver; he said it was not he who had caused the damage; and, secondly, the degree of force which he had used when bringing the handset down on to the receiver. The way in which the appellant himself when giving evidence described the situation was this:

'I went to the telephone box to call a taxi. I put two pence on the slot—not in, but on—I picked up the headset [that must have been the handset]; I heard a tone . . . I did not know it was necessary to put two pence in before dialling. I dialled two or three times without success. I put the headset down, hard. It did not fit on to the cradle so I put it down hard again. I did not lift it before putting it down the first time. I must have missed the cradle the first time. I did not intend to damage it nor was I reckless as to whether I damaged it or not. It did not occur to me that what I was doing might damage it. I was simply reacting to the frustration which I felt. As I put the telephone down hard for the second time there were the police opening the door.'

. . .

---

[37] [1957] 2 QB 396 (CA).   [38] At 399.   [39] [1979] QB 695 (CA).
[40] [1977] 1 WLR 600, (1977) 63 Cr App R 211.   [41] See Ch. 11 for the law on criminal damage.

The complaint made by counsel for the appellant is that the learned judge misdirected the jury in regard to the necessary mental element on which the jury had to be satisfied before convicting. . . .

[Counsel for the appellant] draws support from a decision of this court, *R v Briggs* [1977] 1 All ER 475. That was a case where the facts were very different from those in the instant case. In the course of the judgment the following passage is to be found ([1977] 1 All ER 475 at 477, 478):

'A man is reckless in the sense required [and that is dealing, of course, with s 1 of the Criminal Damage Act 1971] when he carries out a deliberate act knowing that there is some risk of damage resulting from that act but nevertheless continues in the performance of that act. That being so, it is clear from the three passages to which I have in particular referred that the judge did not give a correct direction to the jury on this aspect of the case. Using the words which he did, he might have cured the defect by explaining to the jury in clear terms that the test to be applied was the test of the state of the appellant's mind, but he did not put that anywhere in his summing-up.'

We are bound by that decision and, indeed, at least so far as the first sentence which I have read is concerned, we would not for one moment wish to disagree even were we able to so do. The test is the test of the defendant's state of mind. But, and in the facts of the instant case it is a substantial 'but', the circumstances of this case are that the appellant was plainly fully aware of all the circumstances of the case. He was fully aware that what he was handling was a telephone handset made of Bakelite or some such material. He was well aware that the cradle on to which he admittedly brought down the handset was made of similar material. He was well aware, of course, of the degree of force which he was using—a degree described by counsel for the appellant before us as slamming the receiver down and—demonstration by counsel whether wittingly or not, was given of a hand brought down from head-height on to whatever the receiving object was.

In those circumstances, it seems to this court that if he did not know, as he said he did not, that there was some risk of damage, he was, in effect, deliberately closing his mind to the obvious—the obvious being that damage in these circumstances was inevitable.

In the view of this court, that type of action, that type of deliberate closing of the mind, is the equivalent of knowledge and a man certainly cannot escape the consequences of his action in this particular set of circumstances by saying, 'I never directed my mind to the obvious consequences because I was in a self-induced state of temper.'

We, accordingly, do not differ from the views expressed in *R v Briggs* [1977] 1 All ER 475 with the exception of adding to the definition these words: 'A man is reckless in the sense required when he carries out a deliberate act knowing or closing his mind to the obvious fact that there is some risk of damage resulting from that act but nevertheless continuing in the performance of that act.' . . .

Appeal dismissed.

What is noticeable here is that the Court of Appeal was willing to stretch recklessness to its limits in order to convict the defendant whom it regarded as blameworthy. Having a risk in the back of your mind is not the same as consciously taking a risk, although the Court of Appeal was willing to accept that it was sufficient to amount to *Cunningham* recklessness.[42]

---

[42] See Part II of this chapter for further discussion.

The risk was unreasonable

This requirement is rarely in dispute. It will be unusual for there to be a case where it is reasonable for the defendant to take a risk that a person will be injured. However, there will be some cases where it is. If the defendant is driving and a child runs out in front of his car and he swerves out of the way, the swerve may pose a risk to other road users, but to swerve would often be regarded as reasonable. It should be stressed that this requirement is object-ive. In other words that whether the risk was a reasonable one to take is to be decided by the standards of the ordinary and reasonable person.[43] Whether the defendant thought it was or was not reasonable to take the risk is irrelevant.

Intoxication and recklessness

Defendants who were voluntarily intoxicated at the time of the offence and therefore failed to foresee a risk which they would have foreseen if they had been sober, will be treated as having foreseen the risk. This means that defendants will not be able to claim that they failed to foresee an obvious risk because they were drunk.[44] If defendants are involuntarily intoxi-cated then there are no special rules, and defendants will be reckless if they foresaw the risk, but if they did not foresee the risk they will not be reckless.[45]

QUESTIONS

1. If a psychologist gave evidence that Mr Parker was so angry that he was not aware of a risk, would he deserve to be acquitted? Is there a clear difference between (a) consciously being aware of a risk; (b) putting a risk to the back of your mind; and (c) not being aware of a risk?

2. Thousands of deaths and injuries occur each year in cars. Anyone driving a car is aware that in driving a car there is a risk they will injure someone. Is it beyond doubt that it is still reasonable to drive cars? What about skiing?

3. Is it justifiable to describe as 'reckless', people who are so drunk that they do not see an obvious risk, but not people who are so angry that they do not see an obvious risk? (We will return to this question in Part II.)

3.2 *CALDWELL* RECKLESSNESS

As already mentioned *Caldwell* recklessness has now been abolished. However, it is useful to know in outline what it was and why the House of Lords decided to abolish it.

DEFINITION

Defendants were *Caldwell* reckless if:

(i) they are aware of a risk OR

---

[43] One important issue will be whether the defendant's behaviour was socially useful. A defendant who harms another while carrying out medical treatment is likely to be acting reasonably, while a defendant who harms another while shooting birds for fun will find it harder to persuade a jury his behaviour was reasonable.

[44] *Bennett* [1995] Crim LR 877 (CA).   [45] *Kingston* [1995] 2 AC 355 (HL) (extracted at p. 722).

(ii) there was an obvious and serious risk AND they failed to consider whether or not there was a risk.

Caldwell recklessness was different from *Cunningham* recklessness because it includes defendants who were not aware of an obvious risk. *Caldwell* recklessness fell into disrepute because it punished defendants for failing to notice a risk which would have been obvious to a reasonable person. The issue was considered in *Elliott v C*,[46] where a 14-year-old girl with learning difficulties set fire to a shed by lighting white spirit. The court stated that Lord Diplock in *Caldwell* had made it clear that the test was whether a reasonable person would have realized that the lighting of the spirit would create a risk of damage to the shed, not whether the risk was obvious to the defendant or obvious to a reasonable person of the defendant's age and mental abilities.[47] As she had failed to consider the risk and it would have been obvious to a reasonable person, she was guilty of criminal damage. The decision caused an outcry amongst academic commentators. Had they been tabloid writers it would have been given the title 'the most hated case in Britain'. The reason for the outrage is this: it can lead to the punishment of a defendant who fails to appreciate a risk that she was incapable of foreseeing. C was liable for failing to foresee a risk that because of her mental condition she may have been incapable of foreseeing. The harshness of this approach is revealed by the following example: a blind person is walking down the pavement and walks into a bicycle left lying on the pavement, damaging it. As the risk would be obvious to an ordinary (sighted) person he would be *Caldwell* reckless as he failed to foresee the risk. This is extraordinary. With this in mind it was not surprising that the House of Lords in *G and R* decided that *Caldwell* recklessness had to go.

R v G and R
[2003] UKHL 50 (HL)[48]

One night two boys, aged 11 and 12, went camping without their parents' permission. In the early hours of the morning they set fire to some newspapers under a wheelie-bin they found outside a supermarket. The fire spread and ultimately burned down the supermarket and adjoining buildings. They were convicted on the basis that it would have been obvious to a reasonable person that what they were doing was posing a risk to property. They unsuccessfully appealed to the Court of Appeal, and then on to the House of Lords.

Lord Bingham of Cornhill

1. The point of law of general public importance certified by the Court of Appeal to be involved in its decision in the present case is expressed in this way:

'Can a defendant properly be convicted under section 1 of the Criminal Damage Act 1971 on the basis that he was reckless as to whether property was destroyed or damaged when he gave no thought to the risk but, by reason of his age and/or personal characteristics the risk would not have been obvious to him, even if he had thought about it?'

---

[46] [1983] 2 All ER 1005 (DC).
[47] *Elliott v C* was followed in *Stephen (Malcolm R)* (1984) 79 Cr App R 334.
[48] [2004] 1 AC 1034; [2003] 3 WLR 1060; [2003] 4 All ER 765; [2004] 1 Cr App R 21; [2004] Crim LR 369.

The appeal turns on the meaning of 'reckless' in that section. This is a question on which the House ruled in *R v Caldwell* [1982] AC 341, a ruling affirmed by the House in later decisions. The House is again asked to reconsider that ruling . . .

28. The task confronting the House in this appeal is, first of all, one of statutory construction: what did Parliament mean when it used the word 'reckless' in section 1(1) and (2) of the 1971 Act? In so expressing the question I mean to make it as plain as I can that I am not addressing the meaning of 'reckless' in any other statutory or common law context. In particular, but perhaps needlessly since 'recklessly' has now been banished from the lexicon of driving offences, I would wish to throw no doubt on the decisions of the House in *R v Lawrence* [1982] AC 510 and *R v Reid* [1992] 1 WLR 793.

29. Since a statute is always speaking, the context or application of a statutory expression may change over time, but the meaning of the expression itself cannot change. So the starting point is to ascertain what Parliament meant by 'reckless' in 1971. As noted above in paragraph 13, section 1 as enacted followed, subject to an immaterial addition, the draft proposed by the Law Commission. It cannot be supposed that by 'reckless' Parliament meant anything different from the Law Commission. The Law Commission's meaning was made plain both in its Report (Law Com No 29) and in Working Paper No 23 which preceded it. These materials (not, it would seem, placed before the House in *R v Caldwell*) reveal a very plain intention to replace the old-fashioned and misleading expression 'maliciously' by the more familiar expression 'reckless' but to give the latter expression the meaning which *R v Cunningham* [1957] 2 QB 396 and Professor Kenny had given to the former. In treating this authority as irrelevant to the construction of 'reckless' the majority fell into understandable but clearly demonstrable error. No relevant change in the mens rea necessary for proof of the offence was intended, and in holding otherwise the majority misconstrued section 1 of the Act.

30. That conclusion is by no means determinative of this appeal. For the decision in *R v Caldwell* was made more than 20 years ago. Its essential reasoning was unanimously approved by the House in *R v Lawrence* [1982] AC 510. Invitations to reconsider that reasoning have been rejected. The principles laid down have been applied on many occasions, by Crown Court judges and, even more frequently, by justices. In the submission of the Crown, the ruling of the House works well and causes no injustice in practice. If Parliament had wished to give effect to the intention of the Law Commission it has had many opportunities, which it has not taken, to do so. Despite its power under *Practice Statement (Judicial Precedent)* [1966] 1 WLR 1234 to depart from its earlier decisions, the House should be very slow to do so, not least in a context such as this.

31. These are formidable arguments, deployed by Mr Perry [counsel for the Crown] with his habitual skill and erudition. But I am persuaded by Mr Newman QC for the appellants that they should be rejected. I reach this conclusion for four reasons, taken together.

32. First, it is a salutary principle that conviction of serious crime should depend on proof not simply that the defendant caused (by act or omission) an injurious result to another but that his state of mind when so acting was culpable. This, after all, is the meaning of the familiar rule *actus non facit reum nisi mens sit rea*. The most obviously culpable state of mind is no doubt an intention to cause the injurious result, but knowing disregard of an appreciated and unacceptable risk of causing an injurious result or a deliberate closing of the mind to such risk would be readily accepted as culpable also. It is clearly blameworthy to take an obvious and significant risk of causing injury to another. But it is not clearly blameworthy to do something involving a risk of injury to another if (for reasons other than self-induced intoxication: *R v Majewski* [1977] AC 443) one genuinely does not perceive the risk. Such a person

may fairly be accused of stupidity or lack of imagination, but neither of those failings should expose him to conviction of serious crime or the risk of punishment.

33. Secondly, the present case shows, more clearly than any other reported case since *R v Caldwell*, that the model direction formulated by Lord Diplock (see paragraph 18 above) is capable of leading to obvious unfairness. As the excerpts quoted in paragraphs 6–7 reveal, the trial judge regretted the direction he (quite rightly) felt compelled to give, and it is evident that this direction offended the jury's sense of fairness. The sense of fairness of 12 representative citizens sitting as a jury (or of a smaller group of lay justices sitting as a bench of magistrates) is the bedrock on which the administration of criminal justice in this country is built. A law which runs counter to that sense must cause concern. Here, the appellants could have been charged under section 1(1) with recklessly damaging one or both of the wheelie-bins, and they would have had little defence. As it was, the jury might have inferred that boys of the appellants' age would have appreciated the risk to the building of what they did, but it seems clear that such was not their conclusion (nor, it would appear, the judge's either). On that basis the jury thought it unfair to convict them. I share their sense of unease. It is neither moral nor just to convict a defendant (least of all a child) on the strength of what someone else would have apprehended if the defendant himself had no such apprehension. Nor, the defendant having been convicted, is the problem cured by imposition of a nominal penalty.

34. Thirdly, I do not think the criticism of *R v Caldwell* expressed by academics, judges and practitioners should be ignored. A decision is not, of course, to be overruled or departed from simply because it meets with disfavour in the learned journals. But a decision which attracts reasoned and outspoken criticism by the leading scholars of the day, respected as authorities in the field, must command attention. One need only cite (among many other examples) the observations of Professor John Smith ([1981] Crim LR 392, 393–396) and Professor Glanville Williams ('Recklessness Redefined' (1981) 40 CLJ 252). This criticism carries greater weight when voiced also by judges as authoritative as Lord Edmund-Davies and Lord Wilberforce in *R v Caldwell* itself, Robert Goff LJ in *Elliott v C* [1983] 1 WLR 939 and Ackner LJ in *R v Stephen Malcolm R* (1984) 79 Cr App R 334. The reservations expressed by the trial judge in the present case are widely shared. The shopfloor response to *R v Caldwell* may be gauged from the editors' commentary, to be found in the 41st edition of *Archbold* (1982): paragraph 17–25, pages 1,009–1,010. The editors suggested that remedial legislation was urgently required.

35. Fourthly, the majority's interpretation of 'recklessly' in section 1 of the 1971 Act was, as already shown, a misinterpretation. If it were a misinterpretation that offended no principle and gave rise to no injustice there would be strong grounds for adhering to the misinterpretation and leaving Parliament to correct it if it chose. But this misinterpretation is offensive to principle and is apt to cause injustice. That being so, the need to correct the misinterpretation is compelling.

36. It is perhaps unfortunate that the question at issue in this appeal fell to be answered in a case of self-induced intoxication. For one instinctively recoils from the notion that a defendant can escape the criminal consequences of his injurious conduct by drinking himself into a state where he is blind to the risk he is causing to others. In *R v Caldwell* it seems to have been assumed (see paragraph 18 above) that the risk would have been obvious to the defendant had he been sober. Further, the context did not require the House to give close consideration to the liability of those (such as the very young and the mentally handicapped) who were not normal reasonable adults. The overruling by the majority of *R v Stephenson* [1979] QB 695 does however make it questionable whether such consideration would have led to a different result.

37. In the course of argument before the House it was suggested that the rule in *R v Caldwell* might be modified, in cases involving children, by requiring comparison not with normal reasonable adults but with normal reasonable children of the same age. This is a suggestion with some attractions but it is open to four compelling objections. First, even this modification would offend the principle that conviction should depend on proving the state of mind of the individual defendant to be culpable. Second, if the rule were modified in relation to children on grounds of their immaturity it would be anomalous if it were not also modified in relation to the mentally handicapped on grounds of their limited understanding. Third, any modification along these lines would open the door to difficult and contentious argument concerning the qualities and characteristics to be taken into account for purposes of the comparison. Fourth, to adopt this modification would be to substitute one misinterpretation of section 1 for another. There is no warrant in the Act or in the *travaux préparatoires* which preceded it for such an interpretation.

38. A further refinement, advanced by Professor Glanville Williams in his article 'Reckless-ness Redefined' (1981) 40 CLJ 252, 270–271, adopted by the justices in *Elliott v C* [1983] 1 WLR 939 and commented upon by Robert Goff LJ in that case is that a defendant should only be regarded as having acted recklessly by virtue of his failure to give any thought to an obvious risk that property would be destroyed or damaged, where such risk would have been obvious to him if he had given any thought to the matter. This refinement also has attractions, although it does not meet the objection of principle and does not represent a correct inter-pretation of the section. It is, in my opinion, open to the further objection of over-complicating the task of the jury (or bench of justices). It is one thing to decide whether a defendant can be believed when he says that the thought of a given risk never crossed his mind. It is another, and much more speculative, task to decide whether the risk would have been obvious to him if the thought had crossed his mind. The simpler the jury's task, the more likely is its verdict to be reliable. Robert Goff LJ's reason for rejecting this refinement was somewhat similar (*Elliott v C*, page 950).

39. I cannot accept that restoration of the law as understood before *R v Caldwell* would lead to the acquittal of those whom public policy would require to be convicted. There is nothing to suggest that this was seen as a problem before *R v Caldwell*, or (as noted above in paragraphs 12 and 13) before the 1971 Act. There is no reason to doubt the common sense which tribunals of fact bring to their task. In a contested case based on intention, the defendant rarely admits intending the injurious result in question, but the tribunal of fact will readily infer such an intention, in a proper case, from all the circumstances and probabilities and evidence of what the defendant did and said at the time. Similarly with recklessness: it is not to be supposed that the tribunal of fact will accept a defendant's assertion that he never thought of a certain risk when all the circumstances and probabilities and evidence of what he did and said at the time show that he did or must have done . . .

41. For the reasons I have given I would allow this appeal and quash the appellants' convictions. I would answer the certified question obliquely, basing myself on clause 18(c) of the Criminal Code Bill annexed by the Law Commission to its Report 'A Criminal Code for England and Wales Volume 1: Report and Draft Criminal Code Bill' (Law Com No 177, April 1989):

'A person acts recklessly within the meaning of section 1 of the Criminal Damage Act 1971 with respect to—

   (i) a circumstance when he is aware of a risk that it exists or will exist;

   (ii) a result when he is aware of a risk that it will occur;

and it is, in the circumstances known to him, unreasonable to take the risk.'

Lord Steyn

45. In my view the very high threshold for departing from a previous decision of the House has been satisfied in this particular case. In summary I would reduce my reasons to three propositions. First, in *Caldwell* the majority should have accepted without equivocation that before the passing of the 1971 Act foresight of consequences was an essential element in recklessness in the context of damage to property under section 51 of the Malicious Damage Act 1861. Secondly, the matrix of the immediately preceding Law Commission recommendations shows convincingly that the purpose of section 1 of the 1971 Act was to replace the out of date language of 'maliciously' causing damage by more modern language while not changing the substance of the mental element in any way. Foresight of consequences was to remain an ingredient of recklessness in regard to damage to property. Thirdly, experience has shown that by bringing within the reach of section 1(1) cases of inadvertent recklessness the decision in *Caldwell* became a source of serious potential injustice which cannot possibly be justified on policy grounds . . .

52. In the case before the House the two boys were 11 and 12 respectively. Their escapade of camping overnight without their parents' permission was something that many children have undertaken. But by throwing lit newspapers under a plastic wheelie bin they caused £1m of damage to a shop. It is, however, an agreed fact on this appeal that the boys thought there was no risk of the fire spreading in the way it eventually did. What happened at trial is highly significant. The jury were perplexed by the *Caldwell* directions which compelled them to treat the boys as adults and to convict them. The judge plainly thought this approach was contrary to common sense but loyally applied the law as laid down in *Caldwell*. The view of the jurors and the judge would be widely shared by reasonable people who pause to consider the matter. The only answer of the Crown is that where unjust convictions occur the judge can impose a lenient sentence. This will not do in a modern criminal justice system. Parliament certainly did not authorise such a cynical strategy.

53. Ignoring the special position of children in the criminal justice system is not acceptable in a modern civil society. In 1990 the United Kingdom ratified the Convention on the Rights of the Child which entered into force September 1990. Article 40.1 provides:

'States Parties recognise the right of every child alleged as, accused of, or recognised as having infringed the penal law to be treated in a manner consistent with the promotion of the child's sense of dignity and worth, which reinforces the child's respect for the human rights and fundamental freedoms of others and *which takes into account the child's age* and the desirability of promoting the child's reintegration and the child's assuming a constructive role in society.' (Emphasis added)

This provision imposes both procedural and substantive obligations on state parties to protect the special position of children in the criminal justice system. For example, it would plainly be contrary to article 40.1 for a state to set the age of criminal responsibility of children at, say, five years. Similarly, it is contrary to article 40.1 to ignore in a crime punishable by life imprisonment, or detention during Her Majesty's pleasure, the age of a child in judging whether the mental element has been satisfied. It is true that the Convention became binding on the United Kingdom after *Caldwell* was decided. But the House cannot ignore the norm created by the Convention. This factor on its own justified a reappraisal of *Caldwell*.

54. If it is wrong to ignore the special characteristics of children in the context of recklessness under section 1 of the 1971 Act, an adult who suffers from a lack of mental capacity or a relevant personality disorder may be entitled to the same standard of justice. Recognising the special characteristics of children and mentally disabled people goes some way towards

reducing the scope of section 1 of the 1971 Act for producing unjust results which are inherent in the objective mould into which the *Caldwell* analysis forced recklessness. It does not, however, restore the correct interpretation of section 1 of the 1971 Act. The accepted meaning of recklessness involved foresight of consequences. This subjective state of mind is to be inferred 'by reference to all the evidence, drawing such inferences from the evidence as appear proper in the circumstances': see Lord Edmund-Davies, citing section 8 of the Criminal Justice Act 1967; at 358E. That is what Parliament intended by implementing the Law Commission proposals.

55. This interpretation of section 1 of the 1971 Act would fit in with the general tendency in modern times of our criminal law. The shift is towards adopting a subjective approach. It is generally necessary to look at the matter in the light of how it would have appeared to the defendant. Like Lord Edmund-Davies I regard section 8 of the Criminal Justice Act 1967, as of central importance. There is, however, also a congruence of analysis appearing from decisions of the House. In *R v Morgan* [1976] AC 182 the House ruled that a defence of mistake must be honestly rather than reasonably held. In *Beckford v The Queen* [1988] AC 130, 145 per Lord Griffiths, the House held that self defence permits a defendant to use such force as is reasonable in the circumstances as he honestly believed them to be. *B (A Minor) v Director of Public Prosecutions* [*sub nom. B (A Child) v DPP*] [2000] 2 AC 428 concerned the offence contrary to section 1(1) of the Children Act 1961 (inciting a girl under 14 to commit an act of gross indecency). The House held that the accused's *honest* belief that a girl was over 14 need not be based on reasonable grounds. Lord Nicholls of Birkenhead observed that (at p 462):

'Considered as a matter of principle, the honest belief approach must be preferable. By definition the mental element in a crime is concerned with a subjective state of mind, such as intent or belief.'

To same effect is *R v K* [2002] 1 AC 462 where it was held that while a girl under the age of 16 cannot in law consent to an indecent assault, it is a defence if the defendant honestly believed she was over 16. It is true that the general picture is not entirely harmonious. Duress requires *reasonable* belief: see Lord Lane CJ in *R v Graham (Paul)* [1982] 1 WLR 294, 300, approved by the House of Lords in *Regina v Howe* [1987] AC 417; *R v Martin* [1989] 1 All ER 652. Duress is a notoriously difficult corner of the law. However, in *Graham* Lord Lane CJ, at p 300, stated that in judging the accused's response the test is:

'. . . have the prosecution made the jury sure that a sober person of reasonable firmness, *sharing the characteristics of the defendant*, would not have responded to whatever he reasonably believed [the threatener] said or did by taking part in the offence.' (Emphasis added)

The age and sex of the defendant (but possibly no other characteristics) are relevant to the cogency of the threat: *R v Bowen* [1997] 1 WLR 372. In regard to provocation a wider view of the impact on defendant has prevailed: *R v Smith (Morgan)* [2001] 1 AC 146 (by a 3:2 majority).

56. These developments show that what Lord Diplock in *Caldwell* described as an 'esoteric meaning' of recklessness (353H) was also consistent with the general trend of the criminal law.

Conclusion On *Caldwell*

57. The surest test of a new legal rule is not whether it satisfies a team of logicians but how it performs in the real world. With the benefit of hindsight the verdict must be that the

rule laid down by the majority in *Caldwell* failed this test. It was severely criticized by academic lawyers of distinction. It did not command respect among practitioners and judges. Jurors found it difficult to understand: it also sometimes offended their sense of justice. Experience suggests that in *Caldwell* the law took a wrong turn.

58. That brings me to the question whether the subjective interpretation of recklessness might allow wrongdoers who ought to be convicted of serious crime to escape conviction. Experience before *Caldwell* did not warrant such a conclusion. In any event, as Lord Edmund-Davies explained, if a defendant closes his mind to a risk he must realise that there is a risk and, on the evidence, that will usually be decisive: 358D. One can trust the realism of trial judges, who direct juries, to guide juries to sensible verdicts and juries can in turn be relied on to apply robust common sense to the evaluation of ridiculous defences. Moreover, the endorsement by Parliament of the Law Commission proposals could not seriously have been regarded as a charter for the acquittal of wrongdoers.

59. In my view the case for departing from *Caldwell* has been shown to be irresistible.

60. I agree with the reasons given by Lord Bingham of Cornhill. I have nothing to add to his observations on self-induced intoxication.

Lord Rodger of Earlsferry

. . .

65. It is no secret that, for a long time, many of the leading academic writers on English criminal law have been 'subjectivists'. By that I mean, at the risk of gross over-simplification, that they have believed that the criminal law should punish people only for those consequences of their acts which they foresaw at the relevant time. Those who subscribe to that philosophy will tend to approve the concept of recklessness in *R v Cunningham* [1957] 2 QB 396. The late Glanville Williams and the late Sir John Smith, who were members of the influential Criminal Law Revision Committee, were two of the most distinguished proponents of such views.

66. Glanville Williams (as well as Edmund-Davies LJ) was also a member of the working party set up by the Law Commission to examine the general principles of the criminal law. In June 1970 they produced a working paper on the mental element in crime. And, not surprisingly, on the matter of recklessness, at pp 48–51, it espoused the subjectivist standpoint. Three of the five Law Commissioners also sat on the working party. A month after publishing that working paper, the Law Commission published their report on property offences. In these circumstances it would have been surprising, to say the least, if they had intended their draft bill to do other than incorporate the concept of recklessness that had been developed in *Cunningham* and subsequent cases. Sitting in *Caldwell* Lord Edmund-Davies was well placed to appreciate all these factors.

67. The same view is reflected, of course, in the definition of recklessness in clause 18(c) of the draft code of criminal law published by the Law Commission in 1989 (Report No 177). Again this is scarcely surprising since much of the work was done by a team of academic lawyers that included Sir John Smith. It goes without saying that there are powerful arguments in favour of the view which the Law Commission favoured.

68. On the other hand it is equally clear that other views are not only possible but have actually been adopted by English judges at different times over the centuries. Their judgments reveal many strands of thinking: J Horder, 'Two Histories and Four Hidden Principles of Mens Rea' (1997) 113 LQR 95. There is therefore no reason to treat the concept of recklessness expounded in *Cunningham* either as being the quintessence of the historic English criminal law on the point or as necessarily providing the best solution in all circumstances.

Indeed in *R v Stephenson* [1979] QB 695, a case on section 1(1) of the 1971 Act, Geoffrey Lane LJ recognised that the subjective approach was problematical in certain situations. Having made it quite clear that in his view the test of recklessness under the 1971 Act remained subjective and that the knowledge or appreciation of risk of some damage must have entered the defendant's mind, he commented, at p 704B–C:

'There is no doubt that the subjective definition of "recklessness" does produce difficulties. One of them which is particularly likely to occur in practice is the case of the person who by self-induced intoxication by drink or drugs deprives himself of the ability to foresee the risks involved in his actions. Assuming that by reason of his intoxication he is not proved to have foreseen the relevant risk, can he be said to have been "reckless"? Plainly not, unless cases of self-induced intoxication are an exception to the general rule. In our judgment the decision of the House of Lords in *R v Majewski* [1977] AC 443 makes it clear that they are such an exception.'

In *Caldwell* just the kind of problem envisaged by Geoffrey Lane LJ arose: the defendant said that he was so drunk that it did not occur to him that there might be people in the hotel whose lives might be endangered if he set fire to it. Part of what Lord Diplock did to confront the kind of difficulty identified by Geoffrey Lane LJ was to adopt a wider definition of recklessness that covered culpable inadvertence. In so doing, as the House now holds, he misconstrued the terms of the 1971 Act.

69. It does not follow, however, that Lord Diplock's broader concept of recklessness was undesirable in terms of legal policy. On the contrary, there is much to be said for the view that, if the law is to operate with the concept of recklessness, then it may properly treat as reckless the man who acts without even troubling to give his mind to a risk that would have been obvious to him if he had thought about it. This approach may be better suited to some offences than to others. For example, in the context of reckless driving the House endorsed and re-endorsed a more stringent version: *R v Lawrence (Stephen)* [1982] AC 510; *R v Reid* [1992] 1 WLR 793. I refer in particular to the discussion of the policy issues by Lord Goff of Chieveley in *Reid* at pp 808H–812C. Moreover, the opposing view, that only advertent risk taking should ever be included within the concept of recklessness in criminal law, seems to be based, at least in part, on the kind of thinking that the late Professor Hart demolished in his classic essay, 'Negligence, *Mens Rea* and Criminal Responsibility' (1961), reprinted in H L A Hart, *Punishment and Responsibility* (1968), p 136.

70. Because the decision in *Caldwell* involved this legitimate choice between two legal policies, I was initially doubtful whether it would be appropriate for the House to overrule it. An alternative way to allow the appeal by re-analysing Lord Diplock's speech and overruling *Elliott v C* [1983] 1 WLR 939 might well have been found. But, for the reasons that I have already indicated, I have come to share your Lordships' view that we should indeed overrule *Caldwell* and set the law back on the track that Parliament originally intended it to follow. If Parliament now thinks it preferable for the 1971 Act to cover culpably inadvertent as well as advertent wrongdoers, it can so enact. The Law Commission recognised that, if codifying the law, Parliament might wish to adopt that approach: *A Criminal Code for England and Wales Vol 2 Commentary* (LC No 177) paras 8.21 and 17.6.

Lord Hutton and **Lord-Browne-Wilkinson** agreed with Lord Bingham.

Appeal allowed.

G and R, then, confirms that for criminal damage *Caldwell* recklessness should not be used and instead a defendant will be reckless if he or she realizes that there is a risk of the harm arising and decides to take that risk, when to do so is unreasonable. In *A-G's Ref (No. 3 of 2003)*[49] the Court of Appeal confirmed that *R and G* has abolished *Caldwell* recklessness not just for criminal damage, but for all crimes which had used *Caldwell* recklessness.

To many *G and R* is a welcome decision removing the unfairness that resulted from using the *Caldwell* test in cases like *Elliott v C*. The decision, however, is certainly not without its critics. One major source of disappointment was the failure of the House of Lords to consider an alternative to either *Caldwell* or *Cunningham* recklessness. Here are two alternatives that their Lordships might have considered:

(i) Defendants would be reckless if they were aware of a risk or failed to consider a risk which should have been obvious to a reasonable person of their age and mental abilities.

(ii) Defendants would be reckless if they were aware of a risk or failed to consider an obvious risk, without a good explanation.[50] This would lead to the acquittal of those who failed to see a risk due to an illness or emergency, but lead to the conviction of those who failed to see the risk due to drunkenness or anger.

As a result of *G and R* critics are concerned that it will be too easy for a defendant to claim that they did not consider a risk to others and so be entitled to acquittal. Indeed if a defendant can persuade the jury that he is an utterly selfish person who gives no thought to other people's welfare then he should be acquitted if he does a dangerous act without thinking about its consequences. It may be that in such cases the jury will simply disbelieve a defendant or convict regardless of the judge's direction. Alternatively it is likely that we will see in the future much weight being placed on the decision in *Parker* (excerpted above at p. 157) and the idea of a risk being 'in the back of a defendant's mind'. You should also note that that although the House of Lords in *G and R* proudly asserted the importance of proving a subjective *mens rea* (i.e. an actual awareness of risk), they also confirmed the rules relating to intoxication whereby a defendant who is voluntary intoxicated can be convicted without awareness of the risk. The House of Lords presented the intoxication rules as a special exception to the normal requirement of having to prove a subjective state of mind, but given the number of crimes committed by intoxicated people it is not clear whether in courtrooms the intoxication rules are in fact the normal rule, rather than an exception.

FURTHER READING

Birch, D. (1988), 'The Foresight Saga: The Biggest Mistake of All?', *Criminal Law Review* 4.

Field, S., and Lynn, M. (1993), 'Capacity, Recklessness and the House of Lords', *Criminal Law Review* 127.

Gardner, S. (1993b), 'Recklessness Refined', *Law Quarterly Review* 109: 21 (a very useful commentary on *Reid*).

Halpin, A. (1998), 'Definitions and Directions: Recklessness Unheeded', *Legal Studies* 18: 294.

—— (2004) *Definition in the Criminal Law* (Oxford: Hart), ch. 3.

Kimel, D. (2004), 'Inadvertent Recklessness in the Criminal Law', *Law Quarterly Review* 120: 548.

---

[49] [2004] 2 Cr App R 367.
[50] This kind of approach indicated by the House of Lords in *Reid* [1992] 3 All ER 673.

Leigh, L. (1993), 'Recklessness after Reid', *Modern Law Review* 56: 208.

Norrie, A. (1996), 'The Limits of Justice: Finding Fault in the Criminal Law', *Modern Law Review* 59: 540.

Williams, G. (1981b), 'Recklessness Redefined', *Cambridge Law Journal* 252.

4 NEGLIGENCE

DEFINITION

If the defendant has behaved in the way in which a reasonable person would not, then he or she is negligent.

There are a large number of crimes for which the *mens rea* is negligence,[51] although most of them are minor crimes of a regulatory nature. There are therefore few reported cases which discuss its meaning. Negligence uses an objective test. In other words the defendant's state of mind is not relevant in deciding whether the defendant is negligent. There is no need to show that the defendant intended or foresaw a risk. What matters is the conduct of the defendant: did the defendant behave in a way which was reasonable in the circumstances? If the defendant behaves in the way in which a reasonable person would not then he or she is negligent. To give a practical example, if a defendant while driving crashes into the car in front, to decide whether or not he or she was negligent you simply ask: would a reasonable person in D's shoes have crashed the car or not. If even a reasonable driver would have crashed then the defendant is not negligent. If the reasonable person would not have been travelling as fast as the defendant or would have braked earlier and avoided the accident then the defendant is guilty.

There are a number of disputes over the meaning of negligence:

(1) What if the defendant has acted as a result of panic or fear? Consider a case where a person is driving a car when suddenly a child runs out in front of him or her and he or she swerves to the right and hits an on-coming car. We might say that in fact it would have been better and reasonable to swerve to the left, where the driver would have hit no-one.[52] Is the driver negligent? The answer seems to be that a defendant is expected to act only as a reasonable driver would do. Even reasonable people reacting to an emergency would not necessarily respond in the way that in retrospect would have been the ideal way of acting. As long as he or she responded in a way that a reasonable person might have done when faced with a similar emergency the defendant will not be negligent.

(2) Is the standard expected of the person 'reasonable' or 'ordinary'? Does negligence require people to live up to the standard of behaviour which we think people *ought* to abide by, or the standard of behaviour that is the norm? In many cases there will be identical tests. But not always. We know that drivers ought always to keep strictly to the speed limits. However, we also know that most drivers do on occasion exceed them. If the driver was driving at 35mph in a 30mph speed zone could he or she claim not to be driving negligently if it could be demonstrated that on that stretch of road most drivers exceeded 30mph?[53] There is no definitive ruling on this question by the courts.

---

[51] As we shall see in Part II, some commentators argue that negligence should not be regarded as a form of *mens rea*.

[52] *Simpson v Peat* [1952] 2 QB 24, 28 (CA) considers a similar example.

[53] Such an argument could not, of course, defeat a charge that he or she was breaking the speed limit.

(3) What if the defendant is unable to act in accordance with the standard of the reasonable person? Simester and Sullivan[54] argue that the defendant should be expected to live up only to the standard expected of a reasonable person with the defendant's physical characteristics, including age, sight, and hearing. So, for example, a blind defendant would be expected to act only as a reasonable blind person would. There is, however, limited case law to support this proposition.[55] It is well established that a learner driver can be convicted of careless driving if he or she is driving at the standard below that expected of the reasonable driver, even if he or she is not doing too badly for the first ever effort at driving.[56] Also the cases of *Elliot v C* and *G and R*[57] suggest that the standard in *Caldwell* recklessness is strictly objective and the defendant is not to be judged by the standard expected of a reasonable person with his or her characteristics. If this is so for recklessness it might also to be true of negligence, however unacceptable that is.[58]

(4) Is it possible to expect the defendant to show a higher standard of behaviour than that expected of the reasonable person? It is clear that if a person is purporting to act in a professional capacity he or she is expected to act as a reasonable professional. For example, a doctor is expected to exercise the skill expected of a reasonable doctor, not just the standard of an ordinary person.[59]

5 GROSS NEGLIGENCE

In relation to manslaughter a defendant's negligence must be labelled gross negligence (in essence really bad negligence) if there is to be a conviction.[60] It must be shown that the defendant killed negligently and that this negligence was so bad as to justify a criminal conviction. Manslaughter is the only offence which requires the negligence to be gross. We will discuss this in detail in Chapter 5.

6 DISTINGUISHING BETWEEN INTENTION, RECKLESSNESS, AND NEGLIGENCE

We are now in a position to define more precisely the difference between intention and recklessness and between recklessness and negligence. The precise boundary between intention and recklessness is that point at which the *Woollin* direction applies: cases where a result was not the defendant's purpose but it was foreseen as virtually certain. It is clear that if the result was the defendant's purpose then the result is intended. If the result is not the defendant's purpose but is foreseen as a possible result of his actions then the defendant is reckless. The borderline between intent and recklessness is where the defendant foresees the result as virtually certain. After *Woollin* it is for the jury to decide whether a person who falls into this hinterland intends or is reckless.

The difference between recklessness and negligence is fairly straightforward. To be reckless the defendant must foresee the result, while for negligence the only question is whether the defendant acted as a reasonable person would. However, the division between the two

---

[54] Simester and Sullivan (2003: 151–2).
[55] *Hudson* [1966] 1 QB 448, 455 provides an *obiter dictum* that might support their argument.
[56] *McCrone v Riding* [1938] 1 All ER 721.   [57] [2002] EWCA Crim 1992.
[58] J.C. Smith (2002: 95) appears to support this view.
[59] *Adomako* [1995] 1 AC 171 (HL).   [60] Ibid.

becomes more complex when *Parker*[61] is raised. There a defendant was found reckless because the knowledge of the risk was in the 'back of his mind'. There is a temptation to conclude that because a risk is one a reasonable person would have known about, the defendant must have known about it really; somewhere in his brain. If this argument is used too readily the division between recklessness and negligence becomes blurred. Further it should recalled that a defendant who is voluntarily intoxicated can be convicted of a recklessness-based crime if the risk was one he would have known about if sober. This can be regarded as a form of negligence-based liability.

7 INTOXICATION

At various points so far we have discussed the impact of intoxication upon intention and recklessness. It is useful now to bring these threads together. Intoxication can be relevant in a criminal case in three ways:

(1) The defendant may seek to rely on his intoxication as evidence that he lacked *mens rea*.[62]

(2) The prosecution may seek to rely on the defendant's intoxication to establish the defendant's *mens rea*.

(3) There are certain crimes that specifically refer to being intoxicated. For example, it is an offence to drive a vehicle while under the influence of drink or drugs.[63] These offences will not be discussed in this book.

To understand the law on intoxication it is necessary to make two important distinctions: between voluntary and involuntary intoxication and between offences of basic and specific intent.

DEFINITION

A summary of the law on intoxication:

Defendants who are involuntarily intoxicated can introduce evidence of their intoxication to persuade the jury that they lacked the *mens rea* of the crime. If, however, the jury finds they had the *mens rea* they will be guilty. If they did not, they are not guilty.

Defendants who are voluntarily intoxicated can introduce evidence of their intoxication to prove that they lacked the *mens rea* in crimes of specific intent and are therefore not guilty. In crimes of basic intent the fact that they were intoxicated when they committed the crime will provide the evidence that they had the necessary *mens rea*.

7.1 INVOLUNTARY AND VOLUNTARY INTOXICATION

In simple terms someone is voluntarily intoxicated if he or she chooses to take substances which he or she knows or ought to know are intoxicating. In fact it is a little more

---

[61] [1977] 2 All ER 760 (CA).

[62] Although the Public Order Act 1986, s. 6(5), specifically states that the defendant has the burden of proving that he was not voluntarily intoxicated for the purposes of that particular offence.

[63] Road Traffic Act 1988, s. 4(2).

complicated than this. It is necessary to distinguish a case where the defendant has taken alcohol or illegal drugs from those where the defendant has taken lawful substances, such as medicines prescribed by a doctor.

Alcohol and illegal drugs

Where the defendant has voluntarily taken a substance and is aware that the substance is alcohol or an illegal drug then he or she is voluntarily intoxicated. This rule even applies where the defendant thought he or she was taking a low-alcohol drink.[64] This was made clear in *Allen*,[65] where the defendant was drinking his friend's home-made wine, which he believed had only a little alcohol in it. In fact it contained a high level of alcohol. He was held to be voluntarily intoxicated. It would be quite different if he had thought that what he was drinking was a non-alcoholic fruit punch, which in fact had alcohol (or drugs) in it. In such a case the defendant would be involuntarily intoxicated. Similarly, a person who was forced to drink alcohol or take drugs against his or her will would be involuntarily intoxicated. A person who is addicted to drugs or alcohol is treated as voluntarily taking the substances.[66]

Legal substances

If the defendant is taking a lawful substance, he is voluntarily intoxicated if he is aware that the substance would have this effect on him. In the case of medicine prescribed by a doctor the defendant will be voluntarily intoxicated if he took the medicine in a way not prescribed by the doctor (e.g. by exceeding the stated dose).[67] In *Hardie*,[68] the defendant was given some out-of-date valium tablets. He was told that the tablets would calm his nerves, and do him no harm. In fact he became intoxicated and caused a fire. He was held to be involuntarily intoxicated. The judgment does not make it clear whether the test is that the defendant is voluntarily intoxicated if he *knew* the substance was intoxicating, or whether the defendant *ought to have known* that the substance was intoxicating.

7.2 OFFENCES OF BASIC AND SPECIFIC INTENT

As is clear from the summary of the law above the distinction between crimes of basic and specific intent is important.[69] Unfortunately the House of Lords' decision which emphasized the distinction (*Majewski*) failed to explain precisely what was meant by it. Subsequently courts, academics, and students have struggled to explain the distinction. The most popular view appears to be that offences of specific intent are those which have intention as their *mens rea*; whereas crimes of basic intent are those for which the *mens rea* element can be satisfied by recklessness.[70] Greater uncertainty surrounds crimes which contain elements of intent and elements of recklessness. For example, rape, where the *mens rea* is an intent to engage in sexual intercourse with negligence as to whether the victim consented.

---

[64] Simester and Sullivan (2003: 567).   [65] [1988] Crim LR 698 (CA).

[66] It is possible that a drug addict or alcoholic could rely on a defence of insanity or diminished responsibility (on a charge of murder) (see the discussion in Ch. 12).

[67] *Quick* [1973] QB 910 (CA).

[68] [1984] 3 All ER 848 (CA).   [69] It is discussed in detail in Horder (2005b).

[70] *Caldwell* [1982] AC 341 (HL). Ward (1986) argues that no one explanation seems able to fit every case.

Commentators are divided on such crimes. Some suggest that the court will decide whether a crime is predominantly one of recklessness or intent and label it one of specific or basic intent accordingly.[71] Others argue that it is simply a case of applying the specific intent rule to the intent part of the crime, but the basic intent rules to the basic intent part. So a defendant who is drunk and therefore believes the victim is consenting is guilty of rape; but a defendant who is so drunk that he does not intend sexual intercourse[72] would have a defence.

7.3 STATING THE PRESENT LAW

Having considered the key distinctions between voluntary and involuntary intoxication and between specific and basic intent, we can now state the present law. This can be summarized by considering four situations:

(1) *A voluntarily or involuntarily intoxicated defendant who has* mens rea *for the offence.* A defendant who is voluntarily or involuntarily intoxicated but has the *mens rea* required for the offence is guilty. This is true for all crimes. As is often said, 'a drunken intent is still an intent', and we can add 'drunken recklessness is still recklessness'. It is not a defence for intoxicated defendants to claim that they would not have committed the offence had they been sober.[73]

(2) *The defendant is involuntarily intoxicated and lacks the* mens rea *for the offence.* In such a case the defendant must be acquitted.[74] So if Barbara asks for an orange juice and is (unknown to her) given an orange juice spiked with a large amount of vodka, and she then becomes so intoxicated that she is unaware of what she is doing and attacks someone, then she is not guilty of an assault. It should be stressed that she will be acquitted because of her lack of *mens rea* and not because of the intoxication itself.

(3) *The defendant is voluntarily intoxicated and lacks the* mens rea *for the offence.* If the defendant is voluntarily intoxicated and lacks the *mens rea* then the effect of the law is that such a defendant will be deemed reckless; but the defendant will be acquitted of an offence requiring intention.[75] It should be noted that in most cases where the defendant is acquitted of an offence requiring intent (e.g. murder) he may be convicted of a lesser offence which requires recklessness (e.g. manslaughter).

(4) *Intoxication to enable the commission of a crime.* If the defendant has taken drink for the purpose of giving herself the courage to commit the crime she is still guilty, even if at the time she lacks the *mens rea*. This was established in *A-G of Northern Ireland v Gallagher*.[76]

---

[71] Simester and Sullivan (2003: 562).

[72] It would be hard to imagine a jury ever believing a defendant who made such a claim.

[73] *Bowden* [1993] Crim LR 379 (CA).

[74] The question is whether or not the defendant had the *mens rea*; not whether the accused was capable of forming it (*Sheehan and Moore* (1974) 60 Cr App R 308 (CA)). In *McKnight and Groark* [1999] Crim LR 669 the Court of Appeal seemed to suggest that the question was whether the drunkenness had rendered the defendant incapable of forming an intention to kill or cause grievous bodily harm. This is, with respect, contrary to so many earlier cases that it must be wrong.

[75] *Sheehan and Moore* (1974) 60 Cr App R 308 (CA).   [76] [1963] AC 349 (HL).

FURTHER READING

Smith, J.C. (1987), 'Intoxication and the Mental Element in Crime' in P. Wallington and R. Merkin (eds.), *Essays in Honour of F.H. Lawson* (London: Butterworths).

Ward, A. (1986), 'Making Some Sense of Self-Induced Intoxication', *Cambridge Law Journal* 45: 247.

White, S. (1989), 'Offences of Basic and Specific Intent', *Criminal Law Review* 271.

8 KNOWLEDGE AND BELIEF

DEFINITION

Knowledge involves a positive belief that a state of affairs exists. A defendant who fears that circumstances may exist and deliberately decides not to make any further inquiries in case his or her suspicions prove well founded will be said to know the circumstances.

For some offences it must be shown that the defendant did an act knowing or believing that a certain state of affairs existed. It should be noted that in cases where the *mens rea* is knowledge, careful consideration should be given to which aspects of the *actus reus* need to be known.[77] For example, the offence of handling stolen goods requires proof that the defendant knew or believed that the goods were stolen.[78] The difference between knowledge and belief appears simply to be based on whether the facts known or believed turned out to be true. If they were true then the defendant knew them to be true, if they were false the defendant believed them to be true.[79] Knowledge requires a positive belief. A suspicion may not be enough.[80] The court in *Reader*[81] makes it clear that belief that property might be stolen is not enough for a belief that it is stolen. This does not mean that the defendant must be absolutely certain that the circumstances exist. If he or she assumes a set of facts to be true and has no serious doubt about them, then that state of mind amounts to knowledge.[82]

If the court decides that the defendant was aware that there was a risk that the circumstances existed, and deliberately decided not to make any further inquiries to find out whether his or her fears are true, then in effect the defendant is presumed to know the facts. This is sometimes known as the doctrine of 'wilful blindness'. The House of Lords in *Westminster CC v Croyalgrange Ltd*[83] explained:

---

[77] *Forbes (Giles)* [2001] UKHL 40, [2001] 4 All ER 97 (HL).

[78] As Shute (2002a) points out, statutes involving knowledge rely on a variety of formulations. A few offences require proof of knowledge (e.g. the Misuse of Drugs Act 1971, s. 8, knowingly permitting or suffering certain drug-related activities). But often offences require knowledge or belief (e.g. using a false instrument contrary to the Forgery and Counterfeiting Act 1981, s. 3: the defendant must know or believe that the instrument he was using was false). Other offences require knowledge or suspicion: e.g. the offence under the Criminal Justice Act 1988, s. 93A(1), which requires proof that the defendant knew or suspected that the person he was assisting was or had been engaged in criminal conduct or had benefited from criminal conduct. An alternative formulation is knowing or having reasonable cause for believing (e.g. under the Firearms 1968, s. 25, it is an offence to offer to sell or transfer ammunition knowing or having reasonable cause for believing that the recipient is drunk or is of unsound mind).

[79] Shute (2002a).　　[80] *Grainge* [1974] 1 All ER 928 (CA); *Forsyth* [1997] 2 Cr App R 299, 320 (CA).

[81] (1977) 66 Cr App R 33 (CA).

[82] *Griffiths* (1974) 60 Cr App R 14 (CA); *Woods* [1969] 1 QB 447 (CCA).

[83] [1986] 2 All ER 353, 359 (HL).

it is always open to the tribunal of fact, when knowledge on the part of a defendant is required to be proved, to base a finding of knowledge on evidence that the defendant had deliberately shut his eyes to the obvious or refrained from enquiry because he suspected the truth but did not want to have his suspicion confirmed.

An example of wilful blindness is if Margaret has a friend, William, whom she knows is a regular burglar and William offers Margaret a television for £10. Margaret may decide to buy the cheap television and not to ask William where he got the television from for fear of hearing that it has been stolen. The court may be willing to find that Margaret knew the goods were stolen and hence could be guilty of knowingly handling stolen goods.

It should be emphasized that knowledge and belief are subjective concepts. The question concerns what the defendant knew, not what a reasonable person would have known.[84] Although knowledge is a subjective concept occasionally a statute specifically asks the jury or magistrates to consider what the defendant ought to have known. For example, a defendant is guilty of an offence under the Protection from Harassment Act 1997 if he ought to know that his behaviour would harass the victim.

9 TRANSFERRED *MENS REA*

The doctrine of transferred *mens rea* is often called the doctrine of transferred malice. That is a misleading label as the doctrine does not apply just to malice, but to any *mens rea*. The doctrine applies where a person aims to harm one person or piece of property but misses and harms another.[85] The classic example of the application is where A shoots at B, but misses and instead kills C. Contrast the following examples:

(1) Darren shoots at Marjorie, intending to kill her, but the bullet misses and kills Anna. If Darren is charged with the murder of Anna, is the intention to kill Marjorie sufficient *mens rea*? The answer is 'yes'. The *mens rea* (intention to kill Marjorie) can be 'transferred' to the *actus reus* (the killing of Anna) to create the offence of murder.

(2) Craig shoots at Nick, misses, and damages Narinda's property. If Craig is charged with criminal damage to Narinda's property the doctrine of transferred *mens rea* does not lead to a conviction. This is because adding together the intention to kill Nick and the damage to Narinda's property does not create an offence.[86] The *actus reus* and *mens rea* are those of different kinds of offences (murder and criminal damage). Although transferred *mens rea* might not assist in this context, this does not mean that Craig has not committed an offence. Craig will be guilty of attempting to kill Nick. Indeed Craig may be guilty of criminal damage, not using transferred *mens rea*, but because he has been reckless as to damaging Narinda's property.

(3) Brian is being attacked by Josh and in order to defend himself throws a brick at Josh. Josh ducks and the brick hits Elizabeth. Brian's intent to injure Josh can be transferred

---

[84] Although the concept of 'wilful blindness' blurs these concepts.

[85] A good recent example of the application of the doctrine is *Mitchell* [1983] 2 All ER 427 (CA).

[86] *Pembiliton* (1874) LR 2 CCC 119. If Craig attempted to damage Nick's property and in fact damaged Narinda's the offence would be made out.

to Elizabeth, and so too can his defence of self-defence. So Brian would be able to use self-defence to any charge relating to Elizabeth's injuries.[87]

(4) Paul shoots dead someone whom he believes to be Helen, his enemy. To his horror he discovers he has shot Jade, who looks like Helen. Here Paul is guilty of Jade's murder. There is no need to rely on the doctrine of transferred *mens rea*. Paul intended to shoot dead the person in front of him and that person did die. Although Paul was mistaken as to that person's identity that mistake is irrelevant to his *mens rea*.

(5) Devina shoots into a crowd, not caring who is killed, and Tanya dies from the shot. Here the law relies on 'general malice': where a defendant does an act intending to kill anyone in the way then the defendant is guilty of murder if he kills someone.[88]

EXAMINATION TIP

When answering a problem question always remember that whenever the doctrine of transferred *mens rea* applies there are always two offences to consider:

(i) an attempt to commit the intended offence; and

(ii) the full offence involving the harm that occurred.

One particularly difficult case on transferred *mens rea* was *Attorney-General's Reference (No. 3 of 1994)*,[89] where the accused stabbed his pregnant girlfriend. As a result of the wound the child was born early and died from the wound. One key issue was whether the defendant could be charged with murder. You might at first think that this case could be resolved by a straightforward application of the doctrine of transferred *mens rea*. The accused's intention to cause grievous bodily harm to the girlfriend can be transferred to the killing of the baby to create the offence of murder. The difficulty with this reasoning is that at the time of the stabbing the foetus was not a person in the eyes of the law. The House of Lords held that it was not possible to transfer the intent to kill from the mother to the child who (at the time of the stabbing) did not yet exist as a legal person.[90] What about arguing that the defendant's intention to kill or cause grievous bodily harm to the girlfriend could be transferred to the child who actually died? The House of Lords described the argument as involving an impermissible 'double transfer': from the mother to the unborn child; from the unborn child to the person it would become in the future. The House of Lords was still able to hold that the defendant was guilty of manslaughter, because (as we shall see in Chapter 5) for that offence there was no need to show an intent to injure any particular person.[91]

10 COINCIDENCE OF *ACTUS REUS* AND *MENS REA*

It is a general principle of criminal law that the requirements of *mens rea* and *actus reus* should coincide in time. So, for example, in a murder case the defendant must intend to kill

---

[87] *Gross* (1913) 77 JP 352.

[88] *Attorney-General's Reference (No. 3 of 1994)* [1998] AC 245 (HL).   [89] Ibid.

[90] Although the foetus is not regarded as a person, it can still be a criminal offence to kill a foetus; see, for example, the offence of procuring a miscarriage contrary to Offences Against the Person Act 1861, s. 58.

[91] Care needs to be taken in drafting the indictment when transferred malice cases are involved (see *Slimmings* [1999] Crim LR 69 (CA)).

or cause grievous bodily harm by doing an act which causes the death of the victim. Consider these examples:

(1) One evening Adele decides to kill Sandy at some point in the future and spends the whole night deciding how to do so. The next morning, driving to work, Adele falls asleep at the wheel of her car and drives into a pedestrian killing him. The pedestrian happens to be Sandy. Adele is not guilty of murder. Although the evening before Adele had the *mens rea* for murder and Adele did actually kill Sandy, the *mens rea* and *actus reus* did not coincide at the same time[92] and so Adele should not be convicted of murder.[93]

(2) Spencer is driving along uttering murderous words about Alison whom he hopes to kill as soon as an opportunity arises. Spencer is not paying attention to his driving and crashes into a bus shelter, killing someone who happens to be Alison. Although you may think that the *actus reus* (the causing of the death of Alison) and the *mens rea* (an intention to kill Alison) existed at the same time, this is not a case of murder. Spencer did not intend to kill *by that act*. In other words, he did not intend to kill Alison with the act that caused her death.

(3) Alex stabs Kate intending to kill her and Kate collapses. Alex repents of his actions and desperately tries to save Kate's life. But despite his best effort she dies. Although it could be argued that at the time of Kate's death Alex did not intend her to die this is in fact irrelevant in the criminal law. The key question is whether at the time Alex did the act which caused the death he had the *mens rea*. At the time of the stabbing Alex had the *mens rea* and so he is guilty of murder.

(4) Johnny is driving his car and begins to feel sleepy. He decides to drive on rather than to stop for a rest. He falls asleep at the wheel and kills a pedestrian. Although at the time when he drove into the pedestrian he was acting involuntarily and so technically 'not driving',[94] his careless driving (in deciding not to stop for a rest and to continue) caused him to fall into an involuntary state, which, in turn, caused the pedestrian's injuries.[95] He is guilty of causing death by dangerous driving.

10.1 'EXCEPTIONS' TO THE COINCIDENCE REQUIREMENT

Despite the requirement that the *mens rea* and *actus reus* coincide the courts have developed ways of flexibly interpreting it, or some would say creating exceptions to it. The case law can be divided into three kinds of cases.

The defendant may have the *mens rea* at one point in time and then later (without *mens rea*) perform the *actus reus*

A good example of this kind of case is *Meli v The Queen*.[96] The appellants as part of a preconceived plan struck a man over the head. They thought he was dead and threw what they thought was his corpse over a cliff. In fact medical evidence established that the blow to the head had not killed the victim, but being thrown over the cliff had. The difficulty was

---

[92] At the time of the killing she was asleep and was not intending anything.
[93] She may be guilty of causing death by dangerous driving.   [94] He was an automaton: see p. 87.
[95] *Kay v Butterworth* (1945) 173 LT 191.   [96] [1954] 1 WLR 228 (PC).

that at the time of the *actus reus* (throwing the body over the cliff) the appellants lacked *mens rea*, although they had had the *mens rea* earlier when they hit the victim. The Privy Council held that they could properly be convicted of murder as their acts were part of a plan and so could be described as 'one transaction'. As long as the act performed with *mens rea* and the act which constituted the *actus reus* could be described as part of one transaction then the defendant could be convicted.[97] The Court of Appeal in *Le Brun*[98] extended this reasoning to a case where there was no preconceived plan. In that case the defendant hit his wife and she collapsed. He then picked her body up to take it inside. He dropped her and she died. It was held that he could be convicted of manslaughter as the hitting and the carrying of the body could be regarded as 'one transaction' or a single 'sequence of events'. Key to this case was the fact that the defendant was carrying his wife inside to hide what he had done. Had he been taking her to a doctor the court might well have decided that there was not one 'sequence of events'.[99]

The approach to cases of this kind was approved by Lord Mustill in *Attorney-General's Reference (No. 3 of 1994)*[100] where he summarized the position:

> The existence of an interval of time between the doing of an act by the defendant with the necessary wrongful intent and its impact on the victim in a manner which leads to death does not in itself prevent the intent, the act and the death from together amounting to murder, so long as there is an unbroken causal connection between the act and the death.

Whether the series of events is part of the same sequence of events or part of an 'unbroken causal connection' is a question of fact for the jury.

The defendant committed the *actus reus* at one point in time (without the necessary *mens rea*), but at a later point in time he has the *mens rea*

An example of such a case is where the defendant while asleep starts a fire, then afterwards realizes what he has done and runs off. The courts have dealt with such cases in two ways:

(1) The prosecution could argue that the defendant's initial act should be seen as a continuing act which is still continuing at the point in time when the *mens rea* arises.

(2) An alternative way of considering such cases is to argue that the defendant's failure to stop the harm he was causing amounted to a criminal omission for which the defendant could be convicted. The most significant case discussing this approach is *Miller* (which is excerpted at p. 91).[101] There it will be recalled that once the defendant has set off a chain of events which poses a danger he is under a duty to act to prevent the danger arising. Once the defendant is aware of the danger but fails to prevent it materializing or mitigate it the *mens rea* and the *actus reus* (the failure to act) coincide.

These arguments were considered in the following case:

---

[97] See also *Moore* [1975] Crim LR 229 (PC) and *Church* [1966] 1 QB 59 (CCA).

[98] [1991] 4 All ER 673 (CA).

[99] An alternative line of reasoning the court adopted was that the original hit was an operating cause of the death in the sense that the attempt to carry her away did not break the chain of causation.

[100] [1998] AC 245, at 265 (HL).   [101] [1968] 3 All ER 442, [1968] 3 WLR 1120, (1968) 52 Cr App R 700.

Fagan v Metropolitan Police Commissioner
[1969] 1 QB 439 (QBD)[102]

The appellant, who was driving his car, was asked by a police officer to pull over. The appellant did so, but ended up on the policeman's foot. The police officer apparently then said: 'Get off, you are on my foot'. The appellant did not move the car. When the police officer repeated the request the appellant eventually did so.

Mr Justice James

The justices at quarter sessions on those facts were left in doubt whether the mounting of the wheel on to the officer's foot was deliberate or accidental. They were satisfied, however, beyond all reasonable doubt that the appellant 'knowingly, provocatively and unnecessarily' allowed the wheel to remain on the foot after the officer said 'Get off, you are on my foot'. They found that, on these facts, an assault was proved.

Counsel for the appellant relied on the passage in *Stone's Justices' Manual* (1968 Edn.), Vol. 1, p. 651, where assault is defined (Viz., 'An assault is an attempt by force, or violence, to do bodily injury to another. It is an act of aggression done against or upon the person of another without his consent; not necessarily against his will, if by that is implied an actual resistance or expression of objection made at the time . . .'). He contends that, on the finding of the justices, the initial mounting of the wheel could not be an assault, and that the act of the wheel mounting the foot came to an end without there being any *mens rea*. It is argued that thereafter there was no act on the part of the appellant which could constitute an *actus reus*, but only the omission or failure to remove the wheel as soon as he was asked. That failure, it is said, could not in law be an assault, nor could it in law provide the necessary *mens rea* to convert the original act of mounting the foot into an assault. Counsel for the respondent argues that the first mounting of the foot was an *actus reus*, which act continued until the moment of time at which the wheel was removed. During that continuing act, it is said, the appellant formed the necessary intention to constitute the element of *mens rea* and, once that element was added to the continuing act, an assault took place. In the alternative, counsel argues, that there can be situations in which there is a duty to act and that, in such situations, an omission to act in breach of duty would in law amount to an assault. It is unnecessary to formulate any concluded views on this alternative.

. . .

To constitute this offence, some intentional act must have been performed; a mere omission to act cannot amount to an assault. Without going into the question whether words alone can constitute an assault, it is clear that the words spoken by the appellant could not alone amount to an assault; they can only shed a light on the appellant's action. For our part, we think that the crucial question is whether, in this case, the act of the appellant can be said to be complete and spent at the moment of time when the car wheel came to rest on the foot, or whether his act is to be regarded as a continuing act operating until the wheel was removed. In our judgment, a distinction is to be drawn between acts which are complete—though results may continue to flow—and those acts which are continuing. Once the act is complete, it cannot thereafter be said to be a threat to inflict unlawful force on the victim. If the act, as distinct from the results thereof, is a continuing act, there is a continuing threat to inflict unlawful force. If the assault involves a battery and that battery continues, there is a continuing act of assault. For an assault to be committed, both the elements of *actus reus*

---

[102] [1983] 2 AC 161 (HL).

and *mens rea* must be present at the same time. The '*actus reus*' is the action causing the effect on the victim's mind: see the observations of Parke, B., in *R. v. St. George* (1840), 9 C. & P. 483 at pp. 490, 493. The '*mens rea*' is the intention to cause that effect. It is not necessary that *mens rea* should be present at the inception of the *actus reus*; it can be superimposed on an existing act. On the other hand, the subsequent inception of *mens rea* cannot convert an act which has been completed without *mens rea* into an assault.

In our judgment, the justices at Willesden and quarter sessions were right in law. On the facts found, the action of the appellant may have been initially unintentional, but the time came when, knowing that the wheel was on the officer's foot, the appellant (i) remained seated in the car so that his body through the medium of the car was in contact with the officer, (ii) switched off the ignition of the car, (iii) maintained the wheel of the car on the foot, and (iv) used words indicating the intention of keeping the wheel in that position. For our part, we cannot regard such conduct as mere omission or inactivity. There was an act constituting a battery which at its inception was not criminal because there was no element of intention, but which became criminal from the moment the intention was formed to produce the apprehension which was flowing from the continuing act. The fallacy of the appellant's argument is that it seeks to equate the facts of this case with such a case as where a motorist has accidentally run over a person and, that action having been completed, fails to assist the victim with the intent that the victim should suffer.

We would dismiss this appeal.

Lord Justice Parker agreed with **Mr Justice James's** judgment.
Mr Justice Bridge handed down a dissenting judgment.

Appeal dismissed.

It is unclear when the *actus reus* occurred

An example of this difficulty is revealed in the rather grizzly facts of *Attorney-General's Reference (No. 4 of 1980)*.[103] Here the defendant slapped his girlfriend, pushed her down the stairs, put a rope around her neck, dragged her back up the stairs, cut her throat, and cut her body into pieces. It was unclear which of these acts had caused her death, although it was clear one of them had! The Court of Appeal held that as long as the defendant had the necessary *mens rea* at the time of each of the possible acts that caused the death he could be properly convicted of murder or manslaughter.

FURTHER READING

Marston, G. (1970), 'Contemporaneity of Act and Intention in Crimes', *Law Quarterly Review* 86: 208.

Sullivan, G.R. (1993b), 'Cause and the Contemporaneity of *Actus Reus* and *Mens Rea*', *Criminal Law Journal* 487.

REVISION TIP

When you come to revise specific criminal offences you will need to learn both the *actus reus* and *mens rea* for those offences. But remember with the *mens rea* that you will need to learn

---

[103] [1981] 1 WLR 705 (CA).

not only whether intention, recklessness, or negligence is required, but for what. So do not just say the *mens rea* for murder is intention. You need to say that the *mens rea* for murder is an intention to kill or cause grievous bodily harm to the victim.

QUESTIONS

1. Peter believes that his enemy, Olive, may possibly be allergic to peanuts. He puts peanut oil on Olive's toothbrush, hoping to kill her. It turns out that Olive is allergic to the oil and after brushing her teeth suffers an allergic reaction and dies. Bob, Olive's friend, wants to terrify Peter to teach him a lesson. He sets fire to Peter's house. Peter dies in the fire.

   Did Peter intend to kill Olive? Did Bob intend to kill Peter?

2. Steve is rollerblading down a pavement. Someone steps out in front of him. Without thinking, he jumps to one side. He crashes into a car and scratches the paintwork.

   Was Steve reckless as to damaging the car? Was he negligent?

PART II: *MENS REA* THEORY

11 GENERAL DISCUSSION ON *MENS REA*

Sanford Kadish has suggested that the existence of *mens rea* shows that the criminal law regards people as autonomous agents who are responsible for the choices they make rather than robots which have malfunctioned and need to be mended.[104] Indeed many commentators see *mens rea* as being at the heart of the criminal law, fulfilling three important roles:

(1) It ensures that censure correctly attaches to a criminal conviction. If a criminal conviction is to signify that society censures an individual for his or her actions then it is not enough just to show that the defendant harmed the victim. He or she must have done so in a blameworthy way.

(2) *Mens rea* is not just about ensuring that only blameworthy people are convicted, but also that they are convicted of the right offence. Many people would draw a clear moral distinction between, for example, an intentional killer and a negligent one. Such distinctions, it is said, should be reflected in the criminal law. Hence we distinguish between murder and manslaughter.

(3) *Mens rea* may also help to define the wrong done to the victim. If you are out shopping and are pushed over your reaction will be different depending on whether you were deliberately or accidentally pushed over. If it was deliberate you will feel you have been attacked; if it was accidental you are likely to find the incident far less traumatic. The intention behind the action in part defines the kind of harm the victim has suffered.

It is interesting to consider what a criminal law would be like if it contained no *mens rea* requirements. Baroness Wootton[105] proposed such a legal system. At the heart of her

---

[104] Kadish (1987b: 3).   [105] Wootton (1963).

thinking was the view that the criminal court was not in a position to assess the blame-worthiness of a defendant. We would need to know far more about human psychology and courts would have to be told far more about defendants' personal history if they were truly to assess blameworthiness.[106] Wootton proposed that offences should simply require proof that the defendant harmed the victim. At the sentencing stage the judge would be free to take into account the defendant's state of mind along with other relevant considerations. Opponents of proposals such as Wootton's point out that under them we would then have to accept that a person could be guilty of a crime even though he or she was entirely blameless for his or her actions. It is true that such a defendant may receive no punishment, but the censuring effect of a conviction itself would be lost. We could not assume that a person found guilty of a crime was morally blameworthy. A person who deliberately killed the victim and a person who killed another through no fault of his or her own would both be guilty of murder.[107] There are, however, benefits to Wootton's approach. It does acknow-ledge the harm done to the victim. Imagine the trauma a rape victim feels when her assailant is acquitted because he was not aware that she was not consenting. Her perception is understandably that the criminal law has failed to acknowledge that from her perspective she was raped, whatever the defendant's state of mind. A further important point is Woot-ton's argument that we must not be over-confident in the law's ability to assess the moral blameworthiness of a defendant.

However, most commentators reject the notion of a criminal law system without *mens rea* and insist that serious criminal offences must require proof of *mens rea*. Professor Williams has argued that the requirement of *mens rea* is 'a mark of advancing civilisation'.[108] Indeed, as we shall see in Chapter 4, the House of Lords[109] has stated that there is a presumption that offences require proof of *mens rea* unless there is clear evidence rebutting that presumption. But before English and Welsh lawyers get too puffed up with pride on the humanity and moral subtlety demonstrated by their criminal legal system's use of *mens rea* three points should be emphasized:

(1) As William Wilson has pointed out, we pride ourselves in not punishing animals, infants, or the insane on the basis that they are not responsible agents. Yet animals that attack other animals or people are liable to be put down; children who commit serious crimes are likely to be taken into state care; and the insane are hospitalized. As Wilson notes, '[t]he rhetoric says that such a response is not a mark of blame and such treatment is not punishment. The reality is that those concerned would hardly know the difference'.[110]

(2) A point which will be made several times in this chapter is that the extent to which criminal law seeks to examine the moral blameworthiness of a defendant's actions is limited. For example, a defendant who argues that his criminal behaviour has more to do with his socio-economic background than personal blameworthiness will have little chance of success before a court.

(3) Although *mens rea* is seen as an important principle in fact many crimes do not require proof of the defendant's state of mind.[111] The large majority of crimes are

---

[106] Some would say that only an omniscient, good God would be in a position to make such a judgement.

[107] Although one could give them markedly different sentences. Indeed, if blameworthiness became irrele-vant such a system logically could return to the practice (common in medieval law) of sentencing animals for criminal offences (Evans (1987))!

[108] G. Williams (1983: 70).   [109] *B v DPP* [2000] 2 AC 428 (HL).   [110] Wilson (2003: 120).

[111] Ashworth and Blake (1996).

negligence-based or are offences of strict liability, which require only proof that the defendant acted in a particular way. Andrew Ashworth suggests that there are thousands of strict liability offences.[112] Even if we consider just the more serious offences which cannot be heard by magistrates and must be tried in the Crown Court, over half of these are offences of strict or objective liability.[113]

Despite these important points the judiciary and many academics place much weight on the significance of *mens rea* and much academic and judicial ink has been spilt trying to define the key *mens rea* terms discussed in Part I.

Some academics have sought to develop a guiding theory for allocating blame.[114] But, it should be emphasized that some commentators are very sceptical about such attempts to find an overarching theory of criminal law.[115] For them the benefits and disadvantages of particular states of mind for particular offences need to be judged on their own merits, without there being any attempt to fit these into an overarching theory.

12 CHOICE/CAPACITY CHARACTER THEORY

The debate over the correct definition of the *mens rea* terms reflects the disputes over the choice, capacity, and character theories. These were mentioned in Chapter 1 and will be discussed in more detail in Chapter 12, so will be mentioned only briefly here:[116]

(1) *The choice theory* centres on an argument that people are responsible for the things they chose to do. People should be guilty of a crime only if they chose effectively to do the *actus reus.*[117]

(2) *The capacity theory* is similar to the choice theory in that it accepts the argument that people are responsible for what they chose to do. But it also accepts that it is proper to punish those who *could* have effectively chosen to act lawfully, but did not.

(3) *The character theory* focuses on the argument that the defendant is responsible for his or her character. If his or her criminal actions reveal character traits that are opposed by the criminal law he or she should be punished.

These different theories suggest different understandings of *mens rea*. The choice theory supports crimes based on intention and *Cunningham* recklessness, but would not support offences based on *Caldwell* recklessness, negligence, or strict liability, where the defendant did not necessarily choose to commit a crime. The capacity theory would also support intention and *Cunningham* recklessness, but would also be willing to support criminal liability for inadvertence, as least in so far as the defendant *could* have appreciated the risk. The capacity theory would therefore support the acquittal of Stephenson,[118] but deplore the conviction of C (in *Elliott v C*[119]). The capacity theory would also be happy for some convictions to be based on negligence, but only where the defendant had the capability of

---

[112] Ashworth (2003: 96).   [113] Lacey and Wells (1998: 18–30).
[114] It should not be forgotten that issues such as burden of proof, the privilege against self-incrimination, and trial by jury have a very important impact on the way the *mens rea* requirements operate in practice.
[115] See e.g. Horder (1993).   [116] See p. 36 and p. 750.   [117] G. Williams (1997).
[118] [1979] QB 695 (CA).   [119] [1983] 1 WLR 939 (QBD).

acting non-negligently.[120] The character theory would be less obsessed with the defendant's foresight or intention than the other theories. Although usually an intentional or *Cunningham* reckless act would indicate bad character, it need not always. The character theory could distinguish between a deliberate killing and a mercy killing, in that arguably the former but not the latter indicates a bad character. Some negligence or strict liability could be supported on the basis that the defendant's actions revealed that he did not care enough about other people.

13 SUBJECTIVE/OBJECTIVE

As we have already seen in Chapter 1, another way of looking at the disputes over *mens rea* terms is to see them as a disagreement between the objectivists and subjectivists.[121] Subjectivists focus on what was going on inside the defendant's mind when he or she committed the crime: what did he or she intend, foresee, know, or believe? Objectivists tend to focus more on the defendant's actions: is what the defendant did unreasonable? Objectivists may consider what a reasonable person in the defendant's shoes would have intended, foreseen, known, or believed.

Although there is sometimes talk of a battle between subjectivism and objectivism it is perfectly sensible to take the view that some offences should be drafted in objective terms and others in subjectivist terms.[122] Generally subjectivists support liability for intention and *Cunningham* recklessness and reject *Caldwell* recklessness, negligence, and strict liability as objectivist, although, as we shall see, it is in fact far more complicated than this.

QUESTIONS

1. Is 'inadvertence' or 'indifference' to a risk, a state of mind or an absence of a state of mind?

2. Read R. Tur (1993), 'Subjectivism and Objectivism: Towards Synthesis' in S. Shute, J. Gardner, and J. Horder (eds.), *Action and Value in Criminal Law* (Oxford: OUP). Do you think it is possible to synthesize subjectivism and objectivism?

14 NORMAL MEANING

One theme that has run through many of the judicial decisions is that *mens rea* words like 'intention' and 'recklessness' should carry their normal, everyday meaning.[123] At first this seems uncontroversial. After all, it is far easier for a jury to give words their normal meaning than some technical legal meaning which they may misunderstand.[124] Further, giving such words their normal meaning helps to make the law predictable and readily understandable to ordinary people. For example, if dishonesty in theft was given a highly technical outdated

---

[120] M. Moore (2000: ch. 7) suggests that liability for negligence could be supported on the basis of unexercised capacity.

[121] See p. 41 for a further discussion on subjectivism and objectivism. [122] Sullivan (2002b: 222–3).

[123] *Brutus v Cozens* [1973] AC 854 (HL).

[124] A point stressed by the Court of Appeal in *Belfon* (1976) 63 Cr App R 59. See also Buxton (1988).

meaning a defendant might justly complain 'how on earth was I meant to know that dishonesty meant that?' Also, giving such words their ordinary meaning enables the law to keep abreast of changes in the moral and cultural climate. Defining dishonesty in terms of the standards expected of the ordinary honest person is said by some to mean that the legal concept of dishonesty is kept in line with current standards of morality.

However, some commentators reject any assumption that the legal meanings and normal meanings of words should be the same.[125] Does the word 'intention', for example, have an everyday meaning? Even if it does is it precise enough to assist in borderline cases?[126]

Behind this debate on whether words should have their normal meaning is a debate over how much power a jury should have. If the judge provides a precise legal definition of the concept the judge (in theory) retains control over the definition of the term.[127] If the jury are to give the term its normal meaning then they retain a degree of discretion in deciding, for example, what the current standards of morality are.[128] The hidden use of references to ordinary language is brought out in the following passage by Nicola Lacey. She has just considered those scholars who seek to clarify the notion of intention using 'conceptual analysis', who, she suggests, appear to believe that if only we could come up with a morally sophisticated definition of intention the difficulties in the law would be resolved. She rejects this because:

> the real source of uncertainty and disagreement in the application of criminal law concepts such as intention is not ultimately to do with the concept, but with practical, moral and political issues. Should this person be convicted, and of what offence?

She then turns to those who believe that giving intention its normal meaning will resolve the problems over the definition of intention:

N. Lacey, 'A Clear Concept of Intention: Elusive or Illusory?' (1993) 56 *Modern Law Review* 621

Ordinary Usage

At the other end of the spectrum, we have the resort in the face of difficulties of definition to 'ordinary usage.' It should be noted that ordinary usage is itself something of a chimera. For just as 'legal usage' is arguably a relatively specific and autonomous area of discourse, many other areas of linguistic usage develop particular, local and technical meanings for 'ordinary' words. And even within these local areas, usage is fluid and often contested. This notwithstanding, the resort to the 'common usage' or the 'ordinary person's understanding' of a particular term is a familiar technique in criminal law—perhaps most famously debated in recent years in the context of the concept of dishonesty under the Theft Act 1968. On the view which appeals to 'ordinary usage,' the attempt to articulate and fix particular conceptual analyses in legislative or judicial form is both unnecessary and misguided. It is unnecessary because, in the case of concepts such as intention, dishonesty, violence and so on, 'ordinary

---

[125] G. Williams (1987).   [126] Gardner and Jung (1991).
[127] Lacey (1993a).   [128] For further discussion on this see Herring (2005b: 44–5).

people' have a clear if unarticulated sense of what these terms mean. So it can simply be left to the jury or the lay magistrate to apply those ordinary understandings to the case at hand. And it is misguided, because part of the function of criminal laws which employ those terms is precisely to bring to bear on the alleged offender the standards of judgment thought to be buried within and reflected by 'ordinary usage': the thought behind the legal proscription in question is the application of a general rather than a technical standard in this respect. The 'ordinary language' view is therefore motivated by at least two concerns: the investment of *mens rea* terms with 'ordinary' or 'common sense' meanings, and the delegation of decision-making power in Crown Court cases to jury rather than judge. In some sense, on this view, the framers of criminal laws articulate definitions of offences in terms of a combination of legal and factual questions. The line between questions of law and those of fact is notoriously hard to draw, but the approach based on 'ordinary language' does appear to make conviction depend, in a wide range of cases, on questions of fact—or what might more accurately be called 'lay evaluation.' We should note the attractions to law makers of the rhetorical force which attaches to legislation framed in terms of 'ordinary' terms which resonate with citizens' pre-legal ideas of wrongdoing.

To set out the view which appeals to 'ordinary language' is already to suggest its main weakness as a tool of legal practice. This lies in its assumption that a settled, widely shared understanding underpins the usage of all or most such terms employed by criminal law. It seems only reasonable to observe that this assumption is undermined by recent case law history. Even giving due weight to the opacity of the trial judges' directions in recent murder cases such as *Moloney, Hancock and Shankland*, and *Nedrick*, it is hardly to be doubted that the return of the jury for further advice about the meaning of 'intention' must be put down not just to bewilderment in the face of legal 'guidelines' but also to uncertainty and disagreement over 'ordinary language.' On all the evidence, and in ordinary terms, could Moloney be said to have intended to kill his stepfather; could Hancock and Shankland be said to have intended to kill or seriously injure the drivers and occupants of the vehicles coming up the motorway? Can at least some 'core' notion of intention be identified, in relation to which 'penumbral' cases can easily be incorporated within 'ordinary' usage?

In the face of this kind of problem, judges and commentators have often favoured an intermediate position in which the resort to ordinary language is buttressed by recourse to conceptual analysis and stipulation. Typically, this has consisted in the incomplete and often negative delineation of the term in question, either in terms of a partial definition, or of judicial guidelines, or both. A good example would be dishonesty under the Theft Act 1968, of which section 2 partially defines dishonesty by excluding three specific instances and including another. This is supplemented at the judicial level by guidelines which set out two questions which the jury has to ask itself in determining whether the defendant is dishonest. These questions mark out the concept without supplying the ultimate standard to be applied. A similar compromise strategy is being worked out in the case of intention, and the recent cases will now be analysed in more depth. My aim is to suggest that the strategy entails a fundamental tension, widely present in criminal law cases. This tension is interesting, because it undermines the traditional doctrinal insistence on the importance and (at least relative) possibility of coherence and consistency of principle in criminal law.

15 INTENT

Although academics have written an enormous amount about intent and its meaning has been a matter of heated debate, in practice intent is rarely relevant in criminal trials.[129] Very few offences require proof that the defendant intended a result. Recklessness or negligence is normally sufficient. Nevertheless intent is an important concept in the criminal law because it is widely regarded as the 'worst' kind of *mens rea*.

But what makes intent the most serious form of *mens rea*? Michael Moore[130] explains that an intended action is one where the actor seeks to control the action and its result in the sense used in moral assessments. In other words a person seeks to exert as great a control as possible over an action and its result where that action is intended.[131] Other commentators have seen an intended act as the ideal conception of a voluntary act.[132] Intention reflects not just a choice to act in a way which will lead to a result, but a wholehearted decision to act in order to bring a result about.[133] If Harry stabs James wanting to kill him he has, to the greatest extent possible, committed himself to James's death. If Ivy stabs Katie, not wanting to kill her but being aware that there is a risk that she may, Ivy associates herself to a lesser extent with Katie's death than Harry did with James's.

Before we look at some of the controversial theoretical issues surrounding intention, there is an important point to make. Much of the discussion of the meaning of intention has occurred in the context of the law of murder. It is all too easy in discussing this topic to confuse the issue 'did D intend to kill V?' with the question 'should D be convicted of murder?' But these are separate questions.

We must now turn to some of the most controversial issues surrounding the concept of intention.

15.1 DISTINGUISHING INDIRECT INTENTION AND DIRECT INTENTION

As you will have gathered from the summary of the law in Part I the greatest area of dispute is over the extent to which a result which is not the actor's purpose, but which was foreseen by him, can be said to be intended by him. There is widespread agreement that if it was the defendant's purpose to cause a result or the defendant wanted the result to occur in order to achieve his purpose then he intended it.[134] We called this the 'core meaning of intention' in Part I of this chapter.[135] As mentioned there, the courts have been troubled by cases of indirect or oblique intention. Commentators have equally been divided on the issue. To assist in understanding the different views taken we will consider four hypothetical cases:

1. *The desperate surgeon.* D, a surgeon, has a wife who is in desperate need of a heart transplant. D removes a heart from a healthy patient (V) and transplants it into his wife. D does not want V to die (his purpose is to save his wife's life), but is aware that if he removes V's heart V will die.

---

[129] Lacey (1993b: 621).   [130] M. Moore (1997: 204ff).   [131] Kessler Ferzan (2002).
[132] Duff (1990a: 113).   [133] Gardner (1998: 227). See also the discussion in Bratman (1999).
[134] e.g. Finnis (1991: 36). M. Moore (1996) argues that if killing is one's aim this is invariably worse than killing as a means to some other end (e.g. obtaining an inheritance).
[135] See the discussion of whether purpose is preferable to want or desire in Goff (1988); Fried (1978); Kugler (2002: ch. 1).

2. *The aeroplane bomber.* D puts a bomb on an aeroplane which carries goods which D has insured. His plan is to blow up the plane in mid-flight and claim the insurance money on the destroyed goods. He knows that if the bomb goes off it is virtually certain that the pilot will die. In due course the bomb goes off, killing the pilot.

3. *The burning father.* D is holding his baby on the top of a burning building. As the flames get very close he throws the baby from the building in a last ditch attempt to save the baby's life, but aware that the baby is almost bound to die as a result of the fall. Unfortunately the baby does indeed die, but miraculously the father is rescued by a helicopter.

4. *The revengeful wife.* D, on discovering that her husband is having an affair with V, sets fire to V's house. Her purpose is to scare V away from her husband, although she knows it is likely that V or her family will be inside and may therefore die.

Four views will be sketched in outline here,[136] but there are nearly as many views on what intention is as there are people who have written on the issue:

The 'pure intention' view[137]

This view is promoted by those who argue that intention should mean purpose, nothing more and nothing less.[138] Supporters point out that it is quite possible to foresee a result as virtually certain but not intend it. You may foresee that by drinking ten dry sherries in the bar you will get a hangover the next morning, but that does not mean that you intend to get a hangover when you drink.[139] John Finnis has written that he may foresee that his lecture will confuse half those attending, but that does not mean he intends them to be confused.[140] As Wilson points out: 'If I pull my child's loose tooth out, knowing this cannot be done without him suffering significant pain, only a passing spaceman from Mars could reach the conclusion that I intended to hurt him.' Although if Wilson is correct in saying this quite a few lecturers in criminal law are Martians!

Looking at our scenarios there is no doubt that under the 'pure intention view' the plane bomber, the burning father, and the revengeful wife did not intend the death of V.[141] More problematic is the desperate surgeon. You might think that the 'pure intention view' would hold that the surgeon's purpose was to save his wife's life and so he did not intend to kill V. However, the argument 'I intended to take V's heart out, but did not intend to kill her' is very unattractive.[142] One possible escape route for supporters of the pure intent view is to say that intending to take someone's heart out simply is intending to kill them, the two consequences are inseparable.[143] There is, in our world, no difference between taking out someone's heart and killing them.

---

[136] The names I have given to these theories are mine.   [137] Finnis (1991: 32).

[138] M. Moore (1999). This narrow view of intention is popular with those who take the view that it is never justifiable intentionally to take someone's life. See e.g. Finnis (1991).

[139] Duff (1990a: 61).   [140] Finnis (1991: 64).

[141] Supporters of this view suggest that if we do not like this conclusion in respect of, say, the plane bomber, then we should change the law on what the *mens rea* for murder is, rather than artificially stretch the law on intention.

[142] Fried (1978: 44).

[143] R. Cross (1967: 224) gives an example of a head-hunter who removes someone's head for his collection, but denying that he intended to kill the 'owner' of the head. For further discussion see Simester (1996a) and (1996b).

Supporters of the pure intention view often support the 'ethical doctrine of double effect', which has been defined by John Keown in the following extract:

J. Keown, *Euthanasia, Ethics and Public Policy* (Cambridge: Cambridge University Press, 2003), 20

According to this ethical tradition, it is permissible to allow a bad consequence to result from one's actions, even if it is foreseen as certain to follow, provided certain conditions are satisfied. Those conditions are identified by the principle of 'double effect.' According to this ethical principle, it is permissible to produce a bad consequence if:

- the act one is engaged in is not itself bad;
- the bad consequence is not a means to the good consequence;
- the bad consequence is foreseen but not intended; and
- there is a sufficiently serious reason for allowing the bad consequence to occur.

The 'moral elbow room' view[144]

Here the view taken is that intention is purpose, but that where a defendant is aware that a result is virtually certain to follow from his actions the jury should be given a discretion to decide whether the mental state is wicked enough to be called intention. This would enable supporters of this view to reach what many people would regard as intuitively the correct result: the plane bomber and the desperate surgeon intended to kill V; the burning father and the revengeful wife did not. In these cases some argue that the defendant's wicked recklessness was tantamount to intention and should therefore be treated as such.[145]

Opponents argue that such a test would produce too much uncertainty. Should the case of the desperate surgeon be left to the jury's deliberation: should we not be clear that that is intention? Leaving cases such as that of the plane bomber to the jury means that there is a danger that different juries may reach different conclusions on different facts, leading to the injustice of inconsistent verdicts. It should be the law, not the whim of the jury, which decides whether a person's state of mind constitutes intention.

The 'oblique intention' view

This view is that a result which is foreseen as virtually certain simply is intended. If a person knows that a result will occur as a result of his acts he intended it. Or at least that state of mind is more appropriately classified as intention than recklessness, even if, strictly speaking, it is not intention.[146] Therefore the desperate surgeon, the plane bomber, and the burning father intended to kill V; but the vengeful wife did not (she saw V's death as likely, not virtually certain). The problem scenario for this view is the burning father. Supporters simply reply that although he intended V's death he should be given a defence to ensure he is not guilty of murder. To opponents of this view, to say that the father intended to kill the child when he had the opposite purpose (to save the baby's life) is unsupportable.[147]

---

[144] The phrase appears in Horder (1995: 687).
[146] Ashworth (2003: 178–80); Simester (1996a).
[145] Horder (2005b: 38).
[147] Duff (1990a: 98); Norrie (1999).

The 'Hyam' view

This view suggests that if a result is foreseen as likely then it is intended. Although it has the support of the majority of the House of Lords in *Hyam*, it in fact has few supporters nowadays. Supporters of this view would decide that in all four of our scenarios the defendants intend to kill. Opponents of the view argue that if foresight of a result is intention then the boundary between intention and recklessness becomes hopelessly blurred.

In the following passage Glanville Williams expresses his support for the 'oblique intention' view:

G. Williams, 'Oblique Intention' [1987] *Cambridge Law Journal* 417 at 424–5

Arguments for recognising oblique intent

That cases of the types mentioned should be treated in the same way as ordinary cases of intention is obvious, but opinions differ between two methods of carrying out the policy. One method would be that already proposed: to relax the definition of intent sufficiently to allow oblique intent as a kind of intent. The other would be to redefine all crimes of intention, when it is desired to bring in oblique intent, by making express provision for it.

The second alternative would involve defining murder, for example, as causing death (i) with intent to cause death or serious injury, or (ii) with knowledge that such death or injury is virtually certain. This would make the law perfectly clear, but the definitions of the relevant crimes would become slightly more cumbrous. There appears to be no possibility that Parliament would now revise the law of murder to make specific provision for this additional mental state (upon which the prosecution would rarely need to rely), and any attempt to do so would reopen the whole thorny issue of risk-taking and murder. And not only murder but also various other crimes requiring intention would need the extended definition.

The first alternative would avoid this drawback. As was shown before, there are solid reasons for saying that oblique intent is recognised in the law as it stands, and if the courts accept this opinion no legislative departures are needed.

The case for taking a broad view of intention is particularly strong where the desired consequence is inseparably bound up with the foreseen though undesired consequence. (i) Consider *Arrowsmith* v. *Jenkins*. A political campaigner commenced to address people on the highway, and continued to do so although she knew that she was causing the highway to be blocked, to a degree that (whether she knew it or not) the law regarded as unreasonable. She was convicted of wilfully obstructing the highway, even though her purpose was to hold a meeting, not to obstruct the highway. In the circumstances, holding the meeting was the same thing as obstructing the highway; they were simply two sides of the same coin. (ii) The following were the facts of a notorious Brighton case of 1871. A woman inserted strychnine into a chocolate and attempted to administer it to V. The chocolate she gave having been found to be poisoned, the woman said that she did not know it, and tried to prove her innocence by showing that poisoned chocolates were circulating in the locality. She did this by introducing strychnine into a confectioner's stock of chocolates; and the buyer of some chocolates died. The poisoner was held guilty of murder; yet her primary intent was to dispel the suspicion against her. She did not want anyone other than V to die, and would not have felt frustrated if, by chance, no one died. In those days the crime of murder was much wider than now; but if the poisoner felt sure that her poisoned chocolates would kill someone, would she not still be rightly convicted of murder on the ground that she intended to kill, notwithstanding that she did not desire to do so?

3 MENS REA: THE MENTAL ELEMENT | 191

A peculiar group of cases are those where the law theoretically requires proof of fact y but the courts regard it as readily satisfied by proof of x. A publisher may be convicted of conspiracy to corrupt public morals, obscenity, or blasphemy, on account of an assumed intent to commit these crimes, if he knowingly publishes matter which the jury find to have a tendency to corrupt public morals, to deprave and corrupt those to whom it is published, etc.; and no evidence is needed to support the jury's conclusion. Strict proof of the purported conclusion would be practically impossible, requiring a large sociological enquiry and a consensus on disputed values. The courts simplify the matter by making the equation $x = y$, x being the physical event that the defendant intends (the publication) and y being the jury's determination that it amounts to y.

In the following extract Antje Pedain considers the example of a terrorist bomber who puts a bomb in a public place, wanting to get publicity, but not caring whether anyone is killed. The traditional analysis is that the terrorist would not be said to intend death or serious injury because he did not want people to die and did not foresee death as a virtual certainty. Pedain argues that in fact this can be regarded as a form of intent.

A. Pedain (2003) 'Intention and the Terrorist Example' *Criminal Law Review* 579–93 at 588

Reverting to the terrorist example who contemplates placing a live bomb in a public place, with a view to giving the authorities prior warning so that they may prevent any real harm ('the risky alternative'), as opposed to placing there a mere unactivated 'hoax bomb' which is not dangerous ('the safe alternative'):

By adopting the first course of conduct, the terrorist can expect to maximise the impact his actual and future demands have on the authorities' behaviour: he will achieve being perceived as dangerous and powerful. The price he pays for achieving these objectives is to place innocent human beings at real risk. By adopting the second course of conduct, he can rest assured that no one is really at risk of loss of life or limb at any time. At the same time, he will probably exert some influence on the authorities' behaviour, not only while they still are under the mistaken impression that the device is dangerous but also afterwards, having realised that he had the means at hand to put people into danger and only decided against doing so this time round. Nevertheless, he might be taken less seriously, viewed as less ruthless and therefore easier to be discounted than in the first example—his illegitimate power gain over the conduct of public affairs will be weaker than in the first scenario. Faced with these 'incompatible alternative possible purposes' of what he can achieve by adopting one course of conduct or the other, our terrorist chooses the first one.

In what sense does the terror bomb-announcer 'not want' anyone to suffer harm as a result of his actions? Only in the sense that in his ideal case scenario, the bomb will be successfully defused and no one will be hurt. Does that mean that he really does 'want harm or serious bodily harm not to happen'? This question, in my view, needs to be answered with reference to what we know would have been the terror bomb-announcer's alternative course of conduct which he has actually rejected to pursue: The one in which he desists from making the bomb live, where he places an actually harmless object in a public place. We also know why he decided against it: because in order to achieve his desired objective, he wanted there to be a real risk of harm resulting from his actions, not just a temporary illusion of such a risk.

Placing a live bomb in a public place was a necessary means to achieving his objective, though having the bomb explode was not (and may have been viewed by him as counter-productive). In other words: The 'creation of the risk' was, for him, a necessary means to an end. The risk itself was important, in fact crucial, for the achievement of his objective; he could not have done without the risk (because otherwise he would have done so).

This means that, on a proper understanding of the situation, and despite the fact that he might in a certain sense have 'failed' to achieve his ends in causing widespread mayhem and anger and having inspired, through aversion to his deed, an aversion to his cause, the terror-bomb-announcer's situation is like Hyam's: one who achieved 'too much' rather than 'something different'. He managed to create the risk, which is what he cared for, but he also managed to have the risk materialise, which is more than he cared for and something which ultimately puts into question the achievement of the wider political target which inspired his deed.

When it comes to the question of intention, that latter disappointment does not matter: what matters is only that, in 'intending wilfully to expose another to the risk of death or grievous bodily harm' (as Lord Hailsham succinctly put it in his much maligned speech in *Hyam*), he embraced the actual mayhem caused by the explosion as a possible outcome of his actions.

Why 'intending to create a risk' is different from being reckless

Does this mean that intention now collapses into recklessness? In my view, it does not. 'Having an intention to expose someone to a risk' is different from 'realising that someone will or might be exposed to a risk'. It expresses something more than that. It expresses—and correctly so, in my opinion, when it comes to drawing the line between intention and subjec-tive recklessness—the particular attitude of the defendant towards the risk whose existence he has realised.

In *Hyam*, the defendant realised that there was a risk that whoever might be inside that house could die or get seriously injured in the fire. As for her attitude towards that possible outcome, she wanted to make sure that her former lover was out of harm's way. About other people who might get hurt she 'didn't give a damn'. This is different—significantly different—from someone who proceeds to act because and only because they 'hope that no-one will get hurt'.

Realisations about probabilities of differing degrees on the part of the defendant matter in practice, but they matter only in so far as they provide an evidential indication for the attitude which the defendant had when performing the act in question. They do not substitute the inquiry into the defendant's attitudes with an inquiry into the defendant's assessment of probabilities. It is true that when we are faced with an agent who realised a particular out-come would be certain, we are inclined to say that this constitutes proof of intention without stopping to ask any further questions, but this is because we do not accept that in such a situation there can be a (meaningful) disjunction between what we achieve and what we want. We cannot 'unwant' what we purposefully set out to achieve, as much as we cannot swallow a piece of cake and 'unwant' its disappearance down our throats. As Horder put it, the certain by-products of our actions are simply 'part and parcel' of what we do, and we need no mysterious 'secondary form' of intention to recognise them as intentional, merely a sound grasp of one of the paradigm cases of primary intention. We have as little patience with the explanations of the killer who knew he killed as with a naughty child, who, found chewing on a piece of chocolate cake and asked to explain what it is doing, swallows and brightly replies: 'Nothing!'

The reason that probabilities matter when an outcome is less than certain is because in such a situation, there is room for meaningfully asking the question: Well, what did you do that for? What were you thinking? It is not because the lesser probability in and of itself provides a kind of counter-indication for the presence of intention.

This is blatantly obvious when it comes to the vast majority of cases in which intention is found to exist: the brutal blow to the head struck with a wish to injure and maim; the ramming of a knife into the victim's body, the serving of the drink laced with some home-made ingredient which will hopefully be sufficient to finish off the victim rather than giving her merely a mild indigestion. In all these cases, death or serious physical harm is, from the perspective of the defendant, the hoped for, but far-from-likely-let-alone-certain result.

What is readily accepted in cases where the unlikely outcome is positively desired is equally true in cases where an unlikely and undesired outcome is nevertheless endorsed. The focus on the degree of probability of the possible outcome—foresight of certainty as opposed to foresight as more or less probable—clouds the issue.

If intending something means to endorse it as the consequence of one's voluntary actions, then the issue is not about whether you endorse it as the certain, the likely, or the unlikely consequence of your behaviour. It is about endorsement as such. The point is whether you give that consequence your blessing. To be completely indifferent to the harm you may be causing is a way of accepting that harm as the possible outcome of your actions. It is a very different state of mind from the one in which you take a gamble on another person's well-being because you trust that the risk you create will not materialise.

'Intention to create a risk' and the failure test

Another way of understanding the distinction between intention and recklessness is by applying Duff's 'failure test' to cases of conscious risk-creation. We intend an outcome as a consequence of our actions not only when we want to bring it about or know that it will come about as a result of what we do, but also when we would perceive ourselves to have failed if our actions subsequently turned out to have been harmless in the sense that in the circumstances nobody was or could have been put at risk of suffering the kind of harm which the law states as the consequence we must have intended.

The reckless actor, for instance the car driver who overtakes another car in blind spot not knowing what he might encounter on the wrong side of the road after the bend, will sigh with relief when he discovers that there was no other car coming, and that consequently he never put anyone at risk at all. He will not think that he failed because (from the perspective of an all-knowing observer or from the actor's perspective after the fact) his actions never put anyone at risk, though from his vantage point of imperfect knowledge while he performed them they appeared to carry a certain risk with them.

By contrast, the actor who intends to create a risk of harm—the terrorist bomb warner, or the defendant in *Hyam*—would consider themselves to have failed if the house never caught fire or if the bomb never could have gone off because of its flawed construction. They would resent the fact that from an ex-post perspective, their actions appear to others impotent and silly, rather than powerful and dangerous.

These are the easy cases—people who only potentially create a risk of harm and would be happy to find they did not really put anyone at risk. However, even actors who create an actual risk of harm and are aware of that—for instance, the driver who overtakes another car in the teeth of oncoming traffic hoping that he will be quick enough to pull back into his own lane to avoid collision—can not be said to 'intend to create a risk of harm' in the sense that he cares for its creation. We are tempted to say 'he must be treated like someone who intends to create the harm' because we know that 'the risk is a certain, not just a possible, consequence of his actions'—so we feel tempted to apply the 'knowledge of certainty equals intention'—line of argument to this case. However knowledge of certainty in regard to risks is not the same as knowledge of certainty in regard to results. Even where the existence of the risk is certain, it still makes sense for us to hope that it will not materialise; that bad results may not occur. Therefore we can still meaningfully disassociate ourselves from the possible harmful result of our actions. But when the result itself is certain, such disassociation is impossible.

Consequently, even the person who knows that their actions create an actual risk of harm to others can be allowed to say that they would not consider themselves to have failed to achieve their purpose had they failed to create that risk: 'I only acted because I thought the risk would not materialise', is what such actors typically say: 'I did not care for there being a risk and wish I could have done what I wanted to do without there being that risk.' The intentional risk-makers cannot say the latter. Creating the risk is the very point of what they are doing. Without there being a consequent risk their actions fail to achieve their objective.

It is true that because these distinctions are drawn in relation to an inner fact or state of mind, there will frequently be insufficient evidence to conclude that a person who did create a significant and obvious risk for others was not merely taking a gamble. This is why many perpetrators who, if the truth were known, did endorse the harm they caused as a consequence of their actions will get away with pleading that they have acted merely recklessly. However that should not confuse us about those cases where there is sufficient evidence of such endorsement to find that the defendant acted intentionally, as did the defendant in *Hyam* and as does the terrorist who warns the authorities about the presence of a live bomb he put in a busy place.

15.2 IS INTENTION AN ISSUE OF FACT OR AN ISSUE OF MORAL RESPONSIBILITY?

Is intention a factual concept or is it one that involves a judgement?[148] In other words is intention a psychological fact: if we could see everything that was going on inside the defendant's mind would we know if there was intent? Or is intention in the nature of a moral judgement: is the defendant's state of mind bad enough to deserve the label 'intention'?[149] In the following passage Alan Norrie discusses these different approaches to intention:

A. Norrie, *Crime, Reason and History* (2nd edn., London: Butterworths, 2002), 47–50

(i) Two approaches to direct and indirect (oblique) intention

It will be helpful if we begin by exploring the meaning of the concept of intention. This is not straightforward for we can identify not one but two conceptions, both of which are relevant

---

[148] Linked to this issue is a debate over the extent to which defences, such as necessity, become merged with the notion of intention.

[149] See Horder (1995a). It should be noted that other *mens rea* terms do involve an element of moral judgement. A person is reckless only if he takes an unjustifiable risk; a person is negligent only if he behaves unreasonably. It would not, therefore, be extremely radical to suggest that intention carries an element of moral judgement. For further discussion of this point see Simester and Chan (1997).

to the law. The first is the one that is favoured by the 'orthodox subjectivists' such as Williams and Smith and Hogan, and which has a prominent position in the law itself. It is a formal, 'factual', psychological definition. The second is a more morally substantive, less factual and psychological, account which is reflected in the work, for example, of Anthony Duff (1990), John Gardner (1998) and Jeremy Horder (2000). Here, the emphasis is not on whether the individual as a matter of fact conceived an intention, revealing psychological control of the ensuing action, but rather whether that person's intention was *in its intrinsic quality* morally good or bad. I argue that this latter understanding is also to be found in or behind the law, often in conflict with the first approach, and that we need to understand this interlacing of conflicting views.

(a) The formal psychological ('orthodox subjectivist') approach

In this approach, the paradigm case is the easiest. To talk of intending to do something is to talk of 'meaning' or 'aiming' to do it. It concerns applying one's mind to a particular task and directing one's action to a particular 'aim', 'end' or (the standard lawyer's synonym) 'purpose' (Smith and Hogan, 1999, 54). Our 'purpose' is what we intend to bring about through our actions.

In perhaps most situations it will be relatively clear that an outcome was the direct product of an individual's purpose. A punch on the nose will normally (though not always) be brought about by an intention to punch someone on the nose, so that outcome and intention are directly linked. But there are other situations in which an outcome will not be directly linked to an intention or purpose (end) but will be either a means to a particular end or a by-product or side-effect of such an end. The outcome is not the product of a direct intention, but emerges *obliquely*, as the consequence of the achievement of a desired end (Williams, 1987). Where the outcome is indirectly achieved as a means to an end or as a side-effect (which may not be desired in itself), can one be said to intend it?

Where the means are *necessary* to the desired end, and knowingly undertaken in that light, it is argued that the individual intends the means as well as the end, even if he does not desire (or like) the means themselves. Where the side-effect is known to be a *certain* by-product of achieving one's purpose, it is also argued that one intends the side-effect in addition to the purpose. This analysis conforms with that of Lord Hailsham in *Hyam* ((1974) at 52) where he stated that 'intention' must 'include the means as well as the end and the inseparable consequences of the end as well as the means . . .' For the 'orthodox subjectivist', this linking of what was intended to matters that were strictly not intended involves no element of artificiality: it is quite acceptable to talk of intentions as being either direct or indirect (oblique) (cf Williams, 1987; Goff, 1988, 45–7; Smith and Hogan, 1999, 55). Where artificiality would enter the analysis would be if the means or side-effect were not a *necessary* consequence but a consequence about which there was a degree of chance or probability of its occurrence. Where a side-effect was known to be likely, possible, or probable, one could say that the person *took the risk* that the consequence would occur, but not that he intended it to occur. In other words, he was *reckless* as to its occurrence . . ., rather than intending it.

Finally, an important point of qualification. In the last paragraph, we spoke of *necessary* means and *certain* side-effects of one's actions. But the world is such that we can never act with one hundred per cent certainty that a particular means will be necessary or that a by-product is bound to be created. The world is full of unanticipatable and unanticipated effects which alter or wreck the best-made calculation. I intend to injure my enemy standing behind a closed window by throwing a stone. In 999 cases out of 1000, I must break the window in order to achieve my purpose. On the occasion in question, by a fluke, the window is thrown open as the stone leaves my hand. Or, I intend to collect the insurance on a parcel on a plane by timing a bomb to explode in mid-air. I know it to be a plane without parachutes or ejector seats. It is as certain as can be that the pilot will be killed but, by a freak, he falls from a great height and lives. Could the stone thrower or the bomb planter claim that the possibility of a fluke or freak stopping the means or side-effect occurring meant that he did not intend it, since it was not *absolutely bound* to happen? Could he rely on the chance in a thousand to say that the means or side-effect was not intended since it was not *genuinely* certain to occur? Could he claim that he very much hoped that the window would be thrown open or the pilot would be saved, and that given the possibility of the outside chance, he therefore did not intend the side-effect?

The answer on this analysis is that our actions and plans are always subject to the intervention of the unexpected and this is as true of our direct purposes as of the means to our ends or side-effects of our purposes. The unexpected may defeat the achievement of our purpose or render our calculation of means and side-effects wrong, but it does not cancel our intentions or purposes whether those are either direct or indirect. We need therefore to qualify the argument about the certainty of means or side-effects by talking of certainty 'for all practical purposes'. Judges have used the phrases 'moral' or 'virtual' certainty to denote a situation where an event will occur 'barring some unforeseen intervention' (*Nedrick* (1986)). The important point to note is that 'virtual certainty' *is* a kind of certainty (the only kind in fact that ever exists) and not a kind of high probability or chance.

(b) The morally substantive approach

Duff's critique of the foregoing approach is that it fails to reflect the way in which we understand wrongdoing. Orthodox subjectivism splits one moral judgment, whether a person directed his moral energies into doing something wrong, into two (subjective and objective) components. The 'objective' component is the harm that constitutes the wrong or the crime, which is measured in terms of the bad consequences it produces. The 'subjective' element is the fault of the wrongdoer, which is judged by whether the objective consequences were *as a matter of fact* known, foreseen or intended. For Duff, this approach is inadequate for it fails to reflect the nature of our moral judgments, in which 'objective' wrongdoing and 'subjective' fault are always combined. Thus to judge harm, we need to know about the *moral* quality of what was intended:

'Both the murder victim and the victim of natural causes suffer death: but the character of the harm that they suffer surely also depends on the way in which they die. One who tries to kill me . . . *attacks* my life and my most basic rights; and the harm which I suffer in being murdered . . . essentially involves this wrongful attack on me— . . . The "harm" at which the law of murder is aimed is thus not just the *consequential* harm of death, but the harm which is *intrinsic* to an attack on another's life'. (Duff, 1990, 113)

And to judge intention, we need to know its moral quality:

'Human actions are purposive: they are done for reasons, in order to bring something about; their direction and their basic structure is formed by the intentions with which their agents act. It is through the intentions with which I act that I engage in the world as an agent, and relate myself most closely to the actual and potential effects of my actions; and the central or fundamental kind of wrong-doing is to *direct* my actions towards evil—to *intend* and to *try* to do what is evil.' (Duff, 1990, 112–13)

The intention to do wrong is not a crime because a person has a psychological intention to do a criminal act, but because that intention manifests moral wrong-doing. The idea that intentions reveal bad moral attitudes leads to less emphasis on the precise forms of intention and more on what they reveal about the wrongdoer's motives. For the orthodox subjectivist, a person is guilty of murder where he intends to kill or cause serious ('grievous bodily') harm, or foresees death or serious injury as a virtual certainty, but not where he foresees death or serious injury as a probability. (These are the law's requirements too.) For the orthodox subjectivist, there is doubt as to whether intending to cause serious harm ('implied malice') is a sufficient alternative mental state to a direct intention to kill. Even foreseeing death as a virtual certainty (indirect intention) smacks to some of a false constructivism because there is no direct link between what was intended and the outcome of death. Only an intention actually to kill truly links with the result. Certainly foreseeing death or serious injury as a probable consequence (reckless killing) does not link what was intended sufficiently to the outcome of death to count as murder.

For Duff, the killer in all these situations may legitimately be convicted of murder. Where there is foresight of virtual certainty of death or serious injury, the killer displays 'an utter indifference to [the victim's] rights or interests' (Duff, 1990, 114). Further, where a person foresees the probability of death by exposing his victim to its serious risk (which English law does not see as murder), Duff argues that it is legitimately charged as murder. Such a person is 'wickedly reckless' and guilty of murder, for death 'is an integral aspect of his intended attack' (Duff, 1990, 177). On the orthodox subjectivist approach, as with the law of murder, such a person is guilty only of reckless manslaughter. With the morally substantive approach, this is not so. The moral quality in the act is more important than a precise distinguishing of different psychological states.

QUESTIONS

1. Larry Alexander (2000) has argued that we should not draw a distinction between intention and recklessness. They both indicate essentially the same vice: insufficient concern for others. He sees the justifiability of the risk as more important than the difference between foresight (recklessness) and purpose (intent). Distinguishing in moral terms the mercy killer and the terrorist risking people's lives in terms of the justifiability of the risk taken is more persuasive than considering the cases in terms of purpose or foresight. Do you agree?

2. Law Commission Report No. 218 (para. 7.14) proposed the following definition of intention in its Criminal Law Bill:

   . . . a person acts

   (a) 'intentionally' with respect to a result when—

      (i) it is his purpose to cause it, or

      (ii) although it is not his purpose to cause it, he knows that it would occur in the ordinary course of events if he were to succeed in his purpose of causing some other result.

   Would this proposal clarify the law?

FURTHER READING

Duff, R.A. (1990a), *Intention, Agency and Criminal Liability* (Oxford: Blackwell).

Finnis, J. (1991), 'Intention and Side-Effects' in R. Frey and C. Morris (eds.), *Liability and Responsibility* (Oxford: OUP).

Gorr, M. (1996), 'Should the Law Distinguish between Intention and (Mere) Foresight', *Legal Theory* 2: 359.

Horder, J. (1995a), 'Intention in the Criminal Law—A Rejoinder', *Modern Law Review* 58: 678.

Kaveny, C. (2004), 'Inferring Intention from Foresight', *Law Quarterly Review* 120: 81.

Kugler, I. (2002), *Direct and Oblique Intention in the Criminal Law* (Aldershot: Ashgate).

—— (2004), 'Conditional Oblique Intention', *Criminal Law Review* 284.

Lacey, N. (1993a), 'A Clear Concept of Intention: Elusive or Illusory?', *Modern Law Review* 56: 621.

—— (1995b), 'In(de)terminable Intentions', *Modern Law Review* 58: 592.

Simester, A. (1996a), 'Moral Certainty and the Boundaries of Intention', *Oxford Journal of Legal Studies* 16: 445.

Tadros, V. (2005), *Criminal Responsibility* (Oxford: OUP), ch. 8.

Williams, G. (1988), 'Oblique Intention', *Cambridge Law Journal* 47: 417.

16 RECKLESSNESS

16.1 SUBJECTIVE AND OBJECTIVE FORMS OF RECKLESSNESS AND INADVERTENCE

As shown in Part I of this chapter there were until recently two kinds of recklessness in English and Welsh criminal law: *Cunningham* recklessness and *Caldwell* recklessness. Neither form of recklessness has escaped criticism.

Criticisms of *Cunningham* recklessness

Cunningham recklessness is too narrow, say some commentators. Can it be right that a defendant who cares so little about other people that he does not consider whether his actions might harm them deserves to be acquitted? Should defendants who are so angry or self-absorbed that they do not notice the risks they are posing to others be acquitted?[150] Indeed, critics point out, it is noticeable that if a defendant fails to notice a risk because he is drunk he is still *Cunningham* reckless: why restrict this to drunkenness? Why not include other blameworthy reasons for failing to see an obvious risk? Critics add that attempts by the courts to include 'putting awareness to the back of your mind'[151] within the concept of recklessness demonstrate that pure *Cunningham* recklessness is too narrow.

Supporters of *Cunningham* recklessness are often supporters of the choice theory. They argue that a defendant cannot be said to have chosen to undertake a risk of which he was unaware. Indeed he cannot be blamed for being indifferent to other people's welfare if he was not aware that they were at risk of being harmed.[152] We can only guess what the defendant's attitude would have been had he been aware of the risk. Michael Moore[153] concludes that there is a fundamental difference between a choice (advert risk) and an unexercised capacity (inadvertent risk). Some supporters of *Cunningham* recklessness are

---

[150] S. Gardner (1993). [151] e.g. *Parker* [1977] 1 WLR 600 (CA).
[152] White (1991: ch. 7). [153] Moore (1996: ch. 1).

willing to accept that a person may be blameworthy for failing to notice an obvious risk, but argue that such a person is not as blameworthy as the person who sees the risk and nevertheless takes it. Inadvertent defendants may deserve blame, but they do not deserve to be classified as reckless.[154]

Criticisms of *Caldwell* recklessness

Caldwell recklessness has many critics. The decision enraged some commentators so much that ordinary standards of etiquette when commenting on judicial decisions were put aside, with Professor Smith calling Lord Diplock's reasoning in the case 'pathetically inadequate'.[155] One particular ground of criticism is based around the decisions in *Elliott v C*[156] and *Coles*.[157] By convicting these defendants on the basis of failing to see a risk which would have been obvious to a reasonable person (even if it would not have been obvious to a reasonable person of those defendants' mental abilities), they are said to go against fundamental principles of justice. Even accepting the moral thrust of *Caldwell* recklessness (we blame a defendant for failing to see a risk which he *should* have seen) such an argument is legitimate only where the defendant could have foreseen the risk. To punish someone for failing to do something he or she was incapable of doing seems manifestly unjust.[158] It is hard to mount a defence of the reasoning in these cases except on the basis that it is more important to protect victims from harm from others than to achieve justice in every case.

Although there is hardly a consensus amongst commentators, it seems that a majority would accept that *Cunningham* recklessness is too narrow, while *Caldwell* recklessness is too wide. Is there a middle way between the two forms? Some commentators have suggested that the decision of the House of Lords in *Reid*[159] hinted at one.[160] In cases of inadvertence we should ask why the defendant failed to see an obvious risk. If the defendant has a good reason (e.g. a sudden emergency) he is not reckless. But if he does not have a good reason (e.g. he is angry) then he is reckless.

We will now consider the writings of two theorists who have sought to develop a middle way between *Cunningham* and *Caldwell* recklessness.

16.2 AN INSUFFICIENT REGARD FOR THE INTERESTS OF OTHERS: VICTOR TADROS

Victor Tadros describes the vice of recklessness as an insufficient regard for the interests of others. In the following passage he explains why he thinks that people can be responsible for the way they form their beliefs that their actions are or are not risky:

V. Tadros, 'Recklessness and the Duty to Take Care' in S. Shute and A. Simester (eds.), *Criminal Law Theory* (Oxford: OUP, 2002), 248–50

We are responsible for our beliefs. That idea, it seems to me, is part of the motivation of many of those who argue for objective recklessness. Some who argue for a very strong form

---

[154] Ferzan (2001); Birch (1988).   [155] J.C. Smith (1981).
[156] [1983] 2 All ER 1005 (DC).   [157] [1995] 1 Cr App R 157 (CA).
[158] Whether on the detailed facts of the particular case C deserved to be punished is discussed in Field and Lynn (1992).
[159] [1992] 3 All ER 673 (HL).   [160] Field and Lynn (1993).

of objective recklessness seem to think that it is the falsity of the defendant's belief that provides the target for criminal liability. But, as we have seen, that one has all of the virtues associated with belief formation in proper balance does not guarantee that one's beliefs will all be true. One can have all of the virtues associated with believing and yet hold false beliefs, even beliefs that most ordinary reasonable people would not hold. For this reason, our responsibility for our beliefs is not sufficient ground for imposing criminal liability in cases where the defendant had a false belief that there was no risk involved in the action that she performed. Consequently, our attention turns from the nature of the belief that is held to the process of belief formation.

To see this, let us return to example (6). [I am driving home to watch the football and I come to a junction. I am about to rush out, not caring that a pedestrian might be killed. However, I suddenly realize that I might damage my lovely new car and consequently look either way, just as a responsible driver would. I form the belief that there is no danger but I fail to notice a pedestrian who unexpectedly dashes in front of my car, and run her over.] In that example, I formed a belief that there was no danger to pedestrians, but that was not a response to my concern for pedestrians but rather my concern for my car. However, I did all that was required of me to ensure that the way was clear; I fulfilled my responsibility. In that case it is wrong to make me criminally liable for the death of the pedestrian. I had *done* as much as could be expected of a truly virtuous person, even though I was not truly virtuous. That I was indifferent to the fate of the pedestrian is not sufficient reason to hold me criminally liable. Fulfilling my responsibility to ensure that the way was clear ought to absolve me of criminal liability even if false beliefs are formed. The falsity of the belief itself is not sufficient evidence of fault. If we are to find fault, we must find it in the process of belief formation. Furthermore, it may be that the defendant has not formed his belief in the way that he ought and yet criminal liability may still be inappropriate. For it must be shown that, in holding a false belief, the defendant manifests the appropriate kind of vice.

It might be thought that the appropriate kind of vice is displayed whenever the defendant has formed an irrational or unreasonable belief about the risks. If that were the case, irrationality or unreasonableness would not simply be descriptions of the nature of the belief itself, regardless of who holds it, but descriptions of the way in which the belief was formed. Such a view might be supported by Joseph Raz's recent analysis of irrational beliefs. 'A belief is irrational', Raz writes, 'if and only if holding it displays lack of care and diligence in one's epistemic conduct'. Showing lack of care and diligence, it might be argued, displays a vice that is central to the imposition of criminal liability. After all, that one fails to take care or be diligent also shows that one is insufficiently motivated by the interests of the individuals who might suffer from one's lack of care and diligence.

However, it is not at all clear that the fact that one holds an irrational belief necessarily shows a vice of this kind. That one holds an irrational belief is not itself evidence of a lack of care on the part of the believer. A number of other vices might result in the formation of an irrational belief. It might be that the defendant is merely stupid or illogical; vices which, whilst in themselves warranting blame, do not give rise to the kind and degree of blame that the imposition of criminal liability expresses. If one has such vices, one can take all the care that is required and yet fail to form rational beliefs. In fact, this argument might even be stretched to include some other failings, such as some instances of arrogance.

Consider *R v Shimmen*, in which a martial arts expert attempted to perform a kick near to a window without breaking it. Suppose that he formed the belief that there was no risk involved at all due to an arrogant belief in his own ability. We might conclude that he had manifested a vice in breaking the window, and consequently attribute responsibility to him for breaking the window. But is it correct to attribute criminal liability to him? The difficulty in doing so is that the criminal law should not be interested in the kinds of vice that Shimmen manifested. That Shimmen was arrogant does not show clearly that Shimmen was 'insufficiently different' to the interests of others. It may be that he cared deeply about the shopkeeper and his window, and was sincerely mortified at having broken it (and not because of a change of heart, motivation, or perspective), but truly (though arrogantly) believed that he was doing nothing to put the window at risk. Shimmen may have been responsible for breaking the window but, at least on this presentation of the facts, he did not display an appropriate vice in breaking the window and consequently he ought not to be made criminally liable for it. He did not show an insufficient regard for the interests of others. And that, as I argued above, is central to the concerns of the criminal law.

These considerations militate against many popular constructions of objective recklessness. For example, accounts that rely on the risks that the defendant ought to have recognized, even those such as Hart's that restrict liability to the capacity of the accused to recognize the risks involved in performing a particular action, are too broad. Defendants such as Shimmen, on my construction of the facts, ought to recognize the risks and have the capacity to recognize the risks. Nevertheless, they ought not to be made criminally liable.

This should help to guide us in formulating an appropriate definition of objective recklessness. An appropriate definition of objective recklessness would focus on the process of belief formation. And it would be required to distinguish between cases of mere irrationality, stupidity, or arrogance and cases where the formation of an irrational belief shows that the defendant was not adequately motivated by the interests of others. In an earlier part of the discussion, I suggested that our responsibility for our beliefs is grounded on two facts. The first fact is that belief formation is governed by norms. There are norms that govern the ways in which we ought to see the world, and to interpret what we see. One important aspect of the intellectual virtues has to do with the system of norms that we ought to apply to the formation of beliefs. The second fact is that we have some control over which evidence we are presented with. There are also norms that apply to evidence-gathering; the intellectual virtues relate to the system of norms we apply to evidence-gathering as well. Might these two facts provide grounds upon which we can construct a test for objective recklessness? It will be no surprise that I think that they can.

However, one caveat is in order. My claim is not that these are the only ways in which belief formation is sufficiently vicious to warrant criminal liability. It may be that the test of objective recklessness can be extended to include other cases, in particular cases where the offending belief is derived from a further belief that was viciously formed. Space does not permit me fully to discuss such cases here, though I will try to illuminate some potential problems for assessing liability in such cases. The two cases that I will concentrate on here are, I think, the central cases. The first is where the individual has sufficient information at his fingertips to form the belief that there is a significant risk of a wrong being done to another but, due to a motivational reason of a particular kind, fails to form the belief that such a wrong will be brought about. The second is where an individual knows that a situation that he is in, or the activity that he is performing, might give rise to particular risks and fails to investigate whether there are such risks. In the next section I will show how these two cases might be appropriate targets for the imposition of criminal liability.

. . .

D. Conclusions

From this discussion, we can derive a test of recklessness that can be applied where the agent has failed to realize the risks that his action created. The agent will be reckless if the following conditions are fulfilled:

(a) the action was of a kind that might carry risks with it according to the beliefs of the individual; and either:

(bi) given those beliefs the agent failed to fulfil his duty of investigating the risks; or

(bii) the agent wilfully blinded himself to the existence of the risks.

Where these conditions are not fulfilled it might well be appropriate to make the defendant civilly liable for any harm that is caused through his risky action. But, for the most part at least, criminal liability is inappropriate. This is because the criminal law, unlike the civil law, is concerned not with distributing losses but with punishing the defendant for harms both for which he is responsible and which manifest the appropriate kind of vice.

This test proposed marks a middle way between purely objective and purely subjective accounts. In favour of objective accounts, there are at least some cases where one can attribute *mens rea* to the defendant despite the fact that she does not recognize the risks involved in what she is doing. If her background beliefs are such that she ought to investigate the risks and she does not perform that investigation adequately, or if she forms a belief that there is no risk for a non-evidential reason, it is appropriate to regard her as reckless for the purposes of the criminal law. On the other hand, the test is sensitive to considerations of the rule of law that subjectivists are concerned with. Citizens are given a fair opportunity to know when they are and are not breaching the criminal law, without being required to go far beyond the call of duty in investigating the risks involved in acting day-to-day. It is only those actions that are already recognized by the defendant as risky that have attached to them burdens of investigation, at least as far as the criminal law is concerned. Furthermore, the central purpose of the criminal law, of punishing those who manifest vices such as cruelty or indifference, is achieved without also making criminals of the stupid, the ignorant, or the clumsy.

16.3 PRACTICAL INDIFFERENCE: ANTHONY DUFF

Anthony Duff[161] has proposed an understanding of recklessness based on the concept of practical indifference:[162]

An appropriate general test of recklessness would be—did the agent's conduct (including any conscious risk-taking, any failure to notice an obvious risk created by her action, and any unreasonable belief on which she acted) display a seriously culpable practical indifference to the interests which her action in fact threatened?

This proposal is an attempt to develop a form of recklessness which is in between *Caldwell* and *Cunningham* recklessness. It is wider than *Cunningham* recklessness but narrower than *Caldwell*. It captures both those who see a risk and take it and those who fail to see a risk because they are practically indifferent to the needs of others.[163] The significance of the term 'practically indifferent' is that Duff is able to argue that inadvertence caused by practical

---

[161] Duff (1990a: 172).   [162] See also Simons (1992) who uses the term 'culpable indifference'.
[163] Gardner and Jung (1991) take the view that advertence to a risk can be described as an example of indifference.

indifference is a subjective state of mind; an attitude of the defendant. Whether or not a defendant notices a risk indicates what his attitude towards such risks is. The failure to notice an obvious risk might indicate that the defendant could not care less whether the risk materialized. He gives as an example a bridegroom who is found drinking in a pub at the time of his wedding and explains that he completely forgot about his big day. Quite simply this is the kind of thing one should not forget about and we can properly assume that he did not regard the wedding as sufficiently important. Duff argues that what we do reflects what we care about. Others reject the argument that an action can encapsulate inadvertence.[164] Ferzan discusses eating an ice-cream cone.[165] Does this show an indifference to whether I gain weight, he asks? It might, or it might in fact be that I debated long and hard within myself whether or not to eat the cone, given its weight-inducing possibility. In the latter case it could hardly be said that I was indifferent to putting on weight, he argues.[166] Another way of considering practical indifference is to ask how would the defendant have acted if he or she had been aware of the risk. If he or she would have acted in the same way then that demonstrates that she has the same lack of concern for others as a person who deliberately takes a risk of harming others.[167]

Although Duff's proposal is attractive it has received its critics. Alan Norrie[168] focuses on the example of rape, which Duff discusses. Duff argues that a man who does not ask a woman whether she consents to sexual intercourse and just assumes that she does is practically indifferent to the woman's interests and can therefore be classified as reckless. Norrie argues that although any right-thinking person would blame such a man, we cannot say that he is necessarily indifferent to the woman's interest. He may hold outrageous views on women's consent to sexual intercourse (e.g. that any woman would want to have sexual intercourse with him), but it does not follow that he is *indifferent* to the woman.[169] He may genuinely care whether or not she consents but believe she consents because he is irresistibly attractive, for example. Norrie argues that Duff is classifying such a man as 'practically indifferent' not because that is actually his state of mind, but because 'we' are appalled at his attitude towards women. Norrie is happy to blame such a defendant, but he says Duff cannot claim that doing so is a subjective test. Norrie argues that Duff moves from the notion that the defendant ought to have realized this risk to the notion that the defendant was indifferent to the risk too quickly. Duff's response to this argument is that he does not accept the argument that we can consider states of mind divorced from actions.[170] In other words the actions of the defendant are the actions of an indifferent person, and hence the defendant is classified as indifferent. This reply will convince only those who agree with Duff's understanding of the meanings of actions. However, most subjectivists do not.[171]

More supportive critics may agree with Duff that the practically indifferent people are blameworthy, but argue that he needs to demonstrate that they are sufficiently blameworthy to be classified along with the advertent as reckless. Brady[172] picks up on Duff's example of the groom in the pub at the time of the wedding and argues that we may blame him, but surely he is not in the same class of blameworthiness as the groom who is drinking while fully aware that the bride and all the guests are waiting for him. In other words, even if inadvertence may be blameworthy, it is not as blameworthy as advertence.[173]

---

[164] Ferzan (2001).   [165] Ibid., 618.
[166] A further difficulty is how the law should deal with a defendant who fails to see a risk due to his racist or sexist beliefs.
[167] Simons (1992).   [168] Norrie (2001: ch. 4).   [169] See also Brady (1996).
[170] Duff (1996: ch. 1).   [171] See further Ferzan (2002).   [172] Brady (1996).
[173] For an alternative analysis based on the notion of 'acceptance' see Michaels (1998).

QUESTIONS

1. Anne finds a gun in a park and for a joke, assuming that it has no bullets in it, fires it at her friend Bertha. In fact there are bullets in the gun, and Bertha's eye is seriously injured. Anne is not guilty of assaulting Bertha (she did not intend and was not *Cunningham* reckless as to the injury). If Bertha were later to die from her injuries Anne might be guilty of manslaughter (she may be grossly negligent). Is this the law being an ass?

2. Is it arguable that for minor crimes such as criminal damage the law is entitled to use a more objective test so that cases can be dealt with more quickly in the courts, while for more serious offences, such as an assault, the law should take more time to ensure that the defendant really is blameworthy and hence a subjective test is used? Is it more justifiable to punish a defendant for indifference when he is doing something which he knows to be particularly dangerous (e.g. driving)?

FURTHER READING

Alexander, L. (2000), 'Insufficient Concern: A Unified Conception of Criminal Culpability', *California Law Review* 88: 931.

Duff, R.A. (1990a), *Intention, Agency and Criminal Liability* (Oxford: Blackwell).

Kessler Ferzan, K. (2002), 'Don't Abandon the Model Penal Code Yet! Thinking Through Simons's *Rethinking*', *Buffalo Criminal Law Review* 6: 185.

Norrie, A. (1992), 'Subjectivism, Objectivism and the Limits of Criminal Recklessness', *Oxford Journal of Legal Studies* 12: 45.

Simons, K. (2002), 'Does Punishment for "Culpable Indifference" Simply Punish for "Bad Character"?', *Buffalo Criminal Law Review* 6: 219.

Tadros, V. (2002a), 'Recklessness and the Duty to take Care' in S. Shute and A. Simester (eds.), *Criminal Law Theory* (Oxford: OUP).

—— (2005), *Criminal Responsibility* (Oxford: OUP), ch. 9.

17 NEGLIGENCE

Although many crimes are based on negligence, nearly all of them concern minor offences which carry a slight stigma, such as motoring offences. As noted in Part I of this chapter liability for negligence does not depend on the state of mind of the defendant but rather what the defendant did: did he or she act in a way in which a reasonable person would not have acted? This has led some commentators to argue that negligence should not be classified as a *mens rea*, a state of mind.[174] Of greater importance is the fact that many commentators feel that it is improper for the criminal law to use negligence.[175]

17.1 OPPOSITION TO THE USE OF NEGLIGENCE IN CRIMINAL LAW

Clearly those who support the choice theory will object to liability based on negligence.[176] Character theorists will find it easier to support the doctrine because a negligent act may

---

[174] e.g. G. Williams (1982).   [175] e.g. Hall (1963); Fine and Cohen (1967); Kenny (1978).
[176] e.g. M. Moore (2000); Brady (1980b); Mackie (1977: 210).

indicate a blameworthy characteristic (e.g. a lack of concern for others). However, Michael Moore argues that a single negligent act does not manifest a careless disposition.[177] A single act of negligence might simply be an accident or forgetfulness. It is only once a pattern of negligent acts develops that we may conclude that the defendant's character is in fact indifference to others. Moore concludes that the character theory cannot explain why an isolated act of negligence is punished.

17.2 SUPPORT FOR THE USE OF NEGLIGENCE IN CRIMINAL LAW

We will now consider the writings of those who seek to support liability for negligence, at least in some cases. Professor Herbert Hart has sought to justify a modified form of negligence. The defendant should be liable if, given his mental and physical capabilities, he had the capacity to see the risk:

H.L.A. Hart, 'Negligence, Mens Rea and the Elimination of Responsibility' in H.L.A. Hart, *Punishment and Responsibility* (Oxford: OUP, 1968), 152–7

What is crucial is that those whom we punish should have had, when they acted, the normal capacities, physical and mental, for doing what the law requires and abstaining from what it forbids, and a fair opportunity to exercise these capacities. Where these capacities and opportunities are absent, as they are in different ways in the varied cases of accident, mistake, paralysis, reflex action, coercion, insanity, etc., the moral protest is that it is morally wrong to punish because 'he could not have helped it' or 'he could not have done otherwise' or 'he had no real choice.' But . . . there is no reason (unless we are to reject the whole business of responsibility and punishment) *always* to make this protest when someone who 'just didn't think' is punished for carelessness. For in some cases at least we may say 'he could have thought about what he was doing' with just as much rational confidence as one can say of any intentional wrong-doing 'he could have done otherwise.'

Of course, the law compromises with competing values over this matter of the subjective element in responsibility. . . .

The most important compromise which legal systems make over the subjective element consists in its adoption of what has been unhappily termed the 'objective standard.' This may lead to an individual being treated for the purposes of conviction and punishment as if he possessed capacities for control of his conduct which he did not possess, but which an ordinary or reasonable man possesses and would have exercised. The expression 'objective' and its partner 'subjective' are unhappy because, as far as negligence is concerned, they obscure the real issue. We may be tempted to say with Dr Turner that just because the negligent man does not have 'the thought of harm in his mind,' to hold him responsible for negligence is *necessarily* to adopt an objective standard and to abandon the 'subjective' element in responsibility. It then becomes vital to distinguish this (mistaken) thesis from the position brought about by the use of objective standards in the application of laws which make negligence criminally punishable. For, when negligence is made criminally punishable, this itself leaves open the question: whether, before we punish, both or only the first of the following two questions must be answered affirmatively.

---

[177] M. Moore (1997: 241).

(i) Did the accused fail to take those precautions which any reasonable man with normal capacities would in the circumstances have taken?

(ii) Could the accused, given his mental and physical capacities, have taken those precautions?

. . . If our conditions of liability are invariant and not flexible, *i.e.* if they are not adjusted to the capacities of the accused, then some individuals will be held liable for negligence though they could not have helped their failure to comply with the standard. In *such* cases, indeed, criminal responsibility will be made independent of any 'subjective element,' since the accused could not have conformed to the required standard. But this result is nothing to do with negligence being taken as a basis for criminal liability; precisely the same result will be reached if, in considering whether a person acted intentionally, we were to attribute to him foresight of consequences which a reasonable man would have foreseen but which he did not. 'Absolute liability' results, not from the admission of the principle that one who has been grossly negligent is criminally responsible for the consequent harm even if 'he had no idea in his mind of harm to anyone,' but from the refusal in the application of this principle to consider the capacities of an individual who has fallen below the standard of care.

It is of course quite arguable that no legal system could afford to individualise the conditions of liability so far as to discover and excuse all those who could not attain the average or reasonable man's standard. It may, in practice, be impossible to do more than excuse those who suffer from gross forms of incapacity, viz. infants, or the insane, or those afflicted with recognisably inadequate powers of control over their movements, or who are clearly unable to detect, or extricate themselves, from situations in which their disability may work harm. Some confusion is, however, engendered by certain inappropriate ways of describing these excusable cases, which we are tempted to use in a system which, like our own, defines negligence in terms of what the reasonable man would do. We may find ourselves asking whether the infant, the insane, or those suffering from paralysis did all that a reasonable man would *in the circumstances* do, taking 'circumstances' (most queerly) to include personal qualities like being an infant, insane or paralysed. This paradoxical approach leads to many difficulties. To avoid them we need to hold apart the primary question (1) What *would* the reasonable man with ordinary capacities have done in these circumstances? from the second question (2), *Could* the accused with *his* capacities have done that? Reference to such factors as lunacy or disease should be made in answering only the second of these questions. This simple, and surely realistic, approach avoids difficulties which the notion of individualising the standard of care has presented for certain writers; for these difficulties are usually created by the mistaken assumption that the only way of allowing for individual incapacities is to treat them as part of the 'circumstances' in which the reasonable man is supposed to be acting. Thus Dr Glanville Williams said that if 'regard must be had to the make-up and circumstances of the particular offender, one would seem on a determinist view of conduct to be pushed to the conclusion that there is no standard of conduct at all. For if every characteristic of the individual is taken into account, including his heredity the conclusion is that he could not help doing as he did.' (The General Part (1st Ed.) p. 82.)

But 'determinism' presents no special difficulty here. The question is whether that individual had the capacity (inherited or not) to act otherwise than he did, and 'determinism' has no relevance to the case of one who is accused of negligence which it does not have to one accused of intentionally killing.

QUESTIONS

1. Is punishing negligence punishing someone for an omission: for failing to act as a reasonable person would have done? Is this legitimate, given the law's general reluctance to punish omissions?

2. Is it more legitimate to punish for negligence when the defendant is doing an activity which is known to be dangerous (e.g. driving, carrying out an operation) than where the defendant is doing something that is not especially risky?

FURTHER READING

Brady, J. (1980b), 'Recklessness, Negligence, Indifference and Awareness', *Modern Law Review* 43: 381.

Fine, B., and Cohen, M. (1968), 'Is Criminal Negligence a Defensible Basis for Penal Liability?', *Buffalo Law Review* 16: 749.

Horder, J. (1997), 'Gross Negligence and Criminal Culpability', *University of Toronto Law Journal* 47: 495.

Huigens, K. (1998), 'Virtue and Criminal Negligence', *Buffalo Criminal Law Review* 1: 431.

Simester, A. (2000), 'Can Negligence be Culpable?' in J. Horder (ed.), *Oxford Essays in Jurisprudence* (Oxford: OUP).

18 INTOXICATION

18.1 INTOXICATION AND CRIME

Alcohol

Many commentators accept that there is a link between alcohol and crime.[178] But the strength of that link is a matter of debate.[179] The following comment summarizes the general opinion: 'alcohol may be neither a necessary nor sufficient *cause* of crime, but may nevertheless *affect* crime'.[180] Consider these statistics which may yet persuade you to take a vow of temperance (!):[181]

(1) two-thirds of homicides were linked to alcohol;

(2) 58 per cent of rapists were intoxicated;[182]

(3) 40–50 per cent of domestic violence offenders were drunk;[183]

(4) 88 per cent of criminal damage cases involved a drunk offender.[184]

(5) In 2003 there were 6, 580 deaths linked to alcohol. That is 11.6 people in every 100,000 each year die in a way linked to alcohol.

(6) Alcohol-related crime costs the UK £7.8 billion a year.[185]

---

[178] Marsh, Bradley, Peck, and Carnibella (2001).
[179] Although for a disturbing account of the levels of drinking among young people and the resultant crime see Richardson and Budd (2003).
[180] Raistrick *et al.* (1999: 54). See also Alcohol Concern (2003).
[181] Home Office (2000d); C. Mirrlees-Black, P. Mayhew, and A. Percy (1996); Hodge (1993).
[182] Alcohol Concern (2005)
[183] Ibid., 129.   [184] Home Office (2000d).   [185] Alcohol Concern (2005).

Although these statistics may indicate a strong connection between alcohol and crime, at least one commentator has expressed the view that given the number of people intoxicated at any given time among the general population it is not surprising that so many offenders are drunk.[186] Another unorthodox response is that crime leads to intoxication rather than the other way round.[187] It may be added that many victims of violent offences were drunk at the time.[188]

Drug misuse

Of course alcohol is a kind of drug, but it is a legal one. There is a well-established link between illegal drug use and crime, although there is some dispute whether serious drug users are usually involved in crime before starting their drug misuse.[189] The link between drug crime and property offences committed to finance a drug habit is well established. One study published in 1996 suggested that crime linked to heroin use cost victims between £580 million and £864 million a year.[190] A recent study suggested that 30 per cent of those arrested were addicted to drugs.[191]

18.2 ALCOHOLISM AND DRUG DEPENDENCY: ILLNESS OR WEAKNESS?

There is much debate over the correct understanding of alcohol and drug dependency. On the one hand there are some who see alcoholism[192] and drug addiction as a kind of illness or disease which should be treated as a medical condition.[193] Others see them as a major social problem caused by people's own character weaknesses (drunkenness being an 'odious and loathsome sin'[194]), requiring a tough response from the criminal justice system.[195] In the terms of a criminal trial there is a debate whether intoxication should be regarded as an aggravating or mitigating factor.[196] It may be that attitudes towards drugs are changing, with at least one commentator controversially suggesting that young people now regard drug misuse as 'normal' behaviour.[197]

18.3 EXPLAINING THE PRESENT LAW ON INTOXICATION

As was seen in Part I, the law's approach to intoxication can be regarded as confusing. In relation to crimes involving intention (specific intent offences) intoxication is simply regarded as part of the evidence the jury can take into account in deciding whether the defendant intended the result.[198] Similarly for recklessness (basic intent offences) and involuntary intoxication the question is simply whether the defendant foresaw the risk, and the involuntary intoxication is simply part of the evidence concerning what the

---

[186] South (1999: 948). [187] Raskin, White, and Gorman (2000). [188] Home Office (2000d).
[189] Hough (1996). [190] Mirrlees-Black, Mayhew, and Percy (1996). [191] Travis (2001).
[192] Some prefer the name 'Dependency Syndrome'.
[193] Jellinek (1961). For a rejection of the 'disease' view see Fingarette (1988).
[194] See the discussion of the history of the law's response towards intoxication in Horder (1997a).
[195] See the excellent discussion in Tomlie (2002).
[196] *Bradley* (1980) 2 Cr App R (S) 12. See further Barlow (1984). [197] H. Parker (1997).
[198] Coles and Jang (1996) suggest from a psychological perspective that intoxication cannot affect a person's intent.

defendant foresaw. The only special legal rule concerns crimes of recklessness where the defendant was voluntarily intoxicated. One explanation is that the defendant is treated as having foreseen the risk (whether or not in fact he did) and therefore reckless. How can we explain the law?

This 'presumption of recklessness' could be explained in this way. A person who takes alcohol or drugs is aware there is a risk that he may behave in an unpredictable way. Behaving in an unpredictable way must include committing a crime. Therefore by drinking or taking drugs the defendant is aware that he runs the risk of carrying out an offence.[199] He is therefore reckless. This reasoning has been criticized on several grounds:

(1) Section 8 of the Criminal Justice Act 1967[200] requires a jury to consider all the evidence before deciding whether the accused foresaw a result. This has been interpreted by some commentators[201] to mean that the jury should not rely on presumptions of foresight.

(2) Even if it is accepted that there is recklessness at the time of the drinking there is no coincidence of the *actus reus* and *mens rea*, as is normally required in the criminal law.[202]

(3) The foresight, as explained in the argument above, is that the defendant is aware that he may commit some crime after drinking. However, normally in offences requiring recklessness it is necessary to show that the defendant foresaw a specific kind of harm (e.g. that she would injure someone).

(4) Some argue that the explanation of the law is unconvincing where the defendant has never drunk alcohol before and is unaware of its potential effects. There are similar problems where the defendant is an experienced drinker who, for example, has had two dry sherries before dinner all his life, without ever committing an offence, but on one night the sherries intoxicate him and he commits a crime.[203] In such cases these defendants may justifiably claim that they did not foresee that they might commit an offence.

In the light of these objections some fall back on the view that the law here is based on public policy. What the law is really doing is deterring drunkenness and protecting people from those who become violent when drunk. Indeed Lord Salmon in *Majewski* explained that the decision was not based on logic, but on 'justice, ethics and common sense'.

An alternative explanation of the present law is that it concerns only the law of evidence. The defendant is prevented from introducing evidence of his intoxication to demonstrate that he did not foresee a risk.[204] If the risk was an obvious one and the defendant is not able to introduce evidence that he did not foresee because he was drunk then the jury will almost inevitably find that he foresaw the risk. But why does this 'rule of evidence' apply to recklessness but not intention (remember the defendant *can* introduce evidence of intoxication to rebut intention)? Jeremy Horder's explanation is that where a crime involves intention that intention is an aspect of the wrong done to the victim.[205] Where that is lacking the kind of wrong done to the victim is missing.[206] Opponents of Horder's analysis argue

---

[199] See e.g. *Bennett* [1995] Crim LR 877.
[200] Quoted above at p. 153.   [201] e.g. Allan (2003: 154–6).
[202] Weight was placed on this argument by the High Court of Australia in *O'Connor* (1980) 54 AJLR 349.
[203] Orchard (1993).   [204] Wells (1982).
[205] Many people would regard a deliberate push as a different kind of wrong from an accidental push.
[206] For further discussion see Gough (1996).

that in the criminal law it is inappropriate to reject relevant evidence. To do so is to base the law on what we know to be a fiction.

18.4 ALTERNATIVES TO *MAJEWSKI*

The opposition to *Majewski* inevitably gives rise to the question whether there are alternative approaches the law could take towards intoxication. Here are some:

(1) There should be no special legal regulations governing intoxication. It would be possible simply to treat intoxication as one piece of evidence that a jury considers to decide whether a defendant had intention or recklessness. So, a drunken defendant who did not foresee a risk would not be reckless. This approach has been adopted by the courts in Australia and New Zealand.[207] In fact in very few cases in those jurisdictions have intoxicated defendants been able successfully to plead that they lacked *mens rea*.[208] It appears that an intoxicated defendant who claims he did not foresee a risk is often disbelieved by the jury.[209] An alternative interpretation is that Australian juries are unwilling to acquit intoxicated defendants and convict them regardless of the judge's direction.

(2) Some who argue that the criminal law should penalize drunkenness could argue that drunkenness should constitute the *mens rea* for any offence.[210] Such a view might be supported on the basis of an individual's 'responsibility . . . to stay sober if his intoxication will jeopardize the lives and safety of others'.[211] Few support this view. Even taking a hostile view of intoxication, convicting a defendant of an intent-based offence, rather than a recklessness-based offence, seems unnecessary.

(3) There should be a new offence of 'causing harm while intoxicated'.[212] The Law Commission Consultation Paper proposed an offence of causing certain kinds of harm while intoxicated to a significant extent.[213] Law Commission Report No. 229 rejected this on the basis of fierce opposition from many respondents to the Consultation Paper. Opponents of the Consultation Paper's approach might argue that such an approach draws an inappropriate distinction between drunken and sober vandals who lack concern towards others.[214]

(4) An argument can be made for a crime of public intoxication.[215] A Home Office report has stated: 'Public drunkenness can give rise to serious problems of disorderly conduct, nuisance, criminal damage and alcohol-related assaults, particularly in the proximity of licensed premises at closing time. In addition, it can create a fear of alcohol-related violence, which impacts on the quality of life for many. The government is determined to tackle these issues.'[216] However, one study suggested that less than 1 per cent of intoxicated people commit serious criminal offences.[217]

(5) An alternative approach is to see the 'problem' as not with intoxication, but with our understanding of intoxication. If our legal system was not so in thrall to subjective

---

[207] Orchard (1993). Australia, South Africa, and Canada have all abandoned the *Majewski* rule.

[208] Orchard (1993).

[209] Indeed in the study reported in Mitchell (1988) not one intoxicated person in the sample acted involuntarily.

[210] Keiter (1997).   [211] Justice David Souter in *State v Dufield* 549 A 2d 1205, 1208 (NH, 1988).

[212] Law Commission Consultation Paper No. 127 (1993). The Butler Committee (1975) proposed an offence of dangerous intoxication.

[213] Virgo (1993) is generally supportive.   [214] Gough (1996).   [215] Ashworth (1980).

[216] Home Office (2000d).   [217] Mitchell (1988).

recklessness and was willing to include within recklessness a concept of failing to foresee an obvious risk for some blameworthy reason then there would be no difficulty in classifying voluntarily intoxicated defendants who fail to foresee an obvious risk as reckless. This argument is developed in the following extract (note that this was written before the abolition of *Caldwell* recklessness):

S. Gardner, 'The Importance of *Majewski'* [1994] *Oxford Journal of Legal Studies* 26

The proposition [that an inadvertent defendant is not reckless] is, of course, supported by the well-known subjectivist platform. But it is clear that that platform is itself far from universally accepted. At the lowest, there seems to be a popular notion that when a person has done some misdeed, to say 'I didn't realize' is not necessarily a satisfactory answer to an accusation of culpability for it: the retort, 'Well, you should have done', is felt supportable. A specific manifestation of this seems to be the further popular idea: that one who fails to realize what he is doing because he is voluntarily intoxicated is not to be exonerated; if anything, the intoxication gives especially sharp focus and added power to the retort. These popular perceptions are probably real enough, but of course one needs to be cautious about founding propositions about legal liability directly upon them. The Law Commission emphasize this point when, in this Consultation Paper, they recognize the popular idea about voluntary intoxication and yet reject it as a basis for the law. Observing that a popular speaker might call the intoxicated perpetrator 'reckless', they warn against the temptation to conclude that the perpetrator is thus 'reckless' in the eyes of the law, so as to merit criminal inculpation. Such a conclusion, they say, would be a 'semantic confusion' between the popular and the legal ideas of recklessness, and should be eschewed.

It may be noted in passing that the Commission's treatment of this point raises an interesting question. It seems clear that the law—most of all the criminal law—cannot simply cast itself adrift of popular thought. There needs to be some theory of a relationship between the two, even if it remains right to say that the constraints of 'being the law' can properly require the law sometimes to shape itself by reference to values lying outside substantive popular thought. More accurately, perhaps there needs to be more than one such theory, or at any rate a single theory with more than one branch. Emphasizing the law's internal values to the exclusion of popular thought—as the Law Commission are doing here—might possibly be an intelligible stance for someone working inside the law, such as a judge. But it is arguable that those addressing the law from outside, such as Parliamentary legislators, can and should strike a different balance. It is arguable, too, that the Law Commission should align itself wholly with neither side; its role should perhaps be to act as translator and mediator between the two? It is problematic that the Commission has, in this Consultation Paper, failed to address these questions at all explicitly, at the same time as predicating part of its argument upon a particular (on the face of it relatively unlikely) answer to them.

However, let us resume our enquiry into the sustainability of the subjectivist foundation upon which the Law Commission's thinking is based. And for the sake of argument, let us accept a bar on reference to popular thought in this enquiry, and confine ourselves to values recognizably inherent in the existing law. The existing law does not support the idea that advertence demands to be the sole representative of recklessness. Instead, it reveals a strong tradition to the effect that a person is reckless not only where he realizes he may be doing the *actus reus*, but also in two other cases. One is where he fails to think about what he may be doing and his failure to think is itself blameworthy. The other is where he mistakenly believes he is not doing the *actus reus* and his mistaken belief is itself blameworthy. Liability may thus arise from advertence, from blameworthy inadvertence and from blameworthy mistake. This thesis may be seen at work in child neglect, for example. Take parents who omit to call a doctor to their sick child, either because it never occurs to them that this might be the right thing to do or because, having thought about it, they decide not to. If their inadvertence or their mistake springs from lack of intelligence they are not liable; but if it springs from callousness towards their child they are liable. Essentially the same approach is used in rape, with its *mens rea* of whether the accused 'cared less' about the woman's wishes. Since the landmark decision of the House of Lords in *Reid*, it has also applied to reckless driving and, it seems, criminal damage and manslaughter. Some of the discussion in *Reid*, too, shows an inclination to use this approach also in the context of non-fatal offences against the person, albeit in the teeth of the contrary decision in *Savage and Parmenter*.

Yoking advertence with blameworthy inadvertence and blameworthy mistake as alternative forms of recklessness is thus well enough established as a tradition within the law. Now inadvertence or mistake as a result of voluntary intoxication must be the archetypal cases of blameworthy inadvertence or blameworthy mistake. These deficient states are known to all as the potential result of intoxication by alcohol or dangerous drugs, and there is a clearly recognized moral stigma upon engendering them in this way. So in recognizing intoxication as a basis of inculpation, *Majewski* may be seen as, far from a doctrinal pariah, very much part of this tradition.

Indeed, one can go further. Not only is *Majewski* conformable in this way with the tradition which culminates in *Reid*. It actually facilitates a more coherent account of the law as a whole. Modern treatments of the criminal law often depict a doctrinal battle over the meaning of recklessness, the opposing claims being those of *Cunningham* and those of *Caldwell*. The picture is apparently alarming, showing that the law is in turmoil, and we are usually invited to conclude that one of the protagonists should be vanquished and expelled from our jurisprudence. But on reflection, we can see that the alleged battle is largely an illusion. For, on the one side, we ought to see that *Cunningham* never in fact takes the field alone. It is always accompanied by *Majewski*. Together they establish liability for advertence and for the blameworthy inadvertence or blameworthy mistake which results from voluntary intoxication. For its part, too, *Caldwell* is not the true representative of the other side: *Reid* now is. And *Reid* establishes liability for advertence and blameworthy inadvertence or blameworthy mistake howsoever arising. There is thus a great deal of common ground between the two sides in the supposed battle. That common ground includes the proposition that liability is not confined to advertence alone: and that intoxicated inadvertence and intoxicated mistakes attract liability too.

In fact, the only dispute in the present law is over whether to allow a finding of blameworthy inadvertence or blameworthy mistake in other cases than voluntary intoxication. The combination of *Cunningham* and *Majewski* reacts only to one (the most important) form of blameworthy inadvertence or blameworthy mistake, whilst *Reid* reacts to other forms of these as well. This dispute lies within quite a narrow compass. In seeking to resolve it, I would suggest that the position taken in *Reid* is the preferable one, for it seems self-evident that there are other kinds of blameworthy reasons for inadvertence and mistake besides intoxication, and there seems no good reason why the law should not react to them too. The approach taken by *Cunningham* and *Majewski* does, however, usefully remind us of one further important question, to which attention will need to be paid. Should the concept of blameworthiness be left at large, to be explicated by the jury in the individual case? Or should it be defined by law, so that we would have an authoritatively declared list of sources of blameworthiness—such as intoxication?

For the moment, though, my point is to conclude that *Majewski* is far from 'illogical or contrary to principle'. On the contrary, the presence of *Majewski* alongside *Cunningham* allows us to produce quite a smoothly principled account of the idea of recklessness as a whole, including the contribution from *Reid*. If *Majewski* were to be removed, replacing it with a new offence of causing harm whilst intoxicated would, of course, go towards restoring the smoothness of present position. But the restoration would be only partial, because culpability for the original offence would still be denied, and it is the present law's position of culpability for the original offence that brings it and *Reid* so close together.

So the existing law is moderately coherent. Greater coherence may, however, still be possible. There seem to be three ways in which it could be attained. The least radical would be to take the present law to its logical conclusion by, as I have suggested, articulating recklessness on the lines in *Reid* across the board, so that *Majewski* is swallowed up in this more general theory of liability for advertence, blameworthy inadvertence and blameworthy mistake.

FURTHER READING

Horder, J. (1995c), 'Sobering Up? The Law Commission on Criminal Intoxication', *Modern Law Review* 57: 534.

Mackay, R. (1995), *Mental Condition Defences in the Criminal Law* (Oxford: OUP), ch. 8.

Sullivan, G.R. (1996a), 'Making Excuses' in A. Simester and A. Smith (eds.), *Harm and Culpability* (Oxford: OUP).

Tolmie, J. (2001), 'Alcoholism and Criminal Liability', *Modern Law Review* 64: 688.

19 MOTIVE

19.1 IS MOTIVE RELEVANT IN THE CRIMINAL LAW?

The courts have been consistent in stating that motive and intention are separate. Indeed it is often said that motive is irrelevant in the criminal law.[218] In *Lynch v DPP*[219] the defendant was told by a group of terrorists that he would be killed if he did not assist in a killing. The House of Lords held that he intended to assist in the killing, even though his motive was to avoid being killed by the terrorists. However, the position is not this straightforward. It seems that in some cases the courts do attach significance to the defendant's motives. Here are three examples:

(1) In *Steane*[220] a defendant who during the war assisted the enemy[221] because he feared that otherwise his family would be sent to a concentration camp was held not to have intended to assist the enemy.

(2) In *Adams*[222] it was held that a doctor who gives pain-relieving drugs to a patient, aware that these may slightly shorten the patient's life span, does not intend to kill the patient.

---

[218] J.C. Smith (2002: 95). *Contra* Wilson (2002: ch. 5).   [219] [1975] AC 653 (HL).
[220] [1947] KB 997 (CA).   [221] This was an offence under special wartime regulations.
[222] *Bodkin Adams* [1957] Crim LR 365. Although see *Cox* (1992) 12 BMLR 38 where a doctor was convicted of attempted murder when he administered drugs to a terminally ill patient. His purpose was to kill the patient and thereby end her suffering.

(3) In *Gillick v West Norfolk and Wisbech AHA*[223] the House of Lords held that a doctor who gave a girl aged under 16 contraceptive advice and pills would not necessarily be committing the offence of aiding and abetting unlawful (underage) sexual intercourse. Even though the doctor might know that as a result of the advice a girl might therefore engage in sexual intercourse, he did not intend to assist her.

It seems that in fact it is misleading to describe motive as irrelevant. There are many ways that motive may in fact be relevant in the criminal law:

(1) Motive may help in establishing what the defendant's purpose is. Often a person's motive is to produce a particular result, in which his or her motive and intention are the same. Indeed Norrie[224] argues that it is difficult to imagine someone having an intention to do something without having a motive. Motive, he suggests, is the driving force behind the intention.

(2) Motive may be relevant in deciding in cases of oblique intention whether the jury will find from virtual certainty and foresight of that virtual certainty that there was intention.[225]

(3) Some offences specifically require proof of motive, for example racially aggravated assaults.[226]

(4) In relation to defences it is important to know whether what motivated the defendant's actions was the justifying reason.[227] For example, in order to plead self-defence defendants must use force in order to defend themselves and not out of revenge.

(5) It is impossible to assess whether the defendant was acting dishonestly for the purpose of property offences without considering the motive of the defendant.

(6) Motive can be relevant at the sentencing stage. As Norrie tersely remarks, 'Having insisted upon a strict legal code so as to protect the liberty of the individual, it transpires that the individual's liberty is ultimately dependent not upon the rule of law at all but on a group of men operating with a wide discretion at the sentencing stage'.[228]

(7) There have been cases where it is widely thought that the jury has acquitted the defendant because they have believed he acted from the best of motives, despite a clear direction from the judge that he is guilty in the eyes of the law.[229]

19.2 ARGUMENTS IN FAVOUR OF TAKING MOTIVE INTO ACCOUNT

It seems odd that if *mens rea* is all about ascertaining the blameworthiness of the defendant that motive is not taken into account. Most people would see a clear difference in moral terms between a contract killer and a mercy killer, but the difference lies in their motivation (not their intention). Even so under the law of murder they are treated identically. Indeed, as

---

[223] [1985] 3 All ER 402 (HL).   [224] Norrie (2001: 36).
[225] Ashworth (2003: 177–80).
[226] Crime and Disorder Act 1998, s. 28(1)(b).   [227] See J. Gardner (1998).
[228] Norrie (2002: 200).   [229] e.g. *Ponting* 11 Feb. 1985 (unreported).

hinted at in Part I, motive may be an even better guide to blameworthiness than intention or recklessness.

Alan Norrie[230] has argued that the line between motives and intention is in fact almost impossible to draw. He argues that once we look at what causes intentions and start looking at motive we inevitably bring in complex social and political explanations for people's actions. For example, once we start to consider greed as a motivation we inevitably have to consider the unequal distribution of goods in our society which nurtures feelings of greed. Norrie argues that the legal system, in not wanting to challenge the social and political status quo, avoids entering such treacherous waters by generally refusing to consider motives. However, he argues, where it is convenient to do so motive can suddenly become relevant again, for example in permitting the doctors in *Gillick* to prescribe contraception to under-16-year-olds.[231]

19.3 ARGUMENTS AGAINST TAKING MOTIVES INTO ACCOUNT

Anthony Duff[232] justifies the statement that motive is irrelevant to the criminal law by redefining what commentators mean by such a statement: motive is relevant only when Parliament has declared it to be relevant as part of the definition of an offence. If Parliament has not so declared it the courts cannot permit the defendant to raise his good motive as a defence. For example, if the government had decided to permit trials of genetically modified crops, but a defendant, opposing the growing of such crops, destroyed them, to permit him a defence to a charge of criminal damage on the basis that the jury or magistrates believed that the defendant was acting from good motives would be to undermine the authority of Parliament. If the defendant objects to the law the way to raise it is through political channels and not by committing crimes and raising the issue by way of a defence. A similar point could be made in relation to euthanasia. The legal response to euthanasia should be decided by Parliament, not by juries deciding on individual cases whether the defendant's motives were good. Duff accepts that such an argument is appropriate only as long as there are suitable channels for individuals to raise their points of view. In relation to those in desperate poverty who steal, the solution to their difficulties is to seek the assistance of welfare provision, that is the 'forum' for dealing with dire poverty, not by committing theft and raising poverty as an issue. Although it should be emphasized that Duff accepts that his argument has legitimacy only providing that the welfare provisions are adequate.

FURTHER READING

Motive:

Ashworth, A. (1996), 'The Treatment of Good Intentions' in A. Simester and A. Smith (eds.), *Harm and Culpability* (Oxford: OUP).

Binder, G. (2002), 'The Rhetoric of Motive and Intent', *Buffalo Criminal Law Review* 6: 1.

Duff, R.A. (1998b), 'Principle and Contradiction in the Criminal Law: Motives and Criminal Liability' in A. Duff (ed.), *Philosophy and the Criminal Law* (Cambridge: Cambridge University Press).

---

[230] Norrie (2002: 170–81).   [231] See further Gardner and Jung (1991).   [232] Duff (1998b).

Horder, J. (2000), 'On the Irrelevance of Motive in Criminal Law' in J. Horder (ed.), *Oxford Essays in Jurisprudence* (Oxford: OUP).

Husak, D. (1989a), 'Motive and Criminal Liability', *Criminal Justice Ethics* 1: 3.

Norrie, A. (2002), *Punishment, Responsibility and Justice* (Oxford: OUP), 170–81.

Knowledge and belief:

Callender, D. (1994), 'Wilful Ignorance, Knowledge and the "Equality Culpability" Thesis', *Wisconsin Law Review* 129.

Shute, S. (2002a), 'Knowledge and Belief in the Criminal Law' in S. Shute and A. Simester (eds.), *Criminal Law Theory* (Oxford: OUP).

Sullivan, G.R. (2002b), 'Knowledge, Belief and Culpability' in S. Shute and A. Simester (eds.), *Criminal Law Theory* (Oxford: OUP).

Wasik, M., and Thompson, M. (1981), ' "Turning a Blind Eye" As Constituting *Mens Rea*', *Northern Ireland Law Quarterly* 32: 328.

20 THE 'CORRESPONDENCE PRINCIPLE'

At the end of Part I of this chapter it was emphasized that when you learn what the *mens rea* of a crime is it is not enough just to learn that intention or recklessness is required, but you should learn what must be intended or foreseen. However, this raises the so-called correspondence principle, which is one of the most controversial issues in criminal law. Imagine an offence of causing grievous bodily harm. If we assume that the offence involves recklessness, what exactly must D foresee: grievous bodily harm; at least actual bodily harm; or any harm however minor? These possibilities reflect three views that could be taken:

(1) *The correspondence principle.* The principle requires the *mens rea* of a crime to match the *actus reus*. In other words the defendant must intend or be *Cunningham* reckless as to the *actus reus*. So in this case the defendant must foresee grievous bodily harm. Anything less will be inadequate.

(2) *The 'proportionality' principle.* The defendant need foresee only an injury which is proportionate to the *actus reus*.[233] It does not matter if the injury is slightly more than that foreseen, but if the injury is in a different league from that foreseen (it is not proportionate) the defendant should not be responsible for it. In our example actual bodily harm is close to grievous bodily harm. If the defendant had only foreseen a touching he should not be guilty of an offence involving grievous bodily harm because that would be of a different degree of seriousness.

(3) *The 'moral threshold' principle.* Supporters of this view simply require that the defendant foresaw some kind of harm. Once the defendant acts, foreseeing that he will injure the victim, he loses the sympathy of the law and is responsible for the harm caused.

There are two questions that may be asked here.

---

[233] Tadros (2002b).

20.1 WHICH PRINCIPLE BEST REFLECTS THE LAW?

Although there may be some fine historical precedent for the correspondence principle,[234] it is in fact honoured far more in the breach than in the observance in current criminal law. Of course all strict liability offences infringe it; even murder (which accepts intention to do grievous bodily harm for the *mens rea*) does not observe it. Of the significant offences against the person only section 18 of the Offences Against the Person Act 1861 (inflicting grievous bodily harm with intent to cause grievous bodily harm) complies with it.

20.2 WHICH PRINCIPLE IS MOST JUSTIFIABLE IN THEORY?

Underlying the debate behind these theories is the notion of 'moral luck', which we will discuss in detail in Chapter 14.[235] Imagine that the defendant picks up a stick and throws it at the victim. What happens next may be described as a matter of luck: the stick may hit the victim; the victim may jump out of the way; a sudden gust of wind may blow the stick out of the way; a passer-by may push the victim out of the way. It is then argued that what the defendant can control is his action and his state of mind, but what happens beyond that is just chance that should not affect his liability. If you are persuaded by this argument a number of consequences follow which we shall discuss at various points in this book (e.g. the argument that attempted crimes and complete crimes should be treated identically[236]). However, the argument is relevant in relation to the correspondence principle, because it holds that a defendant who throws the stick intending actual bodily harm is equally blame-worthy whether it causes actual bodily harm or grievous bodily harm. The level of harm the stick throwing causes is just luck. Therefore the defendant should be guilty only of inten-tionally causing actual bodily harm. He should not be responsible for the higher level of harm that occurred because of his action: that was just bad luck.[237] Michael Moore in his book has gone so far as to say that 'a majority of respectable criminal law theoreticians' take this view.[238]

Those who reject the argument tend to raise a number of arguments:

(1) Most people do not regard the consequences of people's actions as just 'bad luck'. It was not just bad luck that the victim suffered grievous bodily harm; it was because the defendant threw a stick at him! Had he not thrown the stick the chance factors (the wind, the movements of the victim) would not have had a role to play. Jeremy Horder[239] has talked of a defendant 'making his own bad luck'. Many people have sympathy for a defendant who genuinely causes an injury by bad luck (e.g. when she trips over a paving stone and bumps into someone). However, where a person has set out to cause an injury to someone she cannot claim it is an accident, she loses the sympathy of the law, and is now liable for the consequences of her actions.

---

[234] Although J. Gardner (1994) denies that the correspondence has even been part of the law.
[235] Nagel (1979); Mandil (1987); Schulhofer (1974); B. Williams (1981); Honoré (1989); J.C. Smith (1971); Fletcher (1998).
[236] Ashworth (1988).   [237] For a theological perspective see Stern (1999).
[238] The impressive list includes: Kadish (1994); Gobert (1993); Becker (1974); Jarvis Thomson (1989); Ashworth (1988); Gross (1979); Schulhofer (1974); and Feinberg (1970).
[239] Horder (1995d).

(2) Surveys of public opinion indicate that the majority of people questioned do support making people liable for the harms they cause, even if that harm is greater than they foresaw or intended.[240]

(3) Consequences matter to onlookers and to the perpetrator. Nagel,[241] in a famous example, discusses a person who leaves a child in the bath with the tap running to answer the door and chats, forgetting the child. If the child manages to survive we dismiss the action as careless; if the child dies this transforms our judgement and the action becomes appalling. We expect different reactions from onlookers and the defendant depending on the consequence of the act (relief rather than outrage, for example). The fact that the consequences do affect our emotional reaction could be said to indicate that a moral difference exists between the two.

Simester and Sullivan argue that it is important to distinguish between acts where the luck (the risk of harm) is extrinsic or intrinsic to the nature of the act. For those actions which are inherently dangerous the defendant cannot claim that it is just bad luck if someone is injured. For those actions which are not inherently dangerous then it may be regarded as luck whether or not the victim is injured. An example of an intrinsically dangerous act is dangerous driving. Other acts are not inherently dangerous. Simester and Sullivan consider the hypothetical scenario of a secretary who is told to collect blood samples as part of a staff survey, but fails to do so. When a worker later falls ill and a blood transfusion cannot be provided because the worker's blood group is not known this is bad luck: she could not have known that her failure to collect the samples for the survey would have fatal consequences.

In the following extract Michael Moore stresses that we have two reasons for blaming people: culpability and wrongdoing. He admits that culpability is the poorer relation as it is both necessary and sufficient as the basis for punishment, but wrongdoing is neither:

M. Moore, *Placing Blame* (Oxford: OUP, 1997), 213–16

The problem of moral luck, as Nagel frames it, is how we can justify holding people more responsible for causing harm than for merely intending or risking harm when they lack that *control* (over whether the harm occurs or not) we generally require for responsibility.

Moral luck is good when an actor fails to cause the harm he has intended or risked, for the actor gets moral credit for something over which he lacked control; moral luck is bad when the actor does cause the harm he intended or risked, because he gets moral demerits for something over which he lacked control. Nagel's question is how such luck could be justified in the face of our control requirement for responsibility.

The question as Nagel poses it arises only if we think that there is such a thing as moral luck. By this, I do not mean to join Kant *et al.* in denying that wrongdoing has any independent moral significance. I mean that an anti-Kantian here might deny that there is any *luck* involved in being held more responsible for successful wrongdoing than for intended or risked wrong-doing that does not materialize. There undoubtedly is some luck involved in whether we cause the harms we intend or risk, but there will be *moral luck* only vis-à-vis some moral baseline of the normal that places all such luck on the side of the extraordinary.

We do have a criminal law doctrine that explicitly deals with the question of luck with regard to consequences. This is the doctrine of proximate causation. The proximate cause

[240] Robinson and Darley (1995) and (1998).   [241] T. Nagel (1979).

tests in criminal law have as their function the separation of harms in fact caused by a defendant's voluntary act into two camps: those freakishly so caused, in which event the actor is liable only for lesser crimes of attempt, specific intent, or risk-imposition; and those more normally so caused, in which event the actor is liable for the more serious punishments reserved for completed crimes. Sometimes these tests are explicit about their being tests of luck. The Model Penal Code, for example, provides that an act is the cause of a harm when the harm would not have happened but for the act, and (with complications here ignored) the 'actual result is not too remote or accidental in its occurrence to have a just bearing on the actor's liability or on the gravity of his offense'. Even when the proximate cause tests are not explicitly directed to this freakishness or luck question, they implicitly aim at just this factor. The foreseeability test of proximate causation, for example, seems to be aimed at an actor's culpability: could he have foreseen that such a harm would result from his action? In reality, given the well-known conundrum about specifying the details of the harm about which to ask foreseeability questions, what the test really asks is whether the 'freakishness of the facts refuses to be drowned' or not.

Consider some examples of Hart and Honoré's: (1) A defendant culpably throws a lighted cigarette onto some bushes; the bushes catch fire, but would burn themselves out if it were not for a normal evening breeze that comes up, carrying the fire to the forest and burning it down. (2) Same as (1), except that the breeze that comes up is a gale force wind never before seen at this time of year, which wind uproots the burning bushes and carries them to a distant forest, which ignites and burns. (3) Same as (1), except no breeze, normal or abnormal, arises; rather, a would-be extinguisher of the fire in the bushes himself catches fire, and in his agony he runs to the forest, which burns. (4) Same as (1), except a second culpable defendant is the vehicle for transferring the fire from the bushes to the forest: he sees that the fire in the bushes is about to go out, so he pours a gasoline trail from the forest to the burning bushes, in order to burn down the forest, which then occurs.

On the direct cause notion of proximate causation that Hart and Honoré so elegantly explore the initial defendant in (1) and (3) is criminally liable for burning down the forest, whereas in variations (2) and (4) the causal routes from defendant's act to the ultimate harm are too accidental, too fortuitous, too much a matter of chance or luck, for the defendant to be liable for such harm; at most, he can be held only for attempted destruction of the forest, or for risking its destruction.

Notice that the normal breeze in (1), the gale in (2), the movements of the clumsy would-be fire extinguisher in (3), and the actions of the arsonist in (4), are all equally outside the control of the initial fire-starter. In Nagel's sense of 'luck', thus, all cases involve moral luck: bad moral luck in (1) and (3) where the fire-starter is held liable, and good moral luck in (2) and (4), where he is not. Nagel's sense of 'luck' is thus obviously not the same as that employed in the criminal law doctrines of proximate causation and the morality that underlies them, for those doctrines use a different notion of luck to distinguish some as matters of luck and others not.

The notion of luck always involves some baseline of comparison. As the proximate cause tests of the criminal law use the notion, the baseline is the normal way things come about. When a defendant negligently operates a train too fast, so that he cannot stop it before it hits another's railroad car, there is no luck involved in his injuring the second car because that is how such things normally happen. When, however, the same negligently speeding defendant causes the same damage to the same car, but does so because a first collision (which does no damage) throws the defendant against the reverse throttle of his engine, thereby knocking him unconscious, whereupon his engine goes in reverse around a circular track, colliding with the other's car and then causing it damage, there is luck involved because of the abnormal conjunction of events taking place between defendant's act and the harm.

Moral luck, on this concept of luck, would exist whenever the consequence of moral blame or credit is brought on one in an abnormal, freakish, or chance way. If one were truly to blame for someone else's actions over whom one had no control, for example, that would be a case of (bad) moral luck. But if one's blameworthiness only comes about in the normal, non-freakish, not-by-chance way, there is no *moral* luck involved in such blameworthiness, wherever it exists, even if there is luck involved. The crucial question, of course, is to spell out when blameworthiness attaches in a normal, as opposed to an abnormal, way. Nagel thinks that this notion of normalcy is to be fleshed out with his idea of control: blameworthiness for a harm would attach in a normal way only if the agent was in control of all factors causally contributing to that harm. Yet this is surely not the notion of normalcy presupposed by the criminal law's notion of luck. And this last observation is not the observation that Nagel requires *complete* control (of *all* factors) while the criminal law and the morality that underlies it only requires control of *some* factors; rather, the observation is that the notion of control is alien to the criminal law's idea of luck. The baseline is freakishness of causal route, not degree of control by the agent of the intervening factors. For notice again: the actors equally lack any control of the breezes or second agents whose interventions were necessary for the destruction of the forest in scenarios (1) to (4) above. It is the normalcy of causal route that decides the normalcy of moral blameworthiness in such cases, ideas of normalcy to which control is simply irrelevant.

21 INDIVIDUALISM AND *MENS REA*

An interesting critique of the current approach to *mens rea* is that it is over-individualistic. In other words our notions of culpability focus on what the defendant intended or foresaw, rather than considering the defendant within his or her community and society. The argument is developed by Victoria Nourse in the following extract:

V. Nourse (2002), 'Heart and Minds: Understanding the New Culpability', *Buffalo Criminal Law Review* 8: 361.

. . . My second fear is that all this emphasis on the proper 'state of mind' occludes an important assumption shared by most of the participants in this debate—the assumption that it is the individual who is the proper focus of the debate. The common law was, I believe, quite a bit more sensitive to this assumption than are we moderns. When the [American] Model Penal Code drafters eschewed common law formulations, they not only got rid of ambiguous terms, they got rid of an entire structure of culpability. Whether we are looking for desire or acceptance or indifference, the modern debate has followed this trend. It has located culpability in the hearts and minds and capacities of individual defendants. We ask whether we should judge the defendant by his choices or his character or his desires. This focus on the individual must be false or at least incomplete; we don't live in bubbles or on islands. People commit crimes against others; and it is the relation between the 'other' and the 'defendant' that informs most of our judgments about the relative blameworthiness of the parties. We know this, in a sense. We know that for all our focus on individuality, all our attempts to describe defendants more and more particularly, whether it be in terms of their choice or their character or their virtue, that this has only led to reaction—to cries of hyper-individualism and abuse excuse and loss of agency.

It is time to reconsider more actively the assumption that the best way to protect individuals is to describe their hearts or minds, rather than to judge their relations to each other. This, by the way, has nothing to do with communitarianism or antiliberalism; it is simply a call for a 'relational individualism,' a call for the consideration of a different, and more direct (in my view), means to protect individuals. Even those who aim toward radical individuation, those who study mind for a living, recognize that the question of protecting individuals is in determining how an 'individual can stand in a healthy relation to his society,' precisely because the very notion that an individual exists at all depends upon a social world of relations.

A final comment (whose implications await elaboration elsewhere): In the end, crime is about power. Power is a relation, a relation that implies not only our regard for each other but the relation between citizens and state. This is why a criminal code will always be susceptible to public, majoritarian sentiment about culpability and blameworthiness even if drafted with the best intentions to protect individuals from unthinking minoritarian norms. Criminal law scholarship must stop hiding the ball in positivism and descriptivism, pretending to be a science, rather than a set of contingent norms. It must openly navigate the risks to the few and the many, to majorities and minorities, rather than deny that they exist. This navigation is impossible in a state of denial: if all the norms are buried in places that look like they are facts of nature, like passion and time and risk, then normativity will continue to be denied. That doesn't mean that the norms go away, it simply means that they will have more force, propelling us back and forth between apparent lenience and vengeance, abuse excuse and legal moralism, more a victim of a crude and unthinking politics than we ever hoped or desired.

It is not enough, any longer, in my view, to imagine culpability either in the image of a lonely cunning self or a cruel deterministic world. The man on an island needs no criminal law for he is fundamentally alone. The man with no government needs no criminal law since he may simply 'take the law into his own hands.' The criminal law helps to constitute our relation to each other as well as the nation in which we live. Conduct an intellectual experiment: Eliminate mens rea entirely from the criminal law and what do you have? A criminal law used to punish the innocent or the accidental is a hallmark of totalitarian regimes. History, if nothing else, tells us that when rulers seek to oppress their people, they repair easily to the criminal law. There is more at stake in a criminal code than individuals, state of mind, or particular words. The criminal law poses important questions about, quite literally, how we govern each other.

QUESTION

Read Diloff (1998) who poses the following hypothetical:

Andre is undertaking shooting practice at a firing range. His enemy Brett wanders into the range close to the target. Andre fires two shots in quick succession: one at Brett and then one at the target. Evidence later shows that the shot Andre aimed at Brett in fact hit the target and the shot he aimed at the target hit Brett.

Is this a case of murder? If not, how is it different from a transferred malice case?

FURTHER READING

Ashworth, A. (1978), 'Transferred Malice and Punishment for Unforeseen Consequences' in P. Glazebrook (ed.), *Reshaping the Criminal Law* (London: Sweet & Maxwell).

Dillof, A. (1998), 'Transferred Intent: An Inquiry into the Nature of Criminal Culpability', *Buffalo Criminal Law Review* 1: 501.

Horder, J. (1995d), 'A Critique of the Correspondence Principle', *Criminal Law Review* 759.

—— (1997b), 'Questioning the Correspondence Principle—A Reply', *Criminal Law Review* 206.

Mitchell, B. (1999), 'In Defence of the Correspondence Principle', *Criminal Law Review* 195.

Morse, S. (2000), 'The Moral Metaphysics of Causation and Results', *California Law Review* 88: 879.

Nourse, V. (2002), 'Heart and Minds: Understanding the New Culpability', *Buffalo Criminal Law Review* 8: 361.

4

STRICT LIABILITY

PART I: THE LAW

DEFINITION

A defendant is guilty of a strict liability offence if by a voluntary act he or she causes the prohibited result or state of affairs. There is no need to prove that the defendant had a particular state of mind.

1 WHAT IS A STRICT LIABILITY OFFENCE?

Offences of strict liability require proof that the defendant performed the prohibited conduct, but do not require proof that the defendant was blameworthy.[1] For example, in *Harrow London BC v Shah*[2] the defendant was convicted of selling a lottery ticket to a person under the age of 16, even though he was not aware that the purchaser was under 16 nor was it obvious that the person was under that age. In fact nearly half of all criminal offences are in fact offences of strict liability.[3]

Most strict liability offences are minor offences. The criminal law covers a wide range of crimes, from murder at the one end to parking tickets at the other. At the lower end such offences are often regarded by the general public as 'not really' criminal. These 'less serious' offences play the role of regulating people's behaviour so that society can work effectively, rather than indicating that the defendant has behaved in a morally reprehensible way.[4] These regulatory offences often do not require proof of *mens rea*, because they do not carry the weight of moral censure that more serious crimes carry. It should be added that it is possible for an offence to be one of strict liability for some aspects of the *actus reus*, but not others.[5]

Strict liability offences should be distinguished from negligence-based offences where the prosecution must demonstrate that the defendant acted unreasonably. As already indicated for strict liability offences, if the defendant has committed the *actus reus* he or she is guilty

---

[1] e.g. *Callow v Tillstone* (1900) 83 LT 411. For a detailed discussion of the meaning of strict liability see Green (2005).

[2] [2000] Crim LR 692 (DC).

[3] Ashworth and Blake (1996).

[4] A distinction is sometimes drawn between crimes that are *male in se* (the activity is in itself harmful (e.g. killing)) and crimes that are *male prohibita* (where the activity is wrong only because it has been prohibited (e.g. driving on the left hand side of the road)).

[5] *Hibbert* (1869) LR 1 CCR 184.

even if he or she was acting reasonably.[6] The line between a strict liability offence and a negligence-based offence is somewhat blurred where a statute does not require proof that defendants acted unreasonably, but the defendants will have a defence if they can prove they acted with 'due diligence'[7] in avoiding the prohibited harm. These are distinct from negligence offences because the burden of proof lies with the defendants to prove that they were acting reasonably, rather than the prosecution proving they were acting negligently.

2 WHICH OFFENCES ARE STRICT LIABILITY?

The vast majority of strict liability offences are found in statutes, although there may be a few common law strict liability offences.[8] For statutes, the key question for a court is how to interpret a statutory offence if Parliament has not included a *mens rea* requirement. In such a case the court has to decide whether to interpret the crime as one of strict liability or to read in a *mens rea* requirement. If Parliament made it absolutely clear for every offence what the *mens rea* requirement (if any) was the courts' job would be easier. Unfortunately Parliament has not.

The following two cases have recently reinforced the common law that in construing statutory offences there is a presumption against strict liability and in favour of *mens rea*:

B (A Child) v Director of Public Prosecutions
[2000] 2 AC 428 (HL)[9]

B, a 15-year-old boy, repeatedly asked a 13-year-old girl on a bus in Harrow to perform oral sex on him. The girl refused. B was convicted of inciting a child under the age of 14 to commit an act of gross indecency contrary to section 1(1) of the Indecency with Children Act 1960. It was accepted that B honestly believed that the girl was over 14, but the justices ruled that that belief did not provide B with a defence. B appealed on the basis that the justices' ruling was wrong. His appeal was dismissed by the Divisional Court and he appealed to the House of Lords.

Lord Nicholls of Birkenhead

. . . Section 1(1) of [the Indecency with Children Act 1960] makes it a criminal offence to commit an act of gross indecency with or towards a child under the age of 14, or to incite a child under that age to such an act. The question raised by the appeal concerns the mental element in this offence so far as the age ingredient is concerned.

The answer to this question depends upon the proper interpretation of the section. There are, broadly, three possibilities. The first possible answer is that it matters not whether the accused honestly believed that the person with whom he was dealing was over 14. So far as the age element is concerned, the offence created by s 1 of the 1960 Act is one of strict

---

[6] As acknowledged, e.g., by Maurie Kay J in *Barnfather v Islington London Borough Council and another* [2003] EWHC 418 (Admin), [2003] All ER (D) 89 (QBD) at para. 30.

[7] Ashworth (2003: 168) suggests that such statutes might not, strictly speaking, be strict liability offences.

[8] e.g. criminal libel or public nuisance. However, these are rarely charged and there is some debate whether these are strict liability offences or not. See Allen (2003: 100–1).

[9] [2000] 1 All ER 833, [2000] 2 WLR 452, [2000] 2 Cr App R 65, [2000] Crim LR 403.

liability. The second possible answer is that a necessary element of this offence is the absence of a belief, held honestly and on reasonable grounds by the accused, that the person with whom he was dealing was over 14. The third possibility is that the existence or not of reasonable grounds for an honest belief is irrelevant. The necessary mental element is simply the absence of an honest belief by the accused that the other person was over 14.

The common law presumption

As habitually happens with statutory offences, when enacting this offence Parliament defined the prohibited conduct solely in terms of the proscribed physical acts. Section 1(1) says nothing about the mental element. In particular, the section says nothing about what shall be the position if the person who commits or incites the act of gross indecency honestly but mistakenly believed that the child was 14 or over.

In these circumstances the starting point for a court is the established common law presumption that a mental element, traditionally labelled *mens rea*, is an essential ingredient unless Parliament has indicated a contrary intention either expressly or by necessary implication. The common law presumes that, unless Parliament indicated otherwise, the appropriate mental element is an unexpressed ingredient of every statutory offence. On this I need do no more than refer to Lord Reid's magisterial statement in the leading case of *Sweet v Parsley* [1970] AC 132 at 148–149:

'... there has for centuries been a presumption that Parliament did not intend to make criminals of persons who were in no way blameworthy in what they did. That means that, whenever a section is silent as to mens rea, there is a presumption that, in order to give effect to the will of Parliament, we must read in words appropriate to require *mens rea* ... it is firmly established by a host of authorities that mens rea is an essential ingredient of every offence unless some reason can be found for holding that that is not necessary.'

Reasonable belief or honest belief

The existence of the presumption is beyond dispute, but in one respect the traditional formulation of the presumption calls for re-examination. This respect concerns the position of a defendant who acted under a mistaken view of the facts. In this regard, the presumption is expressed traditionally to the effect that an honest mistake by a defendant does not avail him unless the mistake was made on reasonable grounds. Thus, in *R v Tolson* (1889) 23 QBD 168 at 181, Cave J observed:

'At common law an honest and reasonable belief in the existence of circumstances, which, if true, would make the act for which a prisoner is indicted an innocent act has always been held to be a good defence. This doctrine is embodied in the somewhat uncouth maxim "*actus non facit reum, nisi mens sit rea.*" Honest and reasonable mistake stands in fact on the same footing as absence of the reasoning faculty, as in infancy, or perversion of that faculty, as in lunacy. ... So far as I am aware it has never been suggested that these exceptions do not equally apply in the case of statutory offences unless they are excluded expressly or by necessary implication.'

[Lord Nicholls then referred to *Bank of New South Wales v Piper* [1897] AC 383 and *Sweet v Parsley* where statements to similar effect were made.]

The 'reasonable belief' school of thought held unchallenged sway for many years. But over the last quarter of a century there have been several important cases where a defence of honest but mistaken belief was raised. In deciding these cases the courts have placed new, or renewed, emphasis on the subjective nature of the mental element in criminal offences. The courts have rejected the reasonable belief approach and preferred the honest belief approach. When *mens rea* is ousted by a mistaken belief, it is as well ousted by an unreasonable belief as by a reasonable belief. . . .

Considered as a matter of principle, the honest belief approach must be preferable. By definition the mental element in a crime is concerned with a subjective state of mind, such as intent or belief. To the extent that an overriding objective limit ('on reasonable grounds') is introduced, the subjective element is displaced. To that extent a person who lacks the necessary intent or belief may nevertheless commit the offence. When that occurs the defendant's 'fault' lies exclusively in falling short of an objective standard. His crime lies in his negligence. A statute may so provide expressly or by necessary implication. But this can have no place in a common law principle, of general application, which is concerned with the need for a mental element as an essential ingredient of a criminal offence.

The traditional formulation of the common law presumption, exemplified in Lord Diplock's famous exposition in *Sweet v Parsley*, cited above, is out of step with this recent line of authority, in so far as it envisages that a mistaken belief must be based on reasonable grounds. This seems to be a relic from the days before a defendant in a criminal case could give evidence in his own defence. It is not surprising that in those times juries judged a defendant's state of mind by the conduct to be expected of a reasonable person.

[Lord Nicholls referred to *DPP v Morgan* [1976] AC 182 and *R v Williams* (1984) 78 Cr App R 276 and other cases which he stated confirmed the 'honest belief' approach.]

The construction of s 1 of the Indecency with Children Act 1960

In s 1(1) of the 1960 Act Parliament has not expressly negatived the need for a mental element in respect of the age element of the offence. The question, therefore, is whether, although not expressly negatived, the need for a mental element is negatived by necessary implication. 'Necessary implication' connotes an implication which is compellingly clear. Such an implication may be found in the language used, the nature of the offence, the mischief sought to be prevented and any other circumstances which may assist in determining what intention is properly to be attributed to Parliament when creating the offence.

I venture to think that, leaving aside the statutory context of s 1, there is no great difficulty in this case. The section created an entirely new criminal offence, in simple unadorned language. The offence so created is a serious offence. The more serious the offence, the greater is the weight to be attached to the presumption, because the more severe is the punishment and the graver the stigma which accompany a conviction. Under s 1 conviction originally attracted a punishment of up to two years' imprisonment. This has since been increased to a maximum of ten years' imprisonment. The notification requirements under Pt I of the Sex Offenders Act 1997 now apply, no matter what the age of the offender: see Sch 1, para 1(1)(b). Further, in addition to being a serious offence, the offence is drawn broadly ('an act of gross indecency'). It can embrace conduct ranging from predatory approaches by a much older paedophile to consensual sexual experimentation between precocious teenagers of whom the offender may be the younger of the two. The conduct may be depraved by any acceptable standard, or it may be relatively innocuous behaviour in private between two young people. These factors reinforce, rather than negative, the application of the presumption in this case.

The purpose of the section is, of course, to protect children. An age ingredient was therefore an essential ingredient of the offence. This factor in itself does not assist greatly. Without more, this does not lead to the conclusion that liability was intended to be strict so far as the age element is concerned, so that the offence is committed irrespective of the alleged offender's belief about the age of the 'victim' and irrespective of how the offender came to hold this belief.

Nor can I attach much weight to a fear that it may be difficult sometimes for the prosecution to prove that the defendant knew the child was under 14 or was recklessly indifferent about the child's age. . . .

Similarly, it is far from clear that strict liability regarding the age ingredient of the offence would further the purpose of s 1 more effectively than would be the case if a mental element were read into this ingredient. There is no general agreement that strict liability is necessary to the enforcement of the law protecting children in sexual matters. . . .

Is there here a compellingly clear implication that Parliament should be taken to have intended that the ordinary common law requirement of a mental element should be excluded in respect of the age ingredient of this new offence? Thus far, having regard especially to the breadth of the offence and the gravity of the stigma and penal consequences which a conviction brings, I see no sufficient ground for so concluding.

. . .

Accordingly, I cannot find, either in the statutory context or otherwise, any indication of sufficient cogency to displace the application of the common law presumption. In my view the necessary mental element regarding the age ingredient in s 1 of the 1960 Act is the absence of a genuine belief by the accused that the victim was 14 years of age or above. The burden of proof of this rests upon the prosecution in the usual way. If Parliament considers that the position should be otherwise regarding this serious social problem, Parliament must itself confront the difficulties and express its will in clear terms. I would allow this appeal.

Lord Steyn

Concentrating still on the wording of s 1(1) of the 1960 Act, I now address directly the question whether the presumption is *prima facie* applicable. Two distinctive features of s 1(1) must be taken in to account. First, the *actus reus* is widely defined. Unlike the position under ss 14 and 15 of the 1956 Act, an assault is not an ingredient of the offence under s 1(1). Any act of gross indecency with or towards a child under the age of 14, or incitement to such an act, whether committed in public or private, is within its scope. The subsection is apt to cover acts of paedophilia and all responsible citizens will welcome effective legislation in respect of such a great social evil. But it also covers any heterosexual or homosexual contact between teenagers if one of them is under 14. And the *actus reus* extends to incitement of a child under 14: words are enough. The subsection therefore extends to any verbal sexual overtures between teenagers if one of them is under 14: see the telling examples given by Brooke LJ ([1998] 4 All ER 265 at 277) in the instant case. For the law to criminalise such conduct of teenagers by offences of strict liability would be far-reaching and controversial. The second factor is that s 1(1) creates an offence of a truly criminal character. It was initially punishable on indictment by a custodial term of up to two years and by subsequent amendment the maximum term has been increased to ten years' imprisonment. Moreover, as Lord Reid observed in *Sweet v Parsley* [1970] AC 132 at 149, 'a stigma still attaches to any person convicted of a truly criminal offence, and the more serious or more disgraceful the offence the greater the stigma.' Taking into account the cumulative effect of these two factors, I am persuaded that, if one concentrates on the language of s 1(1), the presumption is prima facie applicable. It is, however, now necessary to examine weighty contrary arguments based on the broader context in which s 1(1) must be seen. Since counsel for the Crown adopted as part of his argument the reasoning of the Divisional Court, and in particular the reasoning of Rougier J, it is unnecessary to summarise the judgments. Instead I propose to examine directly the major planks of the reasoning contained in the judgments of the Divisional Court and in the submissions of counsel for the Crown. But I would respectfully record my tribute to the careful and elegant judgments in the Divisional Court.

. . .

Practical difficulties

Counsel for the Crown finally submitted that it would in practice be difficult for the Crown to disprove defences of lack of knowledge of the age of the victim. In my view counsel has overstated the difficulties. After all, the legislature expressly made available such an excuse in the case of the so-called 'young man's defence' under s 6(3). Moreover, as Brooke LJ ([1998] 4 All ER 265 at 277) pointed out, recklessness or indifference as to the existence of the prohibited circumstance would be sufficient for guilt. And in practice the Crown would only have to shoulder the burden of proving that the defendant was aware of the age of the victim if there was some evidential material before the jury or magistrates suggesting the possibility of an honest belief that the child was over 14. In these circumstances the suggested evidential difficulties ought not to divert the House from a principled approach to the problem.

Lord Irvine of Lairg LC, Lord Hutton and **Lord Mackay of Clashfern** handed down speeches agreeing with **Lord Nicholls**.

Appeal allowed

A detailed analysis and discussion of this case can be found in the extract by Jeremy Horder at p. 46.

R v K
[2001] UKHL 41 (HL)[10]

K, aged 26, was charged with indecently assaulting a 14-year-old girl, contrary to section 14 of the Sexual Offences Act 1956. He claimed that the sexual activity between them was consensual and that he believed the girl was 16 as she had told him. The judge indicated that the prosecution would be required to prove that at the time of the incident the defendant did not honestly believe that the girl was 16 or over. The prosecution argued that this direction was wrong and appealed. The Court of Appeal allowed the appeal, but granted leave to appeal to the House of Lords, certified that the following points of law of general public importance were involved in the decision, namely:

'(a) Is a defendant entitled to be acquitted of the offence of indecent assault on a complainant under the age of 16 years, contrary to section 14(1) of the Sexual Offences Act 1956, if he may hold an honest belief that the complainant in question was aged 16 years or over? (b) If yes, must the belief be held on reasonable grounds?'

Section 14 of the 1956 Act reads:

'(1)It is an offence, subject to the exception mentioned in subsection (3) of this section, for a person to make an indecent assault on a woman.

---

[10] [2002] 1 AC 462.

(2) A girl under the age of 16 cannot in law give any consent which would prevent an act being an assault for the purposes of this section.

(3) Where a marriage is invalid under section two of the Marriage Act 1949, or section one of the Age of Marriage Act 1929 (the wife being a girl under the age of 16), the invalidity does not make the husband guilty of any offence under this section by reason of her incapacity to consent while under that age, if he believes her to be his wife and has reasonable cause for the belief.

(4) A woman who is a defective cannot in law give any consent which would prevent an act being an assault for the purposes of this section, but a person is only to be treated as guilty of an indecent assault on a defective by reason of that incapacity to consent, if that person knew or had reason to suspect her to be a defective.'

Lord Steyn

33. It is now possible to face directly the question whether section 14(1) makes it compellingly clear that the supplementation of the text by the presumption is ruled out. The actual decision of the House in *B (A Minor)* [sub nom. *B (A Child) v DPP*] v Director of Public Prosecutions [2000] 2 AC 428 on the meaning of section 1(1) of the Indecency with Children Act 1960 springs to mind. The House concluded that on the statutory provision involved in that case the presumption was not displaced. But the particular wording of section 14(1) gives greater scope for the Crown's argument in the present case. Thus it is noteworthy that subsection (4) of section 14, but not subsection (2), makes specific provision, in the context of consent, for a defence of absence of *mens rea*. Nevertheless, I would hold that in the present case a compellingly clear implication can only be established if the supplementation of the text by reading in words appropriate to require mens rea results in an internal inconsistency of the text. Approaching the problem in this way, one can readily accept that section 14(2) could naturally have provided that a genuine belief by the accused that the girl was over 16 was no defence. Conversely, section 14(2) could have provided that a genuine belief that the girl was under 16 was a defence. In my view a provision of the latter type would not have been conceptually inconsistent with any part of section 14. By contrast, the terms of sections 5 and 6 of the 1956 Act namely offences of having sexual intercourse with girls under 13 (section 5) and with girls under 16 (section 6) are inconsistent with the application of the presumption. The 'young man's defence' under section 6(3) makes clear that it is not available to anybody else. The linked provision in section 5, dealing with intercourse with younger girls, must therefore also impose absolute liability. There is nothing in section 14(1) as clearly indicative of the displacement of the presumption. In these circumstances it cannot in my view be said that there is a compellingly clear implication ruling out the application of the presumption.

34. This is a result which serves the public interest. It would have been a strange result to conclude that Parliament created by section 14(1) offences of strict liability where any heterosexual or homosexual contact takes place between two teenagers of whom one is under 16. Fortunately, the strong presumption of *mens rea* enabled the House to avoid such a result.

35. For these reasons, as well as the reasons given by Lord Bingham of Cornhill, I would allow the appeal.

Lord Millett

40. My Lords, I have had the advantage of reading in draft the speech of my noble and learned friend Lord Bingham of Cornhill, with which I agree. For the reasons he gives I would allow the appeal and answer the certified questions as he proposes.

41. I do so without reluctance but with some misgiving, for I have little doubt that we shall be failing to give effect to the intention of Parliament and will reduce section 14 of the Sexual Offences Act 1956 to incoherence. . . .

44. . . . [T]he age of consent has long since ceased to reflect ordinary life, and in this respect Parliament has signally failed to discharge its responsibility for keeping the criminal law in touch with the needs of society. I am persuaded that the piecemeal introduction of the various elements of section 14, coupled with the persistent failure of Parliament to rationalise this branch of the law even to the extent of removing absurdities which the courts have identified, means that we ought not to strain after internal coherence even in a single offence. Injustice is too high a price to pay for consistency.

Lord Bingham of Cornhill, Lord Nicholls of Birkenhead and **Lord Hobhouse of Woodborough** gave speeches allowing the appeal.

Appeal allowed.

These two decisions of the House of Lords have strengthened the presumption in favour of *mens rea*, and all cases decided prior to these decisions have to be read in the light of them.[11] As a result of these decisions the court will read *mens rea* into a statute unless either:

1. there is clear wording in the statute indicating that the offence is to be one of strict liability;[12] or

2. there is a 'compellingly clear' inference that the offence is to be one of strict liability.[13]

3 WHEN WILL A COURT NOT PRESUME *MENS REA*?

The factors which a court will take into account in deciding whether there is a 'compellingly clear' inference that the offence is to be one of strict liability include the following:

(1) If some sections of a statute refer explicitly to a *mens rea* requirement and others do not that may indicate that those sections which do not are meant to be strict liability.[14] However, this will not be a conclusive factor,[15] as is clear from the decision in *K* itself.

(2) The court will examine not only the statute in question, but also other statutes which cover analogous offences,[16] in an attempt to ascertain the will of Parliament.

(3) The court will consider the social context of the offence.[17] In some cases it has been suggested that the court will consider whether the offence is intended to be 'truly

---

[11] *Kumar* [2005] 1 Cr App R 34. Although see *R v Doring* [2002] EWCA Crim 1695 where the Court of Appeal declined to alter the interpretation of the strict liability offence in the Insolvency Act 1986, s. 216.

[12] For a recent case where it was felt that the statutory words made it clear that the offence was to be one of strict liability see *Kirk and Russell* [2002] Crim LR 756 (CA), which considered the Sexual Offences Act 1956, s. 6.

[13] Although it should be noted that in *R v K* [2001] UKHL 41 Lord Steyn seemed to suggest that the presumption could be rebutted only by specific language. However this is not consistent with his *obiter* refusal to apply the presumption of *mens rea* to s. 5 of the Sexual Offences Act 1956 in *B v DPP* ([2000] 1 All ER 839 at 843g–h) even though there was nothing in the wording of that section that would exclude it.

[14] *Cundy v Le Cocq* (1884) 13 QBD 207; *Pharmaceutical Society of Great Britain v Storkwain Ltd* [1986] 1 WLR 903 (HL); *R v Muhamad* [2002] EWCA Crim 1856; *R v Matudi* [2003] EWCA Crim 697.

[15] *Sherras v De Rutzen* [1895] 1 QB 918 (DC).   [16] *B v DPP* [2000] 2 WLR 452 (HL).

[17] *Gammon (Hong Kong) Ltd v A-G of Hong Kong* [1985] AC 1 (HL).

criminal'. If it is intended not to be 'truly criminal' and more in the nature of a regulatory offence then that may be a factor indicating that the offence is to be one of strict liability. In deciding whether an offence is 'truly criminal' the court will look at the following factors:

(i) The severity of the punishment[18] and the level of stigma that attaches to a conviction for that offence.[19] The lower the maximum sentence the more likely it is that the offence is regulatory. However, in *Howells*[20] the fact that the offence[21] carried five years' imprisonment did not prevent the imposition of strict liability.[22]

(ii) Whether the offence is aimed at preventing a very serious danger. Where an activity involves a potentially grave social harm (e.g. a potentially polluting activity) it is more likely to be an offence of strict liability.[23] Where there is no public danger the offence is less likely to be one of strict liability.

(iii) Whether rendering the offence one of strict liability will assist in discouraging the activity.[24] An argument that being strict liability will make it easier to prove and so easier to enforce will not of itself be sufficient to persuade a court to interpret the offence to be one of strict liability.[25] But if rendering the offence one of strict liability could be said to persuade potential defendants to change their behaviour this would be an argument in favour of strict liability.

(iv) Whether the offence applies generally to members of the public or if it is addressed to a group of professionals or to those who engage in a particular kind of activity.[26] It is less likely to be one of strict liability if the offence is addressed to members of the public at large.

4 WHAT *MENS REA* WILL BE PRESUMED?

If there is no clear evidence that the statute is to be one of strict liability the court will presume *mens rea*. The presumed *mens rea* will be that the defendant will have a defence if the defendant believed (even if unreasonably) that an aspect of the *actus reus* did not exist. This can be made clearer by considering the facts of *B v DPP* where the defendant was charged with the offence of inciting a girl under the age of 14 to commit an act of gross indecency, into which the court decides to presume *mens rea*.[27] Contrast the following states of mind:

(1) D believes the victim is 16. Here he will be not guilty. This is so even if his belief as to her age was unreasonable.

---

[18] *B v DPP* [2000] 2 WLR 452 (HL).
[19] *Barnfather v Islington London Borough Council and another* [2003] EWHC 418 (Admin).
[20] [1977] QB 614 (CA).   [21] Firearms Act 1968, s. 1(1)(a).
[22] In *Matudi* [2003] EWCA Crim 697 the point was made that the wide range of offenders could be guilty of a strict liability offence, ranging from a defendant who deliberately caused the harm to a defendant who was blameless in doing so. A strict liability offence might therefore carry a high maximum sentence which would be appropriate for the defendant who deliberately caused the harm.
[23] e.g. *McCrudden* [2005] EWCA 466; *Alphacell Ltd v Woodward* [1972] AC 824 (HL).
[24] *R v Matudi* [2003] EWCA Crim 697. See also *Lim Chin Aik v R* [1963] AC 160 (PC).
[25] *Barnfather v Islington London Borough Council* [2003] EWHC 418 (Admin).
[26] *Sweet v Parsley* [1970] AC 132 (HL).
[27] It is important to realize that the age of the girl was here an aspect of the *actus reus*.

(2) D has not thought about the age of the victim. D will be guilty. He has a defence only if he honestly believes that the victim is over 14.

(3) D knows the victim is under 14 but believes that she is Tina (his friend's sister) when it is in fact Becca (who looks like Tina). Here his mistaken belief does not relate to an aspect of the *actus reus*, and so he is guilty.

5 THE HUMAN RIGHTS ACT AND STRICT LIABILITY OFFENCES

The courts have so far not accepted an argument[28] that Article 6 of the European Court of Human Rights prohibits the existence of strict liability offences.[29] The fact that a defendant can be convicted without proof of his *mens rea* does not infringe the right to a fair trial. Article 6 requires that the trial procedures will be fair, but cannot be used to challenge the substance of the law.[30]

6 COMMON LAW DEFENCES AND STRICT LIABILITY OFFENCES

As is clear from the definition of a strict liability offence there can be no defence of no *mens rea*; because *mens rea* is not required. But what about other common law defences such as self-defence, duress of circumstances, or insanity? The Court of Appeal in *Backshall*[31] has confirmed that duress is available as a defence to a strict liability offence. Presumably, therefore, so would be self-defence, necessity, or automatism.[32] There seems, however, to be some doubt over insanity. In *DPP v H*[33] McCowan LJ stated:

> The [insanity] defence is based on the absence of *mens rea*, but none is required for the offence of driving with an excess of alcohol. Hence the defence of insanity has no relevance to such a charge as it is an offence of strict liability.

This reasoning has been strongly criticized.[34] Insanity is not an absence of *mens rea*. It is quite possible for a defendant to be insane and yet intend to kill, for example.

7 POSSESSION OFFENCES

Several statutory offences involve possession of, for example, offensive weapons,[35] drugs,[36] and articles for use in burglary, theft, or deception.[37] Strictly speaking these are not strict

---

[28] Arden (1999).

[29] *Muhammed* [2002] EWCA Crim 1856; *Barnfather v Islington London Borough Council* [2003] EWHC 418 (Admin).

[30] See Sullivan (2005) for a detailed argument on the potential impact of the Human Rights Act on strict liability offence.

[31] [1999] Crim LR 662 (CA).   [32] *Hennessey* [1989]2 All ER 9 (CA); *Issit* [1978] RTR 211 (CA).

[33] *The Times*, 2 May 1997; discussed in Ward (1997).   [34] Simester and Sullivan (2003: 178).

[35] Prevention of Crime Act 1953.   [36] Misuse of Drugs Act 1971.   [37] Theft Act 1968, s. 25.

liability offences, but their *mens rea* requirement can be minimal and so are analogous to them. Possession offences, from a theoretical point of view, are problematic. There are two particular difficulties:

(1) Does possession involve an act? The difficulty may be that at the time when the person is arrested in possession of the prohibited thing, she may not be doing anything. This may infringe the so-called 'voluntary act principle', discussed in Chapter 3. It could be argued that possession involves an initial act of taking into possession, followed by failure to divest of possession. An analogy could be drawn with the decision in *Fagan*[38] (excerpted at p. 179) where the defendant (accidentally) parked his car on the victim's foot and then refused to move it off.

(2) Does the word 'possess' include any *mens rea* element? In *Warner v Metropolitan Police Commissioner*[39] the defendant picked up two boxes which he thought contained perfume. In fact they contained drugs and the defendant was charged with possession of drugs. The House of Lords held that if a person possesses a container he possesses the items in the container.[40] There are two exceptions to this:[41]

 (i) If the item has been placed in the defendant's bag or pocket without his or her knowledge and without an opportunity to discover that the item has been placed there then it is not possessed by the defendant.

 (ii) If the accused believed that the container had something in it which was completely different from what was actually there then the defendant does not possess the item. However, the width of this exception is not as wide as may appear, because in *Warner* it was held that perfume was not wholly different from drugs and in *McNamara*[42] it was suggested that pornography was not radically different from cannabis resin, both of which are rather surprising findings.

The House of Lords has recently confirmed the definition of possession in *Warner* in the following decision:

R v Lambert
[2001] UKHL 37 (HL)[43]

The appellant was charged with possession of a class A drug with intent to supply contrary to section 5(3) of the Misuse of Drugs Act 1971. He had picked up a duffel bag containing 2 kilograms of cocaine at a railway station. His defence, based on section 28 of the Misuse of Drugs Act 1971, was that although he had been in possession of the bag he did not know or suspect, or have reason to suspect the nature of the contents of the bag. He was convicted and appealed on the basis that he should not have been required to establish his defence on a balance of probabilities. (The case involved a discussion of

[38] [1969] 1 QB 439.   [39] [1969] 2 AC 256 (HL).

[40] The leading case where drugs are found on or in something which is not a container is *Marriot* [1971] 1 All ER 595 where the defendant possessed a penknife. Unknown to him, the penknife had cannabis attaching to the blade. It was held that unless he was aware that there were substances attaching to the penknife he could not be convicted of possession of the cannabis.

[41] The defendant bears the evidential burden in respect of these exceptions (*McNamara* (1988) 87 Cr App R 270 (CA)).

[42] (1988) 87 Cr App R 270 (CA).   [43] [2001] 3 WLR 206.

the impact of the Human Rights Act on the burden of proof which was discussed in Chapter 1.)

Lord Slynn of Hadley

16. The first question asks whether it is an essential element of the offence of possession of a controlled drug under section 5 of the Misuse of Drugs Act 1971 that the accused knows that he has a controlled drug in his possession. Bearing fully in mind the importance of the principle that the onus is on the prosecution to prove the elements of an offence and that the provisions of an Act which transfer or limit that burden of proof should be carefully scrutinised, it seems to me that the Court of Appeal in *R v McNamara* (1988) 87 Cr App R 246 rightly identified the elements of the offence which the prosecution must prove. I refer in particular to the judgment of Lord Lane CJ, at p 252. This means in a case like the present that the prosecution must prove that the accused had a bag with something in it in his custody or control; and that the something in the bag was a controlled drug. It is not necessary for the prosecution to prove that the accused knew that the thing was a controlled drug let alone a particular controlled drug. The defendant may then seek to establish one of the defences provided in section 5(4) or section 28 of the 1971 Act.

Lord Hope

61. ... I consider the settled law to be correct on this point. As far as the 1971 Act is concerned, there are two elements to possession. There is the physical element, and there is the mental element. The physical element involves proof that the thing is in the custody of the defendant or subject to his control. The mental element involves proof of knowledge that the thing exists and that it is in his possession. Proof of knowledge that the thing is an article of a particular kind, quality or description is not required. It is not necessary for the prosecution to prove that the defendant knew that the thing was a controlled drug which the law makes it an offence to possess. I observe that Mr Owen did not submit that it was necessary for the prosecution to prove that the defendant was aware that the thing was a class A, B or C drug, as the case may be, although the class into which the drug falls will usually be relevant to any sentence he may receive.

Appeal dismissed.

PART II: THE THEORY OF STRICT LIABILITY OFFENCES

8 THE ARGUMENTS FOR AND AGAINST STRICT LIABILITY

We will shortly consider the arguments that can be made for and against a strict liability offence. But first it is important to appreciate the wide range of alternatives available to a legal system which wishes to restrict the need to prove *mens rea*. Here are some:

(1) to require that the defendant was negligent as to the *actus reus*;

(2) to provide a defence for a defendant who can prove that he was not negligent;

(3) to establish special defences based on a legal or evidential burden on the defendant;

(4) only to require that the defendant caused the *actus reus*.

As these alternatives show, if it is decided that the prosecution should not be required to prove any *mens rea* on the defendant's part, strict liability is not the only option by any means.

8.1 ARGUMENTS FOR STRICT LIABILITY OFFENCES

The following are some of the main arguments in favour of strict liability offences:

Protection of the public

The main justification in favour of strict liability offences is that they protect the general public.[44] Most strict liability offences are found in those areas of life which pose a risk to others: for example, the sale of food, medical drugs, and alcohol; the prevention of pollution. The argument is that where a person or company is about to engage in an activity which is potentially dangerous (e.g. an industrial activity that may cause pollution) we want the company not just to take 'reasonable steps' to prevent the harm, but to do everything it possibly can.[45] The imposition of strict liability, rather than negligence, may encourage the company to pull out every stop to prevent pollution.[46] The difficulty with this argument is that it suggests that the law expects people to take unreasonable steps to prevent harm.

Ease of proof

Strict liability offences are easier for the prosecution to prove because there is no need to prove the defendant's state of mind. Imagine, for example, that a motorist could be convicted of speeding only if he knew that he was speeding. It would become almost impossible then to succeed in a prosecution for speeding and court cases would take far longer.[47]

Risk-creating activities

It can be argued that if someone chooses to undertake a dangerous activity the law is justified in requiring him to ensure that he does not harm others. A person performing a dangerous activity should not escape criminal punishment by saying that he did not foresee that the act might harm someone.

---

[44] Levenson (1993). See Wooton (1963) who argues that strict liability should be the norm for all criminal offences.

[45] See *Alphacell Ltd v Woodward* [1972] AC 824 (HL) and Wootton (1981).

[46] See Nemerson (1975) for arguments in favour of strict liability offences when people engage in ultra-hazardous activities.

[47] Michaels (1999: 1137).

Difficulties in convicting corporations

Many strict liability offences involve commercial activities. This means that for many statutory offences the defendant is likely to be a company. As we shall see in Chapter 13 there are real difficulties in demonstrating that a company has *mens rea*. By making such offences strict liability it is far easier to convict companies. However, negligence liability could also be used to assist in the conviction of companies.[48]

8.2 ARGUMENTS AGAINST STRICT LIABILITY OFFENCES

Many opponents of strict liability accept that there is some merit in the points just made but argue that they do not demonstrate why the law must require strict liability, rather than a negligence-based offence or at least one where there is a defence of 'due diligence'.[49] They point out that there is no evidence that strict liability is more effective than negligence-based offences at preventing harmful activities.[50] Opponents argue further that it is unjust to convict defendants who have acted in an entirely reasonable way but unpredictably caused a harm.[51] To convict such defendants weakens the stigma that attaches to a criminal conviction and endangers the distinction between criminal and civil law.[52] Such draconian criminal laws may also have the effect of discouraging people from engaging in socially beneficial commercial activities.[53]

Supporters of strict liability suggest that such concerns are overreactions. Where a defendant is genuinely blameless he will not be prosecuted or if he is only a lower sentence will be imposed.[54] Indeed there is evidence that regulatory agencies charged with enforcing some strict liability offences exercise considerable discretion in deciding whether or not to prosecute.[55] Further, supporters of strict liability offences reply that many of the objections overlook the fact that these offences are not, as the courts have put it, 'truly criminal', to which Professor Smith[56] has replied 'this is a peculiar notion of truth. The truth is that it is a crime.'

In the following extract Andrew Simester considers the moral case against strict liability offences.

A. Simester, 'Is Strict Liability Always Wrong?' in A. Simester (ed.), *Appraising Strict Liability* (Oxford: OUP, 2005) at 33–7.

Intrinsic Objections to Strict Liability

It is, in short, arguable that there are instrumental benefits to be gained from the device of strict liability, although their scope and extent is uncertain. However, assuming they exist, those benefits must be weighed against the intrinsic moral objections to strict liability set out below. In the context of stigmatic crimes, it seems to me that these objections are decisive.

---

[48] Simester and Sullivan (2003: 173).
[49] See Horder (2005) for a detailed argument in favour of a 'due diligence defence'.
[50] Jackson (1991); Richardson (1987); Baldwin (1990); Packer (1962: 109).
[51] Michaels (1999) examines the issue from the perspective of the American Constitution.
[52] P. Robinson (1996a).   [53] *Contra* Brady (1972).   [54] *Smedleys Ltd v Breed* [1974] AC 839.
[55] There are concerns that the agencies are under-funded and unable to enforce the strict liability offences effectively: Ashworth (2003: 167).
[56] J.C. Smith (2002: 125).

Objections Specific to Paradigm (Stigmatic) Crimes

Suppose that the state were to create a crime of 'homicide', defined as a strict liability offence of causing death. Objections to crimes of this type depend, in turn, on the nature of the criminal law. Without dwelling on the familiar analysis, there seem to me to be certain paradigm features associated with the criminalization of μing. *Ex ante*, μing is prohibited and declared to be wrong: citizens are not merely requested but instructed not to. *Ex post*, where D is found to have transgressed, he is convicted of μing and liable to punishment which may be substantial, perhaps including imprisonment. The conviction and the punishment also express censure, to D, Y, and the public at large. As well as suffering hard treatment, D is labelled as a particular sort of criminal (a 'μer'), a labelling that conveys a public implication of culpable wrongdoing.

These paradigm features of the criminal law imply certain objections to making μing a strict liability crime, at least where strict liability leads to conviction of blameless defendants . . .

Wrongful Censure

The main objection to strict liability in stigmatic crimes law is that it involves the conviction and punishment of persons who are not at fault. Morally speaking, it is wrong to convict the innocent. If a person does not deserve to be convicted then he has a right not to be; and his conviction cannot be justified by such consequential considerations as deterrence.

Since both are censorious, this objection applies to both conviction and punishment. The imposition of punishment is, *qua* punishment, justified only when D deserves it, in virtue of culpably having done wrong. Indeed, the imposition of hard treatment cannot count as punishment unless it conveys this message. But in the context of strict liability, the state does not rely on the proposition that D is culpable as a precondition of imposing punishment. So the state cannot claim to be punishing D in accordance with D's desert; it is simply imposing hard treatment in virtue of the fact that μing (an *actus reus*) has occurred.

This criticism may be evaded, in part. Even if μing is a strict liability offence, the quantum of punishment imposed for transgressions might still be related to desert in a criminal legal system that required *sentences* to take account of D's level of culpability, with fault being a post-conviction matter for consideration during sentencing.

However, the same get-out is not available with regard to the conviction itself. Independently of the sanction imposed, the conviction also conveys censure. A conviction for μing has the effect of naming D a criminal (in respect of that particular offence), a branding which is communicated to society as well as to D. Assuming that, if imposed on a strict liability basis, the label 'criminal-μ' continues to retain its stigmatic quality, this amounts to systematic moral defamation by the state. Given the public understanding of that designation, when it labels him a criminal the state is no longer telling the public the truth about D. People have a right not to be censured falsely as criminals, a right that is violated when one is convicted and punished for a stigmatic crime without proof of culpable wrongdoing.

That falsehood is no ordinary lie. There is something especially troubling when wrongful censure is imposed by the state. In ordinary defamation cases, the attack is characteristically private; it may affect D, and even harm D's interests, but it lacks the authoritative voice of the state and normally does not undermine his membership of the community. An act of defamation may bring D into conflict with P, but it normally does not alienate D from society. By contrast, convictions are official. They condemn D on behalf of society as a whole. To say that D has a criminal record is to say that he has been labelled as a reprehensible wrongdoer; that the state has made a formal adverse statement about *him*. Moreover, the statement marks D out in such a way that it becomes appropriate, within the community, for the regard in which he is held to be affected. Certain exclusions, both social and professional, may legitimately follow. As such, the criminal record becomes part of the material that frames D's engagement with his community, with adverse implications for D's ability to live his life—a life that is, in part, defined in terms of D's interactions within, and membership of, his society. The conviction (and indeed the punishment, in its censorious facet) tends not only to censure D for the particular act that is proscribed, but also to undermine D's participation in the society itself.

Censure and Stigma

We can elaborate this concern by distinguishing between censure, which the state expresses through its action of convicting (and punishing) the defendant, and the *effect* of that action, in terms of the stigma that attaches to D and his conduct. Of course, as the foregoing discussion has suggested, one reason why the state ought not falsely to censure D for a serious crime is supplied by the consequences for D's life. But the two do not always go together, and D has a right to be neither falsely censured *nor* falsely stigmatized. Even if D suffers no stigma, the state should not purport to censure him without believing him to be culpable. Telling lies is wrong in itself and not merely because of the consequences.

Consider, on the other hand, an argument that the state is not *really* censuring D, since both the state and D know that fault has not been proved when D is convicted of a strict liability offence. The problem with this 'private colloquy' reasoning is that the state should not ignore the significance of its actions for others. When labelling D guilty of a stigmatic crime, the state is bound by the public meaning of the words it uses. Thus, for example, Parliament cannot legitimately enact an offence of 'paedophilia', defined as 'parking for more than one hour on a central London street'. It cannot do so because that is not what paedophilia means. Even if D understands that the label is a technical usage, the state may not disregard the rest of its audience, and the effect that such a label will have on D's life.

Treating a conviction for 'paedophilia' as highly stigmatic is, of course, a reasonable public response. A more difficult case would arise if the reaction of the public, in terms of stigmatizing D, is unreasonable and far exceeds what is deserved in light of the state's censure. Suppose that, in the public mind, parking offenders (labelled as such) came to be regarded like paedophiles. In that event, a strict liability parking conviction, although not intended as censorious, would be highly stigmatic. Even in this sort of case, at least where the stigma is predictable, it seems to me that the state should take account of the consequences of a conviction for defendants. The offence should no longer involve strict liability.

Rights and Instrumental Reason

Of course, some error in the criminal justice system is unavoidable. When the state convicts a person of a stigmatic offence, it generally requires that guilt be proved beyond reasonable doubt. Inevitably, this leaves open the possibility that a particular defendant, properly convicted on that standard of proof, is not in fact guilty. The defamation and wrongful punishment of such persons is none the less justified. Moreover, it is justified by consequential reasons: in particular, by the need to set an achievable standard of proof if society is to have a practicable criminal justice system at all. It might be thought that an analogy can be drawn between these instrumental considerations, which permit wrongful convictions whenever the criminal proof standard is met, and those set out [earlier in the essay], which support convictions on the basis of strict liability.

But the analogy strikes me as false. Where guilt is proved beyond reasonable doubt in stigmatic crimes, the state convicts in good faith—D is believed to be culpable. Further, although error is systemic it remains unsystematic: the distribution of error is unknown, and we cannot predict the likelihood that any particular conviction is a mistake. By contrast, where strict liability is employed in a stigmatic crime, the state consistently labels D as a culpable wrongdoer without believing this to be true. Moreover, defamation is predictable— there are reasons for thinking that the state is particularly likely to censure and punish D wrongly in that class of cases. Hence, while instrumental considerations of an institutional nature may sometimes be relied upon to justify the risk of good-faith erroneous convictions, arguments of this type seem inadequate to justify strict liability for stigmatic crimes.

8.3 ANALYSING THE ARGUMENTS

In the following extract Laurie Levenson discusses in more detail some of the arguments that can be presented for or against strict liability offences:

L.L. Levenson, 'Good Faith Defenses: Reshaping Strict Liability Crimes' (1993) 78 *Cornell Law Review* 401 at 419–27

B. Justifications for Strict Liability Crimes

1. Public Welfare Offenses

The strict liability doctrine often applies to so-called 'public welfare' offenses or regulatory crimes promulgated to address the dangers brought about by the advent of the industrial revolution. Public welfare offenses include the sale of impure or adulterated foods or drugs, driving faster than the speed limit, the sale of intoxicating liquor to minors, and improper handling of dangerous chemicals or nuclear wastes. Defendants violate these laws regardless of their intent or absence of negligent conduct.

There are several reasons the strict liability doctrine is used to redress invasions of the public welfare. First, the doctrine is employed for these offenses because it shifts the risks of dangerous activity to those best able to prevent a mishap. For example, a pharmaceutical manufacturer is in a unique position to know and control product quality. Strict liability holds the manufacturer liable if that product becomes contaminated for any reason. The risk of mishap is shifted to the manufacturer who can be assured of avoiding liability only by not engaging in the particular high risk activity.

Yet, this reason alone cannot justify the doctrine. The strict liability doctrine is not the only possible method for shifting risk onto the manufacturer. A criminal negligence standard also shifts the risk to the party engaging in the activity and punishes those who act carelessly. Under a negligence standard, a defendant is liable for failure to act as a reasonable person would have under the circumstances, even if he did not intend or appreciate the risks of his activities. Under a negligence standard, if the defendant acts reasonably and harm results, no punishment follows. Nonetheless, the burden to learn and operate within society's standards rests with the defendant.

The strict liability doctrine operates in a fundamentally different way. While both negligence and strict liability shift the burden of risk avoidance to the defendant, only under strict liability are individuals imprisoned even if they take all possible precautions to act reasonably. The sole question for the trier of fact is whether the defendant committed the proscribed act. The jury may not decide whether the defendant could have done anything else to prevent the unlawful act.

Thus, there must be additional reasons for selecting the strict liability doctrine over the negligence standard. Among these reasons is the need by the legislature to assure that juries will treat like cases alike when judging conduct involving public welfare. Juries may be ill-suited to decide what is reasonable in complex high risk activities. For example, in order for juries to decide what is reason-able conduct when dealing with nuclear waste, they would have to be educated on the nuclear industry, the risks posed by it, and the safeguards that might be taken. Legislatures prefer to make this assessment themselves, rather than relying on the competence of juries. Moreover, jurors may be swayed by sympathies or prejudices of a particular case. By dictating what is *per se* unreasonable, an individual jury cannot reassess the standard of reasonableness. Accordingly, a second reason for using the strict liability doctrine is that it assures uniform treatment of particular, high risk conduct.

A third justification often offered for the strict liability doctrine is that it eases the burden on the prosecution to prove intent in difficult cases. Strict liability is based largely on the assumption that an accident occurs because the defendant did not take care to prevent it. No showing of intent or negligence is required, because the fact that a prohibited act occurred demonstrates the defendant's negligence. As with most irrebuttable presumptions, the legislature believes individual inquiries are unnecessary because the overwhelming majority of cases will show that the defendant acted at least negligently. Seen in this light, strict liability is a procedural shortcut to punish those who would be culpable under traditional theories of criminal law.

Fourth, even if the presumption is incorrect in a particular case, legislatures determine that this risk is outweighed by the need for additional protection of society and expeditious prosecution of certain cases. For example, driving in excess of a posted speed limit is typically a strict liability crime. With nearly 398,000 annual traffic cases in one [US] state alone, processing these cases as quickly as possible is important. The most efficient way to process such cases is to presume defendants drive carelessly when exceeding speed limits. The presumption is generally accurate and, even when it is not, the need for public safety and the relatively minor punishment minimizes any concern about injustice.

Finally, the strict liability doctrine is attractive as a powerful public statement of legislative intolerance for certain behavior. By labelling an offense as strict liability, the legislature can claim to provide the utmost protection from certain public harms. By affording no leniency for defendants causing harm, the legislature affirms society's interest in being protected from certain conduct. In this sense, strict liability expresses emphatically that such conduct will not be tolerated regardless of the actor's intent.

. . .

C. Opposition to the Strict Liability Doctrine

Opponents of the strict liability doctrine argue that its justifications are inconsistent with both utilitarian and retributivist theories of punishment. Under utilitarian theory, punishment is justified if it deters unlawful behavior. If punishing those who commit prohibited acts will deter others from acting similarly, punishment is justified. Under the retributivist approach, an individual should be punished for choosing to violate the law. Punishment reflects respect for an individual's autonomy to choose to do 'wrong.' If an individual chooses to transgress the boundaries established to protect society, he 'deserves' punishment.

The strict liability doctrine, especially when applied to defendants misled into committing an unlawful act, is not supported by either theory of punishment. Under retributivist theory, criminal law should hold individuals responsible for only those acts for which they are blame-worthy. An individual is blameworthy, not because of accidental conduct, but because of a conscious and knowing breach of the law. At a minimum, the defendant must have acted below the standard of care that a reasonable person would have exercised under the same conditions. A strict liability defendant punished for an act that he has been misled into committing has not consciously decided to violate society's norms. Accordingly, under classic retributivist theory, this defendant does not 'deserve' to be punished.

Additionally, the strict liability doctrine conflicts with utilitarian theories of punishment. Strict liability laws are inefficient because they tend to overdeter individuals' behavior. If the strict liability defendant can be punished for *any* conduct crossing a certain proscribed line, the defendant will be inclined to abstain from *all* activity that could conceivably result in illegal behavior. In some situations, certain individuals might abstain from entering a high risk industry. In situations such as in *Kantor*, individuals may be deterred from engaging in constitutionally protected activity. Thus, strict liability may deter individuals from engaging in activities that are socially necessary or desirable, constitutionally protected, or both. In this manner, strict liability overdeters conduct.

More fundamentally, the strict liability doctrine violates utilitarian theories of criminal punishment because an individual who has no basis for believing he is engaging in unlawful conduct will not be deterred from engaging in that behavior. If an individual has no indication that he is doing anything wrong until the harmful act is completed, then he has no reason to alter his conduct. Given the conflicts with both the retributivist and utilitarian theories of punishment, it is understandable why opponents of strict liability do not want to use the doctrine against defendants who have made an affirmative effort to comply with the law but have been misled into committing a violation. Classic Anglo-American legal philosophy is that '[i]t is better that ten guilty persons escape than one innocent suffer.' Strict liability theory operates from the opposite perspective. Under the strict liability doctrine, an occasional innocent may be punished to assure the safety of the majority. Thus, the prosecution of good faith defendants under strict liability laws appears to conflict with the most fundamental principles of just punishment.

In the following passage Celia Wells challenges the way strict liability is traditionally discussed. She firmly rejects a view that strict liability crimes should be seen as contrary to the principles that underlie criminal law:

C. Wells, *Corporations and Criminal Responsibility* (2nd edn., Oxford: OUP, 2001), 70–4

2. Culpability and Strict Liability

. . .

The numerous statutory and regulatory offences which do not require proof of recklessness or even negligence, have attracted much criticism. There is generally *little* attempt to relate the criticism to the specific framework of regulation nor to step outside the analytical compartments of act and *mental element*. Legal scholars make their own structures within which to contain, comment, and criticize material which they have *selected*. The Law Commission, for example, frequently uses the expression 'contrary to principle' which both *forecloses* and mystifies criticism. The infrastructure of criminal law marginalizes not *only* statutory and regulatory offences but *also* 'defences' or exceptions to the '*golden* principles'. By this I mean that it is not only in the selection of material (common law, 'serious' offences such as homicide and rape) that the distortion occurs. It is in the analysis, the abstraction of broad principle (all crimes have/must have a subjective mental element) that the corruption begins. A prescriptive aspiration (no person should be guilty without proof of a subjective mental element) is wrapped in a descriptive truth (criminal law is based on such a fundamental principle). While something of a caricature, the pervasiveness of such modes of writing should not be underestimated, and their seductiveness needs to be resisted.

The history of strict liability, for long accepted as a straightforward response to industrialization, has recently been subjected to re-assessment. Singer makes a detailed argument that the 'seminal' case of *Woodrow* and the early Sale of Food and Drugs Acts are not examples of strict criminal liability but represent enforcement against tax evasion and consumer fraud. Strict liability, where it was used in the nineteenth century, was more commonly found in the areas of morals, minors, and drink. The point is an interesting one for it demonstrates how the strength of an orthodoxy does not necessarily reflect the soundness of its origin.

Three approaches to strict liability can be discerned: one is based on deterrence; another is to admit its utility in relation to regulatory offences; while the third casts doubt on the premise that strict liability equals blamelessness.

The use and abuse of strict liability as a deterrent to careless corporate activity are arguments which have been well-rehearsed. As with many deterrence arguments it is singularly difficult to arbitrate; the whole concept is an unattractive one to many and even those who regard it as an important goal of criminal law would find difficulty in empirically demonstrating its efficacy. Added to that, the further difficulty arises with strict liability that the empirical evidence points to the fact that law enforcers rarely prosecute unless they have evidence of fault. This adds fuel in two forms to the opponents of strict liability: it reinforces the argument that strict liability is not necessary to control the waywardness of the entrepreneurial capitalist and in addition it might suggest that the wilful law-breaker is being treated as a luckless innocent.

It is unnecessary to dwell here on the argument from deterrence, other perhaps than to insert a note of surprise that deterrence can be presented in terms of a 'potentially inefficient *or* thoughtless member of society [who might] effectively mend his [*sic*] ways if he knows that no excuse will be allowed'. This pathologizes the notion of deterrence in an unrealistic way. What on any account would be a complex, social, and (in the case of corporations) group psychology of risk awareness *or* aversion cannot be reduced to 'ordinary man in the street' musing. One approach is to adopt different standards for corporations, to accept the inevitability and even utility of strict liability for regulatory offences but to out-law it for private individuals.

'Prosecution for corporate crime often results from the enforcement strategy of a regulatory agency that has been monitoring the company's operations for some time, that sees compliance with the law as its ultimate aim, and that regards criminal prosecution as the last resort. Such an approach, combined with strict liability when the law is enforced, may be defended as an effective crime prevention strategy . . .'

Ashworth goes on to make the point that many companies possess resources on such a scale that it may be justifiable to reverse the procedural balance in favour of the regulatory inspectorates.

Both this argument and that from deterrence suffer the flaw (as Ashworth acknowledges) that embracing strict liability for utilitarian reasons may be counter-productive, that strict liability 'downgrades the importance with which the targeted offences are regarded and that it is socially unjust to deploy the stigmatic process of police and conviction of "real" crime against individuals who commit ordinary offences of a non serious kind, while persisting in the corporate sphere with the often less stigmatic process of regulation and with crimes whose penalties inflict little hardship on convicted companies'.

A third strand of argument pitches strict liability against the 'reality' of the criminal justice process. There is often an assumption that *mens rea* offences are proceeded against with full procedural safeguards, such as proof of fault. The reality in the bulk of prosecutions is of course entirely different. The inducements to plead guilty include removal of the immediate pressure of post-arrest detention, the reduction of potential charges (in quantity and quality), the hope of a lower sentence and so on. When strict liability is discussed, there often lurks an implicit model of the criminal justice process which is based on an ideal rarely achieved. And to this procedural point has to be added, of course, the substantive argument already mentioned that much traditional criminal law departs from the 'golden rule' of subjective *mens rea*.

Strict liability has been frequently assailed for being 'unjust', 'unfair', and therefore morally wrong. It is regarded by some as dissonant with the basic premise of criminal liability—that only a morally blameworthy defendant should be stigmatized, much less imprisoned. It has also been criticized for possibly over-deterring socially beneficial behaviour. Doubt, however, can be cast on the assumption that strict liability (if it were enforced literally) involves conviction of the 'blameless innocent'. It is somewhat secondary to the main argument, but fascinating nonetheless, that the case over which many a first-year student has been asked to weep into their hankies, *Hobbs v. Winchester Corpn* in sympathy with the innocent butcher convicted of selling unsound meat turns out, after all, not to have involved a criminal conviction at all. With some deft detective work, Singer uncovered the real story: local meat inspectors had confiscated and destroyed diseased meat sold by Hobbs, who then sought compensation which the Public Health Act 1875 allowed for a person who sustained damage 'to any matter as to which he is not himself in default'. Hobbs had previously been acquitted of criminal charges of selling unsound meat through lack of knowledge; the burden of proof was reversed on the compensation claim and thus it failed.

What this helps to demonstrate is the necessity of looking behind the curtain of the textbook or case report. In a more radical way, the time-frame in which the moral acceptability of a strict liability principle can be re-examined. As Kelman argues, if we take a broader focus on business activities, the clarity which earlier disclosed an 'innocent' shopkeeper caught by the rigour of strict liability regulation, fades. The choice of a narrow time-frame in which to assess culpability is symptomatic of the use of interpretive constructions in criminal law. A broader time-frame might well disclose that the defendant was aware of the risk of the harm occurring. A second point of significance is made with the use of another 'construct', the conscious legislative choice between rules and standards. Conceding that strict liability 'like all conclusive presumptions ... is inaccurate in particular places', he argues that negligence is not very reliable either and suffers the further disadvantage that 'it may convict innocents for *bad* reasons (e.g. race prejudice in juries) rather than *no* reason (i.e. the accidental over-inclusiveness of the conclusive presumption'. One response to this argument would be to abandon both strict liability and negligence standards; its importance, however, is in highlighting the implication in critics of strict liability that other standards avoid the conviction of the innocent.

QUESTIONS

1. In what circumstances, if any, is the imposition of strict liability justifiable?

2. Jeremy Horder (2002b) has suggested that criminal offences which regulate activities which have intrinsic value for participants (e.g. they are aspects of an individual's vision

of the good life) should not normally be strict liability offences. But offences which regulate activities which have instrumental value (i.e. the activities are not valuable in themselves, but are only a means to another end (e.g. in Horder's view transport)) are more appropriate as being interpreted as strict liability. Do you think this is a helpful distinction?

FURTHER READING

Gardner, J. (2005), 'Wrongs and Faults' in A. Simester (ed.), *Appraising Strict Liability* (Oxford: OUP).

Green, S. (2005), 'Six Senses of Strict Liability: A Plea for Formalism' in A. Simester (ed.), *Appraising Strict Liability* (Oxford: OUP).

Horder, J. (2001), 'How Culpability Can, and Cannot, be Denied in Under-Age Sex Crimes', *Criminal Law Review* 15.

—— (2002b), 'Strict Liability, Statutory Construction and the Spirit of Liberty', *Law Quarterly Review* 118: 459.

—— (2004), *Excusing Crime* (Oxford: OUP), ch. 6.

—— (2005c), 'Whose Values Should Determine When Liability is Strict?' in A. Simester (ed.), *Appraising Strict Liability* (Oxford: OUP).

Husak, D. (1995), 'Varieties of Strict Liability', *Canadian Journal of Law and Jurisprudence* 8: 189.

—— (2005), 'Strict Liability, Justice, and Proportionality' in A. Simester (ed.), *Appraising Strict Liability* (Oxford: OUP).

Jackson, B. (1991), '*Storkwain*: A Case Study in Strict Liability and Self-regulation', *Criminal Law Review* 892.

Levenson, L. (1993), 'Good Faith Defenses: Reshaping Strict Liability Crimes', *Cornell Law Review* 78: 401.

Simester, A. (2005), 'Is Strict Liability Always Wrong?' in A. Simester (ed.), *Appraising Strict Liability* (Oxford: OUP).

Simons, K. (1997), 'Criminal Law: When is Strict Criminal Liability Just?', *Journal of Criminal Law and Criminology* 87: 1075.

Sullivan, G.R. (2005), 'Strict Liability for Criminal Offences in England and Wales Following Incorporation into English Law of the European Convention on Human Rights' in A. Simester (ed.), *Appraising Strict Liability* (Oxford: OUP).

HOMICIDE

PART I: THE LAW

1 GENERAL

Homicide in the criminal law can be divided into the following categories:

(1) Murder.

(2) Manslaughter.

(3) Infanticide.

(4) Causing death by dangerous driving or by careless driving when under the influence of drink or drugs.

The first two categories are by far the most important and so they will be discussed in the greatest detail. The topic of corporate homicide will be discussed in Chapter 13.

2 MURDER

DEFINITION

Actus reus: the unlawful killing of another person in the Queen's peace.

Mens rea: an intention to cause death or grievous bodily harm to the victim.

A person convicted of murder must be given a sentence of life imprisonment.

2.1 *ACTUS REUS*

The *actus reus* of murder is the unlawful killing of another person in the Queen's peace.[1] These terms need a little more amplification.

A person

The victim of homicide must be a person. There are two controversial issues which need to be considered here:

[1] Coke 3 Inst 47.

(1) *When does life begin?* According to the law human life begins at birth. Foetuses or unborn children cannot be the victims of murder or manslaughter because they are not yet people.[2] However, the *actus reus* of murder or manslaughter is made out if the child is injured while in the womb, is then born alive, but dies shortly afterwards from the injuries.[3] The crucial moment at which the foetus becomes a human being is when the child is born alive and is completely outside the mother.[4] The child must be capable of breathing, although need not actually have begun to breathe.[5] Although foetuses are not people, this is not to say that unborn children are not protected by the criminal law until they are born. They are protected by the offences of causing or procuring a miscarriage[6] or child destruction,[7] both of which carry the maximum sentence of life imprisonment.[8]

(2) *When does life end?* If the victim was already dead when he was shot by the defendant, the defendant cannot be guilty of murder.[9] The law accepts the medical definition of death.[10] The basic position is that a person dies once he or she stops breathing, the heart stops pumping blood, and the brain ceases to function; in other words 'brain death'.[11]

Unlawfully

If the defendant is able to rely on the defence of self-defence she has not killed unlawfully.[12] Self-defence will be discussed further in Chapter 12.

Queen's peace

It must be shown that the killing took place in the Queen's peace. What this means is that the killing of enemy aliens during war and under battle conditions is not a criminal homicide.[13] An English court can try a British citizen for murder or manslaughter committed in any country.[14]

Killed

It must be shown that the defendant caused the death of the victim. The law on causation is discussed in Chapter 2. In the context of murder it is necessary to show that the defendant accelerated the victim's death by more than a negligible amount.[15] This is interpreted fairly

---

[2] Although the foetus is not regarded as a person, it can still be a criminal offence to kill a foetus; see, for example, the offence of procuring a miscarriage contrary to Offences Against the Person Act 1961, s. 58.

[3] *Senior* (1832) 1 Mood CC 346.

[4] *Poulton* (1832) 5 C & P 329. There is no need for the umbilical cord to have been cut.

[5] *Enoch* (1830) 5 C & P 539; *Brain* (1834) 6 C & P 349.

[6] Offences Against the Person Act 1861, s. 58. For a detailed discussion of this offence see *R (On the application of Smeaton) v Secretary of State for Health* [2002] Crim LR 664, holding that prescription and supply of the 'morning after pill' did not constitute a criminal offence.

[7] Infant Life (Preservation) Act 1929. This Act applies when the child is capable of being born alive. The Human Fertilisation and Embryology Act 1990, s. 37(1)(a), explains that if a pregnancy has lasted 24 weeks, it is presumed that the child is capable of being born alive.

[8] There is no offence if the procedure is permitted by the Abortion Act 1967.

[9] Although a charge of attempted murder may lie: see Ch. 14.

[10] *Re A (A Minor)* [1992] 3 Med L Rev 303. Dickens (1998) discusses the medical definition of death.

[11] *Malcherek and Steel* [1981] 1 WLR 690 (CA).

[12] *Beckford* [1988] AC 130 (PC).   [13] The example is given by Hale 1 PC 433.

[14] Offences Against the Person Act 1861, s. 9; British Nationality Act 1948, s. 3.

[15] *Adams* [1957] Crim LR 365; *Cox* [1992] BMLR 38.

generously in cases of doctors providing pain-relieving drugs to terminally ill patients. A doctor who provides a dying patient with drugs to ease his or her pain will not have committed the *actus reus* of murder if the drugs shorten the patient's life by a few minutes, although the doctor would if the time involved was days or weeks.[16]

It used to be the law that a defendant was liable for murder only if the victim died within a year and a day of the defendant's actions. The rule gave rise to difficulties, especially where victims were kept alive on life support machines, and was abolished in the Law Reform (Year and a Day Rule) Act 1996.[17]

2.2 MENS REA

The *mens rea* of murder is an intention to kill or cause grievous bodily harm. This was established by *Cunningham*,[18] where the House of Lords upheld the conviction of a defendant who killed a victim by hitting him on the head with a chair. Even though there was no intent to kill, the defendant intended to cause grievous bodily harm, and that was sufficient for a murder conviction. Historically the *mens rea* for murder has been described as 'malice aforethought', although this is a misleading phrase because there is no need to show any kind of malice or ill-will. For example, a mercy killing (where a defendant kills the victim out of compassion) could still involve malice aforethought. There are three issues about the *mens rea* for murder that need elaboration:

Intention

Intention is given the meaning that was discussed in detail in Chapter 3. You should re-read that chapter to obtain a detailed discussion of the law, but it will be summarized again here. Intention is to be given its ordinary meaning or purpose. In most cases it will not be necessary for the judge to give any special direction to the jury on the meaning of intent. In difficult cases where the defendant may not have acted with the purpose of killing or causing grievous bodily harm, but that was an extremely likely result of the defendant's actions, then the jury should be given the *Woollin*[19] direction. That is that the jury may find intention only if the death or grievous bodily harm was a virtually certain result of the defendant's actions and the defendant realized this was so.

Kill or cause grievous bodily harm to the victim

Grievous bodily harm here means really[20] serious harm.[21] The fact that an intention to cause grievous bodily harm is sufficient *mens rea* for murder is controversial. Some commentators think that nothing less than an intention to kill should suffice. We shall discuss this further in Part II.

---

[16] *Adams* [1957] Crim LR 365.
[17] Law Commission Consultation Paper No. 136 (1994) discusses the origins of the rule and the reasons justifying its abolition.
[18] [1982] AC 566 (HL).   [19] [1999] 1 AC 82 (HL).
[20] In *Janjua* [1999] Cr App R 91, the Court of Appeal suggested that it was not a misdirection to describe grievous bodily harm as 'serious harm' in a case where the defendant stabbed the victim with a knife.
[21] *DPP v Smith* [1961] AC 290 (HL).

Although the *mens rea* for murder requires the defendant to intend to kill or cause grievous bodily harm *to the victim*, there is no difficulty in establishing a murder conviction if the defendant intends to kill one person, but in fact kills another. This is because the doctrine of transferred *mens rea* operates and the defendant can be guilty of murder.[22] However, the doctrine of transferred *mens rea* cannot apply in murder if the defendant intended to kill an animal or damage a piece of property, but in fact killed the victim. In such a case there is no murder, although there may be manslaughter.

The *mens rea* of murder, as outlined above, is a product of common law. The most important statutory provision is section 1 of the Homicide Act 1957 which states:

(1) Where a person kills in the course or furtherance of some other offence, the killing shall not amount to murder unless done with the same malice aforethought (express or implied) as is required for a killing to amount to murder when not done in the course or furtherance of another offence.

(2) For the purposes of the foregoing subsection, a killing done in the course or for the purpose of resisting an officer of justice, or of resisting or avoiding or preventing a lawful arrest, or of effecting or assisting an escape or rescue from legal custody, shall be treated as a killing in the course of furtherance of another offence.

As section 1 makes clear, it is no longer sufficient for a murder conviction to show that the defendant killed while committing some other crime.[23] Only an intention to kill or cause grievous bodily harm will do.[24]

QUESTIONS

1. Ralph punches Kirsten, intending to give her a nose bleed. She falls over and bangs her head. Because she has a thin skull she dies. Has Ralph murdered Kirsten?

2. Ewan in a fit of spite forces his former girlfriend, Cameron, who is pregnant, to drink a vile substance. He hopes that the substance will cause the baby to be born seriously disabled. In fact the substance causes Cameron to miscarry. Cameron, overcome with grief, commits suicide. What offences have been committed? (Do not forget to consider here whether the doctrine of transferred *mens rea* could apply.)

3 MANSLAUGHTER: AN INTRODUCTION

Manslaughter is a less serious form of homicide than murder. There are two main kinds of manslaughter:

(1) *Voluntary manslaughter.* These are killings which would be murder but for the existence of defined extenuating circumstances. Here the law is acknowledging that in

---

[22] The doctrine of transferred *mens rea* is discussed at p. 175. At one time it was thought that the doctrine of transferred *mens rea* did not need to be relied on in murder cases because the *mens rea* could be an intention to kill or cause grievous bodily harm (GBH) to anyone, but *Attorney-General's Reference (No. 3 of 1994)* [1997] 3 All ER 936 makes it clear that the *mens rea* for murder is an intention to kill or cause GBH *to the victim* or a general malice (to kill anyone).

[23] This used to be known as constructive malice.   [24] *R v Vickers* [1957] 2 QB 517 (CA).

certain circumstances even though the defendant had the *mens rea* and *actus reus* of murder he or she does not deserve the label 'murderer'.

(2) *Involuntary manslaughter.* These are killings where the defendant does not intend to kill or cause grievous bodily harm but there is sufficient fault to justify criminal liability. The difficulty the courts have found is in defining how little fault is sufficient to justify a manslaughter conviction.

These labels are in fact most misleading. For example, 'involuntary manslaughter' has nothing to do with the concept of involuntariness. Nevertheless the terminology is very widely used.

The following is a complete list of the kinds of manslaughter. The first three are examples of voluntary manslaughter and the last three of involuntary manslaughter:

(1) A defendant who successfully pleads provocation to a charge of murder.

(2) A defendant who successfully pleads diminished responsibility to a charge of murder.

(3) A defendant who successfully pleads suicide pact to a charge of murder.

(4) A defendant convicted of reckless manslaughter.

(5) A defendant convicted of gross negligence manslaughter.

(6) A defendant convicted of constructive (or unlawful act) manslaughter.

EXAMINATION TIP

When answering a problem question on homicide, start by considering whether the defendant has caused the death of the victim. If they have discuss whether the defendant has the *mens rea* of murder. If they have, then consider whether the defendant can rely on a general defence (see Chapter 12) or the defence of provocation or diminished responsibility. If the defendant does not have the *mens rea* of murder examine whether the defendant is guilty of reckless, constructive, or gross negligence manslaughter.

4 PROVOCATION

DEFINITION

Provocation is a defence only to murder, and if successful the defendant will still be guilty of manslaughter.

The defendant must show:

(i) he or she was provoked by something said or done to lose his or her self-control and

(ii) a reasonable person would have done the same thing.

EXAMINATION TIP

Mean examiners have been known to set problem questions which appear to raise issues about the defence of provocation, but the victim is not killed. Remember, provocation is a defence only in a case of murder. If you have a problem question where the defendant could not be guilty of murder you should *not* discuss provocation.

Provocation is a defence only to murder.[25] If the defence is successful then the defendant is still guilty of manslaughter.[26] For other offences, such as assaults, the fact that the defendant was provoked into attacking the victim may be relevant in deciding the appropriate sentence, but it does *not* provide a defence. Even in a case of homicide it is crucial to appreciate that provocation should be considered only if the jury are sure that the defendant is otherwise guilty of murder. If there is evidence from the facts of the case that the defendant was provoked then the prosecution carries the burden of proving that the defence is not made out beyond all reasonable doubt.[27]

Although provocation is a common law partial defence, its operation is governed by section 3 of the 1957 Homicide Act:[28]

> Where on a charge of murder there is evidence on which the jury can find that the person charged was provoked (whether by things done or by things said or by both together) to lose his self-control, the question whether the provocation was enough to make a reasonable man do as he did shall be left to be determined by the jury; and in determining that question the jury shall take into account everything both done and said according to the effect which, in their opinion, it would have on a reasonable man.

As is indicated by section 3, there are two limbs to the defence:

(1) the defendant must show that he or she was provoked to lose his or her self-control and kill by something said or done; and that

(2) a reasonable person would have been provoked to lose his or her self-control and do as the defendant did.

It is important to appreciate that both of these requirements must be satisfied. If an unusually calm defendant facing substantial provocation did not in fact lose his self-control, even though a reasonable person would have done, the defence is not available.

The two limbs of the provocation defence need to be discussed in more detail.

4.1 THE DEFENDANT WAS PROVOKED TO LOSE HIS SELF-CONTROL AND KILL

The need to show that the defendant was provoked to lose his self-control is a subjective question. That is, it requires the jury to look into the mind of the defendant and ask whether the defendant actually lost his self-control, rather than considering whether a reasonable person would have lost his self-control. The issue is not, however, straightforward and there are a number of matters which need to be addressed:

---

[25] Provocation is not a defence to attempted murder: *Bruzas* [1972] Crim LR 367. It is available for a person who is an accomplice to murder: *Marks* [1998] Crim LR 676 (CA).

[26] However, this gives the judge a wide discretion on sentencing, including handing down a non-custodial sentence.

[27] *Cascoe* [1970] 2 All ER 833. This is so even if the defendant does not specifically raise the defence of provocation, if the facts indicate that the defendant was provoked: *Cambridge* [1994] Crim LR 690 (CA); *Scott* [1997] Crim LR 597 (CA).

[28] The Homicide Act 1957, s. 3, does not replace the common law, but supplements and amends it.

The defendant must be provoked

It is not enough for the defendant just to show he lost his self-control. He must show he was provoked by something into losing his self-control. In *Acott*[29] the defendant killed his mother in a frenzied attack. There was clear evidence that he had lost his self-control and killed, but there was no evidence of why that had happened. It appears he had just suddenly 'flipped'. It was held that as there was no evidence of a provoking incident the judge was right not to leave the defence of provocation to the jury.

The provocative trigger must be something said or done

It must be shown that the provocative trigger was something said or done. Words or deeds can amount to provocation,[30] but circumstances on their own cannot. In *Acott*[31] Lord Steyn stated, by way of example, that a person who lost his self-control due to slow down of traffic caused by snow would not be able to use the defence. However, the requirement has been interpreted liberally in some cases. In *Doughty*[32] it was assumed that the crying of a baby could constitute a provocative act: it was something said or done.

The defendant must lose his or her self-control

In understanding the meaning of 'loss of self-control' it is important to recall that to be guilty of murder the defendant must have intended to kill or cause grievous bodily harm. This means that loss of self-control cannot require that the defendant has completely lost control of his or her actions or was so angry that he or she was not aware of what he or she was doing, because if either of these were true then the defendant would not have the *mens rea* or *actus reus* of murder. The Court of Appeal in *Richens*[33] stressed that it is not necessary to show that there was a complete loss of self-control, in the sense that the defendant did not know what he was doing, or was not able to stop himself acting in the way he did. It was sufficient that the defendant was unable to restrain himself.[34]

The defendant must suffer a 'sudden and temporary' loss of self-control

The courts have insisted that provocation should not provide a defence to a defendant who was acting out of a desire for revenge. This concern was expressed by Devlin J in *Duffy*:[35]

> Circumstances which induce a desire for revenge are inconsistent with provocation, since the conscious formulation of a desire for revenge means that a person has the time to think, to reflect, and that would negative a sudden temporary loss of self-control, which is of the essence of provocation.

The basis of the requirement that the defendant has suffered a 'sudden and temporary loss of self-control' is that if there is a gap in time between the provocation and the killing then

---

[29] [1997] 1 All ER 706 (HL).

[30] Section 3 reversed the common law rule that words alone could not amount to provocation: *Holmes v DPP* [1946] AC 588 (HL).

[31] [1997] 2 Cr App R 94, 102.   [32] (1986) 83 Cr App R 319 (CA).   [33] [1993] 4 All ER 877 (CA).

[34] For a strict interpretation of this requirement see *Cocker* [1989] Crim LR 740 (CA).

[35] [1949] 1 All ER 932 at 934.

the law will assume that the defendant killed in anger, not in the heat of passion having lost self-control. This has in recent years come under challenge, particularly in cases involving battered women, where the courts have heard evidence that battered women may suffer a 'slow burn reaction'. This means that they may be provoked, but the anger builds up slowly until suddenly there is an outburst, maybe some time after the provoking incident. This led to a reconsideration of the requirement of a sudden and temporary loss of self-control in the following case:

R v Ahluwalia
[1992] 4 All ER 889 (CA)[36]

Kiranjit Ahluwalia was an Asian woman who had entered an arranged marriage with her husband. She had suffered many years of violence and abuse from him. This included an attempt to kill her. One evening the husband threatened to attack her. That night, while he was asleep Ahluwalia poured petrol over him and set it alight. The husband died from the burns he received. At her trial the judge directed the jury that it had to be shown that Ahluwalia had suffered a sudden and temporary loss of self-control. She appealed, *inter alia*, on the ground that such a direction was incorrect.

Lord Taylor of Gosforth CJ

The phrase 'sudden and temporary loss of self-control' encapsulates an essential ingredient of the defence of provocation in a clear and readily understandable phrase. It serves to underline that the defence is concerned with the actions of an individual who is not, at the moment when he or she acts violently, master of his or her own mind. Mr Robertson suggested that the phrase might lead the jury to think provocation could not arise for consideration unless the defendant's act followed immediately upon the acts or words which constituted the alleged provocation. He submits a direction to this effect would have been inappropriate and inconsistent with a number of authorities (see, for example, *R v Hall* (1928) 21 Cr App R 48, *Lee Chun-Chuen v R* [1963] AC 220 and *Parker v R* [1964] AC 1369).

Nevertheless, it is open to the judge, when deciding whether there is any evidence of provocation to be left to the jury, and open to the jury when considering such evidence, to take account of the interval between the provocative conduct and the reaction of the defendant to it. Time for reflection may show that after the provocative conduct made its impact on the mind of the defendant, he or she kept or regained self-control. The passage of time following the provocation may also show that the subsequent attack was planned or based on motives, such as revenge or punishment, inconsistent with the loss of self-control and therefore with the defence of provocation. In some cases, such an interval may wholly undermine the defence of provocation; that, however, depends entirely on the facts of the individual case and is not a principle of law.

Mr Robertson referred to the phrase 'cooling off period' which has sometimes been applied to an interval of time between the provocation relied upon and the fatal act. He suggests that although in many cases such an interval may indeed be a time for cooling and regaining self-control so as to forfeit the protection of the defence, in others the time lapse has an opposite effect. He submits, relying on expert evidence not before the trial judge, that

---

[36] (1992) 96 Cr App R 133, [1992] Crim LR 63.

women who have been subjected frequently over a period to violent treatment may react to the final act or words by what he calls a 'slow-burn' reaction rather than by an immediate loss of self-control.

We accept that the subjective element in the defence of provocation would not as a matter of law be negatived simply because of the delayed reaction in such cases, provided that there was at the time of the killing a 'sudden and temporary loss of self-control' caused by the alleged provocation. However, the longer the delay and the stronger the evidence of deliberation on the part of the defendant, the more likely it will be that the prosecution will negative provocation.

In the present case, despite the delay after the last provocative act or words by the deceased, and despite the appellant's apparent deliberation in seeking and lighting the petrol, the trial judge nevertheless left the issue of provocation to the jury. His references to 'sudden and temporary loss of self-control' were correct in law. He did not suggest to the jury that they should or might reject the defence of provocation because the last provocative act or word of the deceased was not followed immediately by the appellant's fatal acts.

We consider that the learned judge's direction was in accordance with the well-established law and cannot be faulted.

Mr Robertson's argument in support of this ground of appeal amounted in reality to an invitation to this court to change the law. We are bound by the previous decisions of this court to which reference has been made, unless we are convinced that they were wholly wrong. Where a particular principle of law has been reaffirmed so many times and applied so generally over such a long period, it must be a matter for Parliament to consider any change. There are important considerations of public policy which would be involved should provocation be redefined so as possibly to blur the distinction between sudden loss of self-control and deliberate retribution.

[The Court of Appeal went on to decide that a retrial should be ordered because evidence concerning diminished responsibility was not properly left for consideration by the jury.]

Appeal allowed. Conviction quashed. Retrial ordered.

As the Court of Appeal in *Ahluwalia* made clear, the present law is that while it is still necessary to show that the defendant suffered a loss of self-control as a result of a provocation, the fact that there is a gap in time does not preclude the availability of the defence. It is simply that the longer the time between the provocative incident and the killing the harder it will be to show that there was a 'sudden and temporary loss of self-control' and that this was caused by the provocative incident.[37]

The provocation need not be directed to the defendant, nor come from the victim

Provocation is available even if the provocative act is not done by the victim. That said, it will be hard to show that a reasonable person would have killed X in the face of provocation from Y.[38] Further, the defence is available even if the provocation is aimed at someone else and the defendant loses his self-control. So if Jack shouted a racial insult at George, as a

---

[37] See also *Pearson* [1992] Crim LR 193 (CA); *Bailie* [1995] Crim LR 739 (CA).
[38] *Davies* [1975] QB 691 (CA).

result of which George's wife, Nina, lost her self-control and killed Jack, Nina could rely on provocation. In *Pearson*[39] an older brother discovered that his younger brother had been abused by their father and so helped his brother to kill the father. He was able to rely on provocation.

The provocation can be self-induced

There is some dispute over whether the defence is available if the provocation is self-induced. What would be the law's response if the defendant had racially insulted the victim and in reply the victim had insulted the defendant, who lost his self-control and killed? In other words would it be relevant that the defendant's own acts had caused the provocative words or acts? At one time the Privy Council argued that a defendant could not rely on provocative conduct which was a foreseeable consequence of the defendant's actions.[40] However, this was rejected by the Court of Appeal in *Johnson*[41] which stressed that even if the provocative acts were self-induced the defendant could still seek to use provocation. But it would be up to the jury to decide whether a reasonable person would react to that provocation in the way that the defendant did. In fact, it would be rare that a jury would decide that a reasonable person would respond to a self-induced provocation by killing.[42]

4.2 WOULD A REASONABLE PERSON HAVE ACTED AS THE DEFENDANT DID?

In order to rely successfully on the defence of provocation it is not enough for the defendant just to show that she lost her self-control. It must also be shown that a reasonable person would have reacted to the provocation in the same way as the defendant. This objective[43] question is entirely one for the jury. The judge cannot withdraw the case from the jury on the basis that no jury would sensibly decide that a reasonable person would have killed; although the judge can withdraw the case from the jury on the basis that there was no provocative act.[44] For example, in *Doughty*,[45] where a father killed his baby having been provoked by the crying, although the judge may have felt that no jury could decide that a reasonable man would react in this way, he should not have withdrawn the issue from the jury. It is for the jury, not the judge, to decide how the reasonable man would have reacted.[46]

This objective limb of the test has proved problematic for the law and a number of issues have to be addressed.

Misperceived provocation

The jury should consider how the reasonable person would react to the provocation *as it was understood by the defendant*. If a defendant mishears what was said or misinterprets what was done and believes he has been insulted, he is to be judged on the insult he believed was made, not the words actually used or deeds actually done. There is little case law on this, but

---

[39] *Pearson* [1992] Crim LR 193 (CA).
[40] *Edwards* [1973] AC 648 (PC).   [41] [1989] 1 WLR 740 (CA).
[42] See Ch. 12 for a general discussion of self-induced defences.
[43] For the difference between an objective and subjective question see p. 41.
[44] *Acott* [1997] 1 All ER 706 (HL).   [45] (1986) 83 Cr App R 319 (CA).
[46] Section 3 makes this clear.

the little there is suggests that even if a defendant is unreasonable in his misinterpretation he is still to be judged on the facts as he believed them to be.[47]

Another important point in assessing the nature of the provocative act is that the jury must consider the provocation in the light of the defendant's history.[48] This means that what might appear to be a minor act of provocation, when seen in the light of the history of the event, is deeply insulting. For example, if Alf has repeatedly sexually abused his daughter, Bertha, and one day calls her 'a whore'; this is a far more provocative insult to Bertha, in the context of their relationship, than it would be if he said those words to a stranger. Sometimes the courts have referred to the concept of 'cumulative provocation', where a long series of incidents, each minor in itself, causes the defendant to lose her self-control after being provoked by the 'last straw'.[49]

What characteristics are attached to the reasonable person?

A particularly troublesome issue for the courts has been whether the reasonable person should be endowed with any characteristics of the defendant. Before looking at the present law it is useful to consider why the law does not take the easy approach of just considering how a straightforward normal person would have reacted to the provocation. Two cases have revealed the difficulty with this simple position.

First, in *Bedder v DPP*[50] an impotent man visited a prostitute. The prostitute taunted him about his impotence. He lost his self-control and killed her. The House of Lords explained that the jury should consider how a reasonable man would react to the taunts, and that the reasonable man would not be regarded as impotent. Subsequently it has been accepted that this makes little sense, and that the decision is therefore wrong. The jury can make sense of the provocation only if a reasonable person is endowed with the characteristics which made the provocation provocative. So in *Bedder* it makes no sense to consider how a potent man would react to being called impotent; rather the jury must consider how an impotent man would react to being taunted about his condition. Similarly if a racial insult is uttered it is only sensible to consider how a person of the defendant's race would react to that insult.

Secondly, in *Camplin* a 15-year-old boy was raped by the victim, who then taunted the boy. The House of Lords accepted the argument that a 15-year-old could not be expected to possess the same level of self-control as an adult.

These two cases reveal why the courts have found they cannot take the simple approach and ask simply how would the reasonable person react: we need to give the characteristics of the accused to the reasonable person, in order:

(1) to make a realistic assessment of what would be a reasonable reaction to the provocation; and

(2) to take account of some characteristics of the accused which provide a good explanation of why he or she could not live up to the standard of the reasonable person.

The court have been deeply divided as to which characteristics of the defendant, if any, can be taken into account in deciding whether the reasonable person would have acted as the defendant did. Two main views have been developed in the case law:

---

[47] *Brown* (1776) 168 ER 11; *Letenock* (1917) 12 Cr App R 221.

[48] A point emphasized by Lord Goff in *Morhall* [1996] AC 90 (HL).

[49] Wasik (1982); A. Briggs (1996).   [50] [1954] 1 WLR 1119 (HL).

(1) The Camplin view

Lord Diplock in *Camplin* held:[51]

> a proper direction to a jury ... should state ... that the reasonable man referred to in the question is a person having the power of self-control to be expected of an ordinary person of the sex and age of the accused, but in other respects sharing such of the accused's characteristics as they think would affect the gravity of the provocation to him; and that the question is not merely whether such a person would in like circumstances be provoked to lose his self-control but also whether he would react to the provocation as the accused did.

This test drew a distinction between characteristics of the accused which were relevant when considering the gravity of the provocation (any characteristic which makes the provocation graver for the defendant) and those characteristics which affect the level of self-control (only age and sex). The defendant was permitted to claim that because of his or her characteristics the provocation was more provocative than it would have been otherwise. But the defendant is not permitted to claim that because of his or her characteristics he or she was expected to exercise only a lower degree of self-control than an ordinary person. This may be made clearer by considering the facts of *Roberts*.[52] Roberts was a pre-lingually deaf man who was taunted by others who insulted his intelligence. He was permitted to introduce evidence that deaf people find assumptions that because they are deaf they are stupid particularly provocative, but he was not permitted to introduce evidence that purported to show that pre-lingually deaf people have lower levels of self-control than non-deaf people.

The distinction between allowing characteristics that affect the degree of provocation and characteristics that affect the level of self-control proved problematic, most notably in *Dryden*[53] where the defendant was obsessive and eccentric. The Court of Appeal, following *Camplin*,[54] directed that the jury should consider how a reasonable person who was obsessive and eccentric but with ordinary powers of self-control would react to the provocation. You can imagine the confusion a jury would feel having to apply such a direction. Although in 1995 the House of Lords had confirmed the *Camplin* approach in *Morhall*,[55] the Court of Appeal had been increasingly reluctant to follow it.[56]

(2) The Smith view

The issue went to the House of Lords again in *Smith* and a major reconsideration of the issue was undertaken. The House of Lords, by a majority of three to two, decided that it was for the jury to decide which characteristics of the defendant could be attached to the reasonable person. So, in that case, where the defendant suffered from a depressive illness the jury could ask how a reasonable person suffering from the mental illness would react. Their lordships therefore rejected the distinction between characteristics which could affect the gravity of the provocation and characteristics which could affect the level of self-control expected. Indeed Lord Steyn suggested that it might be easiest for the jury to forget about the reasonable person altogether and ask whether the defendant had 'exercised the degree of

---

[51] [1978] AC 705 (HL).   [52] [1990] Crim LR 122 (CA).   [53] [1995] 4 All ER 987 (CA).
[54] [1978] AC 705 (HL).   [55] [1996] AC 90 (HL).   [56] e.g. *Campbell* [1997] 1 Cr App R 199 (CA).

self-control to be expected of someone in his situation?'[57] The approach of the House of Lords in Smith, then, was much more subjective than that in the *Camplin* test. But notice it was not totally subjective. It was still open for a jury to decide that some characteristics of the defendant would not be relevant. No doubt a jury would be reluctant to consider the defendant's extreme possessiveness towards his girlfriend or his intoxication as relevant factors.[58] Further, even considering all of his characteristics, a jury may still conclude that the defendant could have been expected to control himself.

The leading case is now a decision of the Privy Council, *A-G for Jersey v Holley*, which was heard by nine law lords. It rejected the approach taken by the House of Lords in *Smith* and preferred the *Camplin* approach. The Court of Appeal in *Mohammed*[59] and *James*[60] has accepted that *Holley* represents the current law.

Attorney-General for Jersey v Holley
[2005] UKPC 23[61]

Dennis Holley was a chronic alcoholic. While under the influence of drink he killed his girlfriend and was subsequently charged with her murder. At his trial he sought to rely on the law of provocation. His case was heard under the law of Jersey where the law on provocation was identical to that in England. The judge, in directing the jury, told them that drunkenness that rendered a defendant more susceptible to being provoked was not a factor they could take into account in deciding how a reasonable person would have reacted to a provocation of that gravity.

Lord Nicholls of Birkenhead (giving the speech on behalf of the majority)

1. This appeal from the Court of Appeal of Jersey calls for examination of the law relating to provocation as a defence or, more precisely, as a partial defence to a charge of murder. Jersey law on this subject is the same as English law. In July 2000 the House of Lords considered the ingredients of this defence in the Morgan Smith case (*R v Smith (Morgan)* [2001] 1 AC 146). The decision of the House in that case is in direct conflict with the decision of their Lordships' board in *Luc Thiet Thuan v The Queen* [1997] AC 131.

And the reasoning of the majority in the *Morgan Smith* case is not easy to reconcile with the reasoning of the House of Lords in *R v Camplin* [1978] AC 705 or *R v Morhall* [1996] AC 90. This appeal, being heard by an enlarged board of nine members, is concerned to resolve this conflict and clarify definitively the present state of English law, and hence Jersey law, on this important subject.

. . .

[Lord Nicholls then examined some of the previous case law on provocation]

17. Against this background their Lordships turn to consider the point where the substantial difference in judicial views has emerged. Exceptional excitability or pugnacity is one thing. But what if the defendant is suffering from serious mental abnormality, as in the *Morgan Smith* case where the defendant suffered from severe clinical depression? Is he, for

---

[57] In *Lowe* [2003] EWCA Crim 677 the Court of Appeal approved a direction: 'may the behaviour of Terry Lowe have measured up to the standard of self-control that might reasonably be expected of him, taking into account that he was a 16-year-old boy?'

[58] Pearce [2001] EWCA Crim 2834.   [59] [2005] EWCA Crim 1880.

[60] [2006] EWCA 14.   [61] [2005] 3 WLR 29, [2005] 3 All ER 371, [2005] 2 Cr App R 36.

the purposes of the defence of provocation, to be judged by the standard of a person having ordinary powers of self-control?

18. The view of the minority in the case of *Morgan Smith* is that he is. The standard is a constant, objective standard in all cases. The jury should assess the gravity of the provocation to the defendant. In that respect, as when considering the subjective ingredient of provocation (did the defendant lose his self-control?), the jury must take the defendant as they find him, 'warts and all', as Lord Millett observed. But having assessed the gravity of the provocation to the defendant, the standard of self-control by which his conduct is to be evaluated for the purpose of the defence of provocation is the external standard of a person having and exercising ordinary powers of self-control. That is the standard the jury should apply when considering whether or not the provocation should be regarded as sufficient to bring about the defendant's response to it: see Lord Millett, at p 211.

19. This view accords with the approach applied by their Lordships' board in *Luc Thiet Thuan v The Queen* [1997] AC 131, an appeal from Hong Kong. On a trial for murder the defendant relied on the defences of diminished responsibility and provocation. Medical evidence showed the defendant suffered from brain damage and was prone to respond to minor provocation by losing his self-control and acting explosively. The trial judge directed the jury that this medical evidence was not relevant on the defence of provocation. The jury rejected both defences. The correctness of the judge's direction on provocation was the issue on the appeal. The board, Lord Steyn dissenting, upheld the judge's direction. Lord Goff of Chieveley noted that mental infirmity of the defendant, if itself the subject of taunts by the deceased, may be taken into account as going to the gravity of the provocation. He continued, at p 146:

'But this is a far cry from the defendant's submission that the mental infirmity of a defendant impairing his power of self-control should as such be attributed to the reasonable man for the purposes of the objective test.'

20. The majority view expressed in the *Morgan Smith* case [2001] 1 AC 146 rejects this approach. According to this view, the standard of self-control required by the common law and by the statute is not the constant standard of a person having and exercising ordinary self-control. The required standard is more flexible. The jury should apply the standard of control to be expected of the particular individual. The jury must ask themselves whether the defendant 'exercised the degree of self-control to be expected of someone in his situation' (emphasis added): see Lord Slynn of Hadley, at p 155. Lord Hoffmann expressed the view, at p 163, that the effect of the change in the law made by section 3 of the Homicide Act 1957 was that in future the jury

'were to determine not merely whether the behaviour of the accused complied with some legal standard but could determine for themselves what the standard in the particular case should be.'

Lord Hoffmann continued, at p 173:

'The law expects people to exercise control over their emotions. A tendency to violent rages or childish tantrums is a defect in character rather than an excuse. The jury must think that the circumstances were such as to make the loss of self-control sufficiently excusable to reduce the gravity of the offence from murder to manslaughter. This is entirely a question for the jury. In deciding what should count as a sufficient excuse, they have to apply what they consider to be appropriate standards of behaviour; on the one hand making allowance for human nature and the power of the emotions but, on the other hand, not allowing someone to rely upon his own violent disposition.'

21. **Lord Clyde**, at p 179, expressed the expected standard of self-control in these terms:

'the standard of reasonableness in this context should refer to a person exercising the ordinary power of self-control over his passions which someone in his position is able to exercise and is expected by society to exercise. By position I mean to include all the characteristics which the particular individual possesses and which may in the circumstances bear on his power of control other than those influences which have been self-induced.' (Emphasis added.)

22. This majority view, if their Lordships may respectfully say so, is one model which could be adopted in framing a law relating to provocation. But their Lordships consider there is one compelling, overriding reason why this view cannot be regarded as an accurate statement of English law. It is this. The law of homicide is a highly sensitive and highly controversial area of the criminal law. In 1957 Parliament altered the common law relating to provocation and declared what the law on this subject should thenceforth be. In these circumstances it is not open to judges now to change ('develop') the common law and thereby depart from the law as declared by Parliament. However much the contrary is asserted, the majority view does represent a departure from the law as declared in section 3 of the Homicide Act 1957. It involves a significant relaxation of the uniform, objective standard adopted by Parliament. Under the statute the sufficiency of the provocation ('whether the provocation was enough to make a reasonable man do as [the defendant] did') is to be judged by one standard, not a standard which varies from defendant to defendant. Whether the provocative act or words and the defendant's response met the 'ordinary person' standard prescribed by the statute is the question the jury must consider, not the altogether looser question of whether, having regard to all the circumstances, the jury consider the loss of self-control was sufficiently excusable. The statute does not leave each jury free to set whatever standard they consider appropriate in the circumstances by which to judge whether the defendant's conduct is 'excusable'.

23. On this short ground their Lordships, respectfully but firmly, consider the majority view expressed in the *Morgan Smith* case is erroneous.

Points arising

24. Their Lordships mention some ancillary points. The first is relevant to the facts in the present case. It concerns application of the principles discussed above in circumstances where the defendant acted under the influence of alcohol or drugs and, therefore, at a time when his level of self-control may have been reduced. If the defendant was taunted on account of his intoxication, that may be a relevant matter for the jury to take into account when assessing the gravity of the taunt to the defendant. But the defendant's intoxicated state is not a matter to be taken into account by the jury when considering whether the defendant exercised ordinary self-control. The position is the same, so far as provocation is concerned, if the defendant's addiction to alcohol has reached the stage that he is suffering from the disease of alcoholism.

25. The second point their Lordships wish to mention concerns the three examples given by Lord Steyn in his dissenting opinion in *Luc Thiet Thuan v The Queen* [1997] AC 131, 149. Lord Steyn instanced cases of women who are more prone to lose their self-control because they are suffering from postnatal depression, or 'battered woman syndrome', or a personality disorder. Lord Steyn suggested that, on the majority view of the law expressed in that case, in those three instances the judge would have to direct the jury that on the defence of provocation the evidence of the woman's condition was

admissible on the 'first and subjective inquiry' but not on the 'second and objective inquiry'. Their Lordships respectfully differ. This is not wholly correct. As explained above, the evidence of the woman's condition may be relevant on two issues: whether she lost her self-control, and the gravity of the provocation for her. The jury will then decide whether in their opinion, having regard to the actual provocation and their view of its gravity for the defendant, a woman of her age having ordinary power of self-control might have done what the defendant did. More importantly, in each of these three cases the defendant will in principle have available to her the defence of diminished responsibility. The potential availability of this defence in these cases underlines the importance of not viewing the defence of provocation in isolation from the defence of diminished responsibility. These two defences must be read together to obtain an overall, balanced view of the law in this field.

26. Next, in recent years much play has been made of the 'mental gymnastics' required of jurors in having regard to a defendant's 'characteristics' for one purpose of the law of provocation but not another. Their Lordships consider that any difficulties in this regard have been exaggerated. The question is largely one of presentation. It will be noted that their Lordships have eschewed use of the expression 'characteristics', accompanied as that expression now is with much confusing baggage. The better approach is summarised by Lord Hobhouse of Woodborough in the *Morgan Smith* case [2001] 1 AC 146, 205c–h.

27. The final point is this. In expressing their conclusion above their Lordships are not to be taken as accepting that the present state of the law is satisfactory. It is not. The widely held view is that the law relating to provocation is flawed to an extent beyond reform by the courts: see the Law Commission Report on *Partial Defences to Murder* (Law Com No 290) (2004) (Cm 6301), para 2.10. Their Lordships share this view. But the law on provocation cannot be reformulated in isolation from a review of the law of homicide as a whole. In October 2004 the Home Secretary announced the Government's intention to review the law of murder. Given the importance of this area of the criminal law it is imperative that a review, of all aspects of the law of murder, should be undertaken as soon as possible.

. . . .

Lord Bingham of Cornhill and **Lord Hoffmann** delivered the following dissenting opinion

. . .

44. The reason why provocation was accepted by the judges as a partial defence to a charge of murder has been stated on many occasions over many years. It was a humane concession to human infirmity and imperfection, acknowledgement 'that by reason of the frailty of our nature we cannot always stand upright': see, for example, *R v Hayward* (1833) 6 C & P 157, 159, per Tindal CJ; . . . As was said by Coleridge J in R v Kirkham, at p 117:

'The law requires from him [the defendant] and will allow him to show that there were some mitigating circumstances, which alter the presumed character of the act, because it has at once a sacred regard for human life and also a respect for man's failings, and will not require more from an imperfect creature than he can perform.'

We share the opinion, widely expressed, that the law of homicide stands in urgent need of comprehensive and radical reform. But so long as provocation continues to be recognised as a partial defence to a charge of murder it should be applied consistently with its underlying rationale.

. . .

47. The concept of the reasonable man in this context has been recognised as 'inapt' by Lord Diplock in *Camplin*, at p 716, and by Lord Goff of Chieveley, for the House of Lords, in *R v Morhall* [1996] AC 90, 97–98, for the reason which they gave, that powers of ratiocination bear no obvious relationship to powers of self-control. It may no doubt have been recognition of this inaptness which led Viscount Simon LC to refer in Mancini, at p 9, to 'an ordinary person' and Lord Goddard CJ in *R v McCarthy* [1954] 2 QB 105, 112, to 'an average person'. The public policy underlying adoption of the reasonable man test in the common law doctrine of provocation was to reduce the incidence of fatal violence by preventing a person relying on his own exceptional pugnacity or excitability as an excuse for loss of self-control: see Camplin, p 716, per Lord Diplock, p 726, per Lord Simon of Glaisdale; *Morhall*, at p 98, per Lord Goff of Chieveley. But the reasonable man test, literally applied, is in our opinion subject to an even more fundamental objection. Whatever the position in earlier days, when hot blood and a violent response to perceived injury could be more readily excused, few judges or jurors could now conceive of any circumstances in which a reasonable or ordinary or average person would be provoked to take the life of another with the intent necessary for murder.

. . .

65. The decisions to which we have referred in *Newell, Raven, Ahluwalia, Dryden, Humphreys, Morhall* and *Thornton (No 2)* were, in our respectful opinion, faithful to the principles laid down by the House in *Camplin*. Importantly, they reflected the rationale of the provocation defence, both in its recognition of the sanctity of human life and its allowance for human imperfection. The effect of the decisions was not to abrogate the important safeguard provided by the objective comparison, and there is nothing in these cases to suggest that short temper or undue pugnacity or excitability could begin to excuse the deliberate taking of a human life. The cases do, however, make clear that the objective comparison is a matter for the opinion of the jury, as Parliament had enacted, with such properly expressed judicial guidance as might be appropriate in the particular case. And they make clear, as *Camplin* had done, that the question is not whether the defendant showed such self-control as an abstract hypothetical person would have done but such self-control as would reasonably be expected of a person having such of his attributes as the jury thought relevant in the factual situation in which the defendant actually found himself at the relevant time.

66. We cannot accept that *Luc Thiet Thuan v The Queen* [1997] AC 131 was correctly decided by the majority of the board . . . While Mr Peter Thornton for the respondent in the present appeal, made a number of apt criticisms of the reasoning of the majority, we would respectfully highlight three major points of disagreement, each of them in our view important. (1) The majority judgment gives little or no weight to the rationale of the provocation defence, to which, (as in Bedder) scant reference was made. . . . (2) We cannot reconcile the majority's reading of the speeches in Camplin with what their Lordships said in that case, discussed at some length above. The majority [1997] AC 131, 140–141, attribute to the House in Camplin acceptance of Professor Ashworth's observation ('The Doctrine of Provocation' [1976] CLJ 292, 300) that

'The proper distinction . . . is that individual peculiarities which bear on the gravity of the provocation should be taken into account, whereas individual peculiarities bearing on the accused's level of self-control should not'

leading the majority to conclude, at p 144, that

'there is no basis upon which mental infirmity on the part of the defendant which has the effect of reducing his powers of self-control below that to be expected of an ordinary person can, as such, be attributed to the ordinary person for the purposes of the objective test in provocation.'

There is, however, nothing in the report of argument or the speeches to suggest that the House in *Camplin* was referred to the article of Professor Ashworth, and consideration of the gravity of the provocation cannot rationally and fairly be divorced from consideration of the effect of the provocation on the particular defendant in relation to both limbs of the defence. Otherwise one is not comparing like with like, and is losing sight of the essential question whether, in all the circumstances, the defendant's conduct was to some degree excusable. (3) We would not accept that the defences of diminished responsibility and provocation are as sharply demarcated as the majority, at pp 146–147, suggest. It is note-worthy that Lord Simon in his speech in Camplin [1978] AC 705, 726–727, quoted with approval para 53 of a Working Paper of the Criminal Law Revision Committee on Offences against the Person (August 1976):

'In this country the law on this matter [provocation] has been indirectly affected by the introduction of the defence of diminished responsibility. It is now possible for a defendant to set up a combined defence of provocation and diminished responsibility, the practical effect being that the jury may return a verdict of manslaughter if they take the view that the defendant suffered from an abnormality of mind and was provoked. In practice this may mean that a conviction of murder will be ruled out although the provocation was not such as would have moved a person of normal mentality to kill.'

The neat demarcation favoured by the majority might be persuasive if sections 2 and 3 of the 1957 Act (reproduced in articles 3 and 4 of the Jersey Law) had a common origin, but this is not so: section 2 was based on rules developed in the Scottish courts (not recommended for adoption by the Royal Commission) and section 3 on the recommendation of the Royal Commission already referred to. There is, as Lord Hoffmann pointed out in *R v Smith (Morgan)* [2001] 1 AC 146, 168, nothing to suggest that Parliament considered the possibility of overlap between the two defences. In practice the defences have routinely been advanced in tandem, as in *Newell, Dryden* and *Morhall*. In *R (Farnell) v Criminal Cases Review Commission* [2003] EWHC 835 (Admin), 15 April 2003, Mitchell J considered (para 9 of his judgment) that the two defences of diminished responsibility and provocation were 'certainly not mutually exclusive'. If the jury conclude that the defendant has not discharged the burden imposed upon him to establish that his responsibility for a killing was substantially diminished by an abnormality of mind from which he was suffering (a test heavily criticised by much expert psychiatric opinion: see para 5.44 of the Final Report of the Law Commission on *Partial Defences to Murder* (August 2004) (Law Com No 290) (Cm 6301)) there is no reason of logic or fairness why the jury should not, on appropriate evidence, consider, with reference to both limbs of the provocation defence, whether the prosecution have excluded the possibility that the mental characteristics or personal history of the defendant may have rendered him susceptible to provocation in a way which a person without those charac-teristics and that history might not have been, so as to render his conduct to some degree more excusable.

67. The division of opinion expressed in *Luc Thiet Thuan* [1997] AC 131 was repeated in *R v Smith (Morgan)* [2001] 1 AC 146. We would accept the decision of the majority, for the reasons which they gave and which it is unnecessary to repeat. We are of course aware that the majority decision in *R v Smith (Morgan)* has attracted much adverse comment, and we have already recognised (para 44) that the law of homicide stands in urgent need of

comprehensive and radical reform: see, for example, Blom-Cooper & Morris, *With Malice Aforethought* (2004). We must however administer the law as it is, and we consider that the reasoning of the majority in *Smith (Morgan)* is loyal to the rationale of the provocation defence, faithful to the principles laid down in *Camplin* [1978] AC 705 and consistent with the correct interpretation of section 3 of the 1957 Act which meant, as Lord Diplock pointed out in *Camplin*, at p 716, that the reasonable man test fell to be applied now in the context of a law of provocation significantly different from what it had been before the Act was passed. That the majority reasoning lends itself to clear, sensible and intelligible directions is in our opinion exemplified in the direction of Hallett J quoted by the Court of Appeal in *R v Weller* [2004] 1 Cr App R 1, para 20, and Mantell LJ, giving the judgment of the court, succinctly described what we regard as the correct approach, in paras 16–17:

'16. In our view it is to be concluded from the majority speeches in Smith that the question whether the defendant should reasonably have controlled himself is to be answered by the jury taking all matters into account. That includes matters relating to the defendant, the kind of man he is and his mental state, as well as the circumstances in which the death occurred. The judge should not tell the jury that they should, as a matter of law, ignore any aspect. He may give them some guidance as to the weight to be given to some aspects, provided he makes it clear that the question is one which, as the law provides, they are to answer, and not him.

'17. This approach has the considerable advantage that it is unnecessary to determine whether what has been called a "characteristic" of the accused is an eligible characteristic for the purposes of the second element in provocation, the objective element, or is one of which no account should be taken. It avoids categorising human defects into one category or the other, which would otherwise be necessary and is surely artificial. We refer in particular to the difficulties which arose in *R v Dryden* [1995] 4 All ER 987 and to *R v Humphreys* [1995] 4 All ER 1008. It is all a matter for the jury.'

Lord Carswell delivered the following dissenting opinion

69. I also regret that I do not find it possible to join in the opinion expressed by the majority of the board. I fully agree with the reasons given and the conclusions reached in the dissenting opinion of my noble and learned friends, Lord Bingham of Cornhill and Lord Hoffmann, and wish to add only a few brief reasons of my own.

. . .

71. In developing the criminal law the courts should strive to meet three important criteria: its principles should fit a logical pattern; it should be capable of explanation to a jury; and, above all, it should achieve justice. My concern is that the law of provocation accepted as correct by the majority of the board fails to meet these criteria.

72. The dichotomy expressed by the board in *Luc Thiet Thuan v The Queen* [1997] AC 131, and approved by the majority in the present appeal, was neatly expressed by Professor A J Ashworth in his influential article 'The Doctrine of Provocation' [1976] CLJ 292, 300:

'The proper distinction . . . is that individual peculiarities which bear on the gravity of the provocation should be taken into account, whereas individual peculiarities bearing on the accused's level of self-control should not.'

I cannot myself see any convincing logical ground for this distinction. . . .

73. For the reasons set out in the opinion of Lord Bingham of Cornhill and Lord Hoffmann I consider that the view which they take of the law, in agreement with that of the majority in

R v Smith (Morgan) [2001] 1 AC 146, is consistent with the terms of section 3 of the Homicide Act 1957 and its analogue article 4 of the Homicide (Jersey) Law 1986. I hold the very clear view that the dichotomy between the gravity of the provocation and the level of self-control in reaction cannot readily be made comprehensible to a jury by the directions fashioned by a judge with the greatest care and clarity. I am unable to agree with the majority judgment in the present appeal (para 26) that 'any difficulties in this regard have been exaggerated'. I am rather in wholehearted agreement with the remark of Thomas J in the New Zealand case of *R v Rongonui* [2000] 2 NZLR 385, 446 that most trial judges had seen

'the glazed look in the jurors' eyes as, immediately after instructing them that it is open to them to have regard to the accused's alleged characteristic in assessing the gravity of the provocation, they are then advised that they must revert to the test of the ordinary person and disregard that characteristic when determining the sufficiency of the accused's loss of self-control.'

The formula is not only opaque (per Lord Hoffmann in *R v Smith (Morgan)* [2001] 1 AC 146, 173), but even if it can be comprehended by an intelligent jury, they are more than likely to ask themselves how they can sensibly decide whether an ordinary person would have reacted as the defendant did if he would not have found the acts or words provocative in the first place.

74. That is not to say that the solution adopted by the majority in *R v Smith (Morgan)* is free of difficulties. The most fundamental one is the interpretation of section 3 of the 1957 Act, which gives the appearance of requiring an objective test. Yet once one rejects the notion that the comparison should be made with an abstract, hypothetical reasonable man, there is in my opinion sufficient ground for the majority's solution. It has been said that this gives insufficient weight to the standards of society, but it enables the jury, who for that purpose are a microcosm of society as a whole, to apply their standards of justice. Concerns have also been expressed about the relationship between the defence of diminished responsibility provided for in section 2 of the 1957 Act and that of provocation in section 3. There has been unease at the possibility that a defence of provocation may be made out of an unproved case of diminished responsibility. But the defences are not in my opinion mutually exclusive and in practice they are commonly run in tandem.

This is not unacceptable in principle, for the two defences not only have different historical antecedents, but differ in the burden and standard of proof.

. . .

77. I should not like to leave this case without registering my strong agreement with both the majority and minority that the law of homicide needs comprehensive and fundamental reform. It is a patchwork of rules which makes coherent direction of juries unnecessarily difficult and reflects no credit on our legal system. Judges are bound to apply the law as it is, but that does not prevent one from reminding the world at large and the legislature in particular, that there is a real risk that the present law, containing as it does so many difficulties in its application, may cause injustice in individual cases, even where it is faithfully and correctly communicated to a jury. I do not propose to dilate upon the alternatives, a unified offence of unlawful killing or permitting the jury to return a verdict of murder with mitigating circumstances, allied with the abolition of the mandatory death penalty. They do exist, however, and the adoption of one or other would simplify the law, removing the need for the extended discussion of the minutiae of provocation and the differences of opinion among judges. The latter I genuinely regret, but as the law stands I must join the dissent.

The Privy Council in *Holley* have, therefore, returned to the view in *Camplin*. A defendant's characteristics can be relevant in assessing the gravity of the provocation, but not as affecting the level of self-control. In *Mohammed*[62] the Court of Appeal recently had to consider a case of a father who had killed his daughter. The father was described as a strict, angry, devout Muslim, who lost his self-control on discovering that his daughter was seeing a man. The Court of Appeal explained that the defendant's temperament was relevant in assessing the gravity of the provocation: it was more provocative for a strict, devout Muslim father to discover his daughter was dating, than for a placid non-religious father. But his temperament could not be taken into account in assessing the level of self-control expected of someone facing a provocation of that gravity. His age and sex were the only factors that could be considered as affecting the degree of self-control expected.

We shall see in Part II that the Law Commission have suggested that the law in this area needs to be reformed.

Would the ordinary person have done as the defendant did?

The jury have to decide whether the reasonable person would have done as the defendant did. This was interpreted rather literally in *Clarke*[63] where the Court of Appeal had to deal with a defendant who strangled the victim and then electrocuted her. The Court of Appeal took the view that it must be shown not just that the reasonable person would have killed, but that he or she would have killed the victim in the way in which the defendant did and indeed would have disposed of the corpse in the same way. So in *van Dongen*[64] the Court held that even if a reasonable person might have reacted violently he or she would not have given the victim fifteen head wounds, most of them while the victim was defenceless on the ground.

QUESTIONS

1. Following a brain injury suffered in a car crash Mick finds that he suffers from moments of intense irritability. One day Paul calls him a 'short tempered idiot', following which Mick flies into a terrible rage and kills Paul. Is Mick guilty of murder?

2. Professor Bach is a psychologist who specializes in techniques to control anger. A colleague describes his latest book as 'utter rubbish', Bach loses his temper and kills him. Can the jury expect Bach to exhibit a higher level of self-control than ordinary self-control?

3. Why should gender affect the level of self-control expected?

5 DIMINISHED RESPONSIBILITY

DEFINITION

Diminished responsibility is a defence only to murder and, if successful, reduces the charge to manslaughter.

Diminished responsibility: the defendant must show that he or she suffered from:

---

[62] [2005] EWCA 1880.   [63] [1991] Crim LR 383 (CA).   [64] [2005] Crim LR 971 (CA).

(i)   an abnormality of mind

(ii) arising from

    (a) an arrested or retarded development of the mind; or

    (b) an inherent cause; or

    (c) an injury or disease;

(iii) which substantially impaired the defendant's responsibility for his or her actions.

Diminished responsibility is a defence only to murder.[65] Even then it is only a partial defence. If successfully raised the accused will be acquitted of murder, but convicted of manslaughter.[66] The significance of this is that on sentencing for manslaughter the judge has a discretion as to the appropriate sentence, while for murder only the life sentence can be imposed.

Diminished responsibility is defined in section 2(1) of the Homicide Act 1957:

> Where a person kills or is a party to the killing of another, he shall not be convicted of murder if he was suffering from such abnormality of mind (whether arising from a condition of arrested or retarded development of mind or any inherent causes or induced by disease or injury) as substantially impaired his mental responsibility for his acts and omissions in doing or being a party to the killing.

It should be stressed that if the defendant wishes to raised the defence of diminished responsibility the burden of proof of establishing the defence is on him, but only on a balance of probabilities.[67] This has been held to be consistent with Article 6(2) of the European Convention on Human Rights because the prosecution is required to prove the elements of murder and the burden on the defendant of raising the defence of diminished responsibility rests on him only if he wishes to raise it.[68] Indeed the judge should not instruct the jury about diminished responsibility unless the defendant has consented to it being raised.[69]

In practice if the defendant pleads guilty to manslaughter on the ground of diminished responsibility the prosecution will often accept such a plea and not seek to disprove it.[70] However, the Court of Appeal in *Vinagre*[71] has stated that the prosecution should do this only where there is clear evidence of the defendant's mental abnormality. If there is not the jury should be presented with the evidence and be left to decide whether there is evidence of diminished responsibility or whether the defendant must be convicted of murder.

There are three requirements that must be met if a defendant wishes to rely on diminished responsibility:

(1)   He or she was suffering from an abnormality of mind.

(2)   The abnormality of mind was caused by one of the factors in section 2(1).

---

[65] Diminished responsibility is not a defence to attempted murder: *Campbell* [1997] Crim LR 495 (CA). Diminished responsibility cannot be relied upon if the defendant has been found unfit to plead under the Criminal Procedure (Insanity and Unfitness to Plead) Act 1991: *R v Antoine* [2000] 2 All ER 208 (HL).
[66] Homicide Act 1957, s. 2(3).   [67] Homicide Act 1957, s. 2(2); *Dunbar* [1958] 1 QB 1.
[68] *R v Ali; R v Jordan* [2001] 2 WLR 211 (CA).   [69] *Campbell* (1986) 84 Cr App R 255 (CA).
[70] Dell (1982: 814).   [71] (1979) 69 Cr App R 164 (CA).

(3) As a result of the abnormality his or her responsibility for his or her acts was substantially impaired.

These requirements will now be considered in further detail, although it is worth mentioning at this point that in practice the section has been interpreted flexibly to ensure that those thought deserving of a defence by doctors or lawyers are provided with one.[72]

5.1 'ABNORMALITY OF MIND'

This term was usefully discussed in the following case:

R v Byrne
[1960] 2 QB 396 (CA)[73]

The appellant had strangled a girl in a youth hostel and horrifically mutilated her dead body. Medical evidence showed that the appellant was a sexual psychopath, which meant that he suffered from violent perverted sexual desires which he found it difficult or impossible to control. This mental abnormality was said by expert evidence not to amount to insanity, but was caused by an arrested or retarded development of the mind or inherent causes. The issue for the Court of Appeal was whether this amounted to diminished responsibility.

Lord Parker CJ

It is against that background of the existing law that s. 2 (1) of the Homicide Act, 1957, falls to be construed. . . . 'Abnormality of mind', which has to be contrasted with the time-honoured expression in the *M'Naghten* Rules 'defect of reason', means a state of mind so different from that of ordinary human beings that the reasonable man would term it abnormal. It appears to us to be wide enough to cover the mind's activities in all its aspects, not only the perception of physical acts and matters and the ability to form a rational judgment whether an act is right or wrong, but also the ability to exercise will-power to control physical acts in accordance with that rational judgment. The expression 'mental responsibility for his acts' points to a consideration of the extent to which the accused's mind is answerable for his physical acts which must include a consideration of the extent of his ability to exercise will-power to control his physical acts.

Whether the accused was at the time of the killing suffering from any 'abnormality of mind' in the broad sense which we have indicated above is a question for the jury. On this question medical evidence is, no doubt, of importance, but the jury are entitled to take into consideration all the evidence including the acts or statements of the accused and his demeanour. They are not bound to accept the medical evidence if there is other material before them which, in their good judgment, conflicts with it and outweighs it. The aetiology of the abnormality of mind (namely, whether it arose from a condition of arrested or retarded development of mind or any inherent causes or was induced by disease or injury) does, however, seem to be a matter to be determined on expert evidence. Assuming that the jury

---

[72] For a very thorough consideration of the defence of diminished responsibility see Mackay (1995: ch. 4).
[73] [1960] 3 All ER 1, [1960] 3 WLR 440, (1960) 44 Cr App R 246.

are satisfied on the balance of probabilities that the accused was suffering from 'abnormality of mind' from one of the causes specified in the parenthesis of the subsection, the crucial question nevertheless arises: was the abnormality such as substantially impaired his mental responsibility for his acts in doing or being a party to the killing? This is a question of degree and essentially one for the jury. Medical evidence is, of course, relevant but the question involves a decision, not merely whether there was some impairment of the mental responsibility of the accused for his acts, but whether such impairment can properly be called 'substantial', a matter on which juries may quite legitimately differ from doctors.

Furthermore, in a case where the abnormality of mind is one which affects the accused's self-control, the step between 'he did not resist his impulse' and 'he could not resist his impulse' is, as the evidence in this case shows, one which is incapable of scientific proof. A fortiori, there is no scientific measurement of the degree of difficulty which an abnormal person finds in controlling his impulses. These problems, which in the present state of medical knowledge are scientifically insoluble, the jury can only approach in a broad, common-sense way. This court has repeatedly approved directions to the jury which have followed directions given in Scots cases where the doctrine of diminished responsibility forms part of the common law. We need not repeat them. They are quoted in R. v. Spriggs [1958] 1 Q.B. 270. They indicate that such abnormality as 'substantially impairs his mental responsibility' involves a mental state which in popular language (not that of the M'Naghten Rules) a jury would regard as amounting to partial insanity or being on the border-line of insanity.

It appears to us that the learned judge's direction to the jury that the defence under s. 2 of the Act was not available . . . amounted to a direction that difficulty or even inability of an accused person to exercise will-power to control his physical acts could not amount to such abnormality of mind as substantially impaired his mental responsibility. For the reasons which we have already expressed, we think that this construction of the Act is wrong. Inability to exercise will-power to control physical acts, provided that it is due to abnormality of mind from one of the causes specified in the parenthesis in the subsection, is, in our view sufficient to entitle the accused to the benefit of the section; difficulty in controlling his physical acts, depending on the degree of difficulty, may be. It is for the jury to decide on the whole of the evidence whether such inability or difficulty has, nor as a matter of scientific certainty but on the balance of probabilities, been established and, in the case of difficulty, whether the difficulty is so great as to amount in their view to a substantial impairment of the accused's mental responsibility for his acts. The direction in the present case thus withdrew from the jury the essential determination of fact which it was their province to decide.

As already indicated, the medical evidence as to the appellant's ability to control his physical acts at the time of the killing was all one way. The evidence of the revolting circumstances of the killing and the subsequent mutilations, as of the previous sexual history of the appellant, pointed, we think plainly, to the conclusion that the appellant was what would be described in ordinary language as on the border-line of insanity or partially insane. Properly directed, we do not think that the jury could have come to any other conclusion than that the defence under s. 2 of the Homicide Act, 1957, was made out. The appeal will be allowed and a verdict of manslaughter substituted for the verdict of murder. The only possible sentence, having regard to the tendencies of the appellant, is imprisonment for life. The sentence will, accordingly, not be disturbed.

Appeal allowed. Sentence confirmed.

As *Byrne* makes clear, the notion of an abnormality of the mind involves considering whether the defendant's mind is sufficiently different from a normal mind to be classified as abnormal. This appears to give the jury a wide discretion, although the defendant's abnormality must be established on the basis of medical evidence.[74] What made Byrne's mind abnormal was not his lack of awareness of what he was doing, but that it was impossible or very difficult for him to control his behaviour. The concept of diminished responsibility is therefore quite different from insanity, which involves defendants who do not know what they are doing or do not know that what they are doing is wrong.[75] Although in *Byrne* Lord Parker CJ used the term partial insanity, subsequently the Court of Appeal has warned that in some cases such a term may confuse the jury and should be avoided.[76]

5.2 THE CAUSE OF THE ABNORMALITY OF MIND

It must be shown that the abnormality arose in one of three ways:[77]

(1) *Arrested or retarded development of mind.* To fall into this category the condition must be permanent.[78]

(2) *Any inherent causes.* This covers all mental disorders which do not have an external cause, and includes functional disorders.[79] This category can be interpreted broadly. In *Vinagre*[80] the defendant was found to have killed his wife while suffering from 'Othello syndrome', defined as 'morbid jealousy for which there was no cause'.

(3) *Induced by disease or injury.* This includes organic mental disorder[81] and diseases of the brain. A mental impairment caused by taking medically prescribed pills does not constitute an 'injury'.[82] However the following have been regarded as falling within this category: battered women's syndrome;[83] pre-menstrual syndrome;[84] post-natal depression; and stress produced by caring for a terminally ill relative.[85]

The reason the mental abnormality must result from one of the listed causes is that otherwise a defendant who was intoxicated or acting under a strong emotion (e.g. anger) might be able to argue that he or she was suffering from an abnormality of the mind.[86]

5.3 SUBSTANTIAL IMPAIRMENT OF RESPONSIBILITY

It must be shown that the abnormality of mind substantially impaired the defendant's mental responsibility. When considering this question the jury should bear in mind that diminished responsibility is a partial defence; in other words that a defendant relying on it is not claiming that he was blameless, because even if successful the defendant will still be guilty of manslaughter. What needs to be shown is not necessarily that the defendant was incapable of controlling his behaviour, but rather that it was substantially more difficult for

---

[74] *Dix* (1981) 74 Cr App R 306 (CA).   [75] See Ch. 12 for discussion of insanity.
[76] *Seers* (1984) 79 Cr App R 261 (CA).
[77] If the abnormality is not caused in one of the three ways listed in the statute the defence will not be available: *King* [1965] 1 QB 443 (CA).
[78] *Egan* [1992] 4 All ER 470 (CA).   [79] *Sanderson* (1994) 98 Cr App R 325 (CA).
[80] (1979) 69 Cr App R 104 (CA).   [81] *Sanderson* (1994) 98 Cr App R 325 (CA).
[82] *O'Connell* [1997] Crim LR 683 (CA).   [83] *Hobson* [1998] Cr App R 31 (CA).
[84] *Smith* [1982] Crim LR 531.   [85] Edwards (1988: 456).
[86] Although in *Asher, The Times*, 9 June 1981, where a defendant acting under extreme jealousy was able to rely on the defence of provocation.

him to control his behaviour than it would have been for other people.[87] In practice the jury probably ask themselves whether, in the light of the defendant's mental state, he does not deserve the stigma of murder but rather of manslaughter.[88] With this is mind it is understandable that the jury were willing to convict the Yorkshire Ripper of murder, despite strong evidence that he was a paranoid schizophrenic; but that juries are willing to allow mercy killers, who appear to suffer from no particular mental abnormality, to use the defence.[89] This has led to criticism of diminished responsibility that it is too unpredictable and blurs medical and moral issues, a matter which will be examined in Part II.

5.4 DIMINISHED RESPONSIBILITY AND INTOXICATION

How should a jury deal with a case when at the time of the killing the defendant was both suffering from an abnormality of mind and intoxicated? The House of Lords has recently issued authoritative guidance on this issue.[90]

R v Dietschmann
[2003] UKHL 10 (HL)[91]

Anthony Dietschmann was charged with the murder of Nicholas Davies. At the time of the killing he was drunk, but also suffered from an adjustment disorder caused by grief. At trial he sought to rely on the defence of diminished responsibility. The trial judge directed the jury that diminished responsibility could be relied upon as a defence only if the defendant had satisfied them that if he had not taken drink he would have killed as he did, while suffering from diminished responsibility. The jury convicted Dietschmann. The Court of Appeal dismissed the appellant's appeal.

Lord Hutton (with whom their other Lordships agreed)
[5] . . . The question (which I have divided into two parts) certified by the Court of Appeal as a point of law of general importance is as follows:

'(1) Does a defendant seeking to prove a defence of diminished responsibility under s. 2(1) of the 1957 Act in a case where he had taken drink prior to killing the victim, have to show that if he had not taken drink (a) he would have killed as he in fact did; and (b) he would have been under diminished responsibility when he did so?

'(2) If not, what direction ought to be given to a jury as to the approach to be taken to self-induced intoxication which was present at the material time in conjunction with an abnormality of mind which falls within s. 2(1) of the 1957 Act?'

No issue arises on this appeal in relation to the principle stated as follows by Rose LJ in the judgment of the Court of Appeal in the present case (at [13]):

'The general rule that drink does not give rise to an abnormality of mind due to inherent causes was authoritatively established in *R v Fenton* (1975) 61 Cr App R 261 and confirmed in

---

[87] *Lloyd* [1967] 1 QB 175 (CA) and *Byrne* [1960] 2 QB 396 (CA). [88] Butler Committee (1975).
[89] Prins (1983).   [90] Virgo (2003b) discusses the decision.   [91] [2003] 1 All ER 897.

R v Gittens [1984] 3 All ER 252, [1984] QB 698. In line with those authorities, *R v Tandy* [1989] 1 All ER 267, [1989] 1 WLR 350 established that drink is only capable of giving rise to a defence under s 2 if it either causes damage to the brain or produces an irresistible craving so that consumption is involuntary.'

The Interpretation of s. 2(1) of the 1957 Act

[18] In a case where the defendant suffered from an abnormality of mind of the nature described in s. 2(1) and had also taken alcohol before the killing and where (as the Court of Appeal held in this case) there was no evidence capable of establishing alcohol dependence syndrome as being an abnormality of mind within the subsection, the meaning to be given to the subsection would appear on first consideration to be reasonably clear. I would read the subsection to mean that if the defendant satisfies the jury that, notwithstanding the alcohol he had consumed and its effect on him, his abnormality of mind substantially impaired his mental responsibility for his acts in doing the killing, the jury should find him not guilty of murder but (under sub-s. 3) guilty of manslaughter. I take this view because I think that in referring to substantial impairment of mental responsibility the subsection does not require the abnormality of mind to be the sole cause of the defendant's acts in doing the killing. In my opinion, even if the defendant would not have killed if he had not taken drink, the causative effect of the drink does not necessarily prevent an abnormality of mind suffered by the defendant from substantially impairing his mental responsibility for his fatal acts.

. . .

[41] Therefore I would answer the first part of the certified question in the negative. As regards the second part of the question, without attempting to lay down a precise form of words as the judge's directions are bound to depend to some extent on the facts of the case before him, I consider that the jury should be directed along the following lines:

'Assuming that the defence have established that the defendant was suffering from mental abnormality as described in s. 2, the important question is: did that abnormality substantially impair his mental responsibility for his acts in doing the killing? You know that before he carried out the killing the defendant had had a lot to drink. Drink cannot be taken into account as something which contributed to his mental abnormality and to any impairment of mental responsibility arising from that abnormality. But you may take the view that both the defendant's mental abnormality and drink played a part in impairing his mental responsibility for the killing and that he might not have killed if he had not taken drink. If you take that view, then the question for you to decide is this: has the defendant satisfied you that, despite the drink, his mental abnormality substantially impaired his mental responsibility for his fatal acts, or has he failed to satisfy you of that? If he has satisfied you of that, you will find him not guilty of murder but you may find him guilty of manslaughter. If he has not satisfied you of that, the defence of diminished responsibility is not available to him.'

[43] Accordingly, for the reasons which I have given, I would remit the case to the Court of Appeal for that court to decide whether to allow the appeal and quash the conviction for murder and order a new trial or to substitute a verdict of guilty of manslaughter for the verdict of murder found by the jury and to pass an appropriate sentence for that offence.

Appeal allowed.

So, the House of Lords took a simple approach to cases of drunken defendants who suffer from an abnormality of mind and seek to rely on the defence of diminished responsibility: the jury must simply ask whether, despite the drink, the mental abnormality of mind substantially impaired the defendant's mental responsibility.[92]

As Lord Hutton noted, there are only two circumstances in which the effects of alcohol can themselves be regarded as an abnormality of the mind:

(1) where the taking of alcohol has actually damaged the brain; or

(2) the defendant's taking of alcohol was involuntary. So if the defendant is an alcoholic and suffers irresistible cravings such that every drink of the drinking session was involuntarily taken then it may be possible to claim that the effects of the drink are an abnormality of the mind.[93]

FURTHER READING

Griew, E. (1988), 'The Future of Diminished Responsibility', *Criminal Law Review* 75.

Mackay, R. (1995), *Mental Condition Defences in the Criminal Law* (Oxford: OUP).

—— (2000), 'Diminished Responsibility and Mentally Disordered Killers' in A. Ashworth and B. Mitchell (eds.), *Rethinking English Homicide Law* (Oxford: OUP).

Sparks, R. (1964), ' "Diminished Responsibility" in Theory and Practice', *Modern Law Review* 27: 9.

Sullivan, G.R. (1994b), 'Intoxicants and Diminished Responsibility', *Criminal Law Review* 156.

6 SUICIDE PACT

Section 4 of the Homicide Act 1957 provides that if the defendant kills another in pursuance of a suicide pact he or she is guilty of manslaughter, not murder. The definition of a suicide pact is found in section 4(3):

> a common agreement between two or more persons having for its object the death of all of them, whether or not each is to take his own life, but nothing done by a person who enters into a suicide pact shall be treated as done by him in pursuance of the pact unless it is done while he has the settled intention of dying in pursuance of the pact.

An example of a suicide pact is where a husband and wife agree that they will die together. The plan is that the husband will shoot his wife and then turn the gun on himself. He kills his wife, but a passer-by stops the husband killing himself, or he loses his nerve and cannot do it. In such a case the husband could face a charge of murdering his wife. If he could show that he shot his wife in pursuance of a suicide pact, as defined above, then his charge would be reduced to manslaughter.[94] It should be noted that under section 2(1) of the Suicide Act 1961 there is an offence of aiding, abetting, counselling, or procuring the suicide of another,

---

[92] *Roberts* [2005] EWCA 155.   [93] *Tandy* (1988) Cr App R 45 (CA).
[94] The burden of proof is on the accused: Homicide Act 1957, s. 4(2).

and this carries a maximum penalty of fourteen years.[95] So a person who helps another commit suicide as part of a suicide pact will simply be convicted of this offence, suicide pact being a defence only to a charge of murder. The Law Commission has recommended the abolition of the defence of suicide pact as part of their reform of the law of homicide.[96]

FURTHER READING

Wheat, K. (2000), 'The Law's Treatment of the Suicidal', *Medical Law Review* 8: 182.

7 MERCY KILLING AND EUTHANASIA

Mercy killing and euthanasia are widely used terms to describe situations where the defendant kills a person who is suffering from a terminal illness. The ethical issues are very different where the victim is consenting to the killing and where the victim is not.[97] However, the law is straightforward: there is no defence of mercy killing in English criminal law.[98] It is murder to do an act which significantly shortens a person's life, even if that person is in agony and asks to be killed. The House of Lords has recently confirmed that the Human Rights Act 1998 has not changed the position.[99] There is no 'right to die' under the European Convention on Human Rights. However the following points must be appreciated fully to grasp the present law:

(1) If the patient is competent and asks for treatment to be withdrawn (e.g. asking for a ventilation machine to be switched off) then the doctors must follow the patient's wishes, even if as a result the patient will die. This is because although a patient does not have a right to permit others to do acts which will cause her death, she does have the right to refuse treatment and let 'nature take its course'.[100]

(2) If the patient is incompetent a doctor can withdraw treatment, if to do so would be in a patient's best interests.[101]

(3) It appears to be lawful for a doctor to administer a pain-relieving drug which will shorten the patient's life by a few hours, providing that the doctor's primary purpose is to relieve pain.[102]

(4) Relatives who kill those they have been caring for over a long period of time may be able to rely on the defence of diminished responsibility if they can be shown to have been suffering from an abnormality of the mind.[103]

(5) Suicide is no longer a crime, but assisting someone to commit suicide is an offence.[104]

---

[95] It is also an offence to attempt to commit this offence: *McShane* (1977) 66 Cr App R 97.

[96] Law Commission Consultation Paper No. 177 (2005: 5.69).

[97] House of Lords Select Committee on Medical Ethics (1994: paras. 259–60) opposed the creation of a new defence of mercy killing.

[98] It was proposed in Criminal Law Revision Committee 14th Report, para. 115.

[99] *R (Pretty) v DPP (Secretary of State for the Home Department intervening)* [2002] 1 FCR 1 (HL); upheld in the European Court of Human Rights: *Pretty v UK* [2002] FCR 97.

[100] *Re B (Adult: Refusal of Medical Treatment)* [2002] 2 All ER 449.

[101] *Airedale National Health Service Trust v Bland* [1993] AC 789 (HL). In *An NHS Trust v M; An NHS Trust v H* [2001] 2 FLR 367 it was confirmed that to do so would not infringe the patient's right to life under Art. 2 of the European Convention on Human Rights.

[102] See *Moor* (11 May 1999, unreported), discussed in Arlidge (2000).

[103] Though see *Cocker* [1989] Crim LR 740 (CA).   [104] Suicide Act 1961.

FURTHER READING

Ost, S. (2005), 'Euthanasia and the Defence of Necessity', *Criminal Law Review* 355.

Pretty v Director of Public Prosecutions (Secretary of State for the Home Department intervening) [2001] UKHL 61.

8 INFANTICIDE

The legal term 'infanticide' is a little odd, because it is the name of both an offence and a defence. The prosecution may choose to charge the defendant with infanticide. But if it charges the defendant with murder she can raise infanticide as a defence. If successful, she will be guilty of the offence of infanticide (rather than manslaughter). It is possible for a defendant to be convicted of attempted infanticide.[105]

The offence or defence is described in section 1(1) of the Infanticide Act 1938:

> Where a woman by any wilful act or omission causes the death of her child being a child under the age of twelve months, but at the time of the act or omission the balance of her mind was disturbed by reason of her not having fully recovered from the effect of giving birth to the child or by reason of the effect of lactation consequent upon the birth to the child, then, notwithstanding that the circumstances were such that but for this Act the offence would have amounted to murder, she shall be guilty of . . . infanticide, and may for such an offence be dealt with and punished as if she had been guilty of the offence of the manslaughter of the child.

The offence concerns the voluntary killing of a child under the age of one year by her mother. It is most often used where the defendant kills her child while suffering from post-natal depression.[106] Although section 1(1) talks about the disturbance being caused by the birth of the child, in fact post-natal depression is rarely caused by the birth *per se,* but this is overlooked by the courts.[107] The maximum sentence for the offence is life imprisonment, although most cases are dealt with by a probation order.[108] The defence is available only to mothers. Fathers who kill, suffering from the stresses of parenthood, will need to rely on the defence of diminished responsibility. It should also be noted that the defence is available only if the child killed is under the age of twelve months.

9 CONSTRUCTIVE MANSLAUGHTER

DEFINITION

To be guilty of constructive manslaughter the defendant must be proved to have performed an act which was:

(a) unlawful;

(b) dangerous; and

(c) caused the death of the victim.

---

[105] *Smith* [1983] Crim LR 739.   [106] Mackay (1995: 207–14).   [107] Maier-Katkin and Ogle (1993).
[108] e.g. *Sainsbury and Lewis* [1990] Crim LR 903. See also Mackay (1993: 213–14).

The term constructive manslaughter indicates that the crime is constructed from liability for a lesser crime. It is based on the theory that if a person kills in the course of committing a crime then he deserves to be guilty of manslaughter. This kind of manslaughter is sometimes known as 'unlawful act manslaughter'.

The House of Lords undertook a thorough examination of constructive manslaughter in the following case:

Attorney-General's Reference (No. 3 of 1994)
[1998] AC 245 (HL)[109]

B stabbed his girlfriend (M) whom he knew was pregnant. Sixteen days after the stabbing M went into labour. The child, born grossly premature, managed to survive for 121 days in intensive care but eventually died. B was charged with the murder of the child. The House of Lords held that he could not be convicted of murder (see p. 176 for a discussion of that aspect of the case). In this extract Lord Hope considers whether B could be convicted of constructive manslaughter.

Lord Hope of Craighead

The *actus reus*

I have no difficulty in finding in the facts of this case all the elements which were needed to establish the *actus reus* both of murder and manslaughter. The *actus reus* of a crime is not confined to the initial deliberate and unlawful act which is done by the perpetrator. It includes all the consequences of that act, which may not emerge until many hours, days or even months afterwards. In the case of murder by poisoning, for example, there is likely to be an interval between the introduction of the victim to the poison and the victim's death. There may be various stages in the process between each of which time will elapse. The length of the interval is not now important: Law Reform (Year and A Day Rule) Act 1996. What is needed in order to complete the proof of the crime is evidence of an unbroken chain of causation between the defendant's act and the victim's death. Although we cannot now know, as the Court of Appeal have pointed out, whether the jury would have been satisfied on the issue of causation, there was clearly a sufficient case to go to the jury on this matter. There was a respectable body of medical evidence that the child was born prematurely as a result of the stabbing, and that it was as a result of the prematurity of her birth that she died. It was not disputed that injury to a foetus before birth which results in harm to the child when it is born can give rise to criminal responsibility for that injury. So the fact that the child was not yet born when the stabbing took place does not prevent the requirements for the actus reus from being satisfied in this case, both for murder and for manslaughter, in regard to her subsequent death.

The *mens rea*

The difficult issues all relate to the question whether B had the *mens rea* which would be required for him to be guilty of the child's murder or manslaughter. . . .

---

[109] [1997] 3 All ER 936, [1997] 3 WLR 421, [1998] 1 Cr App R 91, [1997] Crim LR 829.

Murder

I have had the advantage of reading in draft the speech which has been prepared by my noble and learned friend, Lord Mustill. I gratefully adopt his analysis of the rules for the crime of murder and of their historical origin, and I agree entirely with the conclusion which he has reached that the *mens rea* for murder was not present in this case. . . .

Manslaughter

Criminal homicide is divided by common law into two separate crimes of murder and manslaughter. Manslaughter itself can be divided into various categories, depending on the context for the exercise. In regard to *mens rea* it is usually convenient to distinguish between (I) cases where the defendant intended to injure the deceased and (2) cases where the defendant had no such intention. Within the first category there are the cases (a) where he intended to cause grievous bodily harm to his victim but his criminal responsibility is reduced on the ground of provocation at the time of the act; and (b) where he intended to cause only minor harm to the victim but death ensues as a result of his act unexpectedly. Within the second category there are the cases (a) where the defendant's act was not unlawful but the death of the victim was the result of negligence of such a gross nature as to be categorised as criminal; and (b) where the defendant's act was both unlawful and dangerous because it was likely to cause harm to some person. The present case is an example of unlawful act manslaughter. But the placing of it into this category does no more than touch the surface of the problem where the ultimate victim of that act was not the intended victim and, moreover, was not even alive when the unlawful act was perpetrated.
. . .

So far as *mens rea* for the common law crime of manslaughter is concerned, I consider that it is sufficient that at the time of the stabbing B had the mens rea which was needed to convict him of an assault on the child's mother. That was an unlawful act, and it was also an act which was dangerous in the sense indicated by Humphreys J in *Rex v Larkin* (1943) 29 Cr App R 18, 23 in the passage which was quoted with approval by Lord Salmon in *Director of Public Prosecutions v Newbury* [1977] AC 500, 506–507. Dangerousness in this context is not a high standard. All it requires is that it was an act which was likely to injure another person. As 'injury' in this sense means 'harm,' the other person must also be a living person. A person who is already dead cannot be harmed any longer, so injury of the kind which is required is no longer possible. That is why it was held in *Reg v Church* [1966] 1 QB 59 that it was a misdirection for the *jury* to be told simply that it was irrelevant to manslaughter whether or not the appellant believed that the woman whom he, threw into the river was already dead. But in this case injury to another living person—the child's mother—was the inevitable result of B's deliberate and unlawful act. Such was the character of the *mens rea* which B possessed when he committed the initial act in the series of events which resulted in the death of the child.

. . . Nor is it necessary, in order to constitute manslaughter, that the death resulted from an unlawful and dangerous act which was done with the intention to cause the victim to sustain harm. This is because it is clear from the authorities that, although the defendant must be proved to have intended to do what he did, it is not necessary to prove that he knew that his act was unlawful or dangerous. So it must follow that it is unnecessary to prove that he knew that his act was likely to injure the person who died as a result of it. All that need be proved is that he intentionally did what he did, that the death was caused by it and that, applying an objective test, all sober and reasonable people would recognise the risk that some harm would result.

...

The only questions which need to be addressed are (1) whether the act was done intentionally, (2) whether it was unlawful, (3) whether it was also dangerous because it was likely to cause harm to somebody and (4) whether that unlawful and dangerous act caused the death.

I think, then, that the position can be summarised in this way. The intention which must be discovered is an intention to do an act which is unlawful and dangerous. In this case the act which had to be shown to be an unlawful and dangerous act was the stabbing of the child's mother. There can be no doubt that all sober and reasonable people would regard that act, within the appropriate meaning of this term, as dangerous. It is plain that it was unlawful as it was done with the intention of causing her injury. As B intended to commit that act, all the ingredients necessary for *mens rea* in regard to the crime of manslaughter were established, irrespective of who was the ultimate victim of it. The fact that the child whom the mother was carrying at the time was born alive and then died as a result of the stabbing is all that was needed for the offence of manslaughter when actus reus for that crime was completed by the child's death. The question, once all the other elements are satisfied, is simply one of causation. The defendant must accept all the consequences of his act, so long as the jury are satisfied that he did what he did intentionally, that what he did was unlawful and that, applying the correct test, it was also dangerous. The death of the child was unintentional, but the nature and quality of the act which caused it was such that it was criminal and therefore punishable. In my opinion that is sufficient for the offence of manslaughter. There is no need to look to the doctrine of transferred malice for a solution to the problem raised by this case so far as manslaughter is concerned.

As Lord Hope's speech indicates, there are three elements of constructive manslaughter:

(1) The defendant must have done an unlawful act.

(2) The unlawful act must have been dangerous.

(3) The unlawful and dangerous act must have caused the death of the victim.

These will now be considered separately:

9.1 AN UNLAWFUL ACT

It is necessary to show that there is a criminal act. The prosecution in a case of constructive manslaughter should make it clear which criminal offence is being relied upon.[110] It is not enough for the act to be a tort or a breach of contract; the act must be criminal, but not necessarily an act of violence.[111] The defendant must be shown

---

[110] *Jennings* [1990] Crim LR 588. Although *obiter* in *Kennedy* [1999] Crim LR 65 (CA) the Court of Appeal appeared to overlook this and suggested that it was sufficient if the accused's acts were tainted with illegality, even if there was not an identifiable criminal act (relying on *Cato* (1976) Cr App R 41). These *dicta* are inconsistent with the clear statement of Lord Hope in *Attorney-General's Reference (No. 3 of 1994)* [1997] 3 All ER 936 that an unlawful act is an essential element of constructive manslaughter.

[111] *Franklin* (1893) 15 Cox CC 163; *DPP v Andrews* [1937] AC 576 (HL). In *Goodfellow* (1986) 83 Cr App R 23 (CA) criminal damage was the unlawful act.

to have committed both the *actus reus* and the *mens rea* and not have a defence to the crime.[112]

In *Andrews v DPP* a driver killed a pedestrian, while overtaking another car. It was accepted that the defendant was guilty of the offence of dangerous driving. The House of Lords stated that for constructive manslaughter an act which was intrinsically criminal was required and not just 'a lawful act with a degree of carelessness which the legislature makes criminal'.[113] This *dictum* is hard to interpret, but the generally accepted view seems to be that a strict liability offence[114] or an offence of negligence (e.g. dangerous driving) cannot form the basis of constructive manslaughter.[115]

There is some debate whether constructive manslaughter could arise from a criminal omission. There is no clear view. In *Senior*[116] the defendant failed to summon medical help for his child, who later died, and this was accepted as manslaughter. However, subsequently in *Lowe*[117] the defendant also failed to call for medical assistance for a dying child, but the Court of Appeal suggested that constructive manslaughter could not be based on an omission.[118] In practice if the case does involve an omission the prosecution may choose to present the case as one of gross negligence manslaughter, which undoubtedly can be committed by omission.[119]

9.2 DANGEROUS ACT

The unlawful act must be dangerous. This means that the act constitutes a risk of physical injury. A risk of an emotional harm (e.g. fear or panic) is insufficient,[120] unless it is likely that that emotional distress will lead to a physical injury, for example by causing a heart attack.

Dangerousness is to be judged objectively. This means that there is no need to show that the defendant was aware that his act was dangerous; the question is whether a reasonable person in the defendant's shoes would appreciate that it was dangerous.[121] This is demonstrated by *Dawson*.[122] The defendant approached a petrol station which was staffed by a 50-year-old man. The defendant was armed with an imitation gun and the victim suffered a heart attack and died. The jury should have been asked whether a reasonable person in the defendant's shoes would have realized that his actions were likely to create a risk of physical injury.[123] The test is not quite a straightforward objective test. The jury should consider whether a reasonable person in the defendant's shoes *with any special knowledge that the defendant has* would have realized that the victim might suffer a physical injury. So,

---

[112] *Slingsby* [1995] Crim LR 570. The defendant engaged in some rough sexual activity with the victim. The accused wore a signet ring which unintentionally caused her a serious injury. It was held that here the behaviour was consented to and so did not constitute an assault. There could therefore be no conviction for constructive manslaughter.

[113] [1937] AC 576 at 584 (HL).

[114] Although in *Andrews* [2003] Crim LR 477 (CA) the Court of Appeal upheld a conviction for unlawful act manslaughter on the basis of a strict liability issue. The issue was not raised before the court.

[115] *Lamb* [1967] 2 QB 981 (CA). Negligent acts could, in an extreme case, amount to gross negligence manslaughter, which will be discussed later.

[116] [1899] 1 QB 283.   [117] [1973] QB 702 (CA).

[118] Contrast the view of Ashworth (2003: 294–5) with Allen (2003: 312).

[119] *Khan and Khan* [1998] Crim LR 830 (CA).

[120] Although this represents the law on the present authorities, it might be arguable that following the acceptance by the House of Lords in *Ireland* [1998] AC 147 (see p. 338) that actual bodily harm could include psychiatric injuries, it is not impossible that the issue could be open to re-examination.

[121] *Church* [1966] 1 QB 59 (CA).   [122] (1985) 81 Cr App R 150 (CA).

[123] *Watson* [1989] 2 All ER 865 (CA).

if the facts in *Dawson* had been different and the defendant had known that the petrol station attendant had a weak heart, then the court would certainly have found the act dangerous.[124]

An important case in this area is *Lamb*.[125] The accused and his friend were playing with a loaded gun. The accused checked that there was no bullet opposite the firing pin, and pulled the trigger. He had not appreciated that the chamber revolves when shot and so the chamber with a bullet moved to opposite the pin and the gun went off and his friend was shot. It was confirmed that although the act was dangerous (a reasonable person would have known that the gun might go off) there was no unlawful act (he lacked *mens rea*) and so he could not be convicted of manslaughter.[126]

9.3 CAUSATION

It is necessary to show that the unlawful and dangerous act caused the death of the victim. The normal rules of causation apply, for which see Chapter 2.

At one time it was suggested that the defendant's unlawful and dangerous act had to be 'aimed at' the victim.[127] This was rejected by Lord Hope in *Attorney-General's Reference (No. 3 of 1994)*[128] who confirmed that as long as there is an unlawful and dangerous act which causes the victim's death it does not matter if the act was directed towards someone else. So if the defendant pushes one person who falls over and knocks into someone else who also falls over and dies, constructive manslaughter is available.[129]

It must be shown that it was the unlawful and dangerous act of the accused that caused the death of the victim, and not simply that the victim died while the defendant was committing an unlawful and dangerous act. This appears to have been overlooked in *Cato*[130] where the defendant supplied unlawful drugs to the victim and then injected the victim with the drugs as a result of which the victim died. The Court of Appeal suggested that the unlawful act could be seen as the possession.[131] With respect, this is hard to support. The possession did not cause the death. The better basis for a manslaughter conviction, which the Court of Appeal suggested as an alternative analysis, was that the injection by the accused was the offence of poisoning contrary to section 23 of the Offences Against the Person Act 1861. This unlawful and dangerous act was the act that caused the death.[132]

We shall now turn to gross negligence manslaughter, but before doing so note that the concepts of constructive manslaughter and gross negligence manslaughter are not mutually exclusive.[133] In other words it is possible for a person to be guilty of manslaughter of both kinds at the same time.

---

[124] Ibid. However the unreasonable mistaken beliefs of the defendant are not to be attributable to the reasonable person in the defendant's shoes: *Ball* [1989] Crim LR 730.

[125] [1967] 2 QB 981 (CA).

[126] There was no assault because both boys were playing and there was no intention to frighten or cause harm.

[127] *Dalby* [1982] 1 All ER 916 (CA).   [128] [1997] 3 All ER 936 (HL).

[129] This actually happened in *Mitchell* (1983) 76 Cr App R 293 (CA), as a result of which the defendant was convicted of manslaughter.

[130] [1976] 1 WLR 110 (CA).

[131] It is unclear how the possession itself could be regarded as dangerous.

[132] Contrast *Kennedy* [2005] EWCA 685 where a rather strained analysis of causation was used to convict of manslaughter a drug supplier who supplied drugs which the accused took.

[133] *Willoughby* [2004] EWCA Crim 3365.

10 GROSS NEGLIGENCE MANSLAUGHTER

DEFINITION

For gross negligence manslaughter it must be shown that:

1. the defendant owed the victim a duty of care;

2. the defendant breached that duty of care;

3. the breach of the duty caused the death of the victim;

4. the breach was so gross as to justify a criminal conviction.

The leading case on gross negligence manslaughter is the House of Lords decision in *Adomako*.[134]

R v Adomako
[1995] 1 AC 171 (HL)[135]

Adomako was an anaesthetist who failed to notice for six minutes that a tube that supplied oxygen to his patient had become disconnected from the ventilator. As a result, the patient died. He was convicted of gross negligence manslaughter, but appealed on the basis that the judge had misdirected the jury.

Lord Mackay of Clashfern LC

The jury convicted the appellant of manslaughter by a majority of 11 to 1. The Court of Appeal, Criminal Division dismissed the appellant's appeal against conviction but certified that a point of law of general public importance was involved in the decision to dismiss the appeal, namely:

'In cases of manslaughter by criminal negligence not involving driving but involving a breach of duty is it a sufficient direction to the jury to adopt the gross negligence test set out by the Court of Appeal in the present case following *R v Bateman* (1925) 19 Cr App R 8 and *Andrews v DPP* [1937] AC 576 without reference to the test of recklessness as defined in *R v Lawrence* [1982] AC 510 or as adapted to the circumstances?'

[Having quoted from *R v Bateman* (1925) 19 Cr App R 8 and *Andrews v DPP* [1937] AC 576 Lord Mackay continued:]

In my opinion the law as stated in these two authorities is satisfactory as providing a proper basis for describing the crime of involuntary manslaughter. . . . On this basis in my opinion the ordinary principles of the law of negligence apply to ascertain whether or not the defendant has been in breach of a duty of care towards the victim who has died. If such breach of duty is established the next question is whether that breach of duty caused the death of the victim. If so, the jury must go on to consider whether that breach of duty should be characterised as gross negligence and therefore as a crime. This will depend on the seriousness of the breach of duty committed by the defendant in all the circumstances in which the defendant was placed when it occurred. The jury will have to consider whether the

---

[134] For a summary of the law prior to *Adomako* see Ashworth (2003: 297).
[135] [1994] 3 All ER 79, [1994] 3 WLR 288, [1994] Crim LR 757.

extent to which the defendant's conduct departed from the proper standard of care incumbent upon him, involving as it must have done a risk of death to the patient, was such that it should be judged criminal.

It is true that to a certain extent this involves an element of circularity, but in this branch of the law I do not believe that is fatal to its being correct as a test of how far conduct must depart from accepted standards to be characterised as criminal. This is necessarily a question of degree and an attempt to specify that degree more closely is I think likely to achieve only a spurious precision. The essence of the matter, which is supremely a jury question, is whether, having regard to the risk of death involved, the conduct of the defendant was so bad in all the circumstances as to amount in their judgment to a criminal act or omission.

. . .

I consider it perfectly appropriate that the word 'reckless' should be used in cases of involuntary manslaughter, but as Lord Atkin put it 'in the ordinary connotation of that word'. Examples in which this was done, to my mind, with complete accuracy are *R v Stone, R v Dobinson* [1977] QB 354 *and R v West London Coroner, ex p Gray* [1988] QB 467.

In my opinion it is quite unnecessary in the context of gross negligence to give the detailed directions with regard to the meaning of the word 'reckless' associated with *R v Lawrence* [1982] AC 510. The decision of the Court of Appeal, Criminal Division in the other cases with which they were concerned at the same time as they heard the appeal in this case indicates that the circumstances in which involuntary manslaughter has to be considered may make the somewhat elaborate and rather rigid directions inappropriate. I entirely agree with the view that the circumstances to which a charge of involuntary manslaughter may apply are so various that it is unwise to attempt to categorise or detail specimen directions. For my part I would not wish to go beyond the description of the basis in law which I have already given.

In my view the summing up of the learned judge in the present case was a model of clarity in analysis of the facts and in setting out the law in a manner which was readily comprehensible by the jury. The summing up was criticised in respect of the inclusion of the following passage:

'Of course you will understand it is not for every humble man of the profession to have all that great skill of the great men in Harley Street but, on the other hand, they are not allowed to practise medicine in this country unless they have acquired a certain amount of skill. They are bound to show a reasonable amount of skill according to the circumstances of the case, and you have to judge them on the basis that they are skilled men, but not necessarily so skilled as more skilful men in the profession, and you can only convict them criminally if, in your judgment, they fall below the standard of skill which is the least qualification which any doctor should have. You should only convict a doctor of causing a death by negligence if you think he did something which no reasonably skilled doctor should have done.'

The criticism was particularly of the latter part of this quotation in that it was open to the meaning that if the defendant did what no reasonably skilled doctor should have done it was open to the jury to convict him of causing death by negligence. Strictly speaking this passage is concerned with the statement of a necessary condition for a conviction by preventing a conviction unless that condition is satisfied. It is incorrect to treat it as stating a sufficient condition for conviction. In any event I consider that this passage in the context was making the point forcefully that the defendant in this case was not to be judged by the standard of more skilled doctors but by the standard of a reasonably competent doctor. There were many other passages in the summing up which emphasised the need for a high degree of negligence if the jury were to convict and read in that context I consider that the summing up cannot be faulted.

For these reasons I am of the opinion that this appeal should be dismissed and that the certified question should be answered by saying:

'In cases of manslaughter by criminal negligence involving a breach of duty, it is a sufficient—direction to the jury to adopt the gross negligence test set out by the Court of Appeal in the present case following *R v Bateman* (1925) 19 Cr App R 8 and *Andrews v DPP* [1937] AC 576 and it is not necessary to refer to the definition of recklessness in *R v Lawrence* [1982] AC 510, although it is perfectly open to the trial judge to use the word "reckless" in its ordinary meaning as part of his exposition of the law if he deems it appropriate in the circumstances of the particular case.'

. . .

Personally I would not wish to state the law more elaborately than I have done. In particular I think it is difficult to take expressions used in particular cases out of the context of the cases in which they were used and enunciate them as if applying generally. This can I think lead to ambiguity and perhaps unnecessary complexity. The task of trial judges in setting out for the jury the issues of fact and the relevant law in cases of this class is a difficult and demanding one. I believe that the supreme test that should be satisfied in such directions is that they are comprehensible to an ordinary member of the public who is called to sit on a jury and who has no particular prior acquaintance with the law. To make it obligatory on trial judges to give directions in law which are so elaborate that the ordinary member of the jury will have great difficulty in following them, and even greater difficulty in retaining them in his memory for the purpose of application in the jury room, is no service to the cause of justice. The experienced counsel who assisted your Lordships in this appeal indicated that as a practical matter there was a danger in over-elaboration of definition of the word 'reckless'. While therefore I have said in my view it is perfectly open to a trial judge to use the word 'reckless' if it appears appropriate in the circumstances of a particular case as indicating the extent to which a defendant's conduct must deviate from that of a proper standard of care, I do not think it right to require that this should be done and certainly not right that it should incorporate the full detail required in *R v Lawrence* [1982] AC 510.

Appeal dismissed.

The ruling in *Adomako* was recently challenged before the Court of Appeal in *Misra* on two grounds. First, it was said to be inconsistent with the House of Lords' decision in *R v G and R*. Secondly it was argued that it was inconsistent with the European Convention on Human Rights. The Court of Appeal rejected both challenges and confirmed that *Adomako* represents the current law on gross negligence manslaughter.

R v Misra
[2004] EWCA Crim 2375[136]

Amit Misra and Rajeev Srivastava appealed to the Court of Appeal against two convictions for gross negligence manslaughter of Sean Phillips. Mr Phillips had undergone surgery at a hospital, but become infected with staphylococcus aureus. Misra and Srivastava were senior house officers involved in the care of the deceased. The prosecution

---

[136] [2005] 1 Cr App R 21.

alleged that their failure to diagnose and treat the victim's infection caused his death. The essence of the prosecution case was that not only did the appellants fail to diagnose the condition from which the deceased was suffering, but that they failed to even appreciate that their patient was serious ill.

Before the Court of Appeal, the appellants developed two main arguments. The first was that the offence of gross negligence manslaughter was so vague that it contravened Article 5 of the European Convention of Human Rights (see p. 60 for a development of this argument). The second was that following the decision of the House of Lords in *R v G* (see p. 160) the definition of gross negligence manslaughter had to be reassessed.

Judge LJ

. . .

49. No issue arises whether both appellants owed a duty of care to the deceased, or were negligently in breach of it. There was however helpful argument about the nature of the relevant risk. Was it, as the judge directed the jury in the present case 'serious risk to life', or was it much broader, extending to serious risk to safety as well as life? In its original formulation in Bateman, Lord Hewitt CJ referred to 'disregard to the life and safety of others' in the sense of serious injury. In Seymour, the risk was confined to the risk of death. In *Stone* [1977] QB 554 and *West London Coroner, ex parte Gray* [1988] QB 467 reference was made to risks in broader terms, extending to health and welfare. Although Lord Mackay spoke in approving terms of these decisions in a different context, it is clear that his approval was directed to the deployment of the word 'reckless'. He was not addressing, and it would have been inconsistent with his own analysis of the legal principles if he were approving, the wider basis for identifying risk described in *Stone* and *West London Coroner ex parte Gray*. It is also striking that Lord Mackay did not expressly adopt or approve the broader formulation of risk made by Lord Taylor CJ in *Prentice*. Since *Adomako*, this issue has been addressed in this court, in *R v Singh (Gurphal)* [1999] CLR 582 and the Divisional Court in *Lewin v CPS*, unreported, 24 May 2002. In *Gurphal Singh*, this court strongly approved the trial judge's direction in a case of manslaughter by gross negligence that 'the circumstances must be such that a reasonably prudent person would have foreseen a serious and obvious risk not merely of injury, even serious injury, but of death'. In *Lewin*, the Divisional Court applied that direction.

50. Mr David Perry, on behalf of the Attorney General, informed us that, as a matter of policy, when making a decision whether to prosecute for this offence in cases like the present, the Director of Public Prosecutions looks for evidence of an obvious risk of death, and that, if the extent of the risk were limited to the obvious risk of serious injury, and no more, prosecution would not follow.

51. The editors of *Blackstone's Criminal Practice* suggest that the law needs clarification, and that, if it were clarified, some 'degree of symmetry' between murder and manslaughter would be achieved if, for the purposes of gross negligence manslaughter, the risk should extend to grievous bodily harm. Professor Smith took the contrary view, suggesting that 'if we are to have an offence of homicide by gross negligence at all, it seems right that it should be . . . limited. The circumstances must be such that a reasonably prudent person would have foreseen a serious risk, not merely of injury, even serious injury, but of death'.

52. There will, of course, be numerous occasions when these distinctions are entirely theoretical. From time to time, however, they will be of great significance, not only to the decision whether to prosecute, but also to the risk of conviction of manslaughter. In our judgment, where the issue of risk is engaged, *Adomako* demonstrates, and it is now

clearly established, that it relates to the risk of death, and is not sufficiently satisfied by the risk of bodily injury or injury to health. In short, the offence requires gross negligence in circumstances where what is at risk is the life of an individual to whom the defendant owes a duty of care. As such it serves to protect his or her right to life.

. . .

55. It is convenient now to address the argument that the decision in *R v G and Another* should lead us to reassess whether gross negligence manslaughter should now be replaced by and confined to reckless manslaughter. As we have shown, precisely this argument by Lord Williams of Mostyn was rejected in *Adomako*. We also note, first, that Parliament has not given effect to possible reforms on this topic discussed by the Law Commission and, second, notwithstanding that *Adomako* was cited in argument in *R v G and Another*, it was not subjected to any reservations or criticisms. Indeed in his speech Lord Bingham of Cornhill emphasised that in *R v G* he was not addressing the meaning of 'reckless' in any other statutory or common law context than section 1(1)and (2) of the Criminal Damage Act 1971. In these circumstances, although we gave leave to Mr Gledhill to amend his grounds of appeal to enable him to deploy the argument, we reject it.

56. We can now reflect on Mr Gledhill's associated contention that if recklessness is not a necessary ingredient of this offence, the decision in *Attorney General's Reference (No. 2 of 1999)* [2000] QB 796 led to the unacceptable conclusion that manslaughter by gross negligence did not require proof of any specific state of mind, and that the defendant's state of mind was irrelevant. In our judgment the submission is based on a narrow reading of the decision that a defendant may properly be convicted of gross negligence manslaughter in the absence of evidence as to his state of mind. However when it is available, such evidence is not irrelevant to the issue of gross negligence. It will often be a critical factor in the decision (see *R (Rowley) v DPP* [2003] EWHC 693). In *Adomako* itself, Lord Mackay directed attention to 'all' of the circumstances in which the defendant was placed: he did not adopt, or endorse, or attempt to redefine the list of states of mind to which Lord Taylor CJ referred in *Prentice*, which was not in any event 'exhaustive' of possible relevant states of mind. It is therefore clear that the defendant is not to be convicted without fair consideration of all the relevant circumstances in which his breach of duty occurred. In each case, of course, the circumstances are fact-specific.

57. Mr Gledhill nevertheless contended that even so, the problem of *mens rea* remains. This, he argued was a necessary, but absent ingredient of the offence. We have reflected, of course, that if the defendant intends death or really serious harm, and acts in such a way to cause either, and death results, he would be guilty of murder. If he intends limited injury, and causes death, he would be guilty of manslaughter in any event. We are here concerned with the defendant who does not intend injury, but who in all the contemporaneous circumstances is grossly negligent. As a matter of strict language, '*mens rea*' is concerned with an individual defendant's state of mind. Speaking generally, negligence is concerned with his failure to behave in accordance with the standards required of the reasonable man. Looked at in this way, the two concepts are distinct. However the term '*mens rea*' is also used to describe the ingredient of fault or culpability required before criminal liability for the defendant's actions may be established. In *Sweet v Parsley* [1970] AC 132, Lord Reid explained that there were occasions when gross negligence provided the 'necessary mental element' for a serious crime. Manslaughter by gross negligence is not an absolute offence. The requirement for gross negligence provides the necessary element of culpability.

58. We can now return to the argument based on circularity and uncertainty, and the application of Articles 6 and 7 of the ECHR. . . .

[Judge LJ then referred to Lord Mackay's speech in *Adomako*]

59. Mr Gledhill suggested that this passage demonstrated that an additional specific ingredient of this offence was that the jury had to decide whether the defendant's conduct amounted to a crime. If the jury could, or was required to, define the offence for itself, and accordingly might do so on some unaccountable or unprincipled or unexplained basis, to adopt Bacon, the sound given by the law would indeed be uncertain, and would then strike without warning. Mr Gledhill's argument then would be compelling.

60. Looking at the authorities since Bateman, the purpose of referring to the differences between civil and criminal liability, whether in the passage in Lord Mackay's speech to which we have just referred, or in directions to the jury, is to highlight that the burden on the prosecution goes beyond proof of negligence for which compensation would be payable. Negligence of that degree could not lead to a conviction for manslaughter. The negligence must be so bad, 'gross', that if all the other ingredients of the offence are proved, then it amounts to a crime and is punishable as such.

. . .

62. Accordingly, the value of references to the criminal law in this context is that they avoid the danger that the jury may equate what we may describe as 'simple' negligence, which in relation to manslaughter would not be a crime at all, with negligence which involves a criminal offence. In short, by bringing home to the jury the extent of the burden on the prosecution, they ensure that the defendant whose negligence does not fall within the ambit of the criminal law is not convicted of a crime. They do not alter the essential ingredients of this offence. A conviction cannot be returned if the negligent conduct is or may be less than gross. If however the defendant is found by the jury to have been grossly negligent, then, if the jury is to act in accordance with its duty, he must be convicted. This is precisely what Lord Mackay indicated when, in the passage already cited, he said, '. . . The jury must go on to consider whether that breach of duty should be characterised as gross negligence and therefore as a crime' (our emphasis). The decision whether the conduct was criminal is described not as 'the' test, but as 'a' test as to how far the conduct in question must depart from accepted standards to be 'characterised as criminal'. On proper analysis, therefore, the jury is not deciding whether the particular defendant ought to be convicted on some unprincipled basis. The question for the jury is not whether the defendant's negligence was gross, and whether, additionally, it was a crime, but whether his behaviour was grossly negligent and consequently criminal. This is not a question of law, but one of fact, for decision in the individual case.

63. On examination, this represents one example, among many, of problems which juries are expected to address on a daily basis. They include equally difficult questions, such as whether a defendant has acted dishonestly, by reference to contemporary standards, or whether he has acted in reasonable self-defence, or, when charged with causing death by dangerous driving, whether the standards of his driving fell far below what should be expected of a competent and careful driver. These examples represent the commonplace for juries. Each of these questions could be said to be vague and uncertain. If he made enquiries in advance, at most an individual would be told the principle of law which the jury would be directed to apply: he could not be advised what a jury would think of the individual case, and how it would be decided. That involves an element of uncertainty about the outcome of the decision-making process, but not unacceptable uncertainty about the offence itself.

64. In our judgment the law is clear. The ingredients of the offence have been clearly defined, and the principles decided in the House of Lords in Adomako. They involve no uncertainty. The hypothetical citizen, seeking to know his position, would be advised that, assuming he owed a duty of care to the deceased which he had negligently broken, and

that death resulted, he would be liable to conviction for manslaughter if, on the available evidence, the jury was satisfied that his negligence was gross. A doctor would be told that grossly negligent treatment of a patient which exposed him or her to the risk of death, and caused it, would constitute manslaughter.

Appeals dismissed

It is clear from Lord Mackay's speech in *Adomako* that there are four elements of gross negligence manslaughter, which will be considered separately.

10.1 A DUTY

It must be shown that the defendant owed the victim a duty of care.[137] The Court of Appeal in *Wacker*[138] recently confirmed that the 'duty of care' is usually to be given the meaning it has in the tort of negligence.[139] It is not possible to provide a complete analysis of when a duty of care arises under tort law. Much simplified, you owe a duty of care towards anyone who may foreseeably be harmed by your actions. Hence a driver owes a duty of care to other road users; a doctor owes a duty of care to a patient;[140] the captain of a boat owes a duty of care to the crew;[141] and an electrician owes a duty of care to the homeowner whose house he is rewiring.[142] Whether or not there is a duty of care on a given set of facts is a question of law for the judge to decide.[143] In *Willoughby*[144] the Court of Appeal stated: 'Whether a duty of care exists is a matter for the jury once the judge has decided that there is evidence capable of establishing a duty.' These are problematic comments. If it is for the jury to decide what the phrase 'duty of care' means, it is far from clear how the jury are meant to define it. Maybe the best explanation is that the judge should direct the jury in terms: 'if you find the facts to be X then there is a duty of care, while if you find they are Y there is not'.

EXAMINATION TIP

The law can get rather confusing where it is claimed that it was a defendant's failure to act which was grossly negligent. In that case the normal rules on omissions in criminal law apply and it is necessary to show that the defendant was under a duty to act (see p. 87), as well as demonstrating that the defendant was under the tort law duty of care. Fortunately wherever a criminal duty to act arises there will also be a duty of care in tort.

---

[137] The *Adomako* test is to be applied whether the case is about an act or an omission of the defendant: *Litchfield* [1998] Crim LR 507 (CA); *Watts* [1998] Crim LR 833 (CA).

[138] *Wacker* [2003] Crim LR 108 (CA). However, on the special facts of that case (the defendant killed many immigrants, while illegally bringing them into the country) there was no liability in tort because of the doctrine of *ex turpi causa*, which prevents one criminal from suing another criminal for harm caused while pursuing a criminal enterprise together. The Court of Appeal explained that the public policy behind that rule did not bar a criminal conviction.

[139] For an opposing view see Law Commission Report No. 237 (1996: 3.11).

[140] *Adomako* [1995] 1 AC 171 (HL).

[141] *Litchfield* [1998] Crim LR 507 (CA).   [142] *Prentice* [1993] 4 All ER 935 (CA).

[143] *Singh (Gurphal)* [1999] Crim LR 582 (CA).   [144] *Willoughby* [2004] EWCA Crim 3365.

10.2 A BREACH OF A DUTY

It must be shown that the defendant breached her duty of care to the victim. In order to decide whether there is a breach of duty the jury must ask whether the defendant's action fell below the standard expected of the reasonable person. Where the defendant is purporting to exercise a special skill, the test is whether the defendant was exercising the skill expected of a reasonable person possessing that skill. So in *Adomako* the accused had to act as a reasonable anaesthetist. In that case the accused had raised arguments that he was exhausted after a long work shift and was inadequately trained. These did not affect the standard: the jury were not to consider whether it was reasonable for Adomako himself to act as he did; but to consider whether he fell below the standard expected of a reasonable anaesthetist.[145]

10.3 CAUSING THE DEATH

It must be shown that the defendant's breach of the duty caused the victim's death. This is a straightforward application of the rules of causation. The point made in *Hayward*[146] is important. There the defendant was driving a horse and cart without holding the reins when he hit a young girl, killing her. Although he clearly caused the death of the girl, the court found that *his negligence* did not. It was found that even if he had been driving with all due care he would not have avoided hitting her: she ran out in front of him without warning. The simplest way for the jury to consider the question would be to ask: if the defendant had acted reasonably would the victim have been killed?

10.4 GROSS NEGLIGENCE

It must be shown that the defendant's breach of duty was gross. Lord Mackay in *Adomako* explained that the jury should ask themselves whether the defendant's actions or omissions were so bad as to deserve a criminal conviction. The point is that establishing that the defendant was negligent will mean that the defendant could be required to pay compensation to the victim (or his family). The jury must ask whether the law should go further and in addition require punishment for the wrong.[147]

Adomako leaves the jury a wide discretion to decide whether to convict the accused. The jury can take all the facts into account and it is hard to predict how a jury will decide a particular case. It is likely that the jury will consider questions such as: did the defendant foresee that his actions or omissions would cause death?; what were the motives influencing the defendant's actions or omissions?; was the defendant indifferent to the well-being of the victim?; were there any good explanations for why the defendant acted or failed to act as he did? In summary the jury will consider the 'badness' of the defendant's actions.[148]

---

[145] The fact that the victim consented to the activity does not prevent a conviction for gross negligence manslaughter: *Wacker* [2003] Crim LR 108 (CA).

[146] (1908) 21 Cox CC 692.

[147] Although in *Becker*, No. 199905228/Y5, 19 June 2000 the Court of Appeal suggested that referring the jury explicitly to the difference between civil and criminal liability might just confuse them.

[148] *R (On the application of Brenda Rowley) v DPP*, 4 Apr. 2003 (QBD) approved of the use of 'badness' here.

The Court of Appeal in *Attorney-General's Reference (No. 2 of 1999)*[149] made it clear that it is *not* necessary to demonstrate that a defendant foresaw a risk of death before he or she can be convicted of gross negligence manslaughter. However, if the defendant did foresee death it is more likely that the jury will find the negligence to be gross than if he or she did not.

A slightly different question is whether it is possible to convict a person of gross negligence manslaughter if the risk of death was not foreseeable. In *Adomako* itself it is unclear whether Lord Mackay required that a risk of death be foreseeable. At one point he talked about gross negligence involving consideration of 'the risk of death involved', however, he also approved *dicta* in *Stone and Dobinson*[150] and *R v West London Coroner, ex parte Gray*[151] which seemed to suggest that a risk to the health and safety of the victim was sufficient, even if death itself was not foreseeable. In *Singh (Gurphal)*[152] the Court of Appeal approved the trial judge's direction that a risk of death must have been foreseeable by a reasonably prudent person. However, there was no real discussion of the issue in that case, so it may still be open to debate. Whatever the position is it would be a most unusual case where death was not foreseeable but the jury decided that the negligence was gross.

11 SUBJECTIVE RECKLESS MANSLAUGHTER

DEFINITION

Subjective reckless manslaughter: the defendant killed the victim foreseeing a risk of death or serious injury.

If the defendant killed the victim, foreseeing a risk of death or serious injury, then he or she can be convicted of subjective reckless manslaughter.[153] It is, in fact, rare for a case explicitly to rely on subjective reckless manslaughter,[154] because whenever there is subjective reckless manslaughter it will be possible to charge constructive or gross negligence manslaughter and these will be easier to prove. Therefore, although it is generally accepted to exist as a form of manslaughter,[155] there are no cases which discuss its exact definition.

12 PROTECTING LIFE ON THE ROADS

Parliament has created specific offences dealing with the causing of death on the roads.[156]

12.1 CAUSING DEATH BY DANGEROUS DRIVING

Section 1 of the Road Traffic Act 1988 (as amended) reads:[157]

---

[149] [2000] QB 796 (CA).   [150] [1977] QB 354 (CA).   [151] [1988] QB 467.
[152] [1999] Crim LR 582 (CA).
[153] I use the term 'subjective reckless manslaughter' to avoid confusion with *Caldwell* reckless manslaughter which was thought to exist at one time, but has now been replaced with gross negligence manslaughter.
[154] For a rare example see *R v Lidar* No. 99/0339/Y4.
[155] Law Commission Report No. 237 (1996: para. 2.26); Clarkson (2000).
[156] See Mackenna (1970). There is evidence that courts are imposing higher sentences for these offences: Clarkson (2000).
[157] As amended by the Road Traffic Act 1991.

> A person who causes the death of another person by driving a mechanically propelled vehicle dangerously on a road or other public place is guilty of an offence.

'Dangerous driving' is defined in section 2A as where:

> (a) the way he drives falls far below what would be expected of a competent and careful driver, and
>
> (b) it would be obvious to a competent and careful driver that driving in that way would be dangerous.

It would also be dangerous driving if it would be obvious[158] to a competent and careful driver that driving the vehicle in its present state would be dangerous.[159] 'Dangerous' in the Act means that there is a danger of injury to any person or of serious damage to property.[160]

The offence is objective. The defendant is guilty unless he drives as a reasonable person would. It is not a defence for a driver to show that he drove as well as he could, if this was below the standard expected of the reasonable person. Where the prosecution alleges that it was the state of the vehicle which rendered the driving dangerous then what matters is not what the defendant knew, but what would have been known by the reasonable person.[161] However, if the defendant does have any special knowledge this knowledge shall be taken into account in deciding how a reasonable driver would react. So, for example, if the defendant was an expert car mechanic and aware that his car was in a dangerous condition, even if a reasonable person would not have been aware of the defect, the defendant can be convicted.

12.2 CAUSING DEATH BY CARELESS DRIVING WHEN UNDER THE INFLUENCE OF DRINK OR DRUGS

Section 3A(1) of the Road Traffic Act 1988 states:

> (1) If a person causes the death on a road of another person by driving a mechanically propelled vehicle or other public place without due care and attention, or without reasonable consideration for other persons using the road or place, and—
>
> (a) he is, at the time when he is driving, unfit to drive through drink or drugs, or
>
> (b) he has consumed so much alcohol that the proportion of it in his breath, blood or urine at that time exceeds the prescribed limit, or
>
> (c) he is, within 18 hours after that time, required to provide a specimen in pursuance of section 7 of this Act, but without reasonable excuse fails to provide it
>
> he is guilty of an offence.

This offence is self-explanatory.

---

[158] This means evident 'at first glance': *Strong* [1995] Crim LR 428 (CA).

[159] Road Traffic Act 1988, s. 2A(2).

[160] Road Traffic Act 1988, s. 2A(3).   [161] *Roberts and George* [1997] Crim LR 209 (CA).

12.3 MANSLAUGHTER AND DRIVING

There is no reason why a person who kills another while driving cannot be convicted of manslaughter. However, in *Adomako* Lord Mackay suggested it would be rare for a manslaughter charge to be brought following a road death. The most likely circumstances in which such a charge would be brought are where the accused deliberately drove at the victim, using his car as a weapon.

QUESTIONS

1. Charles, a fierce opponent of the European Monetary Union, throws paint at the Prime Minister. The Prime Minister pushes his bodyguard, Evander, in the way. Evander is covered in paint and as a result suffers a nasty rash. Evander is interested in alternative medicine and takes a herb recommended by Hu, a local herbalist. Evander suffers an allergic reaction to the herb and dies. Research just published indicates that one in two million people are known to be allergic to this herb. What offences, if any, have been committed? (Some causation issues are raised in this problem. Remember to consider the potential criminal liability of all 'suspects': Charles, the Prime Minister, and Hu all need to be considered.)

2. One Saturday, Thomas, the President of the International Pogo Stick Society, was travelling down the pavement of a crowded street on his pogo stick. He was jumping carefully when his attention was grabbed momentarily by a striking poster advertising colourful knitwear. When he looked back to where he was going he thought he realized that he was about to crash into Clare. He decided to attempt a highly complex manoeuvre which he thought would avoid the accident. Unfortunately it failed and he landed on top of Clare, killing her, and breaking her valuable watch.

   Clare's fiancé, Michael, who has a mental age of 9 and has difficulties in controlling his temper, had been walking beside Clare. He was so upset at what had happened that he picked up a traffic cone and threw it at Thomas, intending to cause him an unpleasant injury. Thomas parried the cone with his pogo stick, but the cone landed on the head of Alfred, a young child who was passing by. Alfred fell to the ground. Thomas immediately rushed over and attempted to give Alfred mouth-to-mouth resuscitation. Unfortunately it had been a long time since he had attended his first-aid classes, and his efforts resulted in asphyxiating Alfred, who died. What offences, if any, have been committed?

13 CAUSING OR ALLOWING THE DEATH OF A CHILD OR VULNERABLE ADULT

Section 5 of the Domestic Violence, Crime and Victims Act 2004 has created a new offence of causing or allowing the death of a child or vulnerable child. It is useful particularly where a child has died while in the care of adults and it is clear one of the adults killed the child, but it is not clear which one. The section 5 offence is committed if the following are proved:

(i) V (the child or vulnerable adult) has died as a result of an unlawful act of a person who was in the same household as the victim and had frequent contact with him;

(ii) There was a significant risk of serious physical harm being casused to V by the unlawful act;

(iii) Either

    (a) D was the person whose act caused V's death or

    (b) D was, or ought to have been aware that there was a was a significant risk of serious physical harm being carried out to V by an unlawful act and D failed to take such steps as he could reasonably have been expected to have taken to protect V from the risk;

(iv) The killing of V occurred in circumstances which D foresaw or ought to have foreseen.

The offence carries a maximum sentence of 14 years. It is to be noted that its *mens rea* is negligence. The test focuses on what D knew or ought to know. In a case where there has been domestic violence it is hoped that the courts will bear in mind that it might be extremely dangerous for a mother, say, to contact the police about fears over what her abusive partner will do to their child.

PART II: THEORETICAL ISSUES IN HOMICIDE LAW

14 HOMICIDE: THE STATISTICS

Be prepared to be surprised by the statistics on homicide. The popular perception of homicide in England and Wales which is usually created by popular television dramas and 'who-done-it' detective books is far from the reality.[162] Consider the following facts:

(1) In 2004/2005 there were 859 recorded homicides.[163] In 1999/2000 of 764 recorded homicides there were 207 murder convictions and 190 manslaughter convictions and 109 cases awaiting a decision.[164]

(2) The most likely victim of homicide is under the age of one.[165] The least likely age group to be murdered is the 5–16-year-olds.[166]

(3) One-fifth of all homicides occur among current or former partners/spouses.[167] In 2001/2002, 46 per cent of female victims of homicide were killed by a former partner/spouse.[168]

(4) More men than women are victims of homicide.[169]

---

[162] Flood-Page and Taylor (2003: 1). For a useful discussion on how to reduce the number of homicides see Brookman and Maguire (2003).

[163] Nicholas *et al.* (2005: 78)   [164] Home Office (2001b).

[165] Ibid.: the risk for under ones was 82 homicides per million; the risk for the general population was 15 per million in 2001. For a wider picture see Walmsley (1986). For a discussion of the difficulties that can arise in convicting defendants for killing young children see Law Commission Report No. 279 (2003).

[166] Flood-Page and Taylor (2003: 1).   [167] Brookman and Maguire (2003).

[168] Flood-Page and Taylor (2003: 3).

[169] 73% of victims were male: Flood-Page and Taylor (2003: 1).

(5) Men are more likely to be killed by strangers that women. In 72 per cent of cases involving female victims of homicide the main suspect was known to the victim.[170]

(6) The vast majority of killers are men.[171]

The last statistic is perhaps the least surprising, but should be the most shocking. The causes of the links between masculinity and killing are outside the scope of this book, but they are links that must dominate any understanding of homicide in practice.[172] It should be stressed that these statistics are based on the law's definition of homicide. As we shall see later deaths on roads or in workplace 'accidents' are not described as homicides and so not included in the statistics.

15 THE STRUCTURE OF HOMICIDE

Different countries around the world structure their laws on homicide in a variety of ways, the English criminal law recognizing basically two kinds of general homicide: murder and manslaughter.[173] The most serious offence is murder; the next is manslaughter. Then we move on to civil liability, where there is no criminal punishment. The defendant may be required to pay compensation (damages) for the loss caused, but does not suffer the censure attached to a criminal conviction or any form of punishment. At the end of the spectrum is a killing for which the defendant is neither criminally nor civilly liable. Cases where the killing was a pure accident and for which the defendant was not to blame fall within this category.

Under the English and Welsh law because there are only two kinds of homicide each category has to be fairly broad. Lord Hailsham in *Howe*[174] explained: 'Murder, as every practitioner of the law knows, though often described as one of the utmost heinousness, is not in fact necessarily so, but consists of a whole bundle of offences of vastly differing degrees of culpability, ranging from brutal cynical and repeated offences like the so-called Moors murders to the almost venial, if objectively immoral, "mercy killing" of a beloved partner.' Similarly into the category of manslaughter will fall a whole range of killings: from an act just short of murder to a case where a person gently pushes the victim who falls over, bangs her head and dies.[175]

The way that homicide is structured in English and Welsh law is only one of a number of ways in which the law could be organized.[176] Before considering the alternatives it should be noted that there are two main reasons why the law may seek to distinguish killings by using different labels (e.g. murder and manslaughter).[177] This may be done in order to differentiate between serious and less serious killings so that the appropriate level of censure is attached to a conviction.[178] Alternatively, the different categories may be used to manage

---

[170] Ibid.
[171] Clarkson and Keating (1998: 628); Alder and Polk (1996).   [172] Chan (2001: ch. 1).
[173] Infanticide could be included as a third category, but this is rare and can be seen as a defence.
[174] [1987] 2 WLR 568, 581 (HL).
[175] Indeed the fact that manslaughter covers both involuntary and voluntary manslaughter, which have quite different theoretical bases, demonstrates its width: Ashworth and Mitchell (2000). Indeed judges sentencing in cases of manslaughter can face great difficulty in cases where the facts are disputed. The jury's verdict of guilty of manslaughter will not reveal whether they decided that the defendant's state of mind was little short of murder or whether there was merely an intention to frighten the victim: Wasik (1994).
[176] See Pillsbury (1998).   [177] See the discussion in Lacey (2000a).
[178] See Ch. 1 for a discussion of labelling theory.

the sentencing stage. For example, in English law a person convicted of murder *must* be given a life sentence, whereas if a defendant is convicted of manslaughter the judge has a wide discretion to decide the appropriate sentence.[179]

Here are some of the alternative ways of structuring the law on homicide.[180]

15.1 CREATING A WIDE RANGE OF KINDS OF HOMICIDE

It would be possible to develop a far more complex structure, for example, by distinguishing between murders in the first degree, second degree, and third degree, and then having various levels of manslaughter.[181] The degree of murder would depend on the moral blameworthiness of the defendant's state of mind. There could also be a range of partial defences to ensure as accurate a description as possible of the crime committed by the defendant. The advantage would be to have a more finely tuned system, although there would be problems in defining the exact distinction between the different grades of murder.[182]

15.2 LEAVING DISTINCTIONS TO SENTENCING

Rather than widening the range of homicides it could be argued that we should have a single offence of homicide, which would replace murder and manslaughter.[183] The proposal would be that the differences between killings would be dealt with at the sentencing stage, rather than by seeking to distinguish them with different labels. The proposal raises the arguments over the 'fair labelling principle', which was discussed in Chapter 1: is it justifiable to use the same label for offences which differ so much in their level of culpability? Also there is the question whether there is a special stigma attached to a murder conviction, which the law should utilize to signify that these are particularly heinous killings.[184]

15.3 DISTINGUISHING ON THE BASIS OF THE VICTIMS

The law could also seek to distinguish between killings involving particular kinds of victims. For example, there could be special offences of murdering children or police officers.[185] The argument in favour of this proposal is that public opinion regards such killings as more serious than other killings.[186] Others strongly oppose this proposal, arguing that the life of a child or a police officer is no more valuable than the life of anyone else. Therefore,

---

[179] For further discussion see D. Thomas (1978).

[180] These suggestions are not necessary mutually exclusive.

[181] Such a system is used by many states in the United States, explained in Stacy (2001).

[182] See e.g. the detailed proposals for the law on homicide put forward in Pillsbury (1998).

[183] Lord Kilbrandon in *Hyam v DPP* [1975] AC 55, 98.

[184] A point emphasized in the Criminal Law Revision Committee 14th Report (1980), para. 19. See also Morris and Blom-Cooper (1964). In English and Welsh law this is signified by the fact that the life sentence applies automatically to a conviction for murder. For arguments in favour of the abolition of the mandatory life sentence see Select Committee of the House of Lords on Murder and Life Imprisonment (1989); Lane Committee on the Penalty of Murder (1993). However, there is some evidence of support for life imprisonment among the general public see Mitchell (1998), at least for the most serious murders. For a discussion of the death penalty see Hood (2002).

[185] See the Government's proposals that life sentences should mean life in prison for *inter alia* murder of a child following abduction or murders involving sexual or sadistic conduct (Home Office (2003a)).

[186] Although whether this is a reflection of public opinion (as opposed to what the tabloid press would say the public opinion is) is a matter of debate; see Mitchell (2000).

whatever the public opinion is, as a matter of principle it would be improper to treat the deaths of some victims as worse than those of others.[187] In reply it could be argued that in the case of children the child's whole life-span is destroyed, which makes the killing worse than that of an adult; or that the killing of a vulnerable person such as a child indicates a particular viciousness, which deserves a particular stigma.[188]

15.4 LABELLING THE METHOD OF KILLING USED

A murder or manslaughter conviction tells us nothing about the form of the killing. Murder could be by poisoning, shooting, or torture. Some jurisdictions take a different approach and distinguish between homicide based on the method of killing, for example, seeing killing with guns as being particularly serious.[189] The difficulty with such an approach is that the kind of weapon does not necessarily reveal the blameworthiness of the conduct. A stabbing, for example, could be a vicious attack or an accident involving a knife.[190]

16 THE *ACTUS REUS* OF HOMICIDE

Causation is discussed in Chapter 2. The *actus reus* of homicide also raises controversial issues in relation to abortion, euthanasia, or the medical treatment of neonates which will not be considered in this book.

FURTHER READING

Briggs, H. (2002), *Euthanasia, Death with Dignity and the Law* (Oxford: Hart).

Dworkin, R. (1993), *Life's Dominion* (London: Harper Collins).

Kennedy, I., and Grubb, A. (2000), *Medical Law* (London: Butterworths), ch. 17.

Keown, J. (2002), *Euthanasia, Ethics and Public Policy* (Cambridge: Cambridge University Press).

Slansky, S. (2001), 'Neonatal Euthanasia: Moral Consideration and Criminal Liability', *Journal of Medical Ethics* 27: 5.

Tur, R. (2003), 'Legislative Technique and Human Rights: The Sad Case of Assisted Suicide', *Criminal Law Review* 3.

17 NON-HOMICIDAL KILLINGS

There are many more people killed in road and industrial accidents than are murdered or are the victims of manslaughter. For example, over 5,000 people a year are killed on the roads. Levi reports that in 1989 people in Britain had a 100 times greater chance of being killed in the oil and gas industry, and a twelve times greater chance of being killed in the coal mining industry than they did of being the victim of homicide.[191] Not only are these

---

[187] Clarkson (2000).   [188] Ibid.

[189] Mitchell (2000) suggests that the general public do see the method of killing as relevant in assessing its seriousness. The Home Secretary has indicated that cases of murder using a firearm or explosive should be regarded as particularly serious and requiring a sentence of at least 30 years (Home Office (2003)).

[190] *Larkin* (1943) 29 Cr App R 18.   [191] Levi (2002b).

deaths only exceptionally treated as murder or manslaughter, they rarely result in a criminal prosecution for even a minor offence. One study indicated that only one in 4,000 deaths in the workplace resulted in a criminal conviction of any kind.[192]

Critics of the present approach argue that industrial and road killings may involve individuals showing a similar lack of regard for others' lives as those convicted for murder or manslaughter. Indeed it could be argued that if the law wanted to protect people from being killed it would do far better to enforce or increase the regulation of driving and safety at work than fine-tuning the criminal law on homicide. It is not difficult to see why some critical scholars have argued that the law is concerned about protecting lives only if doing so does not involve interfering with the lifestyles of those who enjoy driving fast cars or engaging in dangerous business practices: there is one law for the poor killers and another for the rich ones. That said, the evidence suggests that juries are very reluctant to convict people who kill while driving.[193] So, if there is prejudice here it seems to be a prejudice shared by the general public. Juries may well feel in driving cases, 'there but for the grace of God go I'.[194] Those who support the present law's approach argue that control of driving and industry through regulatory agencies can be more effective in protecting people's lives than the criminal law. Some of these issues and the appropriate form of regulation for corporations are discussed in greater detail in Chapters 4 and 13.

18 THE *MENS REA* FOR MURDER

As is clear from Part I of this chapter, the *mens rea* for murder is an intention to kill or cause grievous bodily harm. There are three main theoretical issues here.

18.1 THE MEANING OF INTENTION

This is discussed in detail in Chapter 3. One point worth emphasizing here is that at the exact borderline between murder and manslaughter (that is between intention and recklessness) the *Woollin* test applies and the jury are given an element of discretion to decide whether or not to find intention from evidence of foresight of virtual certainty.[195] Supporters of the present law argue that this provides the jury with 'moral elbow room'[196] to decide whether the defendant deserves to be called a murderer. However, others such as William Wilson have been concerned about the discretion this gives to juries and have argued that 'Whether someone has committed murder is not a matter of opinion'.[197]

18.2 IS INTENTION THE APPROPRIATE *MENS REA*?

Some have argued that intention is not the most appropriate form of *mens rea* for murder. Relying on intent means that the present law on murder is both under- and overinclusive. Consider these two examples:

(1) A rogue plants a bomb on an aeroplane, having insured the goods on board. His plan is that the plane will explode, the goods be destroyed, and then he will claim money

---

[192] Levi (2002b: 302). See also Carson (1982).

[193] Mackenna (1970). For a psychological explanation of why juries are more sympathetic to drivers see Lloyd-Bostock (1979).

[194] Mackenna (1970).   [195] Horder (1995a).   [196] Ibid.   [197] Wilson (2000: 28).

from the insurance company. However, the bomb has only a 90 per cent chance of working. He may not be able to be convicted of murder. Death or grievous bodily harm was not his purpose and he did not foresee that as virtually certain. However, such a bomber would be regarded by many people as deserving a murder conviction.

(2) A terminally ill woman pleads with her husband to kill her for months on end. The husband finally gives way to her wishes and kills her. He intends to kill her and faces a murder conviction, with its mandatory life sentence.[198]

Do such examples indicate that intention is not the most suitable form of *mens rea* for murder?

Some suggest that, rather than looking at intention, the key questions should be attitude of the defendant.[199] Did he demonstrate a callous contempt for the value of other people's lives? Did the defendant show 'wicked recklessness'?[200] Did the defendant have a 'depraved heart, devoid of social duty, and fatally bent on mischief'?[201] Those who prefer to ask questions such as these argue that merely looking at intention or recklessness is too narrow and does not take into account all the moral and social evaluations that would be considered in making a full assessment of the defendant's blameworthiness.[202] Some people suggest that considering the defendant's attitude towards other people's lives is a better indication of his blameworthiness than considering how likely his action was to cause death.[203]

QUESTIONS

1. What factors do you think the jury *really* take into account in deciding whether a defendant is guilty of murder or manslaughter?

2. Would asking juries to consider whether the defendant's attitude was 'wicked' or 'callous' focus the jury's mind on the really important question or would it lead to injustice, with different juries reaching different conclusions on cases involving similar facts?

3. If a husband, say, kills his terminally ill wife at her request because he cannot bear to see her suffer any more, should he be guilty of murder? If not, should this be because he lacked the *mens rea* for murder, or should the law create a special defence?

18.3 THE FACT THAT INTENTION TO CAUSE GRIEVOUS BODILY HARM IS SUFFICIENT

The fact that an intention to cause grievous bodily harm is sufficient *mens rea* for murder is controversial. Lord Mustill[204] and Lord Steyn[205] have indicated that they would be willing to reconsider the law if an appropriate case was brought before the House of Lords. Lord Mustill in *Attorney-General's Reference (No. 3 of 1994)* stated 'the grievous harm rule is an outcropping of old law from which the surrounding strata of rationalisations have weathered away'.[206] In many ways this is a dispute over the application of the so-called correspondence principle, which is discussed in Chapter 3. Most commentators seem to fall within one of three camps:

---

[198] See *Cocker* [1989] Crim LR 740 (CA).   [199] Pillsbury (1998).
[200] Goff (1988). The phrase comes from Scots law.   [201] Wilson (2000: 29).
[202] Ashworth (2003: 262–7).   [203] Gobert (1995).
[204] *Attorney-General's Reference (No. 3 of 1994)* [1997] 3 All ER 936 at 945–6 (HL).
[205] *Powell* [1997] 4 All ER 545 (HL).   [206] [1998] AC 245 at 258.

(1) A strict understanding of the correspondence principle requires that the *mens rea* should always match the *actus reus*. Those who take this view argue that for murder the only appropriate *mens rea* is an intent to kill.[207] To them the present law is clearly unacceptable.

(2) Those who would be willing to take a more flexible interpretation to the correspondence principle might be happy if the law required the defendant to intend to kill or do a life-threatening act. For example, Lord Steyn in *Powell* recommended that the *mens rea* for murder should be an 'intention to kill or an intention to cause really serious harm coupled with awareness of the risk of death.'[208] Supporters of this view may be concerned that the phrase 'grievous bodily harm' in the present law is too wide—it is possible to cause grievous bodily harm which would be most unlikely to threaten life. For example, if D stabbed P in the leg, but P died because (unknown to D) she was a haemophiliac, D could be convicted of murder, as a stab in the leg could well be regarded as serious harm by a jury. The argument here is that if the defendant is aware that his action might endanger the victim's life, he has taken the victim's life into his hands and cannot complain if he is held fully responsible if death results.

(3) Those who reject the correspondence principle would see an intention to cause serious harm as crossing a moral threshold, at which point the defendant is responsible for creating his own bad luck. This might be used to support the present grievous bodily harm requirement, or could be used to support a wider rule, whereby it is sufficient that the defendant intended to commit an attack against the victim.[209]

In the following passage William Wilson examines the boundary between murder and manslaughter. He starts by considering the extent to which it is justifiable to have an intention to cause grievous bodily harm as the *mens rea* for murder:

W. Wilson, 'Murder and the Structure of Homicide' in A. Ashworth and B. Mitchell (eds.), *Rethinking English Homicide Law* (Oxford: OUP, 2000), 36–44

A. Rough Justice: the GBH–Murder Rule

Recently, Jeremy Horder[210] has encouraged us to take a more positive view of the English model. The fairness of punishment, under this approach, is not a function of the foresight or attitude of indifference, and so on, of the defendant which accompanies his voluntary conduct. Rather, it is a function of the moral implications of his intending to violate an interest of the victim for purposes of assigning moral and criminal responsibility. Although this is not a new idea its particular strength lies in the fact of its conclusions being deduced from an historical examination of largely mainstream doctrine; the same doctrine, in fact, which has led others to criticize the domestic model.

Horder argues that a distinct merit of the domestic system is its rejection of the idea that judgments of correct labelling outside murder's focal cases are tied to degrees of foresight. On the contrary, it is not unfair to censure for an unforeseen harm (death) where that harm is not disproportionate to the harm (GBH) intended. This kind of rough justice is not merely to be tolerated by a rational system of blame and punishment on pragmatic evidential grounds;

---

[207] See the discussion in Criminal Law Revision Committee, 14th Report (1980).
[208] [1999] AC 1, echoing Criminal Law Revision Committee, 14th Report (1980).
[209] J. Gardner (1994a).   [210] Horder (1995a).

it is demanded by it for substantive reasons. Taking responsibility for our actions means that we must take responsibility for the (not disproportionate) consequences of, and circumstances surrounding, our actions since they are implicit in the very concept of action. Implied malice is not then a weak compromise with the contempt-for-life model but rather evinces a moral rationality all of its own and informs, overlaid with a requirement of proportionality between harm intended and harm punished, the doctrinal components of all crimes of violence stretching from psychic assault all the way up to murder. If the intention to assault sustains liability for section 47 but not section 20 of the Offences Against the Person Act 1861, and the intention to inflict bodily injury sustains liability for section 20, the same principle of fairness allows the intention to cause grievous bodily harm to sustain liability for murder, given that a lesser intention (to cause bodily injury) sustains liability for manslaughter.

Taken as a whole, this is a plausible restatement of the ethical foundation of the English approach to crimes of violence. Critics have insisted, however, that its adherents are committed to the existence of a rather under-theorized moral bridge between crimes involving different wrongs and levels of wrongdoing. If there is a bridge it is one which has been 'cobbled together' for reasons of expedience rather than in response to and in furtherance of cogent principles of criminal justice. The idea is rejected that there are thresholds of blame which are so loosely connected to the constituent elements of the crimes themselves. While we may be disposed to insist that the authors of violence take the 'rough with the smooth' a problem left uncatered for is the matter of representative labelling. Both murder and manslaughter will arguably be diminished as offence labels and in their symbolic importance if doctrine strays too far from their paradigm cases. The rough-justice model allows a murder conviction in cases where no realistic threat to life is posed and where, far from intending to kill, the defendant intends not to kill. In such cases, at least, it is arguable that the defendant's intended harm is different in kind as much as degree from that for which punishment is sought. As a matter of labelling-propriety, it seems to follow, therefore, that a restructured law of homicide should pay particular attention to how murder, outside its paradigm case, differentiates itself from manslaughter, given that manslaughter's own paradigm case includes a death attributable to an act of violence falling short of mortal injury. The first and obvious requirement is a cogent notion of serious bodily injury which satisfies the proportionality requirement otherwise than, at present, by default.

One solution offered to this problem of representative labelling is to define serious injury in such a way as to require the injury intended to pose some objective risk of death. Examples of GBH–murder defined in this way include the Indian Code, where the fault element is 'the intention of causing bodily injury to any person' and the bodily injury intended to be inflicted is sufficient in the ordinary course of nature to cause death. By contrast with the subjectivist versions detailed above there is no requirement that the defendant be aware that the injury he intends is mortal. This coheres with the moral thrust of the rough-justice approach. It is what one intends rather than what one foresees which forms the basis of one's responsibility for what occurs. As long, then, as the injury intended is sufficient ordinarily to cause death, for example a blow on the head with an iron bar, a savage beating, or a knife wound to the thorax, liability is incurred. On the practical side, such a formulation pre-empts defences rooted in an attitude of culpability, say rage or intoxication, which is morally comparable to actual foresight and generally obviates evidential problems, particularly in cases of spontaneous, instinctive acts of aggression.

The difficulty posed by such compound tests is that they add little by way of moral or conceptual clarity to the notion of implied 'malice'. The key task, for purposes of fair labelling, is to cut up the murder–manslaughter cake in a way which renders the two wrongs meaning fully distinct and makes it clear exactly how citizens must behave to avoid the relevant prohibition. The simplest way of doing so is to ensure that the harm to be intended for murder is the gravest non-fatal harm bearing its own distinct offence label—which at present is grievous bodily harm. What is clearly important is that grievous bodily harm is defined with sufficient precision for this purpose. Given all the various variables, substantive, procedural, and evidential, which contribute to case outcomes in criminal trials, rough justice is the most we can and should aspire to.

A perhaps more serious problem is that the rough-justice model fails fully to sustain the standard justification for a differentiated homicide, which is that there are certain classes of killing which distinguish themselves from the pack of unlawful killings by the unique heinousness of the deeds which cause them. While the intention to cause grievous bodily harm is clearly capable of forming part of a hierarchical framework stretching from trivial acts of violence up to killing it is less clear how, in cases such as *Hyam*, the intention to frighten or create mortal risks, without more, should contribute to this picture.

So Wilson argues that the present law is justifiable, on the basis that it is fair to hold a person who intends grievous bodily harm responsible for any death that results from his or her actions. But he suggests that 'grievous bodily harm' may be too vague a term to be used to draw the line between those cases where it is or is not appropriate to label a person a murderer. In the following passage he considers whether a person who intentionally exposes someone to mortal danger or a person who risks another's life in the course of a violent crime could properly be labelled a murderer.

W. Wilson, 'Murder and the Structure of Homicide' in A. Ashworth and B. Mitchell (eds.), *Rethinking English Homicide Law* (Oxford: OUP, 2000), 44–6

B. Rough Justice: Risk-Taking

What principles of fairness govern the case where the harm is foreseen but there is no harm, serious or otherwise, intended or where it is impossible to prove such intention? Given that, here again, there are two offence-labels available how is the correct label assigned?

1. Intending to Expose Someone to Mortal Danger

A practical starting point for differentiation is provided by the traditional common-law model since, like the Scots model, it is heavily indebted to common-sense notions of moral heinousness, which sustain the differentiated penal response. It was suggested earlier that this approach in its various guises is unable to locate a cogent socially approved basis for determining the level of depravity required. This can clearly be discerned in the following optimistic and woolly evaluation of the American contempt- for-life approach from one of its supporters:

'. . . a motorist who attempts to pass another on a "blind curve" may be acting with such criminal negligence—at if he causes the death of another in a resulting traffic accident he will be guilty of manslaughter. And such a motorist may be creating fully as great a human hazard as one who shoots into a house or train "just for kicks", who is guilty of murder if loss of life results. The difference is that in the act of the shooter there is an element of viciousness—an extreme indifference to the value of human life—that is not found in the motorist. And it is this viciousness which makes the act (murder).'

A better focus to the problem of indiscriminate risk-taking essayed in this latter analysis has been provided by Lord Hailsham. In *Hyam*, he insisted that intention rather than foresight was the fault element in murder. Mrs Hyam was guilty of murder because, lacking any lawful excuse for what she did, she intended to expose her victim to the serious risk of death or grievous bodily harm. This is both a theoretical improvement upon the unmediated moral judgmentalism of the American model and also, by not conflating moral heinousness with degrees of risk foreseen, upon Lord Diplock's intention/foresight amalgam. For Lord Hailsham risk-taking does not become the fault element in murder simply by crossing a threshold of probability, say from possible to probable. As along as it is the accused's intention to court a serious risk of death the actual degree is unimportant, subject always to the overriding requirement that risk taken be unjustified.

Lord Hailsham's restatement is ultimately unsuccessful since he adopts a broad notion of intention which would deem a consequence intended whether it was desired or foreseen as morally certain. The result is to conflate the intentional with the reckless exposure of a person to the serious risk of death. As Lord Hailsham admits it might conceivably convict of murder the above overtaking motorist, which caused him to try to shore up his analysis by requiring the act to be aimed at someone. However, as Lord Bridge pointed out in *Moloney*, while this might enable the acquittal of the motorist it would also acquit those such as terrorists who aim their life-threatening acts at nobody and are designed solely for the purpose of creating terror-in short the very people which an extended fault element would be designed to catch. A more cogent solution would have been to adopt a notion of intention closer to its focal meaning of aim, purpose, or desire *and* to require the end intended to be exposure to the serious risk of death rather than, in Lord Hailsham's formulation, death or serious injury. The resulting fault element is intending, without lawful excuse, to expose another to the serious risk of death.

The merit of such an approach can best be illustrated by reference to some other classic cases involving killing by risk-taking, falling either side of homicide's dividing line, namely (manslaughter) *Goodfellow, Cato, Hancock and Shankland*, (murder) *Hyam, Commonwealth* v. *Ashburn, Banks* v. *State*. What distinguishes Messrs Hyam and other risk-takers as murderers from Messrs Goodfellow and other risk-takers as manslayers is that the point of their action is to expose the victims to the risk of death. It is in this sense only, but crucially, that their action is victim-centred or, for want of a better expression, 'aimed at' a victim. Looked at another way, which indicates how distinct in terms of moral responsibility the two attitudes are, the (merely) reckless killer acts despite the risk of death. Mrs Hyam, the malignant shooter and the Russian-roulette player act because of it. If there was no risk to life attending their conduct they would not have acted in the way they did; they would have changed their behaviour. Taking the risk thus structures their conduct. In this respect the test bears comparison with Mitchell's value-indifference test, which asks whether the defendant would have acted differently had he known the outcome was to be fatal. As explained earlier, whether or not such a distinguishing test is morally informative, what is quite certain is that proof of the relevant attitude would create substantial evidential difficulties. How could a jury ever be certain that Mrs Hyam, Mr Smith, Messrs Hancock and Shankland, the Russian-roulette player, and so on, would not have acted differently if their guardian angel had allowed them to press the fast forward button? A value-deficit test of murderous risk-taking seems destined to convict no one, or, in common with the *Hancock* test, relies for such a conviction upon jury pragmatism.

This test, by contrast, asks whether the defendant would have acted differently if told that there would be *no* risk of death (that is, that there could be no fatal outcome), for which the circumstantial evidence available, for or against, is likely to be correspondingly stronger. So the shooter would presumably not fire into a carriage or room he knew to be empty. Mrs Hyam would presumably not/did not set fire to the house until assured of the presence of the victim. The Russian-roulette player would presumably insert a bullet if he accidentally discharged the sole bullet against the wall. The terrorist would presumably await a better opportunity to cause the terror intended. In each case, because it is the possibility of the outcome occurring rather than some ulterior agenda which structures the action taken the moral difference between intending to kill some-one and intending to endanger their lives diminishes almost to vanishing point.

Apart from providing necessary focus to the contempt-for-life approach the importance of the proposed refined mental element is that it provides a cogent extension in terms of responsibility to the intention to kill and the intention to cause grievous bodily harm, namely an intention to expose someone to mortal danger. As such it would neatly accommodate cases provided for by the American depraved-heart doctrine without succumbing to its emotionalism and conceptual vagueness. There are nevertheless two strong arguments which can be levelled against this extension. The first is that requiring the risk to be a serious one rather than, say, of the 'more likely than not' variety threatens to designate as murderers some whose risk-taking would widely be considered less heinous than others who would, by the same test, only be guilty of manslaughter. Compare the following examples

Case 1. M., a disgruntled bank employee, blows up the bank's Head Office at a time when the office was closed. He does not desire to expose passing pedestrians to the serious risk of death. This is not his point, which is to revenge himself on the bank by destroying its property. Nevertheless he knows that such an outcome is extremely likely, but he does not care.

Case 2. W. plants a car bomb in a busy street. Her purpose is not to kill but to create a risk of death of sufficient severity to mobilize the police and the media thus creating publicity for her political goals. To minimize the risk of death she provides a very precise bomb warning, which in 90 per cent *of* cases would be sufficient to prevent *loss of* life. Due to the error *of* a bomb-disposal expert the bomb detonates, killing the latter.

It is clearly arguable that there is more responsibility, more blame and more of the 'murderer's' credentials attached to M. than to W. and yet under the refined rough-justice approach it would be the latter who would be guilty of murder. For this reason there is a strong argument either for a separate offence label, say, of causing death by intentional endangerment, or for the support of a further category of murderous reckless killing arising out of the commission of inherently dangerous offences. The latter option will be returned to below. The former is rejected for creating an unnecessarily complex label. Both common law and Scots law have traditionally attached the murder label to cases of wicked recklessness. Domestic law has rejected risk-taking as murder only because of an assumption that it is impossible to draw a clear line between murder and manslaughter. Those who desire to create the risk *of* death show contempt *for* the value of life and so we should not be uneasy with the appropriateness of the label, although, inevitably, given instances will not always record the degree of heinousness which we naturally associate with the label.

The second argument is that the concept of seriousness of risk is too flexible and wide ranging in any event to be morally comparable to murder's focal cases. If a person not only does not intend to kill but acts so as not to kill and reasonably supposes that the manner in which he is acting will not cause death it seems unsatisfactory to label such a person in the same way as someone who kills for the joy of killing. This is not rough justice. It is failed justice. The obvious response to this is that the degrees of risk foreseen must become less relevant to the ascription of responsibility when there is a purposive element. Of course they do not bear at all where the consequence itself (rather than simply the creation of the risk) is directly intended. In this latter case it would not be cogent to argue that, notwithstanding his desire to kill the victim, the actor is not guilty of murder unless the means adopted to produce the outcome were likely to achieve it and the shooter was confident of success. Similarly, as can be seen clearly in the roulette example, the shooter's attitude of mind does not change with the number of bullets only the degree of risk. It is submitted that this allows us to say that the former 'as good as' intended to kill even though the risk foreseen is relatively slight.

2. Risk-Taking the Course of Violent Crime

It was suggested above that there might be cases of indiscriminate risk-taking which match or exceed in terms of heinousness cases where the death issues from action taken in furtherance of an actor's desire to expose the victim to the serious risk of death. It was argued that it would be generally desirable for such cases to be treated as murder if a cogent method of distinguishing risk-taking constitutive of murder from that constitutive of manslaughter could be devised.

A proposal for elevating recklessness above the ordinary is to tie risk-taking constitutive of murder into particularly heinous contexts such as the commission of dangerous felonies. In a number of jurisdictions a criminal context aggravates an intentional killing. There is no obvious reason why such a context should not also aggravate a reckless killing such that it is 'pushed' through a higher 'threshold' of blame. By comparison, a person who drives dangerously to get home for tea, detonates explosives in the lawful demolition of a building or in the attempt to remove a blockage in a collapsed tunnel should expect, at worst, a manslaughter conviction. It is not unreasonable to hold that there is a basic moral distinction between risk-taking motivated by ordinary human goals and those whose attainment inherently requires action taken against the interests of another. Where the criminal context is accompanied or characterized by extremely dangerous activity, it is arguably quite fair, assuming the degree of risk taken was already sufficient for manslaughter, to set this as an appropriate threshold for liability in murder. Consider the following examples, death occurring in each case, as support for such a contention:

Case 3. A., having raped V., throws her into a river to destroy evidence of his involvement.

Case 4. A., a bank robber, fires a shotgun at the feet of pursuing police officers in an attempt to evade arrest.

Case 5. A., having abducted B., keeps her imprisoned in a disused culvert. She dies as a result of the combined effect of lack of water, food, and near-freezing conditions.

Each of these cases involves the defendant in an activity which already involves an attack upon the physical interests of another. It is submitted that it should not be necessary to show further either an intention to cause serious injury or a specific intention to expose the victim to the risk of death. His willingness 'to go the extra distance' should suffice for murder.

The main problem here is in circumscribing the 'unholy' context. To avoid an unfocused return to the excesses of felony-murder and to maintain a clear dividing line between risk-taking as murder and risk-taking as manslaughter it is important to ensure broad parity in terms of moral heinousness with the other fault elements. The simplest way of doing so, and one which would dovetail satisfactorily with GBH-murder, is to require the unlawful object to be the commission of a crime ordinarily involving an attack on or threat to the autonomy or bodily integrity of another or to involve hostile activity in evading capture or lawful arrest. This would mean, say, that robbery, but not arson, could form the subject matter of the revived felony-murder unless the latter was committed for a specified ulterior criminal purpose, say resisting arrest or destroying evidence. Without such a requirement a simple case of arson would too easily convert to murder. Such line-drawing exercises are never satisfactory but it is probably better that whatever line is drawn is clear and morally supportable than to allow individual context to shape the range of relevant felonies. A tentative prototype proposal follows:

Criminal homicide also constitutes murder when—

1 (a) death results from the reckless exposure of another to the serious risk of death; and

(b) D. acted either:

(i) for the purpose of resisting lawful arrest; or

(ii) in the execution of and for the purpose of executing any specified offence, or for the purpose of evading capture or detection following the commission or attempted commission of such offence.

(c) The specified offences are robbery, serious sexual assault, torture, whether or not serious injury was thereby effected or intended, abduction.

The requirement in cl. (b)(ii) that D. be acting 'in the execution of and for the purpose of executing', rather than the more natural 'to facilitate the offence' is to minimize inflationism so as to ensure, say, that those who drive dangerously on the way to commit an offence fall outside the reconstituted felony-murder. Inevitably the requirement would protect others less deserving but, once again, the key task involved in reconstructing an acceptable felony-murder/extreme recklessness amalgam is to ensure a broad parity of culpability amongst those included.

The intended effect of these provisions would be that subject to satisfying the reckless-ness component of cl. I(a) the defendants in *DPP* v. *Smith*, *Vickers*, *DPP* v. *Beard* and *Pagett* (by cl. I(a)(i)) and Cases 3, 4, and 5 are guilty of murder, whether or not an intention to cause grievous bodily harm can be proved. So also a defendant who, lacking express or implied malice, raped another 'to death', or caused death, say by heart failure, in the course of administering controlled torture falling short of grievous bodily harm. On the other hand the defendants in Case 1, *Hancock and Shankland*, *Goodfellow*, and *Hyam* are not. It must be conceded that the provision inflates murder so far beyond its core cases as to threaten the receptivity that some might otherwise have to the overall cogency of the differentiating scheme adopted. This is perhaps a reason in favour of constituting this form of homicide with a separate offence label, say 'killing in the course of a felony', or otherwise leave it to be mopped up by the residual law of manslaughter. As will be seen below the problem of inflationism would be compounded by my suggested fault element.

William Wilson is probably in a minority amongst academic commentators in suggesting that the *mens rea* for murder should be extended in the way he proposes. Critics would argue that murder should be restricted to only the most heinous of crimes, especially in a legal system which imposes a mandatory life sentence for murder, and this means that only those who intend death should be labelled murderers.

In the following extract the Law Commission set out their proposals for amending the law of murder:

Law Commission, Consultation Paper 177, *A New Homicide Act for England and Wales* (London: TSO, 2005)

The Proposed Framework

5.7 The framework that we are provisionally proposing comprises three general homicide offences supplemented by specific offences:

(1) 'first degree murder' (mandatory life sentence);

(2) 'second degree murder' (discretionary life sentence);

(3) manslaughter; (fixed term of years sentence) and

(4) specific homicide offences, such as assisting suicide and infanticide (fixed term of years sentence).

5.8 Some people might prefer to see a greater number of general categories of homicide. However, the need to grade accurately different homicides must be balanced against the need to keep the options before the jury simple. Murder trials often involve a number of different defendants all running different, either inter-dependent or conflicting claims and defences in the alternative. There is also a danger that sub-dividing murder or manslaughter too many times will debase the currency of these terms.

'First Degree Murder'

5.9 The foundation on which our proposed framework rests is that the most serious offence within the framework, and the only one that should attract the mandatory life sentence, should be confined to cases where the offender intended to kill. We provisionally propose the label 'first degree murder' for this offence in order to reflect the seriousness of the offence and the high level of criminality involved in its commission. (As will become apparent, we are provisionally proposing that other forms of killing that are currently classified as murder should be classified as 'second degree murder').

. . .

The scope of 'first degree murder'

Intentional killing

5.10 In Part 1 we referred to the connection between murder and the view that life is sacrosanct. For two reasons, we believe that this connection is best expressed through the creation of an offence that is confined to homicides where it was the offender's intention to kill. (In referring to 'intention to kill' we include cases where the victim's death was integral to what the defendant intended to achieve, even though it was not the motive for his or her conduct. An example is the person who plants a bomb on a vessel, timed to explode in mid ocean, in order to make an insurance claim. The 'virtual certainty' test is a way of testing whether the victim's death was within what the defendant can be regarded as having intended).

5.11 First, as a general rule, the culpability of a person who intentionally kills is significantly greater than that of a person who kills without intending to kill. Killing in a state of mind that does not intend the consequence that marks out homicide should not attract a mandatory life sentence.

. . .

5.13 Secondly, research conducted by Professor Barry Mitchell indicates a very high level of agreement amongst the public that as a general rule the presence of an intention to kill renders a homicide especially serious in comparison to other homicides, including those where there is an intention to cause serious harm. This is a strong but not conclusive argument for creating an offence confined to intentional killing which, in terms of seriousness, is graded above all others and attracts a unique sentence.

5.14 We envisage two main objections to our provisional proposal. First, some may say that limiting 'first degree murder' to intentional killings is too restrictive because it excludes cases where the defendant realised that it was 'highly probable', but not 'virtually certain', that his or her conduct would result in another's death.

5.15 In our provisional view, 'first degree murder' should be confined to those cases where the victim's death was integral to what the offender set out to achieve and should not include cases where there was merely a risk of it happening. Taking a risk, even a high risk, of killing someone is recklessness and is very serious but it is not the same as the deliberate taking of life. Accordingly, we do not believe that 'first degree murder' should encompass cases where the offender believes that it is 'highly probable' that death will occur.

5.16 The second objection that may be made to our provisional proposal is that in some cases it will be difficult to prove that there was an intention to kill. We do not accept, however, that this weakens the case for confining 'first degree murder' to cases where there is an intention to kill. The moral case for confining 'first degree murder' to killings where the defendant intended to kill, together with public support for treating such killings as more serious than others, outweighs any practical difficulties in proving an intention to kill.

. . .

Should 'first degree murder' be further restricted?

Confining 'first degree murder' to premeditated intentional killing

5.18 In some jurisdictions, murder is confined to premeditated killing. Under the scheme that we are proposing, the issue is not whether murder should be confined to premeditated killing but whether '*first degree murder*' should be so confined. We do not believe that it should be.

5.19 First, we believe that there will be cases where the jury will find it difficult to decide whether the murder was premeditated. In some cases, a killing will have been carefully planned. In others, the killing will be a spontaneous reaction. Between the two lies a grey area. Even leaving aside the grey area, in some cases there will be insuperable problems of proof for the prosecution to overcome if it has to prove that a killing was premeditated.

5.20 Secondly, it is better to treat premeditation as a potentially aggravating factor going towards the length of the minimum term of the life sentence. This is how it is currently regarded in English law. This is sensible not least because a factor that has the potential to aggravate the seriousness of an offence will not necessarily do so. It may or may not.

5.21 It will do so in the case of the 'contract' killer but not in the case of a carer who, after careful consideration and out of compassion, kills a terminally ill spouse. So long as the relevance of premeditation is confined to setting the length of the minimum term, the law can distinguish fairly between different cases of premeditated killing. If it influences how offences should be graded, it is a blunt and inefficient instrument.

Confining 'first degree murder' to a restricted range of victims

5.22 In some jurisdictions, the grading of homicides is influenced by the status of the victim. If this approach were adopted, then 'first degree murder' would be confined to, for example, cases where the victim was a child or a police officer on duty. We do not find this an attractive proposition.

5.23 It could lead to difficult issues for the jury to resolve, for example whether a police-man was 'on duty' at the time he or she was killed. More importantly, grading offences according to the status of the victim implies that some victims' lives are intrinsically of more value than the lives of others.

5.24 It is better to acknowledge that some victims are, either on account of their age or because of the work that they do, more vulnerable. Their vulnerability should be recognised by ensuring that their killers receive a longer minimum term than would otherwise be the case. This is what the guidelines that Parliament has laid down are designed to ensure.

5.25 A further reason for not confining 'first degree murder' to either premeditated killing or cases where the victim is of a particular status is that an over-elaborate process of grading would result in a large number of categories of offences resulting in complexity.

Provisional proposal

5.26 We provisionally propose that all unlawful killings committed with an intention to kill should be 'first degree murder' unless the defendant has a partial defence, namely provocation, diminished responsibility or duress. The sentence for the offence should be imprisonment for life.

'Second Degree Murder'

5.27 Under our provisional proposals, 'second degree murder' would be the most serious offence after 'first degree murder' and would attract a discretionary life sentence. The offence would accommodate those cases where the level of criminality is too high to be categorised as manslaughter but is not high enough to merit the mandatory life sentence. It would encompass:

(1) killing where the intention was to cause serious harm (currently murder);

(2) killing through reckless indifference to causing death (currently manslaughter);

(3) intentional killing where a partial defence applies, for example provocation or diminished responsibility (currently manslaughter) or duress (not recognised as a partial defence to murder under the current law).

. . .

Killing where the intention was to cause serious harm

5.28 Although the culpability of the person who intends to cause serious harm is less than that of the person who intends to kill, it is nonetheless high. It is true that a person may intend to cause serious harm (for example, a broken nose) without intending to endanger life. It is arguable that any form of murder should require an intention to endanger life.

5.29 If Parliament were to keep the present two-tier structure of homicide—murder and manslaughter—there would be a strong argument that murder should as a minimum require an intention to endanger life. However, we are provisionally proposing a three-tier system. We think that the second tier should cover cases where the defendant intended to cause serious harm, which in fact results in death. We think that the third tier (which we consider below) should cover cases where the defendant intended to cause some, but not serious, harm, which in fact results in death. It is unnecessary and over complex to introduce an extra tier between 'first degree murder' and 'second degree murder' in order to differentiate cases where there was an intention to endanger life from cases where there was merely an intention to cause serious harm.

Provisional proposal

5.30 We provisionally propose that all unlawful killings committed with an intention to cause serious harm should be 'second degree murder'. The maximum sentence for the offence should be imprisonment for life.

Killing through reckless indifference to causing death

5.31 Reckless indifference to causing death refers to the state of mind of a person who does not intend to cause death but realises that his conduct involves an unjustifiable risk of causing death and goes ahead regardless. It is an attitude of 'too bad' if death results. The offender is willing to tolerate the unjustified death of another. Under the current law, if death ensues, the offender is guilty of manslaughter.

. . .

5.33 We have explained why we believe that 'first degree murder' should not encompass cases of reckless indifference to causing death, including cases where the offender believed that death was the 'highly probable', but not the 'virtually certain', consequence of his or her actions. At the same time, we believe that a death caused by reckless indifference to causing death is so serious that it ought to be classified as 'second degree murder' and not merely manslaughter.

5.34 However, a person should only be guilty of 'second degree murder' by virtue of reckless indifference if his or her indifference was to causing *death*. Under our provisional proposals, 'second degree murder' would be the most serious homicide offence after 'first degree murder'. It should, therefore, require a very high level of culpability. Acting with the *intention* of causing serious harm constitutes a sufficiently high level of culpability and so does acting with reckless indifference to causing death. However, acting with reckless indifference to causing *serious harm*, while deplorable conduct, is not on the same level of criminality. It should be regarded as manslaughter.

5.35 Should a distinction be drawn between the defendant who foresaw another's death as the 'highly probable' consequence of his or her actions and the defendant who foresaw another's death as a 'possible' consequence? We think not. A distinction may admittedly be made in that the latter believed that he or she was exposing the victim to a much lower degree of risk and so is less culpable than the former. However, both defendants foresaw a risk of death occurring from their actions. If both are prepared to kill in pursuit of their objectives, they are morally indistinguishable. Each deserves to be convicted of 'second degree murder'.

5.36 Acting with reckless indifference is worse than acting with reckless *stupidity*. The latter is where a person realises that their conduct might result in death but stupidly believes that the risk is unlikely to turn into reality or genuinely believes that it is justified to run the risk or simply does not realise that there is any risk at all

Provisional proposal

5.37 We provisionally propose that all unlawful killings committed with reckless indifference to causing death should be 'second degree murder'. The maximum sentence for the offence should be imprisonment for life.

FURTHER READING

Blom-Cooper, L., and Morris, T. (2004), *With Malice Aforethought* (Oxford: Hart).

Goff, Lord (1988), 'The Mental Element in the Crime of Murder', *Law Quarterly Review* 104: 30.

Law Commission (2005), Consultation Paper No. 177, *A New Homicide Act for England and Wales* (London: TSO).

Norrie, A. (1999), 'After *Woollin*', *Criminal Law Review* 532.

Simester, A. (1999), 'Murder, *Mens Rea*, and the House of Lords—Again', *Law Quarterly Review* 115: 17.

19 DEFINING THE *MENS REA* FOR MANSLAUGHTER

We have just been discussing the exact boundary between murder and manslaughter; that is the difference between the least serious kind of murder and the most serious kind of manslaughter. This section will discuss the debate at the other end of manslaughter: where the boundary should be drawn between the criminal offence of manslaughter and conduct which is not criminal, but which might attach civil liability (i.e. liability to pay compensation). Is it fair to convict people of manslaughter if they have not foreseen death or serious harm? Consider this scenario: Kian gives Shane a gentle shove. Surprisingly Shane falls over, bangs his head, and dies. 999 times out of a thousand, having been shoved Shane would just have stepped back. At the most Kian might have expected a conviction for assault, with a maximum sentence of six months. However, because Shane has died, Kian could be convicted of constructive manslaughter, one of the most serious of criminal offences, carrying a maximum sentence of life imprisonment. Some would say mere 'bad luck' should not affect someone's criminal liability to such an extent.[211] Others argue that by the fact that the victim has been killed, 'an irrevocable evil has occurred',[212] and this was caused by the defendant's aggressive act, and that this should be acknowledged by a conviction for manslaughter.

In the following passage the Law Commission considers whether the offence of unlawful act manslaughter should be retained:

Law Commission Report No. 237, *Legislating the Criminal Code: Involuntary Manslaughter* (London: HMSO, 1996), paras. 4.35–4.43

Part IV

. . .

4.35 As we saw in Part II, the present law provides that a person is guilty of 'unlawful act manslaughter' if she causes death by committing an act which is a crime in itself, and which carries a foreseeable risk of causing *some* injury to another person. A person who commits a relatively minor assault which unexpectedly causes death is thus guilty of manslaughter.

4.36 Our respondents were divided on the question whether this type of manslaughter, or something very close to it, should continue to exist. A number of different reasons were given. For example, the Law Society, in its response to our consultation paper, was of the view that 'those who commit crimes involving, albeit slight, violence should take the

---

[211] A point emphasized by Law Commission Report No. 237 (1996).   [212] Duff (1990a).

consequences if the results turn out to be more catastrophic than they expected.' Mr Justice Rix agreed: 'It seems to me that once a person undertakes a violent act he sets himself deliberately . . . on a road which is not only seriously antisocial, . . . but potentially leading to calamitous results. . . . [H]e has deliberately embarked on an act of criminal violence, which it is, or ought to be, well known, leads to incalculable consequences.' It is interesting that Rix J described the accused's culpability in terms of failing to advert to a 'well known' risk of causing serious harm: this is similar to the first criterion upon which we insisted in our discussion of 'culpable inadvertence' above.

4.37 Dr John Gardner, in his response, argued that the starting point in assessing criminal liability ought to be *what the actor did and the consequences of her action:*

'The first question, in all cases of culpability, is 'what did the defendant do?', the answer to which will be some concrete action with results and circumstances incorporated into it already, e.g. 'kill'. . . . Then we must ask, naturally, to what extent the culpability is mitigated or moderated by the conditions under which the act was performed, including the accidental nature of the result etc. . . . It is not 'why does the mere fact that someone happens to die add to one's crime, or make a major crime out of an otherwise venal act?', but rather, 'how does the mere fact that one kills accidentally serve to mitigate or otherwise intercede in the wrongness of killing?'

4.38 He did not, however, maintain that *all* killings should be subject to criminal sanction. First, he argued, the defendant must be *culpable in some way,* even if this culpability does not extend to the causing of death. Secondly, principles of justice and the rule of law require that the killer must have some *forewarning that her act will incur some criminal liability.* On his view, then, unlawful act manslaughter is, in principle, perfectly acceptable:

'. . . since the act was plainly dangerous, culpability is not eliminated, and this was still a wrongful killing. Then it is asked what protections are required to make sure that the act must have been criminal under some other heading *as well as* dangerous, so as to put the defendant on legal notice.'

4.39 Unless one accepts moral luck arguments, it is not clear *why* a person ought to be held criminally responsibility for causing death if death or serious injury were the *unforeseeable* consequences of her conduct, just because she foresaw, or it was-foreseeable, that *some* harm would result. Surely a person who, for example, pushes roughly into a queue is morally to blame for the foreseeable consequences of her actions—that a few people might get jostled, possibly even lightly bruised, and that people might get annoyed—but not for causing a death if, quite unexpectedly, she sets in train a series of events which leads to such an outcome. We consider that the criminal law should properly be concerned with questions of moral culpability, and we do not think that an accused who is culpable for causing *some harm* is sufficiently blameworthy to be held liable for the unforeseeable consequence of death.

4.40 One final argument in favour of recommending that a person ought to be liable for causing death, even if death or serious injury were not foreseeable consequences of her action, would be that this would be necessary for the protection of the public. This argument was considered by the Royal Commission on Capital Punishment which, in 1953, recommended the abolition of the doctrine of constructive malice in murder:

'We think it would be generally agreed that any liability for constructive crime offends against modern feeling, and that any departure from a subjective test of criminal liability can be justified, if at all, only if it is clearly established that it is essential for the protection of the public.'

Royal Commission concluded that the public would be adequately protected by the existence of other criminal offences—principally, it has to be said, manslaughter.

. . .

4.42 Since, in the cases here under discussion, the risk of causing death or serious injury was neither foreseen by the accused, nor foreseeable by her, it is difficult to see what deterrent effect would be achieved by imposing criminal liability for causing death which would not be achieved equally by imposing liability for the appropriate non-fatal offence.

Conclusion

4.43 In conclusion, we consider, as a matter of principle, that the criminal law ought to hold a person responsible for unintentionally causing death only in the following circumstances:

(1) when she unreasonably and *advertently* takes a risk of causing death or serious injury; or

(2) when she unreasonably and inadvertently takes a risk of causing death or serious injury, where her failure to advert to the risk is culpable because

    (a) the risk is obviously foreseeable, and

    (b) she has the capacity to advert to the risk.

The Home Office published a Consultation Paper in 2000[213] which accepted the proposals of the Law Commission, but also sought consultation on whether a person who killed someone while intentionally committing another offence should be convicted of manslaughter. There is no sign yet of legislation putting any of this into force. In the 2005 Law Commission Paper the following offence was proposed to replace constructive manslaughter: 'to cause another person's death by a criminal act intended to cause physical harm or by a criminal act foreseen as involving a risk of causing physical harm.'[214]

It should be clear from the above discussion that subjectivists in particular are unhappy with the present state of the law. To them it is objectionable that a defendant can be guilty of manslaughter, even though he did not intend or foresee the death of the victim. The present law on the *mens rea* for constructive manslaughter is well short of the subjectivists' ideal. In relation to constructive manslaughter the defendant needs the *mens rea* only for a criminal offence, which could just be the *mens rea* required for criminal damage, for example.[215] It is even worse in the case of gross negligence, where it is not necessary to show that the defendant foresaw anything. Even objectivists may take the view that the present law is too wide because for constructive manslaughter it is not even necessary to show that a reasonable person has foreseen the risk of death or serious harm. All that needs to be shown is that *some* harm was *foreseeable*.

QUESTIONS

1. Do you agree with the view that the criminal law should start with the fact that the defendant killed the victim and then consider whether there is a reason why the defendant should not be held responsible for the victim's death, or should we focus on

---

[213] Home Office (2000c).   [214] Law Commission (2005: 5.50).

[215] Mitchell (2000) suggests that a conviction in such a case would not accord with the views of the general public.

the defendant and ask whether there is any reason why the defendant should be held responsible for the victim's death (see the two quotations in the Law Commission Report excerpt from J. Gardner (1998))? Read again the material in Chapter 3 on the 'Correspondence Principle' before answering this.

2. Had Dr Adomako's (see p. 280) negligent actions left the victim in a seriously disabled condition, but not killed him, there would have been no criminal liability for any offence. Is it right that the fact that death has been caused means we are more ready to convict a defendant?

Particular controversy surrounds gross negligence manslaughter. Is it appropriate to hold a person criminally responsible when he is not even aware that his actions are liable to cause harm to another?[216] You should re-read the parts of Chapter 3 on when, if at all, it is appropriate to punish people for negligence.

There are some particular concerns about the use of gross negligence manslaughter in *Adomako*:

(1) It is said that the *Adomako* test is circular. This is because if the jury asked a judge: 'How do we know if the defendant's negligence was bad enough to be criminal?', they would have to be told 'It is if you think it is.' The jury are given no guidance on what factors they should take into account in reaching their decision. To supporters of *Adomako* this gives the jury a wide discretion to decide whether the defendant deserves a criminal conviction, using the standards of the community. To opponents it too readily leads to inconsistent verdicts being reached on cases of similar facts. Consider the case of a junior doctor, exhausted after working a ridiculously long shift, who negligently causes the death of a patient. It is not difficult to imagine some juries being very sympathetic to such a defendant and deciding that his negligence is not gross, but other juries being less sympathetic and convicting. As Simon Gardner[217] points out, asking the jury to decide whether a person is tall produces uncertainty because we do not have an agreed idea of at exactly what height someone become tall. But, he suggests, the uncertainty in the *Adomako* test is worse than the uncertainty in the 'tall person' case. This is because with tallness we are agreed on what we are measuring (i.e. height), even if it is unclear exactly where the boundary is between being tall and being short. However, with the *Adomako* test the jury are not given guidance on what criminality is.

(2) Many cases of gross negligence involve people acting in a professional capacity, and some argue that punishing such cases is inappropriate. The point can be made that people such as doctors, managers, or electricians are normally acting for good reasons and are doing things that are socially useful, even if doing them incompetently.[218] Contrast one person shoving another in a queue who is doing nothing of social benefit. To other people this involves treating professional middle-class killers more leniently than others. There is another issue here and that is the concern that punishing the individual in question might disguise the fact that the defendant's employer is in fact the person who really deserves blame. Take the facts of *Adomako*. Adomako claimed he had never been properly trained and that he was exhausted after working extremely long hours. Was not the proper blame in that case to attach to a health system which employs under-trained people and works them to the bone, rather than to the individual himself? By focusing on Adomako's liability such questions can be neatly avoided.

---

[216] See e.g. Alexander (2000).　　　[217] S. Gardner (1995b).　　　[218] Clarkson (2000).

(3) The Crown Prosecution Service has complained that it is particularly difficult for it to decide whether or not to prosecute someone for gross negligence following an 'accident'. In part this is because it is so difficult to predict how a jury will respond to a particular case.[219]

In response to these and other criticisms the Law Commission has recommended a reform of gross negligence manslaughter. Their proposed definition is as follows:[220]

5.41 We are provisionally proposing that a person is guilty of manslaughter through gross negligence if:

(1) that person's conduct causes death;

(2) it would have been obvious to a reasonable person in the defendant's position that the conduct involved a risk of death;

(3) the defendant had the capacity to appreciate that his or her conduct involved a risk of causing death; and

(4) the conduct fell far below what could reasonably be expected in the circumstances. We envisage that a person's reckless stupidity would be evidence that their conduct fell far below what could reasonably be expected in the circumstances.

QUESTIONS

1. Imagine you are working for the Crown Prosecution Service. You are handed a file about two teachers who were in charge of a group of children doing a mountain climbing expedition. The teachers failed to check the weather forecast before they went out and an appalling storm set in. In the terrible conditions a child was separated from the group and died. Should there be a prosecution for gross negligence manslaughter? Is it a relevant consideration that teachers may decide not to volunteer to take school trips if there is a prosecution? Would it be relevant whether the local education authority had failed to issue guidance on school trips?

2. Shriver (2003: 157) writes through a character in a novel: 'I'm tremendously sympathetic with the sort of diligent mother who turns her back for an eye blink—who leaves a child in the bath to answer the door and sign for a package, to scurry back only to discover that her little girl has hit her head on the faucet and drowned in two inches of water. Two inches. Does anyone ever give the woman credit for the twenty-four-minus three-minutes a day that she has watched that child like a hawk? . . . Oh, no. We prosecute these people, we call it, "criminal parental negligence" and drag them to court through the snot and salty tears of their own grief. Because only the three minutes count, those three miserable minutes that were just enough.' In the light of this, is it right to punish people who are normally dedicated to the concerns of others for a moment's inadvertence?

---

[219] See e.g. *R (On the application of Stephens) v DPP* CO/2506/2000, 19 Oct. 2000, where the Crown Prosecution Service's decision not to prosecute for gross negligence manslaughter was challenged by way of judicial review.

[220] Law Commission Consultation Paper No. 177 (2005).

FURTHER READING

Ashworth, A., and Mitchell, B. (eds.) (2000), *Rethinking English Homicide Law* (Oxford: OUP).

Keating, H. (1996), 'The Restatement of a Serious Crime', *Criminal Law Review* 535.

20 PROVOCATION

20.1 THEORY

The provocation defence is one of the most controversial defences in English and Welsh law and has received an enormous amount of academic attention. At the heart of much of the debate is a discussion about what is the theoretical basis of the defence. To simplify matters three versions will be presented here.

The 'pure excuse' view[221]

This view is based on the argument that a defendant who acts having lost self-control is not fully responsible for his actions. Provoked defendants are far less to blame, having killed in the heat of the moment, than those who kill in cold blood.[222] It might be said that provoked defendants did not calmly choose to act in the way they did, or did not have a fair opportunity to act otherwise. However, because defendants in provocation cases had *some* control over their actions they are not granted a complete excuse and are still guilty of manslaughter.[223] This version of the defence of provocation sees it as almost a form of diminished responsibility.[224]

Those who oppose this view might ask, as Andrew Ashworth[225] has done, whether it is right to provide a defence to a person who loses his self-control and kills on being arrested by a police officer. If there is to be no assessment of whether it was right or appropriate to lose self-control such a person would be entitled to a defence. Those who take the pure excuse view might reply that they would be happy to allow a defence in such a case, pointing out that a manslaughter conviction can carry a life sentence. The provocation defence in such a case acknowledges that the killing was not as serious as a callous premeditated killing of the police officer in similar circumstances would be.

The 'justification' view

This approach argues that provocation should be available as a defence when the defendant was partially justified in doing what he or she did. In other words that there was something reasonable about what the defendant did, even if it was not fully justifiable.[226] It is this that distinguishes provocation from diminished responsibility.[227] (See the Horder extract later in

---

[221] The differences between an excuse and a justification are explained in detail in Ch. 15.
[222] G. Mousourakis (1998a).   [223] Smith and Wilson (1993).
[224] For a useful discussion of what loss of self-control means see M. Smith (2001).
[225] Ashworth (1976).
[226] Dressler (2002b: 972) doubts that it is possible to be partially justified: 'Either a person has a right to act in a certain manner or he does not.'
[227] A point stressed by Lord Hobhouse in his dissenting speech in *Smith (Morgan)* [2000] 3 WLR 654.

this chapter which develops this point.) There are two main ways in which commentators have suggested that a provoked killing could be regarded as partially justified:

(1) The victim caused his or her own death by provoking the defendant. In other words both the victim and the defendant must share responsibility for the death. This form of argument has few supporters nowadays, although it may have influenced some judges in the past.[228] Given that now the provocation can come from someone other than the victim and that the provoking act need not be an unlawful one (e.g. the crying of a baby), this explanation lacks force.

(2) In the light of the provoking incident some display of righteous anger was appropriate. If a man confesses to parents that he has molested their child some display of anger or outrage is expected from the parents. Indeed to remain unperturbed in the face of such a confession could be regarded as immoral. It is true that killing may be an overreaction in the face of such provocation, but that is reflected in the fact that the defendant is still convicted of manslaughter and not given a complete defence.[229] The defence acknowledges that there was something good about what the defendant did (he was right to display indignation) even though in killing he used an inappropriate way of demonstrating his anger. Jeremy Horder has recently suggested that the provocation defence should only be available where the defendant was feeling both anger in the face of grave provocation and also fear for her own or another's safety.[230] This proposed change in the law would bring the closer to the defence of lawful defence which we shall discuss in Chapter 12.

The 'reasonable excuse' view

A middle approach between these two views accepts that the basis of the defence is an excuse, namely that the defendant was not in full control of his or her behaviour and therefore it does not necessarily reveal bad character, but that this can provide an excuse only if it was appropriate for the defendant to feel the anger and suffer the loss of self-control.[231] A central part of the provocation defence is therefore an assessment of whether the defendant had a good reason for responding to the provocation as he or she did. In other words the defendant must show not only that she lost self-control, but also that she ought to have displayed her indignation at the provocative act.

In the following passage Joshua Dressler explains what he sees as the theoretical basis of the defence. Of the above positions his view seems to fall within the 'reasonable excuse' view:

J. Dressler, 'Why Keep the Provocation Defense?: Some Reflections on a Difficult Subject' (2002) 86 *Minnesota Law Review* 959 at 972–6

The provocation defense is an excuse defense, albeit a partial one, but one that may (but need not) have a justification-like component. My best effort to explain basic provocation law runs as follows: An intentional homicide is not mitigated to manslaughter unless certain conditions are met. First, there must be a provocative event that results in the actor feeling

---

[228] McAuley (1987).

[229] See Gough (1999) who suggests that proportionality of response is the key requirement in the provocation defence.

[230] Horder (2005a).   [231] J. Gardner (1998b).

rage or some similar overwrought emotion. It is important here to understand why the provocation does—and does not—result in anger. It is not that the provocation 'touches a nerve' as, for example, when a person drops a cup when he is stung on the hand by a wasp. The act of dropping the cup—the wasp almost literally hitting a nerve—is a physiological action (in legal terms, an involuntary act) and not one 'mediated by judgment and reason.' In the provocation context, however, anger is preceded by some judgment by the provoked party, even if it occurs instantly, that he or another to whom he feels an emotional attachment has been wronged in some manner by the provoker. In the ordinary provocation case, for example, when the provoker spits in another's face, uses insulting racial epithets, wrongs the individual by assaulting him, or commits some harm to a loved one, the provoker sends a disparaging message (or, at least, the provoked party reasonably interprets it this way) or commits a seeming injustice, which incites the victim of the provocation to fury.

Fury, however, is not enough to activate the defense. The law considers only some provocations 'adequate' to reduce a homicide to manslaughter. If we believe that the provocation is the type that entitles a person to feel anger, or even more strongly, if we feel that the provocation should make a person feel anger or outrage, e.g., when a person is verbally insulted or spat upon, then we may characterize the emotion as, in some sense, 'justifiable' or, if you will, appropriate. In this very limited way the heat-of-passion doctrine potentially contains a 'justificatory' feature.

The basis for mitigation, however, does not require a finding that the provoked party's anger or outrage is one we find appropriate or of which we approve ('justifiable'). It is enough that we are prepared to 'excuse' the actor for feeling as he does, or perhaps more precisely, we empathize with the actor's feelings. We must remember that the provocation defense is based to a considerable extent on the law's concession to ordinary human frailty; the ultimate question, therefore, is whether we (or the jury) consider the provoked party's anger within the range of expected human responses to the provocative situation. Put somewhat differently, we must decide if the provocative event might cause an ordinary person—one of ordinary and neither short nor saintly temperament—to become enraged or otherwise emotionally overcome.

For example, consider a person's emotional upheaval in being informed by his long-time married paramour that she intends to end the relationship and return to her husband. A jury may be unwilling to think of the man's anger or other passionate emotions as justifiable. After all, the woman had every right—indeed, perhaps a moral duty—to call off the relationship, and thus the man had no right to expect the woman to continue the relationship. A jury, however, could (not necessarily would) consider the man's emotional outburst 'excusable' ('empathizable?'), even if it were not prepared to characterize it as appropriate. That is enough to meet the first ingredient of the provocation defense.

One must keep in mind—although critics of the provocation doctrine often do not—that 'justifying' or 'excusing' the provoked party for his emotional upset does not in itself entitle the defendant to mitigation for a killing. My use of the term 'emotional outburst' in the last paragraph was purposeful: It points us in the direction of why provocation is an excuse defense, and not a justification. The modern defense is not about justifiable and controlled anger as outrage to honor; it is about excusable loss of self-control. It is not enough simply to say that a defendant's anger, which was mediated by judgment and reason, was, in the sense I have explained, justifiable or excusable: The provocation must be so serious that we are prepared to say that an ordinary person in the actor's circumstances, even an ordinarily law-abiding person of reasonable temperament, might become sufficiently upset by the provocation to experience substantial impairment of his capacity for self-control and, as a consequence, to act violently.

Under no circumstances is the provoked killing justifiable in the slightest; indeed, the actor's violent loss of self-control is unjustifiable. Moreover, the loss of self-control is not totally excusable, because the law's assumption is that the provoked party was not wholly incapable of controlling or channeling his anger. If he were totally incapable, a full excuse would be defensible. Instead the defense is based on our common experience that when we become exceptionally angry—remembering that we are not blaming the person for his anger—our ability to conform our conduct to the dictates of the law is seriously undermined, hence making law-abiding behavior far more difficult than in nonprovocative circumstances. It is this understandably greater difficulty to control conduct that appropriately mitigates a provoked actor's blameworthiness, and therefore, his responsibility for a homicide.

Many of the disputes over the elements of provocation in fact reflect a dispute over the correct understanding of provocation.[232] We will consider some of the most controversial issues.

20.2 THE PROVOCATIVE ACT MUST BE SOMETHING SAID OR DONE

As noted in Part I, the present law requires that there must be something said or done which caused the defendant to lose his or her self-control. Some who take the pure excuse view argue that this aspect of the present law is unsatisfactory because as long as the defendant lost his or her self-control it should not matter whether there was something that caused the loss of self-control.[233] However, those who take the justification or reasonable excuse view require there to be a provoking event in order to determine whether the defendant's action or anger was justified. They therefore support the approach of the present law.

John Gardner and Timothy Macklem[234] argue that to amount to provocation which can justify an angry response the provocative act must be accepted by society as the kind of thing which is a provoking insult by the standards of the community. Only then can it provide 'a moral warrant' for the angry reaction. They therefore argue that a crying baby,[235] for example, should never be regarded as a provocative insult. Being called 'gay' could be regarded as an insult, not because one's sexual orientation is properly something to be regarded as shameful, but because in our society the word 'gay' can carry insulting connotations in some circumstances.[236]

20.3 THE REASONABLE PERSON REQUIREMENT

As is clear from Part I, the courts have struggled with the correct way to interpret the reasonable person requirement and in particular to what extent the defendant's characteristics should be relevant in assessing the gravity of the provocation or the level of self-control expected. These difficulties have resulted from a failure to develop a clear idea about what role the reasonable person requirement is to play. Here are some of the alternatives that have been proposed.

---

[232] Dressler (1988b).   [233] J.C. Smith (2002: 366).   [234] Gardner and Macklem (2001b).
[235] *Doughty* (1986) 83 Cr App R 319.   [236] See further Howe (1997).

An evidentiary role

The role of the reasonable person test is no more than a 'double check' to provide evidence that the defendant really lost his or her self-control. If there is evidence that the defendant had lost his or her self-control and that a reasonable person would have then we can be confident that the defendant did truly lose his or her self-control. Those taking such an approach would be happy to consider how a reasonable person with all of the defendant's characteristics would react, because this would provide the most accurate evidence of the defendant's state of mind.

Although this would be an approach a legal system could take it does not seem to explain the way in which the reasonable person test applies in England and Wales. If the jury are convinced that the defendant did lose his self-control, but also decide that a reasonable person would not have done so then the defendant must be convicted of murder. This suggests that the reasonable person test is doing more than playing an evidential role.

Justificatory

Those who see provocation as a justification see the reasonable person test as the key part of the law on provocation, in that it ensures that the defendant's acts were partially justified. If this approach is taken then the defendant's characteristics are relevant only in assessing the gravity of the provocation and are not relevant in assessing the level of self-control expected. So, for example, if a racial insult is hurled, the jury must ask what is an appropriate reaction to that insult. The person's racial background may explain why the insult was aggravating, but it is not relevant in deciding the morally appropriate response to a provocation of that gravity.[237] Those who take this approach would therefore be happy with the law as developed in *Camplin*, but would strongly object to *Morgan Smith*.[238] Once the defendant is able to claim that 'my mental illness meant it was reasonable for me to react to this minor provocation in this excessive way', the justificatory element is lost. As John Gardner and Timothy Macklem[239] argue, if we do not allow a defendant who 'suffers' from a dishonest personality to have a defence, why should we allow it to someone who is short-tempered? In other words just as we require all defendants to live up to the same standards of honesty should we not expect all defendants to live up to the same standards of self-control?

Ensuring the defendant is not at prior fault

As shall be seen in Chapter 10, there is a general principle in the law on defences that an individual cannot rely on a defence which is self-induced. In this context the defence of provocation is available only if the defendant is not to blame for losing his self-control. This approach may be more sympathetic to the use of characteristics for which the defendant is not to blame, for example, age or mental disability, but not characteristics for which the defendant is responsible, for example, being an irritable person.[240] Lord Clyde in *Smith (Morgan)*[241] suggests that we should be asking whether the accused had made reasonable efforts to control himself, bearing in mind the limits of what he can reasonably be expected to do. The difficulty with such an approach is that it requires a distinction to be drawn

---

[237] See Herring (1996). [238] [2000] 3 WLR 654 (HL). [239] Gardner and Macklem (2001a).
[240] See Herring (1996). [241] [2000] 3 WLR 654, at 684.

between characteristics for which a defendant is responsible and those for which he or she is not. Such a distinction is not an easy one to make.

Policy level constraint

Dennis Klimchuk[242] has argued that the reasonable person requirement can be seen as a policy-based constraint. It is there to protect the general public. Although we may be sympathetic to a defendant whose psychological make-up means that it is difficult to control his behaviour, in order to protect the public it is necessary to convict of murder those who kill in the face of minor provocations, even if in moral terms they may be less blameworthy than other killers. There is some difficulty with this explanation in that it is possible to impose a life sentence on a person who successfully pleads provocation, if he poses a danger to the public.

QUESTIONS

1. Giovanni, an Italian, is called 'a wimp' by John. Giovanni flies into a rage and kills John. Which of the following arguments, if any, should the law be sympathetic to?:

    (i) Italian men are well known to be hot-blooded and so Giovanni should be expected to demonstrate only the level of self-control expected of the reasonable Italian man.

    (ii) Italian men are macho and so insults about their masculinity are far more insulting than such insults to English men, and the jury should be instructed to bear this in mind.

    When considering this, note the criticism, below, that the provocation defence tends to encourage racial and gender stereotyping!

2. McHugh J in *Masciantonio* (1994–5) 183 CLR 58 (High Court of Australia) questioned whether it is right to judge a person by the standard expected of 'a white middle class Australian of Anglo-Saxon-Celtic heritage'. Do you agree with the statement? Should people from certain educational, ethnic, cultural or socio-economic backgrounds be expected to have lower (or higher) levels of self-control than others?

3. Jeremy Horder (1992: 126) gives this example: 'Consider the case of a South African defendant brought up in England as a die-hard Afrikaner (let us call him Terreblanche) who fervently believes that coloured people should never speak to a white man on any matter whatsoever unless spoken to first, and that it is the highest form of insult to a white man for coloured people to break this rule of social intercourse. The "provocation" put in evidence by Terreblanche is that the coloured person he passed in the street, let us say, said "Good morning" to him before Terreblanche had said anything to him.' Should the law regard Terreblanche as being provoked?

4. Lord Goff in *Morhall* thought that the jury should be asked to consider how an ordinary person would react to the provocation, whereas the majority in *Smith (Morgan)* preferred to refer to the reasonable man. What is the difference between an ordinary person and a reasonable one? Which is the more appropriate test for provocation?

---

[242] Klimchuck (1994).

20.4 THE GENDERED NATURE OF THE DEFENCE

There has been a substantial amount written claiming that the defence of provocation is based on a male ideal of anger: it too easily provides men who kill with a defence, and is too hard to invoke as a defence for women who kill, especially women who kill partners who have been abusing them.[243] Some points in relation to particular provocation will be raised here, but we will be returning to the question of what defence should be available to a battered woman who kills in Chapter 12 (see pp. 782–785).

The defence is too readily available to men

It is clear that the origins of the defence were gendered. The classic examples of provocations in the nineteenth century included a man finding another man in the act of committing adultery with his wife and the sight of an Englishman being unlawfully deprived of his liberty.[244] More recently there have been cases where men have been able to use the defence claiming that their wife's constant 'nagging' or unfaithfulness has caused them to lose their self-control.[245] In such cases the resulting sentence can be surprisingly low.[246] Some commentators argue that such decisions can reinforce male possessiveness and control of women.

Provocation is difficult for battered women to use

There is clear statistical evidence that the majority of women who kill their partners have been abused by them. Such cases must be considered in the light of the social background and in particular the problem of domestic violence.[247] Government statistics indicate that one women in four will experience domestic violence at some stage in her life[248] and that domestic violence accounts for one-quarter of all violent crime.[249]

Women who have killed their partners following months of abuse have not readily found a defence in the criminal law.[250] As self-defence is not available if the defendant is not facing an imminent threat many such defendants have sought to rely on provocation, but have faced a number of difficulties in doing so, including the following:[251]

(1) Battered women are sometimes said to exhibit a 'slow-burn reaction'. That is, rather than the defendant lashing out in anger in response to a provocation her anger slowly increases until violence is exhibited some time after the provocative incident. The law appears more sympathetic to men 'snapping' at discovering their wife having an affair; but not with women driven to killing after years of abuse. In recent years the law on this area has

---

[243] For discussion on the rates of domestic violence and potential causes see Miles (2001) and Kaganas (2002).

[244] Wells (2000).   [245] *Singh* (1992) 13 Cr App R (S) 123 (CA); Bandalli (1992); McColgan (2000a).

[246] Horder (1989), but see Sentencing Guidelines Council (2005) which recommends that such cases are not treated leniently.

[247] Chan (2001). In Home Office (1999b) the government explains its latest attempts to tackle domestic violence.

[248] In fact it is difficult to get accurate statistics on the rate of domestic violence, and some commentators suggest that the figure is closer to one in three women (Mooney (2000)).

[249] Home Office (1999b).

[250] Edwards (1999); O'Donovan (1993); Chan (1994); Bandalli (1995); Nicolson (1995); Bridgeman and Millns (1998); McColgan (1993).

[251] McColgan (1993).

become more accessible to battered women following *Ahluwalia*, where it was accepted that even if there is a gap in time between the provocative act and the killing the jury may still be persuaded that the defendant suffered a sudden and temporary loss of self-control. It is notable that this greater flexibility in the law was achieved only after the court accepted expert medical evidence of a condition known as Battered Woman's Syndrome (BWS), one of the symptoms of which is 'slow-burn reaction'. In other words the 'slow' reaction of women is seen by the courts not as normal under the circumstances, but as a result of a special medical condition.[252]

(2) Sometimes in cases of battered women the defendant has finally snapped after what appears to be a relatively minor incident. It has therefore been difficult to show that the killing was a reasonable response to the provocation. However, since *Morhall*[253] it has been clear that the provocative act must be seen in the light of the defendant's whole history and, hence, what might appear to be a minor provocation can be seen as the 'last straw' following years of abuse.[254]

(3) There can be difficulty in establishing the loss of self-control requirement. Take the facts of *Ahluwalia*[255] (excerpted in Part I of this chapter). The defendant waited until her abusive husband was asleep, found some petrol, poured it over him, and set him alight, killing him. It may be thought that these acts, far from showing a loss of self-control, reveal a carefully thought-out plan. The cases on loss of self-control[256] suggest that the law presently takes a rather narrow view of loss of self-control, requiring a wild flailing around in anger. If loss of self-control could include a loss of self-restraint or loss of moral self-control, battered women may more easily be able to use the defence. Think of it this way. No doubt Ahluwalia must have wanted to kill her husband on many previous occasions, but managed to control her desires. On this night that 'moral check' was lost. Could this not be regarded as a form of loss of self-control?[257]

(4) There can be difficulties in showing that the defendant responded to the provocation in a reasonable way. For example, the trial judge argued in *Thornton*:[258]

> There are . . . many unhappy, indeed miserable, husbands and wives. . . . But on the whole it is hardly reasonable, you may think, to stab them fatally when there are other alternatives available, like walking out or going upstairs.

In response to such an argument it could be replied that the defendant acted as a reasonable woman suffering from BWS.[259]

It will have been noted that some of the difficulties facing battered women who kill who seek then to rely on provocation have been overcome by the courts' willingness to receive evidence that they suffer from BWS.[260] Nicholson and Sanghvi explain that sufferers of BWS 'develop a number of common characteristics, such as low self-esteem, self-blame for the violence, anxiety, depression, fear, general suspiciousness, and the belief that only they

---

[252] For a sceptical look at BWS see Schopp, Sturgis, and Sullivan (1994).   [253] [1996] AC 90 (HL).
[254] *Thornton (No. 2)* [1996] 1 WLR 1174 (CA).   [255] [1992] 4 All ER 889 (CA).
[256] e.g. *Cocker* [1989] Crim LR 740 (CA).
[257] See the proposed 'self-preservation defence' in Griffiths (2000: 148).
[258] Quoted in *Thornton* [1992] 1 All ER 306, 312 (CA).
[259] *Thornton (No. 2)* [1996] 2 All ER 1023 (CA).
[260] Walker (1989); Kaganas (2002).

can change their predicament'.[261] It is also claimed that the effect of this syndrome is that women suffer 'learned helplessness' such that they see no escape from the violence apart from killing.

Despite the fact that recognition of BWS has meant that battered women have more easily been able to find a defence, some commentators have been very concerned about its use in these cases.[262] The concerns include the following:

(1) Regarding BWS as the cause for the killing disguises other reasons why battered women stay in violent relationships (for example, the lack of refuges available for battered women or the absence of effective legal responses to domestic violence).[263] Also it is arguable that staying in the violent relationship, far from indicating a mental abnormality, may even be a sensible decision. There is evidence that women who leave an abusive partner may be at even greater risk of violence than they would have been had they stayed with him.[264] The emphasis placed on the syndrome also 'individualizes' the problem in that it fails to see domestic violence as part of the wider picture of a society within which violence and oppression against women are permitted, if not encouraged.[265]

(2) Commentators argue that women who kill having suffered long periods of violence and facing the prospect of even more violence are responding reasonably and not acting while suffering from some form of mental abnormality.[266] Indeed many commentators have argued that the law should permit battered women to rely on self-defence rather than provocation.[267] (The availability of self-defence for battered women will be discussed in Chapter 15.)

(3) Focusing the jury's mind on BWS leads the jury to concentrate on the evidence of the expert, rather than the evidence of the woman herself, who is seen as unreliable because she suffers from an abnormality. This can lead to claims that battered women's experiences are being rewritten in a medical discourse in criminal cases.[268]

Other commentators have responded differently and argued that killing an abusive partner, rather than leaving him, is a clearly disproportionate response and that too readily permitting defences to such conduct could be seen as condoning, or even encouraging, it.

20.5 THE CASE FOR THE ABOLITION OF THE DEFENCE

Some commentators take the view that the provocation defence should be abolished. These are some of the arguments that have been used:

(1) Jeremy Horder[269] has engaged on a sustained attack on the provocation defence. He argues that killing in anger is no more worthy of a defence than killing while overcome by greed or envy. In the light of a provocation a display of righteous

---

[261] Nicholson and Sanghvi (1993).   [262] See e.g. Wells (1993) and Sheehy, Stubbs, and Tolmie (1992).
[263] See e.g. Wells (1993) and Sheehy, Stubbs, and Tolmie (1992).
[264] Wilson and Daly (1993).   [265] Hanmer (2000).   [266] Kaganas (2002: 106).
[267] Canadian courts are more willing to use self-defence: *Lavallee* [1990] 1 SCR 852. See also Wells (1994); Norse (1997); Rosen (1986).
[268] Kaganas (2002).   [269] Wells (2000) and Horder (1992).

indignation may be appropriate, but a killing after a loss of self-control is so far in excess of an appropriate response that there is no moral warrant for it. There is, in other words, no good reason for killing in anger, and so it should not provide a defence.

(2) Asking what is a reasonable response for a person with the defendant's characteristics encourages the jury to rely on racial and sexual stereotypes.[270] In *Masciantonio*,[271] an Australian case, the defendant attempted to argue that in considering how a reasonable person would react the jury should consider the fact that he was Italian and was therefore hot-blooded and more prone to lose his self-control. This clearly indicates the ways in which provocation can lead to stereotyping.

(3) The provocation defence invites the defendant to defame the deceased.[272] It encourages the defendant to put forward evidence of insulting behaviour by the deceased. For example, a husband who has killed his wife wanting to use the defence of provocation might to seek to introduce evidence that he was continually insulted and demeaned by his wife to such a point that he lost his self-control. Of course, the deceased, in such a case is unable to respond to such allegations.

(4) The gender bias in the operation of the defence means that it should be abolished.[273] Horder points out that on average 52.5 per cent of women who kill their male partners are able to rely on the defence of provocation, while 30 per cent of men who kill their female partners are able to do so.[274] At first sight these figures might suggest, if anything, that the defence operates in a way that is pro-women. However, this would be misconceived. It must be recalled that the vast majority of women who have killed their partners have been subject to sustained physical abuse, while the number of men who will have been subjected to violence by their partners will be tiny. In the light of this the percentage figures for women look very low and the figures for men look surprisingly high. Although these statistics do provide a strong basis for an argument that provocation be abolished, it must be asked if the defence is removed, what defence will the 52.5 per cent of women who kill their abusive partners and currently use provocation be able to rely upon?[275]

In the following passage, having criticized the way in which the present law on provocation too easily provides a defence for a man who kills his wife who has announced she is leaving him, but finds it hard to provide a defence for a woman who kills a man who has raped her some time after the rape, Victoria Norse goes on to consider whether a preferable form of the defence can be developed:[276]

V. Norse, 'Passion's Progress: Modern Law Reform and the Provocation Defense' (1997) 106 *Yale Law Journal* 1331 at 1389–92

Advocates of abolition face an obvious question: If we abolish the defense, what becomes of the woman who, distraught and enraged, kills her stalker, her rapist, or her batterer?

---

[270] Wells (2000).   [271] (1994–5) 183 CLR 58 (H Ct of Aust).   [272] Wells (2000).
[273] Yeo (1999) argues that it is the operation of the defence, rather than the substantive law, which operates in a gendered way.
[274] Horder (1992: 187).   [275] Sullivan (1993a).
[276] For a rejection of her view see Dressler (2002b).

I suspect that many would say that these women deserve our compassion. The most persuasive scholarly defenses of provocation have all invoked examples, like these, in which the defendant's emotion reflects the outrage of one responding to a grave wrong that the law otherwise punishes. Commentators frequently use examples of men killing their wives' rapists or children who kill abusive parents as clear cases of provoked murder. . . .

The problem comes when we focus on cases in which the emotion is based on less compelling 'reasons'—when women kill their departing husbands or men kill their complaining wives. Under conventional liberal theory, if extreme emotion is shown, these cases should be handled no differently from cases where victims kill their rapists and stalkers and batterers. The quantity or intensity of the emotion provides the excuse, not the reasons for the emotion. This focus on emotion, to the exclusion of reason, reflects a very important assumption made by liberal theories of the defense, that emotion obscures reason. When we distinguish the rapist killer from the departing wife killer, we acknowledge a very different view of emotion, one in which emotion is imbued with meaning. Both the departing wife killer and the rapist killer may be upset, but the meanings embodied in their claims for emotional understanding are quite different. In distinguishing these cases based on the reasons for the claimed emotion, we acknowledge a view of emotion in which emotion is not the enemy of reason but, instead, its embodiment.

. . .

Where does this understanding of emotion lead us? It helps us to see why we might distinguish intuitively the rapist killer from the departing wife killer. In the first case, we feel 'with' the killer because she is expressing outrage in ways that communicate an emotional judgment (about the wrongfulness of rape) that is uncontroversially shared, indeed, that the law itself recognizes. Such claims resonate because we cannot distinguish the defendant's sense of emotional wrongfulness from the law's own sense of appropriate retribution. The defendant's emotional judgments are the law's own. In this sense, the defendant is us. By contrast, the departing wife killer cannot make such a claim. He asks us to share in the idea that leaving merits outrage, a claim that finds no reflection in the law's mirror. In fact, the law tells us quite the opposite: that departure, unlike rape and battery and robbery, merits protection rather than punishment.

This understanding finally allows us to suggest an answer to the paradox with which we continually confront our law students: How can it be that a reasonable person kills in these circumstances and, if a reasonable person would, why not completely exonerate him? The short answer is that 'reasonable men and women' do not kill in these circumstances, but reasonable men and women may well possess emotions that the law needs to protect. Without protecting some emotions, the criminal law contradicts itself. It punishes the very emotions implicit in the law's own judgments that killing and raping and robbing are both wrong and merit retribution. At the same time, protecting emotion does not require us to protect the deed. If we protect the act of killing, the criminal law commits itself to a different contradiction, one in which the State embraces or at least tolerates vigilantism.

We can now see why the provocation defense has always stood on the fence, partially condoning, yet partially exculpating. In every provoked murder case the law risks the embrace of revenge. To maintain its monopoly on violence, the State must condemn, at least partially, those who take the law in their own hands. At the same time, however, some provoked murder cases temper our feelings of revenge with the recognition of tragedy. Some defendants who take the law in their own hands respond with a rage shared by the law. In such cases, we 'understand' the defendant's emotions because these are the very emotions to which the law itself appeals for the legitimacy of its own use of violence. At the same time, we continue to condemn the act because the defendant has claimed a right to use violence that is not his own.

The important point to see here is that the provoked killer's claim for our compassion is not simply a claim for sympathy; it is a claim of authority and a demand for our concurrence. The defendant who asks for our compassion, that we feel 'with him,' asks that we 'share the state of mind that [he] expresses.' He asks that we share his judgments of emotional blame. Precisely because he asks us to embrace those emotional judgments, he asks us to embrace him as legislator, as one who rightly sets the emotional terms of blame and wrongdoing vis-a-vis his victim. When a defendant responds with outrage to wrongs the society otherwise punishes, he asks us to believe that he has legislated nothing. However, when a defendant responds with outrage to conduct society protects, he seeks to supplant the State's normative judgment, to impose his individual vision of blame and wrongdoing not only on the victim, but also on the rest of us.

As should be obvious by now, my theory of the defense is based as much on equality as it is on autonomy. All defendants who kill, with good reason or no reason at all, assert superiority over their victims, the superiority that comes from using the victim as a means rather than an end. But in provoked murder cases we also risk allowing the defendant to assert an emotional and normative superiority. The danger is not only that the defendant will 'use' the victim but also that he will rationalize the 'use' of the victim by claiming that we share in his distribution of emotional blame. When we are sure that the victim would not have shared the killer's emotional judgments (where she left because she was beaten) or when we know that the victim would not have expected punishment for the acts triggering the defendant's outrage (bad cooking, complaints, and messy houses), we see that the defendant's claim for compassion is false. It is a claim that we share in a set of emotional judgments vis-a-vis the victim that are not shared. To embrace such claims is to permit the defendant to sit on a higher normative plane.

. . .

Conventional understandings of criminal law place defenses in two mutually exclusive categories: as excuse or justification. In the excuse category are defenses, such as insanity, that focus on state of mind; these defenses do not embody judgments that what the defendant did was 'right' or 'justified,' but that the defendant was less blameworthy. In the 'justification' category are defenses, such as self-defense or necessity, which assume that what the defendant has done, overall, was 'right' or 'warranted.' Traditionally, 'excuse' and 'justification' have been viewed as mutually exclusive categories: A defendant cannot be both excused and justified because an excused action presupposes that the action was wrong and therefore unjustified. This assumes, however, a crucial feature of the inquiry—that we are evaluating acts and acts alone. To say that an act cannot be both justified and excused is to say something about acts, not emotions. It is perfectly consistent to say that one's emotions are justified or warranted even when one's acts are not. Indeed, as I have noted above, we may easily say that passionate killings are not justified even if we believe that the emotions causing some killings are, in some sense, the 'right' emotion.

It is by focusing on the emotion, rather than the act, that my proposal distinguishes itself quite easily (both in theory and practice) from the traditional model of provocation as partial justification. My proposal does not depend upon the theory that the victim deserves to be punished. Instead, I propose that the law should see the defendant's state of mind (his emotion) as something that, in some cases, it should protect. Unlike a partial justification model, my approach allows the defense to retain many features associated with excuse. The law need not impose an 'objective' standard. It may continue to focus on the defendant's perception of the triggering act, rather than its quality in the abstract—something that the partial justification model rejects. Thus, a defendant who believes she is being stalked, even if she is not, could properly claim her emotion was warranted, based on her perception of the situation. The law may also keep a liberal regard for the defendant's characteristics when they are relevant to the underlying defense—again, something irrelevant to the partial justification model. Thus, a defendant who claims that she killed when enraged by a hate crime obviously raises an issue to which racial, gender, or other characteristics may be relevant, if not crucial. Finally, the law may provide for cases in which emotion builds over time—a position that traditional models typically reject. A defendant who claims that he was sodomized and later outraged by taunts will be allowed to pursue the defense, as would a battered woman who claimed that her outrage and fear developed over time.

. . .

If accepted, this theory should bar many, if not most, provocation claims in intimate homicide cases. It would not be enough for a defendant to claim that a divorce or a protective order or moving out caused her rage. Defendants who ask us for compassion in these cases can point to neither law nor social norm that would punish leaving. My proposal would also bar the defense in cases in which the defendant claimed rage inspired by infidelity. Society is no longer willing to punish adultery. In the absence of such a willingness, the adulterer killer has no claim that his emotions were no different from the emotions to which the law itself appeals to rationalize punishment. This does not mean that infidelity is not emotionally painful. It does mean that those who urge compassion based on infidelity can point to nothing in the law itself that would demand that we have compassion for their violent outrage. The law only suffers contradiction when it refuses to embrace a sense of outrage which is necessary to the law's rationalization of its own use of violence. When the law refuses to jail adulterers, the contradiction operates the other way: We are compelled to ask why it is that private parties may enforce a sense of outrage that society has refused itself.

. . .

To adopt this theory, of course, requires us to reject the idea upon which almost all contemporary theories of the defense are predicated: that we partially excuse because the defendant lacks a full or fair capacity for self-control. Let me be clear about what we reject here: We do not reject self-control to embrace judgment; we reject a disguised judgment for one that is acknowledged. No matter how much we try to tie the defense to behavior, no matter how insistent the rhetoric of subjectivity, decisions applying this defense express judgments about when defendants 'should' exercise self-control. The law can continue to deny this if it chooses, to bury it within the qualities of a reasonable person, but it pays a heavy price—one not only of incoherence, but of intellectual passivity and circularity. To say that we partially excuse provoked murderers to increase men's freedom but that their freedom is a condition of granting the excuse is to indulge in tautology. In this circularity resides a space in which we find ourselves committed to beliefs about men and women and their relationships that the law itself long ago abandoned.

20.6 REFORM OF PROVOCATION

The Law Commission have recommended reform of the defence of provocation. They recommend as follows:

Law Commission, Consultation Paper 177, *A New Homicide Act for England and Wales Overview* (London: TSO, 2005).

Provocation

5.53 In our report Partial Defences to Murder, we recommended that the principles that should govern provocation as a partial defence were:

(1) the defendant must have acted in response to:

   (a) gross provocation (meaning words or conduct, or a combination of both, which caused the defendant to have a justifiable sense of being seriously wronged); or

   (b) fear of serious violence towards the defendant or another; or

   (c) a combination of (1) and (2); and

(2) a person of the defendant's age and of ordinary temperament, i.e. ordinary tolerance and self-restraint, in the circumstances of the defendant might have reacted in the same or a similar way.

5.54 We said that that provocation as a partial defence ought to be available to those who acted in response to a fear of serious violence even if they killed at a time when they were not in imminent danger of serious violence. We also said that it ought to be available to those who could not successfully plead self-defence because, although they killed in response to a threat of imminent violence, they responded with a degree of force that was disproportionate to the threat of violence that they faced.

5.55 We emphasised that the defence ought not to be available:

(1) if the provocation was incited by the defendant for the purpose of providing an excuse to use violence; or

(2) if the defendant acted in considered desire for revenge. However, we also said that, if the defendant responded to fear of serious violence, he or she ought not to be treated as having out of a considered desire for revenge merely because he or she was also angry towards the deceased for the conduct that gave rise to the fear of serious violence.

5.56 Finally, we recommended that a judge should not have to leave the defence to the jury unless there was evidence on which a reasonable jury, properly directed, could conclude that it might apply.

5.57 Because we are now provisionally proposing that provocation should be a defence to 'first degree murder' but not 'second degree murder', we have reconsidered our previous recommendations. In particular, we have examined whether the partial defence of provocation should be restricted to cases in which a person responds to a fear of serious violence.

5.58 'First degree murder' requires an intention to kill, an especially heinous violation of the sanctity of life. There should be compelling reasons for reducing a killing committed with an intention to kill to 'second degree murder'. Arguably, a response to conduct that gives rise to a justifiable sense of being seriously wronged is not a compelling reason. By contrast, it might be thought that acting in response to a fear of serious violence is in principle a more plausible candidate for a partial excuse. It is only one step short of being a complete defence, in the form of self-defence, to a charge of murder.

5.59 Importantly, we are recommending that the judge should not be required to leave the defence to the jury unless he or she believes that there is evidence on which a jury could conclude that the defence might apply. We believe that, in most cases where the defendant acts in response to 'gross provocation' which does not involve a fear of serious violence, a properly directed jury could not conclude that a person of ordinary tolerance and self-restraint might have killed with an intention to kill. In such cases, the judge will not leave the defence to the jury. However, we see no reason why, if the judge believes that on the evidence a properly directed jury could so conclude, the defence should not be left to the jury. Accordingly, we are proposing that the partial defence of provocation should be reformed in the way that we previous recommended.

FURTHER READING

Ashworth, A. (1976), 'The Doctrine of Provocation', *Cambridge Law Journal* 35: 292.

Chan, W. (2001), *Women, Murder and Justice* (Basingstoke: Palgrave).

Dressler, J. (1988b), 'Provocation: Partial Justification or Partial Excuse?', *Modern Law Review* 51: 467.

—— (2002b), 'Why Keep the Provocation Defense?: Some Reflections on a Difficult Subject', *Minnesota Law Review* 86: 959.

Edwards, S. (2004), 'Abolishing Provocation and Reframing Self-Defence', *Criminal Law Review* 181.

Gardner, J., and Macklem, T. (2001a), 'Compassion without Respect? Nine Fallacies in *R v Smith*', *Criminal Law Review* 623.

—— and —— (2001b), 'Provocation and Pluralism', *Modern Law Review* 64: 815.

—— and —— (2004) 'No Provocation without Responsibility', *Criminal Law Review* 213.

Garvey, S. (2005), 'Passion's Puzzle', *Iowa Law Review* 90: 1677

Horder, J. (1992), *Provocation and Responsibility* (Oxford: OUP).

—— (2005a) 'Reshaping the Subjective Element in the Provocation Defence', *Oxford Journal of Legal Studies* 25: 123.

Kaganas, F. (2002), 'Domestic Violence, Gender and the Expert' in A. Bainham, S. Day Sclater, and M. Richards (eds.), *Body Lore and Laws* (Oxford: Hart).

Mackay, R., and Mitchell, B. (2003), 'Provoking Diminished Responsibility: Two Pleas Merging into One', *Criminal Law Review* 745.

—— and —— (2004), 'Replacing Provocation', *Criminal Law Review* 219.

—— and —— (2005), 'But is this Provocation? Some thought on the Law Commission Report on Partial Defences to Murder', *Criminal Law Review* 44.

McColgan, A. (1993), 'In Defence of Battered Women who Kill', *Oxford Journal of Legal Studies* 508.

Mousourakis, G. (1998a), *Criminal Responsibility and Partial Excuse* (Aldershot: Ashgate).

Norrie, A. (2002), 'From Criminal Law to Legal Theory: The Mysterious Case of the Reasonable Glue Sniffer', *Modern Law Review* 65: 538.

Wells, C. (2000), 'Provocation: The Case for Abolition' in A. Ashworth and B. Mitchell (eds.), *Rethinking English Homicide Law* (Oxford: OUP).

21 DIMINISHED RESPONSIBILITY

In order to understand the theoretical basis for diminished responsibility it is important to remember some of the other defences available to a charge of murder. In particular there are the defences of no *mens rea*, automatism, and insanity. So diminished responsibility is not intended for those whose mental abnormality is so severe that they are insane or are non-insane automatons. Indeed it should be emphasized that diminished responsibility is a partial defence: the defendant who successfully raises the defence is still guilty of man-slaughter, with the potential for a life sentence. So, a defendant who successfully raises the defence is not blameless, it is rather that his level of blame is not sufficient to justify a murder conviction. This is not to mean that he is unable to act voluntarily and intentionally, but rather that his moral character is so distorted that he is unable critically to evaluate his conduct.[277]

Peter Sparks[278] has argued that there is a fundamental flaw in the notion of diminished responsibility. He suggests that we ask whether the defendant would have killed had he not suffered from the abnormality of mind. If we decide that the defendant would not, Sparks argues that the defendant should have a complete defence, because it was the abnormality which caused the defendant to commit the crime. However, if we decide that even without the abnormality the defendant would still have killed then he deserves no defence. In other words the defendant's abnormality of mind might justify a complete defence or no defence, but not a partial defence. Supporters of diminished responsibility might argue that this overlooks the possibility that the abnormality of mind made it very difficult, but not impossible, to avoid killing.

21.1 DIMINISHED RESPONSIBILITY IN PRACTICE

The diminished responsibility plea is successful in 90 per cent of cases in which the defendant raises it.[279] This is because in 80 per cent of cases the prosecution does not dispute the defendant's evidence of his mental abnormality.[280] Where the prosecution does challenge the defence it succeeds in 64 per cent of cases.[281]

Key to the successful plea of diminished responsibility is finding medical evidence to support it. However, the emphasis on medical evidence is problematic.[282] Doctors and others have complained that they are expected to give evidence on the basis of the terminology used in the Homicide Act 1957; but that terminology is not medical. Although medical evidence might be able to establish whether the defendant suffered from an abnormality of the mind, it is far harder to give evidence about whether the defendant was suffering a substantial impairment of responsibility. The question of the defendant's responsibility is not a question of medical fact, but rather a moral judgement.[283] It is therefore not properly an issue upon which a doctor can give expert advice.

---

[277] For further discussion see Mackay (2000); Horder (1999); Morse (1993).   [278] Sparks (1964).
[279] Mackay (1995); Dell (1984).   [280] Dell (1984: 26).
[281] Dell (1984: 28); Mackay and Machin (2000).
[282] Mackay (1999) questions whether the Human Rights Act 1998 and Art. 6 of the European Convention on Human Rights require that a defendant's plea of diminished responsibility should be assessed by a group of experts, rather than the jury.
[283] Mackay (2000).

There are some concerns that doctors are willing to supply evidence which may lead to the acquittal of the defendant because they feel that the defendant does not deserve a murder conviction. In *Vinagre*[284] a husband killed his wife, whom he suspected of committing adultery. Psychiatrists gave evidence that the defendant was suffering from 'Othello's syndrome'; described as 'morbid jealousy for which there was no cause'. As this was the evidence of the Crown's psychiatrists not surprisingly the defendant accepted it. Lawton LJ caustically noted, 'There was clear evidence of a killing by a jealous husband which, until modem times, no one would have thought was anything else but murder.'

Often the flexibility of the terminology can work to show compassion for a defendant in an unhappy situation.[285] For example, some cases of mercy killing are brought within diminished responsibility, even though there is not technically an abnormality of mind. The operation of the defence involves what has been described as a 'benevolent conspiracy' between lawyers and doctors to ensure that defendants who do not deserve the stigma of a murder conviction are able to avoid it.[286] The difficulty is that there appears to be inconsistent practice among psychiatrists.[287]

21.2 THE THEORETICAL BASIS OF THE DIMINISHED RESPONSIBILITY DEFENCE

In the following passage Jeremy Horder discusses the relationship between provocation and diminished responsibility. In doing so he provides an interesting account of the two defences. Note that he was writing before the House of Lords had delivered their judgments in *Smith (Morgan)* and the Privy Council in *Holley*. He argues that the two defences need to be seen as completely separate:

J. Horder, 'Between Provocation and Diminished Responsibility' [1999] *Kings College Law Journal* 143

Introduction: Excuses and Exemptions

In murder cases, the legal distinction between the pleas of provocation and diminished responsibility reflects an ethical distinction between a partial excuse for wrongdoing (provocation) and a partial denial of responsibility (diminished responsibility). I shall shortly explain what that ethical distinction is. As the important case of *R v Smith*[288] illustrates, however, like any significant ethical distinction, the distinction's boundaries are contested and difficult to draw. For reasons explored in due course, when the boundary is drawn in the wrong place, cases more properly regarded as ones of diminished responsibility tend to be mistakenly categorised as ones of provocation. Let us begin with the basic ethical distinction. A good place to start is with Gardner's definition of an excuse:

'[T]he gist of an excuse is not that the action was "out of character", in the sense of being a departure from what we have come to expect from the person whose action it is. Quite the contrary, in fact. The gist of an excuse . . . is precisely that the person with the excuse lived up to our expectations.'[289]

This view rightly discounts, by implication, purely subjective bases for an excuse (e.g. '

---

[284] (1979) 69 Cr App R 104.   [285] Mackay (1995: 185).   [286] Bluglass (1980: 10).
[287] Griew (1988).   [288] [1998] 4 All ER 387.   [289] Gardner (1998b).

should be excused for the simple reason that I lost my self-control'). In so far as they have any plausibility whatsoever, such accounts confuse claims to excuse with denials of responsibility. On the contrary, when one is excused, one's wrongful conduct—under duress, or following a provoked loss of self-control—is excused if (other things being equal) it measures up to a standard, if it is—in the relevant sense—within the bounds of reasonableness. We must be careful to dispel an appearance of paradox about this view. One might ask: 'is an excuse not something provided when someone was pressured or provoked into *failing* to come up to a standard?' The answer is no. What is excused, if anything, is the unjustified wrongdoing; and the wrongdoing is excusable, if at all, only if one came up to the relevant standard.

One's eligibility for excuse obviously presupposes that one can conform to the relevant standards in one's conduct. The contrast here is with denials of responsibility, such as pleas of insanity or diminished responsibility. These are based on a (partial) denial of ethical agency in respect of the particular action. This is a claim that judgement of the action in accordance with ordinary ethical (excusatory) standards is inappropriate, because an abnormality of mind means that the defendants in question cannot come up to the relevant standards in their conduct. Partial or complete *exemptions* from liability (insanity) or from labelling as a murderer (diminished responsibility), not excuses, are what are granted to such defendants. Those who act whilst insane or while suffering from diminished responsibility are 'moral objects', persons to whom moral concern and humane treatment are due. Such people are not, though (full) moral agents in respect of their actions: they are not persons whose action(s) can be adequately guided by the moral criteria by which they stand to be judged.

Three Theories of Provocation and Two Theories of Diminished Responsibility

So much for the basic distinction between excuses and (partial) denials of responsibility. What makes the distinction hard to make, at crucial points, is that one can have different views about what it means to be someone who in Gardner's phrase 'lived up to our expectations', for excusatory purposes, just as one can have different views about what it means to be (partly) denying one's responsibility. There are at least three ethically plausible ways of giving sense to Gardner's understanding of excuse, and two such ways of understanding a denial of responsibility. In this regard, I want to distinguish a strong, a moderate, and a weak theory *of* excuses, in Gardner's sense.

'*The strong excuse theory:* defendants should be judged by an ordinary standard of conduct, whatever their individual capacity to reach that standard.'

The strong excuse theory is not ethically implausible, because it can involve shaping our expectations to accommodate individual characteristics, if these do not bear directly on the capacity to reach the standard in question. So, suppose a disabled person has been taunted about his or her disability, lost self-control and killed. On the strong excuse theory, one can take account of this individual characteristic affecting the gravity of the provocation, because one can do this without letting go of the notion that an ordinary standard of self-control must be exercised in the face of such a provocation. According to the strong excuse theory, however, no individual characteristics affecting someone's level of self-control can be taken into account, not even a normal characteristic that may lower the levels, such as youth. According to the strong theory, once over the age of criminal responsibility, principles of justice and equality demand that we are all to be held to the same standards of conduct; those that would be maintained by the ordinary adult. The strong excuse theory was, at least arguably, the theory governing the common law, until the decisions of the House of Lords in

Holmes v *DPP*[290] and *Bedder* v *DPP* wrongly turned it into a theory that disregarded all individual characteristics, whether or not they related to the defendant's capacity for self-control.

'*The moderate excuse theory:* defendant should be judged by an ordinary standard of conduct, unless their capacity to reach the standard is inhibited by natural and normal factor, such as age.'

This is the theory that explicitly guides the reasoning in three crucial decisions of high or the highest authority on the doctrine of provocation, *DPP* v *Camplin, R* v *Morhall* and *Luc Thiet Thuan* v *R*. Taken as a whole, and broadly speaking, these decisions stand for the view that mental infirmities or abnormalities are characteristics which must be ignored when considering what standard of self-control D could reasonably be expected to meet, in the face of the provocation in issue. This is because such characteristics are relevant, if at all, only to the defence of diminished responsibility. According to the moderate excuse theory, however, age must, where relevant be permitted to lower the expected standards of self-control, in the face of the provocation because as Lord Diplock put it *in DPP* v *Camplin* 'to require old heads upon young shoulders is inconsistent with the law's compassion to human infirmity'. It would, moreover, be wholly inappropriate to expect, say, young persons to plead diminished responsibility when they have lost self-control and killed. That defence is for those with abnormalities of mind, and youth—with all its occasional unpredictability—is no mental abnormality.

'*The weak excuse theory:* defendants should be judged by the standards of what could be reasonably be expected of the individual in question.'

A number of recent decisions of the Court of Appeal, the latest of which is *R* v *Smith*, have called the moderate excuse theory into question, hence badly eroding, in particular, the authority of *DPP* v *Camplin*. In answer to the question 'by what yardstick should a defendant's conduct be judged partially excusable or wholly inexcusable, when he or she reacted to provocation by losing self-control and killing the victim?', the Court of Appeal has more-or-less consistently answered, 'by the standards we would expect him or her individually to reach, given all his or her characteristics, *including* any mental abnormalities'. This is clearly a move towards the adoption of the weak excuse theory. The move may in part be prompted by the thought that whilst the strong or moderate excuse theories may be the right theories for complete excuses, provocation is only a partial excuse, rendering murder to manslaughter, and a weak excuse theory may not be out of place for partial excuses. I shall say about this below.

As I shall seek to show, this division of opinion between the higher and lower courts echoes a similar debate that took place in the nineteenth century, in the shadow of the death penalty. The question, made all the more pertinent by the absence of a diminished responsibility defence at that time, concerned the scope of voluntary manslaughter by provocation: should mitigation be extended to the naturally irascible person who killed upon trivial provocation? The law itself ultimately gave as its answer a resounding 'no', endorsing the strong excuse theory outline above. The recent developments just described require us to confront the same question again. This time, we ought to be confronting that question with the benefit of knowing how the defence of diminished responsibility relates to the defence of provocation. The problem is that there is more that one theory of how the defence of diminished responsibility (DR) operates as a defence.

[290] [1946] AC 588 (HL).

'*The narrow DR theory:* diminished responsibility is an exemption from labelling as a murderer, akin to a plea of insanity but shorn of some of technicalities that bedevil the latter defence. It is hence granted only when a defendant's mental abnormality so distorts his or her ethical character, that this distortion is in itself sufficient to make blame largely inappropriate.'

On the narrow DR theory, external factors—duress; provocation; intoxication—that may bring a defendant's mental abnormality into play, leading him or her to kill, are never in themselves relevant to the question whether murder should be reduced to manslaughter. They are, at best, no more than evidence that the abnormality of mind had been brought into play, and was substantially diminishing the defendant's responsibility for his or her conduct. The problem with the narrow DR theory is that if, to be successful in his or her plea, a defendant must be found to have been suffering from a mental abnormality akin to insanity, it is unclear why he or she is still rightly convicted of manslaughter. It is unclear, in other words, why a successful plea only changes the offence label (murder into voluntary manslaughter), and does not affect liability as a whole. Problems of this kind have led the courts to operate with a wide DR theory.

'*The wide DR theory:* the diminished responsibility defence is for those whose mental abnormality led them to experience significant—if not insuperable—difficulties in controlling the conduct through which the victim was killed. Hence, although the defendant must still take some blame for the killing, reduction of the offence from murder to manslaughter may none the less be appropriate, particularly if other mitigating factors are present.'

If the law operates with a weak excuse theory and a wide DR theory, there will be considerable overlap between the defences of provocation and of diminished responsibility. Recall that the standard to which we expect a disordered defendant to conform under the weak excuse theory, is the standard he or she could be expected to meet, given his or her mental disorder. In answer to the question, 'has the defendant met the required standard?' we will (in a roundabout way) then be asking much the same question as the question we ask, under the wide DR theory, when we ask whether the defendant's abnormality of mind was such as to pose the kind of significant conduct-control difficulties that ought to reduce the offence to manslaughter. Does an overlap matter? I suggest that it does, because the moral integrity of each defence is preserved only if such defences are capable of operating largely (but not wholly) independently of one another.

A Summary of the Argument

To preserve the moral integrity of each defence, in reducing murder to manslaughter, we should follow the moderate excuse theory in provocation cases. As we shall see, this means that defendants such as Smith would have to seek to rely on diminished responsibility, rather than on provocation, because there would be much less of an overlap between the two defences that Smith itself supports. Why should this be? The provocation defence has been rightly said to be a defence for those who are 'in a broad sense, mentally normal.' In the provocation context, what this means is that the defendant's ethical make-up must be sufficiently robust to be appropriately judged by reference to the 'quantity and quality' of the provocation received that led to his or her loss of self-control. For people with ordinary powers of self-control, the objective gravity of the provocation (judged in accordance with the *Camplin* test) is, and ought to be, crucial to the success of the plea: the graver the provocation the less ethically reprehensible—albeit still unjustified—the degree of violence in the angry response. An explanation of how one came to respond with disproportionate violence to a trivial provocation is, by definition, an explanation of how one failed to act in accordance with ordinary ethical standards. Except on the strong excuse theory, it does not inevitably follow, however, that all such failures must be channelled into a plea of diminished responsibility, if murderous violence in response to a trivial provocation is to end in a manslaughter verdict.

What marks out the moderate excuse theory as moderate is the way in which it insists that the law treat (in particular) young defendants. A less demanding standard of self-control ought to be expected of a young defendant (depending, obviously on his or her exact age), with the result that disproportionate (murderous) attacks by provoked young persons, in response to an objectively trivial provocation, may none the less sometimes be excused. Why? For the simple reason that the less well-developed powers of self-control of young persons are a reflection of their (naturally) as-yet-incompletely-realised potential to become fully accountable moral agents. Their less well developed powers of self-control can hence be a reflection of their *mental normality*, and are thus appropriately catered for by special treatment, within the confines of a doctrine designed for those who are in Ashworth's phrase 'in a broad sense, mentally normal'. It follows that moderate excuse theorists will hold that a line can and should be drawn between young defendants and mentally disordered defendants who (because of their disorder) overreact to trivial provocations. The fact that the latter rely on a mental abnormality to explain their reactions shows why they should be pleading diminished responsibility rather than provocation. For mentally disordered defendants are claiming that the ordinary moral criteria by which the mentally normal are judged, when they lose control in the face of provocation are not appropriately applied to them. The basis for mitigation claimed by mentally disordered defendants who overact is thus qualitatively different from that which underpins such a claim by young persons. In essence, the former seek to by-pass the standards of accountability set by moral agency, whereas the latter say that such standards are applicable, but must be applied in a less rigorous way.

Suppose, then, that we accept this conclusion, as a consequence of adherence to the moderate excuse theory. There will still be a significant problem facing a mentally disordered person who has (due to his or her disorder) lost self-control and killed, in the face of trivial provocation and who now wishes to plead diminished responsibility. That is that, if the narrow DR theory is held to govern the use of that defence in his or her case, he or she may fall short if its requirements, if his or her mental disorder is not so sever that it warrants reducing murder to manslaughter *in itself*, without regard to the effect of other factors. For example, a defendant is barred from claiming that whilst his or her abnormality of mind was not in itself sufficient to impair his or her mental responsibility (whatever that means), to the extent that murder should be reduced to manslaughter, when considered together with the additional effect of his or her intoxication, it was. Arguably, this approach is too restrictive, in general, even if it is the right approach to the particular cases in which voluntary intoxication is an additional impairing factor. This is especially so, when one is considering only a reduction from murder to manslaughter, rather than a full acquittal. If we apply the wide DR theory, we can produce a result more generous to the mentally abnormal accused person who has overreacted to trivial provocation.

On the wide DR theory, it may be accepted that D's abnormality of mind does not in itself sufficiently substantially impair a defendant's mental responsibility to the point where murder should be reduced to manslaughter. According to the wide DR theory, by way of contrast with the narrow DR theory, it may none the less be the case that when that abnormality is considered together with the additional fact that the defendant was provoked to lose self-control, there were sufficient grounds for the reduction. A reduction from murder to manslaughter, on such 'mixed' grounds, should be a legal possibility. It should, though, be a legal possibility under the aegis of diminished responsibility, and this sets limits to the nature of the 'mixture' of the grounds. Under a wide DR theory, provocation plays a different role in justifying the reduction of murder to manslaughter, in diminished responsibility cases to the role it plays in provocation cases. In diminished responsibility cases, in principle, the mere fact that the defendant was provoked to lose self-control can in itself, without regard to the gravity of the provocation; add sufficient grounds for mitigation to the effect of the abnormality of mind to warrant a manslaughter verdict. It is the different nature of provocation's role in the wide DR theory, and in particular the fact that it can play its role without regard to its objectively judged gravity, that preserves the moral significance of the distinction between such a plea, and a plea of provocation.

21.3 REFORM OF DIMINISHED RESPONSIBILITY

The Law Commission have proposed reform of the defence of diminished responsibility as follows:[291]

5.69 We are provisionally proposing that, in order to establish the partial defence of diminished responsibility, the defendant should have to prove that at the time of the killing:

(1) his or her capacity to

   (a) understand events;

   (b) judge whether his or her actions were right or wrong; or

   (c) control him or herself

   was substantially impaired by an abnormality of mental functioning arising from an underlying condition or developmental immaturity, or both, and

(2) the abnormality of mental functioning or developmental immaturity, or a combination of both, was a significant cause of the defendant's conduct in carrying out the killing.

(3) 'Underlying condition' means a pre-existing mental or physiological condition.

QUESTIONS

1. In the light of the Horder extract, consider whether battered women should use the defence of provocation or diminished responsibility.

2. Do you think a person who kills while suffering diminished responsibility is more or less blameworthy than a person who kills under provocation?

3. Why should 'morbid obsessiveness' not be a relevant characteristic to attribute to the reasonable person as suggested by the majority in *Smith*? Should such a person be able to rely on diminished responsibility?

---

[291] Law Commission Consultation Paper No. 177 (2005: 5.69).

FURTHER READING

Griew, E. (1988), 'The Future of Diminished Responsibility', *Criminal Law Review* 75.

Mackay, R. (1995), *Mental Condition Defences in the Criminal Law* (Oxford: OUP).

—— (2000), 'Diminished Responsibility and Mentally Disordered Killers' in A. Ashworth and B. Mitchell (eds.), *Rethinking English Homicide Law* (Oxford: OUP).

Sparks, R. (1964), 'Diminished Responsibility in Theory and Practice', *Modern Law Review* 27: 9.

Sullivan, G.R. (1994b), 'Intoxicants and Diminished Responsibility', *Criminal Law Review* 156.

6

NON-FATAL NON-SEXUAL OFFENCES AGAINST THE PERSON

PART I: THE LAW

1 INTRODUCTION

This chapter will cover a wide range of offences: from an unwanted touching on an arm to a life-threatening attack. Key to the law is the right to bodily integrity: a person should not be touched against his or her wishes. This right is protected under the common law[1] and Article 8 of the European Convention on Human Rights. The significance the law attaches to this right is revealed by these two cases:

(1) In *Thomas*[2] it was held that the unwanted touching of the bottom of a girl's skirt amounted to a battery. The rubbing of someone's clothing might appear to some to be too trivial a harm to justify the intervention of the criminal law, but it reveals the weight attached to the right not to be touched without one's consent.

(2) The decision of the Court of Appeal in *St George's Healthcare NHS Trust v S*[3] reveals that the right to bodily integrity is protected, even if there may be some very good reasons for infringing it. There a woman in the late stages of labour was advised that she should have a caesarean section operation, without which her life and that of her unborn child were in danger. She refused to consent to the operation, wanting a natural delivery. The hospital authorities, having obtained a court order permitting them to do so, carried out the operation against her will. The Court of Appeal held that the court order should not have been granted. The woman's right to bodily integrity was held to be preciously guarded by the law. Even if her decision might appear to be irrational to others, and even if abiding by her decision might lead to her own death and that of her child, it had to be respected by doctors, as long as the woman was competent.

This chapter will consider how the criminal law protects the right to bodily integrity, although it will not consider sexual offences, which will be examined in Chapter 7.

---

[1] *St George's Healthcare NHS Trust v S* [1999] Fam 26 (CA).
[2] *Thomas* (1985) 81 Cr App R 331 (CA).   [3] [1998] 3 All ER 673, discussed in Herring (1998a).

There are five key offences against the person which will be considered in this chapter:

(1) assault;

(2) battery;

(3) assault occasioning actual bodily harm;

(4) malicious wounding;

(5) wounding with intent.

Some commentators[4] see these as a 'ladder' of offences, starting with the least serious offence of assault, rising to the most serious offence of wounding with intent.

The chapter will then look at some of the other offences against the person which address particular forms of assaults. These include poisoning offences, racially aggravated assaults, and harassment offences.

2 ASSAULT AND BATTERY

Under section 39 of the Criminal Justice Act 1988:

> Common assault and battery shall be summary offences and a person guilty of either of them shall be liable to a fine not exceeding level 5 on the standard scale, to imprisonment for a term not exceeding six months or to both.

Technically assault and battery are two separate crimes.[5] In brief, a battery involves an unlawful and unwanted contact with the body of another, while an assault involves causing another to apprehend the possibility of imminent unlawful contact. Of course, often both crimes can be committed in the same incident. Imagine that the defendant approached a victim and then hit her. There would be an assault when the defendant approached the victim and the victim feared some imminent unlawful touching. There would be a battery when the defendant actually hit her. It should be seen from this brief summary that 'assault' in the legal sense does not correspond to its everyday meaning of an attack.

2.1 ASSAULT

The definition of an assault is as follows:

DEFINITION

Actus reus: the defendant caused the victim to apprehend imminent unlawful force.

Mens rea: the defendant intended or was *Cunningham* reckless that the victim would apprehend imminent unlawful force.

---

[4] Ashworth (2003: 36).

[5] *Taylor, Little* [1992] 1 All ER 708 (CA). This means that if the defendant is charged with an assault and/or a battery these should be charged separately in an indictment. But in *Lynsey* [1995] 3 All ER 654 the Court of Appeal left open the question whether assaults and batteries should be regarded as separate statutory offences.

Although the basic meaning of 'assault' is straightforward, the courts have struggled with the precise parameters of the offence. The following are some of the questions which have troubled the courts.

Can words alone amount to an assault?

The key decision on this question is the House of Lords' decision in *R v Ireland*[6] which is excerpted below. The decision makes it clear that words can constitute an assault. In that case silent telephone calls were held to be assaults. It is clear from Lord Steyn's judgment that what matters is that the defendant has caused the victim to apprehend imminent harm. Exactly how that fear was created is immaterial (be it by acts, silence, writing,[7] or words). In the following extract Lord Steyn also considers precisely what is meant by the term 'imminent' in the definition of an assault. The case concerned a charge of assault occasioning actual bodily harm, but Lord Steyn held that in order to convict someone of that offence it first had to be established that an assault or a battery had been committed.

R v Ireland
[1998] AC 147 (HL)[8]

Robert Ireland made a large number of telephone calls to three women. When they answered he remained silent. The women as a result suffered psychological harm. He pleaded guilty to a charge of assault occasioning actual bodily harm, contrary to section 47 of the Offences Against the Person Act 1861, following the direction of the trial judge that the facts of the case could justify such a conviction. He appealed on the basis that the admitted facts were incapable of amounting to the offence.

Lord Steyn

My Lords, it is easy to understand the terrifying effect of a campaign of telephone calls at night by a silent caller to a woman living on her own. It would be natural for the victim to regard the calls as menacing. What may heighten her fear is that she will not know what the caller may do next. The spectre of the caller arriving at her doorstep bent on inflicting personal violence on her may come to dominate her thinking. After all, as a matter of common sense, what else would she be terrified about? The victim may suffer psychiatric illness such as anxiety neurosis or acute depression. Harassment of women by repeated silent telephone calls, accompanied on occasions by heavy breathing, is apparently a significant social problem. That the criminal law should be able to deal with this problem, and so far as is practicable, afford effective protection to victims is self-evident.

. . .

Reg v Ireland: was there an assault?

It is now necessary to consider whether the making of silent telephone calls causing psychiatric injury is capable of constituting an assault under section 47. The Court of Appeal,

---

[6] [1998] AC 147 (HL), discussed in S. Gardner (1998c) and Herring (1999).
[7] *Constanza* [1997] 2 Cr App R 492 (CA).
[8] [1997] 4 All ER 225, [1997] 3 WLR 534, [1998] 1 Cr App R 177, [1997] Crim LR 810.

as constituted in the *Reg v Ireland* case, answered that question in the affirmative. There has been substantial academic criticism of the conclusion and reasoning in *Reg v Ireland*. . . . Counsel's arguments, broadly speaking, challenged the decision in *Reg v Ireland* on very similar lines. Having carefully considered the literature and counsel's arguments, I have come to the conclusion that the appeal ought to be dismissed.

The starting point must be that an assault is an ingredient of the offence under section 47. It is necessary to consider the two forms which an assault may take. The first is battery, which involves the unlawful application of force by the defendant upon the victim. Usually, section 47 is used to prosecute in cases of this kind. The second form of assault is an act causing the victim to apprehend an imminent application of force upon her: see *Fagan v Metropolitan Police Commissioner* [1969] 1 QB 439, 444D–E.

One point can be disposed of, quite briefly. The Court of Appeal was not asked to consider whether silent telephone calls resulting in psychiatric injury is capable of constituting a battery. But encouraged by some academic comment it was raised before your Lordships' House. Counsel for Ireland was most economical in his argument on the point. I will try to match his economy of words. In my view it is not feasible to enlarge the generally accepted legal meaning of what is a battery to include the circumstances of a silent caller who causes psychiatric injury.

It is to assault in the form of an act causing the victim to fear an immediate application of force to her that I must turn. Counsel argued that as a matter of law an assault can never be committed by words alone and therefore it cannot be committed by silence. The premise depends on the slenderest authority, namely, an observation by Holroyd J to a jury that 'no words or singing are equivalent to an assault:' *Rex v Meade and Belt* (1823) 1 Lew 184. The proposition that a gesture may amount to an assault, but that words can never suffice, is unrealistic and indefensible. A thing said is also a thing done. There is no reason why something said should be incapable of causing an apprehension of immediate personal violence, e.g. a man accosting a woman in a dark alley saying, 'Come with me or I will stab you.' I would, therefore, reject the proposition that an assault can never be committed by words.

That brings me to the critical question whether a silent caller may be guilty of an assault. The answer to this question seems to me to be 'Yes, depending on the facts.' It involves questions of fact within the province of the jury. After all, there is no reason why a telephone caller who says to a woman in a menacing way 'I will be at your door in a minute or two' may not be guilty of an assault if he causes his victim to apprehend immediate personal violence. Take now the case of the silent caller. He intends by his silence to cause fear and he is so understood. The victim is assailed by uncertainty about his intentions. Fear may dominate her emotions, and it may be the fear that the caller's arrival at her door may be imminent. She may fear the possibility of immediate personal violence. As a matter of law the caller may be guilty of an assault: whether he is or not will depend on the circumstance and in particular on the impact of the caller's potentially menacing call or calls on the victim. Such a prosecution case under section 47 may be fit to leave to the jury. And a trial judge may, depending on the circumstances, put a common sense consideration before jury, namely what, if not the possibility of imminent personal violence, was the victim terrified about? I conclude that an assault may be committed in the particular factual circumstances which I have envisaged. For this reason I reject the submission that as a matter of law a silent telephone caller cannot ever be guilty of an offence under section 47. In these circumstances no useful purpose would be served by answering the vague certified question in *Reg v Ireland*.

Having concluded that the legal arguments advanced on behalf of Ireland on section 47 must fail, I nevertheless accept that the concept of an assault involving immediate personal violence as an ingredient of the section 47 offence is a considerable complicating factor in bringing prosecutions under it in respect of silent telephone callers and stalkers. That the least serious of the ladder of offences is difficult to apply in such cases is unfortunate. . . .

Appeals dismissed.

Apprehension of force

If the victim suffers no apprehension there can be no assault. So if the defendant utters vile threats against the victim, which do not perturb the victim at all (e.g. because he or she does not believe for a moment that the defendant will carry them out) there can be no assault.[9]

Does the victim of an assault have to apprehend violence, or is the apprehension of a touching sufficient? Although the House of Lords in *Savage and Parmenter* and in *Ireland and Burstow* defined an assault as involving the apprehension of violence it is well established in the case law that an apprehension that one is about to be stroked or kissed can amount to an assault.[10] What if the threat was not to do something that was actually a touching, but was to cause harm? For example, if the defendant threatened to pour away a victim's medicine which the victim needed, would this amount to an assault? It appears that this would not, because the victim did not foresee that the defendant would be touching her.[11] It is arguable that in the light of the acceptance that actual bodily harm can include a psychological harm (see below, p. 348) apprehension that one might suffer a psychological injury caused by the defendant should be sufficient for an assault.[12]

What does 'imminent' mean?

The victim's apprehension must be of imminent harm. It is well established that a threat to be violent in the distant future (e.g. 'I will beat you up next week') is not an assault.[13] But what about a threat to cause violence in the near future? At one time Glanville Williams suggested that to be an assault the defendant must be 'sufficiently near to apply the force then and there. . . .'[14] However, Lord Steyn in *Ireland* indicated that a fear of violence 'within a minute or two' might be sufficient to constitute an assault.[15] This leaves open the question of exactly where the line is to be drawn: is fear of violence in ten minutes enough, an hour, a day? We can know only when we have further guidance from the courts.

The decision in *Ireland* does not mean that every silent telephone call will amount to an assault. It is not enough just to show that the victim was frightened; it must be shown that the victim apprehended an imminent attack. That said, as Lord Steyn pointed out, if the victim of a silent telephone call gives evidence that she was frightened the jury may

---

[9] Further, because assault is a summary offence there is no offence of attempting to assault.

[10] Horder (1998a).

[11] The closest the courts have come to recognizing that this may be an assault was the argument of the Court of Appeal in *Ireland* ([1997] 2 Cr App R 492 (CA)) that there was an assault because the victim foresaw that she would suffer psychological harm as a result of the telephone calls. For criticism of the reasoning in the Court of Appeal in *Ireland* see Herring (1997).

[12] Wells (1997).

[13] But there are some specific offences that relate to threats to harm in the future e.g. there is an offence of threatening to kill in the Offences Against the Person Act 1861, s. 16.

[14] G. Williams (1982: 174).

[15] See also *Smith v Superintendent of Woking Police Station* (1983) 76 Cr App R 234 (DC).

ask themselves 'what, if not the possibility of imminent personal violence, was the victim terrified about?' Simester and Sullivan[16] have questioned this reasoning, arguing that a person may be terrified without that fear having a particular focus. They point out that a person watching a horror film may feel terror, without that amounting to terror of imminent violence. The difficulty in proving that the victim feared imminent violence in cases involving abusive telephone calls or letters may lead prosecutors to rely on the offences under the Communications Act 2003[17] or the Protection from Harassment Act 1997, which are easier to prove.

EXAMINATION TIP

A warning of a common misunderstanding: for an assault it is necessary to show that the victim had an apprehension of imminent harm. It is not enough to show that as a result of the defendant's actions the victim immediately feared that he or she might be harmed a long time in the future. In other words there must be a fear of imminent harm not an imminent fear of harm in the future.

Is it enough for the victim to fear there may be violence?

Lord Steyn stated that an assault would occur if the victim feared the defendant *might* come round within a minute or two. The significance of this was revealed in *Constanza*[18] where the defendant sent over 800 letters to the victim, repeatedly drove past her home, and on three occasions wrote offensive words on her front door. On 4 and 12 June she received two letters which she interpreted as threatening. It was accepted that when she opened the letters and read them she feared that the defendant might harm her 'at some time not excluding the immediate future'.[19] This was sufficient to amount to an assault, because among her fears was that the defendant might inflict some force imminently.

Must the threat be of a touching from the defendant?

What if the defendant threatens to ask someone else to cause harm to the victim? Could this be an assault? The issue has not been addressed directly by the courts, but the answer is likely to be yes. It is an assault for a defendant to threaten to set an animal on the victim.[20] By analogy, threatening to set a boyfriend on the victim should also be an assault. By contrast, it would seem unlikely for there to be an offence where the defendant simply tells the victim that she is being followed by someone. This is not an assault because, although as a result of what the defendant has said the victim may apprehend imminent force, there is nothing in the nature of a threat in what the defendant has said.

Does the defendant have to intend to carry out the threat?

The fact that the defendant does not intend to carry out the attack does not mean that an act cannot constitute an assault. In *Logdon v DPP*[21] the defendant showed the victim a gun and

---

[16] Simester and Sullivan (2003: 383).   [17] See e.g. *DPP v Collins* [2005] Crim LR 794.
[18] [1997] Crim LR 576 (DC).   [19] [1997] Cr App R 492, 494 (CA).
[20] This was assumed to be the law by the Court of Appeal in *Dume, The Times*, 16 Oct. 1986 (CA).
[21] [1976] Crim LR 121 (DC).

announced he would keep the victim hostage. The defendant argued that he did not intend to carry out his threat, and indeed because the gun was a fake he was not able to and therefore he could not be guilty of an assault. His conviction for assault was upheld because he had created fear of violence in the victim. The facts that he did not intend to carry out the threat and was incapable of doing so provided no defence.

What if the threat is conditional?

What is the position if the defendant says 'unless you retract that insult I will punch you'? The argument could be made that this is not an assault because the victim has it in his or her power to avoid the violence by acting as requested and so cannot apprehend imminent force.[22] However, there are also arguments that the victim is still placed at risk of violence because by acting in a lawful way (e.g. keeping silent) she will still be liable to violence and this should amount to an assault.[23] The courts have not provided clear guidance on this issue.

It is important to distinguish a conditional threat from words which negate a threat. For example, in *Tuberville v Savage*,[24] while holding a sword the defendant stated: 'if it were not assize time, I would not take such language'. Here the defendant was making it clear he was not going to attack the victim. The case has been widely interpreted[25] as one where the defendant's words negatived what would otherwise be an assault (the holding of the sword). Jeremy Horder[26] has argued that in some cases there can be an assault even if the defendant's words negative the threat: if the defendant said to the victim 'if we were alone I would attack you' this might be seen as an implied threat that the moment the other people left an attack would be carried out.

Does an assault require an act?

In *Fagan v MPC*[27] it was suggested by the Divisional Court that an assault requires proof of a positive act and cannot be committed merely by an omission. Consider the following: a man is looking up at a house when he sees a woman come to the window, notice him, and appear frightened. Is it an assault if he remains standing where he is and does not move? The *dicta* in *Fagan* imply that he could not be guilty. However, a strong case can be made for saying that an omission can amount to an assault if the defendant is acting unlawfully.[28] So if a trespasser is suddenly aware that his presence in the victim's garden is startling the victim, he may be committing an offence by remaining there.[29]

What does it mean that the apprehension must be of unlawful force?

The force which the victim apprehends must be unlawful. So, if the apprehended touching would not be a criminal offence, for example because it would be done lawfully in self-defence, then there would be no assault.

---

[22] *Blake v Barnard* (1840) 9 C & P 626; 173 ER 985.
[23] *Read v Coker* (1853) 138 ER 1437.   [24] (1669) 1 Mood Rep 3; 86 ER 684.
[25] Although in fact the court did not resolve the question whether or not there was an assault.
[26] Horder (1998a: 402).   [27] [1969] 1 QB 439 (QBD).
[28] *Smith v Superintendent of Woking Police Station* (1983) 76 Cr App R 234 (DC).
[29] See further Simester and Sullivan (2003: 381).

What is the *mens rea* for an assault?

The defendant must be shown to intend or be *Cunningham* reckless[30] as to the creation of apprehension of imminent unlawful violence. This was made clear in the Court of Appeal's decision in *Venna*,[31] which was approved *obiter* by the House of Lords in *Savage and Parmenter*.[32]

2.2 BATTERY

DEFINITION

Actus reus: the defendant touched or applied force to the victim.

Mens rea: the defendant intended or was *Cunningham* reckless as to touching or applying force to the victim.

A battery can be committed without the victim suffering any kind of injury. So, a touching can constitute a battery.[33] Indeed even touching the clothes that someone is wearing can be.[34] So, the offence of battery does not necessarily involve a harming of the body (as the more serious offences against the person do); it includes an invasion of 'personal space'.[35] This is shown by the fact that a battery can take place even if the victim did not feel the touching.[36]

Again we will consider some of the questions about the meaning of battery which have troubled the courts.

Can the battery be carried out via an object?

There seems little doubt that a battery can be carried out through an object. In *Fagan* the defendant committed a battery by placing his car on the victim's foot and leaving it there. By virtue of similar reasoning it has been well established that spitting on someone[37] or throwing beer on them[38] constitutes a battery.

Can the battery be carried out by omission?

It is clear from *Fagan* (extracted at p. 179) that the courts are willing to find a battery, even if in a sense the case involved an omission. There by placing the car on the policeman's foot and not removing it the defendant was continually committing a battery. However, it is unclear whether the courts would find a battery in the hypothetical scenario posed by Smith and Hogan: 'suppose D is sitting at the corner of a corridor with his legs stretched across it. He hears P running down the corridor and deliberately remains still with the intention that P, on turning the corner, shall fall over his legs'.[39] This is different from *Fagan* where there was an initial act of touching the victim (driving onto the foot) and the omission involving

---

[30] As explained in Ch. 3, this means that the defendant actually foresaw the result (i.e. that the victim would apprehend the imminent harm).

[31] [1975] 3 All ER 788 (CA).   [32] [1992] 1 AC 699 at 736 (Lord Ackner).

[33] *Collins v Wilcock* [1984] 3 All ER 374 (QBD).   [34] *Thomas* (1985) 81 Cr App R 331 (CA).

[35] J. Gardner (1994a: 508).   [36] *Thomas* (1985) 81 Cr App R 331 (CA).

[37] *Smith* (1866) 176 ER 910.   [38] *Savage* [1992] 1 AC 699 (HL).   [39] J.C. Smith (2002: 415).

the failure to move. In Smith and Hogan's hypothetical example, it might be argued that the victim walked into the defendant, rather than the defendant touched the victim. In *DPP v Santa-Bermudez*[40] the defendant was asked by a police officer who was planning to search his clothing whether he had on him any sharp objects. He said he did not, but when the officer put her hand in the pocket she was cut by a needle. The Divisional Court had no difficulty in finding a battery, holding that 'where someone (by act or word or a combination of the two) creates a danger and thereby exposes another to a reasonably foreseeable risk of injury which materializes, there is an evidential basis for the actus reus of an assault occasioning actual bodily harm.'[41]

Does a battery require the application of force?

Must a battery involve the application of force or can a battery be committed indirectly, for example, where a person sets a booby trap which the victim falls into or someone shouts 'fire' in a crowded theatre, having blocked the exists, causing people to be crushed in an attempt to escape?[42] The decisions to date suggest these are batteries.[43] *Obiter* in *Savage* Lord Ackner appeared to suggest otherwise, giving an example of a person who interfered with the braking mechanism of a car so that the driver subsequently had a car accident and was injured.[44] He suggested that that might not amount to a battery (although it could be a wounding). However, later cases have not followed the implication that a battery must involve the direct application of force. In *DPP v K*[45] a schoolboy had placed some acid he had stolen from the science laboratory in a hand-drier. Another pupil used the hand-drier and acid was splashed upon him. It was held that this amounted to a battery, even though the schoolboy had not directly applied the acid. In *Haystead v Chief Constable of Derbyshire*[46] the defendant struck a woman who was holding her baby. As a result of the blows she dropped the baby. The defendant was charged with battering the baby. It was held that he was properly convicted because he had caused unlawful force to be applied to the baby when the baby hit the floor.

These decisions, it is submitted, are correct. Adapting the reasoning in *Ireland* that in cases of assault it does not matter what means the defendant uses to create the apprehension of violence; similarly it should not matter what technique the defendant uses to apply force to a person's body. Throwing a pint of beer at someone and placing a pint of beer on the top of a door so that it falls on them when they open the door seem equally blameworthy and it would be artificial to distinguish between them. There must, however, be something that touches the victim. Lord Steyn in *Ireland* rejected the argument that the silent telephone call constituted a battery; if anything it was an assault. He argued that to hold otherwise would mean that there would be too great a separation between the legal meaning of battery and its ordinary meaning.

Can everyday touchings amount to a battery?

If you were to board a tube train in London during the rush hour inevitably you would touch others and they would touch you. Indeed some touchings are part of everyday life. The law would not regard such touchings as batteries, as the following case demonstrates:

---

[40] [2003] EWHC 2908.   [41] Paragraph 10.   [42] Hirst (1999).
[43] *Martin* (1891) 8 QBD 54 (CCR): shouting 'fire' in a crowded theatre is an assault; *Clarence* (1888) 22 QBD 23 (CCR) *obiter* at 36 (Wills J); causing the victim to fall into a booby trap could be a battery.
[44] [1992] 1 AC 699, 725.   [45] [1990] 1 All ER 331 (DC).   [46] [2000] 3 All ER 890 (CA).

Collins v Wilcock
[1984] 3 All ER 374 (QBD)[47]

Two police officers suspected that two women were soliciting for the purpose of prostitution. They approached the women, but one (the appellant) refused to answer questions and walked away. One police officer took hold of her arm. The appellant responded by scratching the officer, and for that she was later convicted of assaulting a police officer in the execution of her duty, contrary to section 51(1) of the Police Act 1964. She appealed against the conviction on the basis that when the assault occurred the police officer was not acting in the execution of her duty. The key question on appeal was whether in grabbing hold of the appellant the police officer was committing a battery.

Lord Justice Robert Goff

. . . The fundamental principle, plain and incontestable, is that every person's body is inviolate. It has long been established that any touching of another person, however slight, may amount to a battery. So Holt CJ held in 1704 that 'the least touching of another in anger is a battery': see *Cole v Turner* 6 Mod Rep 149, 90 ER 958. The breadth of the principle reflects the fundamental nature of the interest so protected as Blackstone wrote in his Commentaries, 'the law cannot draw the line between different degrees of violence, and therefore totally prohibits the first and lowest stage of it every man's person being sacred, and no other having a right to meddle with it, in any the slightest manner' (see 3 Bl Com 120). The effect is that everybody is protected not only against physical injury but against any form of physical molestation.

But so widely drawn a principle must inevitably be subject to exceptions. For example, children may be subjected to reasonable punishment, people may be subjected to the lawful exercise of the power of arrest and reasonable force may be used in self-defence or for the prevention of crime. But, apart from these special instances where the control or constraint is lawful, a broader exception has been created to allow for the exigencies of everyday life. Generally speaking, consent is a defence to battery and most of the physical contacts of ordinary life are not actionable because they are impliedly consented to by all who move in society and so expose themselves to the risk of bodily contact. So nobody can complain of the jostling which is inevitable from his presence in, for example, a supermarket, an underground station or a busy street nor can a person who attends a party complain if his hand is seized in friendship, or even if his back is (within reason) slapped (see *Tuberville v Savage* (1669) 1 Mod Rep 3, 86 ER 684). Although such cases are regarded as examples of implied consent, it is more common nowadays to treat them as falling within a general exception embracing all physical contact which is generally acceptable in the ordinary conduct of daily life. We observe that, although in the past it has sometimes been stated that a battery is only committed where the action is 'angry, or revengeful, or rude, or insolent' (see 1 Hawk PC c 62, s 2), we think that nowadays it is more realistic, and indeed more accurate, to state the broad underlying principle, subject to the broad exception.

Among such forms of conduct, long held to be acceptable, is touching a person for the purpose of engaging his attention, though of course using no greater degree of physical contact than is reasonably necessary in the circumstances for that purpose. So, for example, it was held by the Court of Common Pleas in 1807 that a touch by a constable's staff on the

[47] [1984] 1 WLR 1172, (1984) 79 Cr App R 229.

shoulder of a man who had climbed on a gentleman's railing to gain a better view of a mad ox, the touch being only to engage the man's attention, did not amount to a battery (see *Wiffin v Kincard* (1807) 2 Bos & PNR 471, 127 ER 713); for another example, see *Coward v Baddeley* (1859) 4 H & N 478, 157 ER 927). But a distinction is drawn between a touch to draw a man's attention, which is generally acceptable, and a physical restraint, which is not. So we find Parke B observing in *Rawlings v Till* (1837) 3 M & W 28 at 29, 150 ER 1042, with reference to *Wiffin v Kincard*, that 'There the touch was merely to engage a man's attention, not to put a restraint on his person.' Furthermore, persistent touching to gain attention in the face of obvious disregard may transcend the norms of acceptable behaviour, and so be outside the exception. We do not say that more than one touch is never permitted for example, the lost or distressed may surely be permitted a second touch, or possibly even more, on a reluctant or impervious sleeve or shoulder, as may a person who is acting reasonably in the exercise of a duty. In each case, the test must be whether the physical contact so persisted in has in the circumstances gone beyond generally acceptable standards of conduct and the answer to that question will depend on the facts of the particular case.

. . . The fact is that the respondent took hold of the appellant by the left arm to restrain her. In so acting, she was not proceeding to arrest the appellant and since her action went beyond the generally acceptable conduct of touching a person to engage his or her attention, it must follow, in our judgment, that her action constituted a battery on the appellant, and was therefore unlawful. It follows that the appellant's appeal must be allowed, and her conviction quashed.

Appeal allowed. Conviction quashed.

Although the decision makes it clear that everyday touchings are not batteries, it is not clear why this is so. There are two possible explanations:

(1) *Implied consent.* When entering crowded places or attending events when touchings are common, a person impliedly consents to the physical contact that results.

(2) *Necessity.* Some everyday touchings are an essential part of life.[48] Modern life would not be possible if it were illegal to touch anyone without their consent. So, it is necessary to create a general exception to the offence of battery to cover 'all physical contact which is generally acceptable in the ordinary conduct of everyday life'.[49]

It may be important which explanation is true. If a man wanting to board a tube train can enter only by squeezing in next to his former wife from whom he is acrimoniously divorced can this be a battery on the basis that, although she may have impliedly consented to touching people when entering the tube, her implied consent cannot extend to him? On the other hand if such touchings are simply not batteries, then the lack of implied consent may not be a defence. Although there is no firm guidance on the issue, Lord Goff in *F v West Berkshire Health Authority*[50] preferred the second view.

---

[48] Try running London Underground after forbidding passengers to touch each other!
[49] Lord Goff in *F v West Berkshire Health Authority* [1990] 2 AC 1, 25 (HL).
[50] [1990] 2 AC 1, 25 (HL).

Must the battery be hostile?

There has been some debate whether a battery must involve a hostile act. The view with the most support in the case law is that there is no need for the touching to be hostile, rude, or aggressive.[51] A person who lovingly strokes another's hair without that person's consent is guilty of a battery. The issue is in doubt in part because Lord Jauncey in *Brown*[52] suggested that a battery must involve hostility. However, he seems to have understood hostility to mean that the act was not consented to,[53] rather than to require the act to be aggressive.

What is the *mens rea* of battery?

The *mens rea* of battery is that the defendant must intend or be *Cunningham* reckless as to the application of force or touching of the victim.

Are the *mentes reae* of assault and battery interchangeable?

What if the defendant intends to commits a battery, but in fact commits an assault?[54] Consider this scenario: Tom approached Sean, who was asleep, intending to touch his hair and Sean suddenly awoke and saw Tom close to him and, terrified, ran away before Tom touched him. Here Tom had the *mens rea* for battery, but committed only the *actus reus* of an assault. But does that matter? The courts are yet to provide a clear answer. One argument is that, as the offences are so closely linked, it is possible to use the *actus reus* of an assault and the *mens rea* of the battery to establish the offence. Another view is that *DPP v Little*[55] shows that the offences are separate and that this distinction needs to be taken seriously. Normally it is not possible to combine the *mens rea* of one offence with the *actus reus* of a different offence.

3 ASSAULT OCCASIONING ACTUAL BODILY HARM

Section 47 of the Offences Against the Person Act 1861 states:

> Whosoever shall be convicted upon an indictment of any assault occasioning actual bodily harm shall be liable . . . to be imprisoned for any term not exceeding five years.

DEFINITION

Actus reus: the defendant must commit an assault or battery which causes the victim to suffer actual bodily harm.

Mens rea: the defendant must intend or be *Cunningham* reckless as to the assault or battery. (**N.B.** There is no need to show that the defendant intended or foresaw actual bodily harm.)

---

[51] *Faulkner v Talbot* [1981] 3 All ER 468 at 471 (CA).   [52] [1994] 1 AC 212 (HL).
[53] The civil law case of *Wilson v Pringle* [1987] QB 237 (CA) also suggested that hostility was required.
[54] For further discussion see J.C. Smith (2002: 419).
[55] [1992] QB 645 (DC).

This offence can be broken down into three elements:

(1) *It must be shown that there was an assault.* This means either an assault or a battery.[56] Both the *mens rea* and *actus reus* of the assault or battery must be shown.

(2) *The victim must suffer actual bodily harm.* The phrase 'actual bodily harm' is used to indicate a level of harm which is greater than a mere touching (a battery).[57] Actual bodily harm has been defined as 'any hurt or injury calculated to interfere with the health or comfort' of the victim.[58] The harm need not be permanent, but it should 'not be so trivial as to be wholly insignificant'.[59] Bruisings, grazes, the causing of tenderness,[60] temporary loss of consciousness,[61] or breaking teeth could be included within actual bodily harm.[62]

The House of Lords in *Ireland*[63] held that psychological injuries could be included in the term 'actual bodily harm', but only if they were medically recognized conditions which involved more than fear, panic, or distress.[64] Although it might be thought to be stretching the meaning of 'bodily' to include psychological, the House of Lords accepted the argument that 'the body' includes all the organs, including the brain.[65] It is important to remember at this point that the offence is not committed if there is no assault. If a man breaks off his engagement, causing his fiancée to suffer depression, there will be no offence under section 47 because he did not commit an assault.

(3) *It must be shown that the actual bodily harm was occasioned by the common assault or battery of the defendant.* 'Occasioned' has been interpreted as meaning the same as caused.[66] In the case of battery this is normally straightforward. If A hits B in the face, that is a battery; if that leaves B with a bruise then clearly there has been an assault (i.e. a battery) which has occasioned actual bodily harm. It is also possible for the offence to involve an assault. A good example is *Roberts*,[67] where the Court of Appeal convicted a defendant who made indecent proposals to a woman in his car; she was so frightened that she jumped out of the car. Here he assaulted her and this assault caused her to jump out of the car and suffer actual bodily harm. In a case like *Ireland*[68] it may be hard to show that the psychological harm was caused by the apprehension of imminent harm rather than by something else.

It should be stressed that the only *mens rea* requirement for an assault occasioning actual bodily harm is intent or *Cunningham* recklessness that the victim will suffer an assault or battery. There is no need to show that the defendant foresaw the actual bodily harm. This was made clear in the House of Lords decision in *Parmenter and Savage*.[69] This offence therefore infringes 'the correspondence principle' (discussed at p. 176).

---

[56] Law Commission Report No. 218 (1993a: para. 12.16).

[57] The fact that the maximum sentence for a s. 47 offence is 5 years indicates that it can cover some reasonably serious incidents.

[58] *Donovan* [1934] 2 KB 498 (CCA).   [59] Hobhouse LJ in *Chan-Fook* [1994] 1 WLR 689 at 696.

[60] *R v Reigate Justices, ex parte Counsell* [1984] 148 JP 193 (QBD).

[61] *T v DPP* [2003] Crim LR 622. In *Smith* [2006] EWHC 94 cutting hair without the victim's consent was said to be actual bodily harm.

[62] According to the Offences Against the Person Charging Standards, relied upon by the Crown Prosecution Service (CPS (1996)). For the significance of such codes see Hoyano, Hoyano, Davis, and Goldie (1997).

[63] [1998] AC 147.

[64] *Burstow* [1998] AC 147 (HL); *Chan-Fook* [1994] 1 WLR 689 (CA).

[65] In *Morris* [1998] 1 Cr App R 386 (CA) there was evidence that the victim suffered anxiety, fear, and sleeplessness. But it was held that this was insufficient to amount to actual bodily harm, because it did not involve a recognized medical condition.

[66] *Roberts* (1972) 56 Cr App R 95 (CA). J. Gardner (1994: 509–10) argues that occasioning has a wider meaning than causation, but he does not cite any cases to support this.

[67] *Roberts* (1972) 56 Cr App R 95 (CA).   [68] [1997] 4 All ER 225 (HL).

[69] [1992] 1 AC 699 (HL).

QUESTION

Alf sends Bertha several threatening text messages, following which Bertha suffers depression. What offences has Alf committed?

Alf will be charged with an assault occasioning actual bodily harm (Offences Against the Person Act 1861, section 47). Clearly the prosecution will want to rely on *Ireland* to show that words can amount to assault, and that the depression can be regarded as actual bodily harm. But the prosecution will face three difficult tasks:

1. The prosecution must show that Bertha as the result of the text message apprehended an imminent use of force. It would not be enough if she was just afraid in a general sense.

2. It must be shown that Alf intended or foresaw that Bertha would apprehend an imminent use of force.

3. It must be shown that Bertha suffered the depression because of the apprehension of imminent force.

4 MALICIOUS WOUNDING

The Offences Against the Person Act 1861, section 20 states:

> Whosoever shall unlawfully and maliciously wound or inflict any grievous bodily harm upon any other person, either with or without any weapon or instrument, shall be liable . . . to imprisonment for a term not exceeding five years.

DEFINITION

Actus reus: the defendant unlawfully either:

(i) wounded the victim; or

(ii) inflicted grievous bodily harm to the victim.

Mens rea: the defendant foresaw that the victim might suffer some harm. (**N.B.** It is *not* necessary to show that the defendant intended or foresaw that the victim would suffer grievous bodily harm.)

The following terms need to be defined in greater detail.

(1) *Unlawfully.* This means that the defendant acted without lawful justification. An example of a lawful justification is where the defendant was acting in self-defence. This will be discussed further in Chapter 12.

(2) *Wound.* This has been interpreted in *C v Eisenhower*[70] to mean a break in the continuity of the whole of the skin.[71] A rupture of an internal blood vessel is not a wound.[72]

---

[70] [1984] QB 331 (DC).

[71] The breaking of just the outer skin is insufficient: *M'Loughlin* (1838) 173 ER 651. The skin comprises two layers: dermis and epidermis. Both must be broken for there to be a wound.

[72] *JCC (A Minor) v Eisenhower* (1984) 78 Cr App R 48 (DC). This means that there may be bleeding without there being a wound.

However, the breaking of an inner membrane which is analogous to skin may constitute a wound. So it is generally accepted that an injury to the inside of a mouth was a wound.[73] The requirement that the whole of the continuation of the skin be broken means that a scratch may draw blood but may not be deep enough for a wound if it only disturbs the outer layer of the skin.

William Wilson has argued that the normal meaning of the word 'wound' is that a wound can occur only if there is a direct application of force.[74] If his argument is correct it would mean that if the defendant terrified the victim into running away and the victim fell over and cut herself, there was no wound. In such a case the defendant caused the victim to suffer a wound, but did not wound the victim.[75] Against Wilson's view is the argument that the use of the words 'either with or without any weapon' in section 20 suggests that the courts should not be too concerned with the way the wound is caused. We await a clear decision from the courts on this issue.

(3) *Grievous bodily harm.* Grievous bodily harm means 'really serious bodily harm'.[76] In deciding whether the harm is really serious it is necessary to consider the totality of the injuries inflicted on the victim. So, if the defendant punched a victim a large number of times, leaving him bruised all over his body, the totality of the bruising could constitute grievous bodily harm, even if each individual bruise would only constituted actual bodily harm.[77] In *Brown and Stratton*[78] the Court of Appeal allowed an appeal after a judge had directed the jury to consider whether the victim regarded the injuries as serious. This was said to be wrong: whether the injuries were really serious was an objective test. It is not quite clear what this means. Clearly just because the victim regards the injuries as serious does not mean that the jury must find them serious. But what is not clear is whether the jury in assessing the seriousness of the harm can take into account the characteristics of the victim. For example, if the defendant injured a concert pianist's finger, which meant that she could not play the piano, could the jury decide that this injury *for this victim* was a serious injury, even if for most people it would not be? In *Bollom*[79] the Court of Appeal held that in assessing whether the injuries were really serious the impact of them on the particular victim should be taken into account.

Grievous bodily harm can include very serious psychological harm.[80] To amount to grievous bodily harm there must be more than serious distress or upset; there must be a serious identifiable clinical condition.[81] For example, a very serious depression could amount to grievous bodily harm.

It is important to note that the statute requires that the injury either be a wound or the infliction of grievous bodily harm. Breaking a collar bone would not be a wound,[82] but may well constitute grievous bodily harm. On the other hand some wounds may not amount to grievous bodily harm. A pinprick may be a wound, but not amount to grievous bodily harm.

---

[73] In *Waltham* (1849) 3 Cox CC 442 a policeman was kicked in the genitals in such a way that the lining membrane of the urethra was ruptured, leading to bleeding. The urethra was held to be, in effect, a continuation of the external skin and so there was a wound.

[74] Wilson (2003: 308).

[75] It should be noted that s. 20 does not include the phrase 'by any means whatsoever', which is found in s. 18.

[76] *DPP v Smith* [1961] AC 290 (HL). But it has been suggested that sometimes it is permissible for the judge simply to define it as 'serious harm': *Janjua* [1999] 1 CAR 91 (CA).

[77] *Grundy* [1977] Crim LR 543 (CA).   [78] [1998] Crim LR 484 (CA).

[79] [2003] EWCA Crim 2846.   [80] *Burstow* [1998] AC 147 (HL).

[81] Hobhouse LJ in *Chan-Fook* [1994] 99 Cr App R 147 at 152 (CA).

[82] *Wood* (1830) 1 Mood CC 278.

(4) *Infliction of grievous bodily harm.* It is necessary to show that the defendant *inflicted* the grievous bodily harm. There is much debate over what inflicted means in section 20, and particularly how it differs from the word 'cause' in section 18. What has been established beyond doubt is that there is no need to demonstrate that there has been an assault in order to establish a conviction under section 20. It used to be thought that inflict had a narrower meaning than cause, in that inflict required the direct application of force, whereas cause meant to bring about in any way.[83] However, in *Burstow*,[84] Lord Steyn explained that although the words cause and inflict were not synonymous, 'in the context of the Act of 1861 there is no radical divergence between the meaning of the two words'.[85] As to the argument that infliction required an application of force to the body, Lord Steyn called this 'absurd'.[86] Lord Hope agreed that in the context of the 1861 Act the words had the same meaning, but suggested that the only difference in meaning was that 'inflict' suggested that the consequence was unpleasant for the victim whereas 'cause' did not. Presumably he meant to suggest that in the context of grievous bodily harm, where inevitably[87] the victim will not find the injury pleasant, the two words have the same meaning. Having decided that for the purposes of the Act inflict and cause are synonymous, their Lordships were able to hold that a serious psychological condition could be inflicted by a defendant pursuing a campaign of harassment against the victim.[88] So the judgments in *Burstow* indicate that inflict now means the same as cause.[89]

(5) *The* mens rea *requirement.* The *mens rea* for section 20 is that the defendant must intend or foresee (*Cunningham* recklessness) that he or she may cause some kind of harm, albeit minor harm. So it is *not* necessary for the prosecution to show that the defendant intended or foresaw grievous bodily harm. It is not even necessary to show that the defendant believed that he or she *would* cause some harm: it is enough if it is proved that the defendant believed he or she *might*.[90]

Quite what harm means in this context is not clear. It clearly covers physical injuries to bodies; but what about psychological injuries? It seems likely that a court would follow *Ireland and Burstow*[91] and hold that a recognizable psychological condition would constitute a harm, but that fear on its own would not.[92] This would mean that a defendant will be guilty if he makes a silent telephone call, foreseeing that the victim may suffer a psychological illness as a result, but the victim, in terror, runs down the stairs of her house, falls, suffering grievous bodily harm. He is guilty because his foresight that the victim would suffer a psychological illness would constitute the *mens rea* for a section 20 charge.

The *mens rea* of malicious wounding was established in the following important decision of the House of Lords:

---

[83] *Clarence* (1888) 22 QBD 23 (CCR).   [84] [1998] AC 147 (HL).
[85] The House of Lords in *Wilson* [1984] AC 242 and *Mandair* [1995] 1 AC 208 had already made it clear that an infliction does not require proof of an assault or a battery.
[86] [1997] 3 WLR 534 at 545 (HL).
[87] But a masochist may not find grievous bodily harm unpleasant. It cannot be that Lord Hope was meaning that a defendant might have a defence on the basis that their victim enjoyed the injuries and so the injuries were not inflicted.
[88] *Burstow* [1998] AC 147 (HL).   [89] This was applied in *Dica* [2004] EWCA Crim 1103.
[90] This was stressed in *Rushmore* (1992) 95 Cr App R 252 (CA) and *DPP v A* [2001] Crim LR 140 (DC).
[91] [1998] AC 147 (HL).   [92] *Sullivan* [1981] Crim LR 46 (CA).

R v Savage; R v Parmenter
[1992] 1 AC 699 (HL)[93]

Susan Savage was convicted of unlawful wounding contrary to section 20 of the Offences Against the Person Act 1861. The charge resulted from an incident when Ms Savage approached Ms Beal in a pub and said 'nice to meet you, darling'. Ms Savage had in her hand a pint of beer. She threw the beer over Ms Beal, the glass slipped out of her hand, broke, and Ms Beal was cut. Philip Parmenter caused injuries to his baby son while playing with him in a vigorous way. He explained that he did not realize that what he was doing would cause injury. He was convicted under section 20 of the Offences Against the Person Act 1861.

Lord Ackner

I. *Is a verdict of guilty of assault occasioning actual bodily harm a permissible alternative verdict on a count alleging unlawful wounding contrary to s 20 of the 1861 Act?*

... The critical question remained: do the allegations in a s 20 charge 'include either expressly or by implication' allegations of assault occasioning actual bodily harm? As to this, Lord Roskill concluded (*R v Wilson* (*Clarence*) [1984] AC 242 at 261):

'If "inflicting" can, as the cases show, include "inflicting by assault", then, even though such a charge may not necessarily do so, I do not for myself see why on a fair reading of s 6(3) these allegations do not at least impliedly include "inflicting by assault". That is sufficient for present purposes, though I also regard it as also a possible view that those former allegations expressly include the other allegations.' (Lord Roskill's emphasis)

I respectfully agree with this reasoning and accordingly reject the submission that *R v Wilson* (*Clarence*) was wrongly decided. I would therefore answer the first of the certified questions in *R v Savage* [whether a verdict of guilty of assault occasioning actual bodily harm is a permissible alternative verdict on a count alleging unlawful wounding contrary to section 20 of the Offences Against the Person Act 1861] in the affirmative. A verdict of guilty of assault occasioning actual bodily harm is a permissible alternative verdict on a count alleging unlawful wounding contrary to s 20 of the 1861 Act.

II. *Can a verdict of assault occasioning actual bodily harm be returned upon proof of an assault together with proof of the fact that actual bodily harm was occasioned by the assault, or must the prosecution also prove that the defendant intended to cause some actual bodily harm or was reckless as to whether such harm would be caused?*

Your Lordships are concerned with the mental element of a particular kind of assault, an assault 'occasioning actual bodily harm'. It is common ground that the mental element of assault is an intention to cause the victim to apprehend immediate and unlawful violence or recklessness whether such apprehension be caused (see *R v Venna* [1976] QB 421). It is of course common ground that Mrs Savage committed an assault upon Miss Beal when she threw the contents of her glass of beer over her. It is also common ground that however the glass came to be broken and Miss Beal's wrist thereby cut, it was, on the finding of the jury, Mrs Savage's handling of the glass which caused Miss Beal 'actual bodily harm'. Was the offence thus established or is there a further mental state that has to be established in relation to the bodily harm element of the offence? Clearly the section, by its terms, expressly imposes no such a requirement. Does it do so by necessary implication? It uses

---

[93] [1991] 4 All ER 698, [1991] 3 WLR 914, (1991) 94 Cr App R 193, [1992] Crim LR 288.

neither the word 'intentionally' nor the word 'maliciously'. The words 'occasioning actual bodily harm' are descriptive of the word 'assault', by reference to a particular kind of consequence.

In neither *R v Savage* not *R v Spratt* nor in *R v Parmenter* was the court's attention invited to the decision of the Court of Appeal in *R v Roberts* (1972) 56 Cr App R 95. This is perhaps explicable on the basis that this case is not referred to in the index to Archbold's *Criminal Pleading, Evidence and Practice* (43rd edn, 1988). The relevant text, states (para 20–117): 'The mens rea required [for actual bodily harm] is that required for common assault', without any authority being provided for this proposition.

It is in fact *R v Roberts* which provides authority for this proposition. Roberts was tried on an indictment which alleged that he indecently assaulted a young woman. He was acquitted on that charge, but convicted of assault occasioning actual bodily harm to her. The girl's complaint was that while travelling in the defendant's car he sought to make advances towards her and then tried to take her coat off. This was the last straw and, although the car was travelling at some speed, she jumped out and sustained injuries. The defendant denied he had touched the girl. He had had an argument with her and in the course of that argument she suddenly opened the door and jumped out. In his direction to the jury the chairman of quarter sessions stated: 'If you are satisfied that he tried to pull off her coat and as a result she jumped out of the moving car then your verdict is guilty.'

It was contended on behalf of the appellant that this direction was wrong since the chairman had failed to tell the jury that they must be satisfied that the appellant foresaw that she might jump out of the car as a result of his touching her before they could convict. . . . Thus, once the assault was established, the only remaining question was whether the victim's conduct was the natural consequence of that assault. The words 'occasioning' raised solely a question of causation, an objective question which does not involve inquiring into the accused's state of mind.

. . . The decision in *R v Roberts* (1972) 56 Cr App R 95 was correct. The verdict of assault occasioning actual bodily harm may be returned upon proof of an assault together with proof of the fact that actual bodily harm was occasioned by the assault. The prosecution are not obliged to prove that the defendant intended to cause some actual bodily harm or was reckless as to whether such harm would be caused.

III. *In order to establish an offence under s 20 of the 1861 Act, must the prosecution prove that the defendant actually foresaw that his act would cause harm, or is it sufficient to prove that he ought so to have foreseen?*
Although your Lordships' attention has been invited to a plethora of decided cases, the issue is a narrow one. Is the decision of the Court of Criminal Appeal in *R v Cunningham* [1957] 2 All ER 412, [1957] 2 QB 396 still good law, subject only to a gloss placed upon it by the Court of Appeal, Criminal Division in *R v Mowatt* [1968] 1 QB 421, or does the later decision of your Lordships' House in *R v Caldwell* [1982] AC 341 provide the answer to this question?

[Having surveyed the case law Lord Ackner concluded:]

[I]n order to establish an offence under s 20 the prosecution must prove either that the defendant intended or that he actually foresaw that his act would cause harm.

IV. *In order to establish an offence under s 20 is it sufficient to prove that the defendant intended or foresaw the risk of some physical harm or must he intend or foresee either wounding or grievous bodily harm?*
It is convenient to set out once again the relevant part of the judgment of Diplock LJ in *R v Mowatt* [1967] 3 All ER 47 at 50, [1968] 1 QB 421 at 426. Having considered Professor Kenny's statement, which I have quoted above, he then said:

'In the offence under s 20 ... for ... which [no] specific intent is required—the word "maliciously" does import ... an awareness that his act may have the consequence of causing some physical harm to some other person. That is what is meant by the "particular kind of harm" in the citation from Professor Kenny's *Outlines Of Criminal Law* (18th edn, 1962, para 158a, p 202). It is quite unnecessary that the accused should have foreseen that his unlawful act might cause physical harm of the gravity described in the section, i.e. a wound or serious physical injury. It is enough that he should have foreseen that some physical harm to some person, albeit of a minor character, might result.' (My emphasis.)

Mr Sedley submits that this statement of the law is wrong. He contends that, properly construed, the section requires foresight of a wounding or grievous bodily harm. He drew your Lordships' attention to criticisms of *R v Mowatt* made by Professor Glanville-Williams and by Professor JC Smith in their textbooks and in articles or commentaries. They argue that a person should not be criminally liable for consequences of his conduct unless he foresaw a consequence falling into the same legal category as that set out in the indictment.

Such a general principle runs contrary to the decision in *R v Roberts* (1972) 56 Cr App R 95, which I have already stated to be, in my opinion, correct. The contention is apparently based on the proposition that, as the *actus reus* of a s 20 offence is the wounding or the infliction of grievous bodily harm, the *mens rea* must consist of foreseeing such wounding or grievous bodily harm. But there is no such hard and fast principle. To take but two examples, the *actus reus* of murder is the killing of the victim, but foresight of grievous bodily harm is sufficient and, indeed, such bodily harm need not be such as to be dangerous to life. Again, in the case of manslaughter death is frequently the unforeseen consequence of the violence used.

The argument that, as ss 20 and 47 have both the same penalty, this somehow supports the proposition that the foreseen consequences must coincide with the harm actually done, overlooks the oft-repeated statement that this is the irrational result of this piecemeal legislation. The Act 'is a rag-bag of offences brought together from a wide variety of sources with no attempt, as the draftsman frankly acknowledged, to introduce consistency as to substance or as to form' (see Professor JC Smith in his commentary on *R v Parmenter* ([1991] Crim LR 43)).

If s 20 was to be limited to cases where the accused does not desire but does foresee wounding or grievous bodily harm, it would have a very limited scope. The mens rea in a s 20 crime is comprised in the word 'maliciously'. As was pointed out by Lord Lane CJ, giving the judgment of the Court of Appeal in *R v Sullivan* [1981] Crim LR 46, the 'particular kind of harm' in the citation from Professor Kenny was directed to 'harm to the person' as opposed to 'harm to property'. Thus it was not concerned with the degree of the harm foreseen. It is accordingly in my judgment wrong to look upon the decision in *R v Mowatt* [1968] 1 QB 421 as being in any way inconsistent with the decision in *R v Cunningham* [1957] 2 QB 396.

My Lords, I am satisfied that the decision in *R v Mowatt* was correct and that it is quite unnecessary that the accused should either have intended or have foreseen that his unlawful act might cause physical harm of the gravity described in s 20, i.e. a wound or serious physical injury. It is enough that he should have foreseen that some physical harm to some person, albeit of a minor character, might result.

In the result I would dismiss the appeal in Savage's case but allow the appeal in Parmenter's case, but only to the extent of substituting, in accordance with the provisions of s 3(2) of the Criminal Appeal Act 1968, verdicts of guilty of assault occasioning actual bodily harm contrary to s 47 of the 1861 Act for the four s 20 offences of which he was convicted.

Savage's appeal dismissed. Parmenter's appeal allowed.

QUESTION

An unintended consequence of *Ireland and Burstow*?

If a husband tells his wife that he has had an affair and therefore she suffers serious depression would the husband be guilty of an offence under section 20?

It would be most surprising if he could be convicted of an offence in such a case. But it seems he can. If the husband realizes that his wife may suffer depression in these circumstances, he has the *mens rea* for the section 20 offence. Further, in the light of *Burstow* he can be said to have inflicted the harm (if inflict means the same as cause). There are three possible ways of avoiding this conclusion. First, it could be argued that the conduct of the defendant was not unlawful. However, unlawful in this context simply means that the defendant successfully pleads one of the law's recognized defences (e.g. duress or self-defence). The husband here cannot plead one of these defences. A second argument is to recall that a defendant is *Cunningham* reckless only if the risk of harm taken was an unreasonable one to take. The husband in admitting adultery could be said to be acting reasonably. A third response is to point out that it is not unusual for offences to be very broadly defined and then leave the prosecution to use the offence sensibly. No sensible officer of the Crown Prosecution Service would charge the husband in this example, even if technically he could be convicted of the offence.

5 WOUNDING WITH INTENT

Section 18 of the Offences Against the Person Act 1861 states:

> Whosoever shall unlawfully and maliciously by any means whatsoever wound or cause any grievous bodily harm to any person . . . with intent . . . to do some grievous bodily harm to any person, or with intent to resist or prevent the lawful apprehension or detainer of any person, shall be guilty of an offence and being convicted thereof shall be liable, . . . to imprisonment for life. . . .

DEFINITION

Actus reus: the defendant unlawfully wounded or caused grievous bodily harm to any person.

Mens rea: either: (i) the defendant intended to cause grievous bodily harm; or (ii) the defendant intended to resist or prevent the lawful apprehension or detention of any person.

The wording of section 18 is very similar to that of section 20, and the meaning of many of the terms used in section 18 has already been discussed. There are four key differences between the section 18 and section 20 offences.

(1) The most important difference is the *mens rea*. The core *mens rea* for section 18 is that the defendant intended to do some grievous bodily harm. Intention here is to be

given the same meaning as that discussed in Chapter 3.[94] The *mens rea* requirement for section 18 is, then, more stringent than that required for section 20. Section
18 requires proof of intention, while recklessness is enough for section 20; section 18
requires proof that grievous bodily harm was intended, while section 20 requires that
some harm was foreseen.

Even if the defendant did not intend grievous bodily harm he can still be convicted
under section 18 if he was intending to prevent or resist an arrest. It is necessary to
show both:

(i) the defendant was *Cunningham* reckless (which is how the courts have interpreted maliciously) probably to causing grievous bodily (but possibly just some)
harm;[95] and

(ii) that he intended to resist or prevent the lawful apprehension or detention of any
person.

As regards (ii) it is no defence to show that the defendant thought the arrest was
unlawful.[96] What must be shown is that the defendant intended to resist or prevent an
apprehension, which was in fact a lawful apprehension. If in fact the arrest was not
lawful then the offence would not be committed.

(2) Section 20 states that the wound or cause of grievous bodily harm can be 'with or
without any weapon or instrument', whereas section 18 states that it can be 'by any
means whatsoever'. It is submitted that the best view is that there is no significance in
this difference in the wording. If there is any difference it could be argued that section
20 requires some kind of direct blow, whereas section 18 requires only proof that the
defendant caused the injuries in any way.[97]

(3) The third difference in the wording of the two sections is that section 20 states that the
defendant must cause injury to 'any other person', while in section 18 the injury must
be caused to 'any person'. It could therefore be argued that if a defendant caused
himself grievous bodily harm intentionally he committed an offence contrary to
section 18; but if he did so recklessly there would be no offence contrary to section 20.
However, no reported prosecution has been brought under section 18 on the basis
that the defendant caused himself grievous bodily harm.

(4) We have already discussed the fact that section 18 requires the defendant to have
caused grievous bodily harm; while section 20 requires proof that the defendant
inflicted grievous bodily harm. After *Ireland and Burstow* and *Dica*[98] it is clear that
inflict and cause mean the same thing.

---

[94] However, it should be recalled that in *Woollin* [1999] 1 AC 82 Lord Steyn explicitly stated that his
discussion of intention was limited to the context of murder. It is therefore not impossible that a court might
feel it appropriate to restrict the meaning of intention in s. 18 to direct intention. However, there would need
to be a very good reason why intention in s. 18 should have a different meaning from intention in murder.
[95] The question was left open in *Morrison* (1989) 89 Cr App R 17 (CA).
[96] *Bently* (1850) 4 Cox 406.
[97] See the discussion at p. 351. See Wilson (2003: 316). See also Gardner (1994a).
[98] [2004] EWCA Crim 1103.

6 MIXING AND MATCHING THE OFFENCES

If a defendant is charged with one of these assaults, but the jury acquits him of that offence, the jury can nevertheless convict the defendant of a lesser assault.[99] So, if the defendant is charged with a section 18 offence the jury can still convict him of an offence under section 20 or 47; if charged with a section 20 offence he can still be convicted of an offence under section 47.[100]

7 POISONING

Two poisoning offences will be considered in detail:[101]

(1) Offences Against the Person Act 1861, section 23, which says:

> Whosoever shall unlawfully and maliciously administer to or cause to be administered to or taken by any other person any poison or other destructive or noxious thing, so as thereby to endanger the life of such person, or so as thereby to inflict upon such person any grievous bodily harm shall be guilty of [an offence], and being convicted thereof shall be liable . . . to imprisonment for any term not exceeding ten years. . . .

DEFINITION

Section 23 of the Offences Against the Person Act 1861

Actus reus: the defendant administered to or caused to be administered to or taken by the victim a poison, noxious, or destructive thing. As a result, he or she (a) endangered the life of the victim or (b) inflicted upon the victim any grievous bodily harm.

Mens rea: the defendant was *Cunningham* recklessness as to the administration of a poison, noxious, or destructive thing. (**N.B.** It does not need to be shown that the defendant intended or foresaw that the victim's life would be endangered or that the victim would suffer any grievous bodily harm.)

(2) Offences Against the Person Act 1861, section 24, which states:

> Whosoever shall unlawfully and maliciously administer to or cause to be administered to or taken by any other person any poison or other destructive or noxious thing, with intent to injure, aggrieve, or annoy such person, shall be guilty of an offence, and being

---

[99] Although in practical terms this is highly convenient, there are theoretical problems with it: see Hare (1993).

[100] Whether the judge informs the jury of the possibility of convicting for the lesser offence is in the judge's discretion. But if the judge fears that the jury will convict the defendant even though they find the offence not proved rather than find him not guilty of anything, the judge must inform the jury of the possibility of the lesser charge: *Maxwell* [1994] Crim LR 848 (CA).

[101] You should also be aware of the Sexual Offences Act 2003, s. 61, which makes it an offence to administer a substance to stupefy a victim to enable the sexual activity with them to take place.

> ... convicted thereof shall be liable to imprisonment for a term not exceeding five years.

DEFINITION

Section 24 of the Offences Against the Person Act 1861

Actus reus: the defendant administered or caused to be administered to or taken by the victim a poison, noxious, or destructive thing.

Mens rea: the defendant was *Cunningham* reckless to the administration of the poison or noxious thing AND intended to injure, aggrieve, or annoy the victim.

Although both sections 23 and 24 have the same basic element (unlawfully and maliciously administering or causing to be administered or be taken by a person any poison or other destructive or noxious thing), they have different aggravating features:

(1) In section 23 it is the effect of the poisoning: there must be the infliction of grievous bodily harm or an endangerment of the victim's life. All that needs to be foreseen is the administration of the poison or noxious thing.

(2) In section 24 it is the intent of the defendant which is the aggravating feature: there must be an intent to injure, aggrieve, or annoy the victim.

7.1 THE MEANING OF 'POISON' OR 'NOXIOUS SUBSTANCE'

'Poison' has been widely interpreted by the courts. It is necessary to distinguish between:

(1) substances which are in their nature poisoning or noxious (e.g. cyanide, sulphuric acid, or heroin). Such substances are poisons or noxious substances whatever quantity is used. To put arsenic in someone's tea is to administer poison to them, even if it is harmless in the amount administered.[102] In *Cato*[103] it was confirmed that heroin is noxious even if taken by a regular user who suffers no direct harm;[104]

(2) substances which are not in their nature harmful. For such substances it must be shown that the substance was administered in a quantity sufficient to be harmful.[105] So placing a large amount of cod liver oil in someone's cappuccino could poison them, even though a very small amount would not.

A noxious substance is a substance which is hurtful, unwholesome, or objectionable.[106] If the substance is not in its nature noxious, it can become noxious if administered in such large doses that it becomes so. In *Marcus*[107] a sedative administered in large quantities became noxious, even though, had it been administered in small quantities, it would not have been harmful (and so not noxious).

The following case discusses further the meaning of 'noxious' and 'poison':

---

[102] *Cramp* (1880) 5 QBD 307 (a case considering the meaning of 'poison' under the Offences Against the Person Act 1861, s. 58 (administration of poison to procure an abortion)).
[103] *Cato* [1976] 1 All ER 260 (CA).   [104] This view was also adopted in *Cramp* (1880) 5 QBD 307.
[105] *Marlow* (1964) 49 Cr App R 49 (CA).
[106] *Marcus* [1981] 2 All ER 833 (CA).   [107] [1981] 2 All ER 833 (CA).

R v Marcus
[1981] 2 All ER 833 (CA)[108]

Lilly Marcus put eight sedative and sleeping tablets into milk which had been delivered to her neighbour's house. She was charged with attempting to cause to be taken by her neighbour or another a noxious thing with intent to injure, aggrieve, or annoy. Evidence at the trial suggested that at the levels put in the milk the drugs would be likely to cause sedation and perhaps sleep. There would be no direct harm, but that if the person who had taken the drugs were to be driving a car, for example, they could be endangered. The defendant appealed against her conviction.

Mr Justice Tudor Evans read the following judgment of the court

Two submissions are made. First, it is said that for a thing to be noxious within the meaning of section 24, it must be noxious in itself. A thing which is intrinsically harmless cannot become noxious or harmful because it is given in excess quantity. In support of this submission, counsel relies upon obiter dicta of Lord Widgery C.J. in *Reg. v. Cato* [1976] 1 W.L.R. 110. Secondly, it is submitted that the word 'noxious' means harmful and that the meaning is necessarily confined to injury to bodily health. The word cannot mean harm involving an impairment of faculties. Counsel submits that on the undisputed evidence there was in fact no risk of injury to bodily health. If any one member of the Laskey family had drunk the milk, or any part of it, he or she would have been sedated or at most would have been caused to fall asleep. . . .

We consider that the words 'noxious thing' mean that the jury has to consider the very thing which on the facts is administered or sought to be administered both as to quality and as to quantity. The jury has to consider the evidence of what was administered or attempted to be administered both in quality and in quantity and to decide as a question of fact and degree in all the circumstances whether that thing was noxious. A substance which may have been harmless in small quantities may yet be noxious in the quantity administered. Many illustrations were put in the course of the argument: for example, to lace a glass of milk with a quantity of alcohol might not amount to administering a noxious thing to an adult but it might do so if given to a child.

. . .

We shall now consider the second submission for the appellant, that the word 'noxious' means harmful in the sense of injury to bodily health. Counsel took us through the relevant sections of the Act. In a number of sections (including section 24) the words 'poison or other destructive or noxious thing' appear. It was submitted that the meaning of the word 'noxious' must take colour from the preceding words. We do not accept that construction. It seems to us, looking at the relevant sections, that the statute is dealing with offences in a declining order of gravity and that by 'noxious' is meant something different in quality from and of less importance than poison or other destructive things.

On this part of his argument, counsel relies upon evidence from the toxicologists on both sides that the dose would do no more harm than cause sedation or possibly sleep and was therefore harmless. In fact, the evidence was not so confined. In the course of his summing up, the judge, having referred to the evidence relating to sedation and sleep, continued:

'Mr. Wilson said that little harm is likely to arise, in his opinion, from the toxicity of the drugs themselves, but there is a danger to someone carrying out normal but potentially hazardous

---

[108] [1981] 1 WLR 774, (1981) 73 Cr App R 49.

operations, for example, driving, whilst their faculties are impaired. You may think that it would not have to be driving, it might be crossing a London street, for example; one could think of a lot of things.'

There was therefore evidence before the jury that the drugs in the quantity in which they were present in the milk were potentially harmful in the sense of being capable of causing injury to bodily health. The result of the evidence was that the milk might have had a direct physical effect on the victim. But we do not consider that the word 'noxious' bears the restricted meaning for which counsel contends.

In the course of his summing up, the judge quoted the definition of 'noxious' from the Shorter Oxford English Dictionary, where it is described as meaning 'injurious, hurtful, harmful, unwholesome.' The meaning is clearly very wide. It seems to us that even taking its weakest meaning, if, for example, a person were to put an obnoxious (that is objectionable) or unwholesome thing into an article of food or drink with the intent to annoy any person who might consume it, an offence would be committed. A number of illustrations were put in argument, including the snail said to have been in the ginger beer bottle (to adapt the facts in *Donoghue v. Stevenson* [1932] A.C. 562). If that had been done with any of the intents in the section, it seems to us that an offence would have been committed.

The judge, when summing up to the jury, reminded them fully of the evidence and directed them that it was a matter of fact and degree for them to decide whether the drugs in the milk were noxious. His direction in law was unexceptionable. The appeal must be dismissed.

Appeal dismissed.

7.2 THE MEANING OF 'ADMINISTER'

'Administration' is widely defined in the statute. It includes the defendant administering the poison, as well as causing the victim to take the poison himself. This seems certainly to cover the situation where the defendant secretly poisoned the victim's drink.[109] More controversial is the suggestion in *Kennedy*[110] that supplying a drug at the request of the victim who then took it himself could constitute administration.[111] In *Gillard*[112] it was accepted that spraying CS gas onto the victim would amount to administering poison. It was confirmed by McNeill J that administration of a poison did not require the substance to enter the victim's body, although it would require contact with the body. So, simply putting poison in an enemy's food would not in itself be an administration, until someone ate the food.

7.3 THE MEANING OF 'MALICIOUSLY'

This has been interpreted to mean *Cunningham* recklessness. That means that the defendant must foresee that his act will cause the poison to be administered. For example, in *Cunningham*[113] the defendant broke a gas pipe in a basement. It was confirmed that the prosecution had to prove that the defendant foresaw that the gas would escape and be

---

[109] *Harley* (1830) 4 C & P 396; *Dale* (1852) 6 Cox CC.   [110] *Kennnedy* [2005] EWCA 685.
[111] Although see the criticisms of this case in Ormerod (2005).
[112] (1988) 87 Cr App R 189 (CA).   [113] [1957] 2 QB 396 (CA).

administered to the victim. One issue which is left unresolved by the case law is whether the defendant has to foresee that the gas will be noxious. In other words is it enough that the defendant foresaw the administration of a substance or must it be shown that the defendant foresaw the administration of a poison or noxious substance?

7.4 THE MEANING OF 'ENDANGERMENT OF LIFE' OR 'CAUSE GRIEVOUS BODILY HARM'

For section 23 it is not necessary to show that the defendant intended or foresaw that the victim would suffer grievous bodily harm or endangerment of life. There is some debate whether the causation of grievous bodily harm or endangerment of life in section 23 must be caused directly by the poisoning. Imagine this: the defendant poisons the victim who then feels drowsy; falls down; and suffers grievous bodily harm. Michael Allen[114] argues that in such a case the offence would not be made out because it would not be the poison itself which caused the harm. However, if 'cause' in this section were to be given its ordinary meaning, there seems little doubt that the causation would be established.

7.5 THE MEANING OF 'WITH INTENT TO INJURE, AGGRIEVE, OR ANNOY'

'Intent' in section 24 is to be given its normal meaning within the criminal law, as set out in Chapter 3. The words 'injure', 'aggrieve', or 'annoy' should be given their ordinary meaning. However, there was some debate over whether it is necessary to show that the intent was to injure, aggrieve, or annoy as a direct result of the poisoning or whether it was sufficient to poison with the intent of injuring, aggrieving, or annoying in some other way. The issue was raised in *Hill*.[115] The defendant gave some tablets to boys aged 11 and 13. They were slimming tablets which had the side effect of causing sleeplessness. The prosecution argued that Hill's plan was that the tablets would mean the boys would stay up late and would therefore be more susceptible to his sexual advances. In fact the defendant made no sexual advances and the boys suffered diarrhoea and vomiting. The House of Lords held that the defendant could properly be convicted of an offence under section 24. An intention of keeping boys awake in order to abuse them could constitute an intention to 'injure aggrieve or annoy' for the purposes of section 24. Lord Griffiths[116] suggested that if a mother gave her children a tablet to keep them awake so that they could welcome their father home this would not amount to the requisite intention. So, in deciding whether there was an intent to injure, aggrieve, or annoy the jury should consider not only the intended effects of the substance, but the overall plan of the defendant.

FURTHER READING

Bell, B., and Harrison, K. (1993), 'R v Savage, DPP v Parmenter and the Law of Assault', *Modern Law Review* 56: 83.

Gardner, S. (1998c), 'Stalking', *Law Quarterly Review* 114: 33.

Hare, I. (1993), 'R v Savage, DPP v Parmenter—A Compelling Case for the Code', *Modern Law Review* 56: 74.

---

[114] Allen (2003: 358).   [115] (1986) 83 CAR 386 (HL).   [116] At 390.

Herring, J. (1998b), 'The Criminalisation of Harassment', *Cambridge Law Journal* 57: 10.

Hirst, M. (1999), 'Assault, Battery and Indirect Violence', *Criminal Law Review* 557.

Horder, J. (1998a), 'Reconsidering Psychic Assault', *Criminal Law Review* 392.

8 OTHER ASSAULT CRIMES

There are a number of other assault offences which will not be covered in this book including assaulting an officer of the court;[117] assaulting a clergyman in the discharge of his duties in a place of worship or burial place;[118] assaulting with intent to rob;[119] assaulting with intent to commit a sexual offence;[120] assaulting with intent to resist arrest; and assaulting a police officer.[121] There are also some important public order criminal offences which are not dealt with here,[122] for example riot, violent disorder, affray, causing harassment, alarm, or distress.

9 RACIALLY AND RELIGIOUSLY AGGRAVATED CRIMES

There has been increasing concern over racially or religiously motivated crimes.[123] There has been an 29 per cent increase in the number of prosecutions for racially aggravated crimes from 2003–4 to 2004–5. In 2004–5 there were 444,660 prosecutions for racially aggravated crimes. The government has decided that crimes with a racial element should be given higher sentences and be specifically labelled as such. The justification for this is that:

> The Government recognizes that racist crime does not simply injure the victim or their property, it affects the whole family and it erodes the standards of decency of the wider community. Trust and understanding built up over many years between communities can be eroded by the climate of fear and anxiety which can surround a racist incident.[124]

The Crime and Disorder Act 1998, sections 28 to 32, created a new category of racially or religiously aggravated crimes.[125]

DEFINITION

1. The defendant has committed one of the following offences:
   (i) common assault;
   (ii) section 47 of the Offences Against the Person Act;
   (iii) section 20 of the Offences Against the Person Act;
   (iv) section 2 of the Protection from Harassment Act 1997;

---

[117] County Courts Act 1984, s. 14(1)(b).   [118] Offences Against the Person 1961, s. 36.
[119] Theft Act 1968, s. 8.   [120] Sexual Offences Act 2003, s. 62.   [121] Police Act 1996, s. 89.
[122] For a useful discussion see: Feldman (2002: ch. 18).   [123] Home Office (1997b).
[124] Home Office (1998a: para. 1.1)
[125] Burney (2003) and Burney and Rose (2002) provide useful discussions of the Act's operation.

(v) section 4 of the Protection from Harassment Act 1997;

(vi) criminal damage;

(vii) sections 4, 4A, and 5 of the Public Order Act 1986.

2. The offence was racially or religiously aggravated.

A person commits an offence under section 29 of the Act[126] if he or she commits one of the offences listed in the box above, which is 'racially or religiously aggravated'.[127]

---

(1) An offence is racially or religiously aggravated . . . if—

(a) at the time of committing the offence, or immediately before or after doing so, the offender demonstrates towards the victim of the offence hostility based on the victim's membership (or presumed membership) of a racial or religious group; or

(b) the offence is motivated (wholly or partly) by hostility towards members of a racial group based on their membership of that group.

(2) In subsection (1)(a) above—

'membership' in relation to a racial or religious group includes association with members of that group; 'presumed' means presumed by the offender.

(3) It is immaterial for the purpose of paragraph (a) or (b) of subsection (1) above whether or not the offender's hostility is also based, to any extent, on any factor not mentioned in that paragraph.

(4) In this section 'racial group' means a group of persons defined by reference to race, colour, nationality (including citizenship) or ethnic or national origins.

(5) In this section 'religious group' means a group of persons defined by reference to religious belief or lack of religious belief.

There are therefore two ways of showing the offence is racially or religiously aggravated:[128]

(1) that under section 28(1)(a) racial or religious hostility was demonstrated during the commission of the offence; or

(2) under section 28(1)(b) that the offence was motivated by D's hostility to V.

Section 28(1)(a) will be relied upon where some racial or religious insult was uttered during the attack. It should be noted that, under this subsection, as long as racial or religious hostility is demonstrated, there is no need to show that the attack was motivated by racial or religious hostility.[129] The sub-section can be relied upon where hostility is demonstrated immediately before or immediately after the attack.[130] The victim need not be aware that the hostility has been demonstrated.[131] Where no insulting words are spoken it may be easier in many cases to rely on section 28(1)(b) if it can be shown that the attack was motivated by

---

[126] As amended by the Anti-Terrorism, Crime and Security Act 2001.

[127] There is no racially aggravated version of s. 18 of the Offences Against the Person Act 1861 because that offence has a maximum sentence of life imprisonment, and so it cannot be given a higher sentence.

[128] The courts have indicated that they are willing to give 'race' a wide interpretation: *White* [2001] EWCA Crim 216, [2001] 1 WLR 1352 (CA).

[129] *DPP v Woods* [2002] EWHC 85 (Admin).

[130] In *Parry v Director Of Public Prosecutions* [2004] EWHC 3112 an admission to police 20 minutes after the attack that it was racially motivated was reagarded as a deomonstration of hostility immediately after the attack.

[131] *Parry v Director of Public Prosecutions* [2004] EWHC 3112.

race or religion. How easily this can be proved may depend on how ready a jury will be to assume that an attack is racially or religiously motivated from the fact that the attacker and victim are of a different race or religion and there is no other apparent reason for the attack.

It should not be assumed that because a racial assault was uttered prior to the attack race was the motivation for the attack. In *DPP v Pal*[132] a caretaker at a community centre, described as being of Asian appearance, ejected the defendant (an Asian youth) from the building. The defendant called the caretaker a 'brown Englishman' and uttered other racial insults and later attacked him. It was held by the Divisional Court that this was not a racially aggravated assault because the assault was motivated by the defendant's anger at having to leave the centre and at what he regarded as the victim's close relationships with whites, rather than his race as such. The court, however, emphasized that simply that the defendant and victim were of the same race did not prevent the assault being racially aggravated. The court gave the example of a white man attacking another white man because he was going out with a black woman. However, in *DPP v McFarlane*[133] *Pal* was said to be heavily dependant on the facts of the case and that normally where a racial insult was uttered during a crime it would be regarded as racially aggravated.[134]

In *Rogers*[135] the defendant assault a group of women calling them 'bloody foreigners'. This was held by the Court of Appeal to be hostility based on a racial group. It was held that the notion of race should be defined widely. In *Attorney-General's Reference (No. 4 of 2004)*[136] it was held that the phrase 'immigrant doctor' could be thought by the jury to be a demonstration of racial hostility.

FURTHER READING

Burney, E. (2003), 'Using the Law on Racially Aggravated Offences', *Criminal Law Review* 28.

—— and Rose, G. (2002), *Racially Aggravated Offences: How is the Law Working?* Home Office Research Study No. 244 (London: Home Office).

Home Office (1997b), *Racial Violence and Harassment: A Consultation Document* (London: Home Office).

Malik, S. (1998), 'Racist Crime: Racially Aggravated Offences in the Crime and Disorder Act 1998, Part II', *Modern Law Review* 62: 409.

10   PROTECTION FROM HARASSMENT ACT 1997

10.1   SECTION 1: HARASSMENT

Under section 1 of the Protection from Harassment Act 1997:

> (1) A person must not pursue a course of conduct—
>
>   (a) which amounts to harassment of another; and
>
>   (b) which he knows or ought to know amounts to harassment of the other.

---

[132] [2000] Crim LR 756 (DC).   [133] [2002] EWHC Admin 485.
[134] See also *Rogers* [2005] EWCA Crim 2863.
[135] [2005] EWCA Crim 2863.   [136] [2005] Crim LR 799 (CA).

(2) For the purposes of this section the person whose course of conduct is in question ought to know that it amounts to harassment of another if a reasonable person in possession of the same information would think the course of conduct amounted to harassment of the other.

(3) Subsection (1) does not apply to a course conduct if the person who pursued it shows—

(a) that it was pursued for the purpose of preventing or detecting crime;

(b) that it was pursued under any enactment or rule of law or to comply with any condition or requirement imposed by any person under any enactment, or

(c) that in the particular circumstances, the pursuit of the course of conduct was reasonable.

DEFINITION

Actus reus: the defendant engaged in a course of conduct which amounted to harassment.

Mens rea: the defendant knew or ought to have known that that conduct amounted to harassment.

The offence can be broken down into the following four elements:[137]

(1) *A course of conduct.* A course of conduct[138] must involve at least two incidents.[139] A single incident, however disturbing, will not constitute the offence.[140] In order to amount to a course of conduct, the two or more incidents must be linked; there must be some nexus between them.[141] The fewer the number of incidents and the further apart in time they are the stronger the linking theme must be before the court will find a course of conduct. The following three cases provide a flavour of how the courts decide whether there is a course of conduct:

(i) In *Lau v DPP*,[142] the defendant slapped the victim and then four months later he threatened the victim's new boyfriend with violence. This was held not to constitute a course of conduct. The incidents were too far apart in time and were different in nature.

(ii) In *Hills*[143] the defendant was violent to his partner twice in the course of six months. It was held not to be a course of conduct because the couple had reconciled and cohabited between the two incidents, thereby severing the link between them.

(iii) In *Kelly v DPP*[144] the defendant left three messages on the victim's voice mail facility in the space of five minutes. The victim listened to them all at the same time. The Divisional Court held that the magistrates were entitled to take the

---

[137] Six months is the maximum sentence of imprisonment.
[138] Conduct is said in s. 7(4) to include speech.   [139] Protection from Harassment Act 1997, s. 7(3).
[140] Although in *Wass v DPP*, CO/1101/00, 11 May 2000 (QBD) the Divisional Court was willing to treat two occurrences within a few minutes of each other as a course of conduct.
[141] *Lau v DPP* [2000] 1 FLR 799 (CA).   [142] [2000] Crim LR 586 (CA).
[143] [2001] Crim LR 318 (CA).   [144] [2003] Crim LR 43 (DC).

view that each call was separate and distinct and therefore could amount to a course of conduct.

(2) *The course of conduct must amount to harassment.* Harassment is said in section 7(2) to include causing the victim alarm or distress. However, because the statute uses the word 'includes' it is clear that it is possible to harass a victim who has not been alarmed or distressed.[145] A Home Office Circular[146] has suggested a very extensive definition of the term: 'harassment is any form of anti-social behaviour which needs to be tackled'. Such a circular is not binding on the courts, but a judge minded to take a wide definition of harassment might be willing to adopt it.

Inevitably the courts have had to draw fine lines between acts of legitimate courting and acts of harassment.[147] In *King v DPP*[148] it was explained that offering a plant to the victim as a gift and writing one letter to the victim asking her whether she was interested in a relationship would not amount to harassment. But in *James*[149] it was held that offering a very valuable gift to a person the defendant hardly knew could be harassment.

It should be noted that the partial definition of harassment in section 7(2) focuses on the effect of the defendant's conduct, rather than describing the conduct itself. So if the conduct causes alarm or distress to the victim, it can amount to harassment, even though most people would not be bothered by the conduct. This approach to the definition of harassment nearly caused problems in *King v DPP*[150] where the defendant (*inter alia*) had been secretly filming the victim. It was held that although the conduct could be described as harassment because, although the victim was not aware of the filming at the time, when she was told by the police what the defendant had been doing she was alarmed and distressed.

(3) *The defendant must know or ought to know that the conduct is harassing.* The section 1 offence contains alternatives of either a subjective or an objective *mens rea.* The defendant is guilty if he knew or ought to know that his conduct amounted to harassment. This is significant. It means that it is no defence for a defendant to claim, 'I thought I was expressing my love for the victim; I did not realize she would find this distressing' if it would have been obvious to a reasonable person that the conduct was harassing. Further, if the defendant was acting in a way which he knew was harassing the victim he can be guilty, even if a reasonable person would not realize that the conduct was harassing. In the following case the Court of Appeal considered whether the reasonable person should be endowed with the characteristics of the defendant (as is done in the defence of provocation, for example). They decided not.

R v Colohan
[2001] EWCA Crim 1251 (CA)[151]

The appellant suffered from schizophrenia. He wrote a number of incoherent, abusive, and threatening letters to his Member of Parliament. The appellant

---

[145] *DPP v Ramsdale* [2001] EWHC Admin 106.   [146] Home Office Circular 28/2001.

[147] There are also, of course, difficulties in distinguishing between legitimate and illegitimate expressions of complaint (*Baron v Crown Prosecution Service*, 13 June 2000, QBD CO/1569/00) or points of view (*Thomas v News Group Newspapers Ltd and another* [2001] EWCA Civ 1233 (CA)).

[148] 20 June 2000, unreported.   [149] *Jones* [2001] EWCA Crim 2235.

[150] 20 June 2000, unreported.   [151] [2001] 2 FLR 757, [2001] Fam L 732.

was, as a result, charged with an offence under sections 1 and 2 of the Protection from Harassment Act 1997. The appellant argued that in considering whether he ought to know that his conduct amounted to harassment, the jury should be told to consider what a reasonable person suffering from schizophrenia would have known (by analogy with the defences of provocation and duress). He also argued that his illness rendered his conduct reasonable under section 1(3)(c).

Mr Justice Hughes

. . .

[17] The question raised by these submissions [the arguments of the appellant's counsel] is one of the proper construction of the Protection from Harassment Act 1997. As the first word of that title suggests, this is an Act whose purpose is significantly protective and preventative. The long title is 'An act to make provision for protecting persons from harassment and similar conduct'.

[18] . . . As is well known, the 1997 Act was passed with the phenomenon of 'stalking' particularly, although not exclusively, in mind. The conduct at which the 1997 Act is aimed, and from which it seeks to provide protection, is particularly likely to be conduct pursued by those of obsessive or otherwise unusual psychological make-up and very frequently by those suffering from an identifiable mental illness. Schizophrenia is only one such condition which is obviously very likely to give rise to conduct of this sort.

[19] We are satisfied that to give the 1997 Act the construction for which Mr Butterfield [counsel for the appellant] contends would be to remove from its protection a very large number of victims and indeed to run the risk of significantly thwarting the purpose of the Act. If such a construction is correct it would prevent the conduct in question from being a breach of s 1 and thus exclude not only suitable punishment for the perpetrator, but also damages, and, more especially, an injunction or restraining order for the protection of the victim. We do not believe that Parliament can have meant the provisions in question to have the meaning for which Mr Butterfield contends. Moreover, as it seems to us, if Mr Butterfield's submission were correct then s 1(2) would have been inserted unnecessarily into the Act.

[20] We agree accordingly with the judge that, except insofar as it requires the jury to consider the information actually in the possession of this defendant, s 1(2) requires the jury to answer the question whether he ought to have known that what he was doing amounts to harassment by the objective test of what a reasonable person would think. Its words, we are satisfied, are abundantly clear.

[21] As to s 1(3)(c), that, we are satisfied, poses even more clearly an objective test, namely whether the conduct is in the judgment of the jury reasonable. There is no warrant for attaching to the word 'reasonable' or via the words 'particular circumstances' the standards or characteristics of the defendant himself.

Appeal dismissed.

(4) *Defences to harassment.* Section 1(3) sets out the statutory defences available to the defendant. The one that is likely to be relied upon the most is subsection (c): that the conduct of the defendant is reasonable. The courts have made it clear that unlawful conduct (e.g. actions in breach of an injunction) will not be regarded as

reasonable.[152] In *Colohan*, discussed above, the defendant sought to argue that his conduct was reasonable, given that he was schizophrenic. The Court of Appeal held that his mental illness did not render his conduct reasonable.

10.2 SECTION 4 OF THE PROTECTION FROM HARASSMENT ACT 1997

Section 4 of the Protection from Harassment Act 1997 states:

> (1) A person whose course of conduct causes another to fear, on at least two occasions, that violence will be used against him is guilty of an offence if he knows or ought to know that his course of conduct will cause the other so to fear on each of those occasions.
>
> (2) For the purposes of this section, the person whose course of conduct is in question ought to know that it will cause another to fear that violence will be used against him on any occasion if a reasonable person in possession of the same information would think the course of conduct would cause the other so to fear on that occasion.
>
> (3) It is a defence for a person charged with an offence under this section to show that—
>
> > (a) his course of conduct was pursued for the purpose of preventing or detecting crime,
> >
> > (b) his course of conduct was pursued under any enactment or rule of law or to comply with any condition or requirement imposed by any person under any enactment, or
> >
> > (c) the pursuit of his course of conduct was reasonable for the protection of himself or another or for the protection of his or another's property.

To establish a conviction under section 4[153] it is not necessary to show that the victim was harassed, but it has to be shown that the accused has undertaken a course of conduct which on at least two occasions led the victim to fear that violence would be used against him. It is not enough to show that the victim is 'seriously frightened' in a general way; there must be a specific fear that violence will be used.[154] It does not need to be shown that the threat was issued against the victim: an ostensible threat to a victim's dog could be interpreted by the victim as a threat of violence against the victim.[155] But, as emphasized in *Henley*,[156] it is not enough for the victim to fear that violence will be used against his family.[157]

FURTHER READING

Finch, E. (2001), *The Criminalisation of Stalking* (London: Cavendish).

—— (2002), 'Stalking the Perfect Stalking Law: An Evaluation of the Efficacy of the Protection from Harassment Act 1997', *Criminal Law Review* 703.

Home Office (1996), *Stalking the Solutions: A Consultation Paper* (London: Home Office).

---

[152] *R v DPP, ex parte Moseley and others*, 23 June 1999, CO/664/99 (QBD).
[153] The maximum sentence of imprisonment is 5 years.   [154] *Henley* [2000] Crim LR 582 (DC).
[155] *R v DPP* [2001] Crim LR 397 (DC).
[156] [2000] Crim LR 582 (CA).   [157] *Caurti v DPP* [2002] Crim LR 131 (DC).

Infield, P., and Platford, G. (2000), *The Law of Harassment and Stalking* (London: Butterworths).

Wells, C. (1997), 'Stalking: The Criminal Law Response', *Criminal Law Review* 463.

11 THREATS OFFENCES

Generally it is not an offence to threaten someone.[158] However, statutes have created some specific offences:

(1) threat to kill;[159]

(2) threat to damage or destroy property belonging to another;[160]

(3) blackmail: making an unwarranted demand with menaces;[161]

(4) threatening violence for the purpose of securing unlawful entry to occupied premises;[162]

(5) threats over the telephone;[163]

(6) bomb hoax;[164]

(7) various kinds of threatening behaviour in public places.[165]

There are many others.

FURTHER READING

Alldridge, P. (1994), 'Threats Offences—a Case for Reform', *Criminal Law Review* 176.

Rothman, J. (2001), 'Freedom of Speech and True Threats', *Harvard Journal of Law and Public Policy* 25: 283.

12 TRANSMITTING DISEASE

There has been much discussion over whether a defendant who passes on a disease can be convicted of an offence.[166] This is now governed by the following two decisions:

R v Dica
[2004] QB 1257 (CA)

Mohammed Dica was aware that he was HIV positive. Nevertheless he had unprotected sexual intercourse with two women who were subsequently diagnosed as HIV positive. He was charged with inflicting grievous bodily harm upon then, contrary to section 20, Offences Against the Person Act 1861. At his trial the judge ruled that the jury could

---

[158] For an excellent discussion see Alldridge (1994).   [159] Offences Against the Person Act 1861, s. 16.
[160] Criminal Damage Act 1971, s. 2.   [161] Theft Act 1968, s. 21.
[162] Criminal Law Act 1977, s. 6.   [163] Telecommunications Act 1984, ss. 42, 43.
[164] Criminal Law Act 1977, s. 51(1).   [165] Public Order Act 1986, ss. 1–5.
[166] See Bronitt (1994); Ormerod and Gunn (1996); Dine and Watt (1998).

convict the defendant even if he was able to show that the women were aware of his condition. In other words the consent of the victims to running the risk of becoming HIV positive provided him with no defence. He was convicted and appealed.

Before the Court of Appeal there were two main questions. First, whether the defendant could be said to have inflicted grievous bodily harm and second, in what circumstances, if any, the consent of the victims were relevant to the charge he faced. As to the first, the Court of Appeal, following the House of Lords decision in *R v Burstow* concluded that the word 'inflict' in section 20 of the Offences Against the Person Act carried the same meaning as the word 'cause'. Any suggestion in the case of *Clarance* that a harm could not be 'inflicted' in the course of consensual sexual intercourse was rejected.

Judge LJ

. . .

37. The present case is concerned with and confined to section 20 offences alone, without the burdensome fiction of deemed consent to sexual intercourse. The question for decision is whether the victims' consent to sexual intercourse, which as a result of his alleged concealment was given in ignorance of the facts of the defendant's condition, necessarily amounted to consent to the risk of being infected by him. If that question must be answered 'Yes', the concept of consent in relation to section 20 is devoid of real meaning.

38. The position here is analogous to that considered in *R v Tabassum* [2000] 2 Cr App R 328. The appellant was convicted of indecently assaulting women who allowed him to examine their breasts in the mistaken belief that he was medically qualified. Rose LJ considered *Clarence*, and pointed out that in relation to the infection suffered by the wife, this was an additional, unexpected, consequence of sexual intercourse, which was irrelevant to her consent to sexual intercourse with her husband. Rejecting the argument that an 'undoubted consent' could only be negatived if the victim had been deceived or mistaken about the nature and quality of the act, and that consent was not negatived 'merely because the victim would not have agreed to the act if he or she had known all the facts', Rose LJ observed, in forthright terms, at p 337, 'there was no true consent'. Again, in *R v Cort* [2004] QB 388, a case of kidnapping, the complainants had consented to taking a ride in a motor car, but not to being kidnapped. They wanted transport, not kidnapping. Kidnapping may be established by carrying away by fraud:

'it is difficult to see how one could ever consent to that once fraud was indeed established. The "nature" of the act here is therefore taking the complainant away by fraud. The complainant did not consent to that event. All that she consented to is a ride in the car, which in itself is irrelevant to the offence and a different thing from that with which Mr Cort is charged' (p 393).

39. In our view, on the assumed fact now being considered, the answer is entirely straightforward. These victims consented to sexual intercourse. Accordingly, the defendant was not guilty of rape. Given the long-term nature of the relationships, if the defendant concealed the truth about his condition from them, and therefore kept them in ignorance of it, there was no reason for them to think that they were running any risk of infection, and they were not consenting to it. On this basis, there would be no consent sufficient in law to provide the defendant with a defence to the charge under section 20.

. . .

40. We must now address the consequences if, contrary to their own assertions, the complainants knew of the state of the defendant's health, and notwithstanding the risks to their own, consented to sexual intercourse. Following Judge Philpot's second ruling, this issue was not considered by the jury. In effect the judge ruled that in law such consent (if any) was irrelevant. Having listened to the exchanges on this topic between Mr Carter-Manning, for the defendant, and the court, and on further reflection, Mr Gadsden for the Crown accepted that this issue should not have been withdrawn from the jury. Although we can take the issue relatively briefly, we must explain why this concession was right.

41. As a general rule, unless the activity is lawful, the consent of the victim to the deliberate infliction of serious bodily injury on him or her does not provide the perpetrator with any defence. Different categories of activity are regarded as lawful. Thus no one doubts that necessary major surgery with the patient's consent, even if likely to result in severe disability (eg an amputation) would be lawful. However the categories of activity regarded as lawful are not closed, and equally, they are not immutable. . . .

42. The present policy of the law is that, whether or not the violent activity takes place in private, and even if the victim agrees to it, serious violence is not lawful merely because it enables the perpetrator (or the victim) to achieve sexual gratification. Judge Philpot was impressed with the conclusions to be drawn from the well-known decision in *R v Brown (Anthony)* [1994] 1 AC 212. Sado-masochistic activity of an extreme, indeed horrific kind, which caused grievous bodily harm, was held to be unlawful, notwithstanding that those who suffered the cruelty positively welcomed it. This decision of the House of Lords was supported in the European Court of Human Rights on the basis that although the prosecution may have constituted an interference with the private lives of those involved, it was justified for the protection of public health: *Laskey, Jaggard and Brown v United Kingdom* (1997) 24 EHRR 39. . . .

[Judge LJ then referred to *R v Donovan* [1934] 2 KB 498, *R v Boyea* (1992) 156 JP 505, *R v Emmett, The Times*, 15 October 1999]

46. These authorities demonstrate that violent conduct involving the deliberate and intentional infliction of bodily harm is and remains unlawful notwithstanding that its purpose is the sexual gratification of one or both participants. Notwithstanding their sexual overtones, these cases were concerned with violent crime, and the sexual overtones did not alter the fact that both parties were consenting to the deliberate infliction of serious harm or bodily injury on one participant by the other. To date, as a matter of public policy, it has not been thought appropriate for such violent conduct to be excused merely because there is a private consensual sexual element to it. The same public policy reason would prohibit the deliberate spreading of disease, including sexual disease.

47. In our judgment the impact of the authorities dealing with sexual gratification can too readily be misunderstood. It does not follow from them, and they do not suggest, that consensual acts of sexual intercourse are unlawful merely because there may be a known risk to the health of one or other participant. These participants are not intent on spreading or becoming infected with disease through sexual intercourse. They are not indulging in serious violence for the purposes of sexual gratification. They are simply prepared, knowingly, to run the risk—not the certainty—of infection, as well as all the other risks inherent in and possible consequences of sexual intercourse, such as, and despite the most careful precautions, an unintended pregnancy. At one extreme there is casual sex between complete strangers, sometimes protected, sometimes not, when the attendant risks are known to be higher, and at the other, there is sexual intercourse between couples in a long-term and loving, and trusting relationship, which may from time to time also carry risks.

48. The first of these categories is self-explanatory and needs no amplification. By way of illustration we shall provide two examples of cases which would fall within the second.

49. In the first, one of a couple suffers from HIV. It may be the man: it may be the woman. The circumstances in which HIV was contracted are irrelevant. They could result from a contaminated blood transfusion, or an earlier relationship with a previous sexual partner, who unknown to the sufferer with whom we are concerned, was himself or herself infected with HIV. The parties are Roman Catholics. They are conscientiously unable to use artificial contraception. They both know of the risk that the healthy partner may become infected with HIV. Our second example is that of a young couple, desperate for a family, who are advised that if the wife were to become pregnant and give birth, her long-term health, indeed her life itself, would be at risk. Together the couple decide to run that risk, and she becomes pregnant. She may be advised that the foetus should be aborted, on the grounds of her health, yet, nevertheless, decide to bring her baby to term. If she does, and suffers ill health, is the male partner to be criminally liable for having sexual intercourse with her, notwithstanding that he knew of the risk to her health? If he is liable to be prosecuted, was she not a party to whatever crime was committed? And should the law interfere with the Roman Catholic couple, and require them, at the peril of criminal sanctions, to choose between bringing their sexual relationship to an end or violating their consciences by using contraception?

50. These, and similar risks, have always been taken by adults consenting to sexual intercourse. Different situations, no less potentially fraught, have to be addressed by them. Modern society has not thought to criminalise those who have willingly accepted the risks, and we know of no cases where one or other of the consenting adults has been prosecuted, let alone convicted, for the consequences of doing so.

51. The problems of criminalising the consensual taking of risks like these include the sheer impracticability of enforcement and the haphazard nature of its impact. The process would undermine the general understanding of the community that sexual relationships are pre-eminently private and essentially personal to the individuals involved in them. And if adults were to be liable to prosecution for the consequences of taking known risks with their health, it would seem odd that this should be confined to risks taken in the context of sexual intercourse, while they are nevertheless permitted to take the risks inherent in so many other aspects of everyday life, including, again for example, the mother or father of a child suffering a serious contagious illness, who holds the child's hand, and comforts or kisses him or her goodnight.

52. In our judgment, interference of this kind with personal autonomy, and its level and extent, may only be made by Parliament.

. . .

54. We have taken note of the various points made by the interested organisations. These include the complexity of bedroom and sex negotiations, and the lack of realism if the law were to expect people to be paragons of sexual behaviour at such a time, or to set about informing each other in advance of the risks or to counsel the use of condoms. It is also suggested that there are significant negative consequences of disclosure of HIV, and that the imposition of criminal liability could have an adverse impact on public health because those who ought to take advice, might be discouraged from doing so. If the criminal law was to become involved at all, this should be confined to cases where the offender deliberately inflicted others with a serious disease.

. . .

Conclusion

58. We repeat that the Crown did not allege, and we therefore are not considering the deliberate infection, or spreading of HIV with intent to cause grievous bodily harm. In such

circumstances, the application of what we may describe as the principle in *Brown* [1994] 1 AC 212 means that the agreement of the participants would provide no defence to a charge under section 18 of the 1861 Act.

59. The effect of this judgment in relation to section 20 is to remove some of the outdated restrictions against the successful prosecution of those who, knowing that they are suffering HIV or some other serious sexual disease, recklessly transmit it through consensual sexual intercourse, and inflict grievous bodily harm on a person from whom the risk is concealed and who is not consenting to it. In this context, *Clarence* has no continuing relevance. Moreover, to the extent that *Clarence* suggested that consensual sexual intercourse of itself was to be regarded as consent to the risk of consequent disease, again, it is no longer authoritative. If however, the victim consents to the risk, this continues to provide a defence under section 20. Although the two are inevitably linked, the ultimate question is not knowledge, but consent. We shall confine ourselves to reflecting that unless you are prepared to take whatever risk of sexually transmitted infection there may be, it is unlikely that you would consent to a risk of major consequent illness if you were ignorant of it. That said, in every case where these issues arise, the question whether the defendant was or was not reckless, and whether the victim did or did not consent to the risk of a sexually transmitted disease is one of fact, and case specific.

Conviction quashed. Retrial ordered.

R v Konzani

[2005] EWCA Crim 706 (CA)

Feston Konzani was convicted of inflicting grievous bodily harm on three different women, contrary to section 20 of the Offences Against the Person Act 1861. He had been warned that he was HIV positive and was aware of the risk that by having unprotected sexual intercourse he could infect his partners. Nevertheless he had sexual relations with three women without informing them of his HIV status.

Judge LJ

41. We are concerned with the risk of and the actual transmission of a potentially fatal disease through or in the course of consensual sexual relations which did not in themselves involve unlawful violence of the kind prohibited in *R v Brown*. The prosecution did not seek to prove that the disease was deliberately transmitted, with the intention required by s 18 of the 1861 Act. The allegation was that the appellant behaved recklessly on the basis that knowing that he was suffering from the HIV virus, and its consequences, and knowing the risks of its transmission to a sexual partner, he concealed his condition from the complainants, leaving them ignorant of it. When sexual intercourse occurred these complainants were ignorant of his condition. So although they consented to sexual intercourse, they did not consent to the transmission of the HIV virus. *Dica* analysed two different sets of assumed facts arising from the issue of the complainants' consent, by distinguishing between the legal consequences if, as they alleged, the truth of his condition was concealed from his sexual partners by *Dica*, and the case that he would have developed at trial if he had not been prevented from doing so by the judge's ruling, that far from concealing his condition from the complainants, he expressly informed them of it, and they, knowing of his condition because he had told them of it, consented to unprotected sexual intercourse with him. There is a critical distinction between taking a risk of the various, potentially adverse and possibly

problematic consequences of sexual intercourse, and giving an informed consent to the risk of infection with a fatal disease. For the complainant's consent to the risks of contracting the HIV virus to provide a defence, it is at least implicit from the reasoning in *R v Dica*, and the observations of Lord Woolf CJ in *R v Barnes* confirm, that her consent must be an informed consent. If that proposition is in doubt, we take this opportunity to emphasise it. We must therefore examine its implications for this appeal.

42. The recognition in *R v Dica* of informed consent as a defence was based on but limited by potentially conflicting public policy considerations. In the public interest, so far as possible, the spread of catastrophic illness must be avoided or prevented. On the other hand, the public interest also requires that the principle of personal autonomy in the context of adult non-violent sexual relationships should be maintained. If an individual who knows that he is suffering from the HIV virus conceals this stark fact from his sexual partner, the principle of her personal autonomy is not enhanced if he is exculpated when he recklessly transmits the HIV virus to her through consensual sexual intercourse. On any view, the concealment of this fact from her almost inevitably means that she is deceived. Her consent is not properly informed, and she cannot give an informed consent to something of which she is ignorant. Equally, her personal autonomy is not normally protected by allowing a defendant who knows that he is suffering from the HIV virus which he deliberately conceals, to assert an honest belief in his partner's informed consent to the risk of the transmission of the HIV virus. Silence in these circumstances is incongruous with honesty, or with a genuine belief that there is an informed consent. Accordingly, in such circumstances the issue either of informed consent, or honest belief in it will only rarely arise: in reality, in most cases, the contention would be wholly artificial.

43. This is not unduly burdensome. The defendant is not to be convicted of this offence unless it is proved that he was reckless. If so, the necessary mens rea will be established. Recklessness is a question of fact, to be proved by the prosecution. Equally the defendant is not to be convicted if there was, or may have been an informed consent by his sexual partner to the risk that he would transfer the HIV virus to her. In many cases, as in *Dica* itself, provided recklessness is established, the critical factual area of dispute will address what, if anything, was said between the two individuals involved, one of whom knows, and the other of whom does not know, that one of them is suffering the HIV virus. In the final analysis, the question of consent, like the issue of recklessness is fact-specific.

44. In deference to Mr Roberts' submission, we accept that there may be circumstances in which it would be open to the jury to infer that, notwithstanding that the defendant was reckless and concealed his condition from the complainant, she may nevertheless have given an informed consent to the risk of contracting the HIV virus. By way of example, an individual with HIV may develop a sexual relationship with someone who knew him while he was in hospital, receiving treatment for the condition. If so, her informed consent, if it were indeed informed, would remain a defence, to be disproved by the prosecution, even if the defendant had not personally informed her of his condition. Even if she did not in fact consent, this example would illustrate the basis for an argument that he honestly believed in her informed consent. Alternatively, he may honestly believe that his new sexual partner was told of his condition by someone known to them both. Cases like these, not too remote to be fanciful, may arise. If they do, no doubt they will be explored with the complainant in cross-examination. Her answers may demonstrate an informed consent. Nothing remotely like that was suggested here. In a different case, perhaps supported by the defendant's own evidence, material like this may provide a basis for suggesting that he honestly believed that she was giving an informed consent. He may provide an account of the incident, or the affair, which leads the jury to conclude that even if she did not give an informed consent, he may

honestly have believed that she did. Acknowledging these possibilities in different cases does not, we believe, conflict with the public policy considerations identified in *R v Dica*. That said, they did not arise in the present case.

45. Why not? In essence because the jury found that the complainants did not give a willing or informed consent to the risks of contracting the HIV virus from the appellant. We recognise that where consent does provide a defence to an offence against the person, it is generally speaking correct that the defendant's honest belief in the alleged victim's consent would also provide a defence. However for this purpose, the defendant's honest belief must be concomitant with the consent which provides a defence. Unless the consent would provide a defence, an honest belief in it would not assist the defendant. This follows logically from *R v Brown*. For it to do so here, what was required was some evidence of an honest belief that the complainants, or any one of them, were consenting to the risk that they might be infected with the HIV virus by him. There is not the slightest evidence, direct or indirect, from which a jury could begin to infer that the appellant honestly believed that any complainant consented to that specific risk. As there was no such evidence, the judge's ruling about 'honest belief' was correct. In fact, the honest truth was that the appellant deceived them.

46. In our judgment, the judge's directions to the jury sufficiently explained the proper implications to the case of the consensual participation by each of the complainants to sexual intercourse with the appellant. The jury concluded, in the case of each complainant, that she did not willingly or consciously consent to the risk of suffering the HIV virus. Accordingly the appeal against conviction will be dismissed.

Appeal dismissed.

DEFINITION

To summarize the ruling in *R v Dica* and *R v Konzani*. If D is HIV positive and has sexual relations with another person and causes that person to become HIV positive then D is guilty:

(i) Of an offence under section 20 of the Offences Against the Person Act 1861 if:

  (a) D is aware that there is a risk that by having sexual relations he or she might cause the other person to suffer some harm (e.g. by becoming HIV positive);

  (b) The victim has not given consent to run the risk of becoming HIV positive.

(ii) Of an offence under section 18 of the Offences Against the Person Act 1861 if D intends to cause the victim to suffer grievous bodily harm as a result of the sexual intercourse. In such a case even if the victim consents to running the risk of acquiring the HIV virus there would be no defence.

The cases still leave quite a number of issues unsettled. It is clear that the victim's consent to run the risk of becoming HIV or catching a STD, but it is not quite clear what that consent involves. What, for example, if the victim knew that her partner was HIV positive, but falsely believed that if she had a shower after sexual intercourse there was no risk of her being infected? Also what if the victim knew the defendant was promiscuous and therefore knew there was a risk of him being infectious; is that sufficient to be consent for the purposes of a section 20 charge? If so, it might be argued that we all know that having unprotected sex carries a risk of acquiring an infection and so there is always consent to running the risk of harm.

QUESTION

Martin is told by his doctor that he may be suffering from a sexually transmitted disease and is warned that he should not engage in sexual relations. He ignores the advice and has sexual intercourse with Steve, not telling Steve that he may be infectious. Steve subsequently discovers that he has caught a sexually transmitted disease from Martin, and suffers depression as a result. What offences has Martin committed? Would your answer be any different if Martin had warned Steve that he may be infectious? (To answer the second question you will need to read the next section of this chapter on consent and assault.)

FURTHER READING

Bronitt, S. (1994), 'Spreading Disease and the Criminal Law', *Criminal Law Review* 21.

Harris, J., and Holm, S. (1995), 'Is There a Moral Obligation Not to Infect Others?', *British Medical Journal* 311: 1215.

Ormerod, D., and Gunn, M. (1996a), 'Criminal Liability for the Transmission of HIV', *Web Journal of Current Legal Issues.*

Pedain, A. (2005), 'HIV and Responsible Sexual Behaviour', *Cambridge Law Journal* 64: 540.

Power, H. (1996), 'Consensual Sex, Disease and the Criminal Law', *Journal of Criminal Law* 60: 412.

Weait, M. (2005a), 'Harm, Consent and the Limits of Privacy', *Feminist Legal Studies* 13: 97.

—— (2005b), 'Knowledge, Autonomy and Consent: *R. v Konzani*', *Criminal Law Review* 763.

—— (2005c), 'Criminal Law and the Sexual Transmission of HIV', *Modern Law Review* 68: 121.

13 CONSENT AND ASSAULT

Can a defendant be guilty of a non-fatal assault against the person if the victim consented to the force being used against them? As we shall see in Part II of this chapter there has been much debate over whether consent should be regarded as a defence to a charge of assault or whether lack of consent should be regarded as a defence. For now it will be assumed that consent is a defence to a charge of assault because that was the view of the majority of the House of Lords in *Brown*.[167]

13.1 TO WHAT OFFENCES AGAINST THE PERSON IS CONSENT A DEFENCE?

This question has been considered by the House of Lords in one of the most controversial judgments of recent years:

---

[167] [1994] 1 AC 212 (HL).

R v Brown (Anthony); Lucas; Jaggard; Laskey; Carter
[1994] 1 AC 212 (HL)[168]

The appellants were a group of sado-masochists who engaged in consensual acts of violence against each other for sexual gratification. Some of the group found pleasure in inflicting the pain, others in receiving it. The appellants were convicted of offences under sections 20 and 47 of the Offences Against the Person Act 1861. The appellants sought to rely on the consent of the 'victims' of these offences as a defence to the charges, but the trial judge ruled that the prosecution was not required to prove that the 'victims' did not consent. The appellants appealed unsuccessfully to the Court of Appeal and then on to the House of Lords.

Lord Templeman

. . . The Court of Appeal upheld the convictions and certified the following point of law of general public importance:

'Where A wounds or assaults B occasioning him actual bodily harm in the course of a sado-masochistic encounter, does the prosecution have to prove lack of consent on the part of B before they can establish A's guilt under section 20 or section 47 of the Offences against the Person Act 1861?'

. . .

In the present case each of the appellants intentionally inflicted violence upon another (to whom I refer as 'the victim') with the consent of the victim and thereby occasioned actual bodily harm or in some cases wounding or grievous bodily harm. Each appellant was therefore guilty of an offence under section 47 or section 20 of the Act of 1861 unless the consent of the victim was effective to prevent the commission of the offence or effective to constitute a defence to the charge. In some circumstances violence is not punishable under the criminal law. When no actual bodily harm is caused, the consent of the person affected precludes him from complaining. There can be no conviction for the summary offence of common assault if the victim has consented to the assault. Even when violence is intentionally inflicted and results in actual bodily harm, wounding or serious bodily harm the accused is entitled to be acquitted if the injury was a foreseeable incident of a lawful activity in which the person injured was participating. Surgery involves intentional violence resulting in actual or sometimes serious bodily harm but surgery is a lawful activity. Other activities carried on with consent by or on behalf of the injured person have been accepted as lawful notwithstanding that they involve actual bodily harm or may cause serious bodily harm. Ritual circumcision, tattooing, ear-piercing and violent sports including boxing are lawful activities.

[Having considered the previous case law Lord Templeman continued:]

My Lords, the authorities dealing with the intentional infliction of bodily harm do not establish that consent is a defence to a charge under the Act of 1861. They establish that the courts have accepted that consent is a defence to the infliction of bodily harm in the course of some lawful activities. The question is whether the defence should be extended to the infliction of bodily harm in the course of sado-masochistic encounters. . . .

The question whether the defence of consent should be extended to the consequences of sado-masochistic encounters can only be decided by consideration of policy and public

---

[168] [1993] 2 All ER 75, [1993] 2 WLR 556, [1993] 1 Cr App R 44.

interest. Parliament can call on the advice of doctors, psychiatrists, criminologists, sociologists and other experts and can also sound and take into account public opinion. But the question must at this stage be decided by this House in its judicial capacity in order to determine whether the convictions of the appellants should be upheld or quashed.

Counsel for some of the appellants argued that the defence of consent should be extended to the offence of occasioning actual bodily harm under section 47 of the Act of 1861 but should not be available to charges of serious wounding and the infliction of serious bodily harm under section 20. I do not consider that this solution is practicable. Sado-masochistic participants have no way of foretelling the degree of bodily harm which will result from their encounters. The differences between actual bodily harm and serious bodily harm cannot be satisfactorily applied by a jury in order to determine acquittal or conviction. Counsel for the appellants argued that consent should provide a defence to charges under both section 20 and section 47 because, it was said, every person has a right to deal with his body as he pleases. I do not consider that this slogan provides a sufficient guide to the policy decision which must now be made. It is an offence for a person to abuse his own body and mind by taking drugs. Although the law is often broken, the criminal law restrains a practice which is regarded as dangerous and injurious to individuals and which if allowed and extended is harmful to society generally. In any event the appellants in this case did not mutilate their own bodies. They inflicted bodily harm on willing victims. Suicide is no longer an offence but a person who assists another to commit suicide is guilty of murder or manslaughter.

The assertion was made on behalf of the appellants that the sexual appetites of sadists and masochists can only be satisfied by the infliction of bodily harm and that the law should not punish the consensual achievement of sexual satisfaction. There was no evidence to support the assertion that sado-masochist activities are essential to the happiness of the appellants or any other participants but the argument would be acceptable if sado-masochism were only concerned with sex, as the appellants contend. In my opinion sado-masochism is not only concerned with sex. Sado-masochism is also concerned with violence. The evidence discloses that the practices of the appellants were unpredictably dangerous and degrading to body and mind and were developed with increasing barbarity and taught to persons whose consents were dubious or worthless.

. . . The dangers involved in administering violence must have been appreciated by the appellants because, so it was said by their counsel, each victim was given a code word which he could pronounce when excessive harm or pain was caused. The efficiency of this precaution, when taken, depends on the circumstances and on the personalities involved. No one can feel the pain of another. The charges against the appellants were based on genital torture and violence to the buttocks, anus, penis, testicles and nipples. The victims were degraded and humiliated sometimes beaten, sometimes wounded with instruments and sometimes branded. Bloodletting and the smearing of human blood produced excitement. There were obvious dangers of serious personal injury and blood infection. Prosecuting counsel informed the trial judge against the protests of defence counsel, that although the appellants had not contracted Aids, two members of the group had died from Aids and one other had contracted an HIV infection although not necessarily from the practices of the group. Some activities involved excrement. The assertion that the instruments employed by the sadists were clean and sterilised could not have removed the danger of infection, and the assertion that care was taken demonstrates the possibility of infection. Cruelty to human beings was on occasions supplemented by cruelty to animals in the form of bestiality. It is fortunate that there were no permanent injuries to a victim though no one knows the extent of harm inflicted in other cases. It is not surprising that a victim does not complain to the police when the complaint would involve him in giving details of acts in which he participated. Doctors of course are subject to a code of confidentiality.

In principle there is a difference between violence which is incidental and violence which is inflicted for the indulgence of cruelty. The violence of sado-masochistic encounters involves the indulgence of cruelty by sadists and the degradation of victims. Such violence is injurious to the participants and unpredictably dangerous. I am not prepared to invent a defence of consent for sado-masochistic encounters which breed and glorify cruelty and result in offences under sections 47 and 20 of the Act of 1861.

. . .

Society is entitled and bound to protect itself against a cult of violence. Pleasure derived from the infliction of pain is an evil thing. Cruelty is uncivilised. I would answer the certified question in the negative and dismiss the appeals of the appellants against conviction.

Lord Jauncey of Tullichettle

In my view the line properly falls to be drawn between assault at common law and the offence of assault occasioning actual bodily harm created by section 47 of the Offences against the Person Act 1861, with the result that consent of the victim is no answer to anyone charged with the latter offence or with a contravention of section 20 unless the circumstances fall within one of the well known exceptions such as organised sporting contests and games, parental chastisement or reasonable surgery. There is nothing in sections 20 and 47 of the Act of 1861 to suggest that consent is either an essential ingredient of the offences or a defence thereto. If consent is to be an answer to a charge under section 47 but not to one under section 20, considerable practical problems would arise. It was held in *Reg v Parmenter* [1992] 1 AC 699 that a verdict of guilty of assault occasioning actual bodily harm is a permissible alternative verdict on a count alleging unlawful wounding contrary to section 20: Lord Ackner, at p 740D. A judge charging a jury in a section 20 case would therefore not only have to direct them as to the alternative verdict available under section 47, but also as to the consequences of consent in relation to that alternative only. Such direction would be more complex if consent was an answer to wounding under section 20 but not to the infliction of grievous bodily harm under the same section. These problems would not arise if consent is an answer only to common assault. I would therefore dispose of these appeals on the basis that the infliction of actual or more serious bodily harm is an unlawful activity to which consent is no answer. . . .

. . . [I]n considering the public interest it would be wrong to look only at the activities of the appellants alone, there being no suggestion that they and their associates are the only practitioners of homosexual sado-masochism in England and Wales. This House must therefore consider the possibility that these activities are practised by others and by others who are not so controlled or responsible as the appellants are claimed to be. Without going into details of all the rather curious activities in which the appellants engaged it would appear to be good luck rather than good judgment which has prevented serious injury from occurring. Wounds can easily become septic if not properly treated, the free flow of blood from a person who is HIV positive or who has Aids can infect another and an inflicter who is carried away by sexual excitement or by drink or drugs could very easily inflict pain and injury beyond the level to which the receiver had consented. Your Lordships have no information as to whether such situations have occurred in relation to other sado-masochistic practitioners . . .

My Lords I have no doubt that it would not be in the public interest that deliberate infliction of actual bodily harm during the course of homosexual sado-masochistic activities should be held to be lawful. . . . If it is to be decided that such activities as the nailing by A of B's foreskin or scrotum to a board or the insertion of hot wax into C's urethra followed by the burning of his penis with a candle or the incising of D's scrotum with a scalpel to the effusion of blood are injurious neither to B, C and D nor to the public interest then it is for Parliament with its accumulated wisdom and sources of information to declare them to be lawful. . . .

There was argument as to whether consent, where available, was a necessary ingredient of the offence of assault or merely a defence. There are conflicting *dicta* as to its effect. In *Reg v Coney* Stephen J referred to consent as 'being no defence,' whereas in *Attorney-General's Reference (No 6 of 1980)* [1981] QB 715 Lord Lane CJ referred to the onus being on the prosecution to negative consent. In *Collins v Wilcock* [1984] 1 WLR 1172, 1177F, Robert Goff LJ referred to consent being a defence to a battery. If it were necessary, which it is not, in this appeal to decide which argument was correct I would hold that consent was a defence to but not a necessary ingredient in assault.

Lord Lowry gave a speech dismissing the appeal

Lord Mustill (dissenting)

My Lords, this is a case about the criminal law of violence. In my opinion it should be a case about the criminal law of private sexual relations, if about anything at all. Right or wrong, the point is easily made. The speeches already delivered contain summaries of the conduct giving rise to the charges under the Offences against the Person Act 1861 now before the House, together with other charges in respect of which the appellants have been sentenced, and no longer appeal. Fortunately for the reader my Lords have not gone on to describe other aspects of the appellants' behaviour of a similar but more extreme kind which was not the subject of any charge on the indictment. It is sufficient to say that whatever the outsider might feel about the subject matter of the prosecutions—perhaps horror, amazement or incomprehension, perhaps sadness—very few could read even a summary of the other activities without disgust. The House has been spared the video tapes, which must have been horrible. If the criminality of sexual deviation is the true ground of these proceedings, one would have expected that these above all would have been the subject of attack. Yet the picture is quite different.

[Lord Mustill considered the case law and potential relevance of the European Convention on Human Rights and continued:]

IV Public Policy

The purpose of this long discussion has been to suggest that the decks are clear for the House to tackle completely anew the question whether the public interest requires section 47 of the Act of 1861 to be interpreted as penalising an infliction of harm which is at the level of actual bodily harm, but not grievous bodily harm; which is inflicted in private (by which I mean that it is exposed to the view only of those who have chosen to view it); which takes place not only with the consent of the recipient but with his willing and glad co-operation; which is inflicted for the gratification of sexual desire, and not in a spirit of animosity or rage; and which is not engaged in for profit.

My Lords, I have stated the issue in these terms to stress two considerations of cardinal importance. Lawyers will need no reminding of the first, but since this prosecution has been widely noticed it must be emphasised that the issue before the House is not whether the appellants, conduct is morally right, but whether it is properly charged under the Act of 1861. When proposing that the conduct is not rightly so charged I do not invite your Lordships' House to endorse it as morally acceptable. Nor do I pronounce in favour of a libertarian doctrine specifically related to sexual matters. Nor in the least do I suggest that ethical pronouncements are meaningless, that there is no difference between right and wrong, that sadism is praiseworthy, or that new opinions on sexual morality are necessarily superior to the old, or anything else of the same kind. What I do say is that these are questions of private morality; that the standards by which they fall to be judged are not those of the criminal law; and that if these standards are to be upheld the individual must enforce them upon himself according to his own moral standards, or have them enforced against him by moral pressures exerted by whatever religious or other community to whose ethical ideals he responds. The point from which I invite your Lordships to depart is simply this, that the state should interfere with the rights of an individual to live his or her life as he or she may choose no more than is necessary to ensure a proper balance between the special interests of the individual and the general interests of the individuals who together comprise the populace at large. Thus, whilst acknowledging that very many people, if asked whether the appellants' conduct was wrong, would reply 'Yes, repulsively wrong,' I would at the same time assert that this does not in itself mean that the prosecution of the appellants under sections 20 and 47 of the Offences against the Person Act 1861 is well founded.

This point leads directly to the second. As I have ventured to formulate the crucial question, it asks whether there is good reason to impress upon section 47 an interpretation which penalises the relevant level of harm irrespective of consent, i.e., to recognise sado-masochistic activities as falling into a special category of acts, such as duelling and prize-fighting, which 'the law says shall not be done.' This is very important, for if the question were differently stated it might well yield a different answer. In particular, if it were to be held that as a matter of law all infliction of bodily harm above the level of common assault is incapable of being legitimated by consent, except in special circumstances, then we would have to consider whether the public interest required the recognition of private sexual activities as being in a specially exempt category. This would be an altogether more difficult question and one which I would not be prepared to answer in favour of the appellants, not because I do not have my own opinions upon it but because I regard the task as one which the courts are not suited to perform, and which should be carried out, if at all, by Parliament after a thorough review of all the medical, social, moral and political issues, such as was performed by the Wolfenden Committee. Thus, if I had begun from the same point of departure as my noble and learned friend, Lord Jauncey of Tullichettle, I would have arrived at a similar conclusion; but differing from him on the present state of the law, I venture to differ.

Let it be assumed however that we should embark upon this question. I ask myself, not whether as a result of the decision in this appeal, activities such as those of the appellants should cease to be criminal, but rather whether the Act of 1861 (a statute which I venture to repeat once again was clearly intended to penalise conduct of a quite different nature) should in this new situation be interpreted so as to make it criminal. Why should this step be taken? Leaving aside repugnance and moral objection, both of which are entirely natural but neither of which are in my opinion grounds upon which the court could properly create a new crime, I can visualise only the following reasons.

(1) Some of the practices obviously created a risk of genito-urinary infection, and others of septicaemia. These might indeed have been grave in former times, but the risk of serious harm must surely have been greatly reduced by modern medical science.

(2) The possibility that matters might get out of hand, with grave results. it has been acknowledged throughout the present proceedings that the appellants' activities were performed as a pre-arranged ritual, which at the same time enhanced their excitement and minimised the risk that the infliction of injury would go too far. Of course things might go wrong and really serious injury or death might ensue. If this happened, those responsible

would be punished according to the ordinary law, in the same way as those who kill or injure in the course of more ordinary sexual activities are regularly punished. But to penalise the appellants' conduct even if the extreme consequences do not ensue, just because they might have done so would require an assessment of the degree of risk, and the balancing of this risk against the interests of individual freedom. Such a balancing is in my opinion for Parliament, not the courts; and even if your Lordships' House were to embark upon it the attempt must in my opinion fail at the outset for there is no evidence at all of the seriousness of the hazards to which sado-masochistic conduct of this kind gives rise. This is not surprising, since the impressive argument of Mr Purnell for the respondents did not seek to persuade your Lordships' to bring the matter within the Act of 1861 on the ground of special risks, but rather to establish that the appellants are liable under the general law because the level of harm exceeded the critical level marking off criminal from non-criminal consensual violence which he invited your Lordships to endorse.

(3) I would give the same answer to the suggestion that these activities involved a risk of accelerating the spread of auto-immune deficiency syndrome, and that they should be brought within the Act of 1861 in the interests of public health. The consequence would be strange, since what is currently the principal cause for the transmission of this scourge, namely consenting buggery between males, is now legal. Nevertheless, I would have been compelled to give this proposition the most anxious consideration if there had been any evidence to support it. But there is none, since the case for the respondent was advanced on an entirely different ground.

(4) There remains an argument to which I have given much greater weight. As the evidence in the present case has shown, there is a risk that strangers (and especially young strangers) may be drawn into these activities at an early age and will then become established in them for life. This is indeed a disturbing prospect, but I have come to the conclusion that it is not a sufficient ground for declaring these activities to be criminal under the Act of 1861. The element of the corruption of youth is already catered for by the existing legislation; and if there is a gap in it which needs to be filled the remedy surely lies in the hands of Parliament, not in the application of a statute which is aimed at other forms of wrongdoing. As regards proselytisation for adult sado-masochism the argument appears to me circular. For if the activity is not itself so much against the public interest that it ought to be declared criminal under the Act of 1861 then the risk that others will be induced to join in cannot be a ground for making it criminal.

. . .

V Conclusion

Accordingly I would allow these appeals and quash such of the convictions as are now before the House.

Lord Slynn of Hadley (dissenting)

The determination of the appeal, however, does not depend on bewilderment or revulsion or whether the right approach for the House in the appeal ought to be liberal or otherwise. The sole question is whether when a charge of assault is laid under the two sections in question, consent is relevant in the sense either that the prosecution must prove a lack of consent on the part of the person to whom the act is done or that the existence of consent by such person constitutes a defence for the person charged.

. . .

My conclusion is thus that as the law stands, adults can consent to acts done in private which do not result in serious bodily harm, so that such acts do not constitute criminal assaults for the purposes of the Act of 1861. My conclusion is not based on the alternative argument that for the criminal law to encompass consensual acts done in private would in itself be an unlawful invasion of privacy. If these acts between consenting adults in private did constitute criminal offences under the Act of 1861, there would clearly be an invasion of privacy. Whether that invasion would be justified and in particular whether it would be within the derogations permitted by article 8(2) of the European Convention on Human Rights, it is not necessary, on the conclusion to which I have come, to decide, despite the interesting arguments address to your Lordships on that question and even on the basis that English law includes a principle parallel to that set out in the European Convention on Human Rights.

. . .

If Parliament considers that the behaviour revealed here should be made specifically criminal, then the Offences against the Person Act 1861 or, perhaps more appropriately, the Sexual Offences Act 1967 can be amended specifically to define it. Alternatively, if it is intended that this sort of conduct should be lawful as between two persons but not between more than two persons as falling within the offence of gross indecency, then the limitation period for prosecution can be extended and the penalties increased where sado-masochistic acts are involved. That is obviously a possible course; whether it is a desirable way of changing the law is a different question.

. . .

Accordingly I consider that these appeals should be allowed and the convictions set aside.

Appeals dismissed.

DEFINITION

Summary of the law following *Brown*:

The consent of the victim is a defence to an assault or battery. But is not a defence to an offence involving actual bodily harm or more serious injury, unless the case falls within one of the following recognized exceptional categories:

1. Sporting activities.
2. Dangerous exhibitions and bravado.
3. Rough and undisciplined horseplay.
4. Surgery.
5. Tattooing and body piercing.
6. Religious flagellation.
7. Consensual intimate acts in the course of which one party is infected with a medical condition, where the victim had consented to run the risk of acquiring the infection.

If the court is persuaded that the defendant's conduct is beneficial to society a court may be persuaded to create a new exceptional category.

In the following case the Court of Appeal returned to the question when the consent of the victim provided a defence to the victim. The decision has led to much debate as to how it can be reconciled with the House of Lords decision in *Brown*:

R v Wilson (Alan)
[1997] QB 47 (CA)[169]

Alan Wilson was convicted of an assault occasioning actual bodily harm on his wife. He had branded his initials on her buttocks with a hot knife, apparently at her request. He appealed against his conviction on the basis that his wife's consent provided him with a defence to the charge.

Lord Justice Russell read the following judgment of the court

. . . At the conclusion of the evidence called by the prosecution, defence counsel submitted that his client had no case to answer. The judge, in a ruling of which we have a transcript, after reviewing the facts and authority, concluded as follows:

'The reality that I have to deal with is that on the face of it the majority in the House of Lords in *Reg v Brown (Anthony)* [1994] 1 AC 212 approved of the dicta in *Rex v Donovan* [1934] 2 KB 498 and that accordingly until such time as the legislature or the European Court do something about it we are now saddled with a law that means that anyone who injures his partner, spouse, or whatever, in the course of some consensual activity is at risk of having his or her private life dragged before the public to no good purpose. Sadly, I take the view that I am bound by the majority in *Reg v Brown* and that I would have to, in those circumstances, direct this jury to convict.'

Counsel for the defendant, in the light of that ruling, did not call his client and did not make any submissions to the jury, who in due course convicted the appellant. The judge conditionally discharged him for a period of twelve months.

It is effectively against that ruling of the judge that the appeal is brought to this court. In the court below, and before us, reference was predictably made to *Rex v Donovan* [1934] 2 KB 498, a decision of the Court of Criminal Appeal, and to *Reg v Brown (Anthony)* [1994] 1 AC 212, a decision of the House of Lords. They are the two authorities to which the trial judge referred in the observations we have cited.

In *Rex v Donovan* [1934] 2 KB 498 the appellant, in private, beat a girl of 17 years of age for the purposes of sexual gratification, with her consent. The act had about it an aggressive element. The court held that consent was immaterial. In *Reg v Brown* [1994] 1 AC 212 the appellants engaged in sado-masochism of the grossest kind, involving inter alia, physical torture, and as Lord Templeman pointed out, at p 236D: 'obvious dangers of serious personal injury and blood infection.' The facts of the case were truly extreme.

We are abundantly satisfied that there is no factual comparison to be made between the instant case and the facts of either *Rex v Donovan* [1934] 2 KB 498 or *Reg v Brown* [1994] 1 AC 212: Mrs Wilson not only consented to that which the appellant did, she instigated it. There was no aggressive intent on the part of the appellant. On the contrary, far from wishing to cause injury to his wife, the appellant's desire was to assist her in what she regarded as the acquisition of a desirable piece of personal adornment, perhaps in this day and age no less understandable than the piercing of nostrils or even tongues for the purposes of inserting decorative jewellery.

In our judgment *Reg v Brown* is not authority for the proposition that consent is no defence to a charge under section 47 of the Act of 1861, in all circumstances where actual bodily harm is deliberately inflicted. It is to be observed that the question certified for their Lordships in

[169] [1996] 3 WLR 125, [1996] 2 Cr App R 241, [1996] Crim LR 573.

Reg v Brown related only to a 'sado-masochistic encounter.' However, their Lordships recognised in the course of their speeches, that it is necessary that there must be exceptions to what is no more than a general proposition. The speeches of Lord Templeman, at p 231, Lord Jauncey of Tullichettle, at p 245, and the dissenting speech of Lord Slynn of Hadley, at p 277, all refer to tattooing as being an activity which, if carried out with the consent of an adult, does not involve an offence under section 47, albeit that actual bodily harm is deliberately inflicted.

For our part, we cannot detect any logical difference between what the appellant did and what he might have done in the way of tattooing. The latter activity apparently requires no state authorisation, and the appellant was as free to engage in it as anyone else. We do not think that we are entitled to assume that the method adopted by the appellant and his wife was any more dangerous or painful than tattooing. There was simply no evidence to assist the court on this aspect of the matter.

Does public policy or the public interest demand that the appellant's activity should be visited by the sanctions of the criminal law? The majority in *Reg v Brown* clearly took the view that such considerations were relevant. If that is so, then we are firmly of the opinion that it is not in the public interest that activities such as the appellant's in this appeal should amount to criminal behaviour. Consensual activity between husband and wife, in the privacy of the matrimonial home, is not, in our judgment, normally a proper matter for criminal investigation, let alone criminal prosecution. Accordingly we take the view that the judge failed to have full regard to the facts of this case and misdirected himself in saying that *Rex v Donovan* [1934] 2 KB 498 and *Reg v Brown* [1994] 1 AC 212 constrained him to rule that consent was no defence.

In this field, in our judgment, the law should develop upon a case by case basis rather than upon general propositions to which, in the changing times in which we live, exceptions may arise from time to time not expressly covered by authority.

We shall allow the appeal and quash the conviction. We conclude this judgment by commenting that we share the judge's disquiet that the prosecuting authority thought it fit to bring these proceedings. In our view they serve no useful purpose at considerable public expense. We gave the appellant leave to appeal against his sentence. Had it been necessary for us to consider sentence we would have granted the appellant an absolute discharge.

Appeal allowed. Conviction quashed.

There has been much dispute over the correct interpretation of this case and how it can be reconciled with *Brown*. To some commentators the difference in the approach of the Court of Appeal in *Wilson* and the House of Lords in *Brown* lies in the fact that the Wilsons were a married couple and that therefore their conduct was more 'acceptable' to the Court of Appeal than the group homosexual behaviour of the appellants in *Brown*. However, the Court of Appeal in *Emmett*[170] rejected such an analysis in convicting a man who had seriously injured his fiancée in the course of alleged sado-masochistic behaviour. The explanation of the difference between the two cases provided by the Court of Appeal in *Emmett* was that in *Wilson* the activity was analogous to the exception that exists for tattooing, whereas the behaviour in *Brown* (and *Emmett* itself) did not fall into one of the exceptional categories of cases. We will discuss this further in Part II.

---

[170] *Emmett*, 18 June 1999 (CA).

So now let us consider what are the categories of exceptional case where consent will provide a defence to an offence involving actual bodily harm or a more serious level of injury:

(1) *Sports.* Consent is usually a defence to injuries received in the course of a sporting event, even if those injuries involve actual bodily harm. It is presumed that by deciding to play the sport the victim has consented to the infliction of the kind of force normally involved in the game.[171] So a rugby player cannot claim that when tackled with the ball he was being unlawfully battered. Even if the injury is committed in the course of a foul the court may well feel that when playing a sport you accept that you will be fouled. However, there comes a point where the kind of force used will not be regarded as the kind of foul you consent to by playing that sport. In *R v Barnes*[172] the Court of Appeal held that if there was a foul 'quite outside what could be expected to occur in the course of a football game'[173] that could be a criminal offence. This requires the court to distinguish 'normal fouls', which are consented to and are not criminal offences, and 'over-the-top fouls', which are beyond what might be expected and are not consented to and can amount to a criminal offence. A jury would probably be willing to convict a player who deliberately fouled the other team's best player in an attempt to injure him.

This exceptional category applies only to organized and regulated sports. Two people who got into a fight with each other in a street would both be convicted of assault: they could not claim they were engaged in a boxing match![174] Some unorganized games could fall within the category of 'rough undisciplined horseplay', which will be discussed below.[175]

(2) *Dangerous exhibitions and bravado.* Under this heading fall activities such as circus acts and stunts (e.g. being a human cannonball, bungee jumping, etc.). In the Canadian Supreme Court decision of *Jobidon*[176] it was suggested that stuntmen agreeing to perform dare-devil activities are engaged 'for the good of the people involved, and often for a wider group of people as well'. Within the 'bravado' heading might be a case where the victim says to the defendant 'my stomach is iron, hit me as hard as you like and it won't hurt' and is then injured by the defendant's punch. No offence would be committed if the court were willing to regard this as an act of bravado by the victim.

(3) *Rough and undisciplined horseplay.* A good example of this exceptional category is *Jones*[177] where the defendant (a schoolboy) and other children were playing around and throwing the victim up in the air. The victim was dropped and suffered a broken arm and ruptured spleen. The defendant's appeal against a conviction for an assault occasioning actual bodily harm was allowed. The Court of Appeal held that the victim had consented (or at least the defendant believed the victim had consented) to the rough horseplay,[178] and that consent to rough horseplay provided a defence to offences involving actual bodily harm. The decision could be based on two justifications. First, that otherwise all around the country there would be thousands of offences taking place in school playgrounds. Rough games are

---

[171] Ormerod and Gunn (1995) provide a useful discussion of the law's response to boxing.
[172] [2005] 1 W.L.R. 910.   [173] Paragraph 28.   [174] *A-G's Reference (No. 6 of 1980)* [1981] QB 715.
[175] In *Erisman* [1988] 1 Hong Kong Law Reports 370 the Hong Kong High Court suggested that injuries caused in a war game involving firing pellets at each other were covered by the rough and undisciplined horseplay exception.
[176] [1991] 2 SCR 714, discussed in Kell (1994).
[177] (1986) 83 Cr App R 375 (CA).   [178] Although not to the injuries.

part of childhood and it would be unrealistic to punish them. Secondly, more positively, that such games are beneficial, being an important part of growing up and encouraging exercise. It should, however, be borne in mind that a line has to be carefully drawn between rough horseplay and bullying.

Jones was extended in *Aitken*[179] where the defendants were members of the Air Force who set fire to the victim after a party. It was held that such conduct could fall within the rough horseplay exception, and so the victim's consent[180] could provide a defence. Similarly students throwing each other off balconies were found to be engaged in rough horseplay and the victim's consent (or the defendant's belief in the victim's consent) provided a defence to a criminal charge.[181]

(4) *Surgery.* This has long been recognized as an activity where a person's consent to the injury renders the act lawful. No one would deny that if an operation is required to improve a patient's health it should be permitted. Even operations which are perhaps more controversial and less obviously beneficial (e.g. cosmetic surgery) are generally accepted to be lawful based on the victim's consent. Statute has made it clear that certain operations (for example, female circumcision) are illegal.[182]

(5) *Tattooing and body piercing.* Tattooing and body piercing for the purpose of personal adornment are permitted. In *Wilson*[183] the Court of Appeal held that 'do it yourself' tattooing, where the husband using a hot knife branded his initials onto his wife's buttocks was included within the exception.

(6) *Religious flagellation.* Lord Mustill in *Brown* indicated that there is an exception for those who use flagellation to express feelings of penitence as part of religious practices.

(7) *Infectious intimate relations.* In *Dica*[184] (excerpted above) the Court of Appeal accepted that if the victim agreed to have sexual relations with the defendant, aware that he was infectious and that therefore there was a risk that the infection would be passed on this consent provided a defence to a charged under section 20 Offences Against the Person Act 1861.

In *Brown* their Lordships indicated that this was not a closed list and that if they were persuaded that it was appropriate to do so they would add in a new category. On the facts of that case they declined to add sado-masochistic activity to the list of exceptions.[185]

13.2 WHAT IS CONSENT?

The meaning of 'consent' will be discussed in detail in Chapter 7, and will only be summarized here.

---

[179] (1992) 95 Cr App R 304.
[180] In *Aitken*, controversially, the Court of Appeal seemed willing to assume the consent of the victim to the horseplay from the fact he had been present at the party where such conduct took place.
[181] *Richardson and Irwin* [1999] Cr App R 392.
[182] Prohibition of Female Circumcision Act 1985.
[183] [1996] 3 WLR 125   [184] [2004] EWCA Crim 1103 (CA).
[185] In *Wacker* [2003] Crim LR 108 (CA) the consent of the victims (who were seeking to enter the UK illegally) to being placed in an inadequately ventilated lorry was no defence to a charge of gross negligence manslaughter.

Express or implied consent

Consent can be express or implied. A wife who kisses her husband first thing in the morning can rely on the husband's implied consent. Even two strangers may be able to rely on implied consent if the touching is seen as part of the normal touchings of everyday life.[186]

Competence

Consent can be given only by a competent person. An adult is presumed to be competent,[187] but the Court of Appeal in *Re MB*[188] explained:

> A person lacks capacity if some impairment or disturbance of mental functioning renders the person unable to make a decision whether to consent to or to refuse treatment. That inability to make a decision will occur when
>
> (a) The person who lacks capacity is unable to comprehend and retain the information which is material to the decision, especially as to the likely consequences of having or not having the treatment in question;
>
> (b) The patient is unable to use the information and weigh it in the balance as part of the process of arriving at a decision.

Although these comments were made in the context of medical treatment, they can be relied upon whenever a court is considering whether a person consented to something being done to them. A court might also refer to section 3 of the Mental Capacity Act 2005 which states:

> a person is unable to make a decision for himself if he is unable—
>
> (a) to understand the information relevant to the decision,
>
> (b) to retain that information,
>
> (c) to use or weigh that information as part of the process of making the decision, or
>
> (d) to communicate his decision (whether by talking, using sign language or any other means).

Where the victim is a child or an adult with learning difficulties the court will be particularly wary of finding that they had the capacity to consent.[189] However, in the case of older children the court may be willing to find that they had sufficient maturity to be able to give effective consent.[190]

---

[186] *Collins v Wilcock* [1984] 3 All ER 374 (CA).

[187] *Re MB (An Adult: Medical Treatment)* [1997] 2 FCR 541 at 553 (CA).

[188] Ibid., at 553–4 (CA), approving *dicta* of Thorpe J in *Re C (Adult: Refusal of Treatment)* [1994] 2 FCR 151, at 156 (FD).

[189] In *Burrell v Harmer* [1967] Crim LR 169 a tattooist tattooed two boys on their arms. He was convicted of an assault occasioning actual bodily harm because the boys were not able to understand what was involved in the tattoo and were unable to give their consent. Now it is an offence to tattoo minors under the age of 18 (except where it is done by a doctor for medical purposes): Tattooing of Minors Act 1969.

[190] *Gillick v West Norfolk and Wisbech AHA* [1986] AC 112 (HL).

Consent given in cases where the victim was 'consenting' due to fear or mistake

The law accepts that even though a victim may appear to consent to the force being used by the defendant that consent may not be true consent. That may be so in the following circumstances:

(1) The 'consent' was given by a victim who was mistaken as to the identity of the defendant.

(2) The 'consent' was given by a victim who was mistaken as to the nature of the proposed act.

(3) The 'consent' was given by a defendant who was so fearful that the 'consent' should be regarded as submission and so ineffective.

What if consent is given to actual bodily harm but less harm is caused?

What if a masochist asked a sadist to cause them actual bodily harm or grievous bodily harm, but in fact the sadist inflicted only a battery? Could the sadist be convicted of a battery, or would the masochist's consent provide a defence? There are *dicta* in *Donovan*[191] and *Boyea*[192] that suggest that consent to actual bodily harm is not lawful consent and therefore is to be ignored. Therefore in our scenario the sadist is guilty of a battery. On the other hand the majority in *Brown* accepted without adding any qualifications that consent was a defence to a battery.

Consent where the extent of harm is not foreseen

What if a defendant believes he or she is committing a battery, to which the victim has consented but in fact what he or she is doing causes actual bodily harm or grievous bodily harm? Is the victim's consent a defence to such an offence? There are three views that have been expressed:

(1) No. In *Attorney-General's Reference (No. 6 of 1980)*[193] it was suggested that if actual bodily harm or more serious injury was caused the victim's consent would not provide a defence.[194]

(2) Not if actual bodily harm was foreseeable. In *Boyea*[195] it was suggested that if actual bodily harm was a foreseeable result of the defendant's actions then the victim's consent would not provide a defence. However, if actual bodily harm was not a foreseeable result the victim's consent could provide a defence, even if actual bodily harm (or a more serious injury) resulted.

(3) Not if actual bodily harm was foreseen by the defendant as a result of his actions. In *Slingsby*[196] Judge J held that if the defendant thought he was committing a battery and had not *foreseen* a more serious injury the victim's consent would still provide a

---

[191] [1934] 2 KB 498 (CA).   [192] [1992] Crim LR 574 (CA).   [193] [1981] 1 WLR 705 (CA).
[194] This approach appears to have been approved in *Andrews* [2003] Crim LR 477, but without a detailed consideration of the issue.
[195] [1992] Crim LR 574 (CA).   [196] [1995] Crim LR 571 (HCt).

defence to any charge involving a more serious injury. However, if the defendant was aware that there was a risk that the victim would suffer a more serious injury than a battery or an assault then he or she cannot rely on the consent of a victim.

We need an authoritative ruling on the question, but the *Slingsby* ruling is most in line with the general approach on *mens rea* in offences against the person, which relies on *Cunningham* recklessness.

13.3 WHAT IF THERE IS NO CONSENT BUT THE DEFENDANT BELIEVES THAT THERE IS CONSENT?

The Court of Appeal in *Jones*[197] confirmed that, in a case where the victim's consent would provide a defence, the defendant will also have a defence if he honestly believes that the victim is consenting, even if in fact the victim is not. This is so even if the defendant's belief was unreasonable. Bizarrely in *Richardson and Irwin*[198] it was held that a drunken belief that the victim had consented to the injury as part of rough horseplay was held to provide a defence. Normally in the criminal law a drunken belief that the victim consented does not provide a defence (e.g. in the context of rape[199]). Many commentators therefore assume that *Richardson and Irwin* is incorrect on this point.[200]

QUESTIONS

1. Simone has sexual intercourse with Bill. She knows she has not recently cut her toenails and that she may therefore scratch Bill during the intercourse. She does indeed give an unpleasant scratch. What offences has Simone committed? (Consider here the *Boyea* and *Slingsby* cases and also whether the scratch may be a wound.)

2. Tom (a tattooist) gives Viv an intimate body piercing. Tom does not normally perform piercings, but found Viv attractive and so agreed to do it. What offences (if any) has Tom committed? (Is this more like *Brown* or *Wilson*?)

FURTHER READING

Allen, M. (1995), 'Consent and Assault', *Journal of Criminal Law* 58: 183.

Bix, B. (1993), 'Assault, Sado-Masochism and Consent', *Law Quarterly Review* 109: 540.

Giles, M. (1994), 'R v Brown: Consensual Harm and the Public Interest', *Modern Law Review* 57: 101.

Leng, R. (1994), 'Consent and Offences Against the Person', *Criminal Law Review* 480.

Roberts, P. (1997a), 'Consent to Injury: How Far Can You Go?', *Law Quarterly Review* 113: 27.

---

[197] [1986] 83 Cr App R 375 (CA).
[198] [1999] 1 Cr App R 392 at 397 (CA), although the judgment is, with respect, rather ambiguous.
[199] *Fotheringham* (1989) 88 Cr App R 206 (CA).
[200] See e.g. Allen (2003: 342).

PART II: THEORETICAL ISSUES ON ASSAULTS

14 THE TRUE NATURE AND EXTENT OF VIOLENT CRIME

In the twelve months to March 2005, 1,184,702 convictions of violence against the person were recorded.[201] But looking at such bald statistics is not particularly useful in assessing the level of violent offending. First, of course, there are many more violent incidents which are not reported. The British Crime Survey findings estimated that in the same period there were 2,412,000 incidents of violence.[202] The chance of being a victim of a violent offence if you were a man aged 14–26 during the year 2004 was 14.6 per cent.[203] Secondly, the harm for which a person is convicted may not reflect the actual offence done to the victim. The process from committal of the crime to conviction is not a straightforward one.[204] A procedure known as down-charging is common. This is where a defendant is ultimately convicted in court for an offence which is lower than the wrong which the victim has alleged. Imagine a case where the victim has been stabbed by the defendant. One might expect this to result in a charge under section 18 or 20 of the Offences Against the Person Act 1861. However, if the prosecution is not confident that it can establish the necessary *mens rea*, it may prefer to charge under section 47 where the *mens rea* is easier to prove. Alternatively there may be a plea bargain where the defendant offers to plead guilty to section 47, but will plead not guilty to section 20. In both these cases the prosecution may, in order to save time and resources, prosecute for the lower offence.

There are particular difficulties in convicting a defendant of the section 18 offence. Only 20 per cent of those charged with section 18 offences are convicted of those offences.[205] This is largely because of the difficulty in proving the necessary intent.[206] This is particularly so because many incidents of violence result from complex and emotionally charged situations where proof of intent can be particularly difficult.[207] Indeed the Crime Prosecution Service Charging Standards suggest using section 18 only where there has been 'a repeated or planned attack; deliberate selection of a weapon or adaption of an article to cause injury, such as breaking a glass before an attack; making prior threats; and using an offensive weapon, against, or kicking, the victim's head.'[208]

The popular image of an assault in the newspapers is probably an attack in a dark alley, but this is only part of the picture.[209] Incidents of violence are in fact common in the home.[210] According to a Home Office Study in 2003/4 there were an estimated 12.9 million incidents of domestic violence in England and Wales commited against women and

---

[201] Povey *et al.* (2001). See also Home Office (2002a) and Home Office (2003d).

[202] Nicholas *et al.* (2005).

[203] Nicholas *et al.* (2005).   [204] Clarkson, Cretney, Davis, and Shepherd (1994).

[205] Collier (1995).   [206] Genders (1999).   [207] Ibid.

[208] Crown Prosecution Service (1996: para. 9.7).

[209] Women's Aid Federation of England (2002) provides much statistical information about domestic violence.

[210] See Herring (2001: ch. 6) for a general discussion of the law's response to domestic violence.

2.5 million against men.[211] In fact 22 per cent of all recorded violent incidents were of domestic violence, although less than 35 per cent of domestic violence incidents are reported to the police. As Anthony Giddens has written:

> The home is, in fact, the most dangerous place in modern society. In statistical terms, a person of any age or of either sex is far more likely to be subject to physical attack in the home than on the street at night.[212]

Shockingly, the British Crime Survey found that one in four women (and one in six men) will be physically assaulted by a current or former partner at some point in their lives.[213]

Until the 1960s domestic violence was barely recognized officially. It was seen as a 'private' or 'domestic' matter, in which the police or the state should not be involved. In fact domestic violence has a significant impact on the state. A 2004 study found the total cost to the economy of domestic violence was £5.8 billion.[214] This suggests that the problem of domestic violence has wider consequences than just for the couple involved.

In the following extract Elizabeth Schneider rejects the argument that the state should not intervene in a case of domestic violence because the case is a private matter. She considers that use of the concept of privacy in this argument is misconceived. She focuses on the notion of privacy as developed by Justice Douglas in the decision *Roe v Wade*[215] (the well-known American abortion case).

E. Schneider, 'The Violence of Privacy' in M. Albertson Fineman and R. Mykitiuk (eds.), *The Public Nature of Private Violence* (New York: Routledge, 1994), 52–4

[In Douglas J's judgment] [t]he right of privacy, a passive right that said the state could not intervene was viewed in contrast with the right to liberty, that emphasized the harms women suffered if they could not get abortions and seemed to imply that the state had an affirmative obligation to ensure that women can exercise their freedom. Douglas's concurring opinion suggests the radical potential of the concept of privacy—articulating it as not only the right to be let alone, but as affirmatively linked to liberty and the right to autonomy, self-expression, and self-determination. The notion of women as agents of their own lives is an important and powerful concept that transcends the common experience of the concept of privacy. . . .

The importance of this more affirmative dimension of privacy is underscored by the problem of woman abuse. The rationale of privacy legitimates and supports violence against women; woman abuse reveals the violence of privacy. Privacy justifies the refusal of the state to intervene, of judges to issue restraining orders, of neighbors and friends to intervene or to call the police, of communities to confront the problem, and of social workers to act. Yet when we look at the more affirmative dimensions that Douglas articulates in *Roe*, we can see the importance of these perspectives in thinking about woman abuse. Battered women seek autonomy, freedom of choice with respect to the basic decisions of life concerning intimate association, freedom from battering and coercion, and freedom to be themselves. They seek the freedom to survive free from violence. We need to begin to articulate these affirmative claims as abortion activists did in *Roe*.

---

[211] Walby and Allen (2004). [212] Giddens (1989).
[213] Home Office (2003d). See also Mirrlees-Black and Bayron (2000); Mirrlees-Black (1999); Hoyle (1998).
[214] Walby (2004). [215] 410 US 479 (US SCt).

Conclusion

The challenge is to develop a right to privacy which is not synonymous with the right to state noninterference with actions within the family (Eisler 1987, pp. 292–93), but which recognizes the affirmative role that privacy can play for battered women. Feminist reconstruction of privacy should seek to break down the dichotomy of public and private that has disabled legal discourse and public policy in this area. Male battering of women is a serious public problem for which we need to accept collective responsibility; it requires a dramatic program of mass public reeducation similar to the drunk driving campaigns over the last several years. At the same time, while claiming woman abuse as a public problem, we do not want to suggest that state intervention is always the answer. Frank Michelman has observed that, even if we understand that the personal is political, this insight does not answer the question of the appropriate boundaries of state intervention (Michelman 1990, p. 1794). Others have detailed the ways in which state intervention will always be problematic for women (Olsen 1985, pp. 858–61), and we can see this in the limitations of legal reforms and the child welfare investigations of battered women on failure-to-protect grounds.

However, we also do not want to reject the genuine values and benefits of privacy for battered women. Thinking about privacy as something that women who have been battered might want makes us think about it differently. Battered women seek the material and social conditions of equality and self-determination that make privacy possible (Copelon 1990–1991, pp. 44–50). Privacy that is grounded on equality, and is viewed as an aspect of autonomy that protects bodily integrity and makes abuse impermissible, is based on a genuine recognition of the importance of personhood more true to the vision of privacy that Douglas evolved. . . . Such a notion of privacy could challenge the vision of individual solution rather than social responsibility for abuse. Conceived differently, privacy could help keep women safe, not battered.

So Schneider argues that understanding the concept of privacy as being about enabling people to live the life they would like to live, free from the intervention of others, means that, far from being an argument for not intervening in a case of domestic violence, it is an argument requiring legal intervention. Indeed some commentators have argued that the state has an obligation to protect people from domestic violence and that a failure to do so amounts to an infringement of their human rights.[216]

In the following passage Victor Tadros examines in what way crimes of domestic violence are different from other assaults.

V. Tadros, 'The Distinctiveness of Domestic Abuse' in R.A. Duff and S. Green (eds.), *Defining Crimes* (Oxford: OUP, 2005), 121–5.

Domestic abuse is clearly demarcated from other instances of violence, both in popular perception and in institutional response, and this might be thought to contribute to an understanding of what is distinctive about it. Domestic abuse is considered a particular kind of social problem, which demands a particular kind of social response that is quite distinct from the response to violence in other contexts. Furthermore, institutional responses to domestic

---

[216] Choudhury and Herring (2006).

abuse are clearly different from institutional responses to other forms of violence. Cases of domestic abuse are probably less likely to result in arrest. The victim is often less willing to see a prosecution go ahead, or to testify if a prosecution does go ahead, than are victims of violence in non-domestic contexts. Domestic abuse may previously have been seen as 'less serious' than other instances of violence by the police and prosecuting services, although recent studies suggest that social and institutional evaluation of domestic abuse may well currently be in the process of change. Some jurisdictions mandate, or at least strongly recommend, arrest and/or prosecution in domestic abuse cases, which may explain some of the changes in trends in policing. This shows that institutions treat violence in the domestic context differently from violence in other contexts, although, of course, this may be in part an attempt to ensure that violence in the domestic context is taken 'as seriously' as violence in other contexts.

And yet, despite the fact that institutional responses to domestic abuse are clearly distinct from responses to other forms of violence, there is very little legal recognition of any distinction between domestic abuse and non-domestic violence, at least as far as offence categories are concerned. The offences prosecuted in cases of domestic abuse are, as we have seen, identical to those prosecuted in violence outside the domestic context.

The fact that the institutions of criminal justice have been seen as relatively ineffective in controlling domestic abuse can contribute to the case for a distinct offence, as we shall see. To pre-empt a fuller argument, it may be that the historic failure properly to respond to domestic abuse should motivate the legislature to consider creating an offence simply for the reason that it would encourage better practice in policing and prosecution. However, that case will be strengthened if there is something distinctively wrongful or harmful about domestic abuse. For this reason, criminological studies into domestic abuse ought to be supplemented by normative analysis. Empirical research alone cannot tell us what constitutes the particular wrong of domestic abuse, if anything. That is a moral question rather than a purely empirical question, albeit (as we shall see) one whose answer may build upon empirical observation.

Obviously the principal way in which domestic abuse is to be distinguished from other forms of violence has to do with the social context in which violence occurs. The term 'domestic' may suggest that the primary distinguishing mark of domestic abuse is its location: it occurs in the family home. However, that is not the best way to understand how domestic abuse is distinctive. Domestic abuse is clearly not marked out by the occurrence of violence in the home: violence in the course of a domestic burglary is not domestic abuse, and violence that takes place between husband and wife in public may still contribute to a pattern of domestic abuse. Domestic abuse takes place in the context of a relationship between the abuser and the abused, and a particularly intimate relationship at that. That is its distinctive feature. To regulate domestic abuse is to regulate relationships, not locations.

This also suggests that, as far as domestic abuse goes, there is no important distinction to be made between the public and the private sphere. That distinction may be important when it comes to regulating freedom of expression, for example, but it is not relevant to distinguishing between different forms of non-consensual violence. To that extent, this essay builds upon the insights of feminist scholars who have mounted a critique of the traditional liberal distinction between public and private. Domestic abuse is not particularly a private matter, both in the sense that it ought to be the subject of political concern, and in the sense that it may occur in public. It is only private in the sense that the relationship may be said to be particularly private. For this reason, the word 'domestic' in the phrase 'domestic abuse' is perhaps unfortunate. There is nothing particularly *domestic* about domestic abuse. Despite this weakness, I will continue to use the term 'domestic abuse' due to its familiarity.

Domestic abuse, then, is characterized by the fact that violence Occurs within the context of a relationship. One difficulty in determining the boundaries of the idea has to do with demarcating which relationships count for the purpose of domestic abuse and which do not. There may be violence between spouses or between parents and children, between non-married partners, between siblings, or between those in more distant familial relationships. But violence may also take place in the context of other ongoing relationships, such as between work colleagues or between friends. Whilst the latter instances of violence may share some of the characteristics of domestic abuse, they do not fall within the popular idea of domestic abuse. Whilst the term 'domestic' is misleading, it does indicate something else that is generally regarded as significant in understanding domestic abuse: the abuse Occurs within the context of the family, or related relationships. As suggested above, if cases of violence at work, bullying at school or violence between friends turn out to constitute the same kind of wrong as domestic abuse, there is no particular wrong of domestic abuse. Domestic abuse would merely be an instance of a broader wrong, the domestic context making a difference that is not sufficiently significant to be marked out by the distinction between offences. I will have more to say about that question later.

However, whilst the relationship between the accused and the victim is one central distinguishing feature of domestic abuse, there are other features of such abuse that mark it out socially. Perhaps the most important of these is that violence in the domestic context is generally seen as being much more likely to be repetitive and systematic than violence in the non-domestic context; indeed, that is considered a reason why the institutional and other social responses to domestic violence ought to be distinct from responses to other forms of violence.

The repetitive nature of the abuse is also part of the paradigm of domestic abuse. There is no doubt that a single instance of violence within the context of a relationship may be very serious. However, at least part of the reason for this is that a particular instance of violence is often predictive of further instances of violence in the context of a relationship. An instance of violence may be seen as indicative of further underlying features of the relationship, particularly of male dominance. A recent Home Office study reports that the average number of incidents of assault perpetrated on a victim of domestic violence is around five per year. A single assault within the context of a relationship is probably not sufficiently distinct from single assaults in other contexts to justify criminalization as a distinct offence. Furthermore, there are good reasons, grounded in the presumption of innocence, for the criminal justice system not to label the perpetrator as a systematic abuser on the basis that one incidence of violence in the domestic context is an indication of a pattern of abuse. The victim of a single instance of violence in a domestic context ought, of course, to have recourse to the law. But the proper offence to charge, in such a case, is assault.

There are two central features of domestic abuse, then. The first is that the abuse occurs within the context of an intimate relationship. The second is that the abuse is systematic. These features of domestic abuse help to explain problems that criminal justice agencies have encountered when dealing with domestic abuse, as well as revealing some of the reasons why their responses have tended to be inadequate.

FURTHER READING

Choudhry, S., and Herring, J. (2006), 'Righting Domestic Violence', *International Journal of Law Policy and the Family* 1.

Clarkson, C., Cretney, S., Davis, G., and Shepherd, J. (1994), 'Assaults: the Relationship between Seriousness, Criminalisation and Punishment', *Criminal Law Review* 4.

Cretney, A., and Davis, G. (1997), 'Prosecuting "Domestic" Assault', *The Howard Journal* 36: 146.

Levi, M. (2002b), 'Violent Crime' in M. Maguire, R. Morgan, and R. Reiner (eds.), *The Oxford Handbook of Criminology* (Oxford: OUP).

Tadros, V. (2005), 'The Distinctivness of Domestic Abuse' in R.A. Duff and S. Green (eds.), *Defining Crimes* (Oxford: OUP), 121–5.

van Brunschot, T. (2003), 'Freedom and Integrity. Relationships and Assault', *British Journal of Criminology* 43: 122.

15 THE NATURE OF AN ASSAULT

There has been some debate over the correct understanding of the essence of the offence of assault. Is the offence about the creation of fear (if so why must the fear be of imminent force?) or is it closer to an attempted battery (if so why can words amount to an assault?)? In the following passage Jeremy Horder suggests that the best way to understand the nature of the assault is as a threatening confrontation:

J. Horder, 'Reconsidering Psychic Assault' [1998] *Criminal Law Review* 392 at 399–402

Assaults as threatening confrontations

It is odd that fear remains comparatively under-analysed by criminal lawyers, as a possible species of harm, as compared with bodily and psychiatric injury (of great concern both to criminal and civil lawyers) or with 'moral offence' (of great concern to liberal political thinkers). As a species of harm, fear has a relatively transitory character inconsistent with its recognition as a kind of 'bodily' harm fur the purposes of the Offences Against the Person Act 1861. None the less, some kinds of fear—perhaps especially the fear of physical mistreatment—unacceptably detract from the kind of 'moral environment' in which people can be expected to flourish in both their public and their private lives. In this, the kind of setback to one's interests that it constitutes, fear shares something with the much-discussed notion of 'offence to others': moral offence. But (crucially), fear of physical interference is not generated by the largely moral disapproval of others' activities that gives rise to the notion of 'offensiveness', and which makes the latter so controversial as a basis for criminalisation. That does not mean, however, that, even if it were permissible, it would necessarily be appropriate to seek to criminalise every means by which an unjustified fear of physical interference is induced in another. So, what is morally significant about the wrong in psychic assault, if not the mere causing (by whatever means) of apprehension?

For Williams, an assault is just one kind of 'unlawful interference with another', but the notion of an 'interference' is, without more, too abstract to be imbued with much of moral significance. Closer to the mark is Gardner's contention that '[i]ts [assault's] essential quality lies in the invasion by one person of another's body space'. This contention suggests something of moral significance in assault other than simply causing fear, namely the invasion of body space, but the problem is that it is difficult to square with cases in which unusual physical proximity (such as 'eyeball-to-eyeball' hostilities) is clearly absent, but where there is nevertheless an undoubted assault, as in *Smith v. Newsam* or *Ireland*.

I suggest that what should be regarded as morally significant about the *actus reus* of a psychic assault is that it is experienced as a threatening *confrontation* by the victim. The victims in, for example, *Smith v. Newsam, Ireland, Thomas v. NUM* and *Smith v. Superintendent of Woking Police Station* were all confronted by a threat. What is, in this regard, to be regarded as a 'confrontation'? To be confronted by a threat, for the purposes of the law of assault, should be to perceive it as it is being made. There is something approaching an analogy here with the importance (albeit now somewhat diminished) still attributed, in limiting claims in tort for damage due to nervous shock, to the fact that the shock resulted from 'the sensory and contemporaneous' observance of the accident or its immediate aftermath. What matters is not physical propinquity to what is happening, but actual perception of what is happening or has just happened: sensory and contemporaneous awareness, involving what Lord Ackner vividly describes as, 'the sudden appreciation by sight or sound of a horrifying event, which violently agitates the mind'. My claim is not, of course, that it is necessarily *worse* to perceive a threat as it is made, to be confronted with the making of it, then it is to receive notification of it (say) by letter. Distinctions of moral significance between offences do not necessarily bear on their relative gravity, just as similar distinctions between defences do not necessarily alter their effect on liability. Consider this analogy. The legal effect of having acted under duress *per minas* is, for most purposes, much the same as having acted under duress of circumstances or conditions of necessity. But the experience of being threatened by another is not the same kind of experience as that of responding to a natural emergency, and different evaluative considerations may be involved in each. My claims are that (i) a psychic assault is the sensory and contemporaneous experience of being threatened, being 'confronted' with a threat, an experience that induces a fear of physical interference—whether or not to be inflicted immediately—being done by the threatener and (ii) that this experience is morally distinct as a form of harm, albeit not necessarily more serious, from receiving a threatening letter or the like.

Understanding psychic assault in this way, we can confidently assert that there was an assault in *Ireland*, just as there was in *Smith v. Newsam* and in *Smith v. Superintendent of Woking Police Station*. For, in *Ireland*, the threat was perceived by the victim as it was made by the defendant (*i.e.* there was 'sensory and contemporaneous' perception: Lord Ackner's 'sudden appreciation by sight or sound of a horrifying event'), inducing a fear of physical interference (Lord Ackner's notion of a violent agitation of the mind) in the former. This morally distinctive element of a fear of physical interference, induced through a confrontation, renders irrelevant the fact that the defendant, in *Ireland*, was clearly unable to implement his implied threat immediately. As explained above, moreover, the emphasis on V's perception of D's words as threatening, as the *actus reus*, also allows us confidently to defend the view that there was an assault in *Light*, as there was in *Tuberville v. Savage*. Following a quarrel, Tuberville laid his hand on his sword and said to Savage: 'If it were not assize-time I would not take such language from you'. It is commonly supposed that the Court held that this was not an assault because (in my terms) Tuberville was setting out a defeating condition: 'the declaration of [Tuberville] was, that he would not assault him, the judges being in town'. The argument I have put forward suggests that the supposed ruling ought now to be questioned. Tuberville's words can only be regarded as a defeating condition if one assumes that threats in assault cases must be of immediate violence. But if one abandons this assumption, Savage had every reason to think Tuberville was setting out a mere suspensory condition: he (Tuberville) might well have been saying that he would attack Savage when the judges left town. If Savage thought this (if he was led by Tuberville's words to fear that Tuberville would attack him at some time in the future), then Savage *was* psychically assaulted when Tuberville uttered his now famous words, because of his 'sensory and contemporaneous' observance of the threat, his 'sudden appreciation by sight or sound of a horrifying event, which violently agitates the mind'.

16 OBJECTIONS TO AND REFORM OF THE OFFENCES AGAINST THE PERSON ACT 1861

There is much unhappiness with the law of offences against the person, particularly the Offences Against the Person Act 1861. After all it is hardly surprising that an 1861 Act has had difficulty dealing with our 'modern' problems of e-mail harassment, racially motivated assaults, stalking, and HIV infection. Professor Ashworth has referred to the Act being 'unprincipled[;] it is expressed in unhelpful language, and it may lead judges to perpetrate manifest distortions in order to secure convictions in cases where there is "obvious" guilt but where the Act falls down'.[217] Lord Ackner has referred to the 'irrational result of this piecemeal legislation'.[218]

The most common areas of complaint about the 1861 Act are as follows:

(1) *Maximum sentences.* The maximum penalty for the section 20 offence (wounding or inflicting grievous bodily harm) is five years, which is the same as that for the section 47 one (assault occasioning actual bodily harm). It seems odd that they should have the same maximum sentence, given that the section 20 offence requires proof of a more serious *actus reus* (grievous, rather than actual bodily harm) and a graver *mens rea* (foresight of some harm, rather than foresight of an assault or battery). In practice, section 20 is treated by prosecutors[219] and the judiciary as more serious than section 47. It appears then that both theory and practice would be better reflected if section 20 had a higher maximum sentence than section 47.

It is also notable that there is a large jump in sentencing from section 20 (five years) to section 18 (life). Andrew Ashworth suggests it should be questioned whether the distinction between intention and recklessness (at least in the context offences which often involve acts of instinctive violence) is sufficient to warrant the difference.[220]

(2) *Correspondence principle.* The correspondence principle has been discussed in detail in Chapter 3. In brief its adherents claim that it is wrong to have an offence where the defendant is guilty even though he or she did not intend or foresee the *actus reus*. For example, a defendant under section 20 should be guilty of causing grievous bodily harm only if he intended or foresaw that his act would produce such a result. As we have seen, the Offences Against the Person Act 1861 does not accord with the correspondence principle in respect of section 47 (there is no need to intend or foresee actual bodily harm) and section 20 (there is no need to intend or foresee grievous bodily harm). However, as noted in Chapter 3, other commentators reject the correspondence principle (see e.g. the extract from John Gardner, below).

(3) *'Wound or grievous bodily harm'.* The *actus reus* of sections 18 and 20 involves wounding *or* causing grievous bodily harm.[221] The complaint is that wounding can involve a minor

---

[217] Ashworth (2003: 337).   [218] *Savage and Parmenter* [1992] 1 AC 699 at 723.
[219] Crown Prosecution Service (1996).   [220] Ashworth (2003: 310).
[221] The complaint is weaker in relation to s. 18, where the defendant must intend grievous bodily harm (even if in fact he wounded).

cut which may essentially heal in minutes and that it is wrong to group it together with grievous bodily harm. It can be argued that there was some justification in 1861 for treating wounding and grievous bodily harm similarly because a cut could (at that time) all too easily turn septic and endanger the victim's life. Therefore treating a break in the skin as equivalent to a life-threatening harm was reasonable. Nowadays those who support the 1861 Act tend to rely on one of two arguments. The first is that a cut, a breaking of the skin, involves a significant invasion of the person. It is not just because of the pain that people dread injections. Thus, although not as painful as a broken arm (say), the invasion of the person's sense of self in a wounding case is significantly worse. The second is that the inclusion of wounding in the offence could be justified as a deterrent to those who use knives or sharp implements in an attack.

(4) *Inflict/cause.* As we saw in Part I there is some dispute over the meaning of the words 'inflict' in section 20 and 'cause' in section 18. Probably the position the law has reached is that inflict means the same as cause, in which case it must be asked why the word 'caused' was not used in both sections. It is certainly confusing that two closely linked sections contain two different words with apparently the same meaning.

(5) *Archaic language.* Some commentators and members of the judiciary feel that the language of the Offences Against the Person Act 1881 is archaic and does not describe the offences covered in accessible and clear language. This has meant, they suggest, that the courts have had to give a strained interpretation of the meaning of the sections' words on occasions. One example might be the inclusion of psychological illnesses within the term 'bodily harm'.

(6) *The need for an assault in section 47.* Why is there a requirement in section 47 of an assault? Why should it not be sufficient simply to prove that the defendant caused the victim actual bodily harm? Horder gives the example of someone who puts acid in another's bath, causing actual bodily harm. In such a case should there be any doubt that there has been an offence under section 47 because it may not be easy to demonstrate that there was a battery or an assault?[222]

Although the Law Commission and many commentators are convinced by these arguments there are few commentators who are willing to stand up for the Offences Against the Person Act 1861. One of the strongest defences of the Act is provided by John Gardner. In the following extract he replies to some of the objections mentioned above. He starts by challenging the claim that the Act is irrational:

J. Gardner, 'Rationality and the Rule of Law in Offences Against the Person' (1994) 53 *Cambridge Law Journal* 502 at 503–11

The rationality argument figures less prominently in the Law Commission's latest report than it does in the consultation paper which preceded it. One can only speculate as to the causes of its demotion, but its spirit certainly lives on in the draft Bill. The spirit of the argument is captured in the Commission's comment that 'sections 18, 20 and 47 of the I861 Act . . . were not drafted with a view to setting out the various offences with which they deal in a logical or graded manner'. The assumption is that the three offences can, in substance, be graded, and that this would be the logical way to define and organise them. Between them they deal

---

[222] In fact, in the light of *DPP v K* [1990] 1 All ER 331 there is likely to be a battery.

with matters which would most naturally be dealt with in a hierarchy of more and less serious offences all conforming to a standard definitional pattern. The irrationality of the 1861 Act lies in its failure to take this natural path, its failure to carry the underlying hierarchy of seriousness over into the actual definition and organisation of the offences. Thus, section 18 should be regarded, in substance, as an aggravated version of section 20; and yet there are miscellaneous differences between the two sections which do not appear to bear any rational relation to the aggravation. Likewise, section 20 should be regarded, in substance, as the more serious cousin of section 47; and yet the two offences are drafted in quite different terms, so that the essential difference in point of seriousness is obscured by a mass of other, utterly irrelevant differences. If the sections were properly graded in definition as they are in substance, then section 18 would surely cover a narrower class of cases than section 20 which would cover a narrower class of cases than section 47; and yet section 47 is, in at least one respect, the narrowest offence of the three, while section 18 is, in at least one respect, broader than section 20. That is surely irrational. The law on such matters should be thoroughly governed, in the Law Commission's words, 'by clear distinctions . . . between serious and less serious cases'.

That a section 18 offence should be regarded, in substance, as a more serious version of a section 20 offence is easy enough to understand. Section 20 covers malicious wounding and the malicious infliction of grievous bodily harm. Section 18 covers malicious wounding and maliciously causing grievous bodily harm, when these things are done with intention to do grievous bodily harm or to prevent or resist arrest. The extra element of intention required for a section 18 offence obviously accounts for the difference between the sentencing maxima (five years' imprisonment under section 20 and life under section 18), and marks a difference in point of seriousness (or potential seriousness) which the Law Commission is rightly anxious to retain in its hierarchy of replacement offences. The Commission has not even felt the need to explain its decision, however, to eliminate the difference in the *causal* elements of sections 18 and 20. Section 20 requires that grievous bodily harm be *inflicted*, whereas for section 18 it need only be *caused*. The law at present tells us that infliction requires violent force. One may cause grievous bodily harm by, for example, passing on an infection or poisoning. But one may not inflict grievous bodily harm in that way. If that is right, one may commit a section 18 offence without using violent means, but a section 20 offence requires such means. This the Commission apparently holds to be a self-evidently irrational point of distinction between the two offences. One may glean the reasons. In the first place the distinction between 'causing' and 'inflicting', as the law presents it, fails the test which the Commission uses to determine what factors may affect the seriousness of a crime in this area of the law. For the Commission, seriousness varies only 'according to the type of injury that [the defendant] intended or was aware that he might cause'. In the second place, and more straightforwardly, the distinction we are looking at appears to operate back to front. The extra element of violence is required for the less serious offence, not the more serious. The distinction is not merely irrational, it may be said, but perverse. Not so. The distinction is easy enough to understand. One must begin by thinking of section 20 as the basic offence, and infliction as the basic mode of causation with which the two offences together are concerned. That is not hard to do. Only someone who mistakes the *harm* in section 20 for the *wrong* in section 20 would think it irrelevant how the harm came about. For the wrong is that of bringing the harm about in that way. In morality, as in law, it matters how one brings things about. It matters, first and foremost, in deciding which wrong one committed. You have not been mugged, although you have been conned, if I trick you into handing over your money by spinning some yarn. You have not been coerced, although you have been manipulated, if I get you to do something by making you think you wanted to do it all along. You have not been killed, although you have been left to die, if a doctor fails to prescribe life-saving drugs. These are matters of intrinsic moral significance. The fact that one inflicted harm rather than merely causing it can be, likewise, a matter of intrinsic moral significance. It is this, among other things, which distinguishes the torturer, who continues to enjoy a distinctive offence all of his own in the Law Commission's proposals, and an offence, moreover, which is still explicitly defined in terms of 'infliction'. The old section 20 builds on the same moral significance, although without restricting attention to the special case of the torturer. Under section 20, that is to say, one does not merely end up grievously harmed. One is a victim of violence. This is the common factor, moreover, which unites the infliction of grievous bodily harm with wounding, accounting for the fact that these sit side by side in a single offence. Thus section 20 is correctly regarded, not merely as a core offence against the person, but as a core crime of violence. Violence is the basic section 20 theme which has to be adapted for the purposes of the more heinous offence under section 18.

That the process of adaptation involves extending the crime to cases where grievous bodily harm comes about other than by violence—cases where it is caused without being inflicted—may sound paradoxical, but it is in fact a natural move to make. The move is connected with the familiar maxim that intended consequences are never too remote. That maxim paints a somewhat exaggerated picture, but to the extent that it speaks the truth it proceeds from the thought that those who intend some result could otherwise enjoy a bizarre kind of mastery over their own normative situation. They could evade a moral or legal rule which is means-specific simply by adopting different means. Since the very fact that one adopts means to some result *entails* that one intends it, this kind of evasion is by definition unavailable to those who do not intend the result. So there is good reason, other things being equal, to withdraw some or all of the means-specificity from a moral or legal rule where its violation consists in the intentional pursuit or achievement of some result. That is precisely what section 18 does. Lest the fact that it does this be summarily dismissed as mere slip of the draftsman's pen, it is worth noting that section 18 explicitly confirms the profound importance of the point by including the words 'by any means whatsoever' in its definition, words which contrast neatly with section 20's infliction-oriented proviso 'with or without any weapon or instrument'. So whether or not one believes that there should be specific crimes of violence among the most basic offences against the person, as soon as one appreciates that section 20 creates such a crime, one can at once grasp the rational explanation for the differences between it and section 18.

None of this contradicts the Commission's view that section 18 should be regarded as the more serious version of section 20. On the contrary, it confirms that view. It merely casts doubt on the Commission's reductive assumption about the kind of variations one should expect to find between the definitions of more serious offences and those of less serious offences. These need not be restricted, as a matter of principle, to variations in the con-figuration of *mens rea* and resulting harm. That is the clear message of the relationship between sections 18 and 20. When we come to relate sections 18 and 20 to section 47, however, the message is quite different. What needs to be uprooted here is the assumption that the former relate to the latter, in substance, as more serious offences to less serious. That assumption needs to be replaced with a sensitivity to the essential qualitative differ-ences between section 47 offences and those covered by sections 18 and 20. They are incomparably different types of offences, with different basic themes. Looking at the 1861 Act one might have thought this obvious. In the first place, section 47 has the same maximum sentence as section 20. That instantly alerts one to the possibility that offences under sections 20 and 47 should be regarded like those under sections 1 and 17 of the Theft Act 1968 (*i.e.* theft and false accounting), as offences which are, in essence, neither more serious nor less serious than each other. In the second place section 47 belongs clearly to its own family of offences, namely those of assault (sections 38 to 47). Since the rest of that family is not treated as having some simple scalar relation to section 18 and 20 offences, one may ask why section 47 should be thought to be any different.

The answer lies, once again, in mistaking the harm for the wrong. Section 47 prohibits assault occasioning actual bodily harm. Because actual bodily harm is plainly a less serious variant of grievous bodily harm, too much focus on the harm can lead one to think that section 47 is, in substance, a less serious variant of section 20. And the harm is obviously where one focuses, at the outset, if one adopts the Law Commission's view that seriousness varies in this context only 'according to the type of injury that [the defendant] intended or was aware that he might cause'. But in fact one should pay attention first, in section 47, to the assault, not the harm. Here we find a major point of distinction between section 47 and section 20. For in spite of the fact that most assaults do involve violence, assault is not a crime of violence. Its essential quality lies in the invasion by one person of another's body space. As every law student knows, such an invasion may take one of two forms. It may take the form of a *mere* assault, an invasion of body space without bodily contact but with the apprehension of its imminence, or it may take the form of a battery, when the contact between the two bodies actually takes place. The Law Commission's own proposed redefinition of assault makes it sound as if the contact, apprehended or actual, must be violent. Their draft provisions speak of 'force' and 'impact'. But this has never been the common law's emphasis, and it distorts the substance of the offence. One may assault someone without violence: by removing their coat or shoes, by sitting too close to them, by stroking their hair, etc. Conversely, one may subject another to violence without assaulting, them: by luring someone into the path of an express train, for example, or by leaving a brick where it will fall on someone's head. These are, not peripheral but central cases. They reveal how far the subject-matter of sections 38 to 47 of the 1861 Act differs, in substance as well as in detail, from that of section 20. The accident of drafting is not so much that the assault crimes in sections 38 to 47 diverge from the crimes of violence in sections 18 and 20. The accident, on the contrary, is that they ever coincide.

It is, of course, no accident that section 47 adds a harm requirement to the element of assault. That is precisely what distinguishes a section 47 assault from an assault *simpliciter*, and from the various other special categories of assault specified n the 1861 Act and elsewhere. It would be a mistake to jump to the conclusion, however, that the harm plays the same logical role in section 47 that it plays in sections 18 and 20. In common with other aggravated assault provisions, but quite unlike sections 18 and 20, section 47 creates a crime of constructive liability, *i.e.* a crime which one commits by committing another crime. Committing a certain crime, *e.g.* assault or dangerous driving, may always carry the risk of harm, or other primary risks. But in a constructive liability context, it also exposes one to secondary risks, risks of additional liability, which one would not have faced but for one's commission of the original crime. Under section 47, those who commit the crime of assault take the risk, not only that it will occasion harm (the primary risk), but also that, if it does, they will have committed a more serious crime (the secondary risk). They likewise take the risk, under section 51 of the Police Act 1964, that their assault will be upon a police officer in the execution of his duty (the primary risk), and that, if it is, they will again have committed the more serious crime of assaulting a police officer in the execution of his duty (the secondary risk). And so on. By committing an assault one changes one's own normative position, so that certain adverse consequences and circumstances which would not have counted against one but for one's original assault now count against one automatically, and add to one's crime.

Constructive offences, although common enough even in modern legislation, are not easily accommodated within the criminal law principles espoused by many contemporary criminal lawyers, and taken for granted by the Law Commission. In particular, such offences violate what Andrew Ashworth calls the 'correspondence principle', whereby every element of the *actus reus* must carry with it a corresponding element of *mens rea*. Fortunately, this 'correspondence principle' is not and never has been a principle of English law. The relevant principle of English law is *actus non facit reum nisi mens sit rea*; no guilty act without a guilty mind. Constructive offences, when they are properly conceived and designed, do not violate this principle. The more basic offences with which they are associated require *mens rea*, and that *mens rea* is naturally carried over into the constructive offence. The guilty act must therefore still be attended by a guilty mind, in line with *actus non facit reum nisi mens sit rea*. What need not be attended by any *mens rea* are the consequences and circumstances, the risk of which one bears because one committed the original crime. For if these were attended by *mens rea*, that would make a nonsense of the idea, at the heart of all constructive liability, that those who embark on crimes, or at least certain risky crimes, change in the process their own normative positions regarding the risks they take. That is why there is no grand departure from principle in the House of Lords' recent, and I would say overdue, confirmation that section 47 of the 1861 Act has no *mens rea* requirement apart from the *mens rea* of assault. It also explains the causal element in section 47, the element of 'occasioning'. The chain of 'occasioning' should be regarded as very elastic, stretching to harms rather more remote than any which are caused or inflicted. You lunge towards me, I step backwards, some one's umbrella trips me up, I fall backwards, a cyclist runs me over. The assault occasions the resulting harm even though it does not cause it. Section 47 liability may therefore arise even though the actual bodily harm comes about by a very indirect route, perhaps involving successive coincidences. In committing an assault, on this view, one bears not only the risk that harm will come about, but also, up to a point, the risk of *how* it will come about. In respect of the harm, then, some of the protection of the doctrine of *novus actus interveniens* is forfeited by the assaulter, along with some of the protection of the doctrine of *mens rea*.

In line with its general principle of offence seriousness, the Law Commission would restore both of these protections. In the process it would remove the section 47 offence from the assault family, drop its constructive elements, and replace it with an offence in the same family as those offences which would serve as replacements for sections 18 and 20. Yet this move is not a replacement of less rational organisation with more, as we can now see, but a choice between two possible rational arrangements in the law of non-sexual and non-fatal offences against the person. After all, we have just supplied a perfectly rational explanation for the main features of the section 47 offence, understood as a variation on the assault theme. There are also, as the Law Commission shows, rational explanations for the features of the proposed replacement for section 47, understood as a variation on the theme of sections 18 and 20. The point is, however, that one cannot have it both ways, since the assault theme (invasion of body space) is not the same as the theme of sections 18 and 20 (personal violence). The Law Commission can make their proposed arrangements seem to have it both ways only by diluting the two themes so that they become harder to distinguish. The violence theme is weakened in the replacements for sections 18 and 20 by the eradication of the 'infliction' paradigm. At the same tine the spatial invasion theme is weakened in the restatement of assault by concentration on 'force' and 'impact'. But this two-way *rapprochement* generates a regrettable loss of discrimination in the law of offences against the person which no amount of rational reordering can compensate. It represents a triumph of reductive thinking. Codification need not be like this. In the law of offences against property, excellently codified during the 1960s and 1970s, we find many different offences involving much the same harms. Whether one is a victim of theft, deception, criminal damage or making off, one is harmed by being deprived of one's belongings. Yet this codification did not seek to eradicate the different themes of the different offences, and turn out some general scale of seriousness. On the contrary, it went out of its way to capture these different themes in precise and differentiated language. That is because, in the realm of property offences, the harm does not capture all that is interesting, or rationally significant, about the wrong. Nor are things any different in the law of offences against the person. In substance, the wrong of an assault crime is different from the wrong of a section 20 crime much as the wrong of theft is different from the wrong of fraud. The two may happen to overlap, even across a large porportion [sic] of their terrain, but one cannot in principle unify them into a neatly scaled family of crimes. Indeed the Law Commission recognises this, in spite of its own inclinations, by preserving distinct offences of poisoning and torture, and by hiving off the sexual offences to a different corner of the codification agenda. One may ask why the basic thematic separation of sections 18 and 20 from section 47 does not also deserve preservation. Certainly the rationality argument does not supply the answer, for there is nothing irrational, to speak of, in either section 47 or sections 18 and 20.

17 PROPOSED REFORMS TO THE OFFENCES AGAINST THE PERSON ACT

The Home Office has proposed replacement of the offences with a more coherent pattern of offences:[223]

(i)   A person is guilty of an offence if he intentionally causes serious injury to another.

(ii) A person is guilty of an offence if he recklessly causes serious injury to another.

(iii) A person is guilty of an offence if he intentionally or recklessly causes injury to another.

(iv) A person acts intentionally with respect to a result if—

    (a) it is his purpose to cause it, or

    (b) although it is not his purpose to cause it, he knows that it would occur in the ordinary course of events if he were to succeed in his purpose of causing some other result.

(v)   A person acts recklessly with respect to a result if he is aware of a risk that it will occur and it is unreasonable to take that risk having regard to the circumstances as he knows or believes them to be.

(vi) Injury means physical injury or mental injury.

(vii) [Save for the offence of intentionally causing serious injury] physical injury does not include anything caused by disease but (subject to that) it includes pain, unconsciousness and any other impairment of a person's physical condition.

---

[223] Home Office (1998c). The proposals were made in 1998, but there have been no signs of the proposals being legislated in the near future.

(viii) A person is guilty of an offence if—

   (a) he intentionally or recklessly applies force to or causes an impact on the body of another, or

   (b) he intentionally or recklessly causes the other to believe that any such force or impact is imminent.

There are two points of particular note about these proposals. The first is that they largely accord with the correspondence principle: a person is only responsible for the degree of injury he foresaw or intended.[224] The second is that the language used is simple and readily comprehensible.

But such praises are, however, exactly the reasons why others oppose the proposals. Jeremy Horder sees the simplicity of the language as a vice.[225] He would prefer a statute which defined precisely the wrong that the defendant had done to the victim (e.g. that it would be an offence if the defendant 'castrates, disables, disfigures, or dismembers ... or removes an internal body part' of a victim). He argues that such a statute would comply with labelling theory (described at p. 19) by accurately and precisely defining the wrong done to the victim. William Wilson adopts this argument but suggests that labels such as baby-beating and fighting at football matches would better capture society's condemnation of activities. As he points out, tabloid newspapers are keen to use such labels, rather than just saying they cause harm, because not all assaults are regarded in the same way.

The strongest objection to Horder's or Wilson's proposals would be the possibility of a defendant appealing unmeritoriously against a conviction, on the basis that he was not charged with precisely the correct kind of assault. For example, using Horder's suggestion, much court time and effort might be spent by a defendant claiming 'I did not disable, I disfigured.' In contrast, by adopting the broader definition 'causing serious injury' in the Home Office's proposals such arguments could be avoided.

QUESTIONS

1. Is it more important to have an offence which accurately describes what the defendant has done to the victim, or to have offences which broadly define the defendant's harm and can be speedily prosecuted?

2. Do you find the distinction John Gardner draws (in the passage above) between the harm done to the victim and the wrong done to the victim a useful one?

FURTHER READING

Clarkson, C. (1994), 'Law Commission Report on Offences Against the Person and General Principles: (1) Violence and the Law Commission', *Criminal Law Reform* 324.

Gardner, J. (1994a), 'Rationality and the Rule of Law in Offences Against the Person', *Cambridge Law Journal* 53: 661.

---

[224] They are perhaps not in perfect accord with the correspondence principle because there is no distinction drawn in (iii) between intentionally and recklessly causing injury. The Law Commission feared that to do so would overcomplicate the law: Law Commission Report No. 218 (1993: 13.4).

[225] Horder (1994b).

Genders, E. (1999), 'Reform of the Offences Against the Person Act: Lessons from the Law in Action', *Criminal Law Review* 689.

Home Office (1998c), *Violence: Reforming the Offences Against the Person Act 1861* (London: Home Office).

Horder, J. (1994b), 'Rethinking Non-fatal Offences Against the Person', *Oxford Journal of Legal Studies* 14: 335.

Smith, J.C. (1998b), 'Offences Against the Person: the Home Office Consultation Paper', *Criminal Law Review* 317.

18 CONSENT

18.1 DEFENCE OR *ACTUS REUS*?

Is it better to regard the consent of the victim as a defence or its absence as an aspect of *actus reus*? In Part I we noted that the House of Lords in *Brown*[226] regarded consent as a defence to a charge of assault. In the following passage Stephen Shute considers how the law should approach that issue. He is considering the Law Commission's consultation paper on consent in the criminal law. Here he is criticizing the assumption in that paper that consent should be regarded as a defence to a criminal offence rather than its absence being an element of the *actus reus*:

S. Shute, 'The Second Law Commission Consultation Paper on Consent (1) Something Old, Something Borrowed: Three Aspects of the Project' [1996] *Criminal Law Review* 684

2. The Offence/Defence Distinction: Something Old

Although the second Consultation Paper courageously breaks new ground in relation to mistaken belief in consent, in other respects it falls solidly behind the doctrinal lead provided by the first Consultation Paper. A striking example is that both Papers take it for granted that consent operates as a 'defence' to certain forms of criminal liability. In this the Commission makes two key assumptions about the structure of criminal law: first, that sound theoretical distinction can be drawn between the offence and the defence elements of a crime; and, second, that consent lies exclusively on the defence side of this theoretical divide. As we shall see, however, these two assumptions are unhappy bedfellows, for the most attractive argument in support of the first inevitably undercuts the plausibility of the second.

The claim that it is possible to distinguish clearly between the offence and defence elements of a crime has not gone unchallenged. Glanville Williams, for example, has argued that the distinction is largely dependent upon accidents of legal drafting and of no analytical importance. Nonetheless, support for the distinction can be derived from the fact that in modern Western legal systems criminal laws are intended to affect the reasoning patterns of those who live under them. This insight allows for the development of a reason-based account of the offence/defence distinction according to which the offence elements of a crime are those things which the law *always* takes there to be a reason 'not to do' and the defence elements are exculpatory provisions which apply only once that initial prohibition has been breached.

[226] [1994] 1 AC 212 (HL).

The explanatory power of such a reason-based account has been well illustrated by Kenneth Campbell in an important article on the topic in which he discusses the example of a government that wishes to make it an offence for a householder to operate a radio receiver without a licence. How, Campbell asks, should such a prohibition be drafted? The answer, he says, depends on whether the government thinks there is always a reason against operating a radio receiver or whether it considers that there is only a reason against operating a radio receiver if one does so without a licence: if the latter, the government should define the offence element of the crime narrowly as 'operating a radio receiver without a licence'; if the former, the offence element of the crime should be 'operating a radio receiver' and the government should then add a special defence for those householders who have a licence.

Campbell's example is instructive. It not only reveals that a reason-based approach can provide a principled way of separating out the offence elements of a crime from the defence elements, but it also shows that the Law Commission is wrong to assume dogmatically that consent must always fall on the defence side of the line. Everything, in fact, depends on the underlying value judgments, which are themselves sensitive to the context in which the issues arise. Sometimes, of course, the foundational value judgments will be obscure, which may make it difficult if not impossible to decide into which category any given element might fall. But on other occasions the value judgments are clear. A crime where this is true is rape and, *pace* the Commission, rape also illustrates that there can be situations where consent (or lack of it) should be seen as an offence element of a crime rather than as a separate I defence. According to the reason-based account outlined above, if there were always a reason against having sexual intercourse, the offence clement of rape should be defined as 'engaging in sexual intercourse' and a special defence should be added to cover those cases where consent was present. However drafting a statute in this way seems wrong. The reason is that it reflects a morality that is foreign to us. We simply do not think that there is always a reason against sexual intercourse. We are much happier, therefore, with a definition of rape which includes consent in the definition of the offence rather than allowing it to operate as a separate defence that only comes into play as an after-thought once the initial prohibition has been breached.

The example of rape should give the Commission pause for thought, especially if its ultimate aim is to provide a comprehensive code to govern all aspects of English criminal law. It is to be hoped, therefore, that in its final Report the Commission will show greater sensitivity to the context in which the issue of consent is set and allow for the possibility that, in some cases at least, consent should be regarded as an offence rather than a defence element of a crime.

18.2 THE DISPUTE OVER *BROWN*

The decision of the House of Lords in *Brown*[227] is one of the most controversial in recent years. It has been greatly criticized, and even the few who are sympathetic to the conclusions reached by the majority are not impressed by the reasoning used.[228] For example, Lord Jauncey's argument that holding the defendants' actions to be lawful would be to give 'judicial imprimatur' to the actions cannot, with respect, be correct. To hold an action lawful does not indicate that the law approves of it. Adultery is not illegal, but this does not mean that it is approved of by the law; indeed adultery is a ground of divorce.

[227] [1994] 1 AC 212 (HL). For useful discussions see Giles (1994) and Bix (1993).
[228] Wilson (2002: ch. 1).

Key to the differences between the speeches of the majority and minority are their starting points:

(1) The majority saw the case as involving violence. One person should not inflict violence upon another unless there are very good reasons for doing so. The provision of sexual pleasure is not sufficient.[229] Indeed the majority went further than they needed in saying that not only does sado-masochistic sex not benefit society, it in fact has the potential to cause serious harms.

(2) The minority saw the case as involving consensual private sexual activity.[230] They argued that unless there are strong reasons to render such conduct unlawful it should be permitted. No reasons had been produced to justify rendering the defendants' conduct unlawful.[231]

The arguments in favour of Brown

The arguments of the majority can be summarized as follows:

(1) Concerns about the participants in sado-masochism.

The majority expressed the following ways in which they believed permitting sado-masochistic sexual activities could harm the participants.

(i) The majority expressed concerns that groups of sado-masochists may be insufficiently organized, leading to non-consensual injuries being caused. For example, if in the middle of the activity one person withdraws his consent,[232] the other, caught up in the sexual excitement of the moment, may continue. There was no evidence that this had occurred with the group in *Brown*, but the majority presumably feared that other groups would be less well run. Lord Jauncey feared that there were particular concerns that this might occur if members of the group had taken alcohol or illegal drugs.[233]

(ii) Lord Templeman was concerned that the results of the appellants' actions were 'unpredictably dangerous'.[234] So because the 'victims' could not be aware of the potential consequences of the activity their consent should be regarded as suspect.

(iii) Lord Templeman suggested that the consent of some participants to sado-masochistic group sex should be regarded as dubious. He had in mind particularly the fact that many of the 'victims' in *Brown* were aged about 21, while the appellants were middle-aged men. These concerns are also found in the

---

[229] Indeed the majority thought there were very good reasons why the activity should not be allowed.

[230] The European Court of Human Rights held that the conviction of the appellants in *Brown* did not infringe their right to respect for their private life under Art. 8 of the European Convention on Human Rights. It was held that the convictions could be justified as necessary in the interests of protecting the health or morals of the public: *Laskey, Jaggard and Brown v UK* (1997) 24 EHRR 39. For a discussion of that case see Moran (1998).

[231] For a very useful article expounding the approach of the minority see Kell (1994).

[232] Apparently in sado-masochistic groups it is common to rely on a special word or phrase which when uttered indicates that the individual no longer consents to the harm being caused.

[233] Although it might be added that the horseplay exception is far more open to misuse in cases of bullying than permitting sado-masochism would be (Padfield (1992)).

[234] Lord Templeman.

writings of some feminist commentators that sado-masochism may in fact disguise incidents of domestic violence or the abuse of vulnerable people.[235]

The response of the minority to these concerns is that it might be better to prosecute whenever the victims did not truly consent rather than to outlaw all sado-masochistic activities.

(2) Concerns that the activities would harm others.

The majority indicated that they were concerned that the activities might lead to harms to members outside the group. Lord Templeman suggested that to permit sado-masochistic activities would 'breed and glorify violence'. It was feared that the activities could overspill into illegal activities against non-consenting victims who were not members of the group. The minority found there was no evidence to suggest that such fears were well founded.

(3) Moral outrage at what the defendants did.

It was clear that the majority of their Lordships felt moral outrage at what the appellants had done. Lord Templeman described the activities as an 'indulgence of cruelty'. He explained that 'infliction of pain is an evil thing'. Lord Lowry referred to the 'perverted and depraved sexual desire' of the appellants.

An argument, not made explicitly by the majority but which could be used to support their approach, is that there is an important taboo in society against deliberately inflicting harm on another. The protection of this taboo is crucial if society is not to slip into barbarism.[236] However, as William Wilson suggests, 'As things now stand, no threat to society's moral integrity is likely to result from the esoteric practices of a group of homosexuals, beyond the odd burst blood vessel suffered by "Outraged of Tunbridge Wells".'[237] But he goes on to suggest that there is 'one fundamental residual moral value' which forms a building block of society and that is that 'hurting people is wrong'.[238] To others in our multi-cultural, multi-faith society we have so many different notions of right and wrong that it is not possible to talk of key moral principles that form the cement of our society.

In the following passage Anthony Duff develops an argument that it is permissible for the state to prohibit dehumanizing behaviour. He starts discussing a point made by Irving Kristol,[239] that we would not be happy to permit a gladiatorial contest which spectators paid to witness.

A. Duff, 'Harms and Wrongs' (2001) 5 *Buffalo Criminal Law Review* 13 at 39–41

If we tried to explain what is so disturbing about the gladiatorial example (apart from the likely further effects of such activities), we might talk not just of 'the objective regrettability of millions deriving pleasure from brutal bloodshed', but of the dehumanization or degradation perpetrated by the gladiators on each other, and by the spectators on the gladiators and on themselves. We might talk in similar terms, though with less emphatic insistence, about the sadomasochism of *R v Brown*. Whilst there were no spectators to degrade or be degraded, we might still say that the participants were degrading or dehumanizing themselves and each

---

[235] Hanna (2001). Other feminist writers do not share these concerns: Pa (2001).
[236] See e.g. Devlin (1965) where Lord Devlin in an academic article has written of the 'moral cement' which holds our society together (see p. 29 for further discussion).
[237] Wilson (1992: 392).   [238] Wilson (2002: ch. 1).   [239] Kristol (1971).

other. This would involve an appeal, in both cases, to a normative conception of 'humanity'—of what it is to be human and to recognize the humanity of others, and of what it is to deny or fail to respect that humanity in others or in oneself.

What makes Kristol's gladiatorial combat dehumanizing and degrading is not just the fact that the participants are trying to kill each other. Though radical pacifists might argue that a proper respect for the humanity of others absolutely precludes trying to kill them, most who take humanity seriously allow that we can respect the humanity even of those whom we try to kill, for instance in a just war. Nor need we think that every kind of individual combat (outside war) in which the participants try to kill each other must be dehumanizing. We might be able to recognize a social practice of dueling or of jousting as one in which the participants can respect each other's humanity. Whether such a practice could be consistent with a mutual recognition of, and respect for, the humanity of the participants would depend on the structure of values and conceptions which forms its social context and which provides the participants (and spectators, if any) with their expected motivations. Can we, for instance, see the practice of jousting as one in which citizens can display those martial virtues on which the defense of their families and country depend? Can we see the practice of dueling as one in which honor can be vindicated and restored between gentlemen? If we can, we can also see these practices as at least consistent with a respect for the humanity of the participants. The participants can respect each other as participants in a noble enterprise. Spectators can watch with admiration these displays of appropriate human excellences.

I do not say that we should see any actual historical practice of jousting or dueling in this light. My point is only that combats to the death are not necessarily inconsistent with a mutual respect for each other's humanity amongst the combatants, or with a due recognition amongst the spectators of the humanity of the participants. Kristol's gladiatorial combats, however, are inconsistent with such respect. They are commercial events. What motivates both promoters and gladiators is the prospect of making money from paying spectators. What the gladiators must do, to earn their pay, is to give the customers what they want; and what they want is not the display of martial virtues that can be admired for their civic worth, but 'brutal bloodshed' that they encourage by 'their bloodthirsty screams'. But the 'brutality' that the spectators are paying to see, and that the gladiators must aim to provide, is (one might say 'by definition') a denial of the humanity of those involved. They are reduced to 'brutes' who must try to maim and kill each other for the amusement of a paying and baying crowd.

The defendants in *R v. Brown* were not performing for paying spectators. But they were (on one reading of sadomasochism), trying precisely to degrade and humiliate each other. They were enacting rituals of torture, which treat the person tortured as, or try to reduce him to, a humiliated and degraded animal. This conduct was, no doubt, set in a larger context in which they treated and respected each other as human equals, and they degraded each other in this way only because each freely consented to it. Nonetheless, what they consented to and sought was treatment that, in itself, denied their humanity.

Of course, much more work is needed to flesh out the normative conception of humanity on which these comments about Kristol's gladiators and *R v. Brown* depend. But I hope I have said enough to make such appeals to 'humanity' familiar and plausible.

The arguments against Brown

The arguments for the approach of the minority were in part rejecting the approach of the majority, as already mentioned above. The minority's view is based on the principle that private consensual activities should be rendered illegal only if it can be shown that such conduct harms society. One point strongly in favour of the minority's approach is that the list of exceptional circumstances in which consent can provide a defence (e.g. surgery, sports) is more easily explained by the approach of the minority than the majority. For example, it is easier to explain that the rough and tumble horseplay, tattooing, and religious flagellation exceptions form the minority's perspective (such actions do not harm society) than it is to explain them from the majority's point of view (such actions are beneficial to society and so the violence is justified). The best response for supporters of *Brown* may be to suggest that what the majority objected to in *Brown* was the *intentional* infliction of harm.[240] The exceptional cases, on this explanation, are explained on the basis that they involve situations where the defendant does not intend to cause the harm but rather to play a sport, take part in rough games, give a tattoo, etc. By contrast, in *Brown* the defendants intended to inflict pain, because if there had been no pain their activities would have been a flop for all concerned.[241] This would also explain the decision in *Wilson*,[242] because in that case it was not part of Mr Wilson's purpose that Mrs Wilson suffer pain.

Some opponents of the decision in *Brown* have seen in the courts' decisions in this area prejudicial attitudes. In particular they reveal what the courts see as appropriately 'manly' behaviour.[243] Real men may set each other alight as part of a prank (*Aitken*), but do not wound each other for sexual pleasure (*Brown*).

In the following passage Paul Roberts approaches the question of the relevance of the victim's consent in a criminal case from a philosophical perspective. He outlines three approaches that could be taken: liberalism, paternalism, and legal moralism:

P. Roberts, 'Appendix C' in Law Commission Consultation Paper No. 139, *Consent in the Criminal Law* (London: HMSO, 1998), C. 39–C. 72

Liberalism and Criminalisation

C. 39 The centrality of autonomy in the liberal's scheme of values gives him a preference for minimal state intervention in people's lives. The liberal is particularly hostile to state intervention through the mechanism of criminal prohibition and regulation, for the obvious reason that criminalisation is the state's most coercive form of social control. What could be more invasive of personal autonomy than a system of prohibitions backed by sanctions, including fines, community service and incarceration, administered and enforced by full-time professional investigators, prosecutors, judges and prison officers? As Raz observes:

'[C]oercion by criminal penalties is a global and indiscriminate invasion of autonomy. Imprisoning a person prevents him from almost all autonomous pursuits. Other forms of coercion may be less severe, but they all invade autonomy, and they all, at least in this world, do it in a fairly indiscriminate way. That is, there is no practical way of ensuring that the coercion will restrict the victims' choice of repugnant options but will not interfere with their other choices.'

C. 40 The criminal law places direct limits on individual freedom which the liberal wants to keep to a minimum. But that there *must be* limits to individual freedom is implicit in the liberal's own position, for the absolute autonomy of one is incompatible with the autonomy

---

240 Herring (2002: 144).
241 See Weait (2005b: 108–10) for some powerful criticism of this way of reading the case.
242 [1996] 2 Cr App R 241.   243 Bibbings (2001).

of any others. Brown's freedom to punch Green in the face is clearly at odds with Green's freedom to go about his business without suffering violent assault. The liberal does not value absolute liberty ('licence'), but rather the maximum individual liberty that is compatible with similar liberty for all. That is, the liberal supports the harm and offence principles, as elaborated and augmented for example by Feinberg, but she cannot countenance criminalisation on any other basis. For the liberal the harm and offence principles exhaust the moral limits of the criminal law.

C. 41 The criminalisation of harm to others has a strong intuitive appeal, as was noted above, but it is necessary to say something more at this point about the Criminalisation of offence. Liberals support the offence principle because some forms of offence can be so extreme and protracted that they unacceptably infringe the autonomy of unwilling observers and are therefore, on liberal principles, legitimate candidates for criminalisation. The liberal is, however, extremely cautious in using the criminal law to this end and will only endorse an offence, principle that is properly qualified and carefully circumscribed. The reason is clear: since just about every conceivable activity might give offence to *somebody*, *everybody's* autonomy would be severely and unacceptably curtailed if the criminal law routinely targeted offensive conduct. This point is deployed with particular force in response to the argument that conduct should be criminalised solely on the basis that people are repelled by the mere thought of it going on in private. In most cases, people who use this argument are not really claiming that they are *offended* by the conduct, but rather that it is evil and should be stopped. This is a legal moralist argument,' to which no liberal would subscribe. But suppose that someone really was offended by the mere thought of, say, consensual 'unnatural sexual intercourse' taking place behind locked doors and closed shutters, to such an extent that his obsession with the thought of it dominated and disrupted his life to a seriously detrimental extent. How would the liberal (or anybody else) deal; with this situation? We would surely say that the cause of that person's malady is his own abnormal sensitivity. We might set about helping him to deal with his illness, but we would not pass criminal laws which indiscriminately restrict the freedom of other people with normal sensibilities. The liberal, at any rate, will only countenance criminalising offence which is extreme and unavoidable, and this can never be said of activity which takes place in private.

Consent and the Harm Principle

C. 42 It follows from the fact that liberalism will only countenance interference with individual liberty in order to prevent harm or serious offence to others that it is inconsistent with liberal principles to criminalise self-injury. Self-injury may be in the actor's interests and contribute to his well-being overall, as where a man cuts: off his finger to prevent the spread of infection, but the liberal will not interfere with his determination to injure himself even where injury is not in his interests. This man chooses, perversely we may think, to set back his own interests, but he does not wrong himself. From the liberal perspective, his conduct is not within the legitimate province of the criminal law. Moreover, a person who genuinely consents to being harmed by another cannot be said to be wronged in the relevant sense either, as Feinberg explains:

'The harm principle will not justify the prohibition of consensual activities even when they are likely to harm the interests of the consenting parties; its aim is to prevent only those harms that are wrongs.'

C. 43 Feinberg poses the question whether a person can ever be wronged by conduct to which he has fully consented, and then proceeds to answer it:

'There is a principle of law which emphatically answers this question in the negative: *Volenti non fit injuria* ("To one who has consented no wrong is done"). This ancient maxim is found in the Roman Law and has a central place in all modem legal systems. Perhaps the earliest arguments for it are found in Aristotle's *Nicomachean Ethics*. One person wrongs another, according to Aristotle, when he inflicts harm on him voluntarily, and a harmful infliction is voluntary when it is not the result of compulsion, and is performed in full awareness of all the relevant circumstances including the fact that the action is contrary to the wish of the person acted upon. Therefore it is impossible for a person to consent to being treated unjustly (wronged) by another, for this would be to consent to being-treated-contrary-to-one's-wishes, which is absurd.'

The liberal position on criminalisation and the effect of consent can be derived directly from the principles contained in the last quotation:

'It follows from these premises that no one can rightly intervene to prevent a responsible adult from voluntarily doing something that will harm only himself (for such a harm is not a "wrong"), and also that one person cannot properly be prevented from doing something that will harm another when the latter has voluntarily assumed the risk of harm himself through his free and informed consent.

'[F]ully valid consent ought to be a defense to all the crimes that are defined in terms of individuals acting on other individuals, including battery, [serious injury] and murder. . . . Collaborative behaviour ought never to be criminal when the collaboration is fully voluntary on both sides and no interests other than those of the collaborative patties are directly or substantially affected. (The latter position excludes as proper crimes sodomy, bigamy, adult incest, prostitution, and mutual fighting, among other things.)'

Paternalism

C. 58 As applied to the proper scope and content of the criminal law, 'legal paternalism' may be defined thus:

Legal Paternalism: It is always a good reason in support of a prohibition that it is probably necessary to prevent harm (physical, psychological, or economic) to the actor himself.

C. 59 The legal paternalist advocates just what the liberal denies: that the state may be justified in using its most coercive powers to force a person to act or forbear to act against his will in order to promote his own self-interest and well-being.

Paternalism Ideals and Values

C. 60 Legal paternalism coheres with those philosophies which place a greater value on the attainment of some objective or end-state than on the ideal of autonomy. The defining feature of legal paternalism is that it justifies criminal prohibitions exclusively on the grounds that they promote an actor's own welfare; that is, it endorses state interference with one's freedom of choice and action *for one's own good* . . . .

Paternalism and Criminalisation

C. 61 The challenge for the legal paternalist in marking out the moral limits of the criminal law is to explain *why* the promotion of an individual's welfare should take precedence over the liberal preference for respecting his or her autonomy. The paternalist faces an up-hill battle because the ideal of liberty/autonomy is greatly treasured by, and deeply ingrained in, the (political) culture of this country. Its effects on public and private thought and action are pervasive and diffuse. Nevertheless, the perfectly familiar notion of a man being mistaken about what is in his own best interests, and consequently acting in a way that is detrimental to his own well-being, lends to the paternalist's argument a degree of plausibility. Suppose a person is about to do something—say, give away all her earthly belongings to a religious sect—which is manifestly against her interests and which she will soon come to regret. Her proposed action will greatly diminish her well-being by effectively closing off most of the valuable options and projects which she might otherwise have used her wealth to pursue. Her decision to divest herself of her property will make her destitute and thoroughly miserable. Is the state impotent in this situation? Is not the liberal's insistence that such people should be left to their fate lofty, detached or even callous? The paternalist seems to have the answer: we should legislate to save people from themselves, to prevent them from doing grave harm to their own welfare. People should therefore be prohibited from assigning all their property to religious sects, and such transactions should be declared null and void for the purposes of the civil law of property.

C. 62 The paternalist argument for criminalisation has a certain plausibility when it is applied to this kind of scenario, and over the years it has attracted some illustrious supporters.' One of these was J S Mill, who held that nobody was free to sell himself into permanent slavery, since that would be to relinquish irrevocably the very freedom that he saw as each person's inalienable birth-right. On closer inspection, however, the paternalist argument is not as attractive as it may at first: appear. When one fries to evaluate paternalistic justifications for criminal prohibitions there are three points that must be borne firmly in mind.

C. 63 First, the paternalist argues from a philosophical slippery slope and is at constant risk of taking a rumble. The fact is that many of us make life-style choices which do not promote our immediate or long-term interests. Smoking certainly falls into this category of choices: for the paternalist it should be a clear target for criminalisation. But the point goes much further. If (as seems plausible) a balanced, healthy diet and regular exercise would be in every person's interests the paternalist has a reason for criminalizing fatty foods and sedentary life-styles. Risk-taking without good reason would also be ruled out. Sky-diving, mountaineering and most contact sports would have to be criminalised. In principle, the paternalist seems to be committed to using the criminal law to turn us all into super-fit, clean-living 'spartans,' whether we like it or not. Paternalism seems less attractive when its implications are made apparent.

C. 64 Secondly, some criminal prohibitions which have intuitive appeal and which are often justified by paternalist arguments are in fact best explained in terms of the harm principle and are therefore perfectly consistent with liberalism. Professor Glanville Williams gave an example of one such prohibition when he explained the rationale behind the criminalisation of duelling. At first sight this appears to be a paternalistic measure: (presumably) men who wanted to defend their honour in the traditional way were prevented from doing so *for their own good*. We are told, however, that many people were in fact hounded into duels against their will because prevailing social expectations effectively robbed them of any say in the matter. Once a man was slighted he was bound to offer a duel and his tormentor was bound to accept the challenge, even if neither wanted to fight. The duelling statute was therefore an exemplar of the harm principle. Far from interfering with people's choices in order to promote their welfare, by 'setting men free from the tyranny of custom' the statute gave effect to their authentic desires not to be injured at the hands of another. The liberal can and does support this type of statute without appealing to paternalistic arguments.

C. 65 And thirdly, the liberal need not be as austere or uncompassionate as the paternalist paints her, because situations in which people might foolishly impair their own welfare do not present a straight choice between criminalisation and inaction. Modern-day liberals follow Mill in pointing out that the state can do a great deal to assist people to make the right choice without reasoning to the coercion of criminal sanctions. The liberal state can educate, inform, remonstrate, persuade and exhort, and provided that it stops short of out-right coercion it retains its liberal credentials.' If, however, a man should freely and voluntarily consent to placing himself in permanent servitude, the consistent liberal will let him have his head. Although the paternalist's solution is apparently attractive in these extreme circumstances, it is purchased only with the sacrifice of autonomy, and that is too high a price for the liberal to pay.

. . .

Legal Moralism

C. 70 The final group of arguments can be grouped under the rubric 'legal moralism'. It will be useful to distinguish two different versions:

(1) *Strict legal moralism:* It can be morally legitimate to prohibit conduct on the ground that it is *inherently immoral*, even though it causes neither harm nor offence to the actor or to others.

(2) *Moral conservatism:* It can be morally legitimate to prohibit conduct on the ground that it will lead to *drastic change in traditional ways of life*, even though it causes neither harm nor offence to the actor or to others.

C. 71 Legal moralism provides justifications for criminalising what Feinberg calls 'free-floating non-grievance evils'. These are evils that do not directly harm or offend anyone. They do not infringe people's rights and therefore do not give any particular individual a legitimate ground for grievance or complaint. Criminal prohibition is aimed directly at what is intrinsically evil, evils that, as it were, 'float free' of human interests. Such evils might include:

(1) violation of social or religious taboos;

(2) sexual immorality, such as fornication or adultery;

(3) moral corruption of character (one's own or that of another);

(4) evil or impure thoughts;

(5) false beliefs;

(6) wanton killing of a spider or fly;

(7) extinction of a species of animal;

(8) extinction of cultural identity through assimilation to another culture;

(9) drastic change in the moral or aesthetic climate;

(10) diminishing good manners, etiquette and social grace;

(11) increasing environmental ugliness or drabness;

(12) diminishing standards of architectural good taste.

C. 72 As we have seen, liberalism is not the view that morality can never be enforced by means of criminal prohibition, for the injunctions against causing harm or serious offence to others are surely moral rules. The distinction between liberalism and legal moralism is not that the moralist enforces morals whilst the liberal does not, but that the liberal will only use

> the criminal law to enforce that part of morality constituted by the harm principles. By contrast, the moralist will in principle use the criminal law to proscribe *any* immorality, even if it causes no harm of offence to anybody.

The Law Commission[244] in its report produced after the decision in *Brown* chose not to adopt wholeheartedly any of the three positions outlined in Roberts's paper.[245] They preferred to take what they described as a pragmatic approach. At the heart of their proposals is the concept of a 'serious disabling injury'. This is defined as:

> any injury or injuries which—
>
> (1) cause serious distress, and
>
> (2) involve the loss of a bodily member or organ or permanently bodily injury, or permanent functional impairment, or serious or permanent disfigurement, or severe and prolonged pain, or serious impairment or mental health, or prolonged unconsciousness;
>
> and in determining whether an effect is permanent, no account should be taken of the fact that it may be remediable by surgery.

The Law Commission's basic approach was that a person should not be able to provide effective consent for a 'serious disabling injury'[246] but could for a lesser injury.[247] But there are three exceptional situations where that basic approach does not apply:

(1) a person may consent to a non-fatal injury which is a seriously disabling injury if it is caused during the course of proper medical treatment or care or approved medical research;

(2) injuries (even if not seriously disabling injuries) caused in the course of a fight (unless the fight is a boxing match or a recognized sport) will be an offence;

(3) the consent of a person under 18 to injuries intentionally caused for sexual, religious, or spiritual purposes should not be valid consent.[248]

QUESTIONS

1. Why should people not be allowed to do anything they like with their bodies?

2. Should the law draw any distinction between a case where a person deliberately injures himself and where he asks someone else to injure him?

3. Can you think of any categories that should be added to the list of exceptional cases where the consent of the victim is a defence to a charge of actual bodily harm?

4. Duff may find sado-masochism dehumanizing, but how could he respond to a participant who claimed he or she found such conduct life enhancing?

---

[244] The work of the Law Commission in this area is discussed in Leng (1994); Shute (1996); Omerod and Gunn (1996).

[245] Paragraph 2.13. See Roberts (1997) for further discussion.   [246] Paragraph 4.47.

[247] If the victim does not actually consent the defendant can have a defence if he believed that the victim was consenting unless it would be obvious to a reasonable person that the victim was not.

[248] Paragraphs 10.52–10.55.

FURTHER READING

Bamforth, N. (1994), 'Sado-Masochism and Consent', *Criminal Law Review* 661.

Kell, D. (1994), 'Social Disutility and Consent', *Oxford Journal of Legal Studies* 14: 121.

Ormerod, D., and Gunn, M. (1996b), 'The Second Law Commission Consultation Paper on Consent: Consent—A Second Bash', *Criminal Law Review* 694.

Roberts, P. (1997b), 'The Philosophical Foundations of Consent in the Criminal Law', *Oxford Journal of Legal Studies* 14: 389.

Shute, S. (1996), 'Something Old, Something New, Something Borrowed . . .', *Criminal Law Review* 684.

Wilson, W. (1995), 'Consenting to Personal Injury: How Far Can You Go?', *Contemporary Issues in Law* 1: 45.

19 STALKING

Several of the recent developments in the law on offences against the person have been a response to the problem of stalking,[249] in particular the Protection from Harassment Act 1997 and the decision of the House of Lords in *Ireland*.[250] Emily Finch, in the leading work on stalking in English and Welsh law, suggests that although it is not possible to provide a definition of stalking it is possible to identify three central characteristics of stalking: 'repeated conduct that is unwanted and which provokes an adverse reaction in the recipient'.[251]

The Protection from Harassment Act 1997 in fact prohibits far more than just stalking; any course of conduct which constitutes harassment is covered.[252] In the following passage Finch seeks to ascertain the essence of harassment, as understood in the Protection from Harassment Act 1997:

E. Finch, 'Stalking the Perfect Stalking Law: An Evaluation of the Efficacy of the Protection from Harassment Act 1997' [2002] *Criminal Law Review* 703 at 705–9

The Scope of the Protection from Harassment Act 1997

The Protection from Harassment Act 1997 created two new criminal offences and a statutory tort of harassment. The basic offence of harassment is a summary offence that carries a maximum penalty of six months' imprisonment whilst the more serious offence of causing fear of violence is triable either way with a maximum penalty of five years' imprisonment. In addition to these offences, the Act also facilitates the imposition of indirect criminal liability on a defendant who contravenes either of the orders that may be made following civil or criminal proceedings. Section 3 provides for criminal proceedings to be taken for breach of

---

[249] See Finch (2001); S. Gardner (1998); C. Wells (1997); Herring (1998b). For a discussion of the psychological aspects of stalking see Mullen, Pathe, and Purcell (2000) and Davis, Frieze, and Maiuro (2000).

[250] [1998] AC 147.

[251] Finch (2001: 80). For a useful discussion of the problems in defining stalking see McAnaney, Curliss, and Abeyta-Price (1993).

[252] Wells (1997); Home Office (1996); Goode (1995). J. Harris (2000) discusses how the Act has been used in practice.

civil injunction as an alternative to the more usual contempt proceedings whilst section 5 introduces the concept of restraining orders. Restraining orders can be attached to any other penalty that is imposed upon conviction and prohibit the defendant from engaging in specific conduct that is deemed likely to amount to further harassment. These provisions indicate the combined aims of the Protection from Harassment Act, which is to punish harassment that has already occurred whilst seeking to prevent any further incidents from taking place.

The combination of civil and criminal proceedings ensures that a victim of harassment has a choice between initiating civil proceedings or invoking the protection of the criminal justice system. Although there is an extent to which the effectiveness of the Act requires a consideration of both civil and criminal provisions, the focus of this article is solely on the extent to which the criminal law provides adequate protection for stalking victims. This will involve a consideration of the relevant provisions and their interpretation by the courts to determine the extent of the protection offered by the Act. This will be followed by an evaluation of efficacy of the protection provided by the Act and a discussion of ways in which the law could be strengthened.

Criminal Harassment

As the focus of the Protection from Harassment Act 1997 was on the wider notion of harassment, this obviated the need to formulate a definition of stalking. Instead, section 1 prohibits harassment, which is defined as a course of conduct that causes harassment to another and which the defendant knows, or ought to know, would amount to harassment. This definition forms the basis of the basic offence of harassment (section 2) and the statutory tort (section 3).

It is clear that this definition of harassment contained in section 1 does reflect the essential characteristics of stalking that have been outlined above. The requirement of a course of conduct, which is defined in section 7(3) as conduct on at least two occasions, reflects the continuing and repeated nature of stalking. The second and third characteristics of stalking, that the conduct is unwanted and engenders an adverse reaction in the victim, are also reflected in the statutory definition of harassment. Thus the question of whether or not any course of conduct amounts to harassment has been made a purely subjective determination. The law does not proscribe certain forms of conduct as harassment *per se* but enables the victim to determine the parameters of acceptable interaction on an individualistic basis. During the enactment of the legislation, it was seen to be essential for the protection of stalking victims that primacy was given to the victim's interpretation of events when attributing liability. This was in recognition that conduct that appears innocuous to an objective observer may assume a more menacing aspect when the history of the relationship of the stalker and victim is taken into account. Accordingly stalking (and harassment more generally) is a context dependant crime as the conduct involved may not be unacceptable *per se* but it becomes so in the particular context in which it occurs.

Therefore it is clear that the essential characteristics of stalking are encapsulated in the definition of harassment contained in section 1. Further analysis of each of the composite elements of the definition is necessary, however, in order to explore the extent of the protection offered to stalking victims by the Act.

Course of Conduct

A 'course of conduct' is defined as conduct on at least two occasions that may include speech. Other than this, there is no statutory guidance as to the parameters of a 'course of conduct'. In particular, it should be noted that there is no requirement that the composite

incidents be unlawful in nature. One of the main impediments to the prosecution of stalkers prior to the introduction of the Protection from Harassment Act was that legal intervention was only possible if the stalker committed a substantive criminal offence. Consequently many stalkers remained immune from arrest and there is evidence to suggest that some stalkers deliberately restricted themselves to lawful conduct, deriving additional satisfaction from the inability of the police to intervene. Therefore, the inclusion of a requirement that the composite incidents be unlawful would have narrowed the scope of the Act to the extent that its utility would have been wholly neutralised. The wide definition is also. valuable to stalking victims in that it does not require that the incidents be of the same nature. Stalkers habitually engage in a diverse range of behaviour during their pursuit of the victim; it is extremely unusual for stalking to involve only a single type of behaviour thus any limitation as to the nature of the conduct would have limited the reach of the law. By requiring only two incidents as a basis for liability, the Act establishes a means of intervention at an early stage of stalking. Not only does this minimise the risk of harm to the victim that can result from protracted victimisation but it may also render the stalker more amenable to abandoning the pursuit of the victim. There is evidence to suggest that a prolonged period of stalking generates a commitment to the pursuit of the victim that is not readily abandoned regardless of the adverse consequences to the stalker hence a means of catching the stalking before such a commitment was established was a central aim of the Act.

The generality of the statutory definition creates a wide notion of a course of conduct that would appear to encompass any two incidents regardless of their nature. The courts have shown some disinclination to adopt such an all-encompassing approach with particular scepticism apparent in relation to the mathematical approach of 'incident plus incident equals harassment':

'The incidents which need to be proven in relation to harassment need not exceed two incidents but . . . the fewer the occasions and the wider they are spread the less likely it would be that a finding of harassment can reasonably be made . . . [t]he broad position must be that if one is left with only two incidents you have to see whether what happened on those two occasions can be described as a course of conduct.'

The Court of Appeal were clear that a charge of harassment based upon only a few incidents must demonstrate some nexus between the incidents before a course of conduct will be established. According to this approach, it will not suffice that there are two incidents involving the same parties unless there is something about the incidents that indicates a degree of connectivity. As Ormerod asserts, one would not describe two visits to a hospital by the same person as a 'course of treatment' in the absence of some other connecting feature, *i.e.* that both visits involved treatment for the same ailment.

Despite the restriction in the scope of the offence of harassment, the requirement of a nexus between the composite elements appears an entirely sensible approach to the definition of a course of conduct. The difficulty lies in identifying the nature of the connecting factor. Clearly, the identity of the parties alone cannot suffice to establish a connection and, in any case, the courts have held that two incidents directed at different victims may constitute a course of conduct. Proximity in the nature and timing of the incidents may be indicative of a nexus but, given the deliberately wide approach of the Act with regard to these factors, they should not be taken as determinative. Logic dictates that there must be some nexus between the incidents but the nature of that nexus is somewhat elusive.

Some insight may be provided by an examination of the approach taken in stalking legislation in the United States where an association between the incidents comprising a course of conduct is required. For example, section 646.9(e) of the Californian Penal Code defines a

course of conduct as 'a pattern of conduct composed of a series of acts over a period of time, however short, evidencing a continuity of purpose'. It is clear from this definition that the nexus between the incidents is provided by the motivation of the stalker in engaging in the conduct hence the elusive factor would appear to be continuity of purpose. The notion that the purpose underlying the conduct may provide the requisite nexus has received some support in English law. For example, in *Baron v. Crown Prosecution Service*, it was held that the defendant's ulterior purpose in sending two letters four months' apart would provide the necessary link between what would otherwise be regarded as two separate incidents. An alternative method of establishing a nexus between what is often wholly disparate conduct can be seen in Australia. State legislation defines stalking by reference to a list of *prima facie* lawful conduct when it is undertaken for a particular prohibited purpose, such as an intention to intimidate or intention to cause apprehension or fear of serious harm. The possibility of incorporating an intention requirement into the Protection from Harassment Act 1997 is outlined in the final section of this article.

This approach to defining a 'course of conduct' represents some limitation to the scope of the Act but it remains a far-reaching definition that encompasses a wide range of stalking cases. As such, it can be regarded as a pragmatic approach that acknowledges that stalking can take many diverse forms. Whilst this clearly enhances the protection available for victims of stalking, it also creates a somewhat low threshold of criminal liability. However, establishing a course of conduct is not the only element of the *actus reus* of the offence; the course of conduct must also amount to harassment of another.

Harassment of Another

In *DPP v. Ramsdale*, the defendant's conviction for harassment was quashed despite evidence that he was responsible for a series of incidents spanning two years. This was due to the finding of the court that only one of these incidents caused the victim to feel harassed. This highlights the fact that a course of conduct, viewed in isolation, is a neutral requirement that implies neither moral or legal culpability. Just as intercourse does not amount to rape unless it is accompanied by an absence of consent, a course of conduct will not engender criminal liability unless it causes the recipient of the conduct to feel harassed.

Section 7(2) states that harassment includes causing fear or distress to the victim. As has already been outlined, whether a course of conduct amounts to harassment is a wholly subjective matter based upon the reaction of the victim. This subjective focus acknowledges that individuals may react in different ways to similar events hence conduct that causes alarm and distress to one person may leave another unperturbed. In terms of offering protection to stalking victims, this approach has much to commend it. The impact of the conduct upon the victim is the decisive factor rather than basing liability on the purpose of the stalker or an objective evaluation of the situation. This enables each individual to determine what conduct they find acceptable and from whom, thus acknowledging the context-dependent nature of stalking. However, this subjective focus does nothing to limit the breadth of the offence caused by the generality of the definition of a 'course of conduct'. Taken in conjunction, these two elements give rise to the potential to impose liability based upon two incidents that nobody other than the victim would view as harassment.

QUESTIONS

1. Do you think it would be better to define harassment in terms of what the defendant does or in terms of the effect of the defendant's conduct on the victim?

2. How can the law draw the line between acceptable standards of 'courtship' and harassment or stalking?

FURTHER READING

Budd, T., and Mattinson, J. (2000), *The Extent and Nature of Stalking: Findings from the 1998 British Crime Survey* (London: HMSO).

Harris, J. (2000), *Evaluation of the Use and Effectiveness of the Protection from Harassment Act 1997* (London: HMSO).

McAnaney, K., Curliss, L., and Abeyta-Price, C. (1993), 'From Imprudence to Crime: Anti-Stalking Laws', *Notre Dame Law Review* 68: 819 (discussing the American responses to stalking).

Walby, J., and Allen, H. (2004), *Assault and Stalking: Findings from the British Crime Survey*, Home Office Research Study 276, (London: Home Office).

20 TRANSMITTING DISEASE AND THE CRIMINAL LAW

As we have seen in Part I, the courts have dealing with cases where a defendant has infected his partner in the course of sexual relations. There has also been much debate over what the law should be.[253] On the one hand there are those who suggest a person who recklessly or intentionally causes another harm should be convicted of a criminal offence, and that should be so even if the means used is disease.[254] However, others argue that the criminalization of infection might work contrary to public health strategies. If a person believes he may be suffering from a sexually transmitted disease we wish him to seek treatment, and not be discouraged from doing so for fear of a criminal prosecution.[255] Nor do we want people to be deterred from taking tests to see if they have a sexually transmitted disease, for fear of its potential impact on their sex life. In the context of HIV there are specific fears that the offence may operate as (or be perceived as) an attack on the gay community.[256]

In the following passage Matthew Weait challenges the way in which the courts have examined this issue. He suggests that sexual activity can be regarded as a joint activity, with each participant being responsible for the potential consequences:

M. Weait, 'Knowledge, Autonomy and Consent: *R v Konzani'* [2005] *Criminal Law Review* 763, 768–71

Given the importance of the principles at stake, the judgment of the Court of Appeal in *Konzani* is disappointing in its exploration of the justifications for the conclusion reached. Such principled justification as exists is to be found in one critical passage, referred to above, where it explains that a complainant's 'personal autonomy is not enhanced if [the defendant]

---

[253] Strickland (2001a) and (2001b).

[254] See the useful discussion in the Canadian Supreme Court case of *Currier* [1998] SCR 371.

[255] Simester and Sullivan (2003: 399). For a detailed discussion of these issues see Final Report of the Australian Legal Working Party of the Intergovernmental Committee on AIDS discussed in S. Bronitt (1992).

[256] Ormerod and Gunn (1996) and Home Office (1998c: para. 3.16).

is exculpated when he recklessly transmits the HIV virus to her through consensual sexual intercourse'. What might this mean, and what merit does it have as a justification for imposing criminal liability via the denial of a defence based on honest belief in consent?

Autonomy means, literally, self-government. In the context of law generally, and in the context of the law as it relates to sexual offences and offences against the person in particular, it suggests the right of a person to be free from unwarranted and unwanted physical interference. Thus the essence of rape law, in which the absence of consent is definitional of the actus reus, is that no legal wrong is done if consent exists, because the partner with whom a person has sexual intercourse is exercising his or her autonomy rather than having it infringed or violated; and where consent operates as a defence to a charge of assault, or causing bodily harm, it reflects the law's recognition that there exists a sphere (albeit one circumscribed by public policy considerations) in which people should be entitled to freedom from liability because to hold otherwise would result in a significant and unjustified diminution of essential human freedoms. It is of critical importance to recognise the distinction. In the former (rape) example the reason why the law does not criminalise the putative defendant is that there is no legally recognised harm committed. However in the latter (assault) example the law protects a putative defendant from criminal liability not on the basis that no recognisable harm has been caused, but because of the context in which it has taken place. It follows that in such circumstances the law is not, at least prima facie, concerned with protecting, or indeed 'enhancing' the autonomy of the person harmed, but rather with protecting the person who harms from the imposition of unjustified liability. Put simply, it is his autonomy (in the sense of his right to be free from unwarranted interference and condemnation by the state) that the law is concerned to protect.

If the principles underpinning this argument are sound then any departure from them demands strong and careful justification. With respect, the Court of Appeal in *Konzani* not only departs from them but fails to provide any such justification. The court indicates that a complainant's autonomy is not enhanced by exculpating a person who recklessly harms her by transmitting HIV (and, by implication, that it is enhanced by denying such a defendant the right to assert an honest belief in her consent to the risk of such harm). In so doing it starts from the premise that, in the context of non-fatal offences against the person at least, it is the autonomy of the person harmed that it is the law's function to protect. However, if this were so then those who recklessly harm people should be denied the defence of consent on the basis of honest belief or otherwise, irrespective of the context in which such harm occurs; and yet case law demonstrates that this is not the case. Without explicitly acknowledging this difficulty, the court identifies the failure of a person to disclose his known HIV positive status, and the deception that is thereby practised on a partner to whom he transmits HIV, as the basis for making the distinction. The nondiscloser may not assert an honest belief in his partner's consent, because the fact of non-disclosure renders her 'consent' uninformed, legally nugatory, and therefore not one on which he is, or should be, entitled to rely. This line of reasoning is emphasised in the court's second reference to the autonomy of a complainant, when it states that this is:

'not normally protected by allowing a defendant who knows that he is suffering from the HIV virus which he deliberately conceals, to assert an honest belief in his partner's informed consent to the risk of the transmission of the HIV virus. Silence in these circumstances is incongruous with honesty, or with a genuine belief that there is an informed consent. Accordingly, in such circumstances the issue either of informed consent, or honest belief in it will only rarely arise: in reality, in most cases, the contention would be wholly artificial.'

What is to be made of the court's deployment of autonomy in this way? While it no doubt has a certain intuitive appeal, it is submitted that the consequences of this line of reasoning are such that it should be rejected.

The court recognised in *Dica* that people should be entitled in principle to consent to the risks associated with sexual intercourse because to deny them this right (and the correlative defence such a right provides to those who expose them to such risks) would amount to an infringement of autonomy that only Parliament should sanction. In *Konzani*, however, the court has made clear that only an informed consent, grounded in knowledge gained from direct or indirect disclosure of a partner's HIV positive status, amounts to consent for these purposes. In effect, therefore, the cumulative ratio of the two cases is not that a person should be entitled to consent to the risks associated with sexual intercourse, but that she should be entitled to consent to such risks as have been directly or indirectly disclosed to her. It is only in the latter context that a defendant's claim of honest belief in consent can, and should, be legally recognised. If this is indeed the ratio, a number of consequences follow.

First, in emphasising that it is only in the most exceptional of cases that nondisclosure to a sexual partner by an HIV positive person will be 'congruent' with an honest belief, the court has, in effect, imposed a standard of reasonable belief in cases where there has been an absence of disclosure. This may be consistent with legislative developments in the law of rape, but if such is the trajectory the law should follow then it is submitted that this should be for Parliament to decide, not—with respect—the Court of Appeal. Secondly, the court has also, in effect, imposed a positive duty of disclosure on people who know they are HIV positive (and who wish to avoid potential criminal liability) before they have sex which carries the risk of transmission. Since there is no reason in principle why this positive duty should be limited to HIV (which is, for those able to access treatment at least, a manageable if life-limiting condition), it should be assumed that it applies to all those who are aware that they are suffering from a serious STI. Given that chlamydia may, if untreated in a woman, lead to infertility, that hepatitis B can lead to severe liver damage, and that syphilis—if untreated—can result in significant mental and physical impairment, it is presumably safer to assume that this positive duty now applies to all those who have been diagnosed with these, and other potentially serious, diseases who wish to avoid the possibility of prosecution and imprisonment. Thirdly, in the absence of any indication to the contrary by the court, disclosure as a precautionary principle ought presumably to be adopted by those that are infected with serious or potentially serious contagious diseases. A passenger with SARS or 'flu' may very well be aware that on a transatlantic 747 flight there could be elderly people or others with impaired immune systems (including people living with HIV). Such people's autonomy is certainly not 'enhanced' if the passenger is able to assert that he honestly believed they would consent to being infected by a virus that results in their developing pneumonia; nor is it 'normally protected', where, knowing that he is suffering from a condition that can cause such an effect, he conceals this information.

These consequences of the court's reasoning may be thought more or less fanciful; but the point is, surely, that in using the language of autonomy so loosely, and in failing to specify precisely what the justification for, and scope of, the decision in *Konzani* is, the Court of Appeal has delivered a judgment that fails abjectly to deal with the core issues which its subject matter raises.

Concluding remarks: public health and criminal law

It is a perfectly legitimate question to ask whether, and if so in what circumstances, a person should be held criminally liable for the transmission of serious disease. The problem is that our answer to that question will inevitably depend on the assumptions we make about the role of the criminal law and the values and principles that inform it. If we start, as is common-place, within the liberal legal tradition that emphasises autonomy, choice, individual responsibility and rationality, which treats causation as unidirectional and a matter of 'com-mon sense', and which resorts to 'public policy' when confronted with hard cases, it is no wonder that the transmission of HIV by people who fail to disclose their HIV positive status to partners who are subsequently infected is constructed as a wrong that should be punished. It is also inevitable, given that criminal trials are concerned only with the finding of facts in, and the application of existing law to, the individual case, and that criminal appeals deal only with the discrete point(s) of law at issue, that the broader context of transmission is occluded and the wider social and epidemiological implications of criminalisation ignored.

Some concrete examples should serve to illustrate why the current approach of the law to the transmission of HIV is a problem. As a result of *Dica* and *Konzani* a person who, knowing his own HIV positive status, recklessly transmits HIV to a sexual partner, commits a criminal offence. He may only escape liability where the person to whom he transmits the virus gave an informed consent to the risk of transmission. The Court of Appeal in *Konzani* has indicated that such consent will, essentially, arise only where there has been prior disclosure. A number of potentially adverse consequences for public health may follow from this. First, by treating recklessness in this context simply as conscious unjustifiable risk-taking, but without clarifying whether the appropriate use of condoms negates recklessness as a matter of law, the Court of Appeal has provided no clear guidance as to whether their use will preclude the possibility of a conviction. It would be useful if such clarification could be provided so that people living with HIV understand the scope of any duty they might have. Secondly, the requirement that a person knows his HIV positive status before he can be treated as reckless may have the effect of dissuading some people from having an HIV test and so accessing available medical care, advice and treatment. While it is to be welcomed that, as a matter of general principle, no liability should be incurred by people who are in fact unaware that they may transmit HIV to their partner(s), and that the alternative (of imposing liability on those who are aware (or ought to be aware) that they may be HIV positive) would cast the net of liability too widely, the courts should recognise, and deal explicitly with, the potential public health consequences of applying the mens rea requirement in this way. Third, by in effect imposing a duty to disclose known HIV status prior to sex which carries the risk of transmission (which, even if prophylaxis is used, remains a possibility) the courts appear to be working on the assumption, implicitly at least, that those who are HIV positive and know this will in fact (if they behave in the rational manner upon which criminal law and the justification for punishment are premised) disclose their status to partners in order to avoid criminal liability. Moreover, as a direct result of this people may assume that sexual partners who do not disclose their HIV positive status are in fact HIV negative—why would they risk a criminal conviction for a serious offence by not doing so? Finally, where an HIV positive person has not disclosed prior to sex, and where transmission may have occurred, that person may be dissuaded from informing his partner of the possibility thereby preventing that partner from accessing post-exposure prophylaxis (i.e. intensive drug treatment that may prevent the virus taking hold) because to do so would in effect amount to confessing the commission of a serious criminal offence.

These consequences demonstrate that if we start from a set of a priori assumptions about the function(s) of criminal law in this context, and treat incidents of HIV transmission simply as an opportunity to apply the principles which have traditionally informed the law relating to non-fatal offences against the person, we risk doing more harm than good. UNAIDS, and many other national and international organisations have—since the early years of the

HIV/AIDS pandemic—emphasised the importance of dealing with the spread of HIV as first and foremost a public health issue in which we are all implicated, and for which we are all ultimately responsible. If legislators, courts, prosecutors and police, resisted the immediate temptation to treat alleged cases of HIV transmission as individualised, momentary and (potentially) blameworthy incidents; if they were willing to acknowledge and treat seriously the mass of sound empirical research which explains the reasons why people fail to disclose their HIV positive status to significant others; and if they were to recognise that the use of the criminal law may serve not only to perpetuate people's anxieties about HIV, but also, critically, to have a negative public health impact, this would—I believe—better serve the public interest in the longer term.

QUESTIONS

1. Do you agree with Weait's suggestion that a person infected with HIV has no cause of complaint under the criminal law against his or her infector? Does Weait's argument work only where the sexual encounter is a 'casual' one or does it also apply in a relationship where the parties have promised to be monogamous? Would you treat a case where a husband failed to disclose to his wife that he had become HIV positive after an adulterous affair differently from a case where a female sex worker failed to disclose the fact that she was HIV positive to her clients? (Weait (2005b)).

2. Should those who support criminal sanctions against those who recklessly transmit HIV also support liability for those who go out in public even if they are suffering from a cold, and may therefore infect others?

3. Spencer (2004) writes 'To infect an unsuspecting person with a grave disease you know you have, or may have, by behaviour that you know involves a risk of transmission, and that you know you could easily modify to reduce or eliminate the risk, is to harm another in [a] way that is both needless and callous. For that reason, criminal liability is justified unless there are strong countervailing reasons. In my view there are not.' Do you agree?

4. Harris and Holm (1995) argue that society is entitled to impose obligations upon those who are infectious, but only if society offers adequate care, support, and treatment for them. Does the inadequacy of society's response to AIDS mean that it loses its entitlement to impose obligations upon those who are HIV positive?

FURTHER READING

Harris, J., and Holm, S. (1995), 'Is there a moral obligation not to infect others?', *British Medical Journal* 311: 1215.

Strickland, C. (2001a), *HIV/AIDS and the Criminal Law in England and Wales: A Comparative Analysis* (London: Cavendish).

—— (2001b), 'Why Parliament should Create HIV Specific Offences', *Web Journal of Current Legal Issues.*

Weait, M. (2001), 'Taking the Blame: Criminal Law, Social Responsibility and the Sexual Transmission of HIV', *Journal of Social Welfare and Family Law* 23: 441.

—— (2005a), 'Harm, Consent and the Limits of Privacy', *Feminist Legal Studies* 13.97.

7

SEXUAL OFFENCES

PART I: THE LAW ON SEXUAL OFFENCES

This chapter will primarily focus on the offences of rape and sexual assault. Other sexual offences will be discussed in outline. This topic can be one of the most difficult to study. Anyone who has experienced the horror of a sexual assault will find the judicial and academic writings unbearably dry. How can such a horrific crime be discussed in such clinical terms? Yet the seriousness of the offences requires them to be subject to careful, but sensitive, analysis.

The law on sexual offences has been transformed by the Sexual Offences Act 2003.[1] That Act changed the previous law set out in the Sexual Offences Act 1956, which was described by the Government as 'archaic, incoherent and discriminatory'.[2] The case law under the 1956 Act must be read in the light of the new legislation, but it will be relied upon by the courts in interpreting some of the terms used by the new legislation.

1 RAPE

Rape is defined in section 1 of the Sexual Offences Act 2003 thus:

> (1) A person (A) commits an offence if—
>
>   (a) he intentionally penetrates the vagina, anus or mouth of another person (B) with his penis,
>
>   (b) B does not consent to the penetration, and
>
>   (c) A does not reasonably believe that B consents.
>
> (2) Whether a belief is reasonable is to be determined having regard to all the circumstances, including any steps A has taken to ascertain whether B consents.[3]

---

[1] For the background to the Act see Home Office (2002b), the White Paper which preceded the Act; Law Commission (2000), the advice of the Law Commission on consent in sexual offences; and Home Office (2000), the Home Office's consultation paper.

[2] Home Office (2002b: 1).

[3] The offence carries a maximum sentence of life.

DEFINITION

Actus reus: the defendant penetrated the vagina, anus, or mouth of the victim with his penis and the victim did not consent to the penetration.

Mens rea:

1. the defendant intended to penetrate the vagina, anus, or mouth of the victim with his penis AND

2. the defendant did not reasonably believe that the victim consented to the penetration.

1.1 WHO CAN COMMIT RAPE?

Can a woman commit rape?

Only a man can commit rape. This is because the offence requires penetration with a penis.[4] If a woman forces a man to engage in sexual intercourse against his will this can amount to a sexual assault[5] or the offence of causing another person to perform a sexual act without consent,[6] but will not be rape. It is possible for a woman to be an accessory to the crime of rape (i.e. to aid, abet, counsel, or procure rape).[7]

Can a husband rape a wife?

A husband can be convicted of raping his wife. This was clear only after the 1994 amendments to the Sexual Offences Act 1956, which put into statutory effect the decision of the House of Lords in *R v R*.[8] The House of Lords rejected the outdated view that on marriage a wife gave irrevocable consent to sexual relations at any time during the marriage and therefore marital intercourse could not be unlawful.[9] The shocking fact that marital rape could not be prosecuted until 1991 is seen by many to be indicative of the slowness of the law to intervene to protect women from sexual assault. The House of Lords decision was confirmed by the European Court of Human Rights in *CR v UK*[10] which rejected an argument that in effect the decision constituted retrospective law-making.[11] In fact the European Court went on to hold that the abandonment of the rule was in conformity with the fundamental objectives of the Convention.[12] The Sexual Offences Act 2003 makes no change to the law and does not provide husbands charged with raping their wives with an automatic defence. Of course, the fact that the parties were married will be relevant as a matter of evidence. For example, a husband may more easily persuade the jury that he believed that his wife was consenting to sexual intercourse than if the victim were a stranger.[13]

---

[4] This includes a surgically created penis (Sexual Offences Act 2003, s. 79(3)).

[5] Sexual Offences Act 2003, s. 3. If she penetrates his anus she can be guilty of assault by penetration (Sexual Offences Act 2003, s. 2).

[6] Sexual Offences Act 2003, s. 4.

[7] In *Cogan and Leak* [1976] QB 217 (CA) it had been suggested a woman can be guilty of rape as the principal if she uses an innocent agent to have sexual intercourse with a woman (see p. 889 for an explanation of the doctrine of innocent agency). However, the case has been heavily criticized and subsequent cases have suggested that it is better in such cases to charge the woman with procuring rape: *DPP v R and B* [1997] 1 Cr App R 36 (CA).

[8] [1991] 4 All ER 481 (HL).   [9] Hale, 1 PC 29.   [10] [1996] 1 FLR 434 (ECtHR).

[11] And therefore infringed Art. 7 of the European Convention on Human Rights.

[12] Indeed the exemption could be said to have infringed the rights of wives under Art. 3 of the Convention.

[13] See Rumney (1999) and Warner (2000) for a discussion of differences in sentencing practice in cases of 'marital rape'.

At what age can a man commit rape?

There used to be a rule under common law that a boy under 14 was incapable of committing sexual intercourse. This was abolished for acts after 20 September 1993 by the Sexual Offences Act 2003, section 1. Of course, to be guilty of rape a boy must be above the age of criminal responsibility (i.e. over the age of 10).

1.2 WHO CAN BE THE VICTIM OF RAPE?

A man or woman can be the victim of rape because anal or oral rape is included within section 1. Section 79(3) of the Sexual Offences Act 2003 makes it clear that a surgically constructed vagina is included within the definition of a vagina. This means that a 'male to female' transsexual who has undergone 'gender reassignment surgery' can be vaginally raped.[14]

1.3 WHAT IS PENETRATION?

To amount to rape the only act that is sufficient is penetration of the anus, vagina,[15] or mouth by the defendant's penis. Penetration with objects or other parts of the body apart from the penis against the victim's consent will not amount to rape, although it would amount to the offence of assault by penetration contrary to section 2 of the 2003 Act.

The definition of rape in the 2003 Act requires only penetration.[16] This makes it clear that there can be rape even if there is no ejaculation. If the defendant tries to penetrate but fails to do so this may amount to attempted rape.[17]

One important issue is whether the *actus reus* of rape is complete once penetration takes place or whether it continues as long as there is penetration. The issue is important in cases where the victim consents to the initial penetration, but then asks the man to withdraw, but he refuses.[18] The Sexual Offences Act 2003 provides a clear answer in section 79(2): 'Penetration is a continuing act from entry to withdrawal.'[19] This means that if the victim withdraws his or her consent after the initial penetration, but the defendant does not withdraw within a reasonable length of time, this can be rape. What exactly is a reasonable time may cause difficulties in some cases and will be left to the 'common sense' of the jury.

1.4 WHAT IS CONSENT?

It is important to appreciate that questions over the victim's consent arise in two contexts in relation to rape. First, as a matter of the *actus reus* it must be shown that the victim did not consent to the penetration. Secondly, as a matter of the *mens rea* it must be shown that the defendant did not reasonably believe that the victim consented. These two questions must be dealt with separately. First we will be looking at the *actus reus* issues: did the victim consent?

---

[14] The technical name for what is colloquially (if perhaps inaccurately) known as a 'sex change operation'.

[15] 'Vagina includes vulva': Sexual Offences Act 2003, s. 79(9).

[16] What exactly will amount to penetration is an issue which is likely to be left to the jury, giving penetration its normal meaning.

[17] See Ch. 14.   [18] See e.g. the facts in *Kaitamaki* [1985] AC 147 (PC).

[19] This is similar to the law prior to the 2003 Act: *Cooper and Schaub* [1994] Crim LR 531 (CA).

EXAMINATION TIP

When answering problem questions in relation to rape it is very easy to merge together the questions: (1) did the victim consent? and (2) did the defendant think the victim was consenting? These must be treated as two separate questions: the first is a matter of the *actus reus* and the second is to do with the *mens rea* of rape.

The 2003 Act defines consent in the following way in section 74:

> . . . a person consents if he agrees by choice, and has the freedom and capacity to make that choice.

This leaves unanswered a lot of questions about the meaning of consent and we will now address these. After the 2003 Act the law is a little complicated because there are circumstances under which consent is presumed to be lacking. Where the presumption does not apply or when deciding whether the presumption has been rebutted the courts will turn back to the basic meaning of consent.

So, in deciding whether or not the victim has consented the following approach is recommended:

EXAMINATION TIP

To decide whether the victim consented ask:

1. Is this a case in which the victim is conclusively presumed to have not consented?

   If YES: The Victim did not consent.

   If NO: Consider question 2.

2. Is this a case in which there is an evidential presumption that the victim did not consent?

   If YES: Then you must consider whether or not the presumption is rebutted. If it is: consider question 3. If it is not: The Victim did not consent.

   If NO: Consider question 3.

3. Did the victim consent under the basic meaning of consent is section 74?

   If YES: The victim did consent

   If NO: The Victim did not consent.

Conclusive presumptions: deception as to the nature or purpose of the act

As suggested by the box above, the place to start is to consider whether this is a case where the conclusive presumptions operate. These are found in section 76:

> **76. Conclusive presumptions about consent**
>
> (1) If in proceedings for an offence to which this section applies it is proved that the defendant did the relevant act and that any of the circumstances specified in subsection (2) existed, it is to be conclusively presumed—

> (a) that the complainant did not consent to the relevant act, and
>
> (b) that the defendant did not believe that the complainant consented to the relevant act.
>
> (2) The circumstances are that—
>
>   (a) the defendant intentionally deceived the complainant as to the nature or purpose of the relevant act;
>
>   (b) the defendant intentionally induced the complainant to consent to the relevant act by impersonating a person known personally to the complainant.

It should be noted that these are conclusive presumptions. So, for example, once it is shown that the defendant intentionally deceived the complainant as to the nature of the act he will be guilty of rape. There is no way that he can rebut the presumption. Note also that when the presumption applies both the *mens rea* and *actus reus* of rape are proved.

We will first consider further the circumstances in which it will be presumed that a victim who is mistaken as to the nature of the act does not consent under section 76(2)(a). The following need to be shown:

(1) *There must be a deception.* If the victim is mistaken as to the nature or purpose of the act but not because of any deception of the defendant's then the statutory presumption does not apply. However, the common law does not require the victim's mistake to be as a result of the defendant's action for the mistake to negate consent. Most notably this means if a friend of the defendant deceived the victim as to the nature of the act, the presumption would not apply. However, no doubt the jury would find there was not consent in its general meaning.

(2) *There must be a deception as to the nature or purpose of the act.* If the victim is mistaken as to the nature of the act there is no true consent. Perhaps the best known example is that in *Williams*[20] in which a singing teacher persuaded his pupil (aged 16) to agree to let him do something that would improve her breathing. She was unaware that in fact he was engaging in sexual intercourse with her. He was convicted of rape. The act she consented to (the assistance in breathing technique) was different in nature from the act the defendant did. The case would have been less straightforward if the victim had understood that they were to have sexual intercourse, but the defendant had persuaded the victim that having sexual intercourse would make her sing better.[21] Although she would then not have been mistaken as to the nature of the act she may have been deceived as to the purpose of the act.[22]

(3) *The deception must be intentional.* The statutory presumption of no consent applies only if the defendant's deception was intentional.

In the following case the Court of Appeal held that the victim was not mistaken as to the nature of the act and so there was no rape. It is likely that a similar result would be reached under the new definition of rape.

---

[20] [1923] 1 KB 340. There have also been cases where women have been persuaded to agree to acts said to be 'medical treatment', but which were in fact sexual intercourse (see e.g. *Case* (1850) 4 Cox 220).

[21] Simester and Sullivan (2003: 412).

[22] Presuming that Williams's purposes were sexual.

R v Linekar
[1995] 3 All ER 69 (CA)[23]

The appellant agreed to have sexual intercourse with a prostitute for the sum of £25. The appellant did not have £25 on him at the time and after intercourse had taken place he made off without paying. The prostitute claimed that she had been raped and the appellant was arrested and charged with rape. The judge directed the jury that if they found either that the appellant had forced himself upon the complainant or tricked her inasmuch as he obtained her consent to intercourse by fraud, namely by falsely pretending that he intended to pay, he was guilty of rape but if the jury concluded that he had originally intended to pay but, having had intercourse, he had then changed his mind, he should be acquitted. The jury found the appellant guilty, and when asked the basis for the verdict the foreman replied that the complainant's consent had been vitiated by fraud because the appellant had at no stage intended to pay. The appellant appealed.

Mr Justice Morland, delivered the following judgment of the court

An essential ingredient of the offence of rape is the proof that the woman did not consent to the actual act of sexual intercourse with the particular man who penetrated her. If the Crown prove that she did not consent to sexual intercourse, rape is proved. That ingredient is proved in the so-called 'medical cases'. The victim did not agree in those cases to sexual intercourse. In *R v Flattery* (1877) 2 QBD 410 she agreed to a surgical procedure which she hoped would cure her fits. In *R v Williams* [1923] 1 KB 340 she agreed to a physical manipulation which would provide her with extra air supply to improve her singing.

In our judgment, it is the non-consent to sexual intercourse rather than the fraud of the doctor or choirmaster that makes the offence rape. Similarly, that ingredient is not proved in the husband impersonation cases because the victim did not consent to sexual intercourse with the particular man who penetrated her. We venture to suggest that at common law it is immaterial whether the penetrator is impersonating a husband, a cohabitee or a lover, as is supported by the Criminal Law Revision Committee in the paragraph that we have quoted.

. . .

In 1888 was decided *R v Clarence* 22 QBD 23, [1886–90] All ER Rep 133. This was the well-known case of the husband who knew that he was suffering from gonorrhoea and his wife did not, and he quite deliberately had sexual intercourse with her with the result that the disease was communicated to her. He was convicted of an indictment charging him with inflicting grievous bodily harm under s 20, and of an assault occasioning actual bodily harm under s 47 of the Offences Against the Person Act 1861. The court of 13 judges, by a majority of nine to four, decided that Clarence was not guilty under either section.

The importance of *Clarence*, in our judgment, is that it exposes the fallacy of the submission that there can be rape by fraud or false pretences. Wills J says (22 QBD 23 at 27):

'That consent obtained by fraud is no consent at all is not true as a general proposition either in fact or in law. If a man meets a woman in the street and knowingly gives her bad money in order to procure her consent to intercourse with him, he obtains her consent by fraud, but it would be childish to say that she did not consent. In respect of a contract, fraud does not destroy the consent. It only makes it revocable.'

[23] [1995] 2 WLR 237, [1995] 2 Cr App R 49, [1995] 2 WLR 237, [1995] Crim LR 320.

Stephen J says (22 QBD 23 at 43–44):

'It seems to me that the proposition that fraud vitiates consent in criminal matters is not true if taken to apply in the fullest sense of the word, and without qualification. . . . Many seductions would be rapes, and so might acts of prostitution procured by fraud, as for instance by promises not intended to be fulfilled. [We interpose to say that that is the situation in this particular appeal.] These illustrations appear to show clearly that the maxim that fraud vitiates consent is too general to be applied to these matters as if it were absolutely true. . . . The only cases in which fraud indisputably vitiates consent in these matters are cases of fraud as to the nature of the act done. As to fraud as to the identity of the person by whom it is done, the law is not quite clear. In *Reg. v. Flattery* ((1877) 2 QBD 410), in which consent was obtained by representing the act as a surgical operation, the prisoner was held to be guilty of rape. In the case where consent was obtained by the personation of a husband, there was before the passing of the Criminal Law Amendment Act of 1885 a conflict of authority. The last decision in England, *Reg. v. Barrow* ((1868) LR 1 CCR 158), decided that the act was not rape, and *Reg. v. Dee* ((1884) 15 Cox CC 579), decided in Ireland in 1884, decided that it was. The Criminal Law Amendment Act of 1885 "declared and enacted" that thenceforth it should be deemed to be rape, thus favouring the view taken in *Reg. v. Dee* . . . they justify the observation that the only sorts of fraud which so far destroy the effect of a woman's consent as to convert a connection consented to in fact into a rape are frauds as to the nature of the act itself, or as to the identity of the person who does the act. There is abundant authority to show that such frauds as these vitiate consent both in the case of rape and in the case of indecent assault. I should myself prefer to say that consent in such cases does not exist at all, because the act consented to is not the act done.'

With that sentence, this court respectfully agrees.

Stephen J went on to say (22 QBD 23 at 44):

'Consent to a surgical operation or examination is not a consent to sexual connection or indecent behaviour. Consent to connection with a husband is not consent to adultery. I do not think that the maxim that fraud vitiates consent can be carried further than this in criminal matters. It is commonly applied to cases of contract, because in all cases of contract the evidence of a consent not procured by force or fraud is essential, but even in these cases care in the application of the maxim is required, because in some instances suppression of the truth operates as fraud, whereas in others at least a suggestion of falsehood is required. The act of intercourse between a man and a woman cannot in any case be regarded as the performance of a contract. . . . The woman's consent here was as full and conscious as consent could be. It was not obtained by any fraud either as to the nature of the act or as to the identity of the agent.'

Those two last sentences, in our judgment, apply clearly to the facts of this case.

Moving to more recent times, there is the highly persuasive authority of *Papadimitropoulos v R* (1957) 98 CLR 249, a decision of the High Court of Australia. The court was presided over by Dixon CJ, and consisted of McTiernan, Webb, Kitto and Taylor JJ. The headnote reads:

'Rape is carnal knowledge of a woman without her consent. Carnal knowledge is the physical act of penetration. It is the consent to such physical act of penetration which is in question upon an indictment for rape. Such a consent demands a perception as to what is about to take place, as to the identity of the man and the character of what he is doing. Once the consent is comprehending and actual, the inducing causes cannot destroy its reality and leave the man guilty of rape. Where a woman consented to sexual intercourse under the belief, fraudulently induced by the man, that she was married to him, Held, that the man was not guilty of rape.'

The facts of that case were that the complainant believed that she had gone through a marriage with the appellant.

In its judgment the court said (at 260–261):

'It must be noted that in considering whether an apparent consent is unreal it is the mistake or misapprehension that makes it so. It is not the fraud producing the mistake which is material so much as the mistake itself. But if the mistake or misapprehension is not produced by the fraud of the man, there is logically room for the possibility that he was unaware of the woman's mistake so that a question of his mens rea may arise. So in *R. v. Lambert* ((1919) VLR 205 at 213) Cussen J. says:—"It is plain that, though in these cases the question of consent or non-consent is primarily referable to the mind of the woman, if she has really a mind, yet the mind of the man is also affected by the facts which indicate want of consent or possible want of capacity to consent". For that reason it is easy to understand why the stress has been on the fraud. But that stress tends to distract the attention from the essential inquiry, namely, whether the consent is no consent because it is not directed to the nature and character of the act. The identity of the man and the character of the physical act that is done or proposed seem now clearly to be regarded as forming part of the nature and character of the act to which the woman's consent is directed. That accords with the principles governing mistake vitiating apparent manifestations of will in other chapters of the law. In the present case the decision of the majority of the Full Court extends this conception beyond the identity of the physical act and the immediate conditions affecting its nature to an antecedent inducing cause—the existence of a valid marriage. In the history of bigamy that has never been done. The most heartless bigamist has not been considered guilty of rape. Mock marriages are no new thing. Before the Hardwicke Marriage Act it was a fraud easily devised and readily carried out. But there is no reported instance of an indictment for rape based on the fraudulent character of the ceremony. No indictment of rape was founded on such a fraud. Rape, as a capital felony, was defined with exactness, and although there has been some extension over the centuries in the ambit of the crime, it is quite wrong to bring within its operation forms of evil conduct because they wear some analogy to aspects of the crime and deserve punishment. The judgment of the majority of the Full Court of the Supreme Court goes upon the moral differences between marital intercourse and sexual relations without marriage. The difference is indeed so radical that it is apt to draw the mind away from the real question which is carnal knowledge without consent. It may well be true that the woman in the present case never intended to consent to the latter relationship. But, as was said before, the key to such a case as the present lies in remembering that it is the penetration of the woman's body without her consent to such penetration that makes the felony. The capital felony was not directed to fraudulent conduct inducing her consent. Frauds of that kind must be punished under other heads of the criminal law or not at all: they are not rape. To say that in the present case the facts which the jury must be taken to have found amount to wicked and heartless conduct on the part of the applicant is not enough to establish that he committed rape. To say that in having intercourse with him she supposed that she was concerned in a perfectly moral act is not to say that the intercourse was without her consent. To return to the central point; rape is carnal knowledge of a woman without her consent: carnal knowledge is the physical fact of penetration; it is the consent to that which is in question; such a consent demands a perception as to what is about to take place, as to the identity of the man and the character of what he is doing. But once the consent is comprehending and actual the inducing causes cannot destroy its reality and leave the man guilty of rape.'

Respectfully applying those dicta to the facts of the present case, the prostitute here consented to sexual intercourse with the appellant. The reality of that consent is not destroyed by being induced by the appellant's false pretence that his intention was to pay the agreed price of £25 for her services. Therefore, he was not guilty of rape.

If anything, the appellant was guilty of an offence under s 3 of the 1956 Act, which was not an alternative that was put to this jury.

In our judgment, the appeal must be allowed and the conviction and sentence quashed.

Appeal allowed.

This decision therefore makes clear that just because the victim has consented to sexual intercourse because of a deception does not mean that she has not consented to the act. What must be shown is that the deception rendered the act fundamentally different in nature from that performed. In *Linekar*, the act of sexual intercourse with the defendant was exactly that to which the victim consented. The deception related to what would happen afterwards (whether she would be paid) and not to the nature of the act itself.[24] Therefore the victim did consent to the sexual intercourse, the court held. It might be arguable that the case would not be decided in the same way since the Sexual Offences Act 2003. It could be said that there was a deception as to the purpose of the act. The purpose for the prostitute was that she was going to get paid and the defendant misled her as to that.

The following case has somewhat muddied the waters as to the meaning of 'nature of the act'. The judgment refers to *Linekar* (extract above), *Clarence* (discussed in the *Linekar* extract), and *Richardson* (summarized at p. 438; below).

R v Tabassum
[2000] 2 Cr App R 328 (CA)[25]

Naveed Tabassum was convicted of three counts of indecent assault. He persuaded two women to allow him to touch their breasts in order to demonstrate how to do a self-examination. He said he was a breast cancer specialist and was running a breast cancer survey. The three women said they had consented only because they thought he was medically qualified. In fact Tabassum had no medical training. Tabassum argued that he had only done what the women had consented to and therefore there could be no indecent assault. On appeal the key question was whether the women had consented to these touchings.

Lord Justice Rose, reading the judgment of the court

. . . In our judgment, the pertinent authorities . . . can properly be analysed in this way. The wife in *Clarence*, and the prostitute in *Linekar*, each consented to sexual intercourse knowing both the nature and the quality of that act. The additional unexpected consequences, of

---

[24] For an argument that this is not actually true see Herring (2002: 192).
[25] [2000] Lloyd's Rep Med 404.

infection in the one case and non payment in the other, were irrelevant to and did not detract from the woman's consent to sexual intercourse.

In *Richardson*, the case proceeded solely by reference to the point on identity. As is apparent from page 205F of the judgment, the prosecution in that case did not at trial or on appeal rely on the nature or quality of the act. In our judgment, the learned judge was entitled to follow the passage in the judgment of Stephen J in *Clarence*, which he cited in the course of his ruling. In the present case the motive and intent of the Defendant were irrelevant (see *R v C* to which reference has already been made.) The nature and quality of the Defendant's acts in touching the breasts of women to whom, in sexual terms he was a stranger, was unlawful and an indecent assault unless the complainants consented to that touching.

On the evidence, if the jury accepted it, consent was given because they mistakenly believed that the Defendant was medically qualified or, in the case of the third complainant, trained at Christies and that, in consequence, the touching was for a medical purpose. As this was not so, there was no true consent. They were consenting to touching for medical purposes not to indecent behaviour, that is, there was consent to the nature of the act but not its quality. *Flattery* and *Harms*, which we have earlier cited, are entirely consistent with that view because, in each of those cases, the woman's consent to sexual intercourse was to a therapeutic, not a carnal, act. . . . . It follows that, in our judgment, the judge's ruling was correct.

Appeal dismissed.

The Court of Appeal appears here to draw a distinction between the nature of the acts and the quality of the acts. Although the victims had consented to being touched in the places where they were touched, they were consenting to medically motivated touchings, not to touchings with some other motivation. If *Tabassum* was heard today the case would be easier because section 76(2)(a) makes it clear that a deception as to the purpose of the act can negate the apparent consent of the victim.

It will be interesting to see how the courts will interpret the phrase 'nature or purpose' of the act. Under the law prior to the Act the question was whether the deception related to the 'nature' of the act. On a wide interpretation of 'purpose' it might be argued that a man who persuades a woman to have sexual intercourse 'in order to express our love for each other', when in fact he does not love her, could be guilty of rape. Many commentators feel that would be going too far.

One interesting point to note is that a literal reading of the subsection does not require the deception to have caused the consent. So, for example, if Dec tells Carol that he wants to have sexual intercourse as an expression of their spiritual union, whereas in fact he has no spiritual purpose in mind, this could fall into section 76(2)(a) even if in fact Carol would have been quite happy to have sex with Dec, even without his spiritual comments.

Conclusive presumption: cases of impersonation

Section 76(2) also creates a conclusive presumption in cases of impersonation. The following points can be made about this subsection:

(1) *There must be an impersonation.* In *Elbekkay*,[26] at night-time, the defendant entered the victim's bedroom. She assumed that he was her boyfriend and so consented to sexual

---

[26] [1995] Crim LR 163 (CA).

intercourse. The defendant realized her mistake, but had sexual intercourse with her. The presumption does not apply in such a case because the defendant had not impersonated the boyfriend (he had said nothing to suggest he was the boyfriend). However, as we shall see, he will still be guilty of rape because under the common law of consent the victim did not consent.

(2) *The impersonation must be of a person known personally to the complainant.* Clearly the presumption would apply where the defendant impersonated the victim's husband, partner, or even friend. But, it seems, the presumption would not apply where the defendant impersonated the victim's favourite film star or pop star. Similarly, if the defendant simply claimed an attribute which he did not have (e.g. that he was rich or was a qualified lawyer) this would not negate consent.

(3) *Rather oddly the subsection seems to apply even if the victim is not taken in by the impersonation.* Consider this: Dave fancies his best friend Mick, but Mick is not interested. Pete (whom Dave does not know) fancies Dave and, learning of Dave's liking of Mick, decides to try to impersonate Mick. When Dave sees Pete he realizes that Pete is not Mick, but agrees to sexual intercourse with him because Pete looks so like Mick he can live out a fantasy. It seems that if section 76 was interpreted literally this would be rape. But that is absurd; the subsection (although it does not say so) is surely meant to apply only where the defendant is taken in by the impersonation.

There are two kinds of cases where the statutory presumption of non-consent does not apply, but the jury may still decide that the victim does not consent under the general meaning of consent:

(1) *Where there is no deception.* In the case of *Elbekkay* [27] (summarized above) the Court of Appeal found that the victim had not consented to sexual intercourse with the defendant, even though the defendant had not in fact impersonated the boyfriend. The victim had consented to sexual relations with her partner, not the defendant. There was therefore no consent.

(2) *Where the mistake is as to the identity of a person not known to the victim.* As already mentioned the statutory presumption applies only where the defendant impersonates someone the victim knew personally. For a long time the common law view was that impersonation only of a spouse could negate consent. However, this was extended to unmarried partners in *Elbekkay.* [28] *Obiter,* McCowan LJ giving the judgment of the court explained that 'The vital point about rape is that it involves the absence of consent. That absence is equally crucial whether the woman believes that the man she is having sexual intercourse with is her husband or another.' The phrase 'or another' may suggest the common law is even wider than the statutory presumption and includes cases of impersonation of anyone.

What we know for sure is that if the victim is mistaken as to an attribute of the defendant, rather than the identity of the person, then that is not rape. So, if the victim met a man at a party who simply claimed to be a well-known actor that mistake would not vitiate the victim's consent. That is because his or her mistake would simply be over an attribute (the man's occupation) rather than his identity. In *Richardson* [29] the defendant purported to be a legitimate dentist when in fact she had been struck off the register of dentists. Patients

---

[27] [1995] Crim LR 163 (CA).   [28] Ibid.   [29] [1999] QB 444 (CA).

who received treatment from her were said not to be mistaken as to her identity: she was the very Diane Richardson they thought she was; they were, however, mistaken as to her attributes (she was not a registered dentist). So there was consent to the dentistry work.

Evidential presumptions

The evidential presumptions are set out in section 75.

---

75. Evidential presumptions about consent

(1) If in proceedings for an offence to which this section applies it is proved—

    (a) that the defendant did the relevant act,

    (b) that any of the circumstances specified in subsection (2) existed, and

    (c) that the defendant knew that those circumstances existed,

the complainant is to be taken not to have consented to the relevant act unless sufficient evidence is adduced to raise an issue as to whether he consented, and the defendant is to be taken not to have reasonably believed that the complainant consented unless sufficient evidence is adduced to raise an issue as to whether he reasonably believed it.

(2) The circumstances are that—

    (a) any person was, at the time of the relevant act or immediately before it began, using violence against the complainant or causing the complainant to fear that immediate violence would be used against him;

    (b) any person was, at the time of the relevant act or immediately before it began, causing the complainant to fear that violence was being used, or that immediate violence would be used, against another person;

    (c) the complainant was, and the defendant was not, unlawfully detained at the time of the relevant act;

    (d) the complainant was asleep or otherwise unconscious at the time of the relevant act;

    (e) because of the complainant's physical disability, the complainant would not have been able at the time of the relevant act to communicate to the defendant whether the complainant consented;

    (f) any person had administered to or caused to be taken by the complainant, without the complainant's consent, a substance which, having regard to when it was administered or taken, was capable of causing or enabling the complainant to be stupefied or overpowered at the time of the relevant act.

(3) In subsection (2)(a) and (b), the reference to the time immediately before the relevant act began is, in the case of an act which is one of a continuous series of sexual activities, a reference to the time immediately before the first sexual activity began.

Where it is proved by the prosecution that one of the sets of facts listed in section 75(2) existed and the defendant was aware they existed, then there is a presumption that the *actus reus* and *mens rea* of rape are established. But, this is only an evidential presumption and it is open to the defendant to introduce evidence that in fact the *mens rea* or *actus reus* of rape did not exist. Where the defendant produces 'sufficient evidence to raise an issue' as to whether the *actus reus* or *mens rea* of rape existed then the presumption is rebutted. The prosecution must then prove beyond reasonable doubt that the *actus reus* and *mens rea* of rape existed. This is all a bit confusing, but the following example may assist:

> The prosecution prove that a minute before D and V had sexual intercourse that D intentionally had hit V. Under section 76(2)(a) this creates a presumption that D is guilty of rape. If the defence introduces no evidence the jury should convict D. However, D may try and introduce evidence to rebut the presumption. He might argue, for example, that after he hit V he immediately apologized, she forgave him and they then had sexual intercourse. If he introduces sufficient evidence to raise an issue about this then the presumption is rebutted. The prosecution must then persuade the jury beyond reasonable doubt that the *actus reus* and *mens rea* of rape existed.

A key issue is what 'introduces sufficient evidence to raise an issue' means. In the example above, if D just gave evidence to the effect that they had made up and had consensual sex, would that be enough? If the answer is 'yes' then that means that it would be very easy to rebut the presumption, the defendant just has to say there was in fact consent, in which case it might well be wondered if it is worth having. On the other hand, if the answer is 'no', what more evidence could D introduce in a case like this, apart from his own eyewitness account? Court guidance on the meaning of 'sufficient evidence is adduced to raise' is eagerly awaited. The Judicial Studies Board has suggested in many cases the presumption will be rebutted.[30]

Section 75(2)(a)–(c) deals with cases where there is a threat of violence or unlawful detention. The following points can be made:

(1) Notice that under section 75(2)(b) it does not need to be shown that the defendant used or threatened violence against the victim. So, if the defendant's friend threatens to beat up the victim unless she 'agrees' to sexual intercourse with the defendant the presumption will apply. Similarly, the threat of violence need not be to the victim, but can be to another. So, if the defendant threatened to beat up the victim's friend unless she agreed to sexual intercourse, the presumption could also apply.

(2) The presumption applies only if the threat is of violence. If the threat is to destroy property, for example, then the presumption does not apply. Also, it seems that threats to cause an emotional harm (e.g. to end a relationship) are not included.

(3) The presumption applies only if the threat is of immediate violence. So the presumption will not apply if the threat is that the victim will be beaten up next week.

Section 75(2)(d)–(e) deals with cases where the victim is incapable of consenting, either because they are asleep, unconscious, or unable to communicate with their consent. It must be said that in these cases it is hard to imagine how the presumption could be rebutted. Perhaps it is plausible that V might ask D to have sex with him while he is asleep.

Under section 75(2)(f) there is an evidential presumption of no consent where 'any person had administered to or caused to be taken by the complainant, without the complainant's consent, a substance which, having regard to when it was administered or taken, was capable of causing or enabling the complainant to be stupefied or overpowered at the time of the relevant act.' This provision clearly deals with cases of drug-assisted rape. It is, however, problematic.[31] The first point to make is that it is very surprising that this is an evidential rather than conclusive presumption. Could there be a scenario in which a

---

[30] Judicial Studies Board (2004).   [31] Finch and Munro (2003 and 2004).

defendant gave the victim stupefying drugs without her consent and then had sexual intercourse with her in which it could be said that the victim consented? Maybe yes, where the victim was given a drug which could have been stupefying, but in fact had no effect. However, the fact that the presumption is evidential means that the defendant can seek to claim that the effect of the drug on the victim's consent was negligible and this might involve the jury in difficult questions about the impact of the drug on the victim's mental state. A second concern is that the evidential presumption only arises where the drug is capable of stupefying or overpowering the victim. The problem here is that the drugs used in this kind of offence can have a range of different effects. Some drugs can have the effect of stupefying the victim, but as Emily Finch and Vanessa Munro point out:

> the drugs may reduce the victim's ability to resist sexual advances, render her unable to communicate her wishes regarding intercourse, or engender an uncharacteristic inclination to participate in sexual activity ... it seems that victims may be induced to agree to intercourse with virtual strangers however uncharacteristic this would be in the absence of the drugs. Moreover, it is likely that they will not appreciate that such behaviour is uncharacteristic, thus, whatever their sober preferences in such matters, they will believe that their consent to intercourse represents their genuine wishes regarding sexual activity at the time.[32]

A third issue, and one which may be of the greatest practical significance is whether alcohol is included within this evidential presumption. It is submitted it certainly should be included. It is a substance which is 'capable of causing or enabling the complainant to be stupefied or overpowered'. Some would be concerned that this throws the net of presumption too widely. But it should be recalled that the presumption would only apply where the victim is given alcohol without her consent. This leaves open the question of where a victim knows she is drinking alcohol, but the defendant has spiked her drunk to make it more alcoholic than she realizes. Surely this is to administer the extra substance without her consent, but the point might be thought debatable. A fourth point worth emphasizing is that the presumption applies even if it was not the defendant who administered the drugs. Finally, it is worth noting that the presumption applies where the substance is capable of stupefying the victim, it does not need to be shown that the substance actually has that effect.

EXAMINATION TIP

A warning:

Do not think that just because the presumption of no consent in sections 75 or 76 does not apply the court must decide that there is consent. For example, if the defendant threatens to burn down the victim's house unless she agrees to sexual intercourse, as a result of which the victim submits to sexual intercourse, there is no threat of violence and so there is no presumption of lack of consent under section 75, BUT it is still open to the jury to decide that the victim did not consent. All sections 75 and 76 are doing is setting out circumstances under which it will be presumed that there is no consent. It is *not* setting out the only circumstances under which a jury can find there is no consent.

---

[32] Finch and Munro (2003: 775).

Consent in its general meaning: introduction

If consent is not found using one of the conclusive or evidential presumptions the jury will need to consider whether there is consent under the general meaning. Section 74 states that a person 'consents if he agrees by choice, and has the freedom and capacity to make that choice'.

Consent in its general meaning: positive consent required

The victim must actively agree to the penetration if it is not to amount to rape.[33] It does not need to be shown that the victim resisted the penetration, or even opposed it. The point is demonstrated by the following cases, decided before the 2003 Act, but which would be decided in the same way after it:

(1) In *Lartner*[34] the victim was asleep throughout the act of intercourse. Although she had not actively opposed or resisted the sexual intercourse she had not positively consented to it and so the *actus reus* of rape was made out.

(2) In *Malone*[35] the victim was so drunk she was unaware that the defendant was having sexual intercourse with her, still the *actus reus* of the offence was made out. However, in a recent widely reported trial the judge directed the jury to return a not guilty verdict, after the victim gave evidence that she was so drunk that she could not remember what happened.[36] It appears that the judge took the view that the prosecution were, as a result of her evidence, unable to establish that there was no consent. The judge is reported to have told the jury that drunken consent is still consent.

Although the fact that consent requires agreement, not just lack of resistance, is important, it should be recalled that the jury must be persuaded beyond reasonable doubt that the victim was not consenting, and so where there is no apparent resistance the prosecution will face a harder job persuading the jury that there was no consent than in a case where the victim made her objections obvious.[37]

It is also crucial to appreciate that the consent question is about the victim's state of mind. In *McFall*[38] (a case decided before the 2003 Act came into force), the victim had been kidnapped by the accused, who then indicated that he wished to have sexual intercourse with her. The victim was so terrified he would kill her that she pretended to consent to the intercourse and even 'faked an orgasm'. Even though she may have appeared to an onlooker to consent, the Court of Appeal was able to find the *actus reus* of rape established because it was clear that subjectively (in her mind) the victim did not consent. Of course, whether the victim appeared to consent will be an important question in relation to the *mens rea* question: whether the defendant believed the victim was consenting.

Consent in its general meaning: capacity to consent?

Section 74 makes it clear that in order to be able to consent the victim must have sufficient capacity to consent. For example, a child or an adult suffering from mental illness or

---

[33] *R v Malone* [1998] 2 Cr App R 447 (CA). [34] [1995] Crim LR 75 (CA).
[35] [1998] 2 CAR 447 (CA). [36] BBCNewsonline (2005e).
[37] A point stressed in Waye (1992). [38] [1994] Crim LR 226.

learning difficulty may not have the capacity to consent. Several groups of people need to be considered separately:

(1) *Children.* The law does not presume that at a particular age a child becomes old enough to be able to consent to sexual penetration. If the child has sufficient maturity and understanding she may be competent to consent. In a case concerning whether an under-16-year-old could validly consent to being given contraceptive advice and treatment[39] the House of Lords held that she could if she was mature enough to understand the issues involved, including the moral ones.[40] The courts are likely to take the same approach in relation to sexual intercourse. It should be noted that even if a child is sufficiently competent to be able to consent, and hence the defendant is not guilty of rape, he may be guilty of one of the other offences under the 2003 Act, such as the rape of a child under the age of 13 under section 5, or one of the abuse of a position of trust offences in sections 16 to 24, which do not require the activities to be without the consent of the victim.

(2) *Mental illness or learning difficulties.* There is little guidance on what level of understanding is necessary before someone's mental limitations mean that he or she lack capacity to consent. A court might be tempted to refer to the medical law (where there has been much more case law) on when a person is competent to consent to medical treatment. In medical law an adult is presumed to be competent,[41] but the Court of Appeal in *Re MB*[42] explained:

> A person lacks capacity if some impairment or disturbance of mental functioning renders the person unable to make a decision whether to consent to or to refuse treatment. That inability to make a decision will occur when:
>
> (a) The person who lacks capacity is unable to comprehend and retain the information which is material to the decision, especially as to the likely consequences of having or not having the treatment in question;
>
> (b) The patient is unable to use the information and weigh it in the balance as part of the process of arriving at a decision.

In relation to physical disabilities the Sexual Offences Act 2003 deals with the issue of consent for those suffering physical and mental disabilities explicitly: where 'because of the complainant's physical disability, the complainant would not have been able at the time of the relevant act to communicate to the defendant whether the complainant consented'.[43] It will be presumed that the victim did not consent, if the defendant is aware that the complainant was suffering from such a disability.

(3) *Others who lack capacity.* What about other people who may lack capacity? Perhaps the most controversial cases will involve victims who are drunk. There is little difficulty with the victim who is so drunk he or she is unaware of what is happening; clearly such a victim

---

[39] *Gillick v West Norfolk and Wisbech Area Health Authority* [1986] AC 112 (HL).

[40] This has become known as *Gillick* competence. See also *Howard* [1965] 3 All ER 684 (CCA) and *Harling* [1938] 1 All ER 307.

[41] *Re MB (An Adult: Medical Treatment)* [1997] 2 FCR 541 at 553 (CA).

[42] Ibid. at 553–4 (CA), approving *dicta* of Thorpe J in *Re C (Adult: Refusal of Treatment)* [1994] 2 FCR 151 at 156 (FD).

[43] Section 75(2)(e).

does not consent. What of the victim who is drunk and loudly consents to sexual inter-course, but whose intoxicated judgement is severely clouded? There is no clear guidance from the case law on this, but presumably the jury would be asked whether the victim's state of mind was sufficiently clear to understand what was happening, consider the issue, and reach a decision.[44] It should be noted that if the defendant has administered a substance to the victim without her consent and this 'stupefies' the victim, then there is an evidential presumption that the victim did not consent under section 75(2)(f).

Consent in its general meaning: consent provided through fear

What if the victim has appeared to agree to sexual intercourse, but only out of fear? Many cases of consent provided through fear will be dealt with under the evidential presumption under section 75(2). But if the case is not, the general meaning of consent must be con-sidered. In section 74 it is emphasized that the agreement must be by choice and the choice must be a free one.

The leading case under the law on 'consent', prior to the 2003 Act, after threats is the following. It is likely that courts in interpreting section 74 will follow its approach:

Regina v Olugboja
[1982] QB 320 (CA)[45]

The defendant and the co-accused L met the complainant and K at a discotheque and offered to take them home. In fact they drove them to L's bungalow. The complainants refused to go in and began to walk away. The defendant went into the bungalow but L followed the girls and raped the complainant in the car. The three returned to the bungalow where L dragged K into a bedroom. The defendant then told the complainant that he was going to have intercourse with her. She told him what had happened in the car and asked him to leave her alone. He told her to take off her trousers. She did and he had intercourse with her. The defendant, who admitted having sexual intercourse with the complainant, was charged with rape. The judge directed the jury that, although the complainant had neither screamed nor struggled, and no direct threat had been made towards her, it was open to the jury to decide that she had submitted, rather than consented, to the sexual intercourse. The defendant was convicted and appealed.

Lord Justice Dunn reading the judgment of the court

The question of law raised by this appeal is whether to constitute the offence of rape it is necessary for the consent of the victim of sexual intercourse to be vitiated by force, the fear of force, or fraud; or whether it is sufficient to prove that in fact the victim did not consent.

. . .

Mrs. Trewella [counsel for the defendant] accepted that submission by the victim did not necessarily involve consent, but the submission must be induced because of fear of violence: see *Reg. v. Day*, 9 C. & p. 722. She submitted that moral or economic pressure or

---

[44] *Lang* (1976) 62 Cr App R 50 (CA).
[45] [1981] 3 All ER 443, [1981] 3 WLR 585, (1981) 73 Cr App R 344.

even blackmail causing a woman to submit to sexual intercourse could never be enough to found a charge of rape. Otherwise she said the film producer who induced an actress to have sexual intercourse by telling her she would not get a part in his new film if she did not, or the man who induced a woman to have sexual intercourse by telling her that if she did not he would tell her fiancé that she had been a prostitute, would be guilty of rape. . . .

Mrs. Trewella submitted that just as the law limits the circumstances in which any person may say he has acted involuntarily owing to duress, which involves threats of death or violence to that person or a close relative, so it is consistent that the common law has limited the circumstances in which a woman who has had sexual intercourse may say that the act was not consensual.

Mrs. Trewella submitted finally that to say, as the judge did, that any constraint upon Jayne's will could negative consent constituted a misdirection. The word 'constraint' includes moral as well as physical pressure and moral pressure is not enough. Even to tell a girl that she would not be taken home until she had sexual intercourse, in the absence of any threat of violence expressed or implied, would not vitiate her consent.

[Dunn LJ went on to consider some earlier cases and the history of the Sexual Offences Act 1956.]

Accordingly in so far as the *actus reus* is concerned the question now is simply: 'At the time of the sexual intercourse did the woman consent to it?' It is not necessary for the prosecution to prove that what might otherwise appear to have been consent was in reality merely submission induced by force, fear or fraud, although one or more of these factors will no doubt be present in the majority of cases of rape.

We do not agree, as was suggested by Mrs. Trewella, that once this is fully realised there will be a large increase in prosecutions for rape. Nor, on the other hand, do we agree with Mr. Brent's submission, on behalf of the Crown, that it is sufficient for a trial judge merely to leave the issue of consent to a jury in a similar way to that in which the issue of dishonesty is left in trials for offences under the Theft Act 1968. In such cases it is sufficient to direct the jury that 'dishonest' is an easily understood English word and it is for them to say whether a particular transaction is properly so described or not. Although 'consent' is an equally common word it covers a wide range of states of mind in the context of intercourse between a man and a woman, ranging from actual desire on the one hand to reluctant acquiescence on the other. We do not think that the issue of consent should be left to a jury without some further direction. What this should be will depend on the circumstances of each case. The jury will have been reminded of the burden and standard of proof required to establish each ingredient, including lack of consent, of the offence. They should be directed that consent, or the absence of it, is to be given its ordinary meaning and if need be, by way of example, that there is a difference between consent and submission; every consent involves a submission, but it by no means follows that a mere submission involves consent: per Coleridge J. in *Reg. v. Day*, 9 C. & p. 722, 724. In the majority of cases, where the allegation is that the intercourse was had by force or the fear of force, such a direction coupled with specific references to, and comments on, the evidence relevant to the absence of real consent will clearly suffice. In the less common type of case where intercourse takes place after threats not involving violence or the fear of it, as in the examples given by Mrs. Trewella to which we have referred earlier in this judgment, we think that an appropriate direction to a jury will have to be fuller. They should be directed to concentrate on the state of mind of the victim immediately before the act of sexual intercourse, having regard to all the relevant circumstances; and in particular, the events leading up to the act and her reaction to them showing their impact on her mind. Apparent acquiescence after penetration does not necessarily involve consent, which must have occurred before the act takes place. In addition to the general direction about consent which we have outlined, the jury will probably be helped in such cases by being reminded that in this context consent does comprehend the wide spectrum of states of mind to which we earlier referred, and that the dividing line in such circumstances between real consent on the one hand and mere submission on the other may not be easy to draw. Where it is to be drawn in a given case is for the jury to decide, applying their combined good sense, experience and knowledge of human nature and modern behaviour to all the relevant facts of that case.

Looked at in this way we find no misdirection by the judge in this case. . . .

Appeal dismissed.

It is crucial to appreciate the width of the decision. It is clear that a victim's apparent consent can be negated by a threat, even if the threat is not of death or serious injury. What the jury must focus on is not the nature of the threat (how much violence was threatened) but the effect of the threat (how great was its effect). The jury must decide, given the effect of the threat, whether the victim was consenting to the penetration. Reluctant acquiescence amounts to consent; submission does not.

It should be re-emphasized that the question is subjective to the victim. The focus is not on what the defendant did or threatened, but, rather, the state of mind of the victim.[46] In *Olugboja* the defendant did not actually utter any threat; what was crucial was that the victim regarded his conduct as threatening; such that she did not truly consent. In fact, a victim could interpret a defendant's actions to be so threatening that she was not truly consenting, even though the defendant did not mean to be threatening.[47]

As we shall see in Part II there has been much academic discussion whether a threat not to provide a benefit (as opposed to a threat to cause harm) can vitiate consent. Some commentators take the view that consent following an offer can, in unusual circumstances, be an invalid consent. They reject the view that a sharp distinction between threats and offers can be drawn. Many commentators have discussed whether the film director has committed rape if he has sexual intercourse with an out-of-work actress to whom he has said 'I will only give you a leading role if you agree to sexual intercourse with me'. Unfortunately the courts are yet to deal with the issue.

Consent in its general meaning: mistaken consent

Where the defendant has deceived the victim as to the nature and purpose of the act the conclusive presumption under section 76 will apply. But there may be other cases where the victim consents while under a mistake where the jury might decide that there was not a genuine consent as is required for section 74. Uncontroversial might be a case where a person other than the defendant deceived the victim as to the nature of the act. Whether other mistakes, which do relate as to the nature of the act itself, will be sufficient to mean there is not real consent, will have to be considered by the courts.

---

[46] See the discussion in *Wellard* (1978) 67 Cr App R 364 at 368 of a case where a man was convicted of rape after pretending to be a security officer and pressuring a girl into having sexual intercourse with him. He threatened to tell the girl's parents that she had been having sexual intercourse with her boyfriend.

[47] In such a case the *mens rea* may be hard to prove.

QUESTIONS

1. The Court of Appeal in *McAllister* [1997] Crim LR 233 suggests that only if improper pressure is used by the defendant may it negate the victim's consent. Can it ever be proper to put pressure on another to engage in sexual intercourse? Would the law have greater certainty if, rather than considering the effect of the threat on the victim, it considered the propriety of the defendant's actions?

2. Max knows that his girlfriend Bertha is emotionally unstable. She does not want to have sexual intercourse until they are married. He threatens to end the relationship unless Bertha agrees to sexual intercourse. Bertha, terrified at the possibility of the ending of the relationship, agrees to sexual intercourse. Is Max guilty of rape?

3. Tricia suggests to her boyfriend Simon that they have sexual intercourse as an expression of their undying love. Simon agrees, even though he has fallen in love with someone else and is simply engaging in sex for carnal pleasure. Is this rape?

4. Tom and Patricia agree to have sexual intercourse, but Patricia makes it clear that she agrees only on condition that Tom wears a condom. Tom proceeds with sexual intercourse but, unknown to Patricia, he is not wearing a condom. Is this rape?

5. Diane agrees to vaginal sexual intercourse with Peter. Peter has anal intercourse with her. Diane later states that she did not consent to anal intercourse. Has Peter committed rape?

1.5 *MENS REA*: AN INTENT TO PENETRATE

As we saw earlier, section 1 of the Sexual Offences Act 2003 sets out the *mens rea* for rape. There are two elements. First, we will discuss the requirement that the defendant must intend to penetrate. Section 1 opens:

> (1) A person (A) commits an offence if—
>
>   (a) he intentionally penetrates the vagina, anus or mouth of another person (B) with his penis, . . .

The *mens rea* aspect of this will only rarely arise in a rape case. If the defendant claims that he did not intend to penetrate the victim it is unlikely that this will be believed. Sexual penetration is not something that is done by accident.[48] One case which is perhaps in doubt is where the defendant intended to engage in vaginal intercourse, but in fact engaged in anal intercourse. It is submitted that as both are the form of *actus reus* of the offence, an intent to penetrate either orifice is sufficient.

1.6 *MENS REA*: THE DEFENDANT DOES NOT REASONABLY BELIEVE THAT THE VICTIM CONSENTS

Section 1 of the Sexual Offences Act 2003 goes on to state the second element of the *mens rea*:

---

[48] If a couple agreed to have a naked cuddle, but not engage in sexual intercourse, it might be possible for there to be accidental penetration.

(1)(c) A does not reasonably believe that B consents.

(2) Whether a belief is reasonable is to be determined having regard to all the circumstances, including any steps A has taken to ascertain whether B consents.[49]

Section 1 makes it clear that the defendant will have the *mens rea* if he has any state of mind apart from one in which he reasonably believes that the victim consents. This includes any of the following three states of mind:

(1) He knows the victim does not consent.

(2) He gives no thought to whether the victim consented. This would cover a case where the defendant had decided to engage in sexual penetration of the victim whatever her wishes and therefore gave no thought to whether the victim consented.

(3) He otherwise does not reasonably believe the victim consents. This may cover a case where the defendant does consider whether the victim consents, but simply does not care whether or not she does. Or he believes the victim is consenting but does not have reasonable grounds for his belief.

The Sexual Offences Act 2003 sets out certain circumstances in which it will be presumed that the defendant knew that the victim did not consent. We have come across these already in considering the meaning of consent:

(1) Under section 75(1) if the defendant knew that any of the circumstances listed in section 75(2) were present then 'the defendant is taken not to have reasonably believed that the complainant consented unless sufficient evidence is adduced to raise an issue as to whether to reasonably believe it'.[50] Section 75(2) includes where the victim was asleep at the time of the act or where violence had been used against the victim. It should be noted that these are evidentiary presumptions. It is therefore open to the defendant to show that he did reasonably believe that the victim consented. For example, he could try to argue that even though he knew the victim had been subjected to violence immediately before the penetration he reasonably believed that she was consenting.

(2) Under section 76 (set out above at p. 429) if the defendant had intentionally deceived the victim as to the nature or purpose of the act, or had impersonated a person known to the victim, then he is presumed not to believe that the victim consented to the act. This is a conclusive presumption.

Section 1 invites the jury to consider whether a reasonable person would believe that the victim was consenting. This asks the jury to imagine a reasonable person in the defendant's shoes: would he believe that the victim is consenting? If the reasonable person would not believe that the victim is consenting the defendant cannot claim to have a reasonable belief that the victim is consenting. In some cases (e.g. where the victim is ferociously resisting) it will be obvious that a reasonable person would not believe that the victim is consenting. Other cases may be more ambiguous (e.g. where the victim is being simply passive in the face of the defendant's 'advances'); or the victim appears to keep changing his or her mind

---

[49] The offence carries a maximum sentence of life.   [50] Sexual Offences Act 2003, s. 75(1).

on the issue of consent to sexual activity. It should be noted that the question is not 'would the reasonable person think the victim might be consenting'; but rather 'would the reasonable person believe the victim is consenting'. So if the reasonable person would conclude, 'I think the victim is consenting, but I am not at all sure' then arguably the defendant cannot have a reasonable *belief* that the victim consented.

Under section 1(2) in deciding whether a belief is reasonable the jury should consider all the circumstances including any steps the defendant has taken in ascertaining whether the victim consents. *Protecting the Public*, the Government White Paper which preceded the Act, suggests that in deciding whether a reasonable person would have a doubt:

> The jury would . . . have to take into account the actions of both parties, the circumstances in which they have placed themselves and the level of responsibility exercised by both.[51]

The jury are also likely to consider issues such as: how long have the defendant and victim known each other?; have they had a sexual relationship in the past?; have they discussed the possibility of sexual relations? Of course, the jury will be careful not to assume that because someone consented to sexual relations in the past that this means they have consented to sexual relations in the future.

One issue which the courts will need in due course to resolve is whether in deciding whether the defendant's belief that the victim consented was reasonable the jury should take into account the characteristics of the defendant and, if so, which characteristics. On the one hand a court may be tempted to go down the route of *Smith (Morgan)*[52] on provocation and allow any relevant characteristic to be considered; on the other hand in *Colohan*,[53] discussing the Protection from Harassment Act 1997, the Court of Appeal refused to accept that the defendant's characteristics rendered his actions or beliefs reasonable. *Protecting the Public* states ' "Reasonable" will be judged by reference to what an objective third party would think in the circumstances.'[54] This appears to imply that the reasonable person should not be given any of the characteristics of the accused. However, the response to all the circumstances in section 1(2) could be to include, for example, the defendant's learning disabilities.

Section 1(2) deals with the situation where a reasonable person would be unsure whether the victim consented. The defendant must act reasonably in ascertaining whether the victim consented in doubtful cases. The most obvious way of resolving a doubt would be for the defendant to ask the victim whether or not she was consenting. But there may be other ways where the couple know each other well.[55]

Presumably a defendant would not reasonably believe that a victim was consenting if he was relying on what someone else has told him. In *DPP v Morgan*[56] the victim's husband told some men that they should have sexual intercourse with his wife. He warned them that she might appear to resist, but that she would be doing this only to heighten her sexual enjoyment. The men went ahead and had intercourse with the wife despite her evident protests.

---

[51] Home Office (2002b: 17).
[52] [2001] AC 146 (HL).   [53] [2001] Crim LR 845 (CA).   [54] Home Office (2002b: 17).
[55] e.g. the couple could have developed a way of communicating concerning sexual matters with certain touches or noises indicating a keenness to engage in sexual intercourse.
[56] [1976] AC 142 (HL).

There is no doubt that such men would now be convicted of rape, because they did not *reasonably* believe that the victim consented.

1.7 INTOXICATION AND THE LAW OF RAPE

The Sexual Offences Act 2003 does not provide for a case where the defendant is intoxicated. On basic principles the defendant will be able to introduce evidence that he was intoxicated to persuade a jury that he did not intend to penetrate the victim. However, it is hard to imagine that a jury will believe him. In relation to the second limb of the *mens rea*, an intoxicated defendant will not be able to rely on an unreasonable intoxicated belief that the victim consented.[57]

1.8 HOW THE 2003 ACT CHANGED THE LAW ON RAPE

These are the most significant changes that the 2003 Act has made to the law on rape:

(1) Penetration of the mouth has been added to the *actus reus* of rape.

(2) Section 1 adds a new category of *mens rea*. The *mens rea* under the old law was that the defendant was guilty if he did not honestly believe that the victim consented. Section 1 means that now a defendant who honestly (but unreasonably) believes that the victim consents to sexual intercourse may be guilty of rape.

(3) Sections 75 and 76 set out the circumstances in which it will be presumed that the victim did not consent. Many of these are similar, but not identical, to the common law rules.

The government has sought through the 2003 Act to ensure that sexual offences do not discriminate on the grounds of sexual orientation.[58] Now whether activities are between a man and a woman, or between two people of the same sex, will be irrelevant for the purposes of the criminal law.

QUESTIONS

1. Lord Lloyd in the debates on the Sexual Offences Bill suggested that rather than section 1 leading to a larger number of convictions it will lead to a larger number of appeals due to its complexity. (HL Debs., col. 860, 13 February 2003.) Do you agree?

2. Brian has a low IQ and is sexually inexperienced. He meets Dawn who appears to be very friendly and accepts an invitation for a cup of tea in his flat. He decides that she must be willing to have intercourse with him. Dawn resists his advances but Brian decides that she must be consenting. Has Brian committed rape?

1.9 ASSESSMENT OF THE SEXUAL OFFENCES ACT 2003

In the following extract Andrew Ashworth and Jennifer Temkin assess the 2003 Act:

---

[57] *Woods* (1982) 74 Cr App R 312 (CA).   [58] Home Office (2002b: 10).

A. Ashworth and J. Temkin, 'The Sexual Offences Act 2003: (1) Rape, Sexual Assaults and the Problems of Consent' [2004] *Criminal Law Review* 328 at 336–46

By introducing a three-track approach to matters of consent and belief in consent—irrebuttable presumptions, rebuttable presumptions, and a general definition of consent—the Act raises a number of questions. Are the three categories intended to reflect some kind of moral hierarchy, so that the most serious cases of non-consent give rise to irrebuttable presumptions and the next most serious to rebuttable presumptions, with the remainder falling within the general definition? Or is the organising principle one of clarity and certainty, so that it is the clearest cases (not necessarily the worst) that give rise to irrebuttable presumptions and the next clearest to rebuttable presumptions, with the remainder falling within the general definition? Or is it a mixture of the two, with an added element of common law history? One would have thought that consideration ought to be given to marking out the worst cases of non-consent by means of irrebuttable presumptions, but that appears not to have happened. Various criticisms may be advanced.

(i) Are the types of fraud that give rise to the conclusive presumptions in s.76(2) the worst cases of non-consent?

A preliminary question here is whether the types of fraud singled out by s.76(2) are necessarily the worst types of deception, compared with deception as to intentions, powers and other matters . . . A more pressing question, however, is whether obtaining compliance by fraud or deception is worse than other ways of avoiding true consent, such as using threats or violence, administering drugs, or taking advantage of a sleeping or unconscious person. Obtaining compliance by using violence or threats of immediate violence seems no less heinous than doing so by deception, and yet the Act creates a conclusive presumption in the latter case and only a rebuttable presumption in the former.

There is also a case to be made for a conclusive presumption in the situation set out in s.75(2)(f), where it is proved beyond doubt that C had a substance administered to her without her consent which was capable of stupefying or overpowering her at the time of the relevant act and D knew this. Of course D must have, as he does under this provision, the opportunity to argue that the presumption does not apply because the substance administered was incapable of causing C to be stupefied or overpowered. But if the stupefying effect is established, it is questionable whether D should be able to argue that C nevertheless consented to the subsequent sexual act and that the drug or alcohol did not in fact prevent her from consenting. Can freedom and capacity to make a choice really exist in any meaningful sense in this situation? The present terms of s.75(2)(f) leave it open to the defence to enter into an impossible area of speculation about the precise effect of the substance on C, a matter which can only confuse the jury and cannot satisfactorily be resolved.

Is there any good reason why it should be the case that, if D deceives C by means of impersonation or as to the nature of the act, non-consent is conclusively proved under s.76, but if D has sex with C when C is asleep or unconscious this supports only a rebuttable presumption? The common law drew no such distinction between these situations. The Home Office Minister, Beverley Hughes, asserted that 'one of the principles behind the proposal [in respect of the presumptions] is that we should take steps to clarify existing case law and incorporate it into statute.' However, it has always been the law that consent must be present at the time of the sexual act. This means that consent is necessarily regarded as absent once it is proved beyond doubt that C was asleep or unconscious at the time sexual intercourse took place. If absence of consent is not conclusively presumed in these situations, as it was at common law, then the law is being taken backwards rather than forwards. This new departure reflects the more far reaching and entirely unfortunate proposal of the Law Commission that consent should be defined as a subsisting, free and genuine agreement, which would have invited the defence to argue that a consent given previously had not been withdrawn.

. . .

(ii) Should the list of circumstances in s.75 be more extensive and non-exhaustive?

In Canada and the Australian jurisdictions which have a statutory list of nonconsent situations, the list is non-exhaustive. The exhaustive list in s.75 leaves no scope for further situations to be added through the common law. Only Parliament will be able to make additions to the list. . . .

7. The absence of reasonable belief in consent

As stated above, under the new Act the mens rea of rape and the accompanying sexual assault offences has radically changed. The requirement of knowledge or reckless knowledge of the absence of consent, supported by the 'couldn't care less' test, has been replaced by the need to prove that 'A does not reasonably believe that B consents' (s.1(1)(c)). Should this be seen as an improvement in the law? To answer this, we need to consider several other questions.

Why was the Morgan approach thought unsatisfactory? This landmark decision was widely applauded by subjectivists for its general effects on the criminal law, since it emphasised that people ought to be judged on the facts as they believed them to be, and not on facts to which they had not given thought. If an offence requires proof of intention or recklessness in respect of a consequence or circumstance, then it is a matter of 'inexorable logic' that a mistaken belief in that respect should negative liability. Whatever the justifications for this as a general approach in the criminal law, it seemed to many that those justifications were outweighed in the case of sexual offences, where the two parties are necessarily in close proximity and where intercourse without consent would be a fundamental violation of the victim. Surely, out of respect for the autonomy and sexual choice of B, A should take the opportunity to be clear that B does consent. In most situations this is an easy thing to do, and there is a strong reason for doing it. This is not to suggest strict liability as to the absence of consent: it is to suggest a requirement that A acted as a reasonable person should have done in the situation in respect of ascertaining consent.

Why was the Bill changed during its parliamentary progress? The Government departed from Setting the Boundaries by opting for a reasonableness standard rather than the 'couldn't care less' test, but the clause as originally drafted was unduly complex. Moreover, its formulation turned on whether the defendant had acted as a reasonable person would, and this was attacked on the ground that a defendant with, for example, a learning disability would be judged by standards he could not attain. The Bill was then amended, so that s.1(2) now states:

'Whether a belief is reasonable is to be determined having regard to all the circumstances, including any steps A has taken to ascertain whether B consents.'

This wording discards the 'reasonable person' in favour of a general test of what is reasonable in the circumstances. The Home Affairs Committee applauded the change as avoiding the 'potential injustice' of a test that would operate regardless of individual characteristics:

'by focussing on the individual defendant's belief, the new test will allow the jury to look at characteristics—such as learning disability or mental disorder—and take them into account.' A different approach would have been to retain the reasonable person standard but to add a defence for those mentally incapable of attaining it. The difficulty with s.1(2) is that it could empty the reasonableness test of most of its content, and justify the kind of direction laid down in the self-defence case of *United States v King*:

'In determining whether it is founded on reasonable grounds, the jury are not to conceive of some ideally reasonable person, but they are to put themselves in the position of the assailed person, with his physical and mental equipment, surrounded with the circumstances and exposed to the influences with which he was surrounded and to which he was exposed at the time.'

Has Parliament replaced the 'couldn't care less' test with one that is more demanding on the prosecution and more favourable to the defence? Much depends on how the phrase 'all the circumstances' comes to be interpreted. The Government's view was that 'it is for the jury to decide whether any of the attributes of the defendant are relevant to their deliberations, subject to directions from the judge where necessary.' Beverley Hughes expressed the matter slightly differently, stating that it would be for the judge 'to decide whether it is necessary to introduce consideration of a defendant's characteristics and which characteristics are relevant. . . . The judge or jury can take into account all or any characteristics and circumstances that they wish to, and it is best that we leave that decision to the judge and jury for each case.' By what standards is it to be decided which character-istics are 'relevant'? Much will depend on the Specimen Directions and the approach of the Court of Appeal. But, as L'Heureux-Dube J. famously stated in *Seaboyer*: 'The content of any relevancy decision will be filled by the particular judge's experience, common sense and/ or logic. . . . This area of the law has been particularly prone to the utilisation of stereotype in the determination of relevance.'

In *Protecting the Public* the Government expressed its concern that the *Morgan* test 'leads many victims who feel that the system will not give them justice, not to report incidents or press for them to be brought to trial.' Accordingly, it decided to alter the test 'to include one of reasonableness under the law'. But the present formulation is unlikely to provide the incentive to report or pursue the case that the Government is seeking. The broad reference to 'all the circumstances' is an invitation to the jury to scrutinise the complainant's behaviour to determine whether there was anything about it which could have induced a reasonable belief in consent. In this respect the Act contains no real challenge to society's norms and stereotypes about either the relationship between men and women or other sexual situ-ations, and leaves open the possibility that those stereotypes will determine assessments of reasonableness. Is B's sexual history to be taken to be a relevant part of the circumstances? In answer to a question raised in Committee, the Minister agreed that the section 'should focus the court's attention on what is happening at the time of the offence' and 'should make the previous sexual history of the complainant far less relevant.' But this does not seem to reflect the natural meaning of the words 'all the circumstances', which contain no limitation to circumstances existing at the time of the event in question. Further, it is true that s.1(2) requires consideration of 'any steps A has taken to ascertain whether B consents', however, if A enquires about consent; B says no, but A concludes that B's 'no' is tantamount to 'yes', is his culturally engendered belief to be regarded as reasonable or not? In deciding what it is 'relevant' to consider, what is to prevent the influence of stereotypes about B's dress, B's frequenting of a particular place, an invitation to have a drink, and so forth?

It therefore seems possible that the new element of absence of reasonable belief in consent, which forms part of the four major offences in the Act, may not impose greater duties on defendants than does the present law. Of course, the prosecution may take advantage of the various presumptions in ss.76 (conclusive) and 75 (rebuttable), as we saw . . . above, but there will be many cases that fall outside that list of circumstances. The Act requires the prosecution to establish beyond reasonable doubt that A did not reasonably believe that B consented. Was the Government right to abandon its proposal for placing the onus of proof on the defence, once the basis for one of the rebuttable presumptions has been established?

8. The question of the burden of proof

. . . The Bill originally contained a provision that evidence resulting from the cross-examination of C was not acceptable for these purposes unless it amounted to an admission of consent. That was dropped, leaving open the possibility that statements by C may be used to discharge the evidential burden. The possibility of harassing cross-examination of C to try and extract such evidence therefore reappears. There will be little to prevent this unless it happens to take the form of an attempt to adduce sexual history evidence which is (somewhat) regulated by s.41 of the Youth Justice and Criminal Evidence Act 1999. Turning specifically to cases where reasonable belief in consent is argued, a defendant who wishes to rebut one of the presumptions can surely satisfy the evidential burden only by adducing sufficient evidence of both the belief and its reasonableness. That means that an explanation for the belief will have to be advanced.

The Government was keen to assert that the reduction of the burden on the defence in reasonable belief cases, from a persuasive to an evidential burden, did not undermine the thrust of the Act. Baroness Scotland stated that 'in order for these presumptions not to apply, the defendant will need to satisfy the judge from the evidence that there is a real issue about consent [or belief in consent] that is worth putting to the jury.' In effect, it comes down to how this is translated into practice. If the evidential burden comes to be applied as Baroness Scotland wishes, this would require defendants to go some way towards establishing consent or reasonable belief: it should be borne in mind that the imposition of an evidential burden in respect of an essential element (consent, reasonable belief in consent) of offences that carry a maximum of life imprisonment (rape, assault by penetration) already places an onus on the defence. If, on the other hand, little more than the defendant's say-so were held sufficient, this would be a purer instantiation of the presumption of innocence but would undermine the government's purpose of 'sending out a very clear message that does shift the balance in favour of the complainant.'

Some would argue that the Government has not shifted the balance in favour of the complainant but has, overall, made the prosecution's task harder. The presumptions will assist only in a restricted range of situations and to take advantage of them the prosecution will have to prove both the existence of a given circumstance and the defendant's knowledge of it. Where the defence satisfies the evidential burden, the prosecution will then bear the full burden of proof. In all other non-listed cases, instead of being able to establish liability through the former test of recklessness, the prosecution will now have to prove absence of belief in consent or that a belief was not reasonable, with all the attendant difficulties which that entails.

9. Consent, deception and threats

We have explained above that s.76 creates two conclusive presumptions of the absence of consent and of belief as to consent where there is deception as to the nature and purpose of the act or the identity of the defendant. But this leaves other cases of deception to be dealt with under the broad definition of consent as agreement by choice (s.74). What if D deceives C into thinking that he will pay her £25 for sex when in fact he has no intention of doing so, and does not? In *Linekar* the Court of Appeal held that this deception was not sufficiently fundamental to negative apparent consent. But the jury had originally convicted and, if left with the words of s.74, might they not conclude that she did not agree 'by choice'? What if D deceives C into thinking that he is not HIV positive when he is? If there is a prosecution for rape, how should the jury be directed on consent? Does the judge simply ask the jury to consider whether C agreed by choice? The defence might argue that C was obviously content to have sex with D and was merely deceived as to one of his attributes. The prosecution might argue that any distinction between essence and attributes is unconvincing in this situation, since plainly C was not content to have sex with D in the actual circumstances and the deception deprived her of true choice. Should the judge rule on this, and, if so, in what way? What if D deceives C as to his qualifications, and then carries out a medical procedure to which C would not have consented if she had known the true facts? The pre-Act position was unclear, and it is uncertain whether a judge, in a prosecution for assault by penetration or sexual assault, should direct the jury on whether this may amount to agreement 'by choice' and, if so, which approach the judge should then take. Indeed, in many of these situations a deception by D may not be required: it is arguable that, if C gives her agreement in ignorance of a key fact, and if D knows of that ignorance and takes advantage of it, it may be concluded that C did not agree by choice.

Similar difficulties arise in relation to threats. Section 75(2)(a) and (b) create rebuttable presumptions of the absence of consent where there are threats of immediate violence against the complainant or another person. This leaves all other cases of threats to be dealt with under the broad definition in s.74. What if there are threats of non-immediate violence (e.g. 'we will come and get you and your family, I have some very nasty friends')? The question is whether the jury thinks that these threats mean that the complainant did not agree by choice. What if D tells his employee C, who has committed a disciplinary offence, that, unless she allows him to cane her, he will terminate her employment? If she agrees, would that amount to agreement by choice if D was charged with sexual assault? Might the phrase 'agree by choice' apply differently if D's demand was for full sex, and the charge was rape? What if a police officer stops a woman motorist for an offence, and offers not to report her if she has sex with him? If she agrees, does she do so 'by choice'? That question will always have to be answered in the circumstances of the case and in relation to the particular complainant, notably the latter's 'freedom and capacity to make that choice'. This is the implication of protecting sexual autonomy: 'a threat which had a devastating effect on one victim might appear trivial to another, and if both had intercourse the latter might be held to have consented when the former did not.'

The difficulties with this aspect of the 2003 Act go further. It is not simply that the statutory definition of consent is vague. There is also the problem that the Act repeals the two previous offences of procuring sex by threats or intimidation and procuring sex by false representations, and does not replace them. This ignores the Report's recommendation that a new offence of obtaining sexual penetration by threats or deception in any part of the world should be created; all that appears in the Act is a new provision confined to protecting mentally disordered persons where inducements, threats or deceptions are used. Apart from that it appears that, when a court is deciding whether a particular deception or threat is sufficient to negative ostensible consent, it is effectively deciding between conviction of a serious offence and a complete acquittal. There is no lesser offence, no middle way. Admittedly, convictions under ss.2 and 3 of the 1956 Act were rare; but, in the unusual case where this issue occurs, the vague terms of s.74 now assume a heightened importance.

2 ASSAULT BY PENETRATION

Under section 2 of the Sexual Offences Act 2003:

2. Assault by penetration

(1) A person (A) commits an offence if—

    (a) he intentionally penetrates the vagina or anus of another person (B) with a part of his body or anything else,

    (b) the penetration is sexual,

    (c) B does not consent to the penetration, and

    (d) A does not reasonably believe that B consents.

(2) Whether a belief is reasonable is to be determined having regard to all the circumstances, including any steps A has taken to ascertain whether B consents.

(3) Sections 75 and 76 apply to an offence under this section.

Much of this offence is self-explanatory and has much in common with the offence of rape, just discussed. It is worth noting that the penetration must be sexual. This means that if a doctor inserts a medical instrument into a patient's vagina or anus as part of medical treatment, without getting the patient's consent, he or she will not be committing this offence.[59]

3 SEXUAL ASSAULT

Section 3 of the Sexual Offences Act 2003 states:

3. Sexual assault

(1) A person (A) commits an offence if—

    (a) he intentionally touches another person (B),

    (b) the touching is sexual,

    (c) B does not consent to the touching, and

    (d) A does not reasonably believe that B consents.

(2) Whether a belief is reasonable is to be determined having regard to all the circumstances, including any steps A has taken to ascertain whether B consents.

(3) Sections 75 and 76 apply to an offence under this section.

---

[59] Although he or she may be committing a battery. Arguably if the doctor was inserting the instrument for sexual purposes this could render the act a sexual one. For the definition of a sexual act see p. 455.

DEFINITION

Actus reus: the defendant touches the victim sexually and the victim does not consent to the touching.

Mens rea: the defendant does not reasonably believe that the victim consents.

A number of points need to be made about this offence.

(1) There must be some touching for there to be a sexual assault. Touching is defined in section 79(8) as including: 'touching (a) with any part of the body, (b) with anything else, (c) through anything'.[60] This means that, for example, if the defendant forced the victim to undress by threatening violence, but did not touch the victim, the offence would not be committed.

(2) The touching must be sexual. Section 78 explains:

> penetration, touching or any other activity is sexual if a reasonable person would consider that—
>
> (a) whatever its circumstances or any person's purpose in relation to it, it is because of its nature sexual, or
>
> (b) because of its nature it may be sexual and because of its circumstances or the purpose of any person in relation to it (or both) it is sexual.

This definition of sexual is notably objective. In other words whether or not an act is sexual does not depend on whether the defendant found it to be sexual. What matters is whether a reasonable person would consider it sexual. However, as section 78(b) makes clear, a reasonable person could take into account the purposes of the defendant in deciding whether or not it is sexual. Contrast these three cases:

(i) A defendant forcibly removes the victim's clothing in public. He does this in order to humiliate her and is not sexually motivated. This *could* still be a sexual assault. The jury might think that the act, looked at as a whole, is sexual, even though the defendant was not acting for sexual purposes.

(ii) An underground train becomes very crowded and a man stands against a woman whom he finds very attractive. His touching of her may be to him very sexually provocative, but this is *not* a sexual assault, as under section 78(a) standing next to someone on a crowded tube is not sexual in its nature. Under section 78(b) a touching which in its nature is not sexual cannot be regarded as sexual because of the defendant's purposes.

(iii) A shopkeeper is found hitting a girl on her shorts.[61] This might be regarded as 'objectively' an ambiguous case. This may be sexual or it may not. If the shopkeeper admits that he was sexually motivated then the reasonable person looking at all the circumstances (including the defendant's sexual purposes) probably would regard the spanking as sexual. However, if the shopkeeper gave evidence

---

[60] Section 79(8) also makes it clear that just because a touching is also a penetration does not prevent it from being a touching.

[61] These were the facts in the case of *Court* [1989] AC 28 (HL).

that he was punishing the girl as he had caught her shoplifting, then the reasonable person might conclude that it was not sexual.[62]

It must be admitted that perhaps inevitably the meaning of sexual is ambiguous and it is not difficult to think of cases where it might be hard to predict whether the jury will think that the reasonable person would regard the act as sexual.

(3) The *mens rea* provisions are identical to those used in relation to rape.

We have one case considering the new offence of sexual assault:

R v H
[2005] EWCA 732[63]

The victim was walking her dog at about 10pm when she encountered the appellant. He asked her the time and then said 'Do you fancy a shag?' She ignored this question and walked away. He grabbed her tracksuit bottoms and tried to pull her towards him. She was able to pull away and run to safety. The appellant was charged with a sexual assault contrary to section 3 of the Sexual Offences Act 2003. At his trial he argued that touching clothing could not amount to a touching as required for the section 3 offence. This argument was rejected, he was convicted and appealed.

Lord Woolf CJ

12. The fact that in section 78(b) there are two different questions which we have sought to identify complicates the task of the judge and that of the jury. If there is a submission of 'no case' the judge may have to ask himself whether there is a case to be left to the jury. He will answer that question by determining whether it would be appropriate for a reasonable person to consider that the touching because of its nature may be sexual. Equally, the judge will have to consider whether it would be possible for a reasonable person to conclude, because of the circumstances of the touching or the purpose of any person in relation to the touching (or both), that it is sexual. If he comes to the conclusion that a reasonable person could possibly answer those questions adversely to the defendant, then the matter would have to be left to the jury.

13. We would suggest that in that situation the judge would regard it as desirable to identify two distinct questions for the jury. First, would they, as 12 reasonable people (as the section requires), consider that because of its nature the touching that took place in the particular case before them could be sexual? If the answer to that question was 'No', the jury would find the defendant not guilty. If 'Yes', they would have to go on to ask themselves (again as 12 reasonable people) whether in view of the circumstances and/or the purpose of any person in relation to the touching (or both), the touching was in fact sexual. If they were satisfied that it was, then they would find the defendant guilty. If they were not satisfied, they would find the defendant not guilty.

14. In that suggested approach the reference to the nature of the touching in the first half refers to the actual touching that took place in that case. In answering the first question, the jury would not be concerned with the circumstances before or after the touching took place, or any evidence as to the purpose of any person in relation to the touching.

. . .

---

[62] He might still be guilty of a battery.
[63] [2005] 2 All ER 859, [2005] 2 Cr App R 9, [2005] 1 WLR 2005, [2005] Crim LR 735.

23. At the end of the prosecution case there was a submission of no case to answer. Two arguments were advanced by Mr West on behalf of the appellant. The first was based upon the interpretation of the statutory provisions of the 2003 Act. He submitted that the touching of the tracksuit bottoms alone did not amount to the touching of another person.

24. The judge rejected that submission. We consider that he was right to do so. Where a person is wearing clothing we consider that touching of the clothing constitutes touching for the purpose of the section 3 offence.

25. As against that approach Mr West relied on section 79(8) (set out above). He submits that under section 79(8)(c) touching through anything (through clothing), if pressure in some form is not brought against the body of the person concerned, cannot be touching; there has to be some form of touching of the body of the individual who is alleged to have been assaulted, even if it be through clothing. Mr West submits that, having regard to the complainant's evidence in this case, there was no such touching.

26. It is important to note that the opening words of section 79(8) are 'Touching includes touching' and in particular 'through anything'. Subsection (8) is not a definition section. We have no doubt that it was not Parliament's intention by the use of that language to make it impossible to regard as a sexual assault touching which took place by touching what the victim was wearing at the time.

Appeal dismissed.

QUESTIONS

1. In *George* [1956] Crim LR 52 a man had a foot fetish and removed the victim's shoes without her consent. Would this now be a sexual assault?

2. George visits his doctor, Steve. Steve finds George very attractive and says (untruthfully) that for medical reasons he needs to conduct an intimate examination of George, to which George consents. Is this a sexual assault?

3. Sam visits her doctor, Cynthia. Cynthia conducts an intimate examination which is medically necessary. However, Cynthia has invited her friend Brian to hide in the surgery so that he can watch such examinations for sexual purposes. Has Brian committed a sexual assault? Has he committed any offence? (You will need to read the rest of the chapter to consider this. Do not forget to consider the issue of Cynthia's consent.)

4 CAUSING SEXUAL ACTIVITY WITHOUT CONSENT

Section 4 of the Sexual Offences Act states:

(1) A person (A) commits an offence if—
  (a) he intentionally causes another person (B) to engage in an activity,
  (b) the activity is sexual,
  (c) B does not consent to engaging in the activity, and
  (d) A does not reasonably believe that B consents.

(2) Whether a belief is reasonable is to be determined having regard to all the circumstances, including any steps A has taken to ascertain whether B consents.

This is similar to sexual assault, but does not require the defendant to have touched the victim. In a case decided under the old law, *Sargeant*,[64] the defendant threatened a young man with a knife and forced him to masturbate into a condom. Under the old law the defendant was convicted of an indecent assault,[65] but he would not commit a sexual assault under the 2003 Act because there was no touching. The defendant would, however, be guilty of causing a person to engage in sexual activity without their consent.

5 PREPARATORY OFFENCES

The Act prohibits certain activities done with intent to enable the defendant to commit a sexual offence. For example, under section 61 it is an offence for the defendant to administer a substance to the victim 'with the intention of stupefying or overpowering [him or her], so as to enable any person to engage in a sexual activity that involves [the victim]' without the consent of the victim. Also if a person is a trespasser[66] in any structure, part of a structure, or any land and intends to commit a sexual offence or does commit any sexual offence he or she commits an offence.[67]

6 SEXUAL OFFENCES DESIGNED TO PROTECT CHILDREN

The Sexual Offences Act 2003 produces a large range of offences which are designed to protect children from harmful sexual acts. It is not possible to discuss them all but here is a summary.

6.1 OFFENCES WHICH ARE VERSIONS OF THE GENERAL OFFENCES

The following are versions of the general sexual offences specifically designed to protect children under the age of 13:

(1) section 5: rape of a child under 13;

(2) section 6: assault of a child under 13 by penetration;

(3) section 7: sexual assault of a child under 13;

(4) section 8: causing or inciting a child under 13 to engage in a sexual activity.

All of these offences are equivalent to the adult version of the offences, but with two key modifications. First there is no *mens rea* requirement, except the intent to penetrate, touch, or cause the victim to engage in an activity. There is no need to show that the defendant was aware that the victim was 13. Secondly, it is no defence to prove that the victim consented to the activity. Where the victim is under 13 his or her consent is irrelevant to these offences.

---

[64] [1997] Crim LR 50 (CA).

[65] That offence required proof only that the defendant did an assault or a battery.

[66] Sexual Offences Act 2003, s. 63.   [67] Ibid.

The government White Paper suggests that where the parties are close in age (e.g. a 13-year-old having sexual relations with a 12-year-old) although the 13-year-old could in theory be convicted of one of these offences, it may be more appropriate for the matter to be treated as an issue of child protection for the social services, rather than being appropriate for the ministrations of the criminal courts.[68]

6.2 OFFENCES DESIGNED SPECIFICALLY TO PROTECT CHILDREN FROM SEXUAL ABUSE

The following are offences designed to protect children from sexual abuse:

(1) section 9: sexual activity with a child;

(2) section 10: causing or inciting a child to engage in a sexual activity;

(3) section 11: engaging in sexual activity in the presence of a child;

(4) section 12: causing a child to watch a sexual act;

(5) section 13: child sex offences committed by children or young persons;

(6) section 14: arranging or facilitating commission of a child sex offence;

(7) section 15: meeting a child following sexual grooming etc.

Most of these offences are self explanatory. But two will now be briefly defined:

Section 9(1):

(1) A person aged 18 or over (A) commits an offence if—

  (a) he intentionally touches another person (B),

  (b) the touching is sexual, and

  (c) either—

    (i)   B is under 16 and A does not reasonably believe that B is 16 or over, or

    (ii) B is under 13.

The section 9 offence is therefore designed to cover sexual touchings even where the victim[69] consents to the touching.[70] The defendant is not guilty if he reasonably believes that the victim is 16 or over unless the victim is under 13. The defendant can be guilty only if he himself is over 18. If the defendant is under 18 he can still be charged under section 13. This means that even consensual touchings between teenagers who are consenting will be criminal offences. The government White Paper explained that although many such touchings will be 'experimental' and so 'the intervention of the criminal law may not be appropriate'; it was useful to create such an offence to deal with cases where the touchings were consented to but there was 'manipulation'.[71]

---

[68] Home Office (2002b: 17). But they argued that if a child has a history of abusing other children the criminal law may well be suitable.

[69] If the victim were under 13 the offence would be committed under s. 7.

[70] If the victim consented then there may also be offence contrary to ss. 5, 6, or 7.

[71] Home Office (2002b: 25).

Section 15: Meeting a child following sexual grooming etc.

(1) A person aged 18 or over (A) commits an offence if—

    (a) having met or communicated with another person (B) on at least two earlier occasions, he—

        (i) intentionally meets B, or

        (ii) travels with the intention of meeting B in any part of the world,

    (b) at the time, he intends to do anything to or in respect of B, during or after the meeting and in any part of the world, which if done will involve the commission by A of a relevant offence,

    (c) B is under 16, and

    (d) A does not reasonably believe that B is 16 or over.

This is the offence described in the statute as 'sexual grooming'.[72] The relevant offences are listed in section 15(2) and include any of the offences in the Sexual Offences Act 2003.

6.3 ABUSE OF POSITION OF TRUST OFFENCES

The Sexual Offences Act 2003 contains a number of offences which involve sexual abuse by a person who is in a position of trust:

(1) section 16: abuse of position of trust: sexual activity with a child;

(2) section 17: abuse of position of trust: causing or inciting a child to engage in sexual activity;

(3) section 18: abuse of position of trust: sexual activity in the presence of a child;

(4) section 19: abuse of position of trust: causing a child to watch a second act.

Typical of these offences is section 16(1):

(1) A person aged 18 or over (A) commits an offence if—

    (a) he intentionally touches another person (B),

    (b) the touching is sexual,

    (c) A is in a position of trust in relation to B,

    (d) where subsection (2) applies, A knows or could reasonably be expected to know of the circumstances by virtue of which he is in a position of trust in relation to B, and

    (e) either—

        (i) B is under 18 and A does not reasonably believe that B is 18 or over, or

        (ii) B is under 13.

The term 'position of trust' is extensively defined in sections 22 and 23. It covers the situation where an adult is looking after people under the age of 18 in certain circumstances. 'Looks after' means being 'regularly involved in caring for, training, supervising, or being in

---

[72] The government was particularly concerned about the use of the internet for grooming purposes (Home Office (2002b: 25)).

sole charge of such persons'.[73] There is a long list of circumstances which this definition includes. It includes, by way of example, the following:

> (4) This subsection applies if A looks after persons under 18 who are accommodated and cared for in one of the following institutions—
>
> (a) a hospital,
>
> (b) an independent clinic,
>
> (c) a care home, residential care home or private hospital,
>
> (d) a community home, voluntary home or children's home,
>
> (e) a home provided under section 82(5) of the Children Act 1989, or
>
> (f) a residential family centre,
>
> and B is accommodated and cared for in that institution.
>
> (5) This subsection applies if A looks after persons under 18 who are receiving education at an educational institution and B is receiving, and A is not receiving, education at that institution.

The defendant to a charge under one of the abuse of trust offences will have a defence in any of the following circumstances:

(1) The defendant proves that he reasonably believed the victim was over 18.[74]

(2) The defendant could not reasonably be expected to know that he was in a position of trust in respect of the victim.[75]

(3) If the defendant is lawfully married to the victim at the time of the offence.[76]

(4) If immediately before the position of trust arose a sexual relationship[77] existed between the defendant and the victim.[78]

6.4 FAMILIAL CHILD SEX OFFENCES

The 2003 Act also creates a number of offences which are designed to protect children from abuse by family members:

(1) section 25: sexual activity with a family member;

(2) section 26: inciting a child family member to engage in sexual activity.

Family relationships are defined in section 27:

> (1) The relation of one person (A) to another (B) is within this section if—
>
> (a) it is within any of subsections (2) to (4), or

---

[73] Section 22(2).

[74] Sections 16(1), 17(1), 18(1). But the defendant is guilty if the victim was in fact under 13.

[75] But only if that is one of the positions of trust defined in s. 21(2)–(5).

[76] Sexual Offences Act 2003, s. 23.

[77] This defence cannot be relied upon if the relationship involved unlawful sexual intercourse.

[78] Sexual Offences Act 2003, s. 24.

    (b) it would be within one of those subsections but for section 67 of the Adoption and Children Act 2002 (c. 38) (status conferred by adoption).

(2) The relation of A to B is within this subsection if—

    (a) one of them is the other's parent, grandparent, brother, sister, half-brother, half-sister, aunt or uncle,

    (b) A is or has been B's foster parent.

(3) The relation of A to B is within this subsection if A and B live or have lived in the same household, or A is or has been regularly involved in caring for, training, supervising or being in sole charge of B, and—

    (a) one of them is or has been the partner of the other's step-parent,

    (b) A and B are cousins, or

    (c) one of them is or has been the other's stepbrother or stepsister, or

    (d) the parent or present or former foster parent or one of them is or has been the other's foster parent.

(4) The relation of A to B is within this subsection if—

    (a) A and B live in the same household, and

    (b) A is regularly involved in caring for, training, supervising or being in sole charge of B.

(5) For the purposes of this section—

    (a) 'aunt' means the sister or half-sister of a person's parent, and 'uncle' has a corresponding meaning;

    (b) 'cousin' means the child of an aunt or uncle;

    (c) a person is a child's foster parent if—

        (i) he is a person with whom the child has been placed under section 23(2)(a) or 59(1)(a) of the Children Act 1989 (c. 41) (fostering for local authority or voluntary organisation), or

        (ii) he fosters the child privately, within the meaning given by section 66(1)(b) of that Act;

    (d) a person is another's partner (whether they are of different sexes or the same sex) if they live together as partners in an enduring family relationship.

    (e) 'step-parent' includes a parent's partner and 'stepbrother' and 'stepsister' include the child of a parent's partner.

6.5 CHILD PROSTITUTION AND CHILD PORNOGRAPHY

The Act also includes provisions which are designed to render illegal the payment for sex with a child,[79] or causing, inciting, controlling, arranging, or facilitating child prostitution or pornography.[80]

---

[79] Sexual Offences Act 2003, s. 47.   [80] Ibid., ss. 47, 48, 49, 52, 53.

7 OFFENCES AGAINST THOSE WITH A MENTAL DISORDER

There is in the 2003 Act a raft of offences designed to protect those with a mental disorder:[81]

(1) section 30: sexual activity with a person with a mental disorder impeding choice;

(2) section 31: causing or inciting a person with a mental disorder impeding choice to engage in sexual activity;

(3) section 32: engaging in sexual activity in the presence of a person with a mental disorder impeding choice;

(4) section 33: causing a person with a mental disorder impeding choice to watch a sexual act;

(5) section 34: inducement, threat, or deception to procure sexual activity with a person with a mental disorder;

(6) section 35: causing a person with a mental disorder to engage in or agree to engage in sexual activity by inducement, threat, or deception;

(7) section 36: engaging in sexual activity in the presence, procured by inducement, threat, or deception, of a person with a mental disorder;

(8) section 37: causing a person with a mental disorder to watch a sexual act by inducement, threat, or deception;

(9) section 38: care workers: sexual activity with a person with a mental disorder;

(10) section 39: care workers: causing or inciting sexual activity;

(11) section 40: care workers: sexual activity in the presence of a person with a mental disorder;

(12) section 41: care workers: causing a person with a mental disorder to watch a sexual act.

The defendant will be guilty of these offences if he knew, or could reasonably be expected to know, that the victim had a mental disorder and that because of it the victim was unable to refuse (be that because she lacked the capacity to make a choice whether to consent, or because she was unable to communicate the decision).

8 PROSTITUTION AND TRAFFICKING

There are a variety of provisions which are designed to deal with prostitution. Sections 52 and 53 prohibit the causing, inciting, or controlling prostitution for gain. Sections 57 to 59 create offences prohibiting the trafficking into, within, or out of the UK in people for the sexual exploitation.

9 INCEST

Section 64 states:

---

[81] 'Mental disorder' is given the definition in the Mental Health Act 1983, s. 1 (Sexual Offences Act 2003, s. 79(6)). Learning disability is not defined in the Act.

(1) A person aged 16 or over (A) commits an offence if—

   (a) he intentionally penetrates another person's vagina or anus with a part of his body or anything else, or penetrates another person's mouth with his penis,

   (b) the penetration is sexual,

   (c) the other person (B) is aged 18 or over,

   (d) A is related to B in a way mentioned in subsection (2), and

   (e) A knows or could reasonably be expected to know that he is related to B in that way.

(2) The ways that A may be related to B are as parent, grandparent, child, grandchild, brother, sister, half-brother, half-sister, uncle, aunt, nephew, or niece . . .

(4) Where in proceedings for an offence under this section it is proved that the defendant was related to the other person in any of those ways, it is to be taken that the defendant knew or could reasonably have been expected to know that he was related in that way unless sufficient evidence is adduced to raise an issue as to whether he knew or could reasonably have been expected to know that he was.

Section 65 creates a similar offence but phrases the offence in terms of the defendant consenting to the penetration. Controversially the Act continues to render illegal sexual activity between adult brothers and sisters.[82] The government White Paper baldly stated: 'Despite involving consensual adults it is generally believed that all such behaviour is wrong and should be covered by the law.'[83] To others, just because some people regard conduct as immoral is not a reason for rendering it illegal.[84]

10 MISCELLANEOUS OFFENCES

The Act also includes a number of miscellaneous offences. These include exposure,[85] voyeurism,[86] intercourse with an animal,[87] and sexual penetration of a corpse.[88] The Bill originally had an offence of sexual activity in public.[89] The last had attracted much comment. The government White Paper reassuringly stated, 'it is not our intention to interfere in everyday behaviour that does not cause offence to the vast majority of people such as kissing or cuddling';[90] nor does it intend to criminalize sexual activity[91] in 'an isolated place where one would reasonably expect not to be observed'. However, such reassurance did not persuade Parliament which rejected the proposed offence.

QUESTIONS

1. Lord Thomas of Gresford in his speech at the second reading of the Bill stated:

'it is important to set out a principle at the beginning: that sex between two consenting adults and, in our culture, in private is a healthy, life-enhancing, pleasurable activity. It should be recognised that in my view a great amount of deviant

---

[82] Morton (2003a).   [83] Home Office (2002b: 26).

[84] Morton (2003a). See further the discussion in Ch. 1 on the enforcement of morality.

[85] Section 66.   [86] Section 67.   [87] Section 69.   [88] Section 70.

[89] Clause 74.   [90] Home Office (2002b: 32).   [91] Ibid.

behaviour takes place because it is not recognised due to guilt, inadequacy and immaturity' [HL Debs., col. 779, 13 February 2003).

Do you think the 2003 Act recognizes such a principle?

2. The Act at several points uses the term 'reasonable'. Do you think in sexual matters there is a community consensus which the jury can rely upon when considering what a reasonable person would do or think?

3. In *Leather* (1993) 14 Cr App R (S) 736 the defendant grabbed the testicles of a police officer to stop him making an arrest. This was held to be an indecent assault. Would it be an offence under the 2003 Act?

FURTHER READING

Finch, E., and Munro, V. (2003), 'Intoxicated Consent and the Boundaries of Drug Assisted Rape', *Criminal Law Review* 773.

—— (2004), 'Intoxicated Consent and Drug Assisted Rape Revisited', *Criminal Law Review* 789.

Selfe, D., and Burke, V. (2001), *Perspectives on Sex, Crime and Society* (London: Cavendish).

Spencer, J. (2004b), 'Child and Family Offences', *Criminal Law Review* 347.

Temkin, J. (2002), *Rape and the Legal Process* (2nd edn., Oxford: OUP).

Temkin, J., and Ashworth, A. (2004), 'Rape, Sexual Assaults and the Problems of Consent', *Criminal Law Review* 328.

Thomas, T. (2000), *Sex Crime* (Cullompton: Willan).

PART II: THE THEORY OF SEXUAL OFFENCES

11 BACKGROUND OF SEXUAL CRIMES

For many people sexual touchings represent not only some of the most wonderful, but also the worst, moments of their lives. This highlights a key dilemma in relation to sexual offences: people need to be protected from the unwanted sexual activity which infringes their right to bodily integrity[92] and sexual autonomy;[93] but at the same time people wish to be free to express themselves sexually without government intrusion.[94] Unfortunately, the history of sexual offences shows a failure to protect victims of rape and sexual assault and a

---

[92] The difference between a right to sexual autonomy and one to sexual integrity is explained in Lacey (1998c).

[93] Sexual autonomy is protected under Art. 8 of the European Convention on Human Rights (*ADT v UK* [2000] Crim LR 1009). For a detailed discussion of sexual autonomy see Schulhofer (1998).

[94] Brants (2001); Coughlin (1998).

willingness to intervene to prohibit what is regarded as immoral sexual activity (especially in cases of same-sex sexual activity).[95]

In the following extract the experiences of victims of sexual crimes are described in an attempt to identify the wrong of forced sex:

S.H. Pillsbury, 'Crimes Against The Heart: Recognizing The Wrongs of Forced Sex'
(2002) 35 *Loyola at Los Angeles Law Review* 845 at 893–5

The victims speak about self-identity: who they are to themselves. They speak of a basic change in their idea of themselves as a unique person, constituted of particular experiences, tendencies and abilities, particular thoughts and feelings. They report that sexual violation does such violence to these aspects of identity that their own thoughts and feelings become alien to themselves.

These accounts point us to an important and insidious aspect of the injury of sexual aggression. They reveal that, in some unexpected fashion, the aggressor overcomes psychic defenses to invade the inner person. Normally we can defend ourselves against hostile physical attacks, and even if we cannot, we can separate harm to the body from harm to the inner self. We can keep our minds intact. Indeed rape victims frequently do this by mentally separating from their bodies during the attack. They watch their bodies being used, becoming observers to themselves. But this works only for a time. Eventually the victim's self, her spirit, must rejoin the body and this requires the spirit's acceptance of what the body has suffered.

The victims' accounts remind us that regardless of the power of our minds, we remain embodied beings, inextricably linked to our physical existences. Our bodily and psychic lives are absolutely intertwined, and more closely than we sometimes realize in this age of virtual exploration and fantasy. A meaningful life requires a joining of body and mind, and when their connection is torn, it takes long and hard work to rebuild. The sometimes overwhelming temptation for victims—to treat the body as tainted, as separate from the self—just prolongs the rapist's act of disregard for personal integrity.

The same point can be made another way. The victim accounts remind us of the importance of sex to gender and personal identity. Whether sexually active or inactive, adults generally see themselves as individuals with a particular sexual identity, which implies certain kinds of relationships with others. An important part of every life story is the individual's development of a particular sexual identity through chosen interactions with others. Among the most powerful influences on that development can be physical sexual contact. When that contact is unwanted, it can wreak havoc on the individual's sense of self and future direction.

Although this injury is internal and individual, it has important social repercussions. Because of the perpetrator's invasion of the victim's self and disruption of identity, because of his disregard for her value, many survivors of rape feel socially devastated. Victims feel the attack has dragged them from a place of social order and comfort to one of indifference and cruelty, where ordinary human bonds do not function. They feel abandoned in a place of utter loneliness:

'It's as though the moment I was hit . . . I was cut off from myself—as though all my connections to the world were slashed.'

---

[95] Selfe and Burke (2001: chs. 1 and 2).

> . . . To summarize: By forcibly using the other's body sexually, the rapist intrudes not just into the body but into the mind, and not just temporarily, but in many cases permanently. A crude and in many ways stupid physical act can violate the individual's sense of self and security, crippling the victim's ability to connect to others. Because the injury is sexual it goes deep into the self; because it goes deep, we should consider it a harm, a crime to the soul.

But it would be wrong to consider sexual crimes just from the perspective of the individual victim.[96] The impact of sexual assaults is not limited to the direct victims, but has a severe impact on the wider female population[97] and the children of victims.[98] One study found that rape is the crime women fear more than any other.[99] *Protecting the Public* opens with the statement:

> Sexual Crime, and the fear of sexual crime, has a profound and damaging effect on the social fabric of communities, and the fight against it is of the highest priority to the Government.[100]

It cannot be ignored that the majority of sexual offences are perpetrated against women.[101] The law's protection of people from sexual assault therefore also exists as part of the wider programme to promote equality of men and women. As Cory J wrote in the Canadian decision of *Osolin*, sexual assault 'is an assault upon human dignity and constitutes a denial of any concept of equality for women'.[102]

12 STATISTICS ON RAPE

In the following extract Andy Myhill and Jonathan Allen summarize the key points from the recent British Crime Survey on rape and sexual assault:

A. Myhill and J. Allen, *Rape and Sexual Assault of Women: Findings from the British Crime Survey* (London: TSO, 2002), 1

- 0.4 per cent of women aged 16 to 59 in England and Wales said they had been raped in the year preceding the 2000 BCS—an estimated 61,000 victims.

- 0.9 per cent of women said they had been subject to some form of sexual victimisation (including rape) in this period.

---

[96] See further the extract by Susan Marshall and Anthony Duff at p. 26.   [97] Thomas (2001).
[98] Morgan and Zedner (1992: ch. 3).
[99] Myhill and Allen (2002: 1). For a wide-ranging study of attitudes among Australians to rape see Esteal (1998).
[100] Home Office (2002b: 1).   [101] Selfe and Burke (2001: 61).
[102] *R v Osolin* [1993] 4 SCR 595 at 669.

- Around 1 in 20 women (4.9 per cent) said they had been raped since age 16, an estimated 754,000 victims. About 1 in 10 women (9.7 per cent) said they had experienced some form of sexual victimisation (including rape since age 6).[103]

- Age is the biggest risk factor for experiencing sexual victimisation; women aged 16 to 24 were more likely to say they had been sexually victimised in the last year than older women.

- Women are most likely to be sexually attacked by men they know in some way, most often partners (32 per cent) or acquaintances (22 per cent). Current partners (at the time of the attack) were responsible for 45 per cent of rapes reported to the survey. Strangers were responsible for only 8 per cent of rapes reported to the survey.

- 18 per cent of incidents of sexual victimisation reported to the survey came to the attention of the police; the police came to know about 20 per cent of rapes. 32 per cent of women who reported rape were 'very satisfied' with the way the police handled the matter, 22 per cent were very dissatisfied.

- Less than two-thirds (60 per cent) of female rape victims were prepared to self-classify their experience as 'rape' and less than three-quarters (70 per cent) of women who self-classified themselves as having been the victim of 'attempted rape' also self-classified this incident.

One statistic that should be added is that in the year 2004/2005 there were 12,867 rapes of women and 1,135 rapes of men.[104]

It should be clear from these statistics that the popular image that rape is committed by a stranger is in fact not the most common form of rape. It is more likely that a victim of rape knows the rapist than she does not.[105] As Morrison Torrey puts it,[106] 'It is a horrifying reality for women; we have more to fear from those who say they love us than from strangers.' One survey reported that 14 per cent of wives said that they had had non-consensual intercourse with their husbands.[107]

The conviction rate for rape is appallingly low. It has fallen from 25 per cent, in 1985, to 5.6 per cent in 2004.[108] There are a range of reasons for this, including: the attitude of the police towards complaints of rape, the *mens rea* requirement, the law on evidence at rape trials; and the atmosphere of rape trials themselves.[109] One of the aims of the Sexual Offences Act 2003 was to increase the rate of rape convictions. Whether it will do so remains to be seen.

A shocking survey recently demonstrated attitudes towards victims of rape which one might have thought would be rarely held nowadays. The ICM poll found that 34 per cent of those questioned in the UK thought that a woman who is partially or totally responsible for being raped if she has behaved in a flirtatious manner[110] and 26 per cent said the same where a woman was wearing 'sexy or revealing clothing'.

---

[103] Other studies have had higher figures. Koss (2002) suggests that 15.4% of women are raped at some point during their lives and a further 12.1% will suffer attempted rape.
[104] Home Office (2001b).   [105] For further discussion see Selfe and Burke (2001: 61).
[106] Torrey (1995: 35).
[107] Painter (1991).   [108] Kelly, Lovett, and Regan (2005: appendix 1).
[109] Kelly, Lovett, and Regan (2005). For a powerful indictment of the treatment of rape in the legal system see Lees (1996). Lacey (2001c) emphasizes that the full legal position of rape cannot be understood without consideration of the law of evidence and the procedure governing rape trials.
[110] Amnesty International (2005).

13 THE NATURE OF RAPE

The government has declared that rape is 'one of the most serious and abhorrent crimes a person can commit'.[111] But exactly what is the wrong that is at the heart of rape?[112] This is a controversial issue and it is one which has a significant impact on many of the hotly debated topics in the law of rape. Here are some of the alternatives.[113]

13.1 THE HISTORICAL EXPLANATION

In the past rape was seen as a wrong against the victim's husband, father, or brother.[114] Rape thereby protected the husband's interest in ensuring a legitimate family line. It is unlikely anyone would seriously propose this understanding of rape in modern times.

13.2 THE AUTONOMY EXPLANATION[115]

This view argues that at the heart of the law is the principle that people have the right to decide with whom to have sexual relations: the right of sexual autonomy.[116] This is why the issue of the consent of the victim plays such an important role in rape trials.

John Gardner and Stephen Shute,[117] supporting this view, posit the example of a defendant who has sex with an unconscious victim who suffers no physical or emotional harm. Such a victim is clearly still raped. This indicates that it is not the physical or emotional consequences of rape which are key to the offence, but the lack of respect shown to the victim's sexual autonomy. As they put it, rape is 'the sheer use of another person'.[118]

Other commentators disagree. Victims speaking of their experiences of rape focus on the tangible physical and psychological harms rather than the intangible notion of sexual autonomy. To focus primarily on autonomy overlooks the bodily violation that occurs in rape.[119]

13.3 RAPE AS VIOLENCE

To some, rape should be regarded as a form of violence.[120] Two reasons are often used to support this view. First, it is claimed that what motivates rape is not sexual desire but a wish to express domination over and hatred of women.[121] Describing rape as a crime of violence, rather than a sex crime, emphasizes this. Secondly, by recognizing rape to be an offence of violence the focus of the crime is moved away from the victim's consent. In rape trials there is always a danger that the victim becomes the person on trial, because the key

---

[111] Home Office (2002b: 21).   [112] Cahill (2001).

[113] A significant omission from this list is economic theories of rape: see Posner (1992), criticized in West (1993a).

[114] Burgess-Jackson (1996: ch. 1).

[115] The leading proponent of this view is Schulhofer (1998). See also Larson (1993).

[116] This is an aspect of the general principle that a person cannot touch another without their consent. See e.g. the analysis of consent in Brett (1998).

[117] Gardner and Shute (2000).   [118] Ibid. at 205.   [119] Cahill (2001).

[120] Brownmiller (1975).

[121] Schwartz and Clear (1980). For views that rape is about sexual desire see Posner (1992) and Baker (1999b).

question becomes whether or not she consented.[122] By focusing on the violence done by the defendant, rather than the state of mind of the victim, rape trials may be less traumatic for victims.[123]

Against this view is the argument that such an approach trivializes rapes where there is no violence, but threats of force or deceptions are used to manipulate the victim into sexual intercourse.[124] In reply, some supporters of the 'rape as violence' view have replied that rapes which involve force are different from 'rapes' where there is no force (which may sometimes deserve to be criminal offences, but not of the same kind as violent rape). In a controversial comment Donald Dripps has argued that the use of force is an essential element in rape. He sees unwanted sex (sex where there is no violence) as not particularly serious:

> . . . People generally, male and female, would rather be subjected to unwanted sex than be shot, slashed, or beaten with a tire iron. . . . Whether measured by the welfare or by the dignity of the victim, as a general matter unwanted sex is not as bad as violence. I think it follows that those who press sexual advances in the face of refusal act less wickedly than those who shoot, or slash, or batter.[125]

This generalization is one that has been widely rejected, especially by commentators who have themselves been raped or sexually abused. However, his suggestion that the law should recognize two kind of sexual offences: forcible rape (rape with the use of force) and expropriation of sexual services (sexual intercourse following deceptions or where the defendant has intercourse with a victim who is saying no but no force is used[126]) has received some support.[127]

13.4 RAPE AS INVASION OF INTEGRITY

This view seeks to combine the best parts of the two theories just discussed.[128] It argues that the harm of rape is not the violence exactly, but rather an invasion of an embodied person.[129] This view is explained further in the following extract by Nicola Lacey:

N. Lacey, 'Unspeakable Subjects, Impossible Rights: Sexuality, Integrity and Criminal Law' (1998) 11 *Canadian Journal of Law and Jurisprudence* **47 at 62–6**

Reinserting the corporeal: from autonomy to integrity?

I have suggested that the primary good which a liberal theory of criminal law would expect the sexual offences to respect is that of sexual autonomy. As usually understood, this idea of what is at issue in the area of sexual harm is one which expresses precisely the elevation of mind over body to which feminist criticism has drawn our attention. In focussing on an individualised notion of consent, rather than the conditions under which choices can be meaningful, the prevailing idea of sexual autonomy *assumes* the mind to be dominant and

---

[122] MacKinnon (1989: 245).   [123] Cahill (2001: 20).   [124] Tong (1984).
[125] Dripps (1992: 1792).   [126] Dripps (1992).
[127] See also Schulhofer (1992: 75). For criticism see e.g Fairstein (1994) and West (1994).
[128] Gibson (1993).   [129] West (1988: 70); Childs (2001); Cornell (1995).

controlling, irrespective of material circumstances. Furthermore, the liberal discourse of autonomy appears to leave no space for the articulation of the affective and corporeal dimensions of *certain* violations of autonomy—in other words, it closes off the possibility of developing a sophisticated conception of sexual harms. While the idea of autonomy as independence seems directly relevant to the wrong of rape, it dominates at the expense of the development of a positive conception of what kinds of sexual relationships matter to personhood.

Might it be possible to reconstruct the idea of autonomy or to find an alternative analytic and normative framework within which to rethink the sexual offences—one which would allow repressed corporeality to be thought and spoken, which would contextualise the victim's and the defendant's encounter more adequately, and which would accord the embodied aspects of human existence their proper place? I should like to suggest that we can draw on the work of two feminist legal theorists, Drucilla Cornell and Jennifer Nedelsky, to make significant progress in just this direction.

In her most recent work, Drucilla Cornell has argued for the importance of what she calls the 'imaginary domain'. The imaginary domain generates the psychic and political space within which sexual equality might be realised. Taking one step back from the quasi-contractual starting point of much recent political theory, Cornell focuses on those conditions under which a human being can pursue her life project of becoming a person. These conditions, Cornell asserts, include a fantasy dimension: the psychic space in which each of us can imagine ourselves as whole persons. The core of a substantial liberalism, in Cornell's view, is the political and legal guarantee that this space will be equally open to all.

Cornell's imaginary domain consists in three elements: bodily integrity, access to symbolic forms sufficient to achieve linguistic skills permitting the differentiation of oneself from others, and the protection of the imaginary domain itself. Central to each of these elements is the fact that a crucial part of existence for all humans is our status as sexed and embodied beings, and our sexual desire: without access to the means of expressing one's desire, and of having one's sexuality accorded such respect as is consistent with a similar respect for others, one can never have the psychic space to pursue the project of personhood. For one is barred from the identification with one's sexual imago which is central to the possibility of imagining oneself as a whole being, worthy of respect and capable of self-esteem.

Might the notion of sexual integrity which we can derive from Cornell's argument consti-tute a better analytic peg on which to hang our framing of sexual offences than the mentalist conception of autonomy? Certainly, the idea of integrity, as developed by Cornell, puts the bodily and affective aspects of sexual life more directly in issue, quite simply because the body is implicated in the relationships which are central to human integrity. Within the language of integrity, the real damage of rape might be expressed more fully, recognising the way in which rape violates its victims' capacity to integrate psychic and bodily experi-ences. Understood in this way, respect for victims' integrity seems an eminently worthy ideal for rape law and its enforcement. But it is also worth thinking carefully about the potential for reconstructing the ideal of autonomy so as to escape its dualistic implications. Many critics of atomistic versions of liberalism, from Marx to the present day, have shown that the idea of autonomy can be reconstructed in positive terms. Autonomy, in this sense, focuses on the capability of persons to realise their life plans as much as on formal choice and the negative freedom not to be interfered with. But even among those who embrace the positive concep-tion of freedom, the emphasis has tended to be on the provision of goods and resources external to the person. Because of its close association with the dominant image of the abstract, choosing subject, the history of the concept of autonomy conduces to the body's concealment.

More recently, however, Jennifer Nedelsky's important work on the concepts of autonomy and rights has demonstrated that these ideas can be reconstructed so as to encompass the body. The core of Nedelsky's argument is that human autonomy is fundamentally premised upon the relational aspects of life—our bodily and psychic dependence upon others. This inevitable relational interdependence renders the very idea of atomistic autonomy non-sensical. Without sustaining and respectful relationships, we cannot realise our personhood; and relationships inevitably implicate the corporeal. Hence the connection between auton-omy and the repression of the body, and the supposed opposition between the feminist prioritising of the body and the liberal value of autonomy, begins to unravel. Embodied autonomy becomes, by contrast, a precondition for the pursuit of personal integrity. In Marilyn Friedman's terms, recent liberal conceptions do recognise the importance of rela-tionships as *external* conditions necessary to the realisation of autonomy, but they fail to acknowledge that certain kinds of relationship may be conditions *internal* to autonomy itself. This is not to deny the importance of autonomy as, on occasion, the power to exclude others or to maintain separateness and privacy, nor is it to deny the importance of distinguishing between connections which are valuable in the sense of fostering personhood and those which may be oppressive. It is, rather, to affirm the need to locate our assessments of autonomy in the context of the relational conditions which obtain between human subjects.

The interdependence of autonomy and integrity may easily be demonstrated. In Cornell's sense, integrity embraces both physical integrity and the affective sense in which access to bodily or sexual integrity also depends on a host of social and psychic conditions. These range from external conditions such as adequate sustenance and medical care through to the conditions of respect for differently embodied subjects, different sexualities—respectful relationships as conditions internal to human integrity. A recognition of the value of integrity invites the incorporation of implications of sexual abuse such as shame, loss of self-esteem, objectification, dehumanisation. These are, of course, features central to the emerging social understandings of the wrong of sexual assault, and ones which have led feminist legal scholars such as Robin West to equate rape with 'murder of the spirit'. When combined with the emphasis on personhood as project—as a process of becoming which has an imaginary dimension and no definite end—the idea of integrity promises to escape the dangers both of essentialising a particular conception of the body and of propagating a vision of feminine empowerment which is premised, paradoxically, on a victim status which accords access to 'truth'. It conduces rather to reflection on the conditions under which a multiplicity of bodies and sexualities can be lived by full citizens, and to the opening up of a political debate about the nature of those conditions.

The right to bodily integrity which Cornell advocates is, in one important sense, impossible: it is not something which can be realised or determined institutionally; rather, it operates as a vision which generates both individual ideals and critical standards for the assessment of existing legal and political arrangements. There is an asymmetry in the imaginary domain: it cannot be captured or realised by institutions, but it can be killed or closed off by them. The vision of sexual integrity is at once a necessary condition for the ongoing project of personhood and an impossible ideal which forms a motivating horizon in political rhetoric.

It is interesting to consider, nonetheless, what a rape law framed around the ideal of sexual integrity and relational autonomy as opposed to proprietary autonomy would look like. I would argue that an analysis in terms of sexual integrity and relational autonomy has implica-tions for each of the features of rape law discussed in this paper; for the definition of rape; for evidential and other aspects of the trial process; and for a rethinking of the symbolic role of the criminalisation of rape. As far as the definition of rape is concerned, the most obvious change would be a move away from the emphasis on lack of consent understood in abstract and asymmetrical terms as the central determinant of sexual abuse. Rather, it conduces to a more complex sexual assault law which articulates a distinctive conception of sexual as opposed to proprietary autonomy, specifying particular conditions under which coercive, violent or degrading sexual encounters should be prohibited. In rethinking the idea of autonomy as integrity, we are led to a rethinking of consent itself in both broader terms and ones which assume a mutuality of relationship and responsibility between victim and defendant. The argument, for example, would unambiguously support the proposal currently being advanced by the British pressure group, Women Against Rape, which calls for a legislative definition of consent in the following terms: 'A person shall not be deemed or presumed to have consented to sexual intercourse if that person agreed to it under coercion, including the use of threat or physical violence . . . economic deprivation, abuse of authority, deception, or threat to the welfare or security of a child.' Even this broad statement of the conditions which may undermine the 'reality' of consent, however, does not address the question of mutuality. This, I would argue, could best be dealt with by moving towards some form of 'positive consent' standard: for example, by the institution of a negligence-based fault standard supplemented by a 'no-negligence' defence. While no such reform is a panacea, it would express far more nearly than does the current law in England and Wales a vision of the parties as presumptively equal partners in sexual encounters, adjusted to account for the asymmetry of possible harms arising out of misunderstandings about mutual willingness.

Even more directly, the analysis of rape in terms of relational autonomy and integrity would necessitate the reform of rules of evidence so as to allow victims more fully to express their own narrative in the court room setting, as well as ensuring that they are able to do so without having the rape trial turned into an at large examination of their sexual history. . . .

Finally, however, it should be noted that the value of sexual integrity would not direct a very great reliance on criminalisation as a mode of protecting the imaginary domain. On the contrary, criminal law is likely to be an effective defender of the imaginary domain at a symbolic rather than an instrumental level: what matters is that the criminal law of rape should express an unambiguous commitment to the positive integrity as well as the full humanity of both rape victims and men accused of rape. In my view, this militates towards the maintenance of a distinctive offence rather than a subsumption of the law of rape within the general law of assault. Though lawyers are inclined to lose sight of this obvious fact, the most important conditions for sexual equality and integrity lie in cultural attitudes rather than coercive legal rules. Nonetheless, as I have argued throughout this paper, legal rules may be inimical to these ideals, and the need to avoid this situation is among the most pressing reasons for rape reform in Britain as elsewhere.

13.5 RAPE AS MORAL INJURY

In the following extract Joan McGregor emphasizes that rape should be seen, not only as an infringement of sexual autonomy, but also a moral harm against the victim as a woman.

Joan McGregor, *Is it Rape?* (Aldershot: Ashgate, 2005), 226–32

So far we have been discussing the harm of rape in terms of undermining the victim's consent which violates her sexual autonomy. Here I would like to consider a different wrong, one with which Jean Hampton (1999) argued that a particular kind of *moral injury* occurs. That moral injury is the expression of disrespect for the value of the victim, in other words, a diminishment of that person's worth. Hampton's argument that this moral injury occurs with all wrong-doing may be difficult to support, whereas the argument that moral injury occurs with *many* types of offenses, particularly sexual offenses, is persuasive. I will support the narrower claim that some offenses involve moral injury. In all cases of nonconsenual sex, besides the physical wounds and psychological harm, the claim is that there is an injury to the person's status as an equal. A moral injury is not the same, Hampton cautions, as the 'material or psychological damage to that over which a person has a right [for example, her possessions, her body, her psychological well-being] and comes about because of a wrongful action' (p. 123). It is an *expression* of inferior status, of diminishment; the act of rape *expresses* that degradation or inferior worth of the victim. Failure to secure consent for sexual activity is an injury to the acknowledgment of the victim's value as a fully fledged person worthy of respect.

The idea of moral injury assumes, Hampton argues, a certain conception of value, like the Kantian conception of value that all persons have equal, intrinsic value. That value is not dependent upon characteristics such as race, gender, or intelligence, or even upon the good deeds one has done, but rather on our capacity for rational autonomy. Each of us is, as Kant said, an end- in-herself, each equally deserving of respect. We are not objects or things but subjects and ends. What moral obligations we owe each other are not dependent on factors about individual characteristics or attributes, but rather we owe each other equal moral consideration because people have intrinsic value. This conception of persons' worth informs liberalism and modern democracy. Each person deserves 'equal concern and respect' as Ronald Dworkin has said.

The concept of moral injury also assumes a certain theory of how human behavior expresses meaning. Some wrongful actions *express* the inferiority of the female victim; they 'say' that the victim is worth less than the offender. The treatment, either intentionally or unintentionally 'means' or provides evidence of the offender's belief in his superiority. Not all wrongful behavior is done intentionally for that purpose, but the fact that the offender treats his victim as inconsequential expresses his belief in his superiority and the inferiority of the recipient of the action. Human behavior is meaningful like language and gets its meaning from conventions in society (not unlike the way words' meanings are conventional). Whether bowing, burping, or shaking hands, actions have a meaning in a social context and are understood by members of society. We understand the meaning of behavior by knowing or learning the conventions of that society. Etiquette or manners of a society are conventional—they are not matters of 'common sense,' as Judith Martin has said. Their primary use is to convey respect for others. Failure to behave according' to the customary standards expresses disrespect for others.

Many of our actions—from sarcastically saying to the restaurant owner as you storm 'That was the best meal I have ever had,' to walking out in the middle of a presentation, to refusing to shake someone's hand—express particular meanings that are conventional. Flaunting conventional behavior can send messages about the value of a person. By loudly walking out on someone's presentation of a paper expresses disrespect and contempt for the speaker. Sometimes one doesn't intend to express a particular meaning and later can be embarrassed to find out what was 'heard.' For instance, imagine that the reason former US president Jimmy Carter didn't shake the black-activist politician Jesse Jackson's hand was that Carter had a cold and didn't want to spread his germs. Nevertheless, what Jackson 'heard' was disrespect as the failure of white men to shake hands with black men in the racist south meant that whites thought themselves as superior. Shaking hands expresses greetings to someone considered an equal (this may explain the fact that until recently it was not the practice for men to shake women's hands) and failure to do so expresses belief in the inferior status of the recipients.

An extremely explicit example of some behaviors conveying meaning about the value of others would be cross burning on a black person's lawn. That action *expresses the meaning* in American society that the actor believes that the occupant *qua* black person is inferior to white people and it carries a threat of violence to come. Other behaviors are less explicit yet their meaning is understood. Since we suppose that persons, as equal agents, are deserving or entitled to certain kinds of treatment that respect their equal worth, human behavior that fails to accord that treatment is a harm to their status as an equal. In not treating persons in the way they are entitled, they are insulted (and when we see disrespectful treatment of others we become indignant). The treatment expresses the message of their inferiority, but they are also harmed by not receiving the kind of treatment they deserve.

This is the kind of harm that Hampton labeled 'moral injury,' which is an expressive harm (see p. 123). Some wrongful actions have, over and above their direct physical or psychological damage, this expression of diminution or degradation of the victim's value. The act does not *actually* degrade or make the person less valuable because, according to the Kantian analysis, that cannot be done. Nothing can literally make a human being less valuable, but people can treat others as if they were less valuable, as if they were inferior. Consider the case in Texas a few years ago in which three white men tied a black man to the back of a pickup truck and dragged him along a dirt road until he was literally pulled apart. The method of killing that man was to intentionally reduce him to a thing or object—treating him like a sack of potatoes. The killing expressed the message 'loud and clear' that the killers thought that their victim, as a black man, was inferior to them and, conversely, that they were superior. The injury, the expressive meaning of the murder was clear and certainly was understood by the African-American community as well as by others.

All murder is wrongful and all murder sends a message of disrespect or devaluation of the victim, but racially motivated murders, murders that are expressing a message of inferiority to all members of a targeted group, inflict a moral injury on all members of that race. The victim is a token for the group; obviously she is harmed in other ways as well, but the moral injury—the expression that her racial group is inferior to the perpetrator's—is an injury to her *qua* member of that group and to its other members. Some of the indignation and anger expressed over racially motivated crimes comes from hearing the message of the inferiority of that racial group. We are angered by the treatment of members of groups that is meant to indicate their inferiority and the superiority of the members of the group from whom the perpetrators come. Racially motivated crimes against African-Americans harm them by expressing the message of inferiority in society that once condoned the unequal status of black people and that, to some extent, still countenances the position of their inferiority.

Rapes express very clearly the message of the inferiority of women. The rapist, whether the violent rapist or the subtler 'date rapist,' sends the message that this woman is for his enjoyment, an object to be used for his pleasure. His actions express her inferiority to him since he does not feel the need to bother to investigate whether she is really consenting, even in the face of evidence that she was not or may not be. Her physical and verbal rejections are not worth investigating as to whether they were 'real' since her interests do not really matter. For him, her wishes and desires are irrelevant. He is superior to her, his desires matter and hers do not, making her an object rather than an equal person. Sending this message is the expressive moral injury of rape. The message of inferiority, of what women are for, is received by all women, not merely by the woman who experiences the rape. Not wanting to diminish the real physical and psychological harms to rape victims, I am not claiming that all women experience those harms, which are very real and serious. But there is something peculiar about rape and the response that women have to other women being raped. They are indignant to the harms of another and have a deep response that goes beyond the worry that they might too be a victim. Women are *resentful* of the treatment. What accounts for that response might just be that women understand or hear the message that is being expressed by the rapist. Being a woman in western (American) society, where sexual violence is high, means being vulnerable to rape and thereby 'hearing' the message about devaluing women. The indignation and resentment, combined with the fear that women have about rape, are based on this moral injury. The prevalence of rape makes the message pervasive. The impotence of the legal response to the epidemic of rape reinforces societal acceptance of the message. The rapist aims, whether consciously or not, to establish his mastery of men over women and the law unwittingly may be supporting him. The message of inferiority is extremely insulting. The harm is intensified due to the pervasiveness of rape, and the legal reinforcement of the message of women's inferiority further denigrates women as a group. Rape is therefore a moral injury to women as a group. Moral injury is objective in that it is not dependent on the victim feeling a particular way or believing she has received dishonoring treatment; although most victims of rape certainly do psychologically experience the message of inferiority, of their diminishment. Being used for someone else's sexual purposes is deeply insulting and humiliating, along with the other harms. Indeed that fact that some victims so internalize the message of devaluation may account for the shame that many feel about *being* a victim of rape. They feel shame because they *feel* less valuable as a person, and the societal response to rape of blaming the victim exacerbates that feeling of inferiority. Society often says to victims of rape 'If you only had not done x, this wouldn't have happened,' where x is 'looking sexy,' or 'dressing a particular way,' or 'drinking alcohol,' or 'went to a man's apartment,' and so on. Saying that moral injury does not require the agent to believe she has been treated as inferior is important since some people so lack self-respect or self-worth that they do not recognize when they have been treated as a thing, and thereby wronged. These individuals, sadly, would not notice when some treatment was sending them a message of inferiority because they see themselves as deserving poor treatment (they may in fact see themselves as inferior). Women with what is called 'battered woman syndrome' often see themselves as not having value and thereby deserving the abusive treatment by their husbands. Nevertheless, the rest of us can recognize when another person is treated as inferior in status to the wrongdoer.

Asking for consent is a requirement for treating another person as an equal, so the failure to get consent before proceeding with a sexual relationship expresses deep disrespect for the victim. What Hampton has proposed is that we see rape as expressing a particular kind of moral injury to the victim—the expression of degradation or diminishment of her status. The meaning of the rape involves the victim's worth and the wrongdoer's worth and we can 'read off' the expression of the offender's superiority. In the case of rape, the diminishment in the victim's worth is tied to group membership. Women are the target of rape in society and women get the message that the rapist sends. In this sense, the moral injury of rape is shared by women as a group.

13.6 THE RADICAL FEMINIST EXPLANATION OF RAPE

The radical feminist explanation is that all male–female sexual relations are a form of rape.[130] All heterosexual sexual relationships are on a continuum of subordination. As Catherine MacKinnon puts it:

[130] Bevacqua (2000) discusses the influence of feminist thinking on reform of rape law.

> The wrong of rape has proved so difficult to define because the unquestionable starting point has been that rape is defined as distinct from intercourse, while for women it is difficult to distinguish between the two under conditions of male dominance.[131]

Robin Morgan, suggesting much, if not all, heterosexual sex can be regarded as involuntary, puts it this way:

> Rape exists any time sexual intercourse occurs when it has not been initiated by the woman out of her own genuine affection and desire. . . . Because the pressure is there, and it need not be a knife blade against the throat; it's in his body language, his threat of sulking, his clenched or trembling hand, his self-deprecating humor or angry put-down or silent self-pity at being rejected. How many millions of times have women had sex 'willingly' with men they did not want to have sex with.[132]

The argument is not that every man who engages in heterosexual sexual intercourse should be arrested and charged with rape.[133] Rather, the argument is that we cannot pretend there is a neat division between 'bad rape' and 'good sexual intercourse'. Certainly one study found that 26 per cent of men and 50 per cent of women reported having engaged in unwanted sexual activity within the two-week period of the study.[134]

Even among feminists this approach has not met with unanimous support. Lynn Henderson argues that a victim of rape knows the difference between rape and consensual intercourse and that to deny a distinction is liable to fail to recognize the rape victim's trauma.[135] Other feminists are concerned that the approach may portray women as weak and incapable of giving true consent.[136]

In the following passage Catherine MacKinnon sets out her views:

C.A. Mackinnon, 'Feminism, Marxism, Method and the State: Toward Feminist Jurisprudence' (1983) 8 *Signs* 635 at 646–7, 649–50

The more feminist view to me, one which derives from victims' experiences, sees sexuality as a social sphere of male power of which forced sex is paradigmatic. Rape is not less sexual for being violent; to the extent that coercion has become integral to male sexuality rape may be sexual to the degree that, and because, it is violent.

The point of defining rape as 'violence not sex' or 'violence against women' has been to separate sexuality from gender in order to affirm sex (heterosexuality) while rejecting violence (rape). The problem remains what it has always been: telling the difference. The convergence of sexuality with violence, long used at law to deny the reality of women's violation, is recognized by rape survivors, with a difference: where the legal system has seen the intercourse in rape, victims see the rape in intercourse. The uncoerced context for sexual expression becomes as elusive as the physical acts come to feel indistinguishable. Instead of asking, what is the violation of rape, explain what is right about sex. If this, in turn, is difficult, the difficulty is as instructive as the difficulty men have in telling the difference when women

---

[131] MacKinnon (1989: 174). [132] Morgan (1980: 134–5). [133] Schulhofer (1992: 56).
[134] See O'Sullivan and Rice Allgeier (1998: 239) and Muehlenhard and Cook (1988: 69). For a general discussion of the evidence see Thomas III (2000).
[135] Henderson (1988: 226). [136] Naffine (1997: 102); Lacey (1998: 49).

see one. Perhaps the wrong of rape has proven so difficult to articulate because the unquestionable starting point has been that rape is definable as distinct from intercourse, when for women it is difficult to distinguish them under conditions of male dominance. . . .

Having defined rape in male sexual terms, the law's problem, which becomes the victim's problem, is distinguishing rape from sex in specific cases. The law does this by adjudicating the level of acceptable force starting just above the level set by what is seen as normal male sexual behaviour, rather than at the victim's or woman's point of violation. Rape cases finding insufficient force reveal that acceptable sex, in the legal perspective, can entail a lot of force. This is not only because of the way the injury itself is defined as illegal. Rape is a sex crime that is not a crime when it looks like sex. To seek to define rape as violent, not sexual, is understandable in this context, and often seems strategic. But assault that is consented to is still assault; rape consented to is intercourse. The substantive reference point implicit in existing legal standards is the sexually normative level of force. Until this norm is confronted as such, no distinction between violence and sexuality will prohibit more instances of women's experienced violation than does the existing definition. The question is what is *seen as* force, hence as violence, in the sexual arena. Most rapes, as women live them, will not be seen to violate women until sex and violence are confronted as mutually definitive. It is not only men convicted of rape who believe that the thing they did different from what men do all the time is get caught.

FURTHER READING

Dripps, D. (1992), 'Beyond Rape: An Essay on the Difference between the Presence of Force and the Absence of Consent', *Columbia Law Review* 92: 1780.

Gardner, J., and Shute, S. (2000), 'The Wrongness of Rape' in J. Horder (ed.), *Oxford Essays in Jurisprudence* (Oxford: OUP).

Lacey, N. (1998c), 'Unspeakable Subjects, Impossible Rights: Sexuality, Integrity and Criminal Law', *Canadian Journal of Law and Jurisprudence* 11: 47.

Naffine, N. (1994), 'Possession: Erotic Love in the Law of Rape', *Modern Law Review* 57: 10.

West, R. (1996), 'A Comment on Consent, Sex and Rape', *Legal Theory* 2: 233.

14 CONSENT AND SEXUAL ACTIVITY

In the English and Welsh law on sexual offences it is the notion of consent which has become central. Lack of consent can transform a 'loving act of sexual intercourse' into 'rape'.[137] But, as will be clear from Part I, there are many difficulties over the meaning of consent.

14.1 WHAT IS CONSENT: IS IT OBJECTIVE OR SUBJECTIVE?

Imagine this: Bill and Ben meet at a night club. Ben has had a lot to drink. Bill soon asks whether Ben would be interested in sexual intercourse. Ben is so drunk he does not understand what is happening, but says 'yes'. Sexual intercourse follows. Did Ben consent?[138]

---

[137] Hurd (1996).

[138] Finch and Munro (2003 and 2004) and Falk (2002) discuss cases where a defendant uses drink or drugs deliberately to enable him to have sexual intercourse with the victim.

Subjectively (looking at his mind) he did not, but objectively (looking at what he said) he did. This is a topic over which there has been much legal and philosophical disagreement.[139] Three main views can be found in the literature.[140]

(1) The 'subjective view' of consent. This sees consent as a state of mind of the victim.[141]

(2) The 'objective view' which sees consent as an outward manifestation by the victim in words or acts which indicate permission is granted to the defendant to do the act. As Nathan Brett[142] puts it: 'To consent is to *act* in a way that has conventional significance in communicating permission.'

(3) The third view is a combination of these views and requires *both* a subjective state of mind of the victim and the expression of that state of mind.

As seen in Part I, English and Welsh law has adopted the 'subjective view'.

14.2 WHAT IS CONSENT: TO WAIVE OR INTEND?

What precisely does it mean to consent? One view is that to consent is to forgo one's complaint against the other's action;[143] while another is that consent requires one to intend the other to act in the particular way.[144] The difference between these views can be revealed by the example of a wife whose husband would like to have sexual intercourse. The wife is reluctant to agree, but does so because she does not want to have a row. Although she may have forgone her complaint, it might be said that she does not intend him to have sexual intercourse. Both of these views reinforce the point that it is difficult to draw a sharp distinction between consent and no consent.[145]

14.3 WHAT IS CONSENT: IS A FAILURE TO VOICE OPPOSITION CONSENT?

As we have seen in Part I, the English and Welsh courts have been consistent in holding that the *actus reus* of rape is made out if a man has sexual intercourse with a woman who is asleep or too drunk to resist. They have stressed that the *actus reus* requires the absence of consent, not the absence of resistance or opposition. However, this is not an uncontroversial approach to take. It is not, for example, adopted in parts of the United States where, if the victim fails to voice any complaint about sexual intercourse, there can be no rape.[146] Stephen Schulhofer in this extract argues that the law must require a positive consent:[147]

S. Schulhofer, 'Taking Sexual Autonomy Seriously: Rape Law and Beyond' (1992) 11 *Law and Philosophy* 35 at 74–7

Consider this parable. A hospitalized athlete, suffering from chronic knee problems, consults a surgeon, who recommends an operation. The athlete is not sure. If the operation is

---

[139] Hurd (1996) and Alexander (1996).   [140] Wertheimer (2000).
[141] e.g. the discussion in Bryant (1989).   [142] Brett (1998: 70).
[143] Alexander (1996). For further discussion see Archard (1998).
[144] Hurd (1996).   [145] Dripps (1992).
[146] Bryden (2000: 319). Many scholars reject this. Kashbhai (1996), e.g., argues strongly for a requirement that there is a positive act of consent.
[147] See also Chamallas (1988) and Mandhane (2001).

successful, he will enjoy a long, fulfilling career with his team. But there are imponderables. The operation carries a risk of a burdensome infection that can be hard to cure. The procedure may not produce the expected benefits. In any event, it is sure to be stressful in the short run. The athlete hesitates. There are clear advantages, clear disadvantages, and lots of uncertainties. What to do? Maybe he should postpone this big step for a while, see how things go without it. The surgeon is encouraging: 'Try it. You'll like it'. Still the athlete is unsure. Now our surgeon becomes impatient. He has spent a lot of time with this case. The athlete's hesitation is becoming tiresome and annoying. So the surgeon signals an anesthesiologist to ready the drugs that will flow through an intravenous tube already in place. One last time the surgeon (a sensitive, modem male) reminds the athlete, 'You don't have to go ahead with this. If you really want me to stop, just say so.' But the athlete, his brain still clouded with doubts, fears, hopes, and uncertainties, says nothing. So the surgeon starts the anesthesia and just does it.

Consent? Of course not. But why not? The athlete was not compelled to submit. Nobody forced him. His 'attitude may be deeply ambivalent', but surgical patients are almost always like that. Surely his silence proves that he was not unwilling. If he really objected, all he had to do was say so!

There are, to be sure, important contextual differences between surgery and sexual intimacy. But even allowing for those differences, it would not be implausible to find 'consent' by the patient. provided we could get ourselves to think of illegal surgery as an offense requiring 'forcible compulsion', and to think of 'nonconsent' in this context as revulsion, aversion, or a clearly crystallized negative attitude.

We do not see matters this way because we are not thinking about a crime of violence. We are thinking about an offense against the patient's autonomy. Moral and intellectual autonomy as well as physical, bodily autonomy must be respected. Both dimensions are important. The athlete's freedom of choice might have been impaired by confinement, time pressure, or professional authority. But even if his intellectual autonomy was unconstrained, even if he remained free to choose, his physical autonomy was unquestionably violated because no choice was ever made. In the surgical context, at least, nonconsent cannot mean aversion or a crystallized negative decision because in our society this kind of intrusion on the person requires unambiguous, positive permission. Nonconsent is simply anything that is not positive consent, anything that is not an affirmative, crystallized expression of willingness. To treat the athlete as a victim is not, of course, to patronize him. It is merely to recognize an obvious violation of the physical autonomy of his person.

Why aren't the same conceptions of autonomy and nonconsent just as appropriate for acts of sexual intimacy? Are the differences in context, and in social and psychological meanings, relevant to the result?

One could imagine a world that required affirmative permission even for a kiss or a hug between intimates. 'May I kiss you?' would be respectful but may sound quaint to modern ears. In many social contexts, men and women can justifiably infer positive willingness even without express consent. Conversely, a kiss or hug known to be unwelcome is undoubtedly battery, a clear offense against the physical autonomy of the person.

What if a man kisses a woman when he knows that she is ambivalent? Should ambivalence in this context, the absence of positive consent, count as *non* consent? My impression of both law and existing social etiquette is that it does not, at least not always. Respect for the individual (and sensitivity to the potentially overbearing character of male physical and social power) arguably should prompt a rethinking of cultural attitudes here. For now there is probably no clear social consensus that a kiss violates the autonomy of an ambivalent recipient.

But intercourse is not a kiss. In our society voluntary touching, hugging, and kissing occur frequently between all sorts of acquaintances and even between virtual strangers (at public ceremonies, for example). Attitudes about such casual, superficial physical contacts have no bearing on the meaning and appropriate limitations on intimate genital contact and, especially, sexual intercourse. These intimate contacts unquestionably involve profound intrusions on the physical and emotional integrity of the individual. For such intrusions, as for surgery, actual permission, nothing less than a crystallized attitude of positive willingness, should ever count as consent.

Though I have no doubt about what autonomy *ought to* mean in this context, my approach might seem inconsistent with some of existing social practice. Since the cases (and massive numbers of judges, prosecutors, and juries) have so often insisted on clear, unequivocal objections to intercourse, in effect equating ambivalence with consent, affirmative permission obviously has not been considered necessary. Intercourse has been treated like a kiss.

But this minimalist attitude toward consent surely does not flow from a casual attitude about the physical and psychological significance of intercourse. On the contrary, present culture recognizes intercourse as a major intrusion on physical autonomy in just the way I have posited. Why then the minimalist attitude toward consent? Its source, I suggest, is the pervasive association of 'rape' with violent misconduct. When the charge is 'forcible compulsion', it can be plausible to view the victim's ambivalence as an appropriate defense, as a kind of 'consent'. But there is still, as in surgery, an unambiguous intrusion on the bodily integrity of the person. As in surgery, nothing less than affirmative permission can warrant such action. The unwarranted contact may not be rape, but it is still a grave personal intrusion that criminal law can appropriately reach.

In sum: intercourse in the face of verbal objections, ambivalence, or silence is intercourse without consent, and it represents a clear offense against the physical autonomy of the person. Even in the complete absence of force, such behavior is 'nonviolent sexual misconduct' and should be punished as such.

Many of the ambiguities of abusive dating situations and the hesitations that complicate acquaintance rape enforcement tend to dissolve under this approach. No standard can eliminate all factual uncertainty or swearing contests. But in the autonomy perspective facts that will often be quite clear—verbal protests, ambivalence, or silence—are by themselves sufficient to establish an unambiguous offense against personal autonomy and an unambiguous basis for criminal punishment.

Donald Husak and George Thomas III take the objective view of consent. They argue that to appreciate what consent is we have to understand the social understandings that surround the event. Therefore, when you put your hand out to stop a taxi, get inside, and ask to be taken somewhere, although you do not explicitly agree to pay that is the social convention that surrounds that activity.[148] They argue that many women feel uncomfortable asking for sex. This is seen as being too forward or distasteful. Various conventions have therefore been developed under which consent may be assumed, even if it is not made explicit.[149] In the light of these conventions they argue that if a woman behaves in a way which would

---

[148] Thomas III and Edelman (2000).

[149] One study of Texan undergraduates claimed that 39.3%, including most of those with sexual experience, had sometimes pretended that they did not want sex when in fact they wanted it, while 60.7% stated they had never said no when they wanted sex (Muehlenhard and Hollabaugh (1988: 872)).

normally be taken to indicate consent that behaviour should be taken as consent, even if in fact that was not her intention and even if she never explicitly said she wanted to have sex. David Bryden provides an example:

> A woman who after being propositioned, walks into her host's bedroom and disrobes, may not have given verbal consent. But she has 'affirmatively' manifested her intentions, and that should suffice.[150]

Husak and Thomas III are quick to add that they hope these conventions change so that men and women can more openly and explicitly discuss sexual matters, but until then it is unfair to punish a man who assumes the normal conventions apply when the woman does not mean them to. They go on to add that if the law were to be changed to require that each party to a sexual encounter must explicitly consent to it, that could have unintended consequences:

> A proposal designed to make it more difficult for men to get away with rape might have the unanticipated effect of making it harder for some women to get what they want.[151]

Making a wider point Joshua Dressler argues:

> Men should be taught in our culture to seek permission, but women should also be taught in our culture to express their wishes, whether it is to invite or reject sexual contact.[152]

In *Protecting the Public* the government sought to adopt a view somewhere between Schulhofer's and Husak and Thomas III's views:

> Human beings have devised a complex set of messages to convey agreement or lack of it. Agreement or lack of agreement is not necessarily verbal, but both parties should understand it. Each must respect the right of the other to demonstrate or say 'no' and mean it. We do not of course wish to formalise such understanding into an unnecessary or semi-contractual agreement; it is not the role of Government or the law to prescribe how consent should be sought and given. It is, however, the role of the law to make it unambiguously clear that intimate sexual acts should only take place with the agreement of both parties.[153]

It might be useful to return to the hypothetical scenario at the start of the Schulhofer extract concerning the athlete and the surgeon. To some commentators this is a convincing analogy, but others disagree.

Some argue that the case for convicting a man who proceeds with sexual intercourse without an explicit consent is stronger than the case of the surgeon. The doctor may have *a good reason* for engaging in the treatment (it is in the patient's best interests) and the doctor could legitimately start with a presumption that the patient will consent (the doctor could

---

[150] Bryden (2000: 397). [151] Husak and Thomas III (1992: 112).
[152] Dressler (1998: 428). [153] Home Office (2002b: para. 29).

presume that the patient will want his doctor to do what is in his best interests). But until a person who is about to engage in sexual contact with another knows what the wishes of the other person are, he does not have a good reason for engaging in the activity nor for assuming that the other consents.[154]

Others argue that the analogy is misleading. Thomas III argues that conventionally patients do not give consent by acquiescence, whereas silence is an established way of granting consent to sexual activity.[155] Another point is made by David Bryden who argues that sex is characterized by spontaneity and that therefore it is different from surgery where all decisions are to be carefully thought out and considered. We can expect a doctor to act professionally and follow reasonable rules; parties engaging in sexual intercourse cannot be expected so to behave.[156]

QUESTIONS

1. A wife in order to please her husband on his birthday agrees to sexual intercourse. She does not really want to have sex, but is willing to put up with it. Her husband knows that this is her state of mind but they have sexual relations. Should this be rape? Does this example suggest requiring a positive desire for sexual intercourse is too strict?

2. Some American colleges and universities, in an effort to encourage students better to communicate about sexual matters, have strict rules requiring explicit consent to be obtained to each stage of a sexual relationship. If such consent is not obtained the actions can be regarded as a sexual offence (see e.g. Harrison, Downes, and Williams (1991)). Would such a regime be a good idea as a national law? Some claim it would rob sexual activity of its spontaneity and passion. Would it? Even if it did, would it be worth it if it reduced the incidence of unwanted sex?

14.4 CONSENT: WHAT IS THE STATUS OF A MISTAKEN CONSENT?

The traditional common law position, as explained in Part I, is that only a mistake of identity (e.g. where the victim incorrectly assumes that the defendant is her boyfriend) or as to the nature of the act (e.g. where the victim consents to a medical operation, but the defendant engages in sexual intercourse) will be sufficient to negate the consent of the victim. To some commentators the courts have been asking the wrong question: rather than asking whether the mistake is sufficiently serious to negate consent, the courts should ask a simpler question: 'is what the defendant did the act which the victim consented to?'[157]

Whatever the question asked the topic has excited much debate. Here are three of the hypotheticals which have attracted much comment:

(1) A girlfriend agrees to sexual intercourse with her boyfriend after he tells her that he loves her. In fact he does not, and plans to leave her as soon as they have had sex.

(2) A woman has sex with a man, who tells her that he is not married. She has moral objections to committing adultery and when she discovers that he is married she is deeply distressed.

---

[154] Herring (2002: 192–3).   [155] Thomas III (2000: 530).   [156] Bryden (2000).
[157] Herring (2002: 194–5).

(3) A man tells a woman that he has been recently tested for AIDS and was found not to be positive. She agrees to have sex with him, but she would not have done if she had known the truth that he been tested positive.

In all of these cases there is no doubt that the man has behaved in a morally reprehensible way, but should he be convicted of a criminal offence? If the criminal law should intervene should these situations be classified as rape or as some kind of lesser sexual offence (e.g. procuring sexual offence by deception)? Here are some views:

(1) At one extreme is the view that '[i]f at the time of the sexual activity a person would not have consented to it had they known all the facts at that time (including the defendant's state of mind) then there is no consent'.[158] Such a view would readily convict all three of the defendants above. Supporters of such an approach tend to emphasize that sexual relationships involve intimacy and trust and therefore there are heightened obligations of a fiduciary nature.[159] This means that the standards of honesty and probity expected between lovers should be higher than those expected between two businesspeople, for example.[160]

Objectors to this view argue that the use of deceptions is common in 'chatting up'. If the view became law, it would lead to the criminalization of an extraordinary amount of sexual activity. Some have argued that protestations of love are known to be analogous to 'commercial puffing'[161] and are not to be taken seriously.[162] The use of ruses and lies to obtain sexual intercourse is all part of the 'sexual game'.[163] Although such replies may overlook the evidence of serious psychological harm caused to those who have been tricked into agreeing to sexual intercourse.[164] There is also an argument that to use this rule would create enormous evidential problems. How do we know if 'I love you' is a lie? What exactly does the phrase mean anyway? How can anyone know if the victim would or would not have agreed to sexual intercourse had she known the truth?[165] At the very least there is often 'confusion and messiness' surrounding the party's expectations, particularly in casual sexual liaisons, and so it is inappropriate to probe too deeply into what may or may not have motivated someone to engage in sex.[166]

Even those who would be willing to accept that the law should criminalize the use of deceptions to obtain consent to sexual intercourse might argue that to label it rape belittles that offence.[167] A man lying about his emotional feelings is so far removed from the violent assault that accompanies the 'normal' understanding of rape that it should be labelled differently.[168] Others argue that rights to sexual autonomy are infringed where deception is used as much as where force is used to enable sexual intercourse to take place.[169]

---

[158] Herring (2002); see also Alldridge (1993); Estrich (1987: 96).

[159] Balos and Fellows (1991); Larson (1993).   [160] Waye (1992).   [161] Bryden (2000: 462).

[162] Jeremy Horder has described as 'trivial' a case where one partner deceives another as to whether he loves her in order to persuade her to consent to sexual intercourse: Horder (1999b: 108). For an article warning of the dangers of over-criminalization in the arena of sexual offences see Bronitt (1991). For a strong rejection of the view that all deceptions are fair 'in love and war' see Larsen (1993: 444).

[163] Alldridge (1993) considers, but rejects, such argments. Schulhofer (1992) talks about the importance of fantasy in sexual matters.

[164] Hecht Schafran (1993).   [165] Schulhofer (1992: 93).

[166] Childs (2001); Bryden (2000). Larsen (1993) and Subotnik (1995) suggest that sexual fraud should be regarded as a tort.

[167] Dripps (1992).

[168] Thomas III (2000).   [169] Balos and Fellows (1991); Estrich (1987); Boyle (2000).

(2) A more moderate view is to argue that we should consider whether the matter about which the victim has made a mistake played 'such a compelling role [in her decision to have sexual relations] that she should be dissociated from her decision on account of it'.[170] This requires the jury to consider how important the lied-about matter was to the victim in reaching his or her decision to engage in sexual intercourse.[171] The difficulty with such a view despite its theoretical attractions is its usability. If it is to be distinguished from view 1, it must be possible to imagine a case where, even though a victim would not have agreed to sexual intercourse without knowing a particular fact, that fact is not regarded as compelling. There is a danger that this will slip into a moral assessment of the victim's reasons for deciding to engage in sexual intercourse.

(3) The common law approach restricts 'rape by deception' to only the most serious cases: those where there is a deception as to the nature of the act or the identity of the person. It might be claimed that this is to impose the law's values as to what is regarded as a fundamental mistake upon the victim. In *Papadimitropoulos*[172] the defendant deceived the victim into believing they had been through a ceremony of marriage and she therefore agreed to engage in sexual intercourse. The Australian High Court held that there was no rape because the victim was not mistaken as to the nature of the act: she knew that they were to engage in sexual intercourse. But to some with religious views (for example) there may be the world of difference between marital sexual intercourse and extra-marital sexual intercourse.

In the following extract I criticize the traditional approach of the law and support the first view, although it is an approach which very few commentators have been willing to adopt.

J. Herring, 'Mistaken Sex' [2005] *Criminal Law Review* 511–24 at 513–15, 523–4

There are four specific criticisms of the common law:

The meaning of an act

The meaning of an act depends very much on the cultural understandings surrounding it. The raising of a finger at a person has multiple meanings, depending on its context. It will be appreciated as an insult, a vote or a greeting, depending on its social significance. Such an act can be described simply in mechanical terms (the lifting of a finger), but such a description is one only used by the most erudite of philosophers. In normal life an act gains its meaning from its context and surrounding circumstances. Take sexual intercourse. This can have a wide variety of meanings for different people which may include the following:

1. It may have special religious significance indicating that the parties are embarking on a spiritual union.

2. The act may simply be an expression and conformation of the love the parties have for each other.

3. The act may simply be one which is entered into for physical pleasure.

4. The act of sexual intercourse may be regarded as solely a procreative act.

The same sexual act will have a different meaning for many people depending on the identity of the partner and the time in their lives. A prostitute may well regard sexual activities with

---

[170] Larsen (1993: 288).   [171] S. Gardner (1996).   [172] (1957) 98 CLR 249 (Aust HC).

her client as completely different from sexual relations with her partner. Similarly a religious person may regard marital intercourse as expression of spiritual union blessed by God, while an extra-marital union as an odious sin. Yet, as we saw in *Linekar* and *Papadimitropolos* the traditional common law would not recognise such distinctions which for these people are of fundamental importance.

Defendant-based approach

The traditional approach asks whether the victim's mistake is sufficient to negate her consent. The proper question should be: is the defendant's act that to which the victim has consented? As argued above once the question is asked in that way the victim's response is unlikely to be: 'I consented to X putting his penis inside my vagina/anus/mouth.' It is likely to be much more complicated than this; more complicated in two ways. First, the act is likely to be understood in the context of what it represents: be that 'a moment of mad fun' or 'an affirmation of our love for each other'. Secondly, the act is likely to be understood in the context of the relationship between the parties. The act will be sited in the individuals' understanding of what has happened in the past and what will happen in the future. In other words we need to move away from the simplistic question, 'did the victim say yes or no'. Instead we should be asking how the victim understood the act that she was consenting to. Nicola Lacey puts the point in this way:

'The victim's consent responds to power by conferring legitimacy, rather than shaping power in its own terms: consent is currently understood not in terms of mutuality but rather in relation to a set of arrangements initiated, by implication, by the defendant, in an asymmetric structure which reflects the stereotypes of active masculinity and passive femininity . . .'

The assumption that sexual conduct is good

A further challenge to the traditional approach is that it starts with an assumption that sexual intimacy is a good thing and that we need to identify and criminalise those aspects of sexual intimacy which are harmful. But we could look at this another way and start by seeking to describe the forms of acceptable sexual connection and criminalise the others as harmful. This might particularly have attraction for those sympathetic to the view which casts doubt on whether a woman can ever be said to consent to sexual intercourse with a man, given the oppression under which women live, particularly in the context of sexual relations. Attempting to define what might be regarded as an acceptable form of sexual intimacy would be an interesting task and there is not space to deal with it here. But it is likely that such relations would involve ideas of reciprocity, integration, responsibility, and mutuality. As the Home Office suggests: 'it is important for society as a whole for sexual relationships to be based on mutual respect and understanding.' Unlike commercial transactions, in sexual relations, people are entitled to expect their partners not to consider solely their own interests but rather engage in a cooperative and mutually beneficial relationship. We are therefore entitled to expect sexual partners to owe each other heightened standards of obligation of a fiduciary nature. It hardly seems onerous to expect lovers to behave in a conscionable way with each other.

Deceit negates free choice

Deceit, as much as force and threats, can 'negate consent'. Deceit, like violence, manipulates people into acting against their will. Like threats deceit restricts the options available to another. It does this by making the other unaware of the options the other has available. For example, a man who deceives his partner as to his identity prevents a partner making a decision about whether to have sex with him. Restricting the information on which a person makes a choice can be as inhibiting of a free choice as making an option unattractive through a threat. Indeed in one sense a deception can be regarded as worse than a threat in that the deception uses the victim's own decision-making powers against herself: rendering her an instrument of harm against herself.

. . . .

In the past it was said:

[A] male [may] make promises that will not be kept, . . . indulge in exaggeration and hyperbole, or . . . assure any trusting female that . . . the ugly frog is really the handsome prince. Every man is free, under the law, to be a gentleman or a cad.

But we should no longer be in an age when the 'gentle art of seduction' is revered and praised; when women or men are sexual objects to be prised open by whatever means comes to hand. It should no longer be enough just to ask did the complainant say 'yes' in relation to the proposed sexual activity. Now the values that should underpin our sexual offences law are those of mutual respect, reciprocity, connection and honesty. If we respect sexual integrity and the importance of being able to choose with whom to have sexual partners then the choice must be one that is free from coercion and fraud. A man who has sexual intercourse with another knowing that that person would not be agreeing to the activity if s/he knew the truth is using that person for his own ends. It is the 'sheer use of another person'. It should be rape.

QUESTIONS

1. Alf agrees to have sex with Angie after:
   (a) Angie impersonates Bertha, Alf's girlfriend, who left him five years ago and whom he has never forgotten.
   (b) Angie impersonates Cecile, a family friend whom Alf vaguely knows.
   (c) Angie impersonates Drew, Alf's favourite film star, about whom he knows everything there is to know.
   (d) Angie pretends to be a devout Christian, Alf agreeing to have sexual relations with Angie only because she shares his religion.

   Should any of these be criminal offences? Can any distinction be drawn between them?

2. Fred agrees to sexual relations with Gloria in the following situations:
   (a) Fred suggests they have sex as a religious act, expressing their spiritual union. Gloria has no idea what he is talking about, but agrees to sex as she fancies Fred.
   (b) Gloria agrees to sexual intercourse after Fred tells her he is sterile. In fact he is not and Gloria becomes pregnant as a result.
   (c) Fred suggests they have sex as a demonstration of their mutual adoration. In fact Fred does not love Gloria.

   Should any of these be criminal offences?

3. Cohen (1991) suggests that if the law on 'rape by deception' is too strict then men will be deterred from making sexual advances. Do you agree? Would this be a bad thing?

4. 'A woman who consents to have sex with a man after he assures her that he is unmarried has the same state of mind whether his representation turns out to be true or merely a credible lie' (Dripps (1996: 114)). Is this a convincing argument for saying that a mistake should never negate consent?

5. 'A man befriends a woman and untruthfully says he loves her. As a result of his declaration she gives him substantial gifts and engages in sexual intercourse. If the facts can be proved there would be little difficulty in obtaining a conviction for obtaining the property (the gifts) by deception. She consented to handing over the property, but the consent was acquired by deception and so provides no defence. Many commentators, however, would deny that he is guilty of rape. But is the right to decide with whom to have sexual contact to be ranked somewhere below the right not to be deprived improperly of one's property?' Herring (2002: 200). Discuss.

14.5 CONSENT AND PRESSURE

What if the victim consents to sexual acts as a result of pressure? Few would disagree that a victim who says 'yes' to sexual intercourse in the face of a threat of death or serious harm cannot be properly said to have consented. But what about lesser threats? What about a threat to cause only a minor physical harm (e.g. slap); or what about a threat to cause emotional harm (e.g. 'I will break off our engagement'); or a financial loss ('I will fire you')? Also as we have seen with mistake cases there is a debate over whether or not sexual intercourse procured by the use of illegitimate threats should be regarded as rape[173] or be criminalized using a different label.[174]

Where should the line be drawn?

To some commentators nothing less than a threat of death or serious injury should do. In all kinds of areas of life people reluctantly do things under pressure. Many people do a job only because they need the income to live a certain lifestyle. The fact that the employer threatens not to pay them if they do not work should not be said to undermine their consent to work.[175] As Donald Dripps puts it, 'Any woman who says "yes" because of the pressures of an unjust world deserves our efforts to make the pressures of the world less unjust. But she also deserves our respect for whatever she chooses'.[176]

To other commentators the key question is not so much the nature of the threat, but the appropriateness of the pressure.[177] Although it is permissible (to say the least) for an employer to threaten not to pay a worker who does not work, it is not for an employer to threaten not to pay a worker who does not engage in sexual intercourse with him or her. This view would require a moral assessment of the pressure used. But it is by no means clear that there are generally accepted moral standards of the kinds of 'seduction techniques' that are permissible.

---

[173] McGregor (1996); Estrich (1987).
[174] Schulhofer (1992) discusses civil remedies that could be relied upon.
[175] Bryan (2000).   [176] Dripps (1994: 142–3).   [177] Waye (1992).

Should a line be drawn between a threat and an offer?

Some commentators have suggested that it is useful to distinguish cases where the defendant has threatened harm to the victim unless she agrees to sexual activity (where the threat may invalidate the 'consent') and cases where the defendant has made an offer to the victim (where an offer will never invalidate a 'consent').[178] Such commentators therefore see a significant difference between these two cases:

(1) An aspiring actress is told by a director that he will give her the leading role in his new film if she agrees to have sexual intercourse. The 'consent' is induced by an offer and therefore it cannot be rape.

(2) An actress is told by a director that he will replace her in the leading role she has been given in his new film unless she agrees to have sexual intercourse with him. The 'consent' is induced by a threat. This could amount to rape if the threat was considered sufficiently serious to negate the effectiveness of the consent.

Other commentators reject such a distinction, arguing that in both cases the level of pressure on the victim will be the same, and it is artificial to consider the distinction between them.[179] Such commentators often take the view that the law should focus on the effect of the threat or offer on the victim, rather than the classification of the threat as an offer or a threat.[180] The difficulty with such a position is that it produces (at least from the defendant's point of view) uncertainty in the law. He may put some pressure on a woman (e.g. 'I will end our relationship unless you agree to sexual intercourse'), and unknown to him the effect of such a threat may be very severe. For example, some commentators have suggested that repeated requests for sexual intimacy can be regarded as intimidatory. Some men would be surprised to hear that. To some extent these concerns can be dealt with by the *mens rea* requirement which we will examine later.

14.6 CONSENT: INTOXICATED MISTAKE

In the following passage Alan Wertheimer summarizes the views that could be taken in a case where the victim of rape was intoxicated at the time of sexual intercourse:

A. Wertheimer, 'Intoxicated Consent to Sexual Relations' (2001) 20 *Law and Philosophy* 373

To facilitate the analysis, let us distinguish among five claims that appear in discussions of this issue. . . . First, it may be argued that if B consents to sexual relations while voluntarily intoxicated, we should regard it as impermissible for A to have sexual relations with B. Call this the *impermissibility claim*. The impermissibility claim represents our all things considered judgment as to whether we should treat B's intoxicated consent as valid. Second, it may be argued that if a woman consents while intoxicated, her consent is *necessarily* invalid because intoxication always undermines 'the capacity requirements of valid consent,

---

[178] See Hirshman and Larson (1998) for a discussion of 'sexual bargaining'.
[179] Chamallas (1998: 820–30).
[180] Schulhofer (1998: 120). Tadros (1999), e.g., suggests that the issue should be whether or not the victim had a fair opportunity to exercise her will.

whether or not B's intoxication is voluntary. Call this the *intoxication claim*. The intoxication claim says that intoxication *entails* invalidity, and so it also entails that we should accept the impermissibility claim? Third, it may be argued that if B's intoxication is itself voluntary or self-induced, then we should treat B as responsible for her intoxicated behavior. Call this the *responsibility claim*. By itself, the responsibility claim says nothing about the validity of B's consent. It is a general claim about one's responsibility for one's intoxicated behavior. The fourth claim connects the responsibility claim to consent. It might be argued that if a woman is responsible for her intoxicated behavior, it follows that her intoxicated consent must be treated as valid. Call this the *responsibility entails validity claim*, or, more briefly, the *validity claim*. If we accept the responsibility claim and the validity claim, then we must treat B's consent as valid, that is, we must say that it is permissible for A to have sexual relations with B if B consents while voluntarily intoxicated. A fifth claim supports the position that we should reject the impermissibility claim by drawing an analogy between intoxicated consent and intoxicated criminal behavior. On this view, if people should be held responsible for wrongful acts committed while intoxicated (including acts of violence against women), then we should also treat B's consent as valid. Call this the *consistency claim*.

QUESTIONS

1. How should the law deal with cases where, although there has been no direct threat, there is a 'power imbalance' between the parties? In the United States there has been much discussion over sexual relationships between university lecturers and their students or between attorneys and doctors and their clients. Should there be a presumption of non-consent in such cases? Should this be dealt with as a breach of professional ethics, rather than a criminal matter?

2. Do the difficulties over the definition of consent indicate that it would be better to formulate the law on sexual offences without reference to consent? Chamallas (1988) suggests asking whether the sexual activity reveals 'mutuality' (see also Pineau (1989)). Is that a useful alternative to consent?

15 *MENS REA* FOR RAPE

Great controversy surrounds the *mens rea* for rape. We will now consider some of the views that have been taken:

(1) *The intent-based view*

It could be argued that it is only rape if the defendant intends that the victim did not consent. This is almost impossible to prove. Very rarely would it be said to be the defendant's purpose that the victim did not consent.[181] It is unlikely that the defendant would regard his enterprise to be a failure if it turned out that the victim consented. This view has received very little support in the academic commentary.

(2) *The subjective recklessness view*

This view requires proof that the defendant knew or believed that the victim did not consent; in other words that the defendant was *Cunningham* reckless as to the victim's lack

---

[181] *Khan* [1990] 2 All ER 783 (CA).

of consent. This view would acquit a defendant who unreasonably took the view that the victim consented, for example because he believed he was irresistible to all women.

(3) *The* Morgan *view*

This view, developed by the House of Lords' decision in *Morgan*,[182] holds that the defendant is guilty unless he positively believes that the victim consented. This is slightly different from the subjective recklessness view because it includes not only the state of mind where the defendant knows that the victim is not consenting; it also includes the victim who does not consider whether the victim consents[183] or not, or 'could not care less'; indeed any state of mind except a clear belief that the victim consents is sufficient.

The *Morgan* decision was controversial.[184] The objection to it is straightforward: it is easy for a man to have reasonable grounds for his belief as to whether the victim consents if he is in any doubt: he just has to ask.[185] If the man gets it wrong he causes the victim an enormous level of harm, so surely requiring him to take such a simple step when risking such a serious harm is not too onerous a duty.[186] As Huigens puts the defendants in *Morgan*, if they believed that Mrs Morgan consented they did so out of 'callousness, immaturity, self-absorption, and stupidity' and those should not provide the basis of a defence.[187] Such arguments tend to lead one to support a negligence-based test for rape.

One of *Morgan*'s few academic supporters, although a very notable one, is Professor John Smith.[188] His view is that a person who has chosen to have intercourse with the victim without her consent is not at the same level of blame as a person who has carelessly not checked whether the victim is consenting. Further, negligence is no longer used for offences against the person and it would be anomalous to introduce it just for the offence of rape.

(4) *The negligence view: 'unreasonable belief'*

This view asks simply whether the defendant's view of the victim's consent was reasonable or not. In other words the question is whether a reasonable person in the defendant's shoes would have reached the decision that the victim was consenting. If the reasonable person would have known that the victim was not consenting then the *mens rea* of rape is made out. This is close to the position reached in the definition of rape in the Sexual Offences Act 2003.

Benefits claimed for the negligence approach are that it may increase the conviction rate for rape which is so low at present.[189] The argument is that it is difficult under the *Morgan* test for the jury to be sure that the defendant did not think that the victim was consenting. Another alleged benefit is that it would mean that the focus would not be so much on what was actually going on in the victim's mind, but rather what a reasonable person would think was the victim's attitude to the proposed sexual activity.[190] This might lead to the prevention of distressing lines of cross-examination in rape trials where the defence seeks to show that in fact the defendant was enjoying what was happening.

---

[182] [1976] AC 182 (HL).

[183] Bryden (2000: 342) argues that it is impossible for a man engaging in sexual intercourse not to avert to the issue of whether the victim consented.

[184] Duncan (1994) deconstructs the judgments in *Morgan*. The government of the day took the issue so seriously that they set up a special committee to examine the decision and its ramifications: the Heilbron Committee (1976).

[185] If the victim expresses assent, then the defendant will have reasonable grounds for his belief.

[186] Pickard (1980); Wells (1982); Charlow (2002).   [187] Huigens (2005: 202).

[188] J.C. Smith (1975).   [189] Home Office (2002b).   [190] Byrnes (1998).

(5) *The negligence view: 'unreasonable formation of belief'*

This approach is similar to one just described, but asks whether the defendant acted reasonably in forming his belief that the victim consented. In other words it looks at his reasoning process, rather than the decision actually reached.[191] Simon Gardner suggests that such an approach may be useful in ensuring that defendants who suffer from mild learning difficulties or who are sexually inexperienced and try their very best to ascertain whether the victim is consenting, but reach the wrong conclusion, are not convicted on the basis that a reasonable person would have known that the victim did not consent.[192] The main difficulty with this approach is that juries in rape trials seem to find it hard enough to decide whether or not the defendant thought the victim consented; they will find it even harder to work out the reasoning process the defendant used in reaching that conclusion.

(6) *Strict liability approach to rape*

It would be possible to argue that rape should be a strict liability offence. In other words, once it is proved that there was penetration without the victim's consent the offence is made out. This would of course be very harsh on defendants who, on perfectly reasonable grounds, believe the victim consents, but in fact it is proved that she did not.[193] Therefore, few commentators are willing to suggest that rape generally should be a strict liability offence. But some commentators suggest that under certain circumstances it is fair to impose strict liability.

In the following extract Balos and Fellows[194] focus on cases sometimes called 'acquaintance rape': cases of alleged rape where the defendant and victim are in some kind of relationship.[195] They suggest that if there is a pre-existing relationship there is a heightened duty on the man to ascertain accurately whether the woman consents to sex. Where the defendant fails to obtain her consent he is guilty even if he was acting reasonably or in good faith. They go further and claim that where the relationship has been characterized by violence any consent given by a woman in such a relationship will be presumed to be invalid:[196]

B. Balos and M.L. Fellows, 'Guilty of the Crime of Trust: Nonstranger Rape' (1991) 75
Minnesota Law Review 599 at 605–10

II. Extending the Confidential Relationship Doctrine to Nonstranger Rapes

. . .

If the civil doctrine of confidential relationship were transported to the criminal arena, proof of a pre-existing relationship would create a presumption that the parties reposed trust in each other and, based on that presumption, the law would require each party to exercise a heightened duty of care. The civil law presumes trust from the fact that one party made a promise to the other. Analogously, the criminal law should presume trust from the fact of familiarity between the parties.

The justification for a presumption of reposed trust regarding unwanted sexual contact is that familiarity encourages a woman to be less wary. Failing to acknowledge the reposed

---

[191] Gardner (1991).   [192] Brett (1998).   [193] Husak and George Thomas III (1992).
[194] Balos and Fellows (1991: 603–4).
[195] See McGregor (2005: ch. 3).   [196] See also Basile (1999).

trust is equivalent to saying that women have a duty to be wary. Not all women, of course, repose trust in every male acquaintance, but this is no reason to deny women a right to trust.

Therefore, a pre-existing relationship between the victim and the defendant should apply to assist, rather than to hinder, the state's prosecution of the crime of rape. The two types of confidential relationships will be considered separately for this purpose. First, this Essay analyzes the prosecution of the crime of rape assuming a trust-type relationship, and then modifies the analysis by assuming a dominant-type relationship between the defendant and the victim.

A. The Trust-Type Relationship

The first way that a pre-existing trust-type relationship changes the prosecution of the crime of rape concerns the mental element of the crime. Different jurisdictions have different definitions and degrees of rape, but the one element common to the crime in all jurisdictions is sexual contact against a person's will. Beyond this, the definition and degree of rape varies based on the nature of the force required, the nature of the sexual contact required, and what constitutes consent. Although some courts have held that the state must prove that the defendant acted recklessly in failing to recognize the victim's nonconsent, others only require the state to show that the defendant's belief regarding consent was unreasonable. The introduction of the confidential relationship doctrine would substantially change the mental element. The standard of attentiveness to the victim's interests would increase as a result of the pre-existing trust relationship. This heightened duty justifies conviction if the evidence establishes that the defendant failed to obtain the victim's consent regardless of the defendant's reasonable or good faith belief.

Conviction is justified based on this heightened standard of attentiveness regardless of the duration of the relationship between the defendant and the victim and regardless of any past sexual intimacy. Application of the confidential relationship doctrine in the rape context acknowledges that the victim reposed trust in the defendant. Evidence of a prolonged intimate relationship indicates that the victim reposed more trust in the defendant than had the relationship been of a shorter more platonic nature. The argument put forward here, however, is that any imposition of trust by the victim should be sufficient to raise the heightened duty.

The second way that the pre-existing trust-type relationship affects the prosecution of the crime of rape is in the meaning that courts accord the term 'consent.' This issue is obviously closely connected to the question of the mental element and the heightened duty imposed on a non-stranger for attentiveness to the victim's interests. Silence or other passive behavior by the victim would not constitute sufficient evidence of consent between non-strangers. The defense of a reasonable, good faith belief that the words or conduct were overt and constituted consent also would not be available to the defendant, because it would undermine the heightened duty that arises out of the pre-existing relationship.

The heightened duty of care imposes an obligation on the defendant to meet a stricter standard of conduct than mere reasonable belief. This duty requires the defendant to inquire as to the victim's desire for sexual contact and the form of contact desired. The defendant's subjective belief that the victim's words or acts constituted consent is not relevant because under the heightened duty of care the defendant has no right to rely on his own belief, but rather has the obligation to listen to the victim.

Another way to reconcile the heightened duty standard with reasonable belief is to think of the heightened duty as transforming the meaning of reasonable belief. Society expects a person in a confidential relationship with another to exercise more responsibility. The failure to meet that responsibility is blameworthy. Thus, a reasonable belief consists of the defendant determining consent based on the victim's positive words or conduct.

The third way that the pre-existing trust-type relationship affects the prosecution of the crime of rape is that the evidence proving the relationship becomes relevant for the purpose of imposing a heightened duty of care on the defendant to determine the victim's consent. A prior relationship will no longer be used, as is the current practice, to infer present consent from the fact of previous consent. Although a defendant may still introduce evidence of a pre-existing relationship with the victim in an attempt to raise questions in the juror's minds about the victim's credibility and morality, the primary purpose of this evidence, as the jury instructions should indicate, would be to impose a heightened duty of care on the defendant.

B. The Dominance-Type Relationship

The legal significance to be accorded evidence showing that the defendant had a pattern of exercising dominance over the victim in their confidential relationship raises serious policy questions. The fact of a pre-existing relationship means that under the trust branch of the confidential relationship doctrine the defendant already has the burden of showing that the victim consented through positive words or positive conduct. Does the added dimension of domination mean that the victim was unable to exercise her free will to engage in sexual relations with the defendant? Should proof of consent through positive words or conduct be irrelevant and should sexual contact between the defendant and the victim be viewed as non-consensual, and thus rape?

Catharine MacKinnon and Andrea Dworkin have argued that women do not have real choices in heterosexual sex because of the systemic presence of male dominance in relationships between men and women and because our male-dominated society eroticizes dominance. Although acknowledging male dominance in heterosexual relationships does not lead to the conclusion that all heterosexual sex should be criminalized, it demands that the criminal law recognize the impossibility of consent in egregious circumstances where a man exercises control over a woman through physical and mental intimidation. The dominance branch of the confidential relationship doctrine is the means by which the courts could acknowledge the impossibility of a victim's consent. If the state shows that the defendant had a history of physically abusing the victim within the definitions used for domestic abuse prosecutions, the defense that the victim consented to the sexual contact with positive words or positive conduct would be unavailable.

This approach acknowledges the myth of a woman's choice under circumstances where survival to the next hour or day is itself a struggle. It might also serve to empower the woman in a dominant-type relationship. In these circumstances, even if her words or conduct affirmatively indicated consent to sex, both she and he would know that this is no defense to a rape complaint. Therefore, the dominance prong of confidential relationship doctrine may both empower the woman to pursue a rape prosecution and create for the man an interest in curtailing his behavior designed to control and dominate her. The argument, however, that an abstract evidentiary rule regarding the law of rape will empower a woman who daily is subjected to intimidation, at best, poses an interesting academic debating point, and, at worst, devalues the intense harm that an abused woman experiences.

Admittedly, applying the dominant-type confidential relationship doctrine in this manner may result in diminishing a woman's selfhood. Application of the trust-type confidential relationship to nonstranger rape empowers a woman to control access to her body. Unless she overtly demonstrates her sexual desires through acts or words, her male acquaintance is denied access. To assume that these same overt words or acts demonstrate consent when the woman has been a victim of physical and mental intimidation, however, is to ignore her life. Essentially, it would remove her right to agree to consensual sex. Once again, the question poses the familiar dilemma between acknowledging a woman's subordination and protecting against it and celebrating her autonomous and actualized self.

One possible solution to this dilemma is that courts could restrict application of the dominance branch of the confidential relationship doctrine to situations where the prosecution shows that the sexual contact occurred within some reasonably short time period after an incident of physical abuse. Only under circumstances of recent physical abuse would proof of the woman's affirmative words or conduct agreeing to sexual contact not be a defense. If a woman were to consent to sex freely or seek sex from her partner, it would likely be during a time period when the man had not been overtly abusive. Limiting application of the dominance-type confidential relationship doctrine to instances when overt abuse recently occurred would validate the woman's sexual choices in those circumstances when the possibility of choice was greatest.

Two reasons, however, mandate against restricting the use of the dominance-type confidential relationship rule. First, it fails to recognize that domination and intimidation persist in a relationship regardless of whether the man has recently or repeatedly manifested that domination and intimidation through physical abuse. Second, the proximate timing of overt physical abuse will become the cornerstone of a batterer's defense to rape and will do little to protect abused women from sexual invasion. It will mean that the only battering that makes a difference will be the overt abuse that occurs near and around the rape. The legal rules would continue to fail to reflect the reality of a battered woman's life.

David Bryden rejects the analogy drawn by Balos and Fellows between the relationship of lovers and other relationships where the law presumes undue influence (such as solicitor/client relationships, for example).[197] He argues that it is wrong to assume that women are weak and powerless in their sexual relations. There is a danger that the Balos and Fellows approach portrays woman as feeble. Their critics might also argue that strict liability is normally restricted to minor offences.[198]

An alternative version of a strict liability approach is that a man who had sexual intercourse with a woman who had manifested some kind of opposition to it (be it verbal or physical) has committed rape. This is so even if at the time of sexual intercourse she appeared to be consenting and he reasonably believed that she was consenting.[199] This approach is controversial, especially in cases where there is a significant gap in time between the 'no' and the subsequent 'yes': may not the woman change her mind as the defendant's seductive techniques take effect?[200] However, what to some are 'seduction techniques' are from another perspective coercive. Susan Estrich, for example, argues that repeated requests for sex are inherently coercive.[201] This reveals a major difficulty in this area. What by some men are regarded as 'normal seduction techniques' appear to some women to be threatening behaviour.[202] It is perhaps the lack of open communication and understanding between the genders which is a key difficulty in tackling the issue of unwanted sex.[203]

---

[197] Bryden (2000: 349). [198] Bryden (2000: 364).
[199] Henderson (1992: 158); Estrich (1987: 102–3).
[200] Bryden (2000: 391). [201] See Ch. 4. [202] Kinports (2001). [203] Weiner (1983).

16 THE *ACTUS REUS* OF RAPE

There has been some debate over the *actus reus* of rape. Should it be restricted to penetration of the vagina, or should it include penetration of the anus and mouth, as the Sexual Offences Act 2003 states? Should rape be restricted to penetration by a penis or should it include penetration with objects or other parts of the body? To some rape has a well-established meaning (penile penetration) which is known to the public and it would cause unnecessary confusion to extend it. Another argument that has been used in favour of the traditional understanding of rape as penile penetration is that it uniquely includes the risk of pregnancy.[204] However, some argue that the public needs to be educated; that the definition of rape is phallo-centric[205] and male-dominated: that from a male point of view whether he is penetrating the victim with his finger or his penis is of great significance. However, from the victim's point of view it is not. Further the public may need to be made more aware of the reality of the rape of men by men[206] or arguably the rape of men by women.[207]

Jennifer Temkin has suggested that we could adopt the Canadian approach, suggesting that first-degree sexual assault should be defined to include penetration involving the penis, vagina, or anus, together with the threat or infliction of serious injury. Second-degree assaults would involve penetration involving the penis, vagina, or anus, following a threat or infliction of injury. Third-degree assaults would cover all other sexual assaults involving penetrations, and fourth-degree assaults cover indecent assault not involving penetration.[208]

In the following passage John Gardner and Stephen Shute seek to support a narrower definition of rape:

J. Gardner and S. Shute, 'The Wrongness of Rape' in J. Horder (ed.), *Oxford Essays in Jurisprudence* (4th series, Oxford: OUP, 2000), 209–12

In many jurisdictions, including ours, what counts as sexual intercourse for the purposes of the crime of rape is limited to (one or another kind of) penetrative violation. Why is penetration so special? Does it count as a special way of using another person? The natural answer, of course, is that it counts as an especially humiliating way of using them. But again the special humiliation seems epiphenomenal. There was no special humiliation in the pure case because there was no humiliation at all in the pure case: the rape was never discovered. If, in more everyday cases, penetrative violations *are* particularly humiliating (or terrifying, confidence-sapping, etc.) in the eyes of those who experience them, then as usual we want to know the reason why. Why do violations of *this* kind have such special import for those who suffer them? One might say, of course, that the law itself contributes something to the special significance of penetration by historically reserving the name of 'rape' for that class of violations. Certainly there is something in that: the historic legal names of some criminal offences have gathered moral import with age, and often do contribute to structuring people's moral thinking. The thinking here goes: rape is (particularly) terrible; rape

---

[204] Naffine (1994) is concerned about any definition of rape which disguises the fact that the victims of rape are predominantly female.

[205] Duncan (1995).

[206] For a discussion of the treatment in the courtrooms of male rape see Rumney (2001b).

[207] Rumney (2001a), referring to Coxell *et al.* (1999); A. Clarke, J. Moran-Ellis, and J. Sleney (2002).

[208] Temkin (2002: 95–109).

is non-consensual penetration; so non-consensual penetration is (particularly) terrible. But this cannot serve *by itself* to justify the law's maintaining its insistence on penetration. Perhaps the old focus on penetration was superstitious or corrupt and the modern law should now be doing its utmost to change the confused moral thinking which that old focus left in its wake. Some aspects of the law of rape or the practice of rape prosecution, such as the marital rape exemption and the institutional blindness to date-rape, as well as the accompanying interest in evidence of the victim's sexual history, are now widely acknowledged to have left a false trail, and hence a false understanding of rape, in public consciousness. Is not the penetration condition, with its crude phallocentrism, in the same camp? Does it not hang over from an era of obsession with female virginity and overbearing preoccupation with the sin of bearing illegitimate children, an era in which women were *officially* regarded as objects (chattels of their fathers and husbands) rather than subjects? So maybe we should dump this condition now? We do not think that the answer is quite so simple.

What is true is that the justification of the penetration condition in the modern law of rape does involve some attention to social meaning. Some associate the Kantian argument we adopted above with a view of morality as a body of eternal verities which one abandons on pain of self-contradiction. In places this was how Kant himself presented the applications of the argument. But in fact the applications of the argument depend on many contingencies, including the social meaning of many actions. Which actions count as paradigms of sheer use-and-abuse of human beings varies, even though the Kantian argument against the sheer use-and-abuse of human beings has enduring force. Often the special symbolism of a particular act or class of acts is tied to the particular symbolism of acts which are regarded as their moral opposites. The special symbolism of penetrative violation is closely associated, in our culture, with the special symbolism of penetrative sexual activity. That latter symbolism may be over-romanticized. It may come of an aspiration to an impossible perfect union of two selves through two bodies, by making the two bodies, in a sense, just one (recall Shakespeare's 'beast with two backs'). Be that as it may, the fact that penetrative sex is regarded as having that significance actually endows it with that significance by changing its social meaning. The social meaning of the subversion of penetrative sex—its subversion in rape—tends to mirror the social meaning of penetrative sex. If the latter is thought of as a perfection of subject-subject relations—through the most complete and literal intertwining of selves—then the former may well come to represent a paradigm of subject–object relations. This is relevant to explaining and justifying the reactions even of those who do not share the aspiration to intertwine selves in this literal way (e.g. those who eschew or avoid penetrative sexual relationships, or those who see them as purely functional). The use of penetration can be a special weapon even against these people, perhaps *especially* against these people. It can become a peculiarly dramatic way of objectifying them, of turning them into mere things to be used, mere means to another's ends. That being so, there is reason for all those who suffer such violations to feel humiliated, whether or not they see particular value, or any value, in consensual penetrative sexual activity. The social meaning of consensual sexual penetration is not necessarily the meaning it has for them, and it is the social meaning of consensual sexual penetration which the rapist exploits by subverting it.

This is not a case against expanding the legal definition of rape to include some kinds of non-penetrative violations, or for discriminating among various kinds of penetration. In fact, it is not an argument for any particular legal definition of rape. It merely points out that the reactions of those who attach particular significance to penetrative violations, or to certain penetrative violations, need not be irrational. They may be supported by symbolic values. Much is left to law-makers and law-interpreters in deciding how best to embody and reflect such symbolic values in a given legal system. Social meanings are often ambiguous, and always have grey areas. Rarely do they set definite boundaries to moral wrongdoing without additional instrumental arguments, and instrumental argument also introduces many contingencies which can affect legal classifications. We showed this already in discussing the 'lack of consent' requirement. The instrumental question of what system of sexual relations would lead to the least use-and-abuse of human beings was an element of the argument. No doubt similar instrumental issues arise in the case of the penetration condition. The point is that although the mere use of people is a timeless evil, the elevation of penetrative non-consensual sexual violation to the status of special paradigm is a longstanding, but culturally conditioned application.

These remarks on the importance of social meaning merit the attention of those who are uneasy about the tendency to associate rape with sex, and in particular the tendency to think of it as a 'sexual offence'. Many campaigners and social researchers tell us that rape typically has nothing to do with sexual desire, and everything to do with a male desire for power over women. Surely it should be regarded as a crime of misogynist aggression, a hate-crime, rather than a sexual offence? We are uneasy about the essentialist view of sexual desire which this critique seems to harbour: Why, we wonder, cannot a misogynist desire to subordinate women be a sexual desire? (Is it because sex is wonderful and misogyny is vile?) But even if we grant the integrity of the assumed contrast between sexual desire and other kinds of desire, the main objection to this line of thought is that it assumes that 'sexual offences' are those offences which are differentiated by the offender's motivations. In our view, the real reason for thinking of rape as a sexual offence has nothing to do with the offender's motivations. It is that rape is a weapon against its victim which trades on the social meaning of sexual penetration. It is a way of taking a paradigm subject-subject relationship—a possibly over-romanticized conception of sexual intimacy—and turning it against someone to make a mere object of her. This does not rule out, and indeed may well suggest, that the perpetrator hates the victim, or what she represents. It is not necessary to deny the connection between rape and sex in order to make this clear. On the contrary, if the connection with sex is dropped and rape is simply labelled as, say, 'aggravated assault', then it seems to us that (for better or worse) we have decided no longer to recognize in law what is *particularly* wrong with rape. True, a rape can *accurately* be labelled as a kind of assault (as the police often label it when conducting their investigations) since the unifying theme of assault crimes is invasion by one of another's personal space, and the rapist clearly does invade his victim's personal space. But this is a wrong incidental to, and usually rather trivial when placed alongside, the most fundamental element of wrongdoing in rape. So the description of rape as an assault, though accurate, is reductive and unrevealing? That most fundamental element of wrongdoing in rape, which differentiates rape from (most) assaults and gives rape a separate theme from the family of assault crimes, is the *sheer use* of the person raped, whether that is how the rapist saw what he was doing or otherwise. To understand how rape counts as sheer use, the social meaning of sexual penetration has to be kept in focus.

Whatever the offender means by it, and indeed whatever it means to its victim, rape is a crime of sexual violation according to its social meaning; and that social meaning is the meaning which is at the heart of rape's wrongness. One may still insist that 'violence' would be a better word here than 'violation'. Would it not at least have more political bite? We doubt whether even this is true. Assimilation of rape to the category of 'violent crime' in the media and in public discussion of crime has, in our view, done more than almost anything else to maintain the public myth that rapists are strangers waiting in dark alleys who subdue their victims by force. But rapists work by many more insidious methods than this and they still wrong their victims by non-consensual objectification of them. As our pure case of rape serves to remind us, and many more common kinds of case amply illustrate, the violation that is rape need not be associated with any kind of violence. Nor are the worst rapes necessarily the most violent rapes. Rapes in breach of trust using subtle threats or surreptitiously administered drugs to forestall any resistance can, in some cases, represent an even more egregious abuse of the person raped and can therefore be worse *qua* rapes (and this still remains true, on our analysis, whether or not these are the rapes that involve the worst experiences for the person raped.

QUESTIONS

1. One survey found that 26 per cent of men and 50 per cent of women in dating relationships reported having engaged in unwanted sexual activity within the two-week period of the study (O'Sullivan and Rice Allgeier (1998). See also Muehlenhard and Cook (1988)). Does this suggest that the law on sexual assault is failing badly?

2. Is there much the criminal law can do to change people's behaviour in sexual matters? Does that mean the law should not try?

3. A recently published survey (BBC Newsonline (2005f)) found one in ten men said that they had used a prostitute. A similar survey in 1990 had found the figure to be one in twenty. Does this tell us anything about attitudes towards sexual relations and sexual crimes?

4. Jeffrie Murphy (1994) suggested rape was analogous to forcing someone to eat sushi or taking something that is normally pleasurable and forcing it upon someone. How can people say such things?

5. Is sex that is unwanted the same as sex that is not consented to?

6. Joan McGregor (2005: 183) writes: 'the problem with fraud in the inducement is that exaggeration and puffery are part and parcel of romantic or sexual relationships. People make themselves sound and appear better in order to impress their partner and entice them into sex. Men drive more expensive cars than they can afford and women wear push-up bras to entice and influence men's choices.' Does this mean we should be reluctant to find deceptions negate consent to sexual relations?

7. Should cases of 'date rape' be given higher or lower sentences than other rapes? (See Rumney (2003) for a discussion of the rape sentencing guidelines.)

FURTHER READING

Archard, D. (1998), *Sexual Consent* (Boulder, Cols.: Westview).

Ayres, I., and Baker, K. (2005), 'A Separate Crime of Reckless Sex', *University of Chicago Law Review* 72: 599

Bryden, D. (2000), 'Redefining Rape', *Buffalo Criminal Law Review*, 3: 317.

Burgess-Jackson, K. (1996), *Rape: A Philosophical Investigation* (Dartmouth: Aldershot).

Denno, D. (1997), 'Sexuality, Rape, And Mental Retardation', *University of Illinois Law Review* 17: 315.

Dripps, D. (1992), 'Beyond Rape: An Essay on the Difference between the Presence of Force and the Absence of Consent', *Columbia Law Review* 92: 1780.

Gardner, S. (1996), 'Appreciating *Olugboja*', *Legal Studies* 16: 275.

Henderson, L. (1992), 'Rape and Responsibility', *Law & Philosophy* 11: 127.

Herring, J. (2005a), 'Mistaken Sex', *Criminal Law Review* 511.

Horder, J. (2001), 'How Culpability Can, and Cannot, Be Denied in Under-age Sex Crimes', *Criminal Law Review* 15.

Huigens, K. (2005), 'Is Strict Liability Rape Defensible?', in R.A. Duff and S. Green (eds.), *Defining Crimes* (Oxford: OUP).

McGregor, J. (2005), *Is it Rape?* (Aldershot: Ashgate).

Moerings, M. (2001), 'The Fight Against Sex with Children' in P. Alldridge and C. Brants (eds.), *Personal Autonomy, the Private Sphere and the Criminal Law* (Oxford: Hart).

Oberman, M. (2000), 'Regulating Consensual Sex with Minors: Defining a Role for Statutory Rape', *Buffalo Law Review* 48: 703.

Power, H. (2003), 'Towards a Definition of the *Mens Rea* of Rape', *Oxford Journal of Legal Studies* 15: 379.

Schulhofer, S. (1998), *Unwanted Sex: The Culture of Intimidation and the Failure of Law* (Cambridge, Mass.: Harvard University Press).

Werthmeimer, A. (2003), *Consent to Sexual Relations* (Cambridge: Cambridge University Press).

West, R. (1993b), 'Legitimating the Illegitimate: A Comment on Beyond Rape', *Columbia Law Review* 93: 1442.

8

THEFT, HANDLING, AND ROBBERY

PART I: THE LAW

1 THEFT

Section 1 of the Theft Act 1968 defines theft:

> A person is guilty of theft if he dishonestly appropriates property belonging to another with the intention of permanently depriving the other of it . . .

The offence can be broken down into five elements.

DEFINITION

The defendant is guilty of theft if he or she:

1. appropriates
2. property
3. belonging to another
4. dishonestly
5. with an intention to permanently deprive.

The *actus reus* of theft is, therefore, appropriating property belonging to another. The *mens rea* is dishonesty and an intention permanently to deprive.

N.B. It should be noted that the law involving the dishonest use of cheques, credit cards, and bank balances is complex and involves a consideration of both the law of theft and deception offences. The cases on theft involving those will therefore be delayed until Chapter 9.

We will now consider these five elements. In order to understand appropriation it is necessary first to understand the meaning of 'property'.

1.1 PROPERTY

Section 4(1) of the Theft Act 1968 defines property as follows:

> 'Property' includes money and all other property, real or personal, including things in action and other intangible property.

This is a wide definition which includes most things that would normally be regarded as property, ranging from cars to pieces of paper. Before we look at things on the borderline of the concept of property, some of the phrases in section 4(1) may need explaining:

(1) Real property is land.

(2) Personal property is property which is not land.

(3) A thing in action (sometimes known as 'a chose in action') means a property right that can be claimed in a court action. A common example of 'a thing in action' is a debt. If someone owes you £50 you do not own £50, but under the law of theft you do have a piece of property in the right to sue the other person for that money.

(4) 'Intangible property' includes patents and copyrights.[1] So a person who purports to sell another's rights under a patent is committing theft.[2]

We will now consider cases on the borderline of what is property for the purposes of theft.[3]

Land

Land cannot be stolen. So moving a garden fence to add an extra foot to your garden will not amount to theft of the land. This straightforward proposition needs clarification in three particular situations:

(1) Where the defendant is acting as a trustee or personal representative. Under section 4(2)(a) there can be theft of land by the defendant:

> when he is a trustee or personal representative, or is authorized by power of attorney, or as liquidator of a company, or otherwise, to sell or dispose of land belonging to another, and he appropriates the land or anything forming part of it by dealing with it in breach of the confidence reposed in him.

This means that if the defendant is a trustee and is authorized to sell some land he can be convicted of theft if he sells more land than he is authorized to do.

(2) Things found on a piece of land (e.g. a tree, a piece of garden furniture) fall into one

---

[1] *Mensah Lartey and Relevey* [1996] Cr App R 143 (CA).

[2] A person who infringes a copyright (e.g. by illegally copying a CD) is not committing theft. This is because he does not appropriate the copyright (he does not act as the copyright holder); he simply infringes the copyright. He may, then, be liable to pay damages in a civil case, but there is no theft.

[3] It is notable that some things are not property under the general law of property and so cannot be stolen. Others things are property under the general law, but s. 4 specifically excludes them from the definition of property for the purposes of the law of theft.

of two categories: they either do or do not form part of the land. Something is part of the land if it is growing on the land (e.g. a rose bush); is a permanent structure (e.g. a garden shed); or is an integral part of such a structure or a fixture (e.g. a roof tile). Things that are moveable (e.g. a piece of garden furniture) are not part of the land. Things that do not form part of the land are property for the purpose of theft.

The law is more complex for things that form part of the land. To understand the law in this area it is necessary to distinguish between those who are in possession of the land, those who are tenants, and those who are not in possession of the land.

(i) Those who are in possession of the land. This includes the owners of the land. For them, not surprisingly, it is no offence to take property which forms part of the land or to sever the property from the land. Therefore (of course) an owner of a house does not commit theft if he or she picks flowers from his or her garden.[4]

(ii) Those who are not in possession of the land (e.g. a trespasser or a person invited onto the land by the owner). Such people are dealt with under section 4(2)(b). There can be theft by a defendant of things forming part of the land:

> . . . when he is not in possession of the land and appropriates anything forming part of the land by severing it or causing it to be severed, or after it has been severed.

So, if a trespasser removed something that formed part of the land (e.g. a garden shed) this would be theft.

(iii) Tenants in possession. It would not be an offence for a tenant to remove something that formed part of the land he was renting unless what he removed was a 'fixture or structure'.[5] A fixture is anything permanently attached to the land. It includes a staircase or a wall, but not a plant or gravel.

(3) Special rules relate to fruits and plants from the land.

Section 4(3) of the Theft Act 1968 states:

> A person who picks mushrooms growing on any land, or who picks flowers, fruit or foliage from a plant growing wild on any land, does not (although not in possession of the land) steal what he picks, unless he does it for reward or for sale or other commercial purposes.

These rules apply only to those who are not in possession of the land. In essence picking wild mushrooms, fruits, or flowers from land is not theft unless it is done for commercial reasons (section 4(3)). There are three important restrictions here. First it should be noted that the section refers specifically to 'picking' and so does not apply to people who dig up whole plants, or cut parts of plants, who are guilty of theft.[6] Secondly, it applies only to wild mushrooms and plants, and so a person who picks cultivated flowers commits an offence. Thirdly, a defendant who is picking wild flowers, etc., for commercial purposes is guilty of an offence. This provision means that someone out for a walk in the countryside who picks a blackberry for a little

---

[4] This is true even if the seeds were planted by the previous owner.
[5] Theft Act 1968, s. 4(2)(c).   [6] Unless they are in possession of the land.

snack is not committing an offence. Someone who picks the blackberries to sell at a market stall is.

Wild creatures

These are dealt with by section 4(4) of the Theft Act 1968, which provides:

> Wild creatures, tamed or untamed, shall be regarded as property; but a person cannot steal a wild creature not tamed nor ordinarily kept in captivity, or the carcase of any such creature, unless either it has been reduced into possession by or on behalf of another person and possession of it has not since been lost or abandoned, or another, or another person is in course or reducing it into possession.

The key distinction drawn in this section is between tamed creatures (e.g. pets); wild creatures kept in captivity (e.g. wild animals kept in a zoo) or reduced into possession (e.g. wild animals which have been trapped); and wild creatures not kept in captivity. Tame animals are treated as property and can be stolen. Similarly wild animals kept in captivity or reduced into possession can be stolen. However, wild animals not kept in captivity are not property and cannot be stolen.

Information

Information is not property.[7] In *Oxford v Moss*[8] a civil engineering student copied an examination paper and then returned it.[9] The Court of Appeal quashed a conviction for theft as confidential information cannot be stolen.[10] The protection of confidential information is found in civil law where injunctions can be obtained to prevent its revelation. It should be noted that the Computer Misuse Act 1990 creates special offences which deal with people accessing confidential information held on computers.

Electricity

It seems that electricity is not property, although there is a specific offence under section 13:[11]

> A person who dishonestly uses without due authority, or dishonestly causes to be wasted or diverted, any electricity shall on conviction on indictment be liable to imprisonment for a term not exceeding five years.

Gas[12] and water in an artificial retainer[13] are property and can be stolen. Water in a stream or a pond is treated as part of the land on which it lies and is dealt with under the rules governing land described above.

---

[7] For further discussion see Weinrib (1988) and G. Hammond (1984). The Supreme Court of Canada in *Stewart* (1988) 59 DLR 1 rejected an argument that confidential information is property.

[8] (1979) 68 Cr App R 183 (CA).   [9] Do not get any ideas!

[10] Law Commission Consultation Paper No. 150 (1997) suggested the creation of an offence of disclosing trade secrets.

[11] Theft Act 1968, s. 13, discussed in *Low v Blease* [1975] Crim LR 513.

[12] *White* (1853) 169 ER 696.   [13] *Ferens v O'Brien* (1883) 11 QBD 21.

Bodies

The traditional view is that bodies, parts of bodies, bodily products, and corpses are not property.[14] However, this view is coming under challenge, and it is now accepted that sometimes these can be property. At present, it appears that there are three circumstances in which bodily matter could amount to property for the purposes of the law of theft.

(1) If a corpse is reduced to another's possession or control it becomes property. So a buried corpse is not property, but if the corpse has been taken into the possession or control of a hospital then it is regarded as property that can be stolen.

(2) Bodily products (such as blood, urine, semen) become property if they are taken into someone's control. In *Welsh*[15] a man gave a urine sample to the police, and then ran off with it. He was convicted of theft of the urine. So blood stored at a blood bank or sperm stored at an infertility clinic can be regarded as property. But bodily products left lying around or disposed of in the normal way are not regarded as theft. So a hairdresser who took hair cut from a pop star and sold it would probably not be committing theft.

(3) If someone has exercised special skills in relation to a corpse or part of a body then that corpse or body part may be transformed into property. This issue was considered in the following case:

R v Kelly and another
[1999] QB 621 (CA)[16]

Anthony-Noel Kelly was an artist who was permitted to visit the Royal College of Surgeons in order to draw anatomical specimens being used by trainee doctors. He asked Neil Lindsay, who was employed at the college as a technician, to remove some body parts. Up to forty were removed without the College's permission and used by Kelly to form casts which were to be the basis of works of art. The body parts were then buried in a field. Kelly and Lindsay were charged with theft. They were convicted, and appealed to the Court of Appeal, primarily on the basis that body parts could not constitute property for the purposes of the law of theft.

Lord Justice Rose

We return to the first question, that is to say whether or not a corpse or part of a corpse is property. We accept that, however questionable the historical origins of the principle, it has now been the common law for 150 years at least that neither a corpse, nor parts of a corpse, are in themselves and without more capable of being property protected by rights (see e.g. Erle J, delivering the judgment of a powerful Court of Crown Cases Reserved in *R v Sharpe* (1857) Dears & B 160 at 163, 169 ER 959 at 960, where he said:

---

[14] *Sharpe* (1857) Dears & B 160. For a detailed discussion of this issue see J.W. Harris (1996b).
[15] [1974] RTR 550. See also *Rothery* [1976] RTR 550. In *Herbert, The Times*, 22 Dec. 1960 a man was convicted of theft after cutting off someone's hair.
[16] [1998] 3 All ER 741, [1999] 2 WLR 384.

'Our law recognises no property in a corpse, and the protection of the grave at common law, as contradistinguished from ecclesiastical protection to consecrated ground, depends upon this form of indictment . . .'

He was there referring to an indictment which charged not theft of a corpse but removal of a corpse from a grave.

If that principle is now to be changed, in our view, it must be by Parliament, because it has been express or implicit in all the subsequent authorities and writings to which we have been referred that a corpse or part of it cannot be stolen.

To address the point as it was addressed before the trial judge and to which his certificate relates, in our judgment, parts of a corpse are capable of being property within s 4 of the Theft Act, if they have acquired different attributes by virtue of the application of skill, such as dissection or preservation techniques, for exhibition or teaching purposes: see *Doodeward v Spence*, in the judgment of Griffith CJ to which we have already referred and *Dobson v North Tyneside Health Authority* [1996] 4 All ER 474 at 479, where this proposition is not dissented from and appears, in the judgment of this court, to have been accepted by Peter Gibson LJ; otherwise, his analysis of the facts of Dobson's case, which appears at that page in the judgment, would have been, as it seems to us, otiose. Accordingly the trial judge was correct to rule as he did.

Furthermore, the common law does not stand still. It may be that if, on some future occasion, the question arises, the courts will hold that human body parts are capable of being property for the purposes of s 4, even without the acquisition of different attributes, if they have a use or significance beyond their mere existence. This may be so if, for example, they are intended for use in an organ transplant operation, for the extraction of DNA or, for that matter, as an exhibit in a trial. It is to be noted that in Dobson's case, there was no legal or other requirement for the brain, which was then the subject of litigation, to be preserved (see the judgment of Peter Gibson LJ [1996] 4 All ER 474 at 479).

Appeals against conviction dismissed. Appeals against sentence allowed.

In some areas Parliament has passed legislation to tackle dishonest dealings with things that are not property for the purposes of theft. For example, the Computer Misuse Act 1990 was passed to protect confidential information on computers and the Human Tissue Acts 1961 governs body parts.[17]

QUESTIONS

1. William Wilson (2002: 425) writes the following: 'Less easy to analyse is the legal position suggested by the recent case of the tennis star whose ejaculate, following oral sex, may have been used to impregnate the recipient [without the tennis player's consent or knowledge]. Even assuming ejaculate was capable of being property for the purpose of the Theft Acts no proprietary rights could sensibly be retained by the ejaculator given the votive nature of the process.' Do you agree?

2. Anne picks some wild blackberries to use in her crumble for her boyfriend. When he arrives at dinner that night he announces that he does not like blackberries. Ann decides to sell the blackberry crumble at her shop the next day. Has she committed theft?

---

[17] Services cannot be stolen. A person who takes a taxi journey and then runs away without paying does not steal the journey, although such conduct is covered in the Theft Act 1978, s. 3.

1.2 BELONGING TO ANOTHER

It is normally straightforward whether the property belongs to another.[18] If there is any doubt the law of property normally readily provides an answer.[19] Sometimes property is deemed to belong to no one. This occurs most obviously where property has been abandoned by the owner, with no interest in its return or treatment.[20] However, there are some borderline cases and these are dealt with by the four subsections in section 5 of the Theft Act 1968:

Section 5(1)

Section 5(1) states:

> Property shall be regarded as belonging to any person having possession or control of it, or having in it any proprietary right or interest (not being an equitable interest arising only from an agreement to transfer or grant an interest).

This means that property does not just belong to the person who owns it, but also belongs to any person who has possession or control of it,[21] or has a proprietary interest in it.[22]

It should be added that the possession or control does not have to be lawful possession or control.[23] In other words, if Tim steals property and then Sam takes the property from Tim, this can still be theft by Sam. The fact that he was taking the property from Tim who did not have lawful possession of it is no defence. A further significance of this is that the owner can be convicted of theft of his own property. At first sight this seems a most peculiar idea, but is quite appropriate in some cases. One example was *Turner (No. 2)*[24] where a defendant drove his car away from a garage where he had left it to be repaired, without paying the bill. He was convicted of theft of his car. The car belonged to another because the garage had lawful control of it.[25]

---

[18] Although see *Sullivan and Ballion* [2002] Crim LR 758 (CA), where the money had been taken from a dead person.

[19] See *Marshall* [1998] 2 Cr App R 282, excerpted below.

[20] So a miss-hit golf ball which the player decides she cannot be bothered to look for is abandoned by her (although the ball may then 'belong to' the owner of the golf course for the purposes of the Theft Act as he or she has 'possession and control' over the ball (*Hibbert v McKiernan* [1948] 2 KB 142)). *Williams v Phillips* (1957) 41 Cr App R 5 held (perhaps surprisingly) that property put in a rubbish bin was not abandoned, in that the owner intended it to be removed by the council refuse collectors and not any passer-by.

[21] Generally a person who owns land controls any property on it, even if he does not know of the property's existence: *Woodman* [1974] QB 754 (CA).

[22] It is beyond the scope of this book to discuss all the circumstances in which someone may acquire a legal or equitable interest in the property.

[23] *Kelly* [1998] 3 All ER 741 (CA).

[24] (1971) 55 Cr App R 336 (CA).   [25] See also *Bonner* [1970] 2 All ER 97 (CA).

Section 5(2)

Section 5(2) states:

> Where property is subject to a trust, the persons to whom it belongs shall be regarded as including any person having a right to enforce the trust, and an intention to defeat the trust shall be regarded accordingly as an intention to deprive of the property any person having that right.

Normally, if property is held on trust it is owned by the beneficiaries. However, this subsection deals with the property of trusts which do not have beneficiaries (e.g. charitable trusts). In such a case the property shall be regarded as belonging to those entitled to enforce the trust (e.g. the Attorney-General in the case of charitable trusts).

Section 5(3)

Section 5(3):

> Where a person receives property from or on account of another, and is under an obligation to the other to retain and deal with that property or its proceeds in a particular way, the property or proceeds shall be regarded (as against him) as belonging to the other.

This subsection deals with the situation where a defendant is given property and is under an obligation to deal with that property in a particular way.[26] Although the defendant is in civil law the owner of the property, if he is under an obligation to the victim to deal with that property in a particular way then the property is treated as belonging to the victim for the purposes of the law of theft. The obligation must be a legal obligation; a moral obligation is not enough.[27]

In the following case the Court of Appeal emphasized that it must be shown that the defendant was obliged to deal with *that property* in a particular way:

R v Hall
[1973] 1 QB 126 (CA)[28]

Geoffrey Hall, a travel agent, received money from some clients by way of deposits for air flights to America. He paid the money into the firm's general account. In fact none of the flights materialized and the money was not refunded. He was convicted of theft, but

---

[26] Sometimes giving property to people and placing them under an obligation to deal with it in a particular way will create a trust and therefore s. 5(1) or (2) can be relied upon as an alternative to s. 5(3). A court will not be sympathetic to arguments that the prosecution case should have been based on s. 5(1), rather than 5(3) or vice versa: see *Hallam and Blackburn* [1995] Crim LR 323 (CA).

[27] *Gilks* (1972) 56 Cr App R 734 (CA). It is for the judge to direct the jury on facts they must find before a legal obligation will arise: *Dunbar* [1995] 1 Cr App R 280 (CA). Whether the obligation is legal or moral is a question of law, not a matter of the defendant's belief: *Dyke and Munro* [2001] EWCA Crim 2184, [2002] 1 Cr App R 30 (CA). Although if the obligation was in fact legal, but the defendant believed it to be moral, this might be a relevant issue for the purposes of dishonesty.

[28] [1972] 2 All ER 1009, [1972] 3 WLR 381, (1972) 56 Cr App R 547.

appealed, arguing that the money did not belong to another and section 5(3) did not apply.

Lord Justice Edmund Davies, reading the judgment of the court

Point (1) turns on the application of s 5(3) of the Theft Act 1968, which provides:

'Where a person receives property from or on account of another, and is under an obligation to the other to retain and deal with that property or its proceeds in a particular way, the property or proceeds shall be regarded (as against him) as belonging to the other.'

Counsel for the appellant submitted that in the circumstances arising in these seven cases there arose no such 'obligation' on the appellant. He referred us to a passage in the Eighth Report of the Criminal Law Revision Committee (*Theft and Related Offences*, Cmnd 2977 (1966), p 127) which reads as follows:

'Subsection (3) [of cl 5 "Belonging to Another"] provides for the special case where property is transferred to a person to retain and deal with for a particular purpose and he misapplies it or its proceeds. An example would be the treasurer of a holiday fund. The person in question is in law the owner of the property; but the subsection treats the property, as against him, as belonging to the persons to whom he owes the duty to retain and deal with the property as agreed. He will therefore be guilty of stealing from them if he misapplies the property or its proceeds.'

Counsel for the appellant . . . submits that the position of a treasurer of a solitary fund is quite different from that of a person like the appellant, who was in general (and genuine) business as a travel agent, and to whom people pay money in order to achieve a certain object—in the present cases, to obtain charter flights to America. It is true, he concedes, that thereby the travel agent undertakes a contractual obligation in relation to arranging flights and at the proper time paying the airline and any other expenses. Indeed, the appellant throughout acknowledged that this was so, although contending that in some of the seven cases it was the other party who was in breach. But what counsel for the appellant resists is that in such circumstances the travel agent 'is under an obligation' to the client 'to retain and deal with . . . in a particular way' sums paid to him in such circumstances. . . .

Nevertheless, when a client goes to a firm carrying on the business of travel agents and pays them money, he expects that in return he will, in due course, receive the tickets and other documents necessary for him to accomplish the trip for which he is paying, and the firm are 'under an obligation' to perform their part to fulfil his expectation and are liable to pay him damages if they do not. But, in our judgment, what was not here established was that these clients expected them 'to retain and deal with that property or its proceeds in a particular way', and that an 'obligation' to do so was undertaken by the appellant. We must make clear, however, that each case turns on its own facts. Cases could, we suppose, conceivably arise where by some special arrangement (preferably evidenced by documents), the client could impose on the travel agent an 'obligation' falling within s 5(3). But no such special arrangement was made in any of the seven cases here being considered. It is true that in some of them documents were signed by the parties; thus, in respect of counts 1 and 3 incidents there was a clause to the effect that the People to People organisation [the appellant's firm] did not guarantee to refund deposits if withdrawals were made later than a certain date; and in respect of counts 6, 7 and 8 the appellant wrote promising 'a full refund' after the flights paid for failed to materialise. But neither in those nor in the remaining two cases (in relation to which there was no documentary evidence of any kind) was there, in our judgment, such a special arrangement as would give rise to an obligation within s5(3).

> It follows from this that, despite what on any view must be condemned as scandalous conduct by the appellant, in our judgment on this ground alone this appeal must be allowed and the convictions quashed. . . .
>
> *Appeal allowed. Conviction quashed.*

Key to the Court of Appeal's reasoning in this case was that the courts did not expect the travel agent to deal with the actual monies handed over in a particular way.[29] The customers expected the travel agent to buy tickets for them, but not using the particular monies they provided.

There are conflicting authorities on people who collect money on behalf of a charitable organization, but then keep the money for themselves. In the leading case of *Wain*[30] a defendant collected money for 'The Telethon Trust' (a charitable trust), but did not pass the proceeds on to a charity and transferred the money into his own account. It was held that the defendant was properly convicted because he was under an obligation to retain, if not the actual notes and coins collected, at least their proceeds.[31]

QUESTION

A mother visiting her son at university is concerned that he is not eating enough green vegetables or fresh fruit and gives him a £10 note, saying, 'you must spend this note on fresh fruit or vegetables and on nothing else'. He spends the money on beer. Has he committed theft?

(In answering this question you will need to ask: was this a legal or moral obligation? Was the obligation to deal with the particular note in a special way? Was there dishonesty (see below)?)

Section 5(4)

Under section 5(4):

> Where a person gets property by another's mistake, and is under an obligation to make restoration (in whole or in part) of the property or its proceeds or of the value thereof, then to the extent of that obligation the property or its proceeds shall be regarded (as against him) as belonging to the person entitled to restoration, and an intention not to make restoration shall be regarded accordingly as an intention to deprive that person of the property or proceeds.

This subsection deals with the situation where the defendant has received property as a result of another's mistake and is under an obligation to restore the proceeds or their value. A good example of where section 5(4) operates is *Attorney-General's Reference (No. 1 of 1983)*[32] where a police officer was overpaid her salary by the police force. She was under an

---

[29] Contrast *Klineberg and Marsden* [1999] 1 Cr App R 427 (CA), discussed in J.C. Smith (1999a).

[30] [1995] 2 Cr App R 660 (CA).

[31] Such cases often involve careful analysis of the legal obligations of the parties. In commercial contexts, this can become highly complex: see e.g. *Re Kumar* [2000] Crim LR 504.

[32] [1985] QB 182 (CA).

obligation to return the money (once she was aware of the overpayment) and therefore the money could be treated as belonging to another (the police force).

DEFINITION

Where A hands to D property on the basis of a mistake, four situations need to be distinguished:

1. The mistake is so fundamental that ownership does not pass. So, although D possesses the property in fact it is still owned by A. There is therefore no difficulty in establishing the 'property belonging to another' requirement if D is charged with theft.

2. The mistake is not so fundamental that ownership does not pass and so D owns the property. But the mistake is sufficient to mean that D is under an obligation to return the money or its proceeds. This means that, relying on section 5(4), the property belongs to A for the purposes of the law of theft and so D can be convicted.

3. The mistake is one that means that D holds the property on trust for A. In such a case A has an equitable interest in the property and the property belongs to A under section 5(1) of the Theft Act, so D can be convicted of theft (see e.g. *Shadrokh-Cigari* [1988] Crim LR 465 (CA); *Hallam and Blackburn* [1995] Crim LR 323 (CA)).

4. The mistake is not significant enough to give rise either to a claim that ownership did not pass, or to a claim that there is a legal obligation to make restoration. In that case the property will belong to D and no theft charge can lie, unless the transfer from A itself can be regarded as dishonest. In that case, after *Hinks* [2000] 3 WLR 1590 (House of Lords), a charge of theft could be brought.

1.3 APPROPRIATION

Appropriation is a key element in the law of theft. Under section 3(1):

> Any assumption by a person of the rights of an owner amounts to an appropriation, and this includes, where he has come by the property (innocently or not) without stealing it, any later assumption of a right to it by keeping or dealing with it as owner.

The House of Lords has had to consider the interpretation of appropriation four times since the 1968 Act was passed. We will be quoting the two most recent and important cases shortly, but first we will summarize its conclusions on two key issues:

(1) There is an appropriation if the defendant has assumed *any* of the rights of the owner. This means that if the defendant has done something that an owner has the right to do then this is an appropriation. It is therefore appropriation to touch someone else's property, offer it for sale,[33] or destroy it. It must be shown that the act is something that only an owner has the right to do. Looking at something is therefore not appropriation, because people other than the owner have the right to do that. Similarly, just making the defendant deal with her property in a particular way does not amount to appropriation.[34] There is no need to show that the victim has lost the

---

[33] *Pitham and Hehl* (1976) 65 Cr App R 45 (CA).   [34] Briggs [2004] Crim LR 495.

property for there to be appropriation; indeed there is no need to show that the victim's property interests have been adversely interfered with. In *Morris*, the defendant appropriated items by switching the sticky labels on items in a shop indicating their price.

This definition of appropriation does mean that theft takes place at an earlier point in time than would be assumed by most people. If a person walks into a supermarket and touches a tin of baked beans intending to steal it, theft is committed there and then. You might have thought that theft would not be committed until the defendant ran out of the store with it, but that is not the law.[35]

(2) Does an act of appropriation have to be one that was not consented to by the victim? The answer is simply no. A touching of a piece of property is an appropriation, whether the victim consented, requested, or objected to the act. The victim's state of mind is irrelevant to whether or not there is appropriation. This was confirmed in the *Gomez* decision. In *Hinks* the House of Lords held that even if the property was handed over by the victim to the defendant as part of a valid gift under the law of property this could amount to an appropriation.

The following decision of the House of Lords is the leading case on the interpretation of appropriation:

R v Gomez
[1993] AC 442 (HL)[36]

Edwin Gomez was the assistant manager of a shop. A customer (an acquaintance of his) offered two stolen cheques as payment for some goods. Gomez was aware the cheques were stolen, but persuaded the manager of the shop to accept them by lying and saying that the cheques were 'as good as cash'. Gomez was charged with theft. At his trial he argued that there was no case to answer because the transfer of the goods had been consented to by the manager and there could therefore be no appropriation. He was convicted, the Court of Appeal allowed his appeal, and the prosecution appealed to the House of Lords.

Lord Keith of Kinkel

The [Court of Appeal] granted a certificate under section 33(2) of the Criminal Appeal Act 1968 that a point of law of general public importance was involved in the decision, namely

'When theft is alleged and that which is alleged to be stolen passes to the defendant with the consent of the owner, but that has been obtained by a false representation, has (a) an appropriation within the meaning of section 1(1) of the Theft Act 1968 taken place, or (b) must such a passing of property necessarily involve an element of adverse [interference] with or usurpation of some right of the owner?'

[Lord Keith analysed the speeches in the House of Lords decision in *Lawrence* [1972] AC 626 and continued]

---

[35] However, it will be difficult for a prosecution to prove that the defendant had the *mens rea* of theft if he is arrested before leaving the shop.

[36] [1993] 1 All ER 1, [1992] 3 WLR 1067, [1993] Crim LR 304.

It will be seen that Viscount Dilhorne's speech contains two clear pronouncements, first that it is no longer an ingredient of the offence of theft that the taking should be without the owner's consent and second, that an appropriation may occur even though the owner has permitted or consented to the property being taken. . . .

[Lord Keith then considered the speech of Lord Roskill in the House of Lords in *Morris* [1984] AC 320 and concluded]:

In my opinion Lord Roskill was undoubtedly right when he said in the course of the passage quoted that the assumption by the defendant of any of the rights of an owner could amount to an appropriation within the meaning of section 3(1), and that the removal of an article from the shelf and the changing of the price label on it constituted the assumption of one of the rights of the owner and hence an appropriation within the meaning of the subsection. But there are observations in the passage which, with the greatest possible respect to my noble and learned friend Lord Roskill, I must regard as unnecessary for the decision of the case and as being incorrect. In the first place, it seems to me that the switching of price labels on the article is in itself an assumption of one of the rights of the owner, whether or not it is accompanied by some other act such as removing the article from the shelf and placing it in a basket or trolley. No one but the owner has the right to remove a price label from an article or to place a price label upon it. If anyone else does so, he does an act, as Lord Roskill puts it, by way of adverse interference with or usurpation of that right. This is no less so in the case of the practical joker figured by Lord Roskill than in the case of one who makes the switch with dishonest intent. The practical joker, of course, is not guilty of theft because he has not acted dishonestly and does not intend to deprive the owner permanently of the article. So the label switching in itself constitutes an appropriation and so to have held would have been sufficient for the dismissal of both appeals. On the facts of the two cases it was unnecessary to decide whether, as argued by Mr. Jeffreys, the mere taking of the article from the shelf and putting it in a trolley or other receptacle amounted to the assumption of one of the rights of the owner, and hence an appropriation. There was much to be said in favour of the view that it did, in respect that doing so gave the shopper control of the article and the capacity to exclude any other shopper from taking it. However, Lord Roskill expressed the opinion, at p. 332, that it did not, on the ground that the concept of appropriation in the context of section 3(1) 'involves not an act expressly or impliedly authorised by the owner but an act by way of adverse interference with or usurpation of those rights.'

While it is correct to say that appropriation for purposes of section 3(1) includes the latter sort of act, it does not necessarily follow that no other act can amount to an appropriation and in particular that no act expressly or impliedly authorised by the owner can in any circumstances do so. Indeed, *Reg. v. Lawrence* [1972] A.C. 626 is a clear decision to the contrary since it laid down unequivocally that an act may be an appropriation notwithstanding that it is done with the consent of the owner. It does not appear to me that any sensible distinction can be made in this context between consent and authorisation.

. . . *Lawrence* makes it clear that consent to or authorisation by the owner of the taking by the rogue is irrelevant. The taking amounted to an appropriation within the meaning of section 1(1) of the Act of 1968. Lawrence also makes it clear that it is no less irrelevant that what happened may also have constituted the offence of obtaining property by deception under section 15(1) of the Act.

In my opinion it serves no useful purpose at the present time to seek to construe the relevant provisions of the Theft Act by reference to the report which preceded it, namely the Eighth Report of the Criminal Law Revision Committee on *Theft and Related Offences* (1966) (Cmnd. 2977). The decision in *Lawrence* was a clear decision of this House upon the construction of the word 'appropriate' in section 1(1) of the Act, which had stood for

12 years when doubt was thrown upon it by obiter dicta in *Morris*. *Lawrence* must be regarded as authoritative and correct, and there is no question of it now being right to depart from it.

It is desirable to say a few words about *Reg. v. Skipp* [1975] Crim. L. R. 114 and *Reg. v. Fritschy* [1985] Crim. L. R. 745. In the first case the defendant, posing as a haulage contractor, was instructed to collect consignments of goods from three different places and deliver them to a certain destination. He collected the goods and made off with them. The Court of Appeal, on his appeal against his conviction for theft upon one count covering all three consignments, on the ground that the count was bad for duplicity in that there were three separate appropriations, held that there had been no appropriation until the last of the goods were loaded, or probably until the defendant deviated from the route to the proper destination. In the second case the defendant was instructed by the owner to collect a quantity of krugerrands in London and deliver them to a safe deposit in Switzerland. Although the short report is not very clear on the matter, it seems that the defendant, having collected the coins, took them to Switzerland and there made away with them. The trial judge directed the jury if at the time he collected the coins the defendant had formed the dishonest intention of keeping them for himself he was guilty of theft. The Court of Appeal overturned the resultant conviction for theft on the ground, following *Morris*, that there had been no appropriation in England because the defendant had there taken possession of the krugerrands with the owner's authority. In my opinion both these cases were inconsistent with *Lawrence* and were wrongly decided.

. . .

My Lords, for the reasons which I have given I would answer branch (a) of the certified question in the affirmative and branch (b) in the negative, and allow the appeal.

Lord Browne-Wilkinson

My Lords, I have read the speech of my noble and learned friend, Lord Keith of Kinkel, with which I agree. I only add a few words of my own out of deference to the contrary view expressed by my noble and learned friend, Lord Lowry, and to consider the cases on thefts from companies to which we were referred in the course of argument.

. . .

The fact that Parliament used that composite phrase—'dishonest appropriation'—in my judgment casts light on what is meant by the word 'appropriation'. The views expressed (obiter) by this House in *Reg. v. Morris* [1984] A.C. 320 that 'appropriation' involves an act by way of adverse interference with or usurpation of the rights of the owner treats the word appropriation as being tantamount to 'misappropriation.' The concept of adverse interference with or usurpation of rights introduces into the word appropriation the mental state of both the owner and the accused. So far as concerns the mental state of the owner (did he consent?), the Act of 1968 expressly refers to such consent when it is a material factor: see sections 2(1)(b), 11(1), 12(1) and 13. So far as concerns the mental state of the accused, the composite phrase in section 1(1) itself indicates that the requirement is dishonesty.

For myself, therefore, I regard the word 'appropriation' in isolation as being an objective description of the act done irrespective of the mental state of either the owner or the accused. It is impossible to reconcile the decision in *Lawrence* (that the question of consent is irrelevant in considering whether there has been an appropriation) with the views expressed in *Morris*, which latter views in my judgment were incorrect.

It is suggested that this conclusion renders section 15 of the Act of 1968 otiose since a person who, by deception, persuades the owner to consent to part with his property will necessarily be guilty of theft within section 1. This may be so though I venture to doubt it. Take for example a man who obtains land by deception. Save as otherwise expressly provided, the definitions in sections 4 and 5 of the Act apply only for the purposes of interpreting section 1 of the Act: see section 1(3). Section 34(1) applies subsection (1) of section 4 and subsection (1) of section 5 generally for the purposes of the Act. Accordingly the other subsections of section 4 and section 5 do not apply to section 15. Suppose that a fraudster has persuaded a victim to part with his house: the fraudster is not guilty of theft of the land since section 4(2) provides that you cannot steal land. The charge could only be laid under section 15 which contains no provisions excluding land from the definition of property. Therefore, although there is a substantial overlap between section 1 and section 15, section 15 is not otiose.

Turning to the company cases, the dictum in *Reg. v. Morris* [1984] A.C. 320 has led to much confusion and complication where those in de facto control of the company have been charged with theft from it. The argument which has found favour in certain of the authorities runs as follows. There can be no theft within section 1 if the owner consents to what is done: *Reg. v. Morris*. If the accused, by reason of being the controlling shareholder or otherwise, is 'the directing mind and will of the company' he is to be treated as having validly consented on behalf of the company to his own appropriation of the company's property. This is apparently so whether or not there has been compliance with the formal requirements of company law applicable to dealings with the property of a company and even to cases where the consent relied on is *ultra vires*: see *Reg. v. Roffel* [1985] V.R. 511 and *Reg. v. McHugh* (1988) 88 Cr. App. R. 385.

In my judgment this approach was wrong in law even if the dictum in *Morris* had been correct. Where a company is accused of a crime the acts and intentions of those who are the directing minds and will of the company are to be attributed to the company. That is not the law where the charge is that those who are the directing minds and will have themselves committed a crime against the company: see *Attorney-General's Reference (No. 2 of 1982)* [1984] Q.B. 624 applying *Belmont Finance Corporation Ltd. v. Williams Furniture Ltd.* [1979] Ch. 250.

In any event, your Lordships' decision in this case, re-establishing as it does the decision in *Reg. v. Lawrence* [1972] A.C. 626, renders the whole question of consent by the company irrelevant. Whether or not those controlling the company consented or purported to consent to the abstraction of the company's property by the accused, he will have appropriated the property of the company. The question will be whether the other necessary elements are present, *viz.* was such appropriation dishonest and was it done with the intention of permanently depriving the company of such property?

. . .

I am glad to be able to reach this conclusion. The pillaging of companies by those who control them is now all too common. It would offend both common sense and justice to hold that the very control which enables such people to extract the company's assets constitutes a defence to a charge of theft from the company. The question in each case must be whether the extraction of the property from the company was dishonest, not whether the alleged thief has consented to his own wrongdoing.

Lord Slynn of Hadley and **Lord Jauncey** concurred with the speeches of **Lord Keith** and **Lord Browne-Wilkinson. Lord Lowry** gave a dissenting judgment.

Appeal allowed.

You may be puzzled why in *Gomez* the prosecution did not charge with the offence of obtaining property by deception, which would arguably more accurately define the offence committed. There is no ready explanation for the prosecutors' course of action.

In the following case the House of Lords had to decide whether *Gomez* meant that even where a transfer of property was one that was valid under civil law it could amount to an appropriation. To understand this case a few basic points on the law of property need to be understood. A transfer of money will be a valid one unless there is a 'vitiating factor'. These include a misrepresentation, the use of undue influence, or the exercise of duress. The case proceeded on the basis that in this case, although the defendant might have dishonestly acquired the money, there were no vitiating factors and so the transaction was a valid gift in civil law:

R v Hinks
[2001] 2 AC 241 (HL)[37]

Karen Hinks made friends with John Dolphin, described as a naïve, trusting man of limited intelligence. Nearly every day for over six months Hinks accompanied Dolphin to his building society where he withdrew £300 (the maximum possible) and then handed over the money to her. The total received by Hinks was over £60,000. An expert psychiatrist gave evidence that it was unlikely that Dolphin had made the decision to hand over the money on his own. Hinks was convicted of theft. She appealed on the basis that the judge should have given the jury a clear direction that there could not be theft if the transfer had constituted a valid gift.

Lord Steyn

I

Since the enactment of the Theft Act 1968 the House of Lords has on three occasions considered the meaning of the word 'appropriates' in section 1(1) of the Act, namely in *Reg v Lawrence (Alan)* [1972] AC 626; in *Reg v Morris (David)* [1984] AC 320; and in *Reg v Gomez* [1993] AC 442. The law as explained in *Lawrence* and *Gomez*, and applied by the Court of Appeal in the present case (*Reg v Hinks* [2000] 1 Cr App R 1) has attracted strong criticism from distinguished academic lawyers: see for example, JC Smith [1993] Crim LR 304 and [1998] Crim LR 904; Edward Griew, The Theft Acts, 7th ed (1995) pp 41–59; ATH Smith, 'Gifts and the Law of Theft' [1999] CLJ 10. These views have however been challenged by equally distinguished academic writers: PR Glazebrook, 'Revising the Theft Acts' [1993] CLJ 191–194: Simon Gardner, 'Property and Theft' [1998] Crim LR 35. The academic criticism of Gomez provided in substantial measure the springboard for the present appeal. The certified question before the House is as follows:

'Whether the acquisition of an indefeasible title to property is capable of amounting to an appropriation of property belonging to another for the purposes of section 1(1) of the Theft Act 1968.'

In other words, the question is whether a person can 'appropriate' property belonging to another where the other person makes him an indefeasible gift of property, retaining no proprietary interest or any right to resume or recover any proprietary interest in the property.

---

[37] [2000] 4 All ER 833, [2000] 3 WLR 1590.

Before the enactment of the Theft Act 1968 English law required a taking and carrying away of the property as the *actus reus* of the offence. In 1968 Parliament chose to broaden the reach of the law of theft by requiring merely an appropriation. . . .

These provisions, and in particular the word 'appropriates' in section 1(1), read with the explanatory provision in section 3(1), have been authoritatively interpreted by the House in *Lawrence* [1972] AC 626 and *Gomez* [1993] AC 442. It will be a matter for consideration whether such earlier rulings are dispositive of the question of law before the House. . . .

VI

Counsel for the appellant submitted in the first place that the law as expounded in *Gomez* and *Lawrence* must be qualified to say that there can be no appropriation unless the other party (the owner) retains some proprietary interest, or the right to resume or recover some proprietary interest, in the property. Alternatively, counsel argued that 'appropriates' should be interpreted as if the word 'unlawfully' preceded it. Counsel said that the effect of the decisions in *Lawrence* and *Gomez* is to reduce the *actus reus* of theft to 'vanishing point' (see Smith & Hogan, *Criminal Law*, 9th ed (1999), p 505). He argued that the result is to bring the criminal law 'into conflict' with the civil law. Moreover, he argued that the decisions in *Lawrence* and *Gomez* may produce absurd and grotesque results. He argued that the mental requirements of dishonesty and intention of permanently depriving the owner of property are insufficient to filter out some cases of conduct which should not sensibly be regarded as theft. He did not suggest that the appellant's dishonest and repellent conduct came within such a category. Instead he deployed four examples for this purpose, namely:

(1) S makes a handsome gift to D because he believes that D has obtained a First. D has not and knows that S is acting under that misapprehension. He makes the gift. There is here a motivational mistake which, it is submitted, does not avoid the transaction. (Glanville Williams, *Textbook of Criminal Law*, 1st ed (1978), p 788.)

(2) P sees D's painting and, thinking he is getting a bargain, offers £100,000 for it. D realises that P thinks the painting is a Constable, but knows that it was painted by his sister and is worth no more than £100. He accepts P's offer. D has made an enforceable contract and is entitled to recover and retain the purchase price. (Smith & Hogan, *Criminal Law*, pp 507, 508.)

(3) A buys a roadside garage business from B, abutting on a public thoroughfare; unknown to A but known to B, it has already been decided to construct a bypass road which will divert substantially the whole of the traffic from passing A's garage. There is an enforceable contract and A is entitled to recover and retain the purchase price. The same would be true if B knew that A was unaware of the intended plan to construct a bypass road. (Compare Lord Atkin in *Bell v Lever Brothers Ltd* [1932] AC 161, 224.)

(4) An employee agrees to retire before the end of his contract of employment, receiving a sure of money by way of compensation from his employer. Unknown to the employer, the employee has committed serious breaches of contract which would have enabled the employer to dismiss him without compensation. Assuming that the employee's failure to reveal his defaults does not affect the validity of the contract, so that the employee is entitled to sue for the promised compensation, is the employee liable to be arrested for the theft the moment he receives the money? (Glanville Williams, 'Theft and Voidable Title' [1981] Crim LR 666, 672.)

My Lords, at first glance these are rather telling examples. They may conceivably have justified a more restricted meaning of section 3(1) than prevailed in *Lawrence* [1972] AC 626 and *Gomez* [1993] AC 442. The House ruled otherwise and I am quite unpersuaded that the House overlooked the consequences of its decision. On the facts set out in the examples a jury could possibly find that the acceptance of the transfer took place in the belief that the transferee had the right in law to deprive the other of it within the meaning of section 2(1)(a) of the Act. Moreover, in such cases a prosecution is hardly likely and if mounted, is likely to founder on the basis that the jury will not be persuaded that there was dishonesty in the required sense. And one must retain a sense of perspective. At the extremity of the application of legal rules there are sometimes results which may seem strange. A matter of judgment is then involved. The rule may have to be recast. Sir John Smith has eloquently argued that the rule in question ought to be recast. I am unpersuaded. If the law is restated by adopting a narrower definition of appropriation, the outcome is likely to place beyond the reach of the criminal law dishonest persons who should be found guilty of theft. The suggested revisions would unwarrantably restrict the scope of the law of theft and complicate the fair and effective prosecution of theft. In my view the law as settled in Lawrence and Gomez does not demand the suggested revision. Those decisions can be applied by judges and juries in a way which, absent human error, does not result in injustice.

Counsel for the appellant further pointed out that the law as stated in *Lawrence* [1972] AC 626 and *Gomez* [1993] AC 442 creates a tension between the civil and the criminal law. In other words, conduct which is not wrongful in ii civil law sense may constitute the crime of theft. Undoubtedly, this is so. The question whether the civil claim to title by a convicted thief, who committed no civil wrong, may be defeated by the principle that nobody may benefit from his own civil or criminal wrong does not arise for decision. Nevertheless there is a more general point, namely that the interaction between criminal law and civil law can cause problems: compare J Beatson and AP Simester, 'Stealing One's Own Property' (1999) 115 LQR 372. The purposes of the civil law and the criminal law are somewhat different. In theory the two systems should be in perfect harmony. In a practical world there will sometimes be some disharmony between the two systems. In any event, it would be wrong to assume on a priori grounds that the criminal law rather than the civil law is defective. Given the jury's conclusions, one is entitled to observe that the appellant's conduct should constitute theft, the only available charge. The tension between the civil and the criminal law is therefore not in my view a factor which justifies a departure from the law as stated in *Lawrence* and *Gomez*. Moreover, these decisions of the House have a marked beneficial consequence. While in some contexts of the law of theft a judge cannot avoid explaining civil law concepts to a jury (e.g. in respect of section 2(1)(a)), the decisions of the House of Lords eliminate the need for such explanations in respect of appropriation. That is a great advantage in an overly complex corner of the law.

VII

My Lords, if it had been demonstrated that in practice *Lawrence* and *Gomez* were calculated to produce injustice that would have been a compelling reason to revisit the merits of the holdings in those decisions. That is however, not the case. In practice the mental requirements of theft are an adequate protection against injustice. In these circumstances I would not be willing to depart from the clear decisions of the House in *Lawrence* and *Gomez*. This brings me back to counsel's principal submission, namely that a person does not appropriate property unless the other (the owner) retains, beyond the instant of the alleged theft, some proprietary interest or the right to resume or recover some proprietary interest. This submission is directly contrary to the holdings in *Lawrence* and *Gomez*. It must be rejected. The alternative submission is that the word 'appropriates' should be interpreted as if the word 'unlawfully' preceded it so that only an act which is unlawful under the general law can be an appropriation. This submission is an invitation to interpolate a word in the carefully crafted language of the Act of 1968. It runs counter to the decisions in *Lawrence* and *Gomez* and must also be rejected. It follows that the certified question must be answered in the affirmative.

VIII

In his judgment my noble and learned friend, Lord Hutton, concluded that the trial judge's summing up on dishonesty was materially defective in particular respects which he lists and that the appeal should be allowed on this ground. In reluctant disagreement with Lord Hutton I take a different view. The House is clearly not confined to the certified question. I agree that in the interests of justice one must look at the matter in the round. It is, however, relevant to bear in mind the context in which the points arise. First, the trial judge was not invited to give such special directions. Secondly, these points were not contained in the written grounds of appeal before the Court of Appeal. Thirdly the points of criticism were not contained in the statement of facts and issues or in the printed cases. Fourthly, the House has not seen transcripts of evidence. The relevance of this factor is that the House is inadequately informed as to the way in which the defence case was deployed before the judge and jury. And a summing up must always be tailored to the particular circumstances of each case.

My Lords, for my part the position would have been different if I had any lurking doubt about the guilt of the appellant on the charges for which she was convicted. In the light of a fair and balanced summing up and a very strong prosecution case, the jury accepted the prosecution case and rejected the appellant's account as untruthful. They found that she had acted dishonestly by systematically raiding the savings in a building society account of a vulnerable person who trusted her. Even if one assumes that the judge ought to have directed more fully on dishonesty I am satisfied that the convictions are entirely safe. In these circumstances it is not necessary and indeed undesirable for the House to pronounce upon what directions should be given on dishonesty in cases akin to the present.

IX

My Lords, I would dismiss the appeal to the House.

Lord Hutton (dissenting)

In a criminal case this House is not confined to the certified question and can consider other points if it is necessary to do so in the interests of justice: see *Attorney-General for Northern Ireland v Gallagher* [1963] AC 349. Therefore the question arises whether it is appropriate in this case for the House to consider the element of dishonesty.

. . .

I therefore turn to consider dishonesty where the defendant contends, as in this case, that she received the money or property as a gift. My Lords, it appears contrary to common sense that a person who receives money or property as a gift could be said to act dishonestly, no matter how much ordinary and decent people would think it morally reprehensible for that person to accept the gift. Section 2(1)(b) of the Act recognises this common sense view by providing:

'(1) A person's appropriation of property belonging to another is not to be regarded as dishonest . . . (b) if he appropriates the property in the belief that he would have the other's consent if the other knew of the appropriation and the circumstances of it . . .'

It follows, *a fortiori*, that a persons appropriation of property belonging to another should not be regarded as dishonest if the other person actually gives the property to him.

... I think that in a case where the prosecution contends that the gift was invalid because of the mental incapacity of the donor it is necessary for the jury to consider that matter. I further consider that the judge must make it clear to the jury that they cannot convict unless they are satisfied (1) that the donor did not have the mental capacity to make a gift and (2) that the donee knew of this incapacity.

. . .

But in my opinion in a case where the defendant contends that he or she received a gift, a direction based only on *Ghosh* is inadequate because it fails to make clear to the jury that if there was a valid gift there cannot be dishonesty, and in the present case there is the danger that, if the gift was not void for want of mental capacity, the jury might nevertheless convict on the basis that ordinary and decent people would think it dishonest for a younger woman to accept very large sums of money which constituted his entire savings from a naive man of low intelligence, and that the woman would have realised this.

Therefore I consider that in this case:

(1) It was necessary for the judge to make clear to the jury that if there was a valid gift the defendant could not be found to be dishonest no matter how much they thought her conduct morally reprehensible.

(2) If the Crown were making the case that the gifts were invalid because Mr Dolphin was mentally incapable of making a gift, it was necessary for the judge to give the jury a specific direction as to what degree of mental weakness would, in the light of the value of the gifts and the other circumstances of the case, make the donor incapable of making a valid gift.

(3) The jury should have been directed that if they were satisfied that Mr Dolphin was mentally incapable of making a gift, they should not convict unless they were satisfied that what the defendant did was dishonest by the standards of ordinary decent people and that the defendant must have realised this.

(4) If the Crown were making the case that the gift was invalid because of undue influence or coercion exercised by the defendant, it was necessary for the judge to give the jury a specific direction as to what would constitute undue influence or coercion.

(5) The jury should have been directed that if they were satisfied that the gifts were invalid by reason of undue influence or coercion, they should not convict unless they were satisfied that what the defendant did was dishonest by the standards of ordinary decent people and that the defendant must have realised this.

The conduct of the defendant was deplorable and it may be that if the issues had been more clearly defined a jury would have been entitled to convict, but in my opinion the summing up was defective in the ways which I have described and the convictions should not stand. I consider, with respect, that the Court of Appeal erred in the present case because at [2000] 1 Cr App R 1, 7F–G it rejected the appellant's submission as to dishonesty by referring to the separate issue of appropriation.

Accordingly, for the reasons which I have stated, I would allow the appeal and quash the convictions.

Lord Hobhouse of Woodborough (dissenting)

. . . The reasoning of the Court of Appeal therefore depends upon the disturbing acceptance that a criminal conviction and the imposition of custodial sanctions may be based upon conduct which involves no inherent illegality and may only be capable of being criticised on grounds of lack of morality. This approach itself raises fundamental questions. An essential function of the criminal law is to define the boundary between what conduct is criminal and what merely immoral. Both are the subject of the disapprobation of ordinary right-thinking citizens and the distinction is liable to be arbitrary or at least strongly influenced by considerations subjective to the individual members of the tribunal. To treat otherwise lawful conduct as criminal merely because it is open to such disapprobation would be contrary to principle and open to the objection that it fails to achieve the objective and transparent certainty required of the criminal law by the principles basic to human rights.

I stress once more that it is not my view that the resort to such reasoning was necessary for the decision of the present case. I would be reluctant to think that those of your Lordships who favour dismissing this appeal have fallen into the trap of believing that, without adopting the reasoning of the Court of Appeal in this case, otherwise guilty defendants will escape justice. The facts of the present case do not justify such a conclusion nor do the facts of any other case which has been cited on this appeal.

. . . The discussion in the present case has been marked by a failure to consider the law of gift. Perhaps most remarkable is the statement of the Court of Appeal [2000] Cr App R 1, 9 that 'a gift may be clear evidence of appropriation.' The making of a gift is the act of the donor. It involves the donor in forming the intention to give and then acting on that intention by doing whatever it is necessary for him to do to transfer the relevant property to the donee. Where the gift is the gift of a chattel, the act required to complete the gift will normally be either delivery to the donee or to a person who is to hold the chattel as the bailee of the donee; money can be transferred by having it credited to the donee's bank account—and so on. Unless the gift was conditional, in which case the condition must be satisfied before the gift can take effect, the making of the gift is complete once the donor has carried out this step. The gift has become the property of the donee. It is not necessary for the donee to know of the gift. The donee, on becoming aware of the gift, has the right to refuse (or reject) the gift in which case it revests in the donor with resolutive effect: see Halsbury's Laws of England, 4th ed reissue, vol. 20 (1993), pp 32–33, paras 48–49 and the cases cited.

What consequences does this have for the law of theft? Once the donor has done his part in transferring the property to the defendant, the property, subject to the special situations identified in the subsections of section 5, ceases to be 'property belonging to another.' However wide a meaning one were to give to 'appropriates,' there cannot be a theft. For it to be possible for there to be a theft there will have to be something more, like an absence of a capacity to give or a mistake satisfying section 5(4). Similarly, where the donee himself performs the act necessary to transfer the property to himself, as he would if he himself took the chattel out of the possession of the donor or, himself gave the instructions to the donor's bank, section 5(1) would apply and mean that that constituent of the crime of theft would at that time have been satisfied.

If one treats the 'acceptance' of the gift as an appropriation, and this was the approach of the judge and is implicit in the judgment of the Court of Appeal (despite their choice of words), there are immediate difficulties with section 2(1)(a). The defendant did have the right to deprive the donor of the property. The donor did consent to the appropriation; indeed, he intended it. There are also difficulties with section 6 as she was not acting regardless of the donors rights; the donor has already surrendered his rights. The only way that these con-clusions can be displaced is by showing that the gift was not valid. There are even difficulties with section 3 itself. The donee is not 'assuming the rights of an owner:' she has them already.

Lord Slynn of Hadley and **Lord Jauncey of Tullichettle** agreed with the speech of **Lord Steyn**.

Appeal dismissed.

These cases are, as we shall see in Part II, remarkably controversial. However, if nothing else, they make for an easy definition of appropriation. The assumption of any of the rights of an owner is appropriation, even if consented to by the victim and even if the transaction is a valid one under civil law.

However, there are a couple of issues which are still uncertain in the law:

(1) *Can an omission amount to an appropriation?* Consider these facts. Ann goes to a supermarket with her toddler. On returning home she notices that her toddler had grabbed a toy from the shelves, which she had not paid for, and has now thrown the toy into the garden. If Ann just leaves the toy lying in the garden could this amount to appropriation? The Court of Appeal is yet to address the issue in detail, but it is submitted that an omission can be an appropriation because section 3(1) describes an appropriation as including 'keeping . . . as owner'.[38] However, to amount to 'keeping . . . as owner' it may be necessary to show that the defendant has kept the property for a significant length of time. In *Broom v Crowther*[39] a defendant purchased a stolen theodolite. He later discovered it was stolen. He told the police, once he had found out that there was doubt over the origins of the theodolite, that he had not touched it, just kept it in his room. The Divisional Court quashed his conviction for theft on the basis that he had not appropriated it since discovering that it was stolen (and thereby becoming dishonest). The court held that he could not be said to be 'keeping . . . as owner' for the purposes of section 3 because he kept it only for a few days.

(2) *Can there be multiple appropriations?* A close reading of section 3 reveals the answer to be as follows. An individual can appropriate a piece of property any number of times until he or she steals it. So if a person leaving a restaurant picks up someone else's umbrella by mistake she will appropriate it every time she uses the umbrella, but once she has the *mens rea* for theft she commits theft just once and does not thereafter continue to steal the property every time she uses it. The significance of this tends to be in jurisdictional issues: in which country did the theft take place? In *Atakpu*[40] the defendants hired a car in Germany. The defendants decided to steal the car, drove it to England, and were arrested in Dover. The Court of Appeal held that the defendants had not committed theft in England. They had appropriated it the moment they dishonestly decided permanently to deprive the owner of the car (somewhere in Germany or Belgium), but once they had stolen the car they were not continuing to steal it wherever they drove it.

---

[38] Indeed a conviction could be justified applying the normal laws relating to omissions.
[39] (1984) JP 592 (DC).
[40] [1994] QB 69 (CA), discussed in Sullivan and Warbrick (1994). See also *Bowden*, 28 May 2002 (CA), suggesting that the time at which a theft was complete was a question for the jury.

(3) *Can there be appropriation by a* bona fide[41] *purchaser?* If a person buys a piece of property, in good faith, unaware that the property is stolen and then becomes aware that the property is stolen are they guilty of theft? This is dealt with by section 3(2):

> Where property or a right or interest in property is or purports to be transferred for value to a person acting in good faith, no later assumption by him of rights which he believed himself to be acquiring shall, by reason of any defect in the transferor's title, amount to theft of the property.

So a person who buys a piece of property in good faith will not become a thief on discovering that the property is stolen. If the purchaser is aware that the property may be stolen when they buy it they are not in good faith and so are guilty. It should be noted that section 3(2) applies only where the defendant has acquired the property by way of a purchase. It therefore does not apply in the case of gifts. A defendant who escapes liability for theft because of section 3(2) may still be guilty of handling stolen goods, an offence which we shall discuss shortly.

QUESTIONS

1. Matthew approaches some American tourists visiting London and offers to sell them Tower Bridge. Is this appropriation of the bridge? Can it therefore be theft?

2. Belinda and Catherine go into a supermarket and decide to steal a tube of toothpaste. They pick up a tube, but then notice that a security guard is close by, and so they return the tube to the shelf and make a quick get away, empty-handed. Have they committed theft?

3. Davina knocks on the door of an elderly man and offers to mow his small lawn for £100. The man thinks the price sounds high but likes the look of Davina and so agrees. She mows the lawn and he gives her £100. Is this theft?

1.4 INTENTION PERMANENTLY TO DEPRIVE

The core meaning of the requirement that the defendant must intend permanently to deprive is straightforward, but it has been extended by section 6 of the Theft Act 1968.

The core meaning of 'intentional deprivation'

The requirement of intentional deprivation means that borrowing does not normally amount to theft. Borrowing a friend's dress without her consent is not theft, even if the dress is stolen on the afternoon before a party at which she had intended to wear the dress. Perhaps more surprisingly, if a person walks into a video rental shop, takes a video without paying for it, intending to return it a week later, this does not amount to theft (although it amounts to another offence[42]). A few points should be stressed about the meaning of the requirement:

---

[41] *Bona fide* means in good faith. [42] e.g. the Theft Act 1978, s. 3.

(1) *Intention.* The defendant must *intend* permanently to deprive the victim of the item. So, if Zhu, who is absent minded, borrows a friend's book, there can be no theft, even though Zhu realizes there is a risk that he may never be able to return the book, unless Zhu intends never to return it.

(2) *Deprivation.* What needs to be shown is that the defendant intended to deprive the victim of the property. It does not need to be shown that the defendant intended to acquire the property. So, snatching an item from a rail passenger and throwing it out of a train window can amount to theft, because the act will deprive the owner of the item, even if there was no intention to gain. This point is backed up by section 1(2) of the 1968 Theft Act which states:

It is immaterial whether the appropriation is made with a view to gain, or is made for the thief's own benefit.

(3) *Replacement of taken goods.* What if the defendant took some property with the intention of replacing it with a similar item? For example, if the defendant took some bank notes from her employer's safe, intending to return the same sum of money in the future? This would still be theft (if the jury found it to be dishonest). The defendant intended to deprive the victim of the notes she took, even though she intended to return their equivalent value.[43] In cases where the defendant intends to provide a replacement for the item taken this will be very relevant in deciding whether there was dishonesty.

(4) *The defendant need not intend to deprive by the act of appropriation.* It does not need to be shown that the defendant intended to deprive the owner of the property *by the act of appropriation.* If Ian moves a tin of baked beans to a shelf by the door of the supermarket so that he can run off with it a few minutes later this is theft, even though that moving is not intended to deprive the owner permanently. It is enough that Ian appropriates the property, while having an intention permanently to deprive the owner of it at some point in the future.

(5) *Conditional intention.* The problem of conditional intention is best explained by an example. In *Easom*[44] the defendant picked up a handbag in a cinema. He looked through it, but decided that there was nothing worth stealing. He was charged with theft of 'one handbag, one purse, one notebook, a quantity of tissues, a quantity of cosmetics and one pen'. He was acquitted on the basis that he could not be said to intend permanently to deprive the victim of any of these items. What he intended was permanently to deprive the victim of whatever he found of value. The general view is that the defendant could have been convicted if the charge had been carefully drafted. If he had been charged with theft of the contents of the handbag he could have been convicted on the basis that he intended permanently to deprive the victim of the contents (if he found them valuable). To avoid any possible difficulties an attempted theft charge may be best in cases of this kind.

Section 6 and the extension to the key meaning of 'permanent deprivation'

Section 6 provides an extended meaning to the phrase 'intending permanently to deprive'. It states:

---

[43] *Velumyl* [1989] Crim LR 299 (CA).
[44] [1971] 2 QB 315, [1971] 2 All ER 945, [1971] 3 WLR 82 (CA).

(1) A person appropriating property belonging to another without meaning the other permanently to lose the thing itself is nevertheless to be regarded as having the intention of permanently depriving the other of it if his intention is to treat the thing as his own to dispose of regardless of the other's rights; and a borrowing or lending of it may amount to so treating it if, but only if, the borrowing or lending is for a period and in circumstances making it equivalent to an outright taking or disposal.

(2) Without prejudice to the generality of subsection (1) above, where a person, having possession or control (lawful or not) of property belonging to another, parts with the property under a condition as to its return which he may not be able to perform, this (if done for purposes of his own and without the other's authority) amounts to treating the property as his own to dispose of regardless of the other's rights.

It must be admitted that the wording of this section is not clear. It appears that the section can apply in the following circumstances:

(1) *Throwing taken items away.* If John snatches the victim's purse and runs off with it, later throwing it into a bin, he may argue that he did not intend to deprive the owner of it because he would have been happy if the victim had recovered the item. John can be convicted of theft relying on section 6(1) because he has 'treated the property as his own' and 'disposed' of it.

(2) *Selling the item back to the victim.* If Tony takes Edward's property and tries to sell it back to him he may try to argue that he did not intend permanently to deprive Edward of it, because Tony intended the victim to buy the property and so get it back. This argument is not available because of section 6(1); in offering the victim's property back to Edward, Tony is treating the property as his own and intending to 'dispose' of it.

(3) *Ransoming property.* If Simon takes a painting from Celia, but tells her he will return it to her if she pays a large sum of money, Simon may try to claim that he did not intend permanently to deprive the victim of the property, because he intended Celia to pay the ransom and recover it. However this situation is covered by section 6(1) and so is theft; Simon has treated the property as his 'own to dispose of'.[45]

(4) *Moving the defendant's property.* Can moving property amount to disposing of or dealing in it? The natural meaning of the word dispose might lead you to think not. But in the surprising decision in *DPP v Lavender* (see below) Tuckey J appeared willing to accept it could.

(5) *Returning property in an impoverished state.* What if the defendant borrowed the victim's season ticket for his local football team and returned it once the season was over? Could the defendant argue that he did not intend permanently to deprive the victim of the ticket? This is covered by section 6(1) which states that if the borrowing is 'equivalent to an outright taking or disposal' then this amounts to an intention permanently to deprive. So although the ticket is returned, it is useless as the season is over and so it is equivalent to it being permanently taken. The defendant can therefore be convicted of theft.

The subsection is not as wide as might at first appear, because the borrowing must be equivalent to an outright taking. So if the season ticket was taken but returned with

---

[45] *Coffey* [1987] Crim LR 498 (CA).

a few games left, it is arguable that those takings are not equivalent to an outright taking. In *DPP v SJ, PI, RC*[46] the defendants took the victim's headphones, snapped them, and returned them. It was held that this could amount to theft. It did not need to be shown that the goodness of the property had been 'completely exhausted' for section 6 to apply; it was enough that the property had lost its practical usefulness. The defendants could therefore be convicted of theft of the headphones.[47]

One question still unanswered is whether the goodness of value of the item is to be judged by the standards of the victim or objectively. If the defendant takes the victim's wedding dress and returns it the day after the wedding then it could be argued that the objective value of the dress is undiminished, even though *to the victim* the taking of the dress was equivalent to an outright taking.

(6) *Pawning the goods.* If the defendant pawns or pledges goods, intending to pay back the debt and hence recover the item, this falls within section 6(2) and the defendant will be treated as intending permanently to deprive.

(7) *Risking the property.* If the defendant gambles the victim's property, or invests it in a risky investment the defendant will be treated as intending to deprive the victim of it.[48]

Director of Public Prosecutions v Lavender
[1994] Crim LR 297 (QBD)

Melvyn Lavender lived with his girlfriend in a house owned by South Holland District Council. The council was asked to replace some damaged doors at the property which it refused to do because the damage was not due to normal wear and tear. Lavender took two doors from a nearby unoccupied council house to use at his girlfriend's house. He was charged with theft of the doors. On appeal the sole question was whether he had an intention permanently to deprive the council of the doors.

Mr Justice Tuckey, giving the judgment of the court

. . . The fact that someone can behave as the respondent did without committing the offence of theft might be thought to be a surprising result. But was it the right result as a matter of law on the facts found by the Justices?

We do not think the second limb of Section 6(1) applies to this case. It is difficult, as a matter of language, to describe the taking of a fixture or fitting from one property and fitting it to another belonging to the same owner without his knowledge or consent, as a borrowing and return. But even if it can be so described, the doors themselves would retain their essential quality ('goodness or virtue') as doors. The fact that in a more general sense they were more useful to the council fitted to 25 Royce Road than 37 Royce Road does not persuade us that this part of the subsection applies. The character of the property the subject of charge did not change as a result of what happened.

But does the first limb apply? The words 'if his intention is to treat the thing as his own to dispose of regardless of the other's rights' have to be read together. The Justices focused on

---

[46] CO/4526/2001. [47] A charge of criminal damage would also lie in such a case.
[48] *Fernandes* [1996] 1 Cr App R 175 (CA).

the words 'to dispose of' and applied a dictionary definition to them. We think that this was too narrow an approach. Following the examples given in *Lloyd*, the disposal referred to is a disposal to the owner. Disposal to a third-party would usually show an intention permanently to deprive and there would, therefore, be no need to invoke Section 6(1). Furthermore, following what was said in *Chan Man Sin*, a disposal in this since includes dealing.

So we think the question in the instant case is did the respondent intend to treat the doors as his own in dealing with the council regardless of their rights? The answer to this question must be yes. There can be no doubt that what the respondent did was regardless of the council's right. Those rights included the right not to have the doors at 25 Royce Road removed, and to require the tenant at 37 Royce Road to replace or pay for the damaged doors. In dealing with the doors regardless of those rights, when he consciously did, the respondent manifested an intention to treat them as his own.

For these reasons we think this appeal should be allowed and the case should be remitted to the Justices for a direction to convict.

Appeal (of the prosecution against acquittal) allowed.

R v Marshall and others
[1998] 2 Cr App R 282 (CA)

The three appellants asked members of the public leaving Victoria underground station for their travel cards or underground tickets. They then resold the tickets on to other customers at a cheap price. They were convicted of theft of the tickets. They appealed on the basis that it could not be said that they intended permanently to deprive London Underground of the tickets.

Lord Justice Mantell, reading the judgment of the court

[Mantell LJ quoted the summary prepared by the appellants' counsel of their argument]

'It is submitted by the Appellants that in the circumstances although there was an assumption of the rights of the owner contrary to section 3 of the Theft Act 1968 which amounted to an appropriation there was nevertheless no intention on their part to deprive London Underground Limited of the said ticket. They intended either to return them directly to London Underground Limited or to do so through the third party buyer without resale to London Underground Limited and without any loss in the virtue of the ticket when returned.'

The argument proceeds:

'The ticket forms are pieces of paper printed over with information about the ticket. When returned to London Underground Limited they had no more and no less value than when they were originally purchased. The return to London Underground, notwithstanding these intervening transactions involved no loss of virtue to London Underground Limited's property.'

It was submitted s 6(1) of the Theft Act 1968 did not apply as that was only to be resorted to where there was a resale of the property to the original owner. It was further submitted that the issuing of a travel ticket was analogous to the drawing of a cheque and that as both were choses in action the reasoning in *R v Preddy* [1996] AC 815 was equally applicable.

It will be seen that the submission made on what is accepted to be the single issue in the appeal depends in part upon the misapprehension that the ticket forms would necessarily find their way back into the possession of London Underground. That was the factual basis upon which the learned Judge ruled. As mentioned, we are content to deal with this appeal on a similar basis.

On this point the judge ruled as follows:

'I am satisfied that the essence of section 6 of the Theft Act 1968 is whether there was an intention to treat the tickets as their own regardless of the owners rights. Mr Taylor has drawn my attention in particular to the cases of *R v Duru* [1972] 58 Cr App Rep 151 and *R v Preddy & Others* [1996] 3 WLR 255 and referred me to the commentary by Professor Smith to the case of *R v Mitchell* (1993) Crim LR p.788. I note that all these cases involved cheques and for my part I am not prepared to extend to the underground what the High Court have found in relation to cheques.'

For the reasons which follow we consider that the judge was right.

[Lord Justice Mantell then quoted section 6(1).]

On its face the subsection would seem apt to cover the facts of the present case. The ticket belongs to London Underground. It has been appropriated by an Appellant. It is the exclusive right of London Underground to sell tickets. By acquiring and re-selling the ticket the Appellant has an intention to treat the ticket as his own to dispose of regardless of London Underground's right. However Mr Taylor and Mr Simpson have reminded us of what was said by Lord Lane, Lord Chief Justice in the case of *R v Lloyd, Bhuee & Ali* [1985] QB 829, [1985] 2 All ER 661, at 666h–j of the latter report:

'Bearing in mind the observation of Edmund Davis LJ in *R v Warner* (1970) 55 Cr App Rep 93, we would try to interpret the section in such a way as to ensure that nothing is construed as an intention permanently to deprive which would not prior to the 1968 Act have been so construed. Thus the first part of section 6(1) seems to us to be aimed at the sort of case were a defendant takes things and then offers them back to the owner for the owner to buy if he wishes. If the taker intends to return them to the owner only upon such payment, then, on the wording of section 6(1) that is deemed to amount to the necessary intention permanently to deprive . . .'

It is submitted, therefore, that the subsection is to be construed narrowly and confined to the sort of case of which Lord Lane gave an example and of which the present is not one. However this court had to consider a similar situation in the case of *R v Fernandes* [1996] 1 Cr App Rep 175 where at p 188 Lord Justice Auld giving the judgment of the court said this:

'In our view section 6(1), which is expressed in general terms, is not limited in its application to the illustrations given by Lord Lane CJ in Lloyd. Nor in saying that in most cases it would be unnecessary to refer to the provision, did Lord Lane suggest it should be so limited. The critical notion, stated expressly in the first limb and incorporated by reference in the second is, whether a defendant intended to "treat the thing as his own to dispose of regardless of the others rights." The second limb of subsection (1) and also subsection (2) are merely specific illustrations of the application of that notion. We consider that section 6 may apply to a person in possession or control of another's property who, dishonestly and for his own purpose, deals with that property in such a manner that he knows he is risking its loss.'

In our judgment and following *Fernandes* the subsection is not to be given the restricted interpretation for the which the Appellants contend.

The principal submission put forward on behalf of the Appellants is that the issuing of the ticket is analogous to the drawing of a cheque in that in each instance a chose in action is created which in the first case belongs to the customer and in the second to the payee. So by parity of reasoning with that advanced by Lord Goff in *R v Preddy & Others* [1996] AC 815 the property acquired belonged to the customer and not London Underground and there can have been no intention on the part of the Appellant to deprive London Underground of the ticket which would in due course be returned to the possession of London Underground. Attractive though the submission appears at first blush we do not think that it can possibly be correct.

'A "chose in action" is a known legal expression used to describe all personal rights of property which can only be claimed or enforced by action, and not by taking physical possession.' (See *Talkington v Magee* [1902] 2 KB 427 per Channell J at 430)

On the issuing of an underground ticket a contract is created between London Underground and the purchaser. Under that contract each party has rights and obligations. Theoretically those rights are enforceable by action. Therefore it is arguable, we suppose, that by the transaction each party has acquired a chose in action. On the side of the purchaser it is represented by a right to use the ticket to the extent which it allows travel on the underground system. On the side of London Underground it encompasses the right to insist that the ticket is used by no one other than the purchaser. It is that right which is disregarded when the ticket is acquired by the Appellant and sold on. But here the charges were in relation to the tickets and travel cards themselves and a ticket form or travel card and, dare we say, a cheque form is not a chose in action. The fact that the ticket form or travel card may find its way back into the possession of London Underground, albeit with its usefulness or 'virtue' exhausted, is nothing to the point. Section 6(1) prevails for the reasons we have given.

The Appellants by their pleas having acknowledged that they were acting dishonestly it seems to us that there is no reason to consider the convictions unsafe and these appeals must be dismissed.

Appeals dismissed.

Offences involving temporary deprivation

Parliament has created some special offences to deal with temporary deprivations which are seen as sufficiently serious to justify a criminal conviction, even if they do not constitute theft. For example, it is an offence to remove property from places open to the public[49] (e.g. a museum, a church); or to take a conveyance (e.g. a car or motorcycle) without authority.[50]

1.5 DISHONESTY

The meaning of dishonesty is a mixture of statute and common law. The starting point is section 2 of the Theft Act 1968, which sets out various circumstances in which the defendant will not be dishonest. If the defendant is not dishonest under section 2 that is the end of the case. He or she must be acquitted. If, however, the defendant is not covered by section 2, then it is necessary to consider the common law definition of theft.

---

[49] Theft Act 1968, s. 11(1).   [50] Ibid., s. 12(1).

Section 2 of the Theft Act 1968

Section 2 states:

> (1) A person's appropriation of property belonging to another is not to be regarded as dishonest—
>
>   (a) if he appropriates the property in the belief that he has in law the right to deprive the other of it, on behalf of himself or a third person; or
>
>   (b) if he appropriates the property in the belief that he would have the other's consent if the other knew of the appropriation and the circumstances of it; or
>
>   (c) (except where the property came to him as trustee or personal representative) if he appropriates the property in the belief that the person to whom the property belongs cannot be discovered by taking reasonable steps.
>
> (2) A person's appropriation of property belonging to another may be dishonest notwithstanding that he is willing to pay for the property.

This section defines three circumstances in which a person is *not* dishonest:

(1) *Section 2(1)(a)*: the defendant's belief that he has the right to deprive the owner of the property. If the defendant believes that he or she is legally entitled to deal with the property as he or she does then there is no dishonesty. This belief does not have to be reasonable, nor does it have to be based on an accurate understanding of the law.[51] The most obvious example of the section applying is where the defendant believes that the property is his or her own. For example, if Susan walks out of a restaurant taking someone else's umbrella, believing it to be her own, she is not dishonest. She believes that she is entitled to deal with the property in this way. However, the subsection is wider than this. In *Skivington*,[52] a man held up a wages clerk, demanding his wife's wages. He believed that he was entitled to demand the money and so there was no theft.[53]

It should be stressed that the subsection applies only where the defendant has a belief (even an unreasonable one) that he or she has the right in law to deal with the property. A belief that morally the defendant is entitled to deal with the property is insufficient. Such a moral belief might possibly lead to a finding of not dishonest on the basis of the common law definition of dishonesty.

(2) *Section 2(1)(b)*: belief that the owner would consent. A defendant is not dishonest if he or she believes that the owner would have consented to the taking. This subsection is most likely to apply where the defendant and the 'victim' are friends. Friends and relatives often use each other's property, knowing or assuming that the other would consent. It should be stressed that the issue here is not whether the owner does in fact consent, but whether the defendant believes that the victim would consent. Again the belief need not be a reasonable one, but it must be a genuine belief.

(3) *Section 2(1)(c)*: belief that the owner could not be found. This section deals with the situation where a person finds property which he or she believes has been abandoned. The key question is whether the owner can be found by taking reasonable steps. If the defendant believes that the owner cannot be found then there is no theft. Again the belief must only be

---

[51] *Small* (1987) 86 Cr App R 170 (CA); *Holden* [1991] Crim LR 478 (CA).
[52] [1968] 1 QB 166.   [53] And therefore no robbery.

genuine; it does not have to be reasonable. Further, the defendant need believe only that *reasonable* steps would not identify the owner. If Elizabeth finds a wallet in a town square and keeps it, she may accept that if she spends the next three weeks knocking on the door of every single house in the town she may find the owner, but to do so would not be reasonable. One difficulty facing Elizabeth is that it may well be regarded as reasonable to hand the wallet in to the police. Another point worth noticing here is that even if Elizabeth is not dishonest when she first picks up the wallet (because she believes it to be abandoned) she may subsequently discover who the owner is (e.g. she sees a notice in a shop announcing that the owner has lost the wallet). If thereafter she appropriates the property she can be convicted of theft.

Section 2(2) reiterates that merely intending to pay for an item does not negate theft. To take a pint of milk delivered to your neighbour's door and leave the cash price for the milk can still be theft. Of course, leaving the money may be part of the defendant's belief that the owner would not object to the taking. Imagine this: D is walking in the countryside and comes across a village shop, but finds no shopkeeper. Desperate for a chocolate bar, D takes the bar, but leaves cash behind. The mere fact that he leaves cash does not mean he is not dishonest. However, he may well be able to persuade the jury that he believed the shopkeeper would have no objection as long as he paid for what he took and so he was not dishonest under section 2(1)(a).

The common law test for dishonesty

If the defendant is not acquitted on the basis of section 2(1) the jury will go on to consider the common law test for dishonesty, set out in *Ghosh*:

R v Ghosh
[1982] QB 1053 (CA)[54]

Deb Baran Ghosh, a surgeon, claimed fees for carrying out operations in circumstances in which the prosecution said he should not have been paid. He was convicted of offences contrary to sections 15(1) and 20(2) of the Theft Act 1968. The judge directed the jury to consider whether the appellant had been dishonest according to contemporary standards of honesty and dishonesty. He appealed on the basis that the judge's direction on dishonesty had been wrong.

Lord Lane CJ, giving the judgment of the court

. . . This brings us to the heart of the problem. Is 'dishonestly' in section 1 of the Theft Act 1968 intended to characterise a course of conduct? Or is it intended to describe a state of mind? If the former, then we can well understand that it could be established independently of the knowledge or belief of the accused. But if, as we think, it is the latter, then the knowledge and belief of the accused are at the root of the problem.

Take for example a man who comes from a country where public transport is free. On his first day here he travels on a bus. He gets off without paying. He never had any intention

---

[54] [1982] 2 All ER 689, [1982] 3 WLR 110, (1982) 75 Cr App R 154.

of paying. His mind is clearly honest; but his conduct, judged objectively by what he has done, is dishonest. It seems to us that in using the word 'dishonestly' in the Theft Act 1968, Parliament cannot have intended to catch dishonest conduct in that sense, that is to say conduct to which no moral obloquy could possibly attach. This is sufficiently established by the partial definition in section 2 of the Theft Act itself. All the matters covered by section 2 (1) relate to the belief of the accused. Section 2 (2) relates to his willingness to pay. A man's belief and his willingness to pay are things which can only be established subjectively. It is difficult to see how a partially subjective definition can be made to work in harness with the test which in all other respects is wholly objective.

If we are right that dishonesty is something in the mind of the accused (what Professor Glanville Williams calls 'a special mental state'), then if the mind of the accused is honest, it cannot be deemed dishonest merely because members of the jury would have regarded it as dishonest to embark on that course of conduct.

So we would reject the simple uncomplicated approach that the test is purely objective, however attractive from the practical point of view that solution may be.

There remains the objection that to adopt a subjective test is to abandon all standards but that of the accused himself, and to bring about a state of affairs in which 'Robin Hood would be no robber': *Reg. v. Greenstein*. This objection misunderstands the nature of the subjective test. It is no defence for a man to say 'I knew that what I was doing is generally regarded as dishonest; but I do not regard it as dishonest myself. Therefore I am not guilty.' What he is however entitled to say is 'I did not know that anybody would regard what I was doing as dishonest.' He may not be believed; just as he may not be believed if he sets up 'a claim of right' under section 2 (1) of the Theft Act 1968, or asserts that he believed in the truth of a misrepresentation under section 15 of the Act of 1968. But if he is believed, or raises a real doubt about the matter, the jury cannot be sure that he was dishonest.

In determining whether the prosecution has proved that the defendant was acting dishonestly, a jury must first of all decide whether according to the ordinary standards of reasonable and honest people what was done was dishonest. If it was not dishonest by those standards, that is the end of the matter and the prosecution fails.

If it was dishonest by those standards, then the jury must consider whether the defendant himself must have realised that what he was doing was by those standards dishonest. In most cases, where the actions are obviously dishonest by ordinary standards, there will be no doubt about it. It will be obvious that the defendant himself knew that he was acting dishonestly. It is dishonest for a defendant to act in a way which he knows ordinary people consider to be dishonest, even if he asserts or genuinely believes that he is morally justified in acting as he did. For example, Robin Hood or those ardent anti-vivisectionists who remove animals from vivisection laboratories are acting dishonestly, even though they may consider themselves to be morally justified in doing what they do, because they know that ordinary people would consider these actions to be dishonest.

Cases which might be described as borderline, such as *Boggeln v. Williams* [1978] 1 W.L.R. 873, will depend upon the view taken by the jury as to whether the defendant may have believed what he was doing was in accordance with the ordinary man's idea of honesty. A jury might have come to the conclusion that the defendant in that case was disobedient or impudent, but not dishonest in what he did.

So far as the present case is concerned, it seems to us that once the jury had rejected the defendant's account in respect of each count in the indictment (as they plainly did), the finding of dishonesty was inevitable, whichever of the tests of dishonesty was applied. If the judge had asked the jury to determine whether the defendant might have believed that what he did was in accordance with the ordinary man's idea of honesty, there could only been one answer—and that is no, once the jury had rejected the defendant's explanation of what happened.

In so far as there was a misdirection on the meaning of dishonesty, it is plainly a case for the application of the proviso to section 2 (1) of the Criminal Appeal Act 1968.

Appeal dismissed.

So then, after *Ghosh*, when the jury have to decide whether or not the defendant is dishonest they must consider two separate questions:

(1) Was what the defendant did dishonest according to the standards of reasonable and honest people?

(2) Would the defendant realize that reasonable and honest people would regard what he did as dishonest?

If the answer to both these questions is 'yes' then the defendant is dishonest. If the answer to either question is 'no' then the defendant is not dishonest.[55]

Although this is the full test for dishonesty the courts have made it clear that it need not be used in every case.[56] Indeed only the first question needs to be asked unless the defendant gives evidence that he thought his conduct was honest according to the standards of ordinary people.[57] Also the *Ghosh* direction is not needed if the case is one of such obvious dishonesty that a jury could not believe a defendant who said he or she thought that the conduct was not dishonest. Three points in particular should be made about this test:

(1) The standards of honesty of the ordinary person are a matter for the jury. It is not for the judge to tell the jury what is or is not dishonest; it is a question for the jury, applying their understanding of contemporary standards.[58] Further, jury members should not ask whether they themselves regard the conduct as dishonest, but consider whether ordinary people would regard it as dishonest.

(2) It is irrelevant whether the defendant believes that his conduct is dishonest; what matters is whether the defendant's conduct was dishonest according to the standards of reasonable and honest people and whether the defendant thought reasonable people would regard his conduct as dishonest. Consider these two examples:

(a) Theresa, a nun, picks up a newspaper left by a man on a train. Her high moral standards mean she feels that she is dishonest because she did not buy her own copy of the paper. The fact that she regards herself as dishonest is irrelevant, because ordinary people would not (I suspect) regard such conduct as dishonest.

(b) Angelina, an ardent anti-fur protester, runs out of an exclusive clothes shop, taking some fur coats without paying for them. She regards this as honest, given the evils of fur trading, but she would probably have to admit that the majority of ordinary honest people would not be enlightened enough to see the goodness in

---

[55] *In Pattni, Dhunna, Soni and Poopalarajah* [2001] Crim LR 570 an argument that the *Ghosh* test was so uncertain that it infringed Art. 7 of the European Convention on Human Rights failed.

[56] *Squire* [1990] Crim LR 341.

[57] *Brennan* [1990] Crim LR 118 (CA); *Buzalek and Schiffer* [1991] Crim LR 130 (CA).

[58] *Feely* [1973] QB 530 (CA). But in a case involving a business person (*R v Goldman* [1997] Crim LR 894 (CA)) it was suggested that the jury consider whether the conduct was dishonest by the standards of the ordinary business person.

her actions and would regard them as dishonest. She would therefore be dishonest under the *Ghosh* test.

(3) There may be a difference between conduct being praiseworthy and being dishonest. Imagine an anti-pornography protester who goes into a 'Private Shop' and runs out with hard-core pornography which he then burns. Although (maybe) the majority of people may be sympathetic to his cause, and may even be impressed by his actions, they could not call them honest.

There is one major difficulty in interpreting the *Ghosh* test: are the facts to be taken as those as understood by the defendant? At first the answer seems clear: yes. Lord Lane appeared to address the issue in *Ghosh*:

> Take the man who comes from a country where public transport is free. On his first day here he travels on a bus. He gets off without paying. He never has any intention of paying. His mind is clearly honest; but his conduct, judged objectively by what he has done, is dishonest.

Lord Lane concludes he is not dishonest because under the second limb he believes most people would regard his conduct as honest.[59] Of course, he cannot believe that most people would regard it as honest to leave a bus without paying in a country where one has to pay for public transport, but as he believes it is free then he is not dishonest. But consider an anti-abortion protester who believes that abortion is murder and so steals equipment from a clinic to prevent abortions. It may well be that most people would think it honest to take some equipment from a clinic in order to stop a person committing murder, but they would not think that abortion was murder. The answer, it seems, is that the facts must be taken as the defendant believes that most people would think them to be.

FURTHER READING

Griew, E. (1995), *The Theft Acts 1968 and 1978* (London: Sweet & Maxwell).

Harris, J.W. (1996b), 'Who Owns My Body?', *Oxford Journal of Legal Studies* 16: 55.

Phillips, E., Walsh, C., and Dobson, P. (2001), *The Law Relating to Theft* (London: Cavendish).

Smith, A. (1976), 'Stealing the Body and its Parts', *Criminal Law Review* 622.

—— (1994), *Property Offences* (London: Sweet & Maxwell).

Smith, J.C. (2001), *The Law of Theft* (London: Butterworths).

Spencer, J. (1977), 'The Metamorphosis of Section 6', *Criminal Law Review* 653.

2 ROBBERY

Section 8 of the Theft Act 1968:

> (1) A person is guilty of robbery if he steals, and immediately before or at the time of doing so, and in order to do so, he uses force on any person or puts or seeks to put any person in fear of being then and there subjected to force.

---

[59] Griew (1985).

> (2) A person guilty of robbery, or of an assault with intent to rob, shall on conviction be liable to imprisonment for life.

In essence robbery is made up of two elements.

(1) It must be shown that the defendant has committed theft. The *mens rea* and *actus reus* of theft must be proved.[60]

(2) It must be shown that the defendant has used or threatened force at the time of the theft. Within this apparently simple requirement there are in fact three elements:

(i) There must be the use of force or threat of force. Force is to be given its ordinary meaning by the jury. However, the level of force need be of only a minimal kind. In *Dawson*[61] it was suggested that a nudge from the defendant while taking someone's wallet amounted to force. The force can be used against the person or against the property, but only if the touching of the property affects the victim's body.[62] There is a fine line to be drawn here: simply pulling property out of a bag would not of itself amount to force; but pulling the item out of the victim's grasp so that the victim's body was moved would amount to robbery. The force need not be used or threatened against the victim of theft. It would be robbery for the defendant to threaten to hit a baby if her father did not hand over his wallet.

(ii) The force must be used in order to steal and not for any other purpose. This means that the defendant must be aware that he is using force and intend to use that force in order to steal. The accidental use of force cannot therefore form the basis of a robbery charge.

(iii) The force must be used at the time of the theft or immediately before it.[63] It is not theft if the force is used simply in order to make a getaway from a scene of a theft. The following case demonstrates the significance of this point.

R v Hale
(1979) 68 Cr App R 415 (CA)[64]

Robert Hale was charged with robbery. He and McGuire knocked on the door of Mrs Carrett. Hale covered Mrs Carrett's mouth to prevent her screaming while McGuire went upstairs and took a jewellery box. They then tied her up before leaving the house. The trial judge had directed the jury that they could convict the appellant of robbery if they felt sure that by use of force or threats of force he had stolen her property. The appellant was convicted, but appealed on the basis that the direction could have indicated to the jury that they were permitted to convict if he had used force to enable him to escape and that was a misdirection.

---

[60] *Forrester* [1992] Crim LR 793 (CA).   [61] [1976] Crim LR 692 (CA).

[62] *Clouden* [1987] Crim LR 56 (CA); *Corcoran v Anderton* (1980) 71 Cr App R 104 (CA).

[63] This can require some careful consideration of when the theft has been completed: *Hale* (1978) 68 Cr App R 415 (CA).

[64] [1979] Crim LR 596.

Lord Justice Eveleigh

In the present case there can be little doubt that if the appellant had been interrupted after the seizure of the jewellery box the jury would have been entitled to find that the appellant and his accomplice were assuming the rights of an owner at the time when the jewellery box was seized. However, the act of appropriation does not suddenly cease. It is a continuous act and it is a matter for the jury to decide whether or not the act of appropriation has finished. Moreover, it is quite clear that the intention to deprive the owner permanently, which accompanied the assumption of the owner's rights was a continuing one at all material times. This Court therefore rejects the contention that the theft had ceased by the time the lady was tied up. As a matter of common-sense the appellant was in the course of committing theft; he was stealing.

There remains the question whether there was robbery. Quite clearly the jury were at liberty to find the appellant guilty of robbery relying upon the force used when he put his hand over Mrs. Carrett's mouth to restrain her from calling for help. We also think that they were also entitled to rely upon the act of tying her up provided they were satisfied (and it is difficult to see how they could not be satisfied) that the force so used was to enable them to steal. If they were still engaged in the act of stealing the force was clearly used to enable them to continue to assume the rights of the owner and permanently to deprive Mrs. Carrett of her box, which is what they began to do when they first seized it.

Taking the summing-up as a whole, and in relation to the particular facts of this case, the jury could not have thought that they were entitled to convict if the force used was not at the time of the stealing and for the purpose of stealing. The learned judge said 'In order to be sure that the person is guilty of robbery you have to be sure they were stealing.' While the use of the words complained of would not serve as an alternative definition of robbery and could, if standing alone, be open to the criticism that the learned judge was arriving at a conclusion of fact which the jury had to decide, those words did not stand alone and this Court is satisfied that there was no misdirection. This appeal is accordingly dismissed.

Appeal dismissed.

3 ASSAULT WITH INTENT TO ROB

This offence was created by section 8(2) of the Theft Act 1968. It must be shown that the defendant committed an assault or battery with the intent to rob.

4 HANDLING STOLEN GOODS

The following are the key provisions of the 1968 Theft Act dealing with the offence of handling stolen goods:

(1) Section 22 of the Theft Act 1968 states:

> (1) A person handles stolen goods if (otherwise than in the course of the stealing) knowing or believing them to be stolen goods he dishonestly receives

> the goods, or dishonestly undertakes or assists in their retention, removal, disposal or realisation by or for the benefit of another person, or if he arranges to do so.

(2) Goods are interpreted in section 34(2)(b):

> 'goods', except insofar as the context otherwise requires, includes money and every other description of property except land, and includes things severed from the land by stealing.

(3) Section 24(2) of the Theft Act 1968 expands the scope of the offence:

> (2) For purposes of these provisions references to stolen goods shall include, in addition to the goods originally stolen and parts of them (whether in their original state or not),
>
> (a) any other goods which directly or indirectly represent or have at any time represented the stolen goods in the hands of the thief as being the proceeds of any disposal or realisation of the whole or part of the goods stolen or of goods so representing the stolen goods; and
>
> (b) any other goods which directly or indirectly represent or have at any time represented the stolen goods in the hands of a handler of the stolen goods or any part of them as being the proceeds of any disposal or realisation of the whole or part of the stolen goods handled by him or of goods so representing them.
>
> (3) But no goods shall be regarded as having continued to be stolen goods after they have been restored to the person from whom they were stolen or to other lawful possession or custody, or after that person and any other person claiming through him have otherwise ceased as regards those goods to have any right to restitution in respect of the theft.
>
> (4) For purposes of the provisions of this Act relating to goods which have been stolen (including sub-sections (1) to (3) above) goods obtained in England or Wales or elsewhere either by blackmail or in the circumstances described in section 15(1) of this Act shall be regarded as stolen; and 'steal', 'theft' and 'thief' shall be construed accordingly.

The maximum sentence is fourteen years' imprisonment. At first this seems surprising as the maximum sentence for theft itself is only seven years. One explanation offered by the courts is that if there were no handlers willing to receive and distribute the goods there would be fewer thefts.[65]

This offence can be broken down into four elements.

---

[65] *Shelton* (1993) 15 Cr App R (S) 415 (CA); *Tokeley-Parry* [1999] Crim LR 578 (CA).

4.1 IT MUST BE SHOWN THAT THE GOODS HAVE BEEN ALREADY STOLEN[66]

It is not necessary for the prosecution to prove who stole the goods, as long as it is clear the goods have been stolen by someone.[67] If the defendant believes the goods to be stolen, but in fact they are not, then the defendant may be guilty of an attempted handling offence.[68] The offence covers not only stolen goods, but also the proceeds of stolen goods. So if Robby steals a car and sells it for £1,000; and then passes the £1,000 to his friend, Lucy, then Lucy can be convicted of handling, if she has the necessary *mens rea*. Section 24(3) (quoted above) provides that goods will cease to be stolen in various situations: most notably where goods have been returned to the person from whom they were stolen or the goods have been recovered by the police.[69] So if a person took from a police car stolen property which had been found by the police the person would not be guilty of handling, but could, of course, be charged with theft.

4.2 IT MUST BE SHOWN THAT THE DEFENDANT HANDLED THE PROPERTY

DEFINITION

It must be shown that the defendant engaged in or arranged one of the following:

(a) receiving the property;

or

(b) undertaking any of the following:
- (i) retention;
- (ii) removal;
- (iii) disposal;
- (iv) realization;

of the goods either by another or for another's benefit

or

(c) assisting in any of the following:
- (i) retention;
- (ii) removal;
- (iii) disposal;
- (iv) realization;

of the goods either by another or for another's benefit.

---

[66] As well as goods that are actually stolen the offence covers handling goods obtained through robbery, burglary, blackmail, and by deception: Theft Act 1968, s. 24(4).

[67] *Forsyth* [1997] 2 Cr App R 299 (CA). Goods would be stolen even if the 'thief' were able to rely on an excuse (e.g. duress) and so not be guilty of the offence of theft.

[68] Criminal Attempts Act 1981, s. 1(2). See *Haughton v Smith* [1975] AC 476 (HL).

[69] *Attorney-General's Reference (No. 1 of 1974)* (1974) 59 Cr App R 203 (CA); *Parker v British Airways Board* [1982] 1 All ER 834 (CA), and *Greater London Metropolitan Police Comr v Streeter* (1980) 71 Cr App R 113 (CA) provide detailed discussion of when property can be said to have entered the lawful possession or custody of the police.

The terms used here are readily understandable and are to be given their normal meaning. But a few points of clarification may assist:

(1) Receiving involves taking goods into your possession or control. This means that the accused must be aware that he has possession or control of the items.[70] If the defendant is not aware when he receives the property that it is stolen, but later becomes aware that it is, then it is better to charge the defendant on the basis of retention, rather than receiving.[71] Merely touching the goods may be insufficient to amount to receiving. In *Hobson v Impett*[72] the defendant helped a thief unload stolen goods from a lorry. This was held not to amount to receiving them.

(2) Assisting has been held to involve help or encouragement and requires more than simply using property that someone else is retaining.[73] Lying to the police about whether there is stolen property on someone's premises is sufficient to amount to assisting another.[74] But in *Brown*[75] it was suggested that a failure to inform the police about where stolen goods were did not amount to assisting in the retention of goods.[76]

(3) The handling must be 'otherwise than in the course of stealing'. This is not to say that a thief cannot also be a handler, but that it must be shown that there was an act of handling which occurred after the theft had taken place.[77] Once all the elements of theft are established the defendant is guilty of theft and he does not continually steal each time he touches the item thereafter.[78] Further, appropriation, once the theft has occurred, can amount to handling.

(4) The defendant must have received the property 'by or for the benefit of another'. If the defendant is not alleged to have received the property, but one of the other forms of handling is being relied upon then it needs to be shown that the defendant acted for the benefit of another. The leading case is the following decision of the House of Lords which decided that the sale of a car to someone could not be said to be for the benefit of another:

R v Bloxham
[1983] AC 109 (HC)[79]

Albert Bloxham agreed to buy a car for £1,300. At that time he did not know that the car had been stolen. He paid £500 on account and agreed to pay the balance once the registration documents were produced. They never were. Eleven months later he suspected that the car had been stolen and so he sold it to a third party for £200. He was charged with handling stolen goods. At his trial he argued that he had not disposed of or realized the car 'for the benefit of another'. The trial judge rejected this argument, holding that the purchaser had gained a benefit in that he had acquired use of the car, if not good legal title to it. He appealed to the Court of Appeal which upheld the trial judge's ruling.

---

[70] *Hobson v Impett* (1957) 41 Cr App R 138.   [71] *Pitchley* (1973) 57 Cr App R 30 (CA).
[72] (1957) 41 Cr App R 138.   [73] *Sanders* (1982) 75 Cr App R 84 (CA).
[74] *Kanwar* (1982) 75 Cr App R 87 (CA).   [75] [1970] 1 QB 105 (CA).
[76] See also *Kanwar* (1982) 75 Cr App R 87 (CA).   [77] *Bosson* [1999] Crim LR 596 (CA).
[78] *Atakpu and Abrahams* [1994] QB 69 (CA).
[79] [1982] 1 All ER 582, [1982] 2 WLR 392, (1982) 74 Cr App R 279.

Lord Bridge of Harwich, delivering a speech with which their other Lordships agreed

. . . The [Court of Appeal] certified the following point of law of general public importance as involved in their decision:

'Does a bona fide purchaser for value commit an offence of dishonestly undertaking the disposal or realisation of stolen property for the benefit of another if when he sells the goods on he knows or believes them to be stolen?'

The full text of s 22(1) of the Theft Act 1968 reads:

'A person handles stolen goods if (otherwise than in the course of the stealing) knowing or believing them to be stolen goods he dishonestly receives the goods, or dishonestly under-takes or assists in their retention, removal, disposal or realisation by or for the benefit of another person, or if he arranges to do so.'

It is, I think, now well settled that this subsection creates two distinct offences, but no more than two. The first is equivalent to the old offence of receiving under s 33 of the Larceny Act 1916. The second is a new offence designed to remedy defects in the old law and can be committed in any of the various ways indicated by the words from 'undertakes' to the end of the subsection . . .

The critical words to be construed are 'undertakes . . . their . . . disposal or realisation . . . for the benefit of another person'. Considering these words first in isolation, it seems to me that, if A sells his own goods to B, it is a somewhat strained use of language to describe this as a disposal or realisation of the goods for the benefit of B. True it is that B obtains a benefit from the transaction, but it is surely more natural to say that the disposal or realisation is for A's benefit than for B's. It is the purchase, not the sale, that is for the benefit of B. It is only when A is selling as agent for a third party C that it would be entirely natural to describe the sale as a disposal or realisation for the benefit of another person.

But the words cannot, or course, be construed in isolation. They must be construed in their context, bearing in mind, as I have pointed out, that the second half of the section creates a single offence which can be committed in various ways. I can ignore for present purposes the concluding words 'or if he arranges to do so', which throw no light on the point at issue. The preceding words contemplate four activities (retention, removal, disposal, realisation). The offence can be committed in relation to any one of these activities in one or other of two ways. First, the offender may himself undertake the activity for the benefit of another person. Second, the activity may be undertaken by another person and the offender may assist him. Of course, if the thief or an original receiver and his friend act together in, say, removing the stolen goods, the friend may be committing the offence in both ways. But this does not invalidate the analysis, and if the analysis holds good it must follow, I think, that the category of other persons contemplated by the subsection is subject to the same limitations in whichever way the offence is committed. Accordingly, a purchaser, as such, of stolen goods cannot, in my opinion, be 'another person' within the subsection, since his act of purchase could not sensibly be described as a disposal or realisation of the stolen goods by him. Equally, therefore, even if the sale to him could be described as a disposal or realisation for his benefit, the transaction is not, in my view, within the ambit of the subsection.

Certified question answered in the negative. Order appealed from reversed. Conviction quashed.

4.3 IT MUST BE SHOWN THAT THE DEFENDANT KNEW OR BELIEVED THAT THE GOODS WERE STOLEN

It must be shown that at the time of the handling the defendant knew or believed that the goods were stolen.[80] The test is subjective. It does not matter whether a reasonable person would have known the goods were stolen. What matters is what the defendant knew.[81] The words knowledge and belief are to be given their normal meaning[82] and the matter should be left to the 'common sense of the jury'.[83]

It should be noted that the defendant must know *or* believe. Clearly, it will be rare for a defendant to *know* goods are stolen. The courts, however, have said that suspicion is not enough; the defendant must conclude that the goods are stolen.[84] The most difficult cases involve the concept of wilful blindness. This is where the defendant decides not to ask any questions and just assumes the goods are legitimate, while he is aware in the 'back of his mind' that there must be question marks over the origins of the goods. The courts have held that such wilful blindness does not amount to knowledge.[85]

4.4 THE DEFENDANT WAS DISHONEST

To convict the defendant of handling the jury must be persuaded that the defendant was dishonest. The *Ghosh* test[86] for dishonesty will be used. However, it will be rare that someone who is handling what he or she knows or believes to be stolen goods will be able to claim successfully that he or she was acting honestly.[87] It may be that a defendant can claim that he was intending to return the goods to the original owner or the police.

FURTHER READING

Shute, S. (2002), 'Knowledge and Belief in the Criminal Law' in S. Shute and A. Simester (eds.), *Criminal Law Theory* (Oxford: OUP).

Spencer, J. (1985), 'Handling, Theft and the Mala Fide Purchaser', *Criminal Law Review* 92.

Sullivan, G. (2002), 'Knowledge, Belief and Culpability' in S. Shute and A. Simester (eds.), *Criminal Law Theory* (Oxford: OUP).

Williams, G. (1985), 'Handling, Theft and the Purchaser who Takes a Chance', *Criminal Law Review* 432.

5 MONEY LAUNDERING OFFENCES

Closely allied to handling offences are those involving money laundering. The Criminal Justice Act 1988, as amended by the Criminal Justice Act 1993, Part III, and the Money

---

[80] For an excellent discussion see Shute (2002).   [81] *Atwal v Massey* [1971] 3 All ER 881.
[82] *Forsyth* [1997] 2 Cr App R 299 (CA).   [83] Waller LJ in *Reader* (1977) 66 Cr App R 33, 36.
[84] *Forsyth* [1997] 2 Cr App R 299 (CA).
[85] *Griffiths* (1974) 69 Cr App R 14. See also *Hall* (1985) 81 Cr App R 260 (CA). There is a special rule of evidence known as the doctrine of recent possession which enables the jury to infer knowledge or belief from the fact that the accused was in possession of goods which had been recently stolen.
[86] See above p. 531.   [87] *Roberts* (1987) 84 Cr App R 117.

Laundering Regulations 1993 contain most of the important money laundering offences. In addition section 24A of the Theft Act 1968 creates an offence of dishonestly retaining a wrongful credit.

PART II: THEFT AND THEORY

6 INTRODUCTION TO PROPERTY OFFENCES

6.1 IN WHAT WAY DO PROPERTY OFFENCES HARM VICTIMS?

It is common when looking at the criminal law to distinguish between property offences and offences against the person. This is understandable as they appear to involve quite different kinds of harm. Indeed property offences are often said to be less serious than offences against the person. In part this is because often lost or damaged property (or at least its equivalent[88]) can be restored, but this is not true in the case of a physical injury.[89] However, it should not be forgotten that property offence can cause great emotional distress to the victim (burglary in particular). Further, the ownership and enjoyment of property are seen by some as an essential aspect of the expression and realization of human personality.[90] In the following passage John Gardner and Stephen Shute discuss why it would be wrong to dismiss property offences as being trivial wrongs and why property rights matter to individuals and society:

J. Gardner and S. Shute, 'The Wrongness of Rape' in J. Horder (ed.), *Oxford Essays in Jurisprudence* (Oxford: OUP, 2000), 199–203

What is our interest in property? Only some brief remarks are possible here. Those who focus on productivity are, fundamentally, on the right track-so long as 'productivity' is construed widely enough to include the provision of shelter, security, comfort, amusement, and other benefits to the property-holder. The importance of property lies basically in the valuable things we Can do with that property that we cannot so easily do without it. This we will call its *use-value*. Aspects of property rights other than the right to use property are basically derivative of the use-value of property. The value of being able to acquire and transfer property, for example, is basically the value of property's ending up where it can best be used. In conditions of global and indiscriminate abundance property rights may lose their basic moral purchase, because in these conditions everyone has more than they can use. The question whether something could best be used by a person other than the person who holds it is less prone to arise, for there is always plenty left to go round. But in times of

---

[88] But not always, e.g., a pet dog.

[89] Under the Powers of the Criminal Courts (Sentencing) Act 2000 a court can order that stolen goods be returned by the defendant to the victim.

[90] Waldron (1988) and Dan-Cohen (2002: ch. 9). Feldman (2002: 14–18) discusses whether property can be regarded as a fundamental human right.

scarcity or of merely local or discriminate abundance (i.e. abundance from which some are excluded, leaving them in conditions of scarcity) the question is always live: could this thing be better used by someone else? The idea of a property right to such things is that, up to a point, the question of where something is better used can least wastefully be settled by leaving the question to the person who already holds the thing. This means that, again up to a point, people are left free to hold property that they do not use. It is still theirs and cannot be taken without their say-so. If others were to take it away from them this might yield a better use for it, but the suboptimal use of a particular thing is justified, up to a point, by the general gains in use-value that are made from a co-ordinating system based on consensual transactions.

We say 'up to a point', but the question on everybody's lips is: up to which point? In the long history of property rights the point has been located in different places by different civilizations and regimes. Some things have been regarded at some times and in some places as incapable of being subject to property rights, or incapable of being subject to certain kinds of strong property rights such as ownership. The tendency to wastefulness by property-holders, their refusal to let things be put to their best use, has often been regarded (no doubt sometimes rightly) as too high a price to pay for the avoidance of the costs associated with alternative methods of distribution and allocation. Some things, the value of which is basically their use-value, have therefore on occasions been taken out of a fully-fledged property regime. Thus, at some times and in some places, housing has been publicly provided for tenancy but not for ownership, TV stations or take-off slots at airports have not been capable of being owned, etc. Meanwhile, some things have been owned but with special regulation inhibiting their use and disposal, such as rent control legislation, restrictions on inheritance, rules against predatory pricing or monopolization, and official scrutiny of hostile takeovers. Since the basic value of property is instrumental, different policies and practices may serve that value more or less effectively at different times and places, depending on other prevailing conditions—for instance, the extent of the public tendency towards decadence, the sluggishness of competition, the degree of scarcity, or the extent of globalization.

However, one observation that may be made regarding large parts of the inhabited world today is that property rights are tending to campaign, in a sense, for their own augmentation and deregulation. The rise of public faith in property-holding as a pat solution to the co-ordination problems associated with the use of things under conditions of scarcity, combined with people's increasing alienation from other human beings, leads people to attach great and ever-growing symbolic importance to the acquisition and holding of property. Increasingly, they come to identify with at least some things they hold as extensions of themselves, tokens of their own personality. The idea of 'sentimental value' has always highlighted this aspect of property holding. But it extends nowadays to much else besides the inherited keepsakes of the past or the gifts of friends and family. In fact, it is increasingly associated more with self-chosen than with other-chosen things. In so far as people regard themselves as autonomous beings, their own choice of property—which house to buy, which ties to wear, which CDs to collect—has an ever more important place in their self-expression. The result is the cultural condition which has come to be known as 'consumerism'. No doubt it has got wildly out of hand. But up to a point—and again the point cannot be settled out of local context—consumerism does effect the moral change which its participants seem to presuppose. They regard property as meaning more, as carrying more significance, than just the significance imported by its use-value. Their regarding it as carrying that significance actually endows it with that significance by changing its social meaning. People are increasingly identifying with what they have. So on top of its basic use-value, much more of what people hold now has what we might call *identification-value*. When property is taken away without the proper consensual process, it is not merely (or even) that the system of optimal use-value is disrupted. It is that people are metaphorically violated by the removal of a part of their extended selves.

Some think that identification-value, and particularly the value which comes of investing autonomous choice in property, suffices on its own to explain why property rights continue to reside in those who make suboptimal use of their property. But property rights can persist even when use-value and identification-value are both missing. Consider what might be regarded as the pure case of burglary. Suppose an estate agent who has keys to my house lets himself in while I am on holiday and takes a pile of my old clothes from the attic, passing them on to a charity shop. I had long since forgotten that the clothes were there, and I had no further use, anyway, for loon pants and kipper ties. The burglary goes forever undiscovered. (The estate agent, who told nobody of what he was doing, falls under a bus as he leaves the charity shop, as he would have done anyway even if my clothes had not been among those he delivered.) Yet my property right is violated. Why is this? After all, I have no interest in these old long-forgotten clothes that comes of either my use of them or my identification with them. But on top of that, as we already indicated, there is the co-ordinating value of property rights in securing use-value and identification-value at large (i.e. for people in general). My having this property right over my old clothes, which is violated by the intruding estate agent, does not come of any use-value or identification-value to me but of the contribution which my having such a property right makes to the perpetuation of a system of optimal use-value coupled, so far as possible, with optimal identification-value. So I have an interest in this property which is basically derivative of the public interest in my having such an interest. . . .

In the last paragraph Gardner and Shute refer to the system of property rights which our society uses. Most members of the public probably assume that the form of ownership of property used in the UK is 'natural'. But it is not impossible to think of other property systems that England and Wales's legal system could adopt. They might emphasize communal ownership[91] of property to a far greater extent than we do,[92] or involve a system of property ownership based on the notion of stewardship which would emphasize the obligations as well as the rights of ownership.[93] Although the protection of property through the criminal law may appear a natural part of any liberal democracy it raises some complex issues. To name but a few:

(1) There is much dispute over what kinds of property should be protected by the criminal law. Lacey and Wells have suggested, 'Criminal law defends not property at large, but certain kinds of—highly unevenly distributed—property. It thereby defends not only property, but the power of certain interests and the authority of the social order.'[94] Those sympathetic to such a point of view point out that interests in a clean environment, effective education, healthy food are not protected by property offences, while 'commercial' interests generally are. From a different perspective others claim that the present law's understanding of property is out of touch with modern commercial practice in inadequately protecting 'new property', such as commercially valuable information or pension rights.

---

[91] Thompson (1989).
[92] J.W. Harris (1996) provides a fascinating discussion of alternative property structures that could be used.
[93] Lucy and Mitchell (1996).   [94] Lacey and Wells (1998: 349).

(2) It is significant that property offences, like the law of property generally, are concerned with the fair and effective transfer, control, and creation of property interests; but are not concerned with the fairness of the distribution of property that results. In other words it would be theft for an impoverished person to pick the pocket of a rich one; but it is not theft for one person to own vast wealth while another has virtually nothing. To those of a Marxist persuasion by ensuring 'fair' transfers, but not fair distribution, the law on property offences reinforces and perpetuates the inequalities within society.[95] The law preventing taking works harshly on the destitute who have nothing, but protects the interests of those who are well provided for.[96] Hence Proudhon[97] famously declared that property was theft.[98] Of course, without any property offences it would not be the case that property was equally distributed, but rather the strongest would be able to take the property of the weak without punishment. But we could alter the purpose of property offences from ensuring that those who have can keep what they have to requiring those who have to give to those who have not.[99] One does not have to be a Marxist to make a strong case that theft can be regarded as morally wrong only if the basic framework of the property law is just.[100]

(3) There is a fine line to be drawn in the law on property offences between what is a civil wrong and what is a crime.[101] For example, if you were to decide to employ a builder and paid her in advance £500 to do some work on your flat, but she carried out only half the job and failed to return the money or complete the job, should your remedy be to sue her in the courts for breach of contract or should this be regarded as a criminal offence? This issue regularly arises in property offences. For example, should a temporary taking be regarded as theft or a matter for civil remedies?

(4) The criminal law is not the only way that society may tackle the problem of wrongful interference with property rights. It can certainly be argued that society's resources would be better spent trying to improve the designs of property such as homes, cars, or mobile phones to make them harder to steal, rather than pouring resources into the prosecution and punishment of thieves.[102]

(5) How should we structure criminal offences? Should we distinguish between the value of property taken (e.g. have offences structured according to the value of the property lost) or by the means by which the property was acquired (e.g. distinguishing a robbery from a burglary)?

We shall start by examining the last of these issues, and the other points will be dealt with later on.

6.2 STRUCTURE OF PROPERTY OFFENCES

As a broad generalization in relation to offences against the person the law is structured according to the level of harm suffered by the victim. Hence the most serious offences

---

[95] Marx and Engels (1967).   [96] L. Murphy (2001).   [97] Proudhon (1994).

[98] See also Christman (1994). Interestingly, there is evidence that property crimes increase at a faster rate when there is low economic growth: Barclay (1995: 5).

[99] No doubt taxation etc. would also be needed to ensure a more equal distribution.

[100] J.W. Harris (1996a: 14).

[101] Contrast the law on gross negligence manslaughter: *Wacker* [2003] Crim LR 108.

[102] See the discussion in Clarke and Mayhew (1980). See also Home Office (2003) and Sutton, Schneider, and Hetherington (2001) for the government's thoughts on property crime prevention.

involve death (murder and manslaughter), and then we move down to less serious offences involving rape, grievous bodily harm, and actual bodily harm, down to the least serious offences of assaults and batteries. For offences against the person the method used to cause the harm is largely immaterial. You are guilty of murder whether you kill the victim by drowning, strangling, or poisoning. However, property offences are different. They are less concerned with the value of property affected by the offence,[103] and instead focus on the method used by the defendant to acquire or deal with the property. Hence a distinction is drawn, for example, between theft, blackmail, robbery, burglary, and offences involving deception, etc. As we shall see, there is much debate over whether these should be seen as different kinds of wrong against a victim, or more or less serious forms of the same wrong.[104] Property offences also seek to protect particular kinds of property which are seen as particularly vulnerable to being abused. For example, there are statutory provisions to protect computers and cars from misuse.[105]

6.3 THE CIVIL LAW/CRIMINAL LAW INTERFACE

At the heart of property offences is the definition of a property right. Inevitably criminal lawyers will turn to civil law to find out answers to questions such as: what is property?; who owns the property?; is the property held on trust?[106] However, the need for the criminal law to interact with the civil law causes tensions. These came dramatically to a head in the House of Lords in *Hinks*, where it was held that a transaction which constituted a valid gift in civil law could be regarded as theft in the criminal law. To some this meant that the law was being two-faced, its criminal face labelling Hinks a thief, but its civil face declaring the transaction to be a valid gift. But there are other difficulties here too. If juries and magistrates are to be able to try cases the law needs to be relatively straightforward and if the law of theft can be understood only by a complete understanding of English property law, juries and magistrates will be unable to do their job. There is also a danger that a criminal trial can get so tied up with the civil law issues that it loses sight of the key issue of the blameworthiness and harmfulness of what the defendant did.[107] Further, the definition of what is property for the purposes of civil law may not coincide with what kinds of activities the criminal law wants to prevent through property offences. These issues in part reflect a difference in the aims of the criminal law and civil law in this area. For civil lawyers certainty of ownership is important; for criminal lawyers the prevention of dishonest conduct may be regarded as more important. The temptation may be for criminal lawyers to seek to free criminal law from the 'shackles of civil law'. But that would create all kinds of problems: if the property offences are not protecting the property interests as understood in civil law, what are they protecting? We shall return to this issue when we consider the case of *Hinks*.

In the following passage Andrew Simester and Bob Sullivan describe what they regard as the essence of theft: the protection of property interests. They, therefore, are strong opponents of the decision in *Hinks*.

---

[103] Historically this has not been so: see Fletcher (1978: 115–20). Of course, the value of the property may well be relevant for sentencing purposes.
[104] That we shall look at in Part II of Ch. 9.   [105] Computer Misuse Act 1990; Theft Act 1968, s. 12.
[106] J.C. Smith (1995).   [107] *Clowes (No. 2)* [1994] 2 All ER 316.

A. Simester and G. Sullivan, 'The Nature and Rationale of Property Offences' in R.A. Duff and S. Green (eds.), *Defining Crimes* (Oxford: OUP, 2005), at 174–6

The essence of theft is to misappropriate, with intent to deprive, property to which one is not legally entitled, and to do so without justification or excuse. As such, theft is concerned directly and primarily with protecting the legal structure of proprietary entitlements. Imagine V, a misanthropic billionaire who has inherited and not created any of his wealth. He has withdrawn all his money from his investments, trusts, and bank accounts and stacked the cash away in cardboard boxes that litter the floors of his grim mansion. He is determined that no-one shall have any use or pleasure from his wealth and has resolved that when his time is nigh, he will immolate himself and his cash. D is V's selfless home-carer, Although paid a pittance by V, out of the goodness of her heart she ministers to V's needs beyond any call of duty. From time to time, she takes cash from one or other of the boxes, never for herself, but to ease the path of friends and acquaintances who are in dire economic straits. There is no profligacy in this: she takes enough, just enough, to stave off the worst consequences of the privations that afflict the people she helps. D is a thief; a thief despite the fact that V knows nothing of D's takings and is unharmed psychologically by what D has done, and despite the fact that, for him, the financial loss is *de minimis* in every conceivable sense. She has misappropriated V's property, usurped his property rights without his consent; no more is required. This conclusion follows, as we shall argue, even where D acts with a degree of selflessness and concern would be vindicated as ethically correct under many versions of communitarian morality.

The example illustrates that the immediate victim of a theft may be harmed in a wholly conventional sense, without suffering any substantive disvalue or setback of human interests. Across a range of different cultures and circumstances, outcomes such as death, injury, physical and emotional pain, extreme discomfort, paralysing fear, bereavement, etc., are unequivocal—and pre-legal—harms. Although it does not follow that the infliction of such harms is always wrong, or that their categoric prohibition is justified, it may readily be agreed without reference to the law that a person who is badly physically or emotionally hurt is, while that condition endures, worse off than when her usual circumstances obtain. By contrast, and while D's conviction for theft may be justified in terms of protecting the proprietary regime itself, V is a victim only formally.

Violations of the ownership, control, or possession of property need not always set back the interests of an agent whose rights have been contravened. Of course, sometimes a loss of property may have devastating consequences for the nature and quality of an agent's life. Yet the accretion of property may have no beneficent effect on the quality of life or moral standing of an agent. Take the misanthropic billionaire: no doubt from Aristotelian and communitarian perspectives his life and moral standing would improve immeasurably if, after some ghostly visitation, he were to give away the bulk of his fortune in well-judged and effective acts of philanthropy. Moreover, it may be argued from these moral perspectives that, absent any re-enactment of *The Christmas Carol*, D, his housekeeper, *should* have taken even more of V's money and redistributed it to the needy. It seems an inversion of sound moral judgment to castigate her as a thief. If she is to be criticised at all, it might be for her failure to take more of his money before he, his mansion, and the money went up in smoke.

6.4 THEFT: THE STATISTICS

The official figures

The 2001–2 British Crime Survey found that theft was the most common offence in England and Wales with 57 per cent of the total crimes measured by the survey involving some kind of theft.[108] Of the 5,527,082 offences recorded in the survey 82 per cent of all crimes were property offences.[109] In 2004/5 there were 3,324,000 thefts.[110] People may be particularly likely to report property offences to the police if the property has been insured and they wish to make a claim on their insurance policies. The sums involved are not small. As already noted, the most common forms of theft involve vehicles. One study looking at the financial cost[111] to victims found it was on average £600 in cases of theft from a vehicle and £3,700–£5,600 in cases of theft of a vehicle.[112]

The reality?

Such official figures as those just quoted give perhaps a rather distorted picture of property wrongdoing. This is because it is clear that not all conduct which fulfils the legal requirements of a property offence is treated in the same way. It has been suggested that few people are entirely truthful with their tax returns.[113] Indeed a full complete disclosure as technically required in the tax return would require some people to provide an extraordinarily lengthy return. Whether these are legitimate points it is certainly true that if the tax authorities suspect that a person has not completed his tax return properly criminal proceedings are rarely brought and the matter is dealt with by 'negotiations' between the individual and the Inland Revenue, normally resulting in the individual paying an agreed sum to the Inland Revenue.[114] In recent years people on public transport who are found by a ticket inspector not to have bought a ticket normally have to buy a ticket with an extra surcharge, rather than the matter going through the courts. During the 2002 Word Cup when the football matches were in the afternoon or morning there were widespread press reports of employees not turning up for work and claiming to be sick, so that they could stay at home and watch the match. Few people suggested that this should be regarded as a criminal offence, but why not?

As these examples indicate, some property offences are dealt with in a way which in effect by-passes the criminal procedure. There is no criminal conviction, although sometimes a sum of money equivalent to a fine may have to be paid.[115] These examples indicate that what is regarded as a property offence is not as straightforward as might at first appear. Our society has effectively licensed certain forms of conduct which technically fall within the definition of a property offence, but which are treated as non-criminal.[116] These points can be further considered with the following two examples:

(1) *Shoplifting* The cost to the retail industry of shoplifting in 2004 was estimated to be £2.13 billion.[117] It has been estimated that in the previous five years 3.5 million people in the UK have engaged in shoplifting.[118] This indicates that the number of incidents reported to

---

[108] Simmons *et al.* (2001: 5).   [109] Simmons *et al.* (2001: 27).   [110] Nicholas (2005: 58).
[111] Broadly defined, including the time taken to deal with the issue etc.
[112] Brand and Price (2000).   [113] Mears (1982).
[114] D. Cook (1989) contrasts the legal responses to tax evasion and benefit fraud.
[115] In some American states an amnesty against criminal conviction is offered if a company admits that it has committed certain kinds of commercial crimes: S. Hammond (2001).
[116] Lacey and Wells (1998: 244).   [117] BRC (2005).   [118] BBC Newsonline (2005c).

the police and dealt with through the courts is tiny.[119] It is not that shoplifting is financially insignificant. You will not be surprised to learn that £830 million is the figure for the annual costs to shops from customer shoplifting in the Retail Crime Survey. You may well be surprised to learn that £640 million is the annual cost of staff theft from shops.[120] There has been some debate whether shoplifting should be dealt with by way of on-the-spot payments of the kind used for those caught using public transport without paying.[121]

(2) 'White-collar crime'.[122] Sutherland has defined a white-collar crime as 'a crime committed by a person of respectability and high social status in the course of his occupation'.[123] Property offences in the public imagination involve the sneaky pickpocket or the masked mugger, and not the suited executive arranging price fixing or malinvesting pension funds.[124] Yet white-collar crimes can involve far larger sums than the traditional crime. Despite this they are less likely to be prosecuted.[125] Not only are 'white-collar criminals' less likely to be prosecuted or convicted; if convicted their sentences may be lower than for analogous offences.[126] Some suggest that the explanation for the lack of prosecution for 'white-collar crime' is the fine line in the business world that has to be drawn between criminal activity and sharp business practices.[127] Certainly the line between acceptable and unacceptable business practices can be said to be in a state of flux.[128] We will discuss business crime in greater detail in Chapter 13.

6.5 WHAT IS PROPERTY?

At the heart of property offences is the concept of property.[129] But how do we decide what things can be regarded as property and what cannot. The answer is not self-evident. Some things are held not to be property because of the anti-social consequences that may result (imagine what might happen if it were decided that the sun could be owned and people could be charged for using sunlight);[130] and other things cannot be property because it is not effectively possible to restrict or control access to them (e.g. to air). So, moral, practical, and legal arguments can operate to mean that something is declared not to be property for the purposes of the law. This means that whether something is regarded as capable of being property can change over time. It is arguable, for example, that bodies and body parts are undergoing a transition from being regarded as non-property to being regarded, in some cases at least, as property.[131]

---

[119] It is interesting that the offence is usually called shoplifting, rather than theft. A. Morris (1987) discusses the fact that shoplifting is one of the few crimes where women and men have similar rates of conviction.

[120] Henry (1978) has been willing to go so far as to suggest that petty pilfering from work has become so normal that it can be regarded as an aspect of job satisfaction.

[121] Huber (1980) discusses the German response to shoplifting which is along these lines.

[122] Nelken (2002). Staple (1993) discusses the work of the Serious Fraud Office.

[123] Sutherland (1983: 8).

[124] See Box (1983) and Sutherland (1983) for further discussions.   [125] Pearce (1978).

[126] Lambiras (2003).

[127] Spalek (2001) discusses the impact of white-collar crimes on its victims.

[128] Hadden (1983).

[129] The leading works include Nozick (1974); Honoré (1961); Waldron (1988); Munzer (1990); Christman (1994); J.W. Harris (1996a); Penner (1996).

[130] Gray (1991).

[131] See further Reich (1964) and his discussion of 'new property' which includes things like pension entitlements and environmental interests.

FURTHER READING

Cross, J. (1991), 'Protecting Confidential Information Under the Criminal Law of Theft and Fraud', *Oxford Journal of Legal Studies* 11: 264.

Dworkin, G., and Kennedy, I. (1993), 'Human Tissue: Rights in the Body and its Parts', *Medical Law Review* 1: 29.

Gold, E. (1996), *Body Parts: Property Rights and the Ownership of Human Biological Matter* (Oxford: OUP).

Green, P. (2003), 'The Concept of White Collar Crime in Law and Legal Theory', *Buffalo Criminal Law Review* 8: 1

Green, S. (2002), 'Plagiarism, Norms, and the Limits of Theft Law: Some Observations on the Use of Criminal Sanctions in Enforcing Intellectual Property Rights', *Hastings Law Journal* 54: 167.

Hammond, G. (1984), 'Theft of Information', *Law Quarterly Review* 100: 252.

Harris, J.W. (1996a), *Property and Justice* (Oxford: OUP), ch. 16.

—— (1996b), 'Who Owns my Body?', *Oxford Journal of Legal Studies* 16: 55.

Herring, J. (2002b), 'Giving, Selling and Sharing Bodies' in A. Bainham, S. Day Sclater, and M. Richards (eds.), *Body Lore and Laws* (Oxford: Hart).

Lipton, J. (2001), 'Protecting Valuable Commercial Information in the Digital Age: Law, Policy and Practice', *Journal of Technology Law and Policy* 6.1: 2.

Matthews, P. (1995), 'The Man of Property', *Medical Law Review* 3: 251.

Weinrib, A. (1988), 'Information and Property', *University of Toronto Law Journal* 38: 117.

Having considered some of the more general issues relating to property offences we now turn to theft and consider some of the controversial issues surrounding the definition of theft.

7 THE DEBATE OVER *GOMEZ*

It will be recalled that the House of Lords in *Gomez*[132] confirmed that an appropriation involved an act of interference with one of the rights of an owner, and that an act could amount to appropriation even if it was consented to or authorized by the victim. The decision was highly controversial. We will now summarize some of the arguments for and against the decision.[133]

7.1 THE CASE FOR *GOMEZ*

In the following passage Simon Gardner sets out his reasons for welcoming *Gomez*:

---

[132] [1993] AC 442 (HL).

[133] See also S. Gardner (1990) and (1998); Cooper and Allen (1993); and Clarkson (1993).

S. Gardner, 'Appropriation in Theft: The Last Word?' (1993) 109 *Law Quarterly Review* 194

[Having explained that the House of Lords in *Gomez* essentially decided the case by following *Lawrence*, Gardner continued:]

In its own terms, this summary resolution is unimpeachable. The only question is whether the answer is desirable from first principles. It is suggested that it is. Most fundamentally, it is submitted that the quality of dishonest conduct is not necessarily altered by the victim's consent. Consider, above all, cases where the victim consents to the taking, but does so in a state of low-level, non-specific confusion. For example, elderly people are often exploited by rogues who dishonestly overcharge them for work, or underpay them for their treasures. The victim in such a case has consented to the taking, and her consent is not obviously vitiated, but it is very possible to sense that the rogue's conduct should be criminal. However, in such circumstances it is not easy to convict for anything except ordinary theft. There can be no conviction for obtaining by deception under section 15 of the Theft Act, for want of a clear deception (*cf. R.* v. *Silverman* (1988) 86 Cr. App. R. 213); nor for the special form of theft established under section 5(4), for want of a true mistake; nor for blackmail or robbery, for want of any pressure. If theft were negatived by the victim's consent, then, such cases would constitute no offence. By their Lordships' decision in *Gomez*, however, theft does lie here. That result is to be applauded.

Another argument in favour of *Gomez* is that, even were we attracted to a requirement of non-consent, we should reject it as making theft difficult of administration by the criminal courts, with their lay judges of fact. Consent is a problematic concept. Even if it simply meant 'saying yes,' difficulties would remain. As the facts in *Lawrence* show, the practical boundaries of 'saying yes' are not altogether clear. And making a victim say 'yes' at the point of a gun would apparently negate theft, and so too robbery. That would be absurd. The answer would have to be that consent means 'true consent'—that is, an owner's 'yes' would be subject to vitiation by such factors as mistake or pressure. This approach is familiar from other branches of the law, above all contract. To adopt it in theft, however, would require magistrates' benches and Crown Courts to handle notions which have been found elusive even in the higher courts on the civil side. Directions on the law would consequently be prone to error, and so to appeal; and even if a direction was sound (or even, perhaps, the more sound it was), the task of applying it might well baffle the lay judges of fact (*cf. Whittaker* v. *Campbell* [1984] Q.B. 318). Neither meaning of 'consent,' therefore, would leave the law of theft in a happy condition, if non-consent were a constituent of the offence.

. . .

Lord Lowry offers a dissenting opinion. His main ground for doing so is that the majority has, he contends, failed to apply the ordinary meaning of the verb 'appropriate.' He cites a dictionary definition of 'appropriate' as 'take possession of, take to oneself, especially without authority,' and concludes from the latter words that a requirement of non-consent is involved. With respect, however there are difficulties about this argument. First, his Lordship fails to consider the word 'especially' in this definition. One could accept the formulation of theft as having no such requirement and still observe that very many thefts will in fact be non-consensual. And secondly, his Lordship's use of dictionaries is selective. He does not attribute the definition he cites, but something similar can be found in the *Concise Oxford Dictionary*. The entries in the larger Oxford dictionaries, for example, omit the crucial reference to an absence of authority.

Lord Lowry has another argument. He maintains that Parliament's intention of a requirement of non-consent in theft can be deduced from the relationship between theft and the offence in section 15 of the Theft Act of obtaining property by deception. It can be contended that the majority's decision in *Gomez* has in effect rendered section 15 otiose, for theft can now lie even where the owner, because deceived, consented to the transfer. Yet this cannot be what Parliament intended. By enacting section 15 as a separate offence, Parliament must have meant it to have a distinctive role. And the point is put beyond doubt by the Eighth Report of the Criminal Law Revision Committee, upon which the Theft Act is based. The Report records that the Committee considered recommending the merger of the two offences, but decided otherwise. To avoid confuting Parliament's intention, then, Lord Lowry argues that theft must be restricted to a narrower, non-consensual meaning. This is an important matter; and the majority's decision does not render it of merely academic interest, for prosecutors and courts will need to work with the *post-Gomez* relationship between theft and section 15. It is important to understand, however, that assertions that, by *Gomez*, section 15 has become otiose do not convey a complete truth.

Lord Browne-Wilkinson offers one point to this effect. He observes that whilst theft does not apply to land (and one might add mushrooms and certain wild animals), section 15 does. However, the power of this argument may not be appreciated outside Lincoln's Inn. The real point is this. What is true after *Gomez* is that all the activities which are covered by section 15 are also, give or take mushrooms and the like, contained within theft. But that is also true of robbery and burglary (in its theft variant). These nevertheless exist as separate offences because the harm suffered by the victim is both a loss of property and a further form of injury as well. In robbery this further injury is the feeling of physical powerlessness. In burglary it is feeling of lost territorial security. Reflecting this combination of loss of property and additional injury, robbery and burglary have always been aggravated forms of theft, each carrying a maximum sentence higher than that for simple theft. It should be noted that in neither case does the simple offence of theft discontinue where the aggravated offence begins. This seems wise, for otherwise an accused could defeat a prosecution for simple theft by showing that, having used force or intrusion, he was in fact guilty of an aggravated offence instead: which would be unedifying. Even though they overlap with theft, therefore, it is impossible to say that the offences of robbery and burglary are otiose. Obtaining by deception fits the same pattern. It too responds to the victim's suffering both a loss of property and an additional injury: in this case a feeling of intellectual vulnerability. It too now carries a higher maximum sentence than simple theft. It thus seems entirely supportable that, after *Gomez*, it should operate in the same way as robbery and burglary, as an aggravated form of the with simple theft allowed to overlap it.

7.2 THE CASE AGAINST *GOMEZ*

The following are some of the reasons why many commentators have opposed the *Gomez* decision.

(1) One of the reasons that has led to *Gomez* suffering such ferocious criticism is that as a result of the decision virtually[134] every offence of obtaining property by deception contrary to section 15 of the Theft Act 1968 is theft.[135] To some this is an unacceptable merging of two

---

[134] Heaton (2001) argues that there are more offences of s. 15 which are not a s. 1 offence than is commonly supposed.

[135] Stuart (1967) reviews the background to the Theft Act 1968. In *Isaac v DPP* [2002] EWHC 2448 Davis J held that it would be wrong to convict a person of both attempted theft and attempted s. 15 for the same incident. The same presumably applies to the full offences.

offences.[136] What is the point in having the section 15 offence if virtually every incidence of it is also covered by the offence of theft? As seen in the extract above, Gardner has a ready response to this: so what? All robberies are theft.[137] He argues that section 15 offences can be seen as theft and deception; just as robbery is theft and the use of force. So the fact that nearly every section 15 offence is also theft need not concern us at all. However, others have rejected this understanding of section 15 as an 'aggravated theft' and argued that there is a fundamental moral difference between the two offences. This argument is made in the following passage by Stephen Shute and Jeremy Horder:

S. Shute and J. Horder, 'Thieving and Deceiving: What is the Difference?' (1993) 56 Modern Law Review 548

. . . In our view, Lord Lowry was right to find continuing significance in a broad distinction between theft and obtaining property by deception, by reference to the Committee Report. The criminal law seeks to find appropriate labels for different kinds of wrongdoers, as part of its 'representative labelling' function. The label 'thief' does not carry the same moral import as the label 'conman,' as the Committee pointed out, and this can have practical significance. Suppose that, in cross-examination, an accused person loses the shield protecting him from questions tending to show that he is of bad character and thus not creditworthy. The law holds, it seems, that evidence only of the *fact* of previous convictions rather than their underlying detail may then be given in evidence by the prosecution. If so, evidence that the accused is a convicted conman would seem to be a far more potent indication of a lack of creditworthiness than evidence merely that the accused is a convicted thief. For, whilst the latter (like the former) is certainly dishonest, the former has been *untruthful* as well, and proven untruthfulness is even more damning evidence of a witness's lack of credibility than proof of dishonesty alone.

. . .

[Having suggested that the concept of the victim's consent is not a helpful way of marking out the distinction between theft and obtaining property by deception the authors continue:]

In our view, a more promising approach is to see the conceptual distinction between theft and obtaining property by deception as resting on the difference between an 'involuntary' and a 'voluntary' transfer of property from victim to offender. We will call this new approach the 'voluntariness' view. Unlike the protean concept of consent, which is shot through with questions of degree, voluntariness in the special sense that we will be using here provides the conceptual solidity needed to distinguish between the two offences. Another advantage of the 'voluntariness' view is that it avoids difficult civil law questions as to title, when considering the meaning of appropriation.

For present purposes, the distinction we are drawing between a voluntary and an involuntary transfer of property is simply the distinction between one's having *given* property and one's having had that property *taken*. Put more generally, it is an exemplar of the difference between *doing something* (the 'giving') and *having something done to one* (the 'taking'). Voluntariness in our sense works as an all or nothing concept. Either the property was given or it was taken: there is nothing in between. So, if my lodger waits until I have gone to work and then departs with my possessions, on the 'voluntariness' view the appropriate charge will be theft. This is because the transfer has occurred independently of my will: my property has been taken. The property is hence properly regarded as having been 'appropriated.' It is,

---

[136] Glazebrook (1993) argues that there is no injustice in convicting a swindler of being a thief.

[137] He could have added that all murders are batteries. Many serious offences include less serious ones.

moreover, lack of voluntariness that matters here, *not* mere lack of knowledge. If, on looking out of my window, I see someone taking my car, the fact that I *know* my car is being taken by a thief does not, on this view, make the act of the thief any less theft. The thief has appropriated my property, precisely because the car has been taken—an involuntary transfer— despite my knowledge of the taking.

Care must be taken in applying the voluntariness view, particularly in cases where the act alleged to constitute the crime is not the actual transfer of the property to the defendant, but some later act. Consider the case where a customer asks the owner of a valuable vase if he may look at it. When the owner hands over the vase the customer makes off with it, as he always intended to do. The voluntariness of the transfer of possession of the vase to the defendant means that, on the 'voluntariness' view, obtaining property by deception is the appropriate charge in relation to that act (since the property was given to the customer). It may also be possible, however, to bring a charge of theft, but not one of obtaining property by deception, in relation to the act following the transfer (the 'making off'). For that act is itself a taking although obviously not if the 'making off' is consensual or authorised.

One limitation on the voluntariness approach, however, comes from the use of the word 'steals' in the definition of robbery given in s 8(1) of the Theft Act 1968. If someone threatens me into handing over my property, it is clear that the property is given to the robber, and is hence voluntary in the sense that we are employing. Yet, for the purposes of s 8, the defendant will be held to have 'stolen' the property and will be guilty of robbery. This cuts across the voluntariness view of appropriation and theft, but arguably it is not so much a defect in the voluntariness approach as a defect in the definition of robbery. So long as a defendant has acquired property by the use or the threatened use of force, it should not matter one jot whether the property was 'appropriated' from the victim or not, and s 8(1) could easily be amended to reflect this fact.

Even if the conceptual basis for the distinction between theft and obtaining property by deception is to be found in the voluntariness of the transfer, a different kind of objection to the attempt to find a basis for the distinction might be made. It has been claimed that the distinction between the two offences is morally 'trivial.' We believe, however, that the distinction between theft and obtaining property by deception does have moral significance, and thus that continuing attempts to locate a clear distinction between the two are worthwhile.

In our view, an argument showing that the distinction has a moral foundation might be formulated along these lines. There is in our society a general social practice of uncoerced voluntary transfers ('givings'), even when they are the product of another's advice, influence or persuasion. A straightforward example would be ordinary buying and selling in the marketplace. The moral significance of this social practice derives from the fact that the voluntariness of the transfer is an essential prerequisite if that transfer is to serve to enhance the transferor's autonomy. By way of contrast, there is generally little of value in involuntary transfers of property ('takings'), which—as in the case of theft—serve mostly to reduce rather than enhance the 'transferor's' autonomy.

This moral difference underpinning the distinction between voluntary and involuntary transfers—between takings and givings—means that, on the voluntariness view, the nature of the wrongdoing in theft has a separate moral foundation from that of obtaining by deception. The wrongful conduct in obtaining by deception is internal to the practice of voluntary transfer. Its wrongfulness centres on the abuse of what should have been an autonomy enhancing transaction. The fraudster abuses the control that he or she has over the information on which victims make their decisions about an admittedly voluntary transfer: the victim's chances of making an authentic choice are deliberately or recklessly undermined by the fraudster The wrongful act in theft, however, is external to the legitimate social practice of voluntary transfers of property. Its wrongfulness centres on the fact that the thief bypasses the entire social practice at the victim's expense. Putting it metaphorically, whereas the thief makes war on a social practice from the outside, the deceiver is the traitor within.

QUESTIONS

1. Often thefts involve the defendant deceiving the victim so that the defendant can take property (e.g. distracting the victim so that he can pick his pocket). Does this mean that the distinctions Horder and Shute are trying to draw are not as firm as they suggest?

2. Are you convinced that voluntariness would be easier to use for a jury or magistrates than the law based on *Gomez*? Is it obvious that robbery is not voluntary in their analysis?

(2) Following *Gomez* an act can amount to an appropriation which is not 'manifestly theftous', to use a phrase of George Fletcher's.[138] In other words an act which appears to be objectively innocent (e.g. picking a tin of baked beans from a supermarket shelf[139]) can become theft if accompanied by the necessary *mens rea*.[140] The argument is that there is a danger that theft could become essentially a 'mind crime'. In Chapter 14, when we will discuss the *actus reus* of attempted offences, we will see that the law is very reluctant to convict defendants unless they have clearly revealed that they intend to commit a crime. These concerns do not seem to have been given weight in the law's definition of appropriation.

(3) Lord Lowry in his dissenting judgment in *Gomez* placed much weight on the view that the decision of the majority is not in line with the view of the Criminal Law Revision Committee, whose report formed the basis of the Theft Act 1968.

8 THE *HINKS* DEBATE

Hinks has been deeply unpopular with many academic commentators, although it is by no means without its supporters.

8.1 THE ARGUMENTS AGAINST *HINKS*

Summarizing the main arguments against *Hinks* the following points can be made:

(1) The case sets up a conflict between the criminal and civil law. The law almost appears to be hypocritical, telling Karen Hinks that at the same time she received a valid gift (in civil law), but she stole it (in criminal law). Lord Steyn in the majority in *Hinks* accepted that there appeared to be a conflict, but that this was acceptable, given the different aims that the civil and criminal laws have. The civil law will place great weight on the importance of certainty of ownership, while the criminal law will seek to penalize dishonest conduct. An alternative response is that if there is a conflict

---

[138] Fletcher (1976). [139] This would, after *Gomez*, be theft. [140] Giles and Uglow (1992).

between civil law and criminal law in cases of this kind, it is civil law which has got it wrong. Elderly and vulnerable people need protection from being exploited by others.

(2) There is much uncertainty following *Hinks*. Whether a transfer amounts to theft now very much depends on whether the action is thought by the jury to be dishonest. Some commentators suggest that the law is challengeable as too uncertain for the purposes of Article 6 of the European Convention on Human Rights.[141] Notably the Law Commission Consultation Paper on Fraud and Deception decided that a general offence of dishonesty may be too vague to be compatible with convention rights.[142]

(3) There is some difficulty in *Hinks* in explaining how it was that Hinks could be said to have appropriated property belonging to another. The difficulty is that the very act of appropriation (receiving the money) was the moment in time when the property ceased to belong to the victim and belonged to Hinks. In other words at exactly the same moment there was appropriation and ownership changed hands. The majority seemed happy to accept that this could still be regarded as appropriating property belonging to another.

These and other objections to the *Hinks* decision are explained in the following extract, although Stephen Shute does not find the objections as powerful as they might appear at first sight:

S. Shute, 'Appropriation and the Law of Theft' [2002] *Criminal Law Review* 450–7

3. Arguments Against *Hinks*

For many this enlargement of the scope of the criminal law to include cases where title passes as a result of an unimpeachable transaction is unjustified. One argument against such an expansion is that it rides roughshod over the intentions of the framers of the Theft Act 1968. . . .

A second objection to the decision in *Hinks* is that it opens the door to inappropriate prosecutions. Counsel for the appellant in *Hinks* offered four examples which, in his view, illustrated the 'absurd and grotesque results' that would follow if the appeal were to be dismissed. Once again Lord Steyn was not convinced. He pointed out that the House of Lords in *Gomez* could not have overlooked the consequences of its decision and he said that, in any event, a prosecution was hardly likely to be brought in such cases and, if it were brought, would be 'likely to founder' because the jury would not be persuaded that there was dishonesty in the required *(Ghosh)* sense of that term or would conclude that under section 2(1)(a) of the Theft Act 1968 the transferee believed that he had a legal right to deprive the transferor of the property.

A third objection to *Hinks* is that it pares down excessively the *actus reus* of theft: indeed, some have argued that the combined effect of *Hinks* and *Gomez* is to reduce the *actus reus* of theft to 'vanishing point'. Of course, as the *actus reus* of the crime shrinks, so the role played by the *mens rea* concept of dishonesty will necessarily increase: it will have to take much more of the strain of filtering out cases that ought not to be regarded as theft from those that are clearly theftuous. This, in turn, generates two interconnecting objections to the *Gomez/Hinks* position: one based on the rule of law; the other on the harm principle.

---

[141] Phillips, Walsh, and Dobson (2001: 50).   [142] Paragraph 5.52.

It is a foundational (although not an unqualified) principle of our criminal law that citizens ought to be able to predict in advance whether or not their actions or omissions will fall foul of criminal prohibitions. Honouring this principle enhances a number of significant rule of law values: it imposes constraints on the use of arbitrary power; it goes some way towards ensuring that state authorities show proper respect for human dignity and autonomy; it assists citizens who wish to plan for the future; and it increases human freedom by allowing citizens to choose effectively between various life options. Relying on dishonesty to take most of the definitional strain in the crime of theft is said to work against these values because it is far from easy to predict in advance whether one's actions will or will not be adjudged dishonest. This difficulty is compounded in English law by the fact that the Court of Appeal has held that dishonesty is a matter for the jury. Unless a trial judge can conclude that there is no evidence upon which the jury could properly regard the defendant as dishonest he must put the issue to them: he cannot direct the jury to convict, nor can he withdraw the issue of dishonesty from them on the basis that the defendant was patently dishonest. Where the jury does require some assistance they should be advised on the basis of the test laid out in *R v. Ghosh* which, if given at all, should be given *ipsissima verba*. . . .

Because different juries may take different views about what the ordinary standards of reasonable and honest people require, the *Ghosh* test is said to be too unpredictable in its outcome to do the work now required or it by *Gomez* and *Hinks*. There are, however, arguments that can be made in its support. Richard Tur, for example, has defended the legal role of 'standard-bearing concepts' like dishonesty on the basis that they help to 'guard against an academic tendency to convert questions of practical moral philosophy into technical questions exclusively determined by the law.' When assessing the strength of this argument much will turn on the empirical question of whether there is in fact an identifiable and vivid community norm of 'dishonesty'. If there is, then the benefits of relying on it to take much of the definitional strain in the crime of theft may be sufficient to outweigh the disadvantages of vagueness and unpredictability that may be inherent in a *Ghosh* direction. If there is not, then the rule of law argument against *Hinks* (and for that matter *Gomez*) may be conclusive, although it should also be remembered that incorporating a thicker concept of appropriation into the law of theft in an attempt to counter excessive reliance on dishonesty may not achieve the desired result of an overall reduction in vagueness and unpredictability: for it could be that a thicker concept of appropriation will throw up as many problems of interpretation for judges or juries as the ruling in *Hinks*.

A connected argument against *Hinks* derives from the role of the liberal 'harm principle'. This states that in a liberal society criminalisation is justified only if it serves to prevent harm. The principle operates as a principle of exclusion: it identifies activities that ought not to be criminalised because their criminalisation cannot be shown to serve the goal of preventing harm. The objection to *Hinks* is that it breaches the harm principle because it expands the scope of the offence of theft to include cases where no civil wrong has been committed. Consider, for example, the case of a shopper who, with theftuous intent, takes an incorrectly priced pair of shoes from a sale rack in the hope that when she reaches the checkout she will be charged the lower amount. What the shopper does, it is argued, is nothing more than a 'harmless preparatory activity'. Yet, following *Gomez* and *Hinks*, she will have committed the crime of theft.

Two points can be made in response to this argument; both are controversial. The first is that there are good grounds for thinking that the conditions of the harm principle are met not only where an activity is itself harmful but also where it is a member of a class of acts that *tend* to cause harm. Hence it is false to conclude that the actions of the dishonest shopper described in the preceding paragraph will not satisfy the requirements of the harm principle:

for even if they were not directly harmful they were clearly members of a class of acts which have a propensity to cause harm. The second point is that, in any case, the harm principle does not say that only harmful wrongs may be criminalised. Rather, it states that even harmless wrongs may be criminalised if criminalisation diminishes their occurrence and if their wider occurrence would detract from other people's prospects—for example, by diminishing some public good, such as people's sense of ease with their living environment, or their ability to enjoy public spaces, or their use of commercial facilities, such as shops, or the degree of mutual respect that prevails in public culture at large. Once the harm principle is understood in this way it becomes possible to see why, even if the main reason for criminalising theft is to protect property rights, it may nonetheless be justifiable to extend the crime of theft to cases where no property right has been infringed. This is because a State's failure to criminalise wrongs that do not infringe property rights may itself undermine those rights or indeed some other public good.

A fourth objection to *Hinks* is that it brings the criminal law into conflict with the civil law. Lord Steyn gave this argument the same short shrift that he had given to arguments based on the possibility of inappropriate prosecutions and the intentions of the framers of the 1968 Act. He agreed that 'in theory the two systems should be in perfect harmony' but said that in 'a practical world' there will sometimes be some disharmony between them, especially as their purposes are 'somewhat different'. He added, moreover, (and in this he was influenced by a closely-argued article written by Simon Gardner) that 'it would be wrong to assume on *a priori* grounds' that if there was a disharmony it was the criminal law rather than the civil law that was defective. He concluded therefore that the tension between the civil and the criminal law was not a factor which justified a departure from the law as stated in *Lawrence* and *Gomez*.

But is this conclusion too quick? Professors Beatson and Simester certainly think that it is. In their view any extension of the law of theft to include unimpeachable transfers 'risks seriously distorting the law of property'. At the heart of their position is the claim that *Hinks* leaves the law on the horns of an uncomfortable dilemma. On the one hand the conflict between civil and criminal law could be resolved by requiring the civil law to yield: the existence of the criminal law wrong could, as it were, 'trump' the normal civil law rules, thus rendering an otherwise valid transaction voidable. But such a solution, Beatson and Simester assert, 'cannot be taken seriously'. Property offences are designed to protect property rights and if we were to allow the law governing property offences to trump civil law rules, that dependence would be broken and property crimes would be left with 'no rationale'. On the other hand if we attempt to avoid this apparently unpleasant consequence by leaving the civil law unchanged we will be impaled on the second horn of the dilemma, for we will have to accept that 'the principle that no-one may benefit by his wrong would [in these circumstances] have immediately to be abandoned'.

Beatson and Simester argue, in other words, that *Hinks* forces us to choose between abandoning a well-founded principle of civil law and divorcing property offences from their underlying rationale. Since each alternative is highly unattractive *Hinks* must, they conclude, have been wrongly decided. But, despite its ingenuity, this argument is mistaken. It is, as we have already seen, false to assume that, if the law allows a property offence to be committed without a property right having been infringed, then the link between property offences and property rights will necessarily have been broken. Beatson and Simester's error arises because they fail to see that even without breaching a recognised proprietary right the criminalised act may nonetheless have had a *tendency* to undermine property rights, either directly by attacking the interests that they protect, or indirectly by weakening an established system of property rights and so threatening the public good that that system represents. In either case the justification for criminalising the act may still be the protection of property rights, even though in this instance no property right has been violated.

For this reason there is no necessary threat to the underlying rationale of property offences if the law of theft is extended to cover otherwise unimpeachable transfers. Nor is there a threat to that rationale if a crime committed in these circumstances is able to 'trump' the normal civil law rules thus rendering an otherwise valid transfer voidable. In fact, the law of property has long since acknowledged such a possibility. It does so by giving legal effect to the principle that 'no-one may benefit from his own wrong'. The principle is both limited in its application and relatively weak: first, it applies only where there has been a 'wrong'; second, even where there has been a wrong, the principle is often redundant because the wrong itself will generate a cause of action that is, on its own, sufficient to strip the wrongdoer of his benefit; third, the principle is of limited weight and hence may easily be overridden or excluded by other considerations; fourth, even where operative, the principle usually works by estopping a wrongdoer from relying on the wrongful transaction rather than by creating a new cause of action in some other party; and, fifth, even when not outweighed, the principle need not require that the wrongdoer be stripped of all the benefits he obtained from his wrongdoing: a partial restitution may be all that is required to meet its demands. That said, however, the 'no benefit principle' comes into its own when a criminal wrong has been committed which is not based on a civil law wrong. In these circumstances, driven by a criminal law wrong but not by a civil law wrong, the principle can result in a thief such as Hinks being stripped of (at least some of) the benefits obtained through her wrongdoing. When this happens the civil law is, in a sense, required to 'yield' to the criminal law: if it had not been for the criminal wrong no restitution would have been possible. But this is not an indication of an unacceptable conflict between the civil and the criminal law. Nor is it an indication that there has been a 'serious distortion' of the law of property. Rather, it is an indication that both the criminal law and the law of property have (wisely) chosen to give legal effect to an important moral proposition.

In the following extract Alan Bogg and John Stanton-Ife take up the argument in the last paragraph of the above extract, that because the transfer was valid in civil law there was no harm to the victim. They suggest that even if a transfer was valid, it can be seen as harmful to the victim if it involves exploitation:

A.L. Bogg and J. Stanton-Ife, 'Theft as Exploitation' (2003) *Legal Studies* 402 at 415–16

The prosecution alleged that after having befriended the victim, Hinks manipulated or coerced him to donate his life savings and a television set to her. The victim . . . was a vulnerable individual of limited intelligence, said to be trusting, generous and exceptionally naïve. The defendant had taken unfair advantage of the victim's vulnerability, and abused his trust, in order to procure the transfer of his property. In taking unfair advantage of the victim and abusing his trust, the defendant had exploited the victim.[143] Exploitation is a wrong, though the degree of wrongfulness will depend on a number of features: the manner in which the victim is used, the characteristics that are utilised, and the way in which the

---

143 On the nature of exploitation, see Feinberg (1988: 176–210).

exploitation allocates gains and losses. It is most wrongful if the manner of use involves coercion, deception or manipulation; if the characteristics used are moral virtues or particular vulnerabilities; and if the exploiter makes extensive gains at the expense of the victim's losses. All of these features were present in *Hinks*: the deployment of manipulation in a predatory and acquisitive manner, the taking advantage of the victim's trust and vulnerability, allowing the defendant to make huge financial gain at the expense of the victim's losses.

Critics may respond in Bogg and Stanton-Ife's arguments by claiming that *Hinks* might have engaged in exploitation and this should be criminal, but it is not the crime of theft.[144]

QUESTIONS

1. If you think the decision in *Hinks* is wrong, should Parliament nevertheless introduce special legislation to protect vulnerable people from financial exploitation (for evidence of the widespread financial abuse of elderly people see Brogden and Nijhar (2000))? Or would such legislation be subject to many of the objections that *Hinks* is?

2. If a company's directors pay themselves such a high salary that it is regarded as dishonest, should they be guilty of theft?

9 TEMPORARY APPROPRIATION

As noted in Part I the present law requires there to be an intention of permanent deprivation for there to be theft. A taking intended to be a borrowing will not be a theft (unless it falls within section 6). The main justification for the law's approach is that borrowings are best dealt with under the civil law and are not sufficiently serious to justify the intervention of the criminal law.[145] Although the victim of a temporary appropriation may have lost the ability to use the item for a period of time that is not as serious as an outright taking.[146]

In the following passage Glanville Williams sets out the case for stating that temporary appropriations should amount to theft:

G. Williams, 'Temporary Appropriation should be Theft' [1981] *Criminal Law Review* 129 at 131–3, 137, 138

The general argument for changing the law

Suppose that a person removes a small piece of sculpture from a private exhibition, or a valuable book from a University library, and returns it after a year. During that time it has of course been lost to its owner; and both the owner and the police have been put to trouble. If the owner has made a claim upon an insurer or bailee, and been compensated on the basis of total loss, he may even find that the insurer or bailee claims the right to sell the article

---

[144] Simester and Sullivan (2005: 180).

[145] Tigar (1984), examining the history of the law of theft, has seen a shift from the protection of possession to the protection of property. This shift may explain why temporary interferences in possession are no longer seen as sufficient to justify the attentions of the criminal law.

[146] Wilson (2002: 23).

when it is recovered, so that the owner loses it. The taker of the article may use it in such a way as to put it at risk, or he may make a profit from it, or he may return it in an impaired condition; and if he is a person of no substance the owner's civil remedy against him will be an insufficient penalty.

The intent required by the present law of theft puts the jury or magistrates in a difficult situation. The taker may himself have no clear idea when he takes the things whether he is going to return it or not. I have recently seen a circular from the librarian of a library for undergraduates pointing out that in the last three years as many books have been lost to the library as have been bought for it. Most of these losses, he thinks, can be accounted for by 'careless borrowing which grows with time into theft. That is to say, people who borrow the books without signing them out, intending but in the end never bothering to return them.'

If a person has gone off with the property of another, and upon being apprehended and charged with theft swears that he meant to return it, is his statement to be accepted or not? To accept it too readily gives guilty defendants an easy line of escape; to reject it carries the risk of convicting people who are technically innocent, even though they are morally guilty because they have taken the article dishonestly. In 1953 an art student removed a bronze statuette of Psyche by Rodin from a picture gallery, but later returned it anonymously with a note saying: 'There was no mercenary intent behind my abduction of this exquisite creature. I merely wished to live with her for a while.' Had he been caught with the statuette, the jury might justifiably have disbelieved his explanation, even though, as the event showed, it was true. Technically, there would have been a miscarriage of justice, though not in the fullest sense of the expression. Why should not the dishonest taking be sufficient to consti-tute the offence of theft, thus relieving the prosecution of a very difficult burden of proof? . . .

In *Warner*,[147] a shop assistant, who had been annoyed by employees next door, took their tools and hid them in the shop. When asked by a policeman about the tools he denied all knowledge of them. When the tools were eventually discovered he explained that he had only meant to keep them for about an hour to get his own back. The jury convicted him of theft, but the conviction was quashed on appeal for misdirection, the Court of Appeal reaf-firming the rule that theft required an intent to deprive the owner permanently. This was a trivial case, and if the defendant had not lied to the police he would probably not have been prosecuted. It illustrates the point, however, that a person may take another's property by way of revenge without committing an offence; and he will not commit an offence even if he causes great loss and keeps the property a considerable time, if he intended to give it back in the end. . . .

The effect of changing the law

If the law is changed in the way here suggested, the result will be to simplify it and to preclude unmeritorious defences. It may also have some small effect upon public morality if it is brought home to people that any dishonest taking is theft. Just as supermarkets now exhibit notices saying that 'shoplifting is theft,' so libraries could announce that 'unauthorised removal of books is theft.' . . .

The objection of triviality

It may be that the reader, while accepting some of the arguments in this article, has throughout been afflicted by one other doubt. Is it seriously suggested that trivial cases of dishonestly using the property of another should be subject to prosecution as theft? The

---

147 (1971) 54 Cr App R 93 (CA).

absurdity of this was an argument that appealed powerfully to the majority of the Criminal Law Revision Committee. It was elaborated by Lord Stonham, speaking for the government, in the debate on the Theft Bill in the House of Lords. He gave, as examples of trivial cases, using one's neighbour's lawn mower against his expressed wishes, taking a book from a public library beyond one's borrowing limit, and using a friend's dinner jacket without his consent.

The argument about trivial cases is frequently used to oppose extensions of the law, but it is never conclusive in itself, because practically every offence covers *some* trivial matters. If an offence is needed to deal with serious misconduct, that is sufficient to justify it. Even the present law could be abused by prosecuting for trivial thefts, but in practice a sensible discretion is generally exercised. The Canadian experience bears out the view that a law of *furtum usus* is unlikely to be used oppressively. . . .

FURTHER READING

Bein, D. (1968), 'The Theft of Use and the Elements of "Intention to Deprive Permanently" in Larceny', *Israel Law Review* 3: 368.

Williams, G. (1981a), 'Temporary Appropriation Should be Theft', *Criminal Law Review* 129.

10 DISHONESTY

As has been indicated in our discussion on *Hinks*, after that decision many commentators feel that appropriation has been almost a token requirement, and that dishonesty has become the key notion in theft. To some this is all the more concerning because of the rather loose definition of dishonesty used by the law. In the following passage Edward Griew sets out some of the arguments against the current law's definition of 'dishonest'.[148] He distinguishes between: the *Feely* question 'was what was done dishonest according to the ordinary standards of reasonable and honest people' and the *Ghosh* question 'must the defendant have realized that what he was doing was dishonest according to those standards?':

E. Griew, 'Dishonesty: The Objections to *Feely* and *Ghosh*' [1985] *Criminal Law Review* 341

A. Objections to the *Feely* question

. . .

A1. More, longer and more difficult trials

If the law is right in principle, so be it; the fact that it tends to multiply and prolong trials cannot be a decisive objection. But as an addition to other objections it is of such practical importance that it should have pride of place. There are several distinct points.

---

[148] S. Henry (1978) discusses the ambiguities amongst public opinion over what is dishonest or not.

(a) The question tends to increase the number of trials. Whereas a different approach to the dishonesty issue might make clear that given conduct was dishonest as a matter of law and therefore constituted an offence, the *Feely* question leaves the issue open. It may be worth a defendant's while to take the chance with the jury. . . .

(b) The question tends to complicate and lengthen contested cases. For it is difficult to say of any evidence relating to the defendant's state of mind or to the special circumstances in which he acted that is irrelevant to the *Feely* case. Moreover, it must be in the interests of some defendants to extend and complicate trials in order to obfuscate the issue. . . .

(c) At the end of a trial the jury may have to be asked not simply whether the defendant acted with the state of mind he claims to have had, or in other circumstances that, as he suggests, may have rendered his act not dishonest, but also (if he may have done so) whether his act with that state of mind, or in those circumstances, was dishonest, was dishonest according to ordinary standards. If these matters are not kept separate the jury may be seriously misled. But their careful separation shows the complexity of the direct that the *Feely* question will dictate in some cases. . . .

(d) The separate matters just referred to, that may need to figure in the judge's direction, must then be handled by the jury in their deliberations. They may find them hard to keep separate. The issues we present to juries should be as simple as possible; jury service, after all, imposes tasks on ordinary people that they are not accustomed to discharge. The *Feely* question involves complications that we are not justified in supposing that all jurors are competent to handle.

A2. Inconsistent decisions

The *Feely* question carries an unacceptable risk of inconsistency of decision. This objection has been voiced by many critics. The problem of inconsistency is likely, of course, to affect only a small proportion of cases. In most cases the issue is one as to the facts: what did D do? What was his state of mind? Once the facts are found there will usually be only one plausible answer to the *Feely* question. It is only a minority of cases that the matter will truly admit of argument. But within this crucial marginal group different juries as the presumptive embodiment of ordinary decent standards, may take different views of essentially indistinguishable cases. The law of the relevant offence will then vary as between different defendants. This must be unacceptable.

A3. Fiction of community norms

The *Feely* question implies the existence of a relevant community norm. In doing so it glosses over difference of age, class and cultural background which combine to give the character of fiction to the idea of a generally shared sense of the boundary between honesty and dishonesty. This is the more obvious in a society with the range of cultural groups that ours now has; and it is the more relevant since jury service was extended to the generality of electors between 18 and 65. It is simply naïve to suppose—surely no on does suppose—that there is, in respect of the dishonesty question, any such single thing as 'the standards of ordinary decent people.' . . .

A4. 'Dishonesty' as an 'ordinary word'

The foregoing objection to the *Feely* question is closely related to another. The jury are to consult their sense of ordinary standards because the word 'dishonestly' is 'in common use.' Jurors in their own lives 'have to decide what is and what is not dishonest'; they do not 'require the help of a judge to tell them what amounts to dishonest.' . . . What must be expressed here is a doubt about the 'ordinary word.' It simply does not follow from the truth that a word such as 'dishonestly' is an ordinary word that all speakers of the language share the same sense of its application or non-application in particular contexts. . . .

A5. Specialised cases

The *Feely* question is in any case unsuitable where the context of the case is a specialised one, involving intricate financial activities or dealings in a specialised market. It is neither reasonable nor rational to expect ordinary people to judge as 'dishonest' or 'not dishonest' conduct of which, for want of relevant experience, they cannot appreciate the contextual flavour. . . .

A6. Ordinary dishonest jurors

The general understanding is that the jury may be taken to represent the 'ordinary decent people' to whom the *Feely* question refers. . . . Yet a vast number of what must surely be theft, handling and minor fraud offences are committed by 'ordinary' even 'ordinary decent,' people such as serve upon juries: theft at work ('perks'), handling stole goods being offered in the neighbourhood ('from off the back of a lorry'), inflation of expenses claims, inaccuracy or concealment in the income tax return. These ordinary people, as jurors, will either apply their own standards, as being the prevalent standards of which they know; or they will demand of their defendants higher standards than they themselves attain. To the extent (if at all) that the former occurs, the Court of Appeal in *Feely* and *Ghosh* will have achieved a reduction in the scope of dishonesty offences which it certainly did not intend. We ought not, on the other hand, to view the latter, presumably more common, occurrence, with complacency. It is perfectly acceptable for the law to require a jury to *apply* a standard higher than its own; it is not acceptable that the law should invite a jury so *impose* such a standard by an act of creative hypocrisy. The law in effect expects many jurors, in relation to very common kinds of offences, to have one conception of ordinary standards outside court and another conception inside. This is disreputable.

A7. 'Anarchic' verdicts

The *Feely* question, offered without qualification to the jury, is 'a question of moral estimation without guidelines' and permits ' "anarchic" verdicts which are not technically perverse.' A jury without stars or compass cannot be accused of bad navigation. The direction it takes may be deplorable, but cannot be wrong. A consequence of this, it has been pointed out, is that members of unpopular groups may receive inadequate protection from the law. . . .

A8. What is 'dishonest' should be a matter of law

Whether an individual defendant was dishonest is, of course, a question for the jury. But it should be so only in the sense that the jury will find the facts upon the strength of which, applying legal principles, they will be able to say whether the defendant acted dishonestly. Whether the facts that they find constitute a case of 'dishonesty' within the meaning of that word in the particular legal context is a matter of legal principle upon which they should be able to turn to the law for clear guidance.

   How that guidance is achieved is not necessarily an easy question. But the fact that it is not easy does not justify a refusal to answer it—whether in general terms of case by case. A decision has to be made about the role that the word 'dishonestly' has in the specification of offences. It might have none except to exclude from the scope of offences cases of claim

of right (as well as any, or any other, cases expressly excluded by statute as not cases of dishonesty). In addition to such excluded cases, however, might be those perceived by the judge as involving 'no moral obloquy'. In any such cases the judge would direct an acquittal, thereby making a precedent for the guidance of other courts. Another suggestion has been that in the case of theft 'dishonestly' might be interpreted to mean 'knowing that the appropriation will or may be detrimental to the interests of the owner in a significant practical way.'

. . .

A9. Dishonesty and defences

Leaving the dishonesty issue to the untutored application of community standards allows the issue a potentially unlimited function. The jury may be unwilling to condemn a defendant's conduct as 'dishonest' because they sympathise with his motive or are inclined to excuse what he did in the difficult circumstances in which he found himself; they may be still less willing if they are prepared to say that his conduct was justified in the circumstances. Thus the jury may create for their defendant a defence of necessity greater than any known to the law or a defence of pressure of circumstances where the law knows only a plea in mitigation. But the law of defences should develop in a disciplined way under judicial control, save indeed to the extent that it is statutorily defined.

. . .

A10. Inconsistency within the Theft Acts

The *Feely* question produces an inconsistency between theft and other offences in relation to a claim of right. One who appropriates property in the belief that he has in law the right to deprive the loser of it does not, as a matter of law, appropriate dishonestly. This principle is statutory. But no corresponding statutory principle is provided for any obtaining offence. The judges might have asserted such a principle, however, and could have been expected to do so but for *Feely* and *Ghosh*. As it is, they seem prepared to trust the jury to achieve the corresponding result for the individualise in response to a *Ghosh* direction. The result is that it is *not* theft to obtain at the point of knife what you think you are entitled to, whereas it *may not* be an offence under section 15 of the 1968 Act to obtain the same property by telling a lie—it is up to the jury to say.

A11. Extent of departure from previous law

. . .

B. Objections to the *Ghosh* question

. . .

B1. More, longer and more difficult trials

Compare objection A1. The *Ghosh* question (a) creates an additional ground for contested trials; (b) justifies the introduction of additional evidence; (c) further complicates the judge's direction; and (d) adds further to the complexity of the jury's task. There is no need to labour these points.

B2. Departure from previous law

. . .

B3. Inept correction of error

. . .

The confusion on this point in the *Ghosh* judgment is clear to see in the treatment of the hypothetical treatment of the hypothetical of a visitor from a foreign country where public transport is free. He travels on a bus without paying. Does he do so dishonestly? The courts says that 'his conduct, judged objectively by what he has done, is dishonest.' The error enters the argument at this point. It cannot be right, as the structure of the court's argument plainly implies, that the visitor's conduct would be regarded as dishonest by ordinary decent standards. If the jury knew that he believed public transport to be free, they would say that, according to ordinary standards, he had not behaved dishonestly. There is no need to go further; his 'state of mind' has already been taken into account. But the court, having declared him dishonest when 'judged objectively,' has to introduce a further 'subjective' element to rescue him. This leads to the question: 'Did he know it was dishonest?'—an entirely unnecessary question.

B4. Mistake of law

The *Ghosh* question 'allows something like a mistake of law to be a defence.' The question is a mere addendum to the *Feely* question; it is the answer to the latter that determines the view to be taken of the defendant's conduct as in principle criminal. The jury's apprehension of current standards makes law for the case; the defendant's misapprehension of those standards is indeed 'something like a mistake of law.' It is not strictly one, of course; his failure to realise that ordinary people would call his conduct dishonest means (taking *Ghosh* literally) that it is not dishonest.

B5. The 'Robin Hood defence'

A person may defend his attack on another's property by reference to a moral or political conviction as passionately held that he believed (so he claims) that 'ordinary decent' members of society would regard his conduct as proper, even laudable. It the asserted belief is treated as a claim to have been ignorant that the conduct was 'dishonest' by ordinary standards (and it has been assumed that it might be so treated), and if the jury think (as exceptionally they might) that the belief may have been held, *Ghosh*, produces an acquittal. The result is remarkable. Robin Hood must be a thief even if he things the whole of the right-thinking world is on his side.

B6. A further threat to standards

A person reared or moving in an environment in which it is generally treated as legitimate to take advantage of certain classes of people—perhaps bookmakers or employers—may plausibly claim that he did not realise that his conduct of which a member of such a class was a victim, was generally regarded as dishonest. It is no acceptable that a claim of that sort should be capable even of being advanced. It has been said that 'the [*Ghosh*] questions presents an even greater threat to the standard of honesty than the [*Feely* question].'

Those who support the present law can point to the fact that since *Ghosh* the meaning of dishonesty has not greatly troubled the courts. Interestingly, when the Law Commission sought comments on whether the law on dishonesty needs to be reformed the Magistrates'

Association were in favour of retaining the present law.[149] Whatever its theoretical problems it seems therefore to have provided a workable definition.[150] What, of course, we do not know is whether juries and magistrates actually follow the *Ghosh* direction, or whether they give dishonesty its 'normal' meaning. What the *Ghosh* test is trying to do is to seek a compromise between having a purely objective test for dishonesty which would simply ask whether the conduct was dishonest by the standards of the ordinary person and a subjective approach which would ask whether the defendant regarded his or her conduct as dishonest.

FURTHER READING

Campbell, K. (1984), 'The Test of Dishonesty in *R. v. Ghosh*', *Criminal Law Journal* 43: 349.

Elliott, D. (1982), 'Dishonesty in Theft: A Dispensable Concept', *Criminal Law Review* 395.

—— (1991), 'Directors' Theft and Dishonesty', *Criminal Law Review* 732.

Halpin, A. (1996), 'The Test for Dishonesty', *Criminal Law Review* 283.

—— (2004), *Definition in the Criminal Law* (Oxford: Hart), ch. 4.

Tur, R. (1985), 'Dishonesty and the Jury' in A. Phillips Griffiths (ed.), *Philosophy and Practice* (Oxford: OUP).

Wasik, M. (1977b), '*Mens Rea*, Motive and the Problem of "Dishonesty" in the Law of Theft', *Criminal Law Review* 543.

QUESTIONS

1. 'Once again the law of theft is in urgent need of simplification and modernization, so that a jury of twelve ordinary citizens do not have to grapple with concepts couched in the antiquated "franglais" of "choses in action", and scarce public resources in time and money are not devoted to hours of semantic argument divorced from the true merits of the case' (Bedlam LJ in *Hallam* [1995] *Criminal Law Review* 323). Do you agree? (In fairness it should be added, as Smith (1995) points out, that the Act uses the phrase 'things in action' not 'choses in action'.)

2. Do you think it possible to provide a better definition of dishonesty than that used in *Ghosh*?

3. Law Commission Report No. 276 (2002: para. 5.9) refers to a MORI poll in 1985 in which only 35 per cent of those questioned thought it dishonest to accept payment in cash to avoid payment of tax. But only 37 per cent of those questioned thought most people would regard it as honest. Does this indicate that it is sensible to leave questions of honesty to the jury?

11 ROBBERIES

The offence of robbery ranges from a carefully planned bank raid to a spur of the moment 'bag snatching'. In the popular imagination robbery has become synonymous with

---

[149] Law Commission Report No. 276 (2002: para. 5.14).

[150] Law Commission Report No. 276 (2002: para. 5.15) stated that there was no evidence that juries were producing inconsistent verdicts on similar facts.

'muggings', which have become a common part of urban life and cause such fear.[151] There is some justification for the fear: in 2004–5 there were 88,710 reported, although the BCS estimates there were 255,000 robberies.[152] The empirical evidence suggests that most robberies are often committed by groups and that two in every five robberies leave the victim with an injury.[153] Mobile phones have come to be closely linked with robberies. In the 2002/3 BCS survey 6.9 per cent of respondents had had their mobile phone stolen in the previous year. The courts have responded, and robberies of mobile phones can now attracted sentences of between three and five years, even for a first offence.[154]

In the following passage Andrew Ashworth outlines some of the difficulties with the legal definition of robbery:

A. Ashworth, 'Robbery Re-assessed' [2002] *Criminal Law Review* 851 at 855–7

The Law on Robbery

Several features of the offence [of robbery] require comment.

First, there are three ways of committing robbery—using force, putting someone in fear, or seeking to put someone in fear. This leaves no doubt about the relevance of imitation weapons to the definition of robbery; but, on the other hand, the various ways of committing the offence are not ranked in order of relative seriousness.

Secondly, and echoing a point already made in relation to statistical classification, the dividing line between robbery and theft is anything but robust. This is not necessarily a criticism of the legal definition, since many offences inevitably have fuzzy edges. But the term 'uses force' has been interpreted so as to include relatively slight force, such as barging into someone or tugging at a handbag in such a way that the owner's hand is pulled downwards. The effect is to label such offences as robbery rather than theft, and to put them in a category which has life imprisonment as the maximum penalty.

And thirdly, robbery is a single offence: 'robbery with violence' and armed robbery are not legal terms of art, however often they may appear in crime novels. The single offence is also extraordinarily broad. The maximum penalty for theft is seven years' imprisonment; but, where force or the threat of force is used in order to steal, the category of robbery covers everything from a push or a raised hand in order to snatch a bag, to the most violent robbery of a security vehicle with guns fired and so forth. The single maximum penalty, life imprisonment, covers the whole range. The contrast with other offences involving violence is stark. Although English law remains in a rather antiquated state, the Offences Against the Person Act 1861 provides a ladder of non-fatal crimes—common assault, assault occasioning actual bodily harm, unlawful wounding or grievous bodily harm, and wounding or grievous bodily harm with intent. The structure is desperately in need of modernisation: most modern penal codes grade their offences of violence according to differences in the seriousness of the harm done and differences in culpability, but current English law does so only imperfectly. However, no one has been heard to suggest that we should have a single offence of violence, such as 'using force on another person', to replace everything from common assault to wounding with intent. That would be rejected on many grounds—sentencing would be at large rather than graduated according to different maxima, the label would fail to distinguish

---

[151] Hall (1978).

[152] According to the British Crime Survey as detailed in J. Smith (2003: ch. 2).

[153] J. Smith (2003: ch. 2).

[154] *Attorney-General's References Nos. 4 and 7 of 2002* [2002] 2 Cr App R (S) 77.

the serious from the not-so-serious, the label would be useless for classification purposes (*e.g.* when assessing an offender's criminal record), and so on.

If we (rightly) reject a single offence of violence, should we not also object to such a broad and undifferentiated offence as robbery, based on using or threatening force of any degree? I would argue that the offence of robbery is objectionable because it fails to mark in a public way the distinction between a mere push and serious violence, and because the label 'robbery' is therefore too vague and too liable to stereotypical interpretations—some may assume that serious violence, or a weapon, was involved when this was not necessarily the case. It is often said that robbery is a serious offence, but that applies only to some robberies. There are some offences that involve a small theft with only slight violence that would not warrant more than a charge of assault or battery. Consideration must be given to dividing the offence, so as to mark out as particularly serious those robberies which involve the use or threat of significant violence.

Such an approach could also have a worthwhile practical and procedural consequence. At present all robberies are triable only on indictment. Again, this results in some offences being tried at a higher level than their separate elements (assault, theft) might warrant. Offences of assault occasioning actual bodily harm and section 20 wounding or grievous bodily harm are triable either way, as are offences of theft. If the essence of the offence would not otherwise justify a higher charge, it is surely questionable whether all robberies should go to the Crown Court. If some offences against the person are summary only or triable either way.

In seeking to define the wrong of robbery Simester and Sullivan suggest that in robbery a defendant 'communicates to [the victim] that, in her eyes, [the victim] matters not as a person but only as a source of wealth.'[155] Further, the crime has a wider social impact in that fear of mugging discourages people to walk freely through public space. They argue that it should not therefore be regarded as an aggravated theft, but rather as having a distinct wrong.

FURTHER READING

Andrews, J. (1966), 'Robbery', *Criminal Law Review* 524.

Ashworth, A. (2002d), 'Robbery Re-assessed', *Criminal Law Review* 851.

Matthews, R. (2002), *Armed Robbery* (Cullompton: Willan).

Smith, J. (2003), *The Nature of Personal Robbery* (London: Home Office).

---

[155] Simester and Sullivan (2005: 194).

9

DECEPTION

PART I: THE LAW ON DECEPTION

This chapter concerns offences which involve deception. The main deception offences are found in the Theft Acts 1968 and 1978. Before we look at them it is useful to consider the meaning of the term 'deception'.

1 WHAT IS A DECEPTION?

A deception is defined in section 15(4) of the Theft Act 1968, which states:

> For the purposes of this section 'deception' means any deception (whether deliberate or reckless) by words or conduct as to fact or as to law, including a deception as to the present intentions of the person using the deception or any other person.

The following are some key points about the meaning of a deception:

(1) *The statement must be untrue.* A statement that is true cannot be a deception.[1] If the defendant makes a statement which he or she believes to be untrue, but which is, in fact, true, there will be no deception, although in such circumstances there may be an attempted deception.

(2) *The victim must be deceived.* If the defendant makes an untruthful statement and the victim is aware the statement is untrue then there is no deception.[2] So if Clarissa tells Jamey that her cakes are made from entirely fresh ingredients and Jamey, knowing this to be untrue, still decides to buy a cake, there is no deception. Again in such a case there may be an attempted deception. Where the allegation is that a company has been deceived it has to be shown that a person whose state of mind represented that of the company (e.g. a senior manager) has been deceived.[3]

---

[1] *Mandry and Wooster* [1973] 1 WLR 1232 (CA).
[2] *Hensler* (1870) Cox CC 570; *Deller* (1952) 36 Cr App R 184.
[3] *Rozeik* [1996] 1 WLR 159 (CA).

The requirement that a victim must be deceived probably means that a machine cannot be deceived.[4] If someone, for example, uses a false coin to obtain a chocolate bar from a vending machine, the correct offence would be theft of the chocolate bar, not obtaining the chocolate bar by deception.[5] However, there is no easy answer to what offence, if any, is committed by a person who uses a credit card which she is not authorized to use to access services on the internet.[6]

(3) *Deceptions can be by means of words or conduct.* The well-known case of *Barnard*,[7] involved a defendant who went into a shop (in the 1830s) wearing an academic cap and gown of the kind typically worn by members of Oxford University at that time. The shopkeeper assumed he was a member of the University and therefore gave a discounted price. It was held that by wearing this garb the defendant was representing that he was a member of the University. As he was not, this amounted to a deception. A more modern example is where a person walks through a staff entrance of a night-club (seeking to avoid payment of the entrance fee). She is representing that she is a member of staff and so this could be deceptive. Of course, if no one sees her enter the nightclub through that entrance then there is no deception because no one was led into thinking something untrue.

(4) *Deceptions can be express or implied.* The deception can be implied from conduct or words. If the defendant offers his car for sale, he will be impliedly saying that he owns the car. If he does not this amounts to a deception. Similarly, as we shall see, when people use credit cards or cheques they are implied to represent that they are authorized to use them.

The straightforward test in deciding whether there is an implied statement is: how would a reasonable person understand the act or words?[8] So, if a person orders a meal at a restaurant a reasonable person will interpret the order as including the implied statement that the diner intends to pay for the meal, and so if that is not his or her true intention then the order will amount to a deception.[9]

It is not always easy to determine whether or not to imply a statement. Consider the following case which concerned whether to imply into a charge for building work a representation that it was a reasonable sum to demand:[10]

R v Silverman
(1987) 86 Cr App R 213 (CA)[11]

Michael Silverman was convicted on several counts of obtaining property by deception under section 15(1) of the Theft Act 1968. The victims were two sisters in their 60s who had come to know and trust Michael Silverman and his firm in carrying out building work. After their mother's death Silverman had recommended various building jobs be

---

[4] *Davies v Flackett* [1973] RTR 8; *Wise and Candy, The Independent*, 21 Aug. 1990; *Goodwin* [1996] Crim LR 262 (CA); *Re Holmes* [2005] Crim LR 229 (DC). See also Law Commission Report No. 276 (2002: para. 3.34).

[5] If no property is acquired from the machine then the defendant may still be guilty of abstracting electricity (Theft Act 1968, s. 13), obtaining services by deception (Theft Act 1978, s. 1), or making off without payment (Theft Act 1968, s. 3).

[6] Law Commission Report No. 276 (2002: para. 3.34).   [7] (1837) 7 C & P 784, 173 ER 342.

[8] Although some representations are implied as a matter of law, e.g. under the Sale of Goods Act 1979.

[9] *DPP v Ray* [1974] AC 370 (HL).

[10] Of course, there is no difficulty where the builder expressly states that the price is a reasonable one: *Jeff and Bassett* (1966) 51 Cr App R 28 (CA).

[11] [1987] Crim LR 574.

done and charged or quoted sums which were grossly excessive. He claimed that there was no deception because he never stated that the fees charged were reasonable.

Lord Justice Watkins

Mr Hopmeier [counsel for the appellant] has argued, first, that the appellant made no representations to the complainants. He had not shrunk from conceding that the appellant was dishonest. He had submitted that the appellant quoted the sisters for the work to be done but that it was open to them either to accept or reject the quotation upon such advice as they might seek and perhaps in the light of tenders by others, and that the appellant was in much the same position as anyone else who is asked to quote for work to be done. He has argued that it is a dangerous concept to introduce into the criminal law that an excessively high quotation amounts to a false representation under s 15 (1) of the Theft Act 1968. In certain circumstances that submission may we think be well founded. But whether a quotation amounts to false representation must depend upon the circumstances.

It seems clear to us that the complainants, far from being worldly wise, were unquestionably gullible. Having left their former home, they relied implicitly upon the word of the appellant about their requirements in their maisonette. In such circumstances of mutual trust, one part depending upon the other for fair and reasonable conduct, the criminal law may apply if one party takes dishonest advantage of the other by representing as a fair charge that which he but not the other knows is dishonestly excessive.

In our view, the Judge, in directing the jury, dealt with the matter accurately at the outset. At p 3 of the transcript he said:

'So what are the essentials about which you have to be sure? Well, there are really four of them and they are these. First of all, the prosecution have got to rove that there was a deception, and the deception alleged here is a false representation that the said sum of £2,875 was a fair and proper charge for the work. The deception must operate on the mind of the person deceived, in this case the two sisters. The second essential is this, that the deception must be made dishonestly, and you, members of the jury, must be satisfied that it was in fact made dishonestly. Thirdly, the prosecution must prove that as a result of that deception the defendant obtained property belonging to another, in this case the cheque. Fourthly, it must be done with the intention of permanently depriving the others, that is to say, the sisters, of it. These are the four essentials which have got to be proved in respect of count 1, and the same four essentials have got to be proved in respect of each count.'

The Judge went on to advise the jury perfectly properly of what he stated was a sensible way of approaching the matter, and referred with equal propriety to the relationship that had obtained between the sisters and the appellant and the firm which had employed him over a very long period of time. He encouraged the jury, rightly, in our view, to regard the matter of establishing the four essentials with the background circumstances very well in mind.

As to directing the jury upon what the prosecution had to prove and the circumstances in which they might succeed, we find no fault whatever in the way in which the Judge directed them. There was material for a finding that there had been false representation although it is true that the appellant had said nothing at the time he made his representations to encourage the sisters to accept the quotations. He applied no pressure upon them, and apart from mentioning the actual prices to be charged was silent as to other matters that may have arisen for question in their minds.

On the matter of representation we have been referred to *DPP v Ray* [1974] AC 370, which concerned someone leaving a restaurant without paying for a meal. At p 379 Lord Reid said:

'So the accused after he changed his mind, must have done something intended to induce the waiter to believe that he still intended to pay before he left. Deception, to my mind, implies something positive'.

Mr Hopmeier submits that nothing positive was done in this case. Lord Reid continued:

'It is quite true that a man intending to deceive can build up a situation in which his silence is as eloquent as an express statement'.

Here the situation had been built up over a long period of time. It was a situation of mutual trust and the appellant's silence on any matter other than the sums to be charged were, we think, as eloquent as if he had said: 'What is more, I can say to you that we are going to get no more than a modest profit out of this'.

There is, we think, no foundation for the criticism of the Judge in the first ground of appeal nor any substance in this ground in law.

. . .

Appeal allowed on other grounds.

(5) *The deception can be as to fact, law, or intention.* Although statements of fact, law, and intention can be deception, some fine lines must be drawn between deceptions and breaches of promise or statement of opinion:

(i) Distinguishing breach of promise and deceptions. Imagine that Adam bought Eve an engagement ring after she said that she intended to marry him. If at the time of the engagement Eve had no intention of marrying Adam this could amount to a deception, and so she could be convicted of obtaining the engagement ring by deception. However, if Eve had, at the time she received the ring, intended to marry Adam, but had later changed her mind and not married him there would be no deception. This is because she had not lied to Adam, just broken her promise.

(ii) Statements of opinion and deception. The problem here can be seen with an example of a publican who puts up a sign saying 'I sell the best grapefruit juice in the world'. This statement could be seen in two ways: either an express represen-tation that this grapefruit juice is the best in the world or a statement of opinion, namely that in the publican's view the grapefruit juice is the best in the world. In this context it is likely that this statement will be seen as one of opinion. In that case there is a deception only if it can be shown that it is not in fact the publican's view.[12] Even if the prosecution could persuade a judge that a different grapefruit juice was better than the one promoted by the publican there would be no deception if the publican was honestly making a statement of opinion, rather than fact.

The more precise the statement and the greater the extent of the knowledge of the speaker the more likely it is that this will not be a statement of opinion, but a statement of fact. A leading auction house which says that a table is seventeenth century is likely to be making a statement of fact; the same statement made by a person selling the table at a village jumble sale may be regarded as making a

---

[12] *Edgington v Fitzmaurice* (1885) 29 Ch D 459; *King* [1979] Crim LR 122 (CA).

statement of opinion. The position may be further complicated by the fact that the court may interpret the statement as one of opinion, but impliedly represent that the defendant has reasonable grounds for his opinion.[13]

(6) *Silence can be deceptive.* Silence can be the basis of a deception because it can amount to an implied statement. Here are two examples from the case law:

(i) In *Firth*[14] a doctor sent some patients to an NHS hospital. The standard practice was that if he was referring private patients to an NHS hospital he would state that they were private, but if they were NHS patients nothing would be said. In this case he said nothing, even though in fact the patients were private. This silence was held to be an implied statement that the patients were NHS patients. As this was untrue it amounted to a deception.[15]

(ii) In *Rai*[16] the defendant applied for a grant to install a downstairs bathroom for his infirm mother. The grant was approved by the council. Shortly afterwards the defendant's mother died, although the defendant did not tell the council this and the building went ahead. It was held that the defendant had deceived the council. Although when he applied for the grant his statement about his mother was true, that statement had become untrue and the defendant's silence amounted to a deception. One way of seeing this case is one of omission. Having made a statement upon which the victim is relying the defendant is under a duty to correct the victim's misunderstanding.[17]

The following case demonstrates how the courts sometimes struggle to find a deception, even though it is clear the defendant is acting dishonestly.

Director of Public Prosecutions v Ray
[1974] AC 370 (HL)[18]

Roger Ray ordered a meal at a Chinese restaurant for himself and three friends. At the time he placed the order he intended to pay for the meal. After eating the meal he changed his mind about paying for it and decided to leave without doing so. The group sat at their table for ten minutes until the waiter went out of the dining area, at which point they left the restaurant at speed. He was convicted of dishonestly obtaining a pecuniary advantage contrary to section 16(1).[19]

Lord Macdermott

[Lord Macdermott explained that the case raised two questions:]
First, do the facts justify a finding that the respondent practised a deception? And secondly, if he did, was his evasion of the debt obtained by that deception?
The first of these questions involves nothing in the way of words spoken or written. If there was deception on the part of the respondent it was by his conduct in the course of an

[13] *Smith v Land & House Property Corp* (1884) 28 Ch D 7.   [14] [1990] Crim LR 326 (CA).
[15] The offence involved obtaining an exemption from liability under the Theft Act 1978, s. 2(1)(c).
[16] [2000] 1 Cr App R 242 (CA).
[17] An analogy could be drawn with *Miller* [1983] 2 AC 161 (HL).
[18] [1973] 3 All ER 131, [1974] 3 WLR 359, (1974) 58 Cr App R 130.
[19] N.B. since this case s. 16 has been amended.

extremely common form of transaction which, because of its nature, leaves much to be implied for conduct. Another circumstance affecting the ambit of this question lies in the fact that, looking only to the period after the meal had been eaten and the respondent and his companions had decided to evade payment, there is nothing that I can find in the discernible conduct of the respondent which would suffice in itself to show that he was then practising a deception. No doubt he and the others stayed in their seats until the waiter went into the kitchen and while doing so gave all the appearance of ordinary customers. But in my opinion, nothing in this or in anything else which occurred after the change of intention went far enough to afford proof of deception. The picture, as I see it, presented by this last stage of the entire transaction, is simply that of a group which had decided to evade payment and were awaiting the opportunity to do so.

There is, however, no sound reason that I can see for restricting the enquiry to this final phase. One cannot, so to speak, draw a line through the transaction at the point where the intention changed and search for evidence of deception only in what happened before that or only in what happened after that. In my opinion the transaction must for this purpose be regarded in its entirety, beginning with the respondent entering the restaurant and ordering his meal and ending with his running out without paying. The different stages of the transaction are all linked and it would be quite unrealistic to treat them in isolation.

Starting then at the beginning one finds in the conduct of the respondent in entering and ordering his meal evidence that he impliedly represented that he had the means and the intention of paying for it before he left. That the respondent did make such a representation was not in dispute and in the absence of evidence to the contrary it would be difficult to reach a different conclusion. If this representation had then been false and matters had proceeded thereafter as they did (but without any change of intention) a conviction for the offence charged would, in my view, have had ample material to support it. But as the representation when originally made in this case was not false there was therefore no deception at that point. Then the meal is served and eaten and the intention to evade the debt replaces the intention to pay. Did this change of mind produce a deception?

My Lords, in my opinion it did. I do not base this conclusion merely on the change of mind that had occurred for that in itself was not manifest at the time and did not amount to 'conduct' on the part of the respondent. But it did falsify the representation which had already been made because that initial representation must, in my view, be regarded not as something then spent and past but as a continuing representation which remained alive and operative and had already resulted in the respondent and his defaulting companions being taken on trust and treated as ordinary, honest customers. It covered the whole transaction up to and including payment and must therefore, in my opinion, be considered as continuing and still active at the time of the change of mind. When that happened, with the respondent taking (as might be expected) no step to bring the change to notice, he practised to my way of thinking a deception just as real and just as dishonest as would have been the case if his intention all along had been to go out without paying.

Holding for these reasons that the respondent practised a deception, I turn to what I have referred to as the second question. Was the respondent's evasion of the debt obtained by that deception?

I think the material before the justices was enough to show that it was. The obvious effect of the deception was that the respondent and his associates were treated as they had been previously, that is to say as ordinary, honest customers whose conduct did not excite suspicion or call for precautions. In consequence the waiter was off his guard and vanished into the kitchen. That gave the respondent the opportunity of running out without hindrance and he took it. I would therefore answer this second question in the affirmative.

I would, accordingly, allow the appeal and restore the conviction.

Lords Pearson and **Morris** gave speeches allowing the appeal. **Lords Reid** and **Hodson** gave dissenting judgments.

Appeal allowed.

As this case indicates the courts will not be reluctant to find a deception where the defendant has been acting dishonestly. As the Law Commission put it:

the courts will usually find a deception has taken place if the defendant has formed a dishonest intent, and then subsequently entered into or continued his dealings with the victim in an apparently honest manner.[20]

FURTHER READING

Smith, A. (1982), 'The Idea of Criminal Deception', *Criminal Law Review* 721.

QUESTIONS

1. Sally has been the gardener of Sid (an extremely wealthy and successful business person). Each month she tells him a fee for the work she has done, which Sid pays without question. Initially she always asked for a reasonable fee. But for the past six months she has asked and been paid at a rate way beyond normal gardening rates. Has she committed an offence? (This raises the question whether *Silverman* applies only where the victim is vulnerable. See also *Jones, The Times*, 15 February 1993.)

2. Alan, a landscape gardener, offers to sell Charlie, another experienced gardener, a rose which he says is 'the best in the world'. At the time that was Alan's view but the next day he sees a new variety of rose which he thinks is even better. He does not tell Charlie this and she buys ten of the roses from him the week after. Has Alan deceived?

2 OBTAINING PROPERTY BY DECEPTION

Section 15(1) of the Theft Act 1968 states:

A person who by any deception dishonestly obtains property belonging to another, with the intention of permanently depriving the other of it, shall on conviction on indictment be liable to imprisonment for a term not exceeding ten years.

DEFINITION

Section 15 of the Theft Act 1968 requires proof that the defendant:

  (i) used a deception

---

[20] Law Commission Report No. 276 (2002: para. 2.22).

(ii) intentionally or recklessly

(iii) to obtain

(iv) property belonging to another

(v) dishonestly

(vi) with the intention of permanently depriving the other of it.

The *actus reus* is, therefore, the use of a deception to obtain property belonging to another.

The *mens rea* is that the defendant intended or was reckless that he or she was making a deception, that the defendant was dishonest, and that the defendant intended permanently to deprive the victim of the property.

2.1 THE ELEMENTS OF THE OFFENCE

This offence requires proof of the following elements:

Deception

This term has already been discussed.

Property

Section 4 of the Theft Act 1968, which defines property,[21] applies to section 15, subject to one exception. That exception is that the complex rules in relation to land do not apply. Therefore one can be convicted of obtaining land by deception, contrary to section 15. It should be noticed that the offence requires proof that the defendant obtains something from the victim, but it is not necessary to show that the victim has suffered a particular loss. In *Ashbee*[22] the defendant was convicted of obtaining passports by deception from the Home Office. The defendants could be convicted of obtaining property by deception even though the Home Office could not be shown to have suffered a particular loss because the defendants had certainly gained property.

Obtaining

A person obtains property if he obtains ownership, possession, or control of it.[23] Obtaining an interest short of full ownership, possession, or control (e.g. a charge over a property) is insufficient.[24] The offence is also made out if, as a result of the defendant's deception, a third party is able to obtain property.[25] It should be noted that use of a deception to enable the defendant to retain property is not an offence. So if Angie visited Michelle and asked for the return of her book which she had lent Michelle, but Michelle lied and said she no longer had it, there would be no offence.

It must be shown that the deception causes the obtaining. This involves finding that the victim handed over the property as a result of the deception. The following points illustrate the key issues contained in that requirement:

---

[21] Section 4 is discussed at pp. 502–505.   [22] [1989] 1 WLR 109.   [23] Theft Act 1968, s. 15(2).
[24] Simester and Sullivan (2003: 519).   [25] *Stonehouse* [1978] AC 55 (HL).

(i)   If the defendant has already obtained the property before the deception is made, then it is not possible to say that the deception caused the obtaining.[26]

(ii) The victim must be deceived. If the defendant makes an untrue statement and the victim is aware that the statement is untrue then the deception cannot be said to have caused the obtaining. In *Miller*[27] this nearly led to the defendant's acquittal. The defendant pretended to be a licensed taxi driver, which he was not, and charged people extortionate sums for their journeys. The victims gave evidence that by the time the journey had come to an end and the defendant had asked for the money they were aware that he was not an authorized taxi driver, but paid the money to avoid trouble. He argued that this evidence indicated that at the time of the obtaining the victims had not been deceived and so he could not be guilty. The Court of Appeal argued that it was open to a jury to decide that, looking at the case in the round, the deception caused the obtaining: the victims would not have got into the 'taxi' in the first place and then later felt pressurized to pay had it not been for the original deception. In this sense the deception could be said to have caused the obtaining.

(iii) It is not a defence to demonstrate that even though the victim did hand over his property as a result of the deception most people would not have been taken in by the deception, or that most people would not have attached significance to the defendant's statement. This was made clear by the Court of Appeal in *Talbott*.[28] So if Nicole bought Ewan's car after he told her (untruthfully) that Tom Cruise had once sat in it, it would be no defence to show that most people would not have cared whether Tom Cruise had travelled in the car, or that most people would have realized that the statement was untrue.

(iv) It must be shown that the victim handed over the property because of the deception and not for some other reason. That said, if the victim is deceived, the courts will be reluctant to believe that the property was handed over to the defendant for some other reason. *Laverty*[29] is therefore an unusual case. There the defendant changed the number plates on a car and sold it to the victim, stating that the number plates were the original ones. The defendant's conviction was quashed on the basis that it had not been shown that the victim had attached any significance to the defendant's statement about the number plates. A similar conclusion will be reached where the victim has decided to check up on the truth of a statement made by the defendant. In such a case it might be said that the victim was relying on his or her own checks rather than the representations of the defendant.[30]

Usually the courts have been willing to assume that the victim did rely on any deception of the defendant. When we discuss cases involving cheques and credit cards we shall see in *Charles*[31] and *Lambie*[32] that the House of Lords was willing to assume that the victims handed over property because of the defendants' implied statements that they were authorized to use the cheques or credit cards. In the following case the issue was also raised. Note the contrast between *Doukas* and the decision in *Rashid*:[33]

---

[26] *Collis-Smith* [1971] Crim LR 716 (CA).   [27] [1992] Crim LR 744 (CA).
[28] [1995] Crim LR 396 (CA).   [29] [1970] 3 All ER 432 (CA).
[30] *Roebuck* (1856) D & B 24, 169 ER 900.   [31] [1977] AC 177 (HL).
[32] [1982] AC 449 (HL).
[33] The House of Lords in *Cooke* [1986] AC 909 (HL) discussed both decisions without clearly stating a preference for one or the other.

R v Doukas
(1978) 66 Cr App R 228 (CA)[34]

Joseph Doukas was charged under section 25 of the Theft Act 1968 (going equipped to cheat, an offence which requires proof of a deception). He was a hotel wine waiter. He took with him to the hotel bottles of wine which he intended to substitute for 'house wine' ordered by guests. The plan was to charge the guests for the wine and pocket the money for it. He submitted there was no case to answer on the basis that it had not been shown that any customer would have been influenced to buy the wine by his (implied) deception that the wine offered was the official hotel wine.

Lord Justice Geoffrey Lane

The prosecution must prove that nexus between the deception and obtaining. It is this . . . ingredient which, as we see it in the present case, is the only point which raises any difficulty. Assuming, as we must, and indeed obviously was the case, the jury accepted the version of the police interviews and accepted that this man had made the confession to which I have referred, then the only question was, would this obtaining have in fact been caused by the deception practised by the waiter?

We have, as in the notice of appeal, been referred to the decision in *Rashid* (1977) 64 Cr. App. R. 201, which was a decision by another division of this Court. That case concerned not a waiter in a hotel, but a British Railways waiter who substituted not bottles of wine for the Railway wine but his own tomato sandwiches for the Railway tomato sandwiches; and it is to be observed in that case the basis of the decision was that the summing up of the learned judge to the jury was inadequate. On that basis the appeal was allowed. But the Court went on to express its views obiter on the question whether in these circumstances it could be said that the obtaining was by virtue of deception and it came to the conclusion, as I say obiter, that the answer was probably no.

Of course each case of this type may produce different results according to the circumstances of the case and according, in particular, to the commodity which is being proffered. But, as we see it, the question has to be asked of the hypothetical customer, 'Why did you buy this wine?' or 'If you had been told the truth, would you or would you not have bought the commodity?' It is, at least in theory, for the jury in the end to decide that question.

Here, as the ground of appeal is simply the judge's action in allowing the case to go to the jury, we are answering that question, so to speak, on behalf of the judge rather than the jury. Was there evidence of the necessary nexus fit to go to the jury? Certainly so far as the wine is concerned, we have no doubt at all that the hypothetical customer, faced with the waiter saying to him: 'This of course is not hotel wine, this is stuff which I imported into the hotel myself and I am going to put the proceeds of the wine, if you pay, into my own pocket,' would certainly answer, so far as we can see, 'I do not want your wine, kindly bring me the hotel carafe wine.' Indeed it would be a strange jury that came to any other conclusion, and a stranger guest who gave any other answer, for several reasons. First of all the guest would not know what was in the bottle which the waiter was proffering. True he may not know what was in the carafe which the hotel was proffering, but he would at least be able to have recourse to the hotel if something was wrong with the carafe wine, but he would have no such recourse with the waiter; if he did, it would be worthless.

It seems to us that the matter can be answered on a much simpler basis. The hypothetical customer must be reasonably honest as well as being reasonably intelligent and it seems to

[34] [1978] 1 All ER 1061, [1978] 1 WLR 372, [1978] Crim LR 177.

us incredible that any customer, to whom the true situation was made clear, would willingly make himself a party to what was obviously a fraud by the waiter upon his employers. If that conclusion is contrary to the *obiter dicta* in *Rashid* (supra), then we must respectfully disagree with those *dicta*.

It is not necessary to examine the question any further as to whether we are differing from *Rashid* (supra) or not. But it seems to us, beyond argument, that the learned judge was right in the conclusion he reached and was right to allow the matter to go to the jury on the basis which he did.

Application refused.

Belongs to another

Section 5(1) (discussed in Chapter 8) applies to section 15,[35] but not the other subsections of section 5. It is not necessary to show that the property belonged to the person to whom the deception was made.

Intention or recklessness

The deception must be deliberate or *Cunningham* reckless,[36] as is clear from section 15(4) of the Theft Act 1968. In other words the defendant must know that the statement is false or know that it may be false.[37]

Dishonesty

There is no definition of dishonesty in the 1968 Theft Act for the purposes of section 15. Section 2 of the 1968 Act, setting out circumstances in which a person will not be dishonest for the purposes of the theft, does not apply to obtaining property by deception. This means that for section 15 dishonesty is simply the *Ghosh* test, discussed in Chapter 8.[38] Although section 2 does not apply to section 15 it is unlikely that a jury, using the *Ghosh* test, would find a person who fell within section 2 to be dishonest.[39] Dishonesty is a less significant factor in cases under section 15 than it is in relation to theft. This is because it will be rare for a jury, having found that the defendant deceived the victim, to then decide that she was honest. Rare, but not impossible. If, for example, the defendant has deceived the victim of property, but intended to compensate the victim for his or her loss, that might negate any dishonesty.[40]

Intention permanently to deprive

This carries exactly the same meaning as in theft and was discussed in Chapter 8.

---

[35] Theft Act 1968, s. 34(1).
[36] An argument that *Caldwell* recklessness should be used was rejected in *Large v Mainprize* [1989] Crim LR 213.
[37] *Staines* (1974) 60 Cr App R 160 (CA).
[38] At pp. 531–534. *Woolven* (1983) 77 Cr App R 231 (CA); *Wood* [1999] Crim LR 564 (CA).
[39] *Wood* [1999] Crim LR 564 (CA). But contrast Griew (1995: 176–7).
[40] *O'Connell* (1992) 94 Cr App R 39 (CA).

2.2 DISTINGUISHING BETWEEN OBTAINING PROPERTY BY DECEPTION AND THEFT

Following the House of Lords decisions in *Gomez*[41] and *Hinks*[42] many cases of obtaining property by deception could also be charged as theft. There are two main circumstances in which an offence may amount to obtaining property by deception, but not theft:[43]

(1) Certain kinds of property cannot be stolen but can be obtained by deception. The most important example of this is land.

(2) If the defendant acquires ownership of the property as the result of a deception, but has not yet been able to possess it, then there may be the section 15 offence, without the section 1 offence. If, for example, the defendant deceives the victim into posting property under a contract in which ownership of the property passes at the moment of posting, but the property is stolen by the postal deliverer and never delivered, then the section 15 offence, but not the section 1 offence, may be committed by the defendant. This is because the defendant would have obtained the property, but not appropriated it.

3 OBTAINING A MONEY TRANSFER

Section 15A of the 1968 Theft Act states:

(1) A person is guilty of an offence if by any deception he dishonestly obtains a money transfer for himself or another.

(2) A money transfer occurs when—

(a) a debit is made to one account,

(b) a credit is made to another, and

(c) the credit results from the debit or the debit results from the credit.

(3) References to a credit and to a debit are to a credit of an amount of money and to a debit of an amount of money.

This offence was created by the Theft (Amendment) Act 1996.[44] It was created to deal with cases where, as a result of a deception, money is transferred from one account to another after, for example, a cheque is paid in, a CHAPS transfer, or a telegraph transfer. The problem with such cases is that in the transfers the money that leaves one bank account is not the same money that enters another bank account, in strict banking law terms. What happens is that the credit balance in one account is reduced and a new thing in action is created in the other. So if the transfer is created by a deception there has not been *property belonging to another* which has been obtained. Now in such cases the defendant should be charged with an offence under section 15A. The offence will be appropriate for all transfers

---

[41] [1992] 3 WLR 1061 (HL).   [42] [2000] 4 All ER 833 (HL).

[43] For a detailed discussion see Heaton (2001).

[44] Passed following Law Commission Report No. 243 (1999).

made by CHAPS order, electronic transfer, or by cheque. However, the section cannot be used if the transfer is conditional, for example, if the recipient cannot deal with the funds until there has been a confirmation from the bank sending the money.[45]

It should be noted that the only *mens rea* offence that is needed is dishonesty. There is no need to prove an intent to retain the credit that has been dishonestly obtained.

4 OBTAINING A PECUNIARY ADVANTAGE BY DECEPTION

Section 16 of the Theft Act 1968 states:

> (1) A person who by any deception dishonestly obtains for himself or another any pecuniary advantage shall on conviction on indictment be liable for a term not exceeding five years.
>
> (2) The cases in which a pecuniary advantage within the meaning of this section is to be regarded as obtained for a person are where—
>
>   (a) [repealed]
>
>   (b) he is allowed to borrow by way of overdraft, or to take out any policy of insurance or annuity contract, or obtains an improvement of the terms on which he is allowed to do so; or
>
>   (c) he is given the opportunity to earn remuneration or greater remuneration in an office or employment, or to win money by betting.

4.1 DECEPTION

This has the same meaning that we have already discussed.

4.2 OBTAINING

This has the same meaning already discussed.

4.3 A PECUNIARY ADVANTAGE

At first sight the idea of 'pecuniary advantage' appears to be a very wide term, but following the repeal of section 16(2)(a) it is now of limited scope. The term now *only* includes:

(1) Overdrafts. The term 'allowed to borrow by way of overdraft' includes the situation where a defendant writes a cheque backed up by a cheque guarantee card in excess of the funds in his account. Under the terms of the cheque guarantee card the bank must honour the cheque. The bank will still be said to 'allow' the defendant to borrow the money, even if it had forbidden the defendant from going overdrawn.[46]

---

[45] *Re Holmes* [2005] Crim LR 229.
[46] *Waites* [1982] Crim LR 369 (CA); *Bevan* [1987] Crim LR 129 (CA).

(2) To take out or improve the terms of insurance and annuities. A clear example of this is where a person obtains life insurance after lying about his or her age.

(3) Opportunities to earn money. This includes where a person has got a job after lying about his qualifications.[47] The section does not cover a person who by a deception is awarded a position that does not carry remuneration.[48] Therefore, if Helena tells the director of a local amateur dramatics production untruthfully that she is an experienced performer and thereby lands a leading role in a production she has not committed this offence. The statute is carefully worded. By using the term 'given the opportunity to earn remuneration' the statute prevents a defendant arguing that she obtained her salary not by the lie she used to get the job, but because of the hard work she did once employed.

(4) Opportunities to win money by betting. Again the use of the word 'opportunity' is important. It means that if a person by deception is able to gamble he is guilty of an offence, even if in fact he does not win the bet. It also prevents the defendant from raising an argument that he won the money because (for example) his horse won, rather than the original deception.

5 OBTAINING SERVICES BY DECEPTION

Section 1 of the Theft Act 1968 states:

(1) A person who by any deception dishonestly obtains services from another shall be guilty of an offence.

(2) It is an obtaining of services where the other is induced to confer a benefit by doing some act, or causing or permitting some act to be done, on the understanding that the benefit has been or will be paid for.

(3) Without prejudice to the generality of subsection (2) above, it is an obtaining of services where the other is induced to make a loan, or to cause or permit a loan to be made, on the understanding that any payment (whether by way of interest or otherwise) will be or has been made in respect of the loan.[49]

The offence can be broken down into the following elements:

(1) *Deception.* This has the meaning described above. If the defendant managed to receive a service without a deception (e.g. by managing to get into a cinema to see a film without buying a ticket and without anyone noticing) there is no section 1 offence.

(2) *Dishonestly.* The *Ghosh* test will govern the meaning of dishonestly here.

---

[47] *Callender* [1992] 3 All ER 51. Although in *McNiff* [1986] Crim LR 57 it was held that a tenancy of a public house was neither an office nor an employment.

[48] The phrase 'employment' has been widely interpreted and includes a contract for services as well as contracts for employment.

[49] Five years' imprisonment is the maximum sentence. Subsection (3) was added by the Theft (Amendment) Act 1996.

(3) *Obtaining a service.* A service is defined as the conferring of a benefit. This is a wide definition. The service can either be conferred by the victim directly on the defendant (e.g. cutting the defendant's hair) or indirectly: permitting the defendant to act (e.g. allowing the defendant to look around an historic building). In *Widdowson*[50] obtaining a van on hire-purchase was obtaining a service, even though it could also be regarded as obtaining property. The defendant is guilty if he deceives the victim into providing a service to himself or someone else.[51] There are a few areas of doubt over the meaning of the word 'service' here:

(i) Can a service be provided by omission? Section 1 states that there must be some 'act or causing some act or permitting some act to be done' which confers the benefit. Simester and Sullivan argue that if D sits in a train and shows a guard an invalid ticket, and as a result the deceived guard allows D to remain on the train, then no benefit has been given as a result of the deception.[52] The deception has meant that D has escaped paying;[53] but it had not caused an act to be done which has provided D with a benefit. Against Simester and Sullivan's view it might be argued that had the guard realized D did not have a valid ticket D would have been removed from the train and that therefore by avoiding this the deception did in effect permit D to enjoy the benefit of the acts of the train driver.

(ii) What is a benefit? As already mentioned, to amount to a service there must be the conferring of a benefit. It could be argued that the word 'benefit' suggests that the service must be beneficial. This seems to be too restrictive. Surely if Sheila obtained a massage as a result of a deception she could not escape criminal liability by arguing that the massage had not been of any use to her. Perhaps it simply requires that the service was of some economic value, whether or not it was experienced as beneficial by the defendant. Professor Smith has argued that the word benefit indicates that the service must at least be lawful.[54] This might mean that if the defendant used a deception to obtain an illegal service (e.g. to view child pornography on the internet) this would not fall within section 1. Professor Griew argues that the word benefit has no meaning and that the word is just used as a 'shorthand' to refer to the service.[55] Phillips, Walsh, and Dobson argue that the 'benefit requirement' is designed to prevent a defendant being convicted of getting the victim by a deception to do an act which benefits only the victim.[56] For example, a defendant would not commit an offence if by deception he or she persuaded the victim to mow his or her own lawn or run ten miles. These activities would not benefit the defendant. The courts are yet to address this dispute. Although it should be noted that if the defendant persuades the victim to do an act which benefits a third party this is covered by section 1.[57]

---

[50] (1986) 82 Cr App R 314 (CA).   [51] *Nathan* [1997] Crim LR 835 (CA).

[52] It would be different if the defendant flashed a ticket to be permitted to board a train.

[53] And he may therefore have committed an offence under the Theft Act 1978, s. 2.

[54] Smith (1997: 4–84). He suggests that this is so where 'the object of the law is to protect D . . . against the act in question.' An analogy could be drawn with the rule that a person cannot be convicted in respect of legislation intended to protect them.

[55] Griew (1995: para. 9.06).   [56] Phillips, Walsh, and Dobson (2001: 218–19).

[57] *Nathan* [1997] Crim LR 835 (CA).

(iii) Is the provision of free services covered by the offence? There is no offence under section 1 if the service is provided for free.[58] For example, if Kylie tells her neighbour Jason, untruthfully, that she has injured her foot and so Jason offers to do her gardening for her, the section 3 offence will not be committed because the service is not provided on the understanding that it has to or will be paid for. If, however, Kylie had offered to pay Jason £2 for the gardening he could be guilty of the offence, if it could be shown that Jason provided the service because of the lie about the injured foot. It is not necessary to show that the understanding was that the defendant was to pay for the service, as long as it was a service which was to be paid for by someone. It is unclear whether a defendant who deceived a victim into providing a service in return for another service would commit the offence.

(iv) Is the provision of loans caused by a deception covered by the offence? There was some doubt whether a mortgage advance could be regarded as a service. The position was clarified by the insertion of subsection (3). This makes it clear that a loan is a service for the purpose of the section.[59]

6 SECTION 2 OF THE THEFT ACT 1978: EVASION OF A LIABILITY BY DECEPTION

Section 2 of the Theft Act 1968 states:

(1) Subject to subsection (2) below, where a person by any deception—

   (a) dishonestly secures the remission of the whole or part of any existing liability to make a payment, whether his own liability or another's; or

   (b) with intent to make permanent default in whole or in part on any existing liability to make a payment, or with intent to let another do so, dishonestly induces the creditor or any person claiming payment on behalf of the creditor to wait for payment (whether or not the due date for payment is deferred) or to forgo payment; or

   (c) dishonestly obtains any exemption from or abatement of liability to make a payment; he shall be guilty of an offence.

(2) For purposes of this section 'liability' means legally enforceable liability; and subsection (1) shall not apply in relation to a liability that has not been accepted or established to pay compensation for a wrongful act or omission.

(3) For purposes of subsection (1)(b) a person induced to take in payment a cheque or other security for money by way of conditional satisfaction of a pre-exiting liability is to be treated not as being paid but as being induced to wait for payment.

(4) For purposes of subsection (1)(c) 'obtains' includes obtaining for another or enabling another to obtain.

---

[58] In many cases where a person by deception is able to get a free service a s. 2 offence will be made out.

[59] The controversial decision of *Halai* [1983] Crim LR 624 no longer represents the law and has been effectively overruled by *Graham* [1997] 1 Cr App R 302 (CA) and *Naviede* [1997] Crim LR 662 (CA).

6.1 DISTINGUISHING BETWEEN THE OFFENCES IN SECTION 2

This is the section of the Theft Act 1978 which causes students the greatest difficulty. The Court of Appeal in *Sibartie*[60] said that the wording of the section should be given its ordinary meaning, but given its complexity this is of little assistance.

It is important to remember that section 2 deals only with cases where there are legally enforceable debts which the victim would be able to enforce but for the deception. So if the defendant by a deception persuades the creditor to let the defendant off a 'debt' which in fact was not legally enforceable under the law of contract, there is no liability under section 2.[61]

The differences between the subsections appear to be as follows:

(1) Subsections (a) and (b) apply where the defendant owes the victim money[62] (i.e. there is a liability), but the defendant is seeking to escape from the debt by using a deception. Subsection (c) applies where the defendant is seeking to use the deception to ensure that the defendant never owes the victim money (i.e. to prevent the debt arising in the first place).

(2) Subsection (a) applies where the victim is persuaded to extinguish all or part of the liability. In other words, as a result of the deception the defendant no longer owes all or part of the debt. By contrast (b) covers the situation where the defendant is persuaded by the deception to wait for payment. So, in (a), but not in (b), the debt is extinguished; in (b) the debt still exists but the victim is persuaded not to enforce it.

(3) In subsection (b) there is an extra requirement, which is not in the other two subsections, and that is that there must be an intent to make permanent default. This may not be as big a difference as at first appears because, if the defendant deceives to ensure the avoidance or extinction of the debt as in (a) or (c), this necessarily implies an intent never to pay.

DEFINITION

Contrasting these three examples may clarify the distinction between the subsections of section 2, Theft Act 1978:

1. Anne walks into a hairdresser's and asks whether she can be given a free haircut because she says (untruthfully) that she is an impoverished student. If the hairdresser is persuaded to give Anne a free haircut this may constitute an offence under section 2(1)(c). By the deception Anne avoids becoming liable to pay money.

2. Ben walks into a hairdresser's, receives a haircut, and when asked to pay untruthfully says that he is an impoverished student and asks whether he can be let off the charge. The hairdresser, feeling sorry for Ben, agrees. Ben may be guilty under section 2(1)(a) because he has persuaded the hairdresser to remit the liability. It would be the same if Ben persuaded the hairdresser to give him a 50 per cent discount by the deception.

3. If Charlie has her haircut and when asked to pay says (untruthfully) that she has left her wallet at home and persuades the hairdresser to let her pay next week (intending

---

[60] [1983] Crim LR 470 (CA).   [61] *Gee* [1999] Crim LR 397 (CA).
[62] This must be a legally enforceable liability: Theft Act 1978, s. 2(2).

never to pay) this may be an offence under section 2(1)(b): by deception Charlie has persuaded the hairdresser to wait for payment, intending never to pay.

We must now look at the offences separately.

6.2 SECTION 2(1)(A)

As already indicated, this subsection is appropriate where the defendant has deceived the victim into 'letting him off' a debt. In order to remit a debt the victim must be aware there is a debt. So, if a diner untruthfully persuades the restaurant owner that he is leaving the restaurant having just looked at the menu but not having eaten any food, when in fact he has eaten a large meal, no section 2(1)(a) offence is committed because the victim believes the defendant owes no money and therefore cannot be said to have remitted a debt.[63]

As William Wilson has pointed out, the phrase 'secure the remission' of the debt is problematic.[64] Contract lawyers will tell you that if someone remits a debt as a result of a deception then the remission may in fact be unenforceable and the debt still payable. If this rather technical approach were adopted the section would have no meaning, because it would be impossible to obtain a secure remission of a debt by a deception in contract law. Arguably therefore 'securing' means persuading the victim to forgive the debt, whether or not the debt is technically remitted in the eyes of contract law. This is how the provision was understood in *Jackson*.[65]

6.3 SECTION 2(1)(B)

There are really two different offences involved in this subsection:

(1) the use of a deception to facilitate delaying payment with the eventual aim of never paying;

(2) persuading the victim to forgo the debt.

As to (1), lying to get a little extra time to pay a debt is far from uncommon. 'The cheque's in the post' has almost become synonymous with saying 'I can't pay you quite now but will be paying very soon.' What prevents such lies amounting to this criminal offence is the requirement that a person who commits it is deceiving while never intending never to pay, rather than deceiving to create a little more time before paying.

It is unclear whether giving the victim a cheque which the defendant knows will be dishonoured is making someone wait for payment. It appears from *Andrews and Hedges*[66] that this can amount to an offence under section 2(1)(b) only where immediate payment for the service or goods is required. If immediate payment was not required, then the victim would be taken to accept the cheque as payment of the debt.

As to inducing the creditor to forgo the debt it is, to be honest, far from clear what this means. One suggestion by Professor Griew is that the phrase 'forgoing payment' means that payment is not demanded but the liability remains.[67] An example of this is where the creditor is persuaded by a deception that there is in fact no liability or that the liability has

---

[63] An offence under s. 3 of the Theft Act 1978 may well be committed in this scenario.
[64] Wilson (2003: 476).   [65] [1983] Crim LR 617 (CA).   [66] [1981] Crim LR 106.
[67] Griew (1995: 10.17).

been met[68] or that the defendant is insolvent and so not worth suing. In *Holt and Lee*[69] the accused were charged with an offence under section 2(1)(b) of an attempt to forgo payment of their bill after being heard planning to pretend that they had already paid their restaurant bill. They argued that they should have been charged under section 2(1)(a) because rather than seeking to forgo payment they were seeking a remission of liability. Reassuringly the Court of Appeal stated that there were many overlapping features of the offences under section 2. The fact that the case could have been brought under section 2(1)(a) did not prevent a conviction under section 2(1)(b), as long as the requirement that there was an intention to make permanent default as required under section 2(1)(b) was proved.

6.4 SECTION 2(1)(C)

This offence is committed when a defendant uses a deception to avoid becoming liable for a payment which he or she would otherwise be liable to make. A common example of obtaining an exemption from liability is pretending be under 16 in order to get a child's price ticket at a cinema.

Another example of section 2(1)(c) is the following case:

R v Sibartie
[1983] Crim LR 470 (CA)

Dhununjay Sibartie was a law student. He was using the London Underground and leaving at Tottenham Court Road. He did not have a ticket which covered his journey, and when he walked past a ticket inspector he 'flashed' a season ticket which did not cover the journey. He was convicted of committing an offence under section 2(1)(c).

Lord Lane CJ

. . .

[Counsel for the appellant] submits that the words in the Theft Act 1978 section 2(1)(c), namely 'dishonestly obtains any exemption from . . . liability to make a payment', are not apt to describe that happened on this occasion. He has drawn our attention to the earlier words in section 16 of the Theft Act 1968, now repealed, and he draws our attention to the words which I have already read in section 2(1)(a) and (b) of the Theft Act 1978. He says that unless you give a meaning to subsection (c) of that section different from the one which the Judge gave, the contents of (a) and (b) are not necessary. What he says in other words is this: that taking into account the wording of (a) and (b), it is plain that subsection (c) is not apt to describe what the appellant in the present case was admitting to do. He submits that subsection (c) deals with a potential liability, or alternatively, a liability created at the time of the fraud, and does not extend to the type of situation with which we are dealing at the moment.

We do not accept those arguments. First of all we consider that there may be a degree of overlapping between these various subsections (a), (b) and (c) and the mere fact that the circumstances of the present case, had the attempt been successful, might have been covered by subsection (b) does not seem to us to be any reason for saying that therefore (c) does not apply.

---

[68] e.g. *Holt and Lee* [1981] 2 All ER 854 (CA).   [69] (1981) 73 Cr App R 96.

What we think is the correct method of approach is this. Taking the words in (c) in their ordinary meaning, would one say that what the appellant was attempting to do fell within the ambit of the words? The jury must have been satisfied, as their verdict indicates, that the appellant dishonestly used his season tickets which did not in fact cover the journey that he was making in an attempt to persuade the ticket collectors that they did cover his journey. Does that amount to an attempt to obtain an exemption from liability to make payment for the journey he had made or was making?

[Counsel for the appellant] contends that there must be some agreement on the part of the creditor to exempt the defendant from liability. He uses as an example the exemption under the General Rate Act, from the necessity or liability to pay full rates where the ratepayer or potential ratepayer says 'I am very poor. Therefore please exempt me from paying what otherwise I would have to pay.'

It seems to us that there is no distinction in principle between that situation and the present one, because here the traveller on the underground is saying, albeit tacitly by waving the season tickets in the air, 'I am the holder of a ticket which authorises me to be making this journey without further payment. Consequently I am not under any liability to pay any more.' In the ordinary meaning of the words it seems to us that that is dishonestly obtaining, or attempting to obtain, an exemption from the liability to pay the excess fare which, if he had been honest, he would have had to pay. As we say, the fact that it may also have been an attempt to commit an offence under subsection (b) is neither here nor there. . . .

Appeal dismissed.

7 MAKING OFF WITHOUT PAYMENT: SECTION 3 OF THE THEFT ACT 1978

Section 3 of the 1978 Act states:

(1) Subject to subsection (3) below, a person who, knowing that payment on the spot for any goods supplied or service done is required or expected from him, dishonestly makes off without having paid as required or expected and with intent to avoid payment of the amount due shall be guilty of an offence.

(2) For purposes of this section 'payment on the spot' includes payment at the time of collecting goods on which work has been done or in respect of which service has been provided.

(3) Subsection (1) above shall not apply where the supply of the goods or the doing of the service is contrary to law, or where the service done is such that payment is not legally enforceable.

(4) Any person may arrest without warrant anyone who is, or whom he, with reasonable cause, suspects to be, committing or attempting to commit an offence under this section.

DEFINITION

The key elements of the section 3 offence are:

1. making off;

2. dishonestly;

3. without having paid as required or expected;

4. knowledge that payment on the spot is required for goods or services;

5. intent to avoid payment.

The *actus reus* is the making off without having paid as required or expected.

The *mens rea* is dishonesty, knowledge that payment on the spot is required for goods and services, and an intent to avoid payment.

N.B. There is no need to prove a deception.

This offence carries a maximum sentence (on indictment) of two years' imprisonment. The offence is designed to deal with people who, for example, having eaten a meal at a restaurant run out without paying, or having taken a taxi ride disappear without paying the fare. Notably the Court of Appeal has recently stated that 'section 3(1) is indeed intended to create a simple and straightforward offence'.[70] The court indicated that it would not be sympathetic to interpretations of section 3 which would introduce unnecessary complexity.

The key elements of the offence are:

7.1 MAKING OFF FROM THE PLACE WHERE PAYMENT WAS EXPECTED

The term 'making off' means simply leaving. In *Brooks and Brooks*[71] the Court of Appeal rejected an argument that the term 'making off' indicated that the defendant surreptitiously left. Boldly walking out of the front door of the restaurant is as much 'making off' as leaving through a toilet window at the back. The defendant must make off from the place where payment was expected. This includes the door of a restaurant or even the side of an ice cream van. In *McDavitt*[72] the defendant was apprehended while walking towards the door of a restaurant. Although it looked as if he was not going to pay it was held that the spot where he was expected to pay was the restaurant door, and so it was not until he walked out of the restaurant that he committed the offence, although he could be guilty of an attempted offence.[73] There does seem to be a gap in the section, in that if the defendant gives a taxi driver some fake money and the taxi driver leaves then arguably the defendant has not 'made off'; it is the victim who has left.[74]

There is some doubt whether a defendant can be said to be 'making off' if the victim has given permission to the defendant to leave. *Hammond,*[75] a first instance decision, appears to suggest that if the owner has consented to the defendant's departure there is no making off. However, it is unclear whether this is so if the victim's consent was obtained by the defendant's deception. If, after a meal at a restaurant, the defendant (falsely) tells the owner that he has no money with him and gives the owner his name and address, saying he will pay later, and the owner therefore lets the defendant leave, can it be said he 'makes off'?

---

[70] *Vincent* [2001] 1 WLR 1172 (CA), para. 11.   [71] (1983) 76 Cr App R 66 (CA).

[72] [1981] Crim LR 843.

[73] *Moberley v Allen, The Times,* 13 Dec. 1991 (DC) it was stated that if there were two places where the defendant could pay then the offence was committed only when the defendant had passed them both.

[74] Bennion (1983a).   [75] [1982] Crim LR 611.

John Spencer[76] argues that it is necessary to distinguish between two cases: where the defendant has left without it being possible to locate him in the future and where the defendant has left when it is possible to discover his whereabouts in the future (e.g. because the defendant has left a piece of paper with his name and address on it). He argues that in the former case there is no making off as the situation is not the kind which the Act was meant to deal with, but the latter is. However, as Sir John Smith argues, this may be to read too much into the phrase 'making off'.[77]

7.2 GOODS SUPPLIED OR SERVICES DONE

The offence requires evidence that goods have been supplied[78] or services[79] done for the defendant. These terms are broadly interpreted to include a wide range of things people pay for, from petrol to parking spaces. However, the wording may provide some defendants with a loophole: if a defendant plays golf but runs away without paying, it may be argued that he has not been provided with services.[80] More significantly, however, there is also some dispute about where a defendant took goods from a self-service supermarket or restaurant: are such goods supplied? Griew argues not,[81] but Smith suggests that the goods are supplied, in that they are 'made available for sale'.[82] As theft is available in such cases it is perhaps not surprising that the courts have not been asked to resolve the dispute. In reality in either case it would be unlikely that a court would take a restrictive interpretation to the offence.

Section 3(3) makes it clear that services or goods must be part of a legally enforceable contract. To make off from a brothel or run away from a café selling illegal drugs without paying for their illegal services would not involve the offence.

7.3 WITHOUT HAVING PAID AS REQUIRED OR EXPECTED

It must be shown that the defendant failed to pay as required or expected. This means that if the 'victim' has broken the contract with the defendant in such a way that the defendant is not obliged to pay for the service or goods the defendant commits no offence if he leaves without paying.[83] For example, if a restaurant serves inedible food and the customer storms out without paying he may not be guilty of a section 3 offence on the basis that he was not required to pay for the food.[84]

There is much debate over the case where the defendant gives as payment a cheque which is subsequently dishonoured.[85] Is that payment as required or expected? In favour of finding the defendant not guilty in such a case is the argument that such conduct would be covered by section 2(1)(b) of the Theft Act 1978 and so there is no need for section 3 to apply. Against such liability is an argument that section 2(3) states that a worthless cheque is not to be regarded as payment for a debt. However, section 2(3) applies only to section 2 and it can be argued that this implies that for section 3 a worthless cheque is to be regarded as

---

[76] Spencer (1983). Contrast Bennion (1983a) and Bennion (1983b). [77] Smith (2002: 5.78).

[78] Goods are defined in the Theft Act 1968, s. 34(2)(b), as: ' "goods" except in so far as the context otherwise requires, includes money and every other description of property except land and includes things severed from the land by stealing'. This definition applies to the Theft Act 1978 (s. 5(2)).

[79] Services are defined in s. 1(2) of the Theft Act 1978.

[80] Griew (1995: 213). [81] Griew (1995: 13.07). [82] Smith (1997: 5.03).

[83] *Troughton v Metropolitan Police* [1987] Crim LR 138 (DC).

[84] Such a person may also claim not to be dishonest: *Aziz* [1993] Crim LR 708 (CA). [85] Syrota (1980).

payment. Even if that argument fails, it could be suggested that the defendant, by paying with an ineffective cheque,[86] has not paid as 'expected or required'.

7.4 DISHONESTY

Dishonesty here has the same meaning as in the *Ghosh* case, discussed at p. 531. It must be shown that there was dishonesty at the time of the making off.

7.5 KNOWING THAT PAYMENT ON THE SPOT IS REQUIRED OR EXPECTED OF HIM

This requirement will be most relevant where the defendant is able to persuade the jury that he thought the goods and services were provided on the basis that he would pay at some point in the future or that another person would pay for the items. Imagine that Bill and Ben are dining at a restaurant, when Bill disappears. Ben is stopped as he walks out of the restaurant. He will have a defence to a charge under section 3 if he can prove that he believed Bill was going to pay for the meal. He did not know that payment was expected *of him*.[87] Ben will also have a defence to a section 3 charge if he lied to the manager and told him that he intended to pay the bill next week and that was why the owner of the restaurant let him leave.[88] This is because Ben was not being required or expected to pay as he made off. It might be different if Ben were allowed to leave the restaurant after saying that he needed to get his wallet from the car, because in such a case he was still expected to pay on the spot.[89] His offence, if any, will be under section 2 of the Theft Act 1978.

The fact that payment on the spot is required means that the defendant is expected to pay at that time and at that particular place. In *Aziz*[90] the defendant took a taxi ride, but refused to pay at the destination. The taxi driver decided to take the defendant back to the start of the journey. On the way back the defendant ran off. The defendant tried to argue that payment was expected at the destination, not when he ran off. However the Court of Appeal rejected this argument: he had left the place where payment was expected (i.e. the taxi) at a time when he was liable to pay the full fare.

7.6 INTENT TO AVOID PAYMENT

Although the section does not specifically state that it must be shown that the defendant intended to avoid payment, this was established in the following case:

R v Allen
[1985] AC 1029 (HL)[91]

Christopher Allen stayed at a hotel and ran up a bill of £1,286 when he left without paying. He was charged under section 3 of the Theft Act 1978. His defence was that he

---

[86] If the cheque is backed up with a cheque guarantee card it may be an effective payment.
[87] *Brooks and Brooks* (1983) 76 Cr App R 66 (CA).
[88] *Vincent* [2001] 1 WLR 1172 (CA).   [89] Ibid., para. 11.   [90] [1993] Crim LR 708 (CA).
[91] [1985] 2 All ER 641, [1985] 3 WLR 107, (1985) 81 Cr App R 200, [1985] Crim LR 739.

intended to pay the bill later. The judge directed the jury that this was no defence. His conviction was quashed on appeal and the Crown appealed to the House of Lords.

Lord Hailsham of St Marylebone LC

In refusing leave to appeal to your Lordships' House, the Court of Appeal certified the following point of law of general public importance:

'Upon a construction of the words "with intent to avoid payment" in section 3(1) of the Theft Act 1978, namely, whether an intention to make permanent default on payment is required.'

. . .

The Crown's contention was that the effect of this section [section 3] is to catch not only those who intend permanently to avoid payment of the amount due, but also those whose intention is to avoid payment on the spot, which, after all, is the time at which, *ex hypothesi*, payment has been 'expected or required', and the time, therefore, when the 'amount' became 'due'.

The judgment of the Court of Appeal, with which I agree, was delivered by Boreham J. He said ([1985] 1 All ER 148 at 154, [1985] 1 WLR 50 at 57):

'To secure a conviction under s 3 of the 1978 Act the following must be proved: (1) that the defendant in fact made off without making payment on the spot (2) the following mental elements: (a) knowledge that payment on the spot was required or expected of him and (b) dishonesty and (c) intent to avoid payment [sc "of the amount due"].'

I agree with this analysis. To this the judge adds the following comment:

'If (c) means, or is taken to include, no more than an intention to delay or defer payment of the amount due, it is difficult to see what it adds to the other elements. Anyone who knows that payment on the spot is expected or required of him and who then dishonestly makes off without paying as required or expected must have at least the intention to delay or defer payment. It follows, therefore, that the conjoined phrase "and with intent to avoid payment of the amount due" adds a further ingredient: an intention to do more than delay or defer, an intention to evade payment altogether.'

My own view, for what it is worth, is that the section thus analysed is capable only of this meaning. But counsel for the Crown very properly conceded that, even if it were equivocal and capable of either meaning, in a penal section of this kind any ambiguity must be resolved in favour of the subject and against the Crown. Accordingly, the appeal falls to be dismissed either if on its true construction it means unambiguously that the intention must be permanently to avoid payment, or if the clause is ambiguous and capable of either meaning. Even on the assumption that, in the context, the word 'avoid' without the addition of the word 'permanently' is capable of either meaning, which Boreham J was inclined to concede, I find myself convinced by his final paragraph, which reads:

'Finally, we can see no reason why, if the intention of Parliament was to provide, in effect, that an intention to delay or defer payment might suffice, Parliament should not have said so in explicit terms. This might have been achieved by the insertion of the word "such" before payment in the phrase in question. It would have been achieved by a grammatical reconstruction of the material part of s 3(1) thus, "dishonestly makes off without having paid and with intent to avoid payment of the amount due as required or expected". To accede to the Crown's submission would be to read the section as if it were constructed in that way. That we cannot do. Had it been intended to relate the intention to avoid "payment" to "payment as required or expected" it would have been easy to say so. The section does not say so. At the very least it contains an equivocation which should be resolved in favour of [the respondent].'

There is really no escape from this argument. There may well be something to be said for the creation of a criminal offence designed to protect, for instance, cab drivers and restaurant keepers against persons who dishonestly abscond without paying on the spot and without any need for the prosecution to exclude an intention to pay later, so long as the original act of 'making off' could be described as dishonest. Unlike that in the present section, such an offence might very well as with the railway ticket offence, be triable summarily, and counsel for the Crown was able to call in aid the remarks of Cumming-Bruce LJ in *Corbyn v Saunders* [1978] 2 All ER 697 at 699, [1978] 1 WLR 400 at 403 which go a long way to support such a view. But, as the Court of Appeal remarked, that decision was under a different statute and a differently worded section which did not contain both the reference to 'dishonestly' and the specific intention 'to avoid payment' as two separate elements in the mens rea of the offence. In order to give the section now under consideration the effect required the section would have to be remodelled in the way suggested by Boreham J in the passage quoted above, or the word 'and' in the ultimate phrase would have to be read as if it meant 'that is to say' so that the required intent would be equated with 'dishonestly' in the early part of the subsection.

Lords Scarman, Diplock, Bridge, and **Brightman** gave speeches agreeing with the Lord Chancellor.

Appeal dismissed.

The decision certainly involves reading words into the statute and could be criticized on the basis that it is too easy a defence for a defendant to raise. It offers no protection from the criminal law to hotel owners whose clients leave without intending to pay.

QUESTIONS

1. Amil, a taxi driver, takes Trish home. Trish gives Amil some notes in payment and he drives off. Later Amil discovers that Trish's notes are in fact in a foreign currency. Has Trish committed any offence? Would your answer be different if it transpired that the notes given by Trish were of greater value than the taxi fare? (Consider here especially: was there any making off? Was payment as expected? Was there dishonesty?)

2. Federico visits a restaurant and orders a pizza. He is so shocked at its low quality that he storms out of the restaurant without paying, having eaten half of it. Has he committed any offence?

3. Paul, a student aged 20, sees a sign in a hairdresser's saying 'free haircuts for the under 16s'. He dresses up in his old school uniform and goes in and has a haircut. The hairdresser assumes he is under 16 and does not ask him to pay. But when he has just left the shop the manager sees him and runs after him demanding payment. Paul is able to run faster and escapes. (Was there a deception here? What was obtained? Did Paul make off without payment?)

4. Chloe, a student, as a rag stunt tells an elderly man in the street that if he donates money to charity, she will give him a kiss. He gives her £1, but she runs off without kissing. Has she committed an offence?

8 CHEQUES, CREDIT CARDS, AND CREDIT BALANCES

This is a topic which has caused enormous confusion to students. It may be reassuring that it has also caused difficulties for the judiciary and academic commentators. It is dealt with here as a separate topic as it can involve a rather complex interaction between various of the property offences we have discussed to date. We will summarize the main points first and shortly in the extract from the article by Russell Heaton the law will be looked at in more detail. We will look at three hypothetical scenarios:[92]

(1) Scott buys a car from Nush, a car dealer. He pays by cheque, backed up by a cheque guarantee card (or as an alternative he pays by credit card), even though Scott has been told by his bank that he must not use the card. Nush is paid by the bank or credit card company.

These are some of the offences that Scott may be guilty of:

(i) Theft. It could, after *Hinks*,[93] be found that Scott has appropriated the car. The key issue is whether or not Scott by using the card was dishonest.

(ii) Obtaining property (the car) by deception from Nush (section 15 of the Theft Act 1968). In considering this charge the following questions will have to be considered:

(a) Is there a deception? In *Charles*[94] it was held that if a person writes a cheque in payment for goods or services he impliedly represents:

- he is the person whose name appears on the cheque;

- he *believes*[95] that in the ordinary course of events the cheque will be honoured (either because there is enough money in the account now, or there will be by the time the cheque is presented).[96]

Where a person uses a cheque guarantee card he represents:

- he is authorized by the bank to use the card.

Where a person uses a credit card then according to the House of Lords in *Lambie* he is implied to represent:[97]

- he is authorized to use the credit card.[98]

(b) Has the obtaining caused the deception? This may be difficult to prove in a case like this. Notice that in this case at the end of the day Nush received the money for the car. The difficulty is that, where a cheque guarantee card or credit card is used, as long as a shopkeeper undertakes certain formalities the bank or credit card issuer guarantees payment. Nush therefore may be concerned only that she has undertaken the formalities and will as a result receive

---

[92] Herring (2005: 317–20) provides an even more extensive discussion.
[93] [2001] 2 AC 241 (HL).   [94] *MPC v Charles* [1977] AC 177 (HL).
[95] So if the defendant thinks that the cheque will be honoured but in fact it is not there is no deception.
[96] The defendant will deceive if he knows there is a real risk that the cheque will be dishonoured: *Greenstein* [1975] 1 WLR 1353 (CA).
[97] *Lambie* [1982] AC 449 (HL).
[98] This would deceive if either he is not the person to whom the card was issued, or he had exceeded his credit card limit in an unauthorized way.

payment. She may not care whether or not Scott is in fact authorized to use the card. However, in *Charles* and *Lambie* the House of Lords was willing to assume in such cases that a shopkeeper did rely on the implied statements. It was an 'irresistible inference' that a shopkeeper would not want to assist another in defrauding his or her bank. So the court is likely to assume that Nush did rely on Scott's implied statements when accepting the cheque or credit card as payment and handing over the car.

The other requirements of the section 15 offence are probably made out as long as the jury found his conduct dishonest.

(iii) Obtaining a pecuniary advantage (an overdraft) by deception (section 16 of the Theft Act 1968). This offence will be committed by Scott against his bank or credit card company. There are two main issues:

    (a) Has Scott been 'allowed' to borrow, given that it was really against the bank's wishes that Scott extended his debt to the bank? In *Waites*[99] the Court of Appeal held that a bank 'allows' someone to borrow if the bank does in fact extend the overdraft facility.

    (b) Does it matter that there was no deception here made to the bank? No. The wording of section 16 makes it clear that if a deception by a defendant causes anyone to provide a pecuniary advantage the offence is made out.[100]

(iv) Obtaining a service by deception (section 1 of the Theft Act 1978). The offence will be committed by Scott against his bank or credit card company. Section 1(3) of the 1978 Act makes it clear that an overdraft is to be regarded as a service.

(2) Steph deceives Jon into writing her a cheque by claiming untruthfully that she needs money to feed her hungry child. Steph is arrested before she can pay the cheque into her bank account.

Here are some of the offences that Steph may be convicted of:

(i) Obtaining the cheque as a piece of paper by deception contrary to section 15 of the Theft Act 1968. There is no doubt that as a piece of paper the cheque is property.[101] The only difficulty is the requirement that Steph must intend permanently to deprive Jon of the piece of paper. The problem is that if Steph pays the cheque into her account the piece of paper will ultimately return to Jon's bank and Jon could get it back. If she is aware of this[102] then Steph commits no offence because she can claim that she did not intend to deprive Jon of the piece of paper.[103]

(ii) Obtaining the cheque as a thing in action by deception contrary to section 15. When Jon writes Steph a cheque he is creating a thing in action: a right for Steph to sue Jon. The thing in action is property for the purposes of the Theft Acts.[104] The problem is that it is not property belonging to another. Steph's right to sue

---

[99] [1982] Crim LR 369 (HL).   [100] *Kovacs* [1974] 1 WLR 370 (CA).

[101] *Arnold* [1997] Crim LR 833 (CA).

[102] She might, of course, not be aware of this banking practice, in which case she could be said to have intended permanently to deprive.

[103] It is arguable that although Jon can recover the piece of paper its usefulness has all gone: it can no longer be used as a piece of paper upon which to write cheques, and so s. 6 of the Theft Act 1968 means that he will be treated as having an intention permanently to deprive.

[104] Theft Act 1968, s. 4(1).

Jon represented by the cheque never belonged to someone else.[105] This reasoning was accepted (*obiter*) by the House of Lords in *Preddy*.[106]

As a result of points (i) and (ii) the Court of Appeal has baldly stated that it is not possible to steal or obtain by deception a cheque.[107]

(iii) Procuring by a deception of a valuable security under section 20(2) of the Theft Act 1968. Prosecutors to date have been reluctant to use this (admittedly rather obscure) offence in this context. However, it is hard to see why Steph could not be said to have committed it.[108]

(3) Guss deceives Sissy into writing him a cheque. Guss pays the cheque into his account.

The comments made above about scenario 2 apply. But the fact that the cheque has been paid in makes a difference because now Guss has committed an offence contrary to section 15A of the Theft Act 1968.[109] Guss could also be charged with theft of the money that has left Sissy's account.[110]

The following case discusses the representations that are implied when a defendant uses a credit card and shows how easily a defendant can find a loophole under the present law:

R v Nabina
[2000] Crim LR 48 (CA)

Nabina had applied for various credit cards, giving false information about his personal details. He then used the cards to obtains goods from various shopping outlets. He was charged with obtaining these goods by deception.

Lord Bingham of Cornhill CJ

In our judgment it is plain that the Crown's case rested on the making of a dishonest representation by the appellant to the various sales outlets. Such a representation could be proved in several ways: by documentary evidence showing the making of the false representation; by evidence from the outlet to which the representation was made; by an admission or evidence by the appellant himself that such representation was made; or by necessary or irresistible inference or perhaps as a matter of law. In this case, however, there was no document; there was no evidence from anyone at any of the outlets; and there was no admission by the appellant—no evidence from him that he made the representation charged. So the case must in our judgment rest on either necessary or irresistible inference or implication of law. It is not enough that an inference was possibly open to the jury because the representation is the crux of the offence and the jury could not convict unless the offence were proved to the criminal standard.

In our judgment the Crown, in seeking to uphold this conviction, face an insuperable problem. The drawing of an inference from the facts proved was a matter for the jury, and the

---

[105] *Davis* (1988) 88 Cr App R 347.
[106] Confirmed by the Court of Appeal in *Clark* [2002] 1 Cr App R 14 (albeit with some reluctance).
[107] Ibid.   [108] Smith (1997: 400).
[109] Inserted by the Theft (Amendment) Act 1996. For an explanation of why the new law was needed see Law Commission Report No. 243 (1996).
[110] *Burke* [2000] Crim LR 413 (CA); *Williams (Roy)* [2001] Cr App R 362 (CA).

jury were never directed to consider whether this ingredient of the offence was met and whether the inference should be drawn or not. We have referred to all the relevant parts of the summing-up, which are almost exclusively concentrated on the alleged representations to the banks. There is in our judgment no direction on the misrepresentations to the outlets or as to what the content of any such misrepresentation may have been. Mr O'Byrne, who represents the Crown on this appeal, while not conceding that the conviction is vitiated by the judge's failure to direct the jury on this point, is nonetheless constrained to acknowledge that there is no clear direction to the jury on this essential ingredient. We have the gravest possible doubt whether the jury could properly, even if fully directed, have regarded the making of the representation charged as a necessary inference from the facts before them. The use of a card to obtain goods and services is of course an everyday act. Broadly speaking, suppliers are concerned to ensure that they will receive payment from the issuers of the card. For that reason it is normal to require a signature from the customer, to compare the signature on the card with the signature on the voucher, and to make sure that the card is not on a stop list. There is, however, in our judgment room for doubt whether a supplier is interested in how a holder comes to be the holder of the card, provided (and this we emphasise) the transaction is one which will be honoured by the issuer of the card. In this connection the observations of Lord Diplock in *Metropolitan Police Commissioner v Charles* [1977] AC 177, 182 are very relevant.

On all these counts there was evidence that the issuer, had it known at the time of issue what it knew later, would not have issued the card. But there was no evidence from any of the issuing institutions that any of the transactions had not been, or would not be, honoured, nor that in the circumstances they regarded the appellant as acting outside the authority which they had respectively conferred on him. It is indeed in our judgment doubtful whether the appellant by his conduct could be said to have represented anything more than that he had authority to bind the bank and that the transaction would be honoured. There is room for argument (to say no more) as to whether such a representation, if made, would have been false.

We refer, as the judge did, to *R v Lambie* [1982] AC 449, and draw attention to the facts on which that case was based. The appellant in that case had been issued with a credit card limited to £200. She had used the card on a number of occasions and had very substantially exceeded her credit limit. The result was that the bank sought to recover the card and she agreed to return it. She did not, however, return the card but continued to use it. She was charged with an offence under section 16(1) of the 1968 Act of obtaining a pecuniary advantage:

'namely the evasion of a debt for which she then made herself liable by deception namely by false representations that she was authorised to use a Barclaycard . . . to obtain goods to the value of £10.35.'

Thus the representation alleged against her was that she falsely represented that she was authorised to use the card. The case against her was that she was not so authorised because she had exceeded the limit and the bank had revoked her authority to use the card by seeking its return. At page 459 of the only speech in the House of Lords, Lord Roskill said:

'My Lords, as the appellant says in paragraph 9 of his printed case, the Court of Appeal (Criminal Division) laid too much emphasis upon the undoubted, but to my mind irrelevant, fact that Miss Rounding said she made no assumption about the respondent's credit standing with the bank. They reasoned from the absence of assumption that there was no evidence from which the jury could conclude that she was "induced by a false representation that the defendant's credit standing at the bank gave her the authority to use the card". But, my Lords, with profound respect to the learned Lord Justice, that is not the relevant question. Following the decision of this House in *R v Charles*, it is in my view clear that the representation arising from the presentation of a credit card has nothing to do with the respondent's credit standing at the bank but is a representation of actual authority to make the contract with, in this case, Mothercare on the bank's behalf that the bank will honour the voucher upon presentation. Upon that view, the existence and terms of the agreement between the bank and Mothercare are irrelevant, as is the fact that Mothercare, because of that agreement, would look to the bank for payment. That being the representation to be implied from the respondent's actions and use of the credit card, the only remaining question is whether Miss Rounding was induced by that representation to complete the transaction and allow the respondent to take away the goods. My Lords, if she had been asked whether, had she known the respondent was acting dishonestly and in truth had no authority whatever from the bank to use the credit card in this way, she (Miss Rounding) would have completed the transaction, only one answer is possible—no. Had an affirmative answer been given to this question, Miss Rounding would, of course, have become a participant in furtherance of the respondent's fraud and a conspirator with her to defraud both Mothercare and the bank.'

Lord Roskill then went on to refer to the fact that whether an inference should be drawn was a matter for the jury.

In that case therefore the customer did not have the actual authority of the bank to warrant that the bank would honour the voucher upon presentation because she was in excess of her limit, and her authority to use the card had been revoked by the bank's request for its return and her agreement to return it. Here, so far as the evidence went, the appellant did have the actual authority of the issuing institutions to warrant that they would honour the vouchers upon presentation because the cards had been issued to the appellant and even if the banks would have been entitled to revoke his authority to use the cards, they had not done so. The appellant relies on the general principle that a contract (here the granting by the issuing company to the appellant of a right to use the card) is voidable until rescinded. In Lambie that contract had been rescinded. Here Mr McCullough for the appellant argues that it had not. Thus, he says, the appellant was entitled to exercise the right conferred on him by the issuers even if those rights had been obtained by dishonestly misleading statements until the issuers terminated the appellant's rights as, on the hypothesis of dishonest misleading, they were undoubtedly entitled to do. But Mr McCullough says that the issuers had not done so, and accordingly the appellant remained a person authorised to bind the bank or (if the language of the indictment is adopted) he remained for purposes of the sales outlet a legitimate holder of the card. There was no evidence that the issuers did not regard the appellant as having authority to bind them. Nor was there evidence that these transactions would not be honoured by the issuers.

On behalf of the Crown Mr O'Byrne did not take fundamental issue with the principles of law on which Mr McCullough relied. He cited no authority which threw doubt on those contentions. He accepted that, in the sense contended for, the appellant was a lawful holder of the cards. But he submitted that that was a rule of the civil law, not of the criminal law, and that this was a case concerned with allegations of dishonesty where different considerations applied. It is of course true that this was a prosecution concerned with dishonesty, but the dishonest misrepresentation alleged against the appellant concerned his civil law rights, and the issue whether the representation was correct or incorrect could not in our judgment be avoided.

> . . . Reluctantly, since it seems clear on all the facts that the appellant certainly was acting in a dishonest manner, we feel compelled to allow this appeal.
>
> *Appeal allowed.*

In the following extract Russell Heaton summarizes the law on cheques.

R. Heaton, 'Cheques and Balances' [2005] *Criminal Law Review* 752–61

Why cheques cannot be stolen or obtained by deception

Chose in action

The first source of problems was the courts' (perhaps understandable) tendency to see cheques as choses in action when they are not. At most a completed cheque form creates and at the same time evidences a chose in action, namely the right of the payee of the cheque to sue its drawer for the stated sum. It is not the chose in action itself since that is intangible property distinct from the physical piece of paper creating and evidencing it. It should also be pointed out that not all cheques create choses in action. Only cheques given for valuable consideration constitute the payee a holder for value under s.27(1) of the Bills of Exchange Act 1882 and thus confer a right to sue the drawer. If D induces P to give him a cheque in his favour by fraudulently claiming he is collecting for a charitable purpose, no chose in action comes into existence. D has given no valuable consideration and acquires no right to sue P, not even a voidable right. Similarly if D takes a cheque form and forges P's signature on it, the 'cheque' is a nullity and, contrary to appearances, does not create a chose in action. On the other hand, if D deceives P into issuing a cheque to him by falsely promising to do something amounting to valuable consideration (e.g. promising to deliver goods when he has no intention to do so), it is thought that the cheque would create a chose in action, albeit one that would be voidable for fraud. Technically, unless and until the underlying contract was rescinded by P, it would be valid so that, until rescission of the contract by P, there is an enforceable chose in action created by the cheque.

Can the chose in action still belong to the victim?

Even where the cheque does create a chose in action, the courts have interpreted *Preddy* as closing the door to any idea that D would steal it or obtain it by deception. The reason is that *Preddy* held that such chose in action, from the moment of its creation by the issue of the signed cheque to the moment of its satisfaction by the cheque being met, would never belong to anyone other than D, the payee. It would not at any time be property 'belonging to another' as required by both theft and obtaining property by deception.

   However, that plausible proposition ignores the very wide meaning given to 'belonging to another' by s.5(1). Property belongs to anyone 'having in it any proprietary right or interest' and that clearly includes equitable interests created by the imposition of constructive trusts. Put simply, the question is whether the law of restitution imposes a constructive trust in respect of the chose in action represented by the cheque upon a defendant who gets that cheque by fraudulently deceiving the victim. If it does, then the beneficiary of that trust, the victim, continues to have a 'proprietary right or interest' in the chose in action created by the cheque which therefore remains 'property belonging to another' throughout. Although the possibility was not raised in *Preddy* which therefore cannot sensibly be regarded as excluding it, it seems unlikely that it will be accepted as a way of outflanking that decision.

Its basis is an obiter dictum of Lord Browne-Wilkinson in *West Deutsche Landesbank Girozentrale v Islington LBC* to the effect that equity imposes a constructive trust on a fraudulent recipient of property obtained by fraud. The circumstances in which a constructive trust will be imposed where there is no fiduciary relationship between the victim and the accused cannot be delineated with any certainty but the underlying rationale seems to be based on the unconscionability of the defendant's conduct. A fraudulent recipient inevitably acts unconscionably but to hold that the victim automatically retains an equitable interest in the property on this account cuts across the rules on rescission and the edifice on which transactions which are voidable for fraud are built. If the victim retains a proprietary interest in the property, that will endure (to the possible prejudice of innocent third parties other than innocent purchasers for value), irrespective of whether rescission is possible. To expect a criminal court to build on such insecure foundations is unrealistic, certainly whilst the civil law remains so unsettled. It therefore seems likely that the courts will use *Preddy* as impliedly ruling out the recognition of an equitable interest where D gets the property by fraudulent misrepresentation.

That said, the Court of Appeal in Re Holmes proved receptive to the *West Deutsche* dictum and considered obiter that the recipient bank held the credit balance in D's account upon a constructive trust for the defrauded victim bank. That credit balance was therefore property belonging to another and was stolen by D when he caused it to be transferred out to various accounts around the world. Surprisingly and unnecessarily, the court relied on the application of s.5(3) whereas a beneficial interest under a constructive trust must surely constitute a 'proprietary right or interest' under s.5(1). However it seems unlikely that such a proposition would be applied to a chose in action created by a cheque. It would look rather odd to say that the victim has a beneficial interest under a constructive trust in the debt which he ostensibly owes to D! Furthermore, to do so would undermine *Preddy*.

The extending provisions in s.5(3) and (4) [Theft Act 1968]

Assuming s.5(1) is excluded, could charges of theft be sustained on the basis of s.5(3) or s.5(4)? In respect of s.5(4), it would appear not. Although D gets the chose evidenced by the cheque by the victim's mistake, he cannot be under the necessary obligation to restore it or its value. The chose itself, the debt owed by the victim to D, cannot 'in the ordinary meaning of the word' be 'restored' to the victim. The victim cannot get it back. All that can happen is that it is extinguished. Equally it is difficult to see how D could be said to be obliged to 'make restoration' of the 'value' of the debt. Restoration requires that the victim gets something back which he had in the first place and D's giving up of the debt which the victim created could not properly be described as restoring either the property or its value.

Section 5(3) can provide a neat way of sidestepping the intricacies of equitable interests though many cases where it is satisfied would disclose an equitable interest under s.5(1). In the context of the chose in action evidenced by a cheque made out to D by the account holder, the key question will be whether D is under a legal obligation to the account holder to retain and deal in a particular way with the debt owed by the account holder to D. This is because D will have received it 'from' the account holder. The clearest case is where a trust is impressed but an obligation can arise from simple contract. However, it is suggested that the mere fact that D persuaded the account holder to write the cheque by a fraudulent deception is insufficient unless it related to what was to happen to the debt represented by the cheque and D was thereby undertaking to use it in that way. For example, there might be an express or implied obligation to pay the cheque into a client or other special account. More naturally, however, such obligation is more likely to arise in respect of the proceeds of the cheque, the credit balance in D's account, so that it would be the 'proceeds' which would be deemed by s.5(3) to 'belong to another' and so the proper subject of the theft charge.

The recent case of *Adams* provides an example of how s.5(3) might come into play. D, an insolvency practitioner, was charged with theft of the chose in action evidenced by a cheque for £50,000 drawn in favour of D by an insolvent person, P, pursuant to an agreement between P and his creditors to pay this sum. The cheque should have been paid into D's client account but was paid into D's office account which was overdrawn well in excess of the agreed limit. D claimed that he was unaware of this cheque and payment of it into his office account until it was drawn to his attention by the police. The implicit basis of the jury's verdict was that they could not be sure he was aware of the receipt of the cheque until after it had been paid into the office account.

The Court of Appeal in *Wills* established that, for s.5(3) to apply, it was insufficient in criminal law for D to be under an obligation: he also had to have 'knowledge of the nature and extent of the obligation.' In *Adams*, therefore, s.5(3) could only be applied when D became aware of the nature of the cheque and that it had been paid into his office account. By this time, the debt represented by the cheque (that owed by P to D) had ceased to exist because it had been discharged by payment of the cheque and, furthermore, there were no proceeds because they had been swallowed up by the excess overdraft. Nonetheless the Court of Appeal affirmed D's conviction for theft of the debt owed by P to D on the basis that s.5(3) deemed this debt to belong to P! D certainly received property (the chose in action) from P and the civil law would impose an obligation of trust owed to P (and P's creditors) to retain and deal with the chose or its proceeds in a particular way. That should be enough to bring s.5(3) into play in respect of the issue of 'belonging to another' and D's lack of knowledge of the receipt and obligation should not be relevant to that question. Of course, D could not be guilty of theft without such knowledge but that is because he would not be dishonest (and in the *Adams* situation lack the necessary intention to permanently deprive).

Whether *Wills* is applied or not, it is difficult to see how a conviction can be sustained. By the time D became aware that the cheque had been wrongly paid into his office account and dishonestly decided not to pay P's creditors, the original chose no longer existed and there were no 'proceeds' of that chose in existence because it appears that D's office account was 'constantly in overdraft in excess of the agreed limit' during the whole period of these events. Quite simply, the original chose in action had ceased to exist by the time D became dishonest and there never existed any 'proceeds' of that chose in action so that there was nothing to steal at that point. The Court's contrary assertion envisages that the 'proceeds' of the cheque miraculously lived on despite having disappeared forever into the bank's coffers in reduction of the overdraft. These ethereal 'proceeds' were apparently appropriated by D after he became dishonest 'by failing to deal with the funds in accordance with his duty . . .' (Although not stated, presumably this is by application of the latter part of s.3(1) since D had 'come by the property without stealing it'). The fact that 'the proceeds of the cheque were unavailable to be dealt with properly' because of the unagreed overdraft made no difference. The court's decision is strong on assertion but weak on explanation and seems untenable.

If the defendant's account had been in credit or within agreed overdraft limits, the decision would have been correct. Although the decision was concerned with theft of the proceeds of the cheque (the 'credit' balance in the bank account) rather than the chose in action represented by the cheque itself, the reasoning could equally be applied to the latter. For example, if D had dishonestly endorsed the cheque to a third party, he would have stolen the chose represented by the cheque. That would have been deemed to belong still to the account holder because D received it from him and was under an obligation to him to retain and deal with it in a particular way, i.e. pay it into his client account (or deal with it in some other legitimate way for the benefit of the account holder's creditors).

The overall conclusion is that, whilst there might be some scope for utilising s.5(3), the courts are likely in most cases to conclude with *Preddy* that the chose in action represented by the cheque does not belong to another and so is incapable of being stolen.

Piece of paper

A cheque, being a piece of paper with print and writing on it, is tangible property and falls squarely within the definition of property capable of being stolen within s.4(1). Unlike the chose in action it creates, the piece of paper does 'belong to another'. Until it is issued, the piece of paper clearly belongs to the victim, who both owns [FN55] and possesses it. When the cheque is issued (whether handed over face to face or sent), the defendant obtains ownership at a time when the property belongs to another.

Intention permanently to deprive

However both theft and obtaining property by deception require proof of an 'intention permanently to deprive' the victim of her property. The House of Lords, obiter, in *Preddy* viewed this as absent on the ground that, at the time of receipt, a defendant's intention will invariably be to return the piece of paper to the victim (or, at least, the paying bank as agent of the victim) because that is the way to realise the cheque's value. Even accepting the blithe assumption that defendants invariably understand the basic workings of the cheque system, a number of arguments can be ranged against such a conclusion. Nonetheless the Court of Appeal accepted and applied it in *Graham* and, for this reason, felt bound to apply it again in *Clark* despite finding Sir John Smith's opposite view 'highly persuasive'. Remarkably the court thought that 'it would be wholly inappropriate . . . to treat the House of Lords' decision in relation to cheques as merely obiter . . .' even though counsel for the defence conceded, as was plainly the case, that it was obiter!

Unfortunately the court, preoccupied with the 'valuable security' issue analysed in the next section, did not consider [FN62] the most telling argument in favour of finding a true intention permanently to deprive. The argument is that D would have a conditional intention permanently to deprive. He would intend to return the cheque only if it was paid, otherwise he would intend to keep it. To put it another way, his intention would be to 'sell' it back to p. P would get it back only by paying for it. It is analogous to a ransom situation where D intends to return the property only if his demand for money is met. There is a confused line of authority starting with *Easom* on whether a conditional intention to permanently deprive would suffice but it is submitted that the implicit imposition of conditions as to the cheque's return such as these must satisfy the requirement of an intention permanently to deprive.

Valuable security

Sir John Smith's argument is that the piece of paper (the cheque form) changes character when it is completed, signed and issued. It ceases to be just an insignificant piece of paper and becomes a piece of paper with a valuable additional characteristic. It is a means of accessing or 'key' to the victim's account. It becomes a 'valuable security'. When a cheque is paid into a bank (the collecting bank), it is returned to the account holder's bank (the paying bank) which must either pay it or return it to the payee via the collecting bank. If the paying bank decides to pay the cheque, it naturally cancels it by stamping across its face so that it ceases to be a form enabling access to P's account. It is no longer a 'valuable security', having done its work. Therefore a defendant, assumed as ever to be versed in the ways of bankers, intends the cheque to return permanently to P (or his agent, the paying bank) when it has lost its status as a valuable security and as a means of accessing the account, and become a relatively insignificant piece of paper. If the cheque continues to be a valuable security because the paying bank decides not to pay it, it will be returned to the collecting bank and then to D. On that basis, Sir John concludes that D does intend to permanently deprive P of a valuable security: the tangible, uncancelled piece of paper.

It has been argued that this seems to regard the same tangible piece of paper as comprising at one and the same time two distinct pieces of tangible property—the piece of paper and the valuable security. However, this is a misconception. There is only one piece of paper. The argument is that when it acquires its status as a valuable security it becomes a different piece of paper and similarly when it ceases to be a valuable security. A blank piece of paper is quite different from the same piece of paper with a sketch by Picasso on it. If D intends to return the piece of paper only after erasing the sketch, can it be doubted that he intends to permanently deprive P of the sketch? Whilst the analogy is not entirely exact, it illustrates that the nature of property is often determined by attributes, the addition or subtraction of which transform it into different property. The question in each case is whether the attribute is so closely identified with the essence of the property as to define its nature. That was the view of the Court of Appeal in *Duru*: The cheque 'is a piece of paper which changes its character completely once it is paid, because it then receives a rubber stamp on it saying it has been paid or at any rate it ceases to be, in its substance, the same thing as it was before: that is, an instrument on which payment falls to be made.' In other words, it ceases to be a valuable security and becomes some other property.

Unfortunately the House of Lords in *Preddy* regarded *Duru*, which they overruled on another point, as wrong on this point too. However, the decision on the point was most definitely obiter and there is no real analysis of the arguments. It is true that the issue was canvassed in the arguments addressed to the House by both counsel but in a misconceived way. It was therefore open to the Court of Appeal to follow a different path. However, that path is effectively closed by the refusal of the Court of Appeal in *Graham* (without any real consideration of the point) and latterly *Clark* to adopt the argument. By contrast, in Australia, the Supreme Court of Victoria refused to follow *Preddy* and adopted Sir John Smith's arguments.

The extending provisions in s.6

The product of a messy compromise, the notorious section 6 'sprouts obscurities at every phrase'. It is only needed where D does not have an actual intention permanently to deprive (where D appropriates the property 'without meaning the other to lose the thing itself'). In such a case D is deemed to intend permanently to deprive but only if it is his 'intention to treat the thing as his own to dispose of regardless of the other's rights'.

The House of Lords barely mentioned s.6 in the judgments in Preddy and it cannot be taken as settling that s.6 is inapplicable in the cheque situation. The basic requirement of s.6 is proof of D's intention 'to treat the thing as his own to dispose of regardless of the other's rights'. This was held in *Clark* to be absent because the defendant was, as the victim 'anticipated, paying it [the cheque] into his own account'. My contention is that such an intention will be present when D appropriates the cheque. As far as D is concerned the cheque is his to dispose of as he wishes. It can be assumed that his intention will be either to pay it directly into his bank account or to 'cash' it via a third party who will pay it into their bank account. In the latter case, there is an intention to dispose of it by sale to the third party, a view supported by *Marshall* and *Downes*. Equally in the former situation, D disposes of the cheque when he presents it to the victim's bank in return for payment. He is passing his interest in the cheque to the paying bank which acts as agent for the victim. The fact that he intends to do what the victim and everyone else expects him to do, namely, pay it into the bank is surely not to the point. According to *Gomez* and *Hinks*, an assumption of the owner's rights is still an appropriation even with the blessing of the owner. Equally an intention to treat the thing as one's own to dispose of regardless of the owner's rights should not be governed by whether D does what is expected by the victim or anyone else. No doubt the railway company in *Marshall*, keeping the ticket touts under surveillance, knew exactly what they were going to do with the tickets they acquired. It is true that the defendants in *Downes* and *Marshall* dealt with the property in a way which the victims would not approve of and it has been argued in contradistinction in support of *Clark* that a defendant who presents a cheque just as the victim authorises and expects does not act 'regardless of the other's rights'. However, the argument seems to confuse the victim's rights over the credit balance in his account (not the subject of the relevant charge in *Clark*) with his rights over the cheque itself. When the victim presents D with the cheque, he cedes control of it to D. Can it be doubted that D would no longer be interested in any rights of P to it and would view the cheque as his to dispose of without regard to P? What happens to the cheque is entirely in his hands! The fact that the victim is happy for him to do what he intends should have no bearing on whether he intends to act 'regardless of the other's rights'. It is nonetheless a denial of the other's rights in respect of the cheque.

Furthermore, as can be seen from Lord Lane C.J.'s opinion in *Lloyd*, the fact that the intention is to return only in exchange for payment surely reinforces the notion that D is intending to treat the cheque as his own to dispose of regardless of the owner's rights.

QUESTIONS

1. Do you think most people are aware of the representations that they make when they use a credit card or cheque? Are most shopkeepers aware of the representations that are made? Notice the comment of the Law Commission that the present law relies on 'constructive deception' (Law Commission Consultation Paper No. 155, ch. 8).

2. Do you think Parliament should pass legislation specifically dealing with cheques, rather than relying on the general law on property offences? (See Law Commission Report No. 276 (2000) for such a proposal.)

FURTHER READING

Greenwood, A. (1981), 'Causation and Credit Card Fraud', *Cambridge Law Journal* 40: 209.

Smith, J. (1997), 'Obtaining Cheques by Deception or Theft', *Criminal Law Review* 396.

Spencer, J. (1979), 'The Theft Act 1978', *Criminal Law Review* 24.

Syrota, G. (1979), 'The Theft Act 1978', *Modern Law Review* 42: 301.

—— (1980), 'Are Cheque Frauds Covered by s.3 of the Theft Act 1978?', *Criminal Law Review* 413.

PART II: THE THEORY OF DECEPTION OFFENCES

9 DECEPTION OFFENCES IN PRACTICE

There were 278,902 recorded offences of fraud and forgery in 2004–5.[111] However, it is accepted that the actual level of criminal fraud and deception is much higher.[112] It often goes unreported to the police due either to victims not being aware that they have been deceived or victims pursuing civil remedies. Also, a significant amount of fraud is under-taken by employees against employers, who may, to avoid unwanted publicity, prefer to deal with the matter internally.

Although there are fewer reported criminal offences of fraud than of theft, one major study indicated that in financial terms the money lost from fraud dwarfed all other kinds of property crime.[113] At the end of the year 2001–2 the Serious Fraud Office was handling seventy-five cases, the total amount involved being £1.75 billion.[114] In 2004 it has been estimated that cases of fraud reported in the press involved £756 million.[115] The insurance company Norwich Union has claimed that fraud costs the UK £16 billion per year.[116] That is £340 per adult per year in the UK. The Centre for Retail Research claims that fraud on UK companies and public agencies costs £15 billion a year.[117] One costly form of fraud is credit card fraud, which constituted 153,281 of the recorded fraud offences in 2001–2. In the year 2003–4 BCS 3.6% of credit card users had been the victim of credit card fraud.[118] It has been estimated that credit card fraud losses amounted to £411 million in 2001.[119] The sums involved in tax fraud and benefit fraud are no doubt even higher.

10 WHAT IS A DECEPTION?

You may think that a deception is a straightforward telling of an untruth. In the following extract Stuart Green suggests there is a need to distinguish between lying and other forms of deception:

S.P. Green, 'Lying, Misleading, and Falsely Denying: How Moral Concepts Inform the Law of Perjury, Fraud, and False Statements' (2001) 53 *Hastings Law Journal* 157

I. Lying, Misleading, and Falsely Denying

Like many distinctions we make in our everyday moral thinking and discourse, the distinctions we make among the concepts of lying, misleading, and falsely denying are far

---

[111] Nicholas *et al.* (2005: 41). In addition to the offences discussed in this chapter there is a wide variety of statutory fraud offences and a couple of common law offences (e.g. cheating the public revenue).
[112] E. Posner (2003) provides a legal analysis of greed which motives much fraud.
[113] Levi (1987).   [114] Serious Fraud Office (2002: 23).   [115] BDO Stoy Hayward (2005).
[116] Norwich Union (2005).   [117] Centre For Retail Research (2003).
[118] Wilson (2005: vii).   [119] APACS (2002).

from sharp. Nevertheless, these concepts are widely used, easily recognized, and generally understood. There are good reasons for thinking that the distinctions among them are based on genuine moral differences.

A. Conceptual Differences Between Lying and Other Forms of Deception

For purposes of this article, I shall use the term 'deception' to refer generally to the communication of a message with which the communicator, in communicating, intends to mislead—that is, the communication of a message that is intended to cause a person to believe something that is untrue. A few points about this definition are worth making.

The first is that there is no deception unless the communicator intends to deceive. Untrue statements made by mistake are not deceptive, although they might cause a listener to be misled. . . . Second, there is no requirement that the message itself be untrue, since 'literally true' statements (a concept that is discussed below) can obviously be deceptive. For example, if Bill is asked where he was on the night of February 3 and says he was 'either in Chappaqua or in the City,' while knowing for certain that he was in the City, he has deceived his questioner into believing that he is unsure about his whereabouts on that night, even though his statement is in fact true. Third, deception can come in a variety of different forms. One can deceive by making a statement, asking a question, issuing a command, stating an opinion, displaying a picture, making a facial expression or gesture, or engaging in various other forms of verbal and non-verbal behavior. Kant gives a famous example: A deceives B into believing that he is headed on a journey by conspicuously packing a suitcase, and hoping that B will draw the intended conclusion.

Lying constitutes a subset of deception, involving a much narrower range of behavior. As generally used, the term lying refers to (intentional) deception that (1) comes in the form of a verifiable assertion, and (2) is 'literally false.' By verifiable assertion, I refer to a statement that has a determinable truth value (i.e., is either true or false, although its truth value may not be known at the time the assertion is made). Because they have no truth value, questions, commands, statements of opinion, greetings, apologies, christenings, and so forth are not capable of being lies, although they can certainly be misleading. . . .

What does it mean for a statement to be 'literally false'? 'Assuming that a sentence is not ambiguous, [its] literal meaning is derived, roughly speaking, by determining the meaning of the individual words . . . and applying the grammatical rules of the language to those words.' The 'literal meaning' of the sentence is to be distinguished from what the speaker intends by the sentence when she utters it. A statement that is literally false is thus one that is false on its face, without reference to the speaker's meaning. . . .

The difference between lying and non-lying verbal deception (which I shall henceforth refer to simply as 'misleading') is, therefore, essentially the difference between (1) asserting what one believes is literally false, and (2) leading the listener to believe something false by saying something that is either true or has no truth value. . . .

B. Caveat Auditor: The Moral Distinction Between Lying and Merely Misleading

Assuming a formal distinction between lying and merely misleading, we need next to ask whether there exists any moral difference between the two concepts. Imagine that Bill, who was in Chappaqua from February 1–5, is asked about his whereabouts on February 3. Is there really any moral difference between his responding, 'no, I was not in Chappaqua on February 3' (a lie), and the statement, 'well, I was in Chappaqua on February 4' (a literally true statement that nevertheless creates the misleading impression that he was not in Chappaqua on February 3)? The fact is, people sometimes go to great lengths to avoid not only telling the truth, but also to avoid lying. If lying and merely misleading were morally equivalent, such behavior would be irrational. How can it be explained?

My claim is that, other things being equal, merely misleading is less wrongful than lying because what I call the principle of caveat auditor, or 'listener beware,' applies to merely misleading but does not apply to lying. Like the principle of caveat emptor, which says that a buyer is responsible for assessing the quality of a purchase before buying, the principle of caveat auditor says that, in certain circumstances, a listener is responsible for ascertaining that a statement is true before believing it.

Lying involves the creation, and simultaneous breach, of a relationship of trust between a speaker and listener. As Charles Fried has put it:

'Lying is wrong because when I lie I set up a relation which is essentially exploitative. . . . Lying violates respect and is wrong, as is any breach of trust. Every lie is a broken promise [which] is made and broken at the same moment. Every lie necessarily implies—as does every assertion—an assurance, a warranty of its truth.'

By making an assertion to B, A tells B that she herself believes what she is saying. As a result, B is justified in putting her faith in A; B need not be on her guard or question A's veracity. If A is mistaken about her assertion, then she is wholly responsible for B's false belief. And if A's untrue statement has been intentional, it is A who is wholly to blame.

Merely misleading involves a very different dynamic. When A merely misleads B without making an assertion, she has not told B that she believes what she is saying is true (since what she is saying is neither true nor false). There is thus no warranty of truth that B could rely on. Again, Kant's bag packer provides a good example. If the bag packer lies and asserts that he is going on vacation, then he will be wholly responsible for the spectator's false belief. But if the bag packer merely acts as if he is going on vacation, and his spectator draws the wrong conclusion from those actions, then the spectator will be partly responsible for his mistaken belief. . . .

Lying and merely misleading can also be distinguished on the grounds that each tends to elicit a different set of reactive emotions, and cause a different set of harms, in its victims. A victim who is deceived by a non-lie feels foolish and embarrassed, presumably because he believes he has contributed to his own harm by drawing unwarranted inferences from misleading premises. By contrast, a victim of lies is much more likely to feel 'brutalized' (in Adler's word) by some external force. . . .

In arguing that lying is distinguishable from other forms of deception, I do not of course mean to suggest either that lying is always wrong or that lying is always worse than other forms of deception. A lie told to avoid some greater harm is not likely to be viewed as wrongful. And non-lying deception about a matter of real importance will be viewed as more wrongful than an outright lie about some trivial concern. Moreover, in some unusual cases, a 'bald-faced' lie may actually seem less objectionable than other forms of deception—with all of their subterfuges, dissembling, and pretense. At this point, my claim is simply that there are real and articulable differences in moral content between lying and other forms of deception, and that, ceteris paribus, lying is more wrongful than merely misleading.

11 WHAT IS WRONG WITH A DECEIT?

In the following extract (from an article which is the text of a lecture) Neil MacCormick seeks to define a deceit and consider exactly what is wrong with deliberately lying to another:

N. MacCormick, 'What is Wrong with Deceit?' (1983) *Sydney Law Review* 5

My question for today about deceit is a question which raises one version of that problem. Is deceiving people wrong because in particular and in general it has bad consequences? Or is it just wrong in itself because it is bad in itself? Or is it both? Is it both wrong because of its tendency to do harm *and* because of its own intrinsic nature?

. . .

Charles Fried, in fact, as one of the contemporary proponents of out and out anti-utilitarianism or anti-consequentialism argues that in its essential nature, subject. to a very few exceptions (here he departs from his leading exemplars Kant and Augustine), lying is always categorically wrong. To be lied to is to have one's rights as a rational agent violated. For one's capability of pursuing a rational life-plan is thereby as plainly impaired as if a secret neuro-surgical operation had tampered with one's brain, implanting therein the causes of false belief. Of course, he does not deny that lying can also have all sorts of bad consequences, and that these matter. Rather, his point is that always even apart from its consequences lying is a categorical wrong and an invasion of rights. Hence even good consequences would not justify it.

Unhappily, Fried's theory is vitiated by weakness and insufficiency of analysis. . . .

Deceit in and of itself need not be a matter of words or even of symbols. One person can deceive another simply by laying false clues. During the second world war the British High Command sought to deceive the German High Command into expecting an invasion of Europe from the South in 1944, by planting bogus documents on the body of a drowned army officer whose body was caused to be washed ashore on to German-held territory. One can, as the British in this case did, deliberately act with a view to causing people to form false opinions, using means calculated and intended to have that effect. To do so is to deceive. Whether or not one does wrong in such case depends upon the relationships between the parties. No one thinks it was wrong for the British to resort to the helps and stratagems of war in 1944. Flapping white sheets in your neighbour's garden in the hope he will think the garden is haunted seems a different case, however. In this case one may well be abusing one's neighbour's attitude of trust and credulity, and either acting against the spirit of courteous mutual regard proper to neighbourly relationships, or failing to do one's part in building such a relationship.

Telling lies, the instance of deceit on which I shall concentrate in this talk, is one special case of deceit. It has this in common with other cases of wrongful deceit. Successful lying always presupposes some 'neighbourly' relationship (in the lawyer's sense) between the liar and the person deceived. To understand the abuse of relationship involved, we need to examine the ingredients of a successful lie. I shall suggest there are eight, the first seven of which are also essential to truthful communication.

The first ingredient is that something must be said or (as lawyers usefully put it) 'represented' by one person to another. For example: 'Jones is a creditworthy person whose assets far exceed his liabilities'. To 'say' or to 'represent' is to utter or otherwise signify a proposition on a matter of fact, a proposition capable of being true or false. (That such propositions can be formulated linguistically depends on linguistic conventions, of course.)

The second ingredient is that what is said or represented must be said seriously, not manifestly in jest or by way of a lawyer's or a philosopher's example, or in some other way unseriously. This conception of saying something seriously is explicable only by reference to the speaker's intention, in a quite complex way. That is, in saying that p he must intend his addressee to recognize that this utterance of p is intended to be recognized as a genuine representation of the fact of the matter as the speaker believes it to obtain, or knows it. Of course, an asserter sometimes does not believe in (or know) what he says; he can be lying. But he must intend the addressee to suppose that he means to be taken seriously, and to be revealing a patent intention to be taken seriously.

The third ingredient is that the addressee must actually recognize that the speaker's utterance of his proposition (or his gesture, or whatever) is intended seriously, and openly so intended.

. . . The fourth is that the addressee, as well as recognizing that the utterance is seriously intended, must actually take it seriously: he must suppose that since the speaker says that *p* and means it seriously there is some reason for supposing that *p* is or may be true. But that, of course, is not enough to suit a liar's purposes. If the matter stops here, the addressee may do no more than allow of the possibility of *p* in framing his future calculations and plans, or he can go-and check up for himself to see whether or not *p* is the case.

The fifth ingredient is therefore that the addressee must adopt a belief that *p* is true on the authority of the speaker's seriously intended assertion; Only then has the lie been successful. . . .

The sixth ingredient follows from the fact that different people have different ranges of information and expertise available to them. Some matters of fact which are important to me (like why my roof is leaking) fall within other people's knowledge or expertise. Whatever they believe in such matters, they have at least better ground for their beliefs than I have for such opinions as I may hold. They have, as against me, the relative authority of superior knowledge, or I think they have. One condition of a hearer taking seriously and deciding to believe what a speaker says to him is that he believes the speaker has this authority of superior knowledge. Let me call this the 'authority condition'.

The seventh ingredient is that the hearer repose confidence or trust in the speaker. I shall not believe what you tell me—even if you do satisfy the authority condition—unless I believe that you are speaking truthfully to me. As a reasonable person, I shall not believe that you are speaking truthfully unless you have, or I think you have, reasons to tell me the truth.

Not everybody always thinks that or has reason to think it. If the British High Command had sent a message to the German High Command telling them to expect an invasion from the south in 1944, they would not have been taken very seriously. Conversely, remember the difficulty the British had in getting Stalin to believe that, Hitler was going to invade Russia in 1941. British intelligence had actually to resort to the expedient of passing their true information through a double agent—for a direct message though honest and truthful would not have been believed. Indeed, it was not believed by its recipient.

The point, then, is that a person's readiness to believe another depends upon his opinion as to the relationship in which he stands with that other. He must regard their relationship as friendly rather than hostile, and as implying some degree of mutual trust and confidence. The liar, to be successful as a deceiver, must therefore act in such a way as to generate or sustain his victim's belief that there is a relationship of real trust between them. Again, of course, the same goes for someone who hopes to pass true information or advice to another. Compare the sad case of the boy who cried 'Wolf!' too often.

Accordingly, a condition of successful lying—as of successful information-giving or advice in good faith—is that some relationship of trust obtain between the parties. Let me call this the 'trust condition'.

. . .

The eighth and final point about lying is that lies are assertions made by a speaker who knows or believes them to be false, made with the intention of deceiving the hearer: that is, of causing him to form a false belief. A lie is successful when it is believed; for then the hearer is deceived. The idea that serious assertions depend upon the speaker's intention, and the ideas which I called the trust condition and the authority condition are, I claim, essential ideas. I claim that they make my account of these matters preferable to Fried's and that of other fashionable writers on the theory of speech-acts.

. . . I think my analysis of the ingredients of successful lying has been essential to saying what is wrong with it. To lie is to utter a statement which one openly intends to be taken seriously as actually believed by oneself, and to be believed by the speaker. It is to do so with the contextual implication that one satisfies the authority condition and the trust condition. It works only if the addressee does accept one's authority and trustworthiness and therefore adopts the relevant belief. Yet one does not, in fact, believe what. one says. Hence even an undetected lie is abusive of the trust of one's hearer. In so far as lying always involves disrespect for persons, there is the gist of the disrespect. What is more, since no one can guarantee non-detection of his lies, there is a standing risk of actual harm to one's addressee *by* his discovery that one has abused his trust. For people set great value on their relation-ships of friendship, trust and confidence, as Dr. Finnis well points out. This is therefore a real harm to them, harmful in proportion to the subjective value set on the particular relationship. Moreover, it is an intended or foreseen harm, since one cannot lie without first establishing some trust and then consciously betraying it.

These factors are also relevant to a general consequentialist or rule-utilitarian argument. Relationships of friendly trust and confidence are of the greatest value to human beings. By being truthful one gives support to such relationships, and by being a liar one does harm to them, so it is generally beneficial to have and to observe a rule against lying.

. . . I must conclude.

I have suggested that lying is always wrong as a breach of a relationship of trust, and that there are general consequentialist reasons supporting a general rule against lying. Yet the law while acknowledging lies as in themselves always wrongful means goes further and treats deceit and lying as outside its scope unless further harmful consequences are aimed at by the deceiver, or result to the victim from reliance on false or even carelessly made misrepresentations, or from reliance on continuing intentions of the speaker.

And of course this is sound legal policy. It reminds us that there are degrees of wrong-doing. Some lies actually are trivial lies and more or less trivially wrong. Some are very harmful and thus very wrongful. They are so in proportion as our statements are intended to be and are in fact relied upon in practical ways and in practical matters. It is not only by its ulterior consequences that deceit is wrongful; but by its ulterior consequences, especially those in the intention and foresight of the deceiver, shall we judge of its seriousness as a wrong.

I hope I have fortified your belief that there is something wrong with deceit; but also that some such wrongs really are wronger wrongs than others. This seems to me obscured by such recent writing as insists that all wrongs are just simply and categorically wrong and there is an end on it. Out and out pure consequentialism may be an indefensible doctrine. But that is no ground for denying the vital relevance of consequences to our judgments of action. To have regard to the consequences of one's conduct is, to my mind, a condition of sanity.

The issue of what is wrong with a deception is raised in the dispute over *Gomez*[120] and *Hinks*,[121] discussed in Chapter 8. It will be recalled that following these cases nearly every offence of obtaining property by deception will also amount to the offence of theft. Simon Gardner in the extract at p. 551 justified this position by arguing that section 15 is simply an aggravated form of theft: it is theft and deception. Shute and Horder reject this argument in

[120] [1993] AC 442 (HL).   [121] [2001] 2 AC 241 (HL).

the extract at p. 553. They suggest that the section 15 offence is a fundamentally different kind of wrong from that involved in theft. They note that one of the key differences is that in an offence of obtaining property by deception the victim is required to play a role in the acquiring of the property.[122] It may be said that the defendant is using the victim as a puppet to acquire the property. This, it is argued, is a different kind of wrong from that the victim suffers in a case of theft.

QUESTIONS

1. Is MacCormick's argument effective only where the defendant and the victim are in a close relationship?

2. Do you think a person who had been deceived out of £100 would be more concerned about the loss of money or the way that they lost it? Does this suggest that there should be no fundamental difference between theft and deception offences?

12 DECEPTION OFFENCES AND CIVIL LAW

It is in the area of deception offences that the line between civil liability and criminal liability becomes particularly acute. The court needs to decide whether the wrong to the victim is best dealt with by a criminal sanction or by providing the victim with a civil remedy. Consider the case of *Allen*,[123] excerpted above, who left the hotel without paying but intended to pay at a later point. The House of Lords held that that was not a criminal offence and that civil remedies were the appropriate response. Similarly in cases under section 2(1)(b) of the Theft Act 1978 the difference between the stalling debtor and the person who never intends to pay is never straightforward. Indeed some commentators argue that section 2 offences are in reality little more than bad breaches of contract.[124]

There are, however, other issues here. In contract law there is a well-known principle: *caveat emptor* ('let the buyer beware').[125] In essence this means that if you are selling something you are (normally) not required to inform the purchaser of any defects in the product you are selling. You must not tell lies, but you are not required to reveal any truths. There is a tension here with cases like *Silverman*[126] (excerpted above) where the Court of Appeal felt that the relationship of mutual trust and confidence that had been built up was sufficient to require the party to speak. There is a danger that silent non-disclosures which would not be regarded as illegitimate under contract law will be regarded as criminal offences. This is another example of the way that, after *Hinks*,[127] a transaction may be regarded as valid under civil law, but criminal.

13 STANDARDS OF HONESTY AMONG THE GENERAL PUBLIC

Another issue highlighted by some of the offences is a tension between the standards of the general public in practice and the standards sought to be upheld by the law.[128] Consider

---

[122] Fletcher (1976: 115–20); Clarkson (1993).   [123] [1985] AC 1029 (HL).
[124] Wilson (2003: 474).   [125] Law Commission Report No. 276 (2002: para. 7.64).
[126] [1987] Crim LR 574 (CA).   [127] [2001] 2 AC 241 (HL).
[128] See also fraudulent claims on insurance policies: Clarke (2000).

Whitehouse and Antoniou,[129] where the court upheld the conviction of obtaining property by deception of two men selling cheap cassette tapes laid out on the ground outside an underground station. The conviction was upheld on the basis that the men were deceiving the public. They were, it was said, representing that the tapes were genuine (presumably in the sense that they had the consent of the owner of the copyright to sell the tapes). They had therefore deceived the public (because the tapes were illegal copies). A cynic might suggest anyone buying cheap cassettes from a stall outside an underground station would be aware they were not purchasing legitimate copies. Indeed many people buying cassettes in such circumstances probably could not care less whether or not they were 'legitimate'.[130] Are such cases really about deceptions or in fact is the law here seeking to prohibit dishonest behaviour?

A rather different example can be found in billing techniques used by lawyers. Most lawyers charge clients by the time they spend on a client's case. A major study of law firms in the United States found widespread abuse of the system, with lawyers claiming to spend far more time on a case than they actually did, even charging for 'thinking about a case' while watching television. The fault, the study suggested, was not just with individual lawyers. The study suggested some firms required lawyers to work fifty chargeable hours a week. Such extraordinarily high expectations are likely to lead to untruthful billing claims. The study claimed that exaggeration of time spent was seen as 'epidemic'.[131] But, interestingly, the behaviour was so widespread it had become normal and acceptable to those involved. Indeed the lawyers interviewed found the idea that inflation of hours spent for billing purposes was financial misconduct preposterous.[132] You may dismiss this, asking what would you expect from an American laywer! But there is evidence that white-collar criminals can come to see as 'normal' conduct which to 'outsiders' appears fraudulent.[133]

QUESTIONS

1. Have you ever lied and thereby made a financial gain? Should that be regarded as criminal?

2. Should the criminal law be used against those who overspend on their credit cards? Is it relevant to the argument that credit card companies are notorious in their hard-sell tactics and encourage the building up of debt?

3. Millett LJ in a recent case on insurance fraud commented that there 'seems to be a widespread belief that insurance companies are fair game, and that defrauding them is not morally reprehensible . . .': *Galloway v Guardian Royal Exchange (UK) Ltd* [1999] Lloyd's Insurance Reports 209. Why are insurance companies seen as 'fair game'?

4. Does the widespread fraud in relation to taxation and benefits mean the law should be more or less strict on fraud in those contexts? (See further Levi (1987: 136–44).)

---

[129] [1989] Crim LR 436.

[130] Davis and Roy (1998) argue that there are dangers that interpreting fraud too widely might criminalize socially beneficial commercial behaviour.

[131] Lerman (1999). See also Ross (1991).   [132] Lerman (1999).

[133] Levi (1987). For a detailed discussion of white-collar crime see R.G. Smith (2003).

14 REFORM OF THE PRESENT LAW ON FRAUD AND DECEPTION OFFENCES

Commentators for some time have been suggesting that all the deception offences could be caught up in one big offence of fraud.[134] As Edward Griew puts it:

> No one wanting to construct a rational, efficient law of criminal fraud would choose to start from the present position. The law . . . is in a very untidy and unsatisfactory condition. The various offences are not so framed and related to each other as to cover, in a clearly organised way and without doubt or strained interpretation, the range of conduct with which the law should be able to deal.[135]

This is not just a theoretical difficulty. The Law Commission[136] in its consideration of the issue names a number of cases where defendants were able to escape from conviction due to the complexity of the law, despite their clear dishonesty: *Duru*,[137] *Halai*,[138] *King*,[139] *Mitchell*,[140] *Manjdadria*,[141] *Mensah, Lartey, and Relevy*,[142] and *Preddy*.[143]

In 2002 the Law Commission produced its report on reform of fraud offences. It rejected a proposal that we should have a general offence of dishonesty or deception. Instead it proposed a new offence of fraud:

Law Commission Report No. 276, *Fraud* (London: TSO, 2002), 5.23–7.10

WOULD A GENERAL DISHONESTY OFFENCE BE DESIRABLE?

The arguments for a general dishonesty offence

5.23 The Crown Prosecution Service favoured the creation of a general offence of fraud based on dishonesty 'because of the flexibility it would offer in prosecuting fraud cases' and 'because it would cover situations where deceit is not used to commit the fraud, or where it is difficult to establish a link between the deception and the outcome or intended outcome.' It argued that flexibility was crucial given the developments in financial markets and the increasing use of new technologies. It further argued that complicated and technical legal arguments could be avoided by a general offence and that clarifying issues might help to simplify complex fraud trials.

5.24 The Serious Fraud Office felt that the unresolved problems of internet fraud, where the fraud consisted of enjoyment of a service delivered over the internet which had legitimately been paid for by another, and fraud in financial markets, specifically Eurobond fraud, highlighted the complexity of modern financial practices. It felt that the speed at which such practices were changing and developing showed 'the need for extreme flexibility in the relevant criminal law'. The Department of Trade and Industry expressly agreed with the views of the CPS and the SFO.

---

[134] Sullivan (1985); J.C. Smith (1995a).
[135] Griew (1995: 141).   [136] Law Commission Report No. 237 (2002: para. 3.19).
[137] [1974] 1 WLR 2 (CA).   [138] [1983] Crim LR 624 (CA).   [139] [1992] QB 20 (CA).
[140] [1993] Crim LR 788 (CA).   [141] [1993] Crim LR 73.   [142] 3 July 1995.
[143] [1986] AC 815 (HL).

The arguments against a general dishonesty offence

Legal certainty and fair warning

. . .

5.28 We continue to believe that a general dishonesty offence, by not requiring as an element some identifiable morally dubious conduct to which the test of dishonesty may be applied, would fail to provide any meaningful guidance on the scope of the criminal law and the conduct which may be lawfully pursued. We do not accept the argument that inherent uncertainty is satisfactorily cured by the promise of prosecutorial discretion. This cannot make a vague offence clear and, while it might ameliorate some of the risks, it does not excuse a law reform agency from formulating a justifiable and properly defined offence. . . .

Human rights

5.29 The principle of maximum certainty is now linked to the question of compatibility with the Human Rights Act 1998. [The Paper discusses potential compatibility with Art. 7 of the European Convention on Human Rights and the views of respondents to their consultation paper.]

   5.33 In the light of these responses, we take the view that general dishonesty offences (such as conspiracy to defraud) could perhaps be found to be compatible with the requirements of article 7. We nonetheless remain of the view that they offend against the principle of maximum certainty.

Fair labelling

. . .

5.35 We take the view that a general dishonesty offence would pay insufficient regard to the principle of fair labelling. It would not explain or reflect to society the nature of the wrong-doing or its scale of harm. The law in this area would lose its educative and declaratory functions.

Effect on other dishonesty offences

5.36 The practical consequence of the inroads into the principles of fair warning and fair labelling can be seen by the potential effect on other dishonesty offences. The widespread use of a general dishonesty offence would render largely academic the boundaries of all other offences of dishonesty. Where a person's conduct fell outside a particular offence because of the specific requirements that Parliament has thought appropriate for that offence, the prosecution would be able to circumvent the difficulty by charging the general dishonesty offence instead. For example, the receipt of stolen goods is not an offence under section 22 of the 1968 Act unless the receiver knows or believes them to be stolen. But some people would say it is dishonest to receive goods which one suspects to be stolen. The prosecution could therefore invite the fact-finders to convict a receiver of the general dishonesty offence without being satisfied of the knowledge or belief that the 1968 Act expressly requires. . . .

Is dishonesty criminal?

5.38 In Consultation Paper No 155, we argued that the case for a general dishonesty offence had to rest on the argument that all dishonest conduct should in principle be criminal. There would be no logical reason to attach criminal sanctions to every form of dishonesty for commercial gain, while giving complete licence to those who use dishonesty for political, emotional, social or sexual gains. On the other hand, if all dishonesty were to be criminalised, it would offend against the principle of minimum criminalisation. People across the jurisdiction tell small lies every day. This will often rightly result in social retribution, but such instances of dishonesty cannot be properly described as criminal. It is simply not appropriate to extend the scope of the criminal law to cover every minor social problem or instance of human frailty. A general dishonesty offence would be based on principles which, if taken to their logical conclusion, would trivialise the law and extend its scope too far.

. . .

A GENERAL DECEPTION OFFENCE

. . .

The concept of deception

6.10 Our informal discussion paper also discussed certain difficulties that currently exist in relation to the concept of deception, and would continue to exist if a new general offence were defined in terms of that concept.

6.11 First, as we explained in Part III above, there is a problem where the victim is indifferent to the truth of the proposition asserted by the defendant to be true, and it is therefore debatable whether he or she can be said to have been *deceived*—for example, where the fraud consists in the unauthorised use of a credit card or similar payment instrument. Our informal discussion paper suggested that this problem would be avoided if the law's focus were shifted away from the mind of the victim on to the conduct of the defendant, and to this end it proposed that the new general offence be defined in terms of 'false pretence' rather than deception. It would still have to be proved that the loss or gain *resulted* from the pretence. In order to meet the argument that a pretence has no effect unless it is believed, however, the paper proposed that it should be sufficient if the victim responded in some way to the actions of the defendant *as a whole* (as distinct from responding to the pretence in particular). even if that response were 'automatic' and not based on any positive belief in the truth of the pretence. This idea attracted only limited support: many respondents argued that it would be less artificial simply to recognise that the element of pretence is not essential in the first place. We are now persuaded by this argument. Misrepresentation is therefore one, but only one, of the ways in which the new fraud offence we recommend in Part VII could be committed.

6.12 Secondly, as we also pointed out in Part III, a requirement of deception cannot be satisfied where no human being is deceived because the defendant's false assertion was made only to a machine. It follows that, at present, it is not normally an offence to obtain services (as distinct from property, the dishonest acquisition of which is theft) by 'deceiving' a machine. Our informal discussion paper proposed to meet this problem by taking the idea of 'automatic' response by a human being and applying it to the literally automatic responses of machines. There was general agreement among respondents that the dishonest obtaining of services from machines should be brought within the criminal law, but again there was some opposition to the idea of doing this by stretching the concept of pretence. We are now persuaded that an offence designed to cover such conduct should be formulated simply in terms of the dishonest obtaining of services, rather than requiring that the services be obtained in a particular way which is analogous (but not identical) to deception. . .

. . .

A FRESH APPROACH

7.4 . . . We think it is possible to devise a general fraud offence which, without relying too heavily on the concept of dishonesty, would nevertheless be sufficiently broad and flexible to catch nearly every case that would today be likely to be charged as a conspiracy to defraud. Conspiracy to defraud would then be virtually redundant (in practice if not in theory), and could safely be abolished.

. . .

7.6 The difficulty that we have encountered in seeking to formulate a satisfactory fraud offence. we believe, results largely from the fact that the concept of fraud developed by the criminal courts has in some respects parted company from the word's ordinary meaning. This is not to say that the courts have overtly treated 'fraud' as a legal term of art. On the contrary, they have purported to analyse its ordinary meaning, and to apply that meaning for the purposes of conspiracy to defraud and of other offences defined as involving an element of fraud. It does not follow that they have always succeeded in accurately stating that meaning. According to the classic definition in *Scott*, for example. fraud includes any dishonest conduct which causes, or exposes another to the risk of, financial loss. This definition is wide enough to include conduct such as shoplifting, robbery or burglary, which a non-lawyer would hardly describe as fraud.

7.7 This divergence between the ordinary and legal meanings of fraud has laid a trap for law reformers. We have tended to assume that a fraud offence worthy of the name must inevitably embrace any conduct which the law currently regards as fraud. even if non-lawyers would not so regard it. Yet there is no need for a fraud offence to catch shoplifting, robbery or burglary, because these activities are adequately dealt with by existing statutory offences. To render conspiracy to defraud dispensable. a new fraud offence needs *only* to catch those kinds of dishonest conduct that an ordinary person would call fraud. The question is: what are the hallmarks of such conduct?

7.8 The classic statement of the nature of fraud is Stephen's:

'I shall not attempt to construct a definition which will meet every case which might be suggested, but there is little danger in saying that whenever the words "fraud" or "intent to defraud" or "fraudulently" occur in the definition of a crime two elements at least are essential to the commission of the crime: namely. first, deceit or an intention to deceive or in some cases mere secrecy; and. secondly. either actual injury or possible injury or an intent to expose some person either to actual injury or to a risk of possible injury by means of that deceit or secrecy.'

7.9 We note first that Stephen did not say these two elements are *sufficient* to constitute fraud: he said that they *at least* are essential. For reasons explained in Part V above, we are now persuaded, contrary to the view we provisionally expressed in Consultation Paper No 155, that the element of *dishonesty* should be essential to (though not sufficient for) criminal liability for fraud. With the addition of this element, Stephen's definition requires:

(1) deceit, intention to deceive or secrecy, *and*
(2) *either*
   (a) actual or possible injury to another *or*
   (b) an intent thereby to cause injury to another or to expose another to a risk of possible injury,
(3) *and* dishonesty.

The Government have responded by producing a Fraud Bill, the main provisions of which are as follows:

FRAUD BILL 2005

1. Fraud

(1) A person is guilty of fraud if he is in breach of any of the sections listed in subsection (2) (which provide for different ways of committing the offence).

(2) The sections are—

    (a) section 2 (fraud by false representation),

    (b) section 3 (fraud by failing to disclose information), and

    (c) section 4 (fraud by abuse of position).

(3) A person who is guilty of fraud is liable—

    (a) on summary conviction, to imprisonment for a term not exceeding 12 months or to a fine not exceeding the statutory maximum (or to both);

    (b) on conviction on indictment, to imprisonment for a term not exceeding 10 years or to a fine (or to both).

(4) Subsection (3)(a) applies in relation to Northern Ireland as if the reference to 12 months were a reference to 6 months.

2. Fraud by false representation

(1) A person is in breach of this section if he—

    (a) dishonestly makes a false representation, and

    (b) intends, by making the representation—

        (i) to make a gain for himself or another, or

        (ii) to cause loss to another or to expose another to a risk of loss.

(2) A representation is false if—

    (a) it is untrue or misleading, and

    (b) the person making it knows that it is, or might be, untrue or misleading.

(3) 'Representation' means any representation by words or conduct as to fact or law, including a representation as to the state of mind of—

    (a) the person making the representation, or

    (b) any other person.

3. Fraud by failing to disclose information

A person is in breach of this section if he—

    (a) dishonestly fails to disclose to another person information which he is under a legal duty to disclose, and

    (b) intends, by failing to disclose the information—

        (i) to make a gain for himself or another, or

        (ii) to cause loss to another or to expose another to a risk of loss.

4. Fraud by abuse of position

(1) A person is in breach of this section if he—

    (a) occupies a position in which he is expected to safeguard, or not to act against, the financial interests of another person,

    (b) dishonestly abuses that position, and

    (c) intends, by means of the abuse of that position—

        (i) to make a gain for himself or another, or

        (ii) to cause loss to another or to expose another to a risk of loss.

(2) A person may be regarded as having abused his position even though his conduct consisted of an omission rather than an act.

5. 'Gain' and 'loss'

(1) The references to gain and loss in sections 2 to 4 are to be read in accordance with this section.

(2) 'Gain' and 'loss'—

    (a) extend only to gain or loss in money or other property;

    (b) include any such gain or loss whether temporary or permanent;

    and 'property' means any property whether real or personal (including things in action and other intangible property).

(3) 'Gain' includes a gain by keeping what one has, as well as a gain by getting what one does not have.

(4) 'Loss' includes a loss by not getting what one might get, as well as a loss by parting with what one has.

    . . .

11. Obtaining services dishonestly

(1) A person is guilty of an offence under this section if he obtains services for himself or another—

    (a) by a dishonest act, and

    (b) in breach of subsection (2).

(2) A person obtains services in breach of this subsection if—

    (a) they are made available on the basis that payment has been, is being or will be made for or in respect of them,

    (b) he obtains them without any payment having been made for or in respect of them or without payment having been made in full, and

    (c) when he obtains them, he knows—

        (i) that they are being made available on the basis described in paragraph (a), or

        (ii) that they might be,

    but intends that payment will not be made, or will not be made in full.

(3) A person guilty of an offence under this section is liable—

    (a) on summary conviction, to imprisonment for a term not exceeding 12 months or to a fine not exceeding the statutory maximum (or to both);

(b) on conviction on indictment, to imprisonment for a term not exceeding 5 years or to a fine (or to both).

(4) Subsection (3)(a) applies in relation to Northern Ireland as if the reference to 12 months were a reference to 6 months.

FURTHER READING

Law Commission (2002), Report No. 276, *Fraud* (London: TSO).

Ormerod, D. (1999), 'A Bit of a Con: The Law Commission's Consultation Paper on Fraud', *Criminal Law Reform* 789.

Sullivan, G.R. (1985), 'Fraud and the Efficacy of the Criminal Law: A Proposal for a Wide Residual Offence', *Criminal Law Reform* 616.

Wilson, D. (ed.) (2005), *Fraud and Technology Crimes* (London: Home Office).

BURGLARY AND BLACKMAIL

PART I: THE LAW

1 BURGLARY

The 'person in the street' probably understands burglary to be the theft of property from someone's house.[1] In fact, the offence is far more complicated than this. It is not limited to theft, but can involve the commission of other crimes inside a home. Further, burglary can involve entering someone's home with an intent to commit certain crimes, even without actually doing so.

Section 9 of the Theft Act 1968 defines the offence of burglary:

> (1) A person is guilty of burglary if—
>   (a) he enters any building or part of a building as a trespasser and with intent to commit any such offence as is mentioned in subsection (2) below; or
>   (b) having entered any building or part of a building as a trespasser he steals or attempts to steal anything in the building or that part of it or inflicts or attempts to inflict on any person therein any grievous bodily harm.
> (2) The offences referred to in subsection (1)(a) above are offences of stealing anything in the building or part of a building in question, of inflicting on any person therein any grievous bodily harm or raping any person therein, and of doing unlawful damage to the building or anything therein.

DEFINITION

It is important to appreciate that there are two kinds of burglary:

1. Section 9(1)(a): entering a building or part of a building as a trespasser with an intent to commit one of the following in the building:
   (a) theft;
   (b) criminal damage; or
   (c) infliction of grievous bodily harm.

---

[1] Lauer (1997) provides a useful discussion of the history of burglary.

2. Section 9(1)(b): having entered a building or part of a building as a trespasser, committing either

   (a) theft or attempted theft; or

   (b) infliction or attempted infliction of grievous bodily harm.

The key difference between the two offences is the time at which the crime is committed:[2]

   (1) Section 9(1)(a) is committed when the defendant enters the building.

   (2) Section 9(1)(b) is committed when, once inside the building, the defendant commits one of the listed crimes.

If a defendant enters as a trespasser, intending to steal property, and once inside does indeed steal property the defendant is guilty of both the forms of burglary. If the burglary is from domestic premises the maximum penalty is fourteen years; whereas if the burglary is from a non-domestic building it is ten years.[3]

Several elements of the offence of burglary need further discussion:

1.1 BUILDING OR PART OF A BUILDING

A building must involve a permanent structure. A twenty-five-foot-long freezer sitting in a farmyard for more than two years was held to be a building,[4] whereas a large container that formed the rear part of a lorry was not.[5] Section 9(4) states that an inhabited vehicle is included within the definition of a building. This is designed to cover houseboats and caravans which are permanently inhabited. To be a building there is no need for the structure to be occupied. A garden shed can therefore be a building.

If the defendant enters a building with the consent of the owner (and so is not a trespasser—see below) but then enters a part of the building which he is not permitted to enter with intent to steal, he or she cannot be guilty of burglary. For example, Victor enters a shop, but once inside walks into the manager's office. He can be charged with burglary when entering the manager's office as a trespasser; he has entered part of the building as a trespasser. To constitute a part of a building there must be some kind of physical mark or barrier. A separate room clearly constitutes a part of building; less obviously a 'no entry' sign or rope could mark off a part of a room.[6]

1.2 ENTRY

What does 'enters' mean? The burglar must enter the building, but this does not mean that all of a burglar's body must enter the building. According to the Court of Appeal in *Brown*[7] there must be is an 'effective entry'.[8] In *Brown* the defendant broke a shop window and stuck the top half of his body through it while investigating the inside of the shop. This was

---

[2] The indictment should make it clear which offence is being charged: *Hollis* [1971] Crim LR 525.
[3] Criminal Justice Act 1991.   [4] *B and S v Leathley* [1979] Crim LR 314.
[5] *Norfolk Constabulary v Seekings and Gould* [1986] Crim LR 167.
[6] *Walkington* [1979] 2 All ER 716 (CA).
[7] It rejected the test in *Collins* [1973] QB 100 that there had to be 'an effective and substantial entry'.
[8] *Brown* [1985] Crim LR 212 (CA).

an effective entry, and so the offence was made out. The Court of Appeal in *Ryan*[9] rejected an argument that the test should be whether there was a sufficient amount of the defendant's body inside to enable him or her to carry out one of the crimes. So if Tim enters a downstairs window he has still 'entered' for the purposes of burglary even if he is intending to steal a painting several floors up. If 'effective' does not mean 'effective to be able to commit one of the listed crimes' it is unclear what it means. It may be that all the phrase is doing is making clear that minimal entry (e.g. just a fingertip) would not be sufficient. The question will now be one for the jury to decide.

It is widely accepted that it is possible to commit burglary by using an object to enter the property, although there is no recent authority on the issue.[10] So if a defendant put a pole through a window and pulled out an item this could be burglary. Further, if the defendant trained his young child[11] (or a dog) to enter other people's houses and steal property, the defendant would be guilty of burglary.[12]

1.3 TRESPASSER

To be guilty of burglary the defendant must enter as a trespasser, being aware that she is a trespasser. The term trespasser is in fact a term used in tort law. If someone enters a piece of land she does not own without legal authorization then *prima facie* she is a trespasser. The most common form of legal authorization is to have the consent of the owner of the land[13] or of the owner's family.[14]

In *Collins*,[15] the key issue was whether the owner's daughter had invited the defendant into the house before he had entered. If she had he could not be convicted of burglary because he was not a trespasser.

R v Collins
[1973] QB 100 (CA)[16]

Stephen Collins had had a good deal to drink and was 'desirous of having sexual intercourse'. On passing the victim's house he noticed her light was on. He fetched a ladder, removed all of his clothes, apart from his socks, and climbed up the ladder. He pulled himself onto the window sill. The victim awoke and saw the outline of a naked male form. She assumed it must be her boyfriend and therefore beckoned him in. He joined her in bed and they had sexual intercourse. It was only when she switched on the light that she discovered he was not her boyfriend. He was charged with burglary with intent to rape. The appellant claimed that he would not have entered the room had the victim not beckoned him in. There was no clear evidence of where on the sill the defendant was when the victim welcomed him in. The judge directed the jury that they had to be satisfied that the appellant entered the room as a trespasser with intent to

---

[9] [1996] Crim LR 320 (CA).   [10] e.g. Simester and Sullivan (2003: 503).
[11] This would be to use an innocent agent.   [12] *Wheelhouse* [1994] Crim LR 756 (CA).
[13] Other forms of legal authorization include police officers entering on the basis of a search warrant or a landlord distraining property for non-payment of rent.
[14] *Robson v Hallett* [1967] 2 QB 939 (CA): the son of the owner invited police officers into the house, and so they were not trespassers.
[15] [1973] QB 100 (CA).   [16] [1972] 2 All ER 1105, [1973] 3 WLR 243, (1972) 56 Cr App R 554.

commit rape. Whether or not he was a trespasser depended on the question: was the entry intentional or reckless?

Lord Justice Edmund Davies delivered the judgment of the court

Under s 9 of the Theft Act 1968, which renders a person guilty of burglary if he enters any building or part of a building as a trespasser and with the intention of committing rape, the entry of the appellant into the building must first be proved. Well, there is no doubt about that, for it is common ground that he did enter this girl's bedroom. Secondly, it must be proved that he entered as a trespasser. We will develop that point a little later. Thirdly it must be proved that he entered as a trespasser with intent at the time of entry to commit rape therein.

The second ingredient of the offence—the entry must be as a trespasser—is one which has not, to the best of our knowledge, been previously canvassed in the courts. Views as to its ambit have naturally been canvassed by the textbook writers, and it is perhaps not wholly irrelevant to recall that those who were advising the Home Secretary before the Theft Bill was presented to Parliament had it in mind to get rid of some of the frequently absurd technical rules which had been built up in relation to the old requirement in burglary of a 'breaking and entering'. The cases are legion as to what this did or did not amount to, and happily it is not now necessary for us to consider them. But it was in order to get rid of those technical rules that a new test was introduced, namely that the entry must be 'as a trespasser'.

What does that involve? According to the learned editors of Archbold (*Criminal Pleading, Evidence and Practice* (37th Edn 1969), p. 572, para 1505):

'Any intentional, reckless or negligent entry into a building will, it would appear, constitute a trespass if the building is in the possession of another person who does not consent to the entry. Nor will it make any difference that the entry was the result of a reasonable mistake on the part of the defendant, so far as trespass is concerned.'

If that be right, then it would be no defence for this man to say (and even were he believed in saying), 'Well, I honestly thought that this girl was welcoming me into the room and I therefore entered, fully believing that I had her consent to go in'. If Archbold is right, he would nevertheless be a trespasser, since the apparent consent of the girl was unreal, she being mistaken as to who was at her window. We disagree. . . . In the judgment of this court, there cannot be a conviction for entering premises 'as a trespasser' within the meaning of s 9 of the Theft Act 1968 unless the person entering does so knowing that he is a trespasser and nevertheless deliberately enters, or, at the very least, is reckless whether or not he is entering the premises of another without the other party's consent.

Having so held, the pivotal point of this appeal is whether the Crown established that the appellant at the moment that he entered the bedroom knew perfectly well that he was not welcome there or, being reckless whether he was welcome or not, was nevertheless determined to enter. That in turn involves consideration as to where he was at the time that the complainant indicated that she was welcoming him into her bedroom. If, to take an example that was put in the course of argument, her bed had not been near the window but was on the other side of the bedroom, and he (being determined to have her sexually even against her will) climbed through the window and crossed the bedroom to reach her bed, then the offence charged would have been established. But in this case, as we have related, the layout of the room was different, and it became a point of nicety which had to be conclusively established by the Crown as to where he was when the girl made welcoming signs, as she unquestionably at some stage did.

. . .

[Having considered the trial judge's direction Edmund Davis LJ continued:]

We are compelled to say that we do not think the trial judge by these observations made it sufficiently clear to the jury the nature of the second test about which they had to be satisfied before the appellant could be convicted of the offence charged. There was no doubt that his entry into the bedroom was 'intentional'. But what the appellant had said was, 'She knelt on the bed, she put her arms around me and then I went in'. If the jury thought he might be truthful in that assertion, they would need to consider whether or not, although entirely surprised by such a reception being accorded to him, this young man might not have been entitled reasonably to regard her action as amounting to an invitation to him to enter. If she in fact appeared to be welcoming him, the Crown do not suggest that he should have realised or even suspected that she was so behaving because, despite the moonlight, she thought he was someone else. Unless the jury were entirely satisfied that the appellant made an effective and substantial entry into the bedroom without the complainant doing or saying anything to cause him to believe that she was consenting to his entering it, he ought not to be convicted of the offence charged. The point is a narrow one, as narrow maybe as the window sill which is crucial to this case. But this is a criminal charge of gravity and, even though one may suspect that his intention was to commit the offence charged, unless the facts show with clarity that he in fact committed it he ought not to remain convicted.

. . . One further matter that was canvassed ought perhaps to be mentioned. The point was raised that, the complainant not being the tenant or occupier of the dwelling-house and her mother being apparently in occupation, this girl herself could not in any event have extended an effective invitation to enter, so that even if she had expressly and with full knowledge of all material facts invited the appellant in, he would nevertheless be a trespasser. Whatever be the position in the law of tort, to regard such a proposition as acceptable in the criminal law would be unthinkable.

We have to say that this appeal must be allowed on the basis that the jury were never invited to consider the vital question whether this young man did enter the premises as a trespasser, that is to say knowing perfectly well that he had no invitation to enter or reckless of whether or not his entry was with permission. . . .

Appeal allowed. Conviction quashed.

There are a number of difficulties with the trespasser requirement:

(1) Withdrawing of permission. If Camilla has permission from Liz to enter her house, but that permission is later withdrawn and Liz asks Camilla to leave, Camilla is a trespasser unless she leaves within a reasonable length of time. However, to be guilty of burglary a person has to enter a building as a burglar. So if Camilla is invited into Liz's house, is then asked to leave, but does so very slowly, and on the way out steals some property there is no burglary (only theft). It should, however, be remembered that if a defendant enters a 'part' of a building as a trespasser that is sufficient for theft. So, if on her slow way out Camilla enters a new part of the building she can be convicted.

(2) Acting in excess of permission. More difficult issues arise where the defendant has been given permission to enter a house for a particular purpose (e.g. to read a gas meter) but acts in excess of this permission (e.g. entering a bedroom). He or she is then trespassing and so can be convicted of burglary. This concept was explained in Smith and Jones (extracted at p. 626).

(3) Consent to enter based on a mistake. What if the defendant is given consent to enter a building on the basis of a fundamental mistake? An example was *Collins*, where the appellant gave consent to the defendant to enter on the assumption that he was her boyfriend. The position in civil law is that if the consent is provided following a fundamental mistake (such as to the identity of the individual) then the consent is invalid; but if the mistake is not fundamental (for example, a mistake over an irrelevant matter) then the consent may still be valid. Presumably the criminal courts would take a similar approach. However, it should be recalled that it must be shown that the defendant knew he was a trespasser. So in the *Collins* case, even though the defendant was a trespasser because the daughter had made a fundamental mistake over his identity, if the defendant honestly believed that he was being invited in, he lacked the *mens rea* element because he did not know he was a trespasser.

(4) The *mens rea* of trespasser. As just mentioned, to be guilty of burglary defendants must know that they are trespassers or be reckless.[17] This was emphasized by Edmund-Davies LJ in *Collins*.[18] This does not require evidence that defendants understand the law of trespass and are aware that they may be committing trespass. Rather, it is enough if the defendants are aware of the facts that render them trespassers (e.g. that they entered a building without the permission of the owner). So, if Edith, staying with a friend, goes out for a drink and on her return stupidly mistakes a neighbour's house for her friend's and enters it and carelessly breaks a chair she is not guilty of burglary because she believes (even if unreasonably) that she has permission to enter.

R v Jones; R v Smith
[1976] 3 All ER 54 (CA)[19]

John Jones and Christopher Smith were charged with burglary. They had entered Smith's father's house and stolen two television sets. At the trial Smith stated that his father had given him unreserved permission to enter his house. The appellants appealed against their conviction on the ground that Smith had not entered his father's house as a trespasser.

Lord Justice James delivered the following judgment of the court

. . . The next ground of appeal relied on by counsel for the appellants in his argument is that which is put forward as the first ground in each of the appellant's grounds. It is the point on which counsel had laid the greatest stress in the course of his argument. The argument is based on the wording of the Theft Act 1968, s 9(1), which provides:

'A person is guilty of burglary if . . . (b) having entered any building or part of a building as a trespasser he steals or attempts to steal anything in the building or that part of it or inflicts or attempts to inflict on any person therein any grievous bodily harm.'

The important words from the point of view of the argument in this appeal are 'having entered any building . . . as a trespasser'.

---

[17] In the *Cunningham* sense.
[18] [1973] QB 100 (CA).   [19] [1976] 1 WLR 672, (1976) 63 Cr App R 47.

It is a section of an Act of Parliament which introduces a novel concept. Entry as a trespasser was new in 1968 in relation to criminal offences of burglary. It was introduced in substitution for, as an improvement on, the old law, which required considerations of breaking and entering and involved distinctions of nicety which had bedevilled the law for some time.

Counsel for the appellants argues that a person who had a general permission to enter premises of another person cannot be a trespasser. His submission is as short and as simple as that. Related to this case he says that a son to whom a father has given permission generally to enter the father's house cannot be a trespasser if he enters it even though he had decided in his mind before making the entry to commit a criminal offence of theft against the father once he had got into the house and had entered that house solely for the purpose of committing that theft. . . .

The decision in *R v Collins* [1973] QB 100 in this court, a decision on the criminal law, added to the concept of trespass as a civil wrong only the mental element of *mens rea*, which is essential to the criminal offence. Taking the law as expressed in *Hillen and Pettigrew v ICI (Alkali) Ltd* [1936] AC 65 and in *R v Collins* n1, it is our view that a person is a trespasser for the purpose of s 9(1)(b) of the Theft Act 1968 if he enters premises of another knowing that he is entering in excess of the permission that has been given to him, or being reckless whether he is entering in excess of the permission that has been given to him to enter, providing the facts are known to the accused which enable him to realise that he is acting in excess of the permission given or that he is acting recklessly as to whether he exceeds that permission, then that is sufficient for the jury to decide that he is in fact a trespasser.

In this particular case it was a matter for the jury to consider whether, on all the facts, it was shown by the prosecution that the appellants entered with the knowledge that entry was being effected against the consent or in excess of the consent that had been given by Mr Alfred Smith to his son Christopher. The jury were, by their verdict, satisfied of that.

Appeals dismissed.

This was a controversial decision because it means that whether a person is a trespasser depends on his or her mental state (i.e. whether at the point of entering he or she intended to commit a crime). Taken to its logical conclusion the *Jones and Smith* rule would mean that every shoplifter was a burglar, because when stealing in a shop the defendant was acting in excess of the permission of the shop owner (shop owners do not invite shoplifters into their shops).[20] It appears from *Walkington*,[21] heard after *Jones and Smith*, that the case will not be extended that far. There the Court of Appeal required proof that the defendant, having entered the shop intending to steal, entered a separate part of the shop he was not permitted to go into.

1.4 THE *MENS REA* FOR BURGLARY

The *mens rea* depends on which form of burglary is charged:

(1) Under section 9(1)(a) it must be shown that the defendant had an intention to commit one of the listed offences *at the time the defendant entered the building*. It should be stressed that if the defendant entered the building intending to steal, but

---

[20] Pace (1985).   [21] [1979] 1 WLR 1169 (CA).

628 | CRIMINAL LAW: TEXT, CASES, AND MATERIALS

once inside decided not to steal the offence was still committed. Likewise if the defendant entered the building not intending to commit theft, but once inside decided to do so, there would be no burglary contrary to section 9(1)(a). What is yet to be decided by the courts is what would happen if the defendant intended to take property from the building and damage it outside. The question is whether the word 'therein' in section 9(1)(b) refers to the place where the property is found or the place where the damage takes place.

(2) Under section 9(1)(b) the *mens rea* of burglary under section 9(1)(b) is the *mens rea* for stealing. Less clear is where the relevant crime is the infliction of grievous bodily harm. Controversially the Court of Appeal in *Wilson and Jenkins*[22] suggested that it does not require the proof of any particular *mens rea*.[23] Many commentators have taken the view that this is incorrect and that at least *Cunningham* recklessness as to the infliction of grievous bodily harm is required.[24]

What if the defendant decides to enter property and see if there is anything that is going to be worth stealing? Such an intent is described as a conditional intent: the defendant has an intent to steal on condition that there is something that is worth stealing. Does such an intent amount to an intent to steal for the purposes of burglary? Yes, it does.[25]

2 AGGRAVATED BURGLARY

Section 10 of the Theft Act 1968 states:

(1) A person is guilty of aggravated burglary if he commits any burglary and at the time has with him any firearm or imitation firearm, any weapon of offence, or any explosive; and for this purpose—

(a) 'firearm' includes an airgun or air pistol, and 'imitation firearm' means anything which has the appearance of being a firearm, whether capable of being discharged or not; and

(b) 'weapon of offence' means any article made or adapted for use for causing injury to or incapacitating a person, or intended by the person having it with him for such use; and

(c) 'explosive' means any article manufactured for the purpose of producing a practical effect by explosion, or intended by the person having it with him for that purpose.

Aggravated burglary involves a defendant who has with him at the time of the burglary a firearm, imitation firearm, a weapon of offence, or an explosive.[26] If the burglary is under section 9(1)(a) then it must be shown that the defendant had the weapon at the time of entry; under section 9(1)(b) it must be shown that the defendant had the weapon at the time of committing the further offence. In other words the defendant must possess the

---

[22] [1983] 1 All ER 1000 (CA), confirmed on other grounds in [1984] AC 242 (HL).

[23] There is no offence of simply inflicting grievous bodily harm under the Offences Against the Person Act 1861.

[24] e.g. J.C. Smith (2002: 640).   [25] *A-G's References (Nos. 1 and 2 of 1979)* [1979] 3 All ER 143 (CA).

[26] Note also the Theft Act 1968, s. 25, on going equipped to steal.

weapon at the time when the offence of burglary is committed.[27] The definition of a 'weapon of offence' is wide. It means that a screwdriver can be regarded as weapon of offence if the defendant intends to use it to injure someone.[28] There is no need to show that the defendant intended to use the item at that particular burglary, as long as there was an intention to use the item against someone on some occasion.[29] However, it must be shown that the defendant was aware that he had the weapon with him at the time of the burglary.[30]

3 TRESPASS WITH INTENT TO COMMIT A SEXUAL OFFENCE

Under section 63 of the Sexual Offences Act 2003:

> (1) A person commits an offence if—
>
>   (a) he is a trespasser on any premises,
>
>   (b) he intends to commit a relevant sexual offence on the premises, and
>
>   (c) he knows that, or is reckless as to whether, he is a trespasser.

Notably, this offence refers to a structure (rather than a building). In section 63(2) it is explained that a structure 'includes a tent, vehicle or vessel or other temporary or movable structure'. The term 'sexual offence' is widely defined in section 62 and includes the Sexual Offences in the 2003 Act (which have been discussed in Chapter 7).

4 BLACKMAIL

DEFINITION

The *actus reus* is: (i) the defendant makes an unwarranted demand
                      (ii) with menaces.

The *mens rea* is: (i) the defendant must act with a view to gain for himself or another or with intent to cause loss to another
                    (ii) the defendant either
                         (a) does not believe that he has reasonable grounds for making the belief or
                         (b) does not believe that the use of menaces is a proper means of reinforcing the demand.

At the heart of the offence of blackmail is the use of threats to acquire property or cause a loss to the victim.[31] In a sense it is a combination of an offence against the person (the creation of fear of an unpleasant consequence) and a property offence (the financial gain to

---

[27] *Francis* [1982] Crim LR 363 (CA); *O'Leary* (1986) 82 Cr App R 341 (CA).

[28] *Kelly* [1993] Crim LR 763.

[29] *Stones* (1989) 89 Cr App R 26 (CA); *Kelly* [1993] Crim LR 763.

[30] *Russell* (1985) 81 Cr App R 315; *Kelly* [1993] Crim LR 763.

[31] Tooher (1978), G. Williams (1975), and Bein (1982) provide useful comparative surveys of blackmail law.

the defendant or loss to the victim). The offence of blackmail is defined in section 21 of the Theft Act 1968:

> (1) A person is guilty of blackmail if, with a view to gain for himself or another or with intent to cause loss to another, he makes any unwarranted demand with menaces; and for this purpose a demand with menaces is unwarranted unless the person making it does so in the belief—
>
> (a) that he has reasonable grounds for making the demand; and
>
> (b) that the use of the menaces is a proper means of reinforcing the demand.
>
> (2) The nature of the act or mission demanded is immaterial, and it is also immaterial whether the menaces relate to action to be taken by the person making the demand.

The key elements of the offence[32] are as follows.

4.1 A DEMAND

The demand can be either oral or written.[33] In most cases of blackmail the demand will be explicit: 'Give me some money or else I'll . . .'; but the demand can also be implicit.[34] If Oliver stopped Archie in a dark street, pointed a knife at him, and said 'Would you like to give some money to a good cause', this could be regarded as as much a demand as a cruder request for money. But if a victim voluntarily offers money without an express or implied demand from the defendant there is no blackmail. For example, if Peter catches Wendy red-handed in committing a theft and Wendy offers Peter £200 if he does not tell the police what he has seen, there is no blackmail.[35]

The word 'demand' is to be given its ordinary meaning.[36] All that is necessary is that the demand is issued. There is no need for the victim to hear or receive the demand.[37] If a letter issuing a demand is put in a post box it is at that point that the offence is committed. Therefore, even if the letter is lost in the post and the victim never receives it, the defendant has still committed the offence.[38]

4.2 WITH A VIEW TO A GAIN OR LOSS

The demand must involve a financial gain to the defendant or a third party, or a financial loss to the victim.[39] This is clarified in section 34(2)(a) of the Theft Act 1968:

> . . . 'gain' and 'loss' are to be construed as extending only to gain or loss in money or other property, but as extending to any such gain or loss whether temporary or permanent; and—

---

[32] The maximum sentence is 14 years.

[33] A written demand might amount to an offence under the Malicious Communications Act 1988.

[34] *Collister and Warhurst* (1955) 39 Cr App R 100 (CA).

[35] Although such acts could amount to incitement to commit an offence under the Criminal Law Act 1967, s. 5.

[36] *Treacy v DPP* [1971] AC 537, 565, per Lord Diplock.   [37] Ibid.   [38] Ibid.

[39] Theft Act 1968, s. 34.

> (i) 'gain' includes a gain by keeping what one has, as well as a gain by getting what one has not; and
>
> (ii) 'loss' includes a loss by not getting what one might get, as well as a loss by parting with what one has.

So a demand that the victim remove his or her clothes in public may involve a loss of dignity, but it cannot form the basis of a blackmail charge as there is no monetary loss.[40] In *Bevans*[41] the defendant demanded that a doctor give him some morphine, threatening to shoot him if he did not. The defendant could be convicted of blackmail because the morphine was of some monetary value.[42]

4.3 MENACES

The demand must be made with menaces. The Court of Appeal in *Lawrence and Pomroy*[43] suggested that a jury need be told only that 'menace' is to have its normal meaning and the judge need not explain the term further. The jury are likely to decide that the menace will involve a threat of 'any action detrimental to or unpleasant to the person addressed'.[44] The threat can be that something unpleasant will occur to the victim or a third party. It seems that the unpleasantness referred to here must not be of a minor nature. Sellers LJ in *Clear*[45] held that to amount to menaces the threats must be 'of such a nature and extent that the mind of an ordinary person of normal stability and courage might be influenced or made apprehensive so as to accede unwillingly to the demand'.

The hardest cases on menaces are those where the victim responds to the defendant's words in an unusual way. Contrast the following two situations:

(1) The defendant says something which most people would not regard as frightening, but because the victim is particularly timid he finds it menacing. That will be a menace if the defendant is aware of the effect of the words on the victim.[46]

(2) The defendant says something which most people would find menacing, but being particularly hard skinned the victim does not find it frightening. This would not in the law be regarded as a menace.

These points were emphasized in the following case:

R v Garwood
[1987] 1 All ER 1032 (CA)[47]

Patrick Garwood believed a Mr Sayed had burgled his house. He asked Sayed for something 'to make it quits'. Sayed went home and got £10 to give to Garwood.

---

[40] A sexual assault may be committed in such a case.　　[41] (1987) 87 Cr App R 64 (CA).

[42] There is some dispute over whether being paid money legally due to you is 'a gain'. Such authority as there is suggests that it is: *Parkes* [1973] Crim LR 358.

[43] (1973) 57 Cr App R 64 (CA).

[44] Lord Wright in *Thorne v Motor Trade Association* [1937] AC 797 at 817 (HL).

[45] [1968] 1 All ER 74, 80 (CA).　　[46] *Clear* [1968] 1 All ER 74 (CA).

[47] [1987] 1 WLR 319, (1987) 85 Cr App R 85, [1987] Crim LR 476.

Garwood was charged with blackmail. When considering their verdict the jury asked the judge whether menaces existed if the appellant appeared more menacing to a timid victim than he would have done to most people. The judge in his reply indicated that menaces can exist even though a person of normal stability would not have found what was said or done threatening, and even though the accused was unaware that the victim was unduly susceptible to threats.

Lord Lane CJ

In the judgment of this court [the judge's direction] might have led the jury to believe that the prosecution had proved the existence of menaces even though a person of normal ability would not have been influenced by the words or actions of the accused and the accused was not aware that the victim was thus unduly susceptible to threats. To that extent we think there was a misdirection.

In our judgment it is only rarely that a judge will need to enter upon a definition of the word menaces. It is an ordinary word of which the meaning will be clear to any jury. As Cairns LJ said in *Reg v Lawrence (Rodney)* (1973) 57 Cr App R 64, 72:

'In exceptional cases where because of special knowledge in special circumstances what would be a menace to an ordinary person is not a menace to the person to whom it is addressed, or where the converse may be true, it is no doubt necessary to spell out the meaning of the word.'

It seems to us that there are two possible occasions upon which a further direction on the meaning of the word menaces may be required. The first is where the threats might affect the mind of an ordinary person of normal stability but did not affect the person actually addressed. In such circumstances that would amount to a sufficient menace: see *Reg v Clear* [1968] 1 QB 670.

The second situation is where the threats in fact affected the mind of the victim, although they would not have affected the mind of a person of normal stability. In that case, in our judgment, the existence of menaces is proved providing that the accused man was aware of the likely effect of his actions upon the victim.

If the recorder had told the jury that Sayed's undue timidity did not prevent them from finding 'menaces' proved, providing that the appellant realised the effect his actions were having on Sayed, all would have been well. The issue before the jury was clear-cut. If they felt sure the thought that the appellant's version might be true, there wee equally plainly no menaces. There was no need for the recorder to have embarked upon any definition of the word. It only served to confuse, as the jury's question showed.

However, if he had given a proper and full answer to the jury's question in the terms which we suggested earlier, the jury could have been in no doubt at all that if Sayed's version was correct—which they must have felt that it was—the appellant must have realised from the moment that the conversation started the effect which his actions and words were having upon Sayed.

This is accordingly eminently a case for the application of the proviso. The appeal against conviction is accordingly dismissed.

Appeal against conviction dismissed.

4.4 THE DEMAND MUST BE UNWARRANTED

It is crucial that the demand be unwarranted. There are two stages to the test. First, the jury must decide whether or not they think the demand is unwarranted. It may be that the demand is perfectly reasonable. For example, most people would think that the threat 'unless you return the bicycle I lent you I will come round to you house and take it' was a warranted demand. However, even if the jury think it unwarranted they must still go on to consider section 21. Section 21(1) explains that the defendant's demand will be unwarranted unless it is made in the belief:

(a) that there are reasonable grounds for making it, *and*

(b) that the use of the menaces is a proper means of enforcing the demand.

If the defendant has the two beliefs mentioned the defendant cannot be guilty of black-mail because the demand will not be unwarranted. However, this is subject to an important caveat. If the defendant is aware that he is threatening to commit a crime, he or she cannot claim that the demand is reasonable.[48] This was made clear in the following case:

R v Harvey, Ulyett and Plummer
(1981) 72 Cr App R 139 (CA)[49]

The appellants had agreed with a 'rogue' named Scott that Scott would sell them a large amount of cannabis for over £20,000. Scott had supplied a tiny amount of cannabis and 'a load of rubbish'. The appellants kidnapped Scott, Scott's wife, and their small child and made threats against them unless their money was returned. At their trial as a defence to the blackmail charge the appellants claimed that they believed their threats to be warranted. The judge directed the jury that a threat to do criminal actions could not be regarded as warranted.

Mr Justice Bingham

For the appellants it was submitted that the learned judge's direction, and in particular the earlier of the passages quoted, was incorrect in law because it took away from the jury a question properly falling within their province of decision, namely, what the accused in fact believed. He was wrong to rule as a matter of law that a threat to perform a serious criminal act could never be thought by the person making it to be a proper means. While free to comment on the unlikelihood of a defendant believing threats such as were made in this case to be a proper means, the judge should nonetheless (it was submitted) have left the question to the jury. For the Crown it was submitted that a threat to perform a criminal act can never as a matter of law be a proper means within the subsection, and that the learned judge's direction was accordingly correct. Support for both these approaches is to be found in academic works helpfully brought to the attention of the Court.

The answer to this problem must be found in the language of the subsection, from which in our judgment two points emerge with clarity:

(1) The subsection is concerned with the belief of the individual defendant in the particular case: '. . . a demand with menaces is unwarranted unless the person making it does so *in the*

---

[48] *Harvey, Ulyett and Plummer* (1980) 72 Cr App R 139 (CA).   [49] [1981] Crim LR 104.

belief . . .' (added emphasis). It matters not what the reasonable man, or any man other than the defendant, would believe save in so far as that may throw light on what the defendant in fact believed. Thus the factual question of the defendant's belief should be left to the jury. To that extent the subsection is subjective in approach, as is generally desirable in a criminal statute.

(2) In order to exonerate a defendant from liability his belief must be that the use of the menaces is a 'proper' means of reinforcing the demand. 'Proper' is an unusual expression to find in a criminal statute. It is not defined in the Act, and no definition need be attempted here. It is, however, plainly a word of wide meaning, certainly wider than (for example) 'lawful.' But the greater includes the less and no act which was not believed to be lawful could be believed to be proper within the meaning of the subsection. Thus no assistance is given to any defendant, even a fanatic or a deranged idealist, who knows or suspects that his threat, or the act threatened, is criminal, but believes it to be justified by his end or his peculiar circumstances. The test is not what he regards as justified, but what he believes to be proper. And where, as here, the threats were to do acts which any sane man knows to be against the laws of every civilised country no jury would hesitate long before dismissing the contention that the defendant genuinely believed the threats to be a proper means of reinforcing even a legitimate demand.

It is accordingly our conclusion that the direction of the learned judge was not strictly correct. If it was necessary to give a direction on this aspect of the case at all (and in the absence of any evidence by the defendants as to their belief we cannot think that there was in reality any live issue concerning it) the jury should have been directed that the demand with menaces was not to be regarded as unwarranted unless the Crown satisfied them in respect of each defendant that the defendant did not make the demand with menaces in the genuine belief both—(a) that he had had reasonable grounds for making the demand; and (b) that the use of the menaces was in the circumstances a proper (meaning for present purposes a lawful, and not a criminal) means of reinforcing the demand.

The learned judge could, of course, make appropriate comment on the unlikelihood of the defendants believing murder and rape or threats to commit those acts to be lawful or other than criminal.

On the facts of this case we are quite satisfied that the misdirection to which we have drawn attention could have caused no possible prejudice to any of the appellants. Accordingly, in our judgment, it is appropriate to apply the proviso to section 2(1) of the Criminal Appeal Act 1968, and the appeals are dismissed.

Appeals against conviction dismissed. Sentences varied.

QUESTIONS

1. In *Harry* [1974] Crim LR 32 a student organizing a 'rag event' wrote to shopkeepers offering immunity from the 'inconvenience' during rag events in return for a contribution to a charity. Could this amount to blackmail?

2. Bill (Angelina's gardener) has borrowed Angelina's bicycle, but he is refusing to return it. Angelina threatens not to pay Bill's salary unless he returns the bicycle. She has very high moral standards and feels that what she has done is in fact unjustifiable. Has she committed blackmail?

3. Eliza tells Higgins that she will tell his wife that he has been committing adultery unless he redecorates her house for free. Is this blackmail?

PART II: BURGLARY AND BLACKMAIL: THEORY

5 BURGLARY: THEORY

5.1 BURGLARY IN PRACTICE

England and Wales top the international league table for domestic burglary. They have a higher burglary rate than the USA and four and a half times the rate of Germany.[50] In the year 2004/5 2.7 per cent of all households were reported to have been burgled,[51] but many burglaries go unreported and it has been estimated that in fact in a year one in twenty households are burgled or suffer an attempted burglary.[52] For the year 2004/5 there were 756,000 burglaries recorded by the British Crime Survey, although only 447,100 recorded burglaries.[53] The fear of burglary is high. In a recent study 17 per cent of those questioned said that they had high levels of worry about burglary.[54] One study even found that fear of burglary was higher than fear of mugging or rape.[55] In fact the rate of burglaries depends very much on where in the country a person lives, their age, and lifestyle.[56] For example, as mentioned above, 2.7 per cent of all households were burgled in the last recorded year, but for single parent households the figure is 6.7 per cent.

The severity of burglary varies. Of the domestic burglaries recorded in the British Crime Survey 2002/2003 in 54 per cent the owner had been at home and in 11 per cent there had been a threat or use of violence.[57] On the other hand, one recent survey indicated that it must not be assumed that every incident of burglary was serious: one quarter of burglaries resulted in no property being taken and there are two attempted burglaries for every three successful ones.[58] Burglary can involve malicious damage, but that is fairly rare.[59]

5.2 WHY IS BURGLARY AN OFFENCE?

Burglaries have a profound effect on the victims: both emotionally[60] and financially:[61]

(1) *Emotional*. One quarter of those who are victims of burglary are 'badly shaken'.[62] A small minority suffer lasting effects, including depression and sleeplessness.

(2) *Financial*. One third of burglaries resulted in losses of over £1,000.[63] For those who are insured the financial loss may be limited, but one recent study reported that only

---

[50] Home Office (2003b).
[51] Nicholas *et al.* (2005: 51). See also Sentencing Advisory Panel (2002: Appendix 2) which discusses the statistics. Forrester, Chatterton, and Pease (1988) is a major study investigating who commits burglaries.
[52] Home Office (2003b).   [53] Povey, Ellis, and Nicholas (2003: 6).
[54] Povey, Ellis, and Nicholas (2003: 8).   [55] Mirrlees-Black and Allen (1998).
[56] Mawby (2001); Barclay and Tavares (2000); Michael (1993).
[57] Allen, Nicholas, Salisbury, and Wood (2003: 44). See also Kershaw (2001).
[58] Kershaw *et al.* (2001).   [59] Budd (1999).
[60] In one study Maguire and Kynch (2000) found that 20% of victims were very much affected and 84% suffered some kind of an emotional reaction. 13% reported difficulty sleeping.
[61] Tarling and Davison (2000).   [62] Maguire and Bennett (1982: 164).   [63] Kershaw (2001).

48 per cent of victims of burglary were insured and of those who were only 69 per cent made a claim as a result of the burglary.[64] Brand and Price's study[65] found that the average loss of property for each burglary was £830, but they argued that the average cost to the country as a whole of each burglary was £2,300, once all the costs to everyone involved was taken into account.

This may demonstrate why victims regard burglary as a serious crime, but what is it that distinguishes burglary from theft?[66] And why should it be burglary to enter as a trespasser intending to steal, even if the defendant does not actually steal? It should be recalled that simple trespass is not a criminal offence, only a civil wrong.[67] Should the law regard the intent of the defendant as sufficient to transform a civil wrong into a serious criminal offence?

Here are some of the explanations for the offence:

(1) *Burglary as aggravated theft.* In the same way that robbery can be classified as theft plus the use of force; burglary can be regarded as theft plus entry as a trespasser. The analogy is not exact because the force (in robbery) is itself a crime; while the aggravating factor in burglary (entering as a trespasser) is only a civil wrong. More significantly, although this explanation may be effective as an explanation of the section 9(1)(b) offence, it is less effective as an explanation of the section 9(1)(a) offence which does not require a theft to actually be committed.

(2) *Violation of the victim's private home.* The wrong of burglary can be seen as the violation of the victim's home.[68] Many people's sense of identity is tied up with their home as a place of security and a private space. Most people would not feel deeply distressed if their garden sheds were broken into, but would if their homes were.[69] Homes are meant to be places of haven from the rigours of the outside world and so to have one's safe place invaded can be particularly disturbing.

(3) *Increased likelihood of harm.* Burglary can be regarded as particularly serious for society because it is a form of theft which is particularly likely to lead to violence.[70] Quite simply, if a householder interrupts a burglary there is more likely to be violence on one side or the other than where a person discovers his pocket is being picked in a public place.[71]

In the following passage Barry Mitchell considers 'multiple wrongdoing'. These are crimes which involve the defendant committing several wrongs at the same time. He considers how the law should address and label such incidents. He uses burglary and robbery as his main examples:

---

[64] Ibid.   [65] Brand and Price (2000).

[66] The maximum sentence for burglary is 10 years; it is 7 years for theft.

[67] There are some forms of trespass which can be criminal. These tend to be linked to public order offences, where a large group of people commit trespass: e.g. Criminal Justice and Public Order Act 1994, ss. 61, 68, and 69.

[68] Maguire and Bennett (1982: 614).

[69] In *Brewster* [1998] 1 Cr App R 220, 225–7 Lord Bingham explained that the psychological harms to victims should be taken into account when sentencing.

[70] Cook and Ludwig (2002) argue that higher rates of gun possession among householders does not mean there are lower rates of burglary.

[71] Anon (1951).

B. Mitchell, 'Multiple Wrongdoing and Offence Structure: A Plea for Consistency and Fair Labelling' (2001) 64 *Modern Law Review* 393 at 394–402

Multiple wrongdoing and the structure and composition of current offences

. . .

Both at common law and in statutory form criminal offences vary considerably in the composition and complexity of their definition. Some are constituted by a single act (or omission) whereas others might be more accurately described as a venture in which the defendant commits several acts. Some are comparatively 'large' in that they contain more than one element of wrongful behaviour, sometimes involving threats to or infringements of very differing kinds of interests, arising out of several acts, and some involve more than one victim. Burglary contrary to section 9(1)(b) requires two wrongful acts—trespass in a building (or part), and some sort of 'further offence' (the infliction or attempted infliction of grievous bodily harm or theft or attempted theft). Indeed, the Criminal Law Revision Committee (hereafter 'CLRC') referred to it as a 'double offence'. The person whose house is 'trespassed' may not be the same person as the victim of the further offence. Robbery also consists of two wrongful acts—stealing and using or threatening to use force against someone. There are either two completed harms—the theft and the use of force against the person—or one complete harm and one threat of harm. The victim of the theft need not also be the victim of the (actual or threatened) violence.

In addition, the scope of some offences is such that their essential nature may appear to vary according to the particular facts of the individual case. Robbery encompasses a wide range of situations in which the harm to either physical integrity or property interests, or both, may vary considerably, and may thus be seen primarily as either a crime of violence or a property offence or a combination of the two. Structurally, the only possible variation in robbery is that force may be either used or threatened (in order to steal). In contrast, the potential variations in burglary are much greater. Although the paradigm case is essentially concerned with protecting property interests—trespassory entry of a building together with the intent to steal or attempted or actual theft—numerous alternative forms combine infringements of property interests with intended/attempted/completed attacks on physical integrity or intended attacks against sexual integrity or property. The potential combination of elements that may constitute anyone instance of the offence are such that one burglary may differ quite markedly from another in the overall nature of the offending. Unlike robbery, burglary requires no causal link between the two elements of wrongdoing. D might enter V1's house as a trespasser and whilst there happen to grievously injure V2: the trespassory entry of a building merely provides the setting for the further offence.

This discussion also demonstrates that the basic nature of the multiple wrongdoing varies. Section 9(1)(a) burglary is fundamentally different from the section 9(1)(b) variety and robbery in that section 9(1)(a) contains one act whereas section 9(1)(b) and robbery inevitably require more than one. The multiple wrongfulness in section 9(1)(a) consists of a wrongful act plus a (separate) wrongful intent, and it is clear that the present law accepts that such an intent may assume particular significance. Thus, for example, possession of a controlled drug is distinguished from possession with intent to supply, which is a much more serious crime.

Occasionally, the law recognises aggravated forms of basic offences. Robbery is effectively an aggravated form of theft. Sometimes the offence label is in the form of 'aggravated [crime]'—for example, when D has with him a firearm, imitation firearm, weapon of offence or explosive when he commits a section 9 burglary, his offence becomes 'aggravated burglary' under section 10. Burglary becomes aggravated under section 10 because the possession of a firearm etc not only intensifies the victim's fear but it also brings the possibility that someone might be killed. This provides the new dimension to D's wrongdoing which, although not necessary, puts him in a stronger position in which to commit the burglary. . . .

Inadequacies of current multiple wrongdoing offences

Whilst the fact that the law has been prepared to recognise multiple wrongdoing offences such as burglary and robbery is welcomed, it is arguable that it has been too restrictive in the way in which these crimes have been construed. For example, the various forms which burglary may take under section 9(1)(a) and (b) is in some respects rather odd. Of the possible ulterior intents in paragraph (a), only two—causing grievous injury and stealing—are required to be attempted or completed in paragraph (b). Thus, if D enters a building as a trespasser and damages property (or attempts to do so), or rapes any person (or attempts to do so), he is not guilty of burglary unless he had the ulterior intent (to damage property or rape any person) when he entered. Whilst rape or attempted rape is clearly a more serious wrong than burglary and arguably thus merits separate recognition, the same cannot automatically be said of damaging property. It appears that burglary is defined in the particular ways that it is simply because they reflect the kinds of situations which came before the Courts, but there is no apparent reason in principle why the offence should be limited to the particular combinations of wrongful behaviour set out in section 9 of the Theft Act 1968.

A strong case can surely be made out for extending section 9(1)(b) to include situations where, having entered as a trespasser, D damages property. There are clear parallels between theft and damage: property which has been stolen may be recovered in sound or poor condition or it may be lost forever. Damaged property mayor may not be reparable. To the victim it does not appear to make any significant difference, either financially or sentimentally, whether the property has been stolen or damaged. Furthermore, whilst rape or attempted rape is inevitably a serious matter, it is arguable that section 9(1)(b) should be extended to incorporate it. One of the essential characteristics of burglary is that it reflects the desire for people to feel safe in their own homes, so that the *combination* of trespass in a building and rape/attempted rape is significant. The obvious counter-arguments are that the element of non-consensual intercourse is so significant that the word 'rape' should not be omitted from the offence label, and that the concept of burglary would become too large and unwieldy. Yet that in turn would seem to question the underlying nature and rationale of the offence. If committing (or attempting or intending to commit) certain former felonies whilst trespassing in a building is perceived as having a distinctive character to justify its existence, it is very likely to encompass a wide range of scenarios, unless there are good reasons for limiting the prohibited offences inside the building. Ultimately, the question is whether our concept of burglary is sufficiently capacious to stretch far enough to include trespassory entry plus rape. . . .

FURTHER READING

Anon (1951), 'A Rationale of the Law of Burglary', *Colorado Law Review* 51: 1009.

Budd, T. (1999), *Burglary of Domestic Dwellings* (London: Home Office).

Mawby, R. (2001), *Burglary* (Cullompton: Willan).

Pace, P. (1985), 'Burglarious Trespass', *Criminal Law Review* 716.

Simester, A., and Sullivan, G.R. (2005), 'The Nature and Rationale of Property Offences' in R.A. Duff and S. Green, *Defining Crimes* (Oxford: OUP), 192–4.

Tarling, R., and Davison, T. (2000), *Victims of Domestic Burglary: A Review of the Literature* (London: Victim Support).

6 BLACKMAIL THEORY

6.1 THE INCIDENCE OF BLACKMAIL

Blackmail is not a crime which often reaches the courts, and only in the most obvious and serious of cases will the police charge the offence.[72] There were 1,475 recorded blackmail offences in the year 2004/5.[73] Nowadays if someone has a secret about someone else they are more likely to sell their story to the press than to use it for blackmail. Despite its rarity in the law reports the crime is one that widely captures the imagination as a popular topic for film and books.[74] Lord Lane dramatically declared that:

> in the calendar of criminal offences blackmail is one of the ugliest . . . because it involves what really amounts, so often, to attempted murder of the soul.[75]

The offence has also produced an impressive array of academic comment. It is this to which we must now turn.

6.2 WHY IS BLACKMAIL A CRIME?

The paradox of blackmail

If Alan tells Samantha 'I am planning to tell your husband that you have been committing adultery', this is not a criminal offence. If Alan says to Samantha 'would you like to give me £100?', this is not an offence. But if he says 'I am going to tell your husband that you have been committing adultery. Would you like to give me £100?', this is an offence. Why should the combination of a threat which in itself is not an offence and a request which in itself is not an offence constitute a crime? In essence blackmail involves a threat to do a completely lawful activity. This then is the paradox of blackmail.

Some possible resolutions of the paradox

The resolution of this conflict has puzzled many commentators. Before we describe their solutions it should be admitted that the difficulty with some, if not all, of the theories is that under them some conduct which is blackmail in the eyes of the law is not explained by the theory, and some conduct which is not blackmail ought to be under the particular theory:[76]

(1) The wrong of blackmail is the manipulation of the mind of the victim. An analogy could be drawn between obtaining property by deception and obtaining property by

---

[72] Coarse (1988: 676) claims that the English law deliberately was drafted widely, in order to leave prosecutors with a discretion to decide whether to prosecute. See also Lindgren (1989a).

[73] Home Office (2005b).

[74] McLaren (2002) provides a modern history of blackmail.

[75] Lord Lane in *R v Hadjou* (1989) 11 Cr App R (S) 29 (CA).

[76] Lindgren (1989). See also C. Williams (1975).

blackmail: both involve the acquisition of property through invalid coercion[77] of the victim. Leo Katz[78] suggests that blackmail is analogous to robbery: it is all about taking property from the victim using immoral means. The difficulty with these theories is that companies use all sorts of means to acquire property from people, for example through manipulative advertising, misleading claims for products, but these, even if regarded as immoral, are not normally criminal.[79]

(2) The wrong of blackmail is causing the victim to fear. Under this theory blackmail is seen as analogous to an assault. The threat in blackmail is to cause the victim serious emotional harm. The difficulty with this theory is that causing someone emotional harm (e.g. by ending a relationship) is not normally criminal, even if one is acting immorally in so doing.[80]

(3) The offence could be seen as a means of protecting privacy.[81] Supporters of this view vigorously deny that one has a right to reveal private information.[82] Michael Gorr bases his explanation of the wrong of blackmail on the argument that it is wrong to reveal personal information.[83] The difficulty with this is that the moral principle is contestable. If you discover your best friend's boyfriend is cheating on her is it morally wrong to tell her?

(4) James Lindgren has suggested that the wrong in blackmail can be identified as the wrong to a third party.[84] His point can be made clearer by considering this hypothetical scenario. Anne is bringing a legal action against Bob. Cath has a document which would enable Bob to win the case. Cath tells Anne that she will destroy the document if Anne pays her some money. Here Cath is wronging Bob. She is using his legal rights to make a gain for herself.[85] The difficulty with this it that it runs counter to the common understanding that blackmail is very much a crime against the person who is threatened. Also other forms of blackmail will not necessarily involve a third party ('I will publish nude photographs of you on the worldwide web', for example).

(5) It could be argued that a blackmailer who suggests that he will keep quiet about some wrong if he is paid thereby becomes complicit in this way.[86] This is a persuasive explanation of some forms of blackmail, especially where the blackmailer is promising not to tell the police about a crime which the victim has committed. However, blackmail may not involve the revelation of an evil. If Jeffrey (who used to be a well-known politician) moves to a new town and wishes to keep his identity secret, and Margaret threatens to reveal his identity unless money is paid, it is hard to see what the evil is in which Margaret is complicit.

(6) George Fletcher sees the notion of domination as being at the heart of blackmail. The blackmailer manages to get in a position of great power over the victim, and what makes the offence serious is that that domination can continue for ever.[87] He suggests that blackmail can be seen as a form of moral slavery. This theory works less well where there has been a single incidence of blackmail (e.g. the defendant destroys the

---

[77] Lamond (1996).   [78] Katz (1993).   [79] Block and McGee (1999).
[80] See further the discussion at p. 355.   [81] Alldridge (1993b).   [82] Scalise (2000).
[83] Gorr (1992).   [84] Lindgren (1993a).
[85] J. Brown (1993) argues that blackmail involves a kind of 'private justice'.
[86] See the discussion in Altman (1993: 1665).   [87] Fletcher (1993).

incriminating photographs after the victim has paid the requested sum and so has no hold over the victim).

(7) Mitchell Berman[88] proposes 'the evidentiary explanation of blackmail'. He argues that society may criminalize conduct that tends both to cause harm and to be undertaken with wrongful motives. We can assume that the revelation of private material for gain is done for morally unacceptable motives, because if there were good motives the defendant would keep silent or reveal the information for free. What is being punished, then, is not the act of blackmail itself, but rather the morally unacceptable motive that normally undermines it. The danger with this argument is that there are all kinds of wrongly motivated conduct which are liable to cause harm but which we do not render illegal (for example, adultery, lying).

(8) Some commentators argue that blackmail produces harmful results to society.[89] The victim may have to turn to crime to meet the demands of the blackmailer.[90] Imagine what a society which had no blackmail law might be like:[91] people would undertake intrusive investigations into the private life of others in the hope of making money from them.[92] But it has been argued that all kinds of things can lead to harmful effects. Fattening foods cause harm to people in society, but we do not outlaw them.[93]

(9) Scott Altman suggests that in fact, although no one of the above theories can explain the present law on blackmail, together they provide a 'patchwork' explanation of the offence.[94]

Some commentators take the view that the difficulties in specifying the wrong of blackmail indicate that there is no good reason justifying the offence, and it should be legalized.[95]

In the following passage Grant Lamond offers his reasons for the offence:

G. Lamond, 'Coercion, Threats and Blackmail' in A. Smith and A. Simester (eds.), *Harm and Culpability* (Oxford: OUP, 1996), 230–4

The puzzle of blackmail, it will be recalled, rests in the impermissibility of demanding something in exchange for abstaining from what would otherwise be a permissible action. It will be apparent by now that an understanding of blackmail requires an appreciation of the normative role played by reasons for action. I will begin this section by drawing some pre-liminary distinctions between the kinds of threats amounting to blackmail before going on to consider the nature of the wrong involved in the offence. As I indicated in the introduction, the discussion will range freely over actions which are immoral for the same reason as blackmail threats are criminal. Not all of these cases would, of course, be appropriate for criminalization. I will, in concluding, turn to the question of criminalization, and offer some observations on the compatibility of blackmail with the harm principle.

Blackmail threats can be divided into three categories. The first covers threats of actions which are impermissible *per se* (i.e., irrespective of the agent's reasons), such as physical violence, the destruction of property, and the publication of defamatory information. The second involves threats to perform actions which the maker is already duty-bound (to

---

[88] Berman (1998).   [89] Murphy (1980); Hardin (1993).

[90] Epstein (1983: 564); Shavell (1993: 1092).   [91] Gordon (1993).

[92] Isenbergh (1993: 1911–15); Shavell (1993: 1092); DeLong (1993).

[93] Block (2000: 351).   [94] Altman (1993).   [95] Block (2000).

someone other than the recipient) to perform. A public official may, for example, threaten to revoke a licence where she is aware that conditions requiring revocation have already been fulfilled. Or an opposing party's witness in a civil suit may threaten to give her evidence truthfully unless she is bought off. Or an individual may threaten to report a crime committed against a third party unless her demand is satisfied. Thirdly, there is the category of threats where the action is permissible but not mandatory: the maker of the threat is not bound to take the action but may do so. This would cover cases such as threats to disclose having seen a person in a public place at a certain time, or to foreclose a mortgage which is in default, or to take one's business elsewhere.

The first two categories of blackmail threats are often regarded as unproblematic. The first category certainly is: it is clearly wrong to intend to commit an independent wrong against the recipient unless a demand is met. But the second category is itself puzzling. Why is the recipient of a blackmail demand regarded as the victim when the maker of the demand threatens to fulfil a duty to a third party, thereby proposing *not* to fulfil her duty if the demand is met? In many cases the recipient is better off for not having his licence revoked, or the testimony given, or the crime reported, and would prefer to do as demanded rather than see the duty to the third party discharged. I will return to this issue below. But it is the third category which is generally regarded as the genuinely puzzling one, for how can it he impermissible to threaten what it is permissible to do?

The first step towards elucidating the nature of blackmail is to appreciate that the actions proposed in the third category are not in fact permissible, because the permissibility of actions rests as much on the reasons her taking them as in their consequences. There is, for instance, nothing *per se* wrong in playing music at a reasonable volume or mowing the lawn on a weekend morning, even though a neighbour finds these activities annoying. Nor is there anything wrong in engaging in commercial competition with another, even if one knows that this will drive the competitor out of business. But to do these things *in order* to bring about the unwelcome effects upon another *is* impermissible. To undertake the actions for that reason is to adopt a course of conduct aimed at diminishing another's well-being rather than at pursuing some acceptable goal. The idea that there is a 'puzzle' of blackmail, therefore, rests on too limited a view of which actions are impermissible.

What is involved in blackmail (and in threats generally) is the intrinsic significance of actions—the fact that there are reasons for taking (or refraining from) an action other than the consequences it will bring about. To those with an instrumentalist or consequentialist cast of mind such reasons can seem inexplicable. But they are a pervasive feature of our lives: they account for why it is important not only that my children are cared for, but that they are cared for *by me*. The reasons for which we adopt a course of action are a constitutive part of the action-part of its internal aspect. It is not merely intentions which can contribute to the description under which an action is taken, it is also the reasons for so intending.

Many impermissible actions, of course, lie beyond legal regulation. There are limits to what can be rightly or practically regulated by law. Many immoralities, such as certain types of lies, are not the appropriate concern of the law. In addition, it is generally impractical for the law to adopt regulatory categories other than those based on the consequences of conduct and/or awareness of those consequences, rather than the reasons for bringing them about. Thus if an action is not sufficiently serious in its actual or potential consequences to warrant legal redress, it will be unusual for the actor's reasons to alter this assessment. This explains why many of the threatened actions involved in blackmail are not themselves subject to legal sanction, despite their impermissibility.

The wrong of blackmail, however, does not rest simply in the fact that what is threatened is impermissible. Instead it relates to the way in which the prospect of this action is used by the

dominant party against the victim. Blackmail involves the attempt to obtain some advantage from the victim, whether in the form of financial advancement, sexual intimacy, or control over the victim's conduct. The dominant party thus seeks to secure an advantage which it is permissible to enjoy only with the victim's consent. It is the effect of such threats upon the validity of the consent so induced which is the key to understanding blackmail.

Consenting is a complex normative activity involving the manifestation of an intention to alter (or permit the alteration) of a normative situation. But a consent is effective only where it is the *valid* exercise of a normative power. Broadly speaking, a normative power exists where there arc reasons for a person to be able to bring about an alteration in her own (and/own or others') normative situation when she intends to do so. A person's normative situation is the set of her rights, duties, privileges, and immunities. Promises, for example, alter the promisor's normative situation by putting her under a duty to the promisee; the same act alters the promisee's normative situation by conferring on him a right to the performance of the promised act. Consent is a common way of granting permissions and transferring rights. There are a variety of reasons which justify normative powers, but a particularly important reason is that it enables individuals to exercise a degree of control over certain states of affairs. In some cases, such as the possession of personal property, the value of enjoying such control is regarded as outweighing the possibility of that control being used unwisely or incorrectly. In other cases the value of an activity is constituted by its being controlled by the participant: sexual intimacy, for example, has value only when participation is both willing and motivated for a particular range of reasons.

Whether a consent is valid depends upon whether the act manifesting the intention to consent is effective in those circumstances to bring about the normative change. One must distinguish, therefore, between the fact that a person intended to consent and the question whether it was valid. Whether a consent induced by a threat is valid is a matter of whether the circumstances are compatible with the purposes for which the power exists, *viz.* enabling the individual to control that state of affairs.

This is sometimes thought to be a matter of whether the consent is 'voluntary' or not, but such an approach does little more than restate the problem. It is of course a useful test where 'involuntariness' refers to physical or psychological compulsion: as consent is an intentional action it cannot he produced by physical compulsion, and it is unlikely that anything other than a fully intentional action would suffice, thereby ruling out psychological compulsion. But as most threats do not produce psychological compulsion this is beside the point. On the other hand, it is incorrect to say that consent must be voluntary in order to be valid if it suggests that the validity turns on the *degree* of pressure (either psychological or factual) under which the party acts. A person facing a hard choice, for example on the brink of bankruptcy, may be under immense pressure, but this does not in itself vitiate any transactions entered in those circumstances. Similarly, the fact that a country defeated in a war has no alternative but to surrender does not of itself affect the validity of that surrender. If 'voluntary' is not used to refer to compulsion, nor to the degree of pressure under which a person acts, it seems merely to describe those circumstances in which a consent will be effective in bringing about the purported normative consequences.

Where a party's consent is secured through his being presented with the choice of avoiding an impermissible action, that consent does not serve the purpose of allowing that party to control a state of affairs. Prima facie, therefore, such a consent is defective. There may be countervailing reasons in some cases (or classes of cases) which override this, but otherwise the consent will be invalid. This point is not limited to coercive threats: it also explains the (prima facie) invalidity of consents induced through (i) *offers* not to perform actions which are impermissible *per se* (i.e., irrespective of the offeror's reasons), and

(ii) conditional *warnings* that an impermissible action will be taken if the recipient does not consent to something.

A coercive threat, I have argued, involves the maker of the threat committing herself to bringing about an unwelcome consequence because that consequence is unwelcome to the recipient. It follows that unless the threat is justifiable (or unless there are overriding countervailing reasons), any con- sent it induces is defective. The harm, then, which is involved in the crime of blackmail is the non-consensual obtaining of whatever is demanded from the victim. This explains why blackmail has traditionally been treated as a property crime and its analogues have been located with sexual offences and offences against the person.

QUESTIONS

1. Why should it be blackmail only if the defendant makes an economic gain or another suffers an economic loss? Should it not be blackmail if the defendant threatens to reveal a secret unless the victim takes his or her clothes off?

2. If the victim of blackmail has chosen not to seek the protection of the police before giving in to the threat, should she be protected by the criminal law?

3. Is it possible to distinguish these two cases:

   (i) Jane says to Tom, 'Unless you pay me £100 I will tell your employer about your criminal past.'

   (ii) Jill says to Tim, 'I will give you £100 if you confess to your employer about your criminal past'?

FURTHER READING

Altman, S. (1993), 'A Patchwork Theory of Blackmail', *University of Pennsylvania Law Review* 141: 1639.

Berman, M. (1998), 'The Evidentiary Theory of Blackmail: Taking Motives Seriously', *University of Chicago Law Review* 65: 795.

Block, W. (2000), 'Threats, Blackmail, Extortion and Robbery and Other Bad Things', *Tulsa Law Journal* 35: 333.

Epstein, R. (1983), 'Blackmail, Inc.', *University of Chicago Law Review* 50: 553.

Fletcher, G. (1993), 'Blackmail: The Paradigmatic Crime', *University of Pennsylvania Law Review* 141: 1617.

Gorr, M. (1992), 'Liberalism and the Paradox of Blackmail', *Philosophy and Public Affairs* 21: 43.

Katz, L. (1993), 'Blackmail and Other Forms of Arm-Twisting', *University of Pennsylvania Law Review* 141: 1567.

Lamond, G. (1996), 'Coercion, Threats and the Puzzle of Blackmail' in A.P. Simester and A.T.H. Smith (eds.), *Harm and Culpability* (Oxford: OUP).

CRIMINAL DAMAGE

PART I: THE LAW ON CRIMINAL DAMAGE

Four criminal damages offences are found in the Criminal Damage Act 1971: basic criminal damage, arson, aggravated criminal damage, and aggravated arson.[1] There is also an offence of racially aggravated criminal damage.

1 BASIC CRIMINAL DAMAGE

DEFINITION

The *actus reus* is the destruction of or damage to property belonging to another without lawful excuse.

The *mens rea* is that the defendant intended or was reckless (a) that his or her action would damage or destroy property and (b) that that property belonged to another.

Section 1 of the Criminal Damage Act 1971 states:

> (1) A person who without lawful excuse destroys or damages any property belonging to another intending to destroy or damage any such property or being reckless as to whether any such property would be destroyed or damaged shall be guilty of an offence.

The maximum punishment is ten years' imprisonment.[2] The offence contains the following elements:

---

[1] There are also offences of threatening to damage property (Criminal Damage Act 1971, s. 2, explained in *Cakmak* [2002] Crim LR 581) and possessing property with intent to cause criminal damage to another (Criminal Damage Act 1971, s. 3). There are specific offences involving damage to property under various pieces of legislation: e.g. causing an explosion likely to endanger life or to cause serious injury to property (Explosive Substances Act 1883) or placing wood on railway lines (Malicious Damage Act 1861, s. 2).

[2] Criminal Damage Act 1971, s. 4.

1.1 DAMAGE

The statute uses the terms 'destroy or damage'. The term 'destruction' indicates that following the acts of the defendant the item no longer exists. The term 'damage' therefore suggests that the acts have affected the property, but fall short of destruction. The idea of damage involves either:

(i)   a reduction in the value of the item or

(ii) a reduction in the usefulness of the item.

Either of these will do. Denting the door of a car may not affect the car's usefulness, but it will affect the value of the car and so amount to damage. Removing a sandbag from a wall of sandbags may not affect the value of the sandbags but it will impair their usefulness and so will be damage. An act can constitute damage even if there is no visible effect. If a computer disc had a programme removed this could constitute damage,[3] even though such damage would not be visible to the naked eye. There are a few issues on the meaning of damage over which there is some dispute:

(1) Is minimal damage excluded from the concept? The cases have not been consistent. In *A (A Juvenile) v R*[4] spitting on a police officer's raincoat was held not to amount to damage. It was argued that by simply wiping with a cloth the coat could be returned to its former state and therefore this could not constitute damage. However, other cases seem to take a broader view. Trampling grass on a field was regarded as damaging it;[5] and graffiti on a cell wall which could be removed easily with water was damage.[6] Of course, much depends on the nature of the property: scratching a painting is likely to be regarded as damage, scratching a scaffolding pole may well not be.[7]

(2) Is adding to property damaging it?[8] Again, the courts have not taken a consistent approach. In *Lloyd v DPP*[9] and *Drake v DPP*[10] it was held that putting a wheel clamp on a car did not constitute criminal damage because it did not affect the integrity of the car; rather something is added to the car. However, these cases are controversial. It could be argued that the clamping of the car severely affects its usefulness. Contrast *Hardman v Chief Constable of Avon and Somerset Constabulary*[11] where it was confirmed that painting on a pavement was damage, although such painting did not infringe the 'integrity' of the pavement. Similarly, dumping rubbish on someone's land has been held to damage the land.[12]

(3) How significant is the opinion of the owner of property in deciding whether there was damage? While Lawrence was away on holiday Carol rewallpapered his bedroom without his permission. If when Lawrence returned he was thrilled with the work one would certainly not say the room was damaged. However, if Lawrence was horrified

---

[3] *Cox v Riley* (1986) 83 Cr App R 54 (DC); *Whiteley* (1991) 93 Cr App R 25 (CA), although it should be noted that the Computer Misuse Act 1990 now deals with these offences.

[4] [1978] Crim LR 689.   [5] *Gayford v Chouler* [1898] 1 QB 316 (DC).

[6] *Roe v Kingerlee* [1986] Crim LR 735.   [7] *Morphitis v Salmon* [1990] Crim LR 48 (DC).

[8] It is generally accepted that removing something from property (e.g. taking out an integral part of a machine so that it does not work) is damaging it: *Tacey* (1821) Russ & Ry 452; *Morphitis v Salmon* [1990] Crim LR 48 (DC).

[9] [1992] 1 All ER 982 (DC).   [10] [1994] RTR 411 (DC).   [11] [1986] Crim LR 330.

[12] *Henderson*, 29 Nov. 1984, unreported.

could he claim that it was damaged? There is no case law directly addressing this issue, but it is interesting to note that the defendant's whitewashing over a National Front slogan that a third party had painted on the victim's property was not regarded as damage.[13]

1.2 PROPERTY

This is defined in section 10 of the Act:

> In this Act 'property' means property of a tangible nature, whether real or personal, including money and—
> (a) including wild creatures which have been tamed or are ordinarily kept in captivity, and any other wild creatures or their carcasses if, but only if, they have been reduced into possession which has not been lost or abandoned or are in the course of being reduced into possession; but
> (b) not including mushrooms growing wild on any land or flowers, fruit or foliage of a plant growing wild on any land.

For the purposes of this subsection 'mushroom' includes any fungus and 'plant' includes any shrub or tree.

The notion of property here is very similar to the notion of property in theft. However, property does not have the same meaning in both offences. For example, land can be damaged (for example, by pollution), even though it cannot be stolen. By contrast intangible property, such as patents and copyrights, can be stolen, but not damaged.

1.3 BELONGING TO ANOTHER

It should be stressed that it is not a criminal offence to damage your own property. The Act makes it quite clear that it is an offence under section 1 only to damage property which 'belongs to another'. However, it is an offence to damage your own property if the offence is one contrary to section 1(2) (see below).

Section 10 states:

> (2) Property shall be treated for the purposes of this Act as belonging to any person—
> (a) having the custody or control of it;
> (b) having in it any proprietary right or interest (not being an equitable interest arising only from an agreement to transfer or grant an interest); or
> (c) having a charge on it.
> (3) Where property is subject to a trust, the person to whom it belongs shall be so treated as including any person having a right to enforce the trust.
> (4) Property of a corporation sole shall be so treated as belonging to the corporation notwithstanding a vacancy in the corporation.

---

[13] *Fancy* [1980] Crim LR 171.

1.4 MENS REA

The *mens rea* for the offence is set out in section 1(1): it must be shown that the defendant intended or was reckless as to the damaging of property. The meaning of 'recklessness' was discussed in Chapter 3. It should be noted that the *mens rea* applies to the damage *and* the fact that it belongs to another. This is most relevant in relation to intentional damage: a person who intentionally damages property believing it to be their own does not thereby intentionally damage property belonging to another.

1.5 DEFENCES

In addition to the general defences[14] (e.g. duress) there are some specific defences to criminal damage found in the Act. In section 5 a defendant has a lawful excuse:

> (2) (a) if at the time of the act or acts alleged to constitute the offence he believed that the person or person whom he believed to be entitled to consent to the destruction of or damage to the property in question had so consented, or would have so consented to it if he or they had know of the destruction or damage and its circumstances; or
>
> (b) if he destroyed or damaged or threatened to destroy or damage the property in question . . . in order to protect property belonging to himself or another or a right or interest in property which was or which he believed to be vested in himself or another, and at the time of the act or acts alleged to constitute the offence he believed—
>
> (i) that the property, right or interest was in immediate need of protection; and
>
> (ii) that the means of protection adopted or proposed to be adopted were or would be reasonable having regard to all the circumstances.
>
> (3) For the purpose of this section it is immaterial whether a belief is justified or not if it is honestly held.
>
> (4) For the purposes of subsection (2) above a right or interest in property includes any right or privilege in or over land, whether created by grant, licence or otherwise.[15]

In brief, there is a defence for a defendant who honestly[16] believes that the victim was consenting or would consent to the damage.[17] It is also a defence to damage property in order to protect your own or another's property.[18] It is enough if you act because you believe

---

[14] For which see Ch. 12.

[15] See *Chamberlain v Lindon* [1998] 1 WLR 1252 where the defendant destroyed property to protect a right of way, showing the significance of subs. (4).

[16] As subs. (3) makes clear, the belief does not have to be reasonable. According to *Jaggard v Dickenson* [1980] 3 All ER 716 (DC) a defendant who has a drunken belief that the owner is consenting to the damage has a defence.

[17] This includes where the defendant believes X is the owner and consents, even though X is not the owner. But in *Blake v DPP* [1993] Crim LR 586 (DC) the Divisional Court rejected the defendant's argument that he believed God owned the property and had consented to the damage. Perhaps the best explanation was that the defendant did not believe that God was in the eyes of the law the owner. Another explanation is that God is not a person for the purpose of s. 5(2) (Wilson 2003: 514).

[18] Section 5(2)(b) does not apply if the defendant is acting to protect a person and not property: *Baker and Wilkins* [1997] Crim LR 497 (CA).

that you were protecting the property,[19] even if in fact your property was not at risk or was not your own.[20] However, subsection (2)(b)(i) stresses that it must be shown that the property was in immediate need of protection and subsection (2)(b)(ii) that the protection would be reasonable in all the circumstances. The exact interpretation of these provisions is complex and was considered in the following case, which also summarizes the effect of the earlier decision of *Hunt*:[21]

R v Hill and Hall
(1989) 89 Cr App R 74 (CA)[22]

Valerie Hill and Jennifer Hall were charged under section 3 of the Criminal Damage Act 1971 with having an article intending without lawful excuse to use it to destroy or damage property belonging to another. They sought to rely on a defence under section 5 that they had a lawful excuse in that they were acting to protect property belonging to another. They were found in possession of a hacksaw blade, with which they intended to cut part of the perimeter fence of a United States naval facility in England. They were acting as part of a campaign organized by the Campaign for Nuclear Disarmament aimed at persuading the UK government to abandon nuclear weapons. They claimed that to do so would protect their and their neighbours' property.

Lord Lane CJ

The [trial judge], as I have already indicated, directed the jury to convict on two bases. The first basis was this, that what the applicant did or proposed to do could not, viewed objectively, be said to have been done to protect her own or anyone else's property under section 5(2)(b) which I have just read. It is simply, he concluded, part of a political campaign aimed at drawing attention to the base and to the risks as she described them raised by the presence of the base in Pembrokeshire. It aimed further at having the base removed. He came to the conclusion that the causative relationship between the acts which she intended to perform and the alleged protection was so tenuous, so nebulous, that the acts could not be said to be done to protect viewed objectively.

The second ground was with reference to the provision that the lawful excuse must be based upon an immediate need for protection. In each case the judge came to the same conclusion that on the applicant's own evidence the applicant could not be said to have believed under the provisions of section 5(2)(b)(i) that the property was in immediate need of protection.

. . .

The judge in each case relied upon a decision of this Court in *Hunt* (1978) 66 Cr App R 105. . . . We also have before us a more recent decision of this Court in *Ashford and Smith* (unreported) decided on May 26, 1988, in which very similar considerations were raised to those which exist in the present case. It also has the advantage of having set out the material findings of the Court in *Hunt* which were delivered by Roskill LJ. I am referring to p 4 of the transcript in *Ashford and Smith*, and it will help to set out the basis of the decision not only in *Ashford and Smith* but also in *Hunt* if I read the passage. It runs as follows:

[19] Property here is widely defined and can include an interest in property (e.g. a right of way): *Chamberlain v Lindon* [1998] 1 WLR 1252.
[20] The jury is not therefore required to assess the legitimacy of the defendant's belief: *Jones* [2005] QB 259.
[21] (1977) 66 Cr App R 105 (CA).   [22] [1989] Crim LR 136.

'The judge relied very largely upon the decision of this Court in *Hunt* (1978) 66 Cr App R 105. That was a case in which the appellant set fire to a guest room in an old people's home. He did so, he said, to draw attention to the defective fire alarm system. He was charged with arson, contrary to section 1(1) of the Criminal Damage Act 1971. He sought to set up the statutory defence under section 5(2) by claiming to have had a lawful excuse in doing what he did and that he was not reckless whether any such property would be destroyed. The trial judge withdrew the defence of lawful excuse from the jury and left the issue of recklessness for them to determine. The jury by a majority verdict convicted the appellant. On appeal, held, that, applying the objective test, the trial judge had ruled correctly because what the appellant had done was not an act which in itself did protect or was capable of protecting property; but in order to draw attention to what in his view was an immediate need for protection by repairing the alarm system; thus the statutory defence under section 5(2) of the Act was not open to him; accordingly, the appeal would be dismissed.

Giving the judgment of the Court Roskill LJ said, at p 108: 'Mr Marshall-Andrews' submission can be put thus: if this man honestly believed that that which he did was necessary in order to protect this property from the risk of fire and damage to the old people's home by reason of the absence of a working fire alarm, he was entitled to set fire to that bed and so to claim the statutory defence accorded by section 5(2). 'I have said we will assume in this favour that he possessed the requisite honest belief. But in our view the question whether he was entitled to the benefit of the defence turns upon the meaning of the words "in order to protect property belonging to another".' It was argued that those words were subjective in concept, just like the words in the latter part of section 5(2)(b) which are subjective. 'We do not think that is right. The question whether or not a particular act of destruction or damage or threat of destruction or damage was done or made in order to protect property belonging to another must be, on the true construction of the statute, an objective test. Therefore we have to ask ourselves whether, whatever the state of this man's mind and assuming an honest belief, that which he admittedly did was done in order to protect this particular property, namely the old people's home in Hertfordshire? If one formulates the question in that way, in the view of each member of this Court, for the reason Slynn J gave during the argument, it admits of only one answer: this was not done in order to protect property; it was done in order to draw attention to the defective state of the fire alarm. it was not an act which in itself did protect or was capable of protecting property".'

Then the judgment in *Ashford and Smith*, delivered by Glidewell LJ continued as follows: 'In our view that reasoning applies exactly in the present case. *Hunt* is, of course, binding upon us. But even if it were not, we agree with the reasoning contained in it.'

Now it is submitted by Mr Bowyer to us that the decision in *Hunt* and the decision in *Ashford and Smith* were wrong and that the test is a subjective test. In other words the submission is that it was a question of what the applicant believed, and accordingly, it should have been left to he jury as a matter of fact to decide what it was the applicant did believe.

. . .

That leaves us with the fact that we are bound by the decision in *Hunt*. But we add that we think that *Hunt* was correctly decided, for this reason. There are two aspects to this type of question. The first aspect is to decide what it was that the applicant, in this case Valerie Hill, in her own mind thought. The learned judge assumed, and so do we, for the purposes of this decision, that everything she said about her reasoning was true. I have already perhaps given a sufficient outline of what it was she believed to demonstrate what is meant by that. Up to that point the test was subjective. In other words one is examining what is going on in the applicant's mind.

Having done that, the judges in the present cases—and the judge particularly in the case of Valerie Hill—turned to the second aspect of the case, and that is this. He had to decide as a matter of law, which means objectively, whether it could be said that on those facts as believed by the applicant, snipping the strand of the wire, which she intended to do, could amount to something done to protect either the applicant's own home or the homes of her adjacent friends in Pembrokeshire.

He decided, again quite rightly in our view, that that proposed act on her part was far too remote from the eventual aim at which she was targeting her actions to satisfy the test.

It follows therefore, in our view, that the judges in the present two cases were absolutely right to come to the conclusion that they did so far as this aspect of the case is concerned, and to come to that conclusion as a matter of law, having decided the subjective test as the applicants wished them to be decided.

The second half of the question was that of the immediacy of the danger. Here the wording of the Act, one reminds oneself, is as follows: She believed that 'the property . . . was in immediate need of protection.'

Once again the judge had to determine whether, on the facts as stated by the applicant, there was any evidence on which it could be said that she believed there was a need of protection from immediate danger. In our view that must mean evidence that she believed that immediate action had to be taken to do something which would otherwise be a crime in order to prevent the immediate risk of something worse happening. The answers which I have read in the evidence given by this woman (and the evidence given by the other applicant was very similar) drives this Court to the conclusion, as they drove the respective judges to the conclusion, that there was no evidence on which it could be said that there was that belief.

. . .

Applications refused.

The decision is controversial because it takes a very narrow interpretation of 'acting in order to protect property'. Rather than seeing this test as being about the motive of the defendant (which might be thought to be the natural meaning of the words) the court interpreted it to be asking whether objectively (but on the facts as understood by the defendant) the act could be said to cause the protection of property.

2 ARSON

Arson is to be regarded as a species of criminal damage. Under section 1(3) of the Criminal Damage Act 1971:

An offence committed under this section by destroying or damaging property by fire shall be charged as arson.

The requirements of arson are the same as criminal damage, the only difference being that it must be shown that the damage or destruction was caused by fire.

3 AGGRAVATED CRIMINAL DAMAGE

Under section 1(2) Criminal Damage Act 1971:

> A person who without lawful excuse destroys or damages any property, whether belonging to himself or another—
>
> (a) intending to destroy or damage any property or being reckless as to whether any property would be destroyed or damaged; and
>
> (b) intending by the destruction or damage to endanger the life of another or being reckless as to whether the life of another would be thereby endangered shall be guilty of an offence.

The offence is punishable by life imprisonment.[23]

The *actus reus* of the offence involves destroying or damaging property without lawful excuse. This is similar to the *actus reus* of the basic offence except that the property does not have to belong to another. So, the offence can be committed by the defendant damaging his own property.[24] For example, a defendant who decides to burn down his own house in an attempt to be rehoused, but recklessly forgets that there are still people inside could be guilty of this offence.

There is no need to show that the damage or destruction actually endangers the life of others.[25] In *Sangha*[26] the defendant was convicted of arson contrary to section 1(2)(b) by setting fire to some chairs in a flat with the result that the whole house was burnt down. He was convicted, even though in fact there was (unknown to the defendant) no one in the house, and so there was no risk to people. Because a reasonable person would have thought that there was a risk that people's lives would be endangered he could be convicted.

The *mens rea* is in two parts. First, it must be shown that the defendant intended to destroy or damage the property or was reckless whether or not he did so. This is the same as the *mens rea* requirement for simple criminal damage, discussed above. Secondly, it must be shown that the defendant intended or was reckless to the endangerment of someone's life as a result of the criminal damage. Intention is to be given its usual meaning here, and recklessness refers to *Cunningham* recklessness. It should be stressed that the endangerment to the life must result from the criminal damage. This was established in the following case:

R v Steer
[1988] AC 111 (HL)[27]

Dennis Steer fired several shots at the windows of his former business partner's house. No injuries were caused to those inside. He was charged with damaging property being reckless whether the life of another would be endangered thereby, contrary to section 1(2) of the Criminal Damage Act 1971. The certified question was 'Whether, upon a true construction of section 1(2)(b) of the Criminal Damage Act 1971, the prosecution

---

[23] Section 4.   [24] *Merrick* [1995] Crim LR 802 (CA).   [25] *Dudley* [1989] Crim LR 57.
[26] [1988] 2 All ER 385 (CA).   [27] [1987] 2 All ER 833, [1987] 3 WLR 205, (1987) 85 Cr App R 352.

are required to prove that the danger to life resulted from the destruction of or damage to the property, or whether it is sufficient for the prosecution to prove that it resulted from the act of the defendant which caused the destruction or damage'.

Lord Bridge of Harwich

Under both limbs of s 1 of the 1971 Act it is the essence of the offence which the section creates that the defendant has destroyed or damaged property. For the purpose of analysis it may be convenient to omit reference to destruction and to concentrate on the references to damage, which was all that was here involved. To be guilty under sub-s (1) the defendant must have intended or been reckless as to the damage to property which he caused. To be guilty under sub-s (2) he must additionally have intended to endanger life or been reckless whether life would be endangered 'by the damage' to property which he caused. This is the context in which the words must be construed and it seems to me impossible to read the words 'by the damage' as meaning 'by the damage or by the act which caused the damage'. Moreover, if the language of the statute has the meaning for which the Crown contends, the words 'by the destruction or damage' and 'thereby' in sub-s (2)(b) are mere surplusage. If the Crown's submission is right, the only additional element necessary to convert a sub-s (1) offence into a sub-s (2) offence is an intent to endanger life or recklessness whether life would be endangered simpliciter. It would suffice as a ground for dismissing this appeal if the statute were ambiguous, since any such ambiguity in a criminal statute should be resolved in favour of the defence. But I can find no ambiguity. It seems to me that the meaning for which the respondent contends is the only meaning which the language can bear.

The contrary construction leads to anomalies which Parliament cannot have intended. If A and B both discharge firearms in a public place, being reckless whether life would be endangered, it would be absurd that A, who incidentally causes some trifling damage to property, should be guilty of an offence punishable with life imprisonment, but that B, who causes no damage, should be guilty of no offence. In the same circumstances, if A is merely reckless but B actually intends to endanger life, it is scarcely less absurd that A should be guilty of the graver offence under s 1(2) of the 1971 Act, B of the lesser offence under s 16 of the Firearms Act 1968.

Appeal dismissed.

This case, then, establishes that it must be shown that it is damage to property that endangers the victim's life, rather than, for example, the missile thrown by the defendant.[28] It does not need to be shown that the property which endangers the life of the other is the same as the property which is damaged. An example given in *Attorney-General's Reference (No. 3 of 1992)*[29] was where cutting the rope of a crane (property A) causes a load to fall onto the roof of a car (property B) which endangers life.

3.1 DEFENCES

The defences in section 5 do not apply to section 2: this is not surprising because it is rarely excusable to damage property being aware that doing so will endanger someone's life.

[28] For an application of *Steer*, see *Webster* [1995] 2 All ER 168 (CA).
[29] (1994) 98 Cr App R 383 (CA).

However, the offence does use the phrase 'without lawful excuse', which implies the general defences, such as private defence, are available.

4 RACIALLY AGGRAVATED CRIMINAL DAMAGE

Section 30(1) of the Crime and Disorder Act 1998 states:

> A person is guilty of an offence under this section if he commits an offence under section 1(1) of the Criminal Damage Act 1971 . . . which is racially or religiously aggravated for the purposes of this section.

The notion of racial or religious aggravation was discussed at pp. 362–4.

QUESTIONS

1. Ivy places a leaf over part of a nude statue in her local park. At her trial she produces a petition which suggests that nearly 80 per cent of the inhabitants in her town think that the statue is now improved. Has she committed criminal damage? (Do not forget to consider the *mens rea* issues as well as the question of whether or not there is damage.)

2. Janice is concerned that people are driving too quickly through her village. She puts some glass out in the road next to a sign warning that there is glass on the road. Several cars are not able to stop in time and their tyres are punctured. Has she committed criminal damage?

3. Brian is an organic farmer. His neighbour (Sid) decides to plant genetically modified (GM) crops as part of a government trial. Brian, having carefully researched the issue, believes that material from the GM crops is likely to come over onto his land and 'contaminate' his crops. One night, he sets fire to Sid's GM crops, destroying them. What offences have been committed?

FURTHER READING

Elliot, D. (1997), 'Endangering Life by Destroying or Damaging Property', *Criminal Law Review* 382.

Stalworthy, M. (2000), 'Damage to Crops', *New Law Journal* 150: 728 and 801.

5 COMPUTER CRIME: COMPUTER MISUSE ACT 1990

The Computer Misuse Act 1990 is designed to protect information kept on computers. The term 'computer' is not defined in the Act. No doubt any attempted definition would rapidly become out of date. The courts appear to have taken a broad interpretation of the word 'computer', and it has been held to include electronic personal organizers, boxes attached to televisions which control access to cable television channels,[30] and cash registers.[31]

---

[30] *Maxwell-King* [2001] 2 Cr App R (S) 136 (CA).
[31] *Attorney-General's Reference (No. 1 of 1991)* [1993] QB 94 (CA).

5.1 SECTION 1: UNAUTHORIZED ACCESS TO COMPUTER MATERIAL

This offence is designed to punish people who try to gain access to unauthorized data:

1(1) A person is guilty of an offence if—

(a) he causes a computer to perform any function with intent to secure access to any program or data held in any computer;

(b) the access he intends to secure is unauthorized; and

(c) he knows at the time when he causes the computer to perform the function that that is the case.

(2) The intent a person has to have to commit an offence under this section need not be directed at—

(a) any particular program or data;

(b) a program or data of any particular kind; or

(c) a program or data held in any particular computer.

The *actus reus* of the offence is simply causing a computer to 'perform any function'. This could include switching a computer on.[32] It should be emphasized that there is no need to show that the defendant actually reached unauthorized material, only that he intended to do so. The *mens rea* requirement can be broken down into three elements:

(1) *An intention to secure access to any program or data on any computer.* The phrase secure access is narrower than may be at first assumed. Section 17(2) states:

A person secures access to any program or data held in a computer if by causing a computer to perform any function he—

(a) alters or erases the program or data;

(b) copies or moves it to any storage medium other than that in which it is held or to a different location in the storage medium in which it is held;

(c) uses it; or

(d) has it output from the computer in which it is held (whether by having it displayed or in any other manner);

and references to access to a program or data (and to an intent to secure such access) shall be read accordingly.

This seems to means that simply intending to look at unauthorized data on a computer does not infringe section 1. Once seeing the data the defendant must intend to do one of the four things listed in the section with the data, using a computer.[33] It is made clear in section 1(2) of the Computer Misuse Act that there is no need to prove

---

[32] Simply looking at a computer screen would not be enough.

[33] In *Zezev* [2002] Crim LR 648; [2002] EWHC Admin 589 it was held that sending an e-mail that purported to come from one person but in fact came from another would cause a computer to record information that manifestly affected its reliability and therefore did fall within s. 17.

an intent to obtain access to any particular program or data. In other words the offence is committed if a defendant is entering the computer just to see what she can find. Further, it does not matter whether the defendant is trying to reach data on the computer she is using, or attempting to reach data on another computer using her own computer.[34]

(2) *The intended access to the data must be unauthorized.* To be authorized to access data it must be shown that the defendant was either entitled to control access to that data or had been given authority to access the information by a person who was able to control access to it.[35] It may be that a defendant is permitted access to some parts of a computer's database, but this is no defence if she is attempting to reach other parts of the database. For, example in *R v Bow Street Metropolitan Stipendiary Magistrate, ex parte United States (No. 2)*[36] an employee of a credit card company was allotted certain customers and permitted to access data held about them on her company's computer. She accessed information about other customers. This constituted an offence under section 1 of the Act.

Similarly it may be that a defendant is authorized to access data for one purpose but not another.[37] So, if a defendant is permitted access to data only for work purposes but accesses the data for his or her own reasons then this will be seen as unauthorized access.[38] Further, a person may be entitled to view certain data, but not to amend it. Again, in such a case amending the data could infringe section 1.

(3) *The defendant knows that he or she is not authorized to access the program or data.* It should be noted that this knowledge is based on a subjective test.

5.2 SECTION 2: UNAUTHORIZED ACCESS WITH INTENT

The offence in section 2 is a more serious one than that in section 1. It requires proof that a defendant committed an offence under section 1 and in addition that he or she intended to commit or facilitate the commission of a serious arrestable offence (e.g. theft).[39]

5.3 SECTION 3: UNAUTHORIZED MODIFICATION OF COMPUTER MATERIAL

The *actus reus* of this offence, under section 3(1), is 'any act which causes an unauthorised modification of the contents of any computer'; the *mens rea* is:
an intent to cause a modification to the contents of any computer and by so doing—

(a) to impair the operation of any computer;

(b) to prevent or hinder access to any program or data held in any computer; or

(c) to impair the operation of any such program or the reliability of any such data.

---

[34] *Attorney-General's Reference (No. 1 of 1991)* [1993] QB 94 (CA).
[35] Computer Misuse Act 1990, s. 17(5).   [36] [2000] AC 216 (HL).
[37] *Ellis v DPP (No. 1)* [2001] EWHC Admin 362 confirmed that a person may be authorized to use a computer, but not the program on the computer.
[38] *R v Bow Street Metropolitan Stipendiary Magistrate, ex p United States (No. 2)* [2000] 2 AC 216.
[39] e.g. theft.

It is also necessary to show that the defendant knew that the modification that was intended was unauthorized. Thus a defendant has a defence if she was authorized to modify a program to some extent but by mistake modified much more than she intended.

This section is clearly aimed at people who alter computer data with intent to corrupt a program or alter a database (e.g. by means of a virus[40]). The intent does not need to be directed towards any particular computer or data. Modification is defined as including removal of any program or data on a computer and includes adding to the contents or erasing them. It also includes temporary modification (section 3(5)). The section does not cover those who inhibit access to data. In other words a virus that does not modify the data, but makes access to it harder or impossible does not appear to fall under the scope of the Act.[41]

FURTHER READING

Law Commission (1989), Report No. 186, *Computer Misuse* (London: HMSO).

Wasik, M. (1991), *Crime and the Computer* (Oxford: OUP).

PART II: THEORETICAL ISSUES ON CRIMINAL DAMAGE

6 CRIMINAL DAMAGE THEORY

We will briefly examine here some issues of particular theoretical interest in relation to criminal damage. Discussion of recklessness can be found in Chapter 3.

6.1 STATISTICS

Nineteen per cent of all recorded crime is criminal damage,[42] but the British Crime survey (interviewing members of the public) suggested that criminal damage makes up 25 per cent of crime that actually takes place. There were 2,564,000 incidents of criminal damage recorded by the BCS in 2004/5, with criminal damage to vehicles making up 1,564,000 of those offences.[43] In that year there were 48,035 reported incidents of arson.[44] Arson is a particularly harmful crime. In *an average week* arsonists start 3,600 fires which result in two deaths, sixty casualties, and £40 million worth of damage.[45]

6.2 WHAT IS SPECIAL ABOUT DAMAGING PROPERTY?

It might be argued that we should have a single offence of wrongful interference with property interests that could cover both theft and criminal damage. However, Simester and

---

[40] Akdeniz (1996). [41] All Party Parliamentary Internet Group (2004); Klang (2003).
[42] Simmons *et al.* (2002: 5). [43] Nicholas *et al.* (2005: 59). [44] Ibid.
[45] Office of the Deputy Prime Minister (2003: 1).

Sullivan have argued that criminal damage is different from theft or other offences involving property interests for two reasons. First it is often linked with offences against the person. They explain that 'many typical instances of criminal damage involve forms of vandalism employing percussive force, fire, or explosions, conduct that may well cause alarm and concern even to bystanders lacking any proprietary interest in the property being damaged.'[46] Second, criminal damage such as vandalism can contain an expressive dimension: communicating a contempt for society or the victim.[47]

6.3 SHOULD IT BE AN OFFENCE TO DAMAGE YOUR OWN PROPERTY?

At first it might be assumed that a fundamental aspect of ownership is that one is free to destroy one's own property.[48] Some argue that an artist has creative rights in his or her property even once it has been sold.[49] For example, the American Visual Artists Rights Act 1990 disallows destruction of an original or limited-edition and signed work where the artist is of recognized stature and his or her reputation would be harmed.[50] Thus, in *Martin v City of Indianapolis*[51] the artist obtained damages where the city council had purchased his sculpture, but later bulldozed it down in order to develop the land.

6.4 THE DEFINITION OF DAMAGE

In our materialistic society the destruction or damaging of property can be seen as positively nihilistic. However, there are, as can be seen in Part I, several situations where it will be unclear whether property has been damaged. One interesting example is graffiti:

M.A. Gomez, 'The Writing on our Walls: Finding Solutions through Distinguishing Graffiti Art from Graffiti Vandalism' (1993) 26 *University of Michigan Journal of Law Reform* 633 at 634–5, 650–3

Different motivations drive different types of graffiti, and graffiti cannot be understood or controlled without an understanding of the motivations behind its creation. Although they cannot capture fully the entire spectrum of graffiti, two particular classifications encompass most types of graffiti and the motivations behind it. First, 'graffiti art' describes graffiti-type works that exhibit many of the characteristics of pieces normally termed 'high art' or 'folk art.' The more intricate works of graffiti entitled 'pieces' belong in this category because they result from a desire to create artwork. Second, 'graffiti vandalism' describes those mere scrawlings that are motivated by a desire to mark territory, create notoriety, or show one's defiance of the law and society. Graffiti termed 'gang graffiti' or 'tags' belong in this category. These works are done most often without the permission of the property owner and possess few of the qualities of pieces normally deemed 'high art' or 'folk art.' Although graffiti possessing the characteristics of both art and vandalism is difficult to classify under

---

[46] Simester and Sullivan (2005: 184).   [47] Ibid.

[48] See Lutz and Bonomolo (1997) for a discussion of cases where people damage their family's property on the breakdown of the marriage.

[49] Halpern (1997).   [50] Discussed in Santilli (1997).   [51] 192 F 3d 608 (7th Circ 1999).

the above scheme, the distinction is useful nonetheless because it recognizes that such works are stimulated by both types of motivations.

. . . From the viewpoint of many of those who consider graffiti to be vandalism, all graffiti is vandalism regardless of a piece's artistic value. For these opponents, there is no room for differentiation between mere scrawls or a mural. Graffiti is ugly, indicative of decay, invites crime and additional graffiti, and is done by criminals who should be punished. Graffiti should be eliminated even when it is on private property or was commissioned. Such a view leaves no room for the preservation of even the more intricate pieces of graffiti recognized as art. Opponents are against any encouragement of, or support for, graffiti and often claim that any write-up of graffiti incidents by the press encourages more vandalism. Opponents fail to appreciate what graffiti represents to the youth culture and what motivates the writer. Their only solution is to outlaw all graffiti and punish all writers.

Those who consider some graffiti to be art often differentiate more carefully between types of graffiti. Graffiti art proponents recognize that some pieces have extraordinary merit and deserve recognition. Proponents recognize that the motivation of many writers is not to deface property intentionally, but rather to express themselves or to gain respect by the only means that are accessible to them.

Graffiti's most ardent proponents often fail to acknowledge, however, that the art form often results in the defacing of property. At the same time, many proponents do recognize that defacing property is wrong. They therefore work to prevent writers from vandalizing public and private property by creating alternative outlets for writers' energies. Such alternatives include work on commissioned property or participation in sponsored exhibitions and programs which hone skills and can help writers find employment or win scholarships.

6.5 THE JUSTIFICATION FOR AGGRAVATED CRIMINAL DAMAGE

Why should endangering life by criminal damage be regarded as a particular offence. There are two points here. First, why should endangering life normally not be an offence, but becomes one if done through criminal damage? Secondly, if the defendant causes criminal damage, reckless as to endangering lives, why should it matter how the endangerment occurred (i.e. whether it occurred because of the damage to property or otherwise)? One commentator has described that distinction as 'a dismal one'.[52] In the following extract the problems with the offence of aggravated criminal damage are described in greater detail:

D. Elliot, 'Endangering Life by Destroying or Damaging Property' [1997] *Criminal Law Review* 382, 389–92

Endangerment

Although the reading of section 1(2)(b) in *Steer* is capable of producing distinctions which Lord Taylor C.J. described as 'dismal', it must be noted that Lord Bridge of Harwich, who gave the leading speech in the House of Lords, felt that a contrary construction would lead to anomalies which Parliament could not have intended. 'If A and B both discharge firearms in a public place, being reckless whether life would be endangered, it would be absurd that A,

---

[52] Wilson (2003: 519).

who incidentally causes trifling damage to property, should be guilty of an offence punishable by life imprisonment, but that B, who caused no damage, should be guilty of no offence'. His Lordship rejected as irrational, indeed perverse, any intention of Parliament in section 1(2) to create a general offence of endangering life intentionally or recklessly, however the danger was caused, with a necessary, albeit insignificant, ingredient that some damage to property should also be caused.

Thus one absurdity is avoided, but only at the cost of submitting to another, the one described by Lord Taylor C.J. Nor is this the end of the anomalies lurking in the subsection. For not only does endangerment 'thereby' not mean 'by the act of the defendant'; it also does not mean 'by the damage caused by the defendant'. It means 'by the damage about which he was intentional or reckless', if that is different from the damage he did. Sometimes, but not always, the result produced by this rule is straightforward enough. In *Dudley* D threw a firebomb against a house in which there was a family against whom he had a grievance. Because the blaze was very quickly extinguished by the family, only trivial damage was done to the outside of the door. D's argument that no jury could properly find that the actual damage to the door was intended or likely to endanger life, was rejected by the trial judge, McCullough J. His ruling was upheld on appeal, Staughton L.J. stating that the words 'destruction or damage' in section 1(2)(b) refer back to the destruction or damage which has to be intended by D in section 1(2)(a) or as to which he has to be reckless. This decision was approved in *Webster*, Lord Taylor C.J. remarking that otherwise the gravamen of an offence involving damage by a missile would depend not on D's intention but on whether he was a good shot in seeking to carry it out. Moreover, as was pointed out by Staughton L.J. in *Dudley*, if it were otherwise, injustice would be done in a case where someone was reckless only as to trivial damage, but by some mishap caused danger to life. The decisions in *Dudley* and *Webster* remove the possibility of that injustice. It is only where D is intentional or reckless as to endangerment from the damage he intentionally or recklessly causes that he is guilty of the aggravated offence.

It is the same where endangerment results from damage to a different property from the property attacked. If D does an act which is intended or likely to damage property A, and achieves damage to property B which endangers life, he will be guilty of the simple offence as to property B, if both properties belong to another. He has damaged property belonging to another (property B), intending or being reckless as to whether any 'such' property (i.e. property belong to another–property A) would be damaged. For him to be guilty of the aggravated offence (when, of course, the ownership of either property would be irrelevant), 'it is sufficient to prove that the defendant was reckless as to whether [property B] was damaged and reckless as to whether the life of another would be endangered by the damage to [property B]'. So says Schiemann J. in *Att.-Gen.'s Reference (No. 3 of 1992)*, and the example he gives is one where D cuts a rope by which a heavy object is suspended, so that the object falls and hits the roof of a passing car, which roof collapses, killing the driver. It is sufficient if D was reckless as to whether cutting the rope would damage the car and was reckless as to whether the life of the driver would be endangered by damage to the car.

But although that is sufficient to make D guilty of the aggravated offence, it may not be necessary. If D intended or was reckless as to whether property A would be damaged by his act, and as to whether that damage would endanger life, that is enough even though no endangerment arises from any damage to property A, because A is not in fact damaged. D has damaged property B (*actus reus*) with the appropriate *mens rea*: intending or being reckless as to whether any property (i.e. property A) would be damaged and intending or being reckless as whether life would be endangered thereby (i.e. by damage to property A). The crime is complete once property B is damaged, and the fact that D intended or was reckless as to a completely different result is irrelevant. No endangerment by any damage is needed; no damage to the property attacked by D is needed. The only 'injustice' avoided by the cases of *Dudley* and *Webster* is the conviction of an accused who intentionally or recklessly damaged property in circumstances where no endangerment by any damage to property was intended or likely.

D throws a stone at a moving car, intending it to crash and thereby endanger the lives of the occupants, the stone misses and breaks a window in an empty house. He is guilty of the aggravated offence, having damaged the window with the appropriate *mens rea*. The fact that neither the damage he did nor endangerment from the damage he did was intended or likely is neither here nor there.

7 THE THEORY OF COMPUTER CRIMES

Given that the criminal law is generally rather reluctant to protect confidential information, the Computer Misuse Act looks anomalous. Why is it an offence to copy personal information without authority from a computer but not a filing cabinet?[53] There are four particular reasons suggested by the Law Commission[54] why it might be thought that information held on computers needs special protection by the criminal law. First, it is very hard to safeguard information stored on a computer, particularly as often the information is intended to be accessed by a number of authorized people. By contrast information on paper can be kept in a safe or other secure place. Secondly, the ease of destroying or corrupting data on a computer means they deserve protection, particularly as it is not always possible for the owner of the computer to realize that the data have been looked at. Thirdly, the highly confidential nature of the kind of information kept on computers (often concerning many members of the public) is such that it needs particular protection. Fourthly, it may be better to deter people from searching for confidential information because of the temptation to use it for fraudulent purposes once they have found it. Whether these are convincing or not is a matter for debate.[55]

In the following extract Neal Katyal considers whether there is a justification for having criminal offences directed specifically at computer crime (or cybercrime as he calls it):

N.K. Katyal, 'Criminal Law in Cyberspace' (2001) 149 *University of Pennsylvania Law Review* 1003 at 1005–6

Underlying the 'cybercrime is not different' position is a worry about a unique form of geographic substitution. The concern is that disproportionately punishing activity in either realspace or cyberspace will induce criminals to shift their activities to that sphere in which the expected punishment is lower. For example, if the electronic theft of one million dollars warrants five years imprisonment, and the physical theft of one million dollars warrants ten years imprisonment, criminals are likely to opt for the electronic theft. Such analysis is, however, incomplete. Beccaria and Becker have observed that the expected penalty for criminal activity is not only the sentence in the criminal code, but also a function of the

---

[53] See the discussion in Card and Ashworth (2000: 336–8).
[54] Law Commission Report No. 186 (1989). See also Fearon (2004).
[55] See further Essen (2002).

probability that one will get caught. . . . To the extent that cybercrimes are easier to get away with, sentences might be increased to compensate for this lower probability.

In addition to the probability of being caught, another variable overlooked by the 'cyber-crime is not different' camp is the perpetration cost of engaging in crime. A bank robbery in realspace, for example, consumes tremendous criminal resources. A robber has to hire lookouts and firepower, garner inside knowledge about the bank, and so on. Profits will be split among five, six, or even more people. A computer theft, by contrast, involves fewer resources and may even be accomplished by a single person sitting down at a computer. Because cybercrime requires fewer resource inputs and less investment to cause a given level of harm, the law might approach these crimes differently.

These variations suggest that cyberspace is a unique medium for three reasons. First, and most importantly, the use of computers and other equipment is a cheaper means to per-petrate crime. Criminal law must be concerned not only with punishing crime ex post, but with creating ex ante barriers to inexpensive ways of carrying out criminal activity. . . .

Second, cybercrime adds additional parties to the traditional perpetrator-victim scenario of crime. In particular, much cybercrime is carried out through the use of Internet Service Providers ('ISPs'), such as America Online. Government should consider imposing responsi-bilities on such third parties because doing so promotes cost deterrence. Third parties can develop ways to make criminal activity more expensive and may be able to do so in ways that the government cannot accomplish directly. The same logic sometimes can apply to victims of cybercrime; law can develop mechanisms to encourage optimal victim behavior as well. . . .

Third, and more generally, a host of thorny problems arise because most activities that occur in cyberspace are invisible to third parties—and sometimes even to second parties. In a space where crimes are invisible, strategies that focus on trying to prevent crime by maintaining public order, such as 'broken windows' policing, are of limited utility (though some insights can be adapted to cyberspace). Social norms cannot operate as effectively to prevent crime on the net because its users are not necessarily constrained by the values of realspace.

On the other side of the ledger, the danger of overly aggressive law enforcement is multi-plied in cyberspace. Each new major cybercrime leads law enforcement to push for changes to the technical infrastructure to create better monitoring and tracing. If these monitoring mechanisms are hidden in private hardware and software, however, some contend that public accountability may be undermined. A similar point can be made about enforcement by police: Because police are invisible on the internet, the potential for entrapment or other forms of police misconduct may be greater. The ultimate effect of this loss of police visibility may be to poison legitimate activity on the net because confidence in communication may be undermined. An internet user will not be sure that he is talking to a friend and not a government interloper seeking evidence of criminal activity. Because the technology of law enforcement is not well understood among the public, citizens will fear the net and its potential advantages will be stymied. Consider the public uproar over a third prominent news item from this year: the discovery that the Federal Bureau of Investigation ('FBI') has a system, with the poorly chosen title of 'Carnivore,' which allows it to examine private e-mails.

QUESTIONS

1. Do you think graffiti should be regarded as criminal damage or cultural expression?

2. Why are not pollution and environmental offences regarded as criminal damage?

3. Are there any good reasons why the temporary unauthorized use of a computer should be a criminal offence when it is not for other property?

FURTHER READING

All Party Parliamentary Internet Group (2004), *Revision of the Computer Misuse Act* (London: APIG)

Grabosky, P., Smith, R., and Dempsey, G. (2003), *Electronic Theft* (Cambridge: Cambridge University Press).

Hancock, D. (2001), 'To What Extent Should Computer Related Crimes Be the Subject of Specific Legislative Attention?', *Albany Law Journal of Science and Technology* 12: 97.

Katyal, N. (2001), 'Criminal Law in Cyberspace', *University of Pennsylvania Law Review* 149: 1003.

Thomas, D., and Loader, B. (2000), *Cybercrime* (London: Routledge).

DEFENCES

PART I: THE LAW

Even if the prosecution has been able to prove the *actus reus* and *mens rea* of an offence all is not lost for the defendant. He or she may still be able to rely on a defence. For example, even though the defendant is proved to have intentionally caused the victim grievous bodily harm he may still be acquitted if he was acting under duress. However, there is no straightforward definition of a defence. Criminal lawyers disagree on what should or should not be regarded as a defence, as we shall see in Part II of this chapter. In particular there is dispute whether some claims amount to a defence or in fact to a denial of the *actus reus* or *mens rea*. For example, one of the best known defences in criminal law, self-defence, has been held by the courts in fact to amount to a denial of the *actus reus*. In this chapter a wide definition of defences will be used, to include any claim often said to be defence.

There are also many different ways of classifying the defences, which we will outline in Part II. Not everyone, therefore, will agree with the classification used in this chapter, but one has to be chosen. This section will discuss the defences in the following order:

(1) Defences based on the finding that the defendant acted in a permissible way:
    1. private defence;
    2. necessity;
    3. chastisement;
    4. consent.

(2) Defences based on the pressure exerted upon the defendant by another:
    5. duress;
    6. coercion;
    7. entrapment;
    8. superior orders.

(3) Defences based on the defendant's mental condition:
    9. automatism;
    10. insanity;
    11. diminished responsibility;
    12. provocation;
    13. infancy;

14. intoxication;

15. mistake.

1 PRIVATE DEFENCE AND THE PREVENTION OF CRIME

1.1 THE LEGAL SOURCE OF THE DEFENCE

DEFINITION

The requirements of private defence are:

1. The defendant was (or believed he was) facing an unjust threat from the victim.

2. The defendant used a level of force against the threat (or the threat as it was believed to be) which was reasonable in the circumstances.

A complete defence is available to those who use force in order to defend themselves or another person from an unjustified attack.[1] Unfortunately there is no agreement over the correct name for this defence. Textbooks have used the terms self-defence, private defence, and lawful defence. Self-defence is probably the phrase most familiar to the person in the street, although it is misleading because the defence also applies if the defendant is protecting someone else from an attack. In this book the term private defence will be used.

Further confusion in English law results from the fact that the defence has two separate legal sources:[2]

(1) At common law a person has a defence if he is defending himself or another[3] from an attack.

(2) Under section 3 of the Criminal Law Act 1967:

> (1) A person may use such force as is reasonable in the circumstances in the prevention of crime, or in effecting or assisting in the lawful arrest of offenders or suspected offenders or of persons unlawfully at large.
>
> (2) Subsection (1) above shall replace the rules of the common law on the question when force used for a purpose mentioned in the subsection is justified by that purpose.

Fortunately the courts have held that the rules governing common law private defence and section 3 co-exist.[4] In other words the legal rules are the same whichever form of the defence is used.[5] Therefore courts and commentators usually talk about self-defence or private

---

[1] In Part II an argument will be made that it is more accurate to say that self-defence arises when defendants defend themselves from unjustified threats, rather than attacks.

[2] There are also some statutes that provide a defence in a particular context (e.g. the Criminal Damage Act 1971: see Ch. 11).

[3] *Duffy* [1967] 1 QB 63 (CA).

[4] Technically the s. 3 defence is not available where the 'attacker' is not committing a crime (if, e.g., he or she is a child).

[5] *Cousins* [1982] QB 526 (CA). For a detailed discussion of the relationship see Harlow (1974).

defence, without saying whether they are talking about the statutory or common law version.

1.2 TO WHAT CRIMES IS PRIVATE DEFENCE A DEFENCE?

Can a defendant seek to rely on private defence as a response to any charge? The answer is unclear. Some cases suggest that private defence appears to be available only to a defendant who is charged with a crime that involves the use of force and so is not available to a defence such as possession or parking on a double yellow line. This was stressed in *Renouf*.[6] However, in that case a generous view was taken of what amounted to force. The defendant was charged with reckless driving after forcing a car carrying offenders off the road. This was said to amount to a use of force.[7] The requirement that the offence involve one of force was confirmed in *Blake v DPP*,[8] where a vicar wrote with a felt-tip pen on a pillar near the Houses of Parliament. He argued he was seeking to prevent the first Iraq war and therefore relied on section 3 of the Criminal Law Act 1967. However, because *inter alia*[9] the writing did not involve the use of force it was held that the defence could not be relied upon.

There are other cases which suggest that the defence of private defence can be used even where no force is used. This was suggested by the recent decision of *DPP v Bayer*.[10] This view is preferable, because it seems unjustifiable to allow a defendant to use force to avoid a threat, but not to take a non-forceful, but illegal, way of escaping a threat. It should be noted that in cases where the defendant has not used force duress of circumstances may provide a defence.[11]

1.3 WHAT NEEDS TO BE SHOWN TO ESTABLISH THE DEFENCE?

The key elements of the defence have been summarized in a recent notorious case. The defendant shot two young men who were burgling his house. The key issue was whether the question for the jury should have been whether the amount of force used was reasonable by the standards of the ordinary person, or whether it was sufficient to show that the defendant believed the level of force to be reasonable:

R v Martin (Anthony)
[2001] EWCA Crim 2245 (CA)[12]

Anthony Martin shot at two men who had entered his isolated house at night. He had been burgled several times in the past. Both men were wounded and one of the two died from his wounds. Martin was convicted of murder. On appeal his counsel

---

[6] [1986] 2 All ER 449 (CA).

[7] In *R v Cousins* [1982] 2 All ER 115, 117 Milmo J appeared to reject the *Renouf* restriction, holding that 'if force is permissible, something less, for example, a threat, must also be permissible if it is reasonable in the circumstances'. In that case private defence was held to be a defence to a charge of a threat to kill.

[8] [1993] Crim LR 586.

[9] He also failed to show that the threat was imminent and that the writing was done with the purpose of directly preventing damage to property.

[10] [2004] Crim LR 663.   [11] See *Backshall* [1999] 1 Cr App R 35 (CA).   [12] [2002] 2 WLR 1.

sought to introduce new evidence that the appellant was suffering from a psychiatric condition which was relevant to show (i) Martin was suffering from diminished responsibility at the time of the killing and (ii) because of his condition he was more likely genuinely to believe that he was about to be attacked than an ordinary person would be.

Lord Woolf CJ handed down the following judgment of the court

The law relating to self-defence

4. There was no dispute that Mr Martin had shot the two men. Mr Martin's defence to the principal offences with which he was charged was that he was acting in self-defence. When this defence is raised, the prosecution has the burden of satisfying the jury so that they are sure that the defendant was not acting in self-defence. A defendant is entitled to use reasonable force to protect himself, others for whom he is responsible and his property: see *Beckford v The Queen* [1988] AC 130.

5. In judging whether the defendant had only used reasonable force, the jury has to take into account all the circumstances, including the situation as the defendant honestly believes it to be at the time, when he was defending himself. It does not matter if the defendant was mistaken in his belief as long as his belief was genuine.

6. Accordingly, the jury could only convict Mr Martin if either they did not believe his evidence that he was acting in self-defence or they thought that Mr Martin had used an unreasonable amount of force. These were issues which were ideally suited to a decision of a jury.

7. As to the first issue, what Mr Martin believed, the jury heard his evidence and they could only reject that evidence if they were satisfied it was untrue. As to the second issue, as to what is a reasonable amount of force, obviously opinions can differ. It cannot be left to a defendant to decide what force it is reasonable to use because this would mean that even if a defendant used disproportionate force but be believed he was acting reasonably he would not be guilty of any offence. It is for this reason that it was for the jury, as the representative of the public, to decide the amount of force which it would be reasonable and the amount of force which it would be unreasonable to use in the circumstances in which they found that Mr Martin believed himself to be in. It is only if the jury are sure that the amount of force which was used was unreasonable that they are entitled to find a defendant guilty if he was acting in self-defence.

8. These features of the defence of self-defence are critical to the outcome of this appeal. They are difficult to criticise and mean that Mr Martin is faced with the fact that the jury must have decided that when he shot the two men, he was either not acting in self-defence or, if he was, he used excessive force.

9. What has been the subject of debate is whether a defendant to a murder charge should be convicted of murder if he was acting in self-defence but used excessive force in self-defence. It is suggested that such a defendant should be regarded as being guilty of manslaughter and not murder. He would not then have to be sentenced to life imprisonment but usually instead to a determinate sentence the length of which would be decided upon by the judge, having regard to the circumstances of the offence. If it is thought that this should be the law then the change would have to be made by Parliament. It was not even suggested on this appeal that it would be open to this court by judicial decision to bring about such a change. However, even in the case of a life sentence for murder the circumstances of the offence are taken into account. The Home Secretary, having considered the recommendations of the trial judge and the Lord Chief Justice of the day, fixes the tariff period, that

is the period which has to elapse before a defendant can be recommended for parole by the Parole Board.

. . .

[Lord Woolf examined the new psychiatric evidence and continued:]

65. Mr Wolkind [Counsel for Martin] relied on the recent decision of the House of Lords in *R v Smith (Morgan)* [2001] 1 AC 146. This was also a provocation case that Mr Wolkind contended could be applied to the similar issues which arise when a defendant relies on self-defence. In that case Smith was relying upon evidence that he suffered from clinical depression. There was no dispute that the evidence was admissible and relevant on the issue as to whether he was provoked, the subjective issue. The problem was as to whether the evidence was admissible as being relevant on the objective issue of loss of self-control. As to this the majority of their Lordships came to the conclusion that the jury were entitled to take into account some characteristic, whether temporary or permanent, which affected the degree of control which society could reasonably expect of a defendant and which it would be unjust not to take into account.

66. Is the same approach appropriate in the case of self-defence? There are policy reasons for distinguishing provocation from self-defence. Provocation only applies to murder but self-defence applies to all assaults. In addition, provocation does not provide a complete defence; it only reduces the offence from murder to manslaughter. There is also the undoubted fact that self-defence is raised in a great many cases resulting from minor assaults and it would be wholly disproportionate to encourage medical disputes in cases of that sort. Lord Hobhouse of Woodborough in his dissenting speech in Smith recognized that in relation to self-defence too generous an approach as to what is reasonable could result in an 'exorbitant defence' (p 195). Lord Hoffmann also appeared conscious of this. As a matter of principle we would reject the suggestion that the approach of the majority in Smith in relation to provocation should be applied directly to the different issue of self-defence.

67. We would accept that the jury are entitled to take into account in relation to self-defence the physical characteristics of the defendant. However, we would not agree that it is appropriate, except in exceptional circumstances which would make the evidence especially probative, in deciding whether excessive force has been used to take into account whether the defendant is suffering from some psychiatric condition.

. . .

[Lord Woolf also rejected an argument that the psychiatric evidence could have been relevant to the jury in assessing the reliability of Martin's evidence.]

74. For these reasons the fresh medical evidence has no bearing on the jury's rejection of Mr Martin's contention that he was entitled to be acquitted on the grounds that he was acting in self-defence. The position as to the fresh evidence relating to diminished responsibility is different. Here the evidence is admissible and relevant. The jury did not have the opportunity of considering this issue. Although the issue was never raised at the trial this was because the evidence was not then available to Mr Martin. Mr Martin is entitled to rely on the evidence for the purposes of his appeal (*R v Weekes (Stephen)* [1999] 2 Cr App R 520). The conviction for murder must therefore be quashed.

Conviction for murder quashed. Conviction for manslaughter substituted.

The elements of private defence can be listed as follows:

(1) The victim must pose a threat.

(2) The threat must be unjustified.

(3) The use of force must be necessary.

(4) The degree of force must be reasonable.

(5) The defendant must be acting in order to defend himself or another or property.

These will be considered separately.

The victim must pose a threat

The victim must pose a risk to the defendant or someone else. Contrast these two examples:

(a) Brenda is in desperate need of a heart transplant. Her husband Cyril kills Edwin, a patient in the hospital where Brenda is staying, hoping that Edwin's heart can be transplanted to Brenda.

(b) Fred returns home to find Gavin, a burglar, about to shoot Fred's wife, Harriet. The only way to stop Gavin is to shoot him dead, which Fred does.

In these hypothetical cases both Cyril and Fred killed in order to save the lives of their wives. In both cases they believed that the only way to save their wives' lives was to do the killing. However, Fred, but not Cyril, can use private defence. This is because Gavin was posing a threat to Harriet, but Edwin was not posing a threat to Brenda.[13]

There is no doubt that the defence applies whether the threat is being posed to the defendant or to another person. But there is doubt whether it is possible to use the defence when protecting property. The answer, it seems, is that it is all a matter of what the jury consider reasonable. The jury in the *Martin* case must have taken the view that it was not reasonable for Mr Martin to kill in order to prevent people burgling his house.[14] It may, however, be less controversial to suggest it is reasonable to injure someone to protect your home or a priceless work of art.[15]

The threat must be unjustified

Just because his or her attacker may not be committing an offence does not prevent a defendant relying on self-defence. A defendant can plead self-defence if she uses force against a child or sleepwalker who is attacking her, even though the child or sleepwalker was not committing a crime.[16] However, the threat must be unjust. If Mark attacks Jim and Jim defends himself by using force on Mark, Mark cannot then use further force against Jim and argue that this was in 'self-defence against Jim's attack'. Here Jim's use of force was reasonable and justified; therefore Mark cannot use self-defence as a defence against it. In *Jones*[17] a crime committed in an attempt to stop the Iraq war could not be justified on the

---

[13] These were easy cases. In Part II we shall look at cases where it is far harder to tell whether or not the victim was posing a threat.

[14] Tony Martin may have been unlucky in this respect. There is evidence that juries and prosecuting authorities tend to be very sympathetic to defendants who kill protecting their homes: Lanham (1998). Surveys of public opinion suggest a majority of people feel that they should be able to use force to protect their homes (Robinson and Darley (1995: 60)). There is even some old authority which suggests that a person can kill to protect themselves from being illegally removed from their home: *Hussey* (1924) 18 Cr App R 160.

[15] Still less controversial is the suggestion that one can harm someone's property in order to protect one's own. In *Workman v Cowper* [1961] 2 QB 143 the defendant was entitled to kill a dog who was posing a risk to others.

[16] It is therefore inaccurate to suggest that there must be an unlawful attack.   [17] [2005] QB 259.

basis of private defence because the act of going to war in Iraq was not an offence under English law.

The use of force must be necessary

It must be shown that it was necessary to use force. This means that it must have been reasonable for the defendant to use force, rather than escape from the threat in some way. In other words if the defendant could have escaped from the threat peacefully but unreasonably failed to do so then he will not be able to use the defence.[18] This requirement can be easily misunderstood. We will now consider three points about this requirement:

(1) The defendant does not have a 'duty to retreat'.[19] So, if a jury decided it was reasonable *either* to try and retreat or to stay and ward off the attack, the defendant could still rely on the defence. The question is not would a reasonable person have retreated, but rather was it reasonable for the defendant to use force.[20] Clearly if the defendant tried unsuccessfully to escape from the threat and then used force to repel the attack the jury are particularly likely to find that the defendant was acting reasonably.[21]

(2) The law does permit the defendant to take 'a pre-emptive strike',[22] if to do so is reasonable.[23]

(3) It is not absolutely necessary to show that the attack is imminent or immediate.[24] If Kim is kidnapped by a violent terrorist gang she may use force to escape if she notices that all but one guard have fallen asleep even if she is not facing an imminent threat. This is because her use of force was reasonable in that it would probably be her only chance to escape. That said, in the vast majority of cases it will be reasonable to use force only in the face of an imminent attack.

These examples show that the necessity requirement can be summarized with a simple question: was it reasonable for the defendant to use force, rather than escape?

The use of force must be reasonable

The defendant can successfully use the defence only if the level of force was reasonable in the face of the threat as perceived by the defendant. It should be stressed that the question is whether a reasonable person would say that the level of force was reasonable,

---

[18] *Fagan* [1972] NI 80.   [19] *Bird* [1985] 1 WLR 816 (CA).   [20] *McInnes* [1971] 3 All ER 295 (CA).

[21] *Bird* [1985] 2 All ER 513 (CA).

[22] *Beckford* [1988] AC 130, 414 (PC). Lanham (2005) points out some of the inconsistencies between the law of self-defence and the law prohibiting the possession of offensive weapons.

[23] In *Attorney-General's Reference (No. 2 of 1983)* [1984] QB 456 (CA) the defendant prepared some petrol bombs during a time of widespread rioting. He was charged with making explosive substances contrary to the Explosive Substances Act 1883, s. 4. However, it was held that he had a lawful object in making the bombs (defending himself and his property) and therefore had not committed the offence (although the court indicated that the holding of the bombs was in fact illegal and potentially an offence under the Explosives Act 1875). It should be noted that the circumstances in that case (an area of London suffering night after night from rioting) were unusual. In less compelling circumstances arming oneself against a foreseen attack might not provide a defence: *Evans v Hughes* [1972] 1 WLR 1452 (DC).

[24] *Attorney-General for Northern Ireland's Reference (No. 1 of 1975)* [1977] AC 105 (HL).

not whether the defendant thought the level of force used by the defendant was reasonable.[25] Consider this example: Tony takes Ian's wallet. As Tony runs away Ian pulls out a gun and shoots him dead. Ian thinks it is reasonable for him to shoot a pickpocket dead in order to protect his property. If Ian is charged with Tony's murder and he seeks to rely on private defence, the question is: was it reasonable for Ian to shoot Tony dead in these circumstances, *not* did Ian think it was reasonable for him to shoot Tony dead in these circumstances.

When the jury have to decide whether the amount of force used was reasonable it would be wrong to think that it is only reasonable to use force that is less than the amount of force threatened. Many commentators take the view that it is reasonable to cause greater harm in self-defence than is threatened. For example, many (but by no means all) commentators think it may be reasonable for a woman to kill a person who is about to rape her.[26] However, where the amount of force inflicted in self-defence is far greater than the harm threatened the jury may conclude that it is at an unreasonable level. Causing a serious injury in order to protect your property is likely to be unreasonable.[27]

Sometimes it is suggested that the defendant must use a level of force which is proportionate to the threat. This is a useful concept, but the jury should remember that they are in the 'calm analytical atmosphere of the court room'[28] and that the defendant reacting to a sudden attack 'cannot weigh to a nicety the exact measure of his necessary defensive action'.[29] The courts seem therefore to prefer simply asking whether or not the use of force was reasonable, rather than considering whether the use of force was precisely proportionate.

The defendant must be acting in order to defend himself or another or property

A defendant who is acting, not in order to defend himself or another, but solely out of revenge or retaliation will not be able to rely on the defence.[30] This is part of what has become known as 'the *Dadson*[31] principle': the defendant cannot rely on the justifying circumstances of his or her actions of which he or she is not aware. The principle applies if Simone sees her enemy, Peter, and shoots him dead, but, unknown to Simone, Peter was about to attack her. Had Simone known she was about to be attacked she could have used self-defence. But as she did not know this she cannot rely on the defence. The requirement also meant that defendants in *Ayliffe v DPP*[32] who caused criminal damage while protesting against the Iraq war could not rely on private defence. Their actions were about protest not defending people or property.

---

[25] *Owino* [1995] Crim LR 743 (CA); *DPP v Armstrong-Braun* [1999] Crim LR 416; *Shaw* [2001] UKPC 26, [2001] 1 WLR 1519 (PC); *Martin* [2002] 2 WLR 1 (CA).

[26] Fletcher (1998: 138).

[27] The Criminal Law (Amendment) (Protection of Property) Bill 2005 would have allowed the use of force to protect property unless the amount of force was grossly disproportionate. However, the Bill was 'talked out' and will not become law.

[28] *Attorney-General for Northern Ireland's Reference (No. 1 of 1975)* [1977] AC 105, 138, per Lord Diplock.

[29] Lord Morris in *Palmer* [1971] AC 814, 832 (PC).

[30] *Bird* [1985] 1 WLR 816 (CA).

[31] *Dadson* (1850) 4 Cox CC 358; *Chapman* (1988) 89 Cr App R 190 (CA).   [32] [2005] 3 All E.R. 330.

1.4 WHAT ABOUT DEFENDANTS WHO THINK THEY ARE BEING ATTACKED BUT ARE NOT?

The position is that defendants are to be judged on the facts as he or she believed them to be. So if, for example, the defendant is approached by a person who is out for a jog and believes the jogger is in fact about to attack her and so pushes the jogger, she can rely on self-defence to an assault charge. The jury must ask whether, on the facts as perceived by the defendant, the level of force was reasonable.[33] This was established in *Gladstone Williams*,[34] and was confirmed by the Privy Council in *Beckford v R*.[35] Since then this has been accepted as part of the law.[36] In *Williams* the defendant saw what he thought was a mugging and intervened using force against the 'mugger'. In fact the 'mugger' was carrying out a 'citizen's arrest' on someone who was (or may have been) a criminal. The defendant was charged with assault occasioning actual bodily harm. It was held that he could raise the defence of private defence if he honestly believed that he was intervening to prevent a crime, even if in fact he was not. More importantly the court held that it was not necessary to show that the defendant had reasonable grounds for his belief. So even if the belief was an absurd one, as long as it was the genuine belief of the defendant he could rely on the defence. Of course the more absurd the belief the more reluctant the jury may be to believe that it was the genuine belief of the defendant. As we shall see in Part II this is a controversial approach for the law to take, not least because it appears to provide a defence to a racist defendant who attacked a black man he believed was about to attack him simply because of his race.

1.5 SELF-INDUCED PRIVATE DEFENCES?

If the defendant caused the attack in the first place then he may not be able to rely on the defence. For example, if the defendant provoked the attack deliberately with the hope of being able to argue that any violence was used in self-defence then he cannot rely on the defence.[37] This does not meant that the defence is unavailable simply because the defendant went to a place where he knew that he might be attacked and indeed was.[38] The defence will be denied only where the defendant deliberately sought out an attack.

1.6 EXCESSIVE USE OF FORCE

As the House of Lords in *Clegg*[39] has confirmed, there is no defence if the defendant is justified in using some force, but uses an excessive degree of violence. Their Lordships rejected an argument that if a defendant is charged with murder and has used excessive force in self-defence he should be convicted of manslaughter. The House of Lords held that the creation of such a defence would be a matter for Parliament.

---

[33] There are a few statutory provisions which set out different rules. For example, the offence of child abduction is committed unless the defendant believes that the defendant had *reasonable* grounds to believe he was entitled to detain a child. A defendant who honestly, if unreasonably, believed he was entitled to detain a child could not seek to use s. 3 of the Criminal Law Act 1967 as a defence: *R v Baker and Wilkins* [1997] Crim LR 497 (CA).

[34] (1984) 78 Cr App R 276 (CA).   [35] [1988] AC 130 (PC).

[36] e.g. *Owino* [1995] Crim LR 743 (CA).   [37] *Malnik v DPP* [1989] Crim LR 451.

[38] *Field* [1972] Crim LR 435 (CA).   [39] [1995] 1 AC 482 (HL).

1.7 HAS THE HUMAN RIGHTS ACT 1998 CHANGED THE LAW?

Andrew Ashworth has suggested that the law on private defence may be challenged under the Human Rights Act, at least in the case of murder. He points to Article 2 of the European Convention on Human Rights, which protects the right to life:

1. Everyone's right to life shall be protected by law. No one shall be deprived of his life intentionally save in the execution of a sentence of a court following his conviction of a crime for which this penalty is provided by law.

2. Deprivation of life shall not be regarded as inflicted in contravention of this Article when it results from the use of force which is no more that absolutely necessary:

    (a) in the defence of any person from unlawful violence;

    (b) in order to effect a lawful arrest[40] or to prevent the escape of a person lawfully detained;

    (c) in action lawfully taken for the purpose of quelling a riot or insurrection.

Article 2 makes it clear in paragraph 2(a) that the taking of life is permissible if it is in the defence of a person. However, the European Court has interpreted paragraph 2(a) to mean that it can be relied upon only where the force is absolutely necessary and strictly proportionate.[41] The Court has accepted that paragraph 2(a) can apply in a case where a person mistakenly believes someone is in need of defence, but only if that mistaken belief is based on good reasons.[42] However, in deciding what constitutes a good reason the Court will take into account the fact that a decision to use force may have had to be made in the heat of the moment.[43] This suggests two ways in which the law on self-defence in English and Welsh law falls short of that expected in the European Convention on Human Rights:

(1) the level of force that may be used: the killing must be absolutely necessary and strictly proportionate according to the European Court; but only reasonable under the English and Welsh law;

(2) whether the defence can be used if the defendant mistakenly believes he or another is being attacked: only if that mistake is based on a good reason according to the European Court; but as long as it is genuinely held under English and Welsh law.

In the following passage Fiona Leverick summarizes her argument that the law on self-defence will need to be reconsidered in the light of the Human Rights Act:

---

[40] As J.C. Smith (1994) points out, the suggestion that one can kill in order to arrest someone is bizarre. In 'the course of' rather than 'in order to' might have been better wording.

[41] *Andronicou and Constantinou v Cyprus* (1998) 25 EHRR 491 (ECtHR).

[42] *McCann v UK* (1996) 21 EHRR 97 (ECtHR) and *Andronicou and Constantinou v Cyprus* (1998) 25 EHRR 491 (ECtHR). In *McCann* the European Court of Human Rights explained that law enforcement operations must be organized so as to 'minimise to the greatest extent possible, recourse to lethal force'.

[43] *Andronicou and Constantinou v Cyprus* (1998) 25 EHRR 491 (ECtHR).

F. Leverick, 'Is English Self-defence Law Incompatible with Article 2 of the ECHR?'
[2002] *Criminal Law Review* 347 at 361

The purpose of this paper was to assess the claim that in allowing an honest unreasonable mistake to ground an acquittal on the basis of self-defence, English law is contrary to Article 2 of the ECHR. The reason for this claim is that, in allowing the unreasonably mistaken defendant to escape punishment in this way, English law fails to respect the right to life of the person who, through no fault of their own, is mistaken for an attacker. An examination of relevant case law leads to the conclusion that the substance of English law does indeed contravene Article 2. It had been suggested that because killing in self-defence is not an intentional killing, Article 2 does not apply. Regardless of the theoretical merits of this suggestion, it can be dismissed as it has consistently been held that self-defensive killing *does* fall to be assessed under Article 2. Further, an examination of relevant cases shows that the court has consistently required that a mistaken belief in the need to use self-defensive force be based on good reasons. It is also clear, from cases such as *A v. United Kingdom* and *X and Y v. Netherlands*, that a violation of the Convention can take place when there has been a failure on the part of the State to provide a criminal law sanction that protects its citizens from the violent acts of other individuals, regardless of whether these individuals were State officials or private citizens. This is not to say that the Convention would necessarily require English law to convict the unreasonably mistaken self-defender of murder. It may be that a conviction for a lesser offence, such as manslaughter, is sufficient. Consideration of the degree of punishment appropriate in such circumstances is outside the scope of this paper. The point is that English law as it stands at present contains no sanctions *whatsoever* for the defendant who deprives another of her life in the unreasonable belief that she was an attacker.

The argument against this view is that the criminal law is simply stating that a defendant who kills believing himself to be under attack does not deserve punishment. It is not in any sense authorizing or permitting the defendant to take the victim's life. It is not, therefore, showing a lack of respect for the victim's life, but rather attempting to assess the blameworthiness of the defendant. The criminal law does not criminalize all negligence killings. And after all we do not say that the defence of insanity fails to protect the right to life of those who are killed by the insane.[44]

Of course Article 2 is not relevant in cases of non-deadly force.[45] However, in non-fatal cases Articles 3 or 8 may be relevant because they require protection of citizens from torture or inhuman or degrading treatment, and interferences with their physical or moral integrity.[46]

FURTHER READING

Ashworth, A. (1975), 'Self-defence and the Right to Life', *Cambridge Law Journal* 34: 272.

Leverick, F. (2002a), 'Is English Self-defence Law Incompatible with Article 2 of the ECHR?', *Criminal Law Review* 347.

[44] Although one could reply that, while the law on self-defence might affect the way someone acted (and therefore offered great or less protection for the right to life), the law on insanity clearly cannot affect how a defendant acts.

[45] Ashworth (2003: 137).

[46] *X and Y v Netherlands* (1986) 8 EHRR 235. In that case the fact that procedural rules meant that a man could not be charged in connection with a sexual assault on a mentally ill 16-year-old meant that the state had failed adequately to protect her right to respect for her private life under Art. 8.

—— (2002b), 'The Use of Force in Public or Private Defence and Article 2: A Reply to Professor Sir John Smith', *Criminal Law Review* 963.

Smith, J.C. (1989), *Justification and Excuse in the Criminal Law* (London: Sweet & Maxwell), ch. 4.

—— (2002), 'The Use of Force in Public or Private Defence and Article 2', *Criminal Law Review* 958.

2 NECESSITY

2.1 THE MEANING OF NECESSITY

Unfortunately there has been some confusion over the terminology used in relation to the defence of necessity in criminal law.[47] The term has been used in at least three different senses:

(1) The majority of the academic materials have used the term necessity to refer to a defence that the defendant did 'the lesser of two evils': in other words that the defendant was in a situation which meant that whatever he did would result in harm being caused and the defendant chose the course of action which resulted in the least harm.

(2) Some cases have used the term 'necessity' to mean duress of circumstances.[48]

(3) Sometimes necessity is used to describe an overarching doctrine which explains self-defence, duress, and the 'lesser of two evils',[49] the overarching theme being that the defendant was placed in an emergency of some kind and what the defendant did was necessary to avoid a harm.

In this book necessity will be used in the first sense (the lesser of two evils).

It should be stated immediately that the courts have not accepted a general defence of necessity. The straightforward claim, 'I broke the law but there would have been even worse consequences had I obeyed the law', will not in itself lead to an acquittal.[50] However, there are plenty of examples where the defence of necessity *in effect* is recognized, even if it is not called necessity or recognized as a general defence.

2.2 CASES DENYING THE EXISTENCE OF A GENERAL DEFENCE OF NECESSITY

The courts have been consistent in denying a general defence of necessity. In *Southwark LBC v Williams*[51] the Court of Appeal held that homeless people seeking temporary refuge in empty accommodation had committed trespass. They could not rely on a defence that the trespass was a lesser wrong than their suffering. Lord Denning explained:

---

[47] Schopp (1998: ch. 6); Brudner (1987); S. Gardner (1991b).
[48] *Martin* (1989) Cr App R 343 (CA), but not all: see *Cichon v DPP* [1994] Crim LR 918.
[49] Walker LJ in *Re A (Children)(Conjoined Twins: Surgical Separation)* [2001] 2 WLR 480 (CA).
[50] *Quayle* [2005] EWCA Crim 1415.   [51] [1971] 1 Ch 734 (CA).

> if hunger were once allowed to be an excuse for stealing, it would open a door through which all kinds of lawlessness and disorder would pass. . . . If homelessness were once admitted as a defence to trespass, no one's house could be safe. Necessity would open a door which no man could shut.[52]

To similar effect, in *Kitson*[53] a drunk man who had fallen asleep in the back of car awoke to find the car moving down a hill, and he steered the car to safety, avoiding any injury. He was still convicted of a drink-driving offence. The fact that the man was acting in a way society would have wanted him to act was welcomed. He was still guilty of the offence.[54]

One of the most famous cases in English law is often used to stress that necessity is not a defence to murder: *Dudley and Stephens*.[55] There three men and a boy were shipwrecked in an open boat with no food or water. After several days the men killed the boy who was now very ill. They ate him and therefore managed to survive until they were rescued. In essence the three men claimed that had they not eaten the cabin boy all four of them would have died. Therefore the killing of the cabin boy was the lesser of two evils. Their defence failed and they were convicted of murder and sentenced to death, although their sentences were commuted to six months' imprisonment. The exact *ratio decidendi* of the case has been much debated, although in *Howe*[56] the House of Lords has regarded the case as one setting down the general rule that necessity is not a defence to murder. However, as we shall see in *Re A (Children)(Conjoined Twins: Surgical Separation)*,[57] the majority of the Court of Appeal gave the decision a narrower interpretation.

Despite the denial of a general defence of necessity in fact a limited defence of necessity is recognized at common law and in some statutes.

2.3 THE LIMITED DEFENCE OF NECESSITY AT COMMON LAW

Despite the denial of a general defence of necessity the courts have been willing to accept a defence of necessity in special defined circumstances:

(1) Where the defendant damages or steals another's property in the public interest (e.g. in order to create a fire break he pulls down someone's house).[58]

(2) Where the defendant damages the defendant's property or interferes with another's property in order to save his own person or property (e.g. where the defendant damages another's property to prevent the spread of fire onto his own land).[59]

(3) Where actions taken for the benefit of another person where that person is unable to consent. In *Re F (Mental Patient: Sterilisation)*[60] the doctrine was relied upon to authorize the sterilization of a mentally ill woman. The House of Lords found that the operation would be in her best interests and that she was unable to consent; necessity

---

[52] *Southwark LBC v Williams* [1971] 2 All ER 175, 179.   [53] (1955) 39 Cr App R 66 (CA).
[54] For a recent confirmation see *Pommell* [1995] 2 Cr App R 607 (CA) and *Shayler* [2001] 1 WLR 2206 (CA).
[55] (1884) 14 QBD 273.   [56] [1987] AC 417 (HL).
[57] [2001] 2 WLR 480 (CA). Huxtable (2002) discusses a second conjoined twins case.
[58] *Re F (Mental Patient: Sterilisation)* [1989] All ER 434, 564–5 (HL).
[59] Ibid.   [60] [1990] 2 AC 1 (HL).

could therefore be relied upon. Another example Lord Goff gave in that case was of a defendant who pushed a person out of the way of an oncoming vehicle. He was careful to limit this principle to cases where the 'victim could not consent' (e.g. was incompetent) or there was no time to obtain the victim's consent (e.g. the cases where a person was about to be run over).[61] Where the victim is competent and able to give consent and refuses to do so then it is unlawful to provide treatment to that patient, even if to do so would be in their best interests.[62]

(4) It is permissible for a police constable to direct people to break traffic regulations if that is necessary and reasonable to protect life or property.[63] Further, obeying such a direction does not infringe the law.

(5) A very limited category of necessity as a defence to murder was recognized in *Re A (Children) (Conjoined Twins: Surgical Separation)*.[64] Although their Lordships were willing to recognize the availability of necessity on the highly unusual facts of that particular case, it is difficult to discover a general principle. The case is excerpted below:

Re A (Children) (Conjoined Twins: Surgical Separation)
[2001] Fam 147 (CA)[65]

Jodie and Mary were conjoined twins, born joined at the lower abdomen. Jodie was described as a bright and alert baby. Mary however had a 'primitive brain', no effective heart or lung function, and was alive only because a common artery enabled Jodie to circulate the blood for both of them. Jodie was capable of living independently of Mary, but Mary could not exist apart from Jodie. Doctors at the hospital wished to perform an operation which would separate the twins. If performed, the operation would lead to the death of Mary, but it was hoped it would save the life of Jodie. The parents of the twins refused to consent to the operation. The hospital applied to the court for a declaration that the operation would be lawful. The judge concluded that the operation would be in the best interests of both twins because Mary's continued existence was harmful to Jodie. The case was taken to the Court of Appeal. (This case raises complex issues of medical and family law. The extracts here will focus on the criminal law aspects, but they are only part of the court's reasoning.)

Lord Justice Ward

[Having decided that if the doctors performed the operation and Mary were to die they would intentionally kill Mary, which would be murder, Ward LJ went on to consider whether there was any defence the doctors could rely on:]

---

[61] In *R v Bournewood Community and Mental Health NHS Trust* [1998] 3 All ER 289 (HL) it was held that the detention of a mentally ill patient, who was not detained within the Mental Health Act 1983, was justified by the defence of necessity.

[62] *St George's Healthcare NHS Trust v S* [1999] Fam 26 (CA).

[63] *Johnson v Phillips* [1975] 3 All ER 682. The case involved a police officer who directed a driver to reverse the wrong way down a one-way street to enable an ambulance to attend an incident.

[64] [2001] 2 WLR 480 (CA).   [65] [2001] 2 WLR 480.

7. Unlawfully

7.1 The search for settled principle

The search for settled principle is difficult where the law is as uncertain in this area as Brooke LJ's masterly analysis has shown it to be. Doing the best I can, I have come to these conclusions.

7.2 Necessity

Necessity in the *R v Dudley and Stephens'* sense arises where A kills B to save his own life. The threat to A's life is posed by the circumstances, rather than an act of threat by B on A in conventional self-defence terms.

7.3 Duress

Similar considerations apply to duress. There is, of course, a difference between them but as Lord Hailsham of St Marylebone LC said in *R v Howe* [1987] 1 AC 417 at 429:

'This, however, is, in my view a distinction without a relevant difference, since on this view duress is only that species of the genus of necessity which is caused by wrongful threat. I cannot see that there is any way in which a person of ordinary fortitude can be excused from one type of pressure on his will rather than the other.'

7.4 The policy of the law

The policy of the law is to prevent A being judge in his own cause of the value of his life over B's life or his loved one C's life, and then being executioner as well. The policy of the law was expressed in similar terms in Hale's *Pleas of the Crown* (1 Hale PC (1778) 51), and Blackstone's *Commentaries on the Laws of England* (4 Bl Com (1857 edn) 28). Blackstone wrote that a man under duress 'ought rather to die himself than escape by the murder of an innocent'. The sanctity of life and the inherent equality of all life prevails. . . .

   [Ward LJ also quoted from *Howe* to support this proposition]

7.5 A legal duty?

The first important feature is that the doctors cannot be denied a right of choice if they are under a duty to choose. They are under a duty to Mary not to operate because it will kill Mary, but they are under a duty to Jodie to operate because not to do so will kill her. . . .

7.6 The effect of a conflict of duty

. . .

   What are the doctors to do if the law imposes upon them a duty which they cannot perform without being in breach of Mary's right to life if at the same time the respecting of her right puts them in breach of the equally serious duty of respecting Jodie's right to life? A resort to a sanctity of life argument does not enable both rights to receive the equal protection the doctrine is supposed to provide each of them equally. In those circumstances it seems to me that the law must allow an escape through choosing the lesser of the two evils. The law cannot say, 'heads I win, tails you lose'. Faced as they are with an apparently irreconcilable conflict, the doctors should be in no different position from that in which the court itself was placed in the performance of its duty to give paramount consideration to the welfare of each child. The doctors must be given the same freedom of choice as the court has given itself and the doctors must make that choice along the same lines as the court has done, giving the sanctity of life principle its place in the balancing exercise that has to be undertaken. The respect the law must have for the right to life of each must go in the scales and weigh equally but other factors have to go in the scales as well. For the same reasons that led to my concluding that consent should be given to operate so the conclusion has to be that the carrying out of the operation will be justified as the lesser evil and no unlawful act would be committed.

I should emphasise that the doctors do not cease to owe Mary a duty of care, they must continue to furnish such treatment and nursing care as may be appropriate to ensure that she suffers the least pain and distress and retains the greatest dignity until her life comes to an end.

7.7 Offending the sanctity of life principle

The second reason why the right of choice should be given to the doctors is that the proposed operation would not in any event offend the sanctity of life principle. That principle may be expressed in different ways but they all amount to the same thing. Some might say that it demands that each life is to be protected from unjust attack. Some might say as the joint statement by the Anglican and Roman Catholic bishops did in the aftermath of the Bland judgment that because human life is a gift from God to be preserved and cherished, the deliberate taking of human life is prohibited except in self-defence or the legitimate defence of others. The Archbishop defines it in terms that human life is sacred, that is inviolable, so that one should never aim to cause an innocent person's death by act or omission. I have added the emphases. The reality here—harsh as it is to state it, and unnatural as it is that it should be happening—is that Mary is killing Jodie. That is the effect of the incontrovertible medical evidence and it is common ground in the case. Mary uses Jodie's heart and lungs to receive and use Jodie's oxygenated blood. This will cause Jodie's heart to fail and cause Jodie's death as surely as a slow drip of poison. How can it be just that Jodie should be required to tolerate that state of affairs? One does not need to label Mary with the American terminology which would paint her to be 'an unjust aggressor', which I feel is wholly inappropriate language for the sad and helpless position in which Mary finds herself. I have no difficulty in agreeing that this unique happening cannot be said to be unlawful. But it does not have to be unlawful. The six-year-old boy indiscriminately shooting all and sundry in the school playground is not acting unlawfully for he is too young for his acts to be so classified. But is he 'innocent' within the moral meaning of that word as used by the Archbishop? I am not qualified to answer that moral question because, despite an assertion—or was it an aspersion—by a member of the Bar in a letter to The Times that we, the judges, are proclaiming some moral superiority in this case, I for my part would defer any opinion as to a child's innocence to the Archbishop for that is his territory. If I had to hazard a guess, I would venture the tentative view that the child is not morally innocent. What I am, however, competent to say is that in law killing that six-year-old boy in self-defence of others would be fully justified and the killing would not be unlawful. I can see no difference in essence between that resort to legitimate self-defence and the doctors coming to Jodie's defence and removing the threat of fatal harm to her presented by Mary's draining her life-blood. The availability of such a plea of quasi self-defence, modified to meet the quite exceptional circumstances nature has inflicted on the twins, makes intervention by the doctors lawful.

8. Conclusion

For these reasons, very shortly expressed, I conclude that the operation which I would permit can be lawfully carried out.

Lord Justice Brooke

Conclusion

I have considered very carefully the policy reasons for the decision in *R v Dudley and Stephens*, supported as it was by the House of Lords in *R v Howe*. These are, in short, that there were two insuperable objections to the proposition that necessity might be available as a defence for the Mignonette sailors. The first objection was evident in the court's questions: who is to be the judge of this sort of necessity? By what measure is the comparative value of lives to be measured? The second objection was that to permit such a defence would mark an absolute divorce of law from morality.

In my judgment, neither of these objections are dispositive of the present case. Mary is, sadly, self-designated for a very early death. Nobody can extend her life beyond a very short span. Because her heart, brain and lungs are for all practical purposes useless, nobody would have even tried to extend her life artificially if she had not, fortuitously, been deriving oxygenated blood from her sister's bloodstream.

It is true that there are those who believe most sincerely—and the Archbishop of Westminster is among them—that it would be an immoral act to save Jodie, if by saving Jodie one must end Mary's life before its brief allotted span is complete.

For those who share this philosophy, the law, recently approved by Parliament, which permits abortion at any time up to the time of birth if the conditions set out in s 1(1)(d) of the Abortion Act 1967 (as substituted) are satisfied, is equally repugnant. But there are also those who believe with equal sincerity that it would be immoral not to assist Jodie if there is a good prospect that she might live a happy and fulfilled life if this operation is performed. The court is not equipped to choose between these competing philosophies. All that a court can say is that it is not at all obvious that this is the sort of clear-cut case, marking an absolute divorce from law and morality, which was of such concern to Lord Coleridge and his fellow judges.

There are sound reasons for holding that the existence of an emergency in the normal sense of the word is not an essential prerequisite for the application of the doctrine of necessity. The principle is one of necessity, not emergency: see Lord Goff (in *Re F (mental patient: sterilisation)* [1990] 2 AC 1 at 75), the Law Commission in its recent report (Law Com No 218 (1993), paras 35.5 to 35.6), and Wilson J in *Perka v R* (1984) 13 DLR (4th) 1 at 33.

There are also sound reasons for holding that the threat which constitutes the harm to be avoided does not have to be equated with 'unjust aggression', as Professor Glanville Williams has made clear in s 26.3 of the 1983 edition of his book. None of the formulations of the doctrine of necessity which I have noted in this judgment make any such requirement: in this respect it is different from the doctrine of private defence.

If a sacrificial separation operation on conjoined twins were to be permitted in circumstances like these, there need be no room for the concern felt by Sir James Stephen that people would be too ready to avail themselves of exceptions to the law which they might suppose to apply to their cases (at the risk of other people's lives). Such an operation is, and is always likely to be, an exceptionally rare event, and because the medical literature shows that it is an operation to be avoided at all costs in the neonatal stage, there will be in practically every case the opportunity for the doctors to place the relevant facts before a court for approval (or otherwise) before the operation is attempted.

According to Sir James Stephen, there are three necessary requirements for the application of the doctrine of necessity: (i) the act is needed to avoid inevitable and irreparable evil; (ii) no more should be done than is reasonably necessary for the purpose to be achieved; and (iii) the evil inflicted must not be disproportionate to the evil avoided.

Given that the principles of modern family law point irresistibly to the conclusion that the interests of Jodie must be preferred to the conflicting interests of Mary, I consider that all three of these requirements are satisfied in this case.

Finally, the doctrine of the sanctity of life respects the integrity of the human body. The proposed operation would give these children's bodies the integrity which nature denied them.

For these reasons I, too, would dismiss this appeal.

Lord Justice Robert Walker

Of the many real and imagined examples put before the court it is worth mentioning two incidents which really did happen, although neither was the subject of a court decision. One is the awful dilemma which faced the commander of an Australian warship, in peacetime, when a very serious fire occurred in the engine room. He ordered the engine room to be sealed off and flooded with inert gas, in order to save the ship and the rest of the crew, although the order meant certain death for anyone who was still alive in the engine room. The other is the equally awful dilemma of a mountaineer, Simon Yates, who held his fellow-climber, Joe Simpson, after he had slipped and was dangling on a rope over a precipice at 19,000 feet in the Andes. Yates held Simpson for an hour, unable to recover him and becoming increasingly exhausted. Yates then cut the rope. Almost miraculously Simpson landed on a snowy ice bridge 100 feet below, and survived. When they met again Simpson said to Yates, 'You did right'. This incident is mentioned in Professor Smith's 1989 Hamlyn Lectures, *Justification and Excuse in the Criminal Law* (1989) (p 79).

The House of Lords has made clear that a doctrine of necessity does form part of the common law: see *Re F (mental patient: sterilisation)* [1990] 2 AC 1 (especially in the speech of Lord Goff ([1990] 2 AC 1 at 74–78) and *R v Bournewood Community and Mental Health NHS Trust, ex p L (Secretary of State for Health)* [1999] 1 AC 458. In the latter case Lord Goff said:

'The concept of necessity has its role to play in all branches of our law of obligations—in contract (see the cases on agency of necessity); in tort (see *Re F*); in restitution (see the sections on necessity in the standard books on the subject) and in our criminal law. It is therefore a concept of great importance. It is perhaps surprising, however, that the significant role it has to play in the law of torts has come to be recognized at so late a stage in the development of our law.' (See [1999] 1 AC 458 at 490.)

. . .

In truth there is no helpful analogy or parallel to the situation which the court has to consider in this case. It is unprecedented and paradoxical in that in law each twin has the right to life, but Mary's dependence on Jodie is severely detrimental to Jodie, and is expected to lead to the death of both twins within a few months. Each twin's right to life includes the right to physical integrity, that is the right to a whole body over which the individual will, on reaching an age of understanding, have autonomy and the right to self-determination: see the citations from Bland's case collected in *St George's Healthcare NHS Trust v S* [1999] Fam 26 at 43–45.

In the absence of Parliamentary intervention the law as to the defence of necessity is going to have to develop on a case by case basis, as Rose LJ said in *R v Abdul-Hussain*. I would extend it, if it needs to be extended, to cover this case. It is a case of doctors owing conflicting legal (and not merely social or moral) duties. It is a case where the test of proportionality is met, since it is a matter of life and death, and on the evidence Mary is bound to die soon in any event. It is not a case of evaluating the relative worth of two human lives, but of undertaking surgery without which neither life will have the bodily integrity (or wholeness) which is its due. It should not be regarded as a further step down a slippery slope because the case of conjoined twins presents an unique problem.

There is on the facts of this case some element of protecting Jodie against the unnatural invasion of her body through the physical burden imposed by her conjoined twin. That element must not be overstated. It would be absurd to suggest that Mary, a pitiful and innocent baby, is an unjust aggressor. Such language would be even less acceptable than dismissing Mary's death as a 'side-effect'. Nevertheless, the doctors' duty to protect and save Jodie's life if they can is of fundamental importance to the resolution of this appeal.

Declaration accordingly.

It will be noted that Brooke LJ quoted with approval three requirements for the defence of necessity:

(1) the act is needed to avoid inevitable and irreparable evil;

(2) no more should be done than is reasonably necessary for the purpose to be achieved; and

(3) the evil inflicted must not be disproportionate to the evil avoided.

The difficulty with these three requirements is that they would have provided a defence for the defendants in *Dudley and Stephenson*, although all the members of the Court of Appeal were in agreement that that decision was correct. It may therefore be safest to state that the present approach of the courts is that necessity was available on the facts of *Re A*, and may be in analogous cases, but the courts will develop the law on a case-by-case basis. Discussion of how courts might develop a more principled approach to necessity in these kinds of cases can be found in Part II of this chapter.

2.4 IMPLIED RECOGNITION OF NECESSITY

Although necessity is rarely recognized expressly, Peter Glazebrook has argued that there is 'concealed defence of necessity'. He argues that, even in cases where it is not openly recognized as a defence, the principle that a person should not be guilty of doing the lesser of two evils influences the courts' reasoning. Indeed there are very few cases where a defendant is convicted after doing an act which was the lesser of two evils.[66] In some cases where the defendant has done the lesser of two evils no prosecution is brought;[67] in others the magistrates or jury acquit even if technically an offence was committed. Peter Glazebrook had argued that there is a general principle of statutory interpretation:

. . . that it requires clear and unambiguous language before the courts will hold that a statutory provision was intended to apply to cases in which more harm will, in all probability, be caused by complying with it than by contravening it.[68]

---

[66] *Kitson* (1955) 39 Cr App R 66 (CA) and *Dudley v Stephens* (1884) 14 QBD 273 are arguably two such cases.

[67] See the 'Herald of Free Enterprise Case' discussed at p. 786.   [68] Glazebrook (1972: 93).

In fact this is probably part of the normal rule that a statute should be interpreted in such a way as to give effect to the purpose of the statute. An example may be *Bourne*[69] where the defendant (a surgeon) was charged under section 58 of the Offences Against the Person Act 1861 with unlawfully procuring a miscarriage. The surgeon had performed an abortion on a suicidal 14-year-old who had been the victim of rape. MacNaughten J held that because the doctor had performed the operation in order to save the girl's life he had not acted unlawfully. Without saying so explicitly MacNaughten J appears to have been reading the defence of necessity into the word 'unlawful' in the statute.[70]

2.5 DURESS OF CIRCUMSTANCES

In some cases where the defendant does the lesser of two evils he will be able to rely on the defence of necessity. As will be discussed below, duress of circumstances provides a defence where the defendant reasonably believes that the circumstances are such that unless he commits a crime he or another will suffer death or serious injury and that a reasonable person in the same situation would have committed the crime. This defence clearly overlaps to some extent with necessity. Being faced with the threat of death which the defendant avoids by driving through a red light would fall under the defence of duress of circumstances. It would also be said to be the lesser of two evils. However, duress of circumstances is in some sense narrower and in some sense wider than necessity. It is narrower in that duress of circumstances is not available in order to avoid a threat less than death or grievous bodily harm, although necessity (if recognized) may provide a defence if the crime committed involved less harm than that threatened. Duress of circumstances is wider than a necessity defence would be, in that it covers the situation where the defendant reasonably believed there to be a threat of death or serious injury even if there was in fact no such threat. A necessity defence would not cover such a situation.[71] Further, if the defendant was threatened with grievous bodily harm unless he or she caused grievous bodily harm, although the two kinds of harm may be the same and so he or she may not be able to rely on necessity, he or she may be able to rely on duress of circumstances and argue that a reasonable person would have given in to the threat.

FURTHER READING

Alldridge, P. (1989), 'Duress, Duress of Circumstances and Necessity', *New Law Journal* 139: 911.

Elliott, D. (1989), 'Necessity, Duress and Self-Defence', *Criminal Law Review* 611.

Gardner, S. (2005), 'Direct Action and the Defence of Necessity', *Criminal Law Review* 371.

Glazebrook, P. (1972), 'The Necessity Plea in English Criminal Law', *Cambridge Law Journal* 31: 87.

Ost, S. (2005), 'Euthanasia and the Defence of Necessity', *Criminal Law Review* 355.

---

[69] [1938] 3 All ER 615.
[70] See also *Cichon v DPP* [1994] Crim LR 918 and *Gillick v West Norfolk and Wisbech AHA* [1986] AC 112 (HL).
[71] Unless the necessity defence was modified to cover the case where the defendant reasonably believed that he was acting in doing the lesser of two evils.

3 CHASTISEMENT

In the past the common law defence of lawful chastisement permitted one person to hit another over whom they exercised power. This covered the chastisement of apprentices, children, or servants. Nowadays the defence has been restricted to the chastisement of children and is available only to parents and those who have parental responsibility for the child. Even in this category chastisement has been restricted. It is available only if the chastisement is reasonable. The law in this area is now dominated by the European Convention on Human Rights. In *A v UK*[72] before the European Court of Human Rights, a man had been acquitted of assaulting his step-son by hitting him with a garden cane. He successfully relied on his defence of lawful chastisement. The child claimed that the state had failed to protect his rights under Article 3 of the European Convention on Human Rights to be protected from torture and inhuman and degrading treatment. The European Court agreed. As a result, in interpreting whether the chastisement is reasonable the jury (or magistrates) should be instructed that if it amounts to torture or degrading or inhuman treatment they should convict the accused.[73] The government has undertaken a review of the present law on the corporal punishment of children.[74] As a result, section 58 of the Children Act 2004 provides:

(1) In relation to any offence specified under subsection (2), battery of a child cannot be justified on the ground that it constituted reasonable punishment.

(2) The offences referred to in subsection (1) are—

    (a) an offence under section 18 or 20 of the Offences Against the Person Act 1861 (wounding and causing grievous bodily harm)

    (b) an offence under section 47 of that Act (assault occasioning actual bodily harm);

    (c) an offence under section 1 of the Children and Young Person Act 1861.

In effect then reasonable chastisement will only provide an offence to an assault or battery. Any punishment involving greater force than this will be unlawful. Critics of the new law may complain that it fails to give sufficient guidance to parents because the line between a battery and actual bodily harm is so unclear. Others might complain that the law still allows parents to hit children in a way which would be a criminal offence if done to an adult.

FURTHER READING

Department of Health (2000), *Protecting Children, Supporting Parents: A Consultation Document on the Physical Punishment of Children* (London: Department of Health).

Newell, P. (2002), 'Global Progress on Giving Up the Habit of Hitting Children' in B. Franklin (ed.), *The New Handbook of Children's Rights* (London: Routledge).

Orentlicher, D. (1998), 'Spanking and Other Corporal Punishment of Children by Parents: Overvaluing Pain, Undervaluing Children', *Houston Law Review* 35: 1478.

Rogers, J. (2002), 'A Criminal Lawyer's Response to Chastisement', *Criminal Law Review* 98.

---

[72] (1998) 27 EHRR 611 (ECtHR).   [73] *R v H* [2002] 1 Cr App R 59 (CA).
[74] Department of Health (2000).

4 CONSENT

This defence was discussed in Chapter 6.

5 DURESS

DEFINITION

Duress is a defence to all crimes except murder, attempted murder, and certain forms of treason. To establish the defence a defendant must show that:

1. He or she committed the crime because of threats of death or grievous bodily harm.

2. A reasonable person would have acted as the defendant did.

5.1 TERMINOLOGY

There are two forms of duress that are recognized in the law: duress by threats and duress by circumstances. There is no difference in the legal requirements between them and the distinction is made to help clarify the law. Duress by threats occurs where one person commits a crime after another person has threatened to kill or injure someone if he does not commit a crime. For example, Alf is kidnapped by a terrorist and told he will be killed unless he sets fire to a building. If Alf does what he is told and is charged with arson he can plead the defence of duress by threats. Duress of circumstances arises where no one has specifically told the defendant to commit the crime but the circumstance are such that the defendant believes that unless he commits a crime he or others will suffer death or serious injury. For example, Brian while driving his car is approached by a man wielding a gun. He fears he is about to be shot and drives away in a dangerous manner. In such a case Brian may rely on the defence of duress of circumstances to a charge of dangerous driving. Sometimes it can be difficult to decide whether a case was one of duress by circumstance or duress by threats,[75] but as the rules governing the two defences are identical[76] it does not matter in practice which it is.

5.2 TO WHAT CRIMES IS DURESS A DEFENCE?

It has been established[77] that duress is available to all crimes, except murder, attempted murder, and certain forms of treason.[78] The leading case establishing that duress is not a defence to murder is *Howe*:

---

[75] See e.g. *Cole* [1994] Crim LR 582 (CA).

[76] *Willer* (1986) 83 Cr App R 224 (CA); *Conway* (1988) 88 Cr App R 159 (CA); *Martin* (1989) Cr App R 343 (CA).

[77] The burden of proof is on the prosecution to disprove the defence once the defendant has introduced evidence that he acted under duress: *Giaquinto* [2001] EWCA Crim 2696 (CA). The significance of this is that if, e.g., the jury thought that a reasonable person in the defendant's shoes might possibly have acted as the defendant did they should acquit because the defence has not been disproved.

[78] A detailed discussion on the availability of duress and treason is found in J.C. Smith (2002: 223–4).

R v Howe and others
[1987] AC 417 (HL)[79]

The House of Lords heard a number of conjoined appeals. Michael Howe and John Bannister appealed against their convictions for murder. They claimed that they joined in two brutal assaults on young men which culminated in their deaths only because they had been told by an older man with a substantial criminal record that if they did not they would suffer violence. They understood him to mean they would be killed. Cornelius Burke and William Clarkson were convicted of murdering a man known as Button. Burke admitted he shot Button but said he did so only after Clarkson had threatened him with violence and that in any event the gun went off unintentionally. In both cases the key question was whether duress was a defence to murder.

Lord Hailsham of St Marylebone LC

I begin by affirming that, while there can never be a direct correspondence between law and morality, an attempt to divorce the two entirely is and has always proved to be doomed to failure, and, in the present case, the overriding objects of the criminal law must be to protect innocent lives and to set a standard of conduct which ordinary men and women are expected to observe if they are to avoid criminal responsibility. [Lord Hailsham then cited and discussed *Dudley v Stephens* (1884) 14 QBD 273]

In general, I must say that I do not at all accept in relation to the defence of duress that it is either good morals, good policy or good law to suggest, as did the majority in *Lynch's* case and the minority in *Abbott v R*, that the ordinary man of reasonable fortitude is not to be supposed to be capable of heroism if he is asked to take an innocent life rather than sacrifice his own. Doubtless in actual practice many will succumb to temptation, as they did in *R v Dudley and Stephens*. But many will not, and I do not believe that as a 'concession to human frailty' (see Smith and Hogan *Criminal Law* (5th edn, 1983) p 215) the former should be exempt from liability to criminal sanctions if they do. I have known in my own lifetime of too many acts of heroism by ordinary human beings of no more than ordinary fortitude to regard a law as either 'just or humane' which withdraws the protection of the criminal law from the innocent victim and casts the cloak of its protection on the coward and the poltroon in the name of a 'concession to human frailty'.

I must not, however, underestimate the force of the arguments on the other side, advanced as they have been with such force and such persuasiveness by some of the most eminent legal minds, judicial and academic, in the country.

First, amongst these is, perhaps, the argument from logic and consistency. A long line of cases, it is said, carefully researched and closely analysed, establish duress as an available defence in a wide range of crimes, some at least, like wounding with intent to commit grievous bodily harm, carrying the heaviest penalties commensurate with their gravity. To cap this, it is pointed out that, at least in theory, a defendant accused of this crime under s 18 of the Offences against the Person Act 1861, but acquitted on the grounds of duress, will still be liable to a charge of murder if the victim dies within the traditional period of one year and a day. I am not, perhaps, persuaded of this last point as much as I should. It is not simply an anomaly based on the defence of duress. It is a product of the peculiar *mens rea* allowed on a charge of murder which is not confined to an intent to kill. More persuasive, perhaps, is the

---

[79] [1987] 1 All ER 771, (1987) 85 Cr App R 32, [1987] Crim LR 480.

point based on the availability of the defence of duress on a charge of attempted murder, where the actual intent to kill is an essential prerequisite. It may be that we must meet this casus omissus in your Lordships' House when we come to it. It may require reconsideration of the availability of the defence in that case too.

I would, however, prefer to meet the case of alleged inconsistency head on. Consistency and logic, though inherently desirable, are not always prime characteristics of a penal code based like the common law on custom and precedent. Law so based is not an exact science. All the same, I feel I am required to give some answer to the question posed. If duress is available as a defence to some of the most grave crimes why, it may legitimately be asked, stop at murder, whether as accessory or principal and whether in the second or the first degree? But surely I am entitled, as in the view of the Common Serjeant in the instant case of Clarkson and Burke, to believe that some degree of proportionality between the threat and the offence must, at least to some extent, be a prerequisite of the defence under existing law. Few would resist threats to the life of a loved one if the alternative were driving across the red lights or in excess of 70mph on the motorway. But, to use the Common Serjeant's analogy, it would take rather more than the threat of a slap on the wrist or even moderate pain or injury to discharge the evidential burden even in the case of a fairly serious assault. In such a case the 'concession to human frailty' is no more than to say that in such circum-stances a reasonable man of average courage is entitled to embrace as a matter of choice the alternative which a reasonable man could regard as the lesser of two evils. Other con-siderations necessarily arise where the choice is between the threat of death or *a fortiori* of serious injury and deliberately taking an innocent life. In such a case a reasonable man might reflect that one innocent human life is at least as valuable as his own or that of his loved one. In such a case a man cannot claim that he is choosing the lesser of two evils. Instead, he is embracing the cognate but morally disreputable principle that the end justifies the means.

I am not so shocked as some of the judicial opinions have been at the need, if this be the conclusion, to invoke the availability of administrative as distinct from purely judicial remedies for the hardships which might otherwise occur in the most agonising cases . . . [Lord Halisham went on to discuss *Dudley and Stephens*.]

Appeals dismissed.

This case then establishes that duress is not a defence to murder. By a majority of three to two the House of Lords in *Gotts*[80] decided that duress was not a defence to attempted murder. It is unclear whether the defence applies to incitement or conspiracy to murder.[81] The Law Commission have recommended that duress should be a partial defence to murder.[82]

5.3 WHAT ARE THE ELEMENTS OF THE DEFENCE OF DURESS?

The two key elements of duress are set out by Lane LCJ in *Graham*, in a statement which was approved by the House of Lords in *Howe*:

---

[80] [1992] 2 AC 412 (HL).

[81] The Court of Appeal in *Gotts* seemed to indicate duress was not available to these crimes as they were a further stage removed from the death than an attempt.

[82] Reducing the charge form 'first degree murder' to 'second degree murder' (Law Commission (2005: 5.85)

(1) Was [D], or may he have been, impelled to act as he did because, as a result of what he reasonably believed [E] had said or done, he had good cause to fear that if he did not so act [E] would kill him or . . . cause him serious physical injury?

(2) If so, have the prosecution made the jury sure that a sober person of reasonable firmness, sharing the characteristics of [D], would not have responded to whatever he reasonably believed [E] said or did by [committing the crime]?

We will now look at these requirements in further detail:

The defendant must act because of a threat of death or serious injury

This requirement contains a number of separate elements:

(1) *The defendant must act because of the threat or the circumstances.* The defendant must act because of the threats or circumstances and not for other reasons. It would be in only rather bizarre circumstances that the defendant would commit a crime following threats of death or serious harm, but not because of the threats. The issue is most relevant in cases where the defendant is facing a variety of threats, only some of which are of death or serious harm. In *Valderrama-Vega*[83] the defendant was facing three pressures when he committed his offence: he had been threatened with disclosure of his homosexual tendencies; he was under severe financial pressures; and there were threats of death or serious injury. Only the threats of death or serious injuries could form the basis of a defence of duress. The Court of Appeal held that he could still rely on the defence of duress as long as the threats of death or serious injury were for him a substantial reason for committing the crime. They did not have to be the only reason.

A case which raises a different aspect of this requirement is *DPP v Bell*,[84] where the defendant was in fear of his life and therefore drove off in a car, even though he had consumed excess alcohol. It was held that even if the defence had been available for his initial driving away he had to desist from the crime (the driving) once the threat was no longer potent. By continuing to drive having escaped from the danger area he was from then on not acting because of the threat and so could not rely on the defence of duress.

(2) *The threat must be one of death or grievous bodily harm.* Duress is available only if the threat was of death or serious harm.[85] A lesser kind of threat will not suffice.[86] So threats to property, reputation, or of minor injury[87] cannot form the basis of a duress defence, even where the defendant has committed a very minor crime.[88]

---

[83] [1985] Crim LR 220 (CA).   [84] [1992] RTR 335.

[85] *Graham* [1982] 1 All ER 801 (CA), approved by the House of Lord in *Howe* [1987] AC 417 (HL). In *Steane* [1947] KB 997 (CA) a threat of false imprisonment was held to be sufficient, but this has not been subsequently confirmed.

[86] A defendant who drove while intoxicated in order to acquire a pain killer for his daughter who was ill, but not seriously so, could not successfully rely on the defence of duress of circumstances: *DPP v Hicks* [2002] All ER (D) 285 (QBD). Although s. 5(2)(b) of the Criminal Damage Act 1971 provides a defence to a charge of criminal damage for lesser threats.

[87] In *R v A*, 12 May 2003 (CA) the Court of Appeal doubted whether a threat to punch in the face was sufficient to be a threat of serious harm.

[88] For criticism of the law in this regard see Herring (1999).

There is some doubt whether a threat to cause a serious psychological injury would be sufficient. The House of Lords in *Burstow* explained that the phrase grievous bodily harm in the Offences Against the Person Act 1861 included serious psychological illnesses. This might be used to argue that a threat to cause a serious psychological injury could form the basis for a duress defence. However, this argument was rejected in *Baker and Wilkins*,[89] where the Court of Appeal emphasized that only a threat of death or physical injury would suffice.

(3) *The threat can be of death or serious harm to anyone.* At one time it was thought that for duress to provide a defence the threat must be directed towards the defendant or his close family.[90] It is now clear that the defence can be available if the defendant fears that anyone for whom the defendant reasonably regards himself responsible.[91] This might include a close friend or a child he was looking after. Of course, the identity of the person who is in danger from the threat will be relevant when considering whether a reasonable person would give in to the threat.[92]

(4) *The threat must not come from the defendant himself.* This point was stressed in *Rodger and Rose*[93] where the defendants were charged with offences connected with escaping from prison. They sought to rely on the defence of duress. They argued that they had become so depressed because of the conditions in prison that they would have committed suicide had they not escaped. They were therefore facing a threat of death. The Court of Appeal held that duress was not available because the threat of death did not come from a source extraneous from the defendants.

(5) *The defendant can rely on what he reasonably believed to be a threat.* What if the defendant had thought that he was facing a threat, but in fact he was not? The direction in *Graham* makes it clear that the defendant must have reasonable grounds to believe that the threat had been made.[94] In *Cairns*[95] it was confirmed that if the defendant reasonably believed there was a threat of death or grievous bodily harm, the defence may be available, even if there is in fact no such threat.[96] Lord Bingham in *R v Z*[97] held that the defence of duress is only available if the defendant both genuinely and reasonably believes the threat to have been made.

QUESTION

It appears, then, that in cases of private defence if the defendant unreasonably believes that he is being attacked he can have a defence (*Williams*). But in cases of duress if the defendant unreasonably believes he is being threatened he cannot rely on the defence (*Graham*). Can you think of any reasons why this should be so?

---

[89] [1997] Crim LR 497 (CA).   [90] *Ortiz* (1986) 83 Cr App R 173 (CA).

[91] *R v Z* [2005] UKHL 22, para. 19; *Abdul-Hussain* [1999] Crim LR 570 (CA).

[92] A vague threat to the general public will not be sufficient: see *Shayler* [2001] EWCA Crim 1977, [2001] 1 WLR 2206 (CA). The case went to the House of Lords ([2002] UKHL 11, [2002] 2 All ER 477) which did not discuss the duress issues.

[93] [1998] 1 Cr App R 143 (CA).

[94] This was approved by Lord Bingham in *R v Z* [2005] UKHL 22, para. 23.

[95] [1999] 2 Cr App R 137 (CA).

[96] See also *Safi* [2003] Crim LR 721.

[97] [2005] UKHL 22, para. 23.

The reasonable person must have responded to the threat in the way the defendant did

In considering this issue there are various factors to be examined:

(1) *The jury must decide that the reasonable person must have responded to the threat as the defendant did.* The jury, in deciding how a reasonable person would respond to the threat, are likely to consider how severe the threat was and how grave the required crime. In other words the jury are likely to consider whether the defendant responded in a way which was proportionate to the threat.[98] However, the jury will appreciate the terror felt by a person facing a threat of death or serious injury. The defendant is not expected to behave in an especially heroic way, but simply in a reasonable way.

(2) *What characteristics of the defendant should be attributed to the reasonable person?* The leading case is *Bowen*:

R v Bowen
[1996] 4 All ER 837 (CA)[99]

Cecil Bowen was convicted of obtaining services by deception. He accepted the key facts alleged by the prosecution but claimed that he had acted as he did only because two men had accosted him in a pub and threatened that he and his family would be petrol-bombed if he did not assist in the plan. He was also told that his family would be attacked if he sought the assistance of the police. There was some evidence that he had an IQ of 68 (which would be in the lowest 2 per cent of the population) and unusually suggestible. The question was whether the jury should have been directed to consider the response to the threat of a reasonable person with an IQ of 68.

Lord Justice Stuart-Smith read the judgment of the court

The classic statement of the law is to be found in the judgment of the Court of Appeal in *Graham* (1982) 74 Cr App R 235. At p 240 Lord Lane CJ, giving the judgment of the Court [stated]:

'Whether the words "in his situation" comprehend more than the surrounding circumstances, and extend to the characteristics of the defendant himself, it is difficult to say, and for that reason we would not recommend without qualification the adoption of that solution. We think that there should be an objective element in the requirements of the defence so that in the final event it will be for the jury to determine whether the threat was one which the defendant in question could not reasonably have been expected to resist. This will allow the jury to take into account the nature of the offence committed, its relationship to the threats which the defendant believed to exist, the threats themselves and the circumstances in which they were made, and the personal characteristics of the defendant. The last consideration is, we feel, a most important one. Threats directed against the weak, immature or disabled person, may well be much more compelling than the same threats directed against a normal healthy person.

---

[98] Lord Hailsham in *Howe* [1987] AC 417, 432.   [99] [1997] 1 WLR 372, [1996] 2 Cr App R 157.

'As a matter of public policy, it seems to us essential to limit the defence of duress by means of an objective criterion formulated in terms of reasonableness. Consistency of approach in defences to criminal liability is obviously desirable. Provocation and duress are analogous. In provocation the words or actions of one person break the self-control of another. In duress the words or actions of one person break the will of another. The law requires a defendant to have the self-control reasonably to be expected of the ordinary citizen in his situation. It should likewise require him to have the steadfastness reasonably to be expected of the ordinary citizen in his situation. So too with self-defence, in which the law permits the use of no more force than is reasonable in the circumstances. And, in general, if a mistake is to excuse what would otherwise be criminal, the mistake must be a reasonable one.

'It follows that we accept Mr Sherrard's submission that the direction in this case was too favourable to the appellant. The Crown having conceded that the issue of duress was open to the appellant and was raised on the evidence, the correct approach on the facts of this case would have been as follows: (1) Was the defendant, or may he have been, impelled to act as he did because, as a result of what he reasonably believed King had said or done, he had good cause to fear that if he did not so act King would kill him or (if this is to be added) cause him serious physical injury? (2) If so, have the prosecution made the jury sure that a sober person of reasonable firmness, sharing the characteristics of the defendant, would not have responded to whatever he reasonably believed King said or did by taking part in the killing? The fact that a defendant's will to resist has been eroded by the voluntary consumption of drink or drugs or both is not relevant to this test.'

This formulation was approved by the House of Lords in *R v Howe* [1987] AC 417 (see per Lord Mackay of Clashfern at pp 65, 66 respectively).

But the question remains, what are the relevant characteristics of the accused to which the jury should have regard in considering the second objective test?

[Lord Justice Stuart-Smith reviewed the decisions in *Emery* (1993) 14 Cr App R(S) 394; *Hegarty* [1994] Crim LR 353; *Horne* [1994] Crim LR 584; *Hurst* [1995] 1 Cr App R 82; *Morhall* [1996] AC 90 and continued:]

What principles are to be derived from these authorities? We think they are as follows:

(1) The mere fact that the accused is more pliable, vulnerable, timid or susceptible to threats than a normal person are not characteristics with which it is legitimate to invest the reasonable/ordinary person for the purpose of considering the objective test.

(2) The defendant may be in a category of persons who the jury may think less able to resist pressure than people not within that category. Obvious examples are age, where a young person may well not be so robust as a mature one; possibly sex, though many woman would doubtless consider they had as much moral courage to resist pressure as men; pregnancy, where there is added fear for the unborn child; serious physical disability, which may inhibit self protection; recognized mental illness or psychiatric condition, such as post traumatic stress disorder leading to learned helplessness.

(3) Characteristics which may be relevant in considering provocation, because they relate to the nature of the provocation, itself will not necessarily be relevant in cases of duress. Thus homosexuality may be relevant to provocation if the provocative words or conduct are related to this characteristic; it cannot be relevant in duress, since there is no reason to think that homosexuals are less robust in resisting threats of the kind that are relevant in duress cases.

(4) Characteristics due to self-induced abuse, such as alcohol, drugs or glue-sniffing, cannot be relevant.

(5) Psychiatric evidence may be admissible to show that the accused is suffering from some mental illness, mental impairment or recognized psychiatric condition provided persons generally suffering from such condition may be more susceptible to pressure and threats and thus to assist the jury in deciding whether a reasonable person suffering from such a condition might have been impelled to act as the defendant did. It is not admissible simply to show that in the doctor's opinion an accused, who is not suffering from such illness or condition, is especially timid, suggestible or vulnerable to pressure and threats. Nor is medical opinion admissible to bolster or support the credibility of the accused.

(6) Where counsel wishes to submit that the accused has some characteristic which falls within (2) above, this must be made plain to the judge. The question may arise in relation to the admissibility of medical evidence of the nature set out in (5). If so, the judge will have to rule at that stage. There may, however, be no medical evidence, or, as in this case, medical evidence may have been introduced for some other purpose, e.g. to challenge the admissibility or weight of a confession. In such a case counsel must raise the question before speeches in the absence of the jury, so that the judge can rule whether the alleged characteristic is capable of being relevant. If he rules that it is, then he must leave it to the jury.

(7) In the absence of some direction from the judge as to what characteristics are capable of being regarded as relevant, we think that the direction approved in Graham without more will not be as helpful as it might be, since the jury may be tempted, especially if there is evidence, as there was in this case, relating to suggestibility and vulnerability, to think that these are relevant. In most cases it is probably only the age and sex of the accused that is capable of being relevant. If so, the judge should, as he did in this case, confine the characteristics in question to these.

How are these principles to be applied in this case? Miss Levitt [counsel for Bowen], accepts rightly in our opinion, that the evidence that the appellant was abnormally suggestible and a vulnerable individual is irrelevant. But she submits that the fact that he had, or may have had, a low IQ of 68 is relevant since it might inhibit his ability to seek the protection of the police. We do not agree. We do not see how low IQ, short of mental impairment or mental defectiveness, can be said to be a characteristic that makes those who have it less courageous and less able to withstand threats and pressure. Moreover, we do not think that any such submission as is now made, based solely on the appellant's low IQ, was ever advanced at the trial. Furthermore, it is to be noted that in two places . . . the judge told the jury that if they thought the appellant passed the subjective test they should acquit him. We are quite satisfied that in the circumstances of this case the judge's direction was sufficient. He directed the jury to consider the only two relevant characteristics, namely age and sex. It would not have assisted them, and might well have confused them, if he had added, without qualification, that the person of reasonable firmness was one who shared the characteristics of the appellant.

For these reasons, the appeal will be dismissed.

Appeal dismissed.

To clarify the implications of this judgment it is useful to distinguish two questions:

(a) which characteristics can be taken into account;

(b) for what purposes are characteristics relevant?

As to (a) *Bowen* provides a reasonably clear description of how a trial judge should decide whether a characteristic can be ascribed to the reasonable person. It must be shown:

(i) the characteristic provides a reason for failing to live up to the standards of the reasonable person. Hence low IQ was not relevant, but post-traumatic stress disorder may be.[100] There is no reason why those with low IQ should be less brave than those with higher IQ.[101] Contrast a person suffering with post-traumatic stress disorder who does have a good reason why they cannot be expected to be as brave as an ordinary person.

(ii) the characteristic must not be self-induced (e.g. intoxication).[102] One issue yet to be resolved is whether *Smith (Morgan)*[103] may be applied in relation to duress. Notably Lord Lane CJ in *Graham* (quoted with approval in *Bowen*) controversially suggested that the defences of provocation and duress were analogous. If *Smith (Morgan)* (a House of Lords case on provocation[104]) were held to apply by analogy to duress this would mean that the jury could take into account any characteristic that a jury believed to be relevant. Although the rejection of *Smith* in *Holley* makes that unlikely.

As to question (b), although the Court of Appeal judgment was ostensibly looking at characteristics which affect the level of firmness that can be expected the court in its list of potentially relevant characteristics included pregnancy and physical disability. But surely these characteristics do not affect the level of bravery that can be demonstrated? What this may indicate is that characteristics may be ascribed to the reasonable person in duress for three different reasons:

(i) to affect the level of firmness expected;

(ii) to affect the ability of the defendant to escape from the threat (e.g. physical disability);

(iii) to affect the gravity of the threat (e.g. pregnancy).

Although the Court of Appeal did not say so explicitly it appears that characteristics may be relevant in any of these three ways. In *Bowen*, the Court of Appeal, perhaps, did not give as much consideration as it might have to the question whether the defendant's low IQ led him to think the threat was more serious than it was or to fail to see a way of escaping from the threat.

(3) *The defendant must take any reasonable opportunity to escape from the threat.* The defendant must have taken any opportunity to escape from the threat that a reasonable person would have taken, for example by seeking police protection. In *Heath*[105] the defendant was threatened with violence unless he helped transport drugs in a few days' time. He was told that he could not rely on duress as a defence because

---

[100] The criticisms of this are discussed in Part II of this chapter. There is a fine line between timidity produced by suffering violence and suffering from post-traumatic stress disorder. However, for a mental characteristic to be relevant it must be a medically recognized illness: *Moseley*, 21 Apr. 1999 (CA).

[101] Though see *Antar* [2004] EWCA Crim 2708 where the defendant's very low IQ and learning difficulties were held to be admissible characteristics.

[102] *Flatt* [1996] Crim LR 576 (CA).   [103] [2000] 3 WLR 654 (HL).

[104] This case is discussed at p. 255.

[105] [2000] Crim LR 109 (CA). See also *Harmer* [2002] Crim LR 401 (CA).

he could have escaped from the threat by seeking assistance from the police or moving to relatives in Scotland.[106]

(4) *The threat must be of imminent harm.* In the following case, *Abdul-Hussain,*[107] the Court of Appeal stressed that the threat of death or serious injury had to be imminent. This did not mean that the harm had to be immediate, but it did have to be something due in the very near future:

R v Abdul-Hussain; Aboud; Hasan; Naji; Muhssin; Hosham
[1999] Crim LR 570 (CA)

The appellants were Shiite Muslims who had offended Sadam Hussein's Iraqi regime. They had escaped to Sudan, but had overstayed their visas and were threatened with being returned to Iraq. Members of their families in Iraq had been killed or tortured. They hijacked an aeroplane and eventually arrived in England. They were charged with and convicted of hijacking. One issue on appeal was whether duress was only available if the appellants were facing an imminent threat.

Lord Justice Rose

In the light of the submissions made to us, we derive the following propositions from the relevant authorities:

1. Unless and until Parliament provides otherwise, the defence of duress, whether by threats or from circumstances, is generally available in relation to all substantive crimes, except murder, attempted murder and some forms of treason (*R v Pommell* [1995] 2 Cr App Rep 607 at 615C). Accordingly, if raised by appropriate evidence, it is available in relation to hijacking aircraft; although, in such cases, the terror induced in innocent passengers will generally raise issues of proportionality for determination, initially as a matter of law by the judge and, in appropriate cases, by the jury.

2. The courts have developed the defence on a case-by-case basis, notably during the last 30 years. Its scope remains imprecise (*Howe,* 453G–454C; *Hurst* [1995] 1 Cr App R 82 at 93D).

3. Imminent peril of death or serious injury to the defendant, or those to whom he has responsibility, is an essential element of both types of duress (see *Southwark LBC v Williams* [1971] 1 Ch 734 per Lord Justice Edmund-Davies at 746A; *Loughnan,* by the majority at 448 and the dissentient at 460; and *Cole* at page 10).

4. The peril must operate on the mind of the defendant at the time when he commits the otherwise criminal act, so as to overbear his will, and this is essentially a question for the jury (*Hudson and Taylor* at 4; and *Lynch* at 675F. It is to be noted that in *Hudson and Taylor* Lord Parker CJ presided over the Court, whose reserved judgment was given by Widgery LJ (as he then was).)

---

[106] However, it seems that there are some cases in which the defendant may be able to persuade the jury that seeking police protection was not reasonable (e.g. if the gang is particular vicious: see *Hudson* [1971] 2 All ER 244 (CA), although doubt was cast on that case in *R v Z*, [2005] UKHL 22, at para. 27). The Court of Appeal in *Heath* [2000] Crim LR 109 (CA) was less sympathetic to an argument that because the defendant was a drugs user it was not reasonable for him to seek the assistance of the police.

[107] [1999] Crim LR 570 (CA).

5. But the execution of the threat need not be immediately in prospect (*Hudson and Taylor* at 425). If in *Cole* the Court had had the advantage of argument, as to the distinction between imminence, immediacy and spontaneity which has been addressed to us, it seems unlikely that the second half of the paragraph at page 10 of the judgment which we have cited would have been so expressed. If, and in so far as anything said in *Cole* is inconsistent with *Hudson and Taylor*, we prefer and are, in any event, bound by *Hudson and Taylor*, as, indeed, was the Court in *Cole*.

6. The period of time which elapses between the inception of the peril and the defendant's act, and between that act and execution of the threat, are relevant but not determinative factors for a judge and jury in deciding whether duress operates (*Hudson and Taylor; Pommell* at 616A).

7. All the circumstances of the peril, including the number, identity and status of those creating it, and the opportunities (if any) which exist to avoid it are relevant, initially for the judge, and, in appropriate cases, for the jury, when assessing whether the defendant's mind was affected as in 4 above. As Lord Morris of Borth-y-Gest said in Lynch at 675F in the passage previously cited, the issue in *Hudson and Taylor* was 'whether the threats were so real and were at the relevant time so operative and their effect so incapable of avoidance that, having regard to all the circumstances, the conduct of the girls could be excused.'

8. As to 6 and 7, if Anne Frank had stolen a car to escape from Amsterdam and been charged with theft, the tenets of English law would not, in our judgment, have denied her a defence of duress of circumstances, on the ground that she should have waited for the Gestapo's knock on the door.

9. We see no reason of principle or authority for distinguishing the two forms of duress in relation to the elements of the defence which we have identified. In particular, we do not read the Court's judgment in *Cole* as seeking to draw any such distinction.

10. The judgment of the Court, presided over by Lord Lane CJ and delivered by Simon Brown LJ, in *Martin*, at 345 to 346 (already cited) affords, as it seems to us, the clearest and most authoritative guide to the relevant principles and appropriate direction in relation to both forms of duress. Subject to questions of continuance (which did not arise and as to which, see *Pommell* at 615D), it clearly reflects Lord Lane's judgment in *R v Graham* (1982) 74 Cr App R 235 at 241, which was approved by the House of Lords in *Howe* in 458G. It applies a predominantly, but not entirely, objective test, and this Court has recently rejected an attempt to introduce a purely subjective element divorced from extraneous influence (see *Rodger and Rose*, 9 July 1997).

11. Clauses 25 and 26 of the Law Commission's draft Criminal Law Bill do not represent the present law. Accordingly, reference to those provisions is potentially misleading (see the forceful note by Professor Sir John Smith QC [1998] Crim LR 204, with which we agree).

Applying these principles to the present case, we are satisfied that the learned judge was lead into error as to the applicable law. We have considerable sympathy with him. No submissions were addressed to him as to the distinction between imminence, immediacy and spontaneity, and he sought to follow the judgment of this Court in *Cole*, where, likewise, no such submissions had been advanced.

In our judgment, although the judge was right to look for a close nexus between the threat and the criminal act, he interpreted the law too strictly in seeking a virtually spontaneous reaction. He should have asked himself, in accordance with *Martin*, whether there was evidence of such fear operating on the minds of the defendants at the time of the hijacking as to impel them to act as they did and whether, if so, there was evidence that the danger they feared objectively existed and that hijacking was a reasonable and proportionate response to it. Had he done so, it seems to us it that he must have concluded that there was evidence for the jury to consider.

We stress that the prosecution did not seek to rely on a want of proportionality or to contend that duress was not capable of applying after the plane had landed at Larnaca.

It follows that, in our judgment, in the light of how he was invited to approach the matter, the judge should have left the defence of duress for the jury to consider. . . .

We express no view as to proportionality or the continued availability of duress after Larnaca because, as we have said, these matters were not relied on before the judge and because, more significantly, there is no sufficient material before us as to the evidence on these matters. In any event, having concluded, for the reasons given, that the judge was wrong to withdraw the defence from the jury, the convictions of the appellants at the first trial must be regarded as unsafe. Their appeals are therefore allowed and their convictions quashed.

For the fourth time in 5 years this Court emphasises the urgent need for legislation to define duress with precision.

Appeal allowed.

(5) *The defendant must have good cause to believe that the threat could be carried out.* The *Graham* direction makes it clear that the defendant must have good cause to believe that the threat could be carried out. If therefore Nick said he was going to kill the Queen unless Mary committed a robbery the jury may require some convincing that Mary had good cause to believe that the threat would be carried out. Although, no doubt, in deciding whether or not Mary had good cause to believe the threat the jury would take into account the pressurized position in which she found herself.

(6) *The defendant must not have put himself in a position in which he could have been threatened in this way.* If defendants put themselves into a position where the threat could be made against them then the defence of duress is not available. So the defence is not available if the defendant associates with criminals in circumstances in which he knows or ought to know that he could become subject to compulsion to commit a crime. This was confirmed in the following decision of the House of Lords

R v Z (in some reports R v Hassan)
[2005] UKHL 22[108]

The defendant, Aytach Hasan, sought to rely on a defence of duress in response to a charge of burglary. It was alleged that he had entered the victim's house, claiming that the victim had telephoned for a prostitute. He produced a knife and took £4,000 from a safe. Hasan claimed that he had only done this in response to threats of violence from

[108] [2005] 4 All ER 685.

one Sullivan, for whom he worked and who had a reputation as a violent man. One issue considered by the House of Lords concerned the admissibility of various statements by the defendants. The issue of concern to substantive criminal law was the direction of judge that the defendant could not rely on threats by a man known as S because he had associated with him and therefore put himself in a position in which he knew that he was likely to be subjected to threats. The defendant was convicted and appealed.

Lord Bingham of Cornhill

18. Where duress is established, it does not ordinarily operate to negative any legal ingredient of the crime which the defendant has committed. Nor is it now regarded as justifying the conduct of the defendant, as has in the past been suggested. . . . Duress is now properly to be regarded as a defence which, if established, excuses what would otherwise be criminal conduct: *Director of Public Prosecutions for Northern Ireland v Lynch* [1975] AC 653, 671, 680, 710–711 and *R v Hibbert* (1995) 99 CCC (3d) 193, 204, 213–214 and 219, paras 21, 38 and 47, per Lamer CJC.

19. Duress affords a defence which, if raised and not disproved, exonerates the defendant altogether. It does not, like the defence of provocation to a charge of murder, serve merely to reduce the seriousness of the crime which the defendant has committed. And the victim of a crime committed under duress is not, like a person against whom a defendant uses force to defend himself, a person who has threatened the defendant or been perceived by the defendant as doing so. The victim of a crime committed under duress may be assumed to be morally innocent, having shown no hostility or aggression towards the defendant. The only criminal defences which have any close affinity with duress are necessity, where the force or compulsion is exerted not by human threats but by extraneous circumstances, and, perhaps, marital coercion under section 47 of the Criminal Justice Act 1925.

. . .

21. Having regard to these features of duress, I find it unsurprising that the law in this and other jurisdictions should have been developed so as to confine the defence of duress within narrowly defined limits. Most of these are not in issue in this appeal, but it seems to me important that the issues the House is asked to resolve should be approached with under-standing of how the defence has developed, and to that end I shall briefly identify the most important limitations.

(1) Duress does not afford a defence to charges of murder (*R v Howe* [1987] AC 417), attempted murder (*R v Gotts* [1992] 2 AC 412) and, perhaps, some forms of treason: Smith & Hogan, *Criminal Law*, 10th ed (2002), p 254. The Law Commission has in the past (eg in Criminal Law: Report on Defences of General Application (1977) (Law Com No 83; HC 556), paras 2.44–2.46) recommended that the defence should be available as a defence to all offences, including murder, and the logic of this argument is irresistible. But their recom-mendation has not been adopted, no doubt because it is felt that in the case of the gravest crimes no threat to the defendant, however extreme, should excuse commission of the crime. . . .

(2) To found a plea of duress the threat relied on must be to cause death or serious injury. . . .

(3) The threat must be directed against the defendant or his immediate family or someone close to him: Smith & Hogan, *Criminal Law*, 10th ed, p 258. In the light of recent Court of Appeal decisions such as *R v Conway* [1989] QB 290 and *R v Wright* [2000] Crim LR 510, the current (April 2003) specimen direction (no 49) of the Judicial Studies Board suggests that the threat must be directed, if not to the defendant or a member of his immediate family, to a

person for whose safety the defendant would reasonably regard himself as responsible. The correctness of such a direction was not, and on the facts could not be, in issue on this appeal, but it appears to me, if strictly applied, to be consistent with the rationale of the duress exception.

(4) The relevant tests pertaining to duress have been largely stated objectively, with reference to the reasonableness of the defendant's perceptions and conduct and not, as is usual in many other areas of the criminal law, with primary reference to his subjective perceptions. It is necessary to return to this aspect, but in passing one may note the general observation of Lord Morris of Borth-y-Gest in *Director of Public Prosecutions for Northern Ireland v Lynch* [1975] AC 653, 670:

'it is proper that any rational system of law should take fully into account the standards of honest and reasonable men. By those standards it is fair that actions and reactions may be tested.'

(5) The defence of duress is available only where the criminal conduct which it is sought to excuse has been directly caused by the threats which are relied upon.

(6) The defendant may excuse his criminal conduct on grounds of duress only if, placed as he was, there was no evasive action he could reasonably have been expected to take. It is necessary to return to this aspect also, but this is an important limitation of the duress defence and in recent years it has, as I shall suggest, been unduly weakened.

(7) The defendant may not rely on duress to which he has voluntarily laid himself open. The scope of this limitation raises the most significant issue on this part of this appeal, and I must return to it.

. . .

23. . . . It is evident that the judge, very properly, based himself on the Judicial Studies Board's specimen direction as promulgated in August 2000. That specimen direction included the words, adopted by the judge, 'he genuinely believed'. But the words used in *R v Graham (Paul)* and approved in *R v Howe* were 'he reasonably believed'. It is of course essential that the defendant should genuinely, ie actually, believe in the efficacy of the threat by which he claims to have been compelled. But there is no warrant for relaxing the requirement that the belief must be reasonable as well as genuine. There can of course be no complaint of this departure from authority, which was favourable to the defendant.

. . .

28. . . . It should . . . be made clear to juries that if the retribution threatened against the defendant or his family or a person for whom he reasonably feels responsible is not such as he reasonably expects to follow immediately or almost immediately on his failure to comply with the threat, there may be little if any room for doubt that he could have taken evasive action, whether by going to the police or in some other way, to avoid committing the crime with which he is charged.

29. . . . [T]he certified question on this part of the case . . . is: 'Whether the defence of duress is excluded when as a result of the accused's voluntary association with others: (i) he foresaw (or possibly should have foreseen) the risk of being subjected to any compulsion by threats of violence, or (ii) only when he foresaw (or should have foreseen) the risk of being subjected to compulsion to commit criminal offences, and, if the latter, (iii) only if the offences foreseen (or which should have been foreseen) were of the same type (or possibly of the same type and gravity) as that ultimately committed.' The Crown contend for answer (i) in its objective form. The defendant commends the third answer, omitting the first parenthesis.

. . .

37. The principal issue between the Crown on one side and the appellant and the Court of Appeal on the other is whether *R v Baker* correctly stated the law. To resolve that issue one must remind oneself of the considerations outlined in paras 18–22 above. The defendant is seeking to be wholly exonerated from the consequences of a crime deliberately committed. The prosecution must negative his defence of duress, if raised by the evidence, beyond reasonable doubt. The defendant is, ex hypothesi, a person who has voluntarily surrendered his will to the domination of another. Nothing should turn on foresight of the manner in which, in the event, the dominant party chooses to exploit the defendant's subservience. There need not be foresight of coercion to commit crimes, although it is not easy to envisage circumstances in which a party might be coerced to act lawfully. . . .

38. There remains the question, which the Court of Appeal left open . . ., whether the defendant's foresight must be judged by a subjective or an objective test: ie does the defendant lose the benefit of a defence based on duress only if he actually foresaw the risk of coercion or does he lose it if he ought reasonably to have foreseen the risk of coercion, whether he actually foresaw the risk or not? I do not think any decided case has addressed this question, and I am conscious that application of an objective reasonableness test to other ingredients of duress has attracted criticism: see, for example, D W Elliott, 'Necessity, Duress and Self-Defence' [1989] Crim LR 611, 614–615, and the commentary by Professor Ashworth on *R v Safi* [2003] Crim LR 721, 723. The practical importance of the distinction in this context may not be very great, since if a jury concluded that a person voluntarily associating with known criminals ought reasonably to have foreseen the risk of future coercion they would not, I think, be very likely to accept that he did not in fact do so. But since there is a choice to be made, policy in my view points towards an objective test of what the defendant, placed as he was and knowing what he did, ought reasonably to have foreseen. I am not persuaded otherwise by analogies based on self-defence or provocation for reasons I have already given. The policy of the law must be to discourage association with known criminals, and it should be slow to excuse the criminal conduct of those who do so. If a person voluntarily becomes or remains associated with others engaged in criminal activity in a situation where he knows or ought reasonably to know that he may be the subject of compulsion by them or their associates, he cannot rely on the defence of duress to excuse any act which he is thereafter compelled to do by them. It is not necessary in this case to decide whether or to what extent that principle applies if an undercover agent penetrates a criminal gang for bona fide law enforcement purposes and is compelled by the gang to commit criminal acts.

39. I would answer this certified question by saying that the defence of duress is excluded when as a result of the accused's voluntary association with others engaged in criminal activity he foresaw or ought reasonably to have foreseen the risk of being subjected to any compulsion by threats of violence.

. . .

Baroness Hale of Richmond

76. . . . The principle is that someone who voluntarily accepts the risk of being placed in the 'do it or else' dilemma should not be allowed to use that dilemma as an excuse (even if in some circumstances it might amount to mitigation). There are, however, two other questions.

77. The first is that the cases tend to talk about exposing oneself to the risk of 'unlawful violence'. That, it seems to me, is not enough. The foreseeable risk should be one of duress: that is, of threats of such severity, plausibility and immediacy that one might be compelled to

do that which one would otherwise have chosen not to do. The battered wife knows that she is exposing herself to a risk of unlawful violence if she stays, but she may have no reason to believe that her husband will eventually use her broken will to force her to commit crimes. For the same reason, I would say that it must be foreseeable that duress will be used to compel the person to commit crimes of some sort. I have no difficulty envisaging circumstances in which a person may be coerced to act lawfully. The battered wife knows very well that she may be compelled to cook the dinner, wash the dishes, iron the shirts and submit to sexual intercourse. That should not deprive her of the defence of duress if she is obliged by the same threats to herself or her children to commit perjury or shoplift for food.

78. But this brings me to a concern which I have had throughout this case. It is one thing to deny the defence to people who choose to become members of illegal organisations, join criminal gangs, or engage with others in drug-related criminality. It is another thing to deny it to someone who has a quite different reason for becoming associated with the duressor and then finds it difficult to escape. I do not believe that this limitation on the defence is aimed at battered wives at all, or at others in close personal or family relationships with their duressors and their associates, such as their mothers, brothers or children. The Law Commission's Bills all refer to a person who exposes himself to the risk 'without reasonable excuse'. The words were there to cater for the police infiltrator (see Law Com No 83, para 2.37) but they are also applicable to the sort of association I have in mind. The other elements of the defence, narrowly construed in accordance with existing authority, are more than adequate to keep it within bounds in such cases.

Lord Steyn, **Lord Rodger of Earlsferry**, and **Lord Brown of Eaton-under-Heywood** gave speeches agreeing with **Lord Bingham** on the duress issue.

(7) *Internal duress cannot be relied upon.* Defendants cannot rely on threats that come from within themselves. This point was made in the following decision.

R v Quayle
[2005] EWCA Crim 1415

Barry Quayle and two others were suffering various illnesses which caused them severe pain. They were arrested after it was found that they were growing cannabis for personal use. They were charged with possession of cannabis contrary to the Misuse of Drugs Act 1971. The defendants raised the defence of necessity. This was based on the argument that the use of cannabis was necessary to avoid serious injury and pain. Their defence was not left to the jury by the trial judge and an appeal was made to the Court of Appeal.

Mance LJ

56. The necessitous medical use on an individual basis which is at the root of the defences suggested by all the appellants and Mr Ditchfield is in conflict with the purpose and effect of the legislative scheme. First, no such use is permitted under the present legislation, even on doctor's prescription, except in the context of the ongoing trials for medical research purposes. Secondly, the defences involve the proposition that it is lawful for unqualified individuals to prescribe cannabis to themselves as patients or to assume the role

of unqualified doctors by obtaining it and prescribing and supplying it to other individual 'patients'. This is contrary not only to the legislative scheme, but also to any recommendation for its change made by the Select Committee and Runciman Reports. Further, it would involve obvious risks for the integrity and the prospects of any coherent enforcement of the legislative scheme. A parallel but lawful market in the importation, cultivation, prescription, supply, possession and use of cannabis would have to come into existence, which would not only be subject to no medical safeguards or constraints, but the scope and legitimacy of which would in all likelihood be extremely difficult to ascertain or control. Mr Fitzgerald cited to us Lord Scarman's ringing endorsement in *McLoughlin v. O'Brien* [1983] AC 410, 430B–D of the courts' role in developing, formulating and applying principle, ending with the words:

'By concentrating on principle the judges can keep the legal system clear of policy problems which neither they, nor the forensic process which it is their duty to operate, are equipped to resolve. If principle leads to results which are thought to be socially unacceptable, Parliament can legislate to draw a line or map out a new path.'

Accepting every word of that, we consider that in the present context it cuts in the opposite direction to that for which Mr Fitzgerald contends. Neither judges nor juries are well equipped to resolve issues as to when and how far the deliberate policy of clear legislation should give way in a particular case to countervailing individual hardship, or as to what the overall effect of such derogations would be on the whole legislative scheme.

. . .

72. *Extraneous circumstances*. Lord Bingham spoke in *Hasan* of the need for 'a just and well-founded fear', while accepting that threats of death or serious injury will suffice. He noted that the relevant requirements had been defined objectively, and went on (with the majority of the House) to apply the same approach when he decided that the defence was not available if the defendant ought reasonably to have foreseen the risk of coercion. It is by 'the standards of honest and reasonable men' therefore that the existence or otherwise of such a fear or such threats falls to be decided. We have observed that Lord Bingham did not address or comment on the case of *Safi*, in which this court held that what matters is not whether there was actually a threat of torture, but whether there was a reasonable perception of such a threat. But that still involves an objective test based on external events, conduct or words about which evidence would have to be produced or given. It is also notable that Lord Bingham described the criminal defence which he thought had a close affinity with duress by threats as 'necessity . . . by extraneous circumstances'.

73. There is therefore considerable authority pointing towards a need for extraneous circumstances capable of objective scrutiny by judge and jury and as such, it may be added, more likely to be capable of being checked and, where appropriate, met by other evidence. Lord Bingham's dictum fits in this regard with dicta in *Abdul-Hussain*, the decision in *Rodger & Rose* and Lord Woolf's dicta in *Shayler* speaking of a 'fundamental ingredient' of 'some external agency' as well as with the non-counsel decision in *Brown*.

74. The appellants' objection to any such distinction is that it means, for example, that the commission of an offence could be excused if it was to avoid the realisation of a danger of one's wife committing suicide (cf *Martin*), but not if in that case it had been the wife herself who, realising that she would commit suicide unless she drove her son to school, had driven while disqualified (cf *Rodger & Rose*). Likewise, they suggest, the distinction could deny a defence of necessity to a person at risk of serious injury or perhaps pain, but allow it potentially to a parent or carer responsible for the well-being of such a person; and in circumstances like those in *Rodger & Rose*, a compassionate warder with responsibility for the prisoner, could release the prisoner, if he was able to detect the risk of suicide in time; while

in cases such as the present, a person in or at risk of serious injury or pain could not himself engage in cultivation, possession or use of cannabis for medical purposes, but a parent or carer responsible for his upkeep could cultivate or obtain and administer cannabis to him or her for such purposes. The appellants suggest that none of these distinctions can stand scrutiny, so that *Rodger & Rose* must be regarded as a special case based on policy considerations.

75. We accept that it is right to remember the context of the decision in *Rodger & Rose*. Any court was, we think, bound to recognise the incongruous penal results and the risk of abuse that would result from recognising a defence of necessitous escape from prison based on danger that the prisoner escaping would commit suicide if he remained in custody. But, on that basis, the suggestion that a prison officer in a situation like that in *Rodger & Rose* might legitimately free a prisoner is we think likely to run into problems at a more basic level of legislative policy, which in our view the cases before us also present (see paragraphs 54–58 above). Nevertheless, although the court in *Rodger & Rose* adverted to considerations of policy when it said that the suggested defence was undesirable, it did so not to justify a particular exception in this context to the defence, but in support of a generally expressed common law exception, based on the undesirability of introducing 'an entirely subjective element divorced from any extraneous influence' into the defence. On the authorities (cf. paragraph 73 above), the requirement of an objectively ascertainable extraneous cause has a considerable, and in our view understandable, basis. It rests on the pragmatic consideration that the defence of necessity, which the Crown would carry the onus to disprove, must be confined within narrowly defined limits or it will become an opportunity for almost untriable and certainly peculiarly difficult issues, not to mention abusive defences. On that basis, we consider that the Crown's first narrow point, namely that, for the defence of necessity of circumstances to be potentially available, there must be extraneous circumstances capable of objective scrutiny by judge and jury, is valid.

76. *Pain.* It is, however, submitted on behalf of Messrs. Quayle . . . Wales and Kenny that any such test is satisfied in all their cases both because of the objectively ascertainable facts giving rise to the pain they suffer actually, or would suffer if they were not to use cannabis, whether from their afflictions or from taking alternative lawful medicaments, and because pain is capable of some degree of objective scrutiny and is not wholly subjective. In addressing this submission, we do not gain any real assistance from cases from other areas of the law, where distinctions may or may not have been drawn between injury and harm or pain.

77. The reason why we would not accept the submission is that the law has to draw a line at some point in the criteria which it accepts as sufficient to satisfy any defence of duress or necessity. Courts and juries have to work on evidence. If such defences were to be expanded in theory to cover every possible case in which it might be felt that it would be hard if the law treated the conduct in question as criminal, there would be likely to be arguments in considerable numbers of cases, where there was no clear objective basis by reference to which to test or determine such arguments. It is unlikely that this would lead overall to a more coherent result, or even necessarily to a more just disposition of any individual case. There is, on any view, a large element of subjectivity in the assessment of pain not directly associated with some current physical injury. The legal defences of duress by threats and necessity by circumstances should in our view be confined to cases where there is an imminent danger of physical injury. In reaching these conclusions, we recognise that hard cases can be postulated, but these, as Lord Bingham said, can and should commonly be capable of being dealt with in other ways. The nature of the sentences passed in the cases before us is consistent with this.

78. It is also submitted that the present cases involve not merely pain, but a risk of serious physical or psychological injury as a result of pain, or as a result of the alternative medicines which would have to be taken if cannabis was not. We have in the case of *Quayle* already given our reasons for rejecting on the facts Mr Fitzgerald's submission that there was any relevant risk of suicide in that case (paragraph 2(vi) above). In the case of *Wales*, the judge is criticised for failing to explain that serious pain could amount to serious injury because of its psychological consequences, but there does not appear to have been any evidence which could have justified such a case. Mr Wales did describe the pain he suffered as 'life-threatening' and the judge reminded the jury of this, although it does not appear to have been Mr Wales's case that there was an actual risk of suicide. His case on the facts was that cannabis helped him cope with the pain, without side effects, while the prescribed medicines had side-effects (stopping him eating) and, on the expert evidence that he called, also involved medical risks such as a general risk of peritonitis. We do not see in the evidence any basis on which a jury could be asked to conclude that Mr Wales faced any imminent risk of serious injury sufficient to justify him taking cannabis on a regular basis. Further, if there was such a case, it was left to the jury. Finally, in the case of *Kenny*, the evidence did not suggest any risk other than that of pain, and the criticism is that that risk should have been left to the jury.

79. *Imminence and immediacy.* We consider that these requirements represent another reason why, even at the detailed level, it is difficult to accept that there could be any success-ful defence of necessity in the cases of *Quayle Wales* and *Kenny*. Their defences amount to saying that it is open to defendants on a continuous basis to plan for and justify breaches of the law. However, we need not express a view whether that would have alone justified a judge in refusing to leave their defences to a jury. The requirements of imminence and immediacy mean, in any event, in our view that the judge was right to refuse to leave any defence of necessity to the jury in *Taylor* and *Lee*, and that the defence should not have been left to the jury in *Ditchfield*. In each of these three cases, the defendant was taking a deliberately considered course of conduct over a substantial period of time, involving con-tinuous or regular breaches of the law. In each case, the defendant was not the immediate sufferer and had every opportunity to reflect and to desist. The compassionate grounds which may well have motivated Mr Taylor and Ms Lee and which the jury evidently accepted did motivate Mr Ditchfield cannot avoid the fact that they deliberately chose to act contrary to the law on a continuous basis.

80. We note in passing that the court in *Southwark L.B.C. v. Williams* refused to recognise a defence of necessity raised by squatters in answer to a claim to recover possession of properties owned by the council. The evidence was that there were no homes for the squatters, they had been living in 'quite deplorable conditions' and the empty council properties in which they then squatted had been vandalised by the council to make them unfit for habitation, but that they had entered and lived there in an orderly way and repaired them after entry. Nevertheless, the court upheld summary possession orders, 'for the sake of law and order', as Lord Denning put it, and because the circumstances 'do not . . . consti-tute the sort of emergency to which the plea [of necessity] applies', as Edmund Davies LJ said. Megaw LJ agreed with both judgments on this aspect. The case is an old one, and the law has developed, so that we need not consider it further. But the underlying theme, that a continuous and deliberate course of otherwise unlawful self-help is unlikely to give rise to the defence has itself, in our view, continuing relevance.

81. The point made in paragraphs 79–80 may also be viewed in another way. Where there is no imminent or immediate threat or peril, but only a general assertion of an internal motivation to engage in prohibited activities in order to prevent or alleviate pain, it is also

difficult to identify any extraneous or objective factors by reference to which a jury could be expected to measure whether the motivation was such as to override the defendant's will or to force him to act as he did. If the response is that the defendant was not forced, but chose to act as he did, then the considerations mentioned in the previous paragraph apply.

Appeal dismissed.

FURTHER READING

Buchanan, A., and Virgo, G. (1999), 'Duress and Mental Abnormality', *Criminal Law Review* 517.

Horder, J. (1992), 'Autonomy, Provocation and Duress', *Criminal Law Review* 706.

Smith, K. (1999), 'Duress and Steadfastness: In Pursuit of the Unintelligible', *Criminal Law Review* 363.

6 COERCION

DEFINITION

The defence of coercion is available to any crime, apart from murder and treason. Only wives who commit crimes in the presence of their husbands can rely on the defence. The defendant must show that she committed the crime unwillingly as a result of pressure put on her by her husband.

This is a very limited defence which is analogous to duress. The defence is governed by section 47 of the Criminal Justice Act 1925:

Any presumption of law that an offence committed by a wife in the presence of her husband is committed under the coercion of the husband is hereby abolished, but on a charge against a wife for any offence other than treason or murder, it shall be a good defence to prove that the offence was committed in the presence of, and under the coercion of, the husband.

The defence is available to any crime other than treason or murder.[109] The two key elements of the defence are as follows:

(1) *Coercion is available as a defence to wives who commit crimes in the presence of their husbands.* It is not available to husbands;[110] nor women who are cohabiting outside marriage with the coercer; nor even to a woman who reasonably believes she has entered a valid marriage where in fact her marriage is void.[111] The wife must show that she carried out the crime in her husband's presence. The courts are yet to consider what exactly is meant by presence here. Would it include being in the same house, but not the same room, as the wife?

---

[109] Arguably this includes attempted murder by analogy with *Gotts* [1992] 2 AC 412 (HL) which held that duress is not a defence to attempted murder.

[110] Although a husband pressurized by his wife into committing a crime by a threat of death or serious injury could, of course, use the defence of duress.

[111] *Ditta* [1988] Crim LR 43 (CA).

(2) *The defendant must show her husband coerced her into committing the crime.* The defendant must prove on the balance of probabilities that the husband compelled her to commit the crime unwillingly. There is no need to show that there was a threat of violence. Any kind of threat, badgering, or use of pressure is sufficient.[112]

7 ENTRAPMENT

DEFINITION

It is not a defence for the defendant to show that he committed the offence only because he was trapped by the police into committing it.

If a plain-clothes police officer poses as a person keen to acquire drugs and approaches a suspected drug dealer and the drug dealer supplies drugs can the alleged dealer be convicted of a drugs offence?[113] You may think the answer is obviously 'yes'. But the defendant might not have supplied drugs unless requested to do so by the police officer. In *Sang*[114] the defendant claimed that he would not have committed the offence of dealing with counterfeit currency had he not suffered constant persuasion and insistence of an undercover police officer. The House of Lords rejected an argument that there was a defence of entrapment. However, their Lordships expressed their disapproval of using police officers as *agents provocateurs*.[115] Although entrapment does not provide a general defence, evidence obtained inappropriately can be excluded under the law on evidence,[116] or even lead to a reduction in sentence.[117] In *Looseley*[118] the House of Lords held that it was appropriate to halt a trial for abuse of process where undercover officers had approached a person whom they had no grounds for suspecting to be involved in drugs and given him cheap cigarettes, before asking him for drugs. However, their Lordships added that it would not be necessary to halt a trial for abuse of process where there were reasonable grounds to suspect that the defendant was a drug dealer and the officers had merely given the defendant an opportunity to commit the offence. The key test is 'whether the police conduct preceding the commission of the offence was no more than might be expected from others in the circumstance'.[119]

Cases of entrapment must now be considered in the light of the Human Rights Act 1998. The issue of entrapment was considered by the European Court of Human Rights in *Teixeira de Castro v Portugal*.[120] The defendant, who had no criminal record, was introduced to two police officers. They asked him to buy heroin for them, which he did. He was sentenced to six years' imprisonment. The European Court held that the defendant's right to a fair trial under Article 6 was infringed by the police action. The distinction was drawn between where the undercover police officers were approached by a defendant (which was not illegitimate) and where the undercover police approached a defendant and proposed the commission of an offence (which was illegitimate).[121] This distinction appears to reflect that made in *Looseley*.

---

[112] *Shortland* [1996] 1 Cr App R 116 (CA).
[113] For a thorough discussion of the issue see Ashworth (2002a).   [114] [1980] AC 402 (HL).
[115] Choo (1993) argues there should be a defence of entrapment.
[116] Section 78 of the Police and Criminal Evidence Act 1984 (see *Smurthwaite* [1998] Crim LR 751) and the common law: *Latif* [1996] 1 All ER 353 (HL).
[117] *Springer* [1999] 1 Cr App R (S) 217 (CA).   [118] [2001] 4 All ER 897 (HL).
[119] For further discussion see Ashworth (2002b).   [120] [1998] Crim LR 751 (ECtHR).
[121] See also *Lewis* [2005] Crim LR 797.

8 SUPERIOR ORDERS

Superior orders has never been recognized as a defence in English and Welsh law.[122] So a police officer or soldier who commits a crime has no defence by claiming 'I was only following orders.' Although it has never been directly in issue in an English or Welsh case there are *obiter* statements in the House of Lords and the Privy Council denying the existence of the defence in *Clegg*[123] and *Yip*.[124] Of course, the fact that the defendant was acting under superior orders could in extreme cases form the basis of a defence of duress or lack of *mens rea*.[125]

9 AUTOMATISM

DEFINITION

To plead automatism a defendant needs to show:

(i) he had suffered a complete loss of voluntary control;

(ii) this was caused by an external factor;

(iii) he was not at fault in losing capacity.

Automatism occurs when a defendant suffers a complete loss of self-control caused by an external factor.[126] A popular example is a defendant who is hit on the head by a rock and then loses all awareness of what he is doing and injures someone. Such a defendant will be able to rely on the defence of automatism.

Automatism involves more than a claim that the individual lacked *mens rea* (which he did). It is a claim that he is not acting:[127] it is a denial of the *actus reus*.[128] The significance of this is that automatism is a defence even to a crime of strict liability which has no *mens rea* requirement.

The three elements of automatism will be considered separately.

9.1 A COMPLETE LOSS OF VOLUNTARY CONTROL

The Court of Appeal in the following cases emphasizes that to rely on automatism there must be a *complete* loss of voluntary control:

Attorney-General's Reference (No. 2 of 1992)
[1994] QB 91 (CA)[129]

The respondent was the driver of a heavy goods lorry. He had been driving six out of the preceding twelve hours and covered 343 miles when he steered onto the hard shoulder

---

[122] Brownlee (1989).   [123] [1995] 1 All ER 334 (HL).
[124] [1994] 2 All ER 924, 928 (PC).   [125] See e.g. *James* (1837) 8 C & P 131, 173 ER 429.
[126] If the defendant brings credible evidence raising the possibility of automatism the prosecution must show that beyond reasonable doubt the accused was not acting as an automaton.
[127] Mackay (1995: ch. 1).
[128] *Hill v Baxter* [1958] 1 QB 277. See p. 122 for further discussion of this point.
[129] [1993] 4 All ER 683, [1993] 3 WLR 982, (1993) 97 Cr App R 429, [1994] Crim LR 692.

of a motorway. He crashed into a stationary white van. Two people were killed. The tyre marks indicated that the respondent's lorry had braked only at the very last minute. At his trial on a charge of causing death by reckless driving, the respondent produced evidence from a psychologist (Professor Brown) that he was suffering from a condition known as 'driving without awareness' caused by repetitive visual stimuli which created a trance-like state. The respondent claimed this amounted to automatism and that therefore he was not driving. He was acquitted by the jury, but the Attorney-General referred the case to the Court of Appeal.

Lord Taylor of Gosforth CJ

This is a reference pursuant to s 36 of the Criminal Justice Act 1972 whereby Her Majesty's Attorney General seeks the opinion of this court on a point of law following an acquittal on indictment. The point is defined in the reference as follows:

'Whether the state described as "driving without awareness" should, as a matter of law, be capable of founding a defence of automatism.'

This formulation relates to expert evidence given in the particular case. However, we take the point more generally to raise the question: 'What are the requirements and limits of the defence of automatism?'

. . .

[Lord Taylor referred to defence evidence of Professor Brown about the condition of driving without awareness and stated:]

Despite his phrase 'driving without awareness', Professor Brown agreed that the driver's body would still be controlling the vehicle, that there would be subconscious motivation to his steering and that, although 'largely unaware of what was happening ahead' and 'largely unaware of steering either', the unawareness was not total. Asked if nothing intrudes into the driver's consciousness when he is in this state, the professor said: 'I would not go so far as to say nothing, but very little.' There must, as a matter of common sense, be some awareness if, as Professor Brown accepted, the driver will usually be caused to 'snap out' of the condition by strong stimuli noticed by his eyes.

The contention on behalf of the Attorney General is that on the evidence given by Professor Brown, even taken at its highest, there was no basis for leaving the defence of automatism to the jury. Mr Jones QC [counsel for the Crown] submits that automatism as a defence in a driving case arises only where there is such total destruction of voluntary control that the defendant cannot be said to be driving at all. He cited *Hill v Baxter* [1958] 1 QB 277 at 283, in which Lord Goddard CJ said:

'I agree that there may be cases where the circumstances are such that the accused could not really be said to be driving at all. Suppose he had a stroke or an epileptic fit, both instances of what may properly be called Acts of God; he might well be in the driver's seat even with his hands on the wheel, but in such a state of unconsciousness that he could not be said to be driving.'

Pearson J gave as examples an epileptic fit, a coma, a blow on the head from a stone thrown up from the roadway and an attack by a swarm of bees so that the driver is—

'prevented from exercising any directional control over the vehicle and any movements of his arms and legs are solely caused by the action of the bees. In each of these cases it can be said that at the material time he is not driving and therefore not driving dangerously. Then suppose that the man in the driving seat falls asleep. After he has fallen asleep he is no longer driving, but there was an earlier time at which he was falling asleep and therefore failing to perform the driver's elementary and essential duty of keeping himself awake and therefore he was driving dangerously.' (See [1958] 1 QB 277 at 286.)

In *Bratty v A-G for Northern Ireland* [1963] AC 386 at 409 a defence of automatism due to an attack of psychomotor epilepsy was raised. Lord Denning said of the *actus reus*:

'No act is punishable if it is done involuntarily: and an involuntary act in this context—some people nowadays prefer to speak of it as "automatism"—means an act which is done by the muscles without any control by the mind such as a spasm, a reflex action or a convulsion; or an act done by a person who is not conscious of what he is doing such as an act done whilst suffering from concussion or whilst sleepwalking.'

The extent of the loss of control is crucial in the present case. Mr Jones referred to three other authorities in support of his proposition that automatism requires there to be total destruction of voluntary control and that impairment or reduction of voluntary control is insufficient.

[Lord Taylor then referred to *Watmore v Jenkins* [1962] 2 QB 572; *Roberts v Ramsbottom* [1980] 1 All ER 7; and *Broome v Perkins* [1987] RTR 321.]

. . .

We were referred to a number of decisions drawing a distinction between insane automatism and non-insane automatism: *R v Quick, R v Paddison* [1973] QB 910, *R v Sullivan* [1984] AC 156, *R v Hennessy* [1989] 2 All ER 9 and *R v Burgess* [1991] 2 QB 92. The effect of those decisions is that if the defence of automatism is said to arise from internal causes so as to bring the defendant within the M'Naghten Rules, then if it succeeds the verdict should be one of not guilty by reason of insanity (see *M'Naghten's Case* [1843–60] All ER Rep 229). An epileptic seizure (in *R v Sullivan*), a stress disorder, prone to recur and lacking the features of novelty or accident (in *R v Hennessy*) and sleepwalking (in *R v Burgess*) were all regarded as internal causes. If, however, automatism is said to arise from an external cause, for example a stone hitting the driver on the head, then a successful defendant is entitled to be acquitted.

Here, Mr Pert [counsel for the respondent] argues that the precipitating cause of the condition described by Professor Brown was the external factor of motorway conditions. However that may be, the proper approach is that prescribed by Lord Lane CJ in *R v Burgess* [1991] 2 QB 92 at 96 as follows:

'Where the defence of automatism is raised by a defendant two questions fall to be decided by the judge before the defence can be left to the jury. The first is whether a proper evidential foundation for the defence of automatism has been laid. The second is whether the evidence shows the case to be one of insane automatism, that is to say a case which falls within the M'Naghten Rules, or one of non-insane automatism.'

The first of those questions is the one raised by this reference. In our judgment, the 'proper evidential foundation' was not laid in this case by Professor Brown's evidence of 'driving without awareness'. As the authorities cited above show, the defence of automatism requires that there was a total destruction of voluntary control on the defendant's part. Impaired, reduced or partial control is not enough. Professor Brown accepted that someone 'driving without awareness' within his description, retains some control. He would be able to steer the vehicle and usually to react and return to full awareness when confronted by significant stimuli.

Accordingly, in our judgment the learned recorder ought not to have left the issue of automatism to the jury in this case and the answer to the point of law as formulated is No.

The requirement that there be a *complete* loss of self-control appears to be very harsh. It would deny a defence to a person who had only a vague awareness of what was happening to him. Some commentators have suggested that this strict approach should be limited to driving offences[130] or crimes of strict liability,[131] and that for other crimes it is not necessary to show that there was a complete lack of control.[132] However, there is nothing in the judgment of the Court of Appeal in *Attorney-General's Reference (No. 2 of 1992)* that explicitly restricts their discussion to driving offences.

9.2 AN EXTERNAL FACTOR

If a person acts while unaware of what he is doing such a person may either be an automaton or be insane.[133] The distinction between the two is whether the person's mental state was caused by an internal or external factor:

(1) If it is caused by an internal factor the person is classified as insane.

(2) If it is caused by an external factor the person has the complete defence of automatism.

It can be extremely difficult to tell whether a factor was an internal or external one. Examples of external factors are a blow to the head or the taking of prescribed medication. Internal factors include mental illnesses.[134] It used to be thought that sleepwalking was an external factor, but recently it was held by the Court of Appeal in *Burgess*[135] to be an example of insanity, because it is a mental condition (an internal factor) which predisposes a person to sleepwalking.[136] It is clear that the everyday tensions and pressure will not constitute external factors.

Contrasting the following two cases may well illustrate the difference between internal and external factors:

(1) The Canadian Supreme Court in *Rabey*[137] held that a defendant who suffered a disassociated state and killed his former girlfriend was not an automaton. He sought to plead automatism, arguing that his lack of awareness was caused by an external factor (his girlfriend telling him she was leaving him). The Supreme Court held that this was a case of insanity; the reasoning being that many people have boy- or girlfriends leaving them without it leading to complete lack of awareness, suggesting that it was the mental state of the defendant, rather than the girlfriend's actions which caused his mental state.

---

[130] Simester and Sullivan (2003: 101).   [131] Wilson (2003: 227).

[132] Indeed in *Stripp* (1978) 69 Cr App R 318 (CA) and *Broome v Perkins* (1987) 85 Cr App R 321 (CA) automatism was available, even though the defendants were described as 'semi-conscious'. See also *R v T* [1990] Crim LR 256.

[133] Some commentators use the terminology 'sane and insane automatism'.

[134] *Sullivan* [1983] 2 All ER 673 (HL).   [135] [1991] 2 QB 92 (CA).

[136] *Burgess* [1991] 2 QB 92 (CA). Contrast the approach of the Canadian courts to sleepwalking in *Parks* (1992) 95 DLR (4th) 27. Legal and medical issues surrounding sleepwalking are found in Ebrahim *et al.* (2005) and Wilson *et al.* (2005).

[137] (1980) 15 CR (3d) 225, a decision approved by the English Court of Appeal in *Burgess* [1991] 2 QB 92 (CA).

(2) In *R v T*[138] a woman had been raped and the rape was held to be an external factor. Rape could not be described as part of the 'ordinary stresses and disappointments of life'.[139]

9.3 THE DEFENDANT WAS NOT AT FAULT IN CAUSING THE CONDITION

The defendant cannot plead automatism if he is responsible for causing his condition. So, if the defendant's mental state is caused by taking alcohol or an illegal drug he cannot plead automatism.[140] There may be other ways in which the defendant is responsible for his condition and so will not be able to rely on the defence.[141] For example, if the defendant is a diabetic and is aware that if he does not eat adequate food he may enter a state of lack of awareness, but refrains from eating when symptoms first appear, he may be held responsible for his condition.[142] It seems, although there is no definitive case law on the question, that the test is subjective: was the defendant aware that his actions or inactions would cause his mental condition; rather than asking whether the defendant *ought* to have been aware that his actions or inactions would cause his mental condition?

EXAMINATION TIP

A popular scenario for problem questions involves a defendant who is both intoxicated and suffers automatism (e.g. a drunk defendant who falls down, bangs his head, and suffers concussion).

Stripp indicates that the key question is whether the defendant's state was caused predominantly by his intoxication or by his concussion. If it was the concussion then he would be able to plead automatism, if the voluntary intoxication he would not (see also *Burns* and *Lipman*).

10 INSANITY

It is crucial to distinguish between two[143] different claims in relation to insanity:

(1) A claim that a defendant was insane at the time he committed the offence.

(2) A claim that the defendant was insane at the time of the trial and so unable effectively to defend himself.

As we shall discuss in Part II there are many difficulties with the law's treatment of insanity.

---

[138] [1990] Crim LR 256.

[139] In *Hennessy* [1989] 2 All ER 9 (CA) it was held that stress, anxiety, and depression could not constitute external factors.

[140] *Lipman* [1970] QB 152 (CA).

[141] This has been particularly relevant in driving cases e.g. *Broome v Perkins* (1987) 85 Cr App R 321 (CA); *Isitt* (1978) 67 Cr App R 44 (CA); *Marison* [1996] Crim LR 909 (CA).

[142] *Quick* [1973] QB 910 (CA).

[143] The defendant's mental condition can be taken into account when deciding the appropriate sentence. This is an issue of sentencing law and will not be considered in this book.

10.1 INSANITY AT THE TIME OF THE ALLEGED OFFENCE

The definition of insanity

The issue of the defendant's insanity at the time of the crime can be raised in three ways:

(1) The defendant straightforwardly claims he was insane at the time of the offence.

(2) The defendant raises a defence of no *mens rea* or automatism, but the judge decides that the evidence discloses a defence of insanity. The judge may then instruct the jury to consider the issue of insanity.[144]

(3) If the defendant raises a plea of diminished responsibility then the prosecution is entitled to rebut the defence by producing evidence of insanity.[145]

DEFINITION

A defendant who wishes to plead that he was insane at the time of the offence must demonstrate that he was suffering from a defect of reason caused by a disease of the mind which meant that either:

(i) he did not know the nature or quality of his actions; or

(ii) he did not know that what he was doing was wrong.

If successful in his plea the defendant will be found 'not guilty, but insane'.

The following decision of the House of Lords is one of the leading (and most controversial) cases on the meaning of insanity. The key issue was whether the defendant was to be labelled insane or whether he could rely on the defence of automatism. As we have seen, automatism is available only where the cause of the mental condition is an external one. This led the House of Lords in this case to conclude that an epileptic defendant could not rely on automatism and therefore was labelled insane:

R v Sullivan
[1984] 1 AC 156 (HL)[146]

Patrick Sullivan was visiting an 80-year-old friend of his when he had an epileptic seizure, during which he kicked his friend in the head, inflicting grievous bodily harm. He admitted causing the injuries but sought to rely on the defence of automatism. The trial judge ruled that the facts revealed insanity, rather than automatism. In order to avoid being found not guilty by reason of insanity (and compulsory detention in a special hospital) Mr Sullivan pleaded guilty to an assault occasioning actual bodily harm. He was convicted and sentenced to probation under medical supervision. He appealed against the conviction on the basis that the judge's ruling was incorrect and he should have been able to plead the defence of automatism. The Court of Appeal dismissed his appeal and the case went to the House of Lords.

---

144 *Thomas* [1995] Crim LR 314 (CA).
145 Section 6 of the Criminal Procedure (Insanity) Act 1964. In such a case the burden of proving insanity will be on the prosecution: *Bastian* [1958] 1 WLR 413.
146 [1983] 2 All ER 673, [1983] 1 WLR 123, (1983) 77 Cr App R 176.

Lord Diplock

My Lords, the appellant, a man of blameless reputation, has the misfortune to have been a lifelong sufferer from epilepsy. There was a period when he was subject to major seizures known as grand mal but as a result of treatment which he was receiving as an out-patient of the Maudsley Hospital from 1976 onwards, these seizures had, by the use of drugs, been reduced by 1979 to seizures of less severity known as petit mal, or psychomotor epilepsy, though they continued to occur at a frequency of one or two per week.

. . .

Their expert evidence, which was not disputed by the prosecution, was that the appellant's acts in kicking Mr Payne had all the characteristics of epileptic automatism at the third or post-ictal stage of petit mal, and that, in view of his history of psychomotor epilepsy and the hospital records of his behaviour during previous seizures, the strong probability was that the appellant's acts of violence towards Mr Payne took place while he was going through that stage.

The evidence as to the pathology of a seizure due to psychomotor epilepsy can be sufficiently stated for the purposes of this appeal by saying that after the first stage, the prodram, which precedes the fit itself, there is a second stage, the ictus, lasting a few seconds, during which there are electrical discharges into the temporal lobes of the brain of the sufferer. The effect of these discharges cause him in the post-ictal stage to make movements which he is not conscious that he is making, including, and this was a characteristic of previous seizures which the appellant had suffered, automatic movements of resistance to anyone trying to come to his aid. These movements of resistance might, though in practice they very rarely would, involve violence.

. . .

My Lords, for centuries, up to 1843, the common law relating to the concept of mental disorders as negativing responsibility for crimes was in the course of evolution, but I do not think it necessary for your Lordships to embark on an examination of the pre-1843 position. In that year, following the acquittal of one Daniel M'Naghten for shooting Sir Robert Peel's secretary, in what today would probably be termed a state of paranoia, the question of insanity and criminal responsibility was the subject of debate in the legislative chamber of the House of Lords, the relevant statute then in force being the Criminal Lunatics Act 1800, an Act 'for the safe custody of Insane Persons charged with Offences', which referred to persons who were 'insane' at the time of the commission of the offence, but contained no definition of insanity. The House invited the judges of the courts of common law to answer five abstract questions on the subject of insanity as a defence to criminal charges. The answer to the second and third of these questions combined was given by Tindal CJ on behalf of all the judges, except Maule J, and constituted what became known as the *M'Naghten* Rules. The judge's answer is in the following well-known terms (see *M'Naghten's Case* [1843–60] All ER Rep 229 at 233):

'. . . the jurors ought to be told in all cases that every man is to be presumed to be sane, and to possess a sufficient degree of reason to be responsible for his crimes, until the contrary be proved to their satisfaction and that to establish a defence on the ground of insanity, it must be clearly proved that, at the time of the committing of the act, the party accused was labouring under a defect of reason, from disease of the mind, as not to know the nature and quality of the act he was doing or, if he did know it, that he did not know he was doing what was wrong.'

Although the questions put to the judges by the House of Lords referred to insane delusions of various kinds, the answer to the second and third questions (the *M'Naghten* Rules) is perfectly general in its terms. It is stated to be applicable 'in all cases' in which it is sought 'to establish a defence on the ground of insanity'. . . .

The *M'Naghten* Rules have been used as a comprehensive definition for this purpose by the courts for the last 140 years. Most importantly, they were so used by this House in *Bratty's case*. That case was in some respects the converse of the instant case. Bratty was charged with murdering a girl by strangulation. He claimed to have been unconscious of what he was doing at the time he strangled the girl and he sought to run as alternative defences non-insane automatism and insanity. The only evidential foundation that he laid for either of these pleas was medical evidence that he might have been suffering from psychomotor epilepsy which, if he were, would account for his having been unconscious of what he was doing. No other pathological explanation of his actions having been carried out in a state of automatism was supported by evidence. The trial judge first put the defence of insanity to the jury. The jury rejected it they declined to bring in the special verdict. Thereupon, the judge refused to put the alternative defence of automatism. His refusal was upheld by the Court of Criminal Appeal of Northern Ireland and subsequently by this House.

The question before this House was whether, the jury having rejected the plea of insanity, there was any evidence of non-insane automatism fit to be left to the jury. The *ratio decidendi* of its dismissal of the appeal was that the jury having negatived the explanation that Bratty might have been acting unconsciously in the course of an attack of psychomotor epilepsy, there was no evidential foundation for the suggestion that he was acting unconsciously from any other cause.

In the instant case, as in *Bratty's case*, the only evidential foundation that was laid for any finding by the jury that the appellant was acting unconsciously and involuntarily when he was kicking Mr Payne was that when he did so he was in the post-ictal stage of a seizure of psychomotor epilepsy. The evidential foundation in the case of Bratty, that he was suffering from psychomotor epilepsy at the time he did the act with which he was charged, was very weak and was rejected by the jury. The evidence in the appellant's case, that he was so suffering when he was kicking Mr Payne, was very strong and would almost inevitably be accepted by a properly directed jury. It would be the duty of the judge to direct the jury that if they did accept that evidence the law required them to bring in a special verdict and none other. The governing statutory provision is to be found in s 2 of the Trial of Lunatics Act 1883. This says 'the jury shall return a special verdict'.

My Lords, I can deal briefly with the various grounds on which it has been submitted that the instant case can be distinguished from what constituted the *ratio decidendi* in *Bratty's case*, and that it falls outside the ambit of the *M'Naghten* Rules.

First, it is submitted the medical evidence in the instant case shows that psychomotor epilepsy is not a disease of the mind, whereas in *Bratty's case* it was accepted by all the doctors that it was. The only evidential basis for this submission is that Dr Fenwick said that in medical terms to constitute a 'disease of the mind' or 'mental illness', which he appeared to regard as interchangeable descriptions, a disorder of brain functions (which undoubtedly occurs during a seizure in psychomotor epilepsy) must be prolonged for a period of time usually more than a day, while Dr Taylor would have it that the disorder must continue for a minimum of a month to qualify for the description 'a disease of the mind'.

The nomenclature adopted by the medical profession may change from time to time. Bratty was tried in 1961. But the meaning of the expression 'disease of the mind' as the cause of 'a defect of reason' remains unchanged for the purposes of the application of the *M'Naghten* Rules. I agree with what was said by Devlin J in *R v Kemp* [1957] 1 QB 399 at

407 that 'mind' in the *M'Naghten* Rules is used in the ordinary sense of the mental faculties of reason, memory and understanding. If the effect of a disease is to impair these faculties so severely as to have either of the consequences referred to in the latter part of the rules, it matters not whether the aetiology of the impairment is organic, as in epilepsy, or functional, or whether the impairment itself is permanent or is transient and intermittent, provided that it subsisted at the time of commission of the act. The purpose of the legislation relating to the defence of insanity, ever since its origin in 1880, has been to protect society against recurrence of the dangerous conduct. The duration of a temporary suspension of the mental faculties of reason, memory and understanding, particularly if, as in the appellant's case, it is recurrent, cannot on any rational ground be relevant to the application by the courts of the *M'Naghten* Rules, though it may be relevant to the course adopted by the Secretary of State, to whom the responsibility for how the defendant is to be dealt with passes after the return of the special verdict of not guilty by reason of insanity.

. . .

The only other submission in support of the appellant's appeal which I think it necessary to mention is that, because the expert evidence was to the effect that the appellant's acts in kicking Mr Payne were unconscious and thus 'involuntary' in the legal sense of that term, his state of mind was not one dealt with by the *M'Naghten* Rules at all, since it was not covered by the phrase 'as not to know the nature and quality of the act he was doing'. Quite apart from being contrary to all three speeches in this House in *Bratty's case*, the submission appears to me, with all respect to counsel, to be quite unarguable. Dr Fenwick himself accepted it as an accurate description of the appellant's mental state in the post-ictal stage of a seizure. The audience to whom the phrase in the *M'Naghten* Rules was addressed consisted of peers of the realm in the 1840s when a certain orotundity of diction had not yet fallen out of fashion. Addressed to an audience of jurors in the 1980s it might more aptly be expressed as: he did not know what he was doing.

My Lords, it is natural to feel reluctant to attach the label of insanity to a sufferer from psychomotor epilepsy of the kind to which the appellant was subject, even though the expression in the context of a special verdict of not guilty by reason of insanity is a technical one which includes a purely temporary and intermittent suspension of the mental faculties of reason, memory and understanding resulting from the occurrence of an epileptic fit. But the label is contained in the current statute, it has appeared in this statute's predecessors ever since 1800. It does not lie within the power of the courts to alter it. Only Parliament can do that. It has done so twice it could do so once again.

Sympathise though I do with the appellant, I see no other course open to your Lordships than to dismiss this appeal.

Appeal dismissed.

So, here the House of Lords confirmed that a defendant is presumed to be sane and approved the definition of insanity found in the *M'Naghten*[147] Rules, first set out in 1843. This definition can be broken down into three requirements:

(1) *Disease of the mind.* The phrase 'disease of the mind' is to be given its normal meaning;[148] it is not a medical term. What must be shown is that the defendant was suffering from a disease which affected the functioning of the mind. There is no need,

[147] (1843) 10 Cl & F 200.   [148] *Kemp* [1957] 1 QB 399, 406.

therefore, to show that it was a disease of the brain as such.[149] This means that diabetes, for example, can amount to a disease of the mind if it produces a malfunctioning of the brain. Lord Denning in *Bratty*[150] suggested that a disease of the mind was a mental disorder which manifested itself in violence and was prone to reoccur. However, these *dicta* have since been rejected[151] and it is clear that a 'disease of the mind' need not be prone to recur nor manifest itself in violence.

It should also be stressed that just because there was a malfunctioning of the mind it does not follow that this was a disease. If the defendant was hit on the head by a brick and suffers concussion there might be no disease and so the concussion could not amount to a disease of the mind.

(2) *Defect of reason.* It must be shown that the disease of the mind gave rise to a defect of reason: the defendant's power of reasoning must be impaired. It is not enough to show that the power of reasoning was available but not used. Someone who absent-mindedly was unaware what she was doing cannot rely on insanity.[152]

(3) *The defendant did not know the nature and quality of his act or that it was wrong.* It must be shown that as a result of the defect of reason caused by the disease of the mind either (i) the defendant did not know the nature or quality of his act or (ii) he did not know it was wrong:

(i) *Not knowing the nature and quality of the act.* This requires proof that the defendant did not know what he was doing. This would be so in the following situations:

(a) The defendant had no awareness of what was happening.[153] For example, the defendant was suffering from a seizure of some kind.

(b) The defendant was aware what he was doing, but was deluded as to the material circumstances of his actions, rendering the act fundamentally different. For example, a defendant who thought he was killing a monstrous creature when in fact he was killing a person.

(c) A person who was unaware of the consequences of his act, for example he was unaware that his act would kill the victim. Stephen gave the example of a person who cut off the head of someone who was asleep because 'it would be great fun to see him looking for it when he woke up'.[154]

(ii) *Not knowing that the act is wrong.* There is much uncertainty about the meaning of 'wrong' here. Wrong may mean that the act was morally wrong, or may mean that the act was illegal. The leading case is *Windle*,[155] which preferred illegality as the test, because what was or was not immoral was too uncertain. However, some commentators argue that *Windle* should not be regarded as a strong authority and that a subsequent court could depart from it.[156] Indeed recently in *DPP v Harper*[157] it was suggested that *Windle* applied only to murder cases and in all

---

[149] *Kemp* [1957] 1 QB 399.   [150] [1963] AC 386 (HL).   [151] *Sullivan* [1984] AC 156 (HL).
[152] In any event absent-mindedness is not a disease of the mind: *Clarke* [1972] 1 All ER 219. Of course, absent-minded people may well be able to plead that they have no *mens rea*.
[153] *Sullivan* [1983] 2 All ER 673 (HL).   [154] Stephen (1887: 166).   [155] [1952] 2 QB 826 (CA).
[156] The argument is that the discussion on this issue was *obiter* and that it ignored earlier authorities in favour of the 'immorality' view (e.g. *Codère* (1916) 12 Cr App R 21).
[157] [1998] RTR 200.

other cases wrong meant immoral, although no explanation was offered for the distinction.[158]

The Human Rights Act 1998 and the definition of insanity

Article 5 of the European Convention on Human Rights states:

> Everyone has the right to liberty and security of person. No one shall be deprived of his liberty save in the following cases and in accordance with the procedures prescribed by law; . . .
>
> (c) the lawful detention . . . of persons of unsound mind . . .

The European Court of Human Rights in *Winterwerp v Netherlands*[159] explained that:

'In the Court's opinion, except in emergency cases, the individual concerned should not be deprived of his liberty unless he has been reliably shown to be of 'unsound mind'. The very nature of what has to be established before the competent national authority—that is, a true mental disorder—calls for objective medical expertise. Further, the mental disorder must be of a kind or degree warranting compulsory confinement. What is more, the validity of the continued confinement depends upon the persistence of such a disorder.'[160]

In the light of this decision on Article 5 the present law on the detention of those found not guilty by reason of insanity could be challenged under the Human Rights Act. The following arguments could be made:

(1) As already noted, the legal definition of insanity is far wider than the medical concept of mental disorder. It is certainly arguable that the detention of an epileptic who has been found not guilty by reason of insanity infringes Article 5 because such a person is not 'of unsound mind'.

(2) The *Winterwerp* requirement that there be 'objective medical expertise' could be used to challenge the English law on the basis that the doctors under English law have to use the legal, not medical, understanding of mental disorder.[161]

(3) A defendant is presumed sane unless the contrary is proved. The burden of proving the defence falls on the defendant on the balance of probabilities.[162] This is a departure from the normal rules governing defences, where the prosecution must disprove any defence raised by the defendant. The placing of the burden of proof on the defendant may be challengeable as contrary to the presumption of innocence that is protected under Article 6(2) of the European Convention on Human Rights.[163]

---

[158] It should also be noted that research indicates that, in practice, trial judges direct the jury simply to consider whether the defendant was aware their acts were wrong. Presumably juries interpret this to mean morally wrong (Mackay (1990); Mackay and Kearns (1999)).

[159] 2 EHRR 387 (1979).   [160] At para. 39.

[161] It has only been since s. 1 of the Criminal Procedure (Insanity and Unfitness to Plead) Act 1991 that the jury, before finding insanity, must hear evidence from at least two registered medical practitioners. At least one of the doctors must be approved as having 'special experience in the diagnosis or treatment of mental disorder'. In part the statute was passed in order to comply with Art. 5 of the European Convention.

[162] *Bratty v A-G for Northern Ireland* [1963] AC 386 (HL).

[163] *Kebilene* [1999] 3 WLR 972 (HL) makes it clear that reverses of the burden of proof are challengeable under the 1998 Act.

Insanity and offences of strict liability

Recently in *DPP v Harper*[164] it was held that insanity was not a defence to a strict liability offence.[165] However, most commentators take the view that the decision is wrong. First, it made no reference to an earlier decision, *Hennessy*,[166] which had stated that insanity was a defence to a strict liability offence. Secondly, the reasoning used in *DPP v Harper* is suspect. It was claimed that insanity is a denial of *mens rea*;[167] however, if that was all insanity was there would be no need to have a special defence of insanity because any defendant who was legally insane would simply be able to claim they lacked the *mens rea* of the offence.

Insanity and intoxication

The leading case on insanity and intoxication is *Lipman*.[168] There the defendant took LSD and (he claimed) as a result had an hallucination in which he was attacked by a many-headed monster. He killed the monster. On recovering, he discovered that in fact he had killed his girlfriend. He was not permitted to plead insanity because it was his voluntary intoxication, rather than any disease of the mind, which had caused him to be unaware of the nature of his acts. If, however, a defendant can show that although intoxicated it was his disease of the mind that caused his lack of awareness then insanity may be available (*Burns*[169]).

10.2 A CLAIM THAT THE DEFENDANT WAS INSANE AT THE TIME OF THE TRIAL

When the accused is brought up for trial he may be found unfit to plead under sections 4 and 4A of the Criminal Procedure (Insanity) Act 1964.[170] The key issue is whether the accused is able to understand the charge and the difference between a plea of guilty and of not guilty. The accused must also be able to challenge jurors, to instruct counsel, and understand the evidence.[171] In summary the defendant's mental capabilities must be sufficient for him to be able to conduct his defence adequately.[172] Once it has been determined that the defendant is unfit to stand trial the judge has a wide discretion as to the appropriate course of action (except in the case of murder[173]). The 1991 Act includes disposals ranging from an absolute discharge to admission to hospital with a restraining order.

A controversial decision is *Podola*[174] which concerned a defendant who suffered from hysterical amnesia which prevented him from remembering events, but whose mind was otherwise completely normal. It was held that he was fit to plead. The case was difficult

---

[164] [1998] RTR 200, discussed in Ward (1997).

[165] Driving with excess alcohol in his blood: Road Traffic Act 1988, s. 5(1)(a).

[166] (1989) 89 Cr App R 10 (CA).

[167] The reasoning was that, as insanity was simply a denial of *mens rea*, that was no defence to an offence of strict liability, which requires no *mens rea*.

[168] [1970] 1 QB 152 (CA).   [169] (1984) 79 Cr App R 173 (CA).

[170] As amended by the Criminal Procedure (Insanity and Unfitness to Plead) Act 1991.

[171] *Robertson* [1968] 1 WLR 1767.   [172] Grubin (1993); Duff (1994).

[173] When the court must order detention in hospital (Criminal Procedure (Insanity) Act 1964, s. 5(3)).

[174] [1960] 1 QB 325 (CA).

because on the one hand the defendant was at a clear disadvantage in presenting his defence because he could not remember what happened. On the other hand he was fully mentally competent at the time of the trial. Indeed if Podola had been unfit to plead it would probably have meant that a defendant who was so drunk during the commission of the crime that he could not recall what happened would also be able to claim to be unfit to plead.

The issue of fitness to plead can be raised by the defence, the prosecution, or the judge.[175] Once the issue is raised it must be decided by the jury.[176] Before a defendant is found unfit the jury must receive written or oral evidence of two or more registered medical practitioners (at least one of whom is approved by the Home Secretary as having expertise in mental disorder).[177] The jury must consider whether or not the defendant did the 'act' alleged. The explanation for this requirement is that it would be unfair if a defendant who was unfit to stand trial was somehow presumed to have committed the offence alleged without there being some evidence that he did. Therefore if the jury are not convinced that there is sufficient evidence that he did the 'act' alleged the jury must simply acquit the defendant, like any other person found not to have committed the *actus reus*.

This has produced some difficult questions about what the 'act' means. The Court of Appeal has held that it means that the *actus reus* but not the *mens rea* of the offence must be proved.[178] But there are some difficult lines to be drawn. Some of the decisions to date on the meaning of act here found the following:

(1) When considering a charge of murder the jury did not have to find that the defendant intentionally killed the victim.[179]

(2) When considering whether the defendant did the act in question the jury should not examine whether the defendant might have been able to raise the defence of provocation.[180]

(3) In *Antoine* in the House of Lords it was confirmed that diminished responsibility could not be raised by a defendant following a finding that she was unfit to stand trial.[181]

Although a definitive ruling is awaited, it seems likely that a jury could consider whether or not the defendant was acting in self-defence, because (as we shall see) the courts have held that where successful a plea of self-defence negates the *actus reus* of the offence.

In the following case the House of Lords held that the procedure under the 1964 Act was compatible with the European Convention on Human Rights.

---

[175] *MacCarthy* [1967] 1 QB 68 (CA).   [176] Section 4(5) of the Criminal Procedure (Insanity) Act 1964.
[177] Section 4(6) of the Criminal Procedure (Insanity) Act 1964. There are two points in time at which the defendant's sanity can be raised: (1) it may be considered by a jury at the start of the trial; (2) once the prosecution has presented its case. This will be appropriate where it is unclear whether the prosecution has sufficient evidence to make out its case. The jury will be invited to consider whether the prosecution has established a case which the defence must answer. If not the defendant must be acquitted. If it has a jury will consider the defendant's fitness to plead.
[178] *Attorney-General's Reference (No. 3 of 1998)* [2000] QB 401 (CA).
[179] *Grant* [2002] 2 WLR 1409 (CA).
[180] The reasoning that persuaded the Court of Appeal is that in cases of provocation it is necessary to consider the effect of words and conduct on the mind of the defendant, but if the defendant is unfit to stand trial the jury cannot effectively do this because they will not be able to hear evidence from him.
[181] *R v Antoine* [2001] 1 AC 340 (HL).

R v H (Fitness to Plead)
[2003] HRLR 19 (HL)

The appellant was charged with two offences of indecent assault committed against a girl aged 14. A jury was convened to decide whether he was fit to stand trial. It was decided that he was unfit. At a further hearing a different trial found that the appellant had committed the acts alleged. He was absolutely discharged and registered as a sex offender. The appellant appealed against the finding of the second jury, arguing that the procedure was incompatible with Article 6 of the European Convention on Human Rights. The Court of Appeal dismissed the appeal.

Lord Bingham of Cornhill

1. . . . The certified question is:

'Is the procedure defined by s.4A of the Criminal Procedure (Insanity) Act 1964 compatible with an accused person's rights arising under Art.6(1), 6(2) and 6(3)(d) of the European Convention for the Protection of Human Rights and Fundamental Freedoms? In particular:

  (i) Does the procedure in so far as:

    (a) it provides for an acquittal of the accused person in the circumstances defined by s.4A(1) of the Act;

    (b) it provides for a finding that the accused 'did the act' which constitutes the actus reus of the crime; amount to the 'determination' of a criminal charge for the purposes of Art.6(1)?

  (ii) Does a finding that an accused person 'did the act' which constitutes the *actus reus* of the crime of indecent assault, being a crime of basic intent, violate the presumption of innocence afforded by Art.6(2)?'

The legislative history

2. . . . Over time, and in various statutes, certain rules came to be recognized and given effect:

  (1) Those found to have been insane when committing the offence charged against them should not be convicted and punished in the same way as a sane defendant.

  (2) Those found to be unfit to plead should not stand trial in the same way as a defendant who is fit to plead.

  (3) Trial procedures are necessary to determine whether an accused person was insane when committing the offence charged and (as the case may be) whether he is fit to stand trial.

  (4) These are issues appropriate (where the defendant is charged on indictment) to be determined by a jury, subject to the direction of a judge.

  (5) Even though a person may be found not to have been responsible for his conduct because insane or (as the case may be) may be found unfit to stand trial in the ordinary way, such person may nonetheless represent a continuing threat to members of the public such that, in the interest of public safety, the detention of such person may be justified.

The challenge which underlay all the relevant legislative provisions was on the one hand, to treat the accused person in a fair and humane way and on the other, to protect the public against the risk of danger posed by a person who could not (because of insanity) be held fully responsible for his conduct or could not (because of unfitness to plead) be tried in the ordinary way to decide whether he was guilty or not. . . .

14. It was not suggested by the appellant that the s.4A procedure was incompatible with the Convention even if it did not involve the determination of a criminal charge. His argument depended on making good his premise that the procedure did involve the determination of a criminal charge. Thus the crucial issue dividing the parties was whether the procedure did or did not involve the determination of a criminal charge. . . .

18. It would be highly anomalous if s.4A, introduced by amendment for the protection of those unable through mental unfitness to defend themselves at trial, were itself to be held incompatible with the Convention. It is very much in the interest of such persons that the basic facts relied on against them (shorn of issues concerning intent) should be formally and publicly investigated in open court with counsel appointed to represent the interests of the person accused so far as possible in the circumstances. The position of accused persons would certainly not be improved if s.4A were abrogated. In my opinion, however, the argument is plainly bad in law. Whether one views the matter through domestic or European spectacles, the answer is the same: the purpose and function of the s.4A procedure is not to decide whether the accused person has committed a criminal offence. The procedure can result in a final acquittal, but it cannot result in a conviction and it cannot result in punishment. Even an adverse finding may lead, as here, to an absolute discharge. But if an adverse finding leads to the making of a hospital order, there is no bar to a full criminal trial if the accused person recovers, an obviously objectionable outcome if the person has already been convicted. The s.4A procedure lacks the essential features of criminal process as identified in *Customs and Excise Commissioners v City of London Magistrates' Court* [2000] 1 W.L.R. 2020 at 2025.

19. . . . It is, indeed, difficult if not impossible to conceive of a criminal proceeding which cannot in any circumstances culminate in the imposition of any penalty, since it is the purpose of the criminal law to proscribe, and by punishing to deter, conduct regarded as sufficiently damaging to the interests of society to merit the imposition of penal sanctions.

20. . . . I would also endorse the observation of my noble and learned friend Lord Hutton *in R. v Antoine* [2001] 1 A.C. 340 at 375–376 where, recognising the search for balance which is inherent in the Convention, he said:

'The purpose of s.4A, in my opinion, is to strike a fair balance between the need to protect a defendant who has, in fact, done nothing wrong and is unfit to plead at his trial and the need to protect the public from a defendant who has committed an injurious act which would constitute a crime if done with the requisite *mens rea*. The need to protect the public is particularly important where the act done has been one which caused death or physical injury to another person and there is a risk that the defendant may carry out a similar act in the future. I consider that the section strikes this balance by distinguishing between a person who has not carried out the *actus reus* of the crime charged against him and a person who has carried out an act (or made an omission) which would constitute a crime if done (or made) with the requisite *mens rea*.'

. . . The procedure under s.4A must always, of course, be conducted with scrupulous regard for the interests of the accused person, but the procedure if properly conducted is fair and it was not suggested that the procedure was not properly conducted in this case.

21. I would answer the general opening question posed by the Court of Appeal by ruling that the s.4A procedure laid down by the 1964 Act as amended is compatible with the rights of an accused person under Art.6(1), (2) and (3) of the Convention. I would answer each of the particular questions (i) and (ii) in the negative.

FURTHER READING

Baker, E. (1994), 'Human Rights and M'Naughten, and the 1991 Act', *Criminal Law Review* 84.

Duff, A. (1994), 'Fitness to Plead and Fair Trials', *Criminal Law Review* 419.

Horder, J. (1993b), 'Pleading Involuntary Lack of Capacity', *Cambridge Law Journal* 52: 298.

Mackay, R. (1995), *Mental Condition Defences in the Criminal Law* (Oxford: OUP) is the leading work on English law on this topic.

—— and Kearns, G. (1999), 'More Fact(s) about the Insanity Defence', *Criminal Law Review* 714.

—— and —— (2000), 'An Upturn in Unfitness to Plead? Disability in Relation to the Trial under the 1991 Act', *Criminal Law Review* 532.

11 DIMINISHED RESPONSIBILITY

This is a defence only to a charge of murder. It is discussed at p. 265.

12 PROVOCATION

This is a defence only to a charge of murder. It is discussed at p. 250.

13 CHILDREN

Some children are exempt from criminal liability. It is necessary to distinguish between two age groups:

13.1 CHILDREN BELOW THE AGE OF 10

A child below the age of 10 cannot be convicted of a criminal offence.[182] This is an absolute rule. However deliberate or unpleasant the act committed by a child if he has not yet reached his tenth birthday he cannot be guilty. A child who commits a serious offence may be taken into care by the local authority, but this is a civil, not criminal, matter. One way of understanding the law's approach is to say that a child who commits a crime under the age of 10 needs the protection and support of social workers, rather than deserving the punishment and stigma of a criminal conviction.

---

[182] Children and Young Persons Act 1933, s. 50.

13.2 A CHILD AGED 10 TO 14

A child aged between 10 and 14 can be convicted of a crime.[183] Section 34 of the Crime and Disorder Act 1998 abolished the common law presumption that a child between 10 and 14 was *doli incapax*, meaning that a child was not capable of committing a crime because he or she did not know the difference between right and wrong.[184] Section 34 states:

> **Abolition of rebuttable presumption that a child is *doli incapax***
> The rebuttable presumption of criminal law that a child aged 10 or over is incapable of committing an offence is hereby abolished.

Unfortunately the effect of this provision is unclear. There are two possible interpretations:

(1) Children aged over 10 have no exemption or defence based on their age.

(2) Children aged between 10 and 14 are no longer *presumed* to be *doli incapax*, but they can introduce evidence that they are. If the court is persuaded that the defendant did not know the difference between right and wrong then the court can find her *doli incapax* and she cannot be convicted.[185]

View (1) is the more popular amongst commentators and it appears to have been the intention of Parliament, but we await definitive clarification from the courts.[186]

14 INTOXICATION

Technically intoxication is a not a defence, although it is often spoken of as such. We have discussed in Chapter 3[187] the effect of intoxication on the law's understanding of *mens rea*. Here we shall consider whether there should be a special defence for those who commit crimes with the necessary *mens rea*, after being involuntarily intoxicated. The leading case is *Kingston*:

R v Kingston
[1995] 2 AC 355 (HL)[188]

Barry Kingston was in dispute with two former business associates. They hired Kevin Penn to photograph Kingston in compromising situations with a boy so that they could blackmail him. Penn lured a 15-year-old boy to his flat, gave him a drink which allegedly contained sedative drugs and some cannabis. The boy fell asleep on a bed and remembered nothing until he woke the next morning. Penn then invited Kingston to his

---

[183] In *T v UK* [2000] Crim LR 187 (ECtHR) the European Court of Human Rights rejected an argument that punishing children aged 10 was contrary to Art. 3 of the European Convention.

[184] For a detailed discussion of the criminal liability of young people see Crofts (2003).

[185] Walker (1999). This seemed to be the view of the Solicitor General (HL Debs., vol. 16, col. 596, 1997).

[186] There are special procedures, courts, and sentencing practices in relation to young people which are not covered in this book.

[187] At p. 171.

[188] [1994] 3 All ER 353, [1994] 3 WLR 519, [1994] Crim LR 846, (1994) 99 Cr App R 286.

flat and gave him some coffee. Kingston claimed that unknown to him Penn had drugged the coffee. Penn then showed Kingston the naked boy on the bed and Kingston and Penn assaulted him. Penn photographed and taped the indecent assault. Kingston's defence was based on the fact that he had been involuntarily intoxicated. Although he admitted he had paedophilic tendencies, he claimed to have always been able to keep these under control. Kingston explained that the drugs Penn had put in his coffee had caused him to lose his inhibitions and commit the offence. The trial judge directed the jury that if they found the defendant had intentionally assaulted the boy he was guilty, even if that intent had been induced by the drugs administered by Penn. On appeal to the Court of Appeal his conviction was quashed on the basis that if drugs were surreptitiously administered to a person who was thereby caused to lose his inhibitions and form an intent which he would not otherwise have formed this was not a criminal intent. The issue was referred to the House of Lords.

Lord Mustill

The starting point is the verdict of guilty coupled with the judge's direction on the necessity for intent. This implies that the majority either (a) were sure that the respondent had not involuntarily taken a drug or drugs at all or (b) were sure that whatever drug he may have taken had not had such an effect on his mind that he did not intend to do what he did. We are therefore not concerned with what is picturesquely called automatism; nor was it suggested that the effect of the drug was to produce a condition of temporary insanity. What then was said to have been the induced mental condition on which the respondent relies? Inevitably, since the judge's ruling meant that whatever medical evidence there may have been was not developed we cannot be sure. Still, the general nature of the case is clear enough. In ordinary circumstances the respondent's paedophiliac tendencies would have been kept under control, even in the presence of the sleeping or unconscious boy on the bed. The ingestion of the drug (whatever it was) brought about a temporary change in the mentality or personality of the respondent which lowered his ability to resist temptation so far that his desires overrode his ability to control them. Thus we are concerned here with a case of disinhibition. The drug is not alleged to have created the desire to which the respondent gave way, but rather to have enabled it to be released. The situation is therefore different from that which led to the acquittal of the accused in the first of the Scottish cases to which I shall refer, where the drug directly brought about the violent conduct with which he was charged.

On these facts there are three grounds on which the respondent might be held free from criminal responsibility. First, that his immunity flows from general principles of the criminal law. Secondly, that this immunity is already established by a solid line of authority. Finally, that the court should, when faced with a new problem acknowledge the justice of the case and boldly create a new common law defence.

It is clear from the passage already quoted that the Court of Appeal adopted the first approach. The decision was explicitly founded on general principle. There can be no doubt what principle the court relied upon, for at the outset the court recorded the submission of counsel for the respondent that 'the law recognizes that, exceptionally, an accused person may be entitled to be acquitted if there is a possibility that, although his act was intentional, the intent itself arose out of circumstances for which he bears no blame' (see [1994] QB 81 at 87). The same proposition is implicit in the assumption by the court that if blame is absent the necessary *mens rea* must also be absent.

My Lords, with every respect I must suggest that no such principle exists or, until the present case, had ever in modern times been thought to exist. Each offence consists of a prohibited act or omission coupled with whatever state of mind is called for by the statute or rule of the common law which creates the offence. In those offences which are not absolute the state of mind which the prosecution must prove to have underlain the act or omission— the 'mental element'—will in the majority of cases be such as to attract disapproval. The mental element will then be the mark of what may properly be called a 'guilty mind'. The professional burglar is guilty in a moral as well as a legal sense; he intends to break into the house to steal, and most would confidently assert that this is wrong. But this will not always be so. In respect of some offences the mind of the defendant, and still less his moral judgment, may not be engaged at all. In others, although a mental activity must be the motive power for the prohibited act or omission the activity may be of such a kind or degree that society at large would not criticise the defendant's conduct severely or even criticise it at all. Such cases are not uncommon. Yet to assume that contemporary moral judgments affect the criminality of the act, as distinct from the punishment appropriate to the crime once proved, is to be misled by the expression '*mens rea*', the ambiguity of which has been the subject of complaint for more than a century. Certainly, the 'mens' of the defendant must usually be involved in the offence; but the epithet 'rea' refers to the criminality of the act in which the mind is engaged, not to its moral character. If support from the commentators for this proposition is necessary it may be found in Smith and Hogan *Criminal Law* (7th edn, 1992), pp 79–80, *Glanville Williams Textbook of Criminal Law* (2nd edn, 1983), p 221 and also p 75 and *Russell on Crime* (12th edn, 1964), vol 1, pp 80, 86.

. . . I would therefore reject that part of the respondent's argument which treats the absence of moral fault on the part of the appellant as sufficient in itself to negative the necessary mental element of the offence.

. . .

His second ground is more narrow, namely that involuntary intoxication is already recognized as a defence by authority which the House ought to follow.

[Lord Mustill referred to a variety of English and Commonwealth authorities, none of which he found persuasive support for the Court of Appeal's view.]

. . .

To recognize a new defence of this type would be a bold step. The common law defences of duress and necessity (if it exists) and the limited common law defence of provocation are all very old. Since counsel for the appellant was not disposed to emphasise this aspect of the appeal the subject was not explored in argument, but I suspect that the recognition of a new general defence at common law has not happened in modern times. Nevertheless, the criminal law must not stand still, and if it is both practical and just to take this step, and if judicial decision rather than legislation is the proper medium, then the courts should not be deterred simply by the novelty of it. So one must turn to consider just what defence is now to be created.

. . .

My Lords, since the existence or otherwise of the defence has been treated in argument at all stages as a matter of existing law the Court of Appeal had no occasion to consider the practical and theoretical implications of recognising this new defence at common law, and we do not have the benefit of its views. In their absence, I can only say that the defence appears to run into difficulties at every turn. In point of theory, it would be necessary to reconcile a defence of irresistible impulse derived from a combination of innate drives and external disinhibition with the rule that irresistible impulse of a solely internal origin (not necessarily any more the fault of the offender) does not in itself excuse although it may be a

symptom of a disease of the mind: see *A-G for the State of South Australia v Brown* [1960] AC 432. Equally, the state of mind which founds the defence superficially resembles a state of diminished responsibility, whereas the effect in law is quite different. It may well be that the resemblance is misleading, but these and similar problems must be solved before the bounds of a new defence can be set.

On the practical side there are serious problems. Before the jury could form an opinion on whether the drug might have turned the scale witnesses would have to give a picture of the defendant's personality and susceptibilities, for without it the crucial effect of the drug could not be assessed; pharmacologists would be required to describe the potentially disinhibiting effect of a range of drugs whose identity would, if the present case is anything to go by, be unknown; psychologists and psychiatrists would express opinions, not on the matters of psychopathology familiar to those working within the framework of the Mental Health Acts but on altogether more elusive concepts. No doubt as time passed those concerned could work out techniques to deal with these questions. Much more significant would be the opportunities for a spurious defence. Even in the field of road traffic the 'spiked' drink as a special reason for not disqualifying from driving is a regular feature. Transferring this to the entire range of criminal offences is a disturbing prospect. The defendant would only have to assert, and support by the evidence of well-wishers, that he was not the sort of person to have done this kind of thing, and to suggest an occasion when by some means a drug might have been administered to him for the jury be sent straight to the question of a possible disinhibition. The judge would direct the jurors that if they felt any legitimate doubt on the matter—and by its nature the defence would be one which the prosecution would often have no means to rebut—they must acquit outright, all questions of intent, mental capacity and the like being at this stage irrelevant.

My Lords, the fact that a new doctrine may require adjustment of existing principles to accommodate it, and may require those involved in criminal trials to learn new techniques, is not of course a ground for refusing to adopt it, if that is what the interests of justice require. Here, however, justice makes no such demands, for the interplay between the wrong done to the victim, the individual characteristics and frailties of the defendant, and the pharmacological effects of whatever drug may be potentially involved can be far better recognized by a tailored choice from the continuum of sentences available to the judge than by the application of a single yea-or-nay jury decision. To this, there is one exception. The mandatory life sentence for murder, at least as present administered, leaves no room for the trial judge to put into practice an informed and sympathetic assessment of the kind just described. It is for this reason alone that I have felt any hesitation about rejecting the argument for the respondent. In the end however I have concluded that this is not a sufficient reason to force on the theory and practice of the criminal law an exception which would otherwise be unjustified. For many years mandatory sentences have impelled juries to return merciful but false verdicts, and have stimulated the creation of partial defences such as provocation and diminished responsibility whose lack of a proper foundation has made them hard to apply in practice. I do not think it right that the law should be further distorted simply because of this anomalous relic of the history of the criminal law.

All this being said, I suggest to your Lordships that the existing work of the Law Commission in the field of intoxication could usefully be enlarged to comprise questions of the type raised by this appeal, and to see whether by statute a merciful, realistic and intellectually sustainable statutory solution could be newly created. For the present, however, I consider that no such regime now exists, and that the common law is not a suitable vehicle for creating one. . . .

Appeal allowed.

This decision makes it clear that if a defendant has the necessary *mens rea* for an offence the fact that he only committed it because he was involuntarily intoxicated provides no defence. It is, however, not clear what would happen in a case where the defendant was involuntarily intoxicated and committed a strict liability or negligence-based offence. Lord Mustill's reasoning appears to indicate that the defendant would still be guilty, but this is by no means beyond doubt.

15 MISTAKE

It is in fact technically incorrect to see mistake as a special category of defence.[189] Rather, a mistake can be a particular way of denying that the defendant has *mens rea* or asserting that the defendant has a defence, such as self-defence. Consider these four examples:

(1) *The mistake negates* mens rea. Anna was out shooting rabbits and she saw something she thought was a rabbit and shot at it. In fact it was Tom who was hiding in some bushes, who died from the shot. Anna would have a defence of no *mens rea* to a charge of murder. Her mistake meant that she did not have an intention to kill or cause grievous bodily harm to a person.

(2) *The mistake does not negate* mens rea. Eva is a terrorist. She shoots Damien dead. Eva believes that Damien is a government minister, but she is mistaken and Damien is in fact a member of the public. Here Eva is guilty of murder, but her mistake did not negate her *mens rea* (she did intend to kill a person), nor did her mistake give rise to a defence.[190]

(3) *The mistaken belief forms the basis of a defence.* Elizabeth mistakenly believes that Richard is about to attack her and so she stabs him dead. Elizabeth will be able to rely on the defence of self-defence.[191]

(4) *A mistake of law provides no defence.* Grace buys some cannabis. She misunderstands an inaccurate report in a tabloid newspaper and believes that it is no longer an offence to possess cannabis. She is charged with possession of cannabis. It is no defence for her to claim that she thought what she was doing was legal.

We will now consider these examples in further detail.

15.1 A MISTAKE WHICH MAY NEGATE *MENS REA*

The simple question to ask in these cases is whether in the light of the mistake the defendant had the required *mens rea* or recklessness. The leading case on this area of the law is now *DPP v B*,[192] which was discussed in Chapter 4. There their Lordships confirmed that, unless a statutory offence states otherwise, if the defendant can demonstrate that he honestly (even if unreasonably) believed that an element of the *actus reus* did not exist then he can have a defence.

---

[189] A point stressed by Lord Hailsham in *Morgan* [1976] AC 182, 214 (HL).
[190] See *R v Ellis, Street and Smith* (1987) 84 Cr App R 235 (CA) for a less straightforward case.
[191] *Beckford* [1998] AC 130 (PC). [192] [2000] 2 WLR 452 (HL).

What if the reason for the defendant's mistake which led to his lack of *mens rea* is intoxication? The correct view, it is submitted, is to follow the general approach for intoxication. For example, in cases of voluntarily intoxication the mistaken belief can be introduced as evidence of no *mens rea* in cases of specific intent, but otherwise will not provide a defence. So in a murder case if the defendant was so drunk he thought the victim was a deer and shot him this could provide a defence: there was no intent to kill or seriously injure a person. This defendant would still be convicted of manslaughter. In cases of involuntary intoxication the drunken mistake can provide a defence if that mistake negates *mens rea*.[193]

15.2 MISTAKES AND DEFENCES

The law is not straightforward in cases where a defendant wishes to rely on a defence, such as self-defence or consent, but is mistaken as to one of the elements of the defence. An example is a defendant who uses force against a person he believes is attacking him, but who is not. The easiest way to deal with cases is to consider each defence separately and to consider three kinds of mistake:

(1) Reasonable mistakes. A mistake that a reasonable person in the defendant's shoes might have made.

(2) An unreasonable mistake. A mistake that a reasonable person would not have made.

(3) A drunken mistake. A mistaken belief reached by someone who is drunk.

Now we shall consider each defence separately and how they deal with these three different kinds of mistake:

Lawful defence

(1) Reasonable mistakes: the defendant is to be judged on the facts as he believed them to be.[194] So if the defendant believes he is being attacked when he is not then the jury must ask themselves whether the amount of force used was reasonable assuming the facts to be as the defendant believed them to be. If it was the defendant can use lawful defence.

(2) Unreasonable mistakes: the defendant's belief that he is being attacked does not have to be reasonable.

(3) Drunken mistakes: a defendant cannot rely on a drunken belief that he is being attacked.[195] The question the jury must ask themselves is whether the drunkenness caused the mistake. This will be done by considering whether the defendant would have made the same mistake had he been sober. If he would have done then he can rely on lawful defence, but if he would not then he may not.

---

[193] *Kingston* [1995] 2 AC 355 (HL).
[194] *Williams* (1984) 78 Cr App R 276 (CA); *Beckford* [1988] AC 130 (PC).
[195] *Hatton* [2005] EWCA 2951; *O'Grady* [1987] 3 WLR 321 (CA); *O'Connor* [1991] Crim LR 135 (CA).

Duress

(1) Reasonable mistakes: the defendant can rely on duress (by threats or circumstances) if he has reasonable grounds for believing that the threats have been made or the threatening circumstances exist, even if in fact there is no such threat.[196]

(2) Unreasonable mistakes: the defendant probably[197] must have reasonable grounds for believing that the threat of death or serious injury has been made and that it will be carried out. If he does not have reasonable grounds he cannot rely on the defence.

(3) Drunken belief: an unreasonable drunken belief that the defendant is being threatened will not provide a defence.

Consent

(1) Reasonable mistakes: if the defendant mistakenly believes that the victim was consenting to the use of force, in circumstances in which consent would have provided a defence, then the defendant has a defence.

(2) Unreasonable mistakes: there is no need for the defendant to show that the belief in consent was reasonably held.[198]

(3) Drunken beliefs: general principles suggest that a drunken belief that the victim was consenting will not provide a defence.[199] There are, however, two cases which suggest that a drunken belief that the victim was consenting could provide a defence:

(i) In *Richardson and Irvin*[200] the Court of Appeal suggested that a drunken mistaken belief that the victim was consenting to rough horseplay could provide a defence to a charge of assault occasioning actual bodily harm.

(ii) In *Jaggard v Dickenson*[201] a drunken woman believed she was breaking the window of her friend's house so she could get in. In fact the house belonged to a stranger. It was held that her drunken mistaken belief that the owner would have consented provided a defence to criminal damage under section 5(2) and (3) of the Criminal Damage Act 1971.[202]

It is arguable that these two cases, neither of which was argued in depth, should not be regarded as conclusive. The conflict between the case law requires a decision from the Court of Appeal to clarify the present state of the law.

Provocation

(1) Reasonable mistakes: if a defendant mishears or misinterprets what is said or done and as a result loses his self-control he can rely on provocation.

(2) Unreasonable mistakes: even if the mistake is an unreasonable one it seems that the defendant can rely on provocation.[203]

---

[196] *Martin* [1989] 1 All ER 652 (CA); *Howe* [1987] 1 All ER 771 (HL); *Graham* [1982] 1 WLR 294 (CA).

[197] See the discussion at p. 689.   [198] *Morgan* [1976] AC 182 (HL).

[199] *Fotheringham* (1989) 88 Cr App R 206 (CA).   [200] [1999] 1 Cr App R 392 (CA).

[201] [1981] QB 527 (QBD).

[202] Section 5(2) of the Criminal Damage Act 1971 provides a defence to a person who causes criminal damage, believing that the owner would have consented to the damage if he had known of the circumstances of the damage. Section 5(3) of the Act states: 'For the purposes of this section it is immaterial whether a belief is justified or not if it is honestly held.'

[203] *Letenock* (1917) 12 Cr App R 221.

(3) Intoxicated mistakes: there is little recent authority on this, but there is one case, now nearly 100 years old, which suggests that even if a drunken defendant mistakenly believed he is being insulted he can rely on the defence.[204]

15.3 MISTAKES OF LAW

In considering mistakes of law it is necessary to distinguish between mistakes of law that negate *mens rea* and those which do not:

(1) *Mistakes of law which do not negate* mens rea. There is a well-known legal maxim: ignorance of the law is no excuse (*ignorantia juris neminem excusat*). So it is no defence to a charge of rape that the defendant did not know that it was a criminal offence to have sexual intercourse with someone without her consent.[205]

There are two exceptions to the principle:

(i) A person has a defence if he is charged with an offence created by a statutory instrument which has not been publicized[206] or a government Order if the person affected is unaware of the Order.[207]

(ii) If a person intends to do an act and seeks advice from a state agency as to whether the action is lawful and is told (wrongly) that it is lawful then a subsequent prosecution may be halted by a judge as an abuse of process.[208]

(2) *Mistakes of law which do negate* mens rea. A mistake of law can provide a defence if it means that the defendant lacks the *mens rea* of the offence. This is most relevant in property offences. Section 2(1)(a) of the Theft Act 1968, for example, specifically states that a person will not be dishonest if he believes he has, in law, the right to take the property. For example, if Jonathan is charged with the theft of David's car he has a defence if he can persuade the jury that he believed that because David owed him money he was legally entitled to seize his property. The mistake of law will establish that the defendant was not dishonest.[209]

FURTHER READING

Fletcher, G. (1978), *Rethinking Criminal Law* (Boston, Mass.: Little, Brown), ch. 9.

Husak, D., and von Hirsch, A. (1993), 'Culpability and Mistake of Law' in S. Shute, J. Gardner, and J. Horder (eds.), *Action and Value in Criminal Law* (Oxford: OUP).

Tur, R. (1993), 'Subjectivism and Objectivism: Towards Synthesis' in S. Shute, J. Gardner, and J. Horder (eds.), *Action and Value in Criminal Law* (Oxford: OUP).

---

[204] Ibid. Given the age of this authority and the general developments in the law of intoxication and provocation since, the case cannot be regarded as very strong authority.

[205] This rule can produce great unfairness: see *Bailey* (1800) Russ & Ry 1.

[206] Statutory Instruments Act 1946, s. 3(2).   [207] *Lim Chin Aik v R* [1963] AC 160 (PC).

[208] *Postermobile plc v Brent London Borough Council*, 8 Dec. 1997. Technically the offence is committed, but it is not possible to prosecute it.

[209] For another example see *Smith (David)* [1974] QB 354 (CA).

PART II: THE THEORY OF DEFENCES

16 DEFINING DEFENCES

16.1 THE TRADITIONAL APPROACH

There is much dispute over the correct way to classify defences.[210] Perhaps the most popular way is to draw a distinction between:

(1) the *actus reus* of the crime;

(2) the *mens rea* of the crime;

(3) a defence;

(4) mitigation.

The prosecution must prove the *actus reus* and *mens rea* of the offence, and once these have been proved the defendant will be guilty unless he or she is able to establish a defence. It should be noted that some defences are partial defences, meaning that they do not lead to a complete acquittal, but reduce the charge for which the defendant is convicted. A good example is provocation which, if successful, reduces the charge from murder to manslaughter. Matters of mitigation will not affect whether or not the defendant is guilty of the offence charged but will affect the sentence imposed. For example, if the defendant was racially insulted and therefore hit the victim, the provocation will not amount to a defence (remember provocation is a defence only to murder) but it may well mean that the defendant will receive a lower sentence than he would have received had it been an unprovoked assault.[211]

This apparently straightforward classification is beset with difficulties. Glanville Williams has written:

> what we think of as the definition of an offence and what we call a defence can only be regarded as depending largely upon the accidents of language, the convenience of legal drafting, or the unreasoning force of tradition.[212]

Indeed whether a matter raised by the defence is regarded as a denial of *actus reus*, a denial of *mens rea*, or a defence can be hard to tell.[213] Certainly the classification the courts have adopted is not that which you might at first expect: self-defence is regarded by the courts as a denial of *actus reus*, automatism is seen likewise as a denial of *actus reus*. This is not an argument that the classification cannot be supported but it demonstrates that some careful argumentation is needed to define these classifications.[214]

---

[210] For an excellent discussion see Wilson (2002: ch. 9). Robinson (1997: 11) suggests that defences are 'anything that prevents conviction of a defendant'. This is too wide because it would include the death of the defendant before the trial is completed: Husak (1999a).

[211] J. Gardner (1995a). If the defendant is morally blameless such factors may also influence the prosecution in its decision whether or not to prosecute.

[212] Williams (1982: 256).   [213] Husak (1998a).

[214] Of course, the fact that 'bright lines' cannot be drawn does not mean that generally the classification is not useful.

16.2 ALTERNATIVES TO THE TRADITIONAL CLASSIFICATION

In the light of such difficulties some commentators have suggested alternatives or amendments to the traditional classification:

(1) To add an additional category of exemption: those to whom the criminal law is not addressed or who are outside the purview of the criminal law,[215] the argument being that some people lack the moral capacity necessary to be people to whom the law is appropriately addressed. Children and the insane[216] would be two categories of defendant who clearly fell into this classification. Such people cannot be required or expected to comply with the standards expected of the criminal law because they lack the capacity to appreciate those standards or be responsible for their behaviour.[217] Supporters of the traditional classification claim that these 'exemptions' can be brought within the definition of excuses.[218]

(2) To argue that all defences are in essence about redefining the offence definition.[219] All offences would be made up of just two elements: the *actus reus* and *mens rea*, and all defences would be denials of the *actus reus* or *mens rea*. So, the *actus reus* of the offence would be to do X (except in self defence, or acting under duress).

16.3 DOES ANY OF THIS MATTER?

You may by now be beginning to wonder whether any of this matters very much. Why should it matter whether we regard self-defence as a denial of the *actus reus*, the *mens rea*, or a defence? Is that not a matter which is only of interest to those academics who wish to describe criminal law in terms of nicely defined boxes? Well, there is much to be said for such a point of view, and certainly there are grave dangers in expecting criminal law to fit into neat packages. However, there are cases where the distinctions have practical significance. For example, the prosecution has the burden of proving the *actus reus* and *mens rea* elements of the offence. The defence carries the burden of raising the defence. So whether self-defence (say) is an element of the *actus reus* or a defence matters here. If self-defence is a denial of the *actus reus* then it is for the prosecution to prove that the defendant was not acting in self-defence, whereas if it is a defence if the defendant wishes to raise the matter he must introduce evidence of self-defence before the court.[220]

We will now turn to the wealth of material that has been produced examining the philosophical foundations for the defences recognized in the law. As you will see there are many theories that have been put forwards as *the* theory of criminal defences. Perhaps before starting it is worth noting that many commentators[221] warn against adopting a single theory

---

[215] Lacey (2000a).

[216] Robinson (1982) is sceptical about exemptions. He argues that although someone may be insane at the time of the offence, he may not generally be insane. To describe such a person as exempt from the criminal law sometimes and sometimes not creates unnecessary confusion in his view.

[217] See e.g. Horder (1997b) for further discussion.

[218] For arguments against the existence of exemptions see Wilson (2002: 288–9).

[219] Robinson (1982).

[220] Also, in offences of strict liability, where there is no need for the prosecution to prove any *mens rea*, whether an element is regarded as of *actus reus* or *mens rea* is important.

[221] e.g. Horder (1993b).

of criminal culpability. Rather, each defence and each crime needs careful consideration on its own. Certainly no one theory of culpability can explain the criminal law as it stands at present.

FURTHER READING

Alldridge, P. (1983), 'The Coherence of Defences', *Criminal Law Review* 665.

Campbell, K. (1987), 'Offence and Defence' in I. Dennis (ed.), *Criminal Law and Criminal Justice* (London: Sweet & Maxwell).

Fletcher, G. (1978), *Rethinking Criminal Law* (Boston, Mass.: Little, Brown), ch. 10.

Smith, A. (1978), 'On *Actus Reus* and *Mens Rea*' in P.R. Glazebrook (ed.), *Reshaping the Criminal Law* (London: Stevens).

Tadros, V. (2005), *Criminal Responsibility* (Oxford: OUP).

Williams, G. (1982b), 'The Theory of Excuses', *Criminal Law Review* 732.

Wilson, W. (2005), 'The Structure of Criminal Defences', *Criminal Law Review* 371.

17 JUSTIFICATIONS AND EXCUSES

One popular way of analysing defences is to distinguish between justifications and excuses.[222]

DEFINITION

A justification focuses on what the defendant did and claims that what she did was what the law permitted her to do. Normally that is because society has approved of what the defendant has done.

With an excuse the defendant admits that what she did was not permissible, but that she does not deserve to be blamed. This may be because of her mental state, for example.

As Paul Robinson has stated: 'an actor's conduct is justified; an actor is excused' (Robinson (1999: 69)).

The interest in the difference between justifications and excuses in recent times can be traced back to an enormously influential book by George Fletcher. In the following extract from that book he sets out the key differences between a justification and an excuse as he understands it:

G. Fletcher, *Rethinking Criminal Law* (Boston, Mass.: Little, Brown, 1978), 759–62

The notions of justification and excuse have, by now, become familiar figures in our structured analysis of criminal liability. Claims of justification concede that the definition of the offense is satisfied, but challenge whether the act is wrongful; claims of excuse concede that the act is wrongful, but seek to avoid the attribution of the act to the actor. A justification

---

[222] Fletcher (1978: ch. 10); J.C. Smith (1989); Robinson (1982); Williams (1982b); Greenawalt (1984).

speaks to the rightness of the act; an excuse, to whether the actor is accountable for a concededly wrongful act. For all this apparent simplicity, the notions of justification and excuse lend themselves to considerably more refinement. . . .

§10.1.1. The Interactional Effects of Justificatory Claims

The questions of excusing and assessing accountability arise only in the institutional context of deciding whether someone can fairly be held accountable for a wrongful act. In a system of spontaneous justice, such as the early practice of executing nighttime thieves, there is no place for a system of excuses. Susceptibility to private punishment turns solely on the incriminating effect of appearances. The excuses of mistake, accident, necessity and insanity begin to develop only as the process of condemnation and punishment moves from the scene of the deed to the reflective deliberations of the courtroom.

The implications of this point are important. Whether a wrongful actor is excused does not affect the rights of other persons to resist or to assist the wrongful actor. But claims of justification do. In exploring why this is so, we shall discover the way in which claims of justification function in creating and negating the rights of persons in a situation of conflict.

Consider first the right of the victim to resist an aggressive act. Suppose a starving woman enters a grocery store and starts to take a loaf of bread. When the shopkeeper moves to stop her, she explains that she and her baby have not had food in several days; they have no money and she must take the bread. Does the shopkeeper have the right to resist her taking the loaf? The general understanding, according to the Model Penal Code as well as German, French, and Soviet law, is that the privilege to defend property or personal interests depends upon whether the aggression is wrongful or unlawful. If the attempt to take the loaf of bread is merely excused and not justified, the attempted theft is wrongful and the storekeeper may use at least reasonable force to resist the intrusion. On the other hand, if the intrusion is justified, the property owner must tolerate the taking of the bread. This point was recognized in a leading case in the law of torts, in which a ship captain attempted to take shelter from a storm by mooring his ship at a stranger's wharf. The wharf owner's employee prevented them from docking, as a result of which the ship crashed onto the beach. The wharf owner was liable in damages, for the employee's resistance was unjustified. The reason was that the desire to take refuge from the storm was itself justified on the principle of lesser evils; therefore, the wharf owner was required to submit to the intrusion. If in contrast, the intrusion was merely excused, say, on grounds of mistake or insanity, the wharf owner presumably would not have been required to submit. It is worth noting that even when required to tolerate someone else's justifiable intrusion, the owner may collect damages for the loss incurred by the intrusion. If the shopkeeper were required to tolerate the taking of bread from his store, he would have a valid claim under the law of torts for compensation.

It is not transparent why the right to resist should turn on whether the intrusion is justified or excused. Perhaps both should be resisted, perhaps neither. It is easier to see why justified conduct should not be resisted. The determination that the conduct is justified presupposes a judgment about the superior social interest in the conflict. If the superior social interest is represented by the party seeking to moor his ship or the woman attempting to take a loaf of bread, it is also in the social interest to suppress resistance. On the other hand, if the act of taking the bread is merely excused, the woman may not be to blame, but nor is the shopkeeper to blame for her personal condition. It is not clear why the law should require one innocent party to defer to another. If the shop-keeper would not have a duty to give her a loaf of bread, there is no apparent reason why he should let her take it.

Consider the effect of a justification on the rights of third parties to assist the justified actor or to act in his or her place. Claims of justification lend themselves to universalization. That the doing is objectively right (or at least not wrongful) means that anyone is licensed to do it. The only requirement is that the act be performed for the justificatory purpose, namely, to feed the starving mother and child. Excuses, in contrast, are always personal to the actor; one person's compulsion carries no implications about whether third parties will be excused if they act on behalf of the endangered defendant. Thus, if the starving mother's stealing the loaf of bread is justified, a third person should be able to steal the bread for the sake of saving the mother and her child from starvation. If, however, the desperate act of theft is merely excused, no one else would be able to assert that excuse. If other people do assist her in wrongfully overcoming the resistance of the shopkeeper, they would be presumably guilty as accomplices in the theft. Their accessorial liability would not be undercut by the mother's personal excuse.

A valid justification, then, affects a matrix of legal relationships. The victim has no right to resist, and other persons acquire a right to assist- apart from one exception that need not detain us. Excuses, in contrast, do not affect legal relationships with other persons; the excuse is a claim to be raised only relative to the external authority that seeks to hold the actor accountable for the wrongful deed.

17.1 JUSTIFICATIONS

A justification focuses on the act of the defendant and claims that the defendant performed a permissible act.[223] It is sometimes suggested that a justification is a claim that the defendant did the 'right' thing. This would be misleading. Consider this example: Nick is approached by two 7-year-old children who are playing with guns. They point the guns at Nick and place their hands on the triggers. The only way Nick can save himself is to shoot the children dead, which he does. Now, whether what the defendant did is 'right' is a matter of great debate among ethicists. Some people would take the view that he ought to lay down his own life rather than kill 'the innocent children'. However, what is clear is that he is legally permitted to use force in these circumstances. So, it is preferable to say that a justification involves actions that are permissible, rather than actions that are right.[224]

But how does the law decide what a defendant is permitted to do which would otherwise be a criminal offence? A number of different theories have been produced to explain justifications:[225]

(1) *Lesser of two evils.* A justification applies when the defendant has performed the lesser of two evils.[226] In other words an act is justified if it causes more good than harm; there is no 'net societal harm'.[227] There are difficulties with such an explanation. It

---

[223] One issue of some debate concerning justification is whether, if there is a justification, there is still a wrong committed against a victim. One view is that in the case of a justified act the defendant has still wronged the 'victim', but that this wrong has been outweighed by the good consequences flowing from the act. The opposite view is that if the act is justified then it is 'all right' and no legal wrong has been done. See the discussion in Fletcher (1998, ch. 1).

[224] See the discussion in Uniacke (1994) and Schopp (1998). Uniacke suggests a distinction between a strong justification (the act was morally right) and a weak justification (the act was permissible, although morally wrong). Both are justifications for the purpose of the law.

[225] Dressler (1987).

[226] Teichman (1986) suggests that a justification only arises if the defendant has done the greater of two goods.

[227] Robinson (1996b).

appears to provide a defence to a doctor who killed a nurse to use her organs to save two of his patients. It also does not explain why it is permissible to use slightly more force than is threatened to repel an attack.[228]

(2) *Moral forfeiture.* This is the idea that the victim has forfeited his right not to be injured as a result of his morally wrong conduct, thereby authorizing the defendant's use of force against him. This theory is (as we shall see) a popular way of justifying self-defence. By attacking the defendant the victim has forfeited his right not to be injured and therefore the defendant is entitled to use force to repel the victim's attack. The theory works less well in circumstances in which the victim is not morally to blame, but the defendant is still justified in acting (e.g. where the defendant injures a child who is attacking him, or a case of necessity). There are also some commentators who argue that fundamental rights should not be forfeited. We would not be happy with the idea that someone could forfeit his right not to be tortured, should we be any happier with someone losing the right to life?

(3) *Securing legal and moral rights.* Here justifications are seen as upholding the defendant's legal (and moral) rights. Justifications, the argument goes, arise where the defendant is acting in order to protect or promote his rights. For example, in self-defence the defendant is acting in order to promote his right to personal autonomy. There are difficulties with this theory where there is a clash of rights. If after a shipwreck five people are in a life raft suitable for only four people, does each person have a right of autonomy which permits them to force off one of the others? If one is justified in pushing off the other, is the other justified in resisting the force?

(4) *Public authority justification.* Under this theory public officers (e.g. police officers) are given authority on behalf of the state to use force in certain circumstances.

Which view is adopted on the nature of justification can affect your response to two scenarios which have been hotly debated by those interested in this subject:

The case of the unknown justification[229]

This scenario under discussion is best explained by way of an example. Bill sees in the distance his enemy George. He pulls out his gun and shoots George dead. Unknown to Bill, George was in fact about to blow up a bomb which would have killed many people. So in fact Bill's actions produced a net social good, but he was unaware that he was doing so. Was Bill justified in acting the way he did? Commentators are deeply divided on the issue:

(1) *Bill is justified* (the Robinson view). Those who take this view argue that Bill did exactly what we would have wanted him to do. Because of his actions many lives were saved. We should therefore not criminalize him for what he did. The leading exponent of this view is Paul Robinson. His view has the benefit of simplicity: justifications are about what the defendant does, not what he thinks. He argues that it better reflects the common understanding of justification and enables the law to send a clear message about what conduct is permissible.[230] Robinson has been willing to accept that in our scenario Bill might be appropriately convicted of attempted murder: he tried to commit murder, but in fact carried out a lawful killing.[231] Although other

---

[228] Alexander (1999).
[230] Robinson (1996b).
[229] Discussed in Christopher (1995); Robinson (1996b); J. Gardner (1996).
[231] Ibid. He is supported on this by Gross (1979: 199).

commentators have replied that to say an act both is justified and also constitutes a criminal offence of attempt is contradictory.[232]

(2) *Bill is not justified* (the *Dadson* view). This is the view taken in English law, following the *Dadson*[233] case. Only if one acts in a permissible way and for justifying reasons can one claim to be justified.[234] Some commentators have argued that the law does not want to encourage people to break the law if they are not aware of any justifying circumstances.

The case of the mistaken justification

Again this is best explained by an example. Margaret is out for a late night walk. She hears running behind her, turns and see Ronald running towards her. Convinced that Ronald is about to assault her, she shoots him. In fact it turns out that Ronald was out for a jog and intended Margaret no harm. On the facts as Margaret believed them to be she was justified in acting as she did, but on the facts as they actually were she was not justified. Paul Robinson argues that such an actor is not justified.[235] What Margaret did did not produce a net social good. He points out that if a passer-by (Neil) sees what is happening and tries to stop Margaret, because he appreciates that she has made a mistake, then if we hold Margaret justified in her attack Neil will be committing an offence, whereas if we say she is only excused (as Robinson would have it) then Neil is justified.[236] Simester and Sullivan think it is arguable that Margaret in a case like this acts justifiably.[237] She did what was permitted, how society would have wanted her to act, *given her state of mind*.

Deeds v Reasons

These two problems indicate a fundamental dispute over the nature of justification. In essence there are three views. A person is justified because:

(1) his deeds are justified (the 'deeds' view);[238]

(2) he acts for justifiable reasons (the 'reasons' view); or

(3) both his deeds and reasons are justified (the 'deeds and reasons' view).[239]

The practical differences between these views are demonstrated by the following points:

(1) A person who takes the 'deeds' view would find the unknown justified actor justified, but not the mistaken justified actor.

(2) The 'reasons' view would not find the unknown justified actor justified but would find the mistaken justified actor justified.

(3) The 'deeds and reasons' view would find neither the unknown justified nor the mistaken justified actor justified.

---

[232] Wilson (2002: 273).   [233] (1850) 4 Cox CC 358.
[234] Hitchler (1931). Some commentators would add that the justifying circumstances must be one of the reasons for which the defendant acted.
[235] See also Horder (2004: ch. 5) and Ripstein (1996).
[236] Remember that private defence is available only against an unjust threat (see p. 669).
[237] Simester and Sullivan (2003: 543).
[238] Robinson (1996).   [239] Fletcher (1998: 88–9) and J. Gardner (1996).

17.2 EXCUSES

Excuses are often said to be all about removing blame.[240] An excuse accepts that the defendant behaved in an unjustified way, but argues that he is not to blame for his action. Although, as was explained in Chapter 3, the *mens rea* requirements ensure that the defendant was to blame for bringing about the harm to the victim, *mens rea* can do only part of that job. For example, a defendant may intentionally injure a victim, but only do so because he has been threatened with death. Excuses therefore, it is said, complete the picture of the assessment of the defendant's blameworthiness.

So which defences are justifications and which are excuses?

Unfortunately it is not possible to produce a definitive list of which defences are justifications and which are excuses. The courts rarely talk about the distinction between a justification and an excuse, and there is no consensus over the proper classification of some defences. There is a general agreement that automatism and insanity are excuses.[241] Private defence and chastisement are usually seen as justifications.[242] Much more debate surrounds provocation,[243] duress, and mistaken private defence.

In the following passage Jeremy Horder sets out what he sees as the essential elements of an excuse:

J. Horder, *Excusing Crime* (Oxford: Oxford University Press, 2004), 8–12

To be recognizable as such, it is a necessary condition of any claim to excuse that it is an explanation for engagement in wrongdoing (an explanation not best understood as a justification, as a simple claim of involuntariness, or as an out-and-out denial of responsibility) that sheds such a favourable moral light on D's conduct that it seems entirely wrong to convict, at least for the full offence. So defined, claims that are candidates for excuse overlap to some extent with claims treated as claims for mitigation of sentence; but claims that meet the necessary conditions for excuse are by no means just the most pressing of the claims for mitigation of sentence that D might plausibly make. Excuses are morally as well as legally distinctive in character. Excuses excuse the act or omission amounting to wrongdoing, by shedding favourable moral light on what D did through a focus on the reasons that D committed that wrongdoing, where those reasons played a morally 'active' role in D's conduct (meaning that what D did or what happened to D can be subject to critical moral evaluation). So long as those reasons did play a morally active role in D's conduct, it can still be appropriate to speak of the case for 'excusing' D, even when D combines a factor (duress, say, or provocation) with respect to which he or she was morally active, with a factor (mental disorder, say, or involuntariness), with respect to which he or she was morally 'passive'. The existence of a morally active dimension to what happened to D or to what D did, means that the event stands to be evaluated in the light of underlying 'guiding' reasons, reasons that dictate how D *ought* (not) to have behaved, in failing to control his or her nerves, or in losing his or her temper, as well as in striking someone, and so forth. The applicability of guiding reasons gives rise to the critical, judgmental or evaluative element in a claim, making it to at least some extent excusatory, even if its potential for success must sometimes turn in part

---

[240] Kadish (1987a).

[241] Although many commentators would prefer to refer to insanity as an exemption.

[242] There is of course much debate whether chastisement *should* be a defence at all.   [243] See Ch. 5.

on the influence of some morally passive physical or mental weakness or deficiency, on which guiding reasons can have no bearing. I will say more about the excusatory character and potential of reasons with respect to which D is morally active in a moment. It follows, though, that excuses ought to be distinguished from out-and-out denials of responsibility, of the kind constituted by a claim to acquittal focused solely on the effects of a severe mental disorder or deficiency (such as insanity). For, in such cases, guiding reasons—reasons concerned with how D ought to have behaved-have no moral significance, and we cannot judge D's conduct objectively in the light of an applicable moral standard.

Excusatory reasons, with respect to which one is morally active, can be divided into two general kinds, 'explanatory' reasons and 'adopted' reasons. Adopted reasons are reasons that (even in the blink of an eye) one positively chooses to or makes one's mind up to act on, whereas explanatory reasons are not. An explanatory reason is a reason why something happened to one or why one acted in a certain way, whether accidentally (as in the case of clumsiness) *or* intentionally, without choice or decision, but where there was still a morally active dimension to what happened or to what was done. If a dancer accidentally trips, and in so doing, treads on his or her partner's toes, the accident may be treated as a straightforward denial of voluntariness, on the basis that what happened was a freak accident that could have happened to anyone. There is, though, the potential for an excusatory issue to emerge from behind this categorization of what happens to the dancer. Guiding reasons—in the form of reasons not to tread on someone's toes—clearly have a particular moral salience when one is dancing with a partner; and one can seek to guard against accidents. So, there will always potentially be an issue about whether the dancer could reasonably and should have done more to avoid tripping, bearing in mind the need, in context, to keep his or her dance movements fluid, spontaneous and well timed, etc. This is a classic capacity-focused, excusatory issue, where the dancer's plea, 'I could not, in the circumstances, reasonably have been expected to do more to avoid tripping and hence treading on my partner's toes', is an explanatory (excusatory) reason. We should note, further, that the dancer's claim remains in some sense excusatory in character, even if he or she puts the whole episode down to his or her clumsiness. In such a case, the dancer gives a reason why the accident occurred that relates to an individual condition or disposition (the clumsiness), with respect to which he or she should be regarded as to a degree morally active, and hence for the manifestation of which he or she must thus accept some moral responsibility. Even though the clumsy dancer's claim resembles a claim of simple involuntariness, clumsy people can usually try with some prospect of success to be less clumsy, if they absolutely have to (this is the morally active dimension to what the dancer did). So, the issue is whether the dancer could and should have done more to, keep his or her tendencies to clumsiness under control, given the need also to keep his or her dance movements fluid, well timed, and so on. As in the initial example where the dancer simply trips, this issue involves a capacity-focused question of excuse, even though there is now a more 'individualized' character to that question than there is to the question how much, in general, competent dancers should do to avoid treading on their partner's toes. In that regard, the question how much care we can reasonably expect D him- or herself to take is an excusatory question, albeit not the same excusatory question as the question how much care we can expect of competent dancers in general. The distinction between subjective and objective versions of the capacity theory of excuses that this example exploits will be examined in more detail in chapter 3.6 below.

In the case of intentional conduct, when one seeks excuse by putting a killing down to an instantaneous loss of self-control (provocation), or ascribing to the impact of sheer terror an 'instinctive' defensive response that is too heavy-handed (excessive defence), one may also be giving an explanatory reason for the action. In such cases, the phenomenological strength of the desire at the heart of the emotion (the urge to kill; the desire to ensure the attack is thwarted) spontaneously eclipses or bypasses the restraining or moderating power of reason. So the actions taken, albeit intentional, are not chosen: they are not based on 'adopted' reasons. Indeed, in the kind of cases I have in mind, the actions bear some family resemblances to conduct that is involuntary, as in the case, say, of clumsy actions. Nonetheless, there is clearly still an evaluative dimension to what D does. . . . [W]e can still ask whether D should have let his or her temper, or terror, get the better of him or her to the extent that it did. As Derek Parfit puts it, conduct that is, 'not deserving the extreme charge "irrational" [may, nonetheless, be] open to rational criticism'. One must, however, take care with examples of this kind, in general (angry or fearful actions). People who are provoked to anger, or fearful of threats, can sometimes still remain in evaluative control of their consequent conduct throughout, and can hence make genuine-reasoned-choices, even if they are not the choices they would have made in a calm frame of mind. How do all such actions, actions based on an *adopted* reason (a reason D chose to act on) come to be excused, whether or not they are grounded in an emotional reaction?

There are different routes to excuse for such actions, actions based on adopted reasons, which is why it is important to have a broad understanding of the necessary conditions of excuse. Finding an understandable 'rational defect' in a morally salient motivating force or factor behind an action is perhaps the most commonly encountered route to excuse, particularly but not solely where the action is grounded in a strong emotional reaction. In a case of angry or fearful action, D might claim that the phenomenological strength of an understandable emotion (D's 'operating' reason) so diminished in significance any countervailing evaluative considerations that the wrongful course seemed overwhelmingly attractive or proper, in a way it could and should never rationally have done. By way of contrast with the examples discussed in the preceding paragraph, however, in such cases it is still correct to say that D chooses his or her action from the balance of applicable reasons. D's choice hence has some of the hallmarks of a rational choice, but is a defective example of such a choice, for the reasons just given. So, for example, in an excessive defence case, the fulfilment of the necessary conditions for excuse could hinge on a finding that the sheer strength of D's fear made the choice of a heavy-handed course of action as a means of thwarting an attack *seem* entirely rational and proper, but only because of the mental domination achieved by the desire to ensure that the attack is thwarted. To give a different kind of example, a morally salient rational defect in a motivating factor behind the action also underpins the excusatory element in many factual mistake cases where, as things turn out, the mistake leads D into wrong-doing. In such cases, D commonly acts for an adopted reason, deciding on or choosing a course of action in a normal way. So, D's choice appears to have some of the hallmarks of a rational choice. D chooses that course of action, though, in the more-or-less understandably mistaken belief that a state of affairs exists (D's 'auxiliary' reason) that makes a crucial—morally salient—difference to the rational justification for that course of action, when no such state of affairs really exists. So, there is a rational defect lying behind D's choice. These different kinds of rational defects in morally salient motivating forces or factors behind actions can, of course, combine. So, one might be mistaken about the existence or nature of provocation (one kind of rational defect) that then led one into precipitate action following a loss of self-control (another sort of rational defect).

These kinds of mistake cases, in which the existence of a rational defect in a morally salient motivating force or factor behind D's choice does important excusatory work, are very different from cases where the adopted reason for which D commits the wrongdoing reflects a salient *moral* mistake. This happens where, for example, D decides (adopted reason) to abide by the demands of his or her religion as a matter of conscience, even though to do so means

D will perform acts regarded as wrong in law. ... The defect in the motivation for D's choice here is not rational, but moral: he or she simply gets the balance of reasons wrong by sticking to what conscience demands. D (ex hypothesi) understands the demands of his or her religion well enough to know how believers mean them to influence the balance of reasons. So, the excusatory work is now being done by a sense that it is understandable, albeit morally mistaken, to get the balance of reasons wrong by putting conscience-based compliance with religious demands ahead of avoiding legal wrongdoing. Even so, as in all the examples discussed to date, what matters in this category of cases is a capacity-focused question . . . : could and should more have been expected of D, rationally or morally (as the case may be)? This category of case shares something else with those discussed earlier. It is as true of this category of cases as of all the 'adopted reason' cases briefly discussed so far, that the importance to the excuse of the rational or moral defect in a motivating force or factor behind the choice is that the adopted reason is given for doing the very thing that is, in fact, prohibited by law. In other cases . . . the excusatory focus is on reasons for action D adopted to avoid committing wrongdoing, in spite of which the wrongdoing occurred. This is so, for example, when D says he or she should be excused on a 'due diligence' basis (normally, in regulatory cases), because no more could reasonably have been expected than that he or she put in the effort he or she did put in, taking the steps he or she chose to take, to try to ensure that wrongdoing would be avoided. Given that the adopted reasons—the compliance strategy, in effect—bear on steps taken to avoid wrongdoing, rather than being reasons to commit the act involving wrongdoing itself, there is no need for them to manifest some rational or moral defect. Indeed, as we will see in chapter 6 below, it may be that we would not excuse, on a 'due diligence' basis, unless we could find no rational (and still less, moral) fault whatsoever with the compliance strategy D adopted.

Whilst mitigating circumstances can clearly bear on the explanatory or adopted reasons for the act or omission amounting to criminal wrongdoing, there is no necessary conceptual connection between them. It could be right to mitigate a sentence in response to developments after the commission of the act, such as V's forgiveness, or D's co-operation with the authorities. It could also be right to mitigate the sentence in response to, morally, purely passive factors underlying the crime's commission not amounting, as such, to a denial of responsibility, like D's deprived upbringing? Some factors can be mitigating in a non-excusatory way, or can be dealt with as excusatory claims, depending on what it is that 'counts' about them in context. For example, following the definition of the necessary conditions of excuse just given, youth can only be pleaded in an excusatory way if it is tendered as an argument (say) about the understandable nature of the impulsiveness or lack of adequate foresight (i.e. the rational defect in a morally salient motivating force or factor) that lay behind the act itself. Youth can also, though, be relevant to mitigation in a non-excusatory way, i.e. even if it did nothing to shed light on the reasons why D did as he or she did. This would be the case if the court believes that it would be wrong to sentence D for as long a period in prison as someone older, for the same offence, because the impact of the same period of experiencing imprisonment would be disproportionately harsh on a younger person. The example of youth shows, though, that even if a factor can be pleaded in a genuinely excusatory way (in that it meets the necessary conditions for excuse), this obviously does not mean that it ought to gain recognition as a formal excusing condition, rather than being left as a matter for mitigation of sentence. Whether a plea ought to gain recognition as a formal excuse must turn on how significant the sufficiency conditions for an excuse are, in a given kind of case.

17.3 DOES THE DISTINCTION BETWEEN JUSTIFICATIONS AND EXCUSES REALLY MATTER?

You may by now be thinking, does it really matter whether a defence is a justification or an excuse? Well, some commentators certainly think it does. Here are some of the possible points of significance:

(1) Paul Robinson[244] suggests that if the law provides a justification this in effect changes the law. He therefore argues that if a case came before a court in which a man shot his neighbour's dog which was attacking his baby and the court held he was justified in doing this then the law would be changed to the extent that it would now be lawful for a person to shoot a dog which was attacking a baby.[245] By contrast, if a defendant is granted an excuse this is of no wider significance. No two people are identical, so the fact that one person was excused does not mean another will be.[246] A similar point is made by Jeremy Horder,[247] who argues that justification seeks to offer guidance to defendants before they act, while excuses assess the culpability of offenders once they have acted.[248]

(2) If a defendant is attacked by a person who is excused (for example, the defendant is attacked by a person who is sleepwalking) the defendant can lawfully resist the attack.[249] However, if the person using force against the defendant is justified (for example, the defendant is attacked by a police officer who is making a lawful arrest) then the defendant cannot lawfully resist the attack.[250]

(3) You can lawfully assist a person who is justified in using force, but not someone who is only excused.[251] If you assist a police officer to arrest a villain, you will be justified because the police officer is justified. If you assist an insane person attack an innocent person, the insane person can rely on the excuse of insanity, but you will not therefore have an excuse.[252]

(4) Justificatory defences are applicable to offences of strict liability, but excuses are not. Some commentators would wish to modify this statement by stressing that exemption defences (e.g. infancy, insanity) would apply to strict liability offences, even though they are classified as excuses.

(5) Some commentators argue that if the defence is a justification defendants can still rely on a defence if they honestly believe the circumstances were justificatory, even if in fact they were not.[253] However, if defendants are relying on an excuse they must *reasonably* believe the circumstances to be those that provide them with an excuse.

---

[244] Robinson (1982).

[245] It is interesting to note that one of the reasons in *Dudley and Stephens* (1884) 14 QBD 273 the court was unwilling to accept that the defendant had a defence of necessity was that such a verdict might encourage others placed in a similar position to do as the defendants did.

[246] Although an argument could be made that once a particular medical condition gives rise to a defence then all sufferers can be entitled to an excuse.

[247] Horder (2002a).   [248] Robinson (1990).

[249] Guy-Arye (1986) suggests that a person's right to self-defence should not be lost even if the attack he or she is facing is justified or excused.

[250] Unless he is unaware that the other person is a police officer and believes he is a villain who is trying to kill him.

[251] Guy-Arye (1986) also rejects this on the basis that a person intervening to protect someone's life should have a legal defence whether the person whose life he is saving is facing a justified or an excused attack.

[252] *Quick and Paddison* [1973] QB 910 (CA).   [253] Although this is rejected by some.

(6) Some commentators suggest that a defendant who through his own fault put himself in a position where he must choose between the lesser of two evils can rely on a justification (we would still want him to do the lesser of the two evils even though he is responsible for getting himself into that position) but an excuse is not available for a person who has brought about his own excusing state of mind.[254]

(7) Paul Robinson[255] recommends that when the jury acquits a defendant they should be required to make it clear whether they are acquitting the defendant because they thought he was excused or because he was justified or because the prosecution had failed to established the *mens rea* or *actus reus*. This would clarify the basis of the defendant's acquittal and enable the law to send a clear message about the requirements of the criminal law.[256]

(8) You might think that the legal test for a justification would be objective (was the defendant's *act* permissible?), while the legal test for an excuse subjective (was the defendant responsible?), but this is, in fact, rarely so. As this issue raises some interesting points about the nature of a justification and an excuse we will consider this in detail now under a separate heading.

17.4 SHOULD JUSTIFICATIONS BE OBJECTIVE AND EXCUSES SUBJECTIVE?

As just indicated it seems at first sight obvious that justification would be objective (is what the defendant did permissible (or reasonable)) and an excuse subjective (was the defendant's state of mind such that he was responsible for his actions?). However, if you look back at Part I you will find that most of the defences involve a mixture of objective and subjective elements. Why is this?

On the Robinson view all justifications would be purely objective because we would be simply concerned with the defendant's actions. However, on the *Dadson* view the state of mind of the defendant is relevant too. Remember that according to *Dadson* only if the defendant is aware of the justifying circumstances can the defendant plead a justification. So on the *Dadson* understanding of justifications we would expect to see some subjective elements (requiring that the defendant was aware of and acted because of the justificatory reasons).

Some excuses will in their nature be subjective (e.g. insanity), although much controversy surrounds whether all excuses should be purely subjective. Take duress: should the question be whether the defendant felt compelled to give in to the threat? Or whether it was reasonable for the defendant to give in to the threat? Of course those who regard duress as a justification have no difficulty with having the standard of the reasonable person here, but it is also supported by some of those who regard duress as an excuse. How can they support the use of a reasonable person test? Here are two possible explanations:

---

[254] This proposition is contested by some who argue that a justification should not be available where the defendant has acted for the purpose of putting himself in the position where he has to choose between the two evils. E.g. the defendant who deliberately starts a fire so that he can 'justifiably' destroy his neighbour's house in order to avoid the fire spreading.

[255] Robinson (1982).

[256] Robinson suggested that this would open the way for potential detention or other coercive measures under the civil law where the defendant was merely excused.

(1) To claim that one is blameless it is not enough to show that one was not responsible for one's actions, but also that one *ought* not to have been responsible for one's actions.[257] If Alan (a lover of rose bushes) is kidnapped by Charlie and told that she will destroy his rose bush unless he kills Dermot, Alan may feel himself in an awful dilemma and may feel compelled to killed Dermot, but this should not provide him with an excuse. He may feel greatly pressurized, but he should not be. The law values people higher than rose bushes: this should have been an easy choice for Alan. So, the argument goes, in a duress case it must be shown that the defendant acted faced with what he regarded as an appalling dilemma and that he ought to have found it an appalling dilemma.

(2) A different argument would be based on the character theory. If we are to decide that the defendant's actions did not reveal bad character then the objective test is an aspect of this. A person who injures an innocent third party after she has been threatened that she will be killed does not reveal bad character; a person who injures because his rose bush is threatened does.[258]

The following passage looks at several of the issues relating to justifications and excuses which we have been examining. John Gardner argues that there is a closer relationship between justifications and reasons than is often supposed. To claim you have a justification for doing or believing something is to claim you have good reasons for doing or so believing. He suggests reasons must be guiding or explanatory. Guiding reasons are reasons which dictate what you *ought* to do or believe. Explanatory reasons, by contrast, explain *why* you act in a particular way. A person may think their explanatory reasons are guiding reasons but they need not be. In simple terms a person may think he has a good reason for acting, but in fact that reason is not a good one. Gardner argues that to amount to a justification a person must have both guiding and explanatory reasons for being justified, and the guiding reason must correspond with the explanatory reasons. In simple terms you must have a justifiable reason for acting as you did and you must act *because of* that justifying reason. An excuse, he argues is analogous to a justification in that an excused person must act for good explanatory reasons (e.g. believing that she is justified in acting the way she does) and then justify why she (wrongly) thought she was justified:

J. Gardner, 'Justifications and Reasons' in A. Simester and A. Smith (eds.), *Harm and Culpability* (Oxford: OUP, 1996), 118–22

It is widely thought that excuses are more 'subjective' than justifications. In one sense of 'subjective', as we will see, this is perfectly true. But it is not true if we are using the labels 'subjective' and 'objective' to mark the contrast between explanatory and guiding reasons. Over a wide range of cases, excuses, just like justifications, depend on the union of explanatory and guiding reasons. Whenever excuses depend on the union of explanatory and guiding reasons, moreover, they do so precisely because justifications depend on the union of explanatory and guiding reasons. The structure of excuse derives, in other words, from the structure of justification, and thus shares in its combination of subjective (explanatory) and objective (guiding) rationality.

---

[257] Horder (1992: ch. 8) argues that there is justificatory element in excuses. See further Horden (2004).
[258] Ashworth (1973: 161).

Some theorists have associated excuses with character traits. They are mistaken if they think that every excuse is concerned with character. Many excuses are of a technical nature. They relate to levels of skill rather than degrees of virtue. Their gist is that the person claiming them does not possess the skills needed to do better, and should not be expected to possess those skills. Whether one should be expected to possess certain skills, or skills to a certain degree, depends, to some extent, on one's form of life. A doctor who tries to excuse her blundering treatment by claiming lack of diagnostic skill should not get far, whereas an amateur first-aider may be able to extinguish her blame, under similar conditions, by making exactly the same argument. But such excuses, even though they are of great legal import-ance, will not concern us here. Our concern will be with that major group of excuses which do indeed relate to character evaluation. These include excuses very familiar to criminal lawyers, such as excuses based on provocation and duress. Their gist is similar to that of technical excuses. It is that the person claiming them does not possess the virtues needed to do better, and should not be expected to possess those virtues. Again, which virtues one should be expected to possess, and to what extent, depends largely on one's form of life. A police officer is expected to exhibit more fortitude and courage than an ordinary member of the public, a friend is expected to be more considerate and attentive than a stranger, etc. What exactly does this mean? Essentially, it means that where there is a conflict of reasons, some people are expected to act for some reasons, whereas others are expected to act for other, often incompatible and incomparable, reasons. But obviously the need to claim an excuse from one's action arises only if one fails to establish a full justification. A fully justified action needs no excuse. So the point cannot be that those who act with excuse act for undefeated reasons, i.e., that it is alright for them to act for those reasons. That would yield a full justification for their actions. The point must be that there is something suspect about the reasons for which they act. And indeed there is. They are not valid reasons. They are what the person acting upon them takes to be valid reasons, *and justifiably so*. Thus the structure of excuse derives from the structure of justification. To excuse an action is not, of course, to justify that action. Rather, one justifies one's belief that the action is justified.

This explanation of non-technical excuses has to be modified and extended somewhat to accommodate unjustified actions upon justified emotions, attitudes, passions, desires, decisions, etc., as well as unjustified actions upon justified beliefs. Provocation, as Jeremy Horder has explained involves unjustified action out of justified anger. Duress, or a certain central kind of duress, can be similarly analysed as involving unjustified action out of justified fear. But these are, in a sense, derivative cases. Emotions like anger and fear are mediating forces between beliefs and actions. They enhance or constrain the motivating force of certain motivating beliefs. Their justification therefore turns in part on the justification of the beliefs which partly constitute them. Of course, there is still a justificatory gap: an emotion is not fully justified merely by the justification of its cognitive component. But justified emotion (and in similar vein justified attitude or desire or decision) nevertheless entails justified belief. Thus the most basic or rudimentary case of non-technical excuse remains that of unjustified action upon justified belief. One must therefore consider what is needed to make a belief justified. It is of course one of the great problems of epistemology, and we cannot do justice to it here. Suffice it to say that the general account of justification applicable to action is also broadly applicable to belief. One must have an undefeated reason for one's belief, and that must moreover be the reason why one holds the belief. This explains the nature of epistemic faults, such as prejudice, gullibility, and superstition. One cannot understand these faults unless one appreciates that a belief is justified, not only by the reasons there are for holding it, but also by the process of reasoning by which it came to be held, i.e., not only by guiding reasons but also by explanatory reasons. The same facts also explain why a requirement of *reasonableness* has traditionally been imposed upon excuses in the criminal law. It is not enough that one made a mistake as to justification, if it was not a reasonable mistake, it is not enough that one was angry to the point of losing self-control, if one's anger was not reasonable, etc. By 'reasonable' here is meant, in my view, much the same as 'justified'. There must have been an undefeated reason for one's belief, emotion, etc., which also explains why one held the belief or experienced the emotion, etc. The fact that sometimes this element of reasonableness is dispensed with in the law does not show a drift towards a more purely 'subjective' account of excuses, i.e., one depending on explanatory reasons without regard for guiding reasons. It shows, rather, that some excuse-like arguments, in common with some justification-like arguments, may actually serve to negate an element of the offence rather than to excuse or justify its commission. Some mistakes, as the courts put it, may simply serve to negate the mens rea for the particular crime; and if, as may be, the mens rea required is, e.g., knowledge, then of course the reasonableness of one's mistake is neither here nor there. The extent to which legal systems will tolerate such arguments depends on many contingencies about them, including the extent to which and way in which they implement the demand for mens rea. But this has nothing to do with excuses, in which an element of reasonableness, at some level, is conceptually necessitated whether the crime is one of full subjective mens rea or one of no mens rea at all.

Requirements of 'reasonableness' in criminal excuses also sometimes go beyond what the logic of excuses requires, and in that case they normally serve another role. They serve to orientate the law towards general application to people living many different forms of life, rather than tailoring it to suit the expected virtues of a certain kind of person leading a certain kind of life. The debate about the extent to which the reasonable person should be 'individualized' to the characteristics of the defendant in the definition of criminal excuses is partly a debate about the extent to which the criminal law should aspire to this kind of generality. Should the 'reasonable person' in provocation become the 'reasonable police officer' when the defendant is a police officer? Should the 'reasonable person' in cases of drunken mistake become the 'reasonable drunkard'? Once again there is no universal theoretical solution to this problem. Within broad limits, legal systems may quite properly vary in their willingness to individualize excuses and the general principles, if any, upon which they do so. But legal systems cannot, consistent with the logic of (non-technical) excuses, vary in the importance they attach to the combination of guiding and explanatory reasons in the excusatory scheme of things. Thus they cannot altogether eliminate the essential 'objective' dimension of excusatory claims. They cannot ignore the important point that excuses rely on reason, not on the absence of it. That is, they rely on the ability of the person who claims to be excused to believe and feel as reason demands, and because reason demands it. Those people who cannot meet this condition do not need to bother making excuses. Such people are not responsible for their actions, and are free from blame as well as being improper targets for criminal liability, irrespective of both justification and excuse. Justification and excuse both belong to the realm of responsible agency, and that is precisely because both depend, to put it crudely, on the ability to live within reason.

The logical relationship between justification and (non-technical) excuse helps to explain the so-called 'quasi-justificatory drift' of many familiar excuses. In English law this is compounded by the law's cautious insistence on having a belt as well as braces: in general no excuse is accepted into the criminal law which is not also a partial justification, and no justification is accepted which is not also a partial excuse. The drift of the excuse is not so much quasi-justificatory as truly justificatory. But neither of these facts should obscure the crucial conceptual distinction between justification and excuse. Nor should one be distracted by the paradoxical sound of the claim that an action which is justifiably believed to be justified is excused rather than justified. It only goes to show that, as between the concepts of justification and excuse, justification is the more fundamental. The same proposition also brings out the true sense in which excuses may be regarded as more 'subjective' than justifications. For by their nature excuses take the world as the defendant justifiably sees it rather than as it is. They look to what the defendant believes to be applicable reasons for action, so long as she does so on the basis of genuinely applicable reasons for belief. Justifications, meanwhile, look directly to the genuinely applicable reasons for action, without stopping to look for applicable reasons for belief. But in this whole contrast the calk of 'reasons' is talk of guiding reasons. It leaves on one side the fact that, in both justification and excuse, explanatory reasons also playa key role, and that, in this sense and to this extent, each is just as subjective as the other.

17.5 PROBLEMS WITH JUSTIFICATIONS AND EXCUSES

As we have already noted, there are some commentators who deny the usefulness of the distinction between justifications and excuses. Their reasons include the following:

(1) The English and Welsh courts have not placed great weight on the distinction. The general refusal of the courts to engage in an analysis of the defences in terms of justifications and excuses may indicate the distinction lacks practical benefit.

(2) The fact that there is so much debate over whether duress or mistaken self-defence is a justification or excuse indicates that the distinction is too vague to be useful. As Kurt Greenawalt stresses, there is not even agreement over whether justification should be judged on the basis of the facts that occurred or on the facts as they were believed to be.[259]

(3) Some commentators argue that our society lacks agreed moral standards which can be used to assess the justifiability or not of particular actions. The chastisement of children and the hunting of foxes with dogs at present are controversial issues over which there is no consensus. For the law to declare these actions justifiable or not is to impose a moral judgement when society lacks a sufficient consensus on the issue.

The passage by Nicola Lacey to be excerpted shortly considers some of the criticisms of the justification/excuse distinction.

FURTHER READING ON JUSTIFICATIONS AND EXCUSES

Berman, M. (2003), 'Justification and Excuse, Law and Morality', *Duke Law Journal* 53: 1.

Colvin, E. (1990), 'Exculpatory Defences in the Criminal Law', *Oxford Journal of Legal Studies* 10: 381.

Dressler, J. (1984), 'New Thoughts about the Concept of Justification in the Criminal Law', *University of California Los Angeles* 32: 61.

Gardner, J. (1996), 'Justifications and Reasons' in A. Simester and A. Smith (eds.), *Harm and Culpability* (Oxford: OUP).

—— (1998b), 'The Gist of Excuses', *Buffalo Criminal Law Review* 1: 575.

---

[259] Greenawalt (1984).

Greenawalt, K. (1984), 'The Perplexing Borders of Justification and Excuse', *Colorado Law Review* 84: 1897.

Horder, J. (2004), *Excusing Crime* (Oxford: OUP).

Robinson, P. (1982), 'Criminal Law Defenses: A Systematic Analysis', *Colorado Law Review* 82: 199.

—— (1996b), 'Competing Theories of Justification: Deeds v Reasons' in A. Simester and A. Smith (eds.), *Harm and Culpability* (Oxford: OUP).

Smith, J.C. (1989), *Justification and Excuse in the Criminal Law* (London: Sweet & Maxwell).

Weston, P., and Mangiafico, J. (2003), 'The Crimnal Defense of Duress: A Justification, Not an Excuse—and Why it Matters', *Buffalo Criminal Law Review* 8: 833.

Williams, G. (1982b), 'The Theory of Excuses', *Criminal Law Review* 732.

18 CHARACTER, CHOICE, AND CAPACITY

An alternative way of analysing defences is to examine their theoretical foundations.[260] There are three main schools of thought on the theoretical underpinning on defences, which will be outlined next. However, before that it should be stressed that within each school of thought there is a diversity of opinion as to the correct interpretation of the theory and that there are of course, many other theories that have been adopted. Also there are many commentators who decry any attempt to develop one overarching theory of culpability, arguing that there are different forms of culpability that may be appropriate in different kinds of offences. It is preferable, therefore, to consider offences and defences one by one and decide why we have them, rather than seek to force them all to abide by one guiding principle.[261]

First we briefly summarize the main theories.[262] Then we look at one academic's summary of the competing views and then look in more detail at the strengths and weaknesses of the different theories:

(1) *The choice theory.*[263] At the heart of this theory is the view that a defendant should be punished only for what he chose to do. We have seen in Chapter 3 that supporters of this theory tend to prefer subjective forms of *mens rea*: e.g. intention, *Cunningham* recklessness. Under this theory the law should provide a defence to a defendant who did not choose to act in the way he or she did, for example where the defendant is an automaton.

(2) *The capacity theory.* A popular variant of the choice theory is to justify punishment not only for those who chose to commit the harm, but those who could have avoided causing the harm but did not. Applying this theory to defences then, defences apply when the defendant did not and could not have chosen to obey the law. Hence, in the case of insanity the defendant, because of his or her mental illness, was not capable of

---

[260] Considering the theoretical basis for defences in these ways can be complementary to or independent from analysing them in terms of justifications or excuses.

[261] e.g. Horder (1993b).   [262] See for a detailed discussion Horder (2004: ch. 3).

[263] The choice theory has also been called the responsibility principle and the voluntarism principle.

acting otherwise. In the case of duress the defendant either did not choose or could not realistically have chosen to have acted otherwise.

(3) *The character theory.* This theory focuses on an argument that the defendant's criminal act reflects the bad character of the defendant. Here a defence exists when the act does not reveal bad character. So in a case of duress the fact that the defendant acted in the way he did in response to the threats does not reveal bad character on his part if he responded reasonably.

In this next passage Nicola Lacey distinguishes between the capacity view and the reasons view of defences. What she calls the reasons view is a version of the character theory. She also discusses the fragility of the distinction between justifications and excuses:

N. Lacey, 'Partial Defences to Homicide' in A. Ashworth and B. Mitchell (eds.), *Rethinking English Homicide Law* (Oxford: OUP, 2000), 114–19

1. The 'capacity view'

We can usefully distinguish two main traditions in theorizing about defences. The first draws a line between justifying and excusing defences; whilst justifying defences mark out conduct which criminal law does not regard as wrongful, excuses rather mark out situations in which the internal or external conditions under which a defendant acts are such as to displace— partly or completely—the attribution of responsibility for an admittedly wrongful act. In this tradition, the main questions arising about justificatory defences relate to their implications for third-party liability: if an act is genuinely justified, can it be lawfully assisted by third parties, and is it necessarily unlawful to resist it, for example, by self-defending conduct which might itself be justified? For a policy point of view, debate abounds about the implications of expanding justificatory defences given that they (on some interpretaions) give priority to the defendant's view of the wrongfulness of the conduct over the criminal law's.

In relation to excuses, the main questions arise in relation to the sorts of conditions which block an attribution of liability: which sorts of mental disorders or handicaps should prevent us from holding a person genuinely responsible in the sense of having had adequate cognitive and volitional capacities to have had a fair opportunity to do otherwise than she did; under what sorts of external conditions is it incumbent on the law to find that the conduct was not voluntary in the necessary sense? Excuses, on this view are based in internal or external circumstances which significantly affected the scope or the 'fairness of the opportunities available to the defendant to choose or control her conduct such that it is appropriate for the criminal law to make concessions to human frailty or bad luck. Hence discussion ranges over issues such as the balance to be struck between medical and legal criteria; the adequacy of conceptions of 'moral' or 'physical' voluntariness; and the implications of determinism for the relevant idea of capacity and free, responsible agency.

. . .

The capacity-based, subjective view of responsibility along with its concomitant approach to defences has been highly influential in Britain over the last thirty years. . . . In recent criminal law theory, however, some important criticisms have been made both of the framework of justification and excuse and of the capacity-based judgments of voluntariness which have structured debate about excuses. Let me mention just three relevant difficulties. Firstly, it can be argued that the rigid distinctions between judgments of wrongdoing and attributions of responsibility, between acts and actors implied by the distinction between justification and excuse is conceptually and practically fragile. This is primarily because many of the judgments made in the application of both offence definitions and defences are what might be called contextual judgments. In other words, they assess, label, and grade the relevant conduct in an integrated way such that the wrongfulness of the conduct cannot be understood independently of the attitude of the actor. In this sense, though criminal law's judgments are sometimes focussed more clearly on conduct than on agent and vice versa, they are typically engaged in assessing conduct in an 'agent-relative' way.

Secondly, questions have been raised about this framework's location of excuses within a generally capacity-based approach to criminal responsibility: the essence of an excuse, for example, is that it in some sense affects the genuine capacities of the agent to conform her conduct to legal proscriptions. This appears to raise the spectre of determinism. If it can be argued that our actions are either generally causally determined or, more modestly, significantly influenced by environmental factors in a much wider range of cases than is generally, acknowledged by the defences—in cases of extreme social deprivation, for example—then the normal basis for criminal law's judgments and distinctions seem to be precarious.

Thirdly, the capacity-based approach arguably asks criminal courts to make assessments which pose serious practical difficulties: assessments of the genuine capacities, choices, and opportunities of the defendant. The difficulty inherent in such assessments is illustrated by the unevenness with which expert testimony is used on cases, for example, of diminished responsibility and provocation, and by the difficulty which courts find in assessing such evidence. Furthermore, it may be argued that this practically problematic focus on issues of subjective capacity lends to criminal legal judgement a false air of empiricism, directing attention away from the substantive evolution of 'fairness', which is being made (notably in the application of 'reasonableness' criteria) and failing to provide any analysis or rationaliza-tion of that evaluation.

2. The reasons view

Emerging from these criticisms of the first approach, several writers have been developing a different approach which responds persuasively to some of these difficulties and which turns out to be particularly suggestive of the analysis of the partial defences to murder. Writers within this second tradition typically either reject the justification/excuse distinction altogether or regard it as of secondary importance in criminal law. For on this second, 'reasons-based' view, the rationale of defences, whether focused on act, actor, or agent-relative conduct, is to provide for a more sensitive evaluation of the defendant's conduct than is generally captured in offence definitions alone. Hence motive—generally argued to be irrelevant to the definition of offence elements on the capacity view, and acknowledged only as relevant to the specification of certain defences—becomes a central focus on the reasons view.

Another relatively frequent feature of this strand of thinking—which finds its deepest roots in Aristotelian philosophy but which may also be traced to the ideas of philosophers as different as Spinoza and Hume—is its drawing of a distinction between 'exemptions' and 'exculpatory defences'. Exemptions such as insanity and diminished responsibility mark out subjects who are beyond the purview of criminal law's proscriptions and other communica-tions. In contrast, defences such as duress, self-defence, or (perhaps) provocation mark out subjects who have—according to different versions of the theory—acted on reasons which are approved as within the range which would be expected of a normal, socially responsible person, or acted in a way which manifests no disposition to resist or violate the norms or values protected by criminal law.

The evaluation of the defendant's reasons includes, crucially, an evaluation of the emotions which motivated his or her conduct: these emotions are seen not merely as psychological facts but as things about which human beings can be expected to reason. Our emotions, and the ways in which we act upon them, are seen as basic constituents of our character, and this character, *as manifested in our conduct*, is seen—in stark contrast to the capacity approach—as being a proper object of the judgment of a criminal court. Indeed, the defences are seen as importantly concerned with the specification of positively and negatively evaluated emotions, and this in turn opens up an important space for what we might call an immanent critique of the defences: do they, for example, respond even-handedly to the mitigating influence of outrage, fear, self-preservation, panic, despair and so on? This feature of its argument means that the reasons view provides an illuminating perspective on recent debates about the elimination of defences such as provocation, duress, and self-defence.

. . .

One controversial feature of this view of defences is that it implies—indeed, not infrequently, it claims explicitly—that courts are essentially engaged in making evaluation judgments which relate to assessments not so much of the defendant's capacities but of her character. It is important, however, to be clear about the very specific sense in which the reasons approach relates to character. The focus, crucially, is upon the quality of the attitude manifested in the defendant's conduct, evaluated in the light of (a generous interpretation of) the context in which it occurred. It is not, therefore, a globalised evaluation of the person's character; rather it is an evaluative judgment which is *analogous* to the contextualized evaluation of character found in moral discourse. A defendant whose conduct is based on reasons which are thought to be consistent with the attitudes required of good citizens will be exonerated, while one who departs from those standards is seen as justifiably condemned notwithstanding any inquiry into whether she had the capacity to behave in—for example—a less hot-blooded or cowardly way. At an explanatory level, the reasons approach offers one way of rationalizing the widespread application of 'reasonableness' standards in the specification of defences.

We will now consider the capacity and character theories in greater detail.

18.1 THE CAPACITY THEORY

What is it?

The starting point for the capacity theory is that 'a person is not to be blamed for what he has done if he could not help doing it'.[264] In other words it is appropriate to punish only a person who is responsible for his actions.[265] Defences, then, should be available where the defendant lacked a fair opportunity to choose to act otherwise. Michael Moore[266] has argued that the emphasis within the capacity theory on choice and the ability to choose reflects wider attitudes within our society. People regard the ability to choose as an important freedom. We would resent any attempt by the state to restrict our choice on how to live our lives. We want to have our choices respected. Moore argues that it flows from this that we should respect people's bad choices, and that involves making people responsible for them.

---

[264] Hart (1968: 174). For a discussion of the implications of such an approach see Smith and Wilson (1993).
[265] Dressler (1988a: 701).   [266] M. Moore (1999).

Problems with the capacity theory[267]

The following are some of the problems that have been identified with the capacity theory:

(1) A common complaint about the capacity theory is that the consideration of whether the defendant freely chose to commit the crime is too narrow. For example, arguments that the defendant committed the crime as a result of socio-economic pressures will not be countenanced by the court. There is evidence that people in certain socio-economic groups or from particular backgrounds are more likely to commit offences than others. Of course, this does not prove that, for example, being poor causes someone to commit crime. But it does indicate that, at least in statistical terms, people do not start on a level playing field as regards the likelihood that they will commit crime.

(2) Another complaint made about the capacity theory is that in focusing on choice it does not take into account a wide enough range of factors in assessing the defendant's blameworthiness. Other relevant factors, for example, the emotion which led to the defendant acting in the way she did, are irrelevant for the capacity theory.[268] From the point of view of the capacity theory the person who freely chooses to kill his relative in order to end the pain the relative is suffering from the terminal illness is treated in the same way as a person who kills the relative in order to gain an inheritance. The 'choice' element is the same in both. Yet, it is claimed, a proper assessment of the defendant's blameworthiness would regard the two cases as quite different.

(3) John Gardner[269] suggests that the capacity theory is misleading. By asking, for example, in a duress case where the defendant unreasonably gave in to the threat, whether the defendant had the capacity to act more bravely is misconceived. If it is concluded that the defendant was as brave as he could be, then that is a reason for blame—not excuse. He should not be such a cowardly person.

18.2 THE CHARACTER THEORY

What is it?

The character theory assesses criminal liability on the basis of the extent to which the defendant's actions have displayed good or bad character.[270] As Glover has put it, 'to blame a person for an action is more than merely to say that he has brought about something we object to. We disapprove, not merely of the action or its consequences, but of him.'[271] Applying the theory to defences, a defence arises to rebut an inference from the causing of harm to a bad character trait.

The benefits of the character theory are said to be that it enables the law to undertake a sensitive assessment of the defendant's culpability.[272] Its supporters argue that it enables the law to take a wider range of factors than simply the element of choice, which is the focus of the capacity theory.

---

[267] Some of the problems with the capacity theory in relation to *mens rea* were discussed in Ch. 3.

[268] Reilly (1998).   [269] J. Gardner (1998b).

[270] See especially Fletcher (1978: ch. 10); Nozick (1981); Bayles (1982); Lacey (1988a); Arenella (1990); Mousourakis (1998a).

[271] Glover (1970: 64).

[272] See Mousourakis (1998a) for an argument that the character theory can explain some, but not all, defences.

Problems with the character theory

The following are some of the problems that have been identified with the choice theory:

(1) The character theory assumes that people are responsible for their characters. If you disagree with that controversial assumption[273] then the character theory loses its attraction.[274] There may be a temptation for the character theorist to reply that we are responsible for our character because we choose to be the kind of people we are.[275] However, such an argument is in danger of reducing the character theory to a version of the choice theory.

(2) One problem which critics are keen to point to is the difficulty for the character theory of actions which are 'out of character'. Imagine Gwen has worked as a cashier for a company for twenty years. She daily handles large sums of money and has always done so honestly, except on a single occasion when she took a small sum. Do we conclude that Gwen has a dishonest character and should be guilty of theft? Or rather that the fact she has worked for so long without taking money demonstrates her honesty, and the one lapse is 'out of character' and she should therefore have a defence?[276] Duff argues that such a person has shown a character flaw.[277] An honest person would *always* resist the temptation to be dishonest.[278]

(3) Why do we look only to criminal actions to decide whether or not the defendant has exhibited a criminal trait?[279] If everyone who knew a man was willing to state he was a dishonest person, even though he had never actually committed an offence, why, under the character theory, can you not convict such a person? Character theorists could rely on two possible responses:

   (i) Anthony Duff[280] argues that you cannot claim to have a certain characteristic unless you act in a way that reveals that characteristic.[281] You cannot claim to be a brave person unless you have acted at least once in a brave way. In the same way you cannot exhibit a criminal character trait unless you have acted at least once in that criminal way. So although in your private life you may have shown yourself to be a dishonest person unless you act in a criminally dishonest way you have not shown yourself to be dishonest *in a criminal way*.[282]

   (ii) George Fletcher,[283] defending the character theory, replies that an important principle of privacy comes into play to prevent the conviction of a person with a criminally inclined character who has yet to act in a criminal way.

---

[273] See Lelling (1998) for one psychological perspective.

[274] Vuoso (1987).   [275] M. Moore (1998: ch. 6).

[276] e.g. a person who has been kidnapped and 'brainwashed' by his kidnappers into joining their criminal gang.

[277] Duff (1993).

[278] Even dishonest people regularly resist the temptation to be dishonest. This leads to a further difficulty for character theorists. How can one act reveal a character through a single action? Some character theorists suggest that a person is responsible only for stable character traits (Bayles (1982)), but others reject such a requirement (Horder (1993a)).

[279] Brudner (1987).   [280] Duff (1993).   [281] See also J. Gardner (1998b).

[282] Even this may be not be a complete answer: a defendant could be examined by psychiatrists and found to be predisposed to commit criminal acts, even though he is yet to commit any. Should not the character theory be willing to convict such a person because 'we know' he has a criminal character?

[283] Fletcher (1976: 799–802).

Differences between the character and capacity theories

In many situations the character and capacity theories would provide a defence in similar situations. A defendant who lacks the opportunity to comply with the law is not exhibiting bad character. However, there are two categories of cases where the theories may disagree:

(1) Imagine a person who commits a crime while overcome with anger or hatred so that he loses control of himself. It might be thought that the two theories would deal with these in different ways. A character theorist would have little problem in stating there is no defence because killing when overcome with hatred exhibits bad character. The case is perhaps harder for the capacity theorist. Can such a person claim he did not freely choose to act as he did and given his personality (e.g. being particularly short-tempered) he did not have a fair opportunity to act otherwise?

(2) Imagine a person who has had an exemplary life and is widely recognized by his community to be a considerate and kind person. One day his wife is killed in a tragic accident, he drinks too much, and hits a barman. He has never in the past behaved in this way. The choice theorist would have little difficulty in convicting him of an assault. The character theorist has more problems here. In the light of his exemplary behaviour and the unusual circumstances of the assault can we say that his action reflects a character trait? Is not this kind of conduct simply out of character? The temptation is to say that any chosen behaviour is 'in character' (even if an aspect of the person's character we are yet to see) but this becomes very close to the choice theory.

Some commentators have argued that there is no effective difference between the choice and character theories.[284] Take duress. When successful the choice theorists say that there was no meaningful choice made to commit the crime. But how do they decide that a person has not exercised a meaningful choice? Inevitably an important issue is the gravity of the threat. A person facing a dire threat has less freedom of choice than a person facing a minor threat. However, the argument goes, then the questions whether the choice was genuine and whether the choice was one which reflects badly on the defendant's character merge together.

FURTHER READING

Bayles, M. (1982), 'Character, Purpose and Criminal Responsibility', *Law and Philosophy* 1: 5.

Duff, A. (1993), 'Choice, Character and Criminal Liability', *Law and Philosophy* 12: 345.

Duff, R. (2003), 'Virtue, Vice, and Criminal Liability: Do We Want an Aristotelian Criminal Law?', *Buffalo Criminal Law Review* 6: 147

Horder, J. (1993a), 'Criminal Culpability: The Possibility of General Theory', *Law and Philosophy* 12: 193.

Lacey, N. (1988), *State Punishment* (London: Routledge).

Moore, M. (1997), *Placing Blame* (Oxford: OUP).

Tadros, V. (2005), *Criminal Responsibility* (Oxford: OUP).

---

[284] Duff (1993).

19 DETERMINISM

Determinism is the theory that all our actions are determined by factors outside our control. There are many different forms of determinism, ranging from the view that all our actions are predetermined by God, to a view that we are genetically predetermined to do all we do.[285] If determinism is correct, it produces real problems for both the capacity and character theories, and indeed the blaming function of the criminal law.[286] If our actions are predetermined how can we blame people for the 'choices' they make? If our characters are a result of our genes to what extent can we hold people responsible for their characters?

The truth or otherwise of determinism is not known.[287] Perhaps the predominant view is that even if our actions are to a large extent affected by genetic, social, environmental,[288] and other factors outside our control we still have an element of control over our actions.[289] Indeed our society is based on the assumption that we have free will. If we were all predetermined to do what we do our society would be a very different one. Many organizations and people, not least government, spend much time and effort in trying to persuade people to change (or not to change) their behaviour (e.g. advertising). All such activities would be pointless if our actions were predetermined.

A key question, then, is, accepting that to some extent our actions are affected by genetic, social, and economic factors, is the impact of those factors sufficient to justify providing a defence? After all there is evidence that those from deprived social backgrounds are more likely to commit offences than those who are better off. This has led some commentators to argue for a defence of 'rotten social background'.[290] In the following passage Norrie criticizes the law for being willing to accept some kinds of arguments that a defendant acted involuntarily, but not others:

A. Norrie, *Crime, Reason and History* (London: Butterworths, 2002), 171–3

We saw [earlier in his book] that one of the claims to legitimacy made on behalf of criminal law is that it respects and does justice to individuals by punishing them only for their voluntary acts. In the language of retributive philosophy, the individual brings punishment upon himself by the acts he voluntarily undertakes. There are, however, directly political as well as ideological limits to this respect for individuals. The political limits are seen in the ambivalence of the judiciary towards the necessity defence and the about-turn on the application of the duress defence in murder cases. Individual justice confronts political utility in both situations, with the latter imposing limits on the former. The judges shift in these situations from their position as guardians of a logic of individual right to that of being, in Glanville Williams's term (1983, 144), a 'State instrumentality'.

More deeply, there is an ideological limitation on the claim of individual justice which is implicit in Vining's observation (above, Chapter 1) that the law does not know real individuals at all, only abstract images of the individual which populate our thought in the stead of real

---

[285] Wells (1998).   [286] Kelman (1981); Norrie (2000); Kenny (1978).
[287] Ainsworth (2000).   [288] Bazelon (1976).
[289] Aristotle, Nicomachean Ethics Book III, ch. 5; Wolf (1991); Dennett (1984).
[290] Delgado (1985); Bazelon (1976).

human beings. The criminal law's currency of judgment is that of a set of lowest common denominators. All human beings perform conscious acts and do so intentionally. That much is true, and there is logic in the law's denial of responsibility to those who, because of mental illness or other similar factor, lack voluntariness (narrowly conceived) or intentionality. But such an approach misses the social context that makes individual life possible, and by which individual actions are, save in situations of actual cognitive or volitional breakdown, mediated and conditioned. There is no getting away from our existence in families, neighbourhoods, environments, social classes and politics. It is these contexts that deal us the cards which we play more or less effectively. Human beings, it is true, are not reducible to the contexts within which they operate, but nor are they or their actions intelligible without them. This basic truth of the duality of human life, as both individual and social (Norrie, 1996, 2000), is ignored by a practice and philosophy of legal judgment in which context is always regarded as extrinsic to agency. Even where it is admitted, it is as a secondary and exceptional phenomenon added on to the judgment of conduct 'from the outside'. The law focuses its attention on an isolated homunculus, an individual without past or future, a solitary atom capable of acts and intentions and responsible for them. Even if he cannot choose a particular act, he can choose a previous act which takes its place.

A striking illustration comes from the United States. The major cities there have been gripped by an epidemic of drug abuse, which acts as the seedbed of a great volume of crime (including many 'orthodox' duress situations brought about by gang war). The response of the authorities is to erode civil liberties and to convict large numbers of young people in the inner-city areas. This in turn leads to more and worse violence, as in the Los Angeles riots of 1992. As one economist points out, however, the real backdrop to this criminal inflation is the decline in the social and economic infrastructure in the inner city areas, and what this means for 'choice':

'Revisiting Watts nearly a generation after a famous pioneering study of its problems, UCLA industrial relations economist Paul Bullock discovered that conditions had grown far worse since 1965. At the core of community despair was endemic youth unemployment. Bullock observed that the only rational option open to youth—at least in the neo-classical sense of individual economic choice—was to sell drugs. Indeed as power resources in the community have generally declined, ghetto youth, refusing simply to become "expendable", have regrouped around the one social organisation that seems to give them clout: the street gang.' (Davies with Ruddick, 1988, 51–2)

There is a social world 'out there' which rarely finds its way into the courtroom. If judges are concerned about 'charters for terrorists, gangleaders and kidnappers', these are not simply the product of wicked individuals exploiting the law. They are the product of structural and systemic forces, which the law with its individualist focus ignores?

The significance of the duress and necessity defences is that they begin to open up this otherwise hidden world *within legal discourse*. Such situations are in one sense highly unusual and idiosyncratic. They involve a kind of threat that most will never experience. But the fear that stems from such situations is qualitatively no different from a range of other fears which may be equally efficacious for the 'ordinary reasonable man'. These include, in Williams' account, 'fear of economic ills, fear of displeasing others, or any other determinant of choice'. Whether it be a gangleader, someone using violence for political ends, convicts threatening a prisoner with homosexual rape (Vandervort, 1987, 212–13), people stealing out of hunger or breaking into property because they are homeless, or simply living life in 'the ghetto' with no legitimate options, the contexts are all clearly social, and not easily differenti-able. It is this which gives Lord Simon's argument in *Lynch* its cogency when he argues that the law ought to ignore the constraining context of duress, but in so doing, he must deny the concept of individual justice in its extended morally involuntary form.

Imagine a newspaper picture of a major social event such as a riot in which a mass of people stand on a street and throw stones at another group of people (a police force, an army, an opposing group). The picture is in sharp detail and shows the faces and bodily postures of those concerned. Along with the picture goes the kind of standard text of the better newspapers which explains the sequence of events that occurred, and then proceeds to analyse those events in terms of a series of causes and effects of which they are a part. On another page in the same newspaper is an editorial column which addresses the political and social options and structures available to solve the problems of rioting. Now go back to the picture, draw a ring around one stone throwing individual and cut it out. That is effectively what the law does. It is only interested in *this* individual performing *these* acts *at this* time. Everything else, which gives what the individual did meaning, and without which he would not have acted, is irrelevant. But this is the way it has to be if responsibility is to be imputed purely and simply to the individual.

Legal individualism is one-sided and decontextualised, and this has crucial implications for our understanding of legal justice. For Hart (1968, 22), justice requires that the law 'adjusts the competing claims of human beings [by] treat[ing] all alike as persons by attaching special significance to human voluntary action'. There is at the same time more and less truth in this than Hart realises. The law does indeed treat 'all alike as persons', for it is only by decon-textualising individual actions that the multifarious real differences between individuals in society can be ignored. It is only in terms of an abstract category of legal personhood that human beings who are essentially different in terms of background and biography can be treated as the same. Similarly, the law does indeed attach a 'special significance to human voluntary action': the capacity to be at fault for acting in social contexts that are not of one's making. This ideological process of decontextualisation, as we have seen, is deeply political, for it enables fault attribution to take place while silencing the opposing political and ideological reasons that individuals would give for their actions if they could. Necessity and duress are significant precisely because they push at the line between context and agency. In Chapter 6 (p 114), it was argued that the law permits these defences as a kind of safety valve or sealed box to take the pressure off the narrow paradigm of physical involuntari-ness with which it standard operates. We have seen, however, how the law seeks to limit the size and content of this box, lest when opening the lid, it turn out to be veritably Pandora's.

QUESTIONS

1. If we are all predetermined is there any point discussing whether determinism is correct or not because you are predetermined to accept or reject the theory of determinism? You are also predetermined to get whatever mark you will get in your criminal law examination, so why revise?

2. If we accept Norrie's argument with what do we replace the current criminal law?

FURTHER READING

Dershowitz, A. (1994), *The Abuse Excuse and Other Cop-Outs, Sob Stories, and Evasions of Responsibility* (Boston, Mass.: Little, Brown).

Horder, J. (1996), 'Criminal Law: Between Determinism, Liberalism and Criminal Justice', *Current Legal Problems* 96.

Westen, P. (2005), 'Getting the Fly Out of the Bottle: The False Problem of Free Will and Determinism', *Buffalo Criminal Law Review* 8: 599

Williams, B. (1997), 'Moral Responsibility and Political Freedom', *Cambridge Law Journal* 56: 96.

20 THE REJECTION OF AN OVERARCHING THEORY

It should not be thought that every commentator agrees that the kinds of analysis we have been undertaking are useful. Many commentators take the view that it is only useful to consider each defence individually and that any attempt to find some kind of overarching theme explaining the law on defences is not possible and will be unduly restraining. In the following passage Victor Tadros, responding to an article by John Gardner,[291] rejects an argument that all excuses can be classified under the choice or character theory:

V. Tadros, 'The Characters of Excuses' (2001) 21 *Oxford Journal of Legal Studies* 495 at 495–6 and 517–19

Two theories of excuses are currently popular in criminal law theory: the character theory and the capacity theory. In the former, the claim that the defendant makes is 'although I did it, I wasn't really myself. In the latter, the claim is 'I did it but I couldn't have done otherwise. I had no real choice'. For me, both of these claims might, in appropriate circumstances, provide the defendant with an excuse. Neither is exhaustive of the field of excuses and there is no single unifying theory of excuses.

In 'The Gist of Excuses' John Gardner argues that neither of the above claims provides an adequate excuse to absolve the defendant from liability or to mitigate the offence. Independently of the character and capacity that she displays in her action, the character and capacity of the agent plays no role in excusing the defendant from liability for the act that she has performed. The first alternative Gardner calls the 'Humean' view. In that view, the gist of excuses runs as follows: an excuse will be available to the defendant to the extent that her action was no manifestation of her character. This view, Gardner thinks, is untenable. The actions of the defendant constitute rather than evidence her character. Hence, the difference between the character displayed in the action and the character of the agent cannot be drawn. That the character of the agent at the time at which she performed the action (t) was different from her settled character, that the action was 'out of character', may be a reason for mercy. But it is no excuse.

The second alternative Gardner calls the 'Kantian' view. In this view, the gist of excuses runs as follows: an excuse will be available to the defendant insofar as she did all that was within her capacity to do to conform to the law. If the defendant could not have done more to conform her behaviour to the requirements of the criminal law, she ought to be excused. For the criminal law punishes us for the wrongful choices that we make and, in such cases, the defendant had no choice. Against this view, Gardner argues that the capacity that D has to act virtuously at *t* is also no more and no less than the virtue that D has at time t. And this is because one cannot have the capacity associated with a particular virtue whilst at the same time lacking the tendency to be virtuous. Consequently, he continues, the standard

---

apparently to be applied to the agent 'does reduce straightforwardly to the standard of purely predictive expectation, the standard of character which those making the excuse already meet'.

Finally, Gardner argues, even if it is possible to draw a distinction between the standards of character displayed in a particular action and the capacity that the agent has to behave with better character than that, no good grounds for an excuse are provided. The reason, Gardner thinks, is that one's lack of capacity to behave with good character provides no excuse at all. To plead that no more can be expected of one because one possesses some character flaw is no excuse. To those that attempt to claim such an excuse, the reply that is open to us is that such an agent ought not to have had the character flaw that their action displayed; they ought to have lived up to the expectations that we have of those performing the particular role that they are performing, be it friend, soldier, doctor or simply human being. This, for Gardner, provides the 'gist of excuses'. The gist of excuses is that, although the action was wrong, it was also one that came up to the standard of reasonableness for the particular role that the agent was playing. Hence, in contrast to his analysis of *mens rea*. Gardner thinks that excuses can be analysed under a single theory.

In my view, Gardner's gist of excuses, whilst acceptable in itself, is too narrow to provide a complete theory of excuses. The theory might provide one of the characters of excuse, but it does not have universal application. . . .

I have defended two ways in which the character and the capacity of the accused to behave otherwise might have relevance in the realm of excuses beyond of the character and capacity manifested in the particular act performed. These excuses are grounded entirely differently. In the first kind of excuse the defendant claims the following: although I behaved wrongly, I was in a state where my actions did not reflect my settled character. And I was either not responsible for or justified in being in that state. In short, I did it but I was really *not myself*, and for good reason. In the second kind of excuse the defendant claims that, due to some reprehensible characteristic, but a characteristic that is not rightly a target of the criminal law, she could not have done otherwise. It was *really me*, the defendant admits, but I performed the action because of a characteristic which isn't worthy of the kind of blame that is particular to criminal liability.

These are only two of the ways in which an excuse could operate. There are others. . . .

There are many characters of excuse for wrongful action. Some excuses go to questions of reasonableness, some to questions of character, some to questions of capacity and some to questions of situation. There is no single conceptual foundation for these excuses and consequently no obvious restriction on the characters of excuse that might be regarded as acceptable in the criminal law. For this reason it is unlikely that any 'gist' of excuses can be sketched. At best, we can say that excuses in the criminal law ought to be sensitive to the central targets of criminal liability: to questions of character, capacity, the rule of law, the central vices that are the targets of criminal liability and the like. If the claim of the defendant calls into question one or more of these supervisory principles, that seems to me to be sufficient grounds for at least a partial excuse. To exclude questions of capacity and character of the defendant restricts unnecessarily the range of excuses that a defendant might give for her wrongful behaviour.

Contrast the following passage by William Wilson who suggests that all core defences can be fitted within one template.

William Wilson, 'The Structure of Criminal Defences' [2005] *Criminal Law Review* 108 at 111–13

The template common to all core defences is that in the face of an external prompt the actor reacted in such a way as to permit the usual inference to be blocked that he is a person of an anti-social character usually implicit in the fact that he has infringed a legal prohibition. The external prompt performs two key functions. First, it provides criminal excuses with their moral and political validation. It is only in response to crisis that it is plausible to claim that our actions are not authentically ours or, if authentically ours, nevertheless not indicative of censurable indifference to the interests of others. With defences in which the reasonableness of the defendant's reaction is the central claim the external prompt helps to provide moral focus for the claim that the actor's response was excusable, it being of a nature to afford citizens good reason to believe it is justified or excusable to act otherwise than in accordance with the primary norm.

The second element in the standard defence template is a requirement that the defendant's conduct be by way of reaction to the external prompt. It applies both to defences of reasonable reaction and to defences of impaired voluntariness serving to ensure moral and evidential focus to the defendant's claim that he did no wrong (e.g. self-defence) or that the wrong of which he stands accused is not attributable to him (e.g. automatism). And it supplies an objective referent which tailors the relevant defence to the needs of a norm enforcement system. It is not enough simply that the prompt occurred and the defendant acted in a way which might be expected of people subjected to such prompt, nor even that it rendered compliance less easy. In each case a functional relationship between the crime committed and the external prompt is required. With provocation the actor kills because he is provoked, not simply because he loses his temper, or has reason, perhaps compelling reason, to do so. So provocation was not available where the accused, having suspected his wife of infidelity and having decided to kill her, tracked her and, finding her in bed with her lover, killed them both. Provocation, like automatism, is surely a human frailty defence if ever there was one. Killing, even in justified anger, is the antithesis of reasonableness. Killing is the last thing we expect from reasonable people who nurse a justified sense of moral outrage against their cheating partners even were we to concede such a reaction to a battered spouse. Why else is it (relatively) so uncommon relative to the prompt?

More plausibly, provocation is a rare example of an out-of-character defence. Human beings are not paragons of virtue and sometimes our frailty as human beings subverts our reasonableness. The reasonably-to-be-expected-reaction element is to be explained, therefore, as a function of the aberrant nature of the response. If the context is so extreme that the reasonable person might have done likewise why should we doubt that it was anything but a truly one-off? Sometimes reasonable people act against their settled inclinations, but it takes circumstances of extreme stress to provoke such a response. The very plausible reason why a claim that conduct is out of character is not generally exculpatory but is here is that, under conditions of extreme provocation, it is recognised that the most equable temperament can be found wanting. The human psyche is disposed to 'flip' but there are no overarching moral or psychological markers for such an outcome to be objectively 'normal'. If overreacting to objectively provoking behaviour is a sign of a vicious character it is the kind of vicious character to which any ordinary person may have to own up. We cannot expect human beings with the constitutional weaknesses of ordinary human beings always to measure up in times of extreme stress and it would be inappropriate for the state not to recognise this fact.

21 INSANITY

21.1 PROBLEMS WITH THE PRESENT LAW

The position and treatment of mentally disordered people are problematic for society in many areas, not just the criminal law.[292] There are delicate balances to be made between protecting the interests of the mentally disordered person, his carers, and the interests of the wider community.[293] The popular media in particular have portrayed mentally ill people as dangerous. But consider these two findings:

(1) Gunn and Taylor point out that the risk of being killed by a serious mentally ill patient is 'small'. The risk that a mentally ill person will commit suicide is about 100 times greater.[294]

(2) In a study by Norval Morris[295] (1982) a cohort of mentally disordered people with a range of mental illnesses had no greater incidence of criminal offending than a same-sized cohort of people randomly selected from the community. In fact he found that males aged between 14 and 22 from deprived inner-city areas had a far higher incidence of offending behaviour than the mentally disordered group.[296]

Such statements inevitably raise the question whether our society is more concerned with protecting the lives of the sane than the insane. The question is especially pertinent, given the distressingly high number of prisoners in normal prisons who suffer mental illness and are not getting the medical treatment they need.[297]

The difficulties in finding the appropriate response of the criminal law to mental abnormalities include the following:

(1) One issue which may be thought significant is: did the defendant commit the crime because of his mental illness or would he have committed the offence even if he had not suffered from his illness.[298] Unfortunately this kind of question is extremely difficult to answer.[299] As Daniel Robinson puts it, neither neurology nor psychiatry has any 'magic lantern to light up the concealed corners of a defendant's mind'.[300]

(2) It is all too easy to merge the questions: should the defendant be convicted of a criminal offence and should the defendant be detained in order to receive compulsory treatment.[301] There the argument that 'the pubic need to be protected from dangerous people' pressures the law to ensure the detention of mentally ill people even if 'technically' they have not committed an offence. Also there are those who say 'we need to offer treatment to those who are mentally ill', again pressurizing the system to facilitate the detention of the mentally ill, even if no offence has been committed.[302]

(3) There has been much debate over which definition of insanity the court should use. The starting point of the dispute is the source of the definition. Is it a question of medical expertise? A legal issue? Or should insanity be given its 'ordinary meaning', as

---

[292] Mason and Mercer (1999).

[293] Home Office (1999c) discusses the government's proposals regarding 'dangerous' people.

[294] Gunn and Taylor (1993: 335).   [295] Morris (1982).   [296] Bowden (1996).

[297] Home Office (1987); Simpson (1976); Gray, Laing, and Noaks (2002).

[298] Gross (1979).   [299] D. Robinson (1996).   [300] D. Robinson (1996: 237). See also Morse (1996).

[301] Gostin (1986); Gray, Laing, and Noaks (2002).   [302] See Home Office (1999c).

understood by members of the public?[303] At present the legal definition of insanity is different from the medical one. This means that doctors giving evidence have the difficulty of matching the medical diagnoses with the legal terminology used. There is always the fear (or hope?) that doctors will manipulate the legal terminology to reach what in medical terms would be the 'right' result.

(4) Why should someone who is insane receive any special treatment under the law? An immediate answer may be that an insane person will lack the *mens rea* required for an offence, but if this is so he can rely on the defence of 'no *mens rea*' and will not require a special defence of insanity. Michael Moore justified the defence of insanity by arguing that the criminal law is addressed to those who are rational and have the capacity to comply with its rules.[304] A mentally ill person, lacking the capacity to comply with the rules of the law, is exempt from its requirements. However, as mentioned above, deciding whether a mentally ill person could have avoided breaking the law is extremely difficult.[305]

In the following passage Victor Tadros summarizes his objections to the M'Naghten test for insanity

---

V. Tadros, *Criminal Responsibility* (Oxford: OUP, 2005), 347

I have shown that the M'Naghten Rules are both too broad and too narrow. The rules are too broad because they suggest that *any* failure to appreciate the nature and quality of the act or that it was wrong will be sufficient to undermine responsibility. This fails to recognise the possibility that the defendant is fully responsible for his cognitive or evaluative failure. If the defendant has made a cognitive or evaluative error, it is only where the defendant's cognition or evaluation is radically detached from his background beliefs and values that he ought to be entitled to an excuse.

They are too narrow for three reasons. Firstly, they do not provide a defence for those who lack the autonomy to develop coherent and independent lives in general. They fail to appreciate that there may be defendants who understand the nature and quality of the act that they perform, but whose general capacities are sufficiently lacking that they do not have status-responsibility at all. Such defendants ought to be provided with an exemption. . . .

Secondly, the Rules fail to understand the significance of time for responsibility. They fail to appreciate that there may be defendants who have undergone personality change such that the beliefs and desires that they have are not reflective of their settled character. Such defendants may have all of the capacities of a healthy defendant at the time at which the action is performed, but they lack responsibility for their actions on the grounds that when the action was performed *they were not really themselves*.

Thirdly, the Rules do not include a volitional limb. They fail to appreciate that there may be defendants whose desires are radically detached from their system of beliefs and values in such a way that does not reflect on them *qua* agent. If those desires are sufficiently strong that an agent of good character would not be capable of resisting the desire, the defendant ought to be provided with a defence. In short, the argument that I am pressing is that the M'Naghten Rules have two overly broad limbs where there ought to be five narrower limbs to mental disorder defences.

---

[303] D. Robinson (1996). e.g. Morse (1985) suggests directing the jury to consider whether the defendant was 'crazy'.

[304] Moore (1997: ch. 2). See also Bonnie (1983).   [305] Slobogin (2000).

21.2 REFORM OF THE PRESENT LAW

It is unacceptable that epileptics,[306] diabetics,[307] or sleepwalkers[308] are labelled insane when no one with medical expertise would accept that description. In fact the term 'insanity' is not used in this area by medical professionals who prefer to use terms such as mental illness or mental disorder. Further the distinction between external and internal factors, upon which the law's approach places a great deal of weight, can produce arbitrary distinctions. It is not surprising therefore that there have been many calls for reform of the law on insanity.[309] Three contrasting approaches will be examined here:

Abolishing the insanity defence

There are some who have argued that the insanity defence should be abolished. Although this might sound like a surprising suggestion, several American writers have made this argument. Two arguments have been relied upon and will now be mentioned:

(1) The insane defendant should be able to rely on exactly the same defences as a sane defendant.[310] For example, if an insane person lacks *mens rea* he should be not guilty for that reason. If he believes God is telling him to commit a crime or else he will be struck by a thunderbolt he can plead duress. In other words there should be no special defence for insanity. The argument here is that if an insane person lacks the *mens rea* for a crime or has a defence, then like any other citizen he deserves to be acquitted.[311] His sanity becomes simply irrelevant. It should be added that this argument is not seeking to deal with the question of civil detention of those suffering mental illness. So an insane person who commits a crime unaware of what he is doing should be acquitted of a criminal offence but could be required to undergo compulsory treatment under civil law.[312] Those who reject this argument may point to strict liability offences or negligence-based offences where the insane person would (under this proposal) have no defence.

(2) An extreme view, most notably promoted by Thomas Szasz, is that mental illness is a fiction, a convenient myth created by the mentally ill and those who care for them.[313] Szasz argues that 'mental illness' is a form of survival mechanism which people use to cope with life. Few accept his thesis nowadays, especially now that mental illnesses are far more clearly defined than they were when he was writing. However, it is hard to deny his claim that the line between mental illness, eccentricity, and 'normality' is hard to draw. Maybe his thesis would have found greater support if he had claimed that everyone was insane, rather than claiming that everyone was sane! Certainly it is not difficult to find evidence of people classified as 'insane' who in fact should not have been.[314] Further, there is concerning evidence that the rate of mental illness correlates strongly with social and economic circumstances.[315]

---

[306] *Sullivan* [1984] 1 AC 156.   [307] *Hennesy* [1989] 1 WLR 287.   [308] *Burgess* [1991] 2 QB 92.
[309] It is notable that very few defendants seek to rely on the defence of insanity. One study found that from 1975 to 1988 there were only 49 verdicts of 'not guilty by reason of insanity'. In the five years after the Criminal Procedures (Insanity) Act 1991 there were 44 findings of 'not guilty by reason of insanity': Mackay (1990) and Mackay and Kearns (1999).
[310] Morris (1982); Slobogin (2000).   [311] Szasz (1970).   [312] Goldstein (1967).
[313] Szasz (1970).   [314] Rosenhan (1973).   [315] Hill (1983).

Updating the definition of insanity

The Law Commission has proposed the following 'modern' definition of insanity:

Law Commission Report No. 177, *Draft Criminal Code Bill* (London: HMSO, 1989) Clauses 34–40

35. (1) A mental disorder verdict shall be returned if the defendant is proved to have committed an offence but it is proved on the balance of probabilities (whether by the prosecution or by the defendant) that he was at the time suffering from severe mental illness or severe mental handicap.

(2) Subsection (1) does not apply if the court or jury is satisfied beyond reasonable doubt that the offence was not attributable to the severe mental illness or severe mental handicap.

(3) A court or jury shall not, for the purposes of a verdict under subsection (1), find that the defendant was suffering from severe mental illness or severe mental handicap unless two medical practitioners approved for the purposes of section 12 of the Mental Health Act 1983 as having special experience in the diagnosis or treatment of mental disorder have given evidence that he was so suffering.

(4) Subsection (1), so far as it relates to severe mental handicap, does not apply to an offence under section 106(1), 107 or 108 (sexual relations with the mentally handicapped).

34. In this Act—
'mental disorder' means—

(a) severe mental illness; or

(b) a state of arrested or incomplete development of mind; or

(c) a state of automatism (not resulting only from intoxication) which is a feature of a disorder, whether organic or functional and whether continuing or recurring, that may cause a similar state on another occasion;

'return a mental disorder verdict' means—

(a) in relation to trial on indictment, return a verdict that the defendant is not guilty on evidence of mental disorder; and

(b) in relation to summary trial, dismiss the information on evidence of mental disorder;

'severe mental illness' means a mental illness which has one or more of the following characteristics—

(a) lasting impairment of intellectual functions shown by failure of memory, orientation, comprehension and learning capacity;

(b) lasting alteration of mood of such degree as to give rise to delusional appraisal of the defendant's situation, his past or his future, or that of others, or lack of any appraisal;

(c) delusional beliefs, persecutory, jealous or grandiose;

(d) abnormal perceptions associated with delusional misinterpretation of events;

(e) thinking so disordered as to prevent reasonable appraisal of the defendant's situation or reasonable communication with others;

'severe mental handicap' means a state of arrested or incomplete development of mind which includes severe impairment of intelligence and social functioning.

Widening the scope of the insanity defence

In the following passage Peter Arenella argues that it is not only those suffering from mental illness who lack moral responsibility for their actions:

P. Arenella, 'Convicting the Morally Blameless: Reassessing the Relationship between Legal and Moral Accountability' (1992) 39 *University of California at Los Angeles Law Review* 1511

This essay seeks to reclaim the concept of moral agency from classical moral theory and demonstrate why it is a logically and conceptually prior moral blaming condition to that of fair attribution. It does so by attempting to show why the most persuasive conception of a moral agent's necessary attributes cannot be derived solely from an account of the conditions of knowledge, reason, and control that must be satisfied before we can fairly attribute culpable conduct to the actor.

To support this thesis, this essay relies on moral theory and moral psychology to articulate a normative, *character-based* conception of moral agency that reflects our best considered judgments within the liberal paradigm about what it means to be a moral decision maker and what attributes someone must possess to qualify as a morally accountable actor. I will argue that even a threshold conception of moral agency—one suitable for the minimal moral norms implicated by *mala in se* crimes—must include the following character-based attributes: the capacity to care for the interests of other human beings; the internalization of others' normative expectations, including self-identification as a participant in the community's blaming practices; the ability to engage in moral evaluation of one's character and acts, the capacity to respond to moral norms as a motivation for one's choices; and the power to control those firmly entrenched aspects of character that impair one's ability to act in accordance with one's moral judgments. These character-based moral agency attributes presuppose a far more robust account of knowledge, rationality, and control than that required by the criminal law's rational choice conception of moral agency.

By deriving its account of moral agency from its account of the fair attribution condition, the criminal law's conduct-attribution model of moral responsibility starts backwards and offers an incomplete account of when individuals deserve moral blame for their crime. Consequently, the criminal law does not always honor its promise to exempt the morally blameless from criminal liability. It permits the conviction of some offenders who should not qualify as morally accountable actors even though their wrongful conduct is fairly attributed to them.

. . .

Our accounts of *moral* evil presuppose that the wrongdoer has the capacity for moral concern, judgment, and action. We view moral evil as a corruption of this moral potential. Our p-r ['participant-reactive'] attitudes of resentment and blame rest on such presuppositions. We find it difficult to sustain our initial reaction of blame towards an actor who has breached some moral norm when we come to believe that the actor, through no fault of her own, lacked these moral capacities. We blame people not just for morally bad acts, but for the morally objectionable attitudes that (we believe) the actor conveyed through such behavior. But the liberal model of moral responsibility insists that we should not blame someone for failing to show moral concern for the interests of others if the actor is incapable of feeling such concern or acting on its basis.

What enables us to be moral actors who can understand the moral norms implicated by the criminal law? What *threshold* capacities do we need before we are able to use these norms in our practical judgments? . . . I have argued that a moral agent must possess the following character-based abilities and attributes: the capacity to care for the interests of other human beings, the internalization of others' normative expectations (including self-identification as a participant in a culture's moral blaming practices), the possession of p-r attitudes concerning one's own and others' characters and acts, the ability to subject one's non-moral ends and values to moral evaluation, the capacity to respond to moral norms as a motivation for one's choices, and the power to manage those firmly entrenched aspects of character that impair one's ability to make an appropriate moral evaluation of the situation one is in and the choices open to one.

None of these attributes are properties, skills, or capacities whose development is totally a matter of our own responsible choices. Some of them can only develop through time and appropriate interpersonal relations and experiences with adults who nurture us. A child cannot develop the character-management skills listed above until she develops her character, becomes aware of its nature, and learns how to manage those aspects of it that can motivate the wrong types of choices.

As this passage indicates, the drawing of lines between sanity and insanity is far from straightforward. The difficulty is that once courts embark on a consideration of the moral capacity of each defendant cases will take an impractically long time.

FURTHER READING

Bonnie, R. (1993b), 'The Moral Basis of the Insanity Defence', *American Bar Association Journal* 69: 194.

Duff, R.A. (1986), *Trials and Punishments* (Oxford: OUP).

Howard, H. (2003), 'Reform of the Insanity Defence: Theoretical Issues', *Journal of Criminal Law* 67: 51.

Mitchell, E. (2003), *Self-Made Madness* (London: Avebury).

Moore, M. (1997), *Placing Blame* (Oxford: OUP), ch. 12.

Morris, N. (1969), *Madness and the Criminal Law* (Chicago, Ill.: University of Chicago Press).

Morse, S. (1994), 'Culpability and Control', *University of Pennsylvania Law Review* 142: 1587.

Scottish Law Commission (2003), *Discussion Paper on Insanity and Diminished Responsibility* (Edinburgh: The Stationery Office).

Tadros, V. (2001b), 'Insanity and the Capacity for Criminal Responsibility', *Edinburgh Law Review* 5: 325.

22 PRIVATE DEFENCE

22.1 THE MORAL BASIS OF PRIVATE DEFENCE

Why should the criminal law provide a defence to those who use force in order to protect themselves or others from an attack? This is a question which has troubled many lawyers and ethicists. Here are some of the most popular answers.

The forfeiture theory

The forfeiture theory states that by posing a threat to someone the victim (V) has forfeited his right not to have violence used against him. As Hugo Bedau put it, '[the wrongdoer] no longer merits our consideration, any more than an insect or a stone does'.[316] Suzanne Uniacke has developed perhaps the most sophisticated defence of this approach. She explains that a person's right to life or freedom from violence is conditional upon that person not posing a threat to other people. By posing a threat the person forfeits those rights.[317] Although very popular, this theory is not without its critics whose arguments include:

(1) How does the theory explain that once the threat ceases V cannot be killed? So if V has hit D and then runs off the law is clear that D cannot then shoot V. But why not if V has forfeited his or her right to be killed? Uniacke sees no difficulty with this. She claims that once the threat is no longer posed the victim reacquires the right to life. There will, though, be an ambiguous point in time (when the threat is diminishing, but still present) where there may be a legitimate argument about whether or not the right exists.

(2) How can you say a child or insane person forfeits his right by posing a threat? Although the forfeiture theory may have some appeal in saying that a person who chooses to try and kill another chooses to forfeit his right to life, can we say the same if they are children or insane and do not know what they are doing? Supporters of the forfeiture theory divide when faced with this question. Some reply that a right can be forfeited by your actions (in posing the threat) even if you are not morally responsible for your actions. This argument, that a blameless person can forfeit his rights, is controversial. Other supporters of the forfeiture theory accept that the theory has no application where the attackers are innocent. Instead they rely on an alternative theory to deal with such cases. For example, in the innocent attacker case we are faced with two innocent parties, one of whom is going to suffer pain. The recipient of the attack may legitimately prefer his own welfare over that of his equally innocent attacker. But if D is approached by five children all carrying machine guns, unaware of their dangerous nature, can D kill all five children?[318] It is difficult to justify such killing apart from referring to a right to defend yourself, or a theory of forfeiture.

(3) How does the forfeiture requirement explain the proportionality requirement? If I am attacked does my attacker lose all his rights and therefore I have the right to kill him? Supporters of the forfeiture theory reply that on posing a threat to another the attacker loses the right not to have force proportionate to the threatened force used against him. So if I make as if to slap you I do not lose my right to life, but do lose my right not to have moderate force used against me.

Harder for supporters of the forfeiture theory is this: if V tries to kill D and thereby forfeits V's right to life can D kill V in a particularly brutal way? For example if V pulls out a gun and points it at D, if proportionate and necessary D could shoot V to save his life. But if D has two alternatives means of stopping the attack: by shooting V or throwing into V's face acid which will slowly and painfully kill V most

---

[316] Bedau (1968: 570).   [317] Uniacke (1994: ch. 1). See also Jarvis Thomson (1991).
[318] Alexander (1999) discusses this scenario further.

commentators take the view that D must kill in the least painful way. But under the forfeiture theory V has lost his right to life and so D can choose.

Autonomy arguments for self-defence

An alternative theory in support of self-defence focuses not on V and his loss of rights (as the forfeiture theory does) but on D and his right to defend himself.[319] Supporters of such a view argue that it is part of your rights of autonomy that you can defend yourself from an unjust attack.[320] The difficulty with this argument is that it does not make it clear why self-defence is available only in the face of an unjust threat.

In the following passage Sholmit Wallerstein summarises her objections to some of the popular theories supporting self-defence and proposes her own theory based on 'forced consequences'.

S. Wallerstein, 'Justifying the Right to Self-Defense: A Theory of Forced Consequences' (2005) *Virginia Law Review* 91: 999 at 1032–4

The right to self-defense is a derivative right that originates from the core right not to be killed; the purpose of self-defense is to defend this core right. In this Essay I have attempted to find the moral foundations for this right. I have referred to three contemporary theories. Some theorists hold that the moral foundation of self-defense is found in the lesser harmful results of the defensive response. This position entails balancing the interests of the aggressor with those of the defender, taking into consideration the fault of the aggressor as the one who created the threat. In response to criticism, there has been a shift away from showing that in any specific case the killing of the aggressor is a lesser harmful result, and towards referring to the overall beneficial consequences of recognizing the right to self-defense—most importantly, the reassurance to society and the deterrence it provides against aggressive acts. But this modification still leaves the lesser harmful results theory both too strong and too weak—too strong because if it is taken seriously it ought to permit the use of force even when it is unnecessary or disproportionate, and too weak because it is still dependent on the marginal gains achieved by a recognition of the right.

Other theorists justify self-preference by reference to forced choice. One strand of this school of thought uses forced choice as the basis for a justification of a particular distribution of harm rooted in considerations of justice. One consideration is the general fault-based selection principle: The aggressor is alone responsible for forcing the defender into a position in which he must make a choice between lives. A second consideration is present aggression, which creates a moral asymmetry: Because the aggressor can retreat, but the defender cannot, the aggressor cannot disassociate himself from his actions. The second strand of this school of thought advances the idea of forced choice as an excuse. Self-defense is permitted as a necessary response where there is no 'real choice' but to use defensive force. Ryan develops a variation of this view by comparing self-defense to duress.

---

[319] One way of explaining the defence is that it is the responsibility of the state to protect its citizens from violence. If the state is unable to protect the citizen (because there is an imminent attack) then the citizen is able to intervene and use force. See e.g. Dressler (2002a).

[320] Nourse (2001) has distinguished between what she calls the pacifist position, with its focus on the right to life of the victim and stressing requirements of proportionality and necessity, with the libertarian view which focuses on the defendant's right of autonomy.

Both strands are subject to criticism: the second for counter-intuitively explaining self-defense only as an excuse rather than a justification, and the first for giving a limited justification which permits, on its own, only the killing of culpable aggressors. Even when combined with the second strand of excuse, forced choice as a justification fails to distinguish between the justified killing of innocent aggressors and the unjustified killing of innocent bystanders.

A third position—the most common among contemporary theorists—bases the justification for self-defense on some variation of a rights theory. They trace the right to self-defense back to a core right not to be killed, and ground self-defense in the prevailing core right of the defender over that of the aggressor. The various accounts are based on the relationship between one's rights and the duties these rights impose on others. These theories, however, face a substantial difficulty: they need to overcome the problem of forfeiture that they necessarily entail, while providing a justification that does not depend on a prior stance or belief as to whether self-defense is justified under the circumstances (and thus become circular). Instead, a comprehensive and non-circular theory should serve as a guide to deciding which situations are covered by the right to self-defense.

I have examined two possible responses to this problem. The first recognizes a non-absolute right that is dependent on the actions of its owner. The second is to recognize an absolute right of limited scope, the limitation being either factual or moral. The advantage of the second method is its response to the problems of forfeiture. A proper specification would limit the scope of the right so as to exclude all (and only) those situations in which presumably the right is forfeited. It also allows for humanity to be the only precondition of a right, which should not depend on human conduct. Indeed, the first method is rejected for not overcoming the problem of self-preference.

Using the second method, theorists try to develop a careful moral specification that would avoid circularity and set the basis for the asymmetry between the aggressor and the defender. Uniacke suggests that a moral specification is founded on an objective fact, namely, the causal responsibility of the unjust immediate threat. Meanwhile, Rodin holds that the basis for moral specification is the aggressor's fault. I reject the underlying assumption of both justifications, which is that the right not to be killed has a limited scope. Instead, I find support for my position in two consequences of any limited-scope justification. First, in cases of self-defense, a limited-scope justification provides an awkward explanation for the existence of a requirement of proportionality to a threat of injury that does not involve killing. Second, such a justification offers an insufficient explanation for the situations of defenders who use force against their aggressors for reasons other than self-defense.

Given the difficulties found in the various theories, I suggested a different justification based on forced consequences. Consistent with my position that both sides have an absolute unconditional and unqualified right not to be killed, I argued that the right to self-defense is based on other considerations. The justification combines two separate explanations that respond to two distinct situations. In cases of intentional aggressors I adopted the justification strand advanced by the forced choice theory, finding that the side at fault should pay. However, as this justification by itself cannot explain why innocent aggressors also trigger the right to self-defense and why they should be distinguished from bystanders, I offered a distinct justification for the right to self-defense in instances involving innocent aggressors. Given that it is either the aggressor or the defender who would have to pay the costs of the aggressor's bad luck, the aggressor must be the one to pay it. This justification is by definition limited to the latter situation only, and distinguishes between non-culpable and non-agent aggressors on the one hand and bystanders on the other.

The talk of a right to self-defense does not have to limit our inquiry to rights theories alone. On the contrary, rights theories would bring us to a dead-end if the right not to be killed is indeed, as I have argued, an absolute right. The justification for the right to self-defense has to be found elsewhere, in other moral principles that we employ in various fields of life. I hold that an appeal to what I call 'forced consequences' provides a coherent justification of the right to self-defense.

22.2 MISTAKEN PRIVATE DEFENCE

It will be recalled from Part I that under English and Welsh law a defendant who mistakenly believes that he is being attacked can rely on private defence. But why is this? The leading case on the topic was *Beckford*, which focused on the decision of the House of Lords in *Morgan* that unlawfulness is an element of all crimes of violence. As the *mens rea* of a crime must relate to all aspects of the *actus reus* the defendant must intend or be reckless as to the unlawfulness. Therefore, if the person believes the state of affairs to be such that he would have a defence to any criminal charge he lacks the intent or recklessness as to the unlawfulness part of the *actus reus*. Therefore, if a person believed he was acting in self-defence, even if that was based on an unreasonable mistake, he must be acquitted. The validity of this argument is considered by Andrew Simester in the following extract:

A.P. Simester, 'Mistakes in Defences' (1992) 12 *Oxford Journal of Legal Studies* 295

Is an Alteration Desirable?

Finally, it is not at all obvious that a change in the operation of supervening defences is warranted. The most important recent argument for permitting defences such as self-defence to be mounted upon unreasonable mistakes is that made by Horder. In his view,

'[Negligence] is not culpable where the urgent desire in question was of a kind which ethically well-disposed agents might themselves have experienced as dictating that immediate priority be given to the kind of action in satisfaction of the desire that the defendants took, and not to action based on rational considerations.'

Horder thinks that emotions such as fear and compassion are not embraced by orthodox objectivism, and argues that they should be permitted on occasions to displace an actor's rational considerations. In the context of the present law, I have two objections.

First, Horder's theory simply does not accord with the law after either *Morgan* or *Beckford*. For one thing, and whether or not it ought, the law does not allow emotions a free rein in conduct. In cases of provocation we put the reasonable man in jail. Compassion does not entitle one to kill another, even if that other consents. In addition, whereas Horder's model considers that the defendants in *Morgan* should have been convicted even if their mistake were genuine, the majority in the House of Lords made it quite clear that had the defendants really believed that their victim was consenting—however unreasonably—then they would have been acquitted. *Williams* and *Beckford* support this view.

Second, Horder has not done negligence justice. As we noted earlier, he analyses orthodox objectivism as asking whether:

'Even if defendants did not know that there was a risk of wrongdoing occurring as a result of their conduct, were there facts from which they could reasonably have inferred that the risk was present?'

But the objectivist asks another question: in the circumstances, was it reasonable to run that risk? Although a detailed discussion is inappropriate here, it is submitted that Horder has allowed the 'reasonable man' too little sophistication. We usually excuse a prima-facie 'negligent' mistake because it was not unreasonable in the circumstances. To broadly sketch the reasonable man, when we test negligence we generally evaluate a defendant's actions in the light of (i) certain assimilated perceptions and (ii) moral values. The set of perceptions is taken to be that which a reasonable person (with the physical features of the defendant) would have assimilated in those circumstances. The set of moral values is taken to be that of the community; it *includes* the values of compassion and self-preservation. Although the evaluation of acts by a reasonable man is a cogitative process, in each case it must operate given those values and on the defendant's particular circumstances. This is why, as Bernard Williams notes, it is sometimes reasonable to act precipitously. Cogitatively, when one perceives peril, one might conclude that further enquiry into other considerations is unreasonable in the circumstances. The law recognizes emergencies: in *Cordas* v *Peerless Transportation Co*, the defendant was excused since he had acted when confronted by the prospect that he 'would suffer the loss of his brains'. Contrary to Horder's surmise, the legal test of reasonableness is not 'judged from the rational perspective of the cold light of day'. The 'argument from logic', when the logic is correctly understood (as it was in *Morgan*) does not lead to a one-dimensional analysis: when Horder suggests that the negligence above 'is not culpable', he misses completely the point that it is not negligence at all. So much for the argument that negligence cannot encompass emotions or allow for emergencies. Glanville Williams has an alternative line of attack: that it is illogical, or at least 'intellectually incongruous', to require mistakes as to defences to be reasonable where we do not require the same of mistakes as to offensive elements. Williams argues that there is no sensible distinction between person A who shoots his wife, believing her to be a rabbit, and person B who shoots his wife thinking she is a burglar about to attack. But I think that there is a distinction, and that this is why it is meaningful to speak of a prima-facie offence. My killing another person is prima–facie wrongful, and I know that I ought to be very sure of having good reasons for doing so before I embark upon such a course of action. It is quite a different matter when what I think I am doing is not prima-facie wrongful: need no reasons for my conduct. For this reason Glanville Williams' comparison seems to me a poor analogy. Moreover, it is for this reason that the decisions in *Morgan* and *Albert* v *Lavin* are logically consistent.

It is worth noting that the distinction made here also disposes of the traditional arguments against punishment for negligence. Turner and Hall, for instance, have argued that punishment is morally unjustified unless a defendant 'has in his mind the idea of harm to someone'. But even if one accepts such a proposition, it is irrelevant to mistakes supporting defences. Williams' person B has precisely that idea in his mind, and his case is thus quite different from that of person A.

Williams is not done yet. Even if negligence is a flexible standard, which can logically be demanded of mistakes as to defences but not offences, Williams asks why should we make such a demand?

'[I]t is not murder to shoot and kill another by negligence, however gross. But if a person kills another in the convinced but mistaken and unreasonable belief that he himself is about to be killed by the other, he is theoretically guilty of murder, even though on the facts as he believed them to be he would not have been guilty of any crime. Is this not a harsh rule?'

In other words, granted that there is a logical distinction, is there a sufficient moral one? Before responding to this question, we should consider another proposition implicit in

Williams' stance. He clearly assumes that there is a moral difference between (for example) intentional commission of the *actus reus, simpliciter,* and intentional commission of the *actus reus* accompanied by a negligent mistake. Although Williams does not argue it explicitly, the existence of such a distinction is an obvious reason for not requiring defences to be reasonably perceived. Indeed, the difference seems to me grounds for allowing a palliative defence to prima-facie murder, reducing a conviction to manslaughter and a discretionary sentence. But unlike homicide, other *actus rei* are not regulated by variously severe offences, and it is not realistic to argue that they should be—especially since sentences other than for murder are not mandatory. In these cases unreasonable mistakes in defence must be either irrelevant or a complete defence.

We return to Williams' question. It is rhetorical, and the answer is cursorily assumed in *Williams* and in *Beckford*. But it is submitted that negligent mistakes denying *mens rea are* morally different from those claimed in defence. Moreover, and while an opposing position might be argued for seriously (rather than assumed), in my view there is sufficient moral difference to deny that it is unduly harsh to convict in the latter but not the former instance. Here I plainly disagree with Williams, and I think this is in part due to Williams' lenient view of the defendant's deed:

'If the defendant, believing that he has to act urgently in self-defence, kills or wounds a person who is completely innocent, this must be accounted a tragic accident, and it is pointless to punish for it.'

Indeed, Williams views this case *more* leniently than he does negligence *simpliciter.*

'It would be perfectly possible, and would indeed be rational and proper, to say that even if negligently hitting someone is an offence, a person who believes he is being attacked is entitled to act on that belief, whether the belief is negligent or not.'

It is true that policy considerations in the two cases are different, but in my view policy and morality militate in the direction opposite to that suggested by Williams. The reason for this is grounded in the logical distinction I made earlier. A defendant who relies upon a supervening defence knowingly commits a prima-facie offence. In the words of Lord Diplock, and unlike the case where he is unaware that he is committing the *actus reus* at all, '[t]here is nothing unreasonable in requiring a citizen to take reasonable care to ascertain the facts relevant to his avoiding doing a prohibited act'. By contrast with a person (A) who is inadvertently negligent, a defendant (B) who performs the *actus reus* inadvertently recognizes that he is inflicting harm, and knows that his actions require justification. This distinction underlies our requirement of B, but not of, that his mistakes be reasonable. Effectively (and unlike A) B is asserting a liberty, based upon circumstances, to inflict harm knowingly: it does not seem too much to ask for reasonable ascertainment of such circumstances.

If one rationale for *Caldwell* was to strike a better balance between the interests of the attacker and the victim, it is even more relevant here where the offender is aware of the mischief. The law has an important role to play in maintaining community standards, and the words of Lord Simon remain apposite:

'It would hardly seem just to fob off a victim of a savage assault with such comfort as he could derive from knowing that his injury was caused by a belief, however absurd, that he was about to attack the accused.'

Consider also the contention (endorsed by Horder) that negligent rape should be a crime. A rationale for this contention is that what the negligent 'rapist' does advertently is so close to rape that he has good reason to be on his guard; thus the law should acquit for only reasonable mistakes as to consent. It is submitted that the prima-facie offender also has good reason to guard against mistakes. Indeed, he has better reason than the negligent 'rapist': what he does advertently seems obviously closer to an offence than sexual intercourse *simpliciter*.

One must presume of *Beckford* that the Privy Council was not influenced to manipulate law by the apparently unsatisfactory evidence. In that case, the victim was an unarmed man who had his hands in the air and was saying 'don't shoot me'. He was deliberately shot three times. It is hard to regard this as merely a 'tragic accident'. Nevertheless, the accused then claimed a totally unreasonable belief that he was being fired upon, and walked from his appeal a free man.

FURTHER READING

Ashworth, A. (1975), 'Self-Defence and the Right to Life', *Cambridge Law Journal* 36: 272.

Christopher, R. (1998), 'Self-Defense and Objectivity', *Buffalo Criminal Law Review* 1: 537.

Horder, J. (1995b), 'Redrawing the Boundaries of Self-defence', *Modern Law Review* 58: 431.

Lee, C. (1998), 'The Act–Belief Distinction in Self-defense Doctrine: A New Dual Requirement Theory of Justification', *Buffalo Criminal Law Review* 2: 191.

Schopp, R. (1998), *Justification Defences and Just Convictions* (Cambridge: Cambridge University Press).

Segev, R. (2005), 'Fairness, Responsibility and Self-Defense', *Santa Clara Law Review* 45: 383.

Uniacke, S. (1994), *Permissible Killing* (Cambridge: Cambridge University Press).

Wallerstein, S. (2005), 'Justifying the Right to Self-Defense: A Theory of Forced Consequences' (2005) *Virginia Law Review* 91: 999

23 DURESS

There is much debate over the proper basis of the defence of duress. We will look at five possibilities:

(1) The 'no choice' model. This model argues that a defendant in the face of a threat of death or serious injury suffers such panic that he or she is incapable of rational thought. Duress in this model appears to be almost a form of temporary insanity.[321] Opponents of this approach argue that the law must consider whether the defendant ought to have found this such a difficult choice. If David is told that unless he injures his sister his collection of pornography will be burnt and David is so terrified that his beloved pornography collection will be destroyed that he is not able to think clearly and so injures his sister, should he have a defence? Surely not. Accepting that people can act impulsively in a panic, David should not have got into such a panic. This dilemma should not have been a difficult one for him.[322]

(2) The 'lack of choice' model. Here it is said that even though the defendant may have

---

[321] e.g. Widgery LJ in *Hudson and Taylor* [1971] 2 QB 202 (CA). The use of such terminology was rejected in *DPP for Northern Ireland v Lynch* [1975] AC 653, 679 (HL) per Lord Wilberforce.

[322] For an argument along these lines see Morse (1994).

been able carefully to consider the options before choosing to commit a crime he should not be responsible for his choice.[323] As the capacity theory would have it he did not have a fair opportunity to choose to do otherwise.[324]

(3) The 'character' model. The character model suggests that when acting under duress the defendant's behaviour does not reveal a bad character.[325] The model focuses on the appropriateness of the choice the defendant made: was it one which a morally good agent could make? It might be that the defendant made the morally correct choice (e.g. she committed a minor parking offence, to escape from a threat of death) or it was the wrong choice, but bearing in mind that even morally well-disposed agents are affected by panic and fear it is one such an agent might have made and so it does not reflect bad character on his part.[326]

(4) Justification. Here the claim is that duress is a defence where the defendant made a morally permissible choice.[327] As the choice need be only permissible this means that the defendant will be justified if the harm he is required to commit is the same as[328] or less than the harm threatened.

(5) 'No *mens rea*' model.[329] This view is that the defendant did not intend to harm the victim, but rather his purpose was to avoid the threat being carried out.[330] The defendant in a duress case therefore can claim not to have the *mens rea* necessary for an intent-based offence.

Although much has been written in support of these different theories it should be remembered that it is quite possible that more than one of these theories is correct. For example, it could be argued that some defendants who successfully plead duress have a defence on the basis that their choice was justified, and others on the basis that their state of mind was such they were not responsible for that choice.[331]

The view one takes on the correct basis for the defence affects many of the controversial aspects of the definition of the offence.[332] For example, in relation to the debate over which characteristics of the accused should be attributable to the reasonable person test if you take the justification view then you would not want any characteristics of the accused to affect the degree of bravery expected. However, Duff, supporting the character theory, suggests[333] 'we should ascribe to the reasonable person any of the defendant's actual characteristics that affected her response to the threat, *other than* characteristics which involve either some lack of reasonable regard for the law and its values, or a lack of reasonable courage'.

In the following passage Anthony Duff considers some of these explanations for the defence of duress:

R.A. Duff, 'Rule-Violations and Wrongdoings' in S. Shute and A. Simester (eds.), *Criminal Law Theory* (Oxford: OUP, 2002), 63–6

Consider duress, which (as a criminal defence) is standardly portrayed as an excuse. If we take 'acting under duress' to mean something like 'acting under a human threat', this is

---

[323] M. Moore (1987: 1148).   [324] M. Moore (1999).   [325] Richards (1987).
[326] See the discussion in Horder (1994a); Alexander (1999).
[327] Wertheimer (1987), discussed by Honoré (1990).   [328] Wertheimer (1987: 204).
[329] *Paquette* (1997) 70 DLR (3d) 129 (Sup Ct of Canada).
[330] See Ch. 3, Part II, for a discussion of the different forms of *mens rea*.
[331] e.g. Herring (2005b: 391).   [332] K. Smith (1989).   [333] Duff (1996).

surely wrong: some actions under duress are (morally and should be legally) justified by that duress. A bank clerk who hands over £10,000 of the bank's money at gun-point, or a hostage who drives a stolen car at gun-point, commits what would, absent that threat, be a wrong, but should be neither blamed nor convicted if the threat was sufficiently serious and believable: not because she has an excuse, but because in that context her action is not wrong (it is not morally wrong, and should not count as criminal)—because it is justified. We might indeed sometimes commend such an agent for doing 'the right thing' in that situation, and for being clear-headed enough to see what she should do; we might think that it would have been rash or stupid, rather than heroic or courageous, to resist. In other cases we might not commend the action or admire its agent, but would at least think that giving in as this person did was not wrong—that it was morally (and so should be legally) acceptable or permissible, even if not commendable. In either case, however, there is no wrong committed by that agent for which an excuse is needed (though there is of course a wrong committed by the person who made the threat).

This might seem too hasty. It might be argued that to allow duress to justify a normally criminal action would be to permit 'the abrogation of law in the face of threats'; or that this would permit third parties to assist the person under duress to commit the crime, or forbid others to resist the crime; none of which the law should do. But, first, neither we nor the law should require bank clerks to resist robbers at the likely cost of their own lives: they should be permitted (even expected) to hand over the money at gun-point (neither is this to abrogate the law in the face of threats—the law focuses on the threatener). Secondly, even if justifications have the implications claimed by Fletcher and Robinson, I would think it right for another person to assist the bank clerk in giving over the money, and wrong for another to resist that giving over, *unless* that third party could effectively neutralize the threat.

Those who insist that 'duress' is an excuse, however, need not be denying any of this: they could rather be arguing that we should reserve the term 'duress' for cases in which the agent acts unjustifiably, or wrongly, under the influence of a threat, and locate cases of justified action under threat in some other legal category of justification (such as necessity, in so far as that can be a justification). Duress would then count as an excuse, in so far as it provides a defence at all. But what kind of excuse is it?

Sometimes, duress does operate rather like insanity as an excuse. Suppose that someone is subjected to torture to force him to reveal secret information, and finally gives in, in pain and terror, to avoid further agony; or he is subjected to an immediate threat which is so terrifying that he is completely panicked by it, and does what he is told to do. His conduct is not strictly involuntary (if it were, he would not be doing what he must do to avert the threat); it is indeed at least minimally intentional, in that he acts as he does in order to avert the threat. But, in excusing him, we would say that the torture or the threat rendered him incapable of rational practical thought, of ordered as opposed to disordered practical reasoning: his giving in did not display a lack of commitment to the values violated by his action; as far as we know, and as his own later response to what he has done should reveal, he has a proper concern for those values; but the pressure to which he was subjected seriously impaired his capacity to guide his own actions in the light of that commitment. We wish, and he wishes, that he could have resisted (giving in was not justified): but he could not—his 'will' was 'overborne'. Even in this kind of case, duress as an excuse is not grounded in a purely factual claim that 'he could not resist' the threat. The figure of the 'reasonable person', the 'sober person of reasonable firmness', should still play a normative and criterial (as distinct from evidential) role: for we should ask whether a person with the kind of commitment to the values protected by the law (and violated by this action), and with the kind and degree of courage that we can properly demand of citizens, would have been thus affected by such a threat—i.e. whether his being thus affected did or did not reveal a lack of such commitment or courage.

In such cases, we can certainly say that the defence of duress does not provide reasons which could properly guide the agent's actions: if he reasons to himself 'if I am so terrified by a threat that I cannot think straight, the law allows me to give in; I am thus terrified by this threat; so I'll give in', his reasoning undercuts the very claim on which he wants to rely. We can also say, with two qualifications, that we can no longer properly 'attribute' the action, or the wrong, to the agent: the action or wrong (betraying his country) is not properly 'his' as a responsible agent, because he was non-culpably rendered incapable of guiding his actions in the light of what we can suppose to be his own proper commitments.

(The qualifications are, first, that we would not expect someone who had such proper commitments simply to disown the action as something that happened to him: he has still betrayed his country, and we would expect that to matter to him. Secondly, is not clear that the wrong which we do not attribute to him is just the same wrong as we attribute to someone who culpably, without duress, betrays his country; this point will become clearer shortly.)

However, other cases of duress are more problematic. It seems implausible, for instance, that the defendants in *Hudson and Taylor*, who committed perjury under threat of serious injury, were so panicked by the threat that they were rendered incapable of rational thought and action; and implausible to claim that only threats which have such an effect should provide a complete defence, as distinct from mere mitigation of sentence. The exculpatory claim in such cases is, rather, that to have resisted such a threat would have required a kind or degree of 'firmness'—of courage, of commitment to the values at stake in the situation—which we cannot reasonably expect or demand of a citizen; that is, that in giving in to a threat to which even a person of 'reasonable firmness' would have given in, the agent did not display a culpable *lack* of commitment or of courage.

In *this* kind of case we can say that the agent is excused because she 'lived up to' the 'standards of character which were demanded of' her; or because she 'attained . . . society's legitimate expectation of moral strength'. Such claims might sound like justifications rather than excuses—as claiming not, admittedly, that her action was positively right or admirable (resistance would have been the admirable course), but at least that it was permissible: but they need not be justificatory. As Dressler and Gardner explain the defence, its point seems to be analogous to a defence of 'reasonable mistake' (of fact): the agent's 'choice' to give in was 'deficient, but reasonable'; her fear of the threat was 'rationally adequate, in [her] own eyes as well as according to the applicable standards of character, for [her] to commit the wrong', but she 'mistakenly' acts for that reason. This implies that the agent must, at least at the time, *think* her action justifiable: that what excuses her is the reasonableness of that mistaken thought in that situation. That might be true in some cases: in others, however, the agent might realize that she should resist, but cannot bring herself to do so; she does not think her action justified, but is too weak, or lacking in courage, to act as she realizes she should. What excuses her is that the strength or courage required to resist such a threat is more than we can reasonably demand of a citizen: we should not demand that citizens be saints, but it would require a saint-like courage or firmness to resist.

This is not to say that the agent is 'permitted' not to resist (that is, justified in not resisting), or that she does no wrong in giving in—as if, as far as the law is concerned, it does not matter or is up to her whether she resists or not: she should ideally resist, and falls short of the ideal standards of commitment and courage in failing to resist. But what citizens should ideally do is more than we, or the law, can properly *demand* that they do, on pain of condemnation if they do not; and that is why, whilst we do not regard such an agent's action as justified, we excuse her.

In this kind of case, however, we cannot say that the agent is excused because the wrong that she did cannot be properly 'attributed' to her. There is *a* wrong that it would indeed be inaccurate or misleading to attribute to her simply and without qualification: 'committing perjury', insofar as that bare description implies by its silence that this was *the* relevant feature of her action. Her commission of perjury is a wrong which we might instead attribute to those who threatened her and thus brought her to commit perjury, but it is not the wrong that *she* did. What she did, the action we judge, was to 'commit perjury under threat of being seriously injured': we do not condemn her for that action because, although it was wrong in the sense that in committing it she fell short of the ideals (of commitment and courage) to which she should aspire as a citizen, she did not fall short of those standards which we can properly *demand* that citizens attain.

QUESTIONS

1. Lacey and Wells have argued 'the duress defence is designed to excuse people invested with characteristics which are strongly marked as masculine in our society'. Do you agree?

2. The defendant suffers a medical condition which means that he will die unless he takes certain tablets every two hours. He runs out of medicine and asks his doctor for some more. The doctor says he will give the medicine only if the defendant injures his wife, which he does. Can the defendant plead duress? (**N.B.** Is there a threat here, or an offer?)

FURTHER READING

Dressler, J. (1989), 'Exegesis of the Law of Duress: Justifying the Excuse and Searching for its Proper Limits', *Southern California Law Review* 62: 1331.

Duff, A. (2002), 'Rule-Violations and Wrongdoings' in S. Shute and A. Simester (eds.), *Criminal Law Theory* (Oxford: OUP).

Finkelstein, C. (2002b), 'Excuses and Dispositions in Criminal Law', *Buffalo Criminal Law Review* 6: 317.

Horder, J. (1994a), 'Occupying the Moral High Ground: The Law Commission on Duress', *Criminal Law Review* 334.

Norrie, A. (2001), *Crime, Reason and History* (2nd edn., London: Butterworths).

Weston, P., and Mangiafico, J. (2003), 'The Crimnal Defense of Duress: A Justification, Not an Excuse—and Why it Matters', *Buffalo Criminal Law Review* 8: 833.

24 NECESSITY

As mentioned in Part I, by 'necessity' in this book we mean a claim that the defendant did the lesser of two evils, although as such the defence is recognized by English and Welsh law only to a limited extent. The present law recognizes that necessity is available where the offence is committed which promotes the well-being of a 'victim' who is unable to consent. Such cases are based on the principle that if a person is unable to give consent, then others should treat him in a way which promotes his best interests. Such cases tend to be uncontroversial: few would deny that a doctor can operate on a person brought into a hospital unconscious after a car accident.[334]

The reluctance to accept a general 'lesser of two evils' necessity defence at first sight seems hard to justify: how can it be proper to punish someone whose act has caused more good than harm? The answer can be seen by considering an example: a doctor who kills one healthy patient and uses his organs to save three patients. The doctor could argue that killing one person to save three lives was the lesser of two evils, but very few people would regard his conduct as justified.

As the following extract by Simon Gardner demonstrates, there are not just practical difficulties with such a defence, but also political and theoretical ones.

S. Gardner, 'Direct Action and the Defence of Necessity' (2005) *Criminal Law Review* 371 at 379–82

The status of justificatory necessity as a matter of principle

. . .

The standard account of justificatory necessity depicts it as depending on a utilitarian assessment of the competing goods and harms. But making such an assessment is often, perhaps always, an ethically impossible exercise. Consider again *Re A (Children) (Conjoined Twins: Surgical Separation)*. In utilitarian terms, the question has to be: which involved the greater harm, killing Mary in order to save Josie, or allowing both to die? If one has to choose one, it may be hard not to choose the latter. But many, rejecting the medico-economic arguments adduced by Ward L.J., would regard the question as simply unanswerable, and not the less so for being addressed by judges. Or take *Jones*. A utilitarian assessment would require a decision not merely whether the coalition attack on Iraq was legal, but whether on balance it did good or harm; and, if harm, whether more or less harm than that involved in the acts allegedly done and planned by the accused at the airbase. We cannot expect judges to answer a question like that, and it would do no more than brush the difficulty under the carpet to leave it to be decided by the jury. As noted above, a utilitarian assessment does look more possible where human life and limb, or the interests of the state, are not at stake: say in the example given, where I break your £100 window to save my £200 chair from a fire. But to take a utilitarian approach even here is to disregard the value which I, and especially you, may subjectively attach to our property.

It is much more comfortable to think of necessity in terms of the vindication of rights. That is, I should have the defence if, committing what would otherwise be an offence, I act to vindicate a right that is recognised by the law but not otherwise reflected in the offence's definition, and that is superior to any right or interest that the offence exists to protect and that I injure by my action; and no less aggressive course of action (i.e. no course of action likewise calculated to vindicate the right, but less injurious of the rights and interests protected by the offence) was open to me.

Acceptance of this analysis does not destroy all space for an analysis in terms of 'best interests' or of utility. The 'best interests' doctrine will continue to operate in its own special niche. In the general run of necessity cases, an analysis focused on utility will remain viable where the two goods in question are sufficiently comparable. Perhaps the case of breaking a £100 window to save a £200 chair can be handled in this way after all, by suppressing the issue of the parties' subjective valuations as a luxury which cannot be allowed to obstruct

---

[334] Ashworth (1996: 190).

the defence's availability. But where the two goods are not properly comparable and so a utilitarian approach cannot work (as at any rate in cases involving human life and limb), an approach focused on rights will provide a more robust analytical tool.

For in principle, the attraction of the rights analysis is that rights are (one of their raisons d'etre is to be) justiciable, in a way that the all-things-considered balance of advantage is commonly not. It is true that in England, until recently, this attraction existed more in theory than in practice, as it was hard to say whether a right had the necessary quality of recognition by the law. But, without necessarily saying that the Human Rights Act 1998 is the sole means by which rights can be recognised by English law, the coming into force of that Act has certainly meant that this analysis of necessity in terms of rights should be much more capable of ready practical operation.

Say I ruin your coat when, there being no less aggressive alternative, I use it to save a child from drowning. My act should be seen as justified because it is necessary in order to vindicate the child's right to life under Art.2 of the European Convention on Human Rights (ECHR). Or say I 'spring' those terrorism suspects whose detention without trial in Belmarsh Prison was declared unlawful in *A (FC) v Secretary of State for the Home Department*, as infringing Arts 5 and 14 of the ECHR. If there was no less aggressive alternative way to vindicate the detainees' rights, my act should be seen as justified on that ground. On the other hand, if I liberate some laboratory animals so as to save them from vivisection, I have no justification of this kind, as the interest I am promoting is not one recognised as a right by the law: either under the ECHR or, it is suggested, otherwise.

Care will however be needed over the question whether no less aggressive course of action was open to the accused. There is unlikely to be difficulty on this ground with my using your coat to rescue the drowning child, but it may well upset my defence when I 'spring' the Belmarsh detainees. In circumstances not involving an emergency, it should commonly be right to say that quite considerable time should be given for less drastic approaches to be tried, before a self-help approach would be justified.

Necessity and direct action

This last point surely means that the rights analysis of necessity is unlikely often to justify offences committed by way of political direct action. Such offences would be held justified only once democratic approaches had been exhaustively tried and had failed. It is tempting to say that, in the nature of democratic politics, this time might be something approaching never. But recall that the analysis under discussion is about vindicating the rights of particular individuals. The effluxion of the individuals' lives may create a more pressing timetable.

Peter Glazebrook[335] has argued that it unjustifiable to support the 'lesser of two evils' in the circumstances of duress or self-defence, but not in other circumstances. Alan Norrie[336] picks up on this argument and points out that the existing defences are provided for the kinds of cases in which the more powerful people may find themselves (e.g. protecting themselves from mugging) but not in circumstances in which marginalized members of society are likely to find themselves (e.g. needing to steal food to escape hunger). Indeed an argument can be made that the 'rights' theory of necessity (referred to in Simon Gardner's passage excerpted above) lets society off too much. It means that money cannot be stolen from a very rich person in order to pay for a life-saving operation. It upholds and helps

---

[335] Glazebrook (1972).   [336] Norrie (2001).

maintain a society in which some people do not have enough money for the essentials of life and others have more than enough money. Jeremy Horder replies to such arguments by saying that even if this inequality is accepted as unjust the solution lies, not in allowing poor people to steal from rich people, but rather through reforming the taxation and social security systems. Indeed inequalities within society would be more fairly resolved through taxation and social security systems than through permitting the poor to steal (which would be likely to favour the strong or the devious). Horder,[337] however, recognizes that there are some emergencies where such political alternatives are not available. He gives the example of a person trapped in a freezing storm on a mountainside who comes across a log cabin. Horder suggests he should be permitted to break in. This kind of emergency is not one that Parliament could be expected to provide a political solution to. Nor is this cabin scenario a case with wider ramifications. The starving thief scenario gives rise to a number of complex questions: how starving do you have to be to be able to steal and how rich does a person have to be for it to be permissible to steal from him?

FURTHER READING

Brudner, A. (1987), 'A Theory of Necessity', *Oxford Journal of Legal Studies* 7: 338.

Freeman, M. (2001), 'Whose Life is it Anyway?', *Medical Law Review* 9: 259.

Harris, J. (2001), 'Human Being, Persons and Conjoined Twins', *Medical Law Review* 9: 221.

McEwan, J. (2001), 'Murder by Design: The "Feel-Good Factor" and the Criminal Law', *Medical Law Review* 9: 246.

Michalowski, S. (2002), 'Sanctity of Life—are Some Lives more Sacred than Others?', *Legal Studies* 22: 377.

Norrie, A. (2001), *Crime, Reason and History* (London: Butterworths), ch. 8.

Parry, J. (1999), 'The Virtue of Necessity: Reshaping Culpability and the Rule of Law', *Houston Law Review* 36: 397.

Rogers, J. (2001), 'Necessity, Private Defence and the Killing of Mary', *Criminal Law Review* 515.

Schopp, R. (1998), *Justification Defences and Just Convictions* (Cambridge: Cambridge University Press).

Sheldon, S., and Wilkinson, S. (2001), ' "On the Sharpest Horns of a Dilemma": *Re A (Conjoined Twins)*', *Medical Law Review* 201.

Uniacke, S. (2001), 'Was Mary's Death Murder?', *Medical Law Review* 9: 208.

Wilson, W. (2002), *Central Issues in Criminal Law Theory* (Oxford: Hart), ch. 10.

25 ISSUES WHICH FALL BETWEEN THE GAPS OF THE DEFENCES

We will now look at three controversial scenarios that do not fall neatly into any of the established defences.

---

[337] Horder (2000).

25.1 KINGSTON

The case of *Kingston*[338] has been controversial. It will be recalled that the House of Lords held that the defendant, who was involuntarily intoxicated, could still be convicted of an offence providing he has the necessary *mens rea*. The approach of the Court of Appeal, that a defendant who suffered a disinhibition caused by a stratagem of a third party, could have a defence, was rejected. Perhaps the most sophisticated support for providing *Kingston* with a defence comes from G.R. Sullivan:

G.R. Sullivan, 'Making Excuses' in A. Smith and G. Sullivan (eds.), *Harm and Culpability* (Oxford: OUP, 1996), 131–4

The Possibility of Excuse

How can it be said that a state of involuntary intoxication may give rise to a finding of blamelessness if it does not negate the mental element for the offence nor cause conduct to be compelled? If we take Hart's classic epitome of excusing conditions and ask whether Kingston lacked fair opportunity and capacity to conform his conduct to law, we arguably affirm, not refute, the decision of the House of Lords. The fact that his intoxication was involuntary presumptively engages the issue of fair opportunity. Yet a claim of lack of fair opportunity may be said to founder on the fact that D's conduct was at most merely disinhibited and in no sense compelled. Although self-restraint was made more difficult for D, he seemingly remained in possession of sufficient volitional and cognitive resources with which to conform his conduct to law.

The Court of Appeal's decision to excuse D in such circumstances has been plausibly castigated as unprincipled indulgence. Under that court's reasoning, D merely has to adduce evidence that his state of intoxication was involuntary. Unless that evidence is refuted, the prosecution is faced with the onerous task of proving the hypothesis that D, had he been sober, would have committed the offence with which he is charged. A claim that one would not have indulged in some reprehensible conduct but for a state of disinhibition induced by drink or drugs is inherently plausible. Moreover, Lord Taylor, in giving judgment for the Court of Appeal, remarked that involuntary intoxication should be a defence for all crimes of specific or basic intent. In coming to this conclusion, he invoked an analogy with the defence of duress. There is, however, little point of contact between the respective defences apart from the fact that the involuntary intoxication in *Kingston* arose from the machinations of a third party. Duress, of course, arises only for cases of awful dilemma—offend or be killed or seriously hurt—states of psychic compulsion. By contrast, a condition of intoxication falling short of automatism does not make for involuntary conduct, however loosely the term 'involuntary' is employed. Furthermore, duress is not available if the charge be murder. Although that limitation can be cogently criticized for confusing excuse with justification, granted its existence, to allow non-automatous involuntary intoxication as an excuse for all crimes would further undermine what coherence there is in the current provision of defences.

Lord Mustill was, with respect, correct in ruling that, taken by itself, a state of involuntary intoxication cannot excuse. In *Kingston*, *mens rea* was present and the conduct uncompelled. There was a powerful case to answer and, *pace* Lord Taylor, it was an insufficient response for D to maintain that he would not have so acted had he not been surreptitiously

---

[338] [1994] 3 All ER 353 (HL).

drugged. Many states of being—anger, apprehension, fatigue, etc.—may arise quite involuntarily and provide a necessary condition for conduct that otherwise would not have occurred. Ordinarily, such destabilization affords no more than mitigation.

Under the Model Penal Code, involuntary intoxication will found a defence to any crime if it deprived the defendant of 'substantial capacity to conform his conduct to law'. Arguably, a significant diminution in the capacity for self-control should excuse completely if the defendant's condition had more affinity with automatism than with a state of mere disinhibition. Absent a clear-cut state of automatism, however, the line is difficult to draw. Many jurisdictions in the United States which formerly used 'substantial capacity to conform conduct to law' as a limb of a Model Penal Code-inspired insanity test have abandoned it because of the impalpable questions to which it gave rise. The House of Lords was well advised to reject this test as a standard for an involuntary intoxication defence.

Nonetheless, there may have been principled reasons sufficient for the House of Lords to have upheld, rather than reversed, the Court of Appeal. An opportunity may have been missed for creative yet appropriate judicial law-making. Whether a defence should have been provided in *Kingston* depends, it will be argued, on conditions which may, or may not, have been present on the facts of that case. As stated already, disinhibition falling short of automatism cannot *of itself* excuse. But if such a condition arose blamelessly and induced conduct which would not otherwise have occurred, this will attenuate to some extent the culpability of the agent. That culpability would be further attenuated, it will be claimed, if, until the incident in question, the defendant had abstained from practising his paedophilia.

All we know of the defendant in *Kingston* is that he was a homosexual with paedophiliac predilections. The formative influences of sexual preference are obscure. In terms of orientation, our sexuality is something that we have rather than something we have made. If we are dealt a card marked for paedophilia, the most that can be asked of us is that we do not put it into play. The card cannot be surrendered and it would be a barbarity to punish for mere possession. Requiring forbearance in a matter so pervasive and unpredictable as sexual expression is to require a great deal, notwithstanding that the protection of a vulnerable class must always be the overriding concern. If a person of paedophiliac inclinations does not practise his paedophilia, he is entitled to that full dignity and respect which is due to all law-abiding citizens. Indeed, he may claim particular credit for sustaining a non-criminal status. If on a particular occasion he becomes blamelessly disinhibited by drugs and loses self-control when confronted with that temptation he otherwise avoids and resists, it is not obvious that the public interest requires him to suffer the total forfeit of credit which a conviction for a stigmatic offence entails.

The particularity of facts such as those related above renders the consequentialist claims of individual and general deterrence uncompelling. Retributivist claims are less clearly settled. It has already been suggested that his blameless state of disequilibrium must count in his favour, even if only as mitigation. It will be argued more fully below that mitigation may be upgraded to excuse if, until this particular occasion, the defendant had refrained from paedophiliac practices. However, were he a practising paedophile his conduct would not constitute an arguably condonable lapse from a standard he was able otherwise to sustain. Then, at most, he would be a candidate for mitigation. If he is, on the basis outlined above, a candidate for an acquittal, he may yet deservedly be convicted if the conduct for which he claims excuse was very grave, for example a killing. We are dealing with uncompelled conduct perpetrated with *mens rea*. In such cases previous good conduct and a blameless state of disequilibrium may be insufficient to outweigh the culpability evinced by a heinous wrong. We are not dealing with excusatory claims which, if made out, invariably sustain a plea for acquittal. It may depend on what it is the defendant has done.

In essence, this paper attempts to found the claim, adumbrated above, that involuntarily intoxicated persons of previous good character and others in similar case can, if particular conditions be met, be excused for certain crimes. First, however, we should note the view taken by the House of Lords in *Kingston* that such cases are adequately treated by way of mitigation. This standpoint coheres with the unequivocal opinion of Lord Mustill that a conviction for a serious offence need not entail descriptively or prescriptively that the defendant was in any sense at fault. He endorsed a decision of the Privy Council to the effect that an undercover policeman acting with the knowledge and consent of his superiors and without recourse to entrapment or conduct to the prejudice of third parties would be guilty of trafficking in drugs notwithstanding that the 'trafficking' (carrying drugs out of the jurisdiction) was done solely in the interests of law enforcement. It follows that an involuntarily intoxicated person could at most hope for some degree of mitigation—the policeman's conduct seemed justified whereas the cases we are concerned with fall, at most, to be excused.

By contrast with the House of Lords, the view taken here is that a conviction for a stigmatic offence is a sanction in its own right and that sanctions should be confined to the blameworthy. The non-conviction of the blameless should be a pervasive principle of substantive criminal law limited only by the need to theorize and practise criminal law as a system of rules and by the exigencies of forensic practicability. Those limitations entail that many 'normal' life narratives cannot afford grounds of excuse, however exculpatory the force of the narrative may be. But other accounts, not currently represented in standard defences, can be brought within the framework of substantive criminal law. If it can be done it should be done in order to diminish the incidence of unnecessary criminal convictions.

FURTHER READING

Arenella, P. (1992), 'Convicting the Morally Blameless', *University of California Los Angeles Law Review* 39: 1511.

Horder, J. (1993b), 'Pleading Involuntary Lack of Capacity', *Cambridge Law Journal* 52: 298.

25.2 BATTERED WOMEN

What defence, if any, should be available to a woman who kills her sleeping partner following months of violence from him?[339] We shall briefly outline the options that may be available:

(1) *Provocation.* She may seek to argue that she lost her self-control and killed her husband. As we saw in Chapter 5 there can be great difficulties in proving such a defence in cases of this kind: most notably proving there was a loss of self-control; that the loss of self-control was 'sudden and temporary'; and that the defendant's response was reasonable.

(2) *Diminished responsibility.* As discussed in Chapter 5, if the defendant can demonstrate that at the time of the offence she was suffering from an abnormality of mind (e.g. battered women's syndrome (BWS)[340] she may be able to plead the partial defence of

---

[339] Although this is the hypothetical scenario which most commentators discuss, Maguigan's (1991) American research suggests that in fact most battered women kill in the face of an attack.

[340] Some commentators are sceptical about whether BWS exists as a syndrome: Schopp (1998: 95); Schopp, Sturgis, and Sullivan (1994); Burke (2002).

diminished responsibility. Some commentators oppose reliance on this defence, arguing that far from suffering from an abnormal mind the defendant was in fact acting in an entirely reasonable way, given the abuse she had been through.[341] Further, the defence is available only to a charge of murder.

(3) *Duress.* It could be argued that she was responding reasonably to a threat of death or serious violence. Dressler,[342] the leading proponent of this view, suggests that the question the law should ask is whether in the face of the threats of violence to come the defendant acted in a reasonable way. Horder[343] argues that duress is inappropriate because there is no threat which the defendant is giving in to and in cases of duress the person who is killed is innocent, which is not so here.

(4) *Self-defence.* The woman may seek to claim that she was acting in self-defence to prevent future attacks. Due to his great physical strength she could only realistically prevent herself being attacked when he was asleep. The difficulty in English law in using self-defence is twofold. First, she has difficulty in satisfying the 'requirement' that she was defending herself from an imminent attack.[344] Secondly, it could be argued that she had the opportunity to escape from any prospective attack (by leaving the home) and therefore the use of violence was not necessary.

In the following passages Aileen McColgan considers the difficulties battered women face when seeking to use self-defence or other defences:[345]

A. McColgan, 'General Defences' in D. Nicolson and L. Bibbings (eds.), *Feminist Perspectives on Criminal Law* (London: Cavendish, 1999), 221–4

I have argued elsewhere that, at least in those cases in which women kill when in fear for their lives, self-defence/justifiable force is a more appropriate than either provocation or diminished responsibility.[346] This is partly because it fits the facts of cases when women kill abusive partners out of fear for their lives better than defences premised upon the defendant's rage or mental abnormality. In addition, and by contrast with the partial defences of provocation and diminished responsibility, its successful employment results in an acquittal. Satisfaction of the 'imminence' requirement' does not demand immediate threat of attack, but extends to cases in which the threat is not of physical violence itself, but of being placed in a position where escape from such future threatened violence is impossible.

There is every argument that, as a matter of law, many women who kill abusive partners fulfil the 'necessity' requirement of self-defence (of which imminence is a factor). Some would do so on a purely objective test. Others kill in less apparently clear cut circumstances in which, particularly where the woman is not actually being assaulted at the time, some explanation might be required of why she needed to use force. In such cases, evidence of the perceived or actual difficulties of escape from abusive partners would be of benefit to the defence. Women are most likely to suffer fatal attack when they try to escape their abusers

---

[341] Coughlin (1998: 70); Shaffer (1997); Allen (1987). Others argue that BWS too easily provides women with a defence: Derschowitz (2000).

[342] Dressler (2002a).   [343] Horder (2002a).

[344] Horder (2002a) believes there is no requirement of imminence as such, simply a question whether the defendant was acting reasonably.

[345] See also Nourse (2001); McColgan (1993); Zipursky (1996); Fletcher (1996); Ayyildiz (1995).

[346] McColgan (1993).

and it is almost impossible entirely to disappear from the sight of an abusive partner, not least because the courts generally grant batterers access to their children. Even if a woman's perception of the impossibility or futility of escape was adjudged inaccurate, the proper question is *what* she perceived, rather than whether that perception was reasonable. Where there was any significant doubt about the accuracy of such perception, evidence of BWS could be employed if relevant, as it was in Margaret Howell's case, to support the woman's claim that she regarded escape as impossible. But, in many cases, the danger or futility of attempted escape can be made apparent without resort to expert psychological evidence.

The next question concerns the proportionality of, rather than the necessity for, the force used in self-defence. Margaret Howell may have been convicted of manslaughter because her use of a shotgun was regarded as disproportionate to the threat faced by her. However, any assumption that an armed defence is disproportionate to an unarmed attack overlooks the fact hat men are typically much stronger than the women they abuse and that the dozens of women who are killed by their partners every year are most likely to die at their hands, rather than at the receiving end of any other weapon. The irony is that men's ability to kill with their bare hands appears frequently to result in their conviction for manslaughter, rather than murder; prosecutors and juries being more likely to accept that such killings are unintentional or, in any event, less likely to have been premeditated than where weapons are used.

The question of proportionality, like that of necessity, is an objective one. The defendant must, however, be judged on the facts *as she believed them to be*. Evidence that the defendant 'honestly and instinctively' considered her use of force necessary and proportional is to be regarded as 'the most potent evidence' that it actually was.

Domestic violence typically follows a pattern of escalation, with the effect that a woman who has withstood previous assaults may well get to the point where she suspects, on good grounds, that an impending attack may be fatal. Even if (as in some US jurisdictions) a purely objective approach were to be taken, consideration of the typically escalating pattern of domestic violence suggests the accuracy or, at any rate, the reasonableness, of many defendants' perceptions that they had to act in order to avoid an assault of unprecedented severity. Unless we are to condemn many severely abused women to futile (and possibly fatal) attempts to escape their abusers or to passive acceptance of violence which may itself be life-threatening, we must recognize the necessity, on occasion, of using force in self-defence.

The question which arises is why, given the relatively generous contours of the English law of self-defence, so few women who kill their abusive partners manage, apparently regardless of the circumstances of their actions, to secure acquittals. It seems that the difficulty rests not with the formal legal rules, but with informal, almost extra-legal, models of self-defence. These models are constructed in the imagination, owe their contours to 'common sense' or traditional paradigms of human behaviour and operate to block real consideration of situations which, although arguably within the legal defences' contours, do not fit the model. The relative scarcity of female killers has resulted in a paradigmatically male 'ideal model', which requires a spontaneous reaction against an unknown assailant, the defender using only comparable methods of defence (weapon matched to weapon, bare hand to bare hand). Further, aggressive force is incompatible with stereotypical femininity.

The ideal model of self-defence, thus constructed, operates against women, because of their unequal physical size and strength and, in cases of domestic violence, their possible quasi-hostage status. Successful utilisation of the defence will require reconstruction of the ideal model to include women's experience of life and limb-threatening violence.

In the US, where the rules governing self-defence are generally more restrictive than those which prevail in England, substantial numbers of women argue self-defence in relation to the killings of abusive partners. A proportion of those women succeed with the defence. There, lawyers have used evidence that women were suffering from BWS to assist self-defence pleas *by* showing 'the battered woman's perception that danger or great bodily harm [wa]s imminent', sometimes 'in spite of the fact that her battering partner was passive at the time of the offence'. Evidence of BWS has also been used 'to rebut the prosecution's inference that the defendant could have left, rather than kill the spouse' to draw an analogy between the battered woman and a hostage or a prisoner of war and in order to refute prosecution claims that the 'defendant masochistically enjoyed the beatings her ex-husband had given her'.

The increasing use of BWS in the US has proven problematic. Not only have the courts, in general, been prepared to accept BWS evidence only in those cases in which, *independent of it*, the defendant satisfies the (generally very rigorous) requirements for self-defence, but such evidence sometimes serves only to provide another hurdle between the battered woman and acquittal: not only does she have to establish the elements of self-defence in the ordinary way, but she then has also to show that she is properly regarded as suffering from BWS. Where women fail to conform to the stereotypical pattern of the 'battered woman' (where, for example, a woman has defended herself before or was the main breadwinner), this itself appears sufficient to thwart any chance of an acquittal, even where the elements of self-defence appear to be made out.

FURTHER READING

Dressler, J. (2002a), 'Battered Women Who Kill Their Sleeping Tormenters' in S. Shute and A. Simester (eds.), *Criminal Law Theory* (Oxford: OUP).

Horder, J. (1992), *Provocation and Responsibility* (Oxford: OUP), ch. 9.

—— (2002a), 'Killing the Passive Abuser: A Theoretical Defence' in S. Shute and A. Simester (eds.), *Criminal Law Theory* (Oxford: OUP).

Maguigan, H. (1991), 'Battered Women and Self-Defense', *University of Pennsylvania Law Review* 140: 379.

McColgan, A. (1993), 'In Defence of Battered Women who Kill', *Oxford Journal of Legal Studies* 13: 508.

Rosen, C. (1993), 'On Self-Defense, Imminence, and Women Who Kill Their Batterers', *North Carolina Law Review* 71: 371.

Zipursky, B. (1996), 'Self-Defense, Domination and the Social Contract', *University of Pennsylvania Law Review* 145: 579.

25.3 THE ZEEBRUGGE DISASTER

Is it easy to distinguish between a case of duress and a case of self-defence? At first sight it might be thought that the difference is obvious. Contrast these two cases:

(1) Martin kills Olive who is attacking him.

(2) Penelope kills Quinten after she has been told by Robin that unless she does so she will be killed.

In both cases Martin and Penelope are acting in order to protect their lives. But there is a crucial difference: Olive was not blameless; Quinten was. Hence in English and Welsh law duress is not a defence to murder; self-defence is. The law is said by some to be based on the principle that it cannot be justifiable to take an innocent person's life. But a moment's thought should show that it is not as straightforward as this. Is not a child or an insane person who is attacking not 'innocent'? Even leaving aside these problems, can a clear line be drawn between cases where the victim is or is not posing an unjust threat to the defendant?[347] In the following passage Jeremy Horder considers a case which arose during the Zeebrugge ferry disaster, which demonstrates that the distinction between self-defence, duress, and necessity is far from straightforward:[348]

J. Horder, 'Self-Defence, Necessity and Duress: Understanding the Relationship' (1998) 11 *Canadian Journal of Law and Jurisprudence* 143

The following real-life example illustrates the kind of difficulties that can arise. A ferry—the *Herald of Free Enterprise*—bound for Zeebrugge, overturned in heavy seas, trapping the passengers in the sinking ship. A group of passengers stranded in the ship, threatened by the rising waters, were endeavouring to escape by means of a rope ladder to safety. Unfortunately, a man had become stuck on the ladder, paralysed by cold and fear. When he could not be persuaded to move up or down, those nearest to him pushed him from the ladder so that they could make their escape. He was never seen again, and is presumed drowned. No case was ever brought against any of those involved in pushing him from the ladder, but of this and similar cases, Smith and Hogan say:

'The man on the ladder chose himself as the victim by his immobility there. He was preventing the passengers from going where there had a right and a most urgent need to go. He was, unwittingly, imperilling their lives. In [this example] the evil avoided outweighs that caused—one dies instead of two, or instead of many—and there is extreme duress. . . . So, notwithstanding the approval of *Dudley and Stephens* by *Howe*, it would be premature to conclude that necessity can never be a defence to murder.'

This passage conflates a number of claims, and leaves important questions unanswered. Given that the man on the ladder was paralysed by cold or fear, there is no basis for saying that he 'chose' himself as the victim. Moreover, if it is in some sense true that he 'chose himself' as the victim, this remain true whether only one or one hundred lives are saved by knocking him from the ladder; so, on this view, it is not clear why the numbers count. Although Smith and Hogan see this example as illustrating the need for necessity to be a defence to murder, they point out that the man on the ladder was 'unwittingly, imperilling [the] lives' of the other passengers. This might suggest that the example is one of self-defence, like the case of the rope-cutting mountaineer, because the man on the ladder is an unjust threat to others trying to escape. The example is, however, considerably more complex than the mountaineering example, because it involves an *indirect* or contingent threat, and for the difficulties that such threats raise for any account of self-defence, we must turn to Uniacke's consideration of the problem.

The direct threat to the passengers waiting to climb the rope ladder is clearly the rising water. The question is whether, by his immobility on the ladder, the frozen man (as we may call him) became part of the threat, and thus a legitimate focus for self-defensive steps of the kind taken. It seems obvious that in some circumstances someone can become part of a threat where the direct threat (of which they have become part) stems from natural causes.

---

[347] Unaicke (1994: 39). [348] See also Alexander (1999).

Uniacke gives the examples of someone rocking a (sinking) rowing boat, thus increasing the threat to those in the boat, and of someone who panics and tries to light a fire in a cave where others are trapped with a diminishing supply of oxygen. For Uniacke, in these cases the person concerned *exacerbates* the threat, and thus becomes part of it, and is hence a legitimate target for self-defensive measures. For her, this will be true whether they rock the boat, or are about to start a fire, deliberately or accidentally, by analogy with the analysis of people (discussed earlier) who become direct threats accidentally, like the fallen mountaineer or the person thrown down the well. On the other hand, for Uniacke, someone may be neither a direct threat nor an exacerbating factor, but may simply *expose* others to an independent threat. Suppose someone fires a missile at me. Suppose further that I cannot move out of its path, but its path is (unbeknownst to him) currently blocked by Z. If Z bends over to pick something up, thus clearing the missile's path at the crucial moment, Z exposes me to a threat, but is clearly not the source of or part of the threat. Z is thus not a legitimate target for self-defensive measures. However, even where a mere exposure to a threat is concerned, things may be different if the exposure was free, deliberate and informed. So, if Z ducks *in order that* I should be hit by the missile, I will now be acting self-defensively in preventing Z from ducking. Free, deliberate and informed acts may take on an independent normative significance, a significance capable of changing the normative status of my response to a self-defensive one, in such circumstances. Consider conduct 'triggering' a threat, a notion it seems to me that we need to add to Uniacke's notions of exacerbation of, and exposure to, a threat. If someone booby-traps a room so that the next person to touch the door-handle from the outside will electrocute me, a person touching the door-handle does not really expose me to a threat to which I was not already exposed, nor does he or she exacerbate one. He or she 'triggers' the threat. In such a case, it seems unlikely that we would regard force used to prevent someone touching the door handle as self-defensive, unless the touching of the door handle was free, deliberate and informed: *meant to* harm me.

Into which category does the frozen man fall? He seems to be in much the same position as Philippa Foot's famous fat pot-holer who becomes stuck in the exit hole, blocking his colleagues' path from the rising tide. In Uniacke's view, such a person exposes others to a threat, but does not create or exacerbate the threat. And since there is (*ex hypothesi*) no question of the frozen man or the pot-holer intentionally remaining where they are to hinder the others' escape (a free, deliberate and informed act), force is not used against either of them defensively; for only in cases where threats are exacerbated or created ab initio will 'innocent' exacerbations or creations of threats be met with *defensive* force. In Uniacke's analysis much might be thought to depend, however, on what the difference between exacerbation of a threat, and exposure to a threat, turns out to be. The fat pot-holer and the frozen man undoubtedly make an existing threat more likely to engulf those behind them. Does this fact not, then, make these cases ones of exacerbation of a threat, and thus analogous to those of the person who rocks the sinking boat and the person who lights the fire in the airless cave? Whatever the theoretical soundness of Uniacke's distinction between exacerbation of, and exposure to, a threat, it is in practice a difficult distinction to draw. Problems also arise from the way in which Uniacke ties her conception of 'being under threat' to a counter-factual test. She says, 'force can be used in self-defence against a contingent threat which is itself either an attack or an act which would be an attack were it intended to harm or defeat me.' The case of a contingent threat that is itself an attack is the case where Z (above) deliberately ducks to ensure that a missile hits me, deliberately closes the escape-hatch on a sinking ship, or something of that kind, where the free deliberate and informed nature of the act changes the normative significance of steps directed at negating or warding off the contingent threat, making such steps self-defensive. More problematic is the notion that force is used self-defensively against an act that *would be* an attack if it were intended to harm or defeat another. If *Z* (above) bends down to pick up something that he has dropped, thus unwittingly opening up a clear path for the missile aimed at me, this is certainly an act which would be an attack if it were intended to facilitate the missile's path. Yet Uniacke is clear that such an unwitting action would not be prevented *self-defensively*.

. . .

[Later in the article Horder suggests that it is possible to distinguish duress, necessity and self-defence in this way:]

1. In necessity cases, the key issue is the *moral imperative* to act: what matters is whether in the circumstances it was morally imperative to act, even if this might involve the commission of wrongdoing, in order to negate or avoid some other evil.

2. In duress cases, the key issue is the *personal sacrifice D* is being asked to make: should *D* be expected to make the personal sacrifice involved in refusing to give in to a coercive threat, rather than avoid implementation of the coercive threat by doing wrong?

3. In self-defence cases, the key issue is *D's legal permission* to act: where *V* unjustly represented a threat to *D* (normally, although not exclusively, through his—*V's*— conduct), the question is whether necessary and proportionate steps were taken by *D* to negate or avoid the threat. For, *D* has a legal permission to take necessary and proportionate steps to negate or avoid an unjust threat, even if (exceptionally) these involve the use of lethal force.

QUESTIONS

1. Is it possible to distinguish justifications and excuses? Is it useful to do so?

2. Does the choice or character theory better explain the defence of duress?

3. Are there any good reasons for not permitting duress as a defence to murder?

4. Should any defence be available to a woman who kills a partner who has been persistently abusive to her? Which defence should it be?

5. If the Zeebrugge disaster case had come before the courts would any defence be available to the person who pushed the deceased off the ladder?

13

THE CRIMINAL LIABILITY
OF CORPORATIONS

PART I: THE LAW ON CORPORATE CRIMINALITY

1 THE DIFFICULTY IN CONVICTING COMPANIES OF CRIMES

In recent years there has been increasing interest in convicting companies of crimes follow-ing tragedies including the Ladbroke Grove railway crash,[1] the Zeebrugge ferry disaster, and the King's Cross fire. In particular, it has been felt that some of these awful events have been caused by the actions not just of an individual but of a whole company. It is felt that awarding damages in a civil case fails to recognize the severity of wrong that the company as a whole did towards the victims.

Imagine that a train passes through a red light, and as a result there is a crash. It might be easy simply to see the case as one where the train driver should be held responsible and that is the end of the story. However, such an approach may not pay attention to the fault of the train company in ensuring that signals were placed where they were clearly visible to drivers, or in having safety mechanisms on trains that inhibited drivers from passing through red lights.[2] To dismiss the crash as 'just the train driver's fault' would be to take a very narrow view of who is responsible for the accident. It is not difficult to imagine a case where the employee who directly caused the harm was less responsible than the managers who failed to install appropriate safety mechanisms.[3]

Despite the demands for criminal liability there are difficulties in explaining how a com-pany can be guilty of a criminal offence. The company is a legal person,[4] separate from its directors and its shareholders, but there is a real problem in explaining how a company can be said to act or have *mens rea*. For some offences there is no difficulty in convicting a

---

[1] BBC Newsonline (2005b): the CPS have announced no corporate manslaughter charged will be brought in connection with the Ladbroke Grove railway crash due to insufficient evidence.

[2] Reason (1997: 9).

[3] Wells (2001: 161–3).

[4] The Interpretation Act 1978, s. 5 and sch. 1 state that unless a contrary intention appears in every Act of Parliament 'person' includes (*inter alia*) a corporation.

company because Parliament expressly provides for this. For example, according to section 18 of the Theft Act 1968:

> Where an offence committed by a body corporate under section 15, 16 or 17 of this Act is proved to have been committed with the consent or connivance of any director, manager, secretary or other similar officer of the body corporate or any person who was purporting to act in any such capacity, he as well as the body corporate shall be guilty of that offence. . . .

However, where there is no such provision, the courts have attempted to manipulate the concepts of *mens rea* and *actus reus*, as traditionally understood, so that it is possible to say that a company caused a result or intended or foresaw a consequence. The courts have used two techniques for doing this.

2 VICARIOUS LIABILITY

The notion of vicarious liability will be discussed further, later in this chapter. The notion of vicarious liability, as applied to companies, means that a company can be seen as responsible for the offences committed by its employees when acting within the terms of their employment.[5] The benefit of this doctrine is that it avoids the courts having to find the company acting or thinking in a particular way. The *actus reus* and *mens rea* of the employee are assigned to the company. The difficulty in using this doctrine is that the number of crimes that the courts have been willing to hold can be committed vicariously is relatively small and they tend to be less serious offences. Further, a company might readily claim that their employee in committing an offence was acting outside the scope of his or her employment.

3 IDENTIFICATION

Under this doctrine certain employees of the company are regarded as having sufficient status within the corporation to justify being directly identified with it. If someone has sufficient standing within the company to be regarded as representing the 'mind' of the company then his actions and *mens rea* can be regarded as the *actus reus* and *mens rea* of the company.[6] This theory was developed by the House of Lords in *Tesco v Nattrass*.[7] In the following case the Court of Appeal restated the present law:

Attorney-General's Reference (No. 2 of 1999) [2000] QB 796 (CA)[8]

The defendant train-operating company was charged with manslaughter following the Southall rail crash in 1997 in which seven people were killed. The prosecution claimed

---

[5] See *Alphacell Ltd v Woodward* [1972] AC 824 (HL).

[6] Any suggestion that a company could not be convicted of an offence of violence was rejected in *R v Coroner for East Kent, ex parte Spooner* (1989) 88 Cr App R 10 (DC).

[7] [1972] AC 153 (HL). See also *Meridian Global Funds Management Asia Ltd v Securities Commission* [1995] 2 AC 500 (HL).

[8] [2000] 3 All ER 182, [2000] 3 WLR 195, [2000] Crim LR 475.

that the company was grossly negligent in failing to take reasonable care for the safety of the passengers. The only individual prosecuted in connection with the accident was the driver. The defendant company pleaded guilty to breaches of sections 3(1) and 33(1)(a) of the Health and Safety at Work Act 1974 and were fined £1.5 million as a result. On the manslaughter charge Scott Baker J ruled that a company could only be guilty of manslaughter if a human being who could be said to represent the company had committed the *actus reus* and *mens rea* of the offence. The Attorney-General appealed against this ruling. The Court of Appeal was asked two questions. The first related to the definition of gross negligence (the parts of the judgment relating to the definition of gross negligence are discussed at p. 288). The second related to gross negligence manslaughter.

Lord Justice Rose (Vice President)

(2) Can a non-human defendant be convicted of the crime of manslaughter by gross negligence in the absence of evidence establishing the guilt of an identified human individual for the same crime?

. . . As to question 2, Mr Lissack [counsel for the Attorney-General] accepted that policy considerations arise. Large companies should be as susceptible to prosecution for manslaughter as one-man companies. Where the ingredients of a common law offence are identical to those of a statutory offence, there is no justification for drawing a distinction as to liability between the two and the public interest requires the more emphatic denunciation of a company inherent in a conviction for manslaughter. He submitted that the ingredients of the offence of gross negligence manslaughter are the same in relation to a body corporate as to a human being, namely grossly negligent breach of a duty to a deceased causative of his death. It is, he submitted, unnecessary and inappropriate to enquire whether there is an employee in the company who is guilty of the offence of manslaughter who can be properly be said to have been acting as the embodiment of the company. The criminal law of negligence follows the civil law of negligence as applied to corporations: the only difference is that, to be criminal, the negligence must be gross. Of the three theories of corporate criminal liability, namely vicarious liability, identification and personal liability, it is personal liability which should here apply. In the present case, it would have been open to the jury to convict if they were satisfied that the deaths occurred by reason of a gross breach by the defendant of its personal duty to have a safe system of train operation in place. The identification theory, attributing to the company the mind and will of senior directors and managers, was developed in order to avoid injustice: it would bring the law into disrepute if every act and state of mind of an individual employee was attributed to a company which was entirely blameless (see per Lord Reid in *Tesco Supermarkets Ltd v Nattrass* [1972] AC 153 at 169 and per Estey J of the Supreme Court of Canada in *Canadian Dredge Co v The Queen* 19 DLR 314 at 342). Its origins lay in the speech of Viscount Haldane LC in *Lennard's Carrying Co Ltd v Asiatic Petroleum Co Ltd* [1915] AC 705 at 713, and it was developed by the judgment of Denning LJ in *Bolton Engineering v TJ Graham & Sons* [1957] 1 QB 159 at 172 and *Tesco Supermarkets Ltd v Nattrass* in which, at 170E, Lord Reid said:

'A living person has a mind which can have knowledge or intention or be negligent and he has hands to carry out his intentions. A corporation has none of these: it must act through living persons though not always one or the same person. Then the person who acts is not speaking or acting for the company. He is acting as the company and his mind which directs his acts is the mind of the company. There is no question of the company being vicariously liable. He is not acting as a servant, representative, agent or delegate. He is an embodiment of the company or, one could say, he hears and speaks through the persona of the company, within his appropriate sphere, and his mind is the mind of the company. If it is a guilty mind then that guilt is the guilt of the company.'

Before turning to Mr Lissack's submission in relation to personal liability, it is convenient first to refer to the speech of Lord Hoffmann in *Meridian Global Funds Management v Securities Commission* [1995] 2 AC 500, on which Mr Lissack relied as the linchpin of this part of his argument. It was a case in which the chief investment officer and senior portfolio manager of an investment management company, with the company's authority but unknown to the board of directors and managing director, used funds managed by the company to acquire shares, but failed to comply with a statutory obligation to give notice of the acquisition to the Securities Commission. The trial judge held that the knowledge of the officer and manager should be attributed to the company and the Court of Appeal of New Zealand upheld the decision on the basis that the officer was the directing mind and will of the company. The Privy Council dismissed an appeal. In a passage at 506C, Lord Hoffmann, giving the judgment of the Privy Council, said that the company's primary rules of attribution were generally found in its constitution or implied by company law. But, in an exceptional case, where the application of those principles would defeat the intended application of a particular provision to companies, it was necessary to devise a special rule of attribution. At 507B Lord Hoffmann said:

'For example, a rule may be stated in language primarily applicable to a natural person and require some act or state of mind on the part of that person "himself", as opposed to his servants or agents. This is generally true of the rules of the criminal law, which ordinarily impose liability only for the *actus reus* and *mens rea* of the defendant himself. How is such a rule to be applied to a company? One possibility is that the court may come to the conclusion that the rule was not intended to apply to companies at all; for example, a law which created an offence for which the only penalty was community service. Another possibility is that the court might interpret the law as meaning that it could apply to a company only on the basis of its primary rules of attribution, i.e. if the act giving rise to liability was specifically authorised by a resolution of the board or an unanimous agreement of the shareholders. But there will be many cases in which neither of these solutions is satisfactory; in which the court considers that the law was intended to apply to companies and that, although it excludes ordinary vicarious liability, insistence on the primary rules of attribution would in practice defeat that intention. In such a case, the court must fashion a special rule of attribution for the particular substantive rule. This is always a matter of interpretation: given that it was intended to apply to a company, how was it intended to apply? Whose act (or knowledge, or state of mind) was for this purpose intended to count as the act etc of the company? One finds the answer to this question by applying the usual canons of interpretation, taking into account the language of the rule (if it is a statute) and its content and policy.'

Lord Hoffmann then referred to *Tesco Supermarkets Ltd v Nattrass* and *In re Supply of Ready Mixed Concrete (No 2)* [1995] 1 AC 456, Viscount Haldane's speech in *Lennards Co* and Denning LJ's judgment in *Bolton v Graham*. Having at 511A referred to the concept of directing mind and will, he went on to say:

'It will often be the most appropriate description of the person designated by the relevant attribution rule, but it might be better to acknowledge that not every such rule has to be forced into the same formula. Once it is appreciated that the question is one of construction rather than metaphysics the answer in this case seems to their Lordships to be . . . the policy of s 20 of the Securities Amendment Act 1988 is to compel, in fast-moving markets, the immediate disclosure of the identity of persons who become substantial security holders in public issuers. . . . What rule should be implied as to the person whose knowledge for this purpose is to count as the knowledge of the company? Surely the person who, with the authority of the company, acquired the relevant interest. Otherwise the policy of the Act would be defeated. . . . The company knows that it has become a substantial security holder when that is known to the person who had authority to do the deal. It is then obliged to give notice'.

Lord Hoffmann went on to comment that it was not necessary in that case to inquire whether the chief investment officer could be described as the 'directing mind and will' of the company. At 511H he said: 'It is a question of construction in each case as to whether the particular rule requires that the knowledge that an act has been done, or the state of mind in which it was done, should be attributed to the company'.

Mr Lissack's submission that personal liability on the part of the company is capable of arising in the present case was based on a number of authorities in addition to *Meridian*. . . . [Reference was then made to *R v British Steel plc* [1995] IRLR 310, *R v Associated Octel* [1997] IRLR 123 and *In re Supply of Ready Mixed Concrete (No 2)*.]

Mr Lissack submitted that, in accordance with the speech of Lord Hoffmann in *Meridian*, the choice of the appropriate theory depends on the ingredients of the offence itself; and the requirements of both retribution and deterrence point to corporate liability where death is caused through the company's gross negligence. He relied on a passage in Steyn LJ's judgment in the *British Steel* case at 314, 23 where there is reference to the promotion of 'a culture of guarding against the risks to health and safety by virtue of hazardous industrial operations'.

Mr Lissack advanced two subsidiary submissions. First, if, contrary to his primary submission, a corporation cannot be convicted unless an employee embodying the company can be identified as guilty of manslaughter, the presence of such an employee can be inferred: he relied on a passage in the speech of Lord Hoffmann in *Meridian* at 510H which seems to us to afford no support whatever for this submission. We reject it. Secondly, he suggested that aggregation has a role to play, i.e. where a series of venial management failures are aggregated and cumulatively amount to gross negligence, a company may be convicted. There is a tentatively expressed passage in Smith and Hogan 9th edition at p 186, based on an analogy with civil negligence, which supports this suggestion. But there is no supporting and clear contrary judicial authority—see per Bingham LJ in *R v HM Coroner ex parte Spooner* 88 Cr App R 10 at 16: 'A case against a personal defendant cannot be fortified by evidence against another defendant. The case against a corporation can only be made by evidence properly addressed to showing guilt on the part of the corporation as such.' The Law Commission 237 at para 7.33 are against introducing the concept of aggregation. We reject the suggestion that aggregation has any proper role to play.

For the defendant, Mr Caplan submitted, in relation to question 2, that *Adomako* was not concerned with corporate liability. It is necessarily implicit in the Law Commission's recommendation, in LC 237, that Parliament should enact a new offence of corporate killing, that the doctrine of identification still continues to apply to gross negligence manslaughter since *Adomako. Tesco v Nattrass* is still authoritative (see *Seaboard Offshore v Secretary of State for Transport* [1994] 1 WLR 541) and it is impossible to find a company guilty unless its alter ego is identified. None of the authorities since *Tesco v Nattrass* relied on by Mr Lissack supports the demise of the doctrine of identification: all are concerned with statutory construction of different substantive offences and the appropriate rule of attribution was decided having regard to the legislative intent, namely whether Parliament intended companies to be liable. There is a sound reason for a special rule of attribution in relation to statutory offences rather than common law offences, namely there is, subject to a defence of reasonable practicability, an absolute duty imposed by the statutes. The authorities on statutory offences do not bear on the common law principle in relation to manslaughter. Lord Hoffmann's speech in *Meridian* is a restatement not an abandonment of existing principles: see, for example, Lord Diplock in *Tesco v Nattrass* at 200H: 'There may be criminal statutes which upon their true construction ascribe to a corporation criminal responsibility for the acts of servants and agents who would be excluded by the test that I have stated' (viz those exercising the powers of the company under its articles of association). The Law Commission's proposals were made after *Meridian* and the *British Steel* case. Identification is necessary in relation to the actus reus i.e. whose acts or omissions are to be attributed to the company and *Adomako*'s objective test in relation to gross negligence in no way affects this. Furthermore, the civil negligence rule of liability for the acts of servants or agents has no place in the criminal law—which is why the identification principle was developed. That principle is still the rule of attribution in criminal law whether or not mens rea needs to be proved.

. . .

There is, as it seems to us, no sound basis for suggesting that, by their recent decisions, the courts have started a process of moving from identification to personal liability as a basis for corporate liability for manslaughter. In *Adomako*, the House of Lords were, as it seems to us, seeking to escape from the unnecessarily complex accretions in relation to recklessness arising from *Lawrence* [1982] AC 510 and *Caldwell* [1982] AC 341. To do so, they simplified the ingredients of gross negligence manslaughter by restating them in line with Bateman. But corporate liability was not mentioned anywhere in the submissions of counsel or their Lordship's speeches. In any event, the identification principle is in our judgment just as relevant to the actus reus as to mens rea. In *Tesco v Nattrass* at 173D Lord Reid said 'The judge must direct the jury that if they find certain facts proved then, as a matter of law, they must find that the criminal act of the officer, servant or agent, including his state of mind, intention, knowledge or belief is the act of the Company.' In *R v HM Coroner ex parte Spooner*, Bingham LJ at 16 said: 'For a company to be criminally liable for manslaughter . . . it is required that the *mens rea* and the *actus reus* of manslaughter should be established . . . against those who were to be identified as the embodiment of the company itself.' In *R v P & O European Ferries* 93 CAR 72, Turner J, in his classic analysis of the relevant principles, said at 83 'Where a corporation through the controlling mind of one of its agents, does an act which fulfils the prerequisite of the crime of manslaughter, it is properly indictable for the crime of manslaughter.' In our judgment, unless an identified individual's conduct, characterisable as gross criminal negligence, can be attributed to the company the company is not, in the present state of the common law, liable for manslaughter. Civil negligence rules, e.g. as enunciated in *Wilsons & Clyde Coal Co v English* [1938] AC 57, are not apt to confer criminal liability on a company.

None of the authorities relied on by Mr Lissack as pointing to personal liability for manslaughter by a company supports that contention. In each, the decision was dependent on the purposive construction that the particular statute imposed, subject to a defence of reasonable practicability liability on a company for conducting its undertaking in a manner exposing employees or the public to health and safety risk. In each case there was an identified employee whose conduct was held to be that of the company. In each case it was held that the concept of directing mind and will had no application when construing the statute. But it was not suggested or implied that the concept of identification is dead or moribund in relation to common law offences. Indeed, if that were so, it might have been expected that Lord Hoffmann, in *Associated Octel*, would have referred to the ill health of doctrine in the light of his own speech, less than a year before, in *Meridian*. He made no such reference, nor was *Meridian* cited in *Associated Octel*. It therefore seems safe to conclude that Lord Hoffmann (and, similarly, the members of the Court of Appeal Criminal Division in *British Steel* and in *Gateway Food Market*) did not think that the common law principles as to the need for identification have changed. Indeed, Lord Hoffmann's speech in *Meridian*, in fashioning an additional special rule of attribution geared to the purpose of the statute, proceeded on the basis that the primary 'directing mind and will' rule still applies although it is not determinative in all cases. In other words, he was not departing from the identification theory but reaffirming its existence.

This approach is entirely consonant with the Law Commission's analysis of the present state of the law and the terms of their proposals for reform in their Report No 237 published in March 1996. In this report, both the House of Lords decision in *Adomako* and the Privy Council's decision in *Meridian* were discussed. In the light of their analysis, the Law Commission concluded (para 6.27 and following and para 7.5) that, in the present state of the law, a corporation's liability for manslaughter is based solely on the principle of identification and they drafted a Bill to confer liability based on management failure not involving the principle of identification (see clause 4 of the Draft Bill annexed to their Report). If Mr Lissack's submissions are correct there is no need for such a Bill and, as Scott Baker J put it, the Law Commission have missed the point. We agree with the judge that the Law Commission have not missed the point and Mr Lissack's submissions are not correct: the identification principle remains the only basis in common law for corporate liability for gross negligence manslaughter.

We should add that, if we entertained doubt on the matter, being mindful of the observations of Lord Lowry in *C v DPP* at p 28C, we would not think it appropriate for this court to propel the law in the direction which Mr Lissack seeks. That, in our judgment, taking into account the policy considerations to which Mr Lissack referred, is a matter for Parliament, not the courts. For almost four years, the Law Commission's draft Bill has been to hand as a useful starting point for that purpose.

It follows that, in our opinion, the answer to question 2 is 'No'.

The following points then emerge from this case:

(1) Normally it is necessary to find one person who represents the 'mind and will' of the company (e.g. a senior manager) and who has the *mens rea* required for the offence if a company is to be convicted of an offence involving *mens rea*.[9] So in this case whatever complaint there may have been about the management of safety within the company generally if it was not possible to find a senior manager who was sufficiently negligent to justify a conviction for gross negligence manslaughter, the company could not be convicted.

(2) Exceptionally the *mens rea* of a less senior company official can be attributed to the company if the court decides that a statutory offence was intended to apply to companies and that the statute would be unworkable if the identification principle was applied strictly.

(3) The Court of Appeal rejected the so-called 'aggregation theory'. This theory suggested that if it is not possible to find a single director who has the necessary *mens rea* for the offence it is possible to add together (aggregate) the states of mind of

---

[9] *Information Commissioner v Islington Borough Council* [2002] EWHC 1036.

several senior managers to create the *mens rea* required for the offence. This would mean, for example, if one director knew that a particular piece of machinery was liable to malfunction if the factory often got too hot, another director knew that the factory tended to get very hot, and another director knew that operators of the machinery often did not wear their safety gear because it was so hot, it would be possible to add these states of mind together to form a case for, say, gross negligence manslaughter if a worker was subsequently killed using the machinery.

It should be noted that just because the person who performs the *actus reus* of the offence is not senior enough to constitute the 'mind and will' of the company does not mean that the case is at an end. It may be that a manager has been negligent in failing to put in place appropriate checks and safety mechanisms to ensure that the company's employees abided by them.[10]

Who is 'the mind and will of the company'? There can be little difficulty with this where the company is a small company. In *Kite v OLL Ltd*[11] the company was in effect a one-person company and there was no difficulty in finding that the acts and state of mind of the director were those of the company. In relation to larger companies it will be for the jury to decide whether or not the individual was sufficiently senior to justify being described as 'the mind and will of the company'.

It should be noted that the only effective punishment available at present against a company under English and Welsh law is a fine. Therefore where the offence carries a mandatory sentence of imprisonment (e.g. murder) the company cannot be convicted of that offence.[12]

4 REFORM OF THE LAW ON CORPORATE KILLING

The government has announced that it intends soon to introduce a 'clear and effective new law on corporate killing'.[13] The Government has been considering a number of options for reform of the law.[14] The latest draft Bill[15] contains the following offence of corporate manslaughter in clause 13:

> if the way in which any of the organisation's activities are managed or organized by its senior managers—
>
> (a) causes a person's death, and
>
> (b) amounts to a gross breach of a relevant duty of care owed by the organization to the deceased.

A senior manager is defined as a person who 'plays a significant role' in 'the making of decisions about how the whole or a substantial part of its activities are to be managed or organized, or the actual managing or organising' of those activities. In deciding whether there has been a gross breach of duty the jury must consider whether the failure is far below

---

[10] *Seaboard Offshore Ltd v Secretary of State for Transport* [1994] 2 All ER 99 (HL).
[11] 8 Dec. 1994, unreported.   [12] *IRC Haulage Ltd* [1944] KB 551 (CA).
[13] Ten Downing Street (2003).
[14] Home Office (2000c), which itself relied on Law Commission Report No. 237 (1996).
[15] Home Office (2005).

what can reasonably be expected of the organization in the circumstances and can consider whether there has been a breach of relevant health and safety legislation or guidance and the extent of that breach.[16]

FURTHER READING

Clarkson, C. (2005), 'Corporate Manslaughter: Yet More Government Proposals', *Criminal Law Review* 677.

Glazebrook, P. (2002), 'A Better Way of Convicting Businesses of Avoiding Deaths and Injuries?', *Cambridge Law Journal* 61: 405.

Gobert, J. (2002), 'Corporate Killing at Home and Abroad—Reflections on the Government's Proposals', *Law Quarterly Review* 118: 72.

5 VICARIOUS LIABILITY

5.1 WHAT IS VICARIOUS LIABILITY?

Normally a person is not liable in criminal law for the acts of another. One important exception to this rule is vicarious liability where the act, and in some cases even the *mens rea*, of another person is imputed to the defendant.[17] The defendant's conviction does not rest on anything said or done by the defendant, but on the acts and mental state of another. Vicarious liability is therefore different from accessorial liability (see Chapter 15) where a defendant's guilt flows from his acts of assistance to someone who goes on to commit the offence.

5.2 WHICH CRIMES CAN BE COMMITTED VICARIOUSLY?

Most vicarious liability operates where the offence is one of strict liability, but it is not limited to such crimes.[18] Whether an offence can be committed vicariously is a matter of statutory interpretation for each particular offence.[19] Sometimes the statute explicitly makes the offence one of vicarious liability (e.g. where the statute states that the defendant is guilty if he 'or by his servant or agent sell . . .'[20]). However, the court may decide by implication that the offence is one of vicarious liability.[21] The court is likely to do this if it thinks that the imposition of vicarious liability is necessary to give effect to legislation. Commonly in offences which involve the selling of goods the courts have interpreted the word sell to include an employee selling, this being seen as giving the word 'sell' its normal meaning.[22] So in *Tesco Stores Ltd v Brent LBC*[23] it was held that Tesco Ltd had 'supplied' an 18-rated video to a child, although, of course, the video was actually supplied by the check-out assistant. Similarly, it has been held that an employer is in possession of goods which his employee

---

[16] Clause 3(2)

[17] See also Gelsthorpe and Morris (1999) and the discussion of the circumstances in which a parent can be liable for the crimes of his or her children.

[18] *Tesco v Brent* [1972] AC 153 (HL).

[19] *Seaboard Offshore v Secretary of State for Transport* [1993] 3 All ER 25 (HL).

[20] Licensing Act 1964, s. 59(1).   [21] *Mousell Bros v London and North Western Rwy* [1917] 2 KB 836.

[22] *Coppen v Moore (No. 2)* [1898] 2 QB 306.   [23] [1993] 2 All ER 718.

possesses in the course of his employment[24] and uses a car that his employee uses at work.[25] However, it has been held that driving cannot be committed vicariously; only the person in the driving seat can drive the car.[26] It appears that one cannot be guilty as for an attempt[27] or, as an accessory, vicariously.[28]

5.3 FOR WHOSE ACT CAN THE DEFENDANT BE VICARIOUSLY LIABLE?

If the offence is one that can be committed vicariously then the accused is responsible for the acts of anyone employed by him or authorized to act as his agent.[29] The accused will be vicariously liable only for an employee or agent who is acting within the scope of his employment. For example, in *Adams v Camfoni*[30] it was held that a licensee was not guilty of selling alcohol outside the permitted hours when his messenger boy (who had no authority to sell alcohol) had done so.

5.4 WHAT *MENS REA* MUST BE PROVED?

Normally, where an offence which requires *mens rea* is committed vicariously then the defendant himself must be proved to have that *mens rea*. So, if the offence requires knowledge and the act is performed by an agent or employee it must be shown that the accused knew his employee or agent was doing that act. There appears to be one exception to this and that is where the defendant has delegated responsibility to an agent. In that case the *mens rea* of the agent can be transferred to the defendant. The House of Lords in *Vane v Yiannopoullos*[31] doubted the acceptability of transferring the *mens rea* from the employee and agent. In that case a waitress sold wine contrary to the conditions of a restaurant licence, while the accused, the licence holder, was on the premises. It was suggested that the *mens rea* of an employee could only be ascribed to the accused in a case of complete delegation: where the accused employs a person to stand fully in his shoes.[32] This has become known as the 'delegation principle'. However, in *Allen v Whitehead*[33] the owner of a café was convicted of knowingly 'permitting or suffering' prostitutes to meet at his premises. The owner in fact visited the café only once or twice a week, but he had installed a manager to look after the premises. The manager was aware the prostitutes were gathering at the café. The owner was held to have appointed the manager, not just as a person to serve drinks, but as his representative as the person in charge of the café. The owner had therefore delegated responsibility to the manager and so the manager's knowledge could be imputed to the owner. This case was distinguished from *Vane v Yiannopoullos* where the waitress could not be said to be representing the defendant, who indeed was present on the premises.

---

[24] *Melias Ltd v Preston* [1957] 2 QB 380 (CA).
[25] *Green v Burnett* [1955] 1 QB 78. But see *Cambridge County Council v Associated Lead Mills Ltd* [2005] EWHC Civ 1627 for judicial disagreement on whether using an overweight vehicle contrary to Road Traffic Regulation Act 1984, s. 5(1), can be committed vicariously.
[26] *Thornton v Mitchell* [1940] 1 All ER 339.   [27] *Gardner v Akeroyd* [1952] 2 QB 743 (DC).
[28] *Ferguson v Weaving* [1951] 1 KB 814 (DC).   [29] *Quality Dairies (York) Ltd v Pedley* [1952] 1 KB 275.
[30] [1929] 1 KB 95.   [31] [1965] AC 486 (HL).
[32] Followed in *Winson* [1969] 1 QB 371 (CA).   [33] [1930] 1 KB 211.

PART II: THE THEORY OF CORPORATE LIABILITY

6 THEORETICAL ISSUES IN CORPORATE LIABILITY

6.1 THE REALITY OF CORPORATE CRIME

The Health and Safety Executive reports that for the year 2004/5 there were 220 fatal injuries to employees in the workplace, and 361 fatal injuries to members of the public (although about two thirds of these were acts of suicide or trespass onto railway systems).[34]

In 35 per cent of these there was a prosecution by the Health and Safety Executive, but a fine is the normal punishment.[35] But, just looking at workplace deaths the Health and Safety Executive's own research suggests that 70–85 per cent of workplace deaths were preventable, but in fewer than 20 per cent of those cases was there a prosecution for even a health and safety offence.[36] Following the Southall rail disaster which led to seven deaths, a one and a half million pound fine was imposed.[37]

It is, perhaps, not surprising that courts have been reluctant to impose huge fines. In the case of companies running public services there is a concern that such a fine in reality simply means that less is spent on improving those services.[38] If it is a public company it may be that those who really suffer are junior employees and shareholders, and not the senior management, who may be truly to blame.[39]

6.2 THE CLAMOUR FOR CORPORATE LIABILITY

It is only in recent years that concerns about corporate killing have led to calls for companies to be criminally liable. In the following excerpt Nicola Lacey considers why it is that interest in corporate crime has grown:

N. Lacey ' "Philosophical Foundations of the Common Law": Social not Metaphysical' in J. Horder (ed.), *Oxford Essays in Jurisprudence* **(Oxford: OUP, 2000), 33–5**

Four main cultural arguments have been advanced to explain the recent steps towards recognition of corporate manslaughter. The first argument has to do with technological change: the growth of technology is argued to have increased the scope for huge disasters

---

[34] Health and Safety Executive (2006: 2). There were 27,477 major injuries to employees and 14,362 to members of the public.

[35] Clarkson (2000: 151).

[36] Slapper and Tombs (1999). In 2003 the Health and Safety Executive published new guidelines on procedures for investigating health-related death: Health and Safety Executive (2003b).

[37] See Baldwin (2004) for an argument that the government enforcement of regulations is becoming stricter.

[38] It should not be forgotten that companies are often the victims of crime: Gobert and Punch (2003: ch. 1).

[39] Norrie (1991: 101). Gobert (1998) and Fisse (1990) look at the options for punishing companies.

which cause so much harm that there is bound to be a strong social reaction. This change is reinforced, secondly, by developments in mass communications: where such disasters occur, everyone knows about them. Perhaps partly as a result of these two factors, sociologists have also noted a change, thirdly, in attitudes to both risk and responsibility. In the modern world, we are unwilling to ascribe tragedies to fate, chance, the gods; our scientific world view makes us look for causes, and in particular for causal agencies to which we can attribute responsibility—notably human beings. We assume that where such causes can be found, this implies that disasters were avoidable; and this makes us willing to attribute blame. This has led some sociologists to argue that in the late modern world, we become increasingly aware of failings which are proximate to the event but also systemic failings in the corporation's rules and procedures developed over a period of time.

In cases such as the *Herald* sinking, it is then argued that the relative importance of these systemic failings as compared with reckless or negligent individual acts or omissions proximate to the event renders the exclusive prosecution of junior employees who are often most directly involved unfair. Significantly, the Crown Prosecution Service recently proceeded against not only the train driver but also Great Western Trains in pursuing a manslaughter prosecution following the 1997 Southall rail disaster in which seven people were killed. Notwithstanding the fact that the corporate manslaughter charge was dismissed by the trial judge, the Crown Prosecution Service decision, as well as public reaction to the charge's dismissal, appear to signify the emergence of a social sense of corporate responsibility which is not a derivative of individually blameworthy acts. This development does not, of course, determine the normative question whether corporations *should* be held liable in criminal law. But it directly raises the question whether law *could* develop a conceptual framework for corporate liability presupposing a model of the firm which, though avoiding the metaphysical and anthropomorphic mystifications of the 'real entity' theory, goes beyond the 'aggregate/contractual' model to recognize both firms' distinctive capacity for collective action and citizens' interpretation of firms as autonomous and distinctive collectivities operating in the social world and oriented to risk, yet also increasingly intolerant of it. Finally, both the growing social significance of corporations and increasing public knowledge of their operations, as reflected by, for example, levels of media reporting, have engendered a willingness to blame collectivities as well as individuals. Hence we seem to be witnessing the emergence of (or perhaps a return to) a social construction of corporations as bodies who can be genuinely blameworthy, and whom it is both fair and appropriate to hold directly responsible for crime. The close analysis of how disasters such as the *Herald* sinking occur tend to illuminate the diffusion of responsibility and—as in the case of Sheen J's inquiry—single out not only individual.

6.3 SHOULD A COMPANY BE GUILTY OF A CRIME?

A company is regarded as a person in the eyes of the law.[40] It is able therefore to enter contracts and commit torts. But should it be liable for committing a criminal offence? The arguments over this issue can be divided into those that focus on the practical benefits or disadvantages of corporate liability and those that consider the issue from a more theoretical perspective.

---

[40] Wells (2001: ch. 5) provides a useful history of corporate liability within the UK.

Practical issues

On the one side of the argument there are those who argue that if companies are made criminally liable for deaths or serious harms this will create a strong incentive on corporate managers to ensure that adequate safety systems are properly in place and adhered to.[41] However, to others regulation and non-criminal sanctions will be a more effective means of improving safety standards in corporate enterprise than the criminal law.[42] In particular it is claimed that companies will be more willing to own up to mistakes that have been made and open to discussion about safety problems if the stick of a criminal penalty is not held over them.[43]

In the following passage Christopher Clarkson considers whether corporate wrong doing is better dealt with by criminal or civil liability:

C.M.V. Clarkson, 'Corporate Culpability' [1998] 2 *Web Journal of Current Legal Issues*

2. Criminal or Civil Liability

While the use of criminal sanctions against companies is well-established in both England and the United States, there has been a recent movement, emanating from the law and economics literature in the United States, advocating the use of civil, as opposed to criminal, liability against companies (see Khanna 1996; Fischel and Sykes 1996). The gist of the argument here is that civil liability shares many of the same features as criminal liability, namely, both impose liability upon a company, both aim at deterrence and companies suffer a loss of reputation from both (see Khanna 1996, p. 1508). However, civil liability is better able to calculate appropriate levels of damages to maximise deterrence in a cost-efficient manner because 'pursuing corporate criminal liability results in society bearing the higher sanctioning costs of stigma penalties and the increased costs of deterring corporate mis-behaviour created by the procedural protections of criminal law' (Khanna 1996, p. 1533). Overdeterrence can lead to excessive monitoring at the cost of beneficial activities and 'when the penalty exceeds the social harm, the problem of socially excessive product prices and litigation costs again arises' (Fischel and Sykes 1996, p. 325).

However, these claims can, and should, be resisted. Criminal liability differs from civil liability in a least four important respects (see Khanna 1996, p. 1492). First, criminal liability involves stronger procedural protections such as the safeguards under PACE and the requirement for proof beyond reasonable doubt. Secondly, criminal law is enforced by more powerful enforcement agencies, whether it be the police or the HSE, with more resources at their disposal than many private plaintiffs. Thirdly, criminal punishment involves stigma and censure and, fourthly and related to the last point, criminal sanctions have a symbolic and 'message-sending' (Khanna 1996, p. 1492) role. Claims by law and economics academics tend to paint a one-dimensional picture: what is the minimum sanction in terms of a fine or compensation that is most cost-effective in deterring the activity? Even operating within their paradigm of deterrence, this misses the potential deterrent effect of subjection to the criminal process. The more powerful enforcement powers involving, for instance, the ability to detain and question corporate officials and the extra procedural protections emphasising the seriousness of the proceedings, can in themselves operate as a significant deterrent. The fact that private civil litigation depends upon an identifiable victim with the necessary resources to commence litigation weakens the deterrent impact of civil litigation. For

---

[41] Lacey (2000b).   [42] Simpson (2002).   [43] Khanna (1996).

example, with pollution offences there is often no identifiable victim who is aware of being harmed; the threat of a civil or administrative sanction brought by a public body will not have the same deterrent effect. But, more importantly and stepping outside their paradigm, it is now widely accepted that the main function of the criminal law and punishment is to censure wrongdoing and through such blame and denunciation to emphasise the level of rejection of the wrongdoing. Civil liability is ill-suited for this purpose. The massive publicity surrounding the conviction of a company for manslaughter in *Kite and Others* and the failure of the prosecution in the *P & O* case is testament to the power and dramatic weight of a criminal conviction as compared with civil liability.

Can companies be morally responsible?

Much of the debate over whether companies should be found guilty of serious criminal offences has centred on the question: are companies morally responsible for their actions? In the first extract, G.R. Sullivan challenges the theoretical basis for imposing corporate liability, arguing that companies are not 'moral agents' who can be held morally responsible for their actions.[44] However, he argues this does not mean that companies cannot be held criminally responsible.

G.R. Sullivan, 'The Attribution of Culpability to Limited Companies' (1996) 55 *Cambridge Law Journal* 515 at 532–9

(iv) Are corporations real?

The accounts of 'corporate' corporate liability which we have reviewed have been criticised in terms of their foundations and their likely practical effect. Still open is the question of whether corporations are 'real' in the sense that they may be regarded as substantive moral agents. If the conclusion is affirmative, it follows that further attempts should be made to identify and formulate a truly corporate culpability. But if the moral reality of companies cannot be demonstrated, it may be best to employ more straightforward means of deploying the deterrent resources of the criminal law against organisations.

Many writers on corporate liability take the position that an account of corporate behaviour cannot be exhaustively given by reference to the conduct of individuals associated with it. As Professor Wells has put it, the effect of imposing corporate structures on human interaction is to make '2 + 2 = 5': it is in the surplus that we find the quintessence of corporateness. A common way of asserting the reality of this additional substance is to make the ontological claim that the world is not exclusively a natural place but contains non-natural items such as souls, capacities of the will independent of mind and body and so forth. Plato and Hegel and other less eminent idealist philosophers have asserted the transcendent reality of the non-natural. It will be recalled that the nation-state was the most real thing of all for Hege and, more recently, Professor Scruton has argued that forms of association such as companies subsume and transcend the individuals., associated with them. Such an ontology can readily accommodate companies as not merely legally constituted but as actors in the world with their own intentionality and biography.

---

[44] See also Wolf (1985).

It is submitted that this 'idealist' view of companies would provide; an unsuitable founda-tion for corporate criminal liability in English law. It is partly a matter of history and habits of mind. The only flirtation with an organic view of companies- in English law-the theory of identification-does not rest on any assumptions about the metaphysical reality of companies but on a rough and ready anthropomorphism. The most prominent Anglo-American theoretical accounts of the nature of companies, the accounts of Hohfeld and Hart, bypass organic theory entirely and take it as axiomatic that companies are legal as opposed to real entities. None of this might matter if we could be confident that the organic theory is the best account of companies and is the theory that will ultimately prevail. The problem here is how to accommodate those persons, such as Lord Hoffmann, who insist, 'There is in fact no such thing as the company is such, no *ding* and *sich* . . .' Speaking for himself, this writer cannot see how he would ever become convinced of the reality of companies other than by empirically-founded inductive reasoning and, of course, organic theory derived from idealist philosophy lies entirely outside that tradition. A general Anglo-American adoption of organic theory seems unlikely.

However, there are theoretical accounts of companies as moral agents in their own right which are based on a natural account of the world. Perhaps the best known is in Professor French's *Collective and Corporate Responsibility*. French's theory starts from an examination of the way in which organisations of a certain size, complexity and longetivity decide to do things. He maintains that if the *modus operandi* of organisations is examined and properly understood, an agency is revealed which is intrinsic to corporations and not reducible to the agency, individual or collective, of associated individuals.

The key for French is what he terms corporate internal decision procedures. These are characterised by:

a   Internal organisation and/or decision procedures by which courses of concerted action can be chosen.

b   Enforced standards of conduct different from and more stringent than those applying in the wider community.

c   Members filling differing defined roles by virtue of which they exercise powers over other members.

French maintains that over a sufficiency of time, the decision-making processes of a com-pany are capable of generating plans and projects with which an associated individual may have only a contingent relationship. The company, through its procedures, can respond to the world beyond it and adjust and change its plans and projects. Thus it may be (though as a matter of fact rather than necessity) that the company *qua* company may be possessed of an intention which no individual associated with it shares. That intention . . . 1 may be changed or adjusted as circumstances require through corporate decision making procedures. For French this is sufficient for moral agency; *ergo* companies, for him, are moral agents.

A similar account is offered by Professor Dan-Cohen in his *Rights, Persons and Organisa-tions: A Legal Theory for a Bureaucratic Society*. He argues that bureaucratic structures with their capacity to evolve, mutate and reproduce may become, essentially, free-standing entities in their own right. The relationship between these entities and the individuals associated with them becomes contingent rather than necessary. Bureaucratic procedures may become so complex, automatic and self-perpetuating that the role of individual human agency in bureaucratic decision-making may become inscrutable. He makes the ultimate claim that the reality of bureaucratic structures need not depend on any form of human association. Personless corporations may exist not merely as legal constructs but as intelligent, computer-directed decision-making systems.

Fundamentally, the accounts of French and Dan-Cohen are empirical accounts. The intelligence and decision-making capacities of companies that they speak of are located in the natural world alongside the capacities of humans and animals. Consequently their work presents a genuine challenge to those, like the present writer, who insist that an exhaustive treatment of the nature of companies can only be given in legal terms. It does not seek, as earlier idealist theories do, to place the 'reality' of companies in a non-natural realm beyond empirical refutation. Issue, then, can be properly joined. A challenge to the notion of companies as moral agents can be mounted from the perspective of 'methodological individualism'. An adherent of that school would asset that claims that companies are moral agents or 'intelligent machines' are not, on examination, empirical claims at all, merely idealist claims dressed up in empirical garb. Methodological individualism is the assertion that all social and economic phenomena are attributable to human agency and human agency alone. It is most famously associated with Sir Karl Popper's dismissal of the claim that historical laws rather than human agency determine patterns of social and economic development. It is equally well adapted to challenging the claim that human agency may be submerged in social and bureaucratic structures and that these structures may take on an autonomous social reality. Methodological individualism would claim that, without human agency, there is nothing left in economic and social terms. That void will appear, however long-lasting, complex and familiar are the structures that humans impose on their social and economic interactions. Corporations and bureaucracies rest on human agency and do not transmute that agency into some form of non-human phenomena.

The strength of this position is best tested by posing hypothetical circumstances where a claim of a true corporate culpability not derived from human culpability may acquire some initial plausibility. Take a company which has been selling arms to a proscribed country and is likely to be charged with knowingly selling military equipment. French, we will recall, maintains that a company may possess a state of mind in circumstances where no individual associated with it shows a like state of mind. A methodological individualist denies that such a fact can exist, asserting that the only minds which exist are the ones inside our heads. Accordingly, if methodological individualism is correct, the French claim is revealed to be idealist and not empirical. Variations on this arms sales theme will be employed to see if we can, in the manner of French, identify corporate knowledge which is independent of the state of mind of anyone or more individuals associated with the company. Assume company X has well-established sales links with the proscribed country. The proscription comes into force, but company X makes no changes. Orders emanating from the proscribed country are dealt with and arms are despatched in the long familiar way. Nothing is said, let alone discussed, concerning these sales. Yet if anyone within the company is aware of the destination of these weapons, we can fashion a legal rule whereby that person's knowledge is attributed to the company without any theorising along the lines presented by French. Under the identification doctrine, the individual with the requisite knowledge would merely need to be of sufficient status to support a finding, within the doctrine's terms, of knowing selling on the part of the company.

The narrowness of the identification doctrine is a good reason for looking for alternatives to it as a rule of attribution. French's alternative, if properly understood, is to look directly into the company itself and seek a specifically corporate knowledge arising from the company's decision-making structures. Yet the procedures that a company currently has do not arise spontaneously; they are not the equivalent of a virgin birth. The organisational structure is ultimately the product of human agency, however sophisticated and automated a company's procedures may be. Of course, the current board of company X may have inherited and uncritically adopted the current trading patterns of the company; they may be, as it were, on automatic pilot. Yet that very state of affairs is attributable to their agency and is a state of affairs that could be changed or adjusted if they so chose. It is not obvious why one should look for the culpability for an offence within the company structure rather than among those individuals responsible for maintaining that structure and thereby standing in a relationship of responsibility for the decisions generated within it.

The claim that there can be an inherently corporate mental state is made most starkly if we take company X to be one of Dan-Cohen's personless corporations, a company of some future time which can come into legal being, all legal formalities satisfied, as an artificial intelligence system operated by robots. Once the system is set up, it manufactures products, takes and executes orders and so forth without any further human intervention. Because of the sophistication of its programme, company X can respond to the fact that a particular country may not lawfully acquire its products by creating false certification, arranging intermediate destinations for its shipments in order to continue trading with that country. Assume that no human individual, past or present, is in any way at fault for the fact that company X is trading and will continue to trade with a proscribed country: if there is any knowledge present here at all, it can only be the knowledge of company X.

Whether X's system-guided responses can be taken to be states of mind cognate with human states of mind is a contested philosophical question. Yet even if we assume that artificial intelligence is a form of autonomous ratiocination and that an AI system generates genuine states of mind, it is well to remind ourselves that we are not discussing intentionality in its own right but intentionality as a predicate of criminal culpability. Though we have allowed the possibility that there may be non-human systems which can possess intentionality or knowledge, it is, *pace* French, a further and a much larger step to claim that these properties are a sufficient condition for moral agency. We are presented, in another guise, with the familiar problem of the psychopath. It is not possible to speak of guilt or culpability if the entity to be judged lacks any capacity for empathy, unease, remorse, self-doubt or anything that remotely approaches a conscience. It is one thing to employ rules of attribution whereby the genuine culpability of individuals is attributed as a matter of convention to a company in pursuit of whatever gains in welfare such an attribution may bring. It is quite another to declare that culpability has been manifested when the foundations of culpability are nowhere to be found. We have conceded, if only for the sake of argument, that if you take all human (and non-human) animals out of the world you may still be left with some forms of intentionality, but it is doubtful whether we would be left with any forms of guilt.

All that said, an account of society and its institutions which follows methodological individualism to the letter is to some extent an impoverished account. Professor Ernest Gellner, in his opposition to that school, made the telling point that if we were to avoid consistently any holistic account of our institutions and practices, many tales would take much longer in the telling and there would often be a feeling that something important had been left out. 'The team played well' may require little unpacking, yet if we were to redistribute that judgment by way of an account, however meticulous and accurate, of each individual's performance the full story would remain untold. There is something missing-call it wholeness, synergy, whatever-if we refuse to allow the group ever to transcend its individual members.

This point is made with particular force and clarity in Professor John Searle's *The Construction of Social Reality*. He agrees with the methodological individualists that the only intents there are are the intents inside our heads. Any theory that impersonal entities may possess intents is, for him, empirically unfounded and frequently a consequence of conceptual confusion. But recognition of that important truth should not blind us to the pervasiveness and necessity of what he terms 'collective intentionality'. Collective intentionality is his term for those intents that only arise, and necessarily arise, when we interact socially with others. Collective intentionality is mischaracterised if it is presented as a coincidence of respective individual intents. It is an account of the way in which social interactions generate individual intents. The intents flow from the activity or institution to the individual. The coincidence of respective individual intents does not make the institution; it is the other way around. This point is made in an obvious and vivid way by using Searle's example of a game. A resolves that he will tackle B, if B has the ball and attempts to run past him. A has made that resolution because he is playing rugby football. Rugby football requires a collective intention on the part of all the participants to play that game, otherwise the game would not be possible. Once a collective intention to play the game is instituted, it plays a constitutive role in the individual intents formed in the minds of the players. Those individual intents flow downwards from the collective intent to play the game.

Searle draws out the centrality of collective intentionality in the making of our social institutions. Without it, such items as money, ownership and companies would not be possible. It is responsible for many of the intents formed by individuals. Persons who are members of organisations bonded by a collective intent may form individual, anti-social intents which they would not have formed if they had not been members of the organisation. We have rejected the claim that when such an organisation takes a corporate form it becomes a moral agent in its own right. Nor can any systemic claim be made that individuals bear less responsibility for those intents which are generated by a collective intentionality than for those of their intents which are not. Yet we can and should take cognisance of the fact that the collective intentionality associated with a corporate organisation can be an extremely powerful social force.

Consequently, it is entirely appropriate that collective intentionality should be treated as something to which the criminal law can respond and which it can seek to influence. It should not do this by issuing false tokens. It should not say that companies are real and have their own distinctive culpability. It should not, as reactive fault and aggregation do, deem a crime to exist when the constituent elements of the crime have not been established. Nevertheless, the culpability of an individual associated with a company may well have been influenced by the organisational character of the company. Improvement in that character and a deterrent example to other organisations may well be achieved by conventionally assigning the individual's culpability to the company for the purposes of a corporate criminal conviction. Much may also be done by imposing minimum standards for the conduct of companies. These processes should not be side-tracked by seeking the chimera of a corporate culpability disassociated from human culpability. Appropriate standards of safety, pollution control etc. should be formulated and corporate performances assessed in terms of compliance or non-compliance with those standards.

Those who reject arguments of the kind Sullivan makes suggest that companies do have an existence that is distinct from any identifiable employee.[45] It is possible, they argue, for companies to develop a 'corporate ethos'[46] (e.g. that safety issues are (or are not) important) which cannot be traced to a single person or group of people. It is therefore fair to hold a company morally responsible for its acts.[47] It is also possible to argue that even if not morally

---

[45] Certainly the notion of corporate crime appears to be gaining in acceptability among the general public. See generally the discussion in White and Haines (2000: 7) on the role of media in defining crime.

[46] Bucy (1991).

[47] Wells (2001: 65); Gobert and Punch (2003: 46–9); French (1984). For a discussion of how a company can be seen as an actor see Coleman (1974).

responsible a company can be held liable if to do so promotes another important aim of the criminal law: the avoidance of harm.[48]

In the next extract James Gobert and Maurice Punch see fewer difficulties in describing companies as 'citizens' with the moral responsibilities of citizens:

J. Gobert and M. Punch, *Rethinking Corporate Crime* (London: Butterworths LexisNexis, 2003), 35–9

We start from the premise that companies are corporate citizens, with all the responsibilities of citizenship. The issuance of a charter, or, in more modern times, a certificate of incorporation is, for a company, the analogue of a grant of citizenship to a natural person. Companies can also receive licenses to engage in activities denied to ordinary citizens and those companies to which a license is not granted. As the quid pro quo, companies arguably incur various obligations, including the obligation to obey the law and to foster obedience to the law by their staff and officers. However, experience has taught that many companies do not take these obligations seriously, and that when they do not, the criminal justice system has encountered considerable difficulty in holding them to account. Legal violations frequently occur in the course of a company's business and can result in substantial harm, harm which if caused under comparable circumstances by a human offender would lead to a criminal prosecution, a term of imprisonment, and the social condemnation and stigma that accompanies a conviction. Why do not the same consequences flow from a company's violations of the law and why does the criminal justice system encounter such difficulties in holding companies legally accountable for their wrongdoing?

There are a number of possible explanations. These range from a psychological failure to perceive corporate crimes as 'real' crime; to inadequate investigatory mechanisms for detecting when a corporate offence has occurred; to a legal test of liability which fails to recognise the nature of modern corporate decision-making; to rules of evidence and trial procedures which were designed with individuals in mind and may be ill-suited to the trial of a company; and to a scheme of sanctions and penalties that typically amounts to little more than a slap on the wrist of the offender. Each of these failings interrelates with and compounds the others. The bottom line is that the criminal justice system, as presently constituted, fails to deter, detect or meaningfully punish corporate wrongdoing.

Until fairly recently, neither the government nor the public seemed to view corporate crime as being a serious problem, and they still may not see it being as serious a problem as more common forms of crime such as burglary or theft. The government's reluctance to take corporate crime seriously may be borne of self-serving motives. Profitable, albeit law-breaking, companies pay taxes, reduce unemployment and contribute to the international reputation of the state—as well as to the funding of political parties. It is simply not in the government's interest to put such companies out of business. Even the threat of a possible prosecution may prompt a decision to relocate in a more corporate-friendly environment, or stifle the innovation required to compete in a global economy. The message is conveyed and reinforced by business executives turned politicians, and by ex-politicians turned business executives. There is often an incestuous interchange between political and managerial elites, with former executives winding up with ministerial posts and former ministers being appointed as non-executive directors at a range of companies (Useem 1984).

Equally understandable perhaps is the public's lack of concern over corporate crime. Street crime is more visible, more immediate, and more threatening than is corporate crime. The

---

[48] Gobert and Punch (2003: 47).

public does not fear corporate crime as it does street crime. There is a sense of personal violation when one's home is burgled or one's possessions stolen. There is a palpable fear when one is confronted by a violent hooligan or knife-wielding robber. But how many passengers fear, or are even aware, that they are being transported by a train equipped with a faulty or inoperative warning system or a ferry that is defectively designed and subject to capsize? Consequently, there is not the same public outcry to 'do something' about 'crime in the suites' as there is about 'crime in the streets' (Punch 2000). Indeed, particularly with respect to offences against the revenue, the public is often prepared to collude with wrongdoers. Thus, consumers may be willing to pay in cash in exchange for a lower price, well appreciating that the contractor may be seeking to evade paying VAT. Similarly, purchasers are willing to buy goods in a grey market, their desire for a bargain overcoming whatever reservations they might have that they are handling stolen goods and thereby abetting thieves.

The moral ambivalence that permeates this area (Nelken 1997) can be seen in a highly-publicised case from the Netherlands. A well-known family firm, which ran a chain of hotels and motorway restaurants, was prosecuted for tax fraud. The offences had been deliberate and persistent (the family also had a tendency to build motels without proper planning permission and licences), the sums were large (on the order of £70M), and the defendants had displayed an aggressive recalcitrance when dealing with the authorities. They publicly belittled the regulators, compared their methods to those of the Nazi occupiers in the war, blamed the trade unions for betraying them (and argued for their abolition), and posed as socially conscious employers espousing essential 'Dutch' values of industry and thrift. They were, in particular, scathing about the pettiness and irrelevance of rules which were a meddlesome brake on healthy and 'honest' enterprise. On the other hand, the defendants provided much sought-after local employment as well as excellent value to customers. After they were convicted and given prison sentences, there was widespread public outrage that these industrious entrepreneurs should be treated as criminals, even though the amounts involved were astronomical in relation to most conventional crimes (a feature which attracted high sentences Helmer 1997). Interestingly, on appeal the sentences were reduced to terms of community service (Huisman and Niemeijer 1998).

. . .

Public and judicial ambivalence toward corporate criminality fit comfortably with the government's desire not to ruffle the feathers of its tax-paying corporate citizens. Yet the risks that such organisations create by their illegality can cause harm that far exceeds that which could be wrought by the most dangerous of human offenders. The largest industrial accident ever, at Bhopal in India, may have killed as many as 5,000 people and injured over 2,000,000. Although criminal negligence was suspected, the disaster did not lead to a prosecution and conviction, as criminal proceedings were halted following a settlement between Union Carbide and the Indian government (Shrivastava 1987; Fortun 2001).

If a government were committed to curbing corporate crime, it would as a preliminary matter have to allocate the resources to detect offences. In England, however, the responsibility for enforcing most of the criminal laws that control corporate activity is entrusted to regulatory authorities or inspectorates rather than to the police. As part of the 'deregulatory' movement, successive governments have also decreased the funds allotted to these agencies. Furthermore, they are often understaffed. The experience of the Serious Fraud Office, which is neither underfunded nor understaffed, demonstrates that even under the best of circumstances, it is not easy to bring a corporate offender to heel. Business dealings are complex, and the proof of a criminal violation may lie buried in corporate archives and computer data that require years to sift through and make sense of (assuming they have not already been 'cleansed' or shredded). Financial transactions designed to conceal money laundering, for example, may involve the transfer of funds around the world several times over in the space of minutes, yet following the money trail may take years of painstaking work. For an underfunded and understaffed agency, which may receive at best lukewarm support from the government, the problems are acute.

Bringing a criminal prosecution against a corporate wrongdoer can be problematic as well. As we shall discuss in greater detail in the following chapters, a large part of the difficulty lies in devising a test of liability that is suitable for companies. Traditional legal doctrines were developed with respect to human offenders. In superimposing these doctrines on to corporate defendants, the courts have had to locate the corporate mind for purposes of assessing mens rea. For the English judges the company's mind was to be found in the mind of one of its directors, officers and senior managers, persons who could be 'identified' with the company for legal purposes. But even a rudimentary understanding of how corporate decisions are made would indicate the futility of this approach. In a company, ideas that may originate with an individual will be reviewed by working parties, committees, senior managers, vice-presidents in charge of whatever phase of the company's operation is involved, CEOs and, ultimately, a board of directors. The final product may bear little resemblance to the originator's conception. Where responsibility is so diffused, it makes little sense to strive to link decisions with particular individuals.

Tests of corporate criminality that impute human fault to companies are unsatisfying all around. For the company they are unsatisfying because, as an institutional entity, it may not have behaved in a blameworthy manner. The crime may have been in direct contravention of corporate policy, and the company may have tried its best to prevent its commission. In some instances the company may find itself the victim of the crime, yet at the same time be legally liable for its occurrence. For the prosecution, the link between corporate criminal liability and individual criminal liability is unsatisfying for, while it may be obvious that a crime has been committed, it may be impossible to trace responsibility for that harm to a particular individual because of the diffused nature of corporate decision-making. In the final analysis the linkage of corporate fault to human fault is unsatisfying because corporate fault is not the same as human fault, just as the body corporate is distinct from the individuals who are its directors, officers and employees. The goals of a company cannot automatically be equated with the goals of anyone person or combination of persons, nor can one derive the goals of the company by adding together potentially conflicting individual goals. A company has its own distinctive goals, its own distinctive culture, and its own distinctive personality. It is an independent organic entity, and, as such, should be responsible in its own right, directly and not derivatively, for the criminal consequences that arise out of the way that its business is conducted. This is not to preclude prosecutions of individuals when they have committed an offence, but rather to recognise that, in addition to the prosecution of individuals, the company must shoulder its share of the legal blame to the extent that it bears responsibility for an offence. When that responsibility dwarfs that of the individual actor, then a prosecution of the company alone may be warranted.

What is needed is a theory of criminal liability that captures the distinctive nature of corporate fault. We start from the insight that a significant proportion of corporate offences are, in fact, crimes of omission rather than commission. Typically, the company's fault will lie in its failure to have put into place protective mechanisms that would have prevented harm from occurring. It is for this failure that the company bears responsibility for the harm. Recognising that corporate crimes are more often crimes of omission than commission reinforces the poverty of derivative theories of corporate liability that attribute the offences of individuals to a company. While it may be feasible to link wrongful acts to particular actors, it is often impossible to determine who should have done something that was not done. The obligation to put into place systems that would avert crime is *collective* and the failure to do so is a reflection of the way that the company has chosen to conduct its business.

Once a viable legal theory of criminal liability is established, courts need to consider the rules of evidence and criminal procedure that should govern the trial of a corporate defendant. . . .

Finally, there is the issue of sanctions following a conviction. To the company's way of thinking, this may be a more important issue than that of guilt. . . .

6.4 IF THERE IS TO BE CORPORATE CRIME, WHAT FORM SHOULD IT TAKE?

If the law is to make companies liable for their crimes then the next question is what form should that take.[49] One option would be to use the present offences, but develop ways of finding that the company has a *mens rea* or can commit an *actus reus*. Theories such as the aggregation theory attempt to do this. Another would be to reject the idea that a company can be made to be like a person[50] and to pass legislation which creates specific corporate crimes, of the kind the government has proposed.

In the following extract Celia Wells considers some of the alternative forms that corporate criminal liability could take:

C. Wells, *Corporations and Criminal Responsibility* (2nd edn., Oxford: OUP, 2001), 154–60

3. People, Systems, and Culture

In the arguments about the appropriate basis for corporate criminal liability two distinct strands emerge. One line seeks to equate the corporate entity with the individual, to tease out those characteristics of corporations which can be correlated with the essence of individual responsibility. The other exploits the dissimilarities between individuals and the group entity. Corporations are different from human beings, their activities are not merely on a grander scale, their whole existence, function, and formation marks them apart. The contours of their culpability should reflect those differences. Although either route can lead to corporate liability, the second has more potential. Any argument which seeks to equiparate corporate with individual liability has to confront the group difference at some point; efforts to bring out corporate intentionality from corporate policy need to face the complexities of group structures with their lines of authority and internal power distributions. At the same time, the idea that humans are atomistic individuals acting without reference to the groups of which they are a part is unhelpful.

With the concentration on the group/individual comparison, it is easy to lose sight of the culpability criterion itself. Much of the corporate crime literature makes false assumptions about the nature of criminal fault requirements; commentators use 'intention' without acknowledging the alternative of recklessness. Debate about how best to capture corporate

---

[49] Lacey (2000b).　　[50] Wells (2001: 71).

responsibility is often hampered by a failure to distinguish between culpability criteria such as intention and recklessness. This applies as much to discussions of aggregation as to other proposals introduced below. Aggregation is often conceived as a collective 'knowledge'. An attitudinal rather than a cognitive version of recklessness facilitates the attribution of blame to the corporate entity. Recklessness can be found in the practical indifference, the attitude, which an action manifests. A corporate action can be said to display such an indifference when it results from the decisions of its responsible officers. It is necessary then to adjust perceptions not only of groups and of individuals but also of culpability criteria; by so doing it is possible to emerge with a strengthened theory of corporate 'intentionality'. A theory which makes the corporation responsible for itself is also required. The two organizational models of organizational process and bureaucratic process lead to the recognition that responsibility can be found either in the individual corporate worker *or* in the corporate structure itself. The latter can have a number of forms, ranging from aggregate knowledge to full-blown corporate culture liability. It can also embrace compliance.

i. Extending Identification

Since it is proposed that this second holistic type of liability should be additional and not a substitute for derivative forms, it is necessary first to consider whether the current form of identification liability for *mens rea* offences is broad enough in scope. Many commentators regard the *respondeat superior* doctrine which has developed in the US federal courts as too wide for *mens rea* offences; conversely, the UK direct liability scheme is seen as too narrow. There are strong arguments in favour of extending identification so that the corporation is liable for the crimes of those with responsibility for particular spheres. Under the 'responsible officer' theory regional managers, for example, would be included. This is already reflected in Canadian law; as Schroeder J. put it in one case: 'He may have been but a satellite to a major planet, but his position in the galaxy was not an inferior one.' French proposes a test that at least includes anyone with a 'significant degree of autonomy with regard to making corporate decisions and instigating corporate actions'. The identification rule should reflect actual responsibility rather than formal duty. . . .

ii. Aggregation

The aggregation of employees' knowledge means that corporate culpability does: not have to be contingent on one individual employee's satisfying the relevant culpability criterion. Aggregation straddles agency and holistic forms of liability. It is used in the United States but has been rejected in English corporate manslaughter cases. Conceptually or epistemologic-ally the notion of aggregation is problematic if it is taken to mean that the fragmented knowledge of a number of individuals is fitted together to make one culpable whole. This is less of a problem in offences based on recklessness where recklessness is conceived in terms of practical indifference. But even if the knowledge-of-risk model of recklessness were adopted, the difficulties could be overcome. Aggregation needs to be seen as a recognition that individuals within a company contribute to the whole machine; it is the whole which is judged, not the parts. So the question would not be whether employee X's knowledge plus employee Y's knowledge *added up to* recklessness or whatever, but whether, given the information held amongst a number of 'responsible officers', it can be said that the cor-poration itself was reckless. This is no more demanding a feat of the imagination than that required by so-called subjective mental states when the court determines by what can only be a matter of guesswork whether a defendant actually foresaw a risk or actually intended a result.

iii. Going Holistic

The images of the organization emerging from the discussion in section 1 suggest that a pure form of holistic liability is appropriate. Corporations can be seen as diverse and hetero-geneous both within and amongst themselves, but with a core structure through which management exerts or attempts to exert control both over objectives and over attainment. The anthropomorphic image infusing much legal discourse is unhelpful if it is taken to imply that the mind cannot be responsible for the body. But in other ways the physiological metaphor could be used as the basis for a form of liability which better reflects the reality of the corporate organization. Corporate liability in the United Kingdom assumes that only a select few officers exert control or have any managerial autonomy over aspects of the enterprise for which they work. This does not seem borne out by theories of organizations. Thus a widening of primary liability would be indicated. We do not imagine that we are transacting with the managing director of Marks and Spencer when we shop there, nor that when a plane takes off the airline's board of directors has specific knowledge of its activities, route, or condition that day. We do, however, expect that large companies operate according to a set of rules and procedures and that these, particularly in relation to public transport systems, have addressed the potential risks and developed safety procedures to ensure that those risks are minimized.

The two organizational models referred to earlier, those of organizational process and bureaucratic process, suggest that a scheme of corporate liability should recognize that responsibility can both flow from the individual to the corporation and be found in the cor-poration's structures themselves. Current liability reflects the first: the corporation can be vicariously or directly liable for the wrongdoing of individuals within it. The second goes further and demands that liability be placed on the corporation in some instances even though no identifiable individual has committed an offence. This rejects the conventional analysis of identification liability as the only way in which a corporation can be said to act directly and knowingly, supplementing it with the notion that *the corporation* can be responsible for *the corporation's activities*.

Tigar advances the following arguments for a broader starting point. The first is the familiar one that identification is based on unwarranted assumptions about corporate managerial behaviour. Rules of liability should encourage management to have a preventive system: 'Broad rules of corporate criminal liability shape [the corporation's internal culture] towards law-abiding behaviour at all levels of the structure.' Secondly, a point which was mentioned in Chapter 2, the operation of collateral estoppel: corporate liability is a means of promoting, encouraging, and facilitating civil recovery which would otherwise be inaccessible. And lastly, if the only route to criminal liability is through the complicity or acquiescence of top management, then every corporate guilty plea puts management at serious risk of suit by shareholders. Another point can be added, which is that the narrower the system of liability, the more it favours larger enterprises: smaller companies have fewer bureaucratic layers and differentiate less between managerial and operational roles. Reliance on an identification model, even with a lower threshold of 'responsible officer', is insufficient. Concentration on the misdeeds of managerial officers ignores the reality of corporate decision- making. It is clear from what we know of the way large corporations organize themselves that power is both dispersed (within a clear structure) and that this is mediated by informal rules and rivalries. The identification doctrine applied to diffuse corporate structures can result in no one being liable, or improperly reflect the limits of moral responsibility. Management prior-ities set from above 'determine the social context within which a corporation's shop-floor workers make decisions about working practices'.

French has provided a philosophical model through which to justify the imposition of liability on a company for the actions of its subordinate members. A corporation's internal decision structures, its CIDs, are seen as incorporating recognition rules. A CID structure has three elements: an organizational flow-chart, procedural rules, and policies. The first provides the 'grammar' of the corporation, while the last two are 'corporate decision recognition rules'. Corporations then are mini-jurisdictions and their operating policies are broad, general principles. Where the corporate CID structure has contributed to the realization of a risk, an appropriate legal mechanism should be found in response. Again, organization theories reinforce the argument by showing that corporations usually have detailed configurations which place responsibility for specific aspects on different departments. Internal structure and culture affect a company's actions. While some corporate harms are caused by senior management (individually or collectively) engaging knowingly in fraudulent activity or acting recklessly in the sense described above, many occur through a system failure. The relevant question would then be whether the corporation can be blamed because its system, its operating policies, displayed a reckless attitude to safety. P&O's culpability in relation to the Zeebrugge tragedy provides an instructive example. In that case, the relevant issue was the company's failure to develop a safety policy, which was both a cause of the capsize and a large contributory factor in the failure of the prosecution. The very failures which caused the accident allowed the company to slip through the net of responsibility.

Once the idea that a corporation's fault can be approached through its policies is established, refinements such as compliance or reactive fault can be introduced. CIDs can be used both to lead a corporation towards liability but also to give it the opportunity to escape. The corporation should be able to rebut the attribution of corporate responsibility to any act of its high managerial staff on the grounds that it is against established internal policy. Such a defence will not be easy to mount because it will need evidence of the policy plus a lack of any previous examples whereby it has condoned similar failures: in other words, evidence that the illegal conduct was clearly and convincingly forbidden and of the development and implementation of reasonable safeguards designed to prevent corporate crime. Providing the equivalent of a due diligence defence may also counter those who oppose an extension of identification liability beyond the higher directorial echelons. Liability based either, as just discussed, on the company's structures, or on the wrongdoings of any of its employees, could be rebutted by proving that, as an organization, it exercised due diligence to prevent the crime. If the acts of top officials represent the practices and procedures of the corporation, their involvement in corporate criminal activity should almost always defeat a due diligence defence. This could amount to an effective deterrent, since the affirmative defence of due diligence would have to be preceded by the adoption of stringent procedures to combat illegal activity.

This would be a clear recognition that an act is corporate not only because of its form, but because of the policy it instantiates, displays, or manifests. A variation on this is Fisse's concept of reactive fault, that is: 'unreasonable corporate failure to devise and undertake satisfactory preventive or corrective measures in response to the commission of the *actus reus of* the offence.' Focusing on the corporation's reactions would mean unlocking the time-frame of *actus reus/mens rea*; it would also counter the argument that broadening the liability base could have an undesirable effect on the range *of* penalties by 'undercutting' the justification for imposing sanctions more severe than a fine or other monetary penalty. The concept of reactive fault approaches corporate blameworthiness through its CIDs, but extends the enquiry to allow for the situation, one which is probably common, where a corporation fails to adapt its policies in the light of past errors. This could be particularly useful in the areas of health and safety of workers, product safety, and pollution regulation, where it is easy to refute an allegation of recklessness if each 'offence' is considered in isolation.

As I suggested earlier, an advantage claimed for starting with a broad notion of liability based effectively on the actions *of* any corporate employee, which is then limited by proof of reasonable preventive strategies, is that it avoids the extremely difficult line-drawing exercise *of* deciding where in the corporation the threshold for liability should begin. Some clear models have now emerged. There is agency in one form or another-the strict *respondeat superior* version or the responsible officer version—or there is organizational liability which does not depend on the misdeeds *of* a specified individual. Each *of* these can be qualified by a compliance or due diligence component in the form *of* a positive liability requirement, an affirmative defence, or a sentencing discount. Lastly, liability can in some circumstances be imposed on the individual employee or manager as well. A combination *of* these models is probably optimal, none is sufficient in all conditions and circumstances. The Australian Criminal Code Act discussed in Chapter 7 remains the main example *of* legislation aiming to achieve such a combination. John Coffee's somewhat tighter version emphasises the relevance *of* preventive compliance programmes:

'A legal entity, including a corporation, partnership, union, or other form of business association, may be convicted of an offence if:

a.   the offence is an offence (i) for which a legislative purpose to impose liability on such entity is plainly evident or (ii) in absence of such liability, there is significant risk that the legislature's purpose would be frustrated;

b.   the commission of the offence was performed, authorised, requested, commanded, or recklessly tolerated by a senior managerial agent of the entity acting on behalf of the entity within the normal or foreseeable scope of such agent's authority and with an intent to benefit the entity; or;

c.   the offence was a proximate and foreseeable consequence of the entity's failure to devise and implement reasonable preventive, monitoring, or safety controls or precautions, or to adopt and maintain a reasonable compliance programme, which failure under the circumstances constituted a serious departure from the standards and procedures then observed by similarly situated entities or that should have been observed by any such entity.'

Provision should be made to counter the ability of organizations to disappear or to be absorbed into a different enterprise. An important contributory factor cited by relatives of those killed in the *Piper Alpha* oil rig explosion when they eventually abandoned their efforts to mount a private prosecution was the sale of the rig company by its parent company, Occidental. This distinctive capacity of the company to disaggregate, dissolve, or reconstitute itself presents a challenge which is not peculiar to the enforcement of criminal law; plaintiffs in civil actions have this problem too. The range of possible devices which might be used to stay any such corporate escape moves have not been elaborated here. Where such devices fail, then of course the individual directors might be the only appropriate target. An additional, although related, problem is that identified by Collins as 'complex patterns of economic integration'. A construction site, for example, will often be worked by a number of separate capital units, different contractors working together but legally distinct. This creates problems, particularly with regard to recovery for economic loss in tort, but it has wider implications. 'Firms enjoy considerable freedom both in law and in practice to determine the limits of their boundaries.' Any adjustment of legal principles to reflect vertical integration will have clear implications for criminal liability, but it is not a matter to which I have devoted detailed attention here.

QUESTIONS

1. Nowadays many of the large-scale corporate projects involve a number of companies working together (H. Collins (1990)). Have the proposals concerning corporate liability paid sufficient attention to such cases?

2. If you are convinced by the argument that companies should be responsible for crimes why not schools being responsible for crimes of their pupils, universities of their students, families of their children? Cannot schools, universities, and families also have an 'ethos'?

3. Is there a danger that focusing on corporate liability will lead to negligent managers not being prosecuted (see Centre for Corporate Responsibility (2000: 2.1)?

FURTHER READING

Bergman, D. (2000), *The Case for Corporate Responsibility* (London: Disaster Action).

Bovens, M. (1998), *The Quest for Responsibility: Accountability and Citizenship in Complex Organisations* (Cambridge: Cambridge University Press).

Braithwaite, J., and Fisse, B. (1988), 'The Allocation of Responsibility for Corporate Crime', *Sydney Law Review* 11: 468.

—— and —— (1993), *Corporations, Crime and Accountability* (Cambridge: Cambridge University Press).

Clough, J., and Mulhern, C. (2002), *The Prosecution of Corporations* (Oxford: OUP).

Glazebrook, P. (2002), 'A Better Way of Convicting Businesses of Avoiding Deaths and Injuries?', *Cambridge Law Journal* 61: 405.

Gobert, J., and Punch, M. (2003), *Rethinking Corporate Crime* (London: Butterworths).

Slapper, G., and Tombs, S. (1999), *Corporate Crime* (Harlow: Longman).

Sullivan, G.R. (1996b), 'The Attribution of Culpability to Limited Companies', *Cambridge Law Journal* 55: 515.

Wells, C. (2001), *Corporations and Criminal Responsibility* (2nd edn., Oxford: OUP).

14

INCHOATE OFFENCES

PART I: THE LAW ON INCHOATE OFFENCES

1 INCHOATE OFFENCES

DEFINITION

Inchoate offences are ones that seek to deal with defendants who have taken steps towards the commission of an offence but who have not (yet) committed it. The three best known examples are attempts, incitements, and conspiracies.

The word inchoate means 'just begun' or 'undeveloped'. It is used to indicate that a substantive crime has not been committed, but the defendant has taken steps towards committing one or encouraging others to commit one. This chapter will discuss three inchoate offences of general application:

(1) attempts;

(2) incitements;

(3) conspiracies.

In attempts cases the defendant has gone beyond mere preparation and taken steps towards carrying out a complete crime. Incitement involves encouraging others to commit crimes, while conspiracy involves agreeing with others to commit a crime. In each of these offences the defendant has not himself performed the *actus reus* but is sufficiently close to doing so, or persuading others to do so, for the law to find it appropriate to punish him. As we shall in Part II of this chapter there is much debate about the justification for inchoate offences. There are some who emphasize the practical benefit of such offences: they permit the lawful arrest and punishment of those who plan to harm someone else, without having to wait until a victim is actually harmed. There are others who emphasize the moral blameworthiness of such conduct. It can be a matter of luck that, for example, an attempter failed to harm the victim. On the other hand there are those who are concerned that inchoate offences may infringe an important principle of criminal law: wicked thoughts alone do not deserve punishment.[1] It is for this reason that it is not enough that a defendant plans to

---

[1] *Higgins* (1801) 2 East 5.

harm another; he must put these plans into practice, by taking steps to do so, by encouraging or agreeing with others to do so.[2]

2 ATTEMPT

DEFINITION

The *actus reus*: the defendant has done an act which is more than merely preparatory to the commission of the offence.

The *mens rea*: normally an intention to commit the full offence. It is more difficult if the *actus reus* of the full offence requires proof that the defendant did an act in certain circumstances. Then the defendant must intend to do his or her act but need only be reckless as to the circumstances (if the *mens rea* for the full offence requires only recklessness as to the circumstances).

The criminal law on attempts is now governed by section 1(1) of the Criminal Attempts Act 1981: if, with intent to commit an offence to which this section applies, a person does an act which is more than merely preparatory to the commission of the offence, he is guilty of attempting to commit the offence.

2.1 MENS REA

The *mens rea* is a crucial aspect of a criminal attempt. It can be what makes the difference between a harmless act and a criminal offence: Andrew meets William and raises his hand. This may or may not be an attempted assault: it all depends on whether Andrew is intending to punch William or give him a friendly pat on the back.[3] The key *mens rea* requirement for an attempt as stated in section 1(1) is an intent to produce the *actus reus*. So, for example, attempted murder requires an intention to kill.[4] An intention to cause grievous bodily harm is not enough, even though such an intention is sufficient for the full offence of murder. Similarly for attempted criminal damage it must be shown there was an intention to cause criminal damage,[5] even though recklessness is enough for the full offence. However, unfortunately for students, the law is not quite as straightforward as may at first appear. There are the following difficulties.

What does 'intent' mean?

This is governed by *Pearman*.[6] This case confirms that the word intent in the Criminal Attempts Act carries the same meaning as in the common law. In other words it includes direct intent and sometimes indirect intent. The meaning of intent is therefore the same as that set out in Chapter 3, and is dominated by the House of Lords' decision in *Woollin*.

---

[2] For a discussion of 'double inchoate' offences see Zimmerman (2000).

[3] Of course, as always in the criminal law, the jury will very much rely on what the defendant did to decide what he intended to do: *Attorney-General's Reference (No. 1 of 1992)* [1993] 2 All ER 190 (CA).

[4] *Whybrow* (1951) 35 Cr App R 141 (CA).

[5] *Millard and Vernon* [1987] Crim LR 393 (CA). [6] (1984) 80 Cr App R 259 (CA).

What about the circumstances or consequences of the act?

The law here is governed by two leading cases which need careful reading. They appear to suggest that recklessness as to circumstantial aspects of the *actus reus* of the full offence can sometimes be sufficient for an attempt:

R v Khan (Mohammed Iqbal); R v Dhokia; R v Banga; R v Faiz
[1990] 2 All ER 783 (CA)[7]

Mohammed Iqbal Khan, Mahesh Dhokia, Jaswinder Singh Banga, and Navaid Faiz were charged with attempted rape of a 16-year-old girl. The appellants and the victim met at a disco and then went to a house. Inside the house some young men had sexual intercourse with the victim and the appellants attempted unsuccessfully to have sexual intercourse with her. The trial judge directed the jury that if the defendants were reckless as to whether or not the victim would have consented to sexual intercourse they could be convicted of attempted rape. Recklessness here included a 'could not care less' attitude. They appealed on the basis that the jury should have been directed that they could be convicted of attempted rape only if they knew or intended that the victim was not consenting.

Lord Justice Russell

In our judgment an acceptable analysis of the offence of rape is as follows: (1) the intention of the offender is to have sexual intercourse with a woman; (2) the offence is committed if, but only if, the circumstances are that: (a) the woman does not consent; AND (b) the defendant knows that she is not consenting or is reckless as to whether she consents.

Precisely the same analysis can be made of the offence of attempted rape: (1) the intention of the offender is to have sexual intercourse with a woman; (2) the offence is committed if, but only if, the circumstances are that: (a) the woman does not consent; AND (b) the defendant knows that she is not consenting or is reckless as to whether she consents.

The only difference between the two offences is that in rape sexual intercourse takes place whereas in attempted rape it does not, although there has to be some act which is more than preparatory to sexual intercourse. Considered in that way, the intent of the defendant is precisely the same in rape and in attempted rape and the *mens rea* is identical, namely, an intention to have intercourse plus a knowledge of or recklessness as to the woman's absence of consent. No question of attempting to achieve a reckless state of mind arises; the attempt relates to the physical activity; the mental state of the defendant is the same. A man does not recklessly have sexual intercourse, nor does he recklessly attempt it. Recklessness in rape and attempted rape arises not in relation to the physical act of the accused but only in his state of mind when engaged in the activity of having or attempting to have sexual intercourse.

If this is the true analysis, as we believe it is, the attempt does not require any different intention on the part of the accused from that for the full offence of rape. We believe this to be a desirable result which in the instant case did not require the jury to be burdened with different directions as to the accused's state of mind, dependent upon whether the individual achieved or failed to achieve sexual intercourse.

---

[7] [1990] 1 WLR 813, (1990) 91 Cr App R 29.

We recognise, of course, that our reasoning cannot apply to all offences and all attempts. Where, for example, as in causing death by reckless driving or reckless arson, no state of mind other than recklessness is involved in the offence, there can be no attempt to commit it.

In our judgment, however, the words 'with intent to commit an offence' to be found in section 1 of the Act of 1981 mean, when applied to rape, 'with intent to have sexual intercourse with a woman in circumstances where she does not consent and the defendant knows or could not care less about her absence of consent.' The only 'intent,' giving that word its natural and ordinary meaning, of the rapist is to have sexual intercourse. He commits the offence because of the circumstances in which he manifests that intent—i.e. when the woman is not consenting and he either knows it or could not care less about the absence of consent.

Accordingly we take the view that in relation to the four appellants the judge was right to give the directions that he did when inviting the jury to consider the charges of attempted rape.

. . .

Appeals dismissed.

So *Khan* makes it clear that the *mens rea* for attempted rape is that the defendant intends to have sexual intercourse with the victim, being reckless as to whether the victim consents. As a general proposition, if recklessness as to a circumstance is sufficient for the full offence then it is enough for an attempt to commit that offence. The Court of Appeal, however, returned to the issue in the following case in a decision which has proved hard to interpret:

Attorney-General's Reference (No. 3 of 1992)
(1994) 98 Cr App R 383 (CA)[8]

The respondents were charged with attempted aggravated arson. They threw petrol bombs towards a car in which some people were sitting. The petrol bombs missed the car and hit a wall. On a charge of attempted aggravated arson the judge ruled that it had to be proved that the defendants intended to endanger lives in order to be convicted of the offence. The respondents were acquitted and the Attorney-General referred the case to the Court of Appeal.

Mr Justice Schiemann

Turning from the general to the particular, it is convenient to consider, first, attempting to commit the simple offence [criminal damage], which causes no problem, and then to pass on to attempting to commit the aggravated offence, which is what has given rise to this reference.

So far as attempting to commit the simple offence is concerned, in order to convict on such a charge it must be proved that the defendant (a) did an act which was more than merely preparatory to the commission of the offence and (b) he did an act intending to damage any property belonging to another.

---

[8] [1994] RTR 122, [1994] 1 WLR 409, [1994] Crim LR 348.

One way of analysing the situation is to say that a defendant, in order to be guilty of an attempt, must be in one of the states of mind required for the commission of the full offence, and did his best, as far as he could, to supply what was missing from the completion of the offence. It is the policy of the law that such people should be punished notwithstanding that in fact the intentions of such a defendant have not been fulfilled.

If the facts are that, although the defendant had one of the appropriate states of mind required for the complete offence, but the physical element required for the commission of the complete offence is missing, the defendant is not to be convicted unless it can be shown that he intended to supply that physical element. . . .

We turn finally to the attempt to commit the aggravated offence. In the present case, what was missing to prevent a conviction for the completed offence was damage to the property referred to in the opening lines of section 1(2) of the 1971 Act. . . . Such damage is essential for the completed offence. If a defendant does not intend to cause such damage he cannot intend to commit the completed offence. At worst, he is reckless as to whether the offence is committed. The law of attempt is concerned with those who are intending to commit crimes. If that intent cannot be shown, then there can be no conviction.

However, the crime here consisted of doing certain acts in a certain state of mind in circumstances where the first-named property and the second-named property were the same, in short where the danger to life arose from the damage to the property which the defendant intended to damage. The substantive crime is committed if the defendant damaged property in a state of mind where he was reckless as to whether the life of another would thereby be endangered. We see no reason why there should not be a conviction for attempt if the prosecution can show that he, in that state of mind, intended to damage the property by throwing a bomb at it. One analysis of this situation is to say that although the defendant was in an appropriate state of mind to render him guilty of the completed offence the prosecution had not proved the physical element of the completed offence, and therefore he is not guilty of the completed offence. If, on a charge of attempting to commit the offence, the prosecution can show not only the state of mind required for the completed offence but also that the defendant intended to supply the missing physical element of the completed offence, that suffices for a conviction. That cannot be done merely by the prosecution showing him to be reckless. The defendant must intend to damage property, but there is no need for a graver mental state than is required for the full offence.

The learned trial judge in the present case, however, went further than this, and held that not merely must the defendant intend to supply all that was missing from the completed offence—namely, damage to the first-named property—but also that recklessness as to the consequences of such damage for the lives of others was not enough to secure a conviction for attempt, although it was sufficient for the completed offence. She held that before a defendant could be convicted of attempting to commit the offence it had to be shown that he intended that the lives of others should be endangered by the damage which he intended.

She gave no policy for so holding, and there is no case which bound her so to hold. The most nearly relevant case is *Khan* (1990) 91 Cr. App. R. 29. . . .

An attempt was made in argument to suggest that *Khan* was wrongly decided. No policy reasons were advanced for that view, and we do not share it. The result is one which accords with common sense, and does no violence to the words of the statute.

What was missing in *Khan* was the act of sexual intercourse, without which the offence was not complete. What was missing in the present case was damage to the first-named property, without which the offence was not complete. The mental state of the defendant in each case contained everything which was required to render him guilty of the full offence. In order to succeed in a prosecution for attempt, it must be shown that the defendant intended to achieve that which was missing from the full offence. Unless that is shown, the prosecution have not proved that the defendant intended to commit the offence. Thus in *Khan* the prosecution had to show an intention to have sexual intercourse, and the remaining state of mind required for the offence of rape. In the present case, the prosecution had to show an intention to damage the first-named properly, and the remaining state of mind required for the offence of aggravated arson.

. . .

While the learned judge in the instant case opined that *Khan* was distinguishable she did not indicate any policy reasons for distinguishing it. We see none, and none have been submitted to us directly.

We now remind ourselves of the precise question posed by the reference:

'Whether on a charge of attempted arson in the aggravated form contemplated by section 1(2) of the Criminal Damage Act 1971, in addition to establishing a specific intent to cause damage by fire, it is sufficient to prove that the defendant was reckless as to whether life would thereby be endangered.'

We answer it in the affirmative.

The exact interpretation of these two cases is controversial and commentators have disagreed on how to interpret them. Three views have been put forward:

(1) *Recklessness as to circumstances but not consequences.* A defendant must intend to do his or her action and cause the consequences of that action, but can be reckless as to the circumstances of his or her action (e.g. whether the victim in a rape case consents, or whether there were people in the vicinity of the bomb in the *Attorney-General's Reference (No. 3 of 1992)* case whose lives were endangered).

(2) *'Recklessness to circumstances or consequences' test.* A defendant must intend to do his or her action, but can be reckless as to the consequences *or* circumstances of that action if recklessness is sufficient for the complete offence.

(3) *The 'missing element' test.* The defendant must intend to supply the missing element. This test was proposed in the *Attorney-General's Reference* case. It requires the court to decide what is the missing element in the attempt: that is what is missing from the case which, if present, would mean that the full offence had been committed. In *Khan*, for example, if only the defendant had managed to engage in sexual intercourse would there have been the full offence of rape. All the elements of rape, apart from penetration, were present. So the 'missing element' in *Khan* was the actual sexual intercourse. The missing element test requires the defendant to supply that missing element.

As between views (1) and (2) the key question is whether *Attorney-General's Reference (No. 3 of 1992)* extended the *Khan* decision or merely followed it. The debate centres on the holding in the *Attorney-General's Reference* case that recklessness that 'lives be thereby endangered' is sufficient for the offence of attempted aggravated arson. But is the requirement that 'lives be thereby endangered' a consequence or a circumstance? One could argue either way. It is a consequence: there is the act of arson as a result of which lives are put in danger. It is a circumstance: arson was committed in a situation where lives could be endangered. If you think that the endangerment of lives is a consequence then the Court of Appeal appears to have accepted the view that recklessness as to the consequences of a defendant's actions can be sufficient for an attempt. It should be noted that the Court of Appeal in *Attorney-General's Reference* claimed to be following *Khan*, which might support the circumstances only view.

The Court of Appeal in *Attorney-General's Reference* proposed the 'missing element' test. It indicated that it thought it was an easier test for juries to understand, rather than being a difference in the law. However, as point one in the questions box below demonstrates, it is possible to imagine cases where the missing elements test and the *Khan* test would produce a different result.

EXAMINATION TIP

A good answer in an examination would require an explanation of these three possible interpretations of the *mens rea* for an attempt and a consideration of how the three tests might apply. It may be that they would all produce the same result, which they would on the facts of *Khan*, for example. But in other circumstances they produce different results.

QUESTIONS

1. The Court of Appeal in *Attorney-General's Reference (No. 3 of 1992)* suggested that the 'missing element' test was not intended to be different from the *Khan* test. But consider the following scenario: Tim damages a watch, which he thinks belongs to Judith, but in fact belongs to him. The 'missing element' test would be applied thus: all that is preventing this being criminal damage is that the watch does not belong to another. Tim is therefore guilty of attempted criminal damage if he *intends* the watch to belong to another.

    The 'circumstance' test would be applied in this way: the ownership of the watch is a circumstance, and because recklessness is sufficient as to that in the full offence of criminal damage, it is enough for an attempt. Tim is therefore guilty of attempted criminal damage if he is *reckless* as to whether the watch belongs to another.

    Which test should the court use?

2. In *Khan* the Court of Appeal held that *Caldwell* recklessness is sufficient for a circumstance (or maybe consequence). This is controversial because it indicates that a defendant could be guilty of attempting to commit an offence even though a crucial element of it did not cross the defendant's mind. It also might indicate that in a strict liability offence you can be guilty of attempting it without even thinking of a key element. Is it possible to convict someone of attempted dangerous driving as he reverses out of his drive in a car which (unknown to him) is in a dangerous condition?

Conditional intent

What of a case where the defendant has an intent to commit a crime only in certain circumstances. For example, Dave rushes into a bedroom with a gun raised, intending to kill his wife if he finds her in bed with another man. Or Sue rummages through someone's handbag intending to steal anything that she finds of value.

In *Husseyn*[9] the defendant was charged with attempting to steal sub-aqua equipment from a van. He had opened a bag and started to look in it to see if there was anything worth

---

[9] (1978) 67 Cr App R 131 (CA).

taking. The Court of Appeal held that because it could not be said that he had intended to take the sub-aqua equipment he could not be found guilty of attempting to steal it. Subsequently in *Attorney-General's Reference (Nos. 1 and 2 of 1979)* the Court of Appeal explained that a conditional intent (to steal anything that was worth stealing) could form the basis of an attempt charge if the indictment[10] was drafted carefully. In *Husseyn* the correct charge would be attempting to steal 'some or all of the contents of the holdall'. Smith and Hogan have suggested 'attempting to steal from a holdall' would be even better.[11]

2.2 ACTUS REUS

The *actus reus* of an attempt is defined in section 1(1) of the Criminal Attempts Act 1981 as doing an act which is more than merely preparatory to the commission of these offences. These words are to be given their normal meaning.[12] As Smith and Hogan[13] have emphasized, the word 'merely' is key here. It is clear that not every preparatory act constitutes an attack. If Neil buys a knife, planning to use it in a robbery weeks later, he may have begun to prepare for the robbery, but this is mere preparation and he is well short of an attempted robbery. In reality there is no hard and fast rule about when an act may be more than merely preparatory, but the following cases give some indication of the courts' attitudes:

R v Geddes
[1996] Crim LR 894 (CA)

Gary Geddes entered a boys' lavatory block in a school in Brighton. He had no right to be there. He was found in a cubicle with a cider can, a large knife, some rope, some orange toilet paper, and a roll of masking tape. The prosecution alleged that he was planning to kidnap a boy. At his trial it was argued, *inter alia*, that his actions could not constitute an attempt because he had done nothing that was more than merely preparatory. He was convicted and appealed.

Lord Bingham of Cornhill CJ, reading the judgment of the court

In considering the question whether there was evidence before the jury which entitled them to hold that the appellant had done an act which was more than merely preparatory, it is helpful to begin with the judgment given by the Lord Chief Justice in *R v Rowley* (1992) 94 Cr App R 95. In that case the appellant had left notes in public places inviting boys to respond to him. The purpose of the notes was to initiate relationships for the appellant's sexual gratification, although the notes did not in terms say so. One of the charges against the appellant was of attempting to incite a child under 14 to commit acts of gross indecency with him. With reference to that part of the appeal, the Lord Chief Justice said at page 100:

'. . . The effect of that latter subsection [Criminal Attempts Act 1981, s. 4(3)] is that it is for the jury to determine whether the act is more than merely preparatory or not, but only in circumstances upon which the judge has to rule, where there is some evidence fit for their consideration on that issue.'

---

[10] The indictment sets out the charge the defendant must face.   [11] Smith (2002: 332).
[12] *Jones* [1990] 3 All ER 886 (CA).   [13] Smith (2002: 334).

The Lord Chief Justice then went on to deal with the facts of that case.

In so stating the law, Lord Taylor CJ was echoing observations made by Lord Lane CJ in *R v Gullefer (Note)* [1990] 3 All ER 882, [1990] 1 WLR 1063. At page 1065B of the latter report Lord Lane, giving the judgment of this court, said:

'Thus the judge's task is to decide whether there is evidence upon which a jury could reasonably come to the conclusion that the appellant had gone beyond the realm of mere preparation and had embarked upon the actual commission of the offence. If not, he must withdraw the case from the jury. If there is such evidence, it is then for the jury to decide whether the defendant did in fact go beyond mere preparation. That is the way in which the judge approached this case. He ruled that there was sufficient evidence.'

At page 1066C Lord Lane added:

'It seems to us that the words of the Act of 1981 seek to steer a midway course. They do not provide, as they might have done, that the *Reg v Eagleton* test is to be followed, or that, as Lord Diplock suggested, the defendant must have reached a point from which it was impossible for him to retreat before the actus reus of an attempt is proved. On the other hand the words give perhaps as clear a guidance as is possible in the circumstances on the point of time at which Stephen's "series of acts" begin. It begins when the merely preparatory acts come to an end and the defendant embarks upon the crime proper. When that is will depend of course upon the facts in any particular case.'

The judge also considered *R v Campbell* 93 Cr App R 350. That was a case in which the appellant had been convicted of attempted robbery. The evidence showed that he had been loitering outside a sub-post office, equipped in a manner clearly indicating an intention to rob it. But he had been arrested before he had entered the sub-post office and when he was still outside. It was held, allowing the appeal:

'(1) In directing a jury as to an attempt to commit a crime the judge should restrict himself to the definition of an attempt in the Criminal Attempts Act 1981. In the present case the judge had also directed the jury with references to the law obtaining before that Act; that was wholly unnecessary. It is sufficient to direct the jury that before they could convict they must be satisfied so as to feel sure that the defendant intended to commit the offence and that, with that intent, he did an act which was more than an act of preparation to commit the offence. It was for the jury to decide whether the act relied upon by the prosecution was more than merely preparatory.

(2) In considering a submission that the case should be withdrawn from the jury at the close of the prosecution case the judge must form a judgment upon the Crown's evidence and determine whether or not that evidence is safe to be left to the jury. If he considers that the relevant circumstances could not amount to an attempt he should withdraw the matter from the jury. If he concludes that, although the matter is not as conclusive as that, it nevertheless would be unsafe to leave the evidence to the jury, he should direct a verdict of not guilty. It is only if he is satisfied that there is evidence upon which a jury can properly and safely consider whether or not there has been an attempt that he should allow the case to continue.

(3) In the present case a number of acts remained undone and the appellant's acts were indicative of mere preparation, even if he was still of a mind to rob the post office. If a person in such circumstances has not even gained the place where he could be in a position to carry out the offence, it is extremely unlikely that it could ever be said that he had performed an act which could properly be said to be an attempt. It would be

unwise to try to lay down hard and fast rules as to when, in varying circumstances, an attempt has begun. The matter has to be decided on a case by case basis.'

If one were to ask the simple question: did Campbell attempt to rob the post office, the answer would, in our judgment, be no. The evidence was strong that he had an intention of robbing the post office; he was very close in time and space to doing so; but he did not embark on the actual commission of the robbery.

This appeal is concerned not with the correctness of the jury's decision of fact, but the correctness of the judge's ruling of law. Was the evidence summarised in the admissions sufficient in law to support a finding that the appellant did an act which was more than merely preparatory to the commission of the offence charged? The cases show that the line of demarcation between acts which are merely preparatory and acts which may amount to an attempt is not always clear or easy to recognise. There is no rule of thumb test. There must always be an exercise of judgment based on the particular facts of the case. It is, we think, an accurate paraphrase of the statutory test and not an illegitimate gloss upon it to ask whether the available evidence, if accepted, could show that a defendant has done an act which shows that he has actually tried to commit the offence in question, or whether he has only got ready or put himself in a position or equipped himself to do so.

In the present case, as already indicated, there is not much room for doubt about the appellant's intention. Furthermore, the evidence is clearly capable of showing that he made preparations, that he equipped himself, that he got ready, that he put himself in a position to commit the offence charged. We question whether the cider can in the cubicle is of central importance, but would accept that in the absence of any explanation it could lead to the inference that the appellant had been in the cubicle. But was the evidence sufficient in law to support a finding that the appellant had actually tried or attempted to commit the offence of imprisoning someone? Had he moved from the realm of intention, preparation and planning into the area of execution or implementation? In Campbell, which was of course decided on its own facts, it was held that the appellant had not. Here it is true that the appellant had entered the school; but he had never had any contact or communication with any pupil; he had never confronted any pupil at the school in any way. That may well be no credit to him, and may indeed reflect great credit on the vigilance of the school staff. The whole story is one which fills the court with the gravest unease. Nonetheless, we cannot escape giving an answer to the fundamental legal question. . . . So, for this purpose, must the contents of the rucksack, which give a clear indication as to what the appellant may have had in mind, but do not throw light on whether he had begun to carry out the commission of the offence. On the facts of this case we feel bound to conclude that the evidence was not sufficient in law to support a finding that the appellant did an act which was more than merely preparatory to wrongfully imprisoning a person unknown. In those circumstances we conclude that the appeal must be allowed and the conviction quashed.

Appeal allowed.

The Court of Appeal has avoided setting down any definite rule for the jury to apply, other than to say that the words 'more than merely preparatory' should be given their 'plain meaning'. Useful phrases that have been used by the judiciary to describe the *actus reus* of an attempt are 'on the job'[14] or 'embarks on the crime proper'.[15] Here are some indications which may however be gleaned from the facts of some of the cases, although they do not represent hard and fast rules:

---

[14] *Osborn* (1919) 84 JP 63.   [15] *Gullefer* [1990] 3 All ER 882 (CA).

(1) If the defendant has done the last act before completing his offence the *actus reus* of an attempt will be made out.[16] So if A shoots at B, but B ducks and so avoids the bullet, clearly A will have committed the *actus reus* of an attempt.

(2) It is not necessary to show that the defendant has done the 'last act'[17] before committing the actual offence.[18] In other words even though the defendant may still have several actions to complete he may still be guilty of an attempt.

(3) Simply because an act is one of a series of acts which will lead to the commission of the crime does not mean that the act is necessarily sufficient to amount to attempt. Such acts will amount to preparation, but not necessarily more than mere preparation.[19]

(4) In a crime of violence unless the defendant is face to face with the victim it is unlikely that the act will be described as more than mere preparation.[20] Unlikely, but not impossible. No doubt a terrorist who plants a bomb under a victim's car will be held to have committed an attempt to kill, even though he has not met the victim.

When considering the *actus reus* of an attempt it is necessary to consider carefully the *actus reus* of the full offence. In *Toothill*[21] the defendant was charged with attempted burglary (with intent to rape). He had knocked on the door of the potential victim's house and was arrested in the victim's garden. He was guilty of an attempted burglary. This is because he was more than merely preparatory to entering the property as a trespasser (the *actus reus* of burglary).[22]

Attempt by omission

The 1981 Act requires there to be 'an *act* which is more than merely preparatory'. This seems to imply that an omission cannot constitute an attempt.[23] This may seem obvious; but if a parent sees her child drowning and stands by doing nothing, but at the very last minute someone intervenes and rescues the child can the parent be successfully prosecuted for attempting to murder the child? After all, but for the fortunate intervention of the third party the parent would be guilty of murder. We await definitive guidance from the courts on this question.

Is it possible to convict of an attempt if the attempt was successful?

Is it a defence to a charge of attempt if the defendant in fact succeeded? The answer (not surprisingly) is that the defendant can still be convicted of an attempted offence. Section 6(4) of the Criminal Law Act 1967 resolves the issue:

---

[16] *Jones* [1990] 1 WLR 1057 (CA).   [17] A test proposed in *Eagleton* (1855) 6 Cox CC 559.

[18] *Gullefer* [1990] 3 All ER 882 (CA).   [19] *Gullefer* [1991] Crim LR 576 (CA).

[20] Compare *Kelly* [1992] Crim LR 181 and *Campbell* (1990) 93 Cr App R 350 (CA).

[21] [1998] Crim LR 876 (CA).

[22] There are quite a number of cases in which the Court of Appeal has considered the *actus reus* of an attempt. To get a wider flavour of how they approach such cases read: *Jones* (1990) 91 Cr App R 351; *Gullefer* [1990] 3 All ER 882; *Campbell* [1991] Crim LR 268; *Kelly* [1992] Crim LR 181; *Griffin* [1993] Crim LR 514; *Attorney-General's Reference (No. 1 of 1992)* [1993] Crim LR 274; *Tosti* [1997] Crim LR 746; *Nash* [1999] Crim LR 308.

[23] See the discussion of the use of the word 'act' in the Protection from Eviction Act 1977, s. 1, in *Ahmad* (1987) Cr App R 64 (CA).

... where a person is charged on an indictment with attempting to commit an offence or with any assault or other act preliminary to an offence, but not with the completed offence, then (subject to the discretion of the court to discharge the jury with a view to the preferment of an indictment for the completed offence) he may be convicted of the offence charged notwithstanding that he is shown to be guilty of the completed offence.[24]

What can be attempted?

It is possible to convict a defendant of attempting to commit any offence except for the following:

(1) Conspiracy (either common law or statutory conspiracy).[25]

(2) Offences of assisting an arrestable offender or compounding an arrestable offence.[26]

(3) Offences of aiding, abetting, counselling, or procuring the commission of an offence.[27]

(4) Summary only offences. The explanation is that attempting to commit summary only offences (which are in their nature minor crimes) is not sufficiently serious to justify a criminal conviction.[28] However, there are a few summary only offences in respect of which the statute has explicitly stated that it is an offence to attempt to commit them.[29]

(5) Some commentators suggest that offences where there is a more serious offence with the same *actus reus* cannot be attempted: for example, manslaughter. To intend to commit manslaughter one must intend to kill, which is attempted murder. Other commentators argue that the fact that a defendant could also be charged with attempted murder does not preclude a conviction for attempted manslaughter.[30]

(6) There are complex provisions dealing with attempting to commit offences abroad which are not covered here.[31]

2.3 IMPOSSIBLE ATTEMPTS

The cases under consideration here are where a defendant is trying to commit an offence which he or she cannot complete. The following situations need to be distinguished:

(1) '*Legal impossibility*'. The defendant is trying to perform an action which he believes to be illegal, but which is not. This is simply not an offence. In *Taaffe*[32] the defendant imported into the country packages which he believed contained foreign currency. He believed that it

---

[24] *Webley v Buxton* [1977] QB 481 indicates that although s. 6(4) does not apply to summary offences, the common law rule is the same and a defendant can be convicted of an attempt to carry out a summary offence, even if in fact they have committed the full offence.

[25] Criminal Attempts Act 1981, s. 1(4).   [26] Criminal Law Act 1967, ss. 4(1) and 5(1).

[27] *Dunnington* [1984] QB 472 (CA). Although, it should be noted that the Suicide Act 1961, s. 2(1), creates the offence of aiding the commission of suicide, and it is therefore possible to attempt to aid the commission of suicide.

[28] *Bristol Magistrates' Court, ex p E* [1998] 3 All ER 798 (QBD) confirmed that either way offences can be attempted.

[29] e.g. Road Traffic Act 1988 (driving over the prescribed limit).

[30] Simester and Sullivan (2003: 296).   [31] Smith (2002: 316–18).   [32] [1983] 2 All ER 625 (HL).

was illegal to import foreign currency, which it was not. He could not be convicted of attempting to import foreign currency. Similarly, if the defendant believed that taking topless photographs of his wife was an offence he would not be convicted of attempting to commit the imaginary crime. Less straightforward is a case where the mistake is of civil law. For example, the defendant is attempting to damage property which he believes under civil law is someone else's but which in fact is his.[33] There are no cases directly on this situation.

(2) *'Impossibility through ineptitude'*. This is where the defendant is trying to commit a crime but the means he is using are inadequate to commit the offence. The defendant is clearly guilty. For example, Ray tries to poison Lucy's tea, but puts in so little poison that it has no effect on her wellbeing. Clearly Ray is guilty of an attempt if he intended to kill Lucy.

More controversial is a much-debated hypothetical case where D sticks pins into a wax model of V genuinely believing that doing so will release evil powers which will kill V. If D is a devout believer he may believe that sticking the pins into the model of V is as effective as stabbing V. Although there is a widespread view that the use of such 'radically deficient means' to attempt should not amount to an attempted murder, it is in fact hard to explain how it is different from the case where D shoots at V who is such a long way away that there is no way that a bullet could reach him. The best explanation is that offered by Duff who argues that such conduct 'failed to engage with the world as an attempt to commit [the] offence'.[34]

(3) *'Physical impossibility'*. Here the reason for the failure is not the ineffective means used, but is that the crime simply cannot be committed. For example D tries to kill V who he thinks is asleep, but is in fact dead. Or D plants seeds believing they will grow into a cannabis plant, but in fact he grows chives. In these cases the defendant can still be guilty. The law is governed by section 1(2) and (3) of the Criminal Attempts Act 1981:

> (2) A person may be guilty of attempting to commit an offence to which this section applies even though the facts are such that the commission of the offence is impossible.
>
> (3) In any case where—
>
> (a) apart from this subsection a person's intention would not be regarded as having amounted to an intent to commit an offence; but
>
> (b) if the facts of the case had been as he believed them to be, his intention would be so regarded, then, for the purposes of subsection (1) above, he shall be regarded as having had an intent to commit that offence.

The effect of these provisions is that what is key for the law on attempts in this area is the accused's intention. For the purposes of impossible attempts the facts are taken to be the facts as the defendant believed them. So if the defendant believes he is dealing in illegal drugs he can be convicted of an attempted drug-dealing offence, even if in fact what he is selling is chalk. He will be guilty of an attempt to deal in drugs.

---

[33] A slightly different example is *Haughton v Smith* [1975] AC 476 (HL) where the defendant was charged with attempting to handle stole goods. He handled the goods, but unknown to him they were not stolen.

[34] Duff (1996: 398). Probably the term 'facts' in s. 1(3) could not be said to include beliefs as to what the law is.

DEFINITION

The jury must ask whether on the facts as the defendant believed them to be he was doing an act which was more than merely preparatory to the commission of an offence.

So if Max is dead, but Bob believes he is alive and approaches Max, intending to kill him, then the question is whether, if Max had been alive (that being what Bob believed), what Bob did was more than merely preparatory to killing him.

The leading case on impossible attempts is the following:

R v Shivpuri
[1987] AC 1 (HL)[35]

Pyare Shivpuri was arrested by customs officers. He confessed that he was dealing in illegal drugs. However, on further analysis, it was found that the suitcase did not contain illegal drugs but snuff and harmless vegetable matter. He was charged with an attempt to commit the offence of being knowingly concerned in dealing with and harbouring prohibited drugs, contrary to section 170(1)(b) of the Customs and Excise Management Act 1979. He appealed against his conviction on the basis that, as he did not have in his possession an illegal drug, he could not be charged in connection with an attempt to deal in such drugs. The Court of Appeal dismissed his appeal and he then appealed to the House of Lords.

Lord Bridge of Harwich

The certified question granted . . . reads:

'Does a person commit an offence under Section 1, Criminal Attempts Act, 1981, where, if the facts were as that person believed them to be, the full offence would have been committed by him, but where on the true facts the offence which that person set out to commit was in law impossible, e.g., because the substance imported and believed to be heroin was not heroin but a harmless substance?'

[Lord Bridge quoted section 1 of the Criminal Attempts Act 1981 and continued:]
    Applying this language to the facts of the case, the first question to be asked is whether the appellant intended to commit the offences of being knowingly concerned in dealing with and harbouring drugs of class A or class B with intent to evade the prohibition on their importation. Translated into more homely language the question may be rephrased, without in any way altering its legal significance, in the following terms: did the appellant intend to receive and store (harbour) and in due course pass on to third parties (deal with) packages of heroin or cannabis which he knew had been smuggled into England from India? The answer is plainly Yes, he did. Next, did he, in relation to each offence, do an act which was more than merely preparatory to the commission of the offence? The act relied on in relation to harbouring was the receipt and retention of the packages found in the lining of the suitcase. The act relied on in relation to dealing was the meeting at Southall station with the intended recipient of one of the packages. In each case the act was clearly more than preparatory to the commission of the intended offence it was not and could not be more than merely

---

[35] [1986] 2 All ER 334, [1986] 2 WLR 988, [1986] Crim LR 536.

preparatory to the commission of the actual offence, because the facts were such that the commission of the actual offence was impossible. Here then is the nub of the matter. Does the 'act which is more than merely preparatory to the commission of the offence' in s. 1(1) of the 1981 Act (the *actus reus* of the statutory offence of attempt) require any more than an act which is more than merely preparatory to the commission of the offence which the defendant intended to commit? Section 1(2) must surely indicate a negative answer if it were otherwise, whenever the facts were such that the commission of the actual offence was impossible, it would be impossible to prove an act more than merely preparatory to the commission of that offence and sub-ss (1) and (2) would contradict each other.

This very simple, perhaps over-simple, analysis leads me to the provisional conclusion that the appellant was rightly convicted of the two offences of attempt with which he was charged. But can this conclusion stand with *Anderton v Ryan*? The appellant in that case was charged with an attempt to handle stolen goods. She bought a video recorder believing it to be stolen. On the facts as they were to be assumed it was not stolen. By a majority the House decided that she was entitled to be acquitted. I have re-examined the case with care. If I could extract from the speech of Lord Roskill or from my own speech a clear and coherent principle distinguishing those cases of attempting the impossible which amount to offences under the statute from those which do not, I should have to consider carefully on which side of the line the instant case fell. But I have to confess that I can find no such principle.

Running through Lord Roskill's speech and my own in *Anderton v Ryan* is the concept of 'objectively innocent' acts which, in my speech certainly, are contrasted with 'guilty acts'. A few citations will make this clear. Lord Roskill said ([1985] AC 560 at 580):

'My Lords, it has been strenuously and ably argued for the respondent that these provisions involve that a defendant is liable to conviction for an attempt even where his actions are innocent but he erroneously believes facts which, if true, would make those actions criminal, and further, that he is liable to such conviction whether or not in the event his intended course of action is completed.'

He proceeded to reject the argument. I referred to the appellant's purchase of the video recorder and said ([1985] AC 560 at 582): 'Objectively considered, therefore, her purchase of the recorder was a perfectly proper commercial transaction.'

A further passage from my speech stated ([1985] AC 560 at 582–583):

'The question may be stated in abstract terms as follows. Does s 1 of the 1981 Act create a new offence of attempt where a person embarks on and completes a course of conduct, which is objectively innocent, solely on the ground that the person mistakenly believes facts which, if true, would make that course of conduct a complete crime? If the question must be answered affirmatively it requires convictions in a number of surprising cases: the classic case, put by Bramwell B in *R v Collins* (1864) 9 Cox CC 497 at 498, of the man who takes away his own umbrella from a stand, believing it not to be his own and with intent to steal it the case of the man who has consensual intercourse with a girl over 16 believing her to be under that age the case of the art dealer who sells a picture which he represents to be and which is in fact a genuine Picasso, but which the dealer mistakenly believes to be a fake. The common feature of all these cases, including that under appeal, is that the mind alone is guilty, the act is innocent.'

I then contrasted the case of the man who attempts to pick the empty pocket, saying ([1985] AC 560 at 583):

'Putting the hand in the pocket is the guilty act, the intent to steal is the guilty mind, the offence is appropriately dealt with as an attempt, and the impossibility of committing the full offence for want of anything in the pocket to steal is declared by [sub-s (2)] to be no obstacle to conviction.'

If we fell into error, it is clear that our concern was to avoid convictions in situations which most people, as a matter of common sense, would not regard as involving criminality. In this connection it is to be regretted that we did not take due note of para 2.97 of the Law Commission Report, Criminal Law: Attempt and Impossibility in Relation to Attempt, Conspiracy and Incitement (1980) (Law Com no 102) which preceded the enactment of the 1981 Act, which reads:

'If it is right in principle that an attempt should be chargeable even though the crime which it is sought to commit could not possibly be committed, we do not think that we should be deterred by the consideration that such a change in our law would also cover some extreme and exceptional cases in which a prosecution would be theoretically possible. An example would be where a person is offered goods at such a low price that he believes that they are stolen, when in fact they are not if he actually purchases them, upon the principles which we have discussed he would be liable for an attempt to handle stolen goods. Another case which has been much debated is that raised in argument by Bramwell B. in *Reg. v. Collins*. If A takes his own umbrella, mistaking it for one belonging to B and intending to steal B's umbrella, is he guilty of attempted theft? Again, on the principles which we have discussed he would in theory be guilty, but in neither case would it be realistic to suppose that a complaint would be made or that a prosecution would ensue.'

The prosecution in *Anderton v Ryan* itself falsified the Commission's prognosis in one of the 'extreme and exceptional cases'. It nevertheless probably holds good for other such cases, particularly that of the young man having sexual intercourse with a girl over 16, mistakenly believing her to be under that age, by which both Lord Roskill and I were much troubled.

However that may be, the distinction between acts which are 'objectively innocent' and those which are not is an essential element in the reasoning in *Anderton v Ryan* and the decision, unless it can be supported on some other ground, must stand or fall by the validity of this distinction. I am satisfied on further consideration that the concept of 'objective innocence' is incapable of sensible application in relation to the law of criminal attempts. The reason for this is that any attempt to commit an offence which involves 'an act which is more than merely preparatory to the commission of the offence' but which for any reason fails, so that in the event no offence is committed, must ex hypothesi, from the point view of the criminal law, be 'objectively innocent'. What turns what would otherwise, from the point of view of the criminal law, be an innocent act into a crime is the intent of the actor to commit an offence. I say 'from the point of view of the criminal law' because the law of tort must surely here be quite irrelevant. A puts his hand into B's pocket. Whether or not there is anything in the pocket capable of being stolen, if A intends to steal his act is a criminal attempt if he does not so intend his act is innocent. A plunges a knife into a bolster in a bed. To avoid the complication of an offence of criminal damage, assume it to be A's bolster. If A believes the bolster to be his enemy B and intends to kill him, his act is an attempt to murder B if he knows the bolster is only a bolster, his act is innocent. These considerations lead me to the conclusion that the distinction sought to be drawn in *Anderton v Ryan* between innocent and guilty acts considered 'objectively' and independently of the state of mind of the actor cannot be sensibly maintained.

Another conceivable ground of distinction which was to some extent canvassed in argument, both in *Anderton v Ryan* and in the instant case, though no trace of it appears in the speeches in *Anderton v Ryan*, is a distinction which would make guilt or innocence of the crime of attempt in a case of mistaken belief dependent on what, for want of a better phrase, I will call the defendant's dominant intention. According to the theory necessary to sustain this distinction, the appellant's dominant intention in *Anderton v Ryan* was to buy a cheap video recorder her belief that it was stolen was merely incidental. Likewise in the hypothetical case of attempted unlawful sexual intercourse, the young man's dominant intention was to have intercourse with the particular girl his mistaken belief that she was under 16 was merely incidental. By contrast, in the instant case the appellant's dominant intention was to receive and distribute illegally imported heroin or cannabis.

While I see the superficial attraction of this suggested ground of distinction, I also see formidable practical difficulties in its application. By what test is a jury to be told that a defendant's dominant intention is to be recognised and distinguished from his incidental but mistaken belief? But there is perhaps a more formidable theoretical difficulty. If this ground of distinction is relied on to support the acquittal of the appellant in *Anderton v Ryan* it can only do so on the basis that her mistaken belief that the video recorder was stolen played no significant part in her decision to buy it and therefore she may be acquitted of the intent to handle stolen goods. But this line of reasoning runs into head-on collision with s. 1(3) of the 1981 Act. The theory produces a situation where, apart from the subsection, her intention would not be regarded as having amounted to any intent to commit an offence. Section 1(3)(b) then requires one to ask whether, if the video recorder had in fact been stolen, her intention would have been regarded as an intent to handle stolen goods. The answer must clearly be Yes, it would. If she had bought the video recorder knowing it to be stolen, when in fact it was, it would have availed her nothing to say that her dominant intention was to buy a video recorder because it was cheap and that her knowledge that it was stolen was merely incidental. This seems to me fatal to the dominant intention theory.

I am thus led to the conclusion that there is no valid ground on which *Anderton v Ryan* can be distinguished. I have made clear my own conviction, which as a party to the decision (and craving the indulgence of my noble and learned friends who agreed in it) I am the readier to express, that the decision was wrong. What then is to be done? If the case is indistinguishable, the application of the strict doctrine of precedent would require that the present appeal be allowed. Is it permissible to depart from precedent under the 1966 Practice Statement Note ([1966] 3 All ER 77, [1966] 1 WLR 1234) notwithstanding the especial need for certainty in the criminal law? The following considerations lead me to answer that question affirmatively. Firstly, I am undeterred by the consideration that the decision in *Anderton v Ryan* was so recent. The 1966 Practice Statement is an effective abandonment of our pretention to infallibility. If a serious error embodied in a decision of this House has distorted the law, the sooner it is corrected the better. Secondly, I cannot see how, in the very nature of the case, anyone could have acted in reliance on the law as propounded in *Anderton v Ryan* in the belief that he was acting innocently and now find that, after all, he is to be held to have committed a criminal offence. Thirdly, to hold the House bound to follow *Anderton v Ryan* because it cannot be distinguished and to allow the appeal in this case would, it seems to me, be tantamount to a declaration that the 1981 Act left the law of criminal attempts unchanged following the decision in *Haughton v Smith* [1975] AC 476. Finally, if, contrary to my present view, there is a valid ground on which it would be proper to distinguish cases similar to that considered in *Anderton v Ryan*, my present opinion on that point would not foreclose the option of making such a distinction in some future case.

I cannot conclude this opinion without disclosing that I have had the advantage, since the conclusion of the argument in this appeal, of reading an article by Professor Glanville Williams entitled 'The Lords and Impossible Attempts, or Quis Custodiet Ipsos Custodies?'

[1986] CLJ 33. The language in which he criticises the decision in *Anderton v Ryan* is not conspicuous for its moderation, but it would be foolish, on that account, not to recognise the force of the criticism and churlish not to acknowledge the assistance I have derived from it.

I would answer the certified question in the affirmative and dismiss the appeal.

Appeal dismissed.

So in this decision their Lordships overruled their own decision in *Anderton v Ryan*[36] and held that if, on the facts as the defendant believed them to be, the defendant was doing something that was more than merely preparatory to the commission of the offence, he can be convicted of an attempt. *Shivpuri* does much to clarify the law, and it is simple to understand (although it is, of course, always difficult for the jury to work out what was in fact going on inside the defendant's mind). *Shivpuri* was recently applied in the case of *R v S*[37] where it was held that a defendant could be convicted of attempting to aid and abet a suicide even though the victim had no intention of committing suicide, if the defendant believed they did.

There is, however, one significant area of doubt, and that is what 'believe' means here. What if D has sexual intercourse with V who consents to the sexual intercourse, but D is not sure whether V consents. Is this doubt enough for 'believes' in section 1(2)? In other words for the purposes of section 1(2) in deciding whether the defendant had performed an act which was more than merely preparatory on the facts as the defendant believed them to be, are suspected beliefs sufficient?

2.4 ATTEMPTS AND ABANDONMENT

There is no case which yet accepts a defence of abandonment in English criminal law on attempts.[38] So, if the defendant has done an act which is more than merely preparatory, with intent to commit the full offence, but changes his mind and runs off at the very last minute, he could still be guilty of an attempt.[39]

QUESTION

Pete plans to have sexual intercourse with Emily. She has told him that she fancies him and Pete believes that this means she would like to have sexual intercourse with him. Pete kisses Emily, which she does not like, but she keeps quiet. When Pete starts to undress her, Emily pushes him away and says 'please stop'. Pete continues to try to undress her and Emily's opposition become more vocal. Pete then is aware that Emily does not want sex and leaves. Has Pete committed any offences?

FURTHER READING

Buxton, R. (1984), 'Circumstances, Consequences and Attempted Rape', *Criminal Law Review* 365.

Duff, R. (1996), *Criminal Attempts* (Oxford: OUP).

---

[36] [1985] AC 560 (HL).   [37] [2005] EWCA Crim 819.   [38] See further Wasik (1980).
[39] Although the Crown Prosecution Service may decide not to prosecute him or her.

Horder, J. (1994c), 'Varieties of Intention, Criminal Attempts and Endangerment', *Legal Studies* 14: 335.

Smith, K. (1991), 'Proximity at Attempt: Lord Lane's Midway Course', *Criminal Law Review* 576.

Temkin, J. (1976), 'Impossible Attempts: Another View', *Modern Law Review* 39: 55.

Williams, G. (1991b), 'Intents in the Alternative', *Cambridge Law Journal* 50: 120.

3 INCITEMENT

3.1 THE NATURE OF THE OFFENCE OF INCITEMENT

DEFINITION

The Divisional Court and Court of Appeal have accepted the following as an accurate description of the offence of incitement:

A person is guilty of incitement to commit an offence or offences if:

(a) he incites another to do or cause to be done an act or acts which, if done, will involve the commission of the offence or offences by the other; and

(b) he intends or believes that the other, if he acts as incited, shall or will do so with the fault required for the offence or offences.

It is a common law[40] offence[41] to incite someone to commit a crime even if he does not go on and commit it.[42] The offence is about encouraging someone to commit an offence. It is not about causing him to commit it. John would be guilty of incitement if he said to Celia 'You should kill Graham', to which Celia replied 'Certainly not'. Similarly John would be guilty of incitement if Celia replied 'Don't worry, I was going to kill Graham anyway' and killed Graham, without the incitement influencing her at all.[43]

These important points about incitement are emphasized in the following case on incitement, which also discusses two earlier important cases: *Shaw* and *Curr*.

Director of Public Prosecutions v Armstrong
[2000] Crim LR 379 (QBD)

Andrew Armstrong was charged with inciting Gareth Tobin to distribute indecent photographs of children. He had telephoned a man known as 'John' who he believed could send him child pornography. In fact 'John' was an undercover police officer, DC Tobin. Armstrong asked for photographs of girls 'no younger than, say, 12 years old'. At his trial he used two main arguments: (i) he had been making an inquiry about the availability of such material, rather than inciting the distribution of it;

---

[40] There are some specific statutory offences of incitement: e.g. Offences Against the Person Act 1861, s. 4 (incitement to murder); Incitement to Disaffection Act 1934; Incitement to Mutiny Act 1797.

[41] Magistrates' Courts Act 1980, s. 45; Magistrates' Courts Act 1980, s. 2.

[42] *Higgins* (1801) 2 East 5; *Marlow* [1997] Crim LR 897.

[43] Where the person incited goes on to commit the requested offence the defendant can also be convicted of counselling the commission of the offence.

(ii) the person he incited (the police officer) would never have distributed the pornography and so this was an incitement to perform an impossible act, which was not an offence. The magistrate held that there was no case to answer. The prosecution appealed.

Lord Justice Tuckey

The magistrate was referred to the cases of *R v Shaw* [1994] Crim LR 365 and *R v Curr* [1968] 2 QB 944, (1967) 51 Cr App Rep 113. In explaining how he reached his conclusion [that the respondent (Armstrong) had no case to answer] he said:

'(a) The police officer had made it clear in is evidence that he had no intention of supplying the Respondent with child pornography.

(b) Upon reading the cases of *R v Shaw* and *R v Curr*, that these decisions were binding upon me and require the persons to whom the incitement is made to have a parity of mens rea to the inciter.

(c) There was no evidence that the person incited had the required mens rea in that he had no intention of actually supplying child pornography.

(d) Because the evidence of the police office was that the indecent material would not have been supplied I was satisfied that the full offence could not have been committed and was therefore impossible.'

The questions he poses for the court, so far as they are relevant to the points which have been argued before us, are:

'(i) Was I correct to decide that the Respondent had not incited DC Tobin to distribute indecent material because [he] never had any intention of doing so?

(ii) Was I correct in holding in law that the evidence of the police officer meant the offence was impossible to perform?'

Before considering the two authorities referred to by the magistrate, it is helpful to analyse the position from first principles, free from authority. Incitement, like attempt and conspiracy, is an 'auxiliary' (as Lord Diplock would have it) or 'inchoate' (as the authors of text books would have it) offence. It is one of the ways in which criminal responsibility attaches to conduct short of the commission of the full offence. The actus reus of the offence is the indictment by the defendant of another to do something which is a criminal offence. He must do so with the intention that if the other person does as he asks he will commit a criminal offence. That is the mens rea. On this analysis the intention of the person incited is entirely irrelevant. It is put in Archbold at para 33–70 as follows:

'To solicit another to commit a crime is indictable at common law, even though the solicitation or incitement is of no effect.'

Blackstone refers also to the fact that the offence may be committed where the person incited flatly refuses to commit the offence.

The nature of the offence of incitement is accurately defined in the draft Criminal Code produced by the Law Commission in their paper No 177 at clause 47 which says:

'A person is guilty of incitement to commit an offence or offences if:

(a) he incites another to do or cause to be done an act or acts which, if done, will involve the commission of the offence or offences by the other; and

(b) he intends or believes that the other, if he acts as incited, shall or will do so with the fault required for the offence or offences.'

On this analysis of the law there is no principle of parity of mens rea of the kind contended for by the respondent and accepted by the magistrate. Were that to be the law, then all the cases about agent provocateur would have been wrongly decided because in each such case (where often the agent provocateur is a policemen) if it were a defence to the defendant to say: 'Well, the officer never intended to commit the offence which I asked him to commit', there would be no offence of incitement and many people would be in prison for committing such offences who should not be.

I turn to the related topic of impossibility. Obviously if what the person incited is asked to do is not a criminal offence the offence of incitement cannot be committed. There are other situations in which impossibility will still be a defence to a charge of incitement since this offence, unlike conspiracy and attempt, is not the subject of any statutory modification; it exists, as it always has done, as an offence at common law.

The situations in which such a defence arise are helpfully summarised in Smith and Hogan at pages 321 and 322. Having referred to *Director of Public Prosecutions v Nock* [1978] AC 979, [1978] 2 All ER 654, which dealt with the position under the law of conspiracy before the law was amended, the learned authors say:

'The result of these decisions is that impossibility is a general defence at common law. It seems that the only exception is that [the defendant] may be convicted where the impossibility results from the inadequacy of the means used, or to be used, to commit the offence. So, for example, [the defendant] will not be guilty of incitement where:

(i) The subject matter of the offence does not exist. D incites E to steal from P's safe. P's safe is empty.

(ii) The victim of the offence does not exist. D incites E to murder P. P is already dead.

(iii) The subject-matter of the offence lacks some quality which is an element of the offence. D and E believe a certain diamond to have been stolen. D incites E to receive it. It has not been stolen.

(iv) The victim of the offence lacks some quality which is an element of the offence. D and E believe P to be aged fifteen. In fact she is sixteen. D incites E to have sexual intercourse with her.'

With that analysis of the law free from authority, I turn to see whether the two cases referred to by the magistrate compel one to modify the position.

In *R v Shaw* the defendant, S, was charged with incitement to obtain property by deception. He was an after-sales co-ordinator for a company and he incited his senior maintenance controller to accept and pay bogus invoices. His defence was that he set up the scheme not to make a profit for himself, but to disclose to his employers how easily the company's security arrangements could be circumvented. He did not tell his supervisor what his purpose was, but would eventually have done so. The short report of the case in the Criminal Law Review which we have does not set out the precise terms of the charge but it is clear that it alleged that S dishonestly incited K dishonestly to obtain cheques from the company by the means which I have described. The particulars of the offence also said that he had done so with the intention of permanently depriving the company of the cheques. After the jury had been sent out they returned with a note saying that they (or some of them) were not sure whether the prosecution had established that what S had done was with a view to profit for himself. In other words, they (or some of them) were disposed to accept the defence he was running. The Court of Appeal allowed the appeal because the judge, when faced with the note, had not given the jury an adequate direction about that part of the particulars of the offence which alleged that the appellant had done what he had with the intention of permanently depriving his employers by deception. He should have told them that if they thought it possible that S was merely concerned to demonstrate the insecurity of the system the verdict should be not guilty. In a case where the principal issue was dishonesty and the jury were doubtful about whether S had been dishonest one can well understand why the Court of Appeal was concerned with how the judge had dealt with the note. There is nothing in the report which shows why K's mens rea was relevant. But it says:

'Held, allowing the appeal, the jury were concerned with the proof of mens rea both of S and of K, since both had to be considered.'

It is this sentence which enabled Mr Sharpe to make the submissions he did. It has led to much criticism which can be found in Archbold, Blackstone and in the Commentary which immediately follows in the Criminal Law Report. This Commentary says:

'The decision seems to be misconceived. If I tell Bill Sikes, the burglar, about the poor state of security of my employer's premises and encourage him to enter and steal therein, I have surely incited him to commit burglary. I have tried to persuade him to do an act which, when done, will, as I know, be the offence of burglary. How can it possibly be said that I have not incited him to commit the offence? . . .

The court has confused the *mens rea* of incitement with the mens rea of the offence incited.'

. . .

Shaw is a decision of the Court of Appeal and therefore binding on us. It can be explained on its facts in the way I have attempted to do but it can also perhaps be explained because the indictment specifically alleged that S had dishonestly incited K to dishonestly obtain. It is not in my judgment therefore general authority for the proposition that the person incited must act with the same parity of mens rea as the inciter.

R v Curr (supra) is also binding on us. In that case the appellant was a trafficker in Family Allowance books. His practice was to approach a woman with a large family and lend her money on the security of her book. After signing some of the vouchers the woman would hand them over to appellant as security. The appellant had a team of woman agents whom he sent out to cash the vouchers. He kept the proceeds as repayment of the loans and interest and then returned each book to its owner. He was convicted of soliciting to commit a summary offence under the provisions of the Family Allowance Act 1945. The offence charged was that he had solicited a woman unknown to obtain on his behalf from Her Majesty's Postmaster General the sum of £ 2.18s as on account of an allowance, knowing that it was not properly receivable by her. 'Knowing' was an essential ingredient of that offence under the 1945 Act. The court held that the appellant could be guilty of soliciting only if the woman agent knew that the action which she was asked to perform amounted to an offence. In giving the judgment of the court, Fenton Atkinson J said:

'In our view, the argument for the prosecution here gives no effect to the word "knowing" in the section, and in our view the appellant could be guilty on count 3 only if the woman solicited, the woman agent sent to collect the allowance, knew that the action she was asked to carry out amounted to an offence.'

It seems to me that all the court is saying in that case is that what the appellant was doing was something short of asking the woman concerned to commit a criminal offence. He was not inciting her to commit an offence because the offence required her knowledge that she was committing an offence. There is nothing in the judgment to suggest that the court was making any general pronouncement upon whether for the offence of incitement it is necessary to prove that not only the inciter but also the person incited had the *mens rea* to commit the full offence.

It follows from what I have said that I do not see anything in either of these two cases which compels me to conclude that the law is not as I stated it to be in the earlier part of this judgment. And it also follows that I do not think the magistrate was correct when he found that the law requires that the person incited must have parity of *mens rea* with the inciter. Applied to the facts of this case, it was not necessary for the prosecutor to show that the officer intended to supply child pornography to the respondent. His intention was irrelevant. The offence of incitement was committed when he was asked to commit the offence of supplying child pornography with the intention on the part of the respondent that in doing so he would be committing a criminal offence.

The only basis upon which the magistrate found impossibility was that the police officer would not supply the material. In considering whether there is a defence of impossibility the court must look carefully at what it is that the person incited has been asked to do. In this case the officer was asked to supply child pornography. The fact that he did not intend to do so is irrelevant. The request made to the police officer was in general terms for child pornography and one which he could have met from material in the police's possession, as the findings of the magistrate made clear. The officer could therefore have committed the offence which he had been asked to commit. It cannot therefore be said that it was impossible for him to do so. The facts of this case do not fall within any of the categories of impossibility to which I have referred. This is borne out by the decisions in *R v Quail* (1866) 4 F & F 1976 and *R v Fitzmaurice* [1983] QB 1083, 76 Cr App Rep 17 to which we were referred.

For these reasons I think the magistrate reached the wrong conclusion in this case and I would answer 'No' to each of the two questions which he has posed for this court. It must follow that I would quash his decision.

Appeal allowed.

3.2 WHAT IS THE *ACTUS REUS* OF INCITEMENT?

Incitement includes encouragement, suggestion, proposals, requests, persuasion, inducement, or goading someone to commit a crime.[44] The Court of Appeal[45] recently approved the following comment of a South African judge, Holmes JA:[46]

An inciter . . . is one who reaches and seeks to influence the mind of another to the commission of a crime. The machinations of criminal ingenuity being legion, the approach to the other's mind may take many forms, such as a suggestion, proposal, request, exhortation, gesture, argument, persuasion, inducement, goading or the arousal of cupidity.

There must be an act of incitement, but it can be implied or express encouragement. For example, in *Invicta Plastics Ltd v Clare*[47] a company offered for sale a 'radatex', a device to

---

[44] *Race Relations Board v Applin* [1973] QB 815 (CA).   [45] *Goldman* [1997] Crim LR 894 (CA).
[46] *Mkosiyana* (1966) 4 SA 655 at 658.   [47] [1976] RTR 251 (DC).

detect radar traps set by the police to catch speeding motorists. The use of such a device for that purpose is illegal,[48] as the company made clear in its advertising material. It was held that despite the company making it clear that consumers should not use its product illegally, advertising a product which was useful only if used for an illegal purpose was in effect inciting an offence.[49]

Invicta Plastics Ltd v Clare[50] also demonstrates that a defendant can be convicted of an incitement even if the encouragement is addressed to the world at large, rather than a particular person.[51] Similar issues arose in *Marlow*,[52] where the defendant was convicted of inciting an offence contrary to section 19 of the Misuse of Drugs Act 1971 by writing a book which described in some detail how to grow and produce cannabis. Although nowhere in the book did he actually encourage anyone to produce cannabis, practically speaking anyone reading the book would have felt emboldened to do so.

In *Goldman*[53] the defendant replied to an advertisement inviting people to request indecent photographs of children. He was convicted of inciting the distribution of indecent photographs of children.[54] He appealed on the basis that there could be no incitement on the basis that the alleged incitee had invited people to request the illegal activity. The Court of Appeal held that asking for the illegal photographs to be sent was incitement, whether such incitement was welcomed by the person incited or not.

In *O'Shea v Coventry Magistrates' Court, ex p CPS*[55] the defendant had accessed various internet computer sites which displayed child pornography. He was charged with unlawfully inciting another to distribute an indecent photograph of a child. His defence was that he had not incited another person to distribute the images, rather he had caused a computer to show them. The Divisional Court upheld his conviction on the basis that the people behind the internet site had been encouraged to continue running the site. Although it might be questioned whether this is so, given that they might not be aware that the defendant had visited it.

3.3 WHAT MUST BE INCITED?

The offence is established only if the incited act is one that would be an offence if the incited person performed it. There are two points here. First, it is not an offence to incite a person to perform an act which is not criminal. So inciting a person to commit adultery would not constitute an offence. On the other hand the incitement to commit any criminal offence will constitute incitement, except the following:

(1) It is not an offence to incite to conspire: section 5(7) of the Criminal Law Act 1977.[56]

(2) There is some dispute over whether it is an offence to incite an attempt. The fact that attempts are not listed in the Magistrates Courts Act 1980, Schedule 1, seems to

---

[48] Wireless Telegraphy Act 1949, s. 1(1).

[49] Although contrast *James and Ashford* (1986) 82 Cr App R 226 (CA).

[50] [1976] RTR 251 (DC).

[51] A fine line has to be drawn between announcing that one is prepared to facilitate crimes and the encouragement of others to commit crimes. Contrast *James and Ashford* (1985) 82 Cr App R 226 with *Invicta*.

[52] [1997] Crim LR 897 (CA).   [53] [2001] Crim LR 894 (CA).

[54] An offence under s. 1 of the Protection of Children Act 1978.   [55] CO/6342/2003

[56] It seems that it can be an offence to incite to incite: *Sirat* (1985) 83 Cr App R 41. Although the court made it clear that if the terms of the incitement to incite were in effect an incitement to conspire then that would not be an offence because s. 5(7) states it is not an offence to incite to conspire. This rule is required by the wording of the section rather than any sensible policy.

assume there can be no such offence.[57] However, if D incites A to fire a gun which D knows contains blank bullets at B[58] it is not clear why D should not be charged with incitement to attempt.

(3) It seems there is no offence to incite to aid, abet, counsel, or procure an offence.[59]

Secondly, it must be an offence for *the incitee* (that is the person incited) to carry out the act incited.[60] This significance of this was demonstrated in *Whitehouse*.[61] There it was held not to be a common law offence[62] for a man to incite his daughter to have incestuous sexual intercourse with him.[63] If the girl were to perform intercourse this would not amount to an offence *by her*.[64] If the sexual intercourse were to occur, the man would commit incest, but the girl would not.

3.4 WHEN DOES THE OFFENCE TAKE PLACE?

It seems the offence of incitement takes place only once the encouragement has been communicated to the incitee. So, if the defendant writes a letter inciting another to commit an offence and the letter is intercepted before it arrives at the destination then there is no incitement, although there may then be an attempted incitement.[65] As already emphasized, there is no need for the incitee to commit the offence for there to be a conviction for incitement.

3.5 THE *MENS REA* FOR INCITEMENT

The *mens rea* for incitement is that the defendant must intend the incited offence to be committed. He or she must also know any fact or circumstances that is part of the *actus reus* of the offence. So the *mens rea* for incitement to rape is an intention that the incitee will penetrate the victim and knowledge that the victim would not consent to the penetration.

Consider these examples:

(1) D encourages A to stab B in the arm. A does so but because B is (unknown to D) a haemophiliac he dies as a result of the wound. D is guilty only of incitement to wound.[66]

(2) D encourages A to kill B, intending A to do so, but A decides just to wound B. A is guilty of an incitement to kill (**N.B.** not an incitement to commit grievous bodily harm).

---

[57] Law Commission, Draft Criminal Code, cl. 47(5)(b) includes a liability for incitement to attempt.

[58] An example given in Allen (2003: 253).

[59] *Bodin and Bodin* [1979] Crim LR 176, a first instance judgment which was referred to uncritically in *Sirat* (1985) 83 Cr App R 41 (CA). For an argument that incitement to be an accessory should be an offence see Simester and Sullivan (2003: 260).

[60] *Pickford* [1995] QB 203 (CA).

[61] (1977) 65 Cr App R 33 (CA).

[62] It is now a statutory offence under the Sexual Offences Act 2003, s. 10, for a person to incite a child to engage in sexual activity.

[63] This reasoning was recently followed in *R v C* [2005] EWCA Crim 2827.

[64] This is part of the general principle that if a statute is designed to protect a class of people (e.g. children) they cannot be convicted as an accessory to that offence: *Tyrrell* [1894] 1 QB 719.

[65] *Ransford* (1874) 13 Cox CC 9.

[66] He may be an accessory to manslaughter (see Ch. 15).

(3) D encourages A to kill B, but does not believe that A will agree to do so. The question is one of intention. If D intends A to kill B, even if she accepts that it is unlikely that A will do so then D will be guilty of incitement. If, however, D said the words as a joke and did not want A to kill B there is no incitement.

(4) D, with the honest motivation of seeking to show how inadequate his employer's security measures are, incites A to steal company property, without telling A his reasons. Although D is acting honestly he is inciting A to commit a crime: theft. He is therefore guilty of inciting theft.[67]

Although the courts have said that intention is required, Professor Smith[68] has argued that in fact the cases suggest that it is sufficient if the defendant knew that if his advice was followed the commission of an offence would inevitably follow. In other words, foresight of virtual certainty can amount to intention.[69] He points to *Marlow*[70] and suggests that the defendant in publishing the book on how to grow cannabis probably had the aim of making money and may have been indifferent to whether people actually grew cannabis, and yet his conviction was still upheld.[71] Victor Tadros disagrees. He gives the following example:

> [I]n telling Harry that his wife, Jill, is having an affair, John may know that it is virtually certain that Harry will kill Jill. But that might not be sufficient reason to convict John for inciting Harry to kill Jill. Simply by telling Harry the news, John does not associate himself directly with Harry's action and hence, we might argue, ought not to be convicted of incitement.[72]

A difficult case: where the incitee would not be guilty if she were to perform the requested act

The law as stated so far is fairly straightforward. Two situations are more tricky:

(1) What if the incitee would have been able to rely on a defence had she committed the offence? To answer this question it is useful to consider the following scenario. Nicola threatens Bob with grievous bodily harm unless he commits an offence. Bob refuses to do so. Had Bob given in to the threat and committed the act he would not be guilty of an offence, because he could rely on duress. Most commentators appear to take the view that this amounts to incitement by Nicola,[73] but there is no clear case law on this.

(2) What if the incitee would lack the necessary *mens rea* if he committed the offence? For example, Tim incited Brian to damage a book and in so doing assured him (untruthfully) that it was his (Brian's) own book. Brian refuses to do so. In fact, had Brian damaged the book he might have lacked the *mens rea* for criminal damage, but that would not prevent Tim being guilty of incitement.

---

[67] In *Shaw* [1994] Crim LR 365 the Court of Appeal on similar facts denied that there was an incitement, but in *DPP v Armstrong* [2000] Crim LR 379 (excerpted above) the Divisional Court explained that case on the basis of the peculiar wording of the particular indictment before the jury.

[68] J.C. Smith (2002: 294).

[69] See *Woollin* [1999] AC 82 (HL) and the discussion of intention in Ch. 3 of this book.

[70] [1997] Crim LR 897.

[71] A similar point could be made about *Invicta Plastics v Clare* [1976] Crim LR 131 where it could be said that the company's purpose was to sell products.

[72] Tadros (2002: 454).

[73] An analogy with *Bourne* [1976] QB 217 and *Millward* [1994] Crim LR 527 (CA) can be drawn.

There are two issues here. First, is it an offence to incite just the *actus reus* of an offence?[74] There is much dispute over this question and little case law, although by analogy with the cases on accessories[75] (where the courts have held it is possible to be convicted of procuring the commission of just the *actus reus* of the offence) it is arguable that it is an offence to incite a person to perform the *actus reus* of an offence.

The second issue relates to the relevance of the incitee's *mens rea*. The issue arose in the case of *Curr*,[76] discussed in *Armstrong*, excerpted above. *Curr* appeared to suggest that there is no incitement if the incitee would not have had the *mens rea* for the full offence had she gone on to commit it.[77] However, in the view of many commentators *Curr* was wrongly decided and it was disapproved by the Court of Appeal in *R v C*.[78] As has been stressed several times already, whether the person incited went on to commit an offence is irrelevant to the guilt of the incitor, therefore the incitee's *mens rea* if she does go on to commit the offence should likewise be irrelevant. What matters is what the defendant thought would be the state of mind of the person incited if she were to go on to commit the offence.[79] An alternative analysis of these scenarios is that if D believes that the person will commit the offence but without the *mens rea* or with a defence then it would be correct to interpret the offence as attempting to commit (or committing) the offence through an innocent agent.

3.6 INCITEMENT AND IMPOSSIBILITY

If the defendant is inciting someone to commit a crime which it is impossible to commit there is no offence. This is because in *Fitzmaurice*[80] it was held that the common law on impossibility[81] applies to incitements. It is necessary to distinguish between three situations:

(1) Where the crime is not possible. If D incites A to kill X, while X is already dead, there is no offence.[82] This is because it is impossible for A to do what D requested. However, it is important to remember that incitement is committed at the time of the encouragement, not when the offence is committed. Therefore if the offence is possible at the time of the encouragement but subsequently becomes impossible the offence has still been committed. So if D incites A to kill X while X is still alive, the fact that shortly afterwards X dies (rendering the incited offence impossible) provides no defence to a charge of incitement.

(2) Where it is possible to commit the crime but the means that is encouraged to be used is inadequate there can still be liability for an incitement. For example if D incites A to give X a certain powder in order to kill X, but the powder is (unknown to D) in fact

---

[74] Leng (1978).
[75] e.g. *Millward* [1994] Crim LR 527 (CA). [76] [1968] 2 QB 944 (CA).
[77] If A does have intercourse with B and B does not consent then D may be guilty as an accomplice to the rape of B: *Cogan and Leake* [1976] QB 217 (CA).
[78] [2005] EWCA Crim 2827.
[79] The Court of Appeal in *Curr* [1968] 2 QB 944 appears to be a mistaken decision because it acquitted the defendant on the basis that the women incited were not guilty because they lacked the *mens rea*. The court should have considered what D intended or believed at the time he incited the women.
[80] [1983] QB 1083 (CA).
[81] As set out in *Haughton v Smith* [1975] AC 476 (HL); *DPP v Nock* [1978] AC 979 (HL).
[82] *Sirat* (1986) 83 Cr App R 41 at 43.

innocuous then there is incitement.[83] Similarly in *Armstrong*,[84] excerpted above, the fact that the police officer would never have done the requested act does not mean the act is impossible.

(3) Where the action incited is not a crime there can be no incitement. If D incites A to circumcise his son, believing (incorrectly) that it is a criminal offence to circumcise boys,[85] this is not an offence.[86]

QUESTION

Anne says to Liu, 'It would be nice if someone would kill Steve'. She knows that Liu will not do so, but she hopes that Liu will ask someone else to do so. Liu later mentions to Robert that Anne would like someone to kill Steve. She believes that Robert will kill Steve, because she knows Robert wants to impress Anne, but hopes that he will not. In fact Robert decides not to kill Steve. What crimes have been committed?

4 CONSPIRACY

DEFINITION

A conspiracy is an agreement by two or more people to engage in a course of conduct which amounts to a criminal offence (or corrupt public morals or fraud).

4.1 THE NATURE OF CONSPIRACY

It is an offence to conspire to commit:

(1) Any criminal offence,[87] including aiding, abetting, counselling, procuring, or inciting an offence.[88] These are known as statutory conspiracies.

(2) A small number of activities which are not in and of themselves illegal, but which common law has decreed it is an offence to conspire to commit. They are:
   (i) to defraud; and
   (ii) (maybe) to do an act which corrupts public morals.

These are known as common law conspiracies.

The vast majority of conspiracies are, therefore, statutory conspiracies, although a few are common law conspiracies. There is no rational reason why there should be these two categories of conspiracies, except to annoy law students. The distinction is particularly

---

[83] Unless D was aware that the powder was innocuous, in which case he did not have the *mens rea* for an incitement. But there may be liability for the offence of incitement to attempt to kill in such a case (if it is possible to incite an attempt).

[84] [2000] Crim LR 379 (DC).

[85] It is a criminal offence to circumcise girls, but not boys: Prohibition of Female Circumcision Act 1985.

[86] *Taafe* [1984] AC 539 (HL).

[87] The consent of the Director of Public Prosecutions is required before a charge of conspiracy to commit a summary offence can be brought (Criminal Law Act 1977, s. 4(1)). For discussion of agreements to commit offences abroad see Simester and Sullivan (2003: 315–17).

[88] See e.g. *Booth* [1999] Crim LR 144. Although see the discussion in Simester and Sullivan (2003: 273) doubting whether one can conspire to be an accomplice.

unfortunate because the law governing statutory conspiracies and common law conspiracies differs. The basis for the distinction between these two kinds of conspiracy is found in the wording of the Criminal Law Act 1977. Under section 1(1) it is an offence to agree to commit any offence. Section 5(1) and (2) reads as follows:

(1) Subject to the following provisions of the section, the offence of conspiracy at common law is hereby abolished.

(2) Subsection (1) above shall not affect the offence of conspiracy at common law so far as relate to conspiracy to defraud.

This was interpreted by the House of Lords in *Ayres*[89] to mean that all conspiracies which involve an agreement to commit a criminal offence are statutory conspiracies and cannot be common law conspiracies.

4.2 STATUTORY CONSPIRACIES

DEFINITION

To constitute a conspiracy there must be:

1. An agreement.
2. The agreement must be to pursue a course of conduct that will involve the commission of a crime.
3. The parties must intend the offence to be committed.

Section 1(1) of the Criminal Law Act 1977 (as amended by section 5 of the Criminal Attempts Act 1981) provides:

> Subject to the following provisions of this part of this Act, if a person agrees with any other person or persons that a course of conduct shall be pursued which, if the agreement is carried out in accordance with their intentions, either—
>
> (a) will necessarily amount to or involve the commission of any offence or offences by one or more parties to the agreement, or
>
> (b) would do so but for the existence of facts which render the commission of the offence or any offences impossible
>
> he is guilty of conspiracy to commit the offence or offences in question.

This statutory definition indicates that a conspiracy is made up of the following elements:

An agreement

(i) **The need for an agreement?** The key element of the *actus reus* of the offence of conspiracy is an agreement. The parties must have reached a decision to carry out the unlawful plan as a joint project. They must have gone beyond the stage of negotiation and

---

[89] [1984] AC 447 (HL).

reached the stage where there is an agreement.[90] It is not necessary to show that every member of the conspiracy has communicated with every other. What needs to be shown is that the common purpose has been communicated by the defendant to at least one other party to the conspiracy.[91] If Steve is aware that Jonathan and Bryony are conspiring to commit a crime and he does things to help them, this does not make him a conspirator: he must enter some kind of agreement with Jonathan and Bryony.[92] In some cases it can be difficult to decide whether many people happen to be pursuing the same crime independently (e.g. several members of the public carrying out the same kind of fraud on a company) or whether they are acting in concert.[93]

Once the parties have reached an agreement the *actus reus* of a conspiracy has occurred.[94] Therefore, if the parties agree to commit a crime, but then later decide not to go ahead with the plan, they may be convicted of a conspiracy.[95] Indeed the parties can be guilty of a conspiracy even though they have not taken any steps to implement the agreement.[96]

As long as the parties have reached a clear agreement to commit an offence it is not necessary to show that they have agreed all of the details of the plan. Two people may be guilty of conspiring to burgle, even though they are yet to agree where and when they will commit that crime. It is also a conspiracy to reach a conditional agreement. It would, therefore, be a conspiracy to burgle if the agreement was that 'if the house is unoccupied we will burgle it'.[97]

(ii) **Who can be the parties to a conspiracy?** To amount to a conspiracy there must be at least two parties to the agreement. However, agreements between certain people cannot be a conspiracy:

(a) An agreement between a husband and wife[98] is not a conspiracy (Criminal Law Act 1977, section 2(2)(a)).[99] However, an agreement between a wife, a husband, and a third party can be.[100] The explanation for this rule is that the criminal law seeks to protect marital privacy.

(b) An agreement between one person and a person under the age of criminal responsibility cannot amount to a criminal conspiracy.[101]

(c) An agreement between the defendant and the intended victim[102] of the crime is not a criminal conspiracy.[103] So if D agrees with V illegally to cut off V's leg this does not amount to a conspiracy. However, it appears that if D conspires with others that drugs will be supplied to him he can be guilty of a conspiracy.[104]

(d) There can be no conspiracy if the only two parties to the agreement are a company and the director of that company who is solely responsible for the conduct of the company's business.[105]

---

[90] *Walker* [1962] Crim LR 458; *Mills* (1963) 47 Cr App R 49 (CA).

[91] *Ardalan* [1972] 2 All ER 257 (CA).

[92] *Griffiths* (1965) 49 Cr App R 94 (CA); *contra Meyrick* (1929) 21 Cr App R 523 (CA).

[93] A person can be guilty of conspiracy by joining together with others who have already agreed to commit a crime: *Zezev* [2002] Crim LR 648 (CA).

[94] *Hussain, Bhatti and Bhatti* [2002] Crim LR 405 (CA). [95] *Thomson* (1965) 50 Cr App R 1 (CA).

[96] *DPP v Nock* [1978] AC 979 (HL). [97] *O'hAdhmaill* [1996] Crim LR 509 (CA).

[98] This rule does not apply to an unmarried cohabiting couple.

[99] Of course, if a husband and wife go on to commit a crime they will be guilty of the substantive offence.

[100] *Chrastny* [1991] 1 WLR 1381 (CA). [101] Criminal Law Act 1977, s. 2(2)(b).

[102] The word 'victim' is not defined in the Criminal Law Act 1977.

[103] Criminal Law Act 1977, s. 2(2)(c). [104] *Drew* (2000) Cr App R 91 (CA).

[105] *McDonnell* [1966] 1 QB 233.

There must be at least two parties to the agreement who have the necessary *mens rea* for a conspiracy. If only one party has the *mens rea* then there cannot be a conspiracy. For example, if one party but not the other is aware of a fact that makes the proposed course of conduct illegal then there will be no conspiracy. If all parties to the alleged conspiracy are charged together it is not open to the jury to convict only one of them, unless the evidence against that one conspirator is markedly stronger than the evidence against the others, and the jury are convinced the person convicted conspired with someone, even if they are not sure who that was.[106]

An agreement to commit a crime

The conspirators must agree on a course of conduct which constitutes the *actus reus* of a crime. It is possible to conspire to attempt or to conspire to conspire. However, a conspiracy to aid, abet, counsel, or procure an offence is not itself a crime according to *Hollinshead*.[107]

But what exactly must the conspirators know if they are to be said to have agreed to commit a crime?

(1) There is no need to show that the conspirators knew that their proposed course of conduct amounted to a crime.[108]

(2) The parties must intend the consequences of their actions which are parts of the *actus reus*. For example, it is not enough for a charge of a conspiracy to kill to show that the parties agreed to put poison in the victim's cup of tea; they must also intend the victim to die as a result.[109] If the agreement is to put poison in the victim's cup of tea, with the intention of causing discomfort to the victim, but the victim dies, there is no conspiracy to kill[110] simply because the parties did not agree to kill. Even if the conspirators foresaw the risk that their conduct might kill a victim, there is no conspiracy to murder unless they intended the death.[111] Some doubt over the law as stated in this paragraph now exist as a result of the decision in *R v Saskavickas*[112] where it was suggested that recklessness would be sufficient. However, subsequently in *R v Harmer*[113] and *Ali*[114] the court of appeal confirmed the standard approach that the defendants must know or intend the facts to exist.

(3) Knowledge of essential facts. The conspirators must be aware of any circumstances which form part of the *actus reus* and therefore render their proposed conduct illegal or intend those facts to exist.[115] If two people reach an agreement to grow some plants unaware that the plants are cannabis or agree to have intercourse with a woman, being unsure whether or not she will consent, they will not be guilty of a conspiracy

---

[106] Section 5(8) and (9) of the Criminal Law Act 1977; *Roberts* (1983) 78 Cr App R 41.

[107] [1985] 1 All ER 850. The Court of Appeal's decision was confirmed in the House of Lords ([1985] AC 975) which did not address the issue. It is, however, possible to convict someone of conspiring to commit a statutory offence whose *actus reus* involves aiding or abetting something (e.g. aiding and abetting another's suicide: *Reed* [1982] Crim LR 819 (CA)).

[108] *Churchill v Walton* [1967] 2 AC 224 (HL).

[109] An intention to cause grievous bodily harm is therefore insufficient for a conspiracy to murder: *Siracusa* (1990) 90 Cr App R 340, 350. For further discussion see Smith (2002: 301).

[110] Although they may be guilty of murder.

[111] Although there might be a conspiracy to poison: Offences Against the Person Act 1861, ss. 23 and 24.

[112] [2004] EWCA Crim 2686.   [113] [2005] EWCA Crim 1.   [114] [2005] Crim LR 864.

[115] For a discussion of difficulties of rules of statutory interpretation in reaching that conclusion see Simester and Sullivan (2003: 282–5).

because they do not know[116] the circumstantial facts which are essential to the conspiracy. Recently the Court of Appeal applied this reasoning in finding that an agreement to import Class B drugs is not sufficient to justify a conviction for an agreement to import Class A drugs.[117]

(4) Mistaken beliefs of the conspirators. The conspirators will be judged on their planned actions, not what actually happened. For example, if the parties agreed to plant seeds, believing that they would produce cannabis plants, but in fact the seeds were parsnip seeds, they would be guilty of a conspiracy to produce cannabis.

(5) Intention to commit a more serious crime. If D agrees with A to commit crime X, but secretly intends to commit a more serious crime then D will be guilty of conspiring to commit crime X. However, if D agrees with A to commit crime X, but in fact intends to commit a lesser crime (e.g. D agrees with A to kill V, but intends just to beat V up) he will not be guilty of a conspiracy to commit crime X.[118] If they have both agreed to commit an offence, but differ over some details, this will not affect their criminal liability. So if one conspirator thought that the agreement was to produce one kind of class A drug and the other conspirator thought the agreement was to produce a different kind of Class A drug, they could be said to be both guilty of conspiring to produce a Class A drug.[119]

The plan must necessarily involve the commission of a crime by one or more of the parties

Section 1(1) of the Criminal Law Act 1977 makes it clear that the plan must necessarily involve the commission of a crime. There are two points to consider further:

(1) The agreement must be that at least one of the parties to the conspiracy will commit the crime. So if a gang reaches an agreement that its leader will commit a crime, but the leader is not present at the meeting and so is not a party to the agreement, there is no conspiracy.

(2) The proposed course of conduct must necessarily involve the commission of a crime. The word 'necessarily' is problematic.[120] Very few agreements will inevitably involve the commission of the crime, not least because the conspirators are likely explicitly or implicitly to agree that the plan will not go ahead if there is a police officer at the scene of the crime. Fortunately the courts have refused to treat the word 'necessarily' in a strict way. In *Jackson*[121] four members of a gang arranged to shoot one of their members (W) in the leg. W was on trial for burglary and the hope was that the judge would be sympathetic to W because of his leg injury and pass a lower sentence than he would otherwise. They were charged with a conspiracy to pervert the course of justice. The conspirators argued that their plan did not necessarily involve the perversion of justice because W might have been acquitted of the offence. The Court of Appeal focused on the words 'if the agreement is carried out in accordance with their intentions' and held that the question to ask was if the 'plan worked'

---

[116] In the rape example they suspect, but do not know, that the victim will not consent.

[117] *Taylor* [2002] Crim LR 205 (CA), although the Court of Appeal added that if one person thought that the agreement was to produce Class A drugs and the other thought it was to produce Class B there could be no conspiracy.

[118] *Barnard* (1980) 70 Cr App R 28.   [119] *Broad* [1997] Crim LR 666 (CA).

[120] Notably it is omitted from the Draft Criminal Code.   [121] [1985] Crim LR 444 (CA).

would an offence be committed? Here, if the plan 'worked' W would receive a lesser sentence. The Court of Appeal in *Jackson* expressly rejected an argument that necessarily meant inevitably. Indeed the point was made that the conspirators might think that it was extremely unlikely that their plan would work but could still be held to have conspired to commit an offence.

The Court of Appeal in *Jackson* gave as an example of a plan which would not necessarily involve the commission of an offence an agreement by two people to drive to Edinburgh within a certain time which could be achieved if the traffic was especially light, but if the traffic congestion was at normal levels would require the parties to break the speed limits. In *O'hAdhmaill*[122] a man was charged with conspiring to cause an IRA explosion if the peace talks failed. He argued that he had not agreed on a course of conduct which necessarily amounted to an offence. He was convicted which the Court of Appeal subsequently upheld.

QUESTION

Tom and Una agree to rob a bank. Tom suggests that if a police officer tries to arrest them they will kill him. Is this a conspiracy to kill? (Consider whether this is closer to *O'Hadhmaill* or closer to the drivers to Edinburgh discussed in *Jackson*.)

Intention that the plan be carried out

We have already seen that the parties' plan must involve the commission of an offence and that this requires them to know of any facts or circumstances which are aspects of the *actus reus*. However, the *mens rea* for a conspiracy goes further than this and requires each defendant to intend the conspiracy to be carried out. This is so even if the crime is one of strict liability.[123] It appears that foresight of a result as virtually certain can amount to intention, along the lines of the *Woollin* decision.[124]

This intent requirement appears to be straightforward. But this element of the offence was thrown into doubt by the following decision of the House of Lords decision in *Anderson*.[125]

R v Anderson
[1986] AC 27 (HL)[126]

William Anderson was convicted of conspiring with others to effect the escape of Ahmed Andaloussi, a prisoner at Lewes Prison. The prosecution alleged that Anderson had been paid £20,000 for his part in the escape plan. He was to purchase and supply diamond wire of a kind capable of cutting through metal bars. This was to be smuggled into the prison by other conspirators. In fact, shortly after receiving the £20,000 Anderson was injured in a car accident and unable to supply the wire in pursuance of the plan. He claimed that he was going to supply the wire and then escape to Spain,

---

[122] [1996] Crim LR 509 (CA).   [123] Criminal Law Act 1977, s. 1(2).

[124] *Cooke* [1986] AC 909 (HL) where British Rail employees were convicted of a conspiracy to defraud British Rail. The purpose of their plan was to make money for themselves, but they were aware that in doing so they were virtually certain to cause British Rail losses and so could be said to have intended to cause those losses.

[125] [1986] AC 27 (HL).

[126] [1985] 2 All ER 961, [1985] 3 WLR 268, (1985) 81 Cr App R 253, [1985] Crim LR 651.

playing no further role in the escape. He argued before the House of Lords that he lacked the mens rea for a conspiracy because he did not intend the escape plan to come into effect.

Lord Bridge of Harwich

The Court of Appeal, having dismissed his appeal, certified that its decision involved a point of law of general public importance in terms which can conveniently be divided into two parts, since, in truth, there are two separate questions involved:

'[1] Is a person who "agrees" with two or more others, who themselves intend to pursue a course of conduct which will necessarily involve the commission of an offence, and who has a secret intention himself to participate in part only of that course of conduct, guilty himself of conspiracy to commit that offence under Section 1(1) of the Criminal Law Act 1977 [2] if not is he liable to be indicted as a principal offender under Section 8 of the Accessories and Abettors Act 1861?'

The present appeal is brought by leave of your Lordships' House.

Section 1(1) of the Criminal Law Act 1977 has been amended by the Criminal Attempts Act 1981, but the point of construction arising in this appeal is in no way affected by the amendment. It is sufficient, therefore, for the present purposes, to set out the language of the subsection as originally enacted. It provides as follows:

'Subject to the following provisions of this Part of this Act, if a person agrees with any other person or persons that a course of conduct shall be pursued which will necessarily amount to or involve the commission of any offence or offences by one or more of the parties to the agreement if the agreement is carried out in accordance with their intentions, he is guilty of conspiracy to commit the offence or offences in question.'

The 1977 Act, subject to exceptions not presently material, abolished the offence of conspiracy at common law. It follows that the elements of the new statutory offence of conspiracy must be ascertained purely by interpretation of the language of s 1(1) of the 1977 Act. For purposes of analysis it is perhaps convenient to isolate the three clauses each of which must be taken as indicating an essential ingredient of the offence as follows: (1) 'if a person agrees with any other person or persons that a course of conduct shall be pursued' (2) 'which will necessarily amount to or involve the commission of any offence or offences by one or more of the parties to the agreement' (3) 'if the agreement is carried out in accordance with their intentions'.

Clause (1) presents, as it seems to me, no difficulty. It means exactly what it says and what it says is crystal clear. To be convicted, the party charged must have agreed with one or more others that 'a course of conduct shall be pursued'. What is important is to resist the temptation to introduce into this simple concept ideas derived from the civil law of contract. Any number of persons may agree that a course of conduct shall be pursued without undertaking any contractual liability. The agreed course of conduct may be a simple or an elaborate one and may involve the participation of two or any larger number of persons who may have agreed to play a variety of roles in the course of conduct agreed.

Again, clause (2) could hardly use simpler language. Here what is important to note is that it is not necessary that more than one of the participants in the agreed course of conduct shall commit a substantive offence. It is, of course, necessary that any party to the agreement shall have assented to play his part in the agreed course of conduct, however innocent in itself, knowing that the part to be played by one or more of the others will amount to or involve the commission of an offence.

It is only clause (3) which presents any possible ambiguity. The heart of the submission for the appellant is that in order to be convicted of conspiracy to commit a given offence the language of clause (3) requires that the party charged should not only have agreed that a course of conduct shall be pursued which will necessarily amount to or involve the commission of that offence by himself or one or more other parties to the agreement, but must also be proved himself to have intended that that offence should be committed. Thus, it is submitted here that the appellant's case that he never intended that Andaloussi should be enabled to escape from prison raised an issue to be left to the jury, who should have been directed to convict him only if satisfied that he did so intend. I do not find it altogether easy to understand why the draftsman of this provision chose to use the phrase 'in accordance with their intentions'. But I suspect the answer may be that this seemed a desirable alternative to the phrase 'in accordance with its terms' or any similar expression, because it is a matter of common experience in the criminal courts that the 'terms' of a criminal conspiracy are hardly ever susceptible of proof. The evidence from which a jury may infer a criminal conspiracy is almost invariably to be found in the conduct of the parties. This was so at common law and remains so under the statute. If the evidence in a given case justifies the inference of an agreement that a course of conduct should be pursued, it is a not inappropriate formulation of the test of the criminality of the inferred agreement to ask whether the further inference can be drawn that a crime would necessarily have been committed if the agreed course of conduct had been pursued in accordance with the several intentions of the parties. Whether that is an accurate analysis or not, I am clearly driven by consideration of the diversity of roles which parties may agree to play in criminal conspiracies to reject any construction of the statutory language which would require the prosecution to prove an intention on the part of each conspirator that the criminal offence or offences which will necessarily be committed by one or more of the conspirators if the agreed course of conduct is fully carried out should in fact be committed. A simple example will illustrate the absurdity to which this construction would lead. The proprietor of a car hire firm agrees for a substantial payment to make available a hire car to a gang for use in a robbery and to make false entries in his books relating to the hiring to which he can point if the number of the car is traced back to him in connection with the robbery. Being fully aware of the circumstances of the robbery in which the car is proposed to be used he is plainly a party to the conspiracy to rob. Making his car available for use in the robbery is as much a part of the relevant agreed course of conduct as the robbery itself. Yet, once he has been paid, it will be a matter of complete indifference to him whether the robbery is in fact committed or not. In these days of highly organised crime the most serious statutory conspiracies will frequently involve an elaborate and complex agreed course of conduct in which many will consent to play necessary but subordinate roles, not involving them in any direct participation in the commission of the offence or offences at the centre of the conspiracy. Parliament cannot have intended that such parties should escape conviction of conspiracy on the basis that it cannot be proved against them that they intended that the relevant offence or offences should be committed.

There remains the important question whether a person who has agreed that a course of conduct will be pursued which, if pursued as agreed, will necessarily amount to or involve the commission of an offence is guilty of statutory conspiracy irrespective of his intention, and, if not, what is the *mens rea* of the offence. I have no hesitation in answering the first part of the question in the negative. There may be many situations in which perfectly respectable citizens, more particularly those concerned with law enforcement, may enter into agreements that a course of conduct shall be pursued which will involve commission of a crime without the least intention of playing any part in furtherance of the ostensibly agreed criminal objective, but rather with the purpose of exposing and frustrating the criminal purpose of the other parties to the agreement. To say this is in no way to encourage schemes by which police act, directly or through the agency of informers, as agents provocateurs for the purpose of entrapment. That is conduct of which the courts have always strongly disapproved. But it may sometimes happen, as most of us with experience in criminal trials well know, that a criminal enterprise is well advanced in the course of preparation when it comes to the notice either of the police or of some honest citizen in such circumstances that the only prospect of exposing and frustrating the criminals is that some innocent person should play the part of an intending collaborator in the course of criminal conduct proposed to be pursued. The *mens rea* implicit in the offence of statutory conspiracy must clearly be such as to recognise the innocence of such a person, notwithstanding that he will, in literal terms, be obliged to agree that a course of conduct be pursued involving the commission of an offence.

I have said already, but I repeat to emphasise its importance, that an essential ingredient in the crime of conspiring to commit a specific offence or offences under s 1(1) of the 1977 Act is that the accused should agree that a course of conduct be pursued which he knows must involve the commission by one or more of the parties to the agreement of that offence or those offences. But, beyond the mere fact of agreement, the necessary mens rea of the crime is, in my opinion, established if, and only if, it is shown that the accused, when he entered into the agreement, intended to play some part in the agreed course of conduct in furtherance of the criminal purpose which the agreed course of conduct was intended to achieve. Nothing less will suffice nothing more is required.

Applying this test to the facts which, for the purposes of the appeal, we must assume, the appellant, in agreeing that a course of conduct be pursued that would, if successful, necessarily involve the offence of effecting Andaloussi's escape from lawful custody, clearly intended, by providing diamond wire to be smuggled into the prison, to play a part in the agreed course of conduct in furtherance of that criminal objective. Neither the fact that he intended to play no further part in attempting to effect the escape, nor that he believed the escape to be impossible, would, if the jury had supposed they might be true, have afforded him any defence. . . .

Appeal dismissed.

Two particularly controversial points have been made by Lord Bridge in *Anderson*:

(1) The suggestion that a defendant could be convicted of conspiracy, even without intending the agreement to be carried out. There is wide acceptance of the view that this suggestion should not be regarded as an accurate statement of the law. There are three reasons why not:

    (i) On the facts of the case it was true that Anderson did not think that the plot had much chance of success and that he was just in the plan for the money, but neither of these points meant he did not intend the plan to be carried out. From the discussion in Chapter 3 it will be recalled that it is possible to intend a result without thinking one is likely to achieve it and also that motive is not the same as intent. Here he assisted the project of his conspirators knowing that they were going to implement the plan and this was sufficient to constitute intent.[127]

---

[127] Simester and Sullivan (2003: 283).

(ii) Applying Lord Bridge's logic it could be said that the parties conspired to commit a crime, even though none of them intended to carry out the plan! That would be bizarre.

(iii) The Court of Appeal has consistently failed to follow the House of Lords on this point.[128] Further the Privy Council in *Yip Chiu-Cheung* held that it did have to be shown that every alleged conspirator intended the agreement to be carried out.[129]

(2) That a person is guilty of conspiracy if, and only if, it is established that he intended to play some part[130] in the agreed course of conduct. This was a novel suggestion. As mentioned above, the key element of a conspiracy is an agreement, not the carrying out of the plan. The decision would lead to all kinds of difficulty in defining exactly what could be said to constitute carrying out an element of the plan. In *Siracusa* (extracted below) the Court of Appeal doubted whether it was an essential requirement of a conspiracy that each conspirator play some active role:

R v Siracusa and others
(1989) 90 Cr App R 340 (CA)[131]

Four men were charged with conspiracy to contravene section 170(2)(b) of the Customs and Excise Management Act 1979. The case concerned smugglers who were bringing heroin and cannabis into the UK by secreting it inside pieces of Thai and Kashmiri furniture. The appellants appealed against their conviction on the basis that the judge had wrongly directed the jury that the appellants would be guilty of conspiracy if they had agreed on a course of conduct which necessarily amounted to either the importation of cannabis or the importation of heroin.

Lord Justice O'Connor, reading the judgment of the court

[Having considered passages from Lord Bridge's judgment in *Anderson* O'Connor LJ continued:]

We think it obvious that Lord Bridge cannot have been intending that the organiser of a crime who recruited others to carry it out would not himself be guilty of conspiracy unless it could be proved that he intended to play some active part himself thereafter. Lord Bridge had pointed out at p 259 that:

'in these days of highly organised crime the most serious statutory conspiracies will frequently involve an elaborate and complex agreed course of conduct in which many will consent to play necessary but subordinate roles, not involving them in any direct participation in the commission of the offence or offences at the centre of the conspiracy.'

The present case is a classic example of such a conspiracy. It is the hallmark of such crimes that the organisers try to remain in the background and more often than not are not apprehended. Secondly, the origins of all concealed and it is usually quite impossible to establish when or where the initial agreement was made, or when or where other conspirators were

---

[128] *Edwards* [1991] Crim LR 45 (CA); *Ashton* [1992] Crim LR 667 (CA); *Harvey* [1999] Crim LR 70 (CA).
[129] *Yip Chiu-Cheung* [1995] 1 AC 111 (PC), although their Lordships did not refer to *Anderson* [1986] AC 27 (HL). See also *Edwards* [1991] Crim LR 45 (CA) which requires each conspirator to intend the plan to be carried out.
[130] It is far from clear what 'play some part' means.   [131] [1989] Crim LR 712.

recruited. The very existence of the agreement can only be inferred from overt acts. Participation in a conspiracy is infinitely variable: it can be active or passive. If the majority shareholder and director of a company consents to the company being used for drug smuggling carried out in the company's name by a fellow director and minority shareholder, he is guilty of conspiracy. Consent, that is the agreement or adherence to the agreement, can be inferred if it is proved that he knew what was going on and the intention to participate in the furtherance of the criminal purpose is also established by his failure to stop the unlawful activity. Lord Bridge's dictum does not require anything more.

We return to the first sentence of this paragraph in Lord Bridge's speech. He starts by saying: 'I have said already, but I repeat to emphasise its importance. . . .' We have cited what he had already said when dealing with his clause 2. It is clear that he was not intending to say anything different. So when he goes on to say:

' "an essential ingredient in the crime of conspiring to commit a specific offence or offences under section 1(1) of the Act of 1977 is that the accused should agree that a course of conduct be pursued which he knows must involve the commission by one or more of the parties to the agreement of that offence or those offences," he plainly does not mean that the prosecution have to prove that persons who agree to import prohibited drugs into this country know that the offence which will be committed will be a contravention of section 170(2) of the Customs and Excise Act. He is not to be taken as saying that the prosecution must prove that the accused knew the name of the crime. We are satisfied that Lord Bridge was doing no more than applying the words of section 1 of the Criminal Law Act 1977, namely, that when the accused agreed to the course of conduct, he knew that it involved the commission of an offence.'

The *mens rea* sufficient to support the commission of a substantive offence will not necessarily be sufficient to support a charge of conspiracy to commit that offence. An intent to cause grievous bodily harm is sufficient to support the charge of murder, but is not sufficient to support a charge of conspiracy to murder or of attempt to murder.

We have come to the conclusion that if the prosecution charge a conspiracy to contravene section 170(2) of the Customs and Excise Management Act by the importation of heroin, then the prosecution must prove that the agreed course of conduct was the importation of heroin. This is because the essence of the crime of conspiracy is the agreement and in simple terms, you do not prove an agreement to import heroin by proving an agreement to import cannabis.

Appeals against convictions dismissed. Appeals against sentence by Siracusa, Monteleone, and Luciani allowed. Sentences varied. Appeal against sentence by Di Carlo dismissed.

4.3 IMPOSSIBILITY AND STATUTORY CONSPIRACIES

Section 1(1)(b), quoted above, deals with the problem of impossibility where facts exist which render the commission of the agreed offence impossible: the defendants are judged on the facts as they believe them to be. So the defendants are guilty even if what they plan to do is in fact impossible, if they believe their plan to be feasible. So, if Janet and James conspire to kill Michael they are guilty of conspiracy to kill even if Michael is already dead and so their plan is impossible.[132]

---

[132] For an argument that it is not as straightforward as this: see Simester and Sullivan (2003: 285).

4.4 COMMON LAW CONSPIRACIES

The present position is that the only common law conspiracies that exist are conspiracies to defraud and conspiracies to corrupt public morals. Section 12 of the Criminal Justice Act 1987 states:

> (1) If—
>   (a) a person agrees with any other person or persons that a course of conduct shall be pursued; and
>   (b) that course of conduct will necessarily amount to or involve the commission of any offence or offences by one or more of the parties to the agreement if the agreement is carried out in accordance with their intentions,

The fact that it will do so shall not preclude a charge of conspiracy to defraud being brought against any of them in respect of the agreement.

This indicates that a conspiracy to defraud which also involves a criminal offence can be charged as either a statutory conspiracy or a common law conspiracy. Of course, a conspiracy to defraud which does not involve a criminal act can be charged only as a common law conspiracy.

It used to be thought there was also a common law conspiracy to outrage public decency, but in *Gibson*[133] it was confirmed that there was a substantive offence of outraging public decency, and so conspiring to outrage public decency should now be seen as a statutory conspiracy.[134]

Conspiracy to defraud

(1) *Actus reus.* The most widely accepted definition of a conspiracy to defraud is found in Lord Dilhorne's *dicta* in *Scott v Metropolitan Police Commissioner*:[135]

> . . . it is clearly the law that an agreement by two or more by dishonesty to deprive a person of something which is his or to which he is or would be entitled and an agreement by two or more by dishonesty to injure some proprietary right of his, suffices to constitute the offence of conspiracy to defraud.

As this quotation indicates, there are two key elements of a conspiracy to defraud:

(a) The conspiracy must involve dishonesty.

(b) If the agreement were carried out there would be some prejudice to the victim's property rights.[136]

The key notion of a conspiracy to defraud is, then, dishonest deprivation of the victim's proprietary rights. There is no need to show that if the plan was implemented anyone would

---

[133] [1990] 2 QB 619 (CA). See also *Rowley* [1991] 4 All ER 649 (CA).
[134] See also *Lunderbech* [1991] Crim LR 784.
[135] [1975] AC 910 (HL).   [136] *Moses and Ansbo* [1991] Crim LR 617.

deceived, but there must be some property rights of the victims which are threatened.[137] Nor is it necessary to show that the ultimate fraud will be perpetrated by a party to the agreement. In *Hollinshead*[138] the House of Lords held that it was a conspiracy to defraud to produce devices designed to alter readings on electricity meters. The intention was that members of the public (rather than the conspiritors) would use the devices to defraud the electricity companies.

The leading case is *Scott*, but that is now interpreted by the Privy Council in the following case:

Wai Yu-tsang v R
[1992] 1 AC 269 (PC)[139]

Wai Yu-tsang was the chief accountant of a Hong Kong bank. He did not report to the relevant authorities the fact that the bank had not honoured some cheques and he failed to register the dishonouring in the company's accounts. This created a false impression of the bank's financial position. He was charged with conspiring to defraud the bank, its existing and potential shareholders, creditors, and depositors. He claimed to be acting under the instructions of the managing director and acting in order to prevent a run on the bank, and therefore in the best interests of the bank. He appealed to the Privy Council on the basis that the judge's direction on the mental element of a conspiracy to defraud was erroneous. The judge had stated that it was sufficient if the defendant had intentionally imperilled economic interests or threatened financial prejudice of the company, whatever his motive.

Lord Goff of Chieveley, reading the judgment of the court

This authority [*Welham v DPP* [1960] 1 All ER 805] establishes that the expression 'intent to defraud' is not to be given a narrow meaning, involving an intention to cause economic loss to another. In broad terms, it means simply an intention to practise a fraud on another, or an intention to act to the prejudice of another man's right.

. . .

In the context of conspiracy to defraud, it is necessary to bear in mind that such a conspiracy is an agreement to practise a fraud on somebody of (cf *Welham v DPP* [1960] 1 All ER 805 at 815, [1961] AC 103 at 133 per Lord Denning). In *Allsop*'s case (1977) 64 Cr App R 29 what the defendant agreed to do was to present the company with false particulars, in reliance upon which, as he knew, the company would decide whether to enter into hire-purchase transactions. It is then necessary to consider whether that could constitute a conspiracy to defraud, notwithstanding that the defendant's underlying purpose or motive was not to damage any economic interest of the company but to ensure that the transaction went through so that he would earn his commission. Their Lordships can see no reason why such an agreement should not be a conspiracy to defraud the company, substantially for the reasons given by the Court of Appeal. The defendant was, for his own purposes, dishonestly supplying the company with false information which persuaded it to accept risks which it

---

[137] *Adams* [1995] 1 WLR 52 (PC), where the property was information to which a company was entitled.
[138] [1985] AC 975 (HL).
[139] [1991] 4 All ER 664, [1991] 3 WLR 1006, (1991) 94 Cr App R 264, [1992] Crim LR 425.

would or might not have accepted if it had known the true facts. Their Lordships cannot see why this was not an agreement to practise a fraud on the company, because, as Shaw LJ said, it was a dishonest agreement to employ a deceit which imperilled the economic interests of the company.

The attention of their Lordships was drawn to a critique of *Allsop*'s case in Smith and Hogan *Criminal Law* (6th edn, 1988) p 273, to which they have given careful consideration. The learned authors first criticise the reference by the Court of Appeal to *Hyam v DPP*. With this criticism, their Lordships are inclined to agree, doubting whether an authority on the mental element in the crime of murder throws much light on the nature of a conspiracy to defraud. However, the Court of Appeal only felt it necessary to pray in aid Lord Diplock's speech in *Hyam v DPP* in order to circumnavigate the dictum of Lord Diplock in *Scott*'s case, an exercise which their Lordships do not need to embark upon since they consider that dictum to be, for the reasons they have explained, too narrowly expressed. Next, the authors suggest that *Allsop*'s case can be explained on the basis that there was an intention on the part of the defendant to defraud the company, since the intended the company to pay, as indeed it did pay, money for cars which it would not have paid, even though in the outcome if suffered no loss. There is force in this suggestion, as was recognised by the Court of Appeal itself (see 64 Cr App R 29 at 32). But the Court of Appeal was concerned with the question whether the conviction could stand on the basis of the summing up of the trial judge; and their Lordships are now concerned with the correctness of the reasoning of the Court of Appeal on that question (at 31).

Lastly, it is suggested that, on the rationalisation which the authors prefer, the case was not about recklessness, and did not decide that anything less than intention in the strict sense would suffice for conspiracy to defraud. Their Lordships are however reluctant to allow this part of the law to become enmeshed in a distinction, sometimes artificially drawn, between intention and recklessness. The question whether particular facts reveal a conspiracy to defraud depends upon what the conspirators have dishonestly agreed to do, and in particular whether they have agreed to practise a fraud on somebody. For this purpose it is enough for example that, as in *R v Allsop* and in the present case, the conspirators have dishonestly agreed to bring about a state of affairs which they realise will or may deceive the victim into so acting, or failing to act, that he will suffer economic loss or his economic interests will be put at risk. It is however important in such a case, as the Court of Appeal stressed in Allsop's case, to distinguish a conspirator's intention (or immediate purpose) dishonestly to bring about such a state of affairs from his motive (or underlying purpose). The latter may be benign to the extent that he does not wish the victim or potential victim to suffer harm; but the mere fact that it is benign will not of itself prevent the agreement from constituting a conspiracy to defraud. Of course, if the conspirators were not acting dishonestly, there will have been no conspiracy to defraud; and in any event their benign purpose (if it be such) is a matter which, if they prove to be guilty, can be taken into account at the stage of sentence.

In forming this view of the matter, their Lordships draw comfort from the fact that *R v Allsop* has been accepted as good authority by the Supreme Court of Canada in *R v Olan* [1978] 2 SCR 1175 at 1182 per Dickson J delivering the judgment of the court, in a passage subsequently followed by the Supreme Court of Canada in *Vezina v R, Cote v R* [1986] 1 SCR 2 at 22–23 per Lamer J likewise delivering the judgment of the court.

Appeal dismissed.

As this case indicates, although normally a conspiracy to defraud will, if implemented, lead to a financial loss to the victim there are two circumstances in which this need not be shown:

(a) Deceiving a person holding a public office into acting contrary to his public duty would be a conspiracy to defraud.[140]

(b) If the conspirators know that their actions will put at risk the victim's property then they are guilty of a conspiracy to defraud. This is so even where in fact the risk does not materialize and the victim does not suffer a loss.[141] For example, if the conspirators agree to use the victim's money to gamble with this could be a conspiracy to defraud, even if in fact they win the gamble and the victim profits.

(2) *Mens rea.* The *mens rea* for conspiracy to defraud is:

(a) an intention to defraud; and

(b) dishonesty.

At one time it was thought that what needs to be shown is the conspirators' purpose to cause the prejudice to the victim.[142] In *Wai Yu-tsang* it was pointed out that often the conspirators' purpose is to make a profit and they may prefer the victims not to lose out if that is possible. The Privy Council suggested that the defendault's knowledge that his or her conduct might cause loss to the victim was sufficient for the *mens rea*, even if such loss was not their purpose as such.[143] The conspirators must be dishonest. The *Ghosh*[144] definition of dishonesty is used.

Conspiracy to corrupt morals?

There is yet to be an authoritative decision on whether there is a substantive offence of corrupting public morals. If there is such a substantive offence then a conspiracy to corrupt public morals should be charged as a statutory conspiracy, not a common law one. Whether or not there is such a substantive offence was left open in *Shaw v DPP*[145] and has not yet been resolved.[146]

The House of Lords in *Shaw v DPP*[147] held by a majority that it was an offence to conspire to corrupt public morals. The House of Lords upheld the conviction for conspiracy to corrupt public morals of a man who produced a 'Ladies Directory' giving the names, addresses, and talents of prostitutes. In *Knuller v DPP*,[148] the House of Lords upheld the conviction of conspiracy to corrupt public morals of accused who had published a magazine which included advertisements soliciting homosexual acts. In language which would seem surprising if used by their Lordships today they held that such advertisements could corrupt public morals as they could lead to conduct which is 'destructive to the very fabric of society'. However, in deciding whether the offence was committed their Lordships added that 'the jury should be invited, where appropriate, to remember that they live in plural society with a tradition of toleration towards minorities, and that this atmosphere of toleration is itself part of public decency'.[149]

---

[140] e.g. *Welham v DPP* [1961] AC 103 (HL); *Terry* [1984] AC 374 (HL).

[141] *Wai Yu-tsang* [1991] 4 All ER 664 (PC); *Allsop* (1977) 64 Cr App R 29 (CA).

[142] *Scott v MPC* [1975] AC 819 (PC).

[143] *Cooke* [1986] AC 909 (HL).   [144] *Ghosh* [1982] QB 1053 (CA).   [145] [1962] AC 220 (HL).

[146] This was assumed to be a common law offence in *Armhouse Lee Ltd v Chappell and Another, The Independent*, 26 July 1996 (CA).

[147] [1962] AC 220 (HL).   [148] [1973] AC 435 (HL).   [149] *Knuller* [1973] AC 495, 439.

As this implies it will be very rare that an agreement will amount to a conspiracy to corrupt public morals, and the offence is rarely prosecuted.[150] Perhaps an agreement to promote paedophilia or bestiality would be regarded by the jury as sufficient to involve a conspiracy to corrupt public morals.

4.5 IMPOSSIBILITY AND COMMON LAW OFFENCES

According to the House of Lords in *DPP v Nock*[151] impossibility is a defence to a charge of common law conspiracy. However, this is only where the conspiracy could never be achieved; impossibility is not a defence if the means used to achieve the purpose are impossible. So if A and B conspire to project indecent images into the night-time sky, the fact that such a display was not scientifically possible would not prevent the possibility of a conviction for conspiracy to corrupt public morals. An example of where impossibility would be a defence to a common law conspiracy is where A and B intend to defraud V, while V had already died. It should be stressed that impossibility is assessed at the time of the agreement. The fact that the plan subsequently becomes impossible (for example, the company it was planned to defraud has ceased to exist) does not prevent the original conspiracy being committed.

FURTHER READING

Ashworth, A. (1987b), 'Defining Criminal Offences without Harm' in P. Smith (ed.), *Criminal Law: Essays in Honour of J.C. Smith* (London: Butterworths).

Horder, J. (1996b), 'Crimes of Ulterior Intent' in A. Simester and G.R. Sullivan (eds.), *Harm and Culpability* (Oxford: OUP).

Husak, D. (1995b), 'The Nature and Justifiability of Nonconsummate Offenses', *Arizona Law Review* 37: 151.

Law Commission (2002), Report No. 276, *Fraud* (London: TSO).

Orchard, G. (1974), ' "Agreement" in Criminal Conspiracy', *Criminal Law Review* 297.

PART II: THEORY

5 INCHOATE OFFENCES

At first sight inconsummate offences do not fit naturally into the structures of criminal law. After all where is the harm to a victim where there is an attempt or an incitement for example? Are not the offences discussed in Part I in essence punishing people for bad thoughts? These kinds of concerns are addressed by Douglas Husak in the following passage.

---

[150] In *Armhouse Lee Ltd v Chappell and Another, The Independent*, 26 July 1996 (CA) the Court of Appeal held that advertising phone numbers by which sexually explicit words and descriptions could be heard could not be regarded as corrupting public morals.

[151] [1978] AC 979 (HL).

He accepts that there are difficulties in justifying the punishment of a person whose acts are permissible in the sense that they directly are not causing harm. But it is for this reason that the law imposes limitations on the punishment of inchoate (he uses the term non-consummate) offences. He distinguishes between complex inconsumate offences such as attempts or incitement which punish one act (act a[1]) with intent to do another act (act a[2]) and simple inchoate offence which punish a single act which is not harmful in itself but carries dangers, such as possession of a firearm:

D.N. Husak, 'The Nature and Justifiability of Nonconsummate Offenses' (1995) 37
Arizona Law Review 151 at 170–6

Complex nonconsummate offenses proscribe the performance of an act type a[1] when the person bears a given relation to another act-type a[2], the latter of which causes a consummate harm. Some act-tokens a[1], however, might be permissible, especially when considered apart from their relation to a[2]. A person might be liable for attempted arson, for example, simply by lighting a match. How can liability for complex nonconsummate offenses avoid punishing persons whose conduct is permissible? Constraints must be placed on the nature of the relation between a[1] and a[2] before liability may be imposed. Courts and legislatures have developed at least five distinct principles to reduce the likelihood that persons will be punished for conduct that should be placed beyond the reach of the criminal sanction.

The first such principle might be called the *consummate criminal harm* requirement. In order to qualify as a consummate offense, most tokens of the proscribed act-type must create the risk of a consummate harm, that is, the risk that a right will be violated. According to the consummate criminal harm requirement, this consummate harm itself must be criminal, at least when it is brought about intentionally. In other words, a nonconsummate offense proscribing an act-type that creates a risk of some undesirable state of affairs cannot be justified unless a consummate offense proscribing an act-type that intentionally causes that very state of affairs would be justified as well.

The consummate criminal harm requirement can easily escape notice because its truth is obvious in the context of complex nonconsummate offenses. A consummate harm is identified (sometimes implicitly) in the complete description of any complex nonconsummate offense. If the state of affairs to be prevented were not itself a criminal harm, liability for a complex nonconsummate offense should not be imposed. For example, liability for criminal conspiracy requires that persons agree to commit a criminal act-type; persons who agree to perform an act-type that is not proscribed have not committed criminal conspiracy.

The rationale for the consummate criminal harm requirement is evident. It cannot be worse to risk bringing about an undesirable state of affairs than to intentionally bring about that very state of affairs. If the act of intentionally causing a result should not be a criminal offense, there could be no justification to enact a nonconsummate offense to prevent persons from creating a risk of that result. Since, for example, the act of intentionally failing to save money neither is nor ought to be a criminal offense, a nonconsummate offense to prevent persons from engaging in conduct that increases the risk that they will fail to save money would be incompatible with the consummate criminal harm requirement, and must be rejected as an unjustified exercise of state authority.

The second principle to help distinguish justified from unjustified nonconsummate offenses might be called the *high culpability* requirement. In the context of complex nonconsummate offenses, this principle withholds liability from the person who performs a[1] unless he bears a high degree of culpability for the consummate harm a[2]. It is insufficient that the performance of a[1] happens to make the consummate harm more likely. Selling a firearm to another (a[1]), for example, increases the probability that a firearm offense will be committed (a[2]), but a nonconsummate offense to proscribe such a sale cannot be justified on this basis alone. After all, many tokens of the act-type of selling a firearm might be permissible. Thus persons who perform act-tokens of a[1] should not be punished unless they have a high degree of culpability with respect to a[2]. Commentators disagree about how high this degree of culpability must be. . . .

There is ample doubt, of course, that such conduct as selling a gun to make a profit is permissible when the seller knows or consciously disregards the risk that the gun will be used to commit a crime. A comprehensive theory of justified nonconsummate legislation cannot evade the issue of whether act-tokens a[1] are permissible when performed with lesser degrees of culpability with respect to the consummate harm a[2]. In order to defend a theory about the authority of the state to create and enforce nonconsummate offenses, there is need not only for a theory of interests the violation of which amounts to a harm—as George Fletcher has indicated—but also a theory of privileges the exercise of which should be protected from legal interference. Whatever shape this theory may take when lesser degrees of culpability than purpose (or intention) are involved, there can be little doubt that tokens of such act-types as selling a gun to another are impermissible when accompanied by the *purpose* to promote or facilitate a consummate harm.

A third principle to protect permissible conduct from criminal liability might be called the *causal* requirement. Since nonconsummate offenses are designed to reduce the risk of a consummate harm a[2], an obvious question in endeavors to justify such legislation is whether the proscribed conduct a[1] really creates the risk of that harm. Ultimately, this determination is empirical. In the context of most existing complex nonconsummate legislation, however, no one would anticipate the need to collect empirical data to support the conclusion that the proscribed conduct creates a genuine risk. Satisfaction of the causal requirement is typically assured by the high culpability requirement. 'Common sense' indicates that persons who perform an act-token a[1] with the purpose to bring about a consummate harm a[2] increase the probability that that harm will actually occur. Many attempts, for example, succeed. It is barely possible to imagine that persons are so inept that they do not increase the probability of the occurrence of a consummate harm by performing act-tokens of attempt. . . .

Notice that some conduct a[1] should be placed beyond the reach of the criminal sanction even though each of the foregoing three principles is satisfied, that is, even though a person performs a[1] with the purpose or intention to bring about a consummate criminal harm a[2] and thereby increases the probability of that harm. For example, a person may place an order for a disguise intending to use it to commit a robbery, and be more likely to commit a robbery after placing that order, without thereby incurring liability for a nonconsummate offense. Act a[1] might be said to be too distant or remote from the consummate harm to give rise to liability; the causal contribution made by a[1] is insufficiently proximate to the consummate harm a[2]. Thus a fourth principle to limit the authority of the state to enact nonconsummate offenses might be called the *proximity* requirement.

. . .

The proximity principle applies to those complex nonconsummate offenses the descriptions of which explicitly identify a consummate harm, although this requirement is seldom discussed in this context. For example, the risk of the consummate harm of theft is reduced by the creation and enforcement of a complex nonconsummate offense of burglary, defined as entering 'a building or occupied structure' (a[1]) with the 'purpose to commit a crime therein' (a[2]). Presumably, the act of 'approaching an occupied structure' with a comparable purpose is insufficiently proximate to the consummate harm to give rise to liability. In the context of burglary, the distinction between approaching and entering an occupied structure performs the same function as the distinction between preparation and a substantial step in the context of attempt.

A fifth principle to reduce the likelihood that permissible conduct is punished might be called the *persistence* requirement. Most jurisdictions allow liability for some complex non-consummate offenses to be defeated if a person voluntarily abandons whatever contribution he has made to the consummate harm a[2].

6 THE THEORY OF CRIMINAL ATTEMPTS

6.1 WHY DO WE PUNISH ATTEMPTS?

Although you might at first think it is obvious that the law should punish attempts, further thought reveals that it is not a straightforward issue. After all, normally in an attempt no one has actually been harmed, and yet harm is normally seen as an essential element of an offence. In the following extract George Fletcher sets out some of the difficulties in approaching this issue:

G. Fletcher, *Basic Concepts of Criminal Law* (New York: OUP, 1998), 172–4

Historically, the attempt derives from the completed offense. But once attempts came to be recognized as a staple of nineteenth-century criminal prosecutions, theorists began to wonder whether with regard to at least some crimes, the attempt might indeed be the more basic offense. In cases of bringing about harmful consequences—homicide, arson, destruction of property—the actor might do everything in his power to result without succeeding. He might shoot to kill and hit the wall. She might throw a fire bomb with the intent of burning down a house and the bomb turns out to be a dud. He might swing an axe at his enemy and miss. This element of accident in cases of harmful consequences makes one wonder whether the attempt should be regarded as the basic offense and the completed homicide, arson, or battery merely an adventitious after effect of attempting with intent.

Our ordinary sensibilities tell us that, of course, it is worse to kill than to shoot and miss. The successful killer deserves a greater penalty than the unsuccessful attempter. At least that is what the woman on the street—or the man in the Clapham bus, as the English say, thinks. In law as in basketball, the rule usually is: No harm, no foul. No one with ordinary sensibilities would advocate the death penalty for someone who merely tried to kill. And yet many of the leading theorists of criminal law, at least in the English-speaking world, hold the view that the consummation of an intended offense is merely a matter of chance and therefore not a proper basis for aggravating the penalty designated for the attempt.

The basic argument for this position begins with the sensible premise that punishment should be imposed on the basis of blameworthiness or culpability. There follows a more controversial point: The only fair basis for culpability is the actions under one's control—that is, what can one be sure of bringing about with the extensions of one's body. This includes basic actions such as speaking, pulling the trigger of a gun, putting poison in coffee, planting a bomb. It does not include the consequences of these actions that depend on intervening forces of nature. It follows, according to the logic of this argument, that these consequences should not be charged to the account of the culpable actor. This is the reasoning that leads so many thoughtful writers to support the view that the attempt—which is supposedly within the control of the actor—should be the primary offense. The basis for punishment should, therefore, be the attempt and not its fortuitous after effects.

The more traditional way of thinking about crime and responsibility starts with the bringing about of harm and inquires: Who is responsible for this wrong and to what extent? The attempter merely approaches the harm, merely creates a risk of the harm, and therefore should be held liable for a lesser degree of wrongdoing. A lesser degree of wrongdoing implies mitigated punishment.

The search for the primary or basic offense implies, then, two different concepts of crime. The culpability-centered theory focuses exclusively on the actor who has formulated a criminal intent and has started to act upon it. Whether there is an actual victim, whether the action disturbs the peace, is irrelevant. What counts is the potential of the attempt to bring about harm, if it is not halted in its progression toward execution. The evil of the attempt lies primarily in its defiance of the legal norms designed to protect the interests of others.

The harm-centered conception of crime focuses on the victim. The evil of the offense lies in killing, raping, burning, destroying, maiming, threatening—in general in bringing about harm to a concrete individual. When there is no actual but only a potential victim, there is by definition a lesser wrong.

It is true that those who merely attempt but do not cause harm have lesser grounds for remorse and guilt. In *Crime and Punishment* Raskolnikov is properly haunted by the thought of having killed an old lady to take her money. If he tried to kill her and failed, it would be curiously neurotic for him to suffer the same pangs of guilt. Recognizing the role of remorse testifies to the close connection between wrong-doing and victimhood. That there is an actual victim—an irreversible harm to another human being—produces a human response that differs radically from the sense of impropriety that comes simply from violating a norm of the legal *system*.

We will now pick up some of the points that Fletcher makes in his extract. The first is the 'problem of moral luck'.

6.2 'THE PROBLEM OF MORAL LUCK'

Consider the following case reported in *The Times*:

'Widow gave poisoned sherry to man who rejected her', *The Times*, 4 April 2003

A widow served her new man friend sherry laced with weedkiller after he rejected her advances and refused to marry her, a court was told yesterday.

Dilys Goundry, a former nurse and churchwarden, poisoned David Wood, later saying that she had wanted to see him 'writhing in agony'. After he spat out the drink she offered him a cup of milk. But he smelt bleach, grabbed his belongings and fled.

Goundry, 56, was spared a jail sentence at Lincoln Crown Court. Judge Michael Heath, imposing a 12-month community rehabilitation order after she admitted administering poison with intent to injure, told her: 'You were besotted, and the time came when you acted in a manner that was bizarre and out of character. It is plain you developed very strong feelings for Mr Wood that were—sadly so far as you were concerned—not reciprocated.' Goundry had committed a serious offence but before that had been 'essentially a pillar of the community'.

John Pini, for the prosecution, told the court that Goundry's infatuation with Mr Wood was such that she lost two stone in weight to impress him, leaving herself seriously ill with stomach ulcers. She had been so devastated when he refused her advances that she had had to receive psychiatric help.

The pair had met through a lonely hearts column in a local newspaper. Mr Wood had emphasised that he wanted only friendship, but Mr Pini said that by the end of the year it became clear that Goundry wanted more than that.

The poisoning incident had occurred after Mr Wood saw Goundry, now living in Scotland, at her then home in Horsington, Lincolnshire, in July 2000. Mr Pini said: 'They had a meal and Goundry gave him a glass of Harvey's Bristol Cream. He had a sip and immediately felt burning around his lips, mouth and throat. He ran to the lavatory and spat it out. Goundry then returned with a cup of milk, but he smelt bleach, grabbed his belongings and left.'

The court was told that Goundry later confessed to the incident—from which Mr Wood recovered fully—to a friend. She had said: 'I wanted to see the rat writhe in agony before he died. If I can't have him, nobody can.'

Michael Cranmer-Brown, for Goundry, said that she had suffered violence during her 27-year marriage and had been looking forward to a new life. 'What happened was completely out of character. She is a lady who would not want to hurt a fly. She bitterly regrets what she did to him.'

Goundry, from Aberdeenshire, declined to comment after the case.

© *The Times*, 4 April 2003.

Ms Goundry was fortunate her attempt did not succeed, because if it had she would have been guilty of murder and the judge would have had no option but to impose the mandatory sentence of life for murder. It was in fact no thanks to her that it did not. She was 'lucky' that the victim had not taken a larger gulp of the sherry. Should the fact that the victim was wise enough not to take a larger sip or that the poison was not stronger be a reason for rendering her any less guilty than if she had succeeded? Such questions are addressed in the following passage:

A. Ashworth, 'Belief, Intent and Criminal Liability' in J. Eekelaar and J. Bell (eds.), *Oxford Essays in Jurisprudence* (Oxford: OUP, 1987), 16–17

Is A, who shoots at X intending to kill him but misses because X unexpectedly moves, any less culpable than B, who shoots at Y intending to kill him and does so? An external description of both sets of events would probably not suggest that they have 'done' the same thing, whereas an account which paid more attention to the actor's point of view and to matters which lay within the actor's control would suggest that they both intended and tried, to the same extent, to do the same thing. The argument is that, because of the element of uncertainty in the outcome of things which we try to do, it would be wrong for assessments of culpability to depend on the occurrence or non-occurrence of the intended consequences. 'Success or failure . . . makes no difference at all to [an agent's] moral status in relation to his original act. His original act, strictly considered, was simply his trying and *that* is what moral assessment must concern itself with' (Winch, *Ethics and Action*, 1972, p. 139) . . . Moral blame and criminal liability should be based so far as possible on choice and control, on the trying and not on what actually happened thereafter.

What are the reasons for wishing to reduce the influence of chance upon criminal liability? It cannot be doubted that luck plays a considerable part. Actual results also play a considerable part in judgments of others, and tend to dominate assessments in such fields as business, sport, and education. Those who try hard but are unsuccessful often receive less recognition than those who achieve goals (no matter how little effort they put into it). But these are not moral assessments of the individuals or their characters. If one turns to moral and social judgments, it is doubtful whether outcomes should be proper criteria. It may be desirable overall to have fewer bad outcomes and more good outcomes in society, but that does not lead to the conclusion that moral praise and blame should be allocated solely according to result. Indeed, a bad outcome stemming from a good intent may be a better predictor of good outcomes than a good outcome born of a bad intent. From time to time we may praise someone for producing a good result, even though it was not what he was trying to do, but this is more a reflection of our pleasure at the outcome than an assessment of his conduct and character. If we turn to blaming, is it not unacceptable to blame people for causing results irrespective of whether they were caused intentionally, negligently, or purely accidentally? Blaming is a moral activity which is surely only appropriate where the individual had some choice or control over the matter. For this reason the criminal law should seek to minimize the effect of luck upon the incidence and scale of criminal liability.

To Andrew Ashworth, then, the law should not attach significance to matters which are a matter of luck. As the difference between an attempt and successful crime can be regarded as a matter of luck, an argument can be made that all attempts should be treated in the same way as the complete crime. In the following passage Kimberly Kessler considers some of the arguments for or against such an argument:

K. Kessler, 'The Role of Luck in the Criminal Law' (1994) 142 *University of Pennsylvania Law Review* 2183 at 2211–23

Edith shoots at Frank intending to kill him, but Frank ducks. Edith will be guilty of attempted murder. She is just as morally blameworthy as if she had succeeded, yet the criminal law continues to maintain a distinction between attempts and completed crimes.

A. Defining Attempts and Justifying Their Punishment

. . .

We punish attempts for two reasons. The first is that attempts are sometimes seen as a harm in themselves since they may disrupt society and create unrest. Hence, these are activities which deserve to be punished in their own right. The second rationale is that if we want to prevent theharm that will result from a successful attempt, we may want to intervene before the harm is caused.

Although intervention does not necessarily entail punishment, retributivists will justify punishing attempters on the grounds that once the actor has formed the intention to commit the crime and has completed a substantial enough step to manifest her culpability, she is just as culpable as if she had completed the crime. Utilitarians will also want to punish before completion because it will increase deterrence while decreasing the disutility caused by the harmful result.

B. The Argument in Favor of Equivalence

1. Some Preliminaries

Before beginning an analysis of the arguments in favor of treating attempts and completed crimes the same, it is helpful to set some ground rules. We should first distinguish attempts from completed crimes. A completed crime is a successful attempt: John, with intent to kill, shot at Mary; the bullet hit Mary; Mary died. There are then both completed attempts and incomplete attempts. A completed attempt is where the actor has done everything in his power to effectuate his desired results: John, with intent to kill, shot at Mary; the bullet missed Mary; Mary lived. An incomplete attempt is where the actor has not done the last act necessary to complete the crime: John pointed the gun at Mary and shouted, 'I am going to kill you'; the police then burst through the door. For the moment, let us address only the difference between a completed crime and a completed attempt.

. . .

2. Results Do Not Matter

. . . A simpler, less contrived hypothetical is presented by R.A. Duff:

'Pat and Jill each fire a shot at an intended victim, intending to kill her: Jill succeeds in killing her victim, but Pat does not (her victim moves and the shot misses). Is there any difference between their two cases which can justify the distinction which the law draws between them, such that Jill is sentenced to life imprisonment for murder, whereas Pat receives a lighter sentence for attempted murder?'

The answer should be 'no.' After all, the difference between Pat and Jill is luck. And luck is something upon which true responsibility should not depend. Both Pat and Jill intended to kill their victims, and thus, the mens rea element for murder is met. Both also put their intentions into action when they fired their guns, and hence the actus reus element is met. Why should criminal liability then rely on matters out of the agents' control?

C. The Argument That Results Do Matter

Despite the prevalence of fortuity in attempt law, some commentators continue to argue that the fortuitous result of the creation of a harm is relevant.

1. No Harm, No Reason to Punish

One possible argument in favor of results is that no harm has occurred and thus we do not have a reason to punish the defendant. The rationale, however, for punishing may be different than the rationale for initially criminalizing the conduct. Although the original justification for criminalizing murder is that it causes a harm to others, we do criminalize and punish inchoate crimes also. We, as a society, have made the decision to punish acts that will eventually cause a harm even though the harm does not result in that particular case.

2. Fear of Jury Nullification

Another argument in favor of non-equivalence is that if we punish attempts the same as completed crimes, juries will not convict. Schulhofer extensively addresses the research in this area and concludes that such a fear is unfounded. Ashworth, on the other hand, still maintains that this is a practical possibility which should be kept in mind.

Several things about jury nullification should be noted. First, Ashworth's concern about the practical possibility is just that—a practical question. To a retributivist, the possibility of disutility is not a reason not to punish (although the answer might be different if jury nullification threatened our ability ever to punish such wrongdoers.) Further, jurors are not addressing the fairness of the range of sentencing. Before them is one criminal, and jurors will react to the culpability of that person. Unlike cases of strict liability which jurors may feel are unfair, the culpability of the actor will be sufficient to sway the typical juror.

3. With Attempts, Less Punishment Suffices to Satisfy the Retaliatory Urge

Another argument that results should matter is that our retaliatory urge is greater when harm occurs. After all, how does one apply 'an eye for an eye and a tooth for a tooth' if all John did was make an attempt at the eye? This argument presupposes a system of punishment based on retaliation. As Schulhofer notes, however, most jurisdictions do not invoke retaliation as a reason to punish, and 'legal theorists are virtually unanimous in applauding the judgment.'

4. We Want Society to Take Murders Seriously

Society, it is argued, learns what is good and bad by looking at the law. If we teach people that murder and attempted murder are equally wrong, then people will not take a murder as seriously when it happens.

This argument rests on two faulty assumptions. The first is that punishing people equally for trying to kill and killing means the world is no different when someone lives as opposed to when someone dies. This is simply not true. The actor whom we punish is no different, but the death of a human being necessarily takes its toll. Society is intelligent enough to recognize the difference between (1) equating people who try and people who succeed in doing a bad thing (punishing attempts the same as completions) and (2) equating the gravity of the harm that occurs when a murderer does succeed to the absence of harm when she does not (recognizing the difference when a harm occurs and when it does not).

The second faulty assumption is that by punishing attempts and murders the same, society will begin to feel that murders are not as bad—that they are just like attempts. . . .

Murder is condemned by all of society. If attempt begins to be associated with murder, people will not necessarily think that murder is somehow less grave because it is only punished as an attempt. Rather, people will respect that attempt, too, is a serious crime because it is being punished to the same degree as murder.

5. Deterrence: Differential Punishments Create an Incentive to Stop After Attempters Have Already Begun the Act

Another argument advanced for treating completions differently from attempts is that otherwise, once the actor has taken a substantial step, she has no reason not to finish the intended conduct. Indeed, imagine the case of Cara who shoots at David. Cara misses. If she is going to be held guilty of murder, what incentive does she have not to shoot again and finish him off? . . . Further, the actor's wavering over whether to complete the crime will call into question whether she has the sufficient mens rea. Evidence concerning mens rea becomes more necessary the more remote the conduct is from its completion. Finally, how far the actor was willing to go may mitigate or enhance the severity of the punishment.

6. Attempters Do Not Benefit in the Same Way

Some theorists have argued that when the criminal only attempts the crime, she does not receive the fruits of her activities. This argument amounts to one of unjust enrichment. When a criminal succeeds, she is unjustly enriched, which must be rectified; when she fails, this added element of punishment is unnecessary. Ashworth finds this argument unsatisfactory: 'At bottom, it must be said that the principles of profit deprivation and vindicative satisfaction belong to a separate realm of principles ancillary to punishment—chiefly principles of compensation.'

Indeed, whether someone benefits from a crime is not the criminal law's concern. The criminal law's focus is only on deterring others and punishing violators. Thus, if Ken kills Renee and afterward feels no happiness, he cannot argue that since he derived no pleasure from the murder, he should not be punished. Others will still be deterred from committing the crime by looking at the example of his punishment, Ken will be less likely to kill again (specific deterrence), and Ken is a bad person who chose to violate the law and thus deserves to be punished.

7. Attempters Are Not As Dangerous

Nonequivalence theorists also maintain that attempters are not as dangerous as completers. The failure to complete the act may be due to a lack of fixity of purpose; however, even if attempters and completers were punished equally, this lack of success could then have evidentiary weight as to mens rea. Further, only a small minority of people would truly be less dangerous, evinced by their continual failure.

Paul Rothstein maintains that results are necessary to show dangerousness. He argues that there are differences between (1) a gunman who buys a gun but never gets near his intended victim, (2) the gunman who pulls the trigger but death is prevented by the gun's malfunctioning or the victim's wearing a bulletproof vest, and (3) the gunman who kills his victim. The first gunman's mens rea, according to Rothstein, is uncertain. Although this statement may be true, the criminal law already accommodates this reality by imposing a 'substantial step' definition of an act and by requiring the prosecution to prove the mens rea of purpose.

Rothstein further argues the second gunman may have taken the gun's misfiring or the victim's vest into account and so 'he can take credit for these "chance" circumstances in the world that are supposedly "outside his control." ' But doesn't any credit he takes serve as evidence of mens rea? If I fire a gun at Dick, knowing he is wearing a bulletproof vest or knowing my gun misfires, do (can?) I have the purpose of killing him? What if I know there is about a seventy-five per cent chance that Dick is wearing his vest or that the gun will misfire? Doesn't my knowledge of these factors and how I attempt to accommodate them go to my intentions and not to causation? What I knew beforehand has no influence on the world as we know it once I have acted, and what I did to prepare for what I knew is part of my action and mental state.

8. No Harm, No Foul

One response to the equivalence argument is the intuitive sense that a person deserves less punishment when no harm occurs. Smith argues that if one of his sons throws a stone at the dining room window and misses, he will be angry, but if the window is broken, he will be furious. Rothstein discusses this 'feeling' in addressing a hypothetical presented by Judith Thomson: She sets out the example of the person who, by idly tapping his foot on the sidewalk, saves three lives through some freak of nature unknown to him. Professor Thomson says that our judgment of the morality of the foot tapping—neutral morality—is unaffected by the good result. I would say that people, particularly those saved, would feel very kindly disposed toward such a person, at least more so than toward a foot tapper who did not wind up saving anyone.

If Rothstein proves anything with this assertion, it is just how different feelings can be. How can we base a criminal justice system on feelings that vary from person to person?

Further, the reason 'it just matters' may be socially trained, and therefore reversible in future generations. . . .

9. An Alternative Descriptive Theory

Some commentators have argued not only that fortuity does play a role in the law but also that it should. In his Note, Daniel Mandil argues that chance separates paradigmatic from nonparadigmatic crimes. The paradigmatic crime involves an intentional act and the creation of a harm (such as a death). A crime is nonparadigmatic if one of the elements is missing: an attempt is an intended crime without a harm and criminal negligence is a negligent (non-intended) act with harm. Mandil further notes that no liability is created by a negligent act that does not result in harm. Mandil sees these separations as a balance struck between an individual's freedom of action and the sphere in which the state must necessarily interfere. He argues that:

'In the context of harm without intent, the uncontroversial absence of tort liability for uneventful acts of negligence demonstrates the complete dominance of the value of freedom of action over competing social values. . . .'

Like tort law, in cases of criminal negligence, the criminal law generally preserves the supremacy of freedom over other social values—only the existence of isolated reckless endangerment statutes disturbs the congruence.

Mandil, however, is missing the point. He sees the scarcity of criminal-negligence-with-outresulting-harm statutes as defeating the arguments suggesting that the resulting harm should not matter in the criminal law. A descriptive theory may show what the law is currently doing, but it fails to show why this is what the law should be doing. The lack of endangerment laws only illustrates that the criminal law is failing to realize that it is taking fortuity into account—it does not justify doing so.

You should also refer to the discussion on moral luck that we had in Chapter 2 and particularly the extract by Tony Honoré (p. 133) who argues that taking responsibility for our actions is simply part of being human.

FURTHER READING

Ashworth, A. (1988), 'Criminal Attempts and the Role of Resulting Harm under the Code in the Common Law', *Rutgers Law Journal* 19: 725.

Ben-Shahar, O., and Harel, A. (1996), 'The Economics of the Law of Criminal Attempts: A Victim-cantered Perspective', *University of Pennsylvania Law Review* 145: 299.

Blumoff, T. (2003), 'A Jurisprudence for Punishing Attempts Asymmetrically', *Buffalo Criminal Law Review* 6: 951.

Chapman, B. (1988), 'Agency and Contingency: The Case of Criminal Attempts', *University of Toronto Law Journal* 38: 355.

Christopher, R. (2004), 'Does Attempted Murder Deserve Greater Punishment Than Murder? Moral Luck And The Duty To Prevent Harm', *Notre Dame Journal of Law, Ethics and Public Policy* 18: 419.

Duff, R.A. (1996), *Criminal Attempts* (Oxford: OUP).

—— (2005b), 'Criminalizing Endangerment' in R.A. Duff and S. Green (eds.), *Defining Crimes* (Oxford: OUP).

Gobert, J. (1993), 'The Fortuity of Consequences', *Criminal Law Forum* 1: 1.

Jareborg, N. (1993), 'Criminal Attempts and Moral Luck', *Israel Law Review* 27: 213.

Kadish, S. (1994), 'The Criminal Law and the Luck of the Draw', *Journal of Criminal Law and Criminology* 84: 1501.

Kremnitzer, M. (1984), 'The Punishability of Impossible Attempts', *Israel Law Review* 19: 340.

Mandil, D. (1987), 'Chance, Freedom, and Criminal Liability', *Columbia Law Review* 87: 125.

Note (1989), 'The Luck of the Law: Allusions to Fortuity in Legal Discourse', *Harvard Law Review* 102: 1862.

Perlman, M. (1995), 'Punishing Acts and Counting Consequences', *Arizona Law Review* 37: 227.

Shachar, Y. (1987), 'The Fortuitous Gap in Law and Morality', *Criminal Justice Ethics* 6: 12.

6.3 *ACTUS REUS* OF ATTEMPT

When considering the law on attempts it is useful to contrast three different kinds of attempts.

Imagine Michael decides to kill Jane. He finds her and pulls out a gun. Contrast these three alternatives:

(1) Just before Michael is able to shoot a police office grabs him and prevents him firing a gun.

(2) Michael fires a gun but Jane ducks at the last moment and the bullet misses.

(3) Michael fires the gun but, unknown to Michael, Jane is already dead.

All of these three cases are linked by the fact that in none of them is Jane actually harmed by Michael. But they can be distinguished. Ashworth argues that there is an important difference between complete and incomplete attempts.[152] A complete attempt is where the defendant has done everything that he intended to do, but the attempt nevertheless failed. In an incomplete case the defendant has been prevented from completing his course of actions. So case 1 is an example of an incomplete attempt, but cases 2 and 3 are complete attempts.

There is little doubt that a complete attempt would constitute the *actus reus* of an attempt, but in the case of an incomplete attempt where should the line be drawn? Here are some possible approaches the law could take:

---

[152] Jareborg (1993) is not convinced by the placing of any weight on the distinction.

(1) *Last act.*[153] It could be argued that the defendant should not be liable until he has committed the very last act before the offence is committed. This approach leaves the imposition of criminal liability until the very last moment. It would be supported by those who are wary of punishing attempts for fear of depriving the defendant of an opportunity to 'repent' and turn back from the offence. It would also appeal to those who are concerned about convicting people of simply having an 'evil mind'.

(2) *'Unequivocable act'.*[154] It can be argued that what needs to be shown is an act which unequivocally demonstrates that the defendant intends to complete the crime.[155] In other words, that the defendant is close enough to committing the crime that there is no realistic chance of the defendant changing his or her mind.

(3) *The 'substantial step' test.*[156] This test requires proof that the defendant has not simply started on his plan but has gone a significant way down the path. Opponents of this test claim that it will create too much uncertainty.

(4) *Dangerous proximity.* This test requires proof that the defendant came 'proximately close' to committing the offence. To some commentators it is too vague to give practical guidance to the jury.

(5) *'More than merely preparatory'.* This is the test which is adopted by English and Welsh law. It seeks to draw a line between those acts which are mere preparation and those which are embarking on the offence proper. Its difficulty is that in some cases the distinction can be hard to draw.

(6) *The 'first act' test.*[157] This test requires proof that the defendant has simply done the first of a series of acts that the defendant intends will result in the offence being completed. It would appeal to those who see the *mens rea* as the key element of the offence and seek only an external act revealing that mental state. It also has the benefit of being an easy test to use. The difficulty with it is that different crimes require different levels of planning. Sometimes there will be a single act of preparation (e.g. raising a fist in order to assault); in others a larger numbers of actions may be required (e.g. before committing an armed robbery). Therefore, the first act may not be a ready indicator of the blameworthiness of the defendant.[158]

In the following passage Anthony Duff sets out his views on what should be the conduct element of an offence. He proposes that the defendant should have committed the *actus reus* of an attempt if his conduct amounts to embarking on the commission of the offence he intends to commit[159]

A. Duff, *Criminal Attempts* (Oxford: OUP, 1996), 386–91

Against A Broad Law of Attempts

We noted earlier the tension between minimalist and maximalist presumptions about the proper scope of the law of attempts. Minimalists begin with the commission of some

---

[153] *Eagleton* (1855) 6 Cox CC 559, although see the interpretation of this case in *Roberts* [1855] 6 Cox CC 559.

[154] *Davey v Lee* [1968] 1 QB 366. Turner (1933: 237) stated that acts 'must be unequivocally referable to the commission of the specific crime'.

[155] Schulhofer (1974).   [156] Considered and rejected in *Roberts* (1855) 169 ER 836.

[157] *Scofield* [1784] Cald 397.   [158] Stewart (2001: 403).   [159] See also Stewart (2001).

substantive offence as the paradigm of criminality, and seek to capture only conduct that comes close to that paradigm by the general law of attempts: conduct that is 'proximate' to the completion of that offence. Maximalists begin with the assumption that any conduct directed towards the commission of a substantive offence is a candidate for criminalization, and then ask how far beyond the 'first act' the intending criminal need have progressed before we can safely and properly convict her.

This tension is related to that between constitutive and evidential conceptions of the conduct element. Those who see criminal conduct as being constitutive of criminal culpability will naturally favour a minimalist presumption: if what matters is the character of an agent's conduct (as actualizing a criminal intention), we should properly ask how close that conduct must have come to the completion of the offence to be criminalized as an attempt to commit the offence. By contrast, those who see the conduct element as playing only an evidential role will more naturally favour a maximalist presumption: if what matters as the true basis of criminal liability is something (a firm criminal purpose, a dangerous disposition) that is evidenced, but not constituted by, the agent's conduct, then we should ask how far an agent must have progressed in his criminal enterprise if we are to have proper and reliable evidence of his criminality.

An objectivist approach of the kind which I am offering here will favour a minimalist presumption. It portrays criminal conduct as constitutive of I criminality; and as we saw in the last two sections, it insists that, to count as a criminal attempt, conduct must be intimately related to the commission of a complete offence. What relates an agent's conduct to the commission of an offence is partly her intention to commit that offence, but it also matters how close she has come to fully actualizing that intent. The conduct of someone who has so far only reconnoitered a building from which he plans to steal, for example, or only obtained a poison with which he intends to kill someone, is still 'remote' from the commission of theft (or burglary) or murder. We could not yet count her actions as *essentially* larcenous or murderous, or as *attacks* on property or life; there is still too wide a gap between what she has actually done and the commission, of the intended offence.

This is not to say that we should see her conduct simply as, for instance, 'walking round a building', or 'buying arsenic', which are indeed remote from the commission of theft or murder. Given suitable evidence of her criminal intention, we understand her conduct in the light of that intention, as preparation for the theft or murder that she intends to commit; we understand it, and respond to it, as being connected to that intended crime. However, that connection is so far constituted primarily by her intention, and her commission of the crime has so far only a shadowy existence in the public world: it exists in thought (in her intention), but has yet to acquire any very concrete existence in her actions. As her criminal enterprise advances, and her criminal intention is further actualized in action, her prospective commission of the crime becomes less shadowy, more concrete as an active engagement in the world. Her actions connect her more closely to the commission of the crime, and in the end that crime becomes something she is doing, rather than merely something she is intending or preparing to do.

Why should this matter? Why should we demand not merely conduct undertaken with intent to commit an offence (and perhaps corroborative of that intent), but conduct which comes close to the actual commission of the offence? An initial answer is that the law should leave intending criminals a *locus poenitentiae*: the chance to decide for themselves to abandon their criminal enterprises. This matters, because the law should treat and address its citizens as responsible agents. The central value to which this answer appeals is that of individual freedom to determine one's own actions. We must look more carefully at the character of that value.

From one, roughly consequentialist, perspective, individual freedom is a good which the law should seek to maximize. That is, the law should aim to secure to every citizen the maximum possible freedom to determine her own actions and future, by her own choices. This certainly provides *a* strong reason in favour of a narrow law of attempts: the closer to completing the crime the intending criminal must come before he is liable to arrest, conviction, and punishment, the larger his freedom to decide for himself whether to continue his criminal enterprise. On the other hand, freedom, as a consequentialist value, also provides weighty reasons in favour of a broader law of attempts. For if crimes typically impair the freedom of others (and a legal system aiming to maximize freedom will prohibit conduct which impairs freedom), by preventing crime we increase freedom; and if (as is surely plausible) a broader law of attempts would prevent crime more effectively than a narrower law, we could decide the proper scope of the law of attempts only by weighing the increase in freedom which such a law would achieve (by preventing more crimes) against the greater infringements on freedom which its application and enforcement would involve. It is not clear how that weighing could be done, but we cannot be confident that it would favour a narrow law of attempts.

However, to say that the law should treat its citizens as responsible agents is to assert freedom as a categorical limit which should be *respected*, rather than as a consequential good which should be *maximized*. The objection to a wide law of attempts, for instance one which criminalized merely preparatory conduct, is not that it would on balance reduce freedom rather than increase it, but that it would, by failing to respect the freedom and autonomy of those whom it criminalizes, improperly infringe them.

Would it do so? A law which permitted the coercive detention of those who had not yet committed any kind of criminal act, simply on the ground that they were predictably likely to commit a crime, would certainly fail to respect them as responsible agents: it would pre-empt their own autonomous agency, coercing them on the basis of what they would or might do rather than because of anything they had voluntarily done. But a broader law of attempts, for instance one that criminalized 'substantial steps' towards any criminal goal, or 'merely preparatory' action, would not coerce agents *merely* because of what they would or might otherwise do. Rather, it would prohibit actions done with intent to commit a crime; and agents would become liable to the law's coercive attentions only when they flouted such a prohibition by voluntarily (and culpably) embarking on a criminal enterprise. The law would still address and respect them as responsible agents, since it would give them reason to refrain from certain kinds of conduct (that such kinds of conduct are intended and likely to result in the commission of substantive crimes); leave them free to decide for themselves whether to engage in such conduct; and punish them only if they did engage in it.

None the less, a respect for individual freedom is inconsistent with a very broad law of attempts. To respect someone's freedom as a responsible agent is to see and treat her as someone who is in principle susceptible to rational persuasion; this requires that we seek to modify her conduct only by offering her good reasons to modify it for herself. Suppose we know that someone intends to commit, or is preparing to commit or taking initial steps towards committing, a substantive crime. If we have the moral standing to intervene (which we might claim when what he intends is a crime), we can properly do so by trying to dissuade him from continuing in this criminal enterprise: by appealing to the moral reasons for which he ought to obey the law; or perhaps by reminding him of the prudential reasons for desistance provided by the threat of punishment for the substantive crime. In trying thus to persuade him, we treat him as someone who *could* be persuaded to desist for himself, and who still has time (a *locus poenitentiae*) to desist. We should treat him thus, not necessarily because we think that we might in fact persuade him to desist (we might harbour no real hope of this), but because this is what it is to respect him as a responsible agent. If instead we intervene forcibly to prevent him advancing his criminal enterprise, we cease to treat him as a responsible agent: we deny him the freedom to decide for himself whether to desist; we pre-empt his future actions by force, and thus infringe his autonomy. If the law is to treat its citizens as responsible agents, it must leave them free to decide for themselves, not merely whether to embark on a criminal enterprise, but whether to continue with it.

'In the Process of Committing' the Offence

Is this to say that we should adopt the 'last act' test for attempts: that the agent should become criminally liable only when she has done all that she could to complete the crime, or has done something that was intended to complete the crime without further action by her, and which (for all she knew) put it beyond her power to prevent its completion?

I think not. Consider the use of violence in self-defence. If I use violence to *pre-empt* an attack which I believe another person is about to mount, I do arguably fail to treat him as a responsible, autonomous agent: I coerce him, rather than seeking to persuade him. On the other hand, if I use violence in defence of myself or another, to prevent an assailant from carrying through the wrongful attack on which he has already embarked but has not completed, I do not fail to treat him as a responsible, autonomous agent; my violence is now a legitimate response to his wrongful attack.

Any attempt to justify criminal punishme8t by arguing that punishment is relevantly analogous to the use of defensive violence is controversial. I think the analogy has this much force: just as the use of defensive violence against one who has embarked upon a wrongful attack does not fail to respect him as a responsible agent, neither does the use of the criminal law's coercive powers (of arrest, conviction, and punishment) against one who has decisively embarked on the actual commission of a crime fail to treat him as a responsible agent. Like the assailant against whom defensive violence may be used, he could still have desisted voluntarily: a would-be killer who is killed or arrested just before he can pull the trigger could still have decided not to pull it. However, we could say that someone who is not just preparing to commit a crime but 'in the process of committing' it has 'crossed the Rubicon': by committing himself to the crime, he makes himself liable to defensive violence, and to the coercive attentions of the criminal law.

Thus, I suggest we should use the test favoured by the Court of Appeal in interpreting the 1981 Act's demand for a 'more than merely preparatory' act: was the defendant 'in the process of committing', or had he 'embarked on', the offence itself? As we saw, this test reflects a central strand of thought in the pre-1981 law: it accords with one interpretation of Parke B's requirement for an act 'immediately connected with' the commission of the substantive offence; and with Stephen's requirement for an act 'forming part of a series which would constitute [the offence's] actual commission if it were not interrupted'. Although it is much narrower than the *Model Penal Code's* 'substantial step' test, it does fit with. other strands in American law: with the distinction between 'perpetration' and 'preparation', and the idea of 'the commencement of consummation' of the crime.

Only when an intending criminal passes beyond the stage of 'mere preparation' and embarks on the commission of the crime itself does her prospective commission of that crime acquire a sufficiently concrete form as an active engagement in the public world for her to be convicted of attempting to commit it. Only then has she related herself as an agent sufficiently closely to the prospective crime; only then can we bring the coercive powers of the criminal law to bear on her without infringing her status as a responsible agent. This also accords with the ordinary meaning of 'attempt', and with the idea of attempts as attacks: I am 'attempting' to do X only if I am actually engaged in doing X; and an attack is an attempt on some victim or target. We can thus now justify the Law Commission's claim that, by a 'desirable coincidence of social policy and ordinary language', those kinds of conduct that 'the layman would regard as "attempting" to commit an offence' should count in law as criminal attempts.

Duff admits that his proposed test, which is very similar, if not identical, to the one presently used by the courts, is open to a challenge of being indeterminent. To overcome this he suggests Parliament could list some examples of conduct which would constitute an attempt.[160] Duff claims that his test reflects the 'normal' meaning of an attempt, and to some extent this is supported by interviews among members of the public who appear to support the idea that an attempt should be committed shortly before the commission of the offence.[161] Other commentators, including Glanville Williams, are more sceptical about trying to discover the 'normal' meaning of the word attempt.[162] He points out that throughout the criminal law there are divergences between the normal and legal meaning of words.

QUESTIONS

1. Are you convinced by any of the arguments for why the law should punish attempts? Given that the prisons are so overcrowded should not the law focus on offences where victims are directly harmed?

2. Glazebrook (1969) suggests that there is no need to have a special law of attempts if the law defines each substantive crime to include attempt. However, this would be to treat attempts under the same label as the complete offence. To some, this would not recognize the important moral difference between an attempted offence and a complete offence. What do you think?

3. Would the law on attempts be clearer if greater attention was paid to crimes which punish (unsuccessful) attempts on people and those which endanger people? (see Duff (2005b))

6.4 *MENS REA* FOR ATTEMPT

What is the appropriate *mens rea* for an attempt?[163] Again the issue depends in part on whether one takes a subjectivist or an objectivist approach to attempts. To subjectivists, because it is essentially a matter of chance whether or not the attempt succeeds the *mens rea* for the attempt should be the same as that required for a completed offence.[164] For many objectivists an attempt requires an intention to 'make up' for the lower level of harm in an attempt.[165] Other commentators have made reference to the 'normal meaning' of an attempt, which they suggest means intending to produce a certain result.[166]

---

[160] Duff (1996: 394). For further discussion see Culver (1998).   [161] Robinson and Darley (1995: 20–8).
[162] Williams (1991).   [163] White (1991: 15 ff.): Kugler (2002: 202–12).
[164] Robinson (1994: 890–6).   [165] Clarkson and Keating (1998: 478).
[166] Horder (1994). For criticism of appeals to the normal meaning of attempt see Kugler (2002: 202–12).

In the following passage Anthony Duff sets out his view on what the *mens rea* for an attempt should be:

A. Duff, *Criminal Attempts* (Oxford: OUP, 1996), 362–6

13.3 The Fault Element in Attempts: Why A Law of Attempts?

. . .

We have seen that strict subjectivists (if they can justify distinguishing inchoate and substantive offences at all) should require exactly the same fault element for the inchoate offence as for the relevant substantive offence: if recklessness as to the relevant result (as to death, injury, or damage, for example) suffices for a substantive offence, it should also suffice for the inchoate version of that offence. Can (or should) objectivists resist this conclusion? Can they argue that the non-occurrence of the result required for the substantive offence should make a difference, not just to the seriousness of the offence for which the defendant is convicted, or to the severity of the sentence she receives, but to the fault element required for conviction of the inchoate offence? That is, can they justify a general law of *attempts*, rather than a broader law of inchoate crimes?

I have argued that we should interpret the 'intent to commit an offence', which attempts are often said to require, as an intention such that the agent would necessarily commit an offence in carrying it out. To justify the claim that this should be the fault element of the general inchoate offence, I must show two things: first, why that inchoate offence should require intention even when the relevant substantive offence does not; and secondly, why it should not then require intention as to *all* aspects of the substantive offence. This will involve discussing the difference between *attempts* (or attacks) and actions of *endangerment*, and explaining why we should have a general law of attempts (rather than a broader law of endangerment) by showing how the non-occurrence of the prospective harmful result makes a greater difference to the culpable character of actions of endangerment than it does to that of attempts.

Attacks and Endangerments

I suggested earlier that intended action is the paradigm of action and of responsible agency: in so far as we are responsible agents, we are paradigmatically responsible for our intended actions. This suggests that intended criminal action, the intended doing of criminal harm, is the paradigm of criminality. The paradigm of murder, or wounding, is an intended killing or wounding, done without justification or excuse: that must count as murder, or wounding, if anything does; a responsible agent cannot deny responsibility for a death, or wound, which he causes with intent (whereas he might be able to deny culpable responsibility for deaths or wounds which he foresees even as certain side-effects of his action); and we count some actions, which are not intended to kill or wound, as murders, or woundings, in virtue of their closeness or resemblance to this paradigm.

We are of course also culpably responsible and may be criminally liable for harms which we cause recklessly, rather than with intent. Sometimes, indeed, we may see little moral difference between intention and an especially heinous recklessness. . . . More often, however, we will see an agent's culpable responsibility for a harm which she causes as being qualified by the fact that she caused it recklessly rather than with intent. For she did not direct her action towards that harm; and she could consistently have hoped (as one who intends harm could not) not to cause it: her action (and she as its agent) is therefore less intimately related to that harm. We might then (particularly when the harm is very serious) mark this difference between the intending and the reckless agent by convicting the reckless agent of a lesser offence—of manslaughter rather than murder, for instance; or by convicting the reckless agent of the same offence, but mitigating her sentence.

In such cases there is a completed harm, which we ascribe to the agent: what gives her action its normative character, as a culpable killing or wounding for instance, is the fact that it did cause death or injury, as well as her culpable relationship to that death or injury. The same is true, of course, of actions that are intended to, and do, cause harm: they take their character as wrongfully harmful actions partly from the very fact of their success. What, though, if an action does not cause the harm which it was intended to cause, or risked causing? The distinction between intention and recklessness now becomes more significant, as the distinction between *attack* and *endangerment*—*which* is also the distinction between *essentially* and only *potentially* harmful action.

An action constitutes endangerment when it in fact threatens to cause harm; it endangers that which it threatens to harm. The threat may be unintentional and non-culpable (as when a driver whose brakes unexpectedly fail endangers others); endangerment is culpable when it is negligent (the driver failed to check her brakes), or reckless (she knew that her brakes might fail), or intentional (she drives at a pedestrian deliberately, intending to frighten him).

By contrast, intention is central to the notion of attack (as it is to that of attempt). The paradigm or standard case of attack is an action that is intended to cause harm, and that in fact causes or threatens to cause that intended harm: I attack another's life by acting with the intention of killing her, in a way that in fact directly threatens her life; or I attack another's property by acting with the intention of damaging what I know is her property, in a way that in fact threatens her property.

Attacks are essentially, not merely potentially, harmful. Consider actions intended to kill. An action is essentially murderous if murder is part of its intrinsic character, as the agent intends and engages in it: if it would be murder were it completed as the agent intends. That is, the action is essentially murderous if the agent intends [to kill] and the context is such that the killing would be murder. Likewise, an action is essentially homicidal if the agent intends [to kill], in a context such that the killing would be manslaughter rather than murder. To count an action as essentially murderous or homicidal is to say that the actual occurrence of death simply completes what was already its intrinsic character. It was already structured by the prospect of, and already directed towards, causing death: the occurrence of death objectively actualizes or completes that intrinsic character, rather than giving the action a homicidal character which previously it did not have.

By contrast, actions which constitute endangerment are only potentially harmful. An action is potentially murderous or homicidal if it would constitute murder, or manslaughter, were it to cause death, but the actual causation of death is no part of its intrinsic character as the agent conceives and engages in it.

. . .

To ask whether we should have a general law of attempts, defined in terms of an 'intent to commit an offence', is thus to ask whether we should have a general law of attacks rather than of endangerment: should we criminalize essentially harmful actions which in fact cause no harm more readily than those which are only potentially harmful?

Part of the answer to this question lies in the very difference between essentially and potentially harmful action. One who intends to do harm, whose action is essentially harmful, relates himself as an agent as closely as he can to that harm; his action falls short of the paradigm of wrongfully harmful action only in that its harmful character is not completely actualized; and that non-completion of its harmful character is the non-completion of the action itself, as he intends it. By contrast, one whose action is only potentially harmful relates himself less closely, as an agent, to the harm which he risks causing: if the harm does not ensue, his action is complete without causing harm; it is connected to the paradigm of wrongfully harmful action neither by the fact of causing harm nor by its intentional structure. Relatedly, one who intends to do harm cannot hope that that harm will not ensue, nor (without repenting his action) be relieved if it does not; while one who is only reckless as to a risk of harm can (it is consistent with the intentional structure of his action that he will) have such a hope and feel such relief.

It follows that if we should be criminally liable for our actions, in so far as they are culpably related to some criminal harm, we have stronger reason to criminalize actions which are essentially harmful than to criminalize those which are only potentially harmful: to criminalize failed attacks than to criminalize endangerments which cause no actual harm. For the former are more closely related to the harm which they are intended but fail to cause, than are the latter to the harm which they threaten to but do not actually cause.

FURTHER READING

Alexander, L., and Kessler, K. (1997), '*Mens Rea* and Inchoate Crimes', *Journal of Criminal Law and Criminology* 87: 1138.

Duff, A. (1991), 'The Circumstances of an Attempt', *Cambridge Law Journal* 50: 100.

Stannard, J. (1987), 'Making up for the Missing Element: A Sideways Look at Attempts', *Legal Studies* 7: 194.

Sullivan, G.R. (1992), 'Intent, Subjective Recklessness and Culpability', *Oxford Journal of Legal Studies* 12: 380.

Williams, G. (1991b), 'Intents in the Alternative', *Cambridge Law Journal* 50: 120.

6.5 IMPOSSIBLE ATTEMPTS

In many cases of impossible attempts it is unlikely that the defendant will be charged because his conduct will be objectively innocent. If a man has sexual intercourse with a woman with her consent, believing her to be over 13, whereas in fact she is under 13, technically he is guilty of attempt to have sexual intercourse with a girl under 13. In fact because what he has done is 'objectively innocent' it is unlikely the police will ever find out about this unless the man makes a confession. However, where there is evidence that the defendant believes he is committing an offence, even though in fact he is not (e.g. he is found with a bag of white powder and a drug-taking kit, but the white powder is found to be chalk) should there be an offence?

Subjectivists are likely to take the view that the defendant was as blameworthy as if the facts had been true. He has shown a similar contempt for the values the law upholds and seeks to protect what a person who actually commits the offence has done. It could be claimed it is purely 'luck' that the facts were not as the defendant believed them to be. For objectivists the complete lack of harm means that it is illegitimate to punish an impossible attempt. There is no objective or manifest criminality. The House of Lords in *Shivpuri* adopted the subjective view. In the following extract Christopher Clarkson discusses the present state of the law:

C.M.V. Clarkson, *Understanding Criminal Law* (3rd edn., London: Sweet & Maxwell, 2001), 168–70

This decision [*Shivpuri*] has introduced certainty and simplicity into the law and has given effect to the legislative intent behind the Criminal Attempts Act 1981. However, one can only feel unease at the manner in which the decision was reached. It is abundantly plain that the House of Lords was faced with a situation in *Anderton v. Ryan* (1985) where they felt that criminal liability was inappropriate. People who purchase cheap videos thinking that they are stolen when in fact they are not have done nothing wrong other than commit a crime in their minds. On the other hand, the House found itself faced with a defendant in *Shivpuri* (1986) whom they felt clearly had done wrong and deserved punishment. He had agreed in India to receive a suitcase of drugs in England that would be delivered to him by a courier. This he did and then, removing one package from the suitcase, he took it, still following instructions, to a railway station to deliver to a third party. He was there arrested. While one can understand the House of Lords' desire to uphold the conviction in such an obvious case of trafficking in 'drugs', one nevertheless wonders whether important legal principles ought to be altered so freely to meet the exigencies of the case before the court.

While it is possible to justify the existence of a law of attempt (p. 163) and risk-creating offences (pp. 170–173) despite the absence of a direct harm, such justifications presuppose the potential for causing harm in the real world. If I try to shoot and kill you but my gun is broken or try to steal from your empty pocket, I am attacking your legally protected interests (Duff, 1996) and my actions have a real and observable potential for causing harm. But when I stick pins in a doll believing that it will cause your death, I am not realistically threatening your legally protected interests. Similarly, if I handle goods that are not stolen, whose legally protected interests am I attacking? This is pure thought-crime. The distinction drawn in *Anderton v. Ryan* (1985) between 'acting in a criminal way' and 'objectively innocent' acts could, with refinement, have been developed into a workable test enabling a distinction to be drawn between those attempt cases involving a realistic attack on a legally protected interest (where liability is appropriate) and other cases that amount to no more than thought-crime (and where no liability should ensue).

Duff (1996) has suggested that attempt liability is only appropriate if there is some apparent prospect of success, or some apparent ability to commit the crime, as measured by a reasonable observer. If I fire my gun at what I believe is my enemy but is in fact a tree stump and any reasonable person would realise I was firing at a tree stump, there should be no liability. But when I stick my hand in your empty pocket, the reasonable observer will not know the pocket is empty; there is an 'apparent ability' to commit the crime and attempt liability is appropriate. This test raises the problem: how much knowledge must be attributed to this reasonable observer? Clearly, such an observer must know certain general facts about the world, such as that one cannot kill by witchcraft. But, further, the reasonable observer can only make sense of the defendant's actions if she knows something about the meaning of those actions and, often, neutral actions (such as handling a video recorder) only make sense if there is knowledge of the defendant's dominant intention: the intention that drives and explains the action. Duff (1996) distinguishes between such dominant intentions and incidental but mistaken beliefs (which do not explain the defendant's actions but are simply incidentally held beliefs). Mrs Ryan did not have a dominant intention to handle stolen goods; she was not acting in order to handle stolen goods as she might have been if responding to a bet that she would not have the nerve to handle stolen goods. Her dominant intention was to purchase a video recorder that she incidentally believed was stolen. The reasonable observer should only be endowed with knowledge of dominant intentions and not of this incidental belief. Her actions were therefore 'objectively innocent' and she should not be liable. After *Shivpuri* (1986), however, this is not the approach of English law.

The philosophy underlying the Criminal Attempts Act 1981 and the approach adopted by the House in *Shivpuri* (1986) represent 'subjectivism' gone mad. It amounts to no more than punishing people for their guilty intentions. The person who takes his or her own umbrella thinking it belongs to another can now be convicted of attempted theft. The Law Commission (1980) anticipated such problems. Conceding that there would be liability in this situation and in the case of a person buying goods at such a low price that he believed them to be stolen when in fact they were not, it concluded that 'in neither case would it be realistic to suppose that a complaint would be made or that a prosecution would ensue'. This prognosis sadly turned out to be false. *Anderton v. Ryan* (1985) was exactly such a case. A prosecution was brought and under the law as interpreted in *Shivpuri* (1986) criminal liability would ensue. It must surely be a matter of deep regret that English law is now involved in punishing thought-crime.

A further objection is that this extreme lurch into subjectivism is inconsistent with the approach adopted to many other offences where the dictates of fair labelling have ensured that regard be paid to the resulting harm or the realistic prospect of such harm. Some coherence in the approach adopted towards offences is surely desirable. A clearer understanding of the importance of the causing of harm (albeit 'second-order' harm) would have ensured some check on unbridled 'subjectivism' and would have prevented the present situation arising.

QUESTIONS

1. Michael, of deep religious faith, prays that God will strike down his enemy, Brian, with a thunderbolt. He believes God will answer his prayer, but Brian is still alive. Cynthia invites her friend, Sophie, around for a cup of tea. She has prepared poison in the shape of a sugar cube. She intends to put it in Sophie's tea, but by mistake puts a normal sugar cube in Sophie's tea. Are these 'failed attacks'? Can they be distinguished?

2. George Fletcher (1978: 137ff.) expressed the concern that for many cases of impossible attempt the only way the prosecution could get a conviction was if the defendant was foolish or vulnerable enough to confess. Is that a reason against punishing impossible attempts?

3. Duff (1996: 384) discusses the hypothetical example of a person putting pins into a model of the victim, believing that thereby he will release evil powers which will kill the victim. He argues such behaviour cannot amount to an attempt because 'it fails so radically to engage with the world that it does not even amount to a failed attack'. Is that a convincing argument?

FURTHER READING

Fletcher, G. (1978), *Rethinking Criminal Law* (Boston, Mass.: Little, Brown), 137ff.

Temkin, J. (1976), 'Impossible Attempts: Another View', *Modern Law Review* 39: 55.

Williams, G. (1991a), 'Criminal Omissions—The Conventional View', *Law Quarterly Review* 107: 87.

7 CONSPIRACY THEORY

Conspiracy is a controversial offence. In particular, the fact that the offence can be committed simply by a verbal agreement by two or more people to commit the crime, before any steps are taken to implement the plan.[167] In the following extract Fred Abbate sets out some of the principal concerns with the offence and some of its possible justifications:

F.J. Abbate, 'The Conspiracy Doctrine: A Critique' in M. Gorr and S. Harwood (eds.), *Controversies in Criminal Law* (Boulder, Colo.: Westview, 1992), 56–9

. . . Unlike other inchoate crimes, conspiracy has drawn criticism because of what are thought to be its peculiar features:

(1) The conspirational group may be punished for contemplating an objective for which as individuals they could not be punished. A lone person with felonious designs—even known felonious designs—cannot ordinarily be brought to trial. But if he plots with others, he has committed a crime.

(2) In order for a conspiracy to obtain, no formal agreement need be shown to have occurred. A 'tacit understanding' is enough, a 'unity of design and purpose.' Each conspirator need not even know the identity of all the others.

(3) Where the conspiracy is for an unlawful purpose, even if the conspirators have not yet decided on the means to accomplish it, they may still be prosecuted.

(4) Although most conspiracies are secret, openness does not immunize an agreement from prosecution for conspiracy.

(5) 'Each conspirator is liable for all consequences that naturally flow from the conspiracy and for the acts of all who participate with him in executing the unlawful purpose.' The 'acts' at issue need not be the agreed-upon methods, so long as they are in furtherance of the plan.

(6) Although one may join a conspiracy at a date later than that of the original agreement, he is not only liable for all acts done thereafter, but for the original agreement itself.

(7) Under many statutes no 'overt act' in furtherance of the agreement need be shown in order for the charge of conspiracy to be proven.

(8) Certain of the rules of evidence are relaxed in conspiracy trials, and there is often a higher penalty attached to the conspiracy crime than to the completed offense.

. . .

The classical general defense of the conspiracy doctrine is the 'group-danger' rationale. On the assumption that the criminal law has one of its objectives the prevention of harm to the community, the claim is that, since combinations of person with harmful intentions are more dangerous than lone persons with those same intentions, conspiracies themselves must be made a crime. The increased danger, the argument continues, is the result of several factors:

(a) An individual is more likely to carry out his group commitments than his purely private decisions.

---

[167] Law Commission Report (1976: para. 1.5); Dennis (1977).

(b) Having committed himself to others, it is now much more difficult for a person to reverse the original decision, since such a reversal would require the cooperation of others.

(c) There is now increased probability that the harm intended will be produced.

(d) There is now the prospect of a greater amount of harm than that intended by lone individuals.

These factors have been used to justify the state's stepping in at a stage even earlier than it does in the case of attempt. (The 'overt act' required in conspiracy need not be an attempt to carry out the plan.) This point has been expressed by an often quoted study of conspiracy by the *Harvard Law Review*:

'Since one who has decided to commit a crime does not confront the further choice whether to attempt that crime, the deterrent function of the proscription against attempt is not additional to that of the proscription against the completed offense. By contrast, conspiracy is simply a route by which a given criminal object can be approached. Because the antisocial potentialities of this route are peculiarly great, it is arguable that even those who have not been deterred by the penalty for the completed offense should nevertheless by discouraged from embarking upon their criminal venture in concert with others.'

Further,

'. . . the uneasiness produced by the consciousness that such groupings exist is in itself an important antisocial effect. Consequently, the State has an interest in stamping out conspiracy above and beyond its interest in preventing the com- mission of any specific substantive offense. This additional interest may explain, for example, why some courts have imposed cumulative sentences for a conspiracy and for the crime which was its object.'

By calling the group-danger rationale a 'general defense,' I mean to indicate that it seeks to justify conspiracy as a category of crime while still being neutral about the wisdom of the particular features of the doctrine. Indeed, critics of the procedural and other details of the doctrine often wish to retain the category purged of what they consider its objectionable features. Thus, the group-danger justification will not, without further argument, account for, say, the vicarious responsibility aspect of conspiracy law or the relaxation of the rules of evidence.

But does the group-danger rationale even do its general justifying task without problems? Consider (a) and (b) above, which assert that commitments to groups are less likely to be revised or left unaccomplished than individual decisions. Even if true, the argument would justify stepping in and prosecuting only those conspiracies that are based upon certain sorts of commitments of individuals to groups, not all those (as the category is framed at law) that are 'combinations' or 'agreements.' It has been noted that a 'tacit understanding' or 'unity of design and purpose' is all that is required for conspiracy, and although showing these might sometimes provide evidential support for the existence of 'commitment,' quite clearly it need not. From the fact that M and N have agreed to do or have an understanding that they will do A, it surely does not follow that M is in any clear sense 'committed' to N to do A. He may merely, for example, view his consorting with N as a means to carry out his own particular designs.

But even if M is committed to N, it does not follow that he is therefore more committed to the doing of A than he would be as a lone individual. A person who is morally committed to a course of action does not become more committed to it for having joined with others. Nor does his joining involve the clearer likelihood that now he will carry out his intentions. And

882 | CRIMINAL LAW: TEXT, CASES, AND MATERIALS

stressing point (b) will not help much, since M's change of mind does not require the cooperation of others if his original intention to do A was not itself a result of his joining with others.

If we turn to (c) and (d) of the group-danger rationale, there are more questions. The mere addition of heads and hands does not of itself increase the potential for danger, even in cases where 'commitment' is an appropriate description. As a matter of empirical fact, a single (and single-minded) person might be much more dangerous to the public safety than a group. As Goldstein put it:

'More likely, empirical investigation would disclose that there is as much reason to believe that a large number of participants will increase the prospect that the plan will be leaked as that it will be kept secret; or that the persons involved with share their uncertainties and dissuade each other as that each will stiffen the others determination.'

The remark about secrecy (no longer essential to a conspiracy according to the Spock case) suggests another point. The claim, noted above, that is the 'uneasiness' aroused by knowing there are conspiracies afoot which helps justify the state's interference even before attempt, would work just as well as an argument for punishing lone individuals with harmful intentions. If 'uneasiness' is an important antisocial effect, then presumably any uneasiness will do. In addition, a group which has decided to do some harmful act, but has not yet decided upon the means, should cause less uneasiness than one person who has decided upon both, yet the former is as full-blown a conspiracy as is any other. We will take up the question of punishment for intentions in a moment, but the point to be made now is that the 'uneasiness' argument flatly justifies too much.

Nor will the distinction between attempt and conspiracy, as drawn above, hold much promise after closer scrutiny. It is true, of course, that one who has decided to commit a crime does not face the further choice of whether or not to attempt it, so that the proscription against attempts is, so to speak, 'built in' to the proscription against the accomplished objective. But this is also true with regard to certain kinds of conspiracies, namely, those in which the objective by its very nature requires a group effort. Consider a plot to seize and shut down a complicated waterworks. Given the nature of the crime, one does not (if one is rational) intend to do it unless one intends to do it with others. There are not two choices here-the decision to take over the waterworks *and* the decision to do it in concert with others. The conspiracy cannot be labeled a mere 'route by which a given criminal object can be approached,' and the parallel with attempts is obvious.

These objections to the group-danger rationale do not, of course, show that the invoking of it is always out of place. They do, however, show it to be a much weaker general defense than most who employ it seem to think. For the common-law conception of conspiracy is not what is being justified by the rationale, but rather a special sub-class of the category, viz., one where members are strongly committed to the group's cause and to each other, where the members are in actual fact more dangerous in combination than as individuals, where more than mere social uneasiness is the effect of the venture, and where the objective is such that it does not require a group effort by definition.

Clearly the purpose of the offence of conspiracy is to enable the police and prosecution authorities to intervene early and convict a group of criminals before having to wait until they actually commit the offence. However, there is, as Abbate points out, a remarkable contrast with attempts. In attempts law great care is taken not to put the *actus reus* of an attempt too early. Otherwise defendants could be punished for their evil thoughts, rather than what they have done. Hence the English law insists that the defendant has done an act which is more than merely preparatory. By contrast, in conspiracy there is only a need to demonstrate an agreement to commit the offence.[168] The key difference between a conspiracy and an attempt is the number of people involved.[169]

The argument that is most commonly put forward to justify conspiracy is, to use the words of Andrew Ashworth, 'In many cases group behaviour may acquire a momentum of its own, with individuals being afraid to withdraw and participants spurring each other on.'[170] But is there any evidence to support such a claim?[171] This is considered in the following extract which sets out some of the psychological analysis on the impact of groups:

N. Katyal, 'Conspiracy Theory' (2003) 112 *Yale Law Journal* 1307 at 1316–24

1. Psychological Analysis of Social Identity

A wide body of psychological research over the last century reveals that people tend to act differently in groups than they do as individuals. Some of the work is tentative, thereby precluding robust results. Nevertheless, it is generally accepted that groups are more likely to polarize toward extremes, to take courses of action that advance the interests of the group even in the face of personal doubts, and to act with greater loyalty to each other. Much of the most influential research focuses on how group membership changes an individual's personal identity to produce a new social identity. In this process, a person's self-esteem becomes linked to the group's successes and failures. Group members thus tend to refer more to each other than they do to outsiders, listen more to each other, and reward each other more often. . . .

a. Polarization and Risk-Taking

Groups are more likely to have extreme attitudes and behavior. This research began with findings showing 'risky shifts'—predictability in the conformity result in that people take greater risks in groups. Subsequent work found that the phenomenon was not limited to shifts in risk, and that groups polarize in the direction their members were already tending. For example, French students who already liked de Gaulle liked him even more after discussing him in a group, and those who did not like Americans liked them even less after discussing Americans in a group. Once the problem is conceptualized as polarization, it becomes possible to understand why some groups behave with extreme caution.

From one perspective, criminal risk-taking might be good because lawbreakers may commit acts with a high probability of detection. While more empirical research is necessary, there are reasons to doubt that polarization will occur along this dimension. Polarization arises because individuals exaggerate their conformity to perceived traits of a group's social identity. It is therefore possible to have a group of criminals acting more cautiously with respect to what targets to attack, and more riskily with respect to the number of crimes that they commit. A study of active burglars provides some support for this dual shift, for it found that burglars working in groups committed more burglaries and that they were more cautious about which targets to burgle. The study also found that burglars in groups are more likely to be aroused, raising the possibility that group crimes lead to unplanned violence.

---

[168] Dressler (1987: 382).

[169] Bowne (1993: 224) has concerns for the disproportionate use of conspiracy offences on minority groups.

[170] Ashworth (1999: 475). [171] Barloon (1996); Broderick (1985).

b. Acting Against Self-Interest

Groups encourage individuals to submerge their self-interest to that of the group. Some of the most interesting work on this point is being done by two economists, Nobel laureate George Akerlof and his colleague Rachel Kranton. Their model puts forth a theory for why individuals act against their own interests in order to preserve or augment their group identity. Flouting the perceived ideals of the group generates personal anxiety over self-image. Standard economic theory, Akerlof and Kranton underscore, does not take these considerations into account, and therefore has a difficult time explaining activities that are against individual self-interest, such as self-mutilation through tattoos or piercing.

Akerlof and Kranton's work follows from a number of psychological studies about behavior in groups. In a series of famous experiments, Sherif studied group dynamics in a boys' summer camp. Upon arrival, the boys were free to form spontaneous friendships, but after a few days they were split into two groups. Under isolation, the groups 'developed a cohesive structure and they came to strongly prefer the members of their own group.' When the groups were brought together for a tournament, 'overt group hostility . . . [and] minor acts of discrimination and aggression' were found, and 'in-group loyalty, solidarity and cooperation' were at their height.

A second series of experiments, dubbed the 'minimal group' ones, found that even arbitrary formation of groups with no previous history between the members produces similar results. Henri Tajfel's initial studies divided schoolchildren into two groups by showing them some abstract paintings and asking which ones they liked best. The students were told that they were assigned to their groups on the basis of their answers (in actuality they were randomly assigned, and in later experiments, they were not even shown paintings, but assigned by a coin toss or by being told they were in a red or blue group). The subjects were not told who else was in the group and were placed in individual cubicles. They were then asked to award money between the two groups, and Tajfel found that there was significant discrimination in favor of one's own group. Indeed, individuals favored their group even when it was against their absolute self-interest: They gave their group the largest relative gains instead of giving their group and the other group greater absolute gains. This research suggests that the initial decision to agree to conspire is an important pivot point. Once an individual has made such an agreement, group identity can take hold and lead her to submerge self-interest to the group's interest.

c. Dissuasion

Contracts scholars have spoken of a moral obligation to fulfill contracts—an obligation that increases the probability of performance. When A agrees to engage in a crime with B, the agreement thus makes the crime more likely. What is now understood about groups is that, apart from this obligation, groups are far more difficult to dissuade than are individuals because they develop self-serving inferences. Such inferences permit members of groups to justify their conduct as furthering either social or group goals.

One common inference is for group members to believe that other members are more likely to be correct and that nonmembers are more likely to be wrong. Another inference is that group members are fairer than nonmembers. As a result of these and other group biases, members of a group will listen to one another far more than they will listen to other people. Consequently, people in groups are more likely to escalate their commitments to failing courses of action and more likely to continue with these failing courses of action. Chip Heath, in a related finding, discovered that people are far more likely to experience doubts about their performance and disillusionment when they act as individuals compared to when they act in groups.

Dissuasion and disillusionment are critical ways for the government to fight conspiracy. When criminal groups develop self-serving inferences, it reinforces their tendencies toward crime. Members may feel more justified in pursuing criminal activity to help other members and may develop rationalizations (some drug dealers, for example, believe they perform the positive work of pharmacists and steer customers away from violent dealers). Such rationalizations can also thwart cooperation with law enforcement. Consider the recent startling results of two psychologists who found that prisoners' dilemma players induced to feel empathy for the other party cooperate almost fifty per cent of the time even when they know that the other party has already defected. Game theory predicts constant defection, and yet cooperation is manifested repeatedly. Such research explains why many do not defect from conspiracies. The group encourages a feeling of solidarity and cultivates the view that each member needs the cooperation of the others. It is harder to get people to defect— to flip—when they share an identity.

d. Success in Tasks

Studies of group performance appear to be in some tension with each other. On the one hand, some studies show that people perform less well in groups than they do as individuals. For example, German experiments in the nineteenth century found that when the size of a group asked to pull a rope was increased, the total pull exerted would increase, but the amount each participant pulled would drop. Dyads pulled at 93%, trios at 85%, and groups of eight at only 49% of their individual performance levels. Taylorism, a management theory dominant in the early part of the twentieth century, was based on such notions of group inefficiency. More recent work has argued that groups suppress dissent and stifle creativity, an idea captured by Irving Janis's term 'groupthink.'

On the other hand, a number of studies find that groups enhance performance. Early work showed that when word puzzles were provided to individuals and groups, groups performed better. Other research has found that groups tend to have more solutions to problems, to generate them faster, and to find more creative solutions than do individuals. Indeed, a psychological literature review found a 'general consensus . . . that, on average, groups out-perform individuals' on tasks ranging from intellectual problems to decision-making ones.

The findings from these studies are reconcilable in two ways. First, the rope-pulling and other such experiments were beset with what we will later call 'team-production' problems—circumstances in which an individual's input to the team product was not visible and shirking therefore more likely. So, for example, individuals asked to cheer will not do so as loudly in a group as they will on their own, but will cheer as loudly in a group setting if they are told that a computer can discern their individual level of cheering. As we will soon see, team-production analysis will generate many useful insights for conspiracy law by suggesting doctrines that reward shirking. Second, the group-inefficiency studies often slighted social identity. With a shared identity, performance increases markedly. One literature review found that 'loyalty, rule-following and extra-role behaviour increase when employees define themselves in terms of a relevant team or organizational identity' so that when groups are given tasks that 'encourage participants to define themselves in terms of a shared sense of self, group productivity can match that of isolated individuals and may also exceed it.' Conspiracies, which often cultivate such an identity, therefore can be more productive (and impose greater harm) than isolated individuals.

It should be added that not everyone is convinced by arguments that conspiracies make it more likely that the members will commit offences.

The offence of conspiracy is also justifiable on the basis that an offence committed by a group dedicated to the same purpose involves doing the victim a different kind of wrong from that where there is only one offender. However, such an argument, although it may be convincing where a group has actually committed the offence, is hard to justify where there is no offence.[172]

FURTHER READING

Alexander, L., and Kessler, K. (1997), 'Mens Rea and Inchoate Crimes', Journal of Law and Criminology 87: 1138.

Broderick, P. (1985), 'Conditional Objectives of Conspiracies', Yale Law Journal 94: 895.

Dennis, I. (1977), 'The Rationale of Criminal Conspiracy', Law Quarterly Review 93: 39.

Law Commission (2002), Report No. 276, Fraud (London: TSO).

Levi, M., and Smith, A. (2002), Organised Crime and Conspiracy Legislation (London: Home Office).

Robbins, I. (1989), 'Double Inchoate Crimes', Harvard Journal of Legislation 26: 1.

---

[172] Card (1973).

15

COMPLICITY

PART I: THE LAW OF COMPLICITY

1 PRINCIPALS AND ACCOMPLICES

DEFINITION

The principal is the person whose acts or omission amount to the *actus reus* of the offence.

The accomplice is a person who aids, abets, counsels, or procures the principal in the commission of the offence.

This chapter deals with the legal position of those who help or encourage others to commit crimes. The criminal law punishes not only those who directly harm a victim but also those who assist them. So, if Bob stabs Steven to death, Bob is clearly guilty of murder. But if Charles has given Bob the knife; Diana has told Bob where Steven can be found and Edwina has encouraged Bob to kill Steven, then Charles, Diana, and Edwina can all also be guilty in connection with Steven's death. Those who help others commit crimes have been known by a number of different legal terms: accessories, secondary parties, or accomplices.[1]

It must be said at the outset that the law in this area is unclear in places. Professor Ashworth has stated:

> the English law of complicity is replete with uncertainties and conflicts. It betrays the worst features of the common law: what some would regard as flexibility appears here as a succession of opportunistic decisions by the courts, often extending the law, and resulting in a body of jurisprudence that has little coherence.[2]

As this quotation indicates, the subject of this chapter is not an easy one and commentators have struggled to present a clear guide to the present law. Not surprisingly therefore, students find it difficult too.

---

[1] At one point the common law distinguished between principals in the second degree (those who were assisting the principal and were present when the offence was committed) and accessories before the fact (those whose participation was limited to activities before the crime was committed). The law no longer draws this distinction.

[2] Ashworth (2003: 441).

In order to understand the position of accomplices first it is necessary to distinguish them from principals.

1.1 WHO IS THE PRINCIPAL?

The principal is the perpetrator of the crime. That is the person (or people) whose actions constitute the *actus reus* of the offence. For example, in a murder case it is the person whose act caused the death of the victim. By contrast, the accomplice will be the person who assisted or encouraged the principal to commit the crime. This appears a straightforward distinction; but it is important to contrast six different cases:

(1) Val and Ian both stab Sara. The combined effect of the two wounds is that Sara dies. In such a case Val and Ian are guilty as joint principals.[3] It may be that they have different *mens rea* in which case they will be convicted of different offences (e.g. one of murder and one of manslaughter). Alternatively, they may have the same *mens rea* in which case they are guilty of the same crime.

(2) Laurie gives Stephen a knife, telling him to stab Agatha to death, which Stephen does. Stephen is clearly the accomplice and Laurie the principal.

(3) Minnette and Dorothy, acting together, attack Peter. Evidence is unable to establish whether the fatal wound was inflicted by Minnette or Dorothy. They are both liable for murder. This is because it can be said of both Minnette and Dorothy: 'either your stab wound caused Peter's death or you assisted the person whose stab wound caused Peter's death. Therefore, you are guilty of murder, either as the principal or the accomplice.'[4] This law is demonstrated in the rather unusual facts of *Giannetto*[5] (extracted below at p. 889).

(4) Ruth dies in a house occupied by Larry and Susan. It is clear that either Larry or Susan killed Ruth, but it is not clear which of them did. In such a case neither could be convicted as it could not be shown that Larry and Susan must be guilty of murder as either principals or accessories. Only if it could be shown that the killing was by either party and the other party (whoever it was) must have been an accessory, could a conviction of both properly be established.[6]

(5) Dick and Phyllis attack Tom at the same time, but without intending to assist each other or cooperate together. In such a case Dick and Phyllis are each individually responsible for their own actions, but not for each other's.[7] So, if it was established that the cause of death was only the wound inflicted by Dick, Phyllis could not be convicted of murder or manslaughter (but could be guilty of the wounds she inflicted).

(6) Arthur gives Conan some poison, telling Conan it is medicine for Conan's child. Conan, believing Arthur, gives the poison to the child who dies. In such a case Arthur is guilty of murder as the principal and Conan is not guilty of any offence.

---

[3] *Macklin and Murphy's Case* (1838) 2 Lew CC 225.
[4] *Mohan* [1967] 2 AC 187 (PC); *Giannetto* [1997] 1 Cr App R 1 (CA).   [5] [1997] 1 Cr App Rep 1.
[6] *Lane and Lane* (1986) 82 Cr App R 5 (CA); *Giannetto* [1997] 1 CAR 1 (CA). For a discussion of the present law and proposals for reform see Law Commission Consultation Paper No. 279 (2003) and G. Williams (1989b).
[7] *Peters and Parfitt* [1995] Crim LR 501 (CA).

This last example is an example of the 'doctrine of innocent agency', which needs to be considered in further detail.

R v Giannetto
[1997] 1 Cr App R 1 (CA)

Robert Giannetto made threats to his wife Julia Giannetto and paid Welch to kill her. Giannetto was arrested after his wife's death. The prosecution was unable to establish who had killed her. He was convicted of murder on the basis that either he or someone acting on his behalf (maybe Welch) killed her. He appealed on the basis that the judge had failed to indicate to the jury that they had to be unanimous in deciding whether he was the principal or accessory.

Lord Justice Kennedy

Having considered the authorities with some care we are satisfied that in the circumstances of this case the trial judge was right not to direct the jury that before they could convict they must all be satisfied either that the appellant killed his wife or that he got someone else to do so. They were entitled to convict if they were all satisfied that if he was not the killer he at least encouraged the killing, and accordingly this ground of appeal fails.

There are two cardinal principles. The first is that the jury must be agreed upon the basis on which they find a defendant guilty. The second is that a defendant must know what case he has to meet. Where the Crown allege, fair and square, that on the evidence the defendant must have committed the offence either as principal or as secondary offender, and make it equally clear that they cannot say which, the basis on which the jury must be unanimous is that the defendant, having the necessary *mens rea*, by whatever means caused the result which is criminalised by the law. The Crown is not required to specify the means, because the legal definition of the crime does not require it; and the defendant knows perfectly well what case he has to meet. Of course, if (as will very often be so) the Crown nail their colours to a particular mast, their case will, generally, have to be established in the terms in which it is put. Our judgment should give no encouragement to prosecutors casting around for alternative possibilities where the essential evidence does not show a clear case against the defendant. But the facts of the present appeal are by no means an instance of that.

. . .

Appeal dismissed.

1.2 'INNOCENT AGENCY'

An innocent agent is a person whose act causes the harm to the victim, but who is 'innocent': either because he lacks criminal capacity (e.g. he is insane or under the age of criminal responsibility) or he is unaware of the criminal nature of the act he is doing (e.g. a passer-by who touches a booby trap bomb, setting it off). Where an innocent agent is involved the principal is the person who 'causes' the innocent agent to perform the *actus reus* and the innocent agent is not guilty of any crime.

In the case law the best example of innocent agency is *Michael*,[8] where the defendant wished to kill her baby. She delivered poison to her nurse, telling her it was medicine and to administer it to the baby. The nurse decided not to administer the poison and left it on the shelf. A child then took the poison and administered it to the baby and killed him. The child and nurse in this case could be described as 'innocent agents'. Similarly, in *Stringer and Banks*[9] an employer told his employees to type letters and engage in accounting transactions which (unknown to the employees) resulted in fraudulent transfers. The employees were innocent agents and the principal was the employer.

Professor Sir John Smith[10] has suggested that there are some crimes which cannot be committed through an innocent agent because 'it is impossible to say that D has personally committed the *actus reus*'. He suggests bigamy and rape as examples.[11] The argument in favour of this view is that to say a principal has committed rape when he or she used an innocent agent is an artificial description of what he or she has done. By contrast, in a case where the defendant has used an innocent agent to administer poison there is no artificiality in saying that the defendant has poisoned the victim.

FURTHER READING

Alldridge, P. (1990), 'The Doctrine of Innocent Agency', *Criminal Law Forum* 1: 45.

—— (1992), 'Common Sense, Innocent Agency, and Causation', *Criminal Law Forum* 3: 299.

Williams, G. (1992), 'Innocent Agency and Causation', *Criminal Law Forum* 3: 289.

2 COMPLICITY: THE *ACTUS REUS*

DEFINITION

There are five ways that one can be an accomplice:

1. aiding;
2. abetting;
3. counselling;
4. procuring;
5. party to a joint enterprise.

The Accessories and Abettors Act 1861, section 8, states:[12]

> Whosoever shall aid, abet, counsel, or procure the commission of any indictable offence, whether the same be an offence at common law or by virtue of any act passed or to be passed, shall be liable to be tried, indicted, and punished as a principal offender.

---

[8] (1840) 9 C & P 356.   [9] [1991] Crim LR 639 (CA).   [10] J.C. Smith (2002: 142).

[11] However, in *Cogan and Leak* [1976] QB 217 (CA) a husband was convicted of raping his wife through the innocent agency of his friend. The Court of Appeal did suggest that an alternative way of examining the case was to see it as one of procuring rape, and this analysis was also preferred by the Divisional Court in *DPP v K and B* [1997] 1 Cr App R 39 (DC).

[12] As amended by the Criminal Law Act 1977. The Magistrates' Courts Act 1980, s. 44 contains a similar provision for summary offences.

This section makes three points of crucial importance to the law of accomplices:

(1) There must be an offence committed by the principal.[13] The significance of this is that if the accused offers aiding, abetting, counselling, or procuring to the principal, but the principal does not go on to commit an offence then the accused is not guilty as an accessory. Imagine this: Jeeves, a butler to Bertie, knowing that Gussie, a burglar, is intending to burgle Bertie's house, leaves his safe wide open. Jeeves commits no offence if Gussie does not burgle that night because he has a headache.[14] There is no such offence as an attempt to aid, abet, counsel, or procure.[15]

(2) The accomplice is charged with the basic offence. For example, an accused will be charged with murder, even though the allegation is that he has been an accomplice to the murder. This is particularly significant in the context of murder because a mandatory life sentence automatically follows a conviction of murder.

(3) The four forms of being an accomplice are listed in the section: aiding, abetting, counselling, and procuring. It is necessary to prove only that the defendant was an accomplice in one of these four ways.

Let us now consider the meaning of 'aiding', 'abetting', 'counselling', and 'procuring'. The starting point is the following statement of Lord Widgery CJ in *Attorney-General's Reference (No. 1 of 1975)*:[16]

> We approach s. 8 of the 1861 Act on the basis that the words should be given their ordinary meaning, if possible. We approach the section on the basis also that if four words are employed here 'aid, abet, counsel or procure', the probability is that there is a difference between each of those four words and the other three, because, if there were no such difference, then Parliament would be wasting time in using four words where two or three would do.

The significance of this quotation is that it indicates that the words should be given their normal meaning. This is all well and good, but 'abetting', 'procuring', and 'counselling'[17] are not words in common usage and to give them a 'normal' meaning is therefore not straightforward. The second point that Lord Widgery has made is that the four words are to have distinct meanings.[18] Again this is a little problematic; in particular, commentators have struggled to find an independent meaning of the phrase 'to abet' that is not covered by aiding or counselling.[19] Notably other cases (e.g. *Attorney-General v Able*[20]) have suggested that the four words are just synonyms of helping.

---

[13] The Criminal Law Act 1967, s. 1, means that the section is applicable to all offences whether they were formerly felonies or misdemeanours.

[14] He may be guilty of a firearms offence.

[15] In part this is a reflection of the derivative theory of liability. This will be explained in much greater detail in Part II of this chapter, but in simple terms it means that the liability of the accomplice derives from the principal.

[16] [1975] 2 All ER 684 at 686 (CA).

[17] The word 'counselling' is, of course, normally used in the context of giving someone advice or support on emotional issues, but that is not what is meant here.

[18] See Smith (1978) for an argument that the words should not be seen as four separate terms but as capturing the single common law concept of being an accomplice.

[19] Smith and Hogan (2002: 144).   [20] [1984] QB 795 (CA).

2.1 AIDING

Aiding covers offering help or assistance to someone. This includes giving someone a piece of equipment[21] or some information which helps them commit a crime.[22] It is not necessary to show that the assistance was essential to the commission of the crime, nor that without it the crime could not have taken place. Indeed all that is required is that the assistance was of some help to the principal in committing the crime.[23] However, to constitute aiding an act must actually be of assistance in commission of the crime.[24] So if Harold tells Peter that he is going to kill Tim, and Peter (who hates Tim) gives Harold a knife, but Harold does not use the knife but instead shoots Tim, then Peter will not have aided the murder, because his knife in no way assisted it. Two points however should be made about this example. The first is that the provision of the knife may amount to counselling (discussed below). The second is that if the knife gave Harold confidence to commit the crime, even though he did not use it, Peter might still be held to have aided Harold.[25]

Many cases of aiding will involve the parties meeting so the assistance can be provided,[26] but there need be no meeting. Indeed the principal may not even be aware that he has been assisted.[27] If a security guard, disgruntled with his employer, left a property unlocked, hoping that a passing burglar would take advantage of this, which he did, the security guard could be guilty of aiding a burglary.[28]

2.2 ABETTING

To be honest, no one knows what abetting means. Abetting is defined in the *Oxford English Dictionary* as including 'to incite, instigate or encourage'. As will be seen, these terms are those often used to define counselling.[29] If abetting is to be given a special meaning of its own the best suggestion is that of Devlin J in *NCB v Gamble*[30] who proposed that abetting was encouragement at the time of the offence, while counselling was encouragement before the crime took place.[31]

2.3 COUNSELLING

Counselling involves encouraging, inciting, or instigating the offence. This may involve urging someone to commit an offence or simply indicating that the commission of the offence would be desirable. There is no need to show that the counselling caused the offence. In other words, if Ruth suggests to John 'You should go and kill Andy' but John replies 'Don't worry, I was going to anyway',[32] Ruth can still be a counsellor. In *Giannetto*[33] the trial judge suggested that if a man said to a husband that he was about to kill his wife and the husband did 'as little as patting him on the back, nodding, saying "Oh goody"' this would

---

[21] e.g. *Bainbridge* [1960] 1 QB 129 (CA).   [22] e.g. *Attorney-General v Able* [1984] QB 795 (CA).
[23] *Bryce* [2004] 2 Cr App R 35 (CA).   [24] *Attorney-General v Able* [1984] QB 795 (CA).
[25] Similarly a look-out can be an aider, even if in fact he does not see anyone.
[26] *Attorney-General's Reference (No. 1 of 1975)* [1975] QB 773 (CA).
[27] Simester and Sullivan (2003: 190).
[28] There is no English case law on this, although it is widely accepted to be true.
[29] Smith (1978).   [30] [1959] 1 QB 11.
[31] Smith and Hogan (2002: 144). See also Devlin J in *NCB v Gamble* [1959] 1 QB 11.
[32] *Attorney-General v Able* [1984] 1 QB 795 (CA).   [33] [1997] 1 Cr App R 1, 13 (CA).

be sufficient to amount to counselling. The following case demonstrates the key elements of counselling:

R v Calhaem
[1985] QB 808 (CA)[34]

Kathleen Calhaem had become infatuated with her solicitor. The prosecution case was that Calhaem hired a private detective, Julian Zajac, to kill Shirley Rendell, who had been having an affair with the solicitor. Zajac, armed with a hammer, knife, and gun, approached Rendell's house. Zajac testified that he did not intend to kill Rendell, but rather to act out a charade and pretend to Calhaem that he had tried to kill her. However, when Zajac came face to face with Rendell she started to scream and he panicked, went berserk, and killed her with the hammer. Calhaem appealed against her conviction of murder on the basis (inter alia) that the jury should have been directed that, in order to convict her as an accomplice, it had to be shown that her words of counselling were a substantial cause of the killing. Further, it was argued that Zajac at the time of the killing had abandoned the agreement with Calhaem and embarked on an entirely new enterprise of his own. Therefore, Calhaem should not be regarded as an accomplice to the killing.

Lord Justice Parker

The direction given by the judge was, Mr. Carman [counsel for the appellant] submits, wrong in law. He should have directed the jury that, in the case of counselling as in the case of procuring, the counselling must be a 'substantial cause.'

The point is a novel one, on which there is no direct authority. . . .

We must therefore approach the question raised on the basis that we should give to the word 'counsel' its ordinary meaning, which is, as the judge said, 'advise,' 'solicit,' or something of that sort. There is no implication in the word itself that there should be any causal connection between the counselling and the offence. It is true that, unlike the offence of incitement at common law, the actual offence must have been committed, and committed by the person counselled. To this extent there must clearly be, first, contact between the parties, and, secondly, a connection between the counselling and the murder. Equally, the act done must, we think, be done within the scope of the authority or advice, and not, for example, accidentally when the mind of the final murderer did not go with his actions. For example, if the principal offender happened to be involved in a football riot in the course of which he laid about him with a weapon of some sort and killed someone who, unknown to him, was the person whom he had been counselled to kill, he would not, in our view, have been acting within the scope of his authority; he would have been acting entirely outside it, albeit what he had done was what he had been counselled to do.

Appeal dismissed.

In *Bryce*,[35] excerpted below, the Court of Appeal explained that even in counselling there had to be a causal connection between the counselling and the principal's crime, even though that requirement is given a 'broad interpretation'.

---

[34] [1985] 2 All ER 266, [1985] 2 WLR 826, [1985] Crim LR 303.   [35] [2004] 2 Cr App R 35.

QUESTION

J.C. Smith (2002: 147) suggests that as a result of this case there is no need to show a causal connection between the counselling and the killing. Wilson (2003: 587) argues that it must be shown that the counselling is a 'but for' cause of the killing. He points out that in *Calhaem* but for the counselling Zajac would never have met the victim. Whose interpretation is correct? Read again Parker LJ's example involving the football riot.

It should be remembered that it must be shown that the principal goes on to commit the crime. For example, if B encourages A to commit a crime and A says 'Certainly not, what a terrible thing to suggest.' Although in normal language we would say that B encouraged A to commit the offence, in legal terminology this is not so,[36] nor is it possible to convict someone of attempted counselling. However, B is guilty of incitement, which we will discuss later.

2.4 PROCURING

To procure has been defined as 'to produce by endeavour'.[37] In other words, the accomplice has in a sense caused the principal to commit the offence.[38] At least the principal acted as a consequence of the accomplice's acts. A good example of this is *Attorney-General's Reference (No. 1 of 1975)*[39] where B added alcohol to A's drink. When A later drove A was driving with a blood/alcohol concentration higher than the prescribed limit.[40] B's act had procured A to commit a drink driving offence. Another example of procuring is *Millward*[41] where Millward was convicted of procuring the causing of death by dangerous driving by instructing his employee to drive a tractor and trailer, aware that the hitch mechanism between the two was defective. Subsequently the employee drove the tractor and trailer, which became unhitched, causing the death of a passing motorist. These cases should be contrasted with *Beatty v Gillbanks*[42] where the officers of the Salvation Army knew that a meeting in Weston-super-Mare was likely to produce a violent reaction from a group known as the Skeleton Army. Nevertheless, they decided that the meeting should go ahead, and indeed there was a violent reaction from the Skeleton Army, which included the breaking of shop windows. The Salvation Army officers could not be said to have procured the violence. The case may be explained on the basis that the officers were not *endeavouring* to cause the violence of the Skeleton Army or on the basis that, unlike *Attorney-General's Reference (No. 1 of 1975)*[43] and *Millward*,[44] the principals (the Skeleton Army) knew exactly what they were doing and could be said to have made a fully free, deliberate, and informed act in carrying out the violence.

Procuring is closely linked with the doctrine of innocent agency discussed above; the crucial difference being that in procuring the principal is not entirely innocent (e.g. he does have the capacity to commit the crime and has the relevant *mens rea*).

---

[36] *Clarkson* [1971] 3 All ER 344 (CMCA). Similarly there could be no counselling if the principal did not hear the words of encouragement.

[37] *Attorney-General's Reference (No. 1 of 1975)* [1975] 2 All ER 684 at 686 (CA). K.J.M. Smith (1986); Beynon (1987).

[38] *Attorney-General's Reference (No. 1 of 1975)* [1975] 2 All ER 684 at 687 (CA).

[39] [1975] 2 All ER 684 (CA).

[40] Road Traffic Act 1972, s. 6(1). The offence is now found in the Road Traffic Act 1988, s. 5.

[41] [1994] Crim LR 527 (CA).

[42] (1882) 9 QBD 308.   [43] [1975] 2 All ER 684 (CA).   [44] [1994] Crim LR 527 (CA).

2.5 JOINT ENTERPRISE

A joint enterprise arises where two or more people together embark on the commission of a criminal offence. The two parties may expressly agree to commit a particular crime, or this may be an unspoken understanding. A common example is where two people decide to commit a burglary together. Difficult cases arises where, in the course of committing the agreed crime, the principal goes on to commit a different one. As we shall see shortly, some commentators suggest that a joint enterprise is simply a way of aiding, abetting, counselling, or procuring the offence. Others argue, and this is the line the courts have taken, that there are special *mens rea* requirements which attach to accessories which do not apply to joint enterprises, and vice versa. A joint enterprise does not arise if the accused joins in after the principal has committed the offence.[45]

QUESTIONS

1. Professor Sir John Smith has summarized the law: '(i) Procuring implies causation but not consensus; (ii) "abetting" and "counselling" imply consensus but not causation; (iii) "aiding" requires actual help but neither consensus nor causation' (Smith (2002: 147)). Does it make sense to have these differences in the ways of being an accomplice?

2. The cases seem to suggest that acts that are of only minimal significance to the commission of the crime can be the *actus reus* of being an accomplice: saying 'oh goody' or applauding an illegal performance. Is this too little to justify criminalization? (See Part II of this chapter for further discussion on this.)

3. Martin gives Clement seven good reasons why Clement should kill Edith. Clement rejects the suggestions. Dick overhears what Martin has said, is persuaded by his arguments, and kills Edith. What crimes, if any, has Martin committed?

We will now consider some of the wider issues relating to the *actus reus* of accomplice liability.

2.6 TIME ISSUES

Assistance given to the principal once he has finished the offence will not render someone an accomplice. Therefore, helping the principal escape from the scene of the crime will not amount to aiding or abetting. However, agreeing in advance to help the principal escape could be said to be counselling, in that it might encourage the principal to commit the crime. There are special offences governing assistance after a crime has been committed. These will be discussed later.

The *actus reus* of an accomplice is the giving of assistance or encouragement. The *mens rea* must be present at that time. The mental state of the accomplice at the time the principal commits the crime is irrelevant,[46] unless the accomplice has countermanded her assistance or withdrawn from the enterprise (see p. 919 below).

---

[45] *Percival*, 13 May 2003 (CA).   [46] *Bryce* [2004] 2 Cr App R 35(CA).

2.7 OMISSIONS AND ACCOMPLICE LIABILITY

Simply being present at the scene of a crime does not render you guilty as an accomplice.[47] This is because there is no duty to intervene and stop a crime taking place. So in *Clarkson*,[48] where the defendant came across a man committing a rape and simply watched, he was found not to be an accomplice to the rape. This is part of the general rule that omissions do not form the basis of criminal liability.[49] There are, however, some circumstances in which mere presence can render a person an accomplice:

(1) If a police constable requests that citizens assist in the suppression of a breach of the peace and they refuse to do so this can constitute an offence.[50]

(2) If under the normal law on omissions you are under a duty to protect a person in peril and you fail to do so you can be guilty of an offence. For example, a father who stands by while someone injures his child;[51] or a security guard simply watches while people burgle the premises which he is meant to be guarding, then they may be guilty as accessories to the crimes.[52] Arguably in such cases the defendants could also be regarded as principals if their failure to perform their legal duty caused harm to the victims.[53]

(3) Where a person has a legal power to intervene to prevent a crime and fails to do so then he or she may be responsible as an accessory. In *Rubie v Faulkner*[54] a driving instructor was convicted as an accessory to a dangerous driving offence after failing to intervene to prevent his pupil driving dangerously.[55] Examples of when people have a right to control the behaviour of the principal are where they have ownership or control of the property or premises used by the principal or where the principal is an employee of the accessory.[56]

(4) If the person's presence effectively encourages the principal then this may amount to being an accessory, but only if the accomplice is aware that the principal is encouraged by his presence.[57] In *Francom*[58] the victim was subjected to appalling torture in a flat in which the defendant was present. It was held that, given the length of time for which he was present, the jury were entitled to infer that the detendant's presence must have encouraged the principals. Harder are cases where a group of people watch an illegal fight or musical performance.[59] Merely being present does not normally suffice as encouragement in such offences, but applauding or helping arrange the event would constitute counselling.[60]

---

[47] *Coney* (1882) 8 QBD 534; *Atkinson* (1869) 11 Cox CC 330; *Searle* [1971] Crim LR 592 (CA).

[48] [1971] 3 All ER 344 (CMCA).

[49] See the discussion on omissions in Ch. 2.   [50] *Brown* (1841) Car & M 314.

[51] An Australian case supports this proposition: *Russell* [1933] VLR 59.

[52] See also *Forman and Ford* [1988] Crim LR 677 (Crown Ct).

[53] Simester and Sullivan (2003: 195).   [54] [1940] 1 KB 571.

[55] [1907] 1 KB 40. See also *Tuck v Robson* [1970] 1 All ER 1171 (DC) where the landlord of a pub was convicted of aiding and abetting his customers drinking after hours when standing by and watching them do so. In *Du Cros v Lambourne* [1907] 1 KB 40 the owner of a car sat in the passenger seat while a friend drove the car at a dangerous speed. He was convicted as an accomplice.

[56] *J.F. Alford Transport Ltd* [1997] 2 Cr App R 326 (CA).

[57] *Tait* [1993] Crim LR 538 (CA). In *Allan* [1965] 1 QB 130 the defendant, who watched a fight involving a friend, ready to join in if needed, was not liable as an accessory.

[58] [2001] 1 Cr App R 237 (CA).   [59] See *Coney* (1882) 8 QBD 534; *Wilcox v Jeffrey* [1951] 1 All ER 464.

[60] Ibid.; *Allan* [1965] 1 QB 130 (CA).

In these cases the courts will now have to bear in mind the right to freedom of assembly and association protected under the European Convention on Human Rights. This may, in the light of the Human Rights Act 1998, mean that mere presence at an illegal activity without more should not be regarded as sufficient for criminal liability.[61]

In the following case the Court of Appeal discussed further the question when 'doing nothing' can amount to aiding, abetting, counselling, or procuring:

R v J.F. Alford Transport Ltd
[1997] 2 Cr App R 326 (CA)[62]

Drivers for J.F. Alford Transport Ltd pleaded guilty to making false entries onto their tachograph records[63] contrary to section 99(5) of the Transport Act 1968.[64] Alford Transport Ltd, the managing director, and transport manager were convicted of aiding and abetting these offences, on the basis that they had known what the drivers were doing and did nothing to stop them. They appealed on the basis that passive acquiescence could not amount to aiding and abetting.

Lord Justice Kennedy

5. Aiding and abetting?

Section 8 of the Accessories and Abettors Act 1861 provides that anyone who 'shall aid, abet, counsel or procure' the commission of an indictable offence can be tried and sentenced as a principal offender. An offence contrary to section 99(5) of the Transport Act 1968 is an indictable offence. There was no evidence to suggest that any defendant on any occasion counselled or procured the commission of any such offence, so we can concentrate, as the trial did, on aiding and abetting. Mr Hawkesworth [counsel for the appellants] accepts that the judge was right to tell the jury that aiding and abetting meant simply assisting and encouraging, and that before they could convict any of the defendants of aiding or abetting the driver's offence they must be sure that in each case:

(1) the driver committed an offence (that was not in dispute),

(2) Payne and/or Alford, and therefore the company knew full well what the driver was doing, and

(3) one or other of the individual defendants and therefore the company gave positive encouragement to the driver to perform illegal acts.

. . . [I]n order to establish the offence charged the prosecution had at the end of the day to prove beyond reasonable doubt that Mr Alford knew of each tachograph falsification. And before they could invoke section 35 Criminal Justice and Public Order Act 1994 they had to

---

[61] In *Bland* [1988] Crim LR 41 (CA), which concerned the liability of a woman who was living with a drugs dealer, the court admitted it was necessary to balance the social benefits of requiring a drug dealer's cohabitant to inform the police of criminal activities with the importance of private liberty. In that case it was felt that mere presence in the drug dealer's home was insufficient to constitute criminal liability.

[62] [1999] Crim LR 745.

[63] These record the amount of time driven, the distance travelled, speeds, etc.

[64] It appears the drivers were driving for longer periods than legally permitted.

898 | CRIMINAL LAW: TEXT, CASES, AND MATERIALS

adduce prima facie evidence of knowledge on the part of each defendant. Take count 1, where was the evidence to show that either Mr Alford, or Mr Payne knew that on October 14, 1993 driver Collins was going to produce a false tachograph record, either in the way that he did or at all? That difficulty might have been overcome if the relevant driver had been called as witnesses, or if the individual defendants had made relevant admissions, but there was no evidence of that kind. We accept that in *Johnson v Youden* [1950] 1 KB 544, 546, Lord Goddard C.J. said that knowledge may be inferred if a defendant shuts his eyes to the obvious but, as Gibbs C.J. pointed out in the Australian case of *Giorgianni v. R.* (1985) 156 C.L.R. 473 at 483 the dictum of Lord Goddard needs to be understood. Gibbs C.J. accepted that it would be sufficient to infer knowledge if a defendant deliberately refrained from making enquiries the results of which he did not care to have, but, he continued:

'The failure to make such enquiries as a reasonable person would have made is not equivalent to knowledge; it is not enough to render a person liable as a secondary party that he ought to have known all the facts and would have done so if he acted with reasonable care and diligence. That is so even when the offence is one of strict liability, so that the actual perpetrator may be convicted in the absence of knowledge.'

In reality in attempting to prove knowledge on the part of either individual defendant in relation to any count the prosecution faced problems which seem to us, on the evidence presented to court, to be insurmountable. . . .

Mr Hawkesworth submits that even if knowledge on the part of either individual defendant could have been proved this appeal should still succeed because the judge misled the jury as to what was capable of constituting positive encouragement. In support of that submission Mr Hawkesworth invited our attention to the well-known passage from the judgment of Hawkins J. in *Coney* (1882) 8 Q.B.D. 534, 557, which was cited with approval by Megaw L.J. in *Clarkson* (1971) 55 Cr. App. R. 445, 449, [1971] 1 W.L.R. 1402:

'In my opinion, to constitute an aider and abettor some active steps must be taken by word, or action, with the intent to instigate the principal, or principals. Encouragement does not of necessity amount to aiding and abetting, it may be intentional or unintentional, a man may unwittingly encourage another in fact by his presence, by misinterpreted words, or gestures, or by his silence, or non-interference, or he may encourage intentionally by expression, gestures, or actions intended to signify approval. In the latter case he aids and abets, in the former he does not. It is no criminal offence to stand by, a mere passive spectator of a crime, even of a murder. Non-interference to prevent a crime is not itself a crime. But the fact that a person was voluntarily and purposely present witnessing the commission of a crime, and offered no opposition to it, although he might reasonably be expected to prevent and had the power so to do, or at least to express his dissent, might, under some circumstances, afford cogent evidence upon which a jury would be justified in finding that he wilfully encouraged and so aided and abetted. But it would be purely a question for the jury whether he did so or not.'

Mr Hawkesworth submits that even if the individual defendants knew that drivers were altering the tachograph records the most that could be said against the defendants is that they stood by, and he further submits that the trial judge in summing-up wrongly indicated to the jury that passive acquiescence would suffice. For example, he said at p. 10C that it was the prosecution case that where a person like a transport manager or the managing director of the company who had a right to control the actions of his employees deliberately refrained from exercising control, that in effect gave 'positive encouragement to the drivers to perform illegal acts'. The summing-up continues:

'The defence say that passive sitting back, passive permission, is not enough. There must be some positive act of encouragement. The prosecution say that by their actions these two defendants, and therefore the company, were actively encouraging because they were failing to put any sort of control over these drivers.'

That is another example of the judge simply putting the legal arguments and failing to assist the jury as to the approach which the law required them to adopt, but in our judgment, in the context of this case, if the prosecution could show that the individual defendants, or either of them, knew that the drivers were illegally falsifying tachograph records, and if it could be shown that the individual defendants took no steps to prevent misconduct it was open to the jury in the absence of any alternative explanation, to infer that the individual defendant whom they happened to be considering, and thus the company, was positively encouraging what was going on. In other words on the issue of what could amount to positive encouragement the prosecution approach was correct. As Professor Smith puts it at p. 136 of *Smith and Hogan on Criminal Law* (8th ed.):

'Where D has a right to control the actions of another and he deliberately refrains from exercising it, his inactivity may be a positive encouragement for the other to perform an illegal act, and therefore, an aiding and abetting.'

The textbook goes on to give several examples—two will suffice:

'If a licensee of a public house stands by and watches his customers drinking after hours, he is guilty of aiding and abetting them in doing so (*Tuck v Robson* [1970] 1 WLR 741). Again in *Du Cros v. Lambourne* [1907] 1 KB 40 it was proved that D's car had been driven at a dangerous speed but it was not proved whether D or E was driving. It was held that, nevertheless, D could be convicted. If E was driving she was doing so in D's presence, with his consent and approval; for he was in control and could and ought to have prevented her from driving in a dangerous manner. D was equally liable whether he was a principal or an abettor.'

Mr Hawkesworth submitted that in each of those cases it was critical that the aider and abettor was present at the time of the commission of the principal offence. In our judgment nothing turned on actual presence. What mattered was knowledge of the principal offence, the ability to control the action of the offender, and the deliberate decision to refrain from doing so. We accept that in the context of the present case it would have to be proved that the defendant under consideration intended to do the acts which he knew to be capable of assisting or encouraging the commission of the crime, but he need not have intended that the crime be committed. As Devlin J. said in *NCB v Gamble* [1959] 1 QB 11 at 23:

'If one man deliberately sells to another a gun to be used for murdering a third, he may be indifferent whether the third man dies and interested only in the cash profit to be made out of the sale, but he can still be an aider and abettor.'

Thus if the management's reason for turning a blind eye was to keep the drivers happy rather than to encourage the production of false tachograph records that would afford no defence, and if it could be shown that the individual defendants knew that such a record was likely to be produced the supplying of the lorry to the driver could in some ways be compared with the selling of the gun. We therefore conclude that if knowledge could be shown on the part of one of the individual defendants in relation to any given count it would have been open to the jury to find that he positively encouraged the admission of the offence. However, there being no sufficient evidence of knowledge the appeal must succeed.

Appeal allowed.

3 MENS REA

DEFINITION

The *mens rea* requirement for an accomplice is that he does his acts of assistance intending to assist the principal and foreseeing that the principal might go on to commit the offence with the acts of assistance or encouragement.

The Court of Appeal in *Bryce*[65] have indicated that there is a slight difference in the *mens rea* for accomplices in cases where the defendant was aiding, abetting, counselling, or procuring; and cases of joint enterprise and so we will deal with these separately.

3.1 *MENS REA* IN CASES OF AIDING, ABETTING, COUNSELLING, AND PROCURING

For a long time the law on the *mens rea* for accomplices was unclear. Fortunately, the Court of Appeal in *Bryce*[66] has provided authoritative guidance on the issue. Note that at the end of this extract in paragraph 71 Potter LJ provides a useful summary of the law.

R v Bryce
[2004] EWCA Crim 1231[67]

Craig Bryce was charged with aiding, abetting, counselling, and procuring a person called at the trial X, to commit murder. The allegation was that Bryce drove X to a caravan close to the victim's house so that he could wait for a chance to kill the victim. X killed the victim the next day. The trial judge directed the jury that Bryce would be guilty as an accessory if he deliberately assisted X by taking him to the caravan together with the gun, knowing that it was in order to assist X to kill or cause really serious harm or realizing that there was a real possibility that he might do so. The appellant appealed on three grounds: (i) that the judge had left the jury with the impression that any assistance, however, slight would be sufficient to amount to the *actus reus* of being an accessory; (ii) that the judge had failed to direct the jury that there had to be an intention to assist the principal to kill; and (iii) that the judge had failed to make it clear that a person could only be an accessory to murder if at the time of assistance the principal had the necessary intent for murder.

Potter LJ

40. . . . [I]t is necessary to preserve the distinction between the perpetrator and secondary parties because the mental element or *mens rea* for the secondary party is not necessarily the same as for the perpetrator. This stems from the fact that the *actus reus* of being an accessory involves two concepts: (a) an act (or possibly an omission) which aids, abets, counsels or procures (b) the commission by the perpetrator of the principal offence.

---

[65] [2004] 2 Cr App R 35.   [66] [2004] 2 Cr App R 35.   [67] [2004] 2 Cr App R 35.

Mens rea

41. The required *mens rea* is the same for aiding, abetting, counselling and procuring: see *R. v Rook* (1993) 97 Cr.App.R. 327. . . . As stated in Smith & Hogan: *Criminal Law* (10th ed, 2002) at p.145.

'In the modern law, secondary participation almost invariably consists simply in assisting or encouraging the commission of the crime and it is generally irrelevant whether the secondary participant is present or absent or whether his assistance or encouragement was given before or at the time of the offence. The only possible exception may be the procurer who succeeds in causing the principal to commit the crime (as in the *Attorney General's Reference (No. 1 of 1975)* (1975) 61 Cr.App.R. 118) without doing anything which could be fairly described as encouragement or assistance.'

42. As to (a) it is necessary to show firstly that the act which constitutes the aiding, abetting etc was done intentionally in the sense of deliberately and not accidentally and secondly that the accused knew it to be an act capable of assisting or encouraging the crime. In this case, as in most cases, the first requirement will not be in issue. The act of taking X to the caravan with the gun was obviously done deliberately. . . .

43. As to (b), it is now well established that it is not necessary to prove that the secondary party at the time of the act of aiding, abetting etc intended the crime to be committed.

44. As Devlin J. said in *National Coal Board v Gamble* (1958) 42 Cr.App.R. 240 at 250:

'If one man deliberately sells to another a gun to be used for murdering a third, he may be indifferent whether the third man lives or dies and interested only in the cash profit to be made out of the sale, but he can still be an aider and abetter.'

45. Thus, if it is proved that the defendant intended to do the acts of assistance or encouragement, it is no defence that he hoped that events might intervene to prevent the crime taking place. So, where the defendant drove the perpetrator to a place where he knew that the perpetrator intended to murder a policeman, his intentional driving of the car to that place amounted to an aiding and abetting of the offence despite his unwillingness that the killing should take place. . . .

46. It not being necessary to show that the secondary party intended the crime to be committed by the perpetrator, what must be his state of mind vis-à-vis the commission of the crime? As was stated by Lord Goddard CJ in *Johnson v Youden* [1950] 1 K.B. 544 at 546:

'Before a person can be convicted of aiding and abetting the commission of an offence he must at least know the essential matters which constitute that offence.'

He went on to say:

'He need not actually know that an offence has been committed, because he may not know that the facts constitute an offence and ignorance of the law is not a defence. If a person knows all the facts and is assisting another person to do certain things, and it turns out that the doing of those things constitutes an offence, the person who is assisting is guilty of aiding and abetting that offence.'

. . .

48. But does the secondary party actually have to know that the crime will be committed, as this passage suggests, or is something less sufficient? Lord Simon of Glaisdale in *Lynch* at pp. 35 and 698–699 cited Devlin J. in *National Coal Board v Gamble* (1958) 42 Cr.App.R. 240, 247, [1959] 1 Q.B. 11, 20 and continued:

'The act of supply must be voluntary (in the sense I tried to define earlier in this speech), and it must be foreseen that the instrument or other object or service supplied will probably (or possibly and desiredly) be used for the commission of a crime.' (Emphasis added)

49. Those words were uttered in respect of a person participating at the time of the commission of the offence by the actual perpetrator. However, in the context of a person charged as an accessory who has rendered assistance prior to the commission of the crime by the perpetrator, the circumstances in respect of which knowledge is sufficient for liability may go wider than that of the specific crime actually committed. This is because, as pointed out in *Blackstone's Criminal Practice* (2004) at A6.5 (p.75), it is inappropriate and unworkable to require knowledge of the essential matters constituting the offence in a situation where the offence is yet to be committed in the future or by a person of whose precise intentions the accused cannot be certain in advance. It is thus sufficient for the accused to have knowledge of the type of crime in contemplation. Thus where a person supplies equipment to be used in the course of committing an offence of a particular type, he is guilty of aiding and abetting the commission of any such offence committed by the person to whom he supplies the equipment, providing that he knows the purpose to which the equipment is to be put or realises that there is a real possibility that it will be used for that purpose and the equipment is actually used for that purpose: *see R. v Bullock* (1954) 38 Cr.App.R. 151 and *R. v Bainbridge* (1959) 43 Cr.App.R. 194, [1960] 1 Q.B. 129.

. . .

62. Blackstone's Criminal Practice 2004 (paragraph A 5.4, page 73) relying upon the passage from Devlin J. in *National Coal Board v Gamble* which we have already cited, also states that there must be an intention to aid. . . .

63. The authors then consider the authorities such as *R. v Woollin* [1999] 1 Cr.App.R. 8, [1999] A.C. 82 which decide that a person may still intend to do something even though he does not desire it. The authors continue:

'*Gillick v West Norfolk and Wisbech Area Health Authority* [1986] A.C. 112 is an example of a type of case where the uncertainties of the precise meaning of intention effectively confer a perhaps welcome discretion on whether to impose responsibility. That case concerned, *inter alia*, the question of whether a doctor giving contraceptive advice or treatment to a girl under the age of 16 could be liable as accessory to a subsequent offence of unlawful sexual intercourse committed by the girl's sexual partner. The House of Lords held that generally this would not be the case (the action was a civil one for a declaration) since the doctor would lack the necessary intention (even though he realised that his actions would facilitate such intercourse). One rationale for the decision would be that a jury would not infer intention in such circumstances if they thought that the doctor was acting in what he considered to be the girl's best interests.'

Similar reasoning could be applied to a troublesome group of cases involving the supply of articles for use in crime which the recipient already has some sort of civil right to receive. The general position seems to be that this is not aiding and abetting (see, for example, *R. v Lomas* (1913) 9 Cr.App.R. 220 concerning the return of a jemmy to its owner) because the alleged accessory does not intend to aid the offence but rather merely to comply with his supposed civil-law duties. Critics of this general position rightly point out that it can hardly apply to a person returning a revolver to its owner knowing that he is then going to use it to carry out a murder. But here a jury probably would infer intention to aid from the accused's knowledge of the effects of his action, and the flexibility of the notion of intention enables an appropriate solution to be found to situations for which it is difficult to formulate precise rules in advance.

. . .

71. We are of the view that, outside the *Powell* and *English* situation (violence beyond the level anticipated in the course of a joint criminal enterprise), where a defendant, D, is charged as the secondary party to an offence committed by P in reliance on acts which have assisted steps taken by P in the preliminary stages of a crime later committed by P in the absence of D, it is necessary for the Crown to prove intentional assistance by D in the sense of an intention to assist (and not to hinder or obstruct) P in acts which D knows are steps taken by P towards the commission of the offence. Without such intention the *mens rea* will be absent whether as a matter of direct intent on the part of D or by way of an intent sufficient for D to be liable on the basis of 'common purpose' or 'joint enterprise'. Thus, the prosecution must prove:

    (a) an act done by D which in fact assisted the later commission of the offence,

    (b) that D did the act deliberately realising that it was capable of assisting the offence

    (c) that D at the time of doing the act contemplated the commission of the offence by A, i.e. he foresaw it as a 'real or substantial risk' or 'real possibility' and,

    (d) that D when doing the act intended to assist A in what he was doing.

Appeal dismissed.

EXAMINATION TIP

The easiest way to understand the *Bryce* test is to break it down into essentially two elements:

1. The first element relates to what the accomplice thought or intended about his or her own acts. *Bryce* requires that the defendant must have realized that his act could assist the principal and that he intended to assist the principal.

2. The second element relates to the accused's state of mind about the principal's acts. The defendant must have foreseen that there was a real possibility that the principal would commit the crime he did.

Consider Jeeves, a butler, who deliberately leaves Bertie's (his master's) safe unlocked one night. He could have any one of the following states of mind:

    (a) He wants Bertie's safe to be burgled and leaves it open with that hope.

    (b) He does not want Bertie's safe to be burgled but, knowing of a planned burglary, realizes that it is highly likely it will be burgled.

    (c) He does not want Bertie's safe to be burgled, but realizes that there is a risk that it may be.

    (d) He foresees that the safe will be burgled, but because he was told that the burglars intended to take the whole safe away did not think that his acts would be of any assistance. In other words, although he foresaw the principal's crime he did not foresee that his actions would be of assistance.

There is no doubt that in case (a) Bertie is guilty of being an accomplice; (b) is more problematic. Although Bertie foresees the principal might commit the crime, does he intend to assist the principal? It might be said on the basis of *Woollin*[68] (see p. 151) the jury could

---

[68] [1999] 1 AC 82.

find intention. It seems that in case (c) there is no criminal liability. Although he foresees the principal would commit the crime he does not intend to assist the principal. *Woollin* cannot be used because there is no foresight of virtual certainty. In (d) there is certainly no criminal liability because he did not realize his acts would assist the principal.

More needs to be said about the requirement that the accomplice must foresee that the principal might commit the offence. As this element is shared with the *mens rea* for joint enterprise liability it will discussed next.

3.2 *MENS REA* IN CASES OF JOINT ENTERPRISE

In cases of joint enterprise the only *mens rea* requirement is that the accomplice, while engaging in the joint enterprise, foresaw that the principal might commit the offence he did. The leading case is *Powell and English*.

R v Powell and Daniels; R v English
[1999] AC 1 (HL)[69]

The House of Lords heard two appeals. In the first Anthony Powell, Antonio Daniels, and one other man called at the home of a dealer in cannabis. As the dealer opened the door one of the group shot him. The three defendants were charged with murder on the basis of joint enterprise. Powell argued that he was present solely to buy cannabis and had not taken part in the shooting. Daniels did not give evidence but his barrister argued that Powell had fired the shot.

In the second case, Philip English (aged 15 at the time of the offence) and Weddle were charged with the murder of a police sergeant. The prosecution alleged that, as part of a joint enterprise, English and Weddle attacked the sergeant with a wooden post. During the attack Weddle produced a knife and stabbed the victim to death. English claimed that he had fled the scene before Weddle produced the knife.

Both appeals focused on the correct definition of the *mens rea* equired to convict an accessory charged on the basis of a joint enterprise. The certified questions for their Lordships were:

'(i) Is it sufficient to found a conviction for murder for a secondary party to a killing to have realized that the primary party might kill with intent to do so or with intent to cause grievous bodily harm or must the secondary party have held such an intention himself?

(ii) Is it sufficient for murder that the secondary party intends or foresees that the primary party would or may act with intent to cause grievous bodily harm, if the lethal act carried out by the primary party is fundamentally different from the acts foreseen or intended by the secondary party?'

Lord Hutton

My Lords, the first question gives rise, in my opinion, to two issues. The first issue is whether there is a principle established in the authorities that where there is a joint enterprise to

---

[69] [1997] 4 All ER 545, [1997] 3 WLR 959, [1998] 1 Cr App R 261, [1998] Crim LR 48.

commit a crime, foresight or contemplation by one party to the enterprise that another party to the enterprise may in the course of it commit another crime, is sufficient to impose criminal liability for that crime if committed by the other party even if the first party did not intend that criminal act to be carried out. (I shall consider in a later part of this judgment whether the foresight is of a possibility or of a probability.) The second issue is whether, if there be such an established principle, it can stand as good law in the light of the decisions of this House that foresight is not sufficient to constitute the mens rea for murder in the case of the person who actually causes the death and that guilt only arises if that person intends to kill or cause really serious injury.

My Lords, I consider that there is a strong line of authority that where two parties embark on a joint enterprise to commit a crime, and one party foresees that in the course of the enterprise the other party may carry out, with the requisite mens rea, an act constituting another crime, the former is liable for that crime if committed by the latter in the course of the enterprise.

[Lord Hutton then discussed *Reg. v. Smith (Wesley)* [1963] 1 WLR 1200; *Reg. v. Anderson; Reg. v. Morris* [1966] 2 QB 110.]

As a matter of strict analysis there is, as Professor J.C. Smith pointed out in his commentary on *Reg. v. Wakely* [1990] Crim. L. R. 119, 120, a distinction between a party to a common enterprise contemplating that in the course of the enterprise another party may use a gun or knife and a party tacitly agreeing that in the course of the enterprise another party may use such a weapon. In many cases the distinction will in practice be of little importance because as Lord Lane C.J. observed in *Reg. v. Wakely*, at p. 120, with reference to the use of a pickaxe handle in a burglary, 'foreseeability that the pickaxe handle might be used as a weapon of violence was practically indistinguishable from tacit agreement that the weapon should be used for that purpose.' Nevertheless it is possible that a case might arise where a party knows that another party to the common enterprise is carrying a deadly weapon and con- templates that he may use it in the course of the enterprise, but, whilst making it clear to the other party that he is opposed to the weapon being used, nevertheless continues with the plan. In such a case it would be unrealistic to say that, if used, the weapon would be used with his tacit agreement. However it is clear from a number of decisions, in addition to the judgment of the Court of Criminal Appeal in *Reg. v. Smith (Wesley)* [1963] 1 W.L.R. 1200, that as stated by the High Court of Australia in *McAuliffe v. The Queen*, 69 A.L.J.R. 621, 624 (in a judgment to which I will refer later in more detail) 'the scope of the common purpose is to be determined by what was contemplated by the parties sharing that purpose.' Therefore when two parties embark on a joint criminal enterprise one party will be liable for an act which he contemplates may be carried out by the other party in the course of the enterprise even if he has not tacitly agreed to that act.

. . .

[After discussing *Chan Wing-Siu v. The Queen* [1992] 1 AC 34; *McAuliffe v. The Queen*, 69 ALJR 621 Lord Hutton concluded:]

There is therefore a strong line of authority that participation in a joint criminal enterprise with foresight or contemplation of an act as a possible incident of that enterprise is sufficient to impose criminal liability for that act carried out by another participant in the enterprise.

. . .

The second issue which arises on these appeals is whether the line of authority exempli- fied by *Reg. v. Smith* and *Chan Wing-Siu* is good law in the light of the decisions of this House in *Reg. v. Moloney* [1985] A.C. 905 and *Reg. v. Hancock* [1986] A.C. 455.

. . .

My Lords, I recognise that as a matter of logic there is force in the argument advanced on behalf of the appellants, and that on one view it is anomalous that if foreseeability of death or really serious harm is not sufficient to constitute *mens rea* for murder in the party who actually carries out the killing, it is sufficient to constitute *mens rea* in a secondary party. But the rules of the common law are not based solely on logic but relate to practical concerns and, in relation to crimes committed in the course of joint enterprises, to the need to give effective protection to the public against criminals operating in gangs. As Lord Salmon stated in *Reg. v. Majewski* [1977] A.C. 443, 482e in rejecting criticism based on strict logic of a rule of the common law, 'this is the view that has been adopted by the common law of England, which is founded on common sense and experience rather than strict logic.'

In my opinion there are practical considerations of weight and importance related to considerations of public policy which justify the principle stated in *Chan Wing-Siu v. The Queen* [1985] A.C. 168 and which prevail over considerations of strict logic. One consideration is that referred to by Lord Lane C.J. in *Reg. v. Hyde* [1991] 1 Q.B. 134, 139, where he cited with approval the observation of Professor Smith in his comment on *Reg v. Wakely*:

'If B realises (without agreeing to such conduct being used) that A may kill or intentionally inflict serious injury, but nevertheless continues to participate with A in the venture, that will amount to a sufficient mental element for B to be guilty of murder if A, with the requisite intent, kills in the course of the venture. As Professor Smith points out, B has in those circumstances lent himself to the enterprise and by so doing he has given assistance and encouragement to A in carrying out an enterprise which B realises may involve murder.'

A further consideration is that, unlike the principal party who carries out the killing with a deadly weapon, the secondary party will not be placed in the situation in which he suddenly has to decide whether to shoot or stab the third person with intent to kill or cause really serious harm. There is, in my opinion, an argument of considerable force that the secondary party who takes part in a criminal enterprise (for example, the robbery of a bank) with foresight that a deadly weapon may be used, should not escape liability for murder because he, unlike the principal party, is not suddenly confronted by the security officer so that he has to decide whether to use the gun or knife or have the enterprise thwarted and face arrest.

. . .

Therefore for the reasons which I have given I would answer the certified question of law in the appeals of Powell and Daniels and the first certified question in the appeal of English by stating that (subject to the observations which I make in relation to the second certified question in the case of English) it is sufficient to found a conviction for murder for a secondary party to have realised that in the course of the joint enterprise the primary party might kill with intent to do so or with intent to cause grievous bodily harm. Accordingly I would dismiss the appeals of Powell and Daniels.

The second certified question in the appeal of English arises because of the last sentence in the following passage in the trial judge's summing up to the jury to which I have previously referred:

'If he had the knife and English knew that Weddle had the knife, what would have been— must have been—in the mind of English, bearing in mind whatever condition you find that he was in as a result of drink? So you have to ask that question. If he did not know of the knife then you have to consider whether nevertheless he knew that there was a substantial risk that Weddle might cause some really serious injury with the wooden post which was used in the manner which you find it to have been used.'

In *Reg. v. Hyde* [1991] 1 Q.B. 134, as already set out, Lord Lane C.J. stated, at p. 139:

'If B realises (without agreeing to such conduct being used) that A may kill or intentionally inflict serious injury, but nevertheless continues to participate with A in the venture, that will amount to a sufficient mental element for B to be guilty of murder if A, with the requisite intent, kills in the course of the venture.'

However in *Hyde* the attack on the victim took place without weapons and the Crown case was that the fatal blow to the victim's head was a heavy kick. The problem raised by the second certified question is that, if a jury is directed in the terms stated in *Hyde*, without any qualification (as was the jury in English), there will be liability for murder on the part of the secondary party if he foresees the possibility that the other party in the criminal venture will cause really serious harm by kicking or striking a blow with a wooden post, but the other party suddenly produces a knife or a gun, which the secondary party did not know he was carrying, and kills the victim with it.

   Mr. Sallon, for the appellant, advanced to your Lordships' House the submission . . . that in a case such as the present one where the primary party kills with a deadly weapon, which the secondary party did not know that he had and therefore did not foresee his use of it, the secondary party should not be guilty of murder. He submitted that to be guilty under the principle stated in *Chan Wing-Siu* the secondary party must foresee an act of the type which the principal party committed, and that in the present case the use of a knife was fundamentally different to the use of a wooden post.

   My Lords, I consider that this submission is correct. It finds strong support in the passage of the judgment of Lord Parker C.J. in *Reg. v. Anderson; Reg. v. Morris* [1966] 2 Q.B. 110, 120 which I have set out earlier, but which it is convenient to set out again in this portion of the judgment:

'It seems to this court that to say that adventurers are guilty of manslaughter when one of them has departed completely from the concerted action of the common design and has suddenly formed an intent to kill and has used a weapon and acted in a way which no party to that common design could suspect is something which would revolt the conscience of people today.'

The judgment in *Chan Wing-Siu*'s case [1985] A.C. 168 also supports the argument advanced on behalf of the appellant because Sir Robin Cooke stated, at p. 175:

'The case must depend rather on the wider principle whereby a secondary party is criminally liable for *acts by the primary offender of a type* which the former foresees but does not necessarily intend.' (Emphasis added.)

. . .

[After discussing *R v Gamble* [1989] NI 268 Lord Hutton explained:]

   In my opinion this decision was correct in that a secondary party who foresees grievous bodily harm caused by kneecapping with a gun should not be guilty of murder where, in an action unforeseen by the secondary party, another party to the criminal enterprise kills the victim by cutting his throat with a knife. The issue (which is one of fact after the tribunal of fact has directed itself, or has been directed, in accordance with the statement of Lord Parker C.J. in *Reg. v. Anderson; Reg. v. Morris* [1966] 2 Q.B. 110, 120b) whether a secondary party who foresees the use of a gun to kneecap, and death is then caused by the deliberate firing of the gun into the head or body of the victim, is guilty of murder is more debatable although, with respect, I agree with the decision of Carswell J. on the facts of that case.

. . .

   I have already stated that the issue raised by the second certified question in the appeal of English is to be resolved by the application of the principle stated by Lord Parker C.J. in

*Reg. v. Anderson, at p. 120b. Having so stated and having regard to the differing circum-
stances in which the issue may arise I think it undesirable to seek to formulate a more precise
answer to the question in case such an answer might appear to prescribe too rigid a formula
for use by trial judges. However I would wish to make this observation: if the weapon used
by the primary party is different to, but as dangerous as, the weapon which the secondary
party contemplated he might use, the secondary party should not escape liability for murder
because of the difference in the weapon, for example, if he foresaw that the primary party
might use a gun to kill and the latter used a knife to kill, or vice versa.*

In conclusion I would wish to refer to a number of other points which arise from the
submissions in these appeals. The first issue is what is the degree of foresight required to
impose liability under the principle stated in *Chan Wing-Siu* [1985] A.C. 168. On this issue
I am in respectful agreement with the judgment of the Privy Council in that case that the
secondary party is subject to criminal liability if he contemplated the act causing the death as
a possible incident of the joint venture, unless the risk was so remote that the jury take the
view that the secondary party genuinely dismissed it as altogether negligible.

Secondly, as the Privy Council also stated in *Chan Wing-Siu*, in directing the jury the trial
judge need not adopt a set of fixed formulae, and the form of the words used should be that
best suited to the facts of the individual case. . . . I consider that the test of foresight is a
simpler and more practicable test for a jury to apply than the test of whether the act causing
the death goes beyond what had been tacitly agreed as part of the joint enterprise. Therefore, in cases where an issue arises as to whether an action was within the scope of the joint
venture, I would suggest that it might be preferable for a trial judge in charging a jury to
base his direction on the test of foresight rather than on the test set out in the first passage in
Reg. v. Anderson; Reg v. Morris. But in a case where, although the secondary party may have
foreseen grievous bodily harm, he may not have foreseen the use of the weapon employed
by the primary party or the manner in which the primary party acted, the trial judge should
qualify the test of foresight stated in Reg. v. Hyde [1991] 1 Q.B. 134 in the manner stated by
Lord Parker C.J. in the second passage in *Reg. v. Anderson; Reg. v. Morris*.

As I have already observed in referring to the decision in *Reg. v. Gamble* [1989] N.I. 268, in
applying the second passage in *Reg. v. Anderson* there will be cases giving rise to a fine
distinction as to whether or not the unforeseen use of a particular weapon or the manner in
which a particular weapon is used will take a killing outside the scope of the joint venture, but
this issue will be one of fact for the common sense of the jury to decide.

Lord Steyn

. . .

At first glance there is substance in the third argument that it is anomalous that a lesser
form of culpability is required in the case of a secondary party, viz. foresight of the possible
commission of the greater offence, whereas in the case of the primary offender the law
insists on proof of the specific intention which is an ingredient of the offence. This general
argument leads, in the present case, to the particular argument that it is anomalous that the
secondary party can be guilty of murder if he foresees the possibility of such a crime being
committed while the primary can only be guilty if he has an intent to kill or cause really
serious injury. Recklessness may suffice in the case of the secondary party but it does not in
the case of the primary offender. The answer to this supposed anomaly, and other similar
cases across the spectrum of criminal law, is to be found in practical and policy considerations. If the law required proof of the specific intention on the part of a secondary party, the
utility of the accessory principle would be gravely undermined. It is just that a secondary

party who foresees that the primary offender might kill with the intent sufficient for murder, and assists and encourages the primary offender in the criminal enterprise on this basis, should be guilty of murder. He ought to be criminally liable for harm which he foresaw and which in fact resulted from the crime he assisted and encouraged. But it would in practice almost invariably be impossible for a jury to say that the secondary party wanted death to be caused or that he regarded it as virtually certain. In the real world proof of an intention sufficient for murder would be well nigh impossible in the vast majority of joint enterprise cases. Moreover, the proposed change in the law must be put in context. The criminal justice system exists to control crime. A prime function of that system must be to deal justly but effectively with those who join with others in criminal enterprises. Experience has shown that joint criminal enterprises only too readily escalate into the commission of greater offences. In order to deal with this important social problem the accessory principle is needed and cannot be abolished or relaxed. For these reasons I would reject the arguments advanced in favour of the revision of the accessory principle.

Appeal allowed.

The Court of Appeal in the next case developed some of the general principles in *Powell; English*:

R v Uddin
[1999] QB 431 (CA)[70]

Following a driving incident, six men attacked another man with bars and poles, including part of a snooker cue. Abdul Tahid (one of the group) produced a flick knife during the attack and fatally stabbed the victim. The only evidence that any of the group knew about the knife was that of an eyewitness, who stated that someone had shouted 'stab him'. The stabber and Rejan Uddin were convicted of murder. Three of the other defendants were convicted of manslaughter. The appeal was based on the judge's direction to the jury about the degree of knowledge required.

Lord Justice Beldam, giving the judgment of the court

. . . [W]e think that the principles applicable to a case such as the present are as follows.

(i) Where several persons join to attack a victim in circumstances which show that they intend to inflict serious harm and as a result of the attack the victim sustains fatal injury, they are jointly liable for murder; but if such injury inflicted with that intent is shown to have been caused solely by the actions of one participant of a type entirely different from actions which the others foresaw as part of the attack, only that participant is guilty of murder.

(ii) In deciding whether the actions are of such a different type the use by that party of a weapon is a significant factor. If the character of the weapon, e.g. its propensity to cause death, is different from any weapon used or contemplated by the others and if it is used with a specific intent to kill, the others are not responsible for the death unless it is proved that they knew or foresaw the likelihood of the use of such a weapon.

---

[70] [1998] 2 All ER 744, [1998] 3 WLR 1000, [1999] 1 Cr App R 319, [1999] Crim LR 987.

(iii) If some or all of the others are using weapons which could be regarded as equally likely to inflict fatal injury, the mere fact that a different weapon was used is immaterial.

(iv) If the jury conclude that the death of the victim was caused by the actions of one participant which can be said to be of a completely different type to those contemplated by the others, they are not to be regarded as parties to the death whether it amounts to murder or manslaughter. They may nevertheless be guilty of offences of wounding or inflicting grievous bodily harm with intent which they individually commit.

(v) If in the course of the concerted attack a weapon is produced by one of the participants and the others knowing that he has it in circumstances where he may use it in the course of the attack participate or continue to participate in the attack, they will be guilty of murder if the weapon is used to inflict a fatal wound.

(vi) In a case in which after a concerted attack it is proved that the victim died as a result of a wound with a lethal weapon, e.g. a stab wound, but the evidence does not establish which of the participants used the weapon, then if its use was foreseen by the participants in the attack they will all be guilty of murder notwithstanding that the particular participant who administered the fatal blow cannot be identified: see *Reg. v. Powell; Reg. v. English* [1999] 1 A.C. 1. If, however, the circumstances do not show that the participants foresaw the use of a weapon of this type, none of them will be guilty of murder though they may individually have committed offences in the course of the attack.

(vii) The mere fact that by attacking the victim together each of them had the intention to inflict serious harm on the victim is insufficient to make them responsible for the death of the victim caused by the use of a lethal weapon used by one of the participants with the same or shared intention.

As we have said, in the present case there was no evidence upon which the jury could find that before the attack began the others involved knew that Abdul Tahid was carrying a flick knife.

If the jury accepted the evidence of Mr. Tatham who said that whilst in his laundrette on the opposite side of the road from the attack he heard the shout 'Stab him' as the attack began, they could as we have said have concluded that those of the defendants who then took part in the attack did so being aware, or at least foreseeing, that a knife might be used with intent to cause really serious harm. Whether those who having heard the shout attacked the deceased with shortened billiard cues as clubs themselves committed the offence of inflicting grievous bodily harm with intent or not, they would be guilty of murder as secondary parties.

The judge's direction clearly left it to the jury to say whether one of the defendants had gone beyond the common purpose of the concerted attack and he told them that if one of the defendants had done an act which went beyond the agreed plan and they were not sure that the act was one which another defendant knew was a real possibility, the necessary common intention would not have been established. It was suggested that the jury may from this direction have concluded that if a particular defendant had an intention to do really serious harm the existence of that intention was sufficient to make that defendant guilty of murder even though the action of the party who had caused the death went outside the common purpose of the attack. We do not think that the judge's direction was susceptible of this interpretation but we do think that since *Reg. v. Powell; Reg. v. English* [1999] 1 A.C. 1 it is necessary for the jury to have their attention directed particularly to the nature of a weapon used in a concerted or combined attack and to knowledge or foresight of the use of such a weapon.

[Beldam LJ then quoted from *Powell and English*.]

. . .

Whilst the jury were, as we have said, carefully directed to consider whether the actions of any of the defendants went so outside the common purpose that they were not foreseen by the others, the jury's attention was not specifically focused on the use of the knife by Abdul Tahid and whether on the evidence they were sure that the others were aware that he might use it. As we have said, there was evidence from which the jury could conclude that those of the defendants who took part after the shout of 'Stab him' must have been aware that one of them had a knife and might use it with intent to do serious harm. Lord Hutton stressed the lethal nature of a knife as a weapon; it was for the jury to say whether its use in this attack was so different from the concerted actions of hitting the deceased with clubs and kicking him with the shod foot that Tahid's actions went beyond the common purpose.

It was also for the jury to say in each case whether those taking part were aware, whether from the shout or otherwise, that one of their number might use a knife.

We are further troubled by the distinction apparently drawn by the jury between the parts played by the three defendants convicted of manslaughter and the part played by the appellant. If the actions of Tahid did in fact go outside the common purpose of the attack then those who took part aware that a knife might be used were guilty of murder as secondary parties; if they were not aware that a knife might be used they were entitled to be acquitted: see the observations of Lord Hutton in *Reg. v. Powell; Reg. v. English* [1999] 1 A.C. 1. If, however, the use of the knife did not go outside the common purpose of the attack which from the actions of those taking part was plainly to cause Sharp really serious harm, it is difficult to discern the basis for the verdict of manslaughter or the basis on which the participation of those defendants was found by the jury to be different from the participation of the appellant. It is true that each of those defendants convicted of manslaughter gave evidence that they did not know that any of their number had a knife and therefore that it might be used with intent to do serious harm but equally there was no evidence that before the attack began and the shout of 'Stab him,' the appellant knew that Tahid had a knife. In the circumstances of this case we think that it would be unsafe to allow the conviction of the appellant for murder to stand. We think, however, that as there was evidence from which the jury directed in accordance with *Reg. v. Powell; Reg. v. English* could have concluded that the appellant was guilty of murder there should be a retrial.

Retrial ordered.

It is worth emphasizing a number of points about the test developed in *Powell*. What is said here is true for accomplices whether in cases of joint enterprise, or aiding, abetting, counselling, or procuring.:

(1) It is not necessary to show that the accessory wanted the principal to commit this crime or even authorized it.[71] It is enough if the accomplice foresaw that the principal would commit the crime.

(2) The test is subjective: 'what did the defendant foresee?', not 'what ought the defendant to have foreseen?'[72]

---

[71] See also *Clarke* (1985) 80 Cr App R 344 (CA) and *Attorney-General v Able* [1984] 1 QB 795 (CA).
[72] *Blakley and Sutton v DPP* [1991] Crim LR 763 (DC); *Callow v Tillstone* (1900) 83 LT 411; *J.F. Alford Transport Ltd* [1997] 2 Cr App R 326 (CA).

(3) *Powell* makes it clear that it is enough for the defendant to foresee that the principal may, not that he definitely will, go on to commit the offence. It is enough if the accomplice thought there was a real, not negligible, possibility that the principal would commit the offence.

(4) Under the *Powell* test it is the act of the principal, not its consequence, which must be foreseen.[73] Consider this: Anne assists Harry in an attack which kills Catherine. She foresees that Harry will intentionally stab Catherine, but she does not foresee that Catherine will die. Anne will still be liable as an accessory to murder. She foresaw Harry's act which caused the death and foresaw that he would have the *mens rea* for murder. The obverse of this is that the accomplice is not liable if the act of the accused was fundamentally different from any act foreseen by the accomplice. In *English* (excerpted above) two men armed themselves with stakes to attack a police constable. One of them (unknown to the other) had a knife and he stabbed the police constable with it. It was held that the principal's act was not foreseen by the accomplice and so it was 'outside the scope of the joint enterprise', so the accomplice was not liable. In *Reardon*[74] the defendant gave the principal a knife knowing he was going to stab a man to death. In fact the principal went on to stab two men. However, the Court of Appeal upheld his conviction for two murders. The principal had used the knife in a way foreseen by the accomplice, albeit twice. This departure from what was foreseen by the accomplice was not sufficiently serious to render the acts outside the scope of the joint enterprise.

It is not quite clear how far the courts will take this. If the accomplice foresees that the principal will kill the victim in one way should it really matter if the principal kills by a different route?

(5) *Powell* developed a special rule in relation to weapons. If the accomplice knew that the principal had a weapon with him then the accomplice is deemed to foresee that the principal will use that weapon.[75] This principle has received a wide interpretation from the court, in two ways:

(a) In *Powell* Lord Hutton suggested that if it was known that the principal had a gun which he would use to kneecap the victim, but the principal used the gun to shoot the victim elsewhere the accomplice could still be convicted.[76] In other words it is not necessary to see exactly how the weapon will be used.

(b) If the accomplice knew that the principal had a weapon, but the principal used a weapon of a similar kind then the accomplice is still liable. If, for example, Jack knew George had a gun, but George used a knife to kill the victim, then Jack would still be found to have the *mens rea* for an accessory. On the other hand if Kate knew Stephen had a post and he pulled out a knife, Kate would not be responsible. The knife would be regarded as a fundamentally different kind of weapon. It is, of course, difficult to draw a hard and fast test as to what is a similar kind of weapon and what is different. The issue is left to the jury.[77] The case of

---

[73] *Day* [2001] Crim LR 984 (CA); *Neary* [2002] EWCA Crim 1736 (CA).

[74] [1999] Crim LR 392 (CA).

[75] *Cairns* [2002] EWCA Crim 533 applied the rule even though the accomplice knew about the principal's weapon only a few seconds before the attack.

[76] J.C. Smith (2002: 165) is critical of this view.

[77] *Greatrex* [1999] 1 Cr App R 126 (CA); *Sooklal and another v The State* [1999] 1 WLR 2011 (PC).

Uddin, quoted above, provides detailed guidance on this. In *Uddin* the court accepted that a flick-knife was completely different from shortened billiard cues. In *Greatrex and Bates*[78] the Court of Appeal, ordering a retrial, said that a jury may well decide that a metal bar is fundamentally different from a shod foot. But it was stressed that the question is one for the jury. The jury may well be persuaded to draw a distinction between weapons which are generally regarded as fatal and weapons which are not.[79]

It seems that this 'weapons rule' creates only a presumption. In other words, the alleged accomplice will not be guilty if she can persuade the jury that even though she knew that the principal had a gun she did not foresee that the principal would use the gun (e.g. if the principal had promised not to use it).[80]

(6) The accomplice is liable if the principal does an act of the kind intended or foreseen by the accomplice.[81] So, if the defendant gives the principal a screwdriver, foreseeing that he will use it to burgle and in fact the principal uses it to stab someone, the defendant is not liable as an accomplice. The accomplice will not be liable for acts of the principal which are fundamentally different from those foreseen by the accomplice.[82] However, it is not necessary to show that the accomplice knew exactly where or when the principal would commit the offence. In *Maxwell v DPP*[83] the accomplice foresaw that the principal might commit a range of offences. It was held he was guilty because the principal had committed one of the kinds of offences he had foreseen.

Although it does not need to be shown that the defendant foresaw against whom, when, or where the offence was going to take place, if the accomplice offered assistance in order that a particular crime be committed against a particular person and the principal went on deliberately to commit the crime against someone else then the accomplice is not liable. So if Catherine gives Michael a gun, saying 'here is a gun to help you kill your wife' and instead of killing his wife Michael kills his mother-in-law then it seems that Catherine is not liable.

The previous paragraph applies only where the principal deliberately departs from the plan.[84] Where the principal carries out the plan but accidentally someone else is injured then the accomplice can still be liable. Where the principal and accomplice agree to kill X, and the principal shoots at X, but the bullet misses and kills Y the principal and accomplice may both be liable for murder. This is because the act of the principal (the shooting at X) is the act the accomplice foresaw and assisted. In the sixteenth-century case of *Saunders and Archer*[85] the accomplice encouraged the husband to kill his wife by giving her a poisoned apple. The husband gave the apple to his wife. She took the apple and gave it to their child. The husband stood by and watched the child eat the apple and die. It was held that the accomplice was not responsible for the child's death. The crucial point seems to be that the husband was under a duty to protect his child from danger. His failure to intervene to protect the child was his own decision and this was outside the plan with the accomplice.

---

[78] [1999] 1 Cr App R 126 (CA).   [79] *Greatrex* [1999] 1 Cr App R 126 (CA).
[80] *Perman* [1996] 1 Cr App R 24 (CA); *Roberts* [1990] Crim LR 122 (CA).
[81] *Bainbridge* [1960] 1 QB 129 (CA); *Mahmood* [1994] Crim LR 368.
[82] *R v D* [2005] EWCA Crim 1981, para. 38.   [83] (1979) 68 Cr App R 128 (HL).
[84] See also Lord Hutton in *English* [1997] 3 WLR 959 at 981 (HL).   [85] (1573) 2 Plowd 473.

(7) In *Johnson v Youden*[86] it was emphasized that the defendant must foresee or know the circumstances of the act that render the act criminal. Knowledge here includes a defendant who deliberately shuts his or her eyes to the circumstances.[87] So, if Fred gives Pip a hammer to damage some property Fred is guilty as an accessory only if he knows that the property belongs to someone other than Pip. If Fred believes the property belongs to Pip (i.e. he thinks Pip planned to damage his own property) then Fred is not an accessory to criminal damage. Of course, Fred does not need to know matters which are not aspects of the *actus reus* of the offence (e.g. the value of the property).

(8) In *Powell* it was suggested that the accomplice must foresee that the principal will act with the necessary *mens rea* for the offence.[88] So to be liable as an accessory to murder the accomplice must foresee that the principal will act with the intention to kill or cause grievous bodily harm. If the alleged accomplice foresees only that the principal may accidentally kill he cannot be convicted as an accomplice to murder. To some commentators this is unsatisfactory: should not a person who assists another foreseeing he will kill, which indeed he does, not at least be guilty of manslaughter?[89] The Court of Appeal considered the issue in the following case:

R v Day; R v Day
[2001] EWCA Crim 1594 (CA)

Marc Day, Ian Day, and Stephen Roberts were charged with the murder of Paul Gardener, after the three of them had attacked him. Roberts and Ian Day were convicted of murder and Marc Day was convicted of manslaughter. In this extract Laws LJ considers the argument of Marc Day that these verdicts were inconsistent.

Lord Justice Laws

[52] . . . [I]t is not part of the law of joint enterprise that a secondary party, B, must share the *mens rea* of principal offender, A—see *R v Slack* [1989] 1 QB 775 and *R v Hyde* [1991] 1 QB 134 where it was made clear that foresight of what the principal may do is sufficient *mens rea* for the accessory even if there is no actual agreement between him and the principal. In *Powell and English* itself a major question was whether a secondary party in a murder case must be shown to have been actuated by the *mens rea* required in the principal offender, and the question was answered in the negative. The subject matter of a joint enterprise is not a state of mind or intention but an objective act which it is contemplated will or might be done.

[53] That proposition we think provides the key to the right result in a class of case which is not, so far as counsel's researches have revealed, distinctly the subject of any authority. Suppose that the participants in a joint enterprise all propose or foresee the same kind of violence being inflicted on their victim, let it be punching with the possibility of kicking to follow. On that they are at one. But two of them harbour a subjective intention to inflict really serious injury by means of such violence. The third harbours only, or foresees or intends only, that some harm might be done. One of those actuated by an intent to do grievous bodily harm punches or kicks the victim just as all three foresaw. The victim falls and suffers a

---

[86] [1950] 1 All ER 300 (DC).   [87] *J.F. Alford* [1997] 2 Cr App R 236 (CA).

[88] See also *Dunbar* [1988] Crim LR 693 (CA) and *Wan and Chan* [1995] Crim LR 296 (PC).

[89] See also *Stewart and Schofield* [1995] 1 Cr App R 441 (CA); *Gilmour* [2000] 2 Cr App R 407 (CA(NI)).

subdural haemorrhage and dies. The principal is guilty of murder as he had the mens rea required. So also is the accessory who, like him, intended or contemplated the infliction of the serious injury. What of the third adventurer? Mr Fitzgerald submits he must escape altogether because he did not foresee a murderous state of mind would be harboured by his fellows. Yet if his fellows had entertained only an intention to do some harm and otherwise the facts were the same, all three would be guilty of manslaughter. It does not seem to us that that can be right. In such a case there was a joint enterprise at least to inflict some harm, and that is not negated by the larger intentions of the other two adventurers. In our judgment in such a case there is no reason why the participants should not be convicted and sentenced appropriately as their several states of mind dictate. That was what was done here. Marc Day's conviction is perfectly safe. His appeal, like those of the others, is dismissed.

Appeal dismissed

In *Attorney-General's Reference (No. 3 of 2004)*[90] the Court of Appeal suggested that the key issue was whether the act of the principal was 'fundamentally different' from that foreseen by the accomplice. This was to be decided by the jury. If the killing by the principal was fundamentally different then it was outside the scope of the joint enterprise and the defendant could not be liable for it.

3.3 IS THERE A SPECIAL RULE FOR PROCURING?

There has been some debate over whether or not procuring requires an intention that the principle commits the crime. It will be recalled that 'procuring' has been defined as 'to produce by endeavour'.[91] The phrase 'by endeavour' implies that there must be a purpose to produce a result, in other words direct intention.[92] However, the Court of Appeal in *Rook*,[93] while not wanting finally to resolve on the issue, suggested it would be 'odd' if procuring required intention, while the other forms of accessorial liability did not require intention. *Bryce*[94] also implies there is no special *mens rea* for procuring.

3.4 IS THERE A SPECIAL RULE FOR OFFENCES OF STRICT LIABILITY?

The answer is simply no. Although the principal can be convicted without proof of a particular state of mind, the accomplice must have the full *mens rea* required for an accomplice. This was made clear in *Callow v Tillstone*.[95]

3.5 THE EFFECT OF PROVOCATION ON ACCESSORIES

In *McKechnie*[96] the principal was provoked into killing the victim. The Court of Appeal felt that this meant that those with him could not be accessories. The thinking behind this was that the person who lost his or her self-control could no longer be said to be acting in

---

[90] [2005] EWCA Crim 1882.
[91] *Attorney-General's Reference (No. 1 of 1975)* [1975] 2 All ER 684 (CA).
[92] *Blakely and Sutton v DPP* [1991] Crim LR 763 (DC). [93] (1993) 97 Cr App R 327 (CA).
[94] [2004] 2 Cr App R 37. [95] (1900) 83 LT 411. [96] [1992] Crim LR 194 (CA).

consort with others.[97] According to the Court of Appeal in *Marks*,[98] provocation is a defence to an accessory charged with murder. So, if Greg is insulted by Tim and Greg then asks his friend Pete to kill Tim, which Pete does, Greg can rely on the defence of provocation in response to a charge of counselling murder.

3.6 THE SELLING OF DANGEROUS ITEMS

What if a person asks a shop owner to sell him an item which the shopkeeper is aware will be used in the commission of a crime? The position from *NCB v Gamble*[99] appears to be that in such a case the shopkeeper can be guilty as an accomplice:

> If one man deliberately sells to another a gun to be used for murdering a third, he may be indifferent whether the third man lives or dies and interested only in the cash profit to be made out of the sale, but he can still be an aider or abettor.[100]

However, this is clearly not true where the shopkeeper has no idea that the item is being bought for use in a crime. Ashworth[101] supports the law, arguing that it is reasonable to require a shopkeeper not to sell a weapon which he or she knows may be used in a crime. It has been suggested that where the shopkeeper becomes aware of the criminal intent only after the contract for purchase has been made, but before the order is delivered, the shopkeeper is not an accomplice. The reason is that once the contract has been entered into the property belongs to the accomplice and so the shopkeeper has no legal right to deprive the accomplice of it. This seems to be rather circular reasoning: if it is an offence to supply the item surely there is no legal obligation to deliver it. Further, under contract law a contract for an illegal purpose is unenforceable.[102] There seems therefore to be a strong argument for saying that the shopkeeper who knows he is giving someone equipment which will be used in the commission of a crime may be guilty as an accomplice. There is, however, an opposing view which is that a shopkeeper cannot be expected to be responsible for what people do with what they buy in a shop, particularly where the items are everyday items.[103] Should Tescos really instruct their check-out assistants not to sell sharp objects to shady looking characters?

A slightly different scenario is where A has borrowed something from P and is asked by P to return it. If A is aware that P may use the object to commit a crime but nevertheless returns it, and P does indeed use it to commit a crime, has A committed an offence? In *NCB v Gamble*[104] Devlin J suggested, arguing, that returning borrowed goods should be seen as a negative, not a positive, act. He argued: 'A man who hands over to another his own property on demand, although he may physically be performing a positive act, in law is only

---

[97] The Homicide Act 1957, s. 2(4), states that the principal's diminished responsibility does not affect the liability of the accomplice.

[98] [1998] Crim LR 676 (CA).   [99] [1959] 1 QB 11, 20.

[100] *NCB v Gamble* [1959] 1 QB 11. G. Williams (1983: 124) suggests that there should be no accomplice liability for shopkeepers who are selling ordinary goods.

[101] Ashworth (2003: 421). Simester and Sullivan (2003: 202) argue that the interests of potential victims should override any interests of shopkeepers.

[102] A point emphasized in *Garrett v Arthur Churchill (Glass) Ltd* [1970] 1 QB 92, 99 (CA).

[103] G. Williams (1983: 293).   [104] [1959] 1 QB 11.

refraining from detinue.'[105] There is a difference between the shopkeeper and borrower, in that there is no legal duty on the shopkeeper to sell, but there is a duty on the borrower to return property which is not his. However, it may be questioned whether there is a duty to return someone's property in such circumstances. Some argue that in such a case the potential victim's right to protection is more important than any property rights.

QUESTIONS

1. Alfred and Mary decide to commit a burglary. Alfred knows that Mary has a gun, but she promises she will use it only if they are disturbed by the homeowner. They are disturbed by a passing police officer, whom Mary shoots. Consider Alfred's criminal liability.

2. Elizabeth knows that Henry would like to kill Anne. She tells him where Anne can be found. In fact when Henry finds Anne he only hits her on the nose. Discuss Elizabeth's criminal liability.

3. James and John decide to shoplift. James knows that John has a flick-knife in his pocket. When they are stopped by a store detective, John produces a gun (which James did not know he had) and shoots the detective dead. What crimes have been committed?

4 SECONDARY PARTICIPATION AND INCHOATE OFFENCES

The following statements summarize the inter-relation of accomplice and inchoate offences:

(1) It is an offence to incite, conspire, or attempt to commit an offence.

(2) It is not an offence to attempt to aid, abet, counsel, or procure.[106]

(3) It is not an offence to incite or to conspire to aid, abet, counsel, or procure.[107]

(4) It is an offence to aid, abet, counsel, or procure an attempt to commit an offence.[108]

5 CONVICTION OF SECONDARY PARTY AND ACQUITTAL OF PRINCIPAL

Even if the principal has been acquitted it may be appropriate still to convict the accomplice. It is necessary to distinguish between the following scenarios:

(1) The principal has been acquitted because there is insufficient evidence that he committed the offence. In such a case as long as it is clear that *someone* committed the offence and that the accomplice aided, abetted, counselled, or procured him the accomplice can be convicted.[109]

(2) The principal has been acquitted because he has no *mens rea*. In *Cogan and Leak*[110] Mr Leak terrorized his wife into submitting to sexual intercourse with Mr Cogan. He

---

[105] At 20. [106] Criminal Attempts Act 1981, s. 1(4)(b).
[107] *Hollinshead* [1985] 1 All ER 850, 857–8, (CA). The case was considered by the House of Lords ([1985] AC 975) which did not express a view on *Hapgood and Wyatt* (1870) LR 1 CCR 221 (CCR). whether such an offence existed.
[108] *Hapgood and Wyatt* (1870) LR 1 CCR 221 (CCR).
[109] *Hui Chi-Ming* [1991] 3 All ER 897 (PC). [110] [1976] QB 217 (CA).

had told Mr Cogan that Mrs Leak wanted to have sexual intercourse with him. Here, although the principal (Mr Cogan) was acquitted because he lacked *mens rea*, Mr Leak could be convicted of procuring rape. So, even though the principal is acquitted because he lacked *mens rea* the accomplice can still be convicted. The same principle was applied in *Millward*,[111] where the defendant instructed his employee to drive a vehicle on a road. The defendant knew that the vehicle was in a dangerous condition, but the employee did not. The employee was charged with causing death by reckless driving, and the defendant of abetting the causing death by reckless driving. The employee was found to be not reckless and so was acquitted. The defendant could still be convicted of procuring the *actus reus* (the defendant had the *mens rea* necessary to be an accomplice).[112]

(3) The principal has been acquitted because there is no evidence that the *actus reus* was performed. In such a case no one can be convicted as an accomplice. In *Thornton v Mitchell*[113] a bus conductor negligently signalled to the driver of the bus that he should reverse the bus. The bus killed a pedestrian. The driver was acquitted of careless driving: quite simply his driving was not careless. It therefore followed that the conductor could not be convicted of procuring careless driving. It should be stressed this was not a case where the bus driver simply lacked the *mens rea*; he did not commit the *actus reus*: there was no careless driving.[114]

(4) The principal has been acquitted because he has a special defence. An example of such a situation may be *Bourne*.[115] The defendant compelled his wife to have sexual relations with their dog. The defendant was convicted of abetting the wife to commit buggery. This was even though the wife was never charged with buggery and had she been charged with that offence she was likely to be acquitted on the basis of the defence of coercion.[116]

(5) The principal has been convicted of an offence which the accessory could not have committed. For example, a woman has assisted a man in a rape. In such a case the accessory can be convicted.[117] The fact she could not have committed the offence herself is irrelevant.

6 CAN A SECONDARY PARTY EVER BE GUILTY OF A GREATER OFFENCE THAN THE PRINCIPAL?

What is the position if the accomplice has a more serious *mens rea* than the principal? Lord Mackay gave the following example:

> A hands a gun to B informing him that it is loaded with blank ammunition only and telling him to go and scare V by discharging it. The ammunition is in fact live (as A knows) and V is killed. B is convicted only of manslaughter. . . . It would seem absurd that A should thereby escape conviction for murder.[118]

---

[111] [1994] Crim LR 527 (CA).   [112] *DPP v K and B* [1997] 1 Cr App R 36 (DC).
[113] [1940] 1 All ER 339 (KBD).   [114] See also *Loukes* [1996] Crim LR 341 (CA).
[115] (1952) 36 Cr App R 125 (CA). See also *Austin* [1981] 1 All ER 374 (CA).
[116] See Ch. 12.   [117] *Ram and Ram* (1893) 17 Cox CC 609.
[118] *Burke* [1986] QB 626 at 641–2, approved by Lord Mackay in the House of Lords ([1987] AC 417 (HL)).

Lord Mackay added:

> I would affirm [the] view that where a person has been killed and that result is the result intended by another participant, the mere fact that the actual killer may be convicted only of the reduced charge of manslaughter for some reason special to himself does not, in my opinion in any way, result in a compulsory reduction for the other participant.[119]

So in such a case the accomplice would be convicted of a more serious offence than the principal. Glanville Williams has suggested that such cases should be regarded as examples of a 'semi-innocent agent' (although this expression has been disapproved by others).[120] In *Richards*[121] a woman hired E and F to beat up her husband 'bad enough to put him in hospital for a month'.[122] E and F did beat up the husband but were acquitted of wounding with intent to cause grievous bodily harm[123] and convicted of unlawful wounding.[124] It was held that the woman could not be guilty of counselling wounding with intent to cause grievous bodily harm (because she could not be convicted as an accomplice for a more serious offence than that committed by the principal). This reasoning was rejected in *Howe*. If *Richards* was heard today the defendant could be guilty of counselling wounding with intent to cause grievous bodily harm.

7 WITHDRAWAL BY A SECONDARY PARTY

What is the position where the accomplice is aiding, abetting, counselling, or procuring the principal, but then changes his mind and seeks to cease to be part of the criminal enterprise?[125] To escape such liability it is necessary to show that the withdrawal has taken place before the principal has committed the offence.[126] To withdraw from an enterprise it is not enough just to have a change of heart; something must be done. It should be recalled that the *mens rea* for an accessory must be established at the time of the act of assistance, not at the time when the principal commits the offence. So any withdrawal must take place before the act of assistance is effective.

Exactly what amounts to a withdrawal differs from case to case. There are no hard and fast rules governing this area. The overarching test is that the communication of withdrawal must 'serve unequivocal notice upon the other party to the common unlawful cause that if he proceeds upon it he does so without the further aid and assistance of those who withdraw'.[127] The following case examines in further detail the circumstances in which the defence of withdrawal may be available:

---

[119] [1987] 1 All ER 771, 799.

[120] Kadish (1987b: 183) argues that this terminology only adds to the mystery.

[121] [1974] QB 776 (CA).

[122] She hoped by regularly visiting him in hospital she might win back his affections!

[123] Offences Against the Person Act 1861, s. 18.   [124] Ibid., s. 20.   [125] Lanham (1981).

[126] As it is possible to aid, abet, counsel, or procure an attempt.

[127] *Becerra* (1975) 62 Cr App R 212 (CA). In *Baker* [1994] Crim LR 444 (CA) saying 'I'm not doing it', and turning around, and moving a few feet away were far from unequivocal.

R v Rook
[1993] 2 All ER 955 (CA)[128]

Adrian Rook and Andrew Armstrong were recruited by a husband to kill his wife. They were to be paid £15,000 and some jewellery. Rook recruited Mark Leivers to assist. The four met over a two- or three-day period to plan the killing. On the appointed day for the killing Rook could not be found. The husband nevertheless drove his wife to the agreed site and Leivers killed her. Rook gave evidence that he never intended to kill the wife, that his plan was to take the money and disappear. He appealed against his conviction for murder.

Lord Justice Lloyd

[I]f a person gives assistance and encouragement, such as would make him liable as a secondary party, and he then changes his mind, what must he do to make his withdrawal effective? Must he neutralise the assistance he has already given (to use the term adopted by Smith & Hogan, in *Criminal Law* (7th ed. 1992) at p. 154 and by Glanville Williams in *Criminal Law, The General Part* (2nd ed. 1961), para. 127)? Must he at least have done his best to prevent the commission of the crime, by communicating his withdrawal to the other parties, or in some other way? Or is it enough that he should have absented himself on the day?

. . .

Mr. Maxwell [counsel for the Crown] submits that where a person has given assistance, for example by providing a gun, in circumstances which would render him liable as a secondary party if he does not withdraw, then in order to escape liability he must 'neutralise' his assistance. He must, so it was said, break the chain of causation between his act of assistance, and the subsequent crime, by recovering the gun, or by warning the victim to stay away, or by going to the police. Mr. Hockman [counsel for the appellant] submits, on the other hand, that the Crown must prove that the defendant continued ready to help until the moment the crime is committed; and if there is doubt as to the defendant's state of mind on the day in question, or his willingness to provide further help if required, then the jury must acquit.

As between these two extreme views, we have no hesitation in rejecting the latter. In *Croft* (1944) 29 Cr. App. R. 169, [1944] KB 295, the surviving party of a suicide pact was held to be guilty of murder. Lawrence J. giving the judgment of the Court said ([1944] K.B. 295 at 298):

'The authorities, however, such as they are, show, in our opinion, that the appellant, to escape being held guilty as an accessory before the fact, must establish that he expressly countermanded or revoked the advising, counselling, procuring or abetting which he had previously given.'

In *Whitehouse* [1941] 1 W.W.R. 112, 115, Sloan J.A. said:

'Can it be said on the facts of this case that a mere change of mental intention and a quitting of the scene of the crime just immediately prior to the striking of the fatal blow will absolve those who participate in the commission of the crime by overt acts up to that moment from

---

[128] [1993] 1 WLR 1005, (1993) 68 Cr App R 78, [1993] Crim LR 698.

all the consequences of its accomplishment by the one who strikes in ignorance of his companions' change of heart? I think not. After a crime has been committed and before a prior abandonment of the common enterprise may be found by a jury there must be, in my view, in the absence of exceptional circumstances, something more than a mere mental change of intention and physical change of place by those associates who wish to dissociate themselves from the consequences attendant upon their willing assistance up to the moment of the actual commission of that crime. I would not attempt to define too closely what must be done in criminal matters involving participation in a common unlawful purpose to break the chain of causation and responsibility. That must depend upon the circumstances of each case but it seems to me that one essential element ought to be established in a case of this kind: Where practicable and reasonable there must be timely communication of the intention to abandon the common purpose from those who wish to dissociate themselves from the contemplated crime to those who desire to continue in it. What is "timely communication" must be determined by the facts of each case, but where practicable and reasonable it ought to be such communication, verbal or otherwise, that will serve unequivocal notice upon the other party to the common unlawful cause that if he proceeds upon it he does so without the further aid and assistance of those who withdraw. The unlawful purpose of him who continues alone is then his own and not one in common with those who are no longer parties to it nor liable to its full and final consequences.'

In *Becerra* (1976) 62 Cr. App. R. 212 this Court approved that passage as a correct statement of the law. The facts of Becerra were that the victim was killed in the course of a burglary. The appellant had provided the knife shortly before the murder. The court held that the appellant's sudden departure from the scene of the crime with the words 'Come on let's go' was an insufficient communication of withdrawal. So the appellant's conviction as a secondary party to the murder was upheld. In *Whitefield* (1984) 79 Cr. App. R 36, 39, 40, Dunn L.J. stated the law as follows:

'If a person has counselled another to commit a crime, he may escape liability by withdrawal before the crime is committed, but it is not sufficient that he should merely repent or change his mind. If his participation is confined to advice or encouragement, he must at least communicate his change of mind to the other, and the communication must be such as will serve unequivocal notice upon the other party to the common unlawful cause that if he proceeds upon it he does so without the aid and assistance of those who withdraw.'

In the present case the appellant never told the others that he was not going ahead with the crime. His absence on the day could not possibly amount to 'unequivocal communication' of his withdrawal. In his evidence in chief, in a passage already quoted, he made it quite clear to himself that he did not want to be there on the day. But he did not make it clear to the others. So the minimum necessary for withdrawal from the crime was not established on the facts. In these circumstances, as in Becerra, it is unnecessary for us to consider whether communication of his withdrawal would have been enough, or whether he would have had to take steps to 'neutralise' the assistance he had already given.

  Mr. Maxwell rightly drew our attention to a sentence in the judgment of Sloan J.A., already quoted, where he refers to the service of notice on the other party that if he proceeds he does so without further aid from those who withdraw. This may suggest that aid already afforded need not be neutralised. We agree with Mr. Maxwell that this attaches too much importance to a single word. But that is as far as we are prepared to go in this case. We are not prepared, as at present advised, to give our approval to his proposition in its extreme form. In his *Criminal Law, The General Part* (2nd ed., 1961), Glanville Williams quotes at paragraph 127 a graphic phrase from an American authority. (*Eldredge v. U.S.* 62 F 2d 449 (1932) per McDermott J.) 'A declared intent to withdraw from a conspiracy to dynamite a building is not enough. If the fuse has been set he must step on the fuse.' It may be that this goes too far. It may be that it is enough that he should have done his best to step on the fuse. Since this is as much a question of policy as a question of law, and since it does not arise on the facts of the present case, we say no more about it.

Appeal dismissed.

Do not forget that even where the defence of withdrawal succeeds the accused may still be guilty of incitement or conspiracy.

The rules appear to be slightly different where the accessory and principal have joined together spontaneously to commit a crime, rather than formally planned it. In *Mitchell*[129] a fight involving six people broke out in a restaurant. A, B, and D were on one side and U, V, and W on the other. During the fight V was left prostrate. A, B, and D left, but D then returned to beat V further. The Court of Appeal held that where a group simply spontaneously attacks someone it is sufficient to withdraw, simply to walk away; there is no need to communicate a withdrawal. However, *Robinson*[130] restricted *Mitchell*[131] to the facts of its case, and in particular the fact that in *Mitchell* A, B, and D had walked away, ending their attack; and D's return was, in effect, starting a new attack. Where, as in *Robinson*, the parties join together for a spontaneous attack, then there must be a communicated withdrawal if someone wishes to disassociate herself from the attack.

In *O'Flaherty*,[132] however, a gang (including the appellants) attacked a young man. He managed to escape, but some of the gang pursued him and found him. They attacked him again, this time killing him. One appellant claimed that although he was responsible for the injuries suffered during the first attack he was not responsible for the killing as he was not a party to that attack. The Court of Appeal suggested that it was for the jury to consider whether the second attack was in reality a continuation of the first, or a separate incident. However, they suggested the jury's main focus should be on whether the defendant had disengaged himself from the gang by the time the second attack took place by making an effective withdrawal.

8 ACCESSORIES AND VICTIMS

Where a provision in a statute is designed to protect a class of persons it may be construed as impliedly excluding their liability as an accessory. For example, in *Tyrell*[133] a girl under 16 abetted a man to have sexual intercourse with her. It was held that the girl could not be convicted of aiding and abetting the offence against her. The offence was designed to protect under 16-year-olds, not to criminalize them.[134]

---

[129] [1999] Crim LR 496 (CA).   [130] 3 Feb. 2000 (CA).   [131] [1999] Crim LR 496 (CA).
[132] [2004] EWCA Crim 526.   [133] [1894] 1 QB 710 (CCR).
[134] More controversial is where one adult encourages another adult to cause him actual bodily harm (e.g. as part of a sado-masochistic activity). Can the 'victim' here be convicted of aiding and abetting the offence against himself?

9 ASSISTANCE AFTER OFFENCE

There are a number of offences which are committed by those who assist a person after he or she has committed an offence.[135] It is, for example, an offence to impede the apprehension or prosecution of an arrestable offender[136] or to accept money (or other benefits) for not passing on information which would secure the prosecution or conviction of an offender.[137]

QUESTIONS

1. In a South African case, *S v Robinson* (1968)(1) SA 666, P and two others agreed with V that V should be killed by P so that V could escape prosecution for fraud and others could obtain insurance monies. V withdrew his consent to the arrangement, not surprisingly, but P killed him nevertheless. The offence committed was the one planned. However, key to the plan was that the victim consented and this element of consent was missing. Did its absence mean that the two others should be convicted? (The South African court held them liable as accomplices to attempted murder only, because their complicity in murder was dependent on consent.)

2. Paul lends Susan a gun. Susan asks for it back. She looks very angry and Paul fears she may use it to shoot someone, but he still gives it to her. Susan uses the gun to commit a robbery. Is Paul an accessory to the robbery?

FURTHER READING

Dennis, I. (1988), 'Intention and Complicity: A Reply', *Criminal Law Review* 649.

Duff, A. (1990), ' "Can I Help You?" Accessorial Liability and the Intention to Assist', *Legal Studies* 10: 165.

Smith, K. (1991), *A Modern Treatise on the Law of Criminal Complicity* (Oxford: OUP).

—— (2001), 'Withdrawal in Complicity: A Restatement of Principles', *Criminal Law Review* 769.

Sullivan, G.R. (1988), 'Intent, Purpose and Complicity', *Criminal Law Review* 641.

Taylor, R. (1983), 'Complicity and Excuses', *Criminal Law Review* 656.

PART II: ACCESSORIES AND THEORY

10 GENERAL THEORIES OF ACCESSORIAL LIABILITY

The person in the street, when asked to imagine a typical crime, is likely to think of an individual acting alone attacking a victim.[138] In fact, many crimes are committed by people

---

[135] A detailed discussion of the law can be found in J.C. Smith (2002: ch. 9)
[136] Criminal Law Act 1967, s. 4.   [137] Criminal Law Act 1967, s. 5.
[138] Wells (1999) argues that the criminal law is often based on an individualist model which makes it difficult to criminalize group criminal behaviour.

not acting alone but alongside or with the support of others.[139] The involvement and encouragement of others in committing crimes can affect the nature of the crime in a number of ways:

(1) The victim may regard being the victim of an incident involving a number of offenders as more terrifying and therefore more serious.[140]

(2) The offenders may feel that it is harder to withdraw from the criminal enterprise and keep going with it, when acting alone they would have desisted.[141]

(3) Where a group of offenders commits crimes together there is a greater likelihood of by-standers or anyone seeking to prevent the crime being harmed.[142]

(4) The offenders might be encouraged by others to commit an offence which they would otherwise shun. Indeed one criminologist has suggested that 'peer influence is the principal proximate cause of most criminal conduct, the last link in what is undoubtedly a longer causal chain'.[143]

As can be seen from the discussion in Part I of this chapter the law on accessories is in an uncertain state.[144] This is partly because the law has failed to articulate clearly a single theory of accessorial liability. This part will outline three theoretical models which may explain why one person should be criminally responsible for helping or encouraging another to commit a criminal offence. We will then go on to consider how these theoretical models may assist in some of the questions of the *actus reus* and *mens rea* of accessories that have so troubled the courts. It should not, however, be thought that if the law adopted one theoretical model the law would be crystal clear, because practical and policy issues may make the application of the principle undesirable.

10.1 DERIVATIVE THEORY OF ACCESSORIAL LIABILITY

Explanations of the theory

Under the derivative theory of liability the accomplice's liability derives from the offence committed by the principal. Supporters of the derivative theory have struggled to explain precisely what is meant by this, and various ways of explaining the theory have been used. It is said that accomplices are liable because they have associated themselves with the offence which the principal committed.[145] This is not an argument that accomplices cause principals to commit offences, but rather that in moral terms accomplices have placed themselves alongside the principals and identified themselves with the principals' offences.[146] Some commentators have put it in terms of the doctrine of agency: accomplices authorize the principal to commit the offence on behalf of both of them.[147] Joshua Dressler suggests that accomplices forfeit their right to be regarded as responsible only for their own actions by

---

[139] Some offences can be committed only by two or more people, such as the offence of riot (Public Order Act 1986, s. 1).

[140] Ashworth (2002: 412).

[141] Ibid. Dressler (1985: 113) argues that there is no statistical support for the view that offenders in groups commit more serious offences than individuals acting alone.

[142] Ohana (2000).   [143] Warr (2002: 136).

[144] This was admitted in the Law Commission Consultation Paper No. 131 (1993: ch. 1).

[145] American law treats a conspirator as a perpetrator: *Pinkerton v US* 328 US 640 (1946).

[146] Robinson (1997).

[147] Wilson (2002: 198) discusses whether a link can be made with the civil law of agency here.

choosing to assist another in committing a criminal offence.[148] William Wilson puts it in this way:

> If liability here is derivative it derives not so much from any community of purpose between P and A as from the fact that A, being in a position to thwart P's criminal endeavour, failed culpably to do so.[149]

This rather controversial version of the derivative theory attaches liability to the failure of the accomplice to prevent the principal acting. In other words it is a form of liability for omissions.

Criticisms of the theory

Critics of the derivative theory complain that this is all rather vague. It is normally regarded as a fundamental principle of the criminal law that individuals are autonomous agents who are responsible for their own actions but not the actions of others.[150] Only the most powerful of explanations should justify the infringement of such a central principle. It might be suggested that in cases where there is a very strong link between the accomplice's and the principal's acts some of the arguments used have force, but how can a person who offers a small amount of aid (e.g. babysitting for a person who is out burgling) be said to have fully associated herself with the principal's offence?

Does the theory explain the current law?

The following aspects of the current law appear to be in line with the derivative liability:

(1) The accessory is convicted of the same offence as the principal. So a person who assists in a murder is guilty of the offence of murder, and is liable to the mandatory sentence that follows.[151]

(2) If the principal does not commit the *actus reus* of an offence the accomplice is not liable for a complicity offence. If a husband hires a 'hit man' to kill his wife, he is not liable as an accomplice to murder if the 'hit man' does not commit the offence. There is no offence from which the husband's liability can derive.

(3) The *mens rea* for an accessory requires the accomplice to (at least) foresee the kind of act the principal goes on to commit. A person who has not foreseen that the principal will act in the way he does cannot be said to have adopted that act as his or her own.

However, there are other aspects of the law which fit in less well with the theory. For example:

(1) The House of Lords in *Powell*[152] explicitly rejected the notion that the acts of the principal must be authorized by the accomplice, as is envisaged in some ways of explaining the derivative theory of liability.[153]

---

[148] Dressler (1985).   [149] Wilson (2002: 203).   [150] Kadish (1987).

[151] Under the German system the accomplice gets a maximum sentence of three-quarters of what the principal gets (Ashworth 1999: 415). Ashworth objects to this system because he suggests that sometimes the accomplice is more blameworthy than the principal.

[152] [1999] AC 1 (HL).   [153] Especially those which draw an analogy with agency.

(2) The fact that even though the principal is acquitted it is possible still to convict an accomplice (e.g. if the principal has been able to rely on an excuse, or lacks *mens rea*). This, it might be said, has weakened the claim that the accomplice's liability is flowing from the principal's guilt.[154] For example, it might be said that there has been no legal wrong if the principal has sexual intercourse with the victim, honestly believing that the victim consented.

(3) The *dicta* in *Howe*[155] that it is possible for an accomplice to be convicted of a more serious offence than that committed by the principal appear to be a departure from the derivative liability. However, it could be argued that in such cases the liability derives from the act performed by the principal.

(4) The fact that the accomplice does not have to foresee the exact act of the principal may be said to undermine the derivative theory. For example, after *Powell*,[156] if the defendant knew the principal had a weapon, but the principal kills using a different weapon, albeit of a similar kind of dangerousness, the defendant can still be convicted as an accomplice to murder. Can a defendant be said to have authorized or associated himself with an attack which used a weapon the existence of which he was unaware?

In the following extract William Wilson explains some of his concerns about the derivative theory:

W. Wilson, *Central Issues in Criminal Theory* (Oxford: Hart, 2002), 220–4

The criminal law treats the accessory as if he had committed the wrong himself because whether or not he can be deemed causally responsible it is not unfair to hold him accountable. It is for this reason that the accessory is usually punishable within the full range of punishments available for that offence. This is not necessarily so. Under the German system, for example, punishment for secondary parties is formally discounted to reflect their participatory rather than executory status. There is no such formal discounting in common law systems. This reflects the common law's more pragmatic approach which permits much theoretical rubbish to be swept under the carpet. It allows punishment and condemnation of all those who are associated with the offence, which is a good thing. It does not necessitate rules capable of distinguishing fairly and consistently between different levels and forms of participation, which is a bad thing, on the presumed ground that the creation of such rules would pose a serious legislative headache. The absence of such rules, however, means that differentiating degrees and forms of involvement still goes on but becomes a matter of prosecutorial and judicial discretion tailored to questions of individual fault and participatory role. So it allows for the kind of sentencing flexibility which can punish the (non-perpetrating) instigators of crime as severely, or more severely, than their hired-hands, while also allowing the more typical accessory to be punished less severely than the perpetrator. The theoretical problem thus posed is that this undermines the notion that the accessory's liability derives from what the perpetrator, rather than what he himself has done.

---

[154] Kadish (1985).
[155] *Burke* [1986] QB 626 at 641–2, approved by Lord Mackay in the House of Lords [1987] AC 417 (HL). Kadish (1985: 405) explains such cases on the basis that the principal is a 'semi-innocent agent'.
[156] [1999] AC 1 (HL).

The range of problems left uncatered for by this fudging of the theoretical basis to accessorial liability spreads across the whole field of doctrine. Given that some cases of participation are equivalent under one analysis or another to perpetration while others are not, how can this best be instantiated in consistent doctrine? If liability is derivative, how do we deal with those cases where a co-adventurer goes beyond the common purpose if not what was contemplated? How do we deal with those cases where the principal commits a lesser/greater offence than that to which encouragement and assistance are offered? On what basis is it proper to deem a non-perpetrator to be guilty of the primary offence if for one reason or another it is not possible to convict the perpetrator, and so on?

A number of possible solutions may be mooted. An obvious solution is to abandon altogether the derivative basis to accessorial liability, already much disregarded, and render participation in crime an inchoate offence. This is the position adopted by the Law Commission which recommends replacing accessorial liability with two separate inchoate offences, namely assisting and encouraging crime. The advantage is that an inchoate basis to liability attacks the fiction that there is a necessary moral congruence between those who perpetrate crime and those who help or encourage its commission or that the principal was somehow acting as the secondary party's executive agent. It would, however, require complementary provisions for dealing with cases where, as in *Cogan and Leak* or *Bourne*, the secondary party procures the commission of the *actus reus* of the offence by an otherwise innocent or semi-innocent principal. The strong disadvantage of this proposal is that it ignores the intuition that it is often appropriate to ascribe authorship of a crime to someone other than the perpetrator. Such people should not labelled, along with mere mechanical assisters and encouragers, as mere facilitators, but as principals. As Sir John Smith has argued in the context of murder,

'those who are instrumental in bringing about a killing should not have their responsibility set apart from those who directly perpetrate it because . . . (we) feel strongly that D is responsible for those deaths. If we are going to punish him because he bears that responsibility, we are going to punish him for the homicide; and if we are going to punish him for the homicide, then he ought to be charged with, and convicted of, homicide.'

Another possible solution is to retain a form of derivative liability but to tie liability as an accessory not to the principal's mental attitude but to that of the secondary party. Somebody who acts for the purpose of effecting a criminal wrong arguably commits a different wrong from someone who acts for the purpose only of assisting or encouraging another to commit such wrong. This is so although in given instances culpability may be comparable. The wrong most obviously attributable to the uncaring supplier of a murder weapon, whether a private individual or a state licensed corporate arms dealer, is that of being a killer's 'armourer' rather than a party to a killing/murder. So those who help or encourage because they want the substantive offence to take place could be treated as principal offenders. Those who help or encourage because they merely wish to be helpful or encourage the principal offender in the commission of the offence could be treated as facilitators. The problem with this latter approach is that the distinction between these two states of mind will often be paper-thin and certainly sufficiently insubstantial to make for easy prosecutions. Another response would be to hang accessorial liability upon the notion of control. Both instigator and 'principal in the second degree' are prime movers and so easy to associate with the principal's deed. So where A procures P to kill T, A is the prime mover since, although C pulled the trigger on the gun, it was W who pulled the trigger on H's life. Such an analysis is consistent with the rationale for the doctrine of innocent agency. In the former case we have a conscious, purposive agent. In the latter we have an innocent pawn. But both involve, as executor, an agent who does his principal's bidding which should be enough to warrant equal treatment and punishment. The objection to both *mens rea* and control tests is that they do not cover the case of those who, without being in a position to influence the commission of an offence, nevertheless provide crucial assistance so as to put them on an equivalent causal footing with the perpetrator. If a secondary party, say by providing crucial information or supplying an otherwise unobtainable tool necessary for the commission of the crime, is a *sine qua non* of the crime's successful commission should he not, along with the perpetrator be held accountable for the commission of that offence?

An altogether more satisfactory way of dealing with the problem of different degrees of causal influence might be to create a structure of offences reflecting such difference. It seems extraordinary that the common law, unlike say the German system, makes no formal distinction between a person who successfully incites another person to kill her husband and an ordinary retailer who knowingly supplies the murder weapon. This can be done by drawing a distinction between causal and non-causal participation in crime with the former punishable upon an accessorial basis and the latter, involving lesser acts of assistance and encouragement, upon an inchoate basis. It makes obvious sense to require a causal connection in the case of inciting someone to commit a crime, given that the inchoate offence is still available for (non-causal) encouragement. Cases of assistance might though be treated differently since charging an inchoate offence is not an option for (non-causal) acts of assistance and, as explained above, proving even a minimal but for causal connection would be next to impossible in most cases.

10.2 CAUSATION AND ACCOMPLICE LIABILITY

The theory

A second theory is based on the argument that liability for accomplices should be based on a finding that the accomplice partly caused the harm to the victim.[157] This theory, in effect, argues that an accomplice is in effect a joint principal. Accomplices are not, therefore, being punished for the acts of the principal (as the derivative theory suggests), but rather are being punished for their own acts and their contribution towards the harm done to the victim.

Criticism of the causation theory

Critics of the causation theory would say that there are important moral differences between the person who stabbed the victim and the person who supplied the knife.[158] To say they both caused the victim's death is quite simply wrong. Although it may be possible to imagine a case where, morally speaking, both the principal and accessory were equally causally effective in bringing about the death, in many cases there are important moral differences between the two.[159] John Gardner suggests that although an accomplice and a principal may in some cases by their actions produce the same result this does not mean they are morally equivalent:

---

[157] For support for the theory see Dressler (1985) and K. Smith (1991).
[158] For a powerful criticism of the causation theory see Kadish (1985).   [159] J. Gardner (1998: 212).

> The principal in murder acted against one action-reason (the reason not to kill) while the accomplice acted against a different action-reason (the reason not to procure a killing). But both acted against one and the same outcome-reason (the reason not to do anything in consequence of which someone will die).[160]

It is worth noting that even if one is not fully convinced by the causation theory one may want to distinguish accessories whose assistance or encouragement played a tangible role in the harm suffered by the victim and those whose acts had a minimal causal relevance to the offence committed.[161]

Does the current English and Welsh law reflect the theory?

As already indicated, one difficulty with the causation theory of accomplice liability is that under the normal rules of causation an accomplice cannot be said to have caused the principal to commit the crime.[162] If Fred tells Penelope that she should kill Pip and Penelope does so, Fred cannot in English law be said to have caused Pip's death unless Penelope can be regarded as an innocent agent (for example, because she is insane or under the age of criminal responsibility). This is because of the doctrine of *novus actus interveniens*: a free voluntary act of a third party breaks the chain of causation.[163] Supporters of the causation theory of accessorial liability could respond in two ways:

(1) It might be said that the causation theory of complicity is not using causation in the sense of legal causation, but rather factual causation. In other words all that needs to be shown is that without the accomplice's act the offence would not have been committed at the time and in the place that it was committed.[164] Although the doctrine of *novus actus interveniens* explains why the accomplice is not a legal cause, the fact that he is a factual cause generates a good reason for holding him liable.[165] What is required is a moral causal responsibility, not strict legal causal responsibility.[166] Even with that caveat it might be replied that the courts do not even appear to require that the accomplice's actions are even a factual cause.[167] Supporters of the causation approach might reply that such cases are simply wrong.

(2) It might be said that the doctrine of *novus actus interveniens* is honoured as much in the observance as in the breach and need not be regarded as a part of the law on causation. Indeed in the case of an innocent agent we accept that a defendant can be said to have caused a third party to act in a certain way. Chapter 2 considers some of the cases and arguments over the status of the *novus actus interveniens* doctrine.

Joshua Dressler rejects the current approach in Anglo-American law in treating accessories and principals as both liable for the same offence and treating all accessories as equally guilty whether their assistance to the crime was very minor or not. His view is based on a support for the causation theory:

---

[160] Ibid.   [161] Dressler (1985: 133–4).   [162] Kadish (1985).
[163] See Ch. 3 for a full discussion of this doctrine.   [164] K. Smith (1991).   [165] Kadish (1987: 162).
[166] Wilson (2002: 202); Smith (2002: 132).   [167] e.g. *Wilcox v Jeffery* [1951] 1 All ER 464 (DC).

J. Dressler, 'Reassessing the Theoretical Underpinnings of Accomplice Liability: New Solutions to an Old Problem' (1985) 37 *Hastings Law Journal* 91 at 121–30

Substantial Participation Test

The test most similar to the current system and, therefore, most likely to be acceptable is the substantial participation test. This test would require drawing a distinction between two classes of accomplices: 'substantial participants' in the offense committed, who would be convicted of the same crime and punished to the same degree as the preperpetrator, and 'insubstantial participants,' who would be convicted of a lesser degree of the charged offense, or who would at least be entitled to categorically lesser punishment for the same offense.

It must be noted that this approach is not conceptually tied to causation, although its likely effect would be to exclude from the stiffest punishment some persons who are not causally tied to the ultimate harm. Because 'substantial participants' are defined as those who play a major or active part in the commission of the crime, the most peripheral participants, particularly those whose assistance may be little more than psychological encouragement, would be filtered out. Those accomplices whose actions are substantial would be fully punishable.

This approach is certainly preferable to current law because it excludes from full punishment those for whom, according to our clearest moral intuitions, full punishment is inappropriate. It would also separate out those least likely to be dangerous. Nonetheless, a number of objections may be offered to this approach.

The rule is too subjective for a jury to decide that a participant is a 'substantial' participant. It is true, of course, that no bright line separates the 'substantial' participant from the 'insubstantial' one. Juries frequently are required, however, to draw distinctions without any more guidance than their collective common sense. . . .

This approach fails to make the proper moral or utilitarian distinctions for less peripheral parties. This criticism is more significant. The concern here is that 'participation,' if not defined in terms of causation, will still result in morally inappropriate conclusions for precisely the same reasons the current system is unfair: people are not punished for their personal connection with the punishable harm, but for their decision to join the criminal enterprise. In short, forfeiture, with most of the negative components outlined earlier, remains the guiding principle of this test.

The substantial participation test only serves to use the forfeiture doctrine in a slightly more limited fashion. The test still ignores personal identity when the criminal seems to be so significantly involved in the crime that we are less uncomfortable with the idea that the person must forfeit her personal identity. The fact is, however, that active participation might have little to do with causal connection to the harm. Analogizing to a movie, an actor may have little effect on plot development even though she is on the screen frequently. She is like the fifth wheel attached to an automobile. On the other hand, many supporting actors, vital to plot development, are rarely seen on the screen.

Unless we shift our understanding of 'participation' to give it a causal meaning, therefore, this test may foster counter-intuitive results. *A* may provide a chemical crucial to the making of an illegal drug. Without *A*, the crime could not occur. Yet *A* may come on the scene for only a short time, while the manufacturers of the drug, *B* and *C*, are constantly on the scene. *A* probably would be treated, quite properly under this test, as an insubstantial participant. However, *A*'s personal participation in a causal sense seems to justify holding her fully responsible for the results, which could not have occurred without her. . . . It is the causal involvement rather than the amount of time the accomplice is 'visible' that troubles us and makes us feel the participant should be held fully responsible for the harm done. Surely, such a person is apt to be dangerous, perhaps more dangerous than anyone else involved.

The substantial participation test fails. To the extent that the level of participation is based on the amount of time a person is a part of the criminal activity, truly minor characters will be properly filtered out. Beyond that, however, it will fail not only in achieving utilitarian goals, but also in drawing morally correct judgments. The substantial participation test falters because it, like current law, fails to tie liability to causal participation. Trivial participants aside, the test still permits a person to forfeit her right to be judged and punished according to the degree of connection to the harm.

Control or Hegemony Test

The control or hegemony test, which has significant European support, requires that only those persons who actually control, or who seek and possess hegemony over, the other actors in the crime be treated similarly to perpetrators and given full punishment. Anyone else is considered less guilty or less deserving of punishment. This approach has the effect of making the law more consistent with the agency justification of accomplice liability. Not only does the accomplice who controls others fit more properly the idea of the civil principal, or master, but an accomplice who controls others is likely to be a necessary cause of the crime. But for the control or hegemony, the crime would not have occurred. The rule is also preferable to the substantial participation test because it provides more guidance to the jury. Control over the events is easier to define than substantial participation.

Although preferable to the status quo, this approach goes too far because it needlessly excludes from full guilt and punishment others who our intuitions tell us should be treated as fully punishable actors. One can easily posit a situation in which a person who lacks control or hegemony is nevertheless causally tied to the harm and, not incidentally, highly dangerous. The 'brains' behind a bank robbery, for example, may not be able to succeed in the criminal venture without hiring a skilled electrician to turn off the alarm system. Does our moral intuition reject the notion that the electrician should be held fully responsible for the harm that ensues? Should it matter that she is not in control of the other participants or the events? Assuming the requisite mens rea is present, are not all the essential elements of the crime, even as to the electrician, present? If they are, why not fully punish the electrician? From a utilitarian perspective, too, the person willing to use special skills to commit crimes is especially suitable for punishment.

This second approach, then, while making the agency approach more plausible and coherent, goes too far in permitting leniency. It excludes from full punishment too many actors, even as it generally ensures that those who are fully punished deserve it.

Causation Test

Under this test, accomplices fall into two categories: 'causal accomplices' and 'noncausal accomplices.' A causal accomplice is one but for those acts of assistance the social harm would not have occurred when it did. In effect, the causal accomplice is held accountable for their own crime and not for another's. She is a co-perpetrator because all of the essential elements of the crime—a voluntary act, the requisite mens rea, the social harm, and the causal connection—are provable directly against her. Consequently, full punishment is justified.

The noncausal accomplice, on the other hand, renders unnecessary assistance. The social harm would have occurred when it did even without the accomplice's participation. The noncausal accomplice would not be held accountable for the criminal acts of the perpetrator.

Because the test is not founded on either agency or forfeiture doctrine, the noncausal accomplice would be accountable only for the harm actually caused.

Like inchoate harm, a noncausal accomplice's harm is difficult to define. Surely, there is something wrongful and dangerous, whether or not particular harm ensues, in joining others' efforts to cause that harm. Just as the perpetrator who attempts to commit a crime is punished for the unsuccessful effort, the noncausal accomplice deserves to be punished for attempting to assist others to cause harm that would occur even without her assistance. Like the inchoate offenses of conspiracy or attempt, however, such criminal conduct is less harmful than actually causing the result.

The causation approach makes persons guilty of the harm they cause, not for the harm others cause. The same result can be reached by the conceptually less pure approach of holding the noncausal accomplice, like the causal one, accountable for the prepetrator's crime, while categorically mitigating the punishment of the noncausal accomplice.

There are several possible objections to the causation test. *By definition, causation never exists in cases of accomplice law.* This claim was recently advanced by Professor Kadish. If true, it renders meaningless the suggestions for reform based on causation. Kadish relies heavily on the causation analysis of Hart and Honoré, who contend that a voluntary, willed act renders any previous action, human or otherwise, causally irrelevant to the ensuing results. Thus, when A offers a large sum of money to P to kill V, the decision by P to accept the offered money represents the sole cause of V's death. We cannot say, under this theory, that but for the offer by A, P would not have killed V. According to Kadish, 'when we seek to determine the responsibility of one person for the volitional actions of another, the concept of cause is not available to determine the answer.'

Kadish explains that this view of causation is based on the criminal law's notion of moral responsibility. This notion is predicated on the idea that blame and punishment of an actor are justifiable only if we concede the existence of the free will of the actor. As Kadish explains it, this doctrine of free will renders human action fundamentally different from the unwilled responses of nonhuman forces or the actions of coerced humans. Free will makes it impossible to predict how prior conditions will affect that person. '[E]very volitional actor is a wild card.' Forces of nature, however, are predictable:

'Experience teaches us that natural events occur in consequence of some antecedent events. . . . Barring miracles, so long as we know the causal laws we can speak with certainty. . . . We can say in every instance either that the event would not have happened if that condition were not present, or that it would have occurred even if the condition were absent. . . . The laws of cause and effect permit no other conclusion.'

Kadish's points are important. Blame *is* predicated on free will; concepts of causation must take into consideration the difference between human and nonhuman responses to prior conditions. To concede this point, however, does not render meaningless the reforms recommended here. Nor, it should be emphasized, does Kadish claim otherwise. He concedes that causation *can* be broadly conceived to include human responses. He also concedes that when the changes are remote that a secondary party's assistance 'mattered,' traditional accomplice liability seems excessive. One may choose some term other than 'cause' to identify the appropriate distinctions between parties, but the moral arguments this Article espouses remain pertinent.

Kadish's point primarily demonstrates that proof of causation is more difficult when human, rather than natural, forces intervene. In judging accomplices, we really ask whether an accomplice's behavior '*could have* contributed to the criminal action of the principal . . .

[and whether] without the influence or aid [of the accessory] it is *possible* that the principal would not have acted as he did.'

The implication is that conviction is permitted upon a lesser level of proof of sine qua non connection in view of the unpredictable nature of human action. Once the issue is seen as one of burden of proof, the debate shifts. It is not that causation is not morally important. We simply might need to prove it differently or apply a less demanding burden of proof.

In fact, it is not always harder to prove causation when humans rather than inanimate forces intervene. For example, it is probably easier for a jury to conclude that *A*'s paying *P* a million dollars to kill *V* was a cause of the ensuing murder than it is to say that cigarette smoking killed a particular cancer victim. That is, it is easier in the first case than in the second to say that but for the first event, i.e., the million dollar payment or the cigarette smoking, the second event, i.e., the killing or the cancer death, would not have occurred when it did. People reach causal conclusions not only by application of scientific principles that are explained to them by experts, but also by application of personal human experience. In the cigarette smoking case, jurors must rely heavily on the expertise of medical witnesses; in the solicitation situation, however, they can draw upon their own common sense knowledge about how people react to certain human stimuli. Admittedly, humans are less predictable than well-understood scientific forces. Ultimately, however, causation is a common sense principle that we use to reach judgments about a person's moral and legal responsibility for actions. As long as we are prepared to allow juries to reach common sense conclusions about causal responsibility without requiring scientific certainty, we can reaffirm the importance of causation to accomplice liability. We thereby allow the law to reach results that come much closer than current law to apportioning guilt and punishment to the degree of personal causal connection to social harm.

Causal connection is usually nothing more than a fortuity, and it is morally senseless and socially counter-productive to proportion guilt or punishment on such a basis. Although fortuity sometimes plays a significant role in drawing causal lines, the moral importance of drawing distinctions based on the formalities of causation has been recognized consistently in the common-law treatment of perpetrators of harm. Moreover, many states have penal codes that follow the common law on this matter, and statutes that strip causation from accomplice law would be inconsistent with their general penal philosophy.

The utilitarian criticism, although plausible, also lacks serious substance. If the implication of the argument is that the suggested approach is too lenient, it must be remembered that a finding that an actor is a noncausal accomplice does not result in exoneration, but only in mitigation of what may be an otherwise rather severe penalty. Indeed, one general deterrence approach would call for mitigation of punishment of all accomplices; under that theory, the causation test does not go far enough in mitigation. Clearly, current law makes less utilitarian sense than a legal system that comes reasonably close to assuring that the greatest punishment is inflicted upon the criminal masterminds and those who possess necessary specialized skills or instrumentalities.

The causation approach may make philosophical sense, but how is a jury to decide the degree of influence of the accomplice's conduct? This 'difficulty of proof' problem, similar to that of defining substantial participants, exists for many aspects of criminal litigation. . . . Admittedly, causation will not always be easy to prove in the accomplice context. In most cases, however, the facts should make answers rather predictable. In others, common sense should prevail. Lest it be forgotten, if the proposed reforms result in a jury finding of noncausation, the outcome is not acquittal, but less severe punishment. Finally, if the practical problems of proof ultimately seem too severe, a state might shift the burden of persuasion regarding causation to accomplices, requiring them to prove that their assistance was not causally necessary.

. . .

Of the three suggested changes to accomplice law, the best approach treats accomplices the same as perpetrators by evaluating the degree of guilt or punishment on the basis of the harm that the accomplice causes.

10.3 INCHOATE MODEL

The inchoate model proposes that accomplice liability should be seen as an inchoate offence.[168] In other words, the accomplice's liability does not turn on the guilt of the principal, but rather on the act of the defendant in offering assistance to the principal, believing that the act will be one of assistance or encouragement. Crucially the inchoate model does not require that there is a principal who goes on to commit the crime or the accomplice's acts were actually assisting or encouraging the principal. So if Alan asks Brian to kill Alan's wife he can be liable as an accomplice whether Brian says 'certainly not' and reports Alan to the police; whether Brian goes ahead and kills as requested; or whether the evidence establishes that Brian killed Alan's wife but would have done so even if Alan had not asked him to. In other words, being an accessory involves offering what the defendant believes will be assistance or encouragement to commit a crime; what the principal subsequently did would be irrelevant.[169]

The principal argument behind the inchoate model is that once the accomplice has uttered his words of encouragement, or provided his acts of assistance, then whether the principal goes on to commit the crime is outside the accomplice's control and is entirely up to the principal. The chance outcome of the principal's response should not affect the accomplice's moral blameworthiness or criminal liability.[170]

In the following passage John Spencer puts forward the argument in favour of an inchoate model of accessorial liability, which he suggests could be called facilitation.

J. Spencer, 'Trying to Help Another Person Commit a Crime' in P. Smith (ed.), *Criminal Law: Essays in Honour of J.C. Smith* (London: Butterworths, 1987), 148 at 159–63

If I urge you to rob a bank, burn down a house or maim an enemy I am in serious trouble whether or not you do so, because my behaviour amounts to the inchoate offence of incitement. In addition, if you do commit the crime I encouraged I am likely to find myself guilty of your offence as an accessory. But if I furnish help rather than give encouragement it is a different story. If I merely lend you my car for the robbery, or give you the keys to the house, or sell you a handy cosh, or show you how to use it, or discover for you where you will be able to belabour your intended victim alone and unsuspecting, I may or may not be in trouble. If you commit the crime I knew you intended with my help to commit, I am likely to be an accessory, but if you do not, I may well commit no offence at all. I may be guilty of some

---

[168] Spencer (1987) and Buxton (1969).
[169] Law Commission Consultation Paper No. 131 (1993). For a sympathetic discussion of the paper see Giles (1990).
[170] Clarkson (1998).

specific offence of supplying equipment for a particular criminal purpose, for instance, under s 59 of the Offences Against the Person Act 1861, which penalises the supply of drugs or instruments intended to cause abortion. Sometimes the courts will bend the facts, or law, or both, to turn what I have done into incitement, conspiracy or obstructing the police. Failing any of these, however, I am guilty of no offence at all. This is very strange. In either case, I have done all that I have to do to incur criminal liability. It is no fault of mine—or to be accurate, it is not due to any lack of fault on my part—that the crime was never committed. If my behaviour was bad enough to punish where you actually made use of the help I gave you, it was surely bad enough to punish where I fully expected you to use it but you got caught before you had the chance. If you do eventually commit your crime, there seems to be no good reason why the police should have to wait until you have done so before they can proceed against me. In a number of legal systems, including some which derive from English common law, facilitation, like incitement, is generally punished, and is punished as an inchoate offence. The purpose of this essay is to argue that it ought to be so punished in England as well.

. . .

The first objection is that general liability for facilitation would be curiously out of proportion with the liability of the person who is helped. Take the following example. A, wishing to commit a burglary, asks B to lend him a jemmy, and B does so in full knowledge of A's purpose. That night, the police arrest A as he is about to leave his house on burglary bent. A has not yet committed his burglary, nor does his behaviour, which is purely preparatory, amount to an attempt. As he is still 'at his place of abode', he has not even committed the offence under s. 25 of the Theft Act of going equipped. Except for the dubious possibility of a charge of conspiracy to burgle based on an extended reading of *Anderson* A has committed no offence by acquiring the jemmy. So how can we justify convicting B for supplying it?

This is a considerable difficulty, but I think it can be answered by enquiring why, as a matter of policy, the law does not wish to penalize A. The reason, surely, is that he is still a long way from his objective, and has a number of psychological barriers to cross before he reaches it, at anyone of which he may change his mind and abandon his wicked plan. It seems unduly harsh to punish someone who may yet decide to behave himself, and it is practically unwise as well, because if a man stands to be punished as soon as he has begun to carry out his plan, having begun he may think he has nothing to lose by going on. But this reasoning does not apply to B who has knowingly supplied him with help such as advice or equipment. B has done the last act that he is able to do. He has passed his final psychological barrier. There is no question of his changing his mind and simply not doing it: as far as B is concerned the deed is done. So it is neither unjust nor foolish to punish B for helping A when we do not punish A.

. . .

The second objection to a general crime of facilitation is that it would be over-broad and thus oppressive.

Whether or not this is so depends, obviously, on the precise scope of the offence. I am certainly not proposing an offence which would cover a wider range of behaviour than is already caught by the existing law of accessories when the person helped gets as far as committing or attempting the crime for which the help was provided. The proposed offence of facilitation would be wider, of course, but only because it would occur whether or not the ultimate crime was committed or attempted. Thus it would not make the helper guilty where *he* had done any less than he has to do at present. It would only be broader than the existing liability of accessories because there would be no need for any further behaviour by somebody else over whom the helper, once he has helped, has no further control. For anyone who does not find *Bambridge* and the related case law oppressive, it is hard to see what would be harsh or oppressive in a general offence of facilitation. Of course, for those who feel that the law on accessories is already too much, a second helping of the same dish would obviously be unwelcome.

The offence of facilitation which I am proposing would cover two things provided they are done with an appropriately guilty mind, a difficult point which I shall try to deal with later. The first is actually providing another with equipment, advice or other help for use in the commission of a crime. This would make a person guilty in the *Bainbridge* type of case, but irrespective of whether a burglary took place. The second is offering equipment, advice or other assistance which is intended to be helpful in the commission of a crime. This would cover the person who has agreed to supply a particular would-be criminal with equipment, but has not yet done so: the sort of behaviour which the House of Lords pressed into the mould of conspiracy in *Anderson*. It would also cover those who hold themselves out as generally willing to provide equipment, advice or other help to anyone who wants it: like the person who made and marketed the radar-trap detector in *Invicta Plastics Ltd v Clare*, and the 'black box' manufacturer in *Hollinshead*.

Criticism of the inchoate model

The two main criticisms of the inchoate theory are as follows:

(1) It would require an extension of the present range of liability. Many more people would be potentially liable than at present. Of course, in itself this is not an argument against adopting the theory if it was thought that the extra people caught were sufficiently blameworthy to justify a conviction. But with current concerns with over-crowding in prisons and over-criminalization generally there would need to be a good reason for extending the net of accessorial liability even wider.

(2) Many people argue that the inchoate liability for accessory liability is too remote from any harm. If Alf tells Bert that his neighbour is away on holiday aware that Bert, a prolific burglar, may use the information to carry out a burglary, but Bert does not do so, not only is there no victim who suffers harm, there is not even any kind of attack against the victim. When one compares cases of this kind with the debate over the legitimacy of punishing attempted offences, the accessory's acts appear too distant from a tangible harm to justify a criminal conviction.[171]

Does the inchoate theory explain the law on accomplices in England and Wales?

It does not. The law is clear that if a principal does not commit the *actus reus* of an offence then an accomplice cannot be held liable, however much assistance or encouragement may have been offered. Of course, the law already recognizes incitement as an inchoate offence of encouraging another to commit an offence, and that crime is committed whether or not the incitee actually goes ahead and commits the offence. There is at present no comparative offence in relation to assistance.

---

[171] See Ch. 14.

11 THEORIES OF ACCESSORIAL *MENS REA*

What should the *mens rea* for an accessory be? As will be recalled from Part I of this chapter the law is far from clear.[172] The law is in part inevitably complex because of the number of different matters to which the *mens rea* must relate.[173] It must be decided what state of mind an accomplice must have in relation to the following:

(1) the accomplice's act;

(2) the act of the principal;

(3) the state of mind of the principal;

(4) the circumstances in which the principal acts.

Further, it must be decided whether in respect of these it is necessary to prove intention or recklessness or negligence. Three approaches will be outlined here:

11.1 PURPOSE

It could be argued that the prosecution should be required to show that it was the accomplice's intention that the principal commit the crime with the accomplice's assistance or encouragement. Supporters of such an approach may justify it on the basis that in the case of accomplice liability it is difficult to locate a harm to a victim directly caused by the accomplice and therefore it is appropriate to have a higher standard for the *mens rea*. Such an argument is particularly likely to appeal to those who support the inchoate model of liability. Such an approach may also find support from those who are concerned with excessive criminalization.[174]

In the following passage Sanford Kadish offers an explanation of why the law requires intention:

S. Kadish, 'Reckless Complicity' (1997) 87 *Journal of Criminal Law and Criminology* 369 at 391–4

The reason for the law's insistence on intention is not simply that liability for recklessly assisting the crimes of others would be bad public policy in so far as it might threaten the security of lawful conduct. It is also, and I think more importantly, attributable to the individualistic ethic, the belief that people's freedom to act within the law should not be restrained by considerations of wrongs others might commit. This, I suggest, more fully accounts for the law's different treatment of recklessly caused harms and recklessly assisted harms. A person may fairly be held accountable for the former; he caused them, they are what he did. The latter are what someone else did, not he, and he therefore should not be held responsible for them, unless he made them his own by intentionally helping another commit them.

The treatment of criminal liability for omissions in English and American law offers an instructive parallel. The commonly stated ground for not punishing a person for failing to

---

[172] Weiss (2002) provides a summary of the present American law.
[173] Weisberg (2000).   [174] Simester and Sullivan (2003: 212).

prevent harm to others that the person did not cause or have a duty to prevent is the insecurity such a rule would create in the everyday lives of ordinary citizens: how much of their own interests must people sacrifice in order to prevent how much harm to others that is not their doing? Since no line could be drawn with acceptable clarity, ordinary affairs would be rendered insecure and, in the words of Lord Macaulay, 'the whole order of society' would be disturbed. But it is evident that this can only be a partial explanation of the common law's limitations on liability for omissions. After all, the whole order of society is maintained even though people are held liable for harms to others they recklessly cause by their actions. Why should it be otherwise for harms they could but do not prevent? Surely it is a problem to determine just how much of one's own interest need be sacrificed for how much of another's. But the same basic problem is confronted in determining what constitutes reckless action and is solved by the test of gross deviation from the standard of conduct of a reasonable law-abiding person. An analogous test for omissions would perhaps be something like 'gross deviation from the standard of common decency.' Open-ended, but no more so than the standard of reasonableness. What is at work in omissions, then, is the norm of individualism which, while not necessarily denying the virtue of social responsibility, rejects the rightness, not just the imprudence, of coercing it by law. It is this same individualist ethic that strongly influences the traditional reluctance of the law to impose punishment on a person for harms that others cause by actions he does not intentionally assist, even though on a wider communal ethic he may be thought responsible for those actions.

Now for the related self-determinist component of the ethic, which I suggested was primarily conceptual. I can best illustrate this by returning to the earlier discussion of the father who recklessly lends his car keys to his daredevil son, knowing he has not learned to drive, resulting in a fatal accident. As I said earlier most would feel that the father deserves less punishment than the son. Why should this be?

It may be thought that the answer is the lesser probability of the harm happening as a result of his action than as a result of the son's action. For after all, whatever the probability of the son causing a fatal accident, the probability of the father's action resulting in a death is greater since it depends on the further contingency that the son should drive recklessly. But it is curious that we do not react in the same way to differing probabilities when the issue is causation, that is, when contingencies of happenings rather than of human actions intervene between the reckless action and the harm. Why not, if it is probabilities that are determining our sense of deserved punishment for unintended harms? An example: a driver knowingly drives with bald tires and bad brakes over a mountain road in winter, skids and kills someone. Do we at all feel his culpability is diminished because the accident depended on (i) a sudden rain storm, (ii) a drop in temperature which froze the rain on the road, and (iii) the presence of a hitchhiker on the shoulder of the road? I think not. Nor would the intervening events lead a court to deny liability because of the absence of proximate cause: a typical judicial response would be to find that the intervening events were 'foreseeable.' Yet the requirement of the concurrence of each of these events reduced the probability of the accident.

I suggest that the differences in our reactions when it is a volitional human action that intervenes is not the product of perceived differences in probabilities, but of the pervasive conviction, widely manifested in the law, that it simply matters whether the causal route goes through another person, because we perceive human actions as differing from all other natural events in the world. This is what I mean by the conceptual pull of the self-determinist perspective. It is the same way of seeing the world that lies behind novus actus interveniens: human actions cause, they are not caused. So recklessness with respect to a natural happening is not seen to be commensurable with recklessness with respect to another person acting in a certain way. You may be as culpable as another for the harm the other causes if you exercise your will to participate in his action. Otherwise, what he causes is his doing, not yours. The reckless helper does not cause or participate in causing the harm done by the reckless doer. So even if we are prepared to find the helper blameworthy for his reckless contribution to the upshot we are inclined to see his culpability as necessarily less than that of the doer.

As I say, I do not find all this convincing on a rational level, but it does seem to resonate with an ingrained view of the world which makes the causal route through which an upshot occurs a central feature in assessing blame. Where this view comes from is a bit mysterious. I suspect it's a product of our evolutionary development, somewhat like the urge for retribution or the feeling that one who intends a harm deserves less punishment if he fails than if he succeeds. But that's speculation. What I feel more confident about is that the tension exemplified here between the moral distinctions we intuit and those we feel able rationally to defend is a common feature of the landscape of our moral experience and plays an important role in the shaping of our institutions, like the criminal law, which rests upon it.

11.2 RECKLESSNESS

It could be argued that it must be shown that the accomplice foresaw that the principal would go on to commit the crime with the accomplice's acts of assistance or encouragement. Those who adopt this view will accept that this may mean that the accomplice needs to have a lower *mens rea* than that required for the principal. The argument in favour of recklessness is based on some of the ideas behind derivative liability. In particular, the argument that by joining together with the principal, foreseeing that he or she will commit a crime, the accomplice adopts that offence as his or her own.

Those who take the recklessness view divide on the detail of what the defendant needs to foresee. Easy cases are those where the action was agreed in advance: (e.g. 'we will burgle the house, but if the owner appears we will kill him') or where the agreed action was known to be dangerous (e.g. 'we will steal the car and drive it up the motorway as fast as possible'). Harder are cases where what was foreseen and what occurs slightly differ. If the defendant assists the principal foreseeing that the principal will stab the victim to death, should it matter whether the principal in fact shoots the victim?[175]

11.3 THE ACCOMPLICE'S *MENS REA* SHOULD BE THE SAME AS THAT REQUIRED FOR THE PRINCIPAL

This approach is in favour of requiring that the accomplice have the same *mens rea* as that required for a principal. So in a murder case it would be necessary to show that the accomplice intended the victim to suffer death or grievous bodily harm, while in a negligence-based offence, negligence would suffice.[176]

In the following passage Grace Mueller sets out some of the arguments in favour of this view:

---

[175] Clarkson (1998).

[176] English law does not take such a view: see *Callow v Tillstone* (1900) 64 JP 823 where it was held that negligence was insufficient as the basis for liability as an accomplice.

G.E. Mueller, 'The *Mens Rea* of Accomplice Liability' (1988) 61 *Southern California Law Review* 2169 at 2173

A. Justifications for the Full *Mens Rea* Approach

There are several reasons for requiring that an accomplice possess the *mens rea* of the offense before finding him or her guilty. First, as a matter of social policy, people should not have to constantly look over their shoulders to make sure that they have done nothing which might later subject them to criminal liability. 'A pall would be cast on ordinary activity if we had to fear criminal liability for what others might do simply because our actions made their acts more probable.'[177]

Second, since the concept of culpability provides the basis for our criminal justice system, the act requirement is secondary to the mental element. An accomplice's mental state is one of the reasons we punish a non-perpetrator in the first place. In many cases, an act is required primarily as proof that mental culpability exists. Thus, since the notion of culpability is central to our views of just punishment, it seems absurd to punish an accomplice who did not possess the requisite *mens rea*.

The societal goals of deterrence and retribution do not undermine the argument for a full *mens rea* approach. An accomplice who possesses the *mens rea* of the substantive offense will be deterred as much as the perpetrator, since punishment upon conviction is the same. But it is difficult to deter if one cannot anticipate being connected to the crime. Therefore, only the smallest incremental increase in the deterrence may be anticipated if the accomplice is held liable on some lesser *mens rea*. Further, retribution is founded, in part, on culpability. Generally, society wishes to see criminals punished only to the extent that punishment is deserved. Desert is calculated by the level of culpability involved in the crime, and culpability is tied to the criminal's mental state. 'Deeply ingrained in our legal tradition is the idea that the more purposeful is the criminal conduct, the more serious is the offense, and, therefore, the more severely it ought to be punished.'[178]

A final argument for requiring proof of the mens rea of the substantive crime is inversely related to the culpability rationale discussed above. Since, by definition, an accomplice does not carry out the action which constitutes the act requirement for the offense, the requisite culpability can be demonstrated only by proving that the accomplice had the *mens rea* of the substantive offense. In order to demonstrate that the accomplice should be punished, solid proof of culpability is necessary. Those who accept the idea that knowing facilitation or foreseeability is sufficient for liability might argue that more objective criteria are needed, because actually proving subjective *mens rea* is too difficult. This criticism, however, is easily answered. When a perpetrator is charged with a crime that requires a certain mental state, the state looks to proof that this was indeed the accused's state of mind. It then allows the fact finder to decide whether the prosecution has met its burden of persuasion. The same types of evidence should prove as persuasive in the case of an accomplice, even though no equally clear act may be shown from which judges and juries may infer the mental state. These arguments suggest that the law should require proof that an accused accomplice possesses the mens rea of the substantive offense in order to punish the 'correct' people.

---

[177] Kadish (1985: 353).   [178] *Tison v Arizona* 107 S Ct 1676 (1987).

12 THE THEORY OF JOINT ENTERPRISE

Is joint enterprise simply one way of being an accessory or should cases of joint enterprise be regarded as sufficiently different to justify different legal treatment? In the following passage Andrew Simester and Bob Sullivan argue in favour of the latter view:

A.P. Simester and G.R. Sullivan, *Criminal Law Theory and Doctrine* (Oxford: Hart, 2003), 224–6

'Intellectually', said Lord Mustill, 'there are problems with the concept of a joint venture, but they do not detract from its general practical worth. . . .'[179] One may hesitate to distinguish so readily between matters of intelligence and those of practicality, but it is true that the rationale for joint enterprise liability is somewhat unclear. Smith and Hogan claim that joint enterprise is simply an aspect of aiding, abetting, counselling, or procuring, which therefore falls to be 'governed by the ordinary principles of secondary participation.'[180] If that were true, there would certainly be difficulty in explaining the current law. But it is not true. Joint enterprise cannot be explained as a sub-species of assistance and encouragement.

The gist of a joint enterprise is concerted action, or agreement acted out. It is this element of agreement to commit crime A that triggers the doctrines of joint enterprise liability. That this is so is recognised in *Smith (Wesley)*, where Slade J notes that 'the terms "agreement", "confederacy", "acting in concert", and "conspiracy", all pre-suppose an agreement express or by implication to achieve a common purpose. . . .'[181] By contrast, none of aiding, abetting, counselling, or procuring presupposes an agreement or common purpose. S may, for example, render aid without P's knowledge, or she may offer advice to P without endorsing or allying herself with P's conduct ('if you must do it, and I want no part of it and wish you wouldn't, then do at least take these precautions . . .') Similarly, it is enough for abetment if S's encouragement is merely received by P: there is no need for that endorsement to influence P or even be acknowledged.

It is submitted that to analyse joint enterprise as a special case of aiding and abetting is misleading, in terms of both criminal law doctrine and its underlying justification. This is because the *actus reus* and, especially, the *mens rea* requirements of joint enterprise liability *differ* from those applying to participation by assistance or encouragement. There is no need to show a common purpose in standard cases of aiding and abetting. But it is S's commitment to that common unlawful purpose which justifies the law's requiring only that S must foresee the possibility of P's crime, rather than demanding that S must *know* the essential facts—which, as we saw, is required in the standard cases.

Aiding/abetting and joint enterprise are structurally unalike. In cases of aiding and abetting only one crime is at issue: crime A. S directly participates in crime A by her intended act of aiding or abetting that very crime. The wrong which makes S responsible for crime A is that deliberate assistance or encouragement: it is her act of directly associating herself with P's crime. In joint enterprise cases, the wrong is the agreement or confederacy. That agreement (to commit crime A) opens a wider door to liability; it exposes S to conviction for any foreseen crimes B, C, and D, committed by P in the course of executing the agreement. As such, S's connection to crime B is *indirect*. It operates only through the agreement.

---

[179] *Powell; English* [1997] 4 All ER 545, 548 (HL). [180] J.C. Smith (2002: 147).
[181] [1963] 3 All ER 597, 601.

It is important to recognise that aiding, abetting, counselling; and procuring are not doctrines that operate as ends in themselves. They exist as formally-recognised channels via which the law transcends the normal limitations of autonomy, individual responsibility, and causation doctrines in order to associate one person with responsibility for a crime committed by another. There is no reason, therefore, why the law should not recognise complementary doctrines where a similar rationale for extending responsibility applies. Joint enterprise presents just that situation.

Even so, an important policy question remains. Why should the agreement or confederacy make such a difference? Clearly, the law regards the joint unlawful enterprise as upping the ante, such that S becomes liable to be convicted of crimes to which she has in no way contributed.

By entering into an agreement or joint enterprise, S changes her normative position. She becomes, through her own deliberate choice, a participant in a group action to commit a crime. Moreover, her new status has moral significance: she associates herself with the conduct of the other members of the group in a way that the mere aider or abettor, who remains an independent character throughout the episode, does not. The law has a particular hostility to criminal groups: conspiracy to defraud, for example, is an offence even where individual fraud is not. As with the inchoate crime of conspiracy, the rationale is partly one of dangerousness: 'experience has shown that joint criminal enterprises only too readily escalate into the commission of greater offences'. Criminal associations are dangerous. They present a threat to public safety that ordinary criminal prohibitions, addressed to individual actors, do not entirely address. Moreover, the danger is not just of an immediately physical nature. A group is a form of society, and a group constituted by a joint unlawful enterprise is a form of society that has set itself against the law and order of society at large. Individuals offending alone do not do this. Thus concerted wrongdoing imports additional and special reasons why the law must intervene.

13 *ACTUS REUS* ISSUES

It is striking what a wide range of behaviour is covered by the *actus reus* of being an accessory:[182] from on the one hand a bully who compels a weak-minded person into committing a crime on his behalf; to on the other the wife of a burglar who gives him a cup of tea to send him on his way on his nocturnal activities.[183] Indeed the range of activities involved has led several commentators to suggest that it is not possible to provide one set of legal regulations and approaches to deal with the whole range of forms of accessorship.

In fact, under English and Welsh law actions which have only the most limited connection to the ultimate offence can generate accomplice liability. No doubt often those who could be prosecuted as accessories are not. As Sullivan[184] puts it: 'At present, we are governed by a very broad conception of complicity, considerably tempered by a lack of full enforcement.'

The following scenarios give a flavour of the kinds of cases which may be said to be problematic:

---

[182] Glazebrook (1996) argues that the *actus reus* of an offence should be defined in such a way as to include what are presently defined as principals and accessories.

[183] Williams (1990) supports the idea of reducing accessorship to influencing and helping. Help is much easier to understand than aid.

[184] Sullivan (1994: 254).

(1) Michael Allen[185] asks: 'A sees D, a motorist, standing beside a vehicle which has a punctured tyre. He offers to change the tyre. When performing this act of charity he notices that one of the other tyres is partially bald, and therefore illegal. If A completes the task, will he be liable for aiding and abetting D's offence of driving a vehicle on the road with a defective tyre?'

(2) Jerry, a generous host, provides copious amounts of alcohol at his parties. He does so even though he knows that several guests have driven to the party and will drive home with a blood-alcohol level above that permitted. Lord Widgery CJ in *Attorney-General's Reference (No. 1 of 1975)*[186] suggested he did not think such a host would be liable, but it is hard to see why not. Is it any different from a person who tells a groups of friends about a house that is easy to burgle knowing that amongst the group there are likely to be some who will go on to burgle the property?

(3) If a shopkeeper sells something to someone (e.g. a hammer) aware that the person is likely to use that equipment to carry out a crime (e.g. an assault) is the shopkeeper liable as an accomplice if the assault subsequently takes place?[187] Several commentators have expressed concern that if shopkeepers were not permitted to sell anything to someone they thought might possibly use it illegally then this would place a great burden on shopkeepers. Such concerns could be met in two ways: it might be suggested that a distinction could be drawn between ordinary goods, where there would be no liability for shopkeepers, and items which are particularly dangerous (e.g. guns or explosives), where shopkeepers could be expected not to sell the items to those they feared would use them illegally.[188] Others have suggested that the solution is that shopkeepers should be liable only if they sell items with the purpose of assisting in the commission of a crime.[189] That, of course, would be rare.

Other commentators are less concerned with the potential infringement of the rights of shopkeepers.[190] If someone thinks there is a real possibility that the item being sold will be used illegally the shopkeeper should not go ahead with the sale. The rights of the potential victims who may be injured in the possible offence outweigh concerns over interrupting the business activities of shopkeepers.

These examples demonstrate two concerns in particular: everyday common conduct which we would not expect to be an offence (offering a friend a drink) could constitute an offence.[191] Secondly, throwing the net of accomplice liability too wide could effectively constitute liability of omissions and possibly interfere with basic human rights.

14 WITHDRAWAL

As seen in Part I in limited circumstances it is possible to withdraw from a joint enterprise which would render you liable as an accessory. In the following extract K.J.M. Smith seeks to analyse the law on withdrawal for accessories:

---

[185] Allen (2003: 217).   [186] [1975] QB 773 (CA).
[187] For a detailed discussion of the American law on this see Rogers (1998).
[188] Williams (1990).   [189] Ashworth (2003: 421).
[190] Schroth (2000) discusses the relevance of free speech to complicity.
[191] Kadish (1997). For a dramatic example see Glazebrook (2001).

K.J.M. Smith, 'Withdrawal in Complicity: A Restatement of Principles' [2001] *Criminal Law Review* 769 at 772–4

2. What is the rationale for recognising a withdrawal defence in complicity?

Express judicial articulation of some rationales or policies underlying criminal law concepts is a comparative rarity in common law jurisdictions. Judicial treatment of defences in general, and withdrawal in particular, is no exception to this almost systematic reluctance to venture into conceptual justifications. As will be seen when some relevant case law is examined, the differing requirements specified for a successful plea of withdrawal are often consistent with more than one possible underpinning rationale. Before considering the coherence and implications of such requirements, the theoretical possibilities for withdrawal's underlying rationale(s) will be briefly reviewed. Established case law requirements may then be scrutinised alongside such conceptual and policy expectations.

Two types of supporting rationale are imaginable and commonly offered: one focuses on the power of a withdrawal defence to operate as an incentive for an accessory to think again; the second regards withdrawal as cogent evidence of the accessory's lack of, (or, at least, substantially diminished) culpability or future dangerousness. An incentive rationale rests on the belief that providing a route by which an accessory can extricate himself from a criminal enterprise will increase the chances of such a person doing so, thereby reducing the risk of the principal offence being carried out. Reasoning of this nature is of a distinctly quasi-justificatory character. Although withdrawal is unlike more orthodox examples of justification, there is nonetheless a trading of forgiveness of the accessory's earlier undesirable behaviour for the desirable social benefits of reducing the chances of the principal offence occurring. Such claims have impressed, for example, the American Law Institute and the Law Commission which acknowledged the 'social value of encouraging the reversal of the accessory's acts'. However, the reasoning's cogency is suspect. The most compelling ground for scepticism is the key assumption that the actor will be aware of this defence and, thus, capable of being influenced. Few, if any, other criminal law defences are so dependent on this assumption. Moreover, such a well informed and coolly calculating accessory might not set great store by the withdrawal defence if he is equally well informed of his possible residual liability for incitement or conspiracy. Yet, although its credibility is easy to overstate, the incentive rationale does not warrant complete dismissal. It is at least arguable that the clear, long-term establishment of such a defence in any criminal justice system percolates into the general social consciousness and especially the consciousness of those with criminal inclinations.

Can greater credence be given to an argument that the accessory's abandonment of complicity is a decisive indicator of the absence of (or significantly reduced) culpability or dangerousness? Under this rationale withdrawal assumes a quasi-excusatory guise; but unlike excuses generally, here the defendant cannot be said to be subject to some form of internal incapacity or external impairment preventing his actions from being broadly characterised as the free exercise of informed choice. It could be claimed that an accessory lacks full control over the consequences of earlier actions. Yet, he is in this position as a result of his prior culpable behaviour which generally disqualifies an actor from being excused. Rather than excusing an accessory's complicitous actions because of conditions prevailing at the time, here excuse looks to the redemptive quality of the later withdrawing actions: showing either, that the irresolute accessory is not culpable or insufficiently culpable; or that he merits excusing because he has shown himself to be insufficiently socially dangerous to attract a criminal sanction. As will be suggested later, the credibility of such reasoning leans substantially on the accessory's motives for withdrawal.

In sum, the case for accepting withdrawal as a basis for a defence, rather than mitigation of sentence, is not overwhelming. But, at the same time, it is far from lacking reasonably plausible underpinning logic and conceptual coherence. This, combined with the relatively well established credentials of the general principle of a withdrawal defence, argues for its retention in some form.

QUESTIONS

1. Do you think there is a case for abolishing accessorial liability altogether?

2. Why should the *mens rea* requirement for an accessory match that required for the principal?

FURTHER READING

Dressler, J. (1985), 'Reassessing the Theoretical Underpinnings of Accomplice Liability', *Hastings Law Journal* 37: 111.

Glazebrook, P. (1996), 'Structuring the Criminal Code: Functional Approaches to Complicity, Incomplete Offences and General Defences' in A.P. Simester and G.R. Sullivan (eds.), *Harm and Culpability* (Oxford: OUP).

Kadish, S. (1985), 'Complicity, Blame and Cause', *California Law Review* 73: 323.

—— (1997), 'Reckless Complicity', *Journal of Criminal Law and Criminology* 87: 369.

Lanham, D. (2000), 'Primary and Derivative Criminal Liability: An Australian Perspective', *Criminal Law Review* 707.

Law Commission (1993), Consultation Paper No. 131, *Assisting and Encouraging Crime* (London: HMSO).

Smith, K. (1991), *A Modern Treatise on the Law of Criminal Complicity* (Oxford: OUP).

Wilson, W. (2002), *Central Issues in Criminal Theory* (Oxford: Hart), ch. 7.

BIBLIOGRAPHY

ABBATE, F. (1992), 'The Conspiracy Doctrine: A Critique' in M. Gore and S. Harwood (eds.), *Controversies in Criminal Law* (Boulder, Colo.: Westview).

AINSWORTH, P. (2000), *Psychology and Crime* (Harlow: Longman).

AKDENIZ, Y. (1996), 'Section 3 of the Computer Misuse Act 1990—An Antidote for Computer Viruses' *Web Journal of Current Legal Issues.*

ALCOHOL CONCERN (2005), www.alcoholconcern.org.uk/

ALDER, C., AND POLK, K. (1996), 'Masculinity and Child Homicide', *British Journal of Criminology*, 36: 396.

ALEXANDER, D. (1995), 'Twenty Years of Morgan: A Criticism of the Subjectivist View of Mens Rea and Rape in Great Britain', *Pace International Law Review* 7: 207.

ALEXANDER, L. (1996), 'The Moral Magic of Consent (II)', *Legal Theory* 2: 165.

—— (1999), '*Propter Honoris Respectum*: A Unified Excuse of Pre-emptive Self-protection', *Notre Dame Law Review* 74: 1475.

—— (2000), 'Insufficient Concern: A Unified Conception of Criminal Culpability', *California Law Review* 88: 955.

—— (2002), 'Criminal Liability for Omissions' in S. Shute and S. Simester (eds.), *Criminal Law Theory* (Oxford: Oxford University Press).

—— AND KESSLER, K. (1997), '*Mens Rea* and Inchoate Crimes', *Journal of Law & Criminology* 87: 1138.

ALL PARTY PARLIAMENTARY INTERNET GROUP (2004), *Revision of the Computer Misuse Act* (London: APIG)

ALLAN, J., NICHOLAS, S., SALISBURY, H., AND WOOD, M. (2003), 'The Nature of Burglary, Vehicle and Violent Crime' in C. Flood-Page and J. Taylor (eds.), *Crime in England and Wales 2001/2002 Supplementary Volume* (London: Home Office).

ALLDRIDGE, P. (1983), 'The Coherence of Defences', *Criminal Law Review* 665.

—— (1989), 'Duress, Duress of Circumstances and Necessity', *New Law Journal* 139: 911.

—— (1990), 'The Doctrine of Innocent Agency', *Criminal Law Forum* 2: 45.

—— (1992), 'Common Sense, Innocent Agency, and Causation', *Criminal Law Forum* 4: 299.

—— (1993a), 'Sex Lies and the Criminal Law', *Northern Ireland Law Quarterly* 250.

—— (1993b), 'Attempted Murder of the Soul: Blackmail, Privacy and Secrets', *Oxford Journal of Legal Studies* 13: 368.

—— (1994), 'Threats Offences—a Case for Reform', *Criminal Law Review* 176.

—— (2002), 'Making Criminal Law Known' in S. Shute and S. Simester (eds.), *Criminal Law Theory* (Oxford: Oxford University Press).

ALLEN, C. (1991), 'Explaining Violence: Socio-economics and Masculinity' in D. Chappell, P. Grabosky, and H. Strang (eds.), *Australian Violence: Contemporary Perspectives* (Canberra: Australian Institute of Criminology).

ALLEN, F. (1981), *The Decline of the Rehabilitative Idea* (New York: New York Press).

ALLEN, H. (1987), *Justice Unbalanced* (Milton Keynes: Open University Press).

ALLEN, M. (1995), 'Consent and Assault', *Journal of Criminal Law* 58: 183.

—— (2003), *Textbook on Criminal Law* (Oxford: Oxford University Press).

ALLEN, R. (2002), 'Alternatives to Prosecution' in M. Maguire, R. Morgan, and R. Reiner (eds.), *The Oxford Handbook of Criminology* (Oxford: Oxford University Press).

ALTMAN, S. (1993), 'A Patchwork Theory of Blackmail', *University of Pennsylvania Law Review* 141: 1639.

AMNESTY INTERNATIONAL (2005), *Sexual Assaults Research* (London: Amnesty International).

ANDREWS, J. (1966), 'Robbery', *Criminal Law Review* 524.

ANON. (1951), 'A Rationale of the Law of Burglary', *Colorado Law Review* 51: 1009.

—— (1959), 'Developments in the Law—Criminal Conspiracy', *Harvard Law Review* 72: 920.

—— (1986), 'The Cultural Defense in the Criminal Law', *Harvard Law Review* 99: 1293.

APACS (2002), *Fraud in Focus* (London: APACS).

ARCHARD, D. (1998), *Sexual Consent* (Boulder, Colo.: Westview).

ARDEN, J. (1999), 'Criminal Law at the Crossroads: The Impact on Human Rights from the Law Commission's Perspective and the Need for a Code', *Criminal Law Review* 439.

ARENELLA, P. (1990), 'Character, Choice and Moral Agency', *Social Philosophy and Policy* 7: 67.

—— (1992), 'Convicting the Morally Blameless: Reassessing the Relationship Between Legal and Moral Accountability', *University of California Los Angeles Law Review* 39: 1511.

ARLIDGE, P. (2000), 'The Trial of Dr David Moor', *Criminal Law Review* 31.

ASHWORTH, A. (1975), 'Reason, Logic and Criminal Liability', *Law Quarterly Review* 91: 102.

—— (1976), 'The Doctrine of Provocation', *Cambridge Law Journal* 35: 292.

—— (1978), 'Transferred Malice and Punishment for Unforeseen Consequences' in P. Glazebrook (ed.), *Reshaping the Criminal* (London: Stevens).

—— (1980), 'Intoxication and General Defences', *Criminal Law Review* 556.

—— (1987a), 'Belief, Intent and Criminal Culpability' in J. Eekelaar and J. Bell (eds.), *Oxford Essays in Jurisprudence* (Oxford: Oxford University Press).

—— (1987b), 'Defining Criminal Offences Without Harm' in P.F. Smith (ed.), *Criminal Law: Essays in Honour of J.C. Smith* (London: Butterworths).

—— (1988), 'Criminal Attempts and the Role of Resulting Harm Under the Code, and in the Common Law', *Rutgers Law Journal* 19: 725.

—— (1989), 'The Scope of Criminal Liability for Omissions', *Law Quarterly Review* 105: 424.

—— (1996), 'The Treatment of Good Intentions' in A. Simester and A. Smith (eds.), *Harm and Culpability* (Oxford: Oxford University Press).

—— (2000a), 'Victim's Rights, Defendant's Rights and Criminal Procedure' in A. Crawford and J. Goodey (eds.), *Integrating a Victim Perspective within Criminal Justice*, (Aldershot: Ashgate Dartmouth).

—— (2000b), *Sentencing and Criminal Justice* (3rd edn., London: Butterworths).

—— (2000c), 'The Human Rights Act and the Substantive Criminal Law: A Non-minimalist View', *Criminal Law Review* 564.

—— (2000d), 'Is Criminal Law a Lost Cause?', *Law Quarterly Review* 116: 225.

—— (2001), 'Criminal Proceedings after the Human Rights Act', *Criminal Law Review* 855.

—— (2002a), *Human Rights, Serious Crime and Criminal Procedure* (London: Sweet & Maxwell).

—— (2002b), 'Re-drawing the Boundaries of Entrapment', *Criminal Law Review* 161.

—— (2002c), 'Responsibilities, Rights and Restorative Justice', *British Journal of Criminology* 42: 578.

—— (2002d), 'Robbery Re-assessed', *Criminal Law Review* 851.

—— (2003), *Principles of Criminal Law* (4th edn., Oxford: Oxford University Press).

—— (2004), 'Social Control and Anti-Social Behaviour', *Law Quarterly Review* 120: 263.

—— (2005a), *The Criminal Process* (Oxford: Oxford University Press).

—— (2005b), *Sentencing and Criminal Justice* (Cambridge: Cambridge University Press).

—— AND BLAKE, M. (1996), 'The Presumption of Innocence in English Criminal Law', *Criminal Law Review* 306.

—— AND MITCHELL, B. (2000), 'Introduction' in A. Ashworth and B. Mitchell (eds.), *Rethinking English Homicide Law* (Oxford: Oxford University Press).

—— AND STEINER, E. (1990), 'Criminal Omissions and Public Duties: the French Experience', *Legal Studies* 10: 153.

—— AND STRANGE, M. (2003), 'Criminal Law and Human Rights', *European Human Rights Law Review* 2: 139.

AUSTIN, J. (1956), 'A Plea for Excuses', *Proceedings of the Aristotelian Society* 57: 1.

AYRES, I., AND BAKER, K. (2005), 'A Separate Crime of Reckless Sex', *University of Chicago Law Review* 72: 599.

AYYILDIZ, E. (1995), 'When Battered Woman's Syndrome Does Not Go Far Enough: Battered Woman as Vigilante', *Journal of Gender and Law* 4: 148.

BABCOCK, T. (2000), 'The Psychology of Stalking' in P. Infield and G. Platford (eds.), *The Law of Harassment and Stalking* (London: Butterworths).

BAGBY, J. (2000), 'Justifications for State Bystander Intervention Statutes: Why Crime Witnesses Should Be Required to Call for Help', *Indiana Law Review* 33: 571.

BAKER, E. (1994), 'Human Rights, M'Naughten and the 1991 Act', *Criminal Law Review* 84.

BAKER, K. (1999a), 'Review', *Green Bag* 3: 103.

—— (1999b), 'Sex, Rape and Shame', *Boston University Law Review* 79: 663.

BALDWIN, J. (1997), 'Understanding Judge Ordered and Directed Acquittals', *Criminal Law Review* 536.

BALDWIN, R. (1990), 'Why Rules Don't Work', *Modern Law Review* 53: 321.

—— (2004), 'The New Punitive Regulation', *Modern Law Review* 7: 351.

BALOS, B., AND FELLOWS, M. (1991), 'Guilty of the Crime of Trust: Non-stranger Rape', *Minnesota Law Review* 75: 599.

BAMFORTH, N. (1994), 'Sado-Masochism and Consent', *Criminal Law Review* 661.

BANDALLI, S. (1992), 'Battered Wives and Provocation', *New Law Journal* 142: 212.

—— (1995), 'Provocation: A Cautionary Note', *Journal of Law and Society* 22: 398.

BARCLAY, G. (1995), *Digest 3: Information on the Criminal Justice System in England and Wales* (London: Home Office Research and Statistics Department).

—— AND TAVARES, C. (2000), *International Comparisons of Criminal Justice Statistics 1998* (London: Home Office).

BARLOON, J. (1996), 'An Economic Analysis of Group Crime and the Federal Sentencing Guidelines', *Georgia Law Review* 84: 2261.

BARLOW, N. (1984), 'Drug Intoxication and the Principle of Capacitas Rationalis', *Law Quarterly Review* 100: 639.

BARNETT, R. (1977), 'Restitution: A New Paradigm of Criminal Justice', *Ethics* 87: 279.

BASILE, K. (1999), 'Rape by Acquaintance', *Violence Against Women* 5: 1036.

BAYLES, M. (1982), 'Character, Purpose and Criminal Responsibility', *Law and Philosophy* 1: 5.

BAZELON, D. (1976), 'The Morality of the Criminal Law', *Southern Californian Law Review* 49: 385.

BBC NEWSONLINE (2005a), 'Police "solving too few crimes"' 10 March 2005.

BBC NEWSONLINE (2005b), 'Ladbroke evidence "insufficient"' 6 December 2005.

BBC NEWSONLINE (2005c), 'What do people shoplift?' 28 November 2005.

BBC NEWSONLINE (2005d), '"Half of Drivers" admit speeding' 7 February 2005.

BBC Newsonline (2005e), 'Rape Trial Collapses over Consent' 24 November 2005.

BBC Newsonline (2005f), 'Why are more men using prostitutes?' 1 December 2005.

BDO Stoy Hayward (2005), *Fraudtrack 2* (London: BDO Stoy Hayward).

Beatson, J., and Simester, A. (1999), 'Stealing One's Own Property', *Law Quarterly Review* 115: 372.

Becker, B. (1974), 'Criminal Attempt and the Law of Crimes', *Philosophy and Public Affairs* 3: 262.

Beckett, K., and Western, B. (2000), 'Crime Control, American Style: From Social Welfare to Social Control' in P. Green and A. Rutherford (eds.), *Criminal Policy in Transition* (Oxford: Hart).

Bedau, H. (1968), 'The Right to Life', *Monist* 51: 550.

Bein, D. (1968), 'The Theft of Use and the Elements of "Intention to Deprive Permanently" in Larceny', *Israel Law Review* 3: 368.

—— (1982), 'A Guide to Offences of Threats and Blackmail or "How to see the Forest for the Trees" ', *Israel Law Review* 17: 62.

Bell, B., and Harrison, K. (1993), '*R v Savage, DPP v Parmenter* and the Law of Assault', *Modern Law Review* 56: 83.

Bennion, F. (1983a), 'Letter', *Criminal Law Review* 205.

—— (1983b), 'Letter', *Criminal Law Review* 574.

Ben-Shahar, O., and Harel, A. (1996), 'The Economics of the Law of Criminal Attempts: A Victim-Cantered Perspective', *University of Pennsylvania Law Review* 145: 299.

Benyon, H. (1987), 'Causation, Omissions and Complicity', *Criminal Law Review* 539.

Berger, V. (2000), 'Rape Law Reform at the Millennium: Remarks on Professor Bryden's Non-Millennial Approach', *Buffalo Criminal Law Review* 3: 513.

Bergman, D. (2000), *The Case for Corporate Responsibility* (London: Disaster Action).

Berman, M. (1998), 'The Evidentiary Theory of Blackmail: Taking Motives Seriously', *University of Chicago Law Review* 65: 795.

—— (2003), 'Justification and Excuse, Law and Morality', *Duke Law Journal* 53: 1.

Bevacqua, M. (2000), *Rape on the Public Agenda* (Boston, Mass.: Northeastern University Press).

Beyleveld, D. (1998), 'Deterrence Research and Deterrence Policies' in A. von Hirsch and A. Ashworth (eds.), *Principled Sentencing* (Oxford: Hart).

—— , Kirkham, R., and Townend, D. (2002), 'Which Presumption? A Critique of the House of Lords' Reasoning on Retrospectivity and the Human Rights Act', *Legal Studies* 22: 185.

Bibbings, L. (2001), 'Boys will be Boys: Masculinity and Offences against the Person' in D. Nicolson and L. Bibbings (eds.), *Feminist Perspectives on Criminal Law* (London: Cavendish).

BINDER, G. (2002), 'The Rhetoric of Motive and Intent', *Buffalo Criminal Law Review* 6: 1.

BIRCH, D. (1988), 'The Foresight Saga: The Biggest Mistake of All?', *Criminal Law Review* 4.

BIX, B. (1993), 'Assault, Sado-Masochism and Consent', *Law Quarterly Review* 109: 540.

BLOCK, W. (2000), 'Threats, Blackmail, Extortion and Robbery and Other Bad Things', *Tulsa Law Journal* 35: 333.

—— AND McGEE, R. (1999), 'Blackmail from A to Z: A Reply to Joseph Isenbergh's "Blackmail from A to C" ', *Mercer Law Review* 50: 569.

BLOM-COOPER, L., AND MORRIS, T. (2004), *With Malice Aforethought* (Oxford: Hart).

BLUGLASS, R. (1978), 'Infanticide', *Bulletin of the Royal College of Psychiatrists* 14.

BLUMOFF, T. (2003), 'A Jurisprudence for Punishing Attempts Asymmetrically', *Buffalo Criminal Law Review* 6: 951.

BOGG, A., AND STANTON-IFE, J. (2003), 'Theft as Exploitation', *Legal Studies* 23: 402.

BONNIE, R. (1993a), 'The Competence of Criminal Defendants', *University of Miami Law Review* 47: 539.

—— (1993b), 'The Moral Basis of the Insanity Defence', *American Bar Association Journal* 69: 194.

BOVENS, M. (1998), *The Quest for Responsibility: Accountability and Citizenship in Complex Organisations* (Cambridge and New York: Cambridge University Press).

BOWDEN, P. (1996), 'Violence and Mental Disorder' in N. Walker (ed.), *Dangerous People* (London: Blackstone).

BOWEN, J. (1993), 'The Law of Conspiracy in the Context of the FBI's Record of Surveillance of Black Folk in America', *Western State University Law Review* 21: 219.

BOWNES, I., O'GORMAN, E., AND SAYERS, A. (1991), 'Rape—A Comparison of Stranger and Acquaintance Assaults', *Medical Science Law* 31: 102.

BOX, S. (1983), *Power, Crime and Mystification* (Tavistock: Routledge).

BOYLE, C. (2000), 'The Model Penal Code Revisited: What Makes "Model" Sexual Offenses? A Canadian Perspective', *Buffalo Criminal Law Review* 4: 487.

BRADY, J. (1980a), 'Punishing Attempts', *The Monist* 63: 246.

—— (1980b), 'Recklessness, Negligence, Indifference and Awareness', *Modern Law Review* 43: 381.

—— (1996), 'Recklessness', *Law and Philosophy* 15: 102.

BRAITHWAITE, J. (1989), *Crime, Shame and Reintegration* (Cambridge: Cambridge University Press).

—— (1999), 'Restorative Justice; Assessing Optimistic and Pessimistic Accounts' in M. Tonry (ed.), *Crime and Justice A Review of Research* (Chicago, Ill.: Chicago University Press).

—— AND FISSE, B. (1985), 'Varieties of Responsibility and Organisational Crime', *Law and Policy* 7: 315.

—— AND—— (1988), 'The Allocation of Responsibility for Corporate Crime', *Sydney Law Review* 11: 468.

—— AND—— (1993), *Corporations, Crime and Accountability* (Cambridge: Cambridge University Press).

—— AND PETTIT, P. (1990), *Not Just Deserts* (Oxford: Oxford University Press).

BRAND, S., AND PRICE, R. (2000), *Home Office Research Study No. 217, The Economic and Social Costs of Crime* (London: Home Office).

BRANDT, R. (1959), *Ethical Theory* (Englewood Cliffs, NJ: Prentice-Hall).

BRANTS, C. (2001), 'The State and the Nation's Bedrooms: The Fundamental Rights of Sexual Autonomy' in P. Alldridge and C. Brants (eds.), *Personal Autonomy, the Private Sphere and the Criminal Law* (Oxford: Hart).

BRATMAN, M. (1999), *Faces of Intention: Selected Essays on Intention and Agency* (Cambridge: Cambridge University Press).

BRC (2005), *Retail Crime Survey 2003/2004* (London: The Stationery Office).

BRETT, N. (1998), 'Sexual Offenses and Consent', *Canadian Journal of Law and Jurisprudence* 11: 69.

BRIDGEMAN, J., AND MILLNS, S. (1998), *Feminist Perspectives on Law* (London: Sweet & Maxwell).

BRIGGS, A. (1996), 'Provocation Re-Assessed', *Law Quarterly Review* 112: 403.

BRIGGS, H. (2002), *Euthanasia, Death with Dignity, and the Law* (Oxford: Hart).

BRODERICK, P. (1985), 'Conditional Objectives of Conspiracies', *Yale Law Journal* 94: 895.

BRODIE, K. (1995), 'The Obviously Impossible Attempt: A Proposed Revision to the Model Penal Code', *Northern Illinois University Law Review* 15: 237.

BRODY, S. (1976), *The Effectiveness of Sentencing: A Review of the Literature* (Home Office Research Study No. 35) (London: Home Office).

—— (1998), 'How Effective Are Penal Treatments' in A. von Hirsch and A. Ashworth (eds.), *Principled Sentencing* (Oxford: Hart).

BROGDEN, M., AND NIJHAR, P. (2001), *Crime, Abuse and the Elderly* (Cullompton: Willam).

BRONITT, S. (1991), 'Rape and Lack of Consent', *Australian Journal of Criminal Law* 16: 289.

—— (1992), 'Criminal Liability for the Transmission of HIV/AIDS', *Criminal Law Journal* 16: 83.

—— (1993), 'Defending *Giorgianni*', *Criminal Law Journal* 17: 305.

—— (1994), 'Spreading Disease and the Criminal Law', *Criminal Law Review* 17: 21.

BROOKMAN, F., AND MAGUIRE, M. (2003), *Reducing Homicide: A Review of the Possibilities* (London: Home Office).

BROWN, B. (1964), 'The "Ordinary Man" in Provocation: Anglo-Saxon Attitudes and "Unreasonable Non-Englishmen" ', *International and Comparative Law Quarterly* 13: 203.

BROWN, D., AND ELLIS, T. (1994), *Policing Low-Level Disorder: Police Use of Section 5 of the Public Order Act 1986* (London: HMSO).

BROWN, J. (1993), 'Economics: Blackmail as Private Justice', *University of Pennsylvania Law Review* 141: 1935.

BROWNLEE, I. (1989), 'Superior Orders—Time for a New Realism', *Criminal Law Review* 395.

BROWNMILLER, S. (1975), *Against Our Will* (New York: Simon and Schuster).

BRUDNER, A. (1987), 'A Theory of Necessity', *Oxford Journal of Legal Studies* 7: 338.

—— (1993), 'Agency and Welfare in the Penal Law' in S. Shute, J. Gardner, and J. Horder (eds.), *Action and Value in the Criminal Law* (Oxford: Clarendon Press).

—— (1998), 'Owning Outcomes: On Intervening Causes, Thin Skulls, and Fault-undifferentiated Crimes', *Canadian Journal of Law and Jurisprudence* 11: 89.

BRYANT, A. (1989), 'The Issue of Consent in the Crime of Sexual Assault', *Canadian Bar Review* 68: 94.

BRYDEN, D. (2000), 'Redefining Rape', *Buffalo Criminal Law Review* 3: 317.

BUCHANAN, A., AND VIRGO, G. (1999), 'Duress and Mental Abnormality', *Criminal Law Review* 517.

BUCKE, T., AND JAMES, Z. (1998), *Trespass and Protest* (London: Home Office).

BUCY, P. (1991), 'Corporate Ethos: A Standard for Imposing Corporate Criminal Liability', *Minnesota Law Review* 75: 1095.

BUDD, T. (1999), *Burglary of Domestic Dwellings* (London: Home Office).

—— AND MATTINSON, J. (2000), *The Extent and Nature of Stalking* (London: Home Office).

DE BÚRCA, G., AND GARDNER, S. (1990), 'The Codification of the Criminal Law', *Oxford Journal of Legal Studies* 10: 559.

BURGESS-JACKSON, K. (1996), *Rape: A Philosophical Investigation* (Dartmouth: Aldershot).

BURKE, A. (2002), 'Rational Actors, Self-Defense, And Duress: Making Sense, Not Syndromes, out of The Battered Woman', *North Carolina Law Review* 81: 211.

BURNEY, E. (2003), 'Using the Law on Racially Aggravated Offences', *Criminal Law Review* 28.

—— (2005), *Making People Behave* (Cullompton: Willan).

—— AND ROSE, G. (2002), *Racially Aggravated Offences: How is the Law Working?* Home Office Research Study No. 244 (London: Home Office).

BUSUTTIL, A., AND MCCALL SMITH, A. (1990), 'Fright Stress and Homicide', *Journal of Criminal Law* 54: 257.

BUTLER COMMITTEE (1975), *Report of the Committee on Abnormal Offenders* (London: HMSO).

BUXTON, R. (1969), 'Complicity in the Criminal Code', *Law Quarterly Review* 85: 252.

—— (1984), 'Circumstances, Consequences and Attempted Rape', *Criminal Law Review* 365.

—— (2000), 'The Human Rights Act and the Substantive Criminal Law', *Criminal Law Review* 84.

BYRNES, C. (1998), 'Putting the Focus Where it Belongs: Mens Rea, Consent, Force, and the Crime of Rape', *Yale Journal of Law & Feminism* 10: 277.

CAHILL, A. (2001), *Rethinking Rape* (Ithaca, NY: Cornell University Press).

CALLENDER, D. (1994), 'Wiful Ignorance, Knowledge and the "Equality Culpability" Thesis', *Wisconsin Law Review* 129.

CAMPBELL, K. (1984), 'The Test of Dishonesty in *R. v. Ghosh*', *Cambridge Law Journal* 43: 349.

—— (1987), 'Offence and Defence' in I. Dennis (ed.), *Criminal Law and Criminal Justice* (London: Sweet & Maxwell).

—— (2002), 'Two Distinctions that Do Make a Difference: The Act/Omission Distinction and the Principle of Double Effect', *Philosophy* 77: 211.

CANCIO MELIÁ, M. (2004), 'Victim Behavior and Offender Liability', *Buffalo Criminal Law Review* 7: 513.

CANE, P. (2000), 'Fleeting Mental States', *Cambridge Law Journal* 59: 273.

—— (2001), 'Responsibility and Fault: A Relational and Functional Approach to Responsibility' in P. Cane and J. Gardner (eds.), *Relating to Responsibility* (Oxford: Hart).

—— (2002), *Responsibility in Law and Morality* (Oxford: Hart).

CARD, R. (1973), 'The Working Paper on Inchoate Offences: Reform of the Law of Conspiracy', *Criminal Law Review* 674.

CARD, R., AND ASHWORTH, A. (2000), 'Criminal Law' in D. Hayton (ed.), *Law's Futures* (Oxford: Hart).

CARLEN, P. (1984), 'Crime, Inequality and Sentencing' in A. Duff and D. Garland (eds.), *A Reader in Punishment* (Oxford: Oxford University Press).

CARSON, W. (1982), *The Other Price of Britain's Oil* (London: Martin Robertson).

CARVEL, J. (2002), 'Half of All Pupils Admit to Breaking the Law', *The Guardian*, 8 April 2002.

CENTRE FOR CORPORATE ACCOUNTABILITY (2000), *Response to Home Office Consultation Document* (London: Centre for Corporate Accountability).

—— (2003a), *Safety Statistics* (London: Centre for Corporate Accountability).

—— (2003b), *Manslaughter Cases* (London: Centre for Corporate Accountability).

CENTRE FOR PUBLIC LAW AT THE UNIVERSITY OF CAMBRIDGE (1999), *The Human Rights Act and the Criminal Justice and Regulatory Process* (Cambridge: Centre for Public Law).

CENTRE FOR RETAIL RESEARCH (2003), Home Page: www.retailresearch.org

CHAMALLAS, M. (1988), 'Consent, Equality, and the Legal Control of Sexual Conduct', *South California Law Review* 61: 777.

—— AND KERBER, L. (1990), 'Women, Mothers, and the Law of Fright: A History', *Michigan Law Review* 88: 814.

CHAN, W. (1994), 'A Feminist Critique of Self-Defense and Provocation in Battered Women's Cases in England and Wales', *Women and Criminal Justice* 6: 39.

—— (2001), *Women, Murder and Justice* (Basingstoke: Palgrave).

CHAPMAN, B. (1988), 'Agency and Contingency: The Case of Criminal Attempts', *University of Toronto Law Journal* 48: 355.

CHARLOW, R. (2002), 'Bad Acts in Search of a Mens Rea: Anatomy of a Rape', *Fordham Law Review* 71: 263.

CHILDS, M. (2001), 'Sexual Autonomy and Law', *Modern Law Review* 64: 309.

CHOUDHRY, S., AND HERRING, J. (2006), 'Right Domestic Violence', *International Journal of Law Policy and the Family* 20: 1.

CHRISTIE, N. (1998), 'Conflicts as Property' in A. von Hirsch and A. Ashworth (eds.), *Principled Sentencing* (Oxford: Hart).

CHRISTLIEB, T. (1993), 'Why Superseding Cause Analysis Should Be Abandoned', *Texas Law Review* 72: 161.

CHRISTMAN, J. (1994), *The Myth of Property* (New York: Oxford University Press).

CHRISTOPHER, R. (1995), 'Unknowing Justification and the Logical Necessity of the *Dadson* Principle in Self-Defence', *Oxford Journal of Legal Studies* 15: 229.

—— (1998), 'Self Defense and Objectivity', *Buffalo Criminal Law Review* 537.

—— (2004), 'Does Attempted Murder Deserve Greater Punishment Than Murder? Moral Luck And The Duty To Prevent Harm', *Notre Dame Journal of Law, Ethics and Public Policy* 18: 419.

CLARKE, A., MORAN-ELLIS, J., AND SLENEY, J. (2002), *Attitudes to Date Rape and Relation-ships Rape: A Qualitative Study* (London: Home Office).

CLARKE, M. (2000), 'Lies, Damned Lies, and Insurance Claims: The Elements and Effect of Fraud', *New Zealand Law Review* 233.

CLARKE, R., AND MAYHEW, P. (1980), *Designing Out Crime* (London: HMSO).

CLARKSON, C. (1993), 'Theft and Fair Labelling', *Modern Law Review* 56: 554.

—— (1994), 'Law Commission Report on Offences Against the Person and General Prin-ciples: (1) Violence and the Law Commission', *Criminal Law Reform* 324.

—— (1998), 'Complicity, Powell and Manslaughter', *Criminal Law Review* 556.

—— (2000), 'Context and Culpability in Involuntary Manslaughter' in A. Ashworth and B. Mitchell (eds.), *Rethinking English Homicide Law* (Oxford: Oxford University Press).

—— (2001), *Understanding Criminal Law* (3rd edn)., London: Sweet & Maxwell.

—— (2005), 'Corporate Manslaughter: Yet More Government Proposals', *Criminal Law Review* 677.

CLARKSON, C.M.V., 'Corporate Culpability' [1998] 2 *Web Journal of Current Legal Issues.*

——, CRETNEY, A., DAVIS, G., AND SHEPHERD, J. (1994), 'Assaults: The Relationship between Seriousness, Criminalisation and Punishment', *Criminal Law Review* 4.

—— AND KEATING, H. (1998), *Criminal Law, Cases and Materials* (London: Sweet & Maxwell).

CLOUGH, J., AND MULHERN, C. (2002), *The Prosecution of Corporations* (Oxford: Oxford University Press).

COARSE, R. (1988), 'Blackmail', *Virginia Law Review* 74: 655.

COHEN, L. (1991), 'Sexual Harassment and the Law', *Society*, May–June: 1.

COHEN, M. (1979), 'Inciting the Impossible', *Criminal Law Review* 239.

COLEMAN, J. (1974), *Power and the Structure of Society* (New York: WW Norton and Co.).

COLES, E., AND JANG, D. (1996), 'A Psychological Perspective on the Legal Concepts of "Volition" and "Intent" ', *Journal of Law and Medicine* 60.

COLLIER, P. (1995), *Wounding/Assault Offences: From Prosecution to Conviction*, Home Office Research Bulletin No. 37 (London: Home Office).

COLLINS, H. (1982), *Marxism and the Law* (Oxford: Oxford University Press).

—— (1990), 'The Ascription of Legal Responsibility to Groups in Complex Patterns of Economic Integration', *Modern Law Review* 53: 731.

COLVIN, E. (1990), 'Exculpatory Defences in the Criminal Law', *Oxford Journal of Legal Studies* 10: 381.

—— (1991), *Principles of Criminal Law* (2nd edn., Toronto: Thomson).

COOK, D. (1989), *Rich Law Poor Law: Different Response to Tax and Supplementary Benefit Fraud* (Oxford: Oxford University Press).

COOK, P., AND LUDWIG, J. (2000), *The Effects of Gun Prevalence on Gun Ownership* (Washington, DC: National Beaureu of Economic Research).

COOPER, S., AND ALLEN, M. (1993), 'Appropriation after *Gomez*', *Journal of Criminal Law* 57: 186.

COPELON, R. (1988), 'Unpacking Patriarchy: Reproduction, Sexuality, Originalism and Constitutional Change' in J. Lobel (ed.), *A Less than Perfect Union* (New York: Monthly Review Press).

—— (1990), 'Losing the Negative Right to Privacy: Building Sexual and Reproductive Freedom', *New York University Review of Law and Social Change* 18: 15.

CORNELL, D. (1995), *The Imaginary Domain* (London: Routledge).

COUGHLIN, A. (1984), 'Excusing Women', *California Law Review* 82: 1.

—— (1998), 'Sex and Guilt', *Virginia Law Review* 84: 1.

COURTEAU, C. (1998), 'The Mental Element Required for Accomplice Liability', *Louisiana Law Review* 59: 325.

COXALL, A., KING, M., MEZEY, G., AND GORDON, G. (1998), 'Lifetime Prevalence, Characteristics and Associated Problems of Non-consensual Sex in Men: Cross Sectional Survey', *British Medical Journal* 318: 846.

CRESSEY, D. (1953), *Other People's Money* (Glencoe, Ill.: Free Press).

CRETNEY, A., AND DAVIS, G. (1995), *Punishing Violence* (London: Routledge).

—— AND —— (1997), 'Prosecuting "Domestic" Assault: Victims Failing Courts or Courts Failing Victims?', *The Howard Journal* 36: 146.

CRIMINAL LAW REVISION COMMITTEE (1980), *14th Report, Offences Against the Person* (Cmnd. 7844) (London: HMSO).

CROALL, H. (1992), 'Target Women: Women's Victimization and White-collar Crime' in R. Emerson, R. Dobash, and L. Noakes (eds.), *Gender and Crime* (Cardiff: University of Wales Press).

CROCKER, P. (1985), 'The Meaning of Equality for Battered Women who Kill Men in Self Defense', *Harvard Women's Law Journal* 8: 121.

CROFTS, T. (2003), *The Criminal Responsibility of Young People* (Aldershot: Ashgate).

CROSS, J. (1991), 'Protecting Confidential Information Under the Criminal Law of Theft and Fraud', *Oxford Journal of Legal Studies* 11: 264.

CROSS, R. (1967), 'The Mental Element in Crime', *Law Quarterly Review* 83: 215.

CROWN PROSECUTION SERVICE (1996), *The Offences Against the Person Charging Standards* (London: CPS).

CROWN PROSECUTION SERVICE (2005), CPS Publishes Latest Crime and Religious Crime Data (London: CPS).

CULVER, K. (1998), 'Analyzing Criminal Attempts', *Canadian Journal of Law and Jurisprudence* 11: 41.

DAN-COHEN, M. (2000), 'Basic Values and the Victim's State of Mind', *California Law Review* 88: 759.

—— (2002), *Harmful Thoughts* (Princeton, NJ: Princeton University Press).

DAVIS, K., AND ROY, J. (1998), 'Fraud in the Canadian Courts: An Unwarranted Expansion of the Scope of the Criminal Sanction', *Canadian Business Law Journal* 39: 210.

——, FRIEZE, I., AND MAIURO, R. (2000), *Stalking: Perspectives on Victims and Perpetrators* (New York: Springer Publishing).

DAVIS, M. (1986), 'Why Attempts Deserve Less Punishment than Complete Crimes', *Law and Philosophy* 5: 1.

DELGADO, R. (1985), 'Rotten Social Background: Should the Criminal Law Recognise a Defense of Severe Environmental Deprivation?', *Journal of Law and Inequality* 3: 9.

DELL, S. (1982), 'Diminished Responsibility Reconsidered', *Criminal Law Review* 809.

—— (1989), *Murder into Manslaughter* (Oxford: Oxford University Press).

DeLONG, S. (1993), 'Blackmailers, Bribe Takers, and the Second Paradox of Blackmail', *University of Pennsylvania Law Review* 141: 1663.

DENNETT, D. (1976), 'Considerations of Personhood' in A.O. Rorty (ed.), *The Identities of Persons* (Berkeley, Cal.: University of California Press).

—— (1984), *Elbow Room* (Oxford: Oxford University Press).

DENNIS, I. (1977), 'The Rationale of Criminal Conspiracy', *Law Quarterly Review* 93: 39.

—— (1980), 'Duress, Murder and Criminal Responsibility', *Law Quarterly Review* 96: 208.

—— (1987), 'The Mental Element for Accessories' in P. Smith (ed.), *Criminal Law: Essays in Honour of J.C. Smith* (London: Butterworths).

—— (1988), 'Intention and Complicity: A Reply', *Criminal Law Review* 649.

—— (1997), 'The Critical Condition of Criminal Law', *Current Legal Problems* 213.

DENNO, D. (1997), 'Sexuality, Rape, And Mental Retardation', *University of Illinois Law Review* 17: 315.

—— (2002), 'Crime and Consciousness: Science and Involuntary Acts', *Minnesota Law Review* 87: 269.

DEPARTMENT OF HEALTH (2000), *Protecting Children, Supporting Parents: A Consultation Document on the Physical Punishment of Children* (London: Department of Health).

DERBYSHIRE, P. (2000), 'The Mischief of Plea Bargaining and Sentencing Rewards', *Criminal Law Review* 895.

DERSHOWITZ, A. (1994), *The Abuse Excuse and Other Cop-Outs* (Boston, Mass.: Little, Brown).

DEVLIN, P. (1965), *The Enforcement of Morals* (Oxford: Oxford University Press).

DICKENS, B. (1998), 'Death' in I. Kennedy and A. Grubb (eds.), *Principles of Medical Law* (Oxford: Oxford University Press).

DILLOF, A. (1998), 'Transferred Intent: An Inquiry into the Nature of Criminal Culpability', *Buffalo Criminal Law Review* 1: 501.

DINE, J., AND WATT, B. (1998), 'The Transmission of Disease during Consensual Sexual Activity and the Concept of Associative Autonomy', *Web Journal of Current Legal Issues.*

DINGWALL, G. (2002), 'Statutory Exceptions, Burdens of Proof and the Human Rights Act 1998', *Modern Law Review* 65: 40.

DOAK, J. (2003), 'The Victim and the Criminal Process: an Analysis of Recent Trends in Regional and International Tribunals', *Legal Studies* 23: 1.

DOWNES, D., AND ROCK, P. (2003), *Understanding Deviance* (Oxford: Oxford University Press).

DRESSLER, J. (1984), 'New Thoughts About the Concept of Justification in the Criminal Law: A Critique of Fletcher Thinking and Rethinking', *University of California Los Angeles Law Review* 32: 61.

—— (1985), 'Reassessing the Theoretical Underpinnings of Accomplice Liability: New Solutions to an Old Problem', *Hastings Law Journal* 37: 91.

—— (1987), *Understanding Criminal Law* (New York: Matthew Bender).

—— (1988a), 'Reflections on Excusing Wrongdoers: Moral Theory, New Excuses and the Model Penal Code', *Rutger's Law Journal* 19: 671.

—— (1988b), 'Provocation: Partial Justification or Partial Excuse', *Modern Law Review* 51: 467.

—— (1989), 'Exegesis of the Law of Duress: Justifying the Excuse and Searching For its Proper Limits', *South Carolina Law Review* 62: 1331.

—— (1998), 'Where We Have Been, and Where We Might be Going: Some Cautionary Reflections on Rape Law Reform', *Cleveland State Law Review* 46: 409.

—— (2000), 'Some Brief Thoughts (Mostly Negative) About "Bad Samaritan" Laws', 40 *Santa Clara Law Review* 40: 971.

—— (2002a), 'Battered Women Who Kill Their Sleeping Tormenters: Reflections on Maintaining Respect for Human Life while Killing Moral Monsters' in S. Shute and A. Simester (eds.), *Criminal Law Theory* (Oxford: Oxford University Press).

—— (2002b), 'Why Keep the Provocation Defense?: Some Reflections on a Difficult Subject', *Minnesota Law Review* 86: 959.

DRIPPS, D. (1992), 'Beyond Rape: An Essay on the Difference Between the Presence of Force and the Absence of Consent', *Columbia Law Review* 92: 1780.

—— (1993), 'More on Distinguishing Sex, Sexual Expropriation, and Sexual Assault: A Reply to Professor West', *Columbia Law Review* 93: 1460.

—— (1994), 'Men, Women And Rape', *Fordham Law Review* 63: 125.

—— (1996), 'For a Negative, Normative Model of Consent, with a Comment on Preference-Skepticism', *Legal Theory* 2: 143.

DUFF, R.A. (1986), *Trials and Punishments* (Cambridge: Cambridge University Press).

—— (1990a), *Intention, Agency and Criminal Liability* (Oxford: Blackwell).

—— (1990b), ' "Can I Help You?" Accessorial Liability and the Intention to Assist', *Legal Studies* 10: 165.

—— (1990c), 'Auctions, Lotteries and the Punishment of Attempts', *Law and Philosophy* 8: 1.

—— (1991), 'The Circumstances of an Attempt', *Cambridge Law Journal* 50: 100.

—— (1993), 'Choice, Character and Criminal Liability', *Law and Philosophy* 12: 345.

—— (1994), 'Fitness to Plead and Fair Trials', *Criminal Law Review* 419.

—— (1995), 'Recklessness in Attempts (Again)', *Oxford Journal of Legal Studies* 15: 309.

—— (1996), *Criminal Attempts* (Oxford: Oxford University Press).

—— (1998a), 'Law, Language and Community: Some Preconditions of Criminal Liability', *Oxford Journal of Legal Studies* 18: 189.

—— (1998b), 'Principle and Contradiction in the Criminal Law: Motives and Criminal Liability' in A. Duff (ed.), *Philosophy and the Criminal Law* (Cambridge: Cambridge University Press).

—— (2002), 'Rule-Violations and Wrongdoings' in S. Shute and A. Simester (eds.), *Criminal Law Theory* (Oxford: Oxford University Press).

—— (2003), 'Virtue, Vice, and Criminal Liability: Do We Want an Aristotelian Criminal Law?', *Buffalo Criminal Law Review* 6: 147.

—— (2005a), 'Theorizing Criminal Law: a 25th Anniversary Essay', *Oxford Journal of Legal Studies* 25: 353.

—— (2005b), 'Criminalizing Endangerment' in R.A. Duff and S. Green (eds.), *Defining Crimes* (Oxford: Oxford University Press).

—— (2005c), 'Strict Liability, Legal Presumptions, and the Presumption of Innocence' Innocence' in A. Simester (ed.), *Appraising Strict Liability* (Oxford: Oxford University Press).

—— AND GARLAND, D. (1994), 'Introduction: Thinking about Punishment' in A. Duff and D. Garland, *A Reader on Punishment* (Oxford: Oxford University Press).

—— AND GREEN, S. (2005), 'Introduction: The Special Part and its Problems', in A. Duff and S. Green (eds.), *Defining Crimes* (Oxford: Oxford University Press).

—— AND VON HIRSCH, A. (1997), 'Responsibility, Retribution and the "Voluntary"', *Cambridge Law Journal* 56: 103.

DUMMETT, M. (1989), *Truth and other Enigmas* (Cambridge, Mass.: Harvard University Press).

DUNCAN, S. (1994), 'Law as Literature: Deconstructing the Legal Text', *Law and Critique* 5: 3.

—— (1995), 'Law's Sexual Discipline: Visibility, Violence and Consent', *Journal of Law and Society* 22: 326.

DUSTIN, H. (ed.) (2004), *Women and the Criminal Justice System* (Fawcett Society, London, 2004).

DWORKIN, G. (1981), 'Taking Risks, Assessing Responsibility', *Hastings Centre Report*, 26 October.

—— (1999), 'Devlin was Right: Law and the Enforcement of Morality', *William and Mary Law Review* 40: 927.

—— AND KENNEDY, I. (1993), 'Human Tissue: Rights in the Body and its Parts', *Medical Law Review* 1: 29.

DWORKIN, R. (1993), *Life's Dominion* (London: HarperCollins).

EBRAHIM, I, FENWICK, P., WILSON, W., MARKS, R., AND PEACOCK, K. (2005), 'Violence, Sleepwalking and the Criminal Law', *Criminal Law Review* 614.

EDITORIAL (1986), 'The Criminology of Attempts', *Criminal Law Review* 769.

EDMUNDSON, W. (2002), 'Social Meaning, Compliance Conditions, and Law's Claim to Authority', *Canadian Journal of Law and Jurisprudence* 15: 51.

EDWARDS, I. (2004), 'An Ambiguous Participant', *British Journal of Criminology* 44: 967.

EDWARDS, S. (1988), 'Mad, Bad or Pre-menstrual?', *New Law Journal* 138: 456.

—— (1999), 'Battered Women—in Fear of Luc's Shadow', *New Law Journal* 149: 75.

—— (2004), 'Abolishing Provocation and Reframing Self-Defence', *Criminal Law Review* 181.

EISLER, R. (1987), 'Human Rights: Towards an Integrated Theory for Action', *Human Rights Quarterly* 9: 287.

ELLIOTT, D. (1982), 'Dishonesty in Theft: A Dispensable Concept', *Criminal Law Review* 395.

—— (1989), 'Necessity, Duress and Self-Defence', *Criminal Law Review* 611.

—— (1991), 'Directors' Theft and Dishonesty', *Criminal Law Review* 732.

—— (1997), 'Endangering Life by Destroying or Damaging Property', *Criminal Law Review* 382.

EMMERSON, B., AND ASHWORTH, A. (2001), *Human Rights and Criminal Justice* (London: Sweet and Maxwell).

ENKER, A. (1969), 'Impossibility in Criminal Attempts—Legality and the Legal Process', *Minnesota Law Review* 53: 665.

EPSTEIN, R. (1971), 'A Theory of Strict Liability', *Journal of Legal Studies* 2: 151.

—— (1983), 'Blackmail, Inc.', *University of Chicago Law Review* 50: 553.

ESKRIDGE, W. (1995), 'The Many Faces of Sexual Consent', *William and Mary Law Review* 37: 47.

ESSEN, R. (2005), 'Cybercrime: a Growing Problem', *Journal of Criminal Law* 269.

ESTEAL, R. (ed.) (1998), *Balancing the Scales—Rape Law Reform and Australian Culture* (Sydney: Foundation Press).

ESTRICH, S. (1987), *Real Rape* (Cambridge, Mass.: Harvard University Press).

EVANS, E. (1987), *The Criminal Prosecution and Capital Punishment of Animals* (London: Faber and Faber).

FAIRSTEIN, L. (1994), 'Panel Discussion: Men, Women and Rape', *Fordham Law Review* 63: 125.

FALK, P. (2002), 'Rape by Drugs: A Statutory Overview and Proposals for Reform', *Arizona Law Review* 44: 131.

FARRIER, R. (1980), *Drugs and Intoxication* (London: Sweet & Maxwell).

FEARON, G. (2004), 'All Party Internet Report on the Computer Misuse Act', *Computers and Law* 15: 36.

FEINBERG, J. (1970), *Doing and Deserving* (Princeton, NJ: Princeton University Press).

—— (1984), *Harm to Others, The Moral Limits of the Criminal Law* (New York: Oxford University Press).

—— (1986a), *Harm to Self* (New York: Oxford University Press).

—— (1986b), *Offense to Others* (New York: Oxford University Press).

—— (1988), *Harmless Wrongdoing* (New York: Oxford University Press).

—— (1994), 'The Expressive Function of Punishment' in A. Duff and D. Garland (eds.), *A Reader on Punishment* (Oxford: Oxford University Press).

—— (1995), 'Equal Punishment for Failed Attempts: Some Bad But Instructive Arguments Against It', *Arizona Law Review* 37: 117.

—— (2003), *Problems at the Roots of Law* (Oxford: Oxford University Press).

FELDMAN, D. (2002), *Civil Liberties and Human Rights in England and Wales* (Oxford: Oxford University Press).

FENNELL, P. (1992), 'The Criminal Procedure (Insanity and Unfitness to Plead) Act 1991', *Modern Law Review* 55: 333.

FENWICK, H. (2002), 'The Anti-Terrorism, Crime and Security Act 2001: A Proportionate Response to 11 September', *Modern Law Review* 65: 724.

FIELD, S., AND LYNN, M. (1993), 'Capacity, Recklessness and the House of Lords', *Criminal Law Review* 127.

FINCH, E. (2001), *The Criminalisation of Stalking* (London: Cavendish).

—— (2002), 'Stalking the Perfect Stalking Law: An Evaluation of the Efficacy of the Protection from Harassment Act 1997', *Criminal Law Review* 703.

—— AND MUNRO, V. (2003), 'Intoxicated Consent and the Boundaries of Drug Assisted Rape', *Criminal Law Review* 773.

—— AND —— (2004), 'Intoxicated Consent and Drug Assisted Rape Revisited', *Criminal Law Review* 789.

FINE, B., AND COHEN, M. (1968), 'Is Criminal Negligence a Defensible Basis for Penal Liability?', *Buffalo Law Review* 16: 749.

FINEMAN, M. (2004), *The Autonomy Myth* (New York: New Press).

FINGARETTE, H. (1988), *Heavy Drinking—The Myth of Alcoholism as a Disease* (Berkeley, Cal.: University of California Press).

FINKELSTEIN, C. (1999), 'No Harm No Foul? Objectivism and the Law of Attempts', *Law and Philosophy* 18: 69.

—— (2000), 'Positivism and the Notion of an Offense', *California Law Review* 88: 335.

—— (2002a), 'Involuntary Crimes, Voluntarily Committed' in S. Shute and A. Simester (eds.), *Criminal Law Theory* (Oxford: Oxford University Press).

—— (2002b), 'Excuses and Dispositions in Criminal Law', *Buffalo Criminal Law Review* 6: 317.

FINNIS, J. (1991), 'Intention and Side-Effects' in R. Frey and C. Morris (eds.), *Liability and Responsibility* (Cambridge: Cambridge University Press).

FISCHEL, D., AND SYKES, A. (1996), 'Corporate Crime', *Journal of Legal Studies* 25: 319.

FISSE, B. (1990), 'Sentencing Options against Corporations', *Criminal Law Forum* 1: 211.

FITZGERALD, P. (1960), 'A Concept of Crime', *Criminal Law Review* 257.

FLETCHER, G. (1978), *Rethinking Criminal Law* (Boston, Mass.: Little, Brown).

—— (1993), 'Blackmail: The Paradigmatic Crime', *University of Pennsylvania Law Review* 141: 1617.

—— (1994), 'On the Moral Irrelevance of Bodily Movements', *University of Pennsylvania Law Review* 142: 1443.

—— (1996), 'Self-Defense and Relations of Domination: Moral and Legal Perspectives on Battered Women Who Kill', *University of Pittsburgh Law Review* 57: 553.

—— (1998), *Basic Concepts of Criminal Law* (Oxford: Oxford University Press).

—— (2000), 'The Nature and Function of Criminal Theory', *California Law Review* 88: 687.

FLOOD-PAGE, C., AND TURNER, J. (eds.) (2003), *Crime in England and Wales 2001/2002 Supplementary Volume* (London: Home Office).

FOOT, P. (1978), 'The Problem of Abortion and the Doctrine of Double Effect' in P. Foot, *Virtues and Vices* (Oxford: Blackwell).

FORELL, C., AND MATTHEWS, D. (2000), *The Reasonable Woman as a Measure of Man* (New York: New York University Press).

FORRESTER, D., CHATTERTON, M., AND PEASE, K. (1988), *The Kirkholt Burglary Prevention Project, Rochdale* (London: HMSO).

FREEDMAN, D. (1998), 'Restoring Order to the Reasonable Person Test in the Defence of Provocation', *Kings College Law Journal* 26.

FREEMAN, M. (2001), 'Whose Life is it Anyway?', *Medical Law Review* 9: 259.

FREEMAN, S. (1994), 'Act & Crime: Act & Omission: Criminal Liability and the Duty to Aid the Distressed', *University of Pennsylvania Law Review* 142: 1455.

FREID, C. (1978), *Right and Wrong* (Cambridge, Mass.: Harvard University Press).

FRENCH, P. (1984), *Collective and Corporate Responsibility* (New York: University of Columbia Press).

FUMERTON, R., AND KRESS, K. (2001), 'Causation and the Law: Pre-emption, Lawful Sufficiency, and Causal Sufficiency', *Law & Contemporary Problems* 64: 83.

FUNK, T. (1999), 'Justifying Justifications', *Oxford Journal of Legal Studies* 19: 631.

GARCIA-RILL, E., AND BEECHER-MONAS, E. (2001), 'Gatekeeping Stress: The Science and Admissibility of Post-Traumatic Stress Disorder', *University of Arkansas Little Rock Law Review* 24: 9.

GARDNER, J. (1994a), 'Rationality and the Rule of Law in Offences against the Person', *Cambridge Law Journal* 53: 502.

—— (1994b), 'Review of Act and Crime by Michael S. Moore', *Law Quarterly Review* 110: 496.

—— (1996), 'Justifications and Reasons' in A. Simester and A. Smith (eds.), *Harm and Culpability* (Oxford: Oxford University Press).

—— (1998a), 'On the General Part of the Criminal Law' in A. Duff (ed.), *Philosophy and the Criminal Law* (Cambridge: Cambridge University Press).

—— (1998b), 'The Gist of Excuses', *Buffalo Criminal Law Review* 1: 575.

—— (2005), 'Wrongs and Faults' in A. Simester (ed.), *Appraising Strict Liability* (Oxford: Oxford University Press).

—— AND JUNG, H. (1991), 'Making Sense of Mens Rea: Anthony Duff's Account', *Oxford Journal of Legal Studies* 11: 559.

—— AND MACKLEM, T. (2001a), 'Compassion without Respect? Nine Fallacies in *R v Smith*', *Criminal Law Review* 623.

—— AND—— (2001b), 'Provocation and Pluralism', *Modern Law Review* 64: 815.

—— AND——(2004), 'No Provocation without Responsibility', *Criminal Law Review* 213.

—— AND SHUTE, S. (2000), 'The Wrongness of Rape' in J. Horder (ed.), *Oxford Essays in Jurisprudence* (Oxford: Oxford University Press).

GARDNER, S. (1990), 'Is Theft a Rip-Off?', *Oxford Journal of Legal Studies* 10: 441.

—— (1991a), 'Duress in Attempted Murder', *Law Quarterly Review* 107: 389.

—— (1991b), 'Necessity's Newest Inventions', *Oxford Journal of Legal Studies* 11: 125.

—— (1991c), 'Reckless and Inconsiderate Rape', *Criminal Law Review* 172.

—— (1993a), 'Appropriation in Theft: The Last Word', *Law Quarterly Review* 109: 194.

—— (1993b), 'Recklessness Refined', *Law Quarterly Review* 109: 21.

—— (1995a), 'Criminal Defences by Judicial Discretion', *Law Quarterly Review* 111: 177.

—— (1995b), 'Manslaughter by Gross Negligence', *Law Quarterly Review* 111: 22.

—— (1996), 'Appreciating *Olugboja*', *Legal Studies* 16: 275.

—— (1998a), 'Joint Enterprise', *Law Quarterly Review* 114: 202.

—— (1998b), 'Property and Theft', *Criminal Law Review* 35.

—— (1998c), 'Stalking', *Law Quarterly Review* 114: 33.

—— (2005), 'Direct Action and the Defence of Necessity', *Criminal Law Review* 371.

GARLAND, D. (2001), *The Culture of Control: Crime and Social Order in Contemporary Society* (Oxford: Oxford University Press).

GARVEY, S. (2005), 'Passion's Puzzle' *Iowa Law Review* 90: 1677

GELSTHORPE, L., AND MORRIS, A. (1999), 'Much Ado about Nothing—a Critical Comment on Key Provisions Relating to Children in the Crime and Disorder Act 1998', *Child and Family Law Quarterly* 11: 209.

GENDERS, E. (1999), 'Reform of the Offences Against the Person Act Lessons from the Law in Action', *Criminal Law Review* 689.

GIBSON, S. (1993), 'The Discourse of Sex/War', *Feminist Legal Studies* 1: 179.

GIDDENS, A. (1989), *Sociology* (Cambridge: Cambridge University Press).

GILES, M. (1990), 'Complicity—the Problems of Joint Enterprise', *Criminal Law Review* 383.

—— (1994), '*R v Brown*: Consensual Harm and the Public Interest', *Modern Law Review* 57: 101.

—— AND UGLOW, S. (1992), 'Appropriation and Manifest Criminality in Theft', *Journal of Criminal Law* 56: 179.

GINSBURG, D., AND SHECHTMAN, P. (1993), 'Blackmail: An Economic Analysis of the Law', *University of Pennsylvania Law Review* 141: 1849.

GLAZEBROOK, P. (1960), 'Criminal Omissions: The Duty Requirement in Offences Against Person', *Law Quarterly Review* 76: 386.

—— (1972), 'The Necessity Plea in English Criminal Law', *Cambridge Law Journal* 31: 87.

—— (1978), 'Situational Liability' in P. Glazebrook (ed.), *Reshaping the Criminal* (London: Stevens).

—— (1986), 'Thought Crimes: Some Afterthoughts', *Cambridge Law Journal* 45: 363.

—— (1993), 'Revising the Theft Acts', *Cambridge Law Journal* 52: 191.

—— (1996), 'Structuring the Criminal Code: Functional Approaches to Complicity, Incomplete Offences and General Defences' in A. Simester and A. Smith (eds.), *Harm and Culpability* (Oxford: Oxford University Press).

—— (2001), 'On Being Required to be a Policeman', *Cambridge Law Journal* 60: 537.

—— (2002), 'A Better Way of Convicting Businesses of Avoiding Deaths and Injuries?', *Cambridge Law Journal* 61: 405.

GLOVER, J. (1970), *Responsibility* (New York: Routledge).

GOBERT, J. (1993), 'The Fortuity of Consequences', *Criminal Law Forum* 4: 1.

—— (1995), 'Coherence in the Law of Involuntary Manslaughter', *Criminal Law Forum* 6: 435.

—— (1998), 'Controlling Corporate Criminality: Penal Sanctions and Beyond', *Web Journal of Current Legal Issues*.

—— (2002), 'Corporate Killing at Home and Abroad—Reflections on the Government's Proposals', *Law Quarterly Review* 118: 72.

—— AND PUNCH, M. (2003), *Rethinking Corporate Crime* (London: Butterworths).

GOFF, LORD (1988), 'The Mental Element in the Crime of Murder', *Law Quarterly Review* 104: 30.

GOLD, E. (1996), *Body Parts: Property Rights and the Ownership of Human Biological Matter* (Oxford: Oxford University Press).

GOLDSTEIN, A. (1959), 'Conspiracy to Defraud the United States', *Yale Law Journal* 68: 406.

—— (1967), *The Insanity Defence* (New Haven, Conn.: Yale University Press).

—— AND KATZ, J. (1963), 'Abolish the "Insanity Defense"—Why not?', *Yale Law Journal* 72: 853.

GOODE, M. (1995), 'Stalking: A Crime of the Nineties', *Criminal Law Journal* 19: 21.

GOODRICH, P. (1986), *Reading the Law* (Oxford: Blackwell).

GORDON, W. (1993), 'Truth and Consequences: The Force of Blackmail's Central Case', *University of Pennsylvania Law Review* 141: 1741.

GORR, M. (1992), 'Liberalism and the Paradox of Blackmail', *Philosophy and Public Affairs* 21: 43.

—— (1996), 'Should the Law Distinguish Between Intention and (mere) Foresight', *Legal Studies* 2: 239.

GOSTIN, L. (1986), *Mental Health Services—Law and Practice* (London: Shaw and Sons).

GOUGH, S. (1996), 'Intoxication and Criminal Liability: The Law Commission's Proposed Reforms', *Law Quarterly Review* 112: 335.

—— (1999), 'Taking the Heat out of Provocation', *Oxford Journal of Legal Studies* 19: 481.

GOULD, E. (1996), *Body Parts: Property Rights and the Ownership of Human Biological Matter* (Oxford: Oxford University Press).

GRABOSKY, P., SMITH, R., AND DEMPSEY, G. (2003), *Electronic Theft* (Cambridge: Cambridge University Press).

GRAY, K. (1991), 'Property in Thin Air', *Cambridge Law Journal* 50: 252.

GRAY, N., LAING, J., AND NOAKS, L. (2002), *Criminal Justice, Mental Health and the Politics of Risk* (London: Cavendish Publishing).

GREEN, P. (2003), 'The Concept of White Collar Crime in Law and Legal Theory', *Buffalo Criminal Law Review* 8: 1.

GREEN, S. (2002), 'Plagiarism, Norms, and the Limits of Theft Law: Some Observations on the Use of Criminal Sanctions in Enforcing Intellectual Property Rights', *Hastings Law Journal* 54: 167.

—— (2005), 'Six Senses of Strict Liability: A Plea for Formalism' in A. Simester (ed.), *Appraising Strict Liability* (Oxford: Oxford University Press).

GREENAWALT, K. (1984), 'The Perplexing Borders of Justification and Excuse', *Colorado Law Review* 84: 1897.

GREENWOOD, A. (1981), 'Causation and Credit Card Fraud', *Cambridge Law Journal* 40: 209.

GRIEW, E. (1985), 'Dishonesty: The Objections to Feely and Ghost', *Criminal Law Review* 341.

—— (1988), 'The Future of Diminished Responsibility', *Criminal Law Review* 75.

—— (1995), *The Theft Acts 1968 and 1978* (London: Sweet & Maxwell).

GRIFFITHS, S. (2000), 'Women Who Fight Back' in J. Hanmer and C. Itzen (eds.), *Homes Truths About Domestic Violence* (London: Routledge).

GROSS, H. (1979), *A Theory of Criminal Justice* (New York: Oxford University Press).

GRUBIN, D. (1993), 'What Constitutes Fitness to Plead?', *Criminal Law Review* 748.

GUNN, J., AND TAYLOR, P. (1993), *Forensic Psychiatry; Clinical, Legal and Ethical Aspects* (London: Butterworths).

GUR-ARYE, M. (1986), 'Should the Criminal Law Distinguish between Necessity as a Justification and Necessity as an Excuse?', *Law Quarterly Review* 102: 71.

HADDEN, T. (1983), 'Fraud in the City: The Role of the Criminal Law', *Criminal Law Review* 500.

HALL, J. (1963), 'Negligent Behaviour Should be Excluded from Penal Liability', *Columbia Law Review* 63: 632.

HALL, S. (1978), *Policing the Crisis* (Basingstoke: Macmillan).

HALPERN, S. (1997), 'Of Moral Right and Moral Righteousness', *Marqette Intellectual Property Law Review* 1: 65.

HALPIN, A. (1996), 'The Test for Dishonesty', *Criminal Law Review* 283.

—— (1998), 'Definitions and Directions: Recklessness Unheeded', *Legal Studies* 18: 294.

—— (2004), *Definition in the Criminal Law* (Oxford: Hart).

HAMMOND, G. (1981), 'Quantum Physics, Econometric Models and Property Rights to Information', *McGill Law Journal* 27: 47.

—— (1984), 'Theft of Information', *Law Quarterly Review* 100: 252.

—— (1986), 'Electronic Crime in Canadian Courts', *Oxford Journal of Legal Studies* 6: 145.

HAMMOND, S. (2001), *When Calculating the Costs and Benefits when Applying for Corporate Amnesty* (Washington, DC: US Department of Justice).

HAMPTON, J. (1990), 'Mens Rea', *Social Philosophy and Policy* 7: 1.

HANCOCK, D. (2001), 'To What Extent Should Computer Related Crimes be the Subject of Specific Legislative Attention?', *Albany Law Journal of Science and Technology* 12: 97.

HANMER, J. (2000), 'Domestic Violence and Gender Relations' in J. Hanmer and C. Itzen, *Homes Truths About Domestic Violence* (London: Routledge).

HANNA, C. (2001), 'Sex Is Not a Sport: Consent and Violence in Criminal Law', *Boston College Law Review* 42: 239.

HARCOURT, B. (1999), 'The Collapse of the Harm Principle', *Journal of Criminal Law and Criminology* 90: 109.

HARDIN, R. (1993), 'Blackmailing for Mutual Good', *University of Pennsylvania Law Review* 141: 1787.

HARE, I. (1993), '*R v Savage, DPP v Parmenter*—A Compelling Case for the Code', *Modern Law Review* 56: 74.

HARLOW, C. (1974), 'Self-Defence: Public Right or Private Privilege', *Criminal Law Review* 528.

HARR, R., CLARKE, D., AND DeCARLO, N. (1985), *Motives and Mechanisms* (London: Methuen).

HARRIS, J. (2000), *Evaluation of the Use and Effectiveness of the Protection from Harassment Act 1997* (London: Home Office).

—— (2001), 'Human Being, Persons and Conjoined Twins', *Medical Law Review* 9: 221.

HARRIS, J., AND HOLM, S. (1995), 'Is there a moral obligation not to infect others?', *British Medical Journal* 311: 1215.

HARRIS, J.W. (1996a), *Property and Justice* (Oxford: Oxford University Press).

—— (1996b), 'Who Owns my Body?', *Oxford Journal of Legal Studies* 16: 55.

—— (1997), *Legal Philosophies* (2nd edn., London: Butterworths).

HARRISON, P., DOWNES, J., AND WILLIAMS, M. (1991), 'Date and Acquaintance Rape: Perceptions and Attitude Change Strategies', *Journal of College Student Development* 32: 131.

HART, H. (1963), *Law Liberty and Morality* (Oxford: Oxford University Press).

—— (1968), *Punishment and Responsibility. Essays in the Philosophy of Law* (Oxford: Clarendon Press).

—— AND HONORÉ, A. (1985), *Causation in the Law* (2nd edn., Oxford: Oxford University Press).

HASSETT, P. (1987), 'Absolutism in Causation', *Syracuse Law Review* 38: 683.

HAY, D. (1975), 'Property, Authority and the Criminal Law' in D. Hay, P. Linebaugh, and E.P. Thompson, *Albion's Fatal Tree* (London: Penguin).

HAYDEN, A. (2000), 'Imposing Criminal and Civil Penalties for Failing to Help Another: Are "Good Samaritan" Laws Good Ideas?', *New England International and Comparative Law Annal* 6: 27.

HEALTH AND SAFETY EXECUTIVE (2006), *Health and Safety Statistics Highlights* (London: Health and Safety Executive).

HEATON, R. (2001), 'Deceiving without Thieving?', *Criminal Law Review* 712.

—— (2003), 'Dealing in Death', *Criminal Law Review* 497.

—— (2004), 'Principals? No Principles!', *Criminal Law Review* 463.

HECHT SCHAFRAN, L. (1993), 'Writing and Reading About Rape: A Primer', *St John's Law Review* 66: 979.

HEGEL, G. (1967), *Philosophy of Right* (trans. T. M. Knox, Oxford: Oxford University Press).

HEIDENSOHN, F. (2002), 'Gender and Crime' in M. Maguire, R. Morgan, and R. Reiner (eds.), *The Oxford Handbook of Criminology* (Oxford: Oxford University Press).

HEILBRON COMMITTEE (CHAIRMAN DAME ROSE HEILBRON) (1976), *Report of the Advisory Group on the Law of Rape* (Cmnd. 6352, London: HMSO).

HELMER, C. (1999), *De neutralisatie theorie van Sykes en Matza toegepast op witte boorden criminaliteit* (Thesis, Department of Law, University of Utrecht).

HENDERSON, L. (1988), 'What Makes Rape a Crime', *Berkley Women's Law Journal* 193.

—— (1992), 'Rape and Responsibility', *Law & Philosophy* 11: 127.

—— (1997), 'Without Narrative: Child Sexual Abuse', *Virginia Journal of Social Policy and Law* 4: 479.

HENRY, S. (1978), *The Hidden Economy* (London: Martin Robertson).

HERRING, J. (1997), 'Assault by Telephone', *Cambridge Law Journal* 56: 11.

—— (1998a), 'Caesarean Sections and the Right of Autonomy', *Cambridge Law Journal* 57: 438.

—— (1998b), 'The Criminalisation of Harassment', *Cambridge Law Journal* 58: 10.

—— (1999), 'Mondeo Man, Road Rage, and the Defence of Necessity', *Cambridge Law Journal* 58: 268.

—— (2001), *Family Law* (Harlow: Longman).

—— (2002a), *Criminal Law* (Basingstoke: Macmillan).

—— (2002b), 'Giving, Selling and Sharing Bodies' in A. Bainham, S. Day Sclater, and M. Richards (eds.), *Body Lore and Laws* (Oxford: Hart).

—— (2002c), 'Does Yes mean Yes? The Criminal Law and Mistaken Consent to Sexual Activity', *Singapore Law Review* 22: 182.

—— (2005a), 'Mistaken Sex', *Criminal Law Review* 511.

—— (2005b), *Criminal Law* (Basingstoke: Palgrave).

HILL, D. (1983), *The Politics of Schizophrenia* (New York: University Press of America).

HIRST, M. (1999), 'Assault, Battery and Indirect Violence', *Criminal Law Review* 557.

HIRST, P. (1994), 'The Concept of Punishment' in A. Duff and D. Garland (eds.), *A Reader on Punishment* (Oxford: Oxford University Press).

HOBBES, T. (1651), *Leviathan* (London).

HODGE, J. (1993), 'Alcohol and Violence' in P. Taylor (ed.), *Violence in Society* (London: Royal College of Physicians).

HOEBER, P. (1986), 'The Abandonment Defense to Criminal Attempt and Other Problems of Temporal Individuation', *California Law Review* 74: 377.

HOGAN, B. (1986), 'Omissions and the Duty Myth' in P. Smith (ed.), *Criminal Law: Essays in Honour of J.C. Smith* (London: Butterworths).

HOME OFFICE (1987), *Interdepartmental Group into Mentally Disturbed Offenders in the Prison System* (London: Home Office).

—— (1988), *Violence: Reforming the Offences Against the Person Act 1861* (London: Home Office).

—— (1996), *Stalking the Solutions: A Consultation Paper* (London: Home Office).

—— (1997a), *No More Excuses: A New Approach to Tackling Youth Crime in England and Wales* (London: Home Office).

—— (1997b), *Racial Violence and Harassment: A Consultation Document* (London: Home Office).

—— (1998a), *Guide to Racially Aggravated Offences* (London: Home Office).

—— (1998b), *Criminal Statistics, England and Wales 1997* (London: Home Office).

—— (1998c), *Violence: Reforming the Offences Against the Person Act 1861* (London: Home Office).

—— (1999a), *Statistical Bulletin 12/01* (London: Home Office).

—— (1999b), *Living Without Fear: An Integrated Approach to Tackling Violence Against Women* (London: Home Office).

—— (1999c), *Managing Dangerous People with Severe Personality Disorder: Proposals for Policy Development* (London: Home Office).

—— (2000a), *Criminal Statistics 1999* (London: Home Office).

—— (2000b), *Setting the Boundaries* (London: Home Office).

—— (2000c), *Reforming the Law on Involuntary Manslaughter: The Government's Proposals* (London: Home Office).

—— (2000d), *Tackling Alcohol Related Crime, Disorder and Nuisance* (London: Home Office).

—— (2001a), *Criminal Justice: The Way Ahead* (London: The Stationery Office).

—— (2001b), *Criminal Statistics 2000* (Home Office).

—— (2001c), *Statistical Bulletin* (London: Home Office).

—— (2002a), *Criminal Statistics 2001* (London: Home Office).

—— (2002b), *Protecting the Public* (London: Home Office).

—— (2002c), *Statistics on Race and Criminal Justice System* (London: Home Office).

—— (2002d), *Statistics on Women and the Criminal Justice System* (London: Home Office).

—— (2003a), 'Home Secretary Announces Tougher Sentences for Murderers' Press Release 7, May (London: Home Office).

—— (2003b), *The Government's Crime Reduction Strategy* (London: Home Office).

—— (2003c), *Supporting Families: A Consultation Document* (London: Home Office).

—— (2003d), *Domestic Violence Consultation Paper* (London: Home Office).

—— (2005a), Corporate Manslaughter: The Government's Draft Bill for Reform.

—— (2005b), *Criminal Statistics 2004* (London: Home Office).

HONDERICH, T. (1984), *Punishment: The Supposed Justifications* (Harmondsworth: Penguin).

HONORÉ, A. (1961), 'Ownership' in A. Guest (ed.), *Oxford Essays in Jurisprudence* (Oxford: Oxford University Press).

—— (1988), 'Responsibility and Luck', *Law Quarterly Review* 104: 530.

—— (1990), 'A Theory of Coercion', *Oxford Journal of Legal Studies* 10: 94.

—— (1998), *Responsibility and Fault* (Oxford: Hart).

HOOD, R. (1992), *Race and Sentencing* (Oxford: Oxford University Press).

—— (1996), *The Death Penalty* (Oxford: Oxford University Press).

HORDER, J. (1989), 'Sex, Violence and Sentencing in Domestic Provocation Cases', *Criminal Law Review* 546.

—— (1992), *Provocation and Responsibility* (Oxford: Oxford University Press).

—— (1993a), 'Criminal Culpability: The Possibility of a General Theory', *Law and Philosophy* 12: 193.

—— (1993b), 'Pleading Involuntary Lack of Capacity', *Cambridge Law Journal* 52: 298.

—— (1994a), 'Occupying the Moral High Ground? The Law Commission on Duress', *Criminal Law Review* 334.

—— (1994b), 'Rethinking Non-fatal Offences against the Person', *Oxford Journal of Legal Studies* 14: 335.

—— (1994c), 'Varieties of Intention, Criminal Attempts and Endangerment', *Legal Studies* 14: 355.

—— (1995a), 'Intention in the Criminal Law—A Rejoinder', *Modern Law Review* 58: 678.

—— (1995b), 'Redrawing the Boundaries of Self-Defence', *Modern Law Review* 58: 431.

—— (1995c), 'Sobering Up? The Law Commission on Criminal Intoxication', *Modern Law Review* 58: 534.

—— (1995d), 'A Critique of the Correspondence Principle', *Criminal Law Review* 759.

—— (1996a), 'Provocation's "Reasonable Man" Reassessed', *Law Quarterly Review* 112: 35.

—— (1996b), 'Crimes of Ulterior Intent' in A. Simester and A. Smith (eds.), *Harm and Culpability* (Oxford: Oxford University Press).

—— (1997a), 'Two Histories and Four Hidden Principles', *Law Quarterly Review* 113: 95.

—— (1997b), 'Questioning the Correspondence Principle—A Reply', *Criminal Law Review* 206.

—— (1998a), 'Reconsidering Psychic Assault', *Criminal Law Review* 392.

—— (1998b), 'Self-Defence, Necessity and Duress: Understanding the Relationship', *Canadian Journal of Law and Jurisprudence* 11: 143.

—— (1999a), 'Between Provocation and Diminished Responsibility', *Kings College LawJournal* 143.

—— (1999b), 'Consent, Threats and Deception in Criminal Law', *Kings College Law Journal* 104.

—— (2000), 'On the Irrelevance of Motive in Criminal Law' in J. Horder (ed.), *Oxford Essays in Jurisprudence* (Oxford: Oxford University Press).

—— (2001), 'How Culpability Can, and Cannot, Be Denied in Under-age Sex Crimes', *Criminal Law Review* 15.

—— (2002a), 'Killing the Passive Abuser: A Theoretical Defence' in S. Shute and S. Simester (eds.), *Criminal Law Theory* (Oxford: Oxford University Press).

—— (2002b), 'Strict Liability, Statutory Construction, and the Spirit of Liberty', *Law Quarterly Review* 118: 148.

—— (2004), *Excusing Crime* (Oxford: Oxford University Press).

—— (2005a), 'Reshaping the Subjective Element in the Provocation Defence', *Oxford Journal of Legal Studies* 25: 123.

—— (2005b), 'The Classification of Crimes and the Special Part of the Criminal Law' in A. Duff and S. Green (eds.), *Defining Crimes* (Oxford: Oxford University Press).

—— (2005c), 'Whose Values Should Determine When Liability is Strict?' in A. Simester (ed.), *Appraising Strict Liability* (Oxford: Oxford University Press).

HORNSBY, J. (1993), 'On What's Intentionally Done' in S. Shute, J. Horder, and J. Gardner (eds.), *Action and Value in the Criminal Law* (Oxford: Oxford University Press).

—— (1994), 'Action and Aberration', *University of Pennsylvania Law Review* 142: 1719.

HOUGH, M. (1996), *Drugs Misuse and the Criminal Justice System* (London: Home Office).

—— AND MAYHEW, P. (1983), *The British Crime Survey* (London: HMSO).

HOUSE OF LORDS SELECT COMMITTEE ON MEDICAL ETHICS (1993), *Report (Session 1993–1994)* (London: HMSO).

HOWARD, C. (1961), 'What Colour is the "Reasonable Man"?', *Criminal Law Review* 41.

HOWARD, H. (2003), 'Reform of the Insanity Defence: Theoretical Issues', *Journal of Criminal Law* 67: 51.

HOWE, A. (1991), 'The Problem of Privitized Injuries: Feminist Strategies for Litigation' in M. Fineman and N. Thomasden (eds.), *At the Boundaries of Law: Feminism and Legal Theory* (New York: Routledge).

—— (1997), 'More Folk Provoke their own Demise (Homophobic Violence and Sexed Excuses): Rejoining the Provocation Law Debate, Courtesy of the Homosexual Advance Defence', *Sydney Law Review* 19: 336.

HOYANO, A., HOYANO, L., DAVIS, G., AND GOLDIE, S. (1997), 'A Study on the Impact of the Revised Code for Crown Prosecutors', *Criminal Law Review* 556.

HOYLE, C. (1998), *Negotiating Domestic Violence* (Oxford: Oxford University Press).

—— AND TOUNG, R. (2002), *Proceed with Caution: An Evaluation of the Thames Valley Police Initiative in Restorative Cautioning* (York : Joseph Rowntree Foundation).

HUBER, B. (1980), 'The Dilemma of Decriminalisation: Dealing with Shoplifting in West Germany', *Criminal Law Review* 621.

HUDSON, B. (1994), 'Punishing the Poor: A Critique of the Dominance of Legal Reasoning in Penal Policy and Practice' in A. Duff, S. Marsha II, R. Dobash, and R. Dobash (eds.), *Penal Theory and Practice* (Manchester: Manchester University Press).

HUDSON, S. (1980), 'Character Traits and Desires', *Ethics* 90: 539.

HUGHES, G. (1958), 'Criminal Omissions', *Yale Law Journal* 67: 590.

HUIGENS, K. (1998), 'Virtue and Criminal Negligence', *Buffalo Criminal Law Review* 1: 431.

—— (2005), 'Is Strict Liability Rape Defensible?' in R.A. Duff and S. Green (eds.), *Defining Crimes* (Oxford: Oxford University Press).

HURD, H. (1996), 'The Moral Magic of Consent', *Legal Theory* 2: 121.

HUSAK, D. (1989a), 'Motive and Criminal Liability', *Criminal Justice Ethics* 1: 3.

—— (1989b), 'Recreational Drugs and Paternalism', *Law and Philosophy* 8: 353.

—— (1994), 'Ignorance of Law and Duties of Citizenship', *Legal Studies* 14: 105.

—— (1995a), 'The Relevance of the Concept of Action to the Criminal Law', *Criminal Law Forum* 6: 327.

—— (1995b), 'The Nature and Justifiability of Nonconsummate Offenses', *Arizona Law Review* 37: 151.

—— (1997), 'Attempts and the Philosophical Foundations of Criminal Liability', *Criminal Law Forum* 8: 293.

—— (1998a), 'Partial Defenses', *Canadian Journal of Law and Jurisprudence* 11: 167.

—— (1998b), 'Reasonable Risk Creation and Over-inclusive Legislation', *Buffalo Criminal Law Review* 1: 599.

—— (1999a), 'The Function and Structure of the Substantive Criminal Law', *Law and Philosophy* 19: 85.

—— (1999b), 'Does Criminal Liability Require an Act?' in A. Duff (ed.), *Philosophy and the Criminal Law* (Cambridge: Cambridge University Press).

—— (2002), 'Limitations on Criminalization' in S. Shute and A. Simester (eds.), *Criminal Law Theory* (Oxford: Oxford University Press).

—— (2005), 'Strict Liability, Justice, and Proportionality' in A. Simester (ed.), *Appraising Strict Liability* (Oxford: Oxford University Press).

—— AND CALLENDER, D. (1994), 'Wilful Ignorance, Knowledge and the "Equality Culpability" Thesis', *Wisconsin Law Review* 129.

—— AND THOMAS III, G. (1992), 'Date Rape, Social Convention and Reasonable Mistakes', *Law and Philosophy* 11: 109.

—— AND VON HIRSCH, A. (1993), 'Culpability and Mistake of Law' in S. Shute, J. Gardner, and J. Horder (eds.), *Action and Value in the Criminal Law* (Oxford: Oxford University Press).

HUXTABLE, R. (2002), 'Separation of Conjoined Twins: Where Next for Criminal Law', *Criminal Law Review* 459.

INFIELD, P., AND PLATFORD, G. (2000), *The Law of Harassment and Stalking* (London: Butterworths).

ISENBERGH, J. (1993), 'Blackmail from A to C', *University of Pennsylvania Law Review* 141: 1905.

JACKSON, B. (1991), '*Storkwain*: A Case Study in Strict Liability and Self-Regulation', *Criminal Law Review* 892.

JAREBORG, N. (1993), 'Criminal Attempts and Moral Luck', *Israel Law Review* 27: 213.

—— (1995), 'What Kind of Criminal Law Do We Want?' in A. Snare (ed.), *Beware of Punishment* (Oslo: Pax Forlag).

JARVIS THOMSON, J. (1986), *Rights, Restitution and Risk* (Cambridge, Mass.: Harvard University Press).

—— (1991), 'Self-defence', *Philosophy and Public Affairs* 20: 283.

JELLINEK, E. (1969), *The Disease Concept of Alcoholism* (New Haven, Conn.: Millhouse Press).

JOHNSTONE, G. (2002), *Restorative Justice* (Cullompton: Willan).

JONES, A. (1995), 'Insanity, Automatism and the Burden of Proof on the Accused', *Law Quarterly Review* 111: 473.

JONES, O. (2000), 'Law and the Biology of Rape: Reflections on Transitions', *Hastings Women's Law Journal* 11: 151.

JUDICIAL STUDIES BOARD (2004), *Crown Court Bench Book* (London: Judicial Studies Board).

KADISH, S. (1958), 'The Crisis of Overcriminalisation', *Annals* 374: 157.

—— (1968), 'The Decline of Innocence', *Cambridge Law Journal* 26: 273.

—— (1976), 'Respect of Life and Regard for Rights in the Criminal Law', *California Law Review* 64: 871.

—— (1985), 'Complicity, Cause and Blame: A Study in the Interpretation of Doctrine', *California Law Review* 73: 324.

—— (1987a), 'Excusing Crime', *California Law Review* 75: 257.

—— (1987b), *Blame and Punishment* (New York: Macmillan).

—— (1994), 'The Criminal Law and the Luck of the Draw', *Journal of Criminal Law and Criminology* 84: 679.

—— (1997), 'Reckless Complicity', *Journal of Criminal Law and Criminology* 87: 369.

—— (1998), 'Punishment Incommensurability', *Buffalo Criminal Law Review* 1: 691.

KAGANAS, F. (2002), 'Domestic Violence, Gender and the Expert' in A. Bainham, S. Day Sclater, and M. Richards (eds.), *Body Lore and Laws* (Oxford: Hart).

KAMM, M. (1994), 'Action, Omission, and the Stringency of Duties', *University of Pennsylvania Law Review* 142: 1493.

KASUBHAI, M. (1996), 'Destabilizing Power In Rape: Why Consent Theory in Rape Law is Turned on its Head', *Wisconsin Women's Law Journal* 11: 37.

KATYAL, N. (2001), 'Criminal Law in Cyberspace', *University of Pennsylvania Law Review* 149: 1003.

KATZ, L. (1987), *Bad Acts and Guilty Minds* (Chicago, Ill.: University of Chicago Press).

—— (1993), 'Blackmail and other Forms of Arm-Twisting', *University of Pennsylvania Law Review* 141: 1567.

—— (1996), *Ill-Gotten Gains: Evasion, Blackmail, Fraud, and Kindred Puzzles of the Law* (Chicago, Ill.: University of Chicago Press).

—— (2002), 'A Problem Concerning Criminalization', *Buffalo Criminal Law Review* 6: 451.

KAUFMAN, L (1997), 'Legal Recognition of Independent Fetal Rights', *Children's Legal Rights Journal* 17: 20.

KAVENY, C. (2004), 'Inferring Intention from Foresight', *Law Quarterly Review* 120: 81.

KEATING, H. (1996), 'The Restatement of Serious Crime', *Criminal Law Review* 535.

KEITER, M. (1997), 'Just Say No Excuse', *Journal of Criminal Law and Criminology* 87: 402.

KELL, D. (1994), 'Social Disutility and the Law of Consent', *Oxford Journal of Legal Studies* 14: 121.

KELLY, L., AND RADFORD, J. (1987), 'The Problem of Men: Feminist Perspectives on Sexual Violence' in P. Scraton (ed.), *Law, Order and the Authoritarian State* (Oxford: Oxford University Press).

KELLY, L., LOVETT, J. AND REGAN, L. (2005), *A Gap or a Chasm? Attrition in Reported Rape Cases* (Home Office Research Study 293).

KELMAN, M. (1981), 'Interpretive Construction in the Substantive Criminal Law', *Stanford Law Review* 33: 591.

KENNEDY, I., AND GRUBB, A. (2000), *Medical Law* (London: Butterworths).

KENNY, A. (1978), *Freewill and Responsibility* (London: Routledge and Kegan Paul).

KEOWN, J. (2002), *Euthanasia and Public Policy* (Cambridge: Cambridge University Press).

KERSHAW, C., BUDD, T., KINSHOTT, G., MATTINSON, J., MAYHEW, P., AND MYHILL, A. (2001), *The 2000 British Crime Survey* (London: HMSO).

KESSLER, K. (1994), 'The Role of Luck in the Criminal Law', *University of Pennsylvania Law Review* 142: 2183.

KESSLER FERZAN, K. (2001), 'Opaque Recklessness', *Journal of Criminal Law and Criminology* 91: 597.

—— (2002), 'Don't Abandon the Model Penal Code Yet! Thinking Through Simons's Rethinking', *Buffalo Criminal Law Review* 6: 185.

KHANNA, V. (1996), 'Corporate Criminal Liability; What Purpose does it Serve?', *Harvard Law Review* 109: 1477.

KHLIQ, U., AND YOUNG, J. (2001), 'Cultural Diversity, Human Rights and Inconsistency in the English Courts', *Legal Studies* 21: 192.

KIMEL, D. (2004), 'Inadvertent Recklessness in the Criminal Law', *Law Quarterly Review* 120: 548.

KINPORTS, K. (2001), 'Rape and Force: The Forgotten Mens Rea', *Buffalo Criminal Law Review* 4: 755.

KLANG, M. (2003), 'A Critical Look at the regulation of Computer Viruses', *International Journal of Law and IT* 162.

KLIMCHUK, D. (1994), 'Outrage, Self-Control and Culpability', *University of Toronto Law Journal* 44: 441.

—— (1998), 'Causation, Thin Skulls and Equality', *Canadian Journal of Law and Jurisprudence* 11: 115.

Koss, M. (2002), *Acquaintance Rape: A Critical Update on Recent Findings with Application to Advocacy*, vip.msu.edu/theCAT/CAT_Author/MPK/colorado.html.

KREMNITZER, M. (1984), 'The Punishability of Impossible Attempts', *Israel Law Review* 19: 340.

KRISTOL, I. (1971), 'Pornography, Obscenity and the Case for Censorship', *New York Times*, 28 March.

KUGLER, I. (2002), *Direct and Oblique Intention in the Criminal Law* (Aldershot: Ashgate).

—— (2004), 'Conditional Oblique Intention', *Criminal Law Review* 284.

LACEY, N. (1988), *State Punishment* (London: Routledge).

—— (1993a), 'A Clear Concept of Intention: Elusive or Illusory', *Modern Law Review* 56: 621.

—— (1993b), 'Theory into Practice? Pornography and the Public/Private Dichotomy' in A. Bottomley and J. Conaghan (eds.), *Feminist Theory and Legal Strategy* (Oxford: Blackwell).

—— (1995a), 'Contingency and Criminalisation' in I. Loveland (ed.), *The Frontiers of Criminality* (London: Sweet & Maxwell).

—— (1995b), 'In(de)terminable Intentions', *Modern Law Review* 58: 592.

—— (1996), 'Community in Legal Theory: Idea Ideal or Ideology?', *Studies in Law Politics and Society* 15: 105.

—— (1998a), 'Contingency, Coherence and Conceptualism' in A. Duff (ed.), *Philosophy and the Criminal Law* (Cambridge: Cambridge University Press).

—— (1998b), *Unspeakable Subjects* (Oxford: Hart).

—— (1998c), 'Unspeakable Subjects, Impossible Rights: Sexuality, Integrity and Criminal Law', *Canadian Journal of Law and Jurisprudence* 11: 47.

—— (2000a), 'Partial Defences of Homicide' in A. Ashworth and B. Mitchell (eds.), *Rethinking English Homicide Law* (Oxford: Oxford University Press).

—— (2000b), ' "Philosophical Foundations of Common Law": Social not Metaphysical' in J. Horder (ed.), *Oxford Essays in Jurisprudence* (Oxford: Oxford University Press).

—— (2001a), 'In Search of the Responsible Subject', *Modern Law Review* 64: 350.

—— (2001b), 'Beset by Boundaries: The Home Office Review of Sex Offences', *Criminal Law Review* 3.

—— (2001c), 'General Principles of Criminal Law. A Feminist View' in D. Nicolson and L. Bibbings (eds.), *Feminist Perspectives on Criminal Law* (London: Cavendish).

—— (2002), 'Legal Constructions of Crime' in M. Maguire, R. Morgan, and R. Reiner (eds.), *The Oxford Handbook of Criminology* (Oxford: Oxford University Press).

—— AND WELLS, C. (1998), *Reconstructing Criminal Law* (London: Butterworths).

LAMBIRAS, J. (2003), 'White-Collar Crime: Why the Sentencing Disparity Despite Uniform Guidelines?', *Pepperdine Law Review* 30: 459.

LAMOND, G. (1996), 'Coercion, Threats, and the Puzzle of Blackmail' in A. Simester and A. Smith (eds.), *Harm and Culpability* (Oxford: Oxford University Press).

LANE COMMITTEE ON THE PENALTY FOR MURDER (CHAIRMAN SIR GEOFFREY LANE) (1993), *Report of the Committee on the Penalty for Murder* (London: Prison Reform Trust).

LANHAM, D. (1966), 'Defence of Property in the Criminal Law', *Criminal Law Review* 368.

—— (1976), '*Larsonneur* Revisted', *Criminal Law Review* 276.

—— (1981), 'Accomplices and Withdrawal', *Law Quarterly Review* 97: 575.

—— (1988), 'Death of a Qualified Defence?', *Law Quarterly Review* 104: 239.

—— (1999), 'Danger Down Under', *Criminal Law Review* 980.

—— (2000), 'Primary and Derivative Criminal Liability: An Australian Perspective', *Criminal Law Review* 707.

—— (2005), 'Offensive Weapons and Self-Defence', *Criminal Law Review* 85.

LARSON, J. (1993), 'Women Understand so Little, They Call My Good Nature "Deceit": A Feminist Rethinking of Seduction', *Columbia Law Review* 93: 374.

—— (1999), *Hard Bargains: The Politics of Sex* (New York: Oxford University Press).

LAUER, T. (1997), 'Burglary in Wyoming', *Law & Water Law Review* 32: 721.

LAW COMMISSION (1976), Report No. 76, *Conspiracy and Criminal Law Reform* (London: HMSO).

—— (1977), Report No. 83, *Defences of General Application* (London: HMSO).

—— (1988), Working Paper No. 110, *Computer Misuse* (London: HMSO).

—— (1989), Report No. 186, *Computer Misuse* (London: HMSO).

—— (1992), Report No. 218, *Legislating the Criminal Code: Offences against the Person and General Principles* (London: HMSO).

—— (1993), Consultation Paper No. 131, *Assisting and Encouraging Crime* (London: HMSO).

—— (1994), Consultation Paper No. 136, *The Year and a Day Rule in Homicide* (London: HMSO).

—— (1995), Report No. 139, *Consent in the Criminal Law* (London: HMSO).

—— (1996), Report No. 237, *Legislating the Criminal Code: Involuntary Manslaughter* (London: HMSO).

—— (1997), Consultation Paper No. 150, *Misuses of Trade Secrets* (London: HMSO).

—— (1999), Report No. 243, *Offences of Dishonesty: Money Transfers* (London: HMSO).

—— (2000), *Report on Consent in Sex Offences* (London: HMSO).

—— (2002), Report No. 276, *Fraud* (London: HMSO).

—— (2003), Report No. 279, *Children: Their Non-accidental Death or Serious Injury* (London: HMSO).

—— (2005), Consultation Paper No. 177, *A New Homicide Act for England and Wales* (London: TSO).

LEAVENS, A. (1988), 'A Causation Approach To Criminal Omissions', *California Law Review* 76: 547.

LEE, C. (1998), 'The Act–Belief Distinction in Self-Defense Doctrine: A New Dual Requirement Theory of Justification', *Buffalo Criminal Law Review* 2: 191.

LEES, S. (1996), *Carnal Knowledge. Rape on Trial* (London: Hamish Hamilton).

LEIGH, L. (1982), *Strict and Vicarious Liability* (London: Sweet & Maxwell).

—— (1993), 'Recklessness after Reid', *Modern Law Review* 56: 208.

—— (1995), 'Liability for Inadvertence', *Modern Law Review* 58: 457.

LEITENBERG, H., AND SLATZMAN, H. (2003), 'College Women Who Had Sexual Intercourse When They Were Underage Minors (13–15): Age of Their Male Partners, Relation to Current Adjustment, and Statutory Rape Implications', *Sexual Abuse* 15: 135.

LELLING, A. (1998), 'A Psychological Critique of Character-based Theories of Criminal Excuse', *Syracuse Law Review* 49: 35.

LENG, R. (1994), 'Consent and Offences Against the Person', *Criminal Law Review* 480.

LERMAN, L. (1999), 'Blue-chip Bilking: Regulation of Billing and Expense Fraud by Lawyers', *Georgia Journal of Legal Ethics* 12: 205.

LEVENSON, L. (1993), 'Good Faith Defenses: Reshaping Strict Liability Crimes', *Cornell Law Review* 78: 401.

LEVERICK, F. (2002a), 'Is English Self-defence Law Incompatible with Article 2 of the ECHR?', *Criminal Law Review* 347.

—— (2002b), 'The Use of Force in Public on Private Defence and Article 2: A Reply to Professor John Smith', *Criminal Law Review* 963.

LEVI, M. (1987), *Regulating Fraud: White-collar Crime and the Criminal Process* (London: Tavistock).

—— (2000), *The Prevention of Plastic and Cheque Fraud* (London: Home Office).

—— (2002a), 'Economic Crime' in M. McConville and G. Wilson (eds.), *The Handbook of the Criminal Justice Process* (Oxford: Oxford University Press).

—— (2002b), 'Violent Crime' in M. Maguire, R. Morgan, and R. Reiner (eds.), *The Oxford Handbook of Criminology* (Oxford: Oxford University Press).

—— AND SMITH, A. (2002), *Organised Crime and Conspiracy Legislation* (London: Home Office).

LEVRANT, S., CULLEN, F., FULTON, B., AND WOZNIAK, J. (1999), 'Reconsidering Restorative-Justice', *Crime and Delinquency* 45: 3.

LEWIS, J. (1989), 'The Punishment that Leaves Something to Chance', *Philosophy and Public Affairs* 18: 53.

LEWIS, P. (2000), 'The Human Rights Act 1998: Shifting the Burden', *Criminal Law Review* 306.

LIBLING, D. (1978), 'The Concept of Property: Property in Intangibles', *Law Quarterly Review* 94: 103.

LINDGREN, J. (1989a), 'Blackmail: On Waste, Morals, and Ronald Coase', *University of California Los Angeles Law Review* 36: 597.

—— (1989b), 'Secret Rights: A Comment on Campbell's Theory of Blackmail', *Connecticut Law Review* 21: 407.

—— (1993a), 'Blackmail: An Afterword', *University of Pennsylvania Law Review* 141: 1639.

—— (1993b), 'The Theory, History, and Practice of the Bribery-Extortion Distinction', *University of Pennsylvania Law Review* 141: 1695.

LIPKIN, R. (1983), 'Beyond Good Samaritans and Moral Monsters: An Individualistic Justification of the General Legal Duty to Rescue', *University of California Los Angeles Law Review* 31: 252.

LIPTON, J. (2001), 'Protecting Valuable Commercial Information in the Digital Age', *Journal of Technology, Law and Policy* 6.1: 2.

LLOYD-BOSTOCK, S. (1979), 'The Ordinary Man, and the Psychology of Attributing Causes and Responsibility', *Modern Law Review* 42: 143.

LUBAN, D. (1999), 'Contrived Ignorance', *Georgia Law Journal* 87: 957.

Lucas, J. (1980), *On Justice* (Oxford: Oxford University Press).

Lucy, W., and Mitchell, C. (1996), 'Replacing Private Property: The Case for Stewardship', *Cambridge Law Journal* 55: 566.

Lutz, V., and Bonomolo, C. (1997), 'My Husband Just Trashed Our Home; What Do You Mean That's Not a Crime?', *South Carolina Law Review* 48: 641.

MacCormick, N. (1982), *Legal Right and Social Democracy* (Oxford: Oxford University Press).

Mack, E. (1980), 'Bad Samaritanism and the Causation of Harm', *Philosophy and Public Affairs* 9: 230.

Mackay, R. (1988), 'Pleading Provocation and Diminished Responsibility Together', *Criminal Law Review* 411.

—— (1990), 'Fact and Fiction about the Insanity Defence', *Criminal Law Review* 247.

—— (1993), 'The Consequences of Killing Very Young Children', *Criminal Law Review* 21.

—— (1995), *Mental Condition Defences in the Criminal Law* (Oxford: Oxford University Press).

—— (2000), 'Diminished Responsibility and Mentally Disordered Killers' in A. Ashworth and B. Mitchell (eds.), *Rethinking English Homicide Law* (Oxford: Oxford University Press).

—— and Kearns, G. (1999), 'More Fact(s) about the Insanity Defence', *Criminal Law Review* 714.

—— and —— (2000), 'An Upturn in Unfitness to Plead? Disability in Relation to the Trial under the 1991 Act', *Criminal Law Review* 532.

—— and Machin, D. (2000), 'Transfers from Prison to Hospital; An Empirical Study of the Operation of Section 48 of the Mental Health Act 1983', *British Journal of Criminology* 40: 732.

—— and —— (2005), 'But is this Provocation? Some thought on the Law commission report on Partial Defences to Murder', *Criminal Law Review* 44.

—— and Mitchell, B. (2003), 'Provoking Diminished Responsibility: Two Pleas Merging into One', *Criminal Law Review* 745.

—— and —— (2004), 'Replacing Provocation', *Criminal Law Review* 219.

—— and —— (2005), 'But is this Provocation? Some thought on the Law Comission Report on Partial Defences to Murder', *Criminal Law Review* 44.

Mackenna, B. (1970), 'Causing Death by Reckless or Dangerous Driving: A Suggestion', *Criminal Law Review* 67.

Mackie, J. (1977), 'The Grounds of Responsibility' in P. Hacker and J. Raz (eds.), *Law Morality and Society* (Oxford: Clarendon).

—— (1989), 'Morality and Retributive Emotions', *Criminal Justice Ethics* 1: 3.

MacKinnon, C. (1983), 'Feminism, Marxism, Method and the State', *Signs* 8: 635.

—— (1989), *Towards A Feminist Theory of the State* (Cambridge, Mass.: Harvard University Press).

—— (2000), 'Points Against Postmodernism', *Chicago-Kent Law Review* 75: 687.

MAGUIGAN, H. (1991), 'Battered Women and Self-Defense: Myths and Misconceptions in Current Reform Proposals', *University of Pennsylvania Law Review* 140: 379.

MAGUIRE, M. (2002), 'Crime Statistics, Patterns, and Trends' in M. Maguire, R. Morgan, and R. Reiner (eds.) *The Oxford Handbook of Criminology* (Oxford: Oxford University Press).

—— AND BENNETT, T. (1982), *Burglary in a Dwelling* (London: Heinemann).

—— AND KYNCH, J. (2000), *Public Perceptions and Victims' Experiences of Victim Support* (London: HMSO).

MAIER-KATKIN, D., AND OGLE, R. (1993), 'A Rationale for Infanticide Laws', *Criminal Law Review* 903.

MALIK, S. (1998), 'Racist Crime: Racially Aggravated Offences in the Crime and Disorder Act 1998, Part II', *Modern Law Review* 62: 409.

MANDHANE, R. (2001), 'Efficiency or Autonomy?: Economic and Feminist Legal Theory in the Context of Sexual Assault', *University of Toronto Faculty Law Review* 59: 173.

MANDIL, D. (1987), 'Chance, Freedom, and Criminal Liability', *Columbia Law Review* 87: 125.

MANN, T. (1992), 'Punitive Civil Sanctions: The Middle Ground Between Criminal and Civil Law', *Yale Law Journal* 101: 1795.

MARS, G. (1982), *Cheats at Work* (London: Unwin Paperbacks).

MARSH, P., BRADLEY, S., PECK, F., AND CARNIBELLA, A. (2001), *The Measurement and Recording of Alcohol-related Violence and Disorder* (London: The Portman Group).

MARSHALL, S., AND DUFF, A. (1998), 'Criminalisation and Sharing Wrongs', *Canadian Journal of Law and Jurisprudence* 11: 7.

MARSHALL, T. (1998), *Restorative Justice: An Overview* (London: Home Office).

MARSTON, G. (1970), 'Contemporaneity of Act and Intention in Crimes', *Law Quarterly Review* 86: 208.

MARTINSON, R. (1974), 'What Works? Questions and Answers about Prison Reform', *Public Interest* 35: 22.

MARX, K., AND ENGELS, F. (1967), *The Communist Manifesto* (London: Penguin).

MASON, T., AND MERCER, D. (1999), *The Sociology of the Mentally Disordered Offender* (Harlow: Longman).

MATTHEWS, P. (1995), 'The Man of Property', *Medical Law Review* 3: 251.

MATTHEWS, R. (2002), *Armed Robbery* (Cullompton: Willan).

MATTINSON, J., AND MIRRLEES-BLACK, S. (2000), *Attitudes to Crime and Criminal Justice* (London: Home Office).

Mawby, R. (2001), *Burglary* (Cullompton: Willan).

May, L., and Strikwerda, R. (1994), 'Men in Groups: Collective Responsibility for Rape', *Hypatia* 9: 1.

McAnaney, K., Curliss, L., and Abeyta-Price, C. (1993), 'From Imprudence to Crime: Anti-Stalking Laws', *Notre Dame Law Review* 68: 819.

McAuley, F. (1987), 'Anticipating the Past: The Defence of Provocation in Irish Law', *Modern Law Review* 50: 133.

McCall Smith, A. (1993), 'The Duty to Rescue and the Common Law' in M. Menloweand A. McCall Smith (eds.), *The Duty to Rescue. The Jurisprudence of Aid* (Aldershot: Dartmouth).

McColgan, A. (1993), 'In Defence of Battered Women who Kill', *Oxford Journal of Legal Studies* 15: 508.

—— (2000a), 'General Defences' in D. Nicolson and L. Bibbings (eds.), *Feminist Perspectives on Criminal Law* (London: Cavendish).

—— (2000b), *Women Under the Law* (Harlow: Longman).

McConville, M. (2002), 'Plea Bargaining' in M. Maguire and G. Wilson (eds.), *The Criminal Justice Process* (Oxford: Oxford University Press).

McEwan, J. (2001), 'Murder by Design: The "Feel-Good Factor" and the Criminal Law', *Medical Law Review* 9: 246.

McGregor, J. (1996), 'Why When She Says No She Doesn't Mean Maybe and Doesn't Mean Yes', *Legal Studies* 2: 175.

—— (2005), *Is it Rape?* (Aldershot: Ashgate).

McLaren, A. (2002), *Sexual Blackmail: A Modern History* (Cambridge, Mass.: Harvard University Press).

Mead, G. (1991), 'Contracting into Crime: A Theory of Criminal Omissions', *Oxford Journal of Legal Studies* 11: 147.

Mednick, S., Gabrielli, W., and Hutchings, B. (1984), 'Genetic Influences in Criminal Conviction—Evidence Adopted Cohort', *Science* 224: 891.

Melden, A. (1968), 'Willing' in A. White (ed.), *The Philosophy of Action* (Oxford: Oxford University Press).

Menlowe, M. (1993), 'The Philosophical Foundation of a Duty to Rescue' in M. Menlowe and A. McCall Smith (ed.), *The Duty to Rescue. The Jurisprudence of Aid* (Aldershot: Dartmouth).

Menninger, K. (1868), *The Crime of Punishment* (New York: Viking Press).

Michael, A. (1993), *Safe As Houses? Burglary of Homes: An Analysis* (London: Labour Party).

Michaelman, F. (1990), 'Private, Personal But Not Split: *Randin v Rorty*', *Southern California Law Review* 63: 1783.

MICHAELS, A. (1998), 'Acceptance: The Missing Mental State', *Southern California Law Review* 71: 953.

—— (1999), 'Constitutional Innocence', *Harvard Law Review* 112: 828.

MICHALOWSKI, S. (2002), 'Sanctity of Life—are Some Lives more Sacred than Others?', *Legal Studies* 22: 377.

MIERS, D., MAGUIRE, M., GOLDIE, S., SHARPE, K., HALE, C., NETTEN, A., UGLOW, S., DOOLIN, K., HALLAM, A., ENTERKIN, J., AND NEWBURN, T. (2001), *An Exploratory Evaluation of Restorative Justice Schemes* (London: Home Office).

MILES, J. (2001), 'Domestic Violence' in J. Herring (ed.), *Family Law: Issues, Debates and Policy* (Cullompton: Willan).

MILL, J. (1991), 'On Liberty' in J. Mill, *On Liberty and other Essays* (ed. J. Gray, Oxford: Oxford University Press).

MIRRLEES-BLACK, C. (1999), *Domestic Violence* (London: Home Office).

—— AND ALLEN, J. (1998), *Concern about Crime: Findings from the 1998 British Crime Survey* (London: Home Office).

—— AND BAYRON, C. (2000), *Domestic Violence: Findings from the BCS Self-Completion Questionnaire* (London: Home Office).

——, MAYHEW, P., AND PERCY, A. (1996), *The 1996 British Crime Survey* (London: Home Office).

MITCHELL, B. (1996), 'Culpably Indifferent Murder', *Anglo-American Law Review* 25: 64.

—— (1998), 'Public Perceptions of Homicide and Criminal Justice', *British Journal of Criminology* 38: 453.

—— (1999), 'In Defence of the Correspondence Principle', *Criminal Law Review* 195.

—— (2000), 'Further Evidence of the Relationship Between Legal and Public Opinion on the Homicide Law', *Criminal Law Review* 814.

—— (2001), 'Multiple Wrongdoing and Offence Structure: A Plea for Consistency and Fair Labelling', *Modern Law Review* 64: 393.

MITCHELL, C. (1988), 'The Intoxicated Offender—Refuting the Legal and Medical Myths', *International Journal of Law and Psychology* 11: 77.

MITCHELL, E. (2003), *Self-Made Madness* (London: Avebury).

MOERINGS, M. (2001), 'The Fight Against Sex with Children' in P. Alldridge and C. Brants, *Personal Autonomy, the Private Sphere and the Criminal Law* (Oxford: Hart).

MOONEY, J. (2002), 'Revealing the Hidden Figure of Domestic Violence' in J. Hanmer and C. Itzen (eds.), *Home Truths About Domestic Violence* (London: Routledge).

MOORE, A. (1990), 'A Kantian View of Moral Luck', *Philosophy* 65: 297.

MOORE, M. (1984), *Law and Psychiatry* (Cambridge: Cambridge University Press).

—— (1985a), 'Causation and Excuse', *California Law Review* 73: 1091.

—— (1985b), 'The Moral and Metaphysical Sources of the Criminal Law' in J. Pennock and J. Chapman (eds.), *Criminal Justice* (New York: New York Press).

—— (1987), 'The Moral Worth of Retribution' in F. Schoeman (ed.), *Responsibility, Character and the Emotions* (Cambridge: Cambridge University Press).

—— (1990), 'Choice, Character and Excuse' in E. Paul, F. Miller, and J. Paul (eds.), *Crime, Culpability and Remedy* (Oxford: Blackwell).

—— (1993), *Act and Crime* (Oxford: Clarendon).

—— (1994), 'More on *Act and Crime*', *University of Pennsylvania Law Review* 142: 1749.

—— (1996), 'Prima Facie Moral Culpability', *Boston University Law Review* 76: 319.

—— (1997), *Placing Blame* (Oxford: Oxford University Press).

—— (1999), 'Causation and Responsibility', *Social Philosophy and Policy* 16: 1.

—— (2000), 'The Metaphysics of Causal Intervention', *California Law Review* 88: 8127.

MORAN, L. (1998), '*Laskey v The United Kingdom*: Learning the Limits of Privacy', *Modern Law Review* 61: 77.

MORAN, M. (2003), *Rethinking the Reasonable Person* (Oxford: Oxford University Press).

MORGAN, J., AND ZEDNER, L. (1992), *Child Victims* (Oxford: Oxford University Press).

MORGAN, R. (1980), 'Theory and Practice: Pornography and Rape' in L. Lederer (ed.), *Take Back the Night: Women on Pornography* (New York: William Morrow & Co.).

MORRIS, A. (1987), *Women, Crime and Criminal Justice* (Oxford: Blackwell).

—— AND YOUNG, W. (2000), 'The Practice of Family Group Conferences in New Zealand' in A. Crawford and J. Goodey (eds.), *Integrating a Victim Perspective within Criminal Justice* (Aldershot: Ashgate).

MORRIS, H. (1982), 'Persons and Punishment', *The Monist* 52: 475.

—— (1994), 'A Paternalistic Theory of Punishment', in A. Duff and D. Garland (eds.), *A Reader on Punishment* (Oxford: Oxford University Press).

MORRIS, N. (1969), *Madness and the Criminal Law* (Chicago, Ill.: University of Chicago Press).

—— (1982), 'The Criminal Responsibility of the Mentally Ill', *Syracuse Law Review* 33: 477.

—— (1994), ' "Dangerousness" and Incapacitation' in A. Duff and D. Garland (eds.), *A Reader on Punishment* (Oxford: Oxford University Press).

MORRIS, T., AND BLOM-COOPER, L. (1964), *A Calendar of Murder* (London: Joseph).

MORSE, S. (1985a), 'Excusing the Crazy: The Insanity Defense Reconsidered', *South California Law Review* 58: 777.

—— (1985b), 'Psychology, Determinism and Legal Responsibility' in G. Melton (ed.), *Nebraska Symposium on Motivation* (Lincoln, Neb.: University of Nebraska Press).

—— (1993), 'Diminished Capacity' in S. Shute, J. Gardner, and J. Horder (eds.), *Action and Value in the Criminal Law* (Oxford: Oxford University Press).

—— (1994), 'Culpability and Control', *University of Pennsylvania Law Review* 142: 1587.

—— (1996), 'Brain and Blame', *Georgia Law Review* 84: 527.

—— (2000), 'The Moral Metaphysics of Causation and Results', *California Law Review* 88: 879.

—— (2004), 'Reason, Results and Criminal Responsibility', *University of Illinois Law Review* 363.

MORTON, J. (2003a), 'An Imperfect Bill', *Law Society Gazette* 100(9): 17.

—— (2003b), 'The Sexual Offences Bill', *Journal of Criminal Law* 64: 183.

MOUSOURAKIS, G. (1998a), *Criminal Responsibility and Partial Excuse* (Aldershot: Ashgate).

—— (1998b), 'Character, Choice and Criminal Responsibility', *Cahiers de Droit* 39: 51.

MUEHLENHARD, C., AND COOK, S. (1988), 'Men's Self-Reports of Unwanted Sexual Activity', *Journal of Sexual Research* 24: 58.

—— AND HOLLABAUGH, L. (1988), 'Do Women Sometimes Say No When They Mean Yes? The Prevalence and Correlates of Women's Token Resistance to Sex', *Journal of Personality and Social Psychology* 54: 872.

MUELLER, G. (1998), 'The Mens Rea of Accomplice Liability', *Southern California Law Review* 61: 2169.

MUIRFIELD, P. (1999), 'Letter', *Criminal Law Review* 246.

MULLEN, P., PATHE, M., AND PURCELL, R. (2000), *Stalkers and their Victims* (Cambridge: Cambridge University Press).

MUNZER, S. (1990), *A Theory of Property* (Cambridge: Cambridge University Press).

MURPHY, J. (1980), 'Blackmail: A Preliminary Inquiry', *Monist* 63: 156.

—— (1994), 'Some Ruminations on Women, Violence and the Criminal Law' in J. Coleman and A. Buchanan, *Harms's Way* (Cambridge: Cambridge University Press).

MURPHY, J.G. (1979), *Retribution, Justice and Therapy* (Dordrecht: D. Reidel Publishing Company).

—— (1994), 'Marxism and Retribution' in A. Duff and D. Garland (eds.), *A Reader on Punishment* (Oxford: Oxford University Press).

MURPHY, L. (2001), 'Beneficence, Law, and Liberty: The Case of Required Rescue', *Georgia Law Journal* 89: 605.

MYHILL, A., AND ALLEN, J. (2002), *Rape and Sexual Assault of Women the Extent and Nature of the Problem* (London: Home Office).

NAFFINE, N. (1994), 'Possession: Erotic Love in the Law of Rape', *Modern Law Review* 57: 10.

—— (1997), *Feminism and Criminology* (Cambridge: Polity Press).

—— (1998), *Law and the Sexes* (Sydney: Allen and Unwin).

—— (2002), 'In Praise of Legal Feminism', *Legal Studies* 22: 71.

NAGEL, T. (1979), *Mortal Questions* (Cambridge: Cambridge University Press).

NELKEN, D. (1987), 'Critical Criminal Law', *Journal of Law and Society* 14: 105.

—— (2002), 'White-Collar Crime' in M. Maguire, R. Morgan, and R. Reiner (eds.), *The Oxford Handbook of Criminology* (Oxford: Oxford University Press).

NELSON, C. (2001), 'Enraged or Engaged: The Implications of Racial Context to the Canadian Provocation Defence', *University of Richmond Law Review* 35: 1007.

NEMERSON, S. (1970), 'Criminal Liability Without Fault', *Columbia Law Review* 75: 517.

NEWBURN, T., CRAWFORD, A., EARLE, R., GOLDIE, S., HALE, C., MASTERS, G., NETTEN, A., SAUNDERS, R., SHARPE, K., AND UGLOW, S. (2001), *The Introduction of Referral Orders into the Youth Justice System: Second Interim Report* (London: Home Office).

NEWELL, P. (2002), 'Global Progress on Giving Up the Habit of Hitting Children' in B. Franklin (ed.), *The New Handbook of Children's Rights* (London: Routledge).

NICHOLAS, S., POVEY, D., WALKER, A. AND KERSHAW, C. (2005), *Crime in England and Wales 2004/2005* (London: Home Office).

NICOLSON, D. (1992), 'The Citizen's Duty to Assist the Police', *Criminal Law Review* 611.

—— (1995), 'Telling Tales: Gender Discrimination, Gender Construction and Battered Women Who Kill', *Feminist Legal Studies* 3: 185.

—— AND BIBBINGS, L. (eds.) (2001), *Feminist Perspectives on Criminal Law* (London: Cavendish).

—— AND SANGHVI, R. (1993), 'Battered Women and Provocation', *Criminal Law Review* 728.

NORRIE, A. (1991), 'A Critique of Criminal Causation', *Modern Law Review* 54: 685.

—— (1992), 'Subjectivism, Objectivism and the Limits of Criminal Recklessness', *Oxford Journal of Legal Studies* 12: 45.

—— (1996), 'The Limits of Justice. Finding Fault in the Criminal Law', *Modern Law Review* 59: 540.

—— (1998), 'Simulacra of Morality' in R. Duff (ed.), *Philosophy and the Criminal Law* (Cambridge: Cambridge University Press).

—— (1999), 'After *Woollin*', *Criminal Law Review* 532.

—— (2000), *Punishment, Responsibility and Justice* (Oxford: Oxford University Press).

—— (2001), *Crime, Reason and History* (2nd edn., London: Butterworths).

—— (2002), 'From Criminal Law to Legal Theory: The Mysterious Case of the Reasonable Glue Sniffer', *Modern Law Review* 65: 538.

NORWICH UNION (2005), *UK: Fraud costs Britons almost £16 billion annually* (London: Norwich Union).

NOURSE, V. (1997), 'Passion's Progress: Modern Law Reform and the Provocation Defense', *Yale Law Journal* 106: 1331.

—— (2001), 'Self-Defense and Subjectivity', *University of Chicago Law Review* 68: 1235.

—— (2002), 'Hearts and Minds: Understanding the New Culpability', *Buffalo Criminal Law Review* 8: 361.

NOZICK, R. (1974), *Anarchy, State and Utopia* (Oxford: Blackwell).

—— (1981), *Philosophical Explanations* (Cambridge, Mass.: Harvard University Press).

OBERMAN, M. (2000), 'Regulating Consensual Sex with Minors: Defining a Role for Statutory Rape', *Buffalo Law Review* 48: 703.

O'DONOVAN, K. (1993), 'Law's Knowledge: The Judge, The Expert, The Battered Woman and Her Syndrome', *Journal of Law and Society* 20: 427.

OFFICE OF THE DEPUTY PRIME MINISTER (2003), *Arson Control Forum* (London: Stationery Office).

OHANA, D. (2000), 'The Natural and Probable Consequence Rule in Complicity: Section 34A of the Israeli Penal Law', *Israel Law Review* 34: 321.

OLSEN, F. (1985), 'The Myth of State Intervention in the Family', *University of Michigan Journal of Law Reform* 18: 835.

ORCHARD, G. (1974), '"Agreement" in Criminal Conspiracy', *Criminal Law Review* 297.

—— (1993), 'Surviving without *Majewski*—A View from Down Under', *Criminal Law Review* 426.

ORENTLICHER, D. (1998), 'Spanking and Other Corporal Punishment of Children by Parents: Overvaluing Pain, Undervaluing Children', *Houston Law Review* 35: 1478.

ORMEROD, D. (1998), 'Cheating the Public Revenue', *Criminal Law Review* 627.

—— (1999), 'A Bit of a Con? The Law Commission's Consultation Paper on Fraud', *Criminal Law Review* 789.

—— AND FORTSON, R. (2005), 'Drug Suppliers As Manslaughterers (Again)', *Criminal Law Review* 819.

—— AND GUNN, M. (1995), 'The Legality of Boxing', *Legal Studies* 15: 181.

—— AND —— (1996a), 'Criminal Liability for the Transmission of HIV', *Web Journal of Current Legal Issues.*

—— AND —— (1996b), 'The Second Law Commission Consultation Paper on Consent— A Second Bash', *Criminal Law Review* 694.

O'SULLIVAN, L., AND RICE ALLGEIER, E. (1998), 'Feigning Sexual Desire: Consenting to Unwanted Sexual Activity in Heterosexual Dating Relationships', *Journal of Sex Research* 35: 234.

OST, S. (2005), 'Euthanasia and the Defence of Necessity', *Criminal Law Review* 355.

OTLOWSKI, M. (1997), *Voluntary Euthanasia and the Common Law* (Oxford: Clarendon).

OWENS, R. (2003), 'Legal and Psychological Concepts of Mental Status' in R. Bull and D. Carson (eds.), *Handbook of Psychology in Legal Contexts* (Chichester: Wiley).

PA, M. (2001), 'Beyond the Pleasure Principle: The Criminalization of Consensual Sado-masochistic Sex Fall', *Texas Journal of Women and the Law* 22: 51.

PACE, P. (1985), 'Burglarious Trespass', *Criminal Law Review* 716.

PACKER, H. (1962), 'Mens Rea and the Supreme Court', *Supreme Court Review* 107.

PADFIELD, N. (1992), 'Consent and the Public Interest', *New Law Journal* 142: 430.

—— (1995), 'Clean Water and Muddy Causation', *Criminal Law Review* 683.

—— (2000), 'Justice for Those Who Help the Homeless', *New Law Journal* 150: 26.

—— (2004), 'The Anti-Social Behaviour Act 2003: The Ultimate Nanny-State Act?', *Criminal Law Review* 712.

PAINTER, K. (1991), *Wife Rape, Marriage and the Law* (Manchester: Manchester University Press).

PARKER, H. (1997), 'Adolescent Drugs Pathways in the 1990s' in J. Braggins (ed.), *Tackling Drugs Together: One Year On* (London: Centre for Crime and Justice Studies).

PARKER, R. (1984), 'Blame, Punishment, and the Role of Result', *American Philosophical Quarterly* 21: 269.

PARRY, J. (1999), 'The Virtue of Necessity: Reshaping Culpability and the Rule of Law', *Houston Law Review* 36: 397.

PATON, E. (1995), 'Reformulating the Intoxication Rules: The Law Commission's Report', *Criminal Law Review* 382.

PEARCE, F. (1978), *Crimes of the Powerful: Marxism, Crime and Deviance* (London: Pluto Press).

PEDAIN, A. (2003), 'Intention and the Terrorist Example', *Criminal Law Review* 579.

—— (2005), 'HIV and Responsible Sexual Behaviour', *Cambridge Law Journal* 64: 540.

PENNER, J. (1996), *The Idea of Property in Law* (Oxford: Oxford University Press).

PERKINS, R., AND BOYCE, R. (1982), *Criminal Law* (New York: New York Press).

PERLMAN, M. (1995), 'Punishing Acts And Counting Consequences', *Arizona Law Review* 37: 227.

PETTIT, P. (2001), 'The Capacity to Have Done Otherwise: An Agent Centered View' in P. Cane and J. Gardner (eds.), *Relating to Responsibility* (Oxford: Hart).

PHILLIPS, C., AND BOWLING, B. (2002), 'Racism, Ethnicity, Crime and Criminal Justice' in M. Maguire, R. Morgan, and R. Reiner (eds.), *The Oxford Handbook of Criminology* (Oxford: Oxford University Press).

PHILLIPS, E., WALSH, C., AND DOBSON, P. (2001), *Law Relating to Theft* (London: Cavendish).

PICKARD, T. (1980), 'Culpable Mistakes and Rape: Relating Mens Rea to the Crime', *University of Toronto Law Journal* 30: 75.

PILLSBURY, S. (1998), *Judging Evil: Rethinking The Law of Murder and Manslaughter* (New York and London: New York University Press).

—— (2002), 'Crimes against the Heart: Recognizing the Wrongs of Forced Sex', *Loyola of Los Angeles Law Review* 35: 845.

PINEAU, L. (1989), 'Date Rape: A Feminist Analysis', *Law and Philosophy* 8: 217.

POSNER, E. (2003), 'Preferences and Rational Choice: New Perspectives and Legal Implications: The Jurisprudence of Greed', *University of Pennsylvania Law Review* 151: 1097.

POSNER, R. (1985), 'An Economic Theory of the Criminal Law', *Columbia Law Review* 85: 1193.

—— (1992), *Sex and Reason* (Cambridge, Mass.: Harvard University Press).

—— (1993), 'Blackmail, Privacy, and Freedom of Contract', *University of Pennsylvania Law Review* 141: 1817.

—— (1998), 'Optimal Sanctions: Any Upper Limits' in A. von Hirsch and A. Ashworth (eds.), *Principled Sentencing* (Oxford: Hart).

POVEY, D., *et al.* (2001), *Recorded Crime, England and Wales 12 Months to March 2001* (London: Home Office).

——, ELLIS, C., AND NICHOLAS, S. (2003), *Crime in England and Wales 12 Months to September 2002* (London: Home Office).

POWER, H. (1996), 'Consensual Sex, Disease, and the Criminal Law', *Journal of Criminal Law* 60: 412.

—— (2003), 'Towards a Definition of the *Mens Rea* of Rape', *Oxford Journal of Legal Studies* 15: 379.

PRIMORATZ, I. (1999), *Ethics and Sex* (London: Routledge).

PRINS, H. (1983), 'Diminished Responsibility and the Sutcliffe Case: Legal, Psychiatric and Social Aspects', *Medicine, Science and the Law* 23: 17.

—— (2003), *Will They Do it Again?* (London: Routledge).

PROUDHON, P.-J. (1994), *What is Property?* (trans. D. Kelley and B. Smith, Cambridge: Cambridge University Press).

PUNCH, M. (2000), 'Suite Violence: Why Managers Murder and Corporations Kill', *Crime Law and Social Change* 33: 243.

RAISTRICH, D., HODGSON, R., AND RITSON, B. (eds.) (1999), *Tackling Alcohol Together* (London: Free Association Books).

RAITT, F., AND ZEEDYK, S. (2000), *The Implicit Relation of Psychology and Law* (London: Routledge).

RASKIN WHITE, H., AND GORMAN, D. (2000), 'Dynamics of the Drug–Crime Relationship' in National Institute of Justice, *Criminal Justice 2000* (Washington, DC: Department of Justice).

RAZ, J. (1988), *The Morality of Freedom* (Oxford: OUP).

—— (1989), 'Facing Up: A Reply', *South Carolina Law Review* 62: 1153.

REASON, J. (1997), *Managing the Risks of Organizational Accidents* (Aldershot: Ashgate).

REDMAYNE, M. (2002), 'Appeals to Reason', *Modern Law Review* 65: 19.

REED, A., AND SEAGO, P. (2002), *Criminal Law* (2nd edn., London: Sweet & Maxwell).

REICH, C. (1964), 'The New Property', *Yale Law Journal* 73: 733.

REILLY, A. (1997), 'Loss of Self-Control in Provocation', *Australian Law Journal* 21: 320.

—— (1998), 'The Heart of the Matter: Emotion in Criminal Defences', *Ottawa Law Review* 29: 117.

RICHARDS, M. (1998), *Censure Without Sanctions* (London: Waterside Press).

RICHARDS, N. (1987), 'Acting Under Duress', *The Philosophical Quarterly* 37: 21.

RICHARDSON, A., AND BUDD, T. (2003), *Alcohol, Crime and Disorder*, Home Office Research Study No. 263 (London: Home Office).

RICHARDSON, G. (1987), 'Strict Liability for Regulatory Crime: The Empirical Research', *Criminal Law Review* 295.

RIPSTEIN, A. (1996), 'Self-Defense and Relations of Domination: Moral and Legal Perspectives on Battered Women Who Kill: Self-Defense and Equal Protection', *University of Pittsburgh Law Review* 57: 685.

—— (1999), *Equality, Responsibility, and the Law* (Cambridge: Cambridge University Press).

ROBBINS, I. (1989), 'Double Inchoate Crimes', *Harvard Journal of Legislation* 26: 1.

ROBERTS, P. (1997a), 'Consent to Injury: How Far Can you Go?', *Law Quarterly Review* 113: 27.

—— (1997b), 'The Philosophical Foundations of Consent in the Criminal Law', *Oxford Journal of Legal Studies* 17: 389.

—— (2005), 'Strict Liability and the Presumption of Innocence' in A. Simester (ed.), *Appraising Strict Liability* (Oxford: Oxford University Press).

ROBERTSON, G. (1974), *Whose Conspiracy?* (London: National Council for Civil Liberties).

ROBINSON, D. (1996), *Wild Beasts and Idle Humours* (Cambridge, Mass.: Harvard University Press).

ROBINSON, P. (1975), 'A Theory of Justification: Societal Harms as a Prerequisite for Criminal Liability', *University of California Los Angeles Law Review* 23: 266.

—— (1982), 'Criminal Law Defenses: A Systematic Analysis', *Colorado Law Review* 82: 199.

—— (1984), 'Imputed Criminal Liability', *Yale Law Journal* 93: 609.

—— (1985), 'Causing the Conditions of One's Own Defense: A Study in the Limits of Theory in Criminal Law Doctrine', *Virginia Law Review* 71: 1.

—— (1990), 'Rules of Conduct and Principles of Adjudication', *University of Chicago Law Review* 57: 729.

—— (1993), 'Should the Criminal Law Abandon the *Actus Reus/Mens Rea* Distinction?' in S. Shute, J. Gardner, and J. Horder (eds.), *Action and Value in Criminal Law* (Oxford: Oxford University Press).

—— (1994), 'A Functional Analysis of Criminal Law', *Northwestern University Law Review* 88: 857.

—— (1996a), 'The Criminal–Civil Distinction and the Utility of Desert', *Brooklyn University Law Review* 76: 201.

—— (1996b), 'Competing Theories of Justification: Deeds v. Reasons' in A. Simester and A. Smith (eds.), *Harm and Culpability* (Oxford: Oxford University Press).

—— (1997), *Structure and Function in Criminal Law* (Oxford: Oxford University Press).

—— (2002), 'The Modern General Part: Three Illusions' in S. Shute and A. Simester (eds.), *Criminal Law Theory* (Oxford: Oxford University Press).

—— AND DARLEY, J. (1995), *Justice, Liability and Blame: Community Views and the Criminal Law* (Boulder, Colo.: Westview).

—— AND —— (1996), 'The Utility of Desert', *Northwestern University Law Review* 91: 453.

—— AND —— (1998), 'Objectivist Versus Subjectivist Views of Criminality', *Oxford Journal of Legal Studies* 18: 409.

ROBINSON, T. (1997), 'A Question of Intent: Aiding and Abetting Law and the Rule of Accomplice Liability Under 924(c)', *Michigan Law Review* 96: 783.

ROCK, P. (1998), *After Homicide* (Oxford: Clarendon).

RODWELL, D. (2005), 'Problems with the Sexual Offences Act 2003', *Criminal Law Review* 290.

ROGERS, A. (1998), 'Accomplice Liability for Unintentional Crimes: Remaining Within the Constraints of Intent', *Loyola at Los Angeles Law Review* 31: 1351.

ROGERS, J. (2001), 'Necessity, Private Defence and the Killing of Mary', *Criminal Law Review* 515.

—— (2002), 'A Criminal Lawyer's Response to Chastisement in the European Court of Human Rights', *Criminal Law Review* 98.

ROLFES, B. (1998), 'The Golden Thread of Criminal Law—Moral Culpability and Sexual Assault', *Saskatchewan Law Review* 61: 87.

ROORDING, J. (1996), 'The Punishment of Tax Fraud', *Criminal Law Review* 240.

ROSEN, C. (1986), 'The Excuse of Self-Defense: Correcting a Historical Accident of Behalf of Battered Women Who Kill', *American University Law Review* 36: 11.

—— (1993), 'On Self-Defense, Imminence, and Women Who Kill Their Batterers', *North Carolina Law Review* 71: 371.

ROSENHAN, J. (1973), 'On Being Sane in Insane Places', *Science* 179: 250.

ROSS, W. (1991), 'The Ethics of Hourly Billing by Attorneys', *Rutgers Law Review* 44: 1.

ROTHMAN, J. (2001), 'Freedom of Speech and True Threats', *Harvard Journal of Law and Public Policy* 25: 283.

RUMNEY, P. (1999), 'When Rape Isn't Rape: Court of Appeal Sentencing Practice in Cases of Marital and Relationships Rape', *Oxford Journal of Legal Studies* 19: 243.

—— (2001a), 'The Review of Sex Offences and Rape Law Reform: Another False Dawn?', *Modern Law Review* 64: 890.

—— (2001b), 'Male Rape in the Courtroom: Issues and Concerns', *Criminal Law Review* 205.

—— (2003), 'Progress at a Price: The Construction of Non-Stranger Rape in the Millbery Sentencing Guideines', *Modern Law Review* 66: 870.

RYLE, G. (1949), *The Concept of the Mind* (London: Hutchinson's University Library).

RYU, P. (1958), 'Causation in Criminal Law', *University in Pennsylvania Law Register* 106(6): 773.

SANDERS, A., AND YOUNG, R. (2000), *Criminal Justice* (London Butterworths).

SANTILLI, M. (1997), 'United States' Moral Rights Developments in European Perspective', *Marq. Intellectual Property Law Review* 1: 89.

SAUNDERS, A., AND YOUNG, R. (2002), 'From Suspect to Trial' in M. Maguire, R. Morgan, and R. Reiner (eds.), *The Oxford Handbook of Criminology* (Oxford: Oxford University Press).

SAUNDERS, K. (1988), 'Voluntary Acts and the Criminal Law: Justifying Culpability Based on the Existence of Volition', *University of Pittsburgh Law Review* 49: 443.

SCALISE, R. (2000), 'Blackmail, Legality, and Liberalism', *Tulane Law Review* 74: 1483.

SCHACHAR, Y. (1987), 'The Fortuitous Gap in Law and Morality', *Criminal Justice Ethics* 6: 12.

SCHONSHECK, J. (1994), *On Criminalization* (The Hague: Kluwer).

SCHOPP, R. (1991), *Automatism, Insanity, and the Psychology of Criminal Responsibility* (Cambridge: Cambridge University Press).

—— (1998), *Justification Defences and Just Convictions* (Cambridge: Cambridge University Press).

SCHOPP, R., STURGIS, B., AND SULLIVAN, M. (1994), 'Battered Woman Syndrome, Expert Testimony, and the Distinction Between Justification and Excuse', *University of Illinois Law Review* 14: 45.

SCHROTH, M. (2000), 'Reckless Aiding and Abetting: Sealing the Cracks that Publishers of Instructional Materials Fall Through', *Southwestern University Law Review* 29: 567.

SCHULHOFER, S. (1974), 'Harm and Punishment: A Critique of Emphasis on the Results of Conduct in the Criminal Law', *University of Pennsylvania Law Review* 122: 1497.

—— (1992), 'Taking Sexual Autonomy Seriously: Rape Law and Beyond', *Law and Philosophy* 11: 35.

—— (1995), 'The Feminist Challenge In Criminal Law', *University of Pennsylvania Law Review* 143: 2151.

—— (1998), *Unwanted Sex: The Culture of Intimidation and the Failure of Law* (Cambridge, Mass.: Harvard University Press).

SCHWARTZ, M., AND CLEAR, T. (1980), 'Towards a New Law on Rape', *Crime and Delinquency* 26: 129.

SCOTTISH LAW COMMISSION (2003), *Discussion Paper on Insanity and Diminished Responsibility* (Edinburgh: The Stationery Office).

 SEGEV, R. (2005), 'Fairness, Responsibility and Self-Defense', *Santa Clara Law Review* 45: 383.

SELECT COMMITTEE OF THE HOUSE OF LORDS ON MURDER AND LIFE IMPRISONMENT (1989), *Report (1989)*, HL Paper 78 (London: HMSO).

SELFE, D., AND BURKE, V. (2001), *Perspectives on Sex Crime and Society* (2ⁿᵈ edn., London: Cavendish).

SENTENCING ADVISORY PANEL (2002), *Domestic Burglary: The Panel's Advice to the Court of Appeal* (London: Home Office).

SENTENCING GUIDELINES COUNCIL (2005), *Manslaughter by Reason of Provocation Manslaughter by Reason of Provocation* (Sentencing Guidelines Council).

SERIOUS FRAUD SQUAD (2002), *Annual Report 2001/2002* (London: Serious Fraud Squad).

SHAFFER, M. (1997), 'The Battered Woman Syndrome Revisited: Some Complicating Thoughts Five Years After R v Lavallee', *University of Toronto Law Journal* 47: 1.

SHAPIRA, R. (1998), 'Structural Flaws of The "Willed Bodily Movement" Theory of Action', *Buffalo Criminal Law Review* 1: 349.

SHAPLAND, J., WILLMORE, J., AND DUFF, P. (1995), *Victims in the Criminal Justice System* (Aldershot: Gower).

SHAVELL, S. (1985), 'Criminal Law and the Optimal Use of Non-monetary Sanctions as a Deterrent', *Columbia Law Review* 85: 1232.

—— (1993), 'An Economic Analysis of Threats and their Illegality: Blackmail, Extortion, and Robbery', *University of Pennsylvania Law Review* 141: 1877.

SHEEHY, S., STUBBS, J., AND TOMLIE, J. (1992), 'Defending Battered Women on Trial: The Battered Woman Syndrome and its Limitations', *Journal of Criminal Law* 56: 369.

SHELDON, S., AND WILKINSON, S. (2001), '"On the Sharpest Horns of a Dilemma": *Re A (Conjoined Twins)*', *Medical Law Review* 201.

SHRIVASTAVA, P. (1987), *Bhopal: Anatomy of a Crisis* (London: Paul Chapman).

SHRIVER, L. (2003), *We Need to Talk About Kevin* (London: Serpent's Tail).

SHUTE, S. (1992), 'Causation: Foreseeability v Natural Consequences', *Modern Law Review* 55: 584.

—— (1996), 'The Second Law Commission Consultation Paper on Consent: Something Old, Something New, Something Borrowed: Three Aspects of the Project', *Criminal Law Review* 684.

—— (2002a), 'Knowledge and Belief in the Criminal Law' in S. Shute and A. Simester (eds.), *Criminal Law Theory* (Oxford: Oxford University Press).

—— (2002b), 'Appropriation and the Law of Theft', *Criminal Law Review* 450.

SIMESTER, A. (1992), 'Mistakes in Defence', *Oxford Journal of Legal Studies* 12: 295.

—— (1995), 'Why Omissions are Special', *Legal Theory* 1: 311.

—— (1996a), 'Moral Certainty and the Boundaries of Intention', *Oxford Journal of Legal Studies* 16: 445.

—— (1996b), 'Why Distinguish Intention from Foresight' in A. Simester and A. Smith, *Harm and Culpability* (Oxford: Oxford University Press).

—— (1998), 'On the So-called Requirement for Voluntary Action', *Buffalo Criminal Law Review* 1: 403.

—— (1999), 'Murder, *Mens Rea* and the House of Lords—Again', *Law Quarterly Review* 116: 17.

—— (2000), 'Can Negligence be Culpable?' in J. Horder (ed.), *Oxford Essays in Jurisprudence* (Oxford: Oxford University Press).

—— (2005), 'Is Strict Liability Always Wrong?' in A. Simester (ed.), *Appraising Strict Liability* (Oxford: Oxford University Press).

—— AND CHAN, W. (1997), 'Intention Thus Far', *Criminal Law Review* 704.

—— AND SHUTE, S. (1999), 'Letter', *Criminal Law Review* 41.

—— AND —— (2002), 'On the General Part in Criminal Law' in S. Shute and S. Simester, *Criminal Law Theory* (Oxford: Oxford University Press).

—— AND SULLIVAN, G.R. (2003), *Criminal Law Theory and Doctrine* (Oxford: Hart).

—— AND —— (2005), 'The Nature and Rationale of Property Offences' in R.A. Duff and S. Green (eds.), *Defining Crimes* (Oxford: Oxford University Press).

—— AND VON HIRSCH (2002), 'Rethinking the Offense Principle', *Legal Theory* 8: 269.

SIMONS, K. (1990), 'Criminal Law: Mistake and Impossibility, Law and Fact, and Culpability: A Speculative Essay', *Journal of Criminal Law and Criminology* 81: 447.

—— (1992), 'Rethinking Mental States', *Boston University Law Review* 72: 463.

—— (1997), 'Criminal Law: When is Strict Criminal Liability Just?', *Journal of Criminal Law and Criminology* 87: 1075.

—— (2002), 'Does Punishment for "Culpable Indifference" Simply Punish for "Bad Character"?', *Buffalo Criminal Law Review* 6: 219.

SIMPSON, A. (1976), 'The Butler Committee's Report: The Legal Aspects', *British Journal of Criminology* 16: 175.

SIMPSON, S. (2002), *Corporate Crime Law and Social Control* (Cambridge: Cambridge University Press).

SLANSKY, S. (2001), 'Neonatal Euthanasia: Moral Consideration and Criminal Liability', *Journal of Medical Ethics* 27: 5.

SLAPPER, G., AND TOMBS, S. (1999), *Corporate Crime* (Harlow: Longman).

SLOBOGIN, C. (2000), 'An End to Insanity: Recasting the Role of Mental Disability In Criminal Cases', *Virginia Law Review* 86: 1199.

SMART, A. (1987), 'Criminal Responsibility for Failing to do the Impossible', *Law Quarterly Review* 103: 532.

SMART, C. (1990), 'Law's Power, the Sexed Body, and Feminist Discourse', *Journal of Law and Society* 17: 194.

—— (1992), 'The Woman of Legal Discourse', *Social and Legal Studies* 1: 29.

SMITH, A. (1976), 'Stealing the Body and its Parts', *Criminal Law Review* 622.

—— (1978), 'On *Actus Reus* and *Mens Rea*' in P.R. Glazebrook (ed.), *Reshaping the Criminal Law* (London: Sweet & Maxwell).

—— (1982), 'The Idea of Criminal Deception', *Criminal Law Review* 721.

—— (1994), *Property Offences* (London: Sweet & Maxwell).

SMITH, H. (1998), 'The Harm in Blackmail', *Northwestern University Law Review* 92: 861.

SMITH, J. (1997), 'Obtaining Cheques by Deception or Theft', *Criminal Law Review* 396.

—— (2003), *The Nature of Personal Robbery* (London: Home Office).

SMITH, J.C. (1971), 'The Element of Chance in Criminal Liability', *Criminal Law Review* 63.

—— (1978), 'Aid, Abet, Counsel and Procure' in P.R. Glazebrook (ed.), *Reshaping the Criminal Law* (London: Sweet & Maxwell).

—— (1987), 'Intoxication and the Mental Element in Crime' in P. Wallington and R. Merkin (eds.), *Essays in Honour of F.H. Lawson* (London: Butterworths).

—— (1989), *Justification and Excuse in the Criminal Law* (London: Sweet & Maxwell).

—— (1994), 'The Right to Life and the Right to Kill in Law Enforcement', *New Law Journal* 144: 354.

—— (1995a), 'Fraud and Our Criminal Law' in P. Birks (ed.), *Criminal Justice and Human Rights—Pressing Problems and the Law* (Oxford: Oxford University Press).

—— (1995b), 'Conspiracy to Defraud: Some Comments on the Law Commission's Report', *Criminal Law Review* 209.

—— (1997), 'Criminal Liability of Accessories: Law and Law Reform', *Law Quarterly Review* 113: 452.

—— (1998a), 'Commentary on *R v Woollin*', *Criminal Law Review* 890.

—— (1998b), 'Offences Against the Person: The Home Office Consultation Paper', *Criminal Law Review* 317.

—— (1999a), 'Commentary on *R v Klineberg and Marsden*', *Criminal Law Review* 417.

—— (1999b), 'Commentary on *R v Kennedy*', *Criminal Law Review* 65.

—— (2001), *The Law of Theft* (London: Butterworths).

—— (2002), *Smith and Hogan's Criminal Law* (10th edn., London: Butterworths).

SMITH, K. (1986), 'Complicity and Causation', *Criminal Law Review* 663.

—— (1989), 'Must Heroes Behave Heroically?', *Criminal Law Review* 622.

—— (1991), *A Modern Treatise on the Law of Criminal Complicity* (Oxford: Oxford University Press).

—— (1994), 'The Law Commission Consultation Paper on Complicity: (1) A Blueprint for Rationalism', *Criminal Law Review* 239.

—— (1999), 'Duress and Steadfastness: In Pursuit of the Unintelligible', *Criminal Law Review* 363.

—— (2001), 'Withdrawal in Complicity: A Restatement of Principles', *Criminal Law Review* 769.

—— AND WILSON, W. (1993), 'Impaired Voluntariness and Criminal Responsibility: Reworking Hart's Theory of Excuses—the English Judicial Response', *Oxford Journal of Legal Studies* 13: 69.

SMITH, M. (2001), 'Responsibility and Self-Control' in P. Cane and J. Gardner (eds.), *Relating to Responsibility* (Oxford: Hart).

SMITH, P. (2001), 'Legal Liability and Criminal Omissions', *Buffalo Criminal Law Review* 5: 69.

SMITH, R. (2003), *Crime in the Professions* (Aldershot: Ashgate).

SOUTH, N. (1999), *Drugs: Cultures, Controls and Everyday Life* (London: Sage).

SPALEK, B. (2001), *White Collar Crime Victims and the Issue of Trust* (Leicester: The British Criminology Conference).

SPARKS, R. (1964), ' "Diminished Responsibility" in Theory and Practice', *Modern Law Review* 27: 9.

SPENCER, J. (1977), 'The Metamorphosis of Section 6', *Criminal Law Review* 653.

—— (1979), 'The Theft Act 1978', *Criminal Law Review* 24.

—— (1983), 'Letter', *Criminal Law Review* 573.

—— (1985a), 'Motor Vehicles as Weapons of Offence', *Criminal Law Review* 29.

—— (1985b), 'Handling, Theft and the Mala Fide Purchaser', *Criminal Law Review* 92.

—— (1987), 'Trying to Help Another Person Commit a Crime' in P. Smith (ed.), *Criminal Law: Essays in Honour of J.C Smith* (London: Butterworths).

—— (2000), 'The Case for a Code of Criminal Procedure', *Criminal Law Review* 519.

—— (2004a), 'Liability for reckless infection', *New Law Journal* 154: 471.

—— (2004b), 'Child and Family Offences', *Criminal Law Review* 347.

SPICER, R. (1981), *Conspiracy Law, Class and Society* (London: Lawrence & Wishart).

STACY, T. (2001), 'Changing Paradigms in the Law of Homicide', *Ohio State Law Journal* 62: 1007.

STALWORTHY, M. (2000), 'Damage to Crops', *New Law Journal* 150: 728 and 801.

STANKO, E. (1998), *Counting the Costs: Estimating the Impact of Domestic Violence in the London Borough of Hackney* (London: Women's Aid).

—— (2003), *The Meaning of Violence* (London: Routledge).

STANNARD, J. (1987), 'Making Up of the Missing Element: A Sideways Look at Attempts', *Legal Studies* 7: 194.

—— (1992), 'Criminal Causation and the Careless Doctor', *Modern Law Review* 55: 577.

STAPLE, G. (1993), 'Serious and Complex Fraud: A New Perspective', *Modern Law Review* 56: 127.

STAPLETON, J. (2000), 'Perspectives on Causation' in J. Horder (ed.), *Oxford Essays in Jurisprudence* (Oxford: Oxford University Press).

STEPHEN, J. (1887), *Digest of the Criminal Law* (4th edn.) (London: John Murray).

STERN, C. (1999), 'Crime, Moral Luck and the Sermon on the Mount', *Catholic University Law Review* 48: 801.

STEWARD, M., DOBBIN, S., AND GATOWSKI, S. (1996), 'Definitions of Rape: Victims Police and Prosecutors', *Feminist Legal Studies* 3: 159.

STEWART, H. (2001a), 'The Centrality of the Act Requirement for Criminal Attempts', *University of Toronto Law Journal* 51: 399.

—— (2001b), 'Harms, Wrongs, and Set-Backs in Feinberg's Moral Limits of the Criminal Law', *Buffalo Criminal Law Review* 5: 47.

STEWART, M. (1998), 'How Making the Failure to Assist Illegal Fails to Assist: An Observation of Expanding Criminal Omission Liability', *American Journal of Criminal Law* 25: 385.

STRICKLAND, C. (2001a), *HIV/AIDS and the Criminal Law in England and Wales: A Comparative Analysis* (London: Cavendish).

—— (2001b), 'Why Parliament should Create HIV Specific Offences', *Web Journal of Current Legal Issues.*

STUART, R. (1967), 'Law Reform and the Reform of the Law of Theft', *Modern Law Review* 30: 609.

SUBOTNIK, D. (1995), ' "Sue Me, Sue Me, What Can You do Me? I Love You" A Disquisition on Law, Sex, and Talk', *Florida Law Review* 47: 311.

SULLIVAN, G.R. (1985), 'Fraud and the Efficacy of the Criminal Law: A Proposal for a Wide Residual Offence', *Criminal Law Review* 616.

—— (1988), 'Intent, Purpose and Complicity', *Criminal Law Review* 641.

—— (1992), 'Intent, Subjective Recklessness and Culpability', *Oxford Journal of Legal Studies* 12: 380.

—— (1993a), 'Anger and Excuse', *Oxford Journal of Legal Studies* 13: 421.

—— (1993b), 'Cause and the Contemporaneity of *Actus Reus* and *Mens Rea*', *Cambridge Law Journal* 52: 487.

—— (1994a), 'Fault Elements and Joint Enterprise', *Criminal Law Review* 252.

—— (1994b), 'Intoxicants and Diminished Responsibility', *Criminal Law Review* 156.

—— (1996a), 'Making Excuses' in A. Simester and A. Smith (eds.), *Harm and Culpability* (Oxford: Oxford University Press).

—— (1996b), 'The Attribution of Culpability to Limited Companies', *Cambridge Law Journal* 55: 515.

—— (2001), 'Corporate Killing—Some Government Proposals', *Criminal Law Review* 31.

—— (2002a), 'Is Criminal Law Possible?', *Oxford Journal of Legal Studies* 22: 424.

—— (2002b), 'Knowledge, Belief and Culpability' in S. Shute and A. Simester (eds.), *Criminal Law Theory* (Oxford: Oxford University Press).

—— (2005), 'Strict Liability for Criminal Offences in England and Wales Following Incorporation into English Law of the European Convention on Human Rights' in A. Simester (ed.), *Appraising Strict Liability* (Oxford: Oxford University Press).

—— AND WARBRICK, C. (1994), 'Territoriality, Theft and *Atakpu*', *Criminal Law Review* 650.

SUTHERLAND, E. (1983), *White Collar Crime* (New Haven, Conn.: Yale University Press).

SUTTON, M., SCHNEIDER, J., AND HETHERINGTON, S. (2001), *Tackling Theft with the Market Reduction Approach* (London: Home Office).

SYMONS, D. (1979), *The Evolution of Sexuality* (New York: Oxford University Press).

SYROTA, G. (1979), 'The Theft Act 1978', *Modern Law Review* 42: 301.

—— (1980), 'Are Cheque Frauds Covered by Section 3 of the Theft Act 1978?', *Criminal Law Review* 412.

SZASZ, T. (1970), *The Manufacture of Madness* (New York: Dell Publishing).

TADROS, V. (1999), 'No Consent: A Historical Critique of the *Actus Reus* of Rape', *Edinburgh Law Review* 3: 317.

—— (2001a), 'The Character of Excuses', *Oxford Journal of Legal Studies* 21: 495.

—— (2001b), 'Insanity and the Capacity for Criminal Responsibility', *Edinburgh Law Review* 5: 325.

—— (2002a), 'Recklessness and the Duty to Take Care' in S. Shute and A. Simester (eds.), *Criminal Law Theory* (Oxford: Oxford University Press).

—— (2002b), 'The System of the Criminal Law', *Legal Studies* 22: 448.

—— (2005), *Criminal Responsibility* (Oxford: Oxford University Press).

TALTY, B. (1999), 'New Jersey's Strict Liability for Drug-Induced Deaths: The Leap from Drug Dealer to Murderer', *Rutgers Law Journal* 30: 513.

TARLING, R., AND DAVISON, T. (2000), *Victims of Domestic Burglary: A Review of the Literature* (London: Victim Support).

TAYLOR, I. (2002), 'The Political Economy of Crime' in M. Maguire, R. Morgan, and R. Reiner (eds.), *The Oxford Handbook of Criminology* (Oxford: Oxford University Press).

TAYLOR, LORD (1993), 'Judge and Sentencing', *Journal of Law Society of Scotland* 129.

TAYLOR, R. (1983), 'Complicity and Excuses', *Criminal Law Review* 656.

TEICHMAN, J. (1986), *Pacifism and the Just War* (Oxford: Blackwell).

TEMKIN, J. (1976), 'Impossible Attempts: Another View', *Modern Law Review* 39: 55.

—— (1991), 'Do we Need a Crime of Incest?', *Current Legal Problems* 44: 185.

—— (2002), *Rape and the Legal Process* (2nd edn., Oxford: Oxford University Press).

—— AND ASHWORTH, A. (2004), 'Rape, Sexual Assaults and the Problems of Consent', *Criminal Law Review* 328.

TEN DOWNING STREET, THE OFFICE OF (2003), *Press Release*, 20 May (London: The Stationery Office).

THOMAS, D., AND LOADER, B. (2000), *Cybercrime* (London: Routledge).

THOMAS, D.A. (1978), 'Form and Function in Criminal Law' in P.R. Glazebrook (ed.), *Reshaping the Criminal Law* (London: Stevens).

THOMAS III, G. (2000), 'Realism About Rape Law: A Comment on "Redefining Rape" ', *Buffalo Criminal Law Review* 3: 527.

—— AND EDELMAN, D. (2000), 'Consent To Have Sex: Empirical Evidence About "No" ', *University of Pittsburgh Law Review* 61: 579.

THOMAS, T. (2000), *Sex Crime* (Cullompton: Willan).

THOMPSON, E. (1975), *Whigs and Hunters: The Origin of the Black Acts* (London: Allen Lane).

THOMPSON, M. (1989), 'Property in Land: The Case of the Mohegan Indians in the Privy Council', James Ford Lecture.

TIGAR, M. (1984), 'The Law of Property and the Law of Theft', *Texas Law Review* 62: 1443.

TOLMIE, J. (2001), 'Alcoholism and Criminal Liability', *Modern Law Review* 64: 688.

TOMLINSON, E. (2000), 'The French Experience with Duty to Rescue: A Dubious Case for Criminal Enforcement', *New York Law School Journal of International and Comparative Law* 20: 451.

TONG, R. (1984), *Women, Sex, and the Law* (New York: University Press of America).

TOOHER, L.G. (1978), 'Developments in the Law of Blackmail in England and Australia', *International and Comparative Law Quarterly* 27: 337.

TORREY, M. (1995), 'Feminist Legal Scholarship on Rape: A Maturing Look at One Form of Violence Against Women', *William and Mary Journal of Women and Law* 2: 35.

TRAVIS, A. (2001), '30% of Britons Arrested are Drug Users', *The Guardian*, 4 July.

TUR, R. (1985), 'Dishonesty and the Jury' in A. Phillips Griffiths (ed.), *Philosophy and Practice* (Oxford: Oxford University Press).

—— (1993), 'Subjectivism and Objectivism; Towards Synthesis' in S. Shute, J. Gardner, and J. Horder (eds.), *Action and Value in the Criminal Law* (Oxford: Clarendon).

—— (2003), 'Legislative Technique and Human Rights: The Sad Case of Assisted Suicide', *Criminal Law Review* 3.

TURNER, J. (1933), 'Attempts to Commit Crimes', *Cambridge Law Journal* 5: 230.

UNIACKE, S. (1994), *Permissible Killing—The Self-defence Justification of Homicide* (Cambridge: Cambridge University Press).

—— (2001), 'Was Mary's Death Murder?', *Medical Law Review* 66: 208.

UNITED NATIONS (1999), *Draft Declaration on Basic Principles on the Use of Restorative Justice Programmes in Criminal Matters* (New York: United Nations).

USEEM, M. (1984), *The Inner Circle: Large Corporations and the Rise of Business Activity in the US and UK* (New York: Oxford University Press).

VAN BRUNSCHOT, T. (2003), 'Freedom and Integrity. Relationships and Assault', *British Journal of Criminology* 43: 122.

VANDERVORT, L. (1987), 'Social Justice in the Modern Regulatory State; Duress, Necessity and the Consensual Model in Law', *Law and Philosophy* 6: 205.

VICTIM SUPPORT (2002), *Victim Support Annual Review 2002* (London: Victim Support).

VIRGO, G. (1993), 'The Law Commission Consultation Paper on Intoxication and Criminal Liability', *Criminal Law Review* 415.

—— (1995), 'Reconstructing Manslaughter on Defective Foundations', *Cambridge Law Journal* 56: 14.

—— (2003a), 'Constructing Manslaughter in Drug Abuse Cases', *Cambridge Law Journal* 62: 12.

—— (2003b), 'Diminished Responsibility Expanded', *Cambridge Law Journal* 62: 540.

VON HIRSCH, A. (1976), *Doing Justice* (New York: Hill and Wang).

—— (1985), *Past or Future Crimes* (Manchester: Manchester University Press).

—— (1993), *Censure and Sanctions* (Oxford: Oxford University Press).

—— (1996), 'Extending the Harm Principle: "Remote" Harms and Fair Imputation' in A. Simester and A. Smith (eds.), *Harm and Culpability* (Oxford: Oxford University Press).

—— (1998a), 'The Problem of False Positives' in A. von Hirsch and A. Ashworth (eds.), *Principled Sentencing* (Oxford: Hart).

—— (1998b), 'Selective Incapacitation: Some Doubts' in A. von Hirsch and A. Ashworth (eds.), *Principled Sentencing* (Oxford: Hart).

—— AND ASHWORTH, A. (eds.) (1998), *Principled Sentencing* (Oxford: Hart).

—— AND JAREBORG, N. (1991), 'Gauging Criminal Harms: a Living Standard Analysis', *Oxford Journal of Legal Studies* 11: 1.

—— AND MAHER, L. (1998), 'Should Penal Rehabilitationism be Revived', in A. von Hirsch and A. Ashworth (eds.), *Principled Sentencing* (Oxford: Hart).

——, ROBERTS, J., BOTTOMS, A., ROACH, K., AND SCHIFF, M. (2003), *Restorative Justice and Criminal Justice* (Oxford: Hart).

VUOSO, G. (1987), 'Background Responsibility and Excuse', *Yale Law Journal* 96: 1661.

WALBY, J., AND ALLEN, H. (2004), *Assault and Stalking: Findings from the British Crime Survey*, Home Office Research Study 276 (London: Home Office).

WALBY, S. (2004), *The Costs of Domestic Violence* (London: Women and Equality Unit).

WALD, A. (1997), 'What's Rightfully Ours: Toward A Property Theory of Rape'. *Columbia Journal of Law and Social Problems* 30: 459.

WALDRON, J. (1988), *The Right to Private Property* (Oxford: Clarendon).

WALKER, A. (1989), *Terrifying Love: When the Battered Woman Kills* (New York: Harper and Row).

WALKER, N. (1987), *Crime and Criminology* (Cambridge: Cambridge University Press).

—— (1994), 'Reductivism and Deterrence' in A. Duff and D. Garland, *A Reader on Punishment* (Oxford: Oxford University Press).

—— (1998), 'Desert: Some Doubts' in A. von Hirsch and A. Ashworth (eds.), *Principled Sentencing* (Oxford: Hart).

—— (1999), 'The End of an Old Song', *New Law Journal* 64: 1149.

WALKLATE, S. (2001), *Gender Crime and Criminal Justice* (Cullompton: Willam).

WALLERSTEIN, S. (2005), 'Justifying The Right to Self-Defense: A Theory of Forced Consequences', *Virginia Law Review* 91: 999.

WALMSLEY, A. (1986), *Personal Violence* (London: Home Office).

WARD, A. (1986), 'Making Some Sense of Self-induced Intoxication', *Cambridge Law Journal* 47: 247.

—— (1997), 'Magistrates, Insanity and the Common Law', *Criminal Law Review* 796.

WARNER, K. (2000), 'Sentencing in Cases of Marital Rape: Towards Changing the Male Imagination', *Legal Studies* 20: 592.

WARR, M. (2002), *Companions in Crime* (Cambridge: Cambridge University Press).

WARSHAW, R. (1994), *I Never Called It Rape: The Ms. Report on Recognizing, Fighting and Surviving Date and Acquaintance Rape* (2nd edn., London: HarperCollins).

WASIK, M. (1977a), 'Duress and Criminal Responsibility', *Criminal Law Review* 453.

—— (1977b), '*Mens Rea*, Motive and the Problem of "Dishonesty" in the Law of Theft', *Criminal Law Review* 543.

—— (1980), 'Abandoning Criminal Intent', *Criminal Law Review* 785.

—— (1982), 'Cumulative Provocation and Domestic Killing', *Criminal Law Review* 29.

—— (1991), *Crime and the Computer* (Oxford: OUP).

—— (1994), 'Form and Function in the Law of Involuntary Manslaughter', *Criminal Law Review* 883.

—— (2001), *Emmins on Sentencing* (London: Blackstone).

——, GIBBONS, T., AND REDMAYNE, M. (1999), *Criminal Justice* (Harlow: Longman).

—— AND THOMPSON, M. (1981), ' "Turning a Blind Eye" As Constituting *Mens Rea*', *Northern Ireland Law Quarterly* 32: 328.

Waye, V. (1992), 'Rape and the Unconscionable Bargain', *Australian Criminal Law Journal* 16: 94.

Weait, M. (2001), 'Taking the Blame: Criminal Law, Social Responsibility and the Sexual Transmission of HIV', *Journal of Social Welfare and Family Law* 23: 441.

—— (2005a), 'Harm, Consent and the Limits of Privacy', *Feminist Legal Studies* 13: 97.

—— (2005b), 'Knowledge, Autonomy And Consent: *R. v Konzani*', *Criminal Law Review* 763.

—— (2005c), 'Criminal Law and the Sexual Transmission of HIV', *Modern Law Review* 68: 121.

Weiner, R. (1983), 'Shifting the Communication Burden: A Meaningful Consent Standard in Rape', *Harvard Women's Law Journal* 6: 143.

Weinreb, E. (1980), 'The Case of a Duty to Rescue', *Yale Law Journal* 90: 247.

Weinrib, A. (1988), 'Information and Property', *University of Toronto Law Journal* 38: 117.

Weisberg, R. (2000), 'Reappraising Complicity', *Buffalo Criminal Law Review* 4: 217.

Weisburd, D., and Waring, E. (2001), *White-collar Crime and Criminal Careers* (Cambridge: Cambridge University Press).

Weiss, B. (2002), 'What Were They Thinking?: The Mental States of the Aider and Abettor and the Causer Under Federal Law', *Fordham Law Review* 70: 1341.

Wells, C. (1982), 'Swatting the Subjectivist Bug', *Criminal Law Review* 209.

—— (1994), 'Battered Woman Syndrome and Defences to Homicide: Where Now?', *Legal Studies* 14: 266.

—— (1997), 'Stalking; The Criminal Law Response', *Criminal Law Review* 463.

—— (1998), 'Genetics and Criminal Law', *Modern Law Review* 61: 724.

—— (1999), 'Groups, Girls and Fears' in D. Nicolson and L. Bibbings (eds.), *Feminist Perspectives on Criminal Law* (London: Cavendish).

—— (2000), 'Provocation: The Case for Abolition' in A. Ashworth and B. Mitchell (eds.), *Rethinking English Homicide Law* (Oxford: Oxford University Press).

—— (2001), *Corporations and Criminal Responsibility* (Oxford: Oxford University Press).

—— (2004), 'The Impact of Feminist Thinking on Criminal Law and Justice', *Criminal Law Review* 503.

Wertheimer, A. (1987), *Coercion* (Princeton, NJ: Princeton University Press).

—— (2000), 'What Is Consent? and is it Important?', *Buffalo Criminal Law Review* 3: 557.

—— (2001), 'Intoxicated Consent to Sexual Relations', *Law and Philosophy* 20: 373.

—— (2003), *Consent to Sexual Relations* (Cambridge: Cambridge University Press).

West, R. (1988), 'Jurisprudence and Gender', *University of Chicago Law Review* 55: 1.

—— (1993a), 'Sex, Reason, and a Taste for the Absurd', *Georgia Law Journal* 81: 2413.

—— (1993b), 'Legitimating the Illegitimate: A Comment on Beyond Rape', *Columbia Law Review* 93: 1442.

—— (1994), 'Panel Discussion: Men, Women and Rape', *Fordham Law Review* 63: 125.

—— (1996), 'A Comment on Consent, Sex and Rape', *Legal Theory* 2: 233.

WESTEN, P. (2005), 'Getting the Fly out of the Bottle: the False Problem of Free Will and Determinism', *Buffalo Criminal Law Review* 8: 599.

WESTON, P., AND MANGIAFICO, J. (2003), 'The Crimnal Defense of Duress: A Justification, Not an Excuse—and Why it Matters', *Buffalo Criminal Law Review* 8: 833.

WHEAT, K. (2000), 'The Law's Treatment of the Suicidal', *Medical Law Review* 8: 182.

WHITE, A. (1991), *Misleading Cases* (Oxford: Oxford University Press).

WHITE, R., AND HAINES, F. (2000), *Crime and Criminology* (Oxford: Oxford University Press).

WHITE, S. (1989), 'Offences of Basic and Specific Intent', *Criminal Law Review* 271.

WHITEHEAD, E., AND TAYLOR, J. (2002), 'Confidence in the Criminal Justice System' in C. Flood-Page and J. Taylor (eds.), *Crime in England and Wales 2001/2002* (London: Home Office).

WILCZYNSKI, A., AND MORRIS, A. (1993), 'Parents who Kill their Children', *Criminal Law Review* 31.

WILLIAMS, B. (1981), *Moral Luck* (Cambridge: Cambridge University Press).

—— (1990), 'Voluntary Acts and Responsible Agents', *Oxford Journal of Legal Studies* 10: 1.

—— (1997), 'Moral Responsibility and Political Freedom', *Cambridge Law Journal* 56: 96.

—— AND SMART, J. (1973), *Utilitarianism: For and Against* (Berkeley, Cal.: University of California Press).

WILLIAMS, C. (1975), 'Demanding with Menaces: A Survey of the Australian Law of Blackmail', *Melbourne University Law Review* 10: 118.

WILLIAMS, G. (1955), 'The Definition of Crime', *Current Legal Problems* 107.

—— (1957), 'Causation in Homicide', *Criminal Law Review* 429.

—— (1981a), 'Temporary Appropriation Should be Theft', *Criminal Law Review* 129.

—— (1981b), 'Recklessness Redefined', *Cambridge Law Journal* 40: 252.

—— (1982a), 'Offences and Defences', *Legal Studies* 2: 233.

—— (1982b), 'The Theory of Excuses', *Criminal Law Review* 702.

—— (1983a), *Textbook of Criminal Law* (London: Stevens).

—— (1983b), 'Convictions and Fair Labelling', *Cambridge Law Journal* 42: 11.

—— (1985), 'Handling, Theft and the Purchaser who takes a Chance', *Criminal Law Review* 432.

—— (1986), 'The Lords and Impossible Attempts or Quis Custodiet Ipsos Custodes?', *Cambridge Law Journal* 102: 33.

—— (1987), 'What Should the Code do about Omissions?', *Legal Studies* 7: 92.

—— (1988), 'Oblique Intention', *Cambridge Law Journal* 47: 417.

—— (1989a), 'Which of You Did It?', *Modern Law Review* 52: 179.

—— (1989b), '*Finis* for *Novus Actus*', *Cambridge Law Journal* 48: 391.

—— (1990), 'Complicity, Purpose and the Draft Code', *Criminal Law Review* 4.

—— (1991a), 'Criminal Omissions—The Conventional View', *Law Quarterly Review* 107: 87.

—— (1991b), 'Intents in the Alternative', *Cambridge Law Journal* 50: 120.

—— (1991c), 'Wrong Turnings on the Law of Attempt', *Criminal Law Review* 416.

—— (1992), 'Innocent Agency and Causation', *Criminal Law Forum* 2: 289.

WILIAMS, R. (2005a), 'Policy and Principle in Drugs Manslaughter Cases', *Cambridge Law Journal* 64: 66.

—— (2005b), 'Drugs Manslaughter and Unorthodox Doctrine on Causation', *Cambridge Law Journal* 64: 537.

WILSON, D. (ed.) (2005), *Fraud and Technology Crimes* (London: Home Office).

WILSON, M., AND DALY, M. (1993), 'Spousal Homicide Risk and Estrangement', *Violence & Victims* 8: 3.

WILSON, W. (1992), 'Is Hurting People Wrong?', *Journal of Social Welfare and Family Law* 388.

—— (1995), 'Consenting to Personal Injury; How Far Can You Go?', *Contemporary Issues in Law* 1: 45.

—— (1999), 'Doctrinal Rationality after *Woollin*', *Modern Law Review* 62: 448.

—— (2000), 'Murder and the Structure of Homicide' in A. Ashworth and B. Mitchell (eds.), *Rethinking English Homicide Law* (Oxford: Oxford University Press).

—— (2002), *Central Issues in Criminal Theory* (Oxford: Hart).

—— (2003), *Criminal Law* (2nd edn., Harlow: Longman).

—— (2005), 'The Structure of Criminal Defences', *Criminal Law Review* 371.

——, EBRAHIM, I., FENWICK, P. AND MARKS, R. (2005), 'Violence, Sleepwalking and the Criminal Law: The Legal Aspects', *Criminal Law Review* 601.

WINCH, D. (1972), *Ethics and Action* (London: Routledge).

WOLF, S. (1985), 'The Legal and Moral Responsibility in Organisations' in J. Pennock and J. Chapman (eds.), *Criminal Justice* (New York: New York University Press).

—— (1991), *Freedom without Reason* (New York: Oxford University Press).

WOMEN'S AID FEDERATION OF ENGLAND (2002), *Domestic Violence Statistical Factsheet— 2002* (London: Women's Aid).

Wootton, Baroness (1981), *Crime and the Criminal Law* (London: Sweet & Maxwell).

Wright, M. (1991), *Justice for Victims and Offenders* (Buckingham: Open University Press).

—— (1995), 'Victims Mediation and Criminal Justice', *Criminal Law Review* 187.

Wright, R. (1985), 'Causation in Tort Law', *California Law Review* 73: 1735.

—— (1998), 'Causation, Responsibility, Risk, Probability, Naked Statistics and Proof', *Iowa Law Review* 73: 1001.

Yeager, D. (1993), 'A Radical Community of Aid: A Rejoinder to Opponents of Affirmative Duties to Help Strangers', *Washington University Law Quarterly* 71: 1.

Yeo, S. (1997), *Fault in Homicide* (Sydney: Federation Press).

—— (1999), 'The Role of Gender in the Law of Provocation', *Anglo American Law Review* 38: 431.

—— (2000), 'Blameable Causation', *Australian Criminal Law Journal* 24: 144.

Young, A. (1996), *Imagining Crime* (London: Sage)

Young, J. (2002), 'Crime and Social Exclusion' in M. Maguire, R. Morgan, and R. Reiner (eds.), *The Oxford Handbook of Criminology* (Oxford: Oxford University Press).

Young, R. (2000), 'Reparation and Retribution: are they Reconcilable?', *Modern Law Review* 57: 228.

—— (1994), 'Just Cops Doing "Shameful Business" ' in A. Morris and G. Maxwell (eds.), *Restorative Justice for Juveniles* (Oxford: Hart).

Zedner, L. (1994), 'Reparation and Retribution: Are They Reconcilable?', *Modern Law Review* 57: 228.

—— (2002), 'Victims' in M. Maguire, R. Morgan, and R. Reiner (eds.), *The Oxford Handbook of Criminology* (Oxford: Oxford University Press).

Zimmerman, N. (2000), 'Attempted Stalking: An Attempt-To-Almost-Attempt-To-Act', *Northern Illinois University Law Review* 20: 219.

Zipursky, B. (1996), 'Self-Defense, Domination, and the Social Contract', *University of Pittsburgh Law Review* 57: 579.

INDEX

A

Abandonment of attempts 833
Abetting 272–3, 827, 890, 892,
    see also Accomplices
Abnormality of mind, *see*
    Diminished responsibility
Abuse of position, fraud by 619
Abuse of power 6–9
Accomplices
    actus reus 895, 900–3,
        943–3
    articles for crime, supply of
        902–3
    causation 399
    complicity 892
    defined 887
    fair trial 68
    foreseeability 900–15
    fundamentally different acts
        915
    greater offences, commission
        of 918–19
    human rights 68
    inchoate offences 860, 903–4,
        917–18
    intention 903–4
    knowledge 900–15
    mens rea 895, 900–15
    morality 930
    provocation 915–16
    punishment 926–8
    recklessness 937–8
    shopkeepers 916–17
    subjectivism 930
    theory 923–45
    victims 922
    withdrawal 919–22
Acquittals 917–18
Acts of God, *see* Third party
    intervention
Actual bodily harm, assault
    occasioning 347–9
Actus reus
    see also Definitions
    accomplices 895, 900–3,
        942–3

actual bodily harm, assault
    occasioning 347
appropriation 522
attempts 823, 825–7, 869
battery 343–4
causation
    'but for' test 102–3
    general principles 101–2,
        132–44
    key test 103–4
    third party intervention
        104–18
complicity 890–9
consent to assault 406–16
conspiracy to defraud 854–7
constructive manslaughter
    275, 276–7
correspondence principle
    exceptions 176–80
    theory 216–20
culpability principle 36
defences 120–1
defined 85
duty to act
    harm prevention 89–94
    manslaughter 88–91
    requirement to do what is
        reasonable 94–5
harassment 365
incitement 838–9
mens rea 3
murder 245–7
omissions
    acts distinguished 94–100
    appropriation 522
    attempts 826–7
    battery 343–4
    complicity 896–9
    excluded offences 88
    general principles 87–8
    theory 126–31
    third-party intervention
        111
poisoning 357
rape 437–8, 496–9
scope 85–6

situational offences 100
theory
    causation 132–44
    classification of defences
        120–1
    omissions 126–31
    voluntary acts 120–6
third-party responsibility 100
unauthorized access to
    computers 655
voluntary acts 86–7
Aggravated crimes
    burglary 628–9, 636
    criminal damage 652–3,
        659–61
    justification 659–61
    racially or religiously
        aggravated crimes 362–4,
        654
Aiding, *see* Accomplices
Anti-social behaviour 15–16
Appropriation
    actus reus 522
    meaning 511–23
    morality 520–1
    omissions 522
    temporary 560–2
    theft 511–23
    theory 550–60
Arson 160–7, 651
Assault
    actual bodily harm 347–9
    actus reus 410–16
    autonomy 411–12
    battered women 782–5, 793
    belief 390
    capacity 440–2
    consent
        actus reus 410–16
        autonomy 411–12
        capacity 440–2
        criminalization 411–12
        defences 406–16
        duress 389
        exceptions to general rule
            383–7

Assault—*Cont.*
consent—*cont.*
  foreseeability 389–90
  generally 377–87
  meaning 389–90
  medical treatment 387
  mistaken beliefs 389–90
  morality 408–16
  paternalism 413–16
  public interest 379–82
  sado-masochism 377–87
  sport 386
  theory 406–16
definitions 337
disease, transmission of
  420–5
domestic violence 391–5,
  782–5, 793
duress 389
fair labelling 399
foreseeability 389–90
general principles 337–43
harassment 417–20
harm principle 402
medical treatment 387
mens rea 246–7
mistake 389–90
morality 408–16
paternalism 413–16
penetration, by 454
public interest 379–82
reform 404–5, 417–20
rob, with intent to 536
sado-masochism 377–87
sentencing 398
sexual offences 454–8
sport 386
stalking 417–20
statistics 391–2
theft 396–8
theory
  complaints against existing
    law 398–404
  consent 406–16
  disease, transmission of
    420–5
  domestic violence 391–5
  generally 391–406
  harassment 417–20
  reform proposals 404–5
  stalking 417–20
  statistics 391–2

threatening confrontations
  386–8
Assembly, freedom of 59–62
Attempts
  abandonment 833
  actus reus 823, 826–7, 869
  belief 863–4
  consequentialist theories
    861–2
  culpability 874–7
  defined 816–17
  harm principle 867–8
  impossibility 827–33, 877–9
  intention 816–17, 823, 828,
    861–8
  mens rea 817
  objectivism 874–7
  omissions 826–7
  preparatory acts 823
  punishment 861–8
  recklessness 818–22
  scope 827
  subjectivism 874–7
  theory 861–8
Automatism
  defined 706
  insanity distinguished
    709–10
  requirements 706–9
  responsibility, principle of
    11
  subjectivism 710
  voluntary acts distinguished
    87
Autonomy
  see also Voluntary acts
  assault, consent to 411–12
  consent
  to assault 411–12
  to sex 479–83
  diseases through sexual
    activity, transmission of
    421–5
  principle of criminalization
    22–3
  private defence 767–9
  rape 469–73, 479–83

B

Basic intent
  intoxication 173, 208–9
Battered women 782–5, 793

Battery
  actus reus 343–4
  definition 343
  feminist defence theories
    783–5
  general principles
    343–7
  mens rea 346–7
  omissions 343–4
Belief
  attempts 863–4
  consent to assault 390
  dishonesty 530–1
  handling 541
  knowledge distinguished
    174–5
  mens rea 174–5, 225–8, 390,
    426–7, 455–7, 530–1, 541,
    863–4
  rape 426–7, 455–7
  strict liability 225–8
Blackmail
  consent 643
  defined 629
  harm principle 640–1
  menaces 631–2
  privacy 640
  statistics 639
  theory 639–44
Body piercing 387
Burden of proof
  fair trial 66–7
  human rights 62–7
  presumption of innocence
    62–7
  rape 452
  reverse 62–7
  strict liability 235
Burglary
  aggravated 628–9,
    636
  defined 621–2
  fair labelling 636–8
  harm principle 636
  mens rea 627–8
  private life 636
  requirements 622–7
  statistics 635
  theory 635–8
  trespass 623–7
'But for' test
  causation 102–3

C

Capacity
  consent
    assault 388
    sex 440–2
  consequentialist theories of
    punishment 78
  culpability principle 36
  defence theories 747–51
  excuses 757–8
  foreseeability 137–43
  mens rea 183
  rape 428, 440–5
Causation
  accomplices 928–34
  actus reus 101–18
  assault 399
  'but for' test 102–3
  constructive manslaughter
    278
  foreseeability 115–16, 137–42
  general principles 100
  gross negligence
    manslaughter 287–8
  intention 120
  joint responsibility 113–14
  key test 103–4
  medical treatment, refusal of
    116–18
  minimalism 135–44
  natural events 119
  reasonableness 140–3
  subjective culpability 43
  theory
    actus reus 132–44
    coherent approach 135–44
    should consequences
      matter 132–5
  'thin skull' rule
    third-party intervention
      104–18
    foreseeability 115–16
    general principles 104–11
    intention 120
    medical treatment 116–18
    natural events 119
    'thin skull' rule 118–19
    victim's refusal of medical
      treatment 116–18
Censure
  non-consequentialist theories
    of punishment 79

principle of minimum
    criminalization 13
  stigma 238
  strict liability 237–9
  wrongful 237–8
Certainty, *see* Foreseeability
Character
  defence theories 751–3
  duress 773
  excuses 737–40
  mens rea 183
Chastisement 684
Cheques
  deception 595–7, 600–5
Children
  abuse of trust, sexual offences
    and 458–60
  consent to sex 441
  criminal damage 160–7
  criminal responsibility 721–2
  criminalization 721–2
  death of child or vulnerable
    adult, causing or allowing
    290–1
  defences 721
  necessity, conjoined twins
    and 677–82
  pornography 462, 839
  prostitution 462, 463
  rape 441
  recklessness 160–7
  sexual offences
    abuse of trust 460–1
    family situations 461–2
    pornography 462
    prostitution 462
    protection from abuse
      459–60
    rape 441
Choice
  duress 772–3
  forced 767–8
  mens rea 183
  private defence 767–8
Choses in action, theft or
  obtaining by deception of
  600–5
Civil law
  corporate criminality 801–2
  criminal proceedings and 2, 3
  damages, punitive 2
  deception 612

definitions of crime
    distinguished 2
  theft 545–7, 509–13
Civil liberties 15, *see also* Human
  rights
Classification of crimes 3–5
Codification
  advantages 20–1
  disadvantages 21
Coercion 704–5
Companies, *see* Corporate
  criminality
Competence, *see* Capacity
Complicity
  abetting 892
  accomplices
    aiding 892
    defined 887
    greater offences 918–19
    inchoate offences 917
    mens rea 900–15
    provocation 915–16
    shopkeepers 916–17
    victims 922
    withdrawal 919–22
  actus reus 890–9
  aiding 892
  assistance after offence
    922
  counselling 892–4
  innocent agency 889–20
  joint enterprises 895
  omissions 826–9, 896–9
  principals
    acquittal 917–18
    defined 887
    identification 888–9
  procuring
    general principles 894
    intention 915
  strict liability 915
  theory
    accomplices 923–45
    actus reus 942–3
    joint enterprises 941–2
    withdrawal 843–5
  time issues 895
Computer crime
  theory 661–2
  unauthorized access 655–6
  unauthorized access with
    intent 656

Computer crime—*Cont.*
  unauthorized modifications
    656–7
Conduct, *see Actus reus*
Consent, *see also* Rape, consent
  and
  actus reus 406–16
  assault
    actus reus 406–16
    autonomy 411–12
    capacity 388
    criminalization 411–16
    defences 406–16
    duress 389
    exceptions to general rule
      383–7
    foreseeability 389–90
    harm principle 411–15
    intoxication 489–90
    meaning 388–90
    medical treatment 387
    mistaken beliefs 389–90
    morality 408–16
    paternalism 413–16
    public interest 379–82
    sado-masochism 377–87
    sport 386
    theory 406–16
  autonomy 411–12
  blackmail 643
  causing sexual activity
    without 457–8
  children 441
  criminal damage 648–50
  defences 406–16
  definition 389–90
  disease through sexual
    activity, transmission of
    369–76, 387
  duress 389
  foreseeability 389–90
  harm principle 411–15
  intoxication 489–90
  medical treatment 387
  mentally disordered persons
    440–1, 463
  mistake 389–90, 483–7,
    728
  morality 408–16
  necessity 677
  paternalism 413–16
  presumptions 429–39

public interest 379–82
sado-masochism 377–87
sexual offences 398–9, 436–7,
  440–4, 463, 478–90
sport 386
theft
  appropriation 512
  dishonesty 530
  theory 405–16
Consequentialist theories
  attempts 861–2
  determinism 77–8
  mixed theories 81
  non-consequentialist theories
    79–81
  punishment 77–8, 80–1
  rehabilitation 78
Conspiracy
  actus reus 854–7
  common law offences 854–8
  corruption 857–8
  deception 854–7
  defraud, to 854–7
  defined 843
  impossibility 858
  intention 848–53
  mens rea 857
  morality 857–8
  punishment 880
  requirements 843–4
  statutory offences 743–53
  theory 880–6
Constructive manslaughter
  274–8, 310
Conviction rates 52
Corporal punishment 684
Corporate criminality
  civil liability or
    criminalization 801–2
  criminalization 801–2
  culpability 802–6
  general difficulties 789–90
  gross negligence 791–6
  identification of responsible
    officer 790–6
  manslaughter 791–800
  mens rea 790–6
  morality 807–10
  reforms 796–7
  senior managers, definition
    of 796–7
  statistics 799

strict liability 235
theory 799–815
vicarious liability 790, 797–8
Correspondence principle
  actus reus 176–80, 216–20
  assault 398, 402
  culpability 218–20
  exceptions 176–80
  foreseeability 216
  generally 176–7
  mens rea 176–80, 216–20
  morality 216
  proportionality 216
  theory 216–20
Corrupt, conspiracy to 857–8
Counselling 892–4
Credit
  deception 595–605
Criminal codes
  advantages 20–21
  disadvantages 21
Criminal damage
  aggravated 652–3, 654,
    659–61
  arson 160–7
  children 160–7
  consent 648–50
  defences 648–51
  defined 645
  mens rea 648
  private defence 648–51, 671
  property 648
  racially and religiously
    aggravated 654
  recklessness 160–7
  requirements 645–51
  special qualities of offence of
    657–8
  statistics 657
  theory 657–61
Criminal procedure 2–4
Criminalization
  American model 6
  autonomy 22–3
  children 721 –2
  consent to assault 411–16
  corporate criminality 801–2
  dishonesty 615–16
  equal treatment 13–14
  governing principles
    autonomy 22–3
    harm 23–33

practicality 33–5
harm 23–33
omissions 126–31
practicality 33–5
principle of minimum
    prohibitions 12–16
principles 22–3, 33–5
role of defensive model of
    criminal law 7–9
seriousness 14
Crown Prosecution Service
decisions to prosecute
    54
significance of human rights
    56
Culpability
actus reus 36
attempts 874–7
capacity 36
corporate criminality 802–6
correspondence principle
    218–20
critical assessment 39–41
defences 37–8
feminist approach 76
inadvertence or mistake
    210–11
manslaughter 41–6
mens rea 36
objectivism and subjectivism
    contrasted
    general principles
        41–9
    under-age sex offences
        46–9
    voluntary manslaughter
        41–6
sex offences 46–9
strict liability 241–3
subjectivism 41–9

D
Damages, punitive 2
Death by careless driving under
    the influence 290
Death by dangerous driving
    288–9
Death of child or vulnerable
    adult, causing or allowing
    290–1
Deceit, rape and 486–7

Deception
abuse of position, fraud by
    619
actus reus 854–7
cheques 595–7, 600–5
choses in action 600–5
civil law 612
conspiracy 854–7
credit 595–605
defined 570–1
disclose information, fraud by
    failure to 618
evading liability 585–9
fair labelling 615–16
false representation, fraud by
    618
harm 606–12
human rights 615–16
intention 573–4
key points 570–6
making off without payment
    589–95
morality 606–12
obtaining money transfers
    581–2
obtaining pecuniary
    advantages 582–3
obtaining property
    defined 576–7
    requirements 577–80
    theft distinguished 581
obtaining services 583–5,
    619–20
rape 429–37, 449–50, 486–7
reform 614–20
services dishonestly,
    obtaining 583–5, 619–20
sexual offences 429–37
silence as deception 574
standards of honesty
    612–13
statistics 606
theory
    civil law 612
    lying distinguished 606–8
    morality and harm 606–8
    reforms 614–20
    standards of honesty
        612–13
    statistics 606
Defences
actus reus 120–1

automatism
    defined 706
    insanity distinguished
        709–10
    requirements 706–9
    subjectivism 710
capacity 747–51
chastisement 684
children 721
classification 664
coercion 704–5
consent to assault 406–16
criminal damage 648–51
culpability principle 37–8
diminished responsibility 721
duress
    defined 685
    murder 685–7
    requirements 687–704
    scope 685
entrapment 704–5
insanity
    at time of offence 711–17
    at time of trial 717–21
intoxication 722–6, 780–2
justification 734–6
mistake
    consent 728
    duress 728
    law of 729
    mens rea 726, 727, 729
    objectivism 727
    provocation 728–9
necessity
    duress 683
    implied recognition
        682–3
    meaning 675
    medical treatment for
        children 677–82
    scope 675
    special circumstances
        676–7
private defence
    defined 665
    generally 765–72
    human rights 673–4
    requirements 666–71
    scope 666
provocation 721
strict liability 232
superior orders 706

Defences—*Cont.*
  theory
    battered women 783–5
    capacity 747–51
    character 651–3
    classification 730–1
    determinism 754–7
    duress 772–6
    insanity 760–5
    involuntary intoxication
      780–2
    justification and excuses
      732–46
    murder 782–5
    necessity 776–9
    overarching theory,
      rejection of 757–9
    private defence 765–72
    rejection of overarching
      theory 757–9
Definitions
  accomplices 887
  actual bodily harm, assault
    occasioning 347
  actus reus 85
  appropriation 511–23
  assault 337
  attempts 816–17
  automatism 706
  battery 343
  blackmail 629
  burglary 621–2
  'but for' test 102
  consent to assault 383
  conspiracy 843
  constructive manslaughter
    274
  crime
    legal and sociological
      approaches 1–2
    problems with defining 4
  criminal damage 645
  deception 570
  diminished responsibility
    265–6
  duress 685
  entrapment 704–5
  gross negligence
    manslaughter 280–6
  inchoate offences 816
  incitement 834
  insanity 711

intoxication 171
justification 732
knowledge 174–5
malicious wounding 349
mens rea 85, 146–7
murder 245
necessity 675
negligence 169
obtaining money transfers by
  deception 581–2
obtaining pecuniary
  advantages by deception by
  deception 582
obtaining property by
  deception 576–7
obtaining services by
  deception 583–5
omissions 88
principals 887
principle of legality 11
private defence 665
provocation 249
rape 426–7
recklessness 156, 159–60, 169
robbery 488, 534
sexual assault 455
strict liability 223–4
theft 501
third-party intervention 104
voluntary acts 86
wounding with intent 355
Demands, *see* Blackmail
Detention of terrorist suspects
  15
Determinism 754–7 Deterrence
  consequentialist theories of
    punishment 77–8
  strict liability 237
Diminished responsibility
  abnormality of mind 266–9
  battered women 782–3
  defined 265–6
  generally 721
  impairment of responsibility
    269–70
  intoxication 270–2
  murder 245–7, 265–72,
    721
  reform 334
  requirements 265–7
  theory 329–34
Direct action 778

Direct intention
  indirect intention
    distinguished 187–94
Disclose information, fraud by
  failure to 618
Discrimination 60
Disease, transmission of
  369–76, 387, 420–5
Dishonesty
  assault with intent to rob
    536
  belief 530–1
  conspiracy to defraud 854–7
  criminalization 615–16
  deception
    cheques 595–7
    credit 585–605
    defined 570
    evading liability 585–9
    key points 570–6
    making off without
      payment 589–95
    obtaining money transfers
      581–2
    obtaining pecuniary
      advantages 582–3
    obtaining property by
      deception 576–81
    obtaining services 583–5
    theory 606–12
  handling 536–41
  mentally disordered persons
    566
  robbery
    assault with intent to rob
      536
    defined 534
    use or threats of force
      535
  theft
    appropriation 511–23
    belonging to another
      507–11
    defined 501
    'dishonesty' 529–34
    generally 529–34
    intention to permanently
      deprive 523–9, 603
    property 501–6
    theory 562–7
Domestic violence 391–5,
  782–5, 793

Drugs-related offences
  mens rea 208–10
  rape 438–9
Duress
  association with criminals,
    voluntary 696–40
  battered women 793
  character 773
  choice 722–3
  circumstances, of 683
  consent to assault 389
  consent to sex 442–4, 488–9
  defined 685
  foreseeability 699–700
  harm principle 688–9, 694
  internal threats 700–4
  justification 773
  mens rea 773
  mistake 689, 728
  murder 685–7, 697, 782–5
  necessity 683
  objectivism 689–704
  persons against whom threats
    made 697–8
  rape 442–4
  requirements 687–404
  scope 685
  sex offences 442–4, 488–9
  threats 697–8
Duty of care
  gross negligence
    manslaughter 287–8
Duty to act
  actus reus 88–95
  harm prevention 89–94
  manslaughter 88–91
  necessity 677–82
  requirement to do what is
    reasonable 89–94
  scope 88–9

E
Entrapment 704–5
Environmental protection
  harm principle 26
Equal treatment
  principle of minimum
    criminalization 13–14
Euthanasia 273–4
Evading liability by deception
  585–9, 618

Excuses
  adopted reasons 738–9, 741
  capacity theory 757–8
  character theory 757–8
  defences 737–40
  explanatory reasons 738, 740
  intention 738–9
  justifications distinguished
    732–4, 737–40, 746
  mistake 739–40
  morality 737–40
  provocation 759
  rejection of overarching
    theory 757–9
  standard defence template
    758–9
  subjectivism 742–6
  theory 732–4, 737–41, 746,
    757–9
Expression, freedom of 59

F
Fair labelling
  assault 399
  burglary 636–8
  deception 615–16
  defining crime 1
  homicide theory 294
  principle of criminal law 19
Fair trial
  accomplices 68
  burden of proof 66–7
  generally 56, 58, 66–8
  innocence, presumption of
    66–7
False representation, fraud by
  618
Family life
  coercion 704–5
  conspiracy between husband
    and wife 745
  human rights 59
  rape 469
  right to respect for 59
  sexual offences against
    children 461
Fault, *see* Culpability
Feminism, *see* Gender issues
Fitness to plead 717–21
Fixed penalties 53–5
Force, *see* Violence

Foreseeability
  accomplices 900–15
  causation theory 137–43
  consent to assault 389–90
  correspondence principle 216
  duress 699–700
  intention distinguished
    148–9
  potential consequences of
    Human Rights Act 1998
    60–2
  subjective culpability 45
  third-party intervention
    115–17
Fraud, *see* Deception
Freedom of assembly 59–62
Freedom of expression 59

G
Gender issues
  battered women 783–5
  culpability 76
  general principles 72–6
  harm principle 26
  principles 72–6
  provocation 319–21, 322
  rape 476–8
Grievous bodily harm 369–76,
  398–9
Gross negligence
  corporate criminality 791–6
  definition 280–6
  duty of care 287–8
  manslaughter 280–8, 311–12
  medical negligence 282–6
  mens rea 169
  objectivism and subjectivism
    contrasted 48
  omissions 286

H
Handling 536–41
Harassment 364–8, 417–20
Harm principle
  American model 6
  assault 402
  attempts 867–8
  blackmail 640–1
  burglary 636
  consent to assault 411–15

Harm principle—*Cont.*
  criminalization 126–31
  deception 606–12
  defining crime 1
  duress 688–9, 694
  duty of care 89–94
  duty to act 89–94
  environmental protection 26
  future generations, damage
    to 26
  gender issues 26
  intention 193–4
  morality 29–32
  necessity 682, 777
  non-consequentialist theories
    of punishment 80
  possession 26
  potential harms 26
  principle of criminalization
    23–33
  public interest 26
  punishment 23
  rape 26–9
  theft 542–5
Homicide
  see also Manslaughter,
    Murder, Offences against
    the person
  actus reus 294
  diminished responsibility
    329–34
  euthanasia 273–4
  fair labelling 294
  infanticide 274
  intention 295–308
  medical treatment 106–9
  mens rea 295–308
  mercy killing 273–4
  private defence 104–9
  provocation 313–16
  risk 295–308
  road traffic offences
    death by careless driving
      under the influence 290
    death by dangerous
      driving 288–9
  scope 245
  sentencing 293
  statistics 291–2
  subjective reckless
    manslaughter 288
  suicide pacts 272–3

theory
  actus reus 294
  diminished responsibility
    329–34
  legal structures 292–4
  mens rea 295–308
  provocation 313–16
third-party intervention
  medical treatment 106–9
  private defence 104–9
victims 293–4
Human rights
  accomplices 917
  assembly, freedom of 59–62
  burden of proof 62–7
  Crown Prosecution Service
    56
  deception 615–16
  defining crime 1–2
  discrimination 60
  expression, freedom of 59
  fair trial 56, 58, 66–8
  foreseeability 60–2
  freedom of assembly 59–62
  innocence, presumption of
    62–7
  insanity 716
  liberty and security, right to
    57–8
  life, right to 57, 673–4
  mercy killing 273–4
  police 56
  pornography 68
  potential consequences
    burden of proof 62–7
    certainty 60–2
    particular offences 68
  private and family life, right to
    respect for 59
  private defence 673–4
  punishment without law, no
    58–9
  religion 59
  restorative justice 52
  sentencing 56
  significance 55–7
  torture 57

Identification
  corporate criminality 791–6

principals 888–9
Impossibility
  attempts 827–33, 877–9
  conspiracy 858
  incitement 842–3
  subjectivism 87–9
Inadvertence 198–9
Incest 463–4
Inchoate offences
  accomplices 860, 903–4,
    917–18
  attempts
    abandonment 833
    actus reus 823, 826
    defined 817
    impossibility 827–33
    intention 817–18, 823, 828
    mens rea 817
    omissions 826–7
    preparatory acts 823–6
    recklessness 818–22
    scope 827
  conspiracy
    common law offences
      854–8
    defined 843
    impossibility 858
    intention 848–53
    requirements 843–4
    statutory offences 843–53
  defined 816
  incitement
    actus reus 838–9
    defined 834
    impossibility 842–3
    mens rea 840–2
    requirements 834–8
  justification 758–61
  scope 816–17
  theory
    attempts 861–8
    conspiracy 880–6
    justification 758–61
Incitement
  actus reus 838–9
  child pornography,
    distributing 839
  defined 834
  impossibility 842–3 *mens rea*
    840–2
  requirements 834–8
Indifference 48

Indirect intention
  direct intention distinguished
    187–94
Individualism 220–1
Infanticide 274
Infectious diseases 369–76, 387,
  420–5
Innocence, presumption of
  62–7
Innocent agency 889–20
Insanity
  automatism distinguished
    709–10
  defence theories 760–5
  defined 711
  human rights 716
  intoxication 717
  M'Naghten Rules 713–14, 761
  morality 764–5
  reform 762–5
  strict liability 717
  time of offence, at 711–17
  trial, at time of 717–21
Integrity, rape as invasion of
  470–3
Intention
  assault with intent to rob 536
  attempts 816–18, 823, 828,
    861–8
  basic 173, 208–9
  borderline cases 150–5
  causation 120
  computers, unauthorized
    access to 656–7
  consent to sex 479
  conspiracy 848–53
  core meaning 147–9
  deception 573–4
  direct and indirect
    distinguished 187–94
  excuses 738–9
  failure test 193–4
  foreseeability 148–9
  harm, risk of 193–4
  homicide theory 295–308
  intoxication 156
  making off without payment
    592–4
  mens rea theory 187–94
  morality 189, 194–7
  motive 150
  murder 247, 304–7

oblique 187–94
obtaining property by
  deception 581
pre-meditation distinguished
  from 150
procuring 915
rape 455–7, 490
recklessness 170–1, 192–3
specific 173, 208–9
terrorism 191–4
theft 523–9, 603
third-party intervention 119
trespass for sexual offences
  629
unauthorized access to
  computers 656
wounding 355–6
Intoxication
  basic intent 173, 208–9
  careless driving, death by 290
  consent to sex 489–90
  defence theories 722–6,
    780–2
  defined 171
  diminished responsibility
    270–2
  insanity 717
  intention 156, 173, 208–9
  mens rea
    basic and specific intent
      distinguished 173
    present law 173–4
    relevance 162–3
    theory 208–13
    voluntary and involuntary
      acts distinguished 171–2
  mistake 729
  rape 439, 44–2, 448
  recklessness 162–3
  requirements 722–6
  specific intent 173, 208–9
  statistics 207–8
  voluntary acts 171–2

J
Joint enterprises
  complicity 895
  general principles 895
  mens rea 904
  theory 941–2
Joint responsibility 113–14

Justification
  aggravated criminal damage
    659–61
  defences 734–6
  definitions 732
  duress 773
  excuses distinguished 732–4,
    737–40, 746
  inchoate offences 758–61
  necessity 777–8
  mistake 736
  objectivism 742–6
  private defence 669–70,
    767–8
  provocation 313–14, 317
  strict liability 239–40

K
Knowledge
  accomplices 900–15
  belief distinguished 174–5
  defined 174–5
  handling 541
  making off without payment
    592
  mens rea 900–15
  reform 174–5
  unauthorized access to
    computers 656

L
Labelling, see Fair labelling
Learning disabilities, see
  Mentally disordered victims
Legality
  principle of criminal law 11
Liability
  see also Culpability
  evading by deception 585–9
Liberty and security, right to
  57–8
Life
  human rights 57
  necessity 677–82
  private defence 673–5
  right, to 57, 673–4

M
Making off without payment
  589–95

Malice
  mens rea 175–6
  poisoning 360–1
  transferred *mens rea* 175–6
  wounding 349–55
Manslaughter
  constructive 262–7, 274–8,
    310
  corporate criminality
    791–800
  culpability 41–6
  duty of care 88–91
  duty of care 677–82
  duty to act 88–91
  gross negligence 280–8,
    311–12
  homicide theory 289–91
  mens rea 287–91, 310
  objectivism 41–6
  reckless 288
  reform 310
  road traffic offences 290
  scope 248–9
  subjective recklessness
    288
  subjectivism 41–6, 288
  theory 289–90
  unlawful 308–12
  voluntary acts 248–9
Medical treatment
  causation 116–18
  consent to assault 387
  mercy killing 273–4
  necessity 677–82
  omissions and acts
    distinguished 91–100
  private defence 104–6
  refusal of 116–18
  third-party intervention
    106–9, 116–18
Menaces
  blackmail 631–2
Mens rea
  see also Definitions; Strict
    liability
  accomplices 895, 900–15,
    937–40
  actual bodily harm, assault
    occasioning 347
  actus reus 3
  assault and battery 346–7
  attempts 817–22, 863–4

belief
  attempts 863–4
  consent to assault 390
  dishonesty 530–1
  handling 541
  knowledge distinguished
    174–5
  rape 426–74, 455–7
  strict liability 225–8
burglary 627–8
capacity 183
character 183
choice 183
computers, unauthorized
  access to 656
conspiracy 848–53
conspiracy to defraud 857
constructive manslaughter
  275
corporate criminality
  790–6
correspondence principle
  exceptions 176–80
  theory 216–20
criminal damage 648
culpability principle 36
death of child or vulnerable
  adult, causing or allowing
  291
defined 85, 146–7
dishonesty 530–1
drugs 208–10
duress 773
gross negligence 169
harassment 365
handling 541
homicide theory 295–308
incitement 840–2
individualism 220–1
intention
  assault with intent to rob
    536
  attempts 817–18, 823, 828,
    861–8
  borderline cases 150–5
  consent to sex 479
  conspiracy 848–53
  core meaning 147–9
  direct and indirect
    distinguished 187–94
  generally 187–94
  homicide theory 295–308

intoxication 156, 162–3,
    173–4, 208–13
  making off without
    payment 592–4
  malicious wounding 351
  manslaughter 287–91, 310
  mistake 726, 727, 729
  murder 245–7
  obtaining property by
    deception 581
  procuring 915
  rape 455–7, 490
  rob, assault with intent to
    536
  theft 523–9
  theory 187–94
  third-party intervention
    119
  trespass for sexual offences
    629
  unauthorized access to
    computers 656
  wounding 355–6
intoxication
  basic and specific intent
    distinguished 173
  generally 156, 162–3,
    722–6
  present law 173
  voluntary and involuntary
    acts distinguished
    171–2
joint enterprise 895, 904
knowledge
  accomplices 900–15
  belief distinguished
    174–5
  defined 174
  handling 541
  making off without
    payment 592
  unauthorized access to
    computers 656
making off without payment
  592–4
malice, transferred 175–6
malicious wounding 351
manslaughter theory 289–91,
  310
mistake 726, 727, 729
motive 213–15
murder 245, 247

negligence
    defined 169
    generally 204–5
    objective test 169 –70
    rape 491–2
    recklessness and intention
        distinguished 170 –1
objectivism 184
obtaining property by
    deception 481
poisoning 357
private defence 769
rape 426–74, 490–5
recklessness
    accomplices 937–9
    attempts 818–22
    defined 156, 159–60, 169
    disregard of risk (*Caldwell*)
        160–8
    intention and negligence
        distinguished 170 –1
    intoxication 162–3
    objectivism and
        subjectivism contrasted
        48
    obtaining property by
        deception 581
    rape 490–1
    subjectivism 198–9, 288
    unreasonable risk-taking
        (*Cunningham*) 156–9
rob, assault with intent to 536
sexual offences, consent and
    479
strict liability 225–8
subjectivism 43, 47, 184
superior orders 706
theft 523–9
theory
    choice, capacity, or
        character 183
    intention 187–94
    intoxication 208–13
    motive 213–15
    negligence 204
    normal meaning 184–6
    significance 181–3
    subjective or objective
        approach 184
third-party intervention 119
transferred malice 175–6
trespass 626–7, 629

vicarious liability 798
voluntary and involuntary
    acts distinguished 171–2
wounding 355–6
Mentally disordered persons
    consent to sex 440–2, 463
    necessity 677
    rape 441
    recklessness 160
    sexual offences 422, 440–2,
        463
Mercy killing 273–4
Minimalism
    causation theory 135–44
Minimum criminalization,
    principle of 12–16
Mistake
    assault, consent to 389
    assault, to 389–90
    consent 360, 728
        generally 360, 436–7, 444,
            483–7, 728
    culpability 210–11
    defence to dishonesty 566
    duress 689, 728
    excuses 739–40
    identity, mistake as to 436–7
    intoxication 729
    justification 736
    law, of 729
    mens rea 726, 727, 729
    objectivism 727
    private defence 672, 769–72
    provocation 728–9
    rape 430, 433, 436–7, 486
    sex offences, consent and
        436–7, 444, 483–7
    strict liability 225–8
    theft 510–11
M'Naghten Rules 713–14, 761
Money transfers
    obtaining by deception 581–2
Morality
    accomplices 930
    appropriation 520–1
    consent to assault 408–16
    conspiracy to corrupt 857–8
    corporate criminality 807–10
    correspondence principle 216
    deception 606–12
    defining crime 2
    excuses 737–40

harm principle 29–32
    insanity 764–5
    intention 189, 194–7
    necessity 680
    non-consequentialist theories
        of punishment 79–81
    private defence 765–9
    rape as moral injury 473–6
Motive
    intention distinguished 150
    mens rea 213–15
Murder
    actus reus 245–7, 265–72
    definition 245
    diminished responsibility
        abnormality of mind
            266–9
        defined 265–6
        generally 265–65, 326, 621
        impairment of
            responsibility 270
        intoxication 270–2
    duress 685–7, 697, 782–5
    first degree murder 304–5, 326
    intention 247, 304–7
    mens rea 235–6, 245, 247
    necessity 677, 784
    premeditated intentional
        killing 305
    provocation
        defined 249
        generally 249–65, 326, 621
    loss of self-control 250–4
    reasonable reaction 254–64
    recklessness 307
    reform 303–7
    requirements 250
    second degree murder
        306–7, 326

N
Natural events
    causation 119
    third-party intervention 119
Necessity
    cannabis, growing 700–4
    conjoined twins 677–82
    consent 677
    definition 675
    direct action, political 778
    duress 683

Necessity—*Cont.*
  harm 682, 777
  imminence and immediacy
    703
  implied recognition 682–3
  justification 777–8
  life 677–82
  meaning 675
  medical treatment 677–82
  mentally disordered persons
    677
  morality 680
  murder 677, 784
  police 677
  proportionality 216
  public interest 677
  scope 675
  special circumstances 676–7
  threats 680
  utilitarianism 777
  vindication of rights, as
    777–8
Negligence
  defined 169
  gross 48, 169, 280–6, 282–6,
    791–6
  mens rea 169–70, 204, 491–2
  objectivism
    generally 169–70
      subjectivism contrasted 48
  rape 491–2
  recklessness 170–1
  strict liability 239–40
Novus actus interveniens, see
  Third-party intervention

O
Objectivism
  attempts 874–7
  complicity 826–9
  consent to sex 478–9
  criminalization 126–31
  culpability
    subjectivism contrasted
      41–9
    under-age sex offences
      46–9
    voluntary manslaughter
      41–6
  duress 689–704
  gross negligence 48

justification
  generally 742–6
  manslaughter 41–6
  mens rea 184
  mistake 727
  negligence 48, 169–70
  non-consequentialist theories
    of punishment 79–81
  private defence 666–71
  provocation 254–64, 295–6
  recklessness 48, 198–9
  sex offences 46–9, 455–6
  sexual assault 455–6
  subjectivism contrasted 41–9
  under-age sex offences 46–9
Oblique intention 187–94
Obtaining money transfers by
  deception 581–2
Obtaining pecuniary advantages
  by deception 581–2
Obtaining property by
  deception
  defined 576–7
  intention 581
  requirements 577–80
  theft distinguished 581
Obtaining services by deception
  583–5
Offences against the person
  see also Homicide; Sexual
    offences
  assault
    actual bodily harm, assault
      occasioning 347–9
    consent 377–87
    generally 377–43
    theory 391–406
    with intent to rob 536
  battery 343–7
  convictions of lesser offences
    357
  harassment 364–8
  malicious wounding 349–55
  poisoning 357–61
  racially and religiously
    aggravated offences 362–4
  rob, assault with intent to 536
  scope 336–7
  threats 369
  wounding with intent 355–6
Omissions
  see also Duty to act

acts distinguished 94–100
actus reus 87–8, 94–100, 111,
  126–31, 343–4, 522, 826–7,
  896–9
appropriation 522
attempts 826–7
battery 343–4
complicity 896–9
definition 88
excluded offences 88
gross negligence 286
medical treatment 91–100
theory 126–31
third party intervention
  111
Orders, superior 705

P
Paradigm crimes, objections to
  237–9
Paternalism
  consent to assault 413–16
Pecuniary advantage
  obtaining by deception 582–3
Penetration, assault by 545
Poisoning 357–61
Police
  decisions to prosecute 53–4
  entrapment 705
  necessity 677
  significance of human rights
    56
Political direct action 778
Pornography
  children 462, 839
  incitement, distributing child
    pornography and 839
  potential consequences of
    human rights 68
Possession
  harm principle 26
  situational offences 100
  strict liability 232–4
Practical indifference 202–3
Practicality
  principle of criminalization
    33–5
Pre-meditation
  intention distinguished
    150
Pressure, *see* Duress

Presumption of innocence
  potential consequences of
    human rights 62–7
  proportionality 62–7
Principals
  defined 887
  identification 888–9
Principles
  acquittal 917–18
  aims of American model 6
  autonomy 22–3
  criminalization
    autonomy 22–3
    harm 22–3
    practicality 33–5
  critical analysis
    culpability 39–41
    social and economic
      inequality 69–72
  critical assessment 39–41
  fair labelling 19
  feminist approach 72–6
  harm 22–3
  interests to be protected
    16–18
  legality 11
  minimum criminalization
    12–16
  proportionality 13–14, 16–19
  protection against power
    abuse 6–9
  responsibility 11
  sentencing 81–4
  support of public and private
    interests 6–7
Private defence
  autonomy 767–9
  battered women 782–5
  criminal damage 648–51, 671
  defence theories 765–72
  defined 665
  forced choice 767–8
  human rights 673–4
  justification for 669–70,
    767–8
  life 673–5
  medical treatment 104–6
  mens rea 769
  mistake 672, 769–72
  morality 765–9
  objectivism 666–71
  provocation 672

recklessness 769
requirements 666–71
rights theories 768–9
scope 666
subjectivism 666–71
third-party intervention
  104–6
threats 666
Private life
  blackmail 640
  burglary 636
  human rights 59
  right to respect for 59
Procuring
  general principles 894
  intention 915
Property
  criminal damage 648
  obtaining by deception
    defined 576–7
    requirements 577–80
    theft distinguished 581
  theft 501–6
  theory 542–5, 549
Proportionality
  correspondence principle 216
  general principle, as 13–14,
    16–19
  necessity 682
  presumption of innocence
    62–7
  principle of minimum
    criminalization 13–14,
    16–19
  sentencing 14
Proscribed organizations 65
Prosecution
  Crown Prosecution Service
    54
  fixed penalties 53–5
  police decisions 53–4
  public interest 54
Prostitution
  children 422
  statutory offences 463
Provocation
  accomplices 915–16
  battered women 783
  defined 249
  excuses 759
  first-degree murder 326
  gender issues 319–21, 322

generally 721
justification 313–14, 317
loss of self-control 250–64
mistake 728–9
murder 249–65, 621
objectivism 254–64,
  295–6
private defence 672
public interest 317
reasonable reaction 254–64
recklessness 307
reform 303–7, 325–7
requirements 250
second-degree murder 326
theory 313–16, 325–7
Public interest
  aims of criminal law 6–7
  consent to assault 379–82
  decisions to prosecute 54
  harm principle 26
  necessity 677
  provocation 317
  strict liability 235
Public welfare offences
  239–40
Punishment
  see also Sentencing
  accomplices 926–8
  attempts 861–8
  consequentialist and non-
    consequentialist mixed
    theories 81
  consequentialist theories
    77–8, 81
  conspiracy 880
  fixed penalties 53–5
  harm principle 23
  human rights 58–9
  no punishment without law
    58–9
  non-consequentialist theories
    79–81
  strict liability 240–1
  utilitarianism 240–1
Punitive damages 2

R
Racially and religiously
  aggravated crimes
    criminal damage 654
    general principles 362–4

Rape
  see also Rape, consent and
  acts, meaning of 485–7
  actus reus 437–8, 496–9
  alcohol, effect of 439, 441–2
  attitudes to, survey of 468
  autonomy 469–73, 479–83
  belief 426–7, 455–7
  burden of proof 452
  capacity 428, 441
  children 441, 459
  deceit 486–7
  deception 429–37, 452–4
  defined 426–7
  duress 442–4
  evidential presumptions
    437–9, 446
  fear 442–4
  fraud 431–2, 449–50
  gender issues 476–8
  harm principle 26–9
  identity, mistake as to 436–7
  impersonation, cases of
    435–7
  integrity, as invasion of
    470–3
  intention 445–7, 490
  intoxication 448
  mens rea 437–8, 445–8,
    455–7, 490–5
  mental illness or learning
    difficulties 441
  mistake 430, 433, 436–7, 444,
    486
  moral injury, as 473–6
  negligence 491–2
  penetration 428, 445
  reasonable belief in consent,
    no 445–8, 450–2
  recklessness 490
  statistics 467–8
  strict liability 492
  survey of attitudes to 468
  theory
    actus reus 496–9
    consent 478–87
    mens rea 490–5
    nature of offence 469–73
    statistics 467–8
  threats or use of violence 438,
    442–4, 452–4
  violence 469–70

Rape, consent and
  alcohol, effect of 439, 441–2
  belief 426–7, 455–7
  capacity 440–5
  children 441
  deceit 486–7
  deception 429–37, 452–4
  drug–assisted 438–9
  duress 442–4
  evidential presumptions
    437–9, 446
  fear 442–4
  fraud 431–2, 449–50
  generally 428
  identity, mistake as to 436–7
  mens rea 445–8
  mental illness or learning
    difficulties 441
  mistake 430, 433, 436–7, 444,
    486
  positive, requirement for 440
  presumptions 429–39, 446,
    449–54
  reasonable belief in consent,
    no 445–8, 450–2
  statutory presumption 398–9
  subjectivism 478–87
  threats or use of violence 438,
    442–4, 452–4
Receiving, *see* Handling
Recklessness
  accomplices 937–9
  attempts 818–22
  Caldwell 159–68
  children 160–7
  criminal damage 160–7
  Cunningham 160
  defined 156, 159–60, 169
  disregard of risk (*Caldwell*)
    159–68
  intention 170–1, 192–3
  intoxication 162–3
  manslaughter 288
  mental disabilities, persons
    with 160
  mens rea 818–22, 937–9
  murder 307
  negligence 170–1
  objectivism 48, 198–9
  obtaining property by
    deception 581
  private defence 769

  provocation 307
  rape 490
  subjectivism
    objectivism compared
      192–9
    reckless manslaughter 288
    unreasonable risk-taking
      (*Cunningham*) 156–9
Reforms
  assault 404–5
  corporal punishment 684
  corporate criminality 796–7
  deception 614–20
  diminished responsibility
    334
  insanity 762–5
  manslaughter 310
  murder 303–7
  provocation 307, 325–7
Regulatory offences 239–40
Rehabilitation
  consequentialist theories of
    punishment 78
Religion
  flagellation, consent to 387
  human rights 59
  potential consequences of
    human rights 68
Responsibility
  principle of criminal law 11
Restorative justice 49–52, 78
Retribution 79–81, 240–1
Rights theories 768–9
Risk
  disregard of risk (*Caldwell*)
    159–68
  homicide theory 295–308
  knowledge and belief
    distinguished 174–5
  strict liability 235
  unreasonable risk-taking
    (*Cunningham*) 156–9
Road traffic offences
  death by careless driving
    under the influence 290
  death by dangerous driving
    288–9
  homicide 290
Robbery
  assault with intent to rob 536
  defined 488, 534
  theory 568–9

use or threats of force 535
violence 535
Rule of law
principle of criminal law 11

S

Sado-masochism, consent and
377–87
Self defence, *see* Private defence
Sentencing
see also Punishment
assault 398
defensive model of criminal
law, role of 7–9
flexibility 81–4
homicide theory 293
human rights, significance of
56
minimum criminalization,
principle of 14
principles 81–4
proportionality 14
Services
obtaining by deception 583–5
Sexual activity, transmission of
disease through 369–76, 287
Sexual offences
see also Rape
abuse of trust 460–1
age 46–9
assault
generally 454–8, 458
penetration, by 454
autonomy 479–83
capacity 440–2
causing activity without
consent 457–8
children
abuse of trust 460–1
consent 441
family situations 461–2
pornography 462
prostitution 462, 463
protection from abuse
458–60
statutory offences 459–60
consent
autonomy 479–83
capacity 440–2
children 441
duress 442–4, 488–9

intoxication 489–90
mentally disordered
persons 440–2, 463
objectivism 478–9
presumptions about
429–39
deception 429–37
duress 442–4, 488–9
incest 463–4
intoxication 489–90
mentally disordered victims
422, 440–2, 463
miscellaneous offences 464
objectivism 46–9, 455–6,
478–9
penetration, assault by 545
pornography 462
preparatory acts 458
prostitution 463
subjectivism 46–9
theory
background to sexual
crimes 465–7
touching, by 456–7
trafficking 463
trespass with intent 629
Silence as deception 574
Situational offences 100
Specific intent
intoxication 173, 208–9
Sport
consent to assault 386
Stalking 417–20
Statistics
assault 391–2
blackmail 639
burglary 635
conviction rates 52
corporate criminality 799
criminal behaviour, of 9–10
criminal damage 657
deception 606
generally 5, 9–10
homicide 291–2
intoxication 207–8
murder 291–2
rape 467–8
reported and unreported
crimes 9–10
theft 548–9
Stigmatic crimes, objections to
237–9

Strict liability
burden of proof 235
censure 237–9
common law presumption
defined 225
relevant factors 230–1
scope 231–2
complicity 915
corporate criminality 235
culpability 241–3
defences 232
defined 223–4
determinism 237
insanity 717
justifications for 239–40
meaning 223–4
mistaken beliefs 225–8
negligence 239–40
objections to
generally 236–41
paradigm crimes 237–9
paradigm crimes, objections
to 237–9
particular offences 224
possession 232–4
prevalence of offences of 4–5
public interest 235
public welfare offences
239–40
punishment 240–1
rape 492
reform 235
regulatory crimes 239–40
retribution 240–1
stigmatic crimes, objections
to 237–9
theory 235–44
utilitarianism 240–3
Subjectivism
accomplices 930
attempts 874–7
automatism 710
consent to sex 478–87
culpability
objectivism contrasted
41–9
under-age sex offences
46–9
voluntary manslaughter
41–6
excuses 742–6
foreseeability 45

Subjectivism—*Cont.*
  gross negligence 48
  impossibility 87–9
  mens rea 43, 47, 184
    objectivism 41–9
  private defence 666–71
  reckless manslaughter 288
  recklessness 192–9, 288
Suicide pacts 272–3
Superior orders 705
Surgery, consent to 387

T
Tattooing, consent to 387
Terrorism
  intention 191–4
  proscribed organizations 65
  suspects, detention of 15
Theft
  appropriation 511–23
  belonging to another 507–11
  choses in action 600–5
  civil law 509–13, 545–7
  consent 512, 530
  deception, obtaining property
    by 581
  definition 501
  dishonesty 501–23, 529–34,
    603
  harm principle 542–5
  intention permanently to
    deprive 523–9, 603
  mistake 510–11
  obtaining property by
    deception distinguished
    581
  property 501–6
  statistics 548–9
  theory
    appropriation 550–60
    civil and criminal law
      interface 546–7,
      509–13
    dishonesty 562–7
    harm 542–5, 547
    property 549
    statistics 548–9
    structure of offences
      545–6
    temporary appropriation
      560–2

Theory
  accomplices 923–45
  actus reus
    causation 132–44
    classification of defences
      120–1
    complicity 941–2
    omissions 126–31
    voluntary acts 120–6
  appropriation 550–60
  assault
    complaints against existing
      law 398–404
    consent 406–16
    disease, transmission of
      420–5
    domestic violence 391–5
    harassment 417–20
    reform proposals 404–5
    stalking 417–20
    statistics 391–2
    threatening confrontations
      396–8 –8
  attempts 861–8
  battered women 783–5
  blackmail 639–44
  burglary 635–8
  capacity 747–51
  causation 132–44
  character 651—3
  classification of defences
    120–1, 730–1
  complicity
    accomplices 923–45
    actus reus 942–3
    joint enterprises 941–2
    withdrawal 943–5
  computer crime 661–2
  conspiracy 880–6
  corporate criminality
    799–815
  criminal damage 657–61
  deception
    civil law 612
    lying distinguished 606–8
    morality and harm 608–12
    reforms 614–20
    standards of honesty
      612–13
    statistics 606
  defences
    battered women 783–5

  capacity 747–51
  character 751–3
  classification 730–1
  determinism 754–7
  duress 772–6
  insanity 760–5
  involuntary intoxication
    780–2
  justification and excuses
    732–46
  murder 783–5 necessity
    776–9
  private defence 765–72
  rejection of overarching
    theory 757–9
  determinism 754–7
  diminished responsibility
    329–34
  dishonesty 562–7
  duress 722–6
  excuses 732–4, 737–41, 746,
    757–9
  homicide
    actus reus 294
    diminished responsibility
      328–34
    legal structures 292–4
    manslaughter 289–91
    mens rea 295–308
    provocation 313–16
  inchoate offences
    attempts 761–8
    conspiracy 880–6
    justification 858–61
  insanity 760–5
  intoxication 780–2
  joint enterprises 941–2
  justification and excuses
    732–46
  mens rea
    choice, capacity, or
      character 183
    intention 187–94
    intoxication 207–13
    motive 213–15
    negligence 204
    normal meaning 184–6
    recklessness 198–9
    significance 181–3
    subjective or objective
      approach 184
  murder 782–5

necessity 776–9
omissions 126–31
private defence 765–72
property 542, 545, 549
provocation 313–16, 325–7
rape
  actus reus 496–9
  consent 478–87
  mens rea 490–5
  nature of offence 469–73
  statistics 467–8
robbery 568–9
sexual offences 465–7
strict liability 235–44
theft
  appropriation 550–60
  civil and criminal law
    interface 546–7, 509–13
  dishonesty 562–7
  harm 542–5
  property 549
  statistics 548–9
  structure of offences 545–6
  temporary appropriation
    560–2
  voluntary acts 120–6
'Thin skull' rule 118–19
Third parties, *see* Innocent
  agency; Vicarious liability
Third-party intervention
  actus reus 111
  causation 104–11, 115–20
  definition 104
  foreseeability 115–17
  general principles 102
  homicide 106–9
  intention 119
  medical treatment
    generally 106–9
    refusal of 116–18
  natural events 119
  omissions 111

private defence 104–6
theory 104–11, 115–20
'thin skull' rule 118–19
victims' refusal of medical
  treatment 116–18
voluntary acts 109–10
Threats
  see also Blackmail; Duress
  assault 386–8, 396–8
  consent to sex 442–4
  dishonesty 535
  duress 697–8
  necessity 680
  offences against the person
    369
  private defence 666
  rape 438, 442–4, 452–4
  robbery 535
  statutory offences 369
  theory 386–8
Torture
  human rights 57
Touching, sexual assault by
  456–7
Trafficking 463
Trespass
  burglary 623–7
  intending to commit sexual
    offence 629
  mens rea 626–7

U
Utilitarianism 240–3, 777

V
Vicarious liability
  corporate criminality 790,
    797–8
  meaning 797
  mens rea 798
  scope 798

Victims
  accomplices 922
  homicide theory 293–4
  mentally disordered persons
    160, 422, 440–1, 463, 677
  refusal of medical treatment
    116–18
  restorative justice 49–52
  sex, consent to 440–1, 463
Violence
  see also Offences against the
    person
  rape, as 469–70
  robbery 535
Voluntary acts
  see also Autonomy
  actus reus 86–7, 120–6
  automatism 87
  definition 86
  intoxication 171–2
  manslaughter 248–9
  situational offences 100
  theory 120–6
  third-party intervention
    general principles 104–11
    medical treatment 106–9
    private defence 104–6
Vulnerable adult or child,
  causing or allowing death of
  290–1

W
Withdrawal
  accomplices 919–22
  theory 943–5
Witnesses
  role of defensive model of
    criminal law 7
Wounding
  intent 355–6
  malicious 349–55